FOCUS ON SOCIAL PROBLEMS

A CONTEMPORARY READER

SECOND EDITION

Mindy Stombler
GEORGIA STATE UNIVERSITY

Amanda M. Jungels
COLUMBIA UNIVERSITY

NEW YORK   OXFORD
OXFORD UNIVERSITY PRESS

DEDICATION

We dedicate this book to the tireless work of the activists, researchers, journalists, and instructors working to create change in tumultuous times. We hope their work, represented in this collection, inspires our students to enact sociologically grounded social change.

Oxford University Press is a department of the University of Oxford.
It furthers the University's objective of excellence in research, scholarship,
and education by publishing worldwide. Oxford is a registered trade mark of
Oxford University Press in the UK and certain other countries.

Published in the United States of America by Oxford University Press
198 Madison Avenue, New York, NY 10016, United States of America.

Library of Congress Cataloging-in-Publication Data
Names: Stombler, Mindy, editor. | Jungels, Amanda M., editor.
Title: Focus on social problems : a contemporary reader / [edited by] Mindy
    Stombler, Georgia State University, Amanda M. Jungels, Columbia
    University.
Description: Second Edition. | New York : Oxford University Press, 2021. |
    Revised edition of Focus on social problems, [2017] | Summary: "This is
    an undergraduate level reader for students taking courses in social
    problems"— Provided by publisher.
Identifiers: LCCN 2019053061 (print) | LCCN 2019053062 (ebook) | ISBN
    9780190936419 (paperback) | ISBN 9780190936440 (ebook)
Subjects: LCSH: Social problems—United States. | Sociology—United States.
Classification: LCC HN59.2 .F63 2021 (print) | LCC HN59.2 (ebook) | DDC
    306.0973—dc23
LC record available at https://lccn.loc.gov/2019053061
LC ebook record available at https://lccn.loc.gov/2019053062

Printing number: 9 8 7 6 5 4 3 2 1
Printed by Sheridan Books, Inc., United States of America

TABLE OF CONTENTS

* indicates new to this edition
# indicates updated for this edition

PREFACE

Colleges and universities around the country routinely offer courses studying social problems. To get students discussing and thinking critically about how social problems are created, perpetuated, interrelated, and cumulative, faculty often seek engaging readings to spark critical discussion and evoke a sense of moral outrage. These readings, ideally, will show students how to think systemically and critically about the social problems we face today.

We approached the construction of this reader from a unique position. Combined, we've taught Social Problems to thousands of students for more than 30 years. We have worked with new graduate students who are entering the Social Problems classroom as instructors for the first time—Stombler as the director of instruction and Jungels as the former teaching associate at Georgia State University. We have spent years listening to new instructors evaluate and ultimately lament the dearth of quality Social Problems readers. This reader comes from our own frustration with the current offerings, as well as those of our graduate student instructors who are teaching Social Problems for the first time. We share the following goals: to expose our students to a variety of social problems; to help students understand how social problems are defined, constructed, and controlled; to increase students' empirical knowledge about the causes and consequences of social problems; to develop student empathy; and to encourage students to become agents of social change.

We endeavored to compile a collection of readings that is comprehensive, so that any instructor can find readings to supplement the topics they wish to cover in their course. The reader has a strong critical constructionist foundation, so that instructors can use it as a stand-alone text or as a companion to a traditional textbook. We include articles from a wide variety of sources to illustrate how sociologists, other academics, and claims makers recognize and define social problems, conduct relevant research, illustrate the lived experience of social problems, and actively drive social change.

In the introduction to this book, we discuss the sociological imagination, and we develop our constructivist approach to contemporary social problems. We highlight the way that social problems are interrelated and have a cumulative effect on individual actors. We want students to focus their attention on the systems and structures that are at the core of society's issues.

Our readings provide depth but are appropriately leveled for the average undergraduate taking an introductory course. We have edited our selections judiciously, so that students are not reading an excessive amount, nor are they losing important elements or the "heart" of the selection. On occasion, some readings are a bit longer, but we feel they are engaging enough for students to be able to maintain interest. Whereas traditional textbooks are able to offer incredible breadth, our readings provide additional depth on each featured social problem. Our reader focuses predominantly on the social problems plaguing the United States.

FORMAT OF THE BOOK

The second edition of *Focus on Social Problems: A Contemporary Reader* has several features that distinguish it from other textbooks and readers on social problems. The book is composed of 14 chapters, each focusing on a different social problem (except for Chapter 1, newly expanded for the second edition). Chapter 1 introduces students to sociology, the sociological imagination, the social construction of social problems, and how American values of meritocracy, individualism, and consumption influence how we view social problems and their solution. This represents a consolidation of two chapters of readings from the first edition, a choice we made in order to offer expanded readings throughout the remaining chapters. Each chapter in the second edition consists of a selection of full-length readings and "boxes." Full-length readings cover what we consider important topics on a given social problem and address the breadth, depth, causes of, or solutions to that problem. Full-length readings and boxes may be read together or separately. Boxes are generally briefer than readings and are intended to delve into a narrower subject or simply generate reactions and discussion related to the chapter topic without overburdening the reader with additional full-length articles. Reviewers of the first edition shared helpful ideas about new topics and articles to include, and we are grateful for their suggestions. We chose readings and boxes to engage students' sociological imaginations and provide access to recent data and analyses relevant to current social problems. Vetted by our students, our selections are designed to be accessible to undergraduates at an introductory level and to convey information about causes, consequences, and the scope of social problems.

Full-length readings and boxes come from a diverse group of sources: edited versions of academic, peer-reviewed articles and book chapters (for example, from journals such as *Gender & Society, Contexts, Poverty and Public Policy,* and *Sociological Compass,* and books such as *Reel Inequality* and *$2 a Day: Living on Almost Nothing in America*), articles from the popular press (*The New York Times, National Public Radio, Vanity Fair, Scientific American,* and even *Teen Vogue*), blogs (*The Society Pages, LifeHacker*), and reports from nonprofit organizations (Pew Research Center, Urban Institute, Brennan Center for Justice, Institute for Policy Studies, and the Food Chain Workers Alliance). When we were designing this book, we thought about the weight that each type of source should receive. Although we believe academic, peer-reviewed research is critical to a thorough understanding of social problems, the popular press, investigative journalistic pieces, and research from the nonprofit sector offer important and accessible perspectives that both inform, and have been informed by, sociological research.

Previously published works are included alongside those written expressly for this book. We commissioned original pieces for several reasons. Sometimes we couldn't find articles on a given subject that contained all the information we wanted to share with students, so we invited academics to share knowledge they had about a subject. Other times there was a plethora of material from which to choose, and we asked an author to pull together the information that was the most salient and relevant to students. When we wanted to add updates to pieces we published in the first edition, we asked authors of original pieces to update their work, and in other cases we added editor's notes to give additional or new information on statistics or legislation. In order to support instructors, an Instructor's Manual is available through Oxford University Press.

The other feature of our book that sets it apart from others is the inclusion of Activist Interviews. Many of our social problems students complain that courses focusing on social problems, inequality, and injustice are depressing. It is hard for students to envision change; it is even harder for them to see how individuals or small groups could have any meaningful impact. The activists selected for this book represent social change work across the range of social problems covered in our book. We incorporate interviews with activists who are working within different types of organizations or collectives (from the small, local, grassroots organization to large national organizations) and who are doing a wide array of types of work (from interning to field organizing to serving as directors). For the second edition, we added some new activists that are in entry-level positions in their organizations, to help students recognize accessible pathways to participation. We hope that these interviews, as well as the variety of activist experiences contained within them, will demonstrate to students that they too can enact social change in their communities.

NEW TO THIS EDITION

- Expanded introduction: The introduction to the second edition is now a full-length written chapter by Stombler and Jungels that introduces students to the discipline of sociology, the sociological imagination, the role of American cultural values in defining and understanding social problems, the social construction of social problems, and a critical constructionist perspective.
- Each chapter has a newly composed multi-page introduction that helps students draw connections across the chapter's readings.
- Original pieces written for the first edition have been updated with the latest data.
- Activist interviews have been updated, and there are five new interviews as well, maintaining the diversity in experiences, organizations, and identities that characterized this feature in the first edition.
- Over half of the selections are new to the second edition. While maintaining a focus on social problems foundational to U.S. society, we also captured new developments and directions in research on social problems.

ACKNOWLEDGMENTS

Soliciting, curating, and editing a reader that is so broad in scope is a challenging task. We thank our editor, Sherith Pankratz, for her enthusiasm for the second edition and for her low-pressure but unfailing support throughout both editions. Grace Li, our assistant editor, was exceptionally responsive to our needs and maintained order during chaotic times. Thanks as well to Patricia Berube and the folks at SPi Global U.S., Inc. for their patience and attention to detail during the editing process. We also extend our thanks to the following reviewers, whose detailed feedback shaped the book's format and trajectory: Cassidy Cooper, University of Mobile; Martha Copp, East Tennessee State University; Cristen Dalessandro, University of Colorado Boulder; Sarah

Epplen, Minnesota State University-Mankato; Amy Grau, Shawnee State University; Hortencia Jimenez, Hartnell College; Jeffrey Lentz, University of North Georgia; Helen Marie Miamidian, Arcadia University; Christopher Oliver, Tulane University; Erik Withers, University of South Florida; and one anonymous reviewer.

We are grateful to the activists (and their assistants) for taking time out of their incredibly busy schedules to allow us to interview them for the Activist Interview feature of this book. They offered thoughtful responses to our questions, shared heartfelt stories of their motivations, and provided concrete social change strategies for our students. We also thank the authors who wrote original pieces for this book. We know that we were demanding and that you had to endure last-minute requests to incorporate new data, provide multitudes of drafts and revisions, and meet sometimes short deadlines. We appreciate your patience and hard work to make this book the best it could be.

Focus on Social Problems was built in a supportive environment. Thanks to Katie Acosta, Maura Ryan, alithia zamantakis, Dan Pascuiti, Dresden Lackey, Alan Abramowitz, and Denise Milstein for sharing materials, thoughts, and expertise. We thank our Social Problems students (we've had many thousands, combined) for providing valuable feedback on readings and for their excitement and passion for the material we present and discuss. Finally, thanks to our wonderful subject librarian, Mandy Swygart-Hobaugh, and her colleagues, who were always a source of immediate assistance. There are also innumerable colleagues, friends, and co-workers—too many to name here—who acted as sounding boards, suggested content, and were generally supportive when we needed it.

We also thank our family and friends. In particular, Mindy thanks her husband, Nate Steiner, who was his usual sweet and supportive self, maintaining his own paid work and housework while taking over her share as well (and even reading drafts). This book was built on a foundation of his encouragement and patience during stressful times. He also introduced us to the Slack app, which helped us remain organized as we worked. She also thanks her son, Moey Rojas, for his independence (allowing her to work crazy hours) and his contributions to dinnertime discussions on the social problems in the book before he left for college. She thanks her parents, Lynne and Milton Stombler, for their constant support of her endeavors. Finally, she thanks canine Rue for lovingly flanking her throughout the entire process.

Amanda's parents, Robin and Betty Jungels, and her sister Rebecca and brother-in-law Brandon, were constant sources of encouragement over the many months (years!) it took to create this book. She'd also like to thank her partner Jim Holland for his support, encouragement, and for many engaging discussions about the content of the book. Her friends and colleagues in Minnesota, Georgia, Maryland, and New York (and everywhere else!) were also a huge source of support, always offering help when it was needed: a sympathetic ear, a spare bedroom or much-needed break during the final days of compiling the book, or words of encouragement. She is forever grateful for their support. And, of course, she would be remiss if she failed to mention her adorable canine companion, Max Weber, who keeps things exciting, makes sure sociology is a constant presence in her life, and keeps the couch warm.

This project was completed remotely because our careers took us to different states. Thankfully, through the wonders of Internet technology and file sharing, this project was collaborative in a way that neither of us anticipated at the outset. Working on this book was a true labor of love, and we hope you enjoy the result as much as we enjoyed compiling it.

CONTRIBUTOR LIST

THE EDITORS

Mindy Stombler, Ph.D., is a principal senior lecturer of sociology at Georgia State University. She is co-editor of *Sex Matters: The Sexuality and Society Reader*, 5th edition (W. W. Norton). Her past research has focused on the production of sexual collective identities as well as pedagogical issues. She has been teaching Social Problems courses consistently over the past 25 years. She is also the winner of the Southern Sociological Society's Distinguished Contributions to Teaching Award, an award honoring outstanding teaching contributions beyond one's institution, benefiting the discipline as a whole and the American Sociological Association's Teaching and Learning Section's Carla B. Howery Award for Developing Teacher-Scholars, an award honoring significant contributions to teaching sociology through mentoring and training of graduate students both to teach sociology and to make contributions to the scholarship of teaching and learning.

Amanda M. Jungels, Ph.D., is a Senior Assistant Director for Faculty Programs and Services in the Center for Teaching and Learning at Columbia University. She is a past recipient of the Jacqueline Boles Teaching Fellowship and Teaching Associate Award at Georgia State University. Her past research has focused on the social construction of privacy and sexuality and cognitive sociology, and her current work focuses on faculty and educational development, emphasizing inclusive teaching practices.

THE AUTHORS

Michelle Alexander is visiting professor of social justice at Union Theological Seminary. **Dedrick Asante-Muhammad** is a senior fellow of the Racial Wealth Divide Initiative for Prosperity Now.
Amanda Atwell is an early childhood educator. **Amanda K. Baumle** is an associate professor of sociology and department chair at University of Houston.
Kristen Bialik is a senior specialist analyst at Gartner.
Thomas N. Bradbury is a distinguished professor of clinical psychology at the University of California, Los Angeles.
Otis Webb Brawley is a Bloomberg Distinguished Professor at Johns Hopkins University.

Tristan Bridges is an assistant professor of sociology at the University of California, Santa Barbara.

Katharine Broton is an assistant professor of higher education at the University of Iowa.

Bailey A. Brown is a doctoral student in sociology at Columbia University.

Elizabeth S. Cavalier is an associate professor of sociology at Georgia Gwinnett College.

Camille Z. Charles is the Walter H. and Leonore C. Annenberg Professor in the Social Sciences and director of the Center for Africana Studies at the University of Pennsylvania.

Andrew Cohen is a senior editor at the Marshall Project and a fellow at the Brennan Center for Justice.

Chuck Collins is director of the Program on Inequality and the Common Good at the Institute for Policy Studies.

D'Lane R. Compton is an associate professor of sociology at the University of New Orleans.

Craig Considine is a lecturer of sociology at Rice University.

Eleanor Cummins is a science journalist on staff at Popular Science.

Jessie Daniels is a writer and professor of sociology at Hunter College.

Linda Darling-Hammond is the Charles E. Ducommun Professor of Education Emeritus at Stanford University and president and CEO of Learning Policy Institute.

Arthur Delaney is a senior reporter for the Huffington Post.

Matthew Desmond is the Maurice P. During Professor of Sociology at Princeton University.

Robin DiAngelo is an academic, lecturer, and author.

Lisa Dodson is a senior scientist at Brandeis University and a research professor at Boston College.

Douglas B. Downey is a professor of sociology at The Ohio State University.

Petula Dvorak is a local columnist for *The Washington Post*.

Kathryn J. Edin is a professor of sociology and public affairs at Princeton University.

Jessica Fields is a professor of sociology at San Francisco State University.

Food Chain Workers Alliance is a coalition of worker-based organizations whose members work on the food chain, organizing to improve wages and working conditions for all workers along the food chain.

Amanda M. Gengler is an assistant professor of sociology at Wake Forest University.

Benjamin G. Gibbs is an associate professor of sociology at Brigham Young University.

Malcolm Gladwell is a staff writer for *The New Yorker*. He is the author of three *New York Times* best-sellers.

Paul Goldberg is an investigative reporter and is editor and publisher of *The Cancer Letter*.

Sara Goldrick-Rab a professor of higher education policy and sociology at Temple University.

Desmond Goss is a lecturer of sociology at Georgia State University.

Ruth Gourevitch is a research assistant in the Metropolitan Housing and Communities Policy Center at the Urban Institute.

Michael Grabell is a reporter for *ProPublica* whose work has also been published in *The New Yorker*, *The Atlantic*, and *The New York Times*.

Solomon Greene is a senior fellow in the Research to Action Lab and the Metropolitan Housing and Communities Policy Center at the Urban Institute.

Sarah Halpern-Meekin is an associate professor of human development and family studies at the University of Wisconsin-Madison.

Stacy Gorman Harmon is a guest researcher at the Centers for Disease Control and Prevention.

Elis Herman is a health educator with Planned Parenthood Northern California.

Heather R. Hlavka is an associate professor of sociology at Marquette University.

Josh Hoxie is project director of the Opportunity and Taxation for the Program on Inequality and the Common Good at the Institute for Policy Studies.

Wil S. Hylton is a contributing writer at *The New York Times Magazine*.

Jeneen Interlandi is a member of *The New York Times* editorial board and a contributor to *The New York Times Magazine*.

Carolina Izquierdo is a visiting scholar of anthropology at the University of California, Los Angeles.

Brooke Jarvis is a contributing writer to the *The New York Times Magazine* and *The California Sunday Magazine*, and has also written for *The New Yorker*, *GQ*, and *Harper's*.

Allan G. Johnson is a writer, sociologist, public speaker, and trainer around issues of race and gender.

Mel Jones is a writer based in Washington, DC.

Maggie Jones is a contributing writer at *The New York Times Magazine*.

Victor E. Kappeler is a Foundation Professor and dean of the School of Justice Studies at Eastern Kentucky University.

Maria Kefalas is a professor of sociology and criminal justice at St. Joseph's University.

Mimi Kirk is a contributing writer to CityLab; her writing has also appeared in *The Washington Post*, *Foreign Policy*, and *Smithsonian Magazine*.

Wendy Klein is an associate professor of anthropology and linguistics at California State University, Long Beach.

Maria Konnikova is a book author, television producer, and writer, publishing in *The New Yorker* and *The New Republic*.

Miriam Konrad is a senior lecturer emeritus of sociology at Georgia State University.

Rory Kramer is an assistant professor of sociology at Villanova University.

Kiersten Kummerow is a doctoral student in sociology at Georgia State University.

Dresden Lackey is a doctoral student in sociology at Georgia State University.

Sharon LaFraniere is an investigative reporter at *The New York Times*.

Ashley Lamb-Sinclair is a high school instructional coach and the founder and CEO of Curio Learning.

Andrew W. Lehren is a senior editor on the NBC News investigations team.

Paul Rogat Loeb is the author of *The Impossible Will Take a Little While: Hope and Persistence in Troubled Times* and *Soul of a Citizen: Living with Conviction in Challenging Times*.

Wendy Luttrell is a professor of urban education, sociology, and critical social/personality psychology programs at the CUNY-Graduate Center.

Angie Luvara is an assistant professor of sociology at Hampton University.

Elaine McArdle is an author of several books and a journalist who has published in *The Boston Globe* and *Boston Globe Magazine*.

Edward McClelland is an author of several books; his writing has also appeared in *The New York Times*, *Salon*, and *Slate*.

Stephanie Medley-Rath is an assistant professor of sociology at Indiana University Kokomo.

Robinson Meyer is a staff writer at *The Atlantic*.

Claire Cain Miller is a correspondent for *The New York Times*.

Jordan Forrest Miller is a doctoral student in sociology at Georgia State University.

Stefanie Mollborn is a professor of sociology at the University of Colorado Boulder.

Brittany N. Morey is an assistant professor in public health at the University of California, Irvine.

Michael Moss is a Pulitzer Prize-winning investigative reporter and the author of *The New York Times* best-seller *Salt Sugar Fat: How the Food Giants Hooked Us*.

Emanuel Nieves is a senior policy manager at *Prosperity Now*.

Carmen Nobel is the Program Director of Journalist's Resource at the Harvard Kennedy School and has contributed to such publications as *The Boston Globe* and *Inc. Magazine*.

Anna North is a novelist and a senior reporter at *Vox*.

Michael I. Norton is the Harold M. Brierley Professor of Business Administration and Director of Research at Harvard Business School.

Hollie Nyseth Brehm is an assistant professor of sociology at The Ohio State University.

David Pellow is the Dehlsen Professor and Chair of the Department of Environmental Studies at the University of California, Santa Barbara.

Gary W. Potter is a professor and dean of the School of Justice Studies at Eastern Kentucky University.

Monica Potts is a writer based in Manassas, Virginia, and a fellow with the New America Foundation Asset Building Program, whose work has been published in *The American Prospect* and *The New York Times*.

Anastasia Prokos is a chief legislative analyst at the Florida legislature's Office of Program Policy Analysis and Government Accountability.

Watoii Rabii is an assistant professor of sociology at Oakland University.

Kirstin Ralston-Coley is an instructor of sociology at Kennesaw State University.

Jennifer Randles is an associate professor of sociology at California State University, Fresno.

Mark R. Rank is the Herbert S. Hadley Professor of Social Welfare at Washington University in St. Louis.

Eric Ravenscraft is a freelance writer and editor who has published in Lifehacker and How-to Geek.

Brianna Remster is an assistant professor of sociology at Villanova University.

Sarah Rich is a writer based in Oakland, California.

Ashley Rockwell is a doctoral student in sociology at Georgia State University.

Moey Rojas is a student at Swarthmore College.

Elisabeth Rosenthal is editor-in-chief of Kaiser Health News.

Tracey Ross is associate director of the All-In Citites Initiative at PolicyLink.

Zachary Roth is a fellow at the Brennan Center for Justice at New York University's School of Law.

Alina Selyukh is a correspondent at National Public Radio.

Alana Semuels is a staff writer at *The Atlantic*.

H. Luke Shaefer is an associate professor of social work and public policy and director of the Poverty Center at the University of Michigan.

Renee M. Shelby is a doctoral candidate in the School of History and Sociology at Georgia Institute of Technology.

Alicia Shepard is a journalist, book author, and media writer, publishing in *The New York Times*, *The Washington Post*, *American Journalism Review*, and *USA Today*.

Maanvi Singh is a freelance multimedia reporter for outlets such as *National Geographic* and National Public Radio.

Solidarity Research Cooperative is a solutions agency for worker- and community-based organizations.

Danyelle Solomon is Vice President, Race and Ethnicity Policy, at the Center for American Progress.

Southern Poverty Law Center is a nonprofit legal advocacy organization specializing in civil rights and public interest litigation.

Tim Stelloh is a freelance writer working with NBC and publishing in outlets such as *The New York Times*, The Marshall Project, *The New Republic*, and *Businessweek.*

Joseph E. Stiglitz is a university professor at Columbia University.

Emily Stutzman is academic director and an assistant professor at the Institute for Sustainable Practice at Lipscomb University.

Jennifer Sykes is an assistant professor of social relations and policy at Michigan State University.

Laura Tach is an associate professor of policy analysis and management at the Cornell Institute for Public Affairs.

Margaret Talbot is a staff writer for *The New Yorker*.

Melanie Tannenbaum is Chief Communications Science Advisor for Wescott Strategic Communications and a freelance science writer.

Megan M. Tesene is the Associate Director for the Personalized Learning Consortium at the Association of Public and Land-grant Universities.

Erin Thomas is a sociologist at the Centers for Disease Control and Prevention, Emergency Preparedness and Response.

Heather Ann Thompson is a professor of history and of Afroamerican and African Studies at the University of Michigan.

Claudia Tillman is a doctoral student in the Department of Sociology at Georgia State University.

Tara Leigh Tober is a lecturer of sociology at the University of California, Santa Barbara.

Margery Austin Turner is the Senior Vice President for Program Planning and Management at the Urban Institute.

University of Southern California, Department of Nursing is an evidence-based nursing program that prepares family nurse practitioners.

Chris M. Vidmar is a doctoral student in sociology at Georgia State University.

Linda Villarosa is a journalist, an educator, and a contributing writer to *The New York Times Magazine.*

David Wallace-Wells is deputy editor and climate columnist for *New York Magazine.*

Wendy R. Weiser is the Director of the Democracy Program at the Brennan Center for Justice at New York University's School of Law.

Rose Weitz a professor of sociology and of women and gender studies at Arizona State University.

Matt Wilkins is a postdoctoral fellow at Vanderbilt University's Center for Science Outreach.

Elroi J. Windsor is an associate professor of sociology and department chair at the University of West Georgia.

Adia Harvey Wingfield is a professor of sociology at Washington University in St. Louis.

Yolanda Young is a contributing writer for publications such as *USA Today*, *The Washington Post*, and *Essence Magazine.*

Nancy Wang Yuen is an associate professor of sociology at Biola University.

CHAPTER 1

INTRODUCTION
What Is Sociology?

If you're opening this book or enrolled in a sociology class for the first time, you might be wondering: what is sociology, and why would a sociologist study social problems? Even if you have no preexisting training in sociology or have never studied sociology before, don't worry—you are already immersed in the content of sociology on a daily basis, simply because you live in a society.

Sociology is the systematic study of human relationships (formal and informal), social interaction (between groups as small as two people or as large as many millions), and social institutions (e.g., the educational system, political system, economic system, families, health care systems, and more). The scope of what sociologists study varies from small-group dynamics like speech interruption patterns in conversations between women and men, or doctors and patients, to large-scale comparisons of the efficacy of social welfare policies and programs. According to the American Sociological Association, sociologists study "social life, social change, and the causes and consequences of human behavior."[1] Instead of focusing on individual behavior, we explore patterns of behavior to understand how and why people behave the way they do, as well as the result of those actions.

Sociologists often boast that they can study nearly anything. Subfields within sociology include political sociology; aging, children, and youth; medical sociology; labor and labor movements; consumers and consumption; crime, law, and deviance; war, peace, and social conflict; race, gender, and class; sexualities; sociology of the family, of religion, of sport, and of the environment, just to name a few.[2] The number of research topics in the field is nearly limitless, and we use a wide variety of research methods to study them. Mindy Stombler (the first editor of this book), for example, has studied the social structure of and interactions in

---

1   American Sociological Association. n.d. "What Is Sociology?" http://www.asanet.org/about/sociology.cfm.
2   American Sociological Association. n.d. "Current Sections." http://www.asanet.org/sections/list.cfm.

gay fraternities and also fraternity little sister/sweetheart programs at both predominantly Black and predominantly White fraternities, whereas Amanda Jungels (the second editor) has studied men who solicit sex workers, privacy disclosures among sex toy party participants, and suicide and sexual assault among United States Army soldiers. Sociologists may conduct large-scale studies where thousands of people are surveyed; in-depth studies using interviews or observations; analyses of content (such as books or films); or some combination of methods. Just a quick glance through the table of contents of this book—or any course listing at a college or university that offers sociology classes—will give you a good idea of the areas and types of inquiry in which sociologists participate. The uniqueness of sociology is reflected not only in the endless available topics of study, but also in the perspective we use to guide our analyses: the sociological imagination.

THE SOCIOLOGICAL IMAGINATION

Most sociology classes, especially at the introductory level, begin with a discussion of C. Wright Mills's concept of the *sociological imagination*. The sociological imagination is a particular lens we use to view the world, one that encourages us to think like sociologists—to focus on the role social institutions and social structure have in our everyday lives. In fact, the idea of a lens used to view the world is why we decided to name this book *Focus on Social Problems: A Contemporary Reader*. We want readers to be reminded to use the appropriate lens—just as a photographer would—to see the world around them sharply: sometimes focusing closely on a subject, other times zooming out to get a sense of the bigger picture or context.

Mills argued that individuals often have trouble connecting the events of their lives to the larger society in which they live—for instance, how an individual's inability to find a job is connected to our capitalist economic system, where a financial downturn can result in downsizing and a reduction in available jobs. Understanding the history of a society can help explain the current structure of that society, which in turn can help explain how larger social forces affect the individual circumstances of members of the society. Our individual biography is not enough to understand our life chances, according to Mills; instead, we must consider the interplay between the individual and this history. Karen Sternheimer discusses an example of this intersection of history and biography, as described by Malcolm Gladwell in his book *Outliers*:

> [T]he so-called Robber Barons who became America's captains of industry in the late 1800s were mostly born within a few years of each other. People like Andrew Carnegie and John D. Rockefeller were born just a few years apart in the 1830s, as were many other business titans who amassed great wealth. Was there something particularly profitable in the water back then? Lessons taught in school at that time that would have led to their incredible achievements? As Gladwell points out, their timing couldn't have been better. Yes, they likely worked hard and had brilliant business minds. But they also came of age just as the industrial revolution was exploding in America. They were able to get in on the ground floor of advanced capitalism.[3]

---

3   Sternheimer, Karen. 2009. "Biography + History = Opportunity." *Everyday Sociology*. Retrieved on March 23, 2019, from https://nortonbooks.typepad.com/everydaysociology/2009/09/biography-history-opportunity.html.

Bill Gates and Steve Jobs, who were both born in 1955, were similarly influenced by the circumstances of where and when they were born. They both lived near where "supercomputers" (the giant, room-sized predecessors to today's computers and smart phones), were located when few people had access to them. Gates in particular had access to programming classes through his elite private high school, at a time when few colleges had such technology and courses.[4],[5] Of course, both Gates and Jobs worked hard and were visionaries, but without these initial advantages, would they have become two of the most influential figures of our time? The sociological imagination can be a difficult concept to grasp at first. Applying a sociological lens requires looking beyond individual circumstances and instead focusing on the social patterns that contribute to those circumstances, including historical, economic, political, familial, and global forces. Many of us have not been taught to think critically about the social structure (and social institutions) of which we are a part, to question why institutions exist the way they do, or to wonder who benefits from their continued existence or the maintenance of the status quo.

Distinguishing between two concepts, personal troubles and public issues, may help to clarify the sociological imagination. On the one hand, a *personal trouble* refers to an incident or challenge that takes place in a person's life; it "occurs within the character of an individual" and does not extend beyond the person's "immediate relationship with others . . . a trouble is a private matter."[6] *Public issues*, on the other hand, refer to the seemingly impersonal problems that are a result of larger social forces. They "have to do with matters that transcend these local environments of the individual and . . . [instead are the result of] the institutions of an historical society as a whole . . . [that] overlap and interpenetrate to form the larger structure of social and historical life."[7] A classic example, as mentioned above, is unemployment. If a person in a large city is unemployed, then that person's unemployment may be a personal trouble, and we may ask questions about that individual's skills, education level, or work ethic to understand why they are unemployed. But in a society like the United States—with nearly 163 million people in the labor force[8] and an additional 6.2 million unemployed[9]—we must look at the structure of the economy to understand why so many people are unemployed. Is there something about capitalist economies that makes it impossible for all people to be gainfully employed at all times? Employing a sociological imagination means looking beyond personal explanations ("that person is lazy and has a poor work

---

4   National Public Radio. 2008. "'Outliers' Puts Self-Made Success to the Test." November 18. Retrieved on March 23, 2019, from https://www.npr.org/templates/story/story.php?storyId=97117414.

5   Sternheimer, 2009.

6   Mills, C. Wright. 1959 [2000]. *The Sociological Imagination*, Fortieth Anniversary Edition. New York: Oxford University Press, p. 8.

7   Mills, 1959 [2000], pp. 8–9.

8   Bureau of Labor Statistics, U.S. Department of Labor. 2019. "United States Labor Force Statistics, Seasonally Adjusted." Retrieved on March 22, 2019, from https://data.bls.gov/pdq/SurveyOutputServlet?graph_name=LN_cpsbref1&request_action=wh.

9   As of March 2019, when the unemployment rate was 3.8 percent. Bureau of Labor Statistics, U.S. Department of Labor. 2019. "Labor Force Statistics from Current Population Survey, Seasonally Adjusted Unemployment Rate." Retrieved on March 22, 2019, from https://data.bls.gov/cgi-bin/surveymost.

ethic," or "they didn't study hard enough in school and that's why they don't have a job") to social and institutional forces. A sociological approach may argue that capitalism requires some employable, yet currently unemployed, people to be ready to step in and take over the jobs of the currently employed (what Karl Marx called "the reserve army of the poor"). This process helps keep wage demands down (and profits high) and keeps the workers from protesting or forming unions, as there is always the threat that they will be replaced by a member of the "reserve army." Or, rather than blaming the individual, we might look at the environment within which the person was educated and ask a series of questions about their educational experience. Were the schools they attended well funded, with caring and well-trained teachers, proper learning tools (including textbooks and technology), and in buildings that were properly maintained? Was their home life peaceful; their neighborhood safe and free of environmental contamination that can cause long-term health impacts; and did they have access to the resources that lead to successful educational outcomes, like trips to museums, zoos, libraries, after-school activities, or private tutors—the things that many middle- and upper-class children, for example, find easily accessible? Did they have the assistance many young people and their parents need in filling out financial aid forms for college; the funds for college testing preparation to raise their chances of acceptance and scholarships; the guidance and funds necessary to complete the college application and interview process; or the economic resources to secure loans necessary to attend college? Sociologists might also focus on the gatekeepers to gainful employment, inquiring whether they hold any biases based on race, gender, class, sexual identity, sex, or disabilities. These are the questions that arise when we start to think critically about the social nature and structural causes of social problems.

The sociological imagination is relevant to the social problems discussed in this reader because it encourages us to look to the system (our social institutions) as the main sources of social problems (a *system-blame* approach) as opposed to those who are suffering from the problems (a *person-blame* approach). Most of us have been taught to take the person-blame approach: to look at those who are different in some way—the poor, those who have committed crimes, those who are marginalized for one reason or another—and to think of them as the source of the problem, rather than the society itself.[10] We do this despite the fact that those who experience social problems have neither constructed nor controlled the institutions or conditions under which they suffer. Using a system-blame approach requires that we look beyond the individual to see how institutions, structures, and systems of oppression have contributed to the existence and perpetuation of these conditions. A sociological lens asks us to be critical of a system from which many of us acquire our deeply held values, such as individuality and the ideas of meritocracy and freedom of choice. Moreover, it asks us to question whether we benefit from the maintenance of the status quo in any way. Questioning these deeply held assumptions can be uncomfortable and unfamiliar, but it is key to taking a critical and sociological approach to understanding social problems.

Of course, maintaining a strict adherence to either system-blame or person-blame approaches has its consequences. Focusing too much on person-blame can result in leaving the

---

10 Eitzen, Stanley D., Maxine Baca Zinn, and Kelly Eitzen Smith. 2014. *Social Problems*, 13th ed. New York: Pearson Higher Education.

existing power structure and systems of inequality unchallenged and unchanged. Conversely, approaching every problem from a purely system-blame approach can oversimplify social problems wherein individuals are merely the products of their environment, with no free will or responsibility for their actions. Clearly, a balanced approach is needed, and the use of the sociological imagination fosters development of the oft-ignored system-blame approach.

DEFINING A SOCIAL PROBLEM

So what are social problems? Many books and textbooks focus on the sociological study of social problems, and each seems to contain a slightly different definition. For example, Eitzen, Baca Zinn, and Smith[11] define social problems as "societally induced conditions that cause psychic and material suffering for any segment of the population, and acts and conditions that violate the norms and values found in a society." Similarly, Mooney, Knox, and Schacht[12] propose that a social problem is "a social condition that a segment of society views as harmful to members of society and in need of remedy." Treviño[13] offers a slightly different definition, wherein a social problem is "a social condition, event, or pattern of behavior that negatively affects the well-being of a significant number of people (or a number of significant people) who believe the condition, event, or pattern needs to be changed or ameliorated." As you can see, the definitions may vary, but there are some key similarities. At the very least, nearly all definitions include the idea that a social problem is a *social condition* (rather than a purely physical ailment, for example) that causes harm to many people.

Many definitions integrate the role of "claims makers" in bringing the social problem to the attention of the general public or those in power. Claims makers can be individuals or groups, and they can hold a variety of positions in society, including political leaders, members of the media, advocates and activists, community or religious leaders, researchers and academics, or individual people.[14] Claims makers attempt to garner public attention for their social issue in the hopes that increased attention will translate to action on the part of citizens, lawmakers, or those in power, to help change the conditions that caused the problem or to help alleviate the suffering of the victims. This process, called *claims making*, essentially relies on "societal reaction and social definition. From this perspective, social problems come and go as societal reactions and responses to particular conditions change."[15]

Sociologists sometimes include additional elements within their definitions, for example, that social problems need to be recognized by people with power and influence or that people need to be actively trying to correct or ameliorate the condition for it to be defined as

11   Eitzen, Baca Zinn, and Smith, 2014, p. 10.
12   Mooney, Linda A., David Knox, and Caroline Schacht. 2015. *Understanding Social Problems*, 9th ed. Stamford, CT: Cengage Learning, p. 3.
13   Treviño, Javier. 2015. *Investigating Social Problems*. Thousand Oaks, CA: Sage, p. 6.
14   Spector, Malcolm, and John I. Kitsuse. 1977. *Constructing Social Problems*. New Brunswick, NJ: Transaction.
15   Perrin, Robin D., and Cindy L. Miller-Perrin. 2011. "Interpersonal Violence as Social Construction: The Potentially Undermining Role of Claims Making and Advocacy Statistics." *Journal of Interpersonal Violence* 26(15): 3033–49.

a social problem. These additions to definitions stress the importance of power in defining conditions as worthy of change, which reflects the reality that much of our understanding of social problems supports the interests of those who have power in our society. For example, a reading included in this book by Miriam Konrad and Angie Luvara questions why corporate crime is not considered as problematic as street crime, although it is arguably more costly and damaging to society (but more likely to be committed by those in power). Other readings ask why more attention is not paid to growing wealth inequality in America, to employment discrimination against minorities, to the expanding costs but declining quality of our health care system, or to the exploding prison population—all issues that are more likely to affect those with less power in society.

Many discussions of social problems include a comparison between *subjective* and *objective* components of problems. Objective components focus on measurable amounts of harm or the number of people affected by an issue, reasoning that if a large number of people are harmed, then the condition is a social problem. Claims makers often take this approach, using statistics to make the argument that the issue is serious and in need of change. While factual information is essential to understanding the scope and depth of social problems, challenges remain. The objective components rely on concepts on which there is little agreement. How many people is "a large number?" Is 10,000 enough? That might seem like a lot of people, but that is less than 0.003 percent of the population of the United States.[16] Do the conditions need to affect more than 10 percent of the U.S. population (more than 32 million people)? What counts as harm, and what is the threshold we should use to establish whether someone has been harmed? Students often ask us if localized phenomena (like the Flint water crisis) are social problems in and of themselves, since they would seem to impact a smaller number of people than, say, unemployment. We tend to ask them to think more broadly and to see crises such as Flint's as instances of larger social problems—for example, our lack of investment in infrastructure; race and class discrimination; and corporations profiting from—and in some cases causing—environmental degradation.

One of the challenges with relying solely on objective definitions of social problems is that they so often rely on numbers, statistics, and data that can have unclear origins, aren't grounded in sociological research methods, or just don't make sense. Joel Best offers an example in his book *Damned Lies and Statistics*[17]: a statistic which claimed that "every year since 1950, the number of American children gunned down has doubled."

> What makes this statistic so bad? Just for the sake of argument, let's assume that "the number of American children gunned down" in 1950 was one. If the number doubled each year, there must have been two children gunned down in 1951, four in 1952, eight in 1953, and so on. By 1960, the number would have been 1,024. By 1965, it would

---

16 Based on a U.S. population in March 2019 of 328 million people (U.S. Census Bureau. U.S. and World Population Clock. Retrieved on March 22, 2019, from http://www.census.gov/popclock.

17 Best, Joel. 2012. *Damned Lies and Statistics: Untangling Issues from the Media, Politicians, and Activists.* Berkeley, CA: University of California Press, p. 2.

have been 32,768 (in 1965, the FBI identified only 9,960 criminal homicides in the entire country, including adult as well as child victims). By 1970, the number would have passed one million; by 1980, one billion (more than four times the total U.S. population in that year). . . . By 1995 . . . the annual number of victims would have been over 35 trillion—a really big number, of a magnitude you rarely encounter outside economics or astronomy.

It's easy to accept a statistic like the one that confounded Best when we consider the fact that we are often "awestruck" by statistics, and our lack of critical thought imbues them with even more power. Statistics are indeed critical to understanding our social world and the social problems we encounter; otherwise, we would have no idea about how many people were experiencing a given problem. We should therefore approach statistics thoughtfully, rather than accepting them blindly or rejecting them all outright as attempts to manipulate us. This begins by recognizing that, as Best points out, "every social statistic reflects the choices that go into producing it. The key choices involve definition and methodology: whenever we count something, we must first define what it is we hope to count, and then choose the methods by which we will go about counting."[18] When you encounter statistics about social problems—including those in the readings in this book—you should ask yourself:

> What might be the sources for this number? How could one go about producing the figure? Who produced the number, and what interests might they have? What are the different ways key terms might have been defined, and which definitions have been chosen? How might the phenomena be measured, and which measurement choices have been made? What sort of sample was gathered, and how might that sample affect the result? Is the statistic being properly interpreted? Are comparisons being made, and if so, are the comparisons appropriate? Are there competing statistics? If so, what stakes do the opponents have in the issue, and how are those stakes likely to affect their use of statistics? And is it possible to figure out why the statistics seem to disagree, what the differences are in the ways the competing sides are using figures?[19]

In addition to understanding the objective nature of social problems, sociologists also seek to understand their subjective nature, which usually begins with a discussion about how social problems are socially constructed. Social construction is a process in which people generate meanings and understandings of their social world through interacting with one another.[20] Focusing on this aspect of social problems means developing an understanding of how social conditions come to be seen or "discovered" as a problem. This process begins with claims makers identifying a problem in need of resolution and then attempting to bring attention to the problem. These claims makers enter an already crowded field. After all, as

---

18 Best, Joel. 2001. "Promoting Bad Statistics." *Society*, 38(3): 10–15.
19 Best, 2012, p. 169.
20 Berger, Peter L., and Thomas Luckmann. 1966. *The Social Construction of Reality: A Treatise in the Sociology of Knowledge*. New York: Doubleday.

Best argued, "there are many causes and a limited amount of space on the front page of the *New York Times*. Advocates must find ways to make their claims compelling."[21] Claims makers essentially define a social problem: they identify an issue, bring public attention to it, and when members of the society accept these claims, the issue becomes a social problem. As Perrin and Miller-Perrin summarize it: "social problems, then, are essentially 'discovered' through this process of societal reaction and social definition. From this perspective, social problems come and go as societal reactions and responses to particular conditions change."[22]

A classic example of the subjective nature and process of the social construction and "discovery" of a social problem focuses on child abuse. Until the 1960s, there were no laws in the United States protecting children from abuse by their caretakers.[23] Although advances in the rights of children had been made prior to this point, there was little attention to the issue of child abuse from those in the legal, political, or social welfare fields who had "little incentive for interfering with an established power set—the parent over the child."[24] Members of the general public were largely unconcerned with the issue as well, and studies at the time concluded that most people were tolerant of, and even empathetic toward, those who had been accused or convicted of abusing a child.[25] Attempts to deal with child abuse were framed as preventing future harm to society in the form of "future delinquents . . . it was the children, not their abusive guardians, who felt the weight of the moral crusade."[26]

So, although the condition and experience of child abuse had existed for thousands of years, it wasn't until the 1940s and 1950s that pediatric radiologists—those who X-ray children admitted to the hospital with traumatic injuries—first "discovered" child abuse in the form of broken bones and skeletal traumas.[27] An article in the *Journal of the American Medical Association* entitled "The Battered Child Syndrome" labeled child abuse as an "illness" that children might be suffering from, making it more likely that doctors would be willing to "see" abuse, as well as seeing abusive parents as people who needed help. Various social welfare organizations joined in the call for more attention to the issue, arguing that children should be examined for child abuse symptoms; law enforcement advocates argued that child abuse should be criminalized and offenders prosecuted. Buttressed by the "objective" voices of doctors and law enforcement, the media coverage of this "new" condition of child abuse was prolific. In reaction to this increased attention and public outcry, over the course of four years (beginning in 1962), all fifty states had passed legislation to deal with the new problem of child abuse.[28] In this case, radiologists, doctors, social welfare organizations, and law enforcement officials all became claims makers, advocating for a reframing of

21   Best, 2001.
22   Perrin, Robin D., and Cindy L. Miller-Perrin. 2011. "Interpersonal Violence as Social Construction: The Potentially Undermining Role of Claims Making and Advocacy Statistics." *Journal of Interpersonal Violence* 26(15): 3033–49, 3035.
23   Pfohl, Stephen J. 1977. "The Discovery of Child Abuse." *Social Problems* 14(3): 310–23.
24   Pfohl, 1977, p. 314.
25   Pfohl, 1977.
26   Pfohl, 1977, p. 311.
27   Pfohl, 1977.
28   Pfohl, 1977.

our understanding of child abuse from a "private" issue into a social problem that needed public legislative intervention. Because this reframing was successful, we now view child abuse as a serious social problem with individual and societal consequences.

A more contemporary example is the issue of using a cell phone while driving. Although today most people acknowledge that driving while talking on a cell phone is risky and many states have made using a cell phone while driving illegal, in the recent past this was not the case. As Parilla[29] demonstrates, concern about the distraction and possible fatal consequences that come from texting or talking while driving began to increase in the early 2000s, as cell phone use increased and more claims makers (including government officials, celebrities, and members of law enforcement) began to publicly warn about the dangers of distracted driving. Parilla argues that the key to the success of this movement was garnering media attention and support; after all, claims makers had to convince the public that something they did nearly every day was, in fact, dangerous. Garnering support meant relying on shifting definitions (e.g., initially focusing on handheld rather than hands-free devices; then banning cell phone use for new drivers rather than more experienced ones; and, finally, making an increased push against the broader problem of "distracted driving"). The media played an important role in guiding the public's understanding of the issue as a problem. From 1984 to 2010, the period of time during which Parilla reviewed newspaper articles about cell phone use as the cause of traffic accidents, the vast majority of articles presented the claim that driving while on the phone caused accidents but offered no *counterclaim* or alternative discussion about or viewpoint on the issue. Parilla found that only 15 percent of the articles presented a counterclaim (for example, that eating and driving may be the cause of traffic accidents rather than cell phone use).[30] We frequently see counterclaims in discussions of many social problems today (e.g., global warming/climate change), where there is disagreement not only about the scope and impact of the problem, but about whether the issue is a problem at all. This highlights the importance of the media not only in disseminating claims, but also in framing how we understand an issue to be a social problem.

THE ROLE OF AMERICAN CULTURAL VALUES IN DEFINING AND UNDERSTANDING SOCIAL PROBLEMS

One of the challenges in applying a sociological lens to understanding social problems is that you may need to reconcile this lens with the cultural values many of us have absorbed since childhood. These values have become important parts of our belief systems and the way we understand the world, and they influence how we come to understand social problems, in particular, whether we are likely to take a person- or system-blame approach when thinking about causes and solutions to social problems. In this section, we discuss some common American cultural values such as individualism and meritocracy and how they influence our understanding of social problems.

---

29 Parilla, Peter F. 2013. "Cell Phone Use While Driving: Defining a Problem as Worthy of Action." In *Making Sense of Social Problems: New Images, New Issues*, Joel Best and Scott R. Harris, eds. (pp. 27–46). Boulder, CO: Reiner.
30 Parilla, 2013.

American culture has long emphasized the rights and responsibilities of the individual rather than the social group, resulting in an individualistic culture that attributes what happens to individuals to their effort, will, and self-reliance rather than to their social circumstances, random fate, or the actions of others.[31] These are the basic tenets of the American Dream, a term first coined by James Truslow Adams in 1931: "that dream of a land in which life should be better and richer and fuller for every man, with opportunity for each according to his ability or achievement."[32] There are religious, political, economic, historical, and social foundations for the American Dream—far more than we can discuss in this brief introduction—but the crux of the ideology (based partly on our democratic political system) is that America is a land of equality of opportunity, and the only barrier to success people face is themselves. Closely connected to the idea of individualism is the concept of meritocracy. Meritocracy is the idea that individuals' success is based on their individual talent, ability, and desire to work hard—that you get out of the system what you put into it—and that people can move up in the society through this effort.[33]

Americans have a strong belief in meritocracy and individualism. For example, the Pew Research Center found in 2012 that 75 percent of Americans believed "everyone has it in their own power to succeed"; 58 percent agreed that "most people who want to get ahead can make it if they're willing to work hard"; and 90 percent of Americans said they "admire people who got rich through hard work."[34] Americans endorse more individualistic ideologies than do most people around the globe.[35] For example, Americans are less likely to agree with the belief that coming from a wealthy family is "essential or very important to getting ahead" than are people from other countries, and are more likely than people from other countries to say they believe that people get rewarded for intelligence, skill, and hard work.[36]

These beliefs about the value of hard work, individual effort, and self-reliance influence people's perspectives on the causes of social problems and possible solutions. For example, if you believe that with hard work and effort anyone can get ahead, you may be less likely to support programs that support those in poverty, perhaps because you believe they are poor because of their own personal failings. Research on attitudes toward government support for the poor bears this out: Americans are far less likely to support social safety net programs that help support people in need compared to citizens in western Europe. For

---

31   Fischer, Claude S. 2008. "Paradoxes of American Individualism." *Sociological Forum* 23(2): 2.

32   McNamee, Stephen J. 2018. *The Meritocracy Myth*, Fourth Edition. Lanham, MD: Rowan and Littlefield, p. 2.

33   McNamee, 2018.

34   Pew Research Center. 2012. "For the Public, It's Not about Class Warfare, but Fairness." Retrieved on March 22, 2019, from https://www.people-press.org/2012/03/02/for-the-public-its-not-about-class-warfare-but-fairness.

35   Pew Research Center. 2014. "Emerging and Developing Economies Much More Optimistic than Rich Countries about the Future." Retrieved on March 22, 2019, from https://www.pewglobal.org/2014/10/09/emerging-and-developing-economies-much-more-optimistic-than-rich-countries-about-the-future/pg_14-09-04_usindividualism_640-px.

36   Pew Charitable Trusts Economic Mobility Project. "Economic Mobility: Is the American Dream Alive and Well?" Retrieved on March 22, 2019, from https://www.pewtrusts.org/-/media/legacy/uploadedfiles/wwwpewtrustsorg/reports/economic_mobility/empamericandreamreportpdf.pdf.

example, when asked whether it was the responsibility of the government to "care for very poor people who can't take care of themselves," more than 50 percent of Swedes, British, Spanish, and Germans strongly agreed, whereas only 22 percent of Americans strongly agreed.[37] Similarly, 58 percent of Americans said that it was more important for "people to have the freedom to pursue their life's goals" than to have the government "guarantee nobody was in need" (35 percent); these numbers are essentially reversed for citizens of western European countries.[38] The influence of these cultural values can extend to social problems beyond poverty; it's not hard to imagine how strong endorsement of the values of individualism and self-reliance and a belief in meritocracy might impact an individual's perspective on affirmative action, affordable health care, environmental regulation, or criminal rehabilitation programs. Endorsement of the meritocracy ideology also has ramifications for an individual's mental health and sense of self-esteem. Research published in 2017 indicated that young people from racial, ethnic, or economically marginalized backgrounds who grew up believing in the meritocratic ideals of hard work and perseverance showed a decline in self-esteem and an increase in risky behaviors when they were in their early teens. As Erin Godfrey, the lead researcher, described in an interview, kids from privileged positions (either because of their race, class, or gender) believe the system is fair and feel little conflict about whether their success was achieved fairly. But for kids who come from marginalized backgrounds, believing that the system is inherently fair can create challenging questions: "'If the system is fair, why am I seeing that everybody who has brown skin is in this kind of job? You're having to think about that . . . like you're not as good, or your social group isn't as good.'"[39] As you can see, these values have consequences not only for how we view social problems and our fellow citizens, but also how we view our self-worth.

These values of individualism and meritocracy, embodied by the American Dream, act as the foundation for many Americans' value systems. It can therefore be challenging to examine these values or to read materials that demonstrate that these closely held values are falling short of their ideal. Throughout this book, you'll find readings that demonstrate, for example, that there are significant barriers to upward social mobility, especially for people of color; that seeking a higher education and working hard do not always guarantee economic success for individuals or their families; that the social safety net is failing many individuals and communities; and that discrimination and bias still play an active role in our society, no matter how much we strive to provide equality for everyone. We encourage you to approach these readings with an open mind and to use a sociological approach to understanding the causes and consequences of social problems by acknowledging the role that institutions and social structures play in our lives.

---

37 Stokes, Bruce. 2013. "Public Attitudes toward the Next Social Contract." New America Foundation. Retrieved on March 22, 2019, from https://assets.pewresearch.org/wp-content/uploads/sites/2/pdf/Stokes_Bruce_NAF_Public_Attitudes_1_2013.pdf): 5.

38 Stokes, 2013, p. 7.

39 Anderson, Melinda D. 2017. "Why the Myth of Meritocracy Hurts Kids of Color." *The Atlantic*, July 27. Retrieved on March 22, 2019, from https://www.theatlantic.com/education/archive/2017/07/internalizing-the-myth-of-meritocracy/535035.

THEORETICAL FOUNDATIONS

Sociologists use different theoretical perspectives to help them explore the causes and consequences of social problems. As we selected readings to include in this book, several theoretical perspectives guided our choices. Although Mills emphasizes the importance of examining the social structure and social conditions to understand the lived experiences of one's self and others, he did not emphasize the process by which social problems come to be defined and recognized as such. When people interact, share ideas, and begin to create meaning and understandings of a particular situation[40] (as the result of claims making, for example), they are engaging in the social construction of a social problem. Social constructionism, or how we create ideas and define social problems through our interaction, helps us understand part of the "story" of social problems. But we believe that social constructionism, as a theoretical perspective, doesn't go far enough analytically.

Critical constructionism acknowledges that the process by which social problems come to be defined as such is a political process, where the desires of those who have the most power in society (political power, economic power, and so on) hold the most sway in the social problem construction process (see, for example, readings in Chapter 2 by Stiglitz and by Vidmar). This power is defined as the ability to maintain or change the social structure in society. Critical constructionism assumes that those who have the most power will generally influence social structures in such a way as to maintain their power. Furthermore, those who have the most power to shape policy and control institutions (like education, media, or government) have the most resources at their disposal to influence the ideas of everyone in the society, thereby helping shore up their own positions and maintain the status quo. Critical constructionism encourages us to acknowledge that those with the fewest resources must work significantly harder to have their voices heard and that a main avenue to creating change may be to convince those in power that it is in their own interest to solve a social problem.[41]

We also sought to use an intersectional perspective in our selection of readings, recognizing that race, social class, gender, sexual identity, and other categories intersect to create unique experiences of oppression and discrimination within different contexts.[42] For example, Black women are affected by discrimination in ways that may differ from the experiences of both White women and Black men. Further, Black women's class backgrounds and sexual identities can result in different experiences of discrimination *among* Black women.[43] We try to capture the experience of these intersections in readings such as "The Second

---

40 Berger and Luckman, 1966.

41 Heiner, Robert. 2013. *Social Problems: An Introduction to Critical Constructionism*. New York: Oxford University Press.

42 Collins, Patricia Hill. 2000. *Black Feminist Thought*. New York: Routledge; Collins, Patricia Hill. 2004. *Black Sexual Politics*. New York: Routledge; Crenshaw, Kimberlé Williams. 1989. "Demarginalizing the Intersection of Race And Sex: A Black Feminist Critique of Antidiscrimination Doctrine, Feminist Theory, and Antiracist Politics." *University of Chicago Legal Forum* 1(8): 139–67.

43 Collins, 2000; Collins, 2004; Wingfield, Adia Harvey. 2019. "Reclaiming Our Time": Black Women, Resistance, and Rising Inequality." *Gender & Society* 33(3): 1–18.

Racial Wealth Gap," "The Eviction Economy," "The Fault in Our Scores," "Why America's Black Mothers and Babies Are in a Life-and-Death Crisis," and "About Those 79 Cents." These are just some examples of the ways in which the readings in this book foreground how race, class, and gender, in particular, intersect in unique and sometimes particularly virulent ways across a variety of social problems. Although there are many ways to define social problems and theoretical lenses with which to view them, this book is designed to illustrate how social problems come to be defined as such and, more importantly, to share the extent and causes of the social conditions of our society so that you, as changemakers, can approach them from a deep and broad base of sociological knowledge.

SOCIAL CHANGE

The readings in this book will highlight just how entrenched many social problems are in our society; we want you to understand the scope of the conditions (from everyday instances of discrimination and bias to more systemic ones, for example) that create suffering in the lives of those affected directly by social problems.[44] As the readings in this book (and some of the examples mentioned in this introduction) demonstrate, social problems are often interrelated and cumulative in nature. An individual born into poverty may be exposed to hazardous environmental conditions that impede physical and mental development and then go on to attend a poorly funded public school that lacks the resources to teach the vast number of skills needed to succeed in college and in the job market, all of which may damage long-term economic prospects. Individuals who live in an impoverished area with few economic opportunities may turn to petty crime to survive, resulting in arrests or time spent in jail; a criminal record may subsequently affect their ability to get and keep a good job to provide for themselves and their families.

The realization that so many social problems are interrelated and that solutions are often hard to come by may cause students to feel powerless. Yet, it is important to remember that although our actions are constrained by social institutions and the structure of our society, we retain individual and collective agency—the ability to act to create change for ourselves and others. Interviews with activists working to solve social problems begin each chapter in this book. We selected interviewees from a wide range of organizations (national, state, and local), who hold diverse kinds of positions (from interns to directors), and who tackle myriad social problems included in this book. We included these interviews to give you a glimpse into the ways that individuals and groups (small and large) can create social change on issues they are passionate about. After all, humans built the structures that reproduce our social problems, and thus they can also adapt, alter, or replace such structures.

---

44 Best, Joel. 2002. "Constructing the Sociology of Social Problems: Spector and Kitsuse Twenty-Five Years Later." *Sociological Forum* 17(4): 699–706.

CHAPTER 2

WEALTH AND INCOME INEQUALITY

Researchers have documented how since the 1970s, the rich have gotten richer and the poor have gotten poorer as a result of policies and large-scale economic changes. They examined this increasing inequality by measuring growing gaps in income (wages) and wealth (assets like homes and investments, minus debts). For example, in the 1960s, families near the top of the economic ladder had six times the wealth of families in the middle of the ladder, but by 2016, families near the top of the economic ladder had twelve times the amount of wealth as the families in the middle.[1] Americans are concerned about this growing inequality. They know that assets (such as owning a home) offer financial stability, a safety net during emergencies, an ability to invest in education and business opportunities, and support for a healthy retirement. They also know that the costs of this inequality extend beyond individuals' net worth. Gallup surveys indicate that around 60 percent of Americans believe that current income and wealth distributions are unfair. These attitudinal data have remained relatively constant for over three decades.[2] In the first reading in this chapter, Michael I. Norton gauges Americans' understanding of economic inequality in the United States, asking research respondents to estimate current inequality and assess what level of inequality would be "ideal." Despite their concern about wealth inequality, Americans tend to underestimate current levels to a significant extent. While they are not seeking "total equality" as an ideal, they also consistently show support for much more equitable distributions of income and wealth than currently exist.

Both Michael I. Norton and Renee M. Shelby demonstrate that the costs of economic inequality go beyond inherent unfairness and diminishing the life chances of individuals,

---

1 Anon. 2017. "Nine Charts about Wealth Inequality in America (Updated)." Urban.org. Retrieved February 4, 2019, from http://urbn.is/wealthcharts.
2 Newport, Frank. 2015. "Americans Continue to Say U.S. Wealth Distribution Is Unfair." Gallup.Com. Retrieved February 4, 2019, from https://news.gallup.com/poll/182987/americans-continue-say-wealth-distribution-unfair.aspx.

and that the inequality itself damages our economy and society by demotivating lower-wage workers, encouraging unethical behavior, stunting economic growth, intensifying inflation, and compromising democratic principles. Shelby demonstrates how rising economic inequality has led to a society in which few people are able to move up the income and wealth ladders. As the rich get richer and the poor get poorer, the middle class, once economically strong, continues to face hardship and stagnation. Edward McClellan's reading offers a reason for the weakening middle class, arguing that as we've moved from a manufacturing economy (where workers were typically unionized) to a service economy (where they are typically nonunionized), White-collar workers—whose positions now require college degrees—earn low salaries and have no union leverage to bargain for higher wages consistent with middle-class economic stability. These large-scale economic changes in job structure certainly contribute to our increasing economic inequality.

While Americans in general suffer from increasing economic inequality, it is important to note that they do not all suffer equally. Some groups of Americans, owing to past and current patterns of exploitation, fare much worse than others. Researchers have documented a substantial racial wealth gap that has persisted for decades. A recent study of median net worth (assets minus debts) in American households found that nonimmigrant African American households in Boston had an average of $8 in net worth compared to $247,500 for White households![3] Another study found that the average White family had six times more liquid retirement savings compared to average African American and Latinx families.[4] The readings in this chapter by Dedrick Asante-Muhammad et al. and Mel Jones document major gaps in income and wealth inequality by race, discussing their origins, growth, and consequences.

While some groups suffer disproportionately from economic inequality, others have benefited financially and politically as a result. The social movement Occupy Wall Street called attention to the "1 Percent" or the ultra-wealthy in society. The readings on this topic by both Joseph E. Stiglitz and Chris M. Vidmar demonstrate that with income and wealth come an interest in and the power to support policies that enhance one's own financial position, even to the detriment of others and the greater good of society. This manifests particularly in the area of political campaign contributions. Vidmar documents how a small number of ultra-wealthy donors are able to use their economic resources to sway political policies to best serve their own interests, enhancing their power and further increasing economic inequality.

Reducing economic inequality, in the face of large-scale economic changes such as the decline in manufacturing and the increase in globalization, will require political will and some creative policies. An economic system and policies that have favored the wealthy have increased our inequality over time; new policies have the capacity to counter current trends. The American public wants to see change, for the sake of our economy and our democracy.

---

3   Muñoz, Ana Patricia, Marlene Kim, Mariko Chang, Regine O. Jackson, Darrick Hamilton, and William A. Darity Jr. 2015. "The Color of Wealth in Boston." Federal Reserve Bank of Boston. Retrieved February 4, 2019, from https://www.bostonfed.org/publications/one-time-pubs/color-of-wealth.aspx.

4   Anon. 2017a. "Nine Charts about Wealth Inequality in America (Updated)." Urban Institute. Retrieved February 4, 2019, from http://urbn.is/wealthcharts.

SAM NELSON

Sam Nelson is an organizer with Jobs With Justice

What is the mission of your organization, and what types of work do you do in your position?

The mission of Jobs With Justice (JWJ) is to build the power of working-class communities across the United States and internationally. Our central focus is expanding the right to collectively bargain (for example, advocating for things like fair wages, safe working conditions, and high-quality benefits). We believe collective bargaining is central both to working-class people having the ability to control their lives and a healthy democracy. Collective bargaining should not be limited to just workers and their employer, but can be expanded to tenants and their landlords, community residents, and banks or other corporate entities, or communities and the police. We achieve this goal by running strategic campaigns around new forms of worker organization, policy formation, and building coalitions. We also do bread-and-butter solidarity work with workers and communities like turning out to pickets and helping bring community members into union fights (we've recently mobilized with Stop and Shop workers in Massachusetts, Little Big Burger, and Burgerville workers in Portland, Oregon, and University of Illinois-Chicago graduate students on strike in Chicago).

I'm on our organizing team, so I develop and maintain relationships with our local coalitions. I cover retail (scheduling and hours reform, minimum wage, retail worker organizing), e-commerce (worker organizing), and the global supply chain (working with our partners in Asia Floor Wage Alliance, who are supporting Asia workers' attempts to directly negotiate for a living wage with garment brands like Gap and H&M).

How did you first become interested in this type of activism?

It aligned with my long-held vaguely liberal politics. My parents both made sure I kept up with the news (my dad works at a newspaper). Early on, they instilled in me the importance of antiracism, being a good neighbor, etc. But when the recession hit, the material reality of work in the United States hit me. My dad's workplace shrank dramatically, and for years he came home worried about being laid off. The psychological toll of uncertainty combined with the financial toll of not getting raises for years (even though you're doing more and more work), strained everyone in the family, and our family wasn't alone. I resolved to do "activity" things in college to get over some of that feeling of helplessness the recession brought on.

I went to George Washington University (GWU) on a scholarship and loans. I joined an organization on campus called the Progressive Student Union (PSU). It was through PSU and their affiliation with DC Jobs With Justice that I learned about labor movements and workers' rights, and how GWU was violating them every day. I was given tools to actually build power with workers so they could take the lead themselves, and not rely on others to advocate for them.

How did you get your current job?

PSU was an affiliate of the Student Labor Action Project (SLAP), which at the time was the student program of Jobs With Justice. We were also a member of the local DC Jobs With Justice coalition. I had some mentors in the organization who introduced me to that wider world. The national SLAP Coordinator for JWJ at the time taught me a lot of nuts and bolts about how to organize and analyze power. It was through my work in PSU, helping build that organization over about two years, that my mentors helped me develop as a leader. After one of them graduated, he asked me to take his spot on the DC Jobs With Justice steering committee, which decides campaigns, approves new members, and helps coordinate among all the various groups. It was also during that summer that I got an internship at national Jobs With Justice and worked on student organizing around student debt and various other issues. At the time of my graduation, I was deeply integrated into JWJ's extensive national network of activists and organizers. When a job opened up for a position in the national office about a year after I graduated, I applied. I was picked both because of the relationships I had developed and my experience within the organization. I deeply understood what the organization was about and how it functioned.

What strategies do you try to use to enact social change in your area of activism?

The core of JWJ's work is relationship building. If you're not in reciprocal, long-term relationship with the people you are organizing with, you're going to have a hard time. Also at the core is our analysis of power: What is our power? What is the opponent's power? How can we disrupt theirs? We learn this through our national training program so that JWJ activists have a common understanding of these concepts and we're all using the same playbook. From there, strategies depend on what's needed. For example, if it's a policy fight, like the Retail Workers Bill of Rights in San Francisco,[1] we organize groups of workers who would benefit from that policy to help craft it, talk to legislators about it, and integrate other members of the community who may not be directly affected. Then once it's passed, those workers can continue to organize to ensure it is enforced. All strategies are centered on workers leading on their own behalf and setting us up for the next fight through a campaign.

What are the major challenges activists in your field face?

Individual activists face "burnout" a lot. This is hard work. Because of the social justice nature of it, many of us push ourselves to our breaking points. We teach in our training program that we need to practice "self-interest," the idea that you are in a relationship with yourself and the community, so that if you are completely selfless you may burn out and actually harm campaigns.

As with any movement, racism and sexism exist to varying degrees. Some unions tend to be "male, pale and stale" as the saying goes, so it can be a challenge for women organizers and organizers of color to do the work. This is where solidarity is incredibly important within our organizations, so we can stand with our fellow organizers if they are being subjected to racism or sexism internally or externally.

Organizationally, there is the constant issue of funding. Foundation funding sometimes comes with strings attached or ebbs and flows with interest in a certain area, and grassroots funding is a whole body of work unto itself. There's also the reality that worker organizing doesn't get a lot of attention from funders in general. Actually, building power so that workers can confront their bosses and companies isn't always palatable to those with the power and money to fund our efforts.

(*continued*)

What would you consider to be your greatest successes as an activist in this area of activism?

Personally, it's been the work with the Asia Floor Wage Alliance. I've helped build our international program with them, so now we are working in concert, targeting brands that have their clothes manufactured by workers across South and Southeast Asia. We've been able to make interventions at the International Labor Organization, and we've gotten Gap to the table with Asia Floor Wage Alliance to discuss solutions to gender-based violence in their supply chains. We've demonstrated that we can have an international labor movement, but that it takes mutual respect and having the workers in the Global South lead.

What are major misconceptions the public has about activism in general and your issue specifically?

Around activism in general, I'd say it's that we're all trust fund kinds who don't know the real world. Yet I come from a working-class background, as do most of my colleagues. Most people I meet in this work are in it because they know what it's like to have a bad boss or to have your life thrown into disarray because of decisions made by a company you have no control over. Most people are doing this work because they know it's going to take a movement of people affected by these issues to build power collectively so we can solve them.

With the labor movement specifically, it's the idea behind the incredibly problematic term *big labor*, which implies that unions are corrupt, out of touch, or unduly influencing politics. Yet 90 percent of Americans do not belong to unions, and union political contributions pale in comparison to the many multinational companies and their lobbyists and campaign contributions that have immense influence in our political system. Labeling labor unions "just another special interest group" is disingenuous, as unions right now are the only organizations that are composed of working-class people of all faiths, races, genders, and geographies that are trying to make the world better materially. There are problems for sure, and no one will list the problems of the labor movement more readily than those of us in the labor movement, but we know that the alternative is increased power

of companies, and as I said in my experience with the recession, that leads to powerlessness.

Why should students get involved in your line of activism?

The labor movement still skews older, yet young people are the age group most likely to agree with the mission of unions. We need a generational shift that both respects those that came before and allows younger generations to take leadership and change the labor movement for the better. Movements in fast food, tech, and education are all largely led by young people.

If an individual has little money and time, are there other ways they can contribute?

Reading groups are always a good entry point. You can also turn out for a picket line or protest. Have events on campus or in the community where you have speakers come and talk about the movement. Just remember to get outside of your comfort zone.

What ways can college students enact social change in their daily lives?

Students should not simply focus on social change as individuals, but how they can play their part in a movement. At the very base level it's building relationships with your fellow students, but also the workers on your campus. Dining hall workers, bus drivers, janitors, and clerical workers all have stories that may align with yours. Your own personal consumer boycott can't do much, but if you organize your boycott like the Coalition of Immokalee Workers' current boycott of Wendy's or the boycott of Driscoll's Berries last year called by farmworkers in the United States and Mexico, then you amplify your individual influence.

NOTE

1. The Retail Workers Bill of Rights in San Francisco ensured five protections for hourly retail workers in the city: "promoting full time work and access to hours . . . encouraging fair predictable schedules . . . discouraging abusive on-call scheduling practices . . . equal treatment for part-time workers . . . encouraging worker retention and job security." (http://retailworkerrights.com/get-the-facts)

MICHAEL I. NORTON

1. UNEQUALITY

Who Gets What and Why It Matters

How unequal do you think income and wealth are in the United States? How unequal should they be *ideally*? Norton explores the current patterns of income and wealth inequality and discusses how accurate Americans are at estimating current levels of economic inequality. Americans tend both to underestimate economic inequality and to share a common desire for a more equal (and yet not totally equal) society. Norton describes some of the psychological and behavioral costs of economic inequality that should motivate making societal changes to decrease economic inequality.

INTRODUCTION

From Occupy Wall Street to the Tea Party, from slogans like "We are the 99%" to "We are the 47%," from debates about universal health care to the minimum wage, questions about who should get what drive many of the most heated policy debates—and debates at the kitchen table. And these debates are not limited to the United States, as evidenced by movements from Occupy Armenia to Occupy Nigeria to Occupy Seoul and worker strikes around the world demanding higher wages. How countries deal with rising inequality—and how citizens push their governments to address inequality—is a critical issue with trickle-down effects to nearly every other issue, from early childhood education to job training to immigration policy. For each, policymakers and citizens are forced to answer the question: Who should get what?

Income and wealth inequality in the United States have increased dramatically since the 1980s to levels not seen since just before the Great Depression in the 1930s (Keister, 2000; Wolff, 2002). In contrast to previous periods in American history, nearly all of the new income and wealth generated over the last decades has gone to the richest Americans. From 2009 to 2012, the incomes of the top 1% grew by 31.4%, whereas the incomes of the bottom 99% grew only by 0.4%, such that the top 1% got 95% of the income gains in these years (Piketty & Saez, 2014). The Great Recession brought the stark differences in outcomes for rich and poor into sharp contrast. For example, research shows that, while gains in income have little positive impact on people's well-being, losses in income have a much larger negative impact: Getting richer does not feel nearly as good as getting poorer feels bad (Boyce, Wood, Banks, Clark, & Brown, 2013; De Neve et al., 2014). Or compare the enormous bonuses paid to CEOs—even CEOs of underperforming companies—to data suggesting that nearly 50% of Americans report that they would be unable to come up with US$2,000 in 30 days, no matter how many sources they tapped (Lusardi, Schneider, & Tufano, 2011).

But what is the right level of inequality? Economists have used historical data to attempt to determine when and why inequality has positive and negative consequences at the macroeconomic level (see Piketty, 2014). Behavioral scientists—both psychologists and behavioral economists—have taken a different and complementary approach, examining the consequences of inequality at the microlevel: How inequality affects the thoughts, emotions, and behavior of a single person in

Republished with permission of SAGE Publications from Norton, M. I. (2014). Unequality: Who Gets What and Why It Matters. Policy Insights from the Behavioral and Brain Sciences, 1(1), 151–155. https://doi.org/10.1177/2372732214550167.

worlds that are more or less unequal, and how that person's rank in each world—from richest to poorest—further shapes behaviors ranking from cheating to effort to generosity. People strongly believe that the current levels of inequality are unfair, but they rarely want perfect equality (Kiatpongsan & Norton, 2014; Norton & Ariely, 2011). Moreover, people from all walks of life—rich and poor, liberal and conservative—agree far more than they disagree on what America should look like. People exhibit a desire for *unequality*—not too equal but not too unequal.

Two approaches inform what the ideal level of unequality might be. First, my research with my colleagues simply asks citizens directly what they think the right level is: In other words, if people in the United States and all over the world are asked how they think resources such as wealth and income should be distributed among people, what do they think is ideal? These data—laypeople's sense of an ideal distribution—offer one input into understanding the ideal level of inequality. Second, experimental research varies levels of inequality and people's rank in those more-and-less equal distributions, revealing that too much inequality can exert a negative impact on crucial outcomes: overall productivity, decision making (including people's tendency to gamble), and likelihood of engaging in both ethical and unethical behavior. On each of these metrics, inequality comes with costs not just to poor and middle-class Americans, but to the rich as well.

BUILDING A BETTER AMERICA—ONE WEALTH QUINTILE AND WAGE GAP AT A TIME

My recent research takes a novel approach to inequality, focusing not on what is bad about inequality and the bitter debates surrounding inequality, but attempting to show that people all over the world in fact have a strong shared vision of who should get what.

People volunteer to play the "desert island game." Here's how it works: In some domain of inequality—say, wealth— people are asked to step back from the current political climate and from their notions about what policies should be implemented right now, and join a desert island thought experiment—where they get to play the dictator (or social engineer). People consider what they would do if they got to start over

from scratch and decide how things should ideally be distributed among people. How much would you give to the wealthy in your new ideal society? To the middle class? To the poor? These data are the first input to determining who should get what.

Think about the richest 20%—the "top quintile"—of Americans for a moment. In other words, rank all Americans in order and count down from the richest person until you are one-fifth of the way down that list.

Now answer this question:

Of all the wealth in the United States, what percent do you think the richest 20% of Americans own? _____%

Now play the desert island game. How would you answer if you could start over from scratch and build your ideal society?

Of all the wealth in the United States, what percent do you think the richest 20% of Americans should own? _____%

Now compare your two answers. Did you (hypothetically) write the same numbers for both questions? If you are like the vast majority of people who have completed surveys all around the world, you very likely gave a lower percentage for the second question than the first. You may have estimated that the richest 20% owned 60% of the wealth, but felt that ideally they should own 40%.

Before learning what the richest 20% actually own, answer two more questions. This time, think about the poorest 20% of Americans. In other words, rank all Americans in order again but count up from the poorest person until you are one-fifth of the way up the list.

Now answer the same two questions:

Of all the wealth in the United States, what percent do you think the poorest 20% of Americans own? _____%
Of all the wealth in the United States, what percent do you think the poorest 20% of Americans should own? _____%

If you are like most people surveyed, you probably estimated that the poorest 20% of Americans had about 5% of the wealth—and you wanted them to have about 10%.

Now for the answers, according to the latest estimates. Compare these with your answers above. The richest 20% of Americans have about 85% of all the wealth. And the bottom 20%? They have about 0.1%. That is not a typo—not 1% of the wealth, one-tenth of 1%.

In research with more than 5,000 Americans, people dramatically underestimated the current level of wealth inequality, and they wanted greater equality than even these estimates (Norton & Ariely, 2011). In other words, they thought that things were more equal than they are, and they wanted things to be even more equal than they thought they were. Americans believed that the richest 20% had about 60% of the wealth, they wanted them to have about 30%, and in reality, as noted, they have 85%. At the other end, Americans estimated that the poorest 20% had about 4%, they wanted them to have 10%, and in reality they have 0.1%. Note, however, that despite this desire for greater equality, Americans still want some level of inequality: The richest should have more than the poor, just a smaller gap. Australians show the same pattern: a consensus desire for unequality—not too equal, not too unequal (Norton, Neal, Govan, Ariely, & Holland, 2014).

Perhaps importantly from a public policy viewpoint, Americans consistently express a strong—and unexpected—consensus on their views of the right levels of unequality in wealth. Despite a belief that rich and poor Americans, and especially liberal and conservative Americans, would disagree in their ideal levels of who gets what, every group—from richest to poorest, across the entire political spectrum—finds the current level of wealth inequality to be dramatically higher than their ideal level. Every group surveyed desires a more equal America—but again, an unequal America such that the rich have more than the poor.

This same general pattern holds true when examining not wealth but income, in data from thousands of people from 16 countries (including the United States). Respondents estimated the gap in pay between CEOs and unskilled workers and reported what they thought that gap ideally should be (Kiatpongsan & Norton, 2014). The questions are again simple:

How much income do you think the average CEO makes each year? US$_____
How much income do you think the average unskilled worker makes each year? US$_____

And

How much income do you think the average CEO **should** *make each year? US$_____*
How much income do you think the average unskilled worker **should** *make each year? US$_____*

For each pair of questions, we calculated a pay ratio by dividing the first number by the second, which shows how much more people think CEOs currently make, and how much more people think CEOs *should* make.

As with wealth, ideal income gaps between CEOs and unskilled workers are significantly smaller than estimated gaps, and people drastically underestimate actual pay inequality. In each of 16 countries, people's ideal gap was smaller than their estimated gap. Moreover, as with wealth, the actual pay gaps for the 16 countries are dramatically larger than people's estimates and ideals.

Underestimation was larger in the United States than in any other country: The actual pay ratio of CEOs to unskilled workers was 354:1 (meaning that CEOs on average earned 354 times more income), whereas Americans estimated the gap to be 30:1 and reported an ideal ratio of 7:1. As with wealth, people underestimate actual pay gaps, and their ideal pay gaps are even farther from reality than their erroneous estimates. Note also, however, that Americans again express a desire for inequality: CEOs should still make more money than unskilled workers, but the gap should be much smaller than it currently is.

As with wealth inequality, the desire for smaller pay gaps between the rich and poor was a consensus desire. Rich and poor, left wing and right wing, highly educated and less educated—each group believed that smaller gaps in pay were more ideal than the current gaps in the United States and around the world.

THE (NEGATIVE) CONSEQUENCES OF INEQUALITY

Of course, just because Americans report desiring more equal distributions of wealth and income does not necessarily mean that these are the levels policymakers should pursue. In fact, one argument for higher levels of inequality is that inequality can be a motivating positive force in people's lives: People may work harder and better if they know that doing so can improve their outcomes in life and their children's future outcomes. Indeed, the fact that when surveyed, Americans unanimously support some level of inequality offers support for the notion that they, too, believe that complete equality is not the best solution. However, research shows that increasing levels of inequality can have negative consequences for people's behavior, suggesting that while some inequality may be desirable, too much can have negative repercussions. Below are some key findings about the effects of inequality on productivity, decision making, and ethical and unethical behavior.

INEQUALITY AND PRODUCTIVITY

One of the truisms of the benefits of inequality is that higher salaries attract better workers and motivate people to work harder and perform better to reach those incentives. However, research shows that when pay inequality is made public—when workers know where they stand in the distribution—lower paid workers report less job satisfaction, but higher paid workers do not experience any benefit (Card, Mas, Moretti, & Saez, 2012). Similarly, one field experiment showed that when workers are paired and one of them experiences a pay cut—such that one is now making more pay than the other—the lower paid worker exhibits less effort, but the higher paid worker does not increase effort (Cohn, Fehr, & Götte, 2015). If anything, research shows that really large incentives (think of the enormous compensation packages for CEOs) can actually undermine performance. Why? Faced with the opportunity to earn—but simultaneously faced with the threat of squandering—huge bonuses, people choke at very high levels of compensation, performing worse than they did when working toward a more reasonable bonus (Ariely, Gneezy, Loewenstein, & Mazar, 2009). Taken together, these results suggest that pay inequality is demotivating for lower paid workers and is not offset by increases in motivation for higher paid workers—and may even lead to worse performance in both groups.

INEQUALITY AND DECISION MAKING

An emerging body of research also suggests that inequality has negative consequences for decision making, with a particular focus on how the scarcity experienced by the poor contributes to (understandable) decisions to borrow more and save less (e.g., Shah, Mullainathan, & Shafir, 2012). But research shows that the negative effects of inequality on decision making do not accrue merely to the poor.

Take the example of gambling. Research on "last-place aversion" shows that being near the bottom of the distribution can lead people to take unwise risks in an effort to get out of, or avoid being in, last place—such as playing the lottery or forgoing sure cash for the chance at bigger cash that moves them out of last place (Kuziemko, Buell, Reich, & Norton, 2014). In one experiment, people received different amounts of money (from US$1 to US$8) and learned their rank in an "income distribution," with each rank separated by US$1. Then, they had to choose between getting US$0.50 for sure or taking a (very low) chance at winning US$2. Because ranks were separated by just US$1, taking US$0.50 meant staying in your current rank, but gambling for US$2 allowed you the possibility of "leapfrogging" the person above you. People in last place—desperate to escape—were most likely to take this unwise gamble (see also Haisley, Mostafa, & Loewenstein, 2008). But it is not only the experience of being poor that leads to gambling: The experience of being rich can have the same effects on risk-taking. Research has revealed a "house money effect," whereby people who have just experienced a big win are more likely to make risky decisions going forward (Thaler & Johnson, 1990). In sum, research shows that the experience of being both too high and too low in a distribution can impair decision making.

INEQUALITY AND UNETHICAL AND ETHICAL BEHAVIOR

Poor people give a higher percentage of income to charity than people in the middle class, and only the very rich give the same percentage as the poor (Piff, Kraus, Côté, Cheng, & Keltner, 2010). Why? The data suggest that even feeling temporarily rich can lead people to feel less empathy for others, driving their decreased generosity. At the same time, people in the lower middle class can be less generous to the very poor than others and even less generous to the poor than they are to the rich. Why? As with gambling, this behavior is driven by last-place aversion: People in the middle class or just below want to make sure that someone stays below them (Kuziemko et al., 2014). This desire does not just play out in the laboratory. Why do people with wages just above the minimum wage often oppose increasing it? On one hand, they may receive a small raise, but now would have the "last-place" wage. Kuziemko et al. (2014) find exactly this pattern in survey data: Americans making between US$7.26 and US$8.25 are the least likely to support increasing the current minimum wage of US$7.25.

Inequality can lead not only to less generous behavior but also to more unethical behavior. In one experiment, people who discovered they were paid less than others for completing a task were more likely to cheat to make more money (John, Loewenstein, & Rick, 2014). Moreover, the ease with which they could compare their lower wages with the "rich workers" predicted how much they were willing to cheat. And inequality can even make the rich cheat more, in an effort to restore equity. When given a lucky outcome that gives them more cash than someone else, the "rich" will fudge their grading of the "poor" person's test to compensate that poor person more than deserved (Gino & Pierce, 2009). In other words, people who end up at the top sometimes cheat on behalf of the poor because they feel badly about their relative advantage. Taken together, this research suggests that inequality can lead to less generosity and more unethical behavior across the income distribution.

CONCLUSION

The extreme disagreements in the political arena—also reflected in debates among academics—about the optimal level of inequality suggest the importance of determining who gets what. While a number of lenses must be brought to bear on the issue, the illustrative sample of behavioral research summarized here offers some crucial guidance. First, clearly, as inequality increases, a number of negative outcomes occur, both psychological (Norton, 2013) and behavioral—from worse performance to impaired decision making to increased cheating. Second, also clearly, unlike politicians and academics, laypeople from all over the world exhibit a remarkable consensus on what they believe the "right amount" of inequality is, at least for wealth and income: not equal, but much more equal than the current state of affairs. Policies that come closer to achieving this optimal level of *unequality* offer the promise of not only minimizing the negative psychological and behavioral effects of inequality but also creating a set of outcomes for citizens that more closely match the outcomes they desire.

REFERENCES

Ariely, D., Gneezy, U., Loewenstein, G., & Mazar, N. (2009). Large stakes and big mistakes. *Review of Economic Studies*, 76, 451–69.

Boyce, C. J., Wood, A. M., Banks, J., Clark, A. E., & Brown, G. D. (2013). Money, well-being, and loss aversion: Does an income loss have a greater effect on well-being than an equivalent income gain? *Psychological Science*, 24, 2557–62.

Card, D., Mas, A., Moretti, E., & Saez, E. (2012). Inequality at work: The effect of peer salaries on job satisfaction. *American Economic Review*, 102, 2981–3003.

Cohn, A., Fehr, E., & Götte, L. (2015). Fair wages and effort provision: Combining evidence from a choice experiment and a field experiment. *Management Science*, 61, 1741–2011.

De Neve, J., Ward, G. W., De Keulenaer, F., Van Landeghem, B., Kavetsos, G., & Norton, M. I. (2014). *Loss aversion in the macroeconomy: Global evidence using subjective well-being data* (Harvard Business School Working Paper).

Gino, F., & Pierce, L. (2009). Dishonesty in the name of equity. *Psychological Science*, 20, 1153–60.

Haisley, E., Mostafa, R., & Loewenstein, G. (2008). Subjective relative income and lottery ticket purchases. *Journal of Behavioral Decision Making*, 21, 283–95.

John, L. K., Loewenstein, G., & Rick, S. (2014). Cheating more for less: Upward social comparisons motivate the poorly compensated to *cheat*. *Organizational Behavior and Human Decision Processes*, 123, 101–109.

Keister, L.A. (2000). *Wealth in America*. New York: Cambridge University Press.

Kiatpongsan, S., & Norton, M. I. (2014). How much (more) should CEOs make? A universal desire for more equal pay. *Perspectives on Psychological Science*, 9, 587–93.

Kuziemko, I., Buell, R. W., Reich, T., & Norton, M. I. (2014). Last-place aversion: Evidence and redistributive implications. *Quarterly Journal of Economics*, 129, 105–49.

Lusardi, A., Schneider, D., & Tufano, P. (2011). Financially fragile households: Evidence and implications. *Brookings Papers on Economic Activity*, 83–134.

Norton, M. I. (2013). All ranks are local: Why humans are both (painfully) aware and (surprisingly) unaware of their lot in life. *Psychological Inquiry*, 24, 124–25.

Norton, M. I., & Ariely, D. (2011). Building a better America—One wealth quintile at a time. *Perspectives on Psychological Science*, 6, 9–12.

Norton, M. I., Neal, D. T., Govan, C. L., Ariely, D., & Holland, E. (2014). The not-so-common-wealth of Australia: Evidence for a cross-cultural desire for a more equal distribution of wealth. *Analyses of Social Issues and Public Policy*, 14, 339–51.

Piff, P. K., Kraus, M. W., Côté, S., Cheng, B. H., & Keltner, D. (2010). Having less, giving more: The influence of social class on prosocial behavior. *Journal of Personality and Social Psychology*, 99, 771–84.

Piketty, T. (2014). *Capital in the twenty-first century*. Cambridge, MA: Harvard University Press.

Piketty, T., & Saez, E. (2014). Inequality in the long-run. *Science*, 344, 838–43.

Shah, A. K., Mullainathan, S., & Shafir, E. (2012). Some consequences of having too little. *Science*, 338, 682–85.

Thaler, R., & Johnson, E. J. (1990). Gambling with the house money and trying to break even: The effects of prior outcomes on risky choice. *Management Science*, 36, 643–60.

Wolff, E. N. (2002). *Top heavy: The increasing inequality of wealth in American and what can be done about it*. New York: New Press.

RENEE M. SHELBY

2. INCOME INEQUALITY THREATENS THE AMERICAN DREAM

Shelby documents the rise in income and wealth inequality and how, despite our belief in the American Dream, the United States is more economically unequal than comparable nations. Increasing economic inequality clearly hurts individuals, as their life chances are diminished, but Shelby demonstrates how the entire society suffers, as rising inequality stunts economic growth, intensifies inflation, and even compromises democratic principles. The middle class, once economically strong, continues to face hardship and stagnation. The public is becoming increasingly aware of the costs of economic inequality, but it will be challenging to break the current patterns of accumulation.

The American Dream holds that if we work hard, each generation will enjoy a higher standard of living than the one before it. But is your generation going to enjoy a better life than your parents' generation? Perhaps not. According to a 2018 study by the Federal Reserve, Americans born during the 1980s are at risk of becoming a "lost generation" for wealth accumulation.[1] The wealth of households headed by someone born in the 1980s is 34% lower than is expected based on the experiences of earlier generations. Although the Great Recession imposed severe financial losses, the intergenerational gains of Americans born after the 1980s have also stalled due to long-term income and wealth inequality. While the nation has undoubtedly prospered since the 1970s,[2] an increasingly smaller portion of the U.S. population reaps the economic rewards.

INCOME INEQUALITY

When most people think of economic success, they think of income. *Income* is the money a person receives for work, transfers (e.g., gifts, inheritances, government assistance), or from returns on investments.

In the United States, income is highly concentrated among a small group of people. In 2015, the highest earning 10% of Americans received nearly half of all available income (50.5%)—almost as much as the bottom 80% of Americans combined. Yet, the distribution of income is even more densely concentrated than you may think. In 2015, the top 1% of earners took home 22% of all available income.[3] In 1980, the 1% earned only 11% of all income.[4] In just a few decades, the 1% doubled their share of total income. Moreover, a considerable share of the nation's income has gone not just to the top 1%, but to the top 0.01% of earners, who now earn, on average, over $35.1 million per year![5] When compared to the average income for the bottom 80%—a mere $45,500 by comparison—the level of inequality becomes even more apparent.[6]

Despite consistent increases in national productivity, since the 1970s, real wages have stagnated for the majority of Americans. *Real wages* are current wages adjusted for inflation. They provide a valuable measure for comparison because they reflect the actual purchasing power of goods over time. Taking inflation into account is critical because the cost of living has steadily

Original to *Focus on Social Problems: A Contemporary Reader*.

increased almost every year since 1960,[7] making it difficult for individuals to maintain their standard of living without a corresponding wage increase.[8] When we look at real wages over the past 45 years, earnings have had practically zero growth.[9] In 1979, the median income (50th percentile) for male and female workers was $20.27.[10] By 2017, that number increased a whopping 6.1% to a median of $21.50.[11] According to a 2014 study by the Pew Research Center, a little over half of Americans (56%) report that their family's income is "falling behind" the cost of living, and only a mere 5% say their salaries are staying ahead of inflation.[12] And as incomes have stalled, annual work hours have increased. In 1979, the average employee worked 1,687 hours; however, by 2017, annual work hours had crept up to 1,780—an extra 93 hours per year.[13] Despite these extra hours, on average, workers are not receiving much additional economic benefit.

Although we tend to see ourselves as a land of equal economic opportunity, globally, the United States ranks as one of the most economically unequal countries. Income inequality is often measured and compared with the Gini Index—a statistic that represents a nation's income distribution. A Gini coefficient of zero represents perfect equality (everyone in the society earns the same amount), whereas a coefficient of 100 represents extreme inequality (one person earns all the money, and everyone else earns none).[14] In 1979, America's Gini Index coefficient was 34.6.[15] By 2016, it increased to 41.5.[16] In fact, since the 1970s, America's Gini Index coefficient has risen steadily, making U.S. income concentration by far the highest of any other wealthy Western country. For example, compare America's 2016 score to the Gini coefficients of Australia (34.0), Germany (29.0), Canada (32.0), or Sweden (28.0).[17]

In recent years, economists have adopted an additional measure of inequality—the Palma ratio—which illustrates more explicitly the differences between high- and low-income earners. This measure is the ratio of the income of the richest 10% of earners divided by the income of the poorest 40% of earners. It is named for Cambridge economist Jose Gabriel Palma who found that middle-class incomes tend to account for half of gross national incomes, while the remaining half is split between the richest 10% and the poorest 40%. A lower Palma ratio closer to zero indicates that the country has a balance between high and low earners, whereas a Palma ratio greater than zero indicates that income is skewed toward the top. The higher the ratio, the greater the inequality. In 2014, the Palma ratio for the United States was 2.0, which indicates that the richest 10% earned roughly twice as much as the bottom 40%. Contrast this number to the Palma ratios of Australia (1.34), Canada (1.16), Germany (1.03), and Sweden (0.97), all of which have a much more equitable distribution of income. Worldwide, the United States ranks near the middle of all countries worldwide and at the bottom of OECD (the Organisation for Economic Co-Operation and Development) member countries—a consortium of 36 countries dedicated to "help governments foster prosperity and fight poverty through, economic growth and financial stability."[18,19]

Beyond our comparison to other nations, income inequality has many negative sociopolitical consequences. Often, these are direct and tangible, meaning that when a person experiences an economic gain, that person can access more social and political resources. Conversely, when a person suffers a financial loss, social and political resources become more limited. As fewer individuals experience economic gain, their *life chances*—or the number of opportunities a person has to live a good life—shrink. Consequently, examining the broad effects of income inequality is a critical site of investigation.

WEALTH INEQUALITY

Foremost, persistent income inequality drives *wealth inequality*. *Wealth* is the value of a person's assets (cash savings, house, car, etc.) minus their debts (outstanding loans). The United States measures wealth every 10 years through the Census. In 2010, the wealthiest 20% of Americans possessed 84% of all wealth, while the bottom 60% possessed less than 6% of all wealth.[20] While wealth inequality is highly skewed toward the top, it is also highly skewed in terms of race. Within the middle-income quintile—those Americans who earn between $37,201 and $61,328 each year—White households own 8 times as much wealth ($86,100) as Black households ($11,000)[21] and 10 times more wealth than Latino families ($8,600). As wealth may be the most important marker of financial well-being, if we redefined the middle class through wealth, households would need to own between $68,000 and $204,000 of wealth to be classified as middle class. Under these guidelines, a shocking 70% of Black and Latino households would fail to meet the middle-class minimum, while only 40% of White households would fail to meet the middle-class minimum. As most wealth is transferred between generations through inheritances and cash transfers, an increasing number of Americans are being financially left behind as the racial wealth gap persists.

Being able to accumulate wealth is beneficial in that it provides individuals with a cushion against income shocks (such as a job loss or serious injury/illness) and access to desirable neighborhoods and schools. Amassed wealth also increases a person's social status and political influence. Further, if an individual accrues enough wealth, they can live comfortably off dividends (income earned from investments) and will no longer need to work. However, fewer and fewer Americans can do this, while those who are able to do so can continue accumulating their wealth.

STUNTED ECONOMY

On a broader scale, income and wealth inequality also hinder overall economic growth, are linked to rising interest rates, and create unstable and volatile economic conditions.[22,23,24] Since the 1960s, conservative economists and politicians have argued that inequality is unimportant and that it propels the economy forward, a theory colloquially called "trickle-down" or supply-side economics.[25,26] This theory argues that economic growth is achieved by making it easier to produce goods and services and invest in capital. Essentially, when those at the top of the income ladder do well economically, the economic rewards "trickle down" to those at the bottom. Reducing taxes, particularly for the wealthy, has been a cornerstone of supply-side economics. However, new research using Census data has found the supposed benefits of trickle-down economics, such as job creation and the idea that "the rising tide floats all boats," are not supported by data and that economic inequality actually benefits only the super-rich.[27]

This is evident in the recent case study of Kansas, where Governor Sam Brownback reduced the tax rate

for the top 30% of earners in 2012. In 2013, he also reduced the business tax rate for certain types of profits to zero.[28] As some of the largest cuts ever enacted by a state, the Kansas Department of Commerce promoted them nationally with print media ads declaring, "Cut the taxes, cut the cost of doing business and you are left in a perfect state . . . Kansas" and "With one of the most pro-growth tax policies in the country, it's not hard to [become the best]."[29] Brownback claimed the cuts would act as a "shot of adrenaline into the heart of the Kansas economy."[30] At the time, Arthur Laffer, a supply-side economist and member of Ronald Reagan's Economic Policy Advisory Board (1981–1989), asserted that Brownback's policies would benefit the Kansan economy, leading to immediate and long-term growth. In fact, Brownback even hired Laffer to promote the new policies and cited his work as justification for the tax cuts.[31]

Although Brownback asserted on MSNBC's *Morning Joe* (June 19, 2014) that he wanted Kansas to be a "real, live experiment" for supply-side economics, most Kansans have not benefited from this experiment, and the state continues to lag in its recovery from the Great Recession.[32] Indeed, the cuts have not boosted the Kansan economy, and as of 2017, they have generated a $280 million budget deficit from a historic budget surplus.[33,34] Fewer jobs have been added compared to the national trend (the job growth of the United States was 9.4% between 2012 and 2017, and only 4.2% in Kansas), and the Kansas economy also grew more slowly than other Midwestern states and even more slowly than Kansas had grown in previous years. The incomes and earnings of Kansans are now below the national average, and because income tax cuts were aimed at high-income households, the taxes for low-income families were raised to compensate for the state's revenue loss. As revenues have sharply declined, Kansas has had to make cuts in school, health care, and public service funding—critical programs used primarily by lower- and middle-class citizens. As Brownback's experiment clearly failed the state, in June of 2017, the Kansas state legislature passed a bill to raise taxes.[35] Although Brownback vetoed the bill, the legislature persisted and voted to override his veto. The Kansas experiment reveals that supply-side economics produce economic and social inequalities that may persist for years. As the Center on Budget and Policy Priorities declared, "Kansas is a cautionary tale, not a model."

INTENSIFYING INFLATION AND DEBT

In addition to chilling economic growth, rising inequality is positively correlated with inflation.[36] That is, as inequality rises, so does inflation, devaluing the money already in circulation and making it more difficult for the majority of Americans to buy the things they need. When incomes fail to keep pace with inflation and interest rates, families increasingly have to rely on credit, tap into savings and retirement accounts, or take out loans against their current assets to stay afloat. However, while most families own something, their overall amount of debt often cancels out the worth of their property, leaving around 20% of Americans with zero or negative net worth.[37] For Latino households, that number increases to 27%, and for Black households it increases to 30%. In contrast, only 14% of White households have zero net worth. Consequently, many families are forced to live paycheck-to-paycheck, devoting most or all of their income to meeting regular household expenses.[38]

Being "financially vulnerable" is defined as being unable to come up with $2,000 for an emergency within 30 days.[39] A 2016 Federal Reserve survey found that 44% of Americans could not afford an unexpected $400 emergency expense without borrowing money or selling something.[40] This is an improvement from the first 2013 survey, in which a full 50% of Americans could not afford a $400 emergency expense.[41] Consequently, many Americans are unable to accumulate the three-month savings cushion suggested by financial planners (as a protection in the event of job loss, medical emergency, or other financial challenges).

Increasingly, Americans have turned to "payday loans" as a strategy to survive. A payday loan is typically a small loan borrowed at a high interest rate with the expectation that it will be repaid with the borrower's next paycheck. Of the 12 million Americans with a payday loan, 69% reported borrowing to cover basic necessities, such as groceries or rent, and another 16% borrowed to cover an emergency.[42] The average

payday loan borrower earns $30,000 per year[43] and is in the second lowest household income quintile. While payday loans are marketed as being short term, the standard two-week payday loan has an interest rate between 391% and 521%! Given the extremely short repayment period, nearly every borrower must take out subsequent loans just to pay off the initial loan. Consequently, 98% of borrowers get trapped in a cycle of payday debt, taking an average of seven or more loans per year.[44,45]

THE MIDDLE CLASS AND RISING DEBT

Increasingly, the impact of persistent income inequality is affecting middle-class Americans—a group long considered the epitome of upward mobility and a hopeful economic future. Historically, joining the middle class meant having a secure job, owning a home and car, having comprehensive health care, accruing retirement and college savings, and earning enough surplus income to enjoy an annual vacation. Looking at Census data between 2000 and 2014, we see that the proportion of adults in middle-class households shrank in 203 of the 229 U.S. metropolitan areas.[46] During this same time, the number of adults in lower-income households increased in 160 of the 229 areas, and the number of adults in high-income households increased in 172 metropolitan areas. Despite these changes, since 2013, when middle-class optimism was at a clear low,[47] an increasing number of Americans report that their economic well-being has improved, according to a 2018 Federal Reserve Report.[48] Overall, 40% of Americans report they are doing at least "okay" financially—a 10% increase from 2013. While this is a marked improvement, there are important disparities in terms of race. Less than two-thirds of Black and Latino families report they are doing financially "okay" compared to three-fourths of White families.

This shift is remarkable, as self-identification with an economic class is an identity people tend to consider permanent.[49] Further, identification with either the middle or lower classes is highly psychological, given, for example, the language usage and stereotypes common to each. A content analysis of common word associations with the terms "middle" and "lower class" reveals key distinctions. The *Corpus of Contemporary*

American English is a database of speeches, media, and academic texts from 1990 to 2017, totaling more than 560 million words.[50] Notably, statements about the "middle class" are most likely to contain the words "emerging," "burgeoning," "burdened," and "squeezed." In contrast, statements about the "lower class" are likely to include the terms "control," "judgment," "disapproval," and "help." The words associated with the middle class express challenges experienced by external influences, whereas the words associated with the lower class reflect negative views toward the group. Consequently, the cognitive shift required to change one's self-identity from the middle class (whose experience is seen, at worst, as burdened or squeezed) toward the lower class (whose experience is commonly associated with judgment and disapproval) is extraordinary.

While the middle class's waning optimism offers a bleak image of the state of the American Dream, recent data from the Federal Reserve Bank indicate that it is not unwarranted. For the majority of Americans, opportunities to grow earnings wane as workers grow older. Using data from U.S. Social Security Administration records, the Federal Reserve Bank found that, by age 40, most individuals are within about $1,000 of peak lifetime earnings, in which real wages tend to plateau, and the "average earnings growth from ages 35 to 55 is zero."[51] Only one group of Americans defies this trend: the top 20%, who show moderate growth beyond age 40, and the top 1%, who experience wage growth at every age bracket.[52]

Even for young Americans, economic prospects may be dimming, although employment opportunities are improving to their pre-2007 levels. As wages continue to stagnate, this problem is exacerbated for college graduates with student loan debt. In 2003, student loan debt totaled around $240 billion. By 2017, this number swelled to $1.3 trillion, with over 44 million Americans holding outstanding student debt.[53] While increasing student debt is driven by the fact that there are more college students than ever before, the cost of a college education has also far outpaced the standard rate of inflation, particularly at four-year institutions. In real wages, in 1971, the average price of a year of college at a public college was $8,734.[54] By 2016, this number increased 140.1% to $20,967.[55] As more students rely on loans to attend college, outstanding student debt now exceeds credit card, auto

loan, and home-equity debt. A substantial number of student debtors come from middle- and lower-income families who have access to fewer resources. In Sallie Mae's national survey, *How America Saves for College 2017*,[56] low-income households pay for 22% of total education costs with loans; middle-income households pay 21% of total education costs with loans; while high-income households only pay 15% of total education costs with loans. It is perhaps no wonder that the bottom 50% of the income distribution currently holds 75% of total student loan debt.[57]

While college is an important investment, as of 2017, the average borrower now leaves with $37,172 in debt. Consequently, beginning in 2012, student loan borrowers are now less likely than nonstudent loan borrowers to purchase a home by age 30.[58] In part, waning home purchases among those with student debt may be attributed to poor labor markets, whereby graduates expect to earn less and choose not to make large purchases. However, as creditors have tightened their lending restrictions, graduates with student loan debt may also fail to meet new debt-to-income ratio standards and are thus not credit-qualified to make these purchases. According to the Federal Reserve, the credit scores of non-student loan borrowers are on average 15 points higher than those of student loan borrowers at age 25 and 24 points higher at age 30.[59] While some members of Congress (such as Senator Elizabeth Warren of Massachusetts) have tried to reform student loan debt and ease the economic burden to student borrowers and their families, new measures have yet to be adopted. This is in part due to polarized legislative processes that have stalled political solutions to economic inequality. As more and more Americans face economic hardship, those at the top of the income ladder continue to shape the political process in ways that prevent positive change for working and middle-class families.

UPPER-CLASS POLITICAL GAINS

While rising income inequality has limited many families' economic prospects, it also gives the upper class more influence over the political process via major contributions to think-tanks, political campaigns, and lobbying groups. Further, a growing portion of congressional representatives are super-rich themselves, giving elite earners increased, direct control over economic policies. Nearly 50% of congressional members are millionaires, compared to only about 1% of Americans in general; and in 2016, the median net worth of congressional members was $511,000. The 115th Congress (2017–2018) was an astounding 20% richer than the 114th Congress, and 10 of the top 50 richest legislators sit on the Senate Finance or House Ways and Means committees—committees responsible for drafting tax cuts and code changes.[60] It is perhaps no surprise that the tax cuts pushed by President Trump and enacted at the end of 2017 overwhelmingly benefited wealthy Americans—including the super-wealthy members of his cabinet and Congress.

Notably, the increase in the number of congressional millionaires has correlated with a decreasing tax burden for the wealthy over time. Since the 1940s, the tax rates for the super-rich have plummeted. In 1945, a millionaire's tax rate was 66.4%. With Lyndon B. Johnson's tax cuts, it dropped to 55.3%, and it further decreased to 47.7% with Ronald Reagan's cuts. Through 2017, with George W. Bush's cuts still in effect, a millionaire's tax rate was just 32.4%.[61, 62] However, this tax rate is only for payroll wages and differs substantially from minimally taxed *capital gains* (income generated from long-term investments, such as homes, stocks, or bonds). When you sell an investment, the difference between the price you initially paid for the asset and the price you sold the asset for is your capital gain (if the change is positive) or capital loss (if the change is negative). Beginning in the early 1990s, earnings from capital gains began to concentrate toward the top of the income scale, whereby capital gains now comprise a significant portion of wealthier taxpayers' incomes.[63] As payroll wages have stagnated across the nation, earnings from capital gains have skyrocketed. Between 2001 and 2014, the top 0.01% of taxpayers (those with incomes over $10 million) earned 52.6% of their income through capital gains.[64] And with separate tax rates for income and capital gains, top earners can use this loophole to avoid paying their assigned income tax rates. In fact, most of the earnings of individuals on the *Forbes Richest 400* list[65] come from non-job-creating capital gains, with the top tax rate for capital gains capped at a mere 15%.[66] Thus, when capital gains taxes are factored in, the tax rates for the rich and everyone else converge;

so much so, in fact, that the effective tax rate for those earning between $43,000 and $69,000 is nearly the same as for those earning more than $370,000 per year.[67]

THE FADING AMERICAN DREAM

Given that our government is supposed to be of the people, by the people, and for the people, one would think there would be more public outrage over policies that benefit very few at the expense of many. While the Occupy Wall Street movement helped raise awareness of the growing inequality and the policies that support its growth, it has not resulted in new economic policies and regulations that foster equality. However, Americans are beginning to take notice. In a 2011 survey, researchers found that many Americans—Democrats and Republicans, liberals and conservatives—support a more egalitarian model of income distribution in which income is more fairly distributed between upper, middle, and lower classes.[68] This does not mean that every American wants a system in which everyone makes the same amount of money; it just means that Americans are not in favor of the current, clearly skewed system.

In 2014, Princeton survey analysts found that 65% of adults recognize there is a growing gap between rich Americans and everyone else,[69] and 60% feel the economic system unfairly favors the wealthy.[70] However, Americans are not only discouraged about the current economic outlook, but also believe the next generation's prospects are grim. According to a 2017 Pew Research Center survey, 58% of Americans now believe the next generation will be financially worse off than their parents.[71] Yet constituents continue to vote for politicians who do not share their economic interests—leaving few opportunities to change the economic state of affairs. Former Labor Secretary Robert Reich has argued that with sinking wages and growing economic insecurity, many people are so desperate for a job that they are unwilling to cause trouble, such as going on strike, protesting, or voting out politicians who do not support the middle and lower classes, leaving a substantial portion of the country without a political voice.[72] The consequence of this inactive approach has been 40 years of rising inequality.

NOTES

1. Emmons, William R., Ana Hernandez Kent, and Lowell R. Ricketts. 2018. "Essay No. 2: A Lost Generation? Long-Lasting Wealth Impacts of the Great Recession on Young Families." *The Demographics of Wealth, 2018 Series, How Education, Race, and Birth Year Shape Financial Outcomes.* St. Louis, MO: Federal Reserve Bank of St. Louis.

2. Morris, Martina, and Bruce Western. 1999. Inequality in Earnings at the Close of the 20th Century. *Annual Review of Sociology*, 25, 623–57.

3. Saez, Emmanuel. 2015. *The Evolution of Top Incomes in the United States (Updated with 2015 Preliminary Estimates).* Retrieved July 10, 2017, from https://eml.berkeley.edu/~saez/saez-US-topincomes-2015.pdf.

4. Alvaredo, Facundo, Lucas Chancel, Thomas Piketty, Emmanuel Saez, and Gabriel Zucman. 2018. *World Inequality Report.* World Inequality Lab.

5. Saez, Emmanuel. 2015. *The Evolution of Top Incomes in the United States (Updated with 2015 Preliminary Estimates).* Retrieved July 10, 2017, from https://eml.berkeley.edu/~saez/saez-US-topincomes-2015.pdf.

6. Approximate estimate taken from Dungan, Adrian. 2018. *Individual Income Tax Shares, 2015.* Washington, DC: Internal Revenue Service.

7. Bureau of Labor Statistics. 2014. *Consumer Price Indices.* Washington DC: United States Department of Labor.

8. Ashenfelter, Orley. 2012. Comparing Real Wage Rates. *American Economic Review*, 102(2), 617–42.

9. Pollin, Robert. 2009. "Green Growth and Sustainable Development—The U.S. Case." *Paper Presented at the 64th Session of United Nations General Assembly*, October 26, 2009, New York. Retrieved September 15, 2014, from http://www.un.org/en/ga/second/64/pollin.pdf.

10. Donovan, Sarah A., and David H. Bradley. March 15, 2018. *Real Wage Trends, 1979 to 2017.* Washington, DC: Congressional Research Service. Retrieved July 10, 2018 from https://fas.org/sgp/crs/misc/R45090.pdf.

11. Ibid.

12. Pew Research Center. August 2014. "Views of Job Market Tick Up, No Rise in Economic Optimism." http://assets.pewresearch.org/wp-content/uploads/sites/5/2014/09/9-4-14-Economy-release1.pdf.

13. Organisation for Economic Co-operation and Development. 2018. Average Annual Hours Actually Worked per Worker. Retrieved July 10, 2018, from https://stats.oecd.org/index.aspx?DataSetCode=ANHRS#.

14. Bellu, Lorenzo Giovanni, and Paolo Liberati. 2006. *Inequality Analysis: The Gini Index.* Rome, Italy: Food and Agriculture Organization of the United Nations (FAO).

15. The World Bank. 2018. *GINI Index (World Bank Estimate).* Retrieved July 10, 2018, from. https://data.worldbank.org/indicator/SI.POV.GINI?end=2016&start=1979&view=chart&year_low_desc=false.

16. The World Bank, 2018.

17. Central Intelligence Agency. 2013–2014. *The World Factbook.* Washington, DC: Central Intelligence Agency.

18. Calculations were retrieved from the Organisation for Economic Co-Operation and Development on August 30, 2018, from https://stats.oecd.org/Index.aspx?QueryId=66597.

19. Organisation for Economic Co-Operation and Development. 2018. "What We Do and How." Retrieved September 27, 2018, from http://www.oecd.org/about/whatwedoandhow.

20. Norton, Michael, and Dan Ariely. 2011. Building a Better America-One Wealth Quintile at a Time. *Perspectives on Psychological Science*, 6(1), 9–12.

21. Asante-Muhammad, Dedrick, Chuck Collins, Josh Hoxie, and Emanuel Nieves. 2017. *The Road to Zero Wealth: How the Racial Wealth Divide Is Hollowing Out America's Middle Class*. Washington, DC: Institute for Policy Studies and Prosperity Now.

22. Bagchi, Stritha, and Jan Svenjar. 2013. *Does Wealth Inequality Matter for Growth? The Effect of Billionaire Wealth, Income Distribution, and Poverty*. Institute for the Discussion of Labor. IZA Discussion Paper No. 7733, November 2013.

23. Ostry, Jonathan D., Andrew Berg, and Charalambos G. Tsangarides. 2014. *Redistribution, Inequality, and Growth*. Washington, DC: International Monetary Fund.

24. Bruckner, Markus, Kerstin Gerling, and Hans Peter Gruner. 2010. Wealth Inequality and Credit Markets: Evidence from Three Industrialized Countries. *Journal of Economic Growth*, 15, 155–76.

25. Laffer, A. B. 1981. "Supply-side economics." *Financial Analysts Journal*, 37(5): 29–43.

26. Galbraith, John Kenneth. 1982. Recession Economics. *New York Review of Books*, 29(1). Online. Retrieved March 19, 2015, from http://www.nybooks.com/articles/archives/1982/feb/04/recession-economics.

27. Van der Weide, Roy, and Branko Milanovic. 2014. *Inequality Is Bad for Growth of the Poor, But Not for That of the Rich*. Paper Number 6963. Washington, DC: Policy Research Working Paper Series.

28. Hernandez, Raul. June 8, 2017. "Kansas Republicans Scrapped the State's Disastrous Tax Cuts That Look a Lot Like Trump's Plan." Business Insider.com. Retrieved July 10, 2018, from http://www.businessinsider.com/kansas-budget-disaster-tax-reform-repeal-gop-similar-to-trumps-2017–6.

29. Kansas Department of Commerce. 2014. *Tax Cut Ad in Small Business Resource*. Retrieved February 14, 2015, from http://www.motherjones.com/mojo/2014/09/sam-brownback-kansas-tax-cuts-marketing.

30. Hiltzik, Michael. June 7, 2017. "Kansas Legislature Finally Ends Gov. Sam Brownback's Destructive Tea Party Tax Cuts." Retrieved from LA Times.com http://www.latimes.com/business/hiltzik/la-fi-hiltzik-brownback-override-20170607-story.html.

31. Cooper, Brad. January 19, 2012. *Reaganomics Guru Arthur Laffer Touts Brownback Tax Plan at Capitol*. The Kansas City Star Online. Retrieved from http://www.kansascity.com/news/local/article300536/Reagonomics-guru-Arthur-Laffer-touts-Brownback-tax-plan-at-Capitol.html.

32. Leachman, Michael, and Chris Mai. 2014. *Lessons for Other States from Kansas' Massive Tax Cuts*. Washington, DC: Center on Budget and Policy Priorities.

33. Kansas Legislative Research Department. 2013. *Consensus Revenue Estimate*. Retrieved February 14, 2015, from *http://budget.ks.gov/files/FY2015/CRE_Long_Memo-Nov2013.pdf*.

34. Woodall, Hunter. March 1, 2017. "Kansas Tops Revenue Estimates; 2017 Budget Shortfall Dips." The Witchita Eagle.com. Retrieved July 10, 2018, from https://www.kansas.com/news/politics-government/article135796598.html.

35. Hernandez, Raul. June 8, 2017. "Kansas Republicans Scrapped the State's Disastrous Tax Cuts That Look a Lot Like Trump's Plan." Business Insider.com. Retrieved July 10, 2018, from http://www.businessinsider.com/kansas-budget-disaster-tax-reform-repeal-gop-similar-to-trumps-2017–6.

36. Albanesi, Stefania. 2006. Inflation and Inequality. *Journal of Monetary Economics.* 54(4): 1088.

37. Bricker, J., L. J. Dettling, A. Henriques, J. W. Hsu, L. Jacobs, K. B. Moore,. . . and R. A. Windle (2017). Changes in US Family Finances from 2013 to 2016: Evidence from the Survey of Consumer Finances. *Federal Reserve Bulletin*, 103(1): 1–41.

38. Klawitter, Marieka, M., C. Leigh Anderson, and Mary Kay Gugerty. 2013. Savings and Personal Discount Rates in a Matched Savings Program for Low-Income Families. *Contemporary Economic Policy*, 31(3), 468–85.

39. Lusardi, Annamaria, Daniel J. Scheider, and Peter Tufano. 2011. *Financially Fragile Households: Evidence and Implications.* Paper Number 17072. Cambridge, MA: National Bureau of Economic Research.

40. Board of Governors of the Federal Reserve. 2018. *Report on the Economic Well-Being of U.S. Households in 2017.* Washington, DC: The Federal Reserve.

41. Board of Governors of the Federal Reserve. 2014. *Report on the Economic Well-Being of U.S. Households in 2013.* Washington, DC: The Federal Reserve.

42. Kaufman, Alex. 2013. *PayDay Lending Regulation.* Finance and Economics Discussion Series. Divisions of Research and Statistics and Monetary Affairs. Washington, DC: Federal Reserve Board.

43. Urahn, Susan, K., Travis Plunkett, Nick Bourke, Alex Horowitz, Walter Lake, and Tara Roche. 2013. *Payday Lending in America: Policy Solutions. Report 3 in the Payday Lending in America series. A Report from the PEW Charitable Trusts.* Retrieved July 13, 2018, from http://www.pewtrusts. org/-/media/legacy/uploadedfiles/pcs_assets/2013/pewpaydaypolicysolutionsoct2013pdf.pdf? la=en&hash=27299A7591562A9169ADC57C9E261319E01B8C09.

44. Kaufman, Alex. 2013. *PayDay Lending Regulation.* Finance and Economics Discussion Series. Divisions of Research and Statistics and Monetary Affairs. Washington, DC: Federal Reserve Board.

45. Kaufman, 2013.

46. Pew Research Center. May 11, 2016. "America's Shrinking Middle Class: A Close Look at Changes Within Metropolitan Areas."

47. Allstate/National Journal. 2014. Heartland Monitor Poll XXI. Survey. October 22–26, 2014.

48. Board of Governors of the Federal Reserve. 2018. *Report on the Economic Well-Being of U.S. Households in 2017.* Washington, DC: The Federal Reserve.

49. Benson, Michaela. 2014. Trajectories of Middle-Class Belonging: The Dynamics of Place Attachment and Classed Identities. *Urban Studies*, 51(14), 3097–112.

50. Corpus of Contemporary American English. 2018. http://corpus.byu.edu/coca.

51. Guvenen, Fatih, Fatih Karahan, Serdar Ozkan, and Jae Song. 2015. "What Do Data on Millions of U.S. Workers Reveal about Life-Cycle Earnings Risk? Federal Reserve Bank of New York Staff Reports." Staff Report No. 710. New York: Federal Reserve Bank of New York.

52. Guvenen, Karahan, Ozkan, and Song, 2015.

53. Pew Research Center analysis of Federal Reserve Board's 2016 Survey of Household Economics and Decision-making.

54. Controlling for inflation, all estimates are in 2017 dollars.

55. College Board, "Tuition and Fee and Room and Board Charges over Time." Retrieved July 9, 2018, from collegeboard.org.

56. Sallie Mae's National Study of Parents with Children under Age 18. 2017. *How America Saves for College.* Washington, DC: Ipsos Public Affairs.

57. Sallie Mae's National Study, 2017.

58. Brown, Meta, and Sydnee Caldwell. 2013. *Young Student Loan Borrowers Retreat from Housing and Auto Markets*. New York: Federal Reserve Bank.

59. Brown and Caldwell, 2013.

60. Hawkings, David. February, 27, 2018. "Wealth of Congress: Richer Than Ever, But Mostly at the Very Top." Rollcall.com. Retrieved July 23, 2018, from https://www.rollcall.com/news/hawkings/congress-richer-ever-mostly-top.

61. Hungerford, Thomas, L. 2012. *Taxes and the Economy: An Economic Analysis of the Top Tax Rates Since 1945. Congressional Research Service Report for Congress*. Washington, DC: Congressional Research Service.

62. Internal Revenue Service. 2013. U.S. *Individual Income Tax: Personal Exemptions and Lowest and Highest Bracket Tax Rates, and Tax Base for Regular Tax*. New Carrolton, MD: Department of the Treasury.

63. Congressional Budget Office. 2011. *Trends in the Distribution of Household Income Between 1979 and 2007*. Washington, DC: The Congress of the United States.

64. Nunns, James R. March 15, 2017. How Capital Gains Affected Average Income Tax Rates From 2001–2014. Tax Policy Center. Retrieved July 13, 2018 from https://www.taxpolicycenter.org/taxvox/how-capital-gains-affected-average-income-tax-rates-2001–2014.

65. Ali, Mazhar, Brian Miller, Shannon Moriarty, Jessica Mornealt, Tim Sullivan, and Michael Young. 2012. *Born on the Third Base: What the Forbes 400 Really Says about Economic Equality and Opportunity in America*. Boston: United for a Fair Economy.

66. Internal Revenue Service. 2014. *Topic 209—Capital Gains and Losses*. Retrieved September 15, 2014, from http://www.irs.gov/taxtopics/tc409.html.

67. Internal Revenue Service. 2014. *Publication 505: Tax Withholding and Estimated Tax*. New Carrolton, MD: Department of the Treasury.

68. Norton, Michael I., and Dan Ariely. 2011. Building a Better America—One Quintile at a Time. *Perspectives on Psychological Science*, 6(1), 9–12.

69. Pew Research Center. January 2014. *Most See Inequality Growing, But Partisans Differ Over Solutions*. Survey. Retrieved from http://www.people-press.org/files/legacy-pdf/1-23-14 percent20Poverty_Inequality percent20Release.pdf.

70. Pew Research Center, 2014.

71. Stokes, Bruce. 2017. *Global Publics More Upbeat about the Economy: But Many Are Pessimistic about Children's Future*. Pew Research Center. http://www.pewglobal.org/2013/05/01/spring-2013-survey-data.

72. Reich, Robert. January 15, 2014. "Fear Is Why Workers in Red States Vote Against Their Economic Self-Interest." Robert Reich Blog. Retrieved September 15, 2014 from http://robertreich.org/page/5.

THE "MIDDLE-CLASS" MYTH: HERE'S WHY WAGES ARE REALLY SO LOW TODAY

EDWARD MCCLELLAND

Let me tell you the story of an "unskilled" worker in America who lived better than most of today's college graduates. In the winter of 1965, Rob Stanley graduated from Chicago Vocational High School, on the city's Far South Side. Pay rent, his father told him, or get out of the house. So Stanley walked over to Interlake Steel, where he was immediately hired to shovel taconite into the blast furnace on the midnight shift. It was the crummiest job in the mill, mindless grunt work, but it paid $2.32 an hour—enough for an apartment and a car. That was enough for Stanley, whose main ambition was playing football with the local sandlot all-stars, the Bonivirs.

Stanley's wages would be the equivalent of $17.17 today—more than the "Fight For 15" movement is demanding for fast-food workers. Stanley's job was more difficult, more dangerous, and more unpleasant than working the fryer at KFC (the blast furnace could heat up to 2,000 degrees). According to the laws of the free market, though, none of that is supposed to matter. All that is supposed to matter is how many people are capable of doing your job. And anyone with two arms could shovel taconite. It required even less skill than preparing dozens of finger lickin' good menu items, or keeping straight the orders of 10 customers waiting at the counter. Shovelers didn't need to speak English. In the early days of the steel industry, the job was often assigned to immigrants off the boat from Poland or Bohemia.

"You'd just sort of go on automatic pilot, shoveling ore balls all night," is how Stanley remembers the work. Stanley's ore-shoveling gig was also considered an entry-level position. After a year in Vietnam, he came home to Chicago and enrolled in a pipefitters' apprenticeship program at Wisconsin Steel.

So why did Rob Stanley, an unskilled high school graduate, live so much better than someone with similar qualifications could even dream of today? Because the workers at Interlake Steel were represented by the United Steelworkers of America, who demanded a decent salary for all jobs. The workers at KFC are represented by nobody but themselves, so they have to accept a wage a few cents above what Congress has decided is criminal.

The argument given against paying a living wage in fast-food restaurants is that workers are paid according to their skills, and if the teenager cleaning the grease trap wants more money, he should get an education. Like most conservative arguments, it makes sense logically, but it has little connection to economic reality. Workers are not simply paid according to their skills, they're paid according to what they can negotiate with their employers. And in an era when only 6 percent of private-sector workers belong to a union, and when going on strike is almost certain to result in losing your job, low-skill workers have no negotiating power whatsoever.

Granted, Interlake Steel produced a much more useful, much more profitable product than KFC. Steel built the Brooklyn Bridge, the U.S. Navy, and the Saturn rocket program. KFC spares people the hassle of frying chicken at home. So let's look at how wages have declined from middle-class to minimum-wage in a single industry: meat processing.

Slaughterhouses insist they hire immigrants because the work is so unpleasant that Americans won't do it. They hired European immigrants when Upton Sinclair wrote *The Jungle*, and they hire Latin American immigrants today. But it's a canard that Americans won't slaughter pigs, sheep, and cows. How do we know this? Because immigration to the United States was more or less banned from 1925 to 1965, and millions of pigs, sheep, and cows were slaughtered during those years. But they were slaughtered by American-born workers, earning middle-class wages. *Mother Jones* magazine explains what changed:

> [S]tarting in the early 1960s, a company called Iowa Beef Packers (IBP) began to revolutionize the industry, opening plants in rural areas far from union strongholds, recruiting immigrant workers from Mexico, introducing a new division of labor that eliminated the need for skilled butchers, and ruthlessly battling unions. By the late 1970s, meatpacking companies that wanted to compete with IBP had to adopt its business methods—or go out of business. Wages in the meatpacking industry soon fell by as much as 50 percent.[1]

In Nick Reding's book *Methland*, he interviews Roland Jarvis, who earned $18 an hour throwing hocks at Iowa Ham . . . until 1992, when the slaughterhouse was bought out by a company that broke the union, cut wages to $6.20 an hour, and eliminated all benefits. Jarvis began taking meth so he could work extra shifts, and then began dealing the drug to make up for his lost income.

Would Americans kill pigs for $18 an hour? Hell, yes, they would. There would be a line from Sioux City to Dubuque for those jobs. But Big Meat's defeat of Big Labor means it can now negotiate the lowest possible wages with the most desperate workers: usually, Mexican immigrants who are willing to endure dangerous conditions for what would be considered a huge pile of money in their home country. Slaughterhouses hire immigrants not because they're the only workers willing to kill and cut apart

---

1 Schlosser, Eric. 2001. "The Most Dangerous Job in America." *Mother Jones*. Retrieved February 4, 2019, from https://www.motherjones.com/politics/2001/07/dangerous-meatpacking-jobs-eric-schlosser.

(continued)

Edward McClelland, "The "Middle Class" Myth: Here's Why Wages Are Really So Low Today," Salon. December 30th, 2013. Reprinted with permission of the author.

pigs, but because they're the only workers willing to kill and cut apart pigs for low wages, in unsafe conditions.

In Rob Stanley's native South Side, there is more than one monument to the violence that resulted when the right of industry to bargain without the interference of labor unions was backed up by government force. In 1894, President Cleveland sent 2,500 troops to break a strike[2] at the Pullman Palace Car Factory. On Memorial Day 1937, Chicago police killed 10 striking workers outside the Republic Steel plant. The names of those dead are cast on a brass plaque bolted to a flagpole outside a defunct steelworkers' hall. They were as polyglot as a platoon in a World War II movie: Anderson, Causey, Francisco, Popovich, Handley, Jones, Reed, Tagliori, Tisdale, Rothmund.

I first saw those sites on a labor history tour led by "Oil Can Eddie" Sadlowski, a retired labor leader who lost a race for the presidency of the USW in 1977. Sadlowski was teaching a group of ironworkers' apprentices about their blue-collar heritage and invited me to ride along on the bus. Oil Can Eddie had spent his life agitating for a labor movement that transcended class boundaries. He wanted laborers to think of themselves as poets, and poets to think of themselves as laborers.

"How many Mozarts are working in steel mills?" he once asked an interviewer.

In the parking lot of the ironworkers' hall, I noticed that most of the apprentices were driving brand-new pickup trucks—Dodge Rams with swollen hoods and quarter panels, a young man's first purchase with jackpot union wages. Meanwhile, I knew college graduates who earned $9.50 an hour as editorial assistants or worked in bookstores for even less. None seemed interested in forming a union. So I asked Sadlowski why White-collar workers had never embraced the labor movement as avidly as blue-collar workers.

"The White-collar worker has kind of a Bob Cratchit attitude," he explained. "He feels he's a half-step below the boss. The boss says, 'Call me Harry.' He feels he's made it. You go to a shoe store, they got six managers. They call everybody a manager, but they pay 'em all shit."

The greatest victory of the anti-labor movement has not been in busting industries traditionally organized by unions. That's unnecessary. Those jobs have disappeared as a result of automation and outsourcing to foreign countries. In the United States, steel industry employment has declined from 521,000 in 1974 to 150,000 today.

"When I joined the company, it had 28,000 employees," said George Ranney, a former executive at Inland Steel, an Indiana mill that was bought out by ArcelorMittal in 1998. "When I left, it had between 5,000 and 6,000. We were making the same amount of steel, 5 million tons a year, with higher quality and lower cost."

The anti-labor movement's greatest victory has been in preventing the unionization of the jobs that have replaced well-paying industrial work. Stanley was lucky: After Wisconsin Steel shut down in 1980,[3] a casualty of obsolescence, he bounced through ill-paying gigs hanging sheetrock and tending bar before finally catching on as a plumber for the federal government. The public sector is the last bastion of the labor movement, with a 35.9 percent unionization rate. But I know other laid-off steelworkers who ended their working lives delivering soda pop or working as security guards.

Where would high school graduates go today if they were told to pay rent or get out of the house? They might go to KFC, where the average team member earns $7.62 an hour—57 percent less, in real dollars, than Stanley earned for shoveling taconite. (No hourly worker at KFC earns as much[4] as Stanley did.) The reasons given for the low pay—that fast-food work is an entry-level job that was never meant to support a family or lead to a career—are ex post facto justifications for the reality that KFC can get away with paying low wages because it doesn't fear unionization. It's a lot harder to organize workers spread across dozens of franchises than it is to organize a single steel mill.

As Oil Can Eddie pointed out, class consciousness discourages office workers from unionizing. There's a popular discounting company in Chicago called Groupon, where the account executives—who are all expected to have bachelor's degrees—earn $37,800 a year. Adjusted for modern dollars, that's about Stanley's starting wage, without overtime. Because they're educated and sit safely at desks, they don't think of themselves as blue-collar mopes who need to strike for higher pay and better working conditions.

The fact that many of today's college graduates have the same standard of living as the lowest-skilled workers of the 1960s proves that attitude is wrong, wrong, wrong. If we want to restore what we've traditionally thought of as the middle class, we have to stop thinking of ourselves as middle class, no matter how much we earn or what we do to earn it. "Working class" should be defined by your relationship to your employer, not by whether you perform physical labor. Unless you own the business, you're working class.

"The smartest people I ever met were guys who ran cranes in the mill," Oil Can Eddie once said.

They were smart enough, at least, to get their fair share of the company's profits.

2   Smith, Carl. n.d. "Pullman Strike." *Encyclopedia of Chicago.* Retrieved February 4, 2019, from http://www.encyclopedia.chicagohistory.org/pages/1029.html.

3   Brown, Terry. 2008. "The Closing of Wisconsin Steel." *Chicagotribune.Com.* Retrieved February 4, 2019, from https://www.chicagotribune.com/news/nationworld/politics/chi-chicagodays-wisconsinsteel-story-story.html.

4   Anon. n.d. "KFC Hourly Pay." *Glassdoor.* Retrieved February 4, 2019, from https://www.glassdoor.com/Hourly-Pay/KFC-Hourly-Pay-E7860.htm.

CHUCK COLLINS, DEDRICK ASANTE-MUHAMMED,
EMANUEL NIEVES, AND JOSH HOXIE

3. THE EVER-GROWING GAP

Without Change, African American and Latino Families Won't Match White Wealth for Centuries

As more people become concerned about the unequal distribution of wealth in the United States, increasing attention has been paid to the growing racial wealth gap—the large gap in wealth accumulation between White and minority households. This reading discusses the origins, growth, and consequences of the racial wealth gap for communities, families, and the nation as a whole, noting the disproportionate impact of the Great Recession on racial minority wealth. The authors extrapolate from current data, predicting that without policy changes, the gap will never close.

INTRODUCTION

Racial and economic inequality are the most pressing social issues of our time. In the last decade, we have seen the catastrophic economic impact of the Great Recession and an ensuing recovery that has bypassed millions of Americans, especially households of color. This period of economic turmoil has been punctuated by civil unrest throughout the country in the wake of a series of high-profile African American deaths at the hands of police. These senseless and violent events have not only given rise to the Black Lives Matter movement, they have also sharpened the nation's focus on the inequities and structural barriers facing households of color.[1] While these centuries-old problems are once again at the forefront today, much of the recent media and political attention has focused on how structural inequities manifest in the criminal justice system. But confining conversations around racial inequality to criminal justice alone ignores the fact that households of color are also simultaneously facing a slew of economic inequities that exacerbate the social disparities they face.

However, even when these economic inequities do get attention, the focus is often on a single facet of the issue: income. This reading focuses instead on a related but distinct facet of the issue: the essential role that wealth plays in achieving financial security and opportunity. More specifically, this reading makes use of data from the Survey of Consumer Finance (SCF) . . . to examine our country's growing racial wealth divide and the trajectory of that divide. . . . Despite the progress of the civil rights movement, White households have been pulling away from households of color, particularly Black and Latino households, for decades. Today, the lingering effects of generations of discriminatory and wealth-stripping practices have left Latino and Black households owning an average of six and seven times less wealth ($98,000 and $85,000, respectively) than White households ($656,000).

Even more unfortunate, the extreme rise in overall wealth inequality over the past three decades has only served to further compound and exacerbate this racial wealth divide. Over that time, the wealthiest 20% of

Chuck Collins, Dedrick Asante-Muhammed, Emanuel Nieves, Josh Hoxie, The Ever-Growing Gap: Without Change, African-American and Latino Families Won't Match White Wealth for Centuries. August 2016. Reprinted with permission of Prosperity Now (formerly CFED) and the Institute for Policy Studies.

Americans have taken 99.4% of all gains in wealth, while the bottom 80% have been left to split just 0.6% among themselves.[2] As shocking as this disparity in wealth concentration is, it's even more startling when we realize that today, America's richest 400 individuals—with a collective net worth of $2.34 trillion—now own more wealth than the entire Black population, plus one-third of the Latino population, combined.[3]

While income is necessary to meet daily expenses, wealth helps families get through lean times and empowers them to climb the economic ladder. Wealth is money in the bank, a first home, a college degree, and retirement security— it's the countless opportunities afforded by having savings and investments. Unfortunately, when an overwhelming amount of wealth is concentrated in such few hands, not only do highly unequal societies suffer from significant negative social and health outcomes, there are also fewer opportunities available for others to get ahead.[4]

When wealth and opportunity are more evenly distributed, financially vulnerable families are better able to get ahead rather than just scrape by. Imagine that instead of low-wealth Black and Latino families finding themselves unable to deal with fluctuating incomes or how they're going to make it through an unexpected financial emergency, they have the freedom to invest in their children's future aspirations. Or, instead of resorting to selling loose cigarettes or CDs to earn a little more money for their families, Blacks and Latinos have the opportunity to build long-term wealth by owning their own businesses. These are just some of the opportunities lost because of the growing racial and economic inequality we face. This growing wealth divide is no accident. Rather, it is the natural result of public policies past and present that have been either purposefully or thoughtlessly designed to widen the economic chasm between White households and households of color and between the wealthy and everyone else. In the absence of significant reforms, the racial wealth divide—and overall wealth inequality—are on track to become even wider in the future.

THE GROWING RACIAL WEALTH DIVIDE

In telling the story of the country's growing racial wealth divide and the trajectory of that divide, it should be noted that we focus on the average wealth of Black and Latino households rather than median wealth. While the past three decades have seen the average wealth of Latino and Black households increase from $58,000 and $67,000 in 1983 to $98,000 and $85,000 in 2013, respectively, the trends at the median show Latino and Black wealth moving in the wrong direction. In fact, when consumer durable goods are excluded, median wealth for Black and Latino families has gone down over the past thirty years from $6,800 and $4,000 in 1983 to $1,700 and $2,000 in 2013, respectively.[5] If current trends continue, Black and Latino families at the median will never reach the level of wealth of White families today. By utilizing average wealth instead of median wealth, our analysis provides a more conservative look at how the racial wealth divide will develop over the next several decades and beyond.

BLACK AND LATINO HOUSEHOLDS

Over the past three decades, the racial wealth divide between Black and Latino households and White households increased from about $280,000 in 1983 to over $500,000 in 2013. . . . While the racial wealth divide that Black and Latino households face today has been long in the making, the Great Recession further exacerbated the divide as Blacks and Latinos disproportionally bore the brunt of damage brought about by the bursting of the housing bubble. Between 2007 and 2010, the average Black and Latino household lost three and four times more wealth, respectively, than the average White household.[6] Although household wealth is impacted by a multitude of factors, the racial disparities in homeownership are emblematic of the larger racial wealth divide facing Black and Latino households.

Racial Disparities in Homeownership

Despite the collapse of the housing market during the Great Recession, homeownership still remains one of the greatest sources of Americans' wealth. Unfortunately, decades of discriminatory housing policies and market practices, coupled with a recession that disproportionately harmed households of color, have contributed to the fact that today, only 41% of Black households and

45% of Hispanic households own their homes, compared to 71% of White households.[7] Adding to this disparity, even when they do own their homes, Blacks and Latinos build less wealth through homeownership than White homeowners do.[8] Moreover, because inheritances and downpayment assistance are more common in White families, African American families find themselves eight years behind White families on the path toward building home equity.[9]

While housing has been a major driver in the growth of the racial wealth divide, Black and Latino households have also faced numerous other economic inequities that are impacting their wealth position. At the root of this are a number of discriminatory practices—including, among others, employment discrimination, racial discrimination in the criminal justice system, housing segregation, and unequal access to educational opportunities—that have continued into the present even as some acts of past discrimination decline. Today, as a result of this continued cycle of racial injustice, Black and Latino families face a number of barriers toward achieving financial security at almost every turn.

Greater Rates of Unemployment

For many Americans, having a job that pays a decent wage is not only a matter of having the dignity of being able to provide for their families, it's also foundational to longer-term financial security. For Black (8.6%)[10] and Latino workers (5.8%),[11] that foundation is uneven at best, as these workers are unemployed at much higher rates today than their White counterparts (4.4%).[12] Although the lingering effects of the Great Recession have undoubtedly contributed to these inequalities, this has been the unfortunate reality for Black and Latino workers since the 1970s.[13]

Income Inequality and Lower Returns on Income Earned

Even when Latino and Black families are employed, they face a median household income gap that sees them earning about $13,000 and $20,000 less per year, respectively, than the median White household earns ($50,400).[14] Adding to this disparity is the fact that not every dollar earned is equal between these communities. For every dollar White households earn, they see a wealth return of $19.51, whereas Black and Latino

households see a wealth return of just $4.80 and $3.63, respectively, for every dollar they earn.[15]

Limited Ability to Weather a Financial Emergency

Over two-thirds of Black and Hispanic households (67% and 71%, respectively) lack the savings necessary to subsist at the poverty level for three months in the event of an unexpected income disruption, such as a job loss or medical emergency.[16] By comparison, a little over a third of White households are in a similar financial position. Put differently, Black and Latino families face financial insecurity at about double the rate of White families.

Increased Exposure to Wealth-Stripping Products and Services

For low-wealth households, meeting everyday financial needs often means relying on alternative financial services, such as nonbank remittances, prepaid cards, or check cashers. Today, 46% of Black households and 40% of Latino households use these services—more than double the usage rate among White households (18%).[17] While there are a number of reasons why Black and Latino households turn to these services—such as banks moving out of poorer rural areas, high overdraft fees, and mistrust of financial institutions—the reality is that fees and interest associated with these services end up stripping families of much-needed financial resources. In some instances, these services take away as much as 10% of a household's income.[18] For Black and Latino households living on the financial edge, spending this much of their limited resources just to carry out day-to-day financial transactions is a burden they cannot afford.

Lower Educational Attainment and Wealth Insulation

Less than 20% of Black adults and less than 15% of Hispanic adults hold four-year degrees.[19] Unfortunately, even after obtaining a four-year degree, the wealth returns generated by that education are much more valuable to White graduates ($55,869) than for Black ($4,846) and Hispanic ($4,191) graduates.[20] Even more unfortunate is that although education continues to be one of the surest ways to move up the economic ladder, research has found that higher education hasn't provided households of color with the kind of protection against wealth loss one would image it would.[21]

Lower Entrepreneurship Rates and Business Values

Not only are households of color less likely to own businesses than White households, but when they do, the average value of their businesses is significantly lower than the average value of White-owned businesses. On average, White-owned businesses are worth eight times more than the average Black-owned business and four times more than the average Hispanic-owned business.[22]

Nonexistent Retirement Savings

Today, the average Black and Latino household has over $100,000 less in retirement savings than the average White household ($19,049 and $12,329, respectively, compared to $130,472 for White households).[23] Included among the factors that are fueling this disparity are the racial inequities in homeownership—equity from which many retirees depend on—and high student loan debt carried by Black and Latino households.[24] Moreover, making the dignity of a comfortable retirement more difficult for Black and Latino workers to achieve is the fact that these workers are less likely than White workers to have access to and participate in employer-sponsored retirement plans.[25]

ASIAN AMERICAN AND PACIFIC ISLANDERS

While this report focuses on the economic well-being of Blacks and Latinos, Asian American and Pacific Islander (AAPI) and Native American households are facing great economic challenges as well. In fact, despite having greater economic strength than other racial groups, AAPI families lost over half of their wealth in the aftermath of the Great Recession.[26] When it comes to the economic divide between White and Asian households, recent research from the Federal Reserve Bank of St. Louis has found that the racial wealth divide between these two groups is closing rapidly as Asian Americans have steadily seen their income and wealth increase over the years. Today, according to this very same research, Asian households are already surpassing White households in median income and are soon to pass them in median wealth.

However, despite the tremendous progress Asian households have made over the years, our ability to truly understand the state of Asian economic security is greatly hampered by aggregated Asian economic data, which groups multiple AAPI communities under a single racial category.[27] In turn—as recent research has found in Los Angeles[28] and throughout the country[29]—the collective Asian label obscures the different economic realities of dozens of AAPI ethnicities, as well as people with different immigration and citizenship statuses. Moreover, aggregated Asian economic data also conceal the fact that since the wake of the recession, the number of AAPIs living in poverty has increased by more than half a million, an increase of 38%. This increase is much higher than that of the general population (27%), second only to the increase seen within the Latino population (42%).[30]

Native American Households

Similarly, while research shows that Native American households face economic security challenges similar to those of Black and Latino households—including high rates of employment (26%)[31] and poverty (28%)[32]—the economic disparities facing these communities are often overlooked because of limited economic data. In part, this is due to the size of the Native American population (5.4 million individuals, or about 2% of the total U.S. population),[33] which makes it difficult to demonstrate their economic well-being in nationally representative studies.

THE FUTURE OF THE RACIAL WEALTH DIVIDE

Given the fact that over the past 30 years, the racial wealth divide has steadily increased, we can reasonably speculate that the future of this divide will be much worse. Fortunately, we do not have to simply speculate about the future of racial wealth inequality. Extrapolating from past trends, we can estimate what the future of wealth inequality will look like in this country. Unfortunately, it doesn't look good.

THE RACIAL WEALTH DIVIDE IN 2043

For White households, repeating the past 30 years would mean an average wealth increase of $18,368 a year—topping out at $1.2 million. Were Latino households to repeat the past three decades, they would see their wealth increase by only $2,254 a year, for a total of about $165,000. When it comes to Black households, their wealth would only increase by $765 per year, reaching over $107,000 by 2043. By then, the racial wealth divide between White households and Black and Latino households will stand at over a million dollars.

By 2043, the U.S. Census Bureau projects that households of color will account for more than half of the entire U.S. population.[34] By the time people of color become the majority, the racial wealth divide will not just be a racial and social justice issue impacting a particular group of people—it will be the single greatest economic issue facing our country. If these trends continue unabated, the entire U.S. economy will suffer.

In fact, while former Federal Reserve chair (2014–2018) Janet Yellen . . . categorized the relationship between inequality and economic growth as complex and not yet fully understood, she warned that the wealth disparities between White households and households of color—which she called "extremely disturbing"—could have an impact on future consumer spending (a noted indicator of overall economic health).[35] If we look at the annual rates of wealth increase over the next 30 years that we present in this reading, we see a 3% annual increase for Whites, a 2% annual increase for Latinos, and a 1% annual increase for Blacks. If we compare these annual increases to the country's long-term inflation rate, which averages about 3%, it's easy to see that even after 30 years, Whites are holding steady in terms of their buying power while Blacks and Latinos are losing ground.

The Long Road to Reaching Racial Wealth Equity

For any person or group to overcome the extreme economic inequality we face today is a daunting task. For Black and Latino households—who for years have had their wealth and economic opportunity stripped from them—overcoming these inequities seems almost impossible. Regrettably, as we highlighted earlier in this reading, the trends for median wealth among Black, Latino, and White families clearly show that we aren't on a path to reaching racial wealth equality any time soon, if at all. If we continue at similar rates, even after an infinite number of years into the future, the racial wealth gap won't close. If we do nothing, the racial wealth divide will just keep getting worse.

Even if we were on a path toward racial wealth equality between Whites, Blacks, and Latinos, our data show that the end of that road would be a really long way off. Assuming that White wealth remained stagnant at today's levels and average Latino wealth grew at the same pace it has over the past three decades, it would take average Latino families 84 years to amass the same amount of wealth White families have today—that's the year 2097. For Black families, that figure jumps to 228 years, meaning Black families would not reach wealth parity with White households until the year 2241. To put this number in perspective, the amount of time Black families would need to build the wealth White families have today is just 17 years shorter than the 245-year span of slavery in this country. . . .

NOTES

1. Civil Rights Division, Investigation of the Ferguson Police Department (Washington, DC: United States Department of Justice, 2015).
2. Edward N. Wolff, *Household Wealth Trends in the United States, 1962–2013: What Happened over the Great Recession?* (Cambridge, MA: National Bureau of Economic Research, 2014), 51.
3. Chuck Collins and Josh Hoxie, *Billionaire Bonanza: The Forbes 400 and the Rest of Us* (Boston: Institute for Policy Studies, 2015), 17.
4. Richard Wilkinson, "How Economic Inequality Harms Societies," Ted Global, July 2011. For more, see Sam Pizzigati, *Greed and Good: Understanding and Overcoming the Inequality That Limits Our Lives* (Lanham, MD: Rowman & Littlefield, 2014), 311–30. Also see Dr. Stephen Bezruchka's website, Population Health Forum (http://depts.washington.edu/eqhlth), for information

on global and U.S. health and inequality information. See also Stephen Bezruchka and Mary Anne Mercer, "The Lethal Divide: How Economic Inequality Affects Health," in M. Fort, Mary Anne Mercer, and Oscar Gish (eds.), *Sickness and Wealth: The Corporate Assault on Global Health* (Boston: South End Press, 2004), 11–18.

5. Wolff, *Household Wealth Trends*, 60–61.
6. Signe-Mary McKernan, Caroline Ratcliffe, Eugene Steuerle and Sisi Zhang, *Less Than Equal: Racial Disparities in Wealth Accumulation* (Washington, DC: Urban Institute, 2013), 5.
7. Kasey Wiedrich, Lebaron Sims Jr., Holden Weisman, Solana Rice. and Jennifer Brooks, *The Steep Climb to Economic Opportunity* (Washington, DC: CFED, 2016), 11–12.
8. Merrit Gillard, *Homeownership Is Still Out of Reach for Millions of Households* (Washington, DC: CFED, 2016), 3.
9. Thomas Shapiro, Tatjana Meschede and Sam Osoro, *The Roots of the Widening Racial Wealth Gap: Explaining the Black-White Economic Divide* (Waltham, MA: Institute on Assets and Social Policy, Brandeis University, 2013), 3.
10. U.S. Bureau of Labor Statistics, "Table A-2. Employment Status of the Civilian Population by Race, Sex and Age," July 2016, http://www.bls.gov/news.release/empsit.t02.htm.
11. U.S. Bureau of Labor Statistics, "Table A-3. Employment Status of the Hispanic or Latino Population by Sex and Age," July 2016, http://www.bls.gov/news.release/empsit.t03.htm.
12. U.S. Bureau of Labor Statistics," Table A-2."
13. Derek Thompson, "The Workforce Is Even More Divided by Race than You Think," *The Atlantic*, November 6, 2013, www.theatlantic.com/business/archive/2013/11/the-workforce-is-even-more-divided-by-race-than-youthink/281175.
14. Laura Sullivan, Tatjana Meschede, Lars Dietrich, Thomas Shapiro, Amy Traub, Catherine Ruetschlin, and Tamara Draut, *The Racial Wealth Gap: Why Policy Matters* (New York: Demos and Institute for Assets & Social Policy, Brandeis University, 2015), 24.
15. Sullivan et al., 2015, 25.
16. Liquid asset poverty is a measure of the liquid savings households hold to cover basic expenses for three months if they experienced a sudden job loss, a medical emergency, or another financial crisis leading to loss of stable income. For a family of four, that amount is approximately $6,063. "Liquid Asset Poverty Rate," Assets & Opportunity Scorecard, January 2016, http://scorecard.assetsandopportunity.org/latest/measure/liquid-asset-povertyrate.
17. FDIC National Survey of Unbanked and Underbanked Households (Washington, DC: Federal Deposit Insurance Corporation, 2013), 58.
18. Based on 34 million households, earning an average of $25,000 per year, spending a total of $82 billion in 2011. Source: KPMG, Serving the Underserved Market, 2011, as quoted in Providing Non-Bank Financial Services for the Underserved (Washington, DC: U.S. Postal Service Office of the Inspector General, 2014).
19. "Four-Year Degree by Race," Assets and Opportunity Scorecard, January 2016, http://scorecard.assetsandopportunity.org/latest/measure/four-year-degree-by-race.
20. Sullivan et al., 2015, 16.
21. William R. Emmons and Bryan J. Noeth, "Why Didn't Higher Education Protect Hispanic and Black Wealth?," *In The Balance: Perspectives on Household Balance Sheets*, Issue 12, (August 2015), https://www.stlouisfed.org/~/media/publications/in%20the%20balance/images/issue_12/itb_august_2015.pdf
22. "Business Value by Race," Assets & Opportunity Scorecard, January 2016, http://scorecard.assetsandopportunity.org/latest/measure/business-value-by-race.

23. Serena Lei and Fiona Blackshaw, "Nine Charts about Wealth Inequality in America," Urban Institute, February 2015, http://apps.urban.org/features/wealth-inequality-charts.

24. Danny Vinik, "The Alarming Retirement Crisis Facing Minorities in America," *The New Republic*, February 18, 2015, https://newrepublic.com/article/121084/urban-institute-study-minorities-have-built-less-wealth-Whites.

25. Nari Rhee, *Race and Retirement Insecurity in the United States* (Washington, DC: National Institute on Retirement Security, 2013), 3.

26. Maya Rockeymoore and Elvis Guzman, *The Racial Wealth Gap: Asian Americans and Pacific Islanders* (Washington, DC: Center for Global Policy Solutions, 2014), 2.

27. Rockeymoore and Guzman, 2014.

28. Melany De La Cruz-Viesca, Zhenxiang Chen, Paul M. Ong, Darrick Hamilton, and William A. Darity, Jr., *The Color of Wealth in Los Angeles* (Los Angeles: Asian American Studies Center, UCLA, 2016).

29. Alvina Condon, Jane Duong, Joyce Pisnanont, Chhandara Pech, Paul M. Ong, and Melany De La Cruz-Viesca, *Scrimping + Saving: A Report on Financial Access, Attitudes, and Behaviors of Low- and Moderate-Income Asian Americans and Pacific Islanders* (Washington, DC: National Coalition for Asian Pacific American Community Development, 2015).

30. Josh Ishimatsu, *Spotlight: Asian American and Pacific Islander Poverty* (Washington, DC: National Coalition for Asian Pacific American Community Development, 2013), 1.

31. Bryce Covert, "The Unemployment Rate for Native Americans Has Been over 10 Percent For Five Years," *ThinkProgress*, October 2013, http://thinkprogress.org/economy/2013/10/29/2855951/unemployment-nativeamericans/.

32. "Income Poverty Rate," Assets & Opportunity Scorecard, January 2016, http://scorecard.assetsandopportunity.org/latest/measure/income-poverty-rate.

33. "American Indian and Alaska Native Heritage Month: November 2015," U.S. Census Bureau, November 2015, http://www.census.gov/newsroom/facts-for-features/2015/cb15-ff22.html.

34. "New Census Bureau Report Analyzes U.S. Population Projections," U.S. Census Bureau, March 2015, http://www.census.gov/newsroom/press-releases/2015/cb15-tps16.html.

35. Craig Torres, "Yellen Calls Widening Racial Wealth Gap 'Extremely Disturbing,'" Bloomberg, June 22, 2016, http://www.bloomberg.com/news/articles/2016-06-22/yellen-calls-widening-racial-wealth-gap-extremely-disturbing.

THE SECOND RACIAL WEALTH GAP

MEL JONES

He died on a Saturday.

My mother and I had planned to pick my dad up from the hospital for a trip to the park. He loved to sit and watch families stroll by as we chatted about oak trees, Kona coffee, and the mysteries of God. This time, the park would miss him. His skin, smooth and brown like the outside of an avocado seed, glistened with sweat as he struggled to take his last breaths.

In that next year, I graduated from grad school, got a new job, and looked forward to saving for a downpayment on my first home, a dream I had always had but found lofty. I pulled up a blank spreadsheet and made a line item called "House Fund." That same week I got a call from my mom—she was struggling to pay off my dad's funeral expenses. I looked at my "House Fund" and sighed. Then I deleted it and typed the words "Funeral Fund" instead. My father's passing was unexpected. And so was the financial burden that came with it.

For many Millennials of color, these sorts of trade-offs aren't an anomaly. During key times in their lives when they should

(*continued*)

be building assets, they're spending money on basic necessities and often helping out family. Their financial future is a rocky one, and much of it comes down to how much—or how little—assistance they receive. A seminal study published in the *Journal of Washington Economic Monthly Perspectives* on wealth accumulation estimates that as much as 20 percent of wealth can be attributed to formal and informal gifts from family members, especially parents. And it starts early. In college, Black and Hispanic Millennials are more likely to have to work one or two jobs to get through, missing out on opportunities to connect with classmates who have time to tinker around in dorm rooms and go on to found multibillion-dollar companies together. Many of them take on higher levels of student debt than their White peers, often to pay for routine expenses, like textbooks, that their parents are less likely to subsidize. "Student debt is the biggest millstone around Millennials, period, and an even larger and heavier one around the necks of Black Millennials," said Tom Shapiro, director of the Institute on Assets and Social Policy. "It really hits those doing the right thing. [They're] going through all the hoops." He explained that, unlike in previous decades, when college tuition was drastically lower, the risks of educational costs are now passed down to the individual.

Recent polls indicate that a large portion of Millennials receive financial help from parents. At least 40 percent of the 1,000 Millennials (ages 18 to 34) polled in a March USA Today/Bank of America poll get help from parents on everyday expenses. A Clark University poll indicated an even higher number, with almost three-quarters of parents reporting that they provide their Millennial children with financial support. Another survey saw nearly a third of Baby Boomers paying for Millennials' medical expenses. A quarter of Boomers subsidized "other expenses" so that their Millennial offspring could save money. Black and Hispanic Americans are less likely to be the recipients of this type of support.

Ironically, even though Black and Hispanic Millennials are less likely to receive financial support from parents, their parents are more likely than White parents to expect their kids to help financially support them later on. According to the Clark poll, upward of 80 percent of Black parents and 70 percent of Hispanic parents expect to be supported. And most studies show that a primary reason why people of color are unable to save as adults is because they give financial support to close family. This is important because when life emergencies happen, many Millennials won't have the reserve money to cover it. A Millennial who gets regular financial gifts and support from parents will either have the money to cover an emergency themselves or (more likely) have a parent or grandparent cover it so there's no damage to their credit. They won't have to borrow from predatory lending institutions, move into unsafe neighborhoods to save on rent, or start from financial scratch each time. It doesn't even have to be a life emergency. If you have to decide between paying for a professional networking event or a cell phone bill, the latter is likely to win out. It should come as no surprise that Millennials who are free to choose career

development activities over routine expenses are likely to benefit more in the long run. When this happens once or twice on a small scale, it's not a big deal. It's the collective impact of a series of decisions that matters, the result of which is displayed among ethnic and class lines and grounded in historical privilege.

And the help doesn't end when Millennials enter the next stage of adulthood. It's not just young, out-of-work Millennials who get help from parents or family members, according to the USA Today poll: even Millennials making $75,000 or more said they had gotten money from their parents for basic necessities. Twenty percent of parents paid for their children's groceries, and more than 20 percent contributed money for clothing. Even 20 percent of cohabiting Millennials still had a parent paying for expenses like cell phone bills, according to the poll.

Shapiro said the numbers of Millennials receiving support from family are "absolutely underestimated" because many survey questions are not as methodical and specific as those a sociologist might ask. "As much as 90 percent of what you'll hear isn't picked up in the survey," he said. Shapiro's work pays special attention to the role of intergenerational family support in wealth building. He coined the term *transformative assets* to refer to any money acquired through family that facilitates social mobility beyond what their current income level would allow for. And it's not that parents and other family members are exceptionally altruistic either. "It's how we all operate," Shapiro said. "Resources tend to flow to people who are more needy."

Racial disparity in transformative assets became especially striking to Shapiro during interviews with middle-class Black Americans. "They almost always talk about financial help they give family members. People come to them," Shapiro said. But when he asked White interviewees if they were lending financial support to family members, he said, "I almost always get laughter. They're still getting subsidized." These small savings add up over time. Commentary often centers on the dire circumstances Millennials inherited ("It's the recession, stupid!") or the defective attributes of recipients ("Millennials are too entitled!"). But these oversimplified viewpoints miss the point of how some Millennials and their parents are able to weather tumultuous financial terrain in the first place—and more, how intergenerational financial support contributes to the long-term wealth-building capacity of these Millennials.

To many Millennials, the small influxes of cash from parents are a lifeline, a financial relief they're hard pressed to find elsewhere. To researchers, however, it's both a symptom and an exacerbating factor of wealth inequality. In a 2004 *CommonWealth* magazine interview, Shapiro explained that gifts like this are "often not a lot of money, but it's really important money. It's a kind of money that allows families to obtain something for themselves and for their children that they couldn't do on their own" (Keough 2004, p. 73). To be sure, gift-giving parents see it as a step in helping their Millennial children reach financial independence. But the bigger picture is that their support acts as a stabilizing factor now and an inheriting factor later. The Institute on Assets and Social Policy's "The Roots of the Widening Racial Wealth Gap" found that every dollar in financial family support received by a White American yielded 35 cents in wealth growth. For a Black individual, family support is much more essential to their financial trajectory: every one dollar received yielded 51 cents in wealth growth. Millennials of all backgrounds would certainly benefit from increased financial family support, but where you wind up depends a lot on where you started from.

You can't discuss wealth inequality without talking about race; within the American context, they are inseparable. The fact that Millennials of color feel the impact of a precarious financial foundation more acutely is not a surprise. For Black Millennials in particular, studies point to a legacy of discrimination over several centuries that contributed to less inherited wealth passed down from previous generations. This financial disparity stems from continuous shortfalls in their parents' net worth and low homeownership rates among Blacks, which works to create an unlevel playing field. As a result, the median wealth of White households is thirteen times the median wealth of Black households. In addition, the most recent housing bust is estimated to have wiped out half of the collective wealth of Black families—a setback of two generations. "It was just incredible," Shapiro said. "It hit hardest those groups latest to becoming home buyers." Homeownership makes up a large amount of Black families' wealth composition, accounting for over 50 percent of wealth for Blacks, compared with just 39 percent for Whites. Shapiro also pointed out that the people impacted by the housing crisis were likely to be the parents of Millennials.

Even with equal advances in income, education, and other factors, wealth grows at far lower rates for Black households because they usually need to use financial gains for everyday needs rather than long-term savings and asset building. Each dollar in income increase yields $5.19 in wealth for White American households, but only 69 cents for Black American households. In addition, while many Americans don't have adequate savings, the rate is far higher for families of color: 95 percent of African American and 87 percent of Latino middle-class families do not have enough net assets to meet most of their essential living expenses for even three months if their source of income were to disappear. If Millennials of color aren't getting as much financial help, it's because there's just not as much help for their families to give. It's more than just a lack of "pocket money" from parents that impacts Millennials of color. The last significant stop on life's journey is often an economically definitive one too, when parents and grandparents pass away and leave an inheritance.

According to the Institute on Assets and Social Policy, White Americans are five times more likely to inherit than Black Americans (36 percent to 7 percent, respectively). And even when both groups received an inheritance, White Americans received about ten times more. "It's really a double whammy," Shapiro said. On the flip side, Black Millennials and other low-asset groups are much more likely to go into debt when a family member passes away. It's not uncommon for some families to throw bake sales and engage in other fundraising activities to bury their relatives. A 2013 *Washington Post* article noted that "Black families rarely benefited from inheritances and gifts to help them make down payments on homes. The result was that Black families typically bought homes eight years later than Whites, giving them less time to build equity." "That's an eight-year window of not paying rent and building equity," Shapiro said (Fletcher, 2013).

The life cycle of homeownership-related matters is an onerous one for Black Americans to begin with. The researchers Kerwin Charles and Erik Hurst found that Black mortgage applicants were almost twice as likely to be rejected for a loan in the first place, even when credit profile and household wealth were controlled for. The same study found that almost half of White Americans got money from a family source for a home downpayment, while nine in ten Black Americans had to come up with their entire downpayment on their own—which had the effect of disincentivizing younger Black renters from buying. "Even when they were able to buy a home," the *Post* article said, "the typical Black family did not see that property appreciate as much as did the typical White family."

It all adds up to a slice of the racial wealth gap that's hard to grasp because it's made up of many smaller inequalities instead of one massive one. It's not the difference between a silver spoon and a dirt floor, it's the one between textbook money and a campus job. It's not the difference between the 1 percent and the destitute, it's the one between a birthday card from Grandma and paying her hospital bill. The gap in gifts, debts, and inheritances creates a vicious cycle, with large ramifications for many Black Millennials and their financial future. When combined with redlining and unequal returns on income and education, the odds are stacked in a terrible way.

My father left me with many things of value: a love of creation, an affinity for literature, a deep sense of integrity, and a penchant for easily making friends out of strangers. He loved America, despite the times it relegated him to the back doors of its restaurants as a "colored man." He placed glossy graduation photos of me from high school and college in nooks around the house like prized medallions. They symbolized his version of the "American Dream," where his children—his Millennials—would accomplish more than he ever could. For his sake and mine, I hope he's right.

REFERENCES

Fletcher, Michael. 2013. "Study Ties Black-White Wealth Gap to Stubborn Disparities in Real Estate." *The Washington Post*, February 26.
Keough, Robert. 2004. "To Have and Not Have. *Common Wealth* 9(2): 71–79.

JOSEPH E. STIGLITZ

4. OF THE 1%, BY THE 1%, FOR THE 1%

Stiglitz highlights the increasing power and privilege of the richest 1% and calls for change. He discusses how this economic inequality is bad for our country because increasing inequality contributes to decreasing equality of opportunity and a reluctance of the 1% to identify with and spend on the common needs of our society.

It's no use pretending that what has obviously happened has not in fact happened. The upper 1 percent of Americans are now taking in nearly a quarter of the nation's income every year. In terms of wealth rather than income, the top 1 percent control 40 percent. Their lot in life has improved considerably. Twenty-five years ago, the corresponding figures were 12 percent and 33 percent. One response might be to celebrate the ingenuity and drive that brought good fortune to these people, and to contend that a rising tide lifts all boats. That response would be misguided. While the top 1 percent have seen their incomes rise 18 percent over the past decade, those in the middle have actually seen their incomes fall. For men with only high-school degrees, the decline has been precipitous—12 percent in the last quarter-century alone. All the growth in recent decades—and more—has gone to those at the top. In terms of income equality, America lags behind any country in the old, ossified Europe. . . . Among our closest counterparts are Russia with its oligarchs and Iran. While many of the old centers of inequality in Latin America, such as Brazil, have been striving in recent years, rather successfully, to improve the plight of the poor and reduce gaps in income, America has allowed inequality to grow.

Economists long ago tried to justify the vast inequalities that seemed so troubling in the mid-19th century—inequalities that are but a pale shadow of what we are seeing in America today. The justification they came up with was called "marginal-productivity theory." In a nutshell, this theory associated higher incomes with higher productivity and a greater contribution to society. It is a theory that has always been cherished by the rich. Evidence for its validity, however, remains thin. The corporate executives who helped bring on the recession of the [mid-2000s] . . . whose contribution to our society, and to their own companies, has been massively negative—went on to receive large bonuses. In some cases, companies were so embarrassed about calling such rewards "performance bonuses" that they felt compelled to change the name to "retention bonuses" (even if the only thing being retained was bad performance). Those who have contributed great positive innovations to our society, from the pioneers of genetic understanding to the pioneers of the Information Age, have received a pittance compared with those responsible for the financial innovations that brought our global economy to the brink of ruin.

Some people look at income inequality and shrug their shoulders. So what if this person gains and that person loses? What matters, they argue, is not how the pie is divided but the size of the pie. That argument is fundamentally wrong. An economy in which *most* citizens are doing worse year after year—an economy like America's—is not likely to do well over the long haul. There are several reasons for this.

First, growing inequality is the flip side of something else: shrinking opportunity. Whenever we diminish equality of opportunity, it means that we are not using some of our most valuable assets—our people—in the most productive way possible. Second, many of the distortions that lead to inequality—such as those associated with monopoly power and preferential tax treatment for special interests—undermine the efficiency of the economy. This new inequality goes on to create new distortions, undermining efficiency even further. To give just one example, far too many of our most talented young people, seeing the astronomical rewards, have gone into finance rather than into fields that would lead to a more productive and healthy economy. Third, and perhaps most important, a modern economy requires "collective action"—it needs government to invest in infrastructure, education, and technology. The United States and the world have benefited greatly from government-sponsored research that led to the Internet, to advances in public health, and so on. But America has long suffered from an under-investment in infrastructure (look at the condition of our highways and bridges, our railroads and airports), in basic research, and in education at all levels. Further cutbacks in these areas lie ahead.

None of this should come as a surprise—it is simply what happens when a society's wealth distribution becomes lopsided. The more divided a society becomes in terms of wealth, the more reluctant the wealthy become to spend money on common needs. The rich don't need to rely on government for parks or education or medical care or personal security—they can buy all these things for themselves. In the process, they become more distant from ordinary people, losing whatever empathy they may once have had. They also worry about strong government—one that could use its powers to adjust the balance, take some of their wealth, and invest it for the common good. The top 1 percent may complain about the kind of government we have in America, but in truth they like it just fine: too gridlocked to re-distribute, too divided to do anything but lower taxes.

Economists are not sure how to fully explain the growing inequality in America. The ordinary dynamics of supply and demand have certainly played a role: labor-saving technologies have reduced the demand for many "good" middle-class, blue-collar jobs. Globalization has created a worldwide marketplace, pitting expensive unskilled workers in America against cheap unskilled workers overseas. Social changes have also played a role—for instance, the decline of unions, which once represented a third of American workers and now represent about 12 percent.

But one big part of the reason we have so much inequality is that the top 1 percent want it that way. The most obvious example involves tax policy. Lowering tax rates on capital gains, which is how the rich receive a large portion of their income, has given the wealthiest Americans close to a free ride. Monopolies and near monopolies have always been a source of economic power—from John D. Rockefeller at the beginning of the last century to Bill Gates at the end. Lax enforcement of anti-trust laws, especially during Republican administrations, has been a godsend to the top 1 percent. Much of today's inequality is due to manipulation of the financial system, enabled by changes in the rules that have been bought and paid for by the financial industry itself—one of its best investments ever. The government lent money to financial institutions at close to 0 percent interest and provided generous bailouts on favorable terms when all else failed. Regulators turned a blind eye to a lack of transparency and to conflicts of interest.

When you look at the sheer volume of wealth controlled by the top 1 percent in this country, it's tempting to see our growing inequality as a quintessentially American achievement—we started way behind the pack, but now we're doing inequality on a world-class level. And it looks as if we'll be building on this achievement for years to come, because what made it possible is self-reinforcing. Wealth begets power, which begets more wealth. During the savings-and-loan scandal of the 1980s—a scandal whose dimensions, by today's standards, seem almost quaint—the banker Charles Keating was asked by a congressional committee whether the $1.5 million he had spread among a few key elected officials could actually buy influence. "I certainly hope so," he replied. The Supreme Court, in its recent *Citizens United* case, has enshrined the right of corporations to buy government, by removing limitations on campaign spending. The personal and the political are today in perfect alignment. Virtually all U.S. senators, and most of the representatives in the House, are members of the top

1 percent when they arrive, are kept in office by money from the top 1 percent, and know that if they serve the top 1 percent well they will be rewarded by the top 1 percent when they leave office. By and large, the key executive-branch policymakers on trade and economic policy also come from the top 1 percent. When pharmaceutical companies receive a trillion-dollar gift—through legislation prohibiting the government, the largest buyer of drugs, from bargaining over price—it should not come as cause for wonder. It should not make jaws drop that a tax bill cannot emerge from Congress unless big tax cuts are put in place for the wealthy. Given the power of the top 1 percent, this is the way you would *expect* the system to work.

America's inequality distorts our society in every conceivable way. There is, for one thing, a well-documented lifestyle effect—people outside the top 1 percent increasingly live beyond their means. Trickle-down economics may be a chimera, but trickle-down behaviorism is very real. Inequality massively distorts our foreign policy. The top 1 percent rarely serve in the military—the reality is that the "all-volunteer" army does not pay enough to attract their sons and daughters, and patriotism goes only so far. Plus, the wealthiest class feels no pinch from higher taxes when the nation goes to war: borrowed money will pay for all that. Foreign policy, by definition, is about the balancing of national interests and national resources. With the top 1 percent in charge, and paying no price, the notion of balance and restraint goes out the window. There is no limit to the adventures we can undertake; corporations and contractors stand only to gain. The rules of economic globalization are likewise designed to benefit the rich: they encourage competition among countries

for *business*, which drives down taxes on corporations, weakens health and environmental protections, and undermines what used to be viewed as the "core" labor rights, which include the right to collective bargaining. Imagine what the world might look like if the rules were designed instead to encourage competition among countries for *workers*. Governments would compete in providing economic security, low taxes on ordinary wage earners, good education, and a clean environment—things workers care about. But the top 1 percent don't need to care.

CONCLUSIONS

The U.S. now has a campaign finance system where a tiny slice of individuals—31,385 people, not even enough to fill half of a professional football stadium—collectively account for more than a quarter of all individual contributions (that we can trace), even though they represent just one in ten thousand Americans. Every single member of Congress elected in 2012 received a contribution from this group of individuals, and the vast majority of those elected (84 percent) received more money from the "1% of the 1%" than they did from all small donations (under $200).

A tiny sliver of Americans who can afford to give tens of thousands of dollars in a single election cycle have become the gatekeepers of public office in America. Through the growing congressional dependence on their contributions, they increasingly set the boundaries and limits of American political discourse—who can run for office, what their priorities should be and even what can be said in public. And in an era of unlimited campaign contributions, the power of the 1% of the 1% only stands to grow with each passing year.

CHRIS M. VIDMAR

5. THE COST OF ADMISSION

Political Elites and the National Discourse

Vidmar documents the increasing influence of the wealthy in politics through their financing of political campaigns (including influencing who can run for office and win), demonstrating that a small number of very wealthy individuals are able to amplify their own political interests over those of the average citizen. He describes how the political elite, through their contributions, are able to set political agendas and influence the political process in an unfettered way. Vidmar's analysis demonstrates a need for campaign finance reform if we want to move toward more democratic participatory government.

It's no secret that running for office in the United States takes a lot of money, especially at the national level. Effective political campaigns are shockingly expensive and have only gotten more so in recent years. Spending on the 2000 presidential election reached $1.4 billion and ballooned to almost $2.4 billion in 2016 (Center for Responsive Politics 2018). In those same years, total spending on congressional races went from approximately $1.7 billion to just over $4 billion, and spending on the 2018 elections topped $5.7 billion (Center for Responsive Politics 2018). When accounting for all sources of spending (the candidate's campaign, party dollars, outside sources, etc.) the average winner of a Senate race in 2016 had $19.4 million spent on their campaign (Kim 2016). The landmark 2010 U.S. Supreme Court decision *Citizens United vs. the Federal Election Commission*, which greatly deregulated spending toward campaigns, was central to these increases (Drutman 2013).

Perhaps more important than the amount of money spent on campaigns is where that money comes from. If even getting your name on the ballot in any meaningful way requires raising millions in campaign money, then the people who give to politicians effectively control who can run for office. In an ideal democracy, this would mean campaign contributions from a wide variety of citizens in reasonably small amounts, thus reflecting a broad and diverse constituency. But this is not the current case in the United States. Recent elections have seen an increasingly disproportionate concentration of campaign funds from a very small percentage of the population. These political elites have tremendous sway over the political discourse by influencing who can run for office, who is likely to win, and what their agendas look like after they are elected.

POLITICAL ELITES

Tracking where campaign money comes from and where it goes is complicated. Funds can come from individuals or corporations and go to individual candidates, political parties, or outside organizations. To complicate matters even more, recent deregulation has led to increased amounts of untraceable contributions known as "dark money." Two nonprofit organizations, the Sunlight Foundation and the Center for Responsive Politics, have approached this issue by taking a close look at who these elite campaign contributors are, what

Original to *Focus on Social Problems: A Contemporary Reader*.

proportion of campaign funding they are responsible for, and who their money supports. They focus on what they call the 1% of the 1%—the top contributors roughly equal to 0.01% of the U.S. population (around 32,000people). According to their analysis, the proportion of traceable campaign contributions that comes from political elites has grown in recent elections. In 2010, they were responsible for 21% of all disclosed political fundraising (Olsen-Phillips et al. 2015). This rose to 25% in 2012, and in 2014 they were responsible for 29%—a whopping $1.18 billion in contributions (Olsen-Phillips et al. 2015). In 2014, the lowest contribution that would get you into this group was $8,800, and the median contribution was $14,750, but the upper echelon of political elites gave much more (contributions can be to a single source or through multiple channels) (Olsen-Phillips et al. 2015). Each of the top 100 contributors to the 2018 elections gave over $1.6 million, with the top contributor giving $123 million (Center for Responsive Politics 2018). What does it mean for our democracy to have so few responsible for the lifeblood of political campaigning?

With such a strikingly disproportionate level of influence over the political process, these political elites clearly serve as gatekeepers to public office; without their support, what chance would a candidate have? Well, it turns out very little at all. Every single member of Congress in the 2012 and 2014 elections received money from political elites (Drutman 2013; Olsen-Phillips et al. 2015). In 2012, Republicans received 40% more funds than Democrats from political elites, but this gap disappeared in subsequent elections as contributions from political elites have swelled for both parties (Center for Responsive Politics 2018; Drutman 2013; Olsen-Phillips et al. 2015). Contributions from the top 100 elites in 2018 totaled $395 million for Democrats and $343 million for Republicans (Center for Responsive Politics 2018).

Clearly, political elites influence both parties, but who are they? Some inferences might be made about the political elites by their occupations, the sector of the economy they represent, or their stated reasons for contributing (when given). The largest proportion of funds to both parties came from donors who work in finance,

insurance, and real estate (FIRE). Elites in securities and investments gave the most to both parties, and more political elites worked for Goldman Sachs than any other employer (Drutman 2013). After givers from the FIRE sector, Republican donations came largely from miscellaneous businesses and the energy sector, while Democrats saw a large proportion of their donations from lawyers (Drutman 2013). Democrats also had a greater proportion of their funds from ideological contributors—those who gave based on support for a single political issue—compared to Republicans. The influence of the political elites is also gendered: 75% of political elites are men, and only one woman was in the top 20 donors in 2014 (Drutman 2013).

Beyond party breakdowns, where does the money go? In 2014, about 28% of money given by political elites went directly to candidates, roughly 30% went to political parties, and a concerning 31% went to super PACs (Drutman 2013). Since the *Citizens United* decision, this giving from political elites to outside groups—mainly in the form of super PACs—has exploded. These organizations, a type of political action committee, are the main pathway for *unlimited* giving because they are intended to operate without coordinating with parties or campaigns. However, many critics have pointed out that the campaigning they do is often identical in message and approach to "official" party or candidate messages (Sullivan 2014; Wollner 2015). In 2010, political elites gave only $38.6 million to outside organizations such as super PACs, but in 2014 this sum grew to over $373 million (Drutman 2013). Super PACs often use this money to run extensive media campaigns for those candidates the elites favor—and against any that might oppose their interests.

WHY WE SHOULD CARE

In October 2013, then President Obama expressed his concerns about the effect of *Citizens United* and similar actions to deregulate campaign financing:

> There aren't a lot of functioning democracies around the world that work this way, where you can have millionaires and billionaires bankrolling whoever they want, however they want, in some cases undisclosed.

What it means is ordinary Americans are shut out of the process . . . they can entirely skew our politics, and there are a whole bunch of members of Congress right now that privately will tell you, "I know our positions are unreasonable, but we're scared that if we don't go along with . . . [an] extremist agenda, we'll be challenged from the right, and the threats are really explicit." (*New York Times* 2013)

Obama also underscored that this was not a partisan issue—politicians on both sides of the aisle have fallen under the influence of political elites—and that many of the problems in Washington are a result of these funding issues. If politicians rely on the money of political elites to get reelected, they have little choice but to adopt the ideology of those donors on virtually all issues. This ideological functioning makes it difficult to pinpoint the influence of political elites. Rarely is there an overt trading of favors; instead, there is a subtle and continuous control of the political conversation. If a motion or piece of legislation is proposed by a member of Congress that might genuinely benefit their constituency but goes against the interests of the political elites, it is silenced or simply ignored.

This pattern was empirically demonstrated by political scientists Gilens and Page (2014). Through a statistical analysis of 1,779 instances where the public was asked their opinion of policy changes, they found that individual economic elites and organizations held substantial sway over public policy, while the public had little influence. Their conclusion was that Americans "do enjoy many features central to democratic governance such as regular elections . . . [but when] policymaking is dominated by powerful business organizations and a small number of affluent Americans . . . America's claims to being a democratic society are seriously threatened" (Gilens & Page 2014). When a select few can steer the course of politics through unlimited campaign contributions, we have to question the integrity of our system.

In most cases, issues that many Americans agree on simply never enter the discourse. Take, for example, the issue of wealth and income inequality—an issue on which we can safely assume the position of most political elites (since higher-income levels predict greater approval of the current distribution) (Gallup 2015). Surveys have found that 63% of Americans think the distribution of income and wealth in the United States is unfair, and as high as 52% support heavy taxes on the rich to even the distribution (Newport 2015). In regard to corporations, over half (52%) of Americans believe corporations should pay higher taxes, while less than half that number (24%) think corporate tax should be reduced (Fingerhut 2017). Despite this evidence that most Americans think that higher taxes on the rich and corporations would make for a fairer society, the legislative agenda reflects the interests of political elites, with massive tax cuts on corporate profits and capital gains—a primary source of income for the super-rich (Paletta 2018). This is only one obvious issue where the interests of the political elites overpower majority concerns. Social issues such as mass incarceration and criminal justice reform, legalization or decriminalization of prostitution and of certain drugs, reduction of military spending, and the ballooning of student loan debt all show significant public support, but these conversations rarely enter the political conversation, and when they do, they often get little to no traction.

Beyond casting a ballot, contributing to a campaign is the next logical step in influencing politics: if you want to have your concerns addressed, help someone who shares your views get elected. In a regulated way, where donations are spread from a large diverse pool, this system can support a healthy democracy. However, it's clear that deregulation has corrupted this system; wealth now amplifies the voices of political elites, controlling the political discourse and overpowering the needs of common citizens. Understanding these systems is challenging, but at a minimum we need to be critical of campaign messages and learn who is behind them. We may not be able to outspend the political elites, but contacting representatives, engaging in protests, and volunteering for ethical candidates are powerful actions. Most important, we need to send a clear message to our leadership: restore regulations to campaign financing, and rebuild our healthy democracy.

REFERENCES

Center for Responsive Politics. 2018. "Cost of Election | OpenSecrets." Retrieved November 22, 2019, from https://www.opensecrets.org/overview/cost.php.

Drutman, Lee. 2013. "The Political 1% of the 1% in 2012." *Sunlight Foundation*. Retrieved September 28, 2018, from https://sunlightfoundation.com/2013/06/24/1pct_of_the_1pct.

Fingerhut, Hannah. 2017. "Americans Would Rather Raise than Lower Taxes on Corporations, High Incomes." *Pew Research Center*. Retrieved September 29, 2018, from http://www.pewresearch.org/fact-tank/2017/09/27/more-americans-favor-raising-than-lowering-tax-rates-on-corporations-high-household-incomes.

Gilens, Martin, and Benjamin I. Page. 2014. "Testing Theories of American Politics: Elites, Interest Groups, and Average Citizens." *Perspectives on Politics* 12(3): 564.

Kim, Soo Rin. 2016. "The Price of Winning Just Got Higher, Especially in the Senate." *Huffington Post*. Retrieved September 21, 2018, from https://www.huffingtonpost.com/opensecrets-blog/the-price-of-winning-just_b_12888366.html.

New York Times. 2013. "Obama on Citizens United Ruling–YouTube." Retrieved September 29, 2018, from https://www.youtube.com/watch?v=O8ApHBsP5Z0.

Newport, Frank. 2015. "Americans Continue to Say U.S. Wealth Distribution Is Unfair." *Gallup.Com*. Retrieved September 29, 2018, from https://news.gallup.com/poll/182987/americans-continue-say-wealth-distribution-unfair.aspx.

Olsen-Phillips, Peter, Russ Choma, Sarah Bryner, and Doug Weber. 2015. "The Political One Percent of the One Percent: Megadonors Fuel Rising Cost of Elections in 2014." *Sunlight Foundation*. Retrieved January 8, 2019, from https://sunlightfoundation.com/2015/04/30/the-political-one-percent-of-the-one-percent-megadonors-fuel-rising-cost-of-elections-in-2014.

Paletta, Damian. 2018. "Trump Administration Considers Tax Cut for the Wealthy." *Washington Post*. Retrieved September 29, 2018, from https://www.washingtonpost.com/business/economy/trump-administration-considers-tax-cut-for-the-wealthy/2018/07/30/1dbaafbc-9442-11e8-810c-5fa705927d54_story.html.

Sullivan, Sean. 2014. "Super PACs and Campaigns Can't Talk to Each Other. Here's How They Get around It." *Washington Post*. Retrieved October 11, 2018, from https://www.washingtonpost.com/news/the-fix/wp/2014/04/24/super-pacs-and-campaigns-cant-talk-to-each-other-heres-how-they-get-around-it.

Wollner, Adam. 2015. "10 Ways Super PACs and Campaigns Coordinate, Even Though They're Not Allowed To." *The Atlantic*. Retrieved October 11, 2018, from https://www.theatlantic.com/politics/archive/2015/09/10-ways-super-pacs-and-campaigns-coordinate-even-though-theyre-not-allowed-to/436866.

CHAPTER 3

POVERTY

Poverty is a social problem that has been ever present in American society and one that, over the last several decades, we have made great strides in reducing. When the U.S. Census Bureau first began measuring the poverty rate in 1959, 22.4 percent of Americans were living in poverty.[1] Over the next decade, the poverty rate fell over 10 percent to 12.6 percent, where it has remained, fluctuating up and down a few points, since the late 1960s.[2] This dramatic decline in the poverty rate was due in large part to President Johnson's "War on Poverty," a set of initiatives (including Medicaid, Medicare, the food stamp program, and the expansion of Social Security) which still exist today.[3] Despite our success in reducing poverty, millions of Americans still live in poverty, suffering in myriad ways as a result. Sociologists study the causes and consequences of poverty, as well as its solutions, pointing, in particular, to structural reasons for poverty, with possible structural changes as solutions. Yet despite the abundance of research identifying structural causes of poverty, the American public remains divided on the subject. For example, in 2014 the Pew Research Center found that 44 percent of Americans believed that the poor "have it easy because they can get government benefits without doing anything in return," whereas 47 percent said that "poor people have hard lives because government benefits don't go far enough to help them live decently."[4] Perhaps unsurprisingly, these responses varied by income; nearly 40 percent of

1   Edwards, Ashley. 2018. "Poverty Rate Drops for Third Consecutive Year in 2017." *United States Census Bureau.* Accessed on January 20, 2019, from www.census.gov/library/stories/2018/09/poverty-rate-drops-third-consecutive-year-2017.html.
2   Edwards, 2018.
3   Matthews, Dylan. 2014. "Everything You Need to Know about the War on Poverty." *Washington Post*, January 8. Accessed on January 29, 2019, from https://www.washingtonpost.com/news/wonk/wp/2014/01/08/everything-you-need-to-know-about-the-war-on-poverty/?utm_term=.9f048f63f457.
4   Krogstad, Jens Manuel, and Kim Parker. 2014. "Public Is Sharply Divided on Views of Americans in Poverty." *Pew Research Center.* Accessed on January 20, 2019, from www.pewresearch.org/fact-tank/2014/09/16/public-is-sharply-divided-in-views-of-americans-in-poverty.

those with incomes above $50,000 said that poor people have hard lives, whereas more than 66 percent of those who earned less than $20,000 said the poor led hard lives.[5] A sociological examination of the social problem of poverty moves beyond the individual explanations for poverty and looks at the ways in which the structure of American society creates and maintains poverty and questions whether any groups in society benefit from continued poverty. This approach also examines government programs that are intended to reduce and eliminate poverty, asking whether they achieve those goals, how they might be improved, why some Americans oppose these programs, and what other factors might impede an individual or family's path out of poverty.

In addition to the fact that more than 10 percent of Americans are living in poverty at any given time, the majority (60 percent) of Americans experience a bout of poverty at some point in their adult years. As Mark R. Rank discusses in the first reading in this chapter, despite the ubiquity of poverty in American life, Americans have traditionally viewed poverty as the result of individual failings, bad choices, or personal defects such as poor work ethic, inability to curb spending, or lack of education. Rank argues that Americans need to change their thinking about the causes and consequences of poverty—including understanding the structural causes of poverty that are inherent to capitalism—and why we often vilify those in poverty as "undeserving" of our empathy and support. The reading "Perceived Racial Threat and Welfare Backlash in the United States" by Amanda M. Jungels and Jordan Forrest Miller examines these opinions about programs that support the poor in more detail, describing research that reveals the ways in which racial bias contributes to Americans' opposition to benefits for the poor.

In the second reading in this chapter, we turn our attention to a group of Americans whom policymakers and researchers alike frequently overlook: the severely poor. In "$2 a Day: Living on Almost Nothing in America," Kathryn J. Edin and H. Luke Shaefer discuss Americans who live on nearly no income or government benefits, and argue that changing poverty policy—which emphasizes support for the working poor—has contributed to the creation of this extreme poverty in the United States. Kristen Bialik examines data from the Pew Research Center and finds that not only have the number of poor Americans living in severe poverty increased since the Great Recession, those in severe poverty have actually seen their incomes fall, deepening their descent into poverty.

Understanding the structural factors that create and perpetuate poverty is an essential aspect of taking a sociological approach to the problem. In her piece focused on the history and experiences of Native Americans, Ashley Rockwell offers some insight into how a history of racial and cultural oppression can contribute to high poverty rates, and how poverty can result in a number of other social problems such as food insecurity, mental illness and addiction, and lack of access to health care. Rockwell also addresses a common myth about Native Americans in the United States—namely, that many tribes operate wildly successful gaming and casino operations and that individual tribe members are wealthy as a result. The reality of life on Native American reservations counteracts

---

5   Krogstad and Parker, 2014.

this narrative. Rockwell demonstrates that supporting and empowering people on both the individual and the group level is an important way of helping those in poverty to move from surviving to thriving.

Over the course of America's multidecade fight against poverty, a number of programs have been developed to help assist those in poverty, such as subsidized child care, housing, health insurance, and food assistance programs. These programs are not intended to support people until they are securely in the middle class but rather to help them survive; these programs are not sufficiently funded to support the large number of people who qualify for services, and there are often years-long waitlists for benefits.[6] Other challenges that people living in poverty must confront include a number of hidden costs that not only dramatically decrease their ability to get out of poverty but also seem intended to make upward mobilization more difficult and life in poverty more unpleasant. Journalist Eric Ravenscraft details some of these costs, which seem to occur *because* someone is poor rather than *as a result of* poverty. For example, it requires more time, money, and effort to accomplish the same tasks and achieve the same standard of living that middle-class and wealthier Americans take for granted, and whole industries and policies, such as payday loans and bank overdraft fees, have developed seemingly to exploit the poor's desperation and lack of choices. Arthur Delaney discusses another hidden cost of poverty: stigma for receiving and using benefits, borne out of resentment for those who are in need and who may not seem to "deserve" support.

Finally, the last readings in this chapter discuss national programs with the potential to dramatically reduce poverty in the United States. First, Matthew Desmond, who achieved prominence for his Pulitzer Prize-winning book *Evicted: Poverty and Profit in the American City*, discusses how the lack of affordable housing contributes to poverty, and argues that a national affordable housing program would be an enormous first step to ending poverty. In "Hand Up for Lower Income Families," Sarah Halpern-Meekin, Laura Tach, Kathryn J. Edin, and Jennifer Sykes examine a program which is not often viewed as a benefit or support for people in poverty, but which has nonetheless helped raise more than five million children above the poverty line: the earned income tax credit. This popular program, which offers a model of a government program that helps alleviate the psychological and financial stress of poverty while avoiding stigma for recipients. By examining the structural causes of poverty, the reality of the lives of those in poverty, and the difficulty families and individuals face on the road out of poverty, we hope that students are able to better examine this phenomenon from a sociological perspective.

---

6   Flowers, Andrew. 2016. "Why So Many Poor Americans Don't Get Help Paying for Housing." *FiveThirtyEight*, September 16. Accessed on January 20, 2019, from https://fivethirtyeight.com/features/why-so-many-poor-americans-dont-get-help-paying-for-housing.

DESTINY VASQUEZ

Destiny Vasquez is an intern for the National Coalition for the Homeless (NCH) and a member of their Faces of Homelessness Speakers' Bureau.

What is the mission of your organization?

The National Coalition for the Homeless's mission is "to prevent and end homelessness while ensuring the immediate needs of those experiencing homelessness are met and their civil rights protected."

What is your current position in your organization, and what does it entail?

As an intern, I do research on homeless policy and homeless statistics. Recently, I have been researching public housing policies and funding. I am also part of the Faces of Homelessness Speakers Bureau, where I talk about my experience with homelessness and what I have accomplished since overcoming homelessness.

How did you get this position?

I am part of the Cal-State DC Scholars Program at California State University, Fullerton. The program director connected me with the Grassroots Analyst for the National Coalition for the Homeless. After a phone interview, I immediately knew I wanted to intern with NCH.

How did you first become interested in this type of activism?

Living and being homeless in Los Angeles offered me a first-hand perspective of the homeless issue. Growing up, the homeless were and still are a neglected population; it wasn't until I became homeless and lived in a park that I fully comprehended the issue and stigma associated with being homeless. I am always open and honest about the struggles I have overcome, and my homelessness experience is one I share with every individual that I meet.

As an activist in your organization, currently what are your top goals?

My top goals are education, outreach, and policy change. I want to educate others about the real causes of homelessness, as well as the fact that the homeless experience is unique for each individual. Outreach includes engaging with the homeless population by providing basic resources such as clothing, food, water, and human connection. Policy change includes working with congressional and local leaders to further their understanding about the causes of homelessness and what needs to be done to prevent and end homelessness.

What strategies do you try to use to enact social change in your area of activism?

Besides being part of the Faces of Homelessness Speakers Bureau where I speak about my homelessness experience to large groups, I also speak to individuals. I use my life experience with homelessness to educate everyone I come in contact with. I let it be known that homeless individuals are not just an older population; they are also students and children, and they are often members of the working class.

What are the major challenges activists in your field face?

Some challenges homeless activists face are a lack of education that leaders and other community members have on the issue of homelessness, funding for the homeless, and available platforms for activists to communicate about the problem of homelessness. There are many common misconceptions surrounding the issue of homelessness and poverty, and without a proper platform or place at the table to discuss the issues, a roadblock is formed. Homeless individuals are typically not given the time or space to speak about how or why they ended up where they are, and by not being given a platform there is a disparity between what the issue really is and what is being presented to the public. We need more funding to provide affordable housing and to support grassroots organizations that campaign for the homeless.

What would you consider to be your greatest success as an activist?

Personally, my greatest success as an activist is being able to tell my story and let others know that not every homeless story is the same. I experienced homelessness as a child, which is a different experience from being homeless as an adult. Not every homeless individual has an addiction. Some are children, and some grow up in poverty and do not have the resources to get out of poverty. When I share my story, I am able to touch the hearts of people a few years younger or older than myself. For NCH, one of the biggest successes was passage of the McKinney-Vento Homeless Assistance Act of 1987. This piece of legislation paved the way for many programs and provisions for the homeless.

What are major misconceptions the public has about activism in general and your issue specifically?

There is often a negative stereotype about activism in general. In recent years, activism has been seen as violent, and that is just not the real face of activism. There is also resentment from the public when it comes to the issue of homelessness. There are the "not-in-my-backyarders" who make it difficult to advocate and successfully implement shelters or public housing units.

Why should students get involved in your line of activism?

Homelessness is a nationwide issue. Homelessness can also affect anyone during anytime in their life; their socio-economic background may not protect them. Homeless individuals are in every community, and becoming an activist for the homeless is helpful to combat the issue.

If an individual has little money and time, are there other ways they can contribute?

As a university student, I have little time and money to contribute to the cause, but any way I can, I do. I often keep extra articles of clothing in the backseat of my car and water bottles to give to anyone I see that I feel might need them. Organizing clothes drives on campus and donating them to a local shelter is one way. You can call your state representatives and let them know that the issue of homelessness should be a priority.

What ways can college students enact social change in their daily lives?

December 21, typically the coldest and longest night of the year, is reserved as National Homeless Persons' Memorial Day. On this night, communities around the country gather and host a vigil to commemorate those who have died while homeless. By hosting or being part of a vigil, you are letting your community know that these individuals will not be forgotten.

Also, students can simply engage in polite conversation or acknowledge homeless individuals. A friendly face can go a long way. By simply engaging in conversation, you show your peers that the homeless are not to be feared. You are making it socially acceptable to engage with them and creating a path for homeless individuals to become an active member of your community.

MARK R. RANK

RETHINKING AMERICAN POVERTY

When you think of someone living in poverty, how do you imagine they got there? Did they cause their own troubles or are there cultural and economic factors that contributed? Do we think of poverty as a problem that impacts all Americans, either directly or indirectly, or is it a problem that for many people is "out of sight, out of mind"? Rank argues that the way we conceptualize poverty—as caused by individual failing or pathology—informs how we have worked (or in some cases, not worked) to solve the problem. Rank discusses three shifts in thought that are needed if we are to begin addressing the issue of poverty in America and notes that without these changes, many Americans will continue to live in poverty in the wealthiest nation on earth.

It's a fundamental paradox: in America, the wealthiest country on earth, one also finds the highest rates of poverty in the developed world. Whether we examine children's rates of poverty, poverty among working adults, poverty within single parent families, or overall rates of poverty, the story is much the same—the United States has exceedingly high levels of impoverishment. As a result, half of U.S. children will reside in a household that uses food stamps at some point during childhood. Life expectancy in Harlem is shorter than in Bangladesh. The bottom 60 percent of the American population currently holds less than one percent of the financial wealth in the country. And two-thirds of the counties that Black children are growing up in are considered high poverty with respect to impoverished neighborhoods. Although there are several possible explanations for why these conditions exist, the argument developed here is that a major reason has to do with how we as a society have tended to conceptualize the issue of poverty and, based upon this thinking, how we have acted (or better put, failed to act) toward the issue.

The traditional manner of thinking about poverty in the U.S. has viewed impoverishment as largely the result of individual inadequacies and failings. These shortcomings include not working hard enough, failure to acquire sufficient skills, or just making bad decisions. Consequently, the problem of poverty is often seen through a lens of individual pathology. Since individuals are perceived as having brought poverty onto themselves, our collective and societal obligations are seen as limited. The age-old distinction between the deserving versus the undeserving poor reflects this perspective—unless the working-age poor have very good grounds for their poverty, they're deemed largely undeserving of help. Poverty is therefore understood as primarily affecting those who choose not to play by the rules of the game. Ultimately, this perspective reflects and reinforces the myths and ideals of American society: there are economic opportunities for all, individualism and self-reliance are paramount, and hard work is rewarded.

This overall mindset has long influenced both the general public's attitudes toward the poor and much of the policy and academic work analyzing poverty. Nevertheless, it seriously misconstrues the true nature of poverty and fosters a lack of political and social will to address the problem itself. Three major changes are

Published with permission of SAGE Publications from Rank, M. R. (2011). Rethinking American Poverty. Contexts, 10(2), 16–21. https://doi.org/10.1177/1536504211408794.

essential for realistically and proactively reframing American impoverishment.

POVERTY AFFECTS US ALL

A first fundamental shift in thinking is the recognition that poverty affects us all. All too often we view poverty as someone else's problem, or think that poverty is confined to certain areas and neighborhoods (such as inner cities or remote rural areas), and that by avoiding such areas we can simply ignore the issue. The notion is "out of sight, out of mind."

Clearly, this perspective is incorrect and intellectually lazy. In one way or another, poverty affects us all. There are at least two ways of thinking about this. The first is that whether we realize it or not, we pay a steep price for our high rates of poverty. As mentioned earlier, the extent and depth of poverty and economic inequality in the U.S. are far greater than in any other Western industrialized country. As a result, we spend considerably more money than needed on social problems associated with poverty. These include greater health problems, family problems, a less able work force, and so on down a long list. When we speak about homeland security, these are the issues that undermine us and our security as a nation. We wind up paying a tremendous price for quietly allowing so many of our citizens and communities to remain mired in poverty.

As an example, a study by the economist Harry Holzer and colleagues attempted to quantify the annual monetary cost of childhood poverty in the U.S. They calculated the economic costs that growing up in poverty had for future earnings, risk of engaging in crime, and health quality in later life. Their estimate was that the overall cost of childhood poverty was an eye opening $500 billion per year—nearly four percent of this country's GDP. The result is that we end up spending much of our tax dollars and resources on the by-products of poverty, assuredly a more expensive approach over the long term than preventing poverty in the first place. In short, each of us pays dearly in a number of ways for letting poverty exist at such levels, but we too often fail to see this connection.

However, there is also a second way of thinking about poverty as affecting us all. And that comes in considering the chances that an average American will directly encounter poverty at some point during his or her lifetime. As it turns out, the number of Americans who are touched by poverty during adulthood is exceedingly high. My co-author, sociologist Thomas Hirschl and I have estimated that between the ages of 20 and 75, nearly 60 percent of Americans will experience at least one year below the poverty line and three quarters will experience a year either in or near poverty. Perhaps more surprising is the fact that two thirds of Americans between the ages of 20 and 65 will wind up using a social welfare program such as Food Stamps or Medicaid; 40 percent will use such a program in at least five years scattered throughout their working age adulthood.

Consequently, although those in poverty and welfare recipients are routinely vilified and portrayed as members of "marginalized groups" on the fringes of society, most of us will find ourselves below the poverty line and using a social safety net program at some point. After all, during the course of a lifetime, any number of unexpected, detrimental things can happen—job loss, family break ups, or the development of a major health problem. In addition, recent research has shown that this life course risk of poverty and economic instability has been rising since the 1990s. More and more families, including middle class ones, are experiencing greater income volatility, greater instability in the labor market, and a lack of benefits such as health and unemployment insurance. Jobs are no longer as stable as they once were, health care benefits are harder to get, and the safety net has weakened over time. A first shift in thinking therefore asks the question, "Who is at risk of poverty and its consequences?" The answer is: virtually all of us. As a result, each of us has a vested interest in and an imperative for reducing poverty in the U.S.

STRUCTURAL FAILINGS

A second critical change in thinking is a recognition that American poverty is largely the result of failings at the economic and political levels, rather than at the individual level. In the past, we've emphasized individual inadequacies as the major reason for poverty; that is, people aren't motivated enough, aren't working hard enough, have failed to acquire enough skills and education, or have just made bad decisions. These behaviors and attributes are seen as leading people into poverty and keeping them there. And in fact, we tend to confront most social problems in this country as individual pathologies.

In contrast to this perspective, the basic problem lies in a shortage of viable opportunities for all Americans. Certainly, particular individual shortcomings, such as the lack of education or skills, help explain who is more likely to be left out in the competition to locate and secure good opportunities, but they cannot explain why there's a shortage of such opportunities in the first place. In order to answer that question, we must turn to the inability of the economic and political structures to provide the supports and opportunities necessary to lift all of us out of poverty.

The most obvious example is in the mismatch between the number of decent paying jobs and the pool of labor in search of those jobs. Over the past 30 years, the U.S. economy has been producing more and more low-paying jobs, part-time jobs, and jobs without benefits (it's estimated that approximately one third of all jobs are low-paying—less than $11.50 an hour). And of course, beyond those in low-paying jobs, there are millions of unemployed Americans at any point in time. During the recent economic downturn, six to seven people have been competing for every single job opening. Coupled with the country's lack of universal coverage for childcare, health care, and affordable housing, this situation leaves an increasing number of families economically vulnerable.

In class, I often use the analogy of musical chairs to help students recognize this disconnect. Picture a game with ten players, but only eight chairs. When the music stops, who's most likely to be left standing? It will be those who are at a disadvantage in terms of competing for the available chairs (less agility, reduced speed, a bad position when the music stops, and so on). However, given that the game is structured in a way such that two players are *bound* to lose, these individual attributes only explain who loses, not why there are losers in the first place. Ultimately, there are simply not enough chairs for those playing the game. . . . So while characteristics such as deficiencies in skills or education or being in a single parent family help to explain who's at a heightened risk of encountering poverty, the fact that poverty exists in the first place results not from these characteristics, but from a failure of the economic and political structures to provide enough decent opportunities and supports for the whole of society. By focusing solely upon individual characteristics, we can shuffle people up or down in terms of their likelihood to land a job with good earnings, but when there aren't enough of these jobs to go around, somebody will still end up in poverty. We're playing a large-scale version of musical chairs.

The recognition of this dynamic represents a fundamental shift in thinking from the past. It helps explain why the social policies of the last three decades have been largely ineffective in reducing poverty rates. We've spent our attention and resources on altering players' incentives and disincentives through various welfare reform measures, or, in a very limited way, upgrading their skills and ability to compete with various job-training programs, but we've left the structure of the game untouched. Overall rates of poverty do go up and down, but primarily as a result of changes on the structural level (that is, increases or decreases in the number of available opportunities—the "chairs"). In particular, the performance of the economy has been historically important, since, when the economy is expanding, more opportunities are available for the competing pool of labor and their families. The reverse occurs when the economy slows down, as we saw in the 2000s and the economic collapse that began in 2008. To attribute the rise of poverty over the past ten years to individual inadequacies or lowered motivation is absurd. Rather, the increase in poverty has everything to do with deteriorating economic conditions, particularly in the last decade.

Likewise, changes in various social supports and the social safety net affect how well families are able to avoid poverty. When such supports were increased by the War on Poverty initiatives of the 1960s and buoyed by a strong economy, poverty rates declined significantly. Likewise, when Social Security benefits were expanded during the 1960s and 1970s, poverty rates among the elderly dropped sharply. Conversely, when social supports have been eroded, as in the case of children's programs over the past 30 years, rates of poverty among those relying on such services have gone up.

The recognition of poverty as a structural failing also makes it clear why the U.S. has such high rates of poverty when compared to other Western countries. It's not that Americans are less motivated or less skilled than those in other countries, but that our economy has been producing millions of low-wage jobs and our social policies have done relatively little to economically support families compared to other industrialized countries. From this perspective, one key to addressing poverty is to increase the labor market opportunities and social supports available to American households. We must shift our thinking to recognize the fundamental distinction between who loses at the game and why the game produces losers in the first place.

THE MORAL GROUND

Let's turn to the third shift in thinking that's needed to create a more realistic and proactive approach toward poverty. And that is the moral ground on which we view poverty in America must change. In the past, our moral perspective has been rooted in the ethos of individual blame, with a resulting general acceptance of the status quo. In other words, since people bring it upon themselves, poverty's their problem, not mine.

But poverty is a moral problem. It represents an injustice of a substantial magnitude. Severe deprivation and hardship have been documented in countless studies—not to mention millions of human lives. And, as argued earlier, a large portion of this poverty is the result of failings at the structural rather than the individual level, which places much of the responsibility for poverty beyond the poor. However, what makes this injustice particularly grievous is the stark contrast between the wealth, abundance, and resources of America and its levels of destitution. Something is seriously wrong when we find that, in a country with the most abundant resources in the world, there are children without enough to eat, families who cannot afford health care, and people sleeping on the streets for lack of shelter.

It should also be noted that the gap between extreme prosperity and vulnerability has never been wider. The venerable economist Paul Samuelson, writing in the first edition of his introductory economics textbook in 1948, observed that if we were to make an income pyramid out of a child's play blocks, with each layer representing $1,000 of income, the peak would be somewhat higher than the Eiffel Tower, but almost all of us would be within several yards of the ground. By the time of Samuelson's 2001 edition of the textbook, most of us would still be within several yards of the ground, but the Eiffel Tower would now have to be replaced with Mount Everest to represent those at the top. Or consider the distance between the average worker's salary and the average CEO's salary. In 1980, the average CEO of a major corporation earned around 42 times the pay of the average worker. [As of 2011], it is well over 400 times. Adding insult to injury, during the past 30 years, an increasing number of companies have demanded concessions from their workers, including pay cuts and the elimination of health benefits in order to keep their labor costs down, while those at the top have prospered beyond any sense of decency. Patterns of wealth accumulation have become even more skewed. The top one percent of the U.S. population currently owns 42 percent of the country's entire financial wealth, while the bottom 60 percent of Americans are in possession of less than one percent. And while all of these trends have been emerging, our social policies have continued to give more to the well-to-do and less to the economically vulnerable, with the argument that these policies help all Americans through "trickle down economics."

A new way of thinking recognizes this as a moral outrage. Injustice, rather than blame, becomes the moral compass with which to view poverty amidst abundance. The magnitude of such injustice constitutes a strong impetus for change. It signals that a wrong is being committed and cries out for a remedy. A shift in thinking is premised upon the idea that social change is essential for addressing the injustices of poverty. This is in sharp contrast with the old way of thinking, in which the moral focus is upon individual blame. Such thinking simply reinforces the status quo by letting us do little while poverty rates climb. The perspective of injustice exhorts us to actively engage and confront poverty, rather than comfortably settling for widespread impoverishment.

In his last book, *Where Do We Go from Here: Chaos or Community?*, the Rev. Dr. Martin Luther

King, Jr. wrote, "A true revolution of value will soon cause us to question the fairness and justice of many of our past and present policies. We are called to play the Good Samaritan on life's roadside; but that will be only an initial act. One day the whole Jericho road must be transformed so that men and women will not be beaten and robbed as they make their journey through life. True compassion is more than flinging a coin to a beggar; it understands that an edifice that produces beggars needs restructuring. A true revolution of values will soon look uneasily on the glaring contrast of poverty and wealth." This revolution of values must begin with a fundamental shift in how American society understands, and ultimately acts toward, the poverty in which so many of our citizens live. These are the building blocks on which to challenge and confront the paradox of poverty amidst plenty.

PERCEIVED RACIAL THREAT AND WELFARE BACKLASH IN THE UNITED STATES

AMANDA M. JUNGELS AND JORDAN FORREST MILLER

Americans have a long history of holding distorted views about government assistance, in particular about which racial/ethnic groups are most likely to be the recipients of different types of federal assistance. Researchers have found that these misperceptions, based on racial stereotypes, shape our views on whether Americans consider the poor to be deserving of assistance, and so they can influence support for government assistance programs such as welfare, food stamps, Social Security, and public housing. In reality, White recipients vastly outnumber racial and ethnicity minorities in terms of benefiting from government aid. For example, in 2013, 40 percent of Medicaid[1] recipients were White (over 29 million people), and 21 percent were Black (15 million people) (Kaiser Family Foundation 2018), but White survey respondents *perceived* Medicaid as benefiting Black people more than White people (YouGov 2018). Using Census Bureau data, researchers found that more White people without a college degree (6.2 million) were lifted out of poverty by government assistance than were similarly educated Black (2.8 million) or Hispanic people (2.4 million), even though Black and Hispanic communities are disproportionately impacted by poverty (Shapiro, Trisi, & Chaudhry 2017). Welfare has long been regarded as a "racially coded issue" that "plays upon White Americans' negative views of Blacks without explicitly raising the 'race card'" (Gilens 1996). Recent research by Wetts and Willer (2018) can help explain why White Americans oppose welfare programs, even though they are by far the largest recipients of such programs, and the consequences that these racially biased perceptions have on race relations in the United States.

Wetts and Willer's research relied on group position theory, which argues that "certain racial groups in particular social contexts—such as White people in the United States—often come to hold 'a sense of group position,' or an expectation that their racial/ethnic group has a higher-status position than other groups and that this position is associated with greater access to economic, political, and social resources" (Wetts & Willer 2018: 4). Challenges to this White supremacist position could include (perceived) increases in the economic and political power of racial minority groups, as well as historical events that are symbolic of changing race relations, such as the election of the first Black president (Wetts & Willer 2018). Furthermore, this theory posits that people in the dominant group (White people) will react in racially biased ways when they perceive their groups' position and access to resources threatened.

First, Wetts and Willer wanted to understand the historical relevance and accuracy of this theory by examining nationally representative data about welfare attitudes and racial resentment from the years 2000–2012. They hypothesized that White people's opposition to welfare would increase beginning in 2008 as a reaction to the election of Obama (and the related public discourse about the growing electoral power of racial/ethnic minorities) as well as the beginning of the Great Recession. Wetts and Willer's hypothesis was confirmed; they found that Whites' racial resentment began to rise in 2008 and continued rising in 2012 (aligning with Obama's reelection). Moreover, in 2008, racial/ethnic minority group members' attitudes about welfare became *less* oppositional and White people's *more* oppositional, despite the fact that 2008 marked the beginning of a severe economic recession that impacted people of all races.

---

1 Medicaid is a state and government initiative that provides free or low-cost health care coverage to low-income individuals and families.

Original to *Focus on Social Problems: A Contemporary Reader.*

Next, Wetts and Willer conducted an experiment to test whether White people's perceptions of their racial groups' status would impact their attitudes toward welfare. The researchers believed that White people who were led to believe that their racial status was threatened would more strongly oppose welfare than those who believed that White status was not threatened. Participants were presented with varied charts that showed different trends in racial/ethnic diversity in the United States, and were then asked questions about their support for welfare programs (including an imaginary scenario where they were tasked with cutting $500 million from the federal budget and were given a list of nine areas, including welfare, whose budgets they could reduce) and their level of racial resentment. When study participants were presented information suggesting a decline in White majority status, White participants showed an increase in their levels of racial resentment, and were more likely than people of color to propose cutting welfare spending. Moreover, White participants who were shown information indicating that White racial supremacy was in decline cut nearly twice as much from welfare budgets ($51 million) compared to White participants who were shown information that indicated they would still be the dominant racial group ($28 million). In other words, when White participants perceived their economic and political majority status as threatened, their support for welfare programs decreased. Based on previous historical trends, White racial resentment is expected to be higher during times of economic downturns such as the Great Recession, in which there may be perceived threats to resources predominantly controlled and used by White people. After controlling for the effects of economic anxiety at the time, racial resentment was still found to be a significant contributor to opposition to welfare programs (Wetts & Willer 2018).

Finally, Wetts and Willer wanted to test whether White people's opinions about welfare would change if presented with information that showed that White people, rather than racial/ethnic minorities, are the primary beneficiaries of federal assistance programs. They also wanted to test a specific aspect of racial status threat by randomly telling some participants that the racial income gap had either shrunk or grown. The researchers hypothesized that "if threatened Whites show heightened opposition to a welfare program that benefits minorities, but not to a program that benefits Whites, it would be convincing evidence that racial status threats lead Whites to oppose welfare as a result of heightened racial antipathy" (Wetts & Willer 2018: 19). Similar to their previous experiment, participants were shown charts that indicated that either the racial income gap had widened after the Great Recession (i.e., White incomes had returned to previous levels, but Black/Latino incomes had declined and had not recovered) or that the racial income gap was closing (i.e., White people's incomes fell during the Great Recession but Black/Latino incomes had stayed the same, resulting in a narrowing of the gap). Next, participants were shown information about the racial identities of those receiving unemployment insurance and those receiving Temporary Assistance for Needy Families (TANF), a cash assistance program many know as "welfare." Half of the participants were shown information that indicated that most TANF recipients were White and unemployment insurance recipients were Black or Latino; the other half received the opposite information. They were then asked to rate how much they supported each of the programs, and whether they thought the programs were a good use of government resources.

In general, White participants were less supportive of TANF (cash assistance) than of unemployment insurance, regardless of their perceptions of the racial income gap or the race of program beneficiaries. But White participants who were told that the racial income gap was closing showed significantly less support for programs that they believed benefited minorities (Wetts & Willer 2018). Black and Latino participants showed no statistically significant relationship between the racial income gap information, the race of the program beneficiaries, and the participants' attitudes toward welfare programs. Interestingly, participants who were Black and Latino supported a welfare program more if they were shown information that indicated the racial income gap was decreasing (i.e., White incomes were declining) and that White people were the recipients of government assistance (though this relationship was not statistically significant). The researchers hypothesized that "minorities (like Americans generally) may be more likely to see Whites as members of the 'deserving poor' and thus increase support for programs supporting Whites when Whites appear to need them" (Wetts & Willer 2018: 24).

These racially based attitudes have serious ramifications in the public sphere, as public opposition to government assistance can result in stricter requirements for recipients of government assistance, decreased budgets, or elimination of programs altogether (Khazan 2018). Racially driven views about who are the primary beneficiaries of government assistance, and the subsequent attitudes, are held by the most powerful members of government—those deciding which programs receive support and which do not. In March 2017, President Trump met with members of the Congressional Black Caucus, and when a congressional representative told President Trump that his proposed welfare cuts would harm her constituents, "not all of whom are Black," the president replied, "Really? Then what are they?" (Salama 2018).

It is important to understand the underlying causes that drive attitudes about welfare and to consider the role that politicians and the media play in perpetuating racialized and racist ideologies that foster racial resentment. As researcher Rachel Wetts said in an interview in 2018:

> While Whites continue to enjoy many of their historical privileges in this country, much public discourse about race—particularly in the period immediately following the election of Barack Obama—emphasized America's increasing demographic diversity and the declining dominance of White people in this country. . . . While it's true that Whites on average

(continued)

continue to have political and economic advantages relative to African-Americans and Latinos, these larger social trends and high-profile events can create the sense that these advantages are potentially precarious or slipping away. Perceptions don't always match reality. And members of the media and politicians sometimes frame or highlight social trends and events in ways that might make them seem more threatening to Whites' status than they actually are. (DeVega 2018)

Addressing this underlying racial animus is critical, as members of the dominant group may react in political ways to perceived increases in racial equity.

REFERENCES

DeVega, Chauncy. 2018. "White Americans Support Welfare Programs, but Only for Themselves, Says New Research." *Salon.com*, August 1. Retrieved from https://www.salon .com/2018/08/01/white-americans-support-welfare-programs-but-only-for-themselves-says-new-research.

Gilens, Martin. 1996. "'Race Coding' and White Opposition to Welfare." *Social Forces* 90(3): 593–604.

Kaiser Family Foundation. 2018. "Medicaid Enrollment by Race, 2013." Retrieved from https://www.kff.org/medicaid/ state-indicator/medicaid-enrollment-by-raceethnicity/?dataV iew=1&currentTimeframe=0&sortModel=%7B%22colId%22: %22Location%22,%22sort%22:%22asc%22%7D.

Khazan, Olga. 2018. "Racial Resentment Can Motivate Opposition to Welfare." *The Atlantic*, June 5. Retrieved from https://www.theatlantic.com/science/archive/2018/06/ racial-resentment-motivates-opposition-to-welfare/562010.

Salama, Vivian. 2018. "Trump's History of Breaking Decorum with Remarks on Race, Ethnicity." *NBC News*, January 12. Retrieved from https://www.nbcnews.com/news/us-news/ trump-s-history-breaking-decorum-remarks-race-ethnicity-n837181.

Shapiro, Isaac, Danilo Trisi, and Raheem Chaudhry. 2017. "Poverty Reduction Programs Help Adults Lacking College Degrees the Most." *Center on Budget and Policy Priorities*. Retrieved from https://www.cbpp.org/sites/default/files/ atoms/files/2-16-17pov.pdf.

Wetts, Rachel, and Robb Willer. 2018. "Privilege on the Precipice: Perceived Racial Status Threats Lead White Americans to Oppose Welfare Programs." *Social Forces*, 80(4): 789–819.

YouGov. 2018. "Huffpost: Government Programs." Retrieved from http://big.assets.huffingtonpost.com/ tabsHPGovernmentprograms20180116.pdf.

KATHRYN J EDIN AND H. LUKE SHAEFER

7. $2 A DAY

Living on Almost Nothing in America

Many Americans may not be aware that a large number of their fellow citizens are surviving on less than $2 a day. Edin and Shaefer discuss the growing number of families and individuals who survive on such limited resources (and who often don't receive government assistance), and the role that changing poverty policy has had in creating and perpetuating this level of dire poverty in the richest nation in the world.

Deep on the South Side of Chicago, far from the ever-evolving steel skyline of America's third-largest city, sits a small, story-and-a-half White clapboard house clad in peeling paint. That's where Susan Brown lives with her husband, Devin, and their eight-month-old daughter, Lauren, the three of them sharing the home with Susan's grandmother, stepgrandfather, and uncle.[1]

Wooden steps lead up to the age-worn threshold of an enclosed front porch, which slumps noticeably to the left. To enter the house, visitors must sidestep a warped, mold-stained plywood board that covers a large hole in the porch floor. The front door opens into a small, dark room furnished with a worn couch, a shaky wooden coffee table, and a leatherette easy chair with stuffing escaping from the left arm. Up and to the left, you can see a dark patch where the wall meets the ceiling. It seems like the spot is at best damp and at worst crumbling.

The air is dense. It is well above 90 degrees outside, but it feels even hotter inside the house. None of the windows open, although gaps between the frames and their casings let in a little bit of air. The carpeting in the front room has been discolored by footsteps and spills, and its matted surface feels a bit sticky. Where the carpet has worn away, there are the crumbling remains of Black-and-White linoleum. Where the linoleum has worn through, there are the vestiges of once-fine hardwood floors.

At the back of the house, a giant 1980s-era refrigerator dominates a small kitchen outfitted with open shelving and a porcelain sink that may well be a century old. Inside the refrigerator, there are just a few bottles of baby formula that Susan has gotten from the Special Supplemental Nutrition Program for Women, Infants, and Children, called WIC. She says of baby Lauren, "She gets WIC, but it don't last. . . . They give her, like, seven cans, but it's like the *little* cans." Otherwise, she says with a shrug, "we don't have no food in the freezer right now." The fridge groans as it works to keep its mostly empty shelves cold.

In the heart of all the chaos that is inevitable when six people share a cramped, worn three-bedroom home, there is a small dining area sandwiched between the front room and the empty fridge in the back. In it sits a round dining table covered with a pristine White linen tablecloth, intricately embroidered around the edges. Four place settings are outfitted with gold-rimmed china and silver flatware. Four bright White napkins embellished with the same embroidery as the tablecloth have been carefully folded and placed in large crystal goblets. It is hard to imagine a more elegant table at which to share a meal. Yet here it sits— never used, never disturbed—accompanied by a single chair.

This table harks back to a different era, a better time in the life of Susan's family, when owning this house in this part of Chicago signaled the achievement of middle-class African American respectability. Before the economic anchors of this far South Side neighborhood closed down—the steel yards in the 1960s, the historic Pullman railway car company by the early 1980s, and the mammoth SherwinWilliams paint factory in 1995—Roseland was a community with decent-paying, stable jobs. It was a good place to raise your kids.

As the jobs left, the drugs arrived. "It got worse, it's changed," Susan says. "There's too much violence . . . unnecessary violence at that." Given what her family has been through, this is more than a bit of an understatement. Susan's brother was shot in broad daylight just one block away. Her great-grandmother, in whose house they are living, has fled for a meager retirement out West. Susan's family would like nothing more than to find another place to live, safer streets, and a home that isn't crumbling around them. Yet despite all of its ills, this house is the only thing keeping Susan, Devin, and Lauren off the streets. They have spent the past few months surviving on cash income so low that it adds up to less than $2 per person, per day. With hardly a cent to their names, they have nowhere else to go.

Two dollars is less than the cost of a gallon of gas, roughly equivalent to that of a half gallon of milk. Many Americans have spent more than that before they get to work or school in the morning. Yet in 2011, more than 4 percent of all households with children in the world's wealthiest nation were living in a poverty so deep that most Americans don't believe it even exists in this country.

Devin has a high school diploma. A clean record. Some work history. He spent most of the past year working construction gigs off the books for an uncle, until he got a temp job up in the northern suburbs. But that job lasted only a few months, and now he's gone half a year without finding another. After two months at home following the birth of baby Lauren,

Susan began a frantic search for work, but it hasn't been going well. "I've been looking for jobs for forever," she says, clearly demoralized. "It's gonna drive me crazy!" Before she became pregnant with Lauren, Susan earned her GED and spent more than a year in community college, completing the remedial courses that would allow her to finally begin earning credits toward a certification in early childhood education. Yet she can't afford to return to college right now. Somebody has to find work.

Devin speaks with more confidence than Susan. He believes that any day now, things are bound to turn around. On his way to apply for a position at the Save-A-Lot grocery store nearby, his blue jeans are clean and crisp, his short-sleeved button-down shirt pressed. He has heard that there is an opening for part-time work in the produce department, paying $8.50 an hour. Despite six months of rejections, he is confident that he's got this one. At only twenty hours a week, it won't get his family above the poverty line, but it's a start. Now if only Susan can find something. At least child care isn't a worry. Susan's grandmother has had to leave her job to care for her husband, just home after a long hospitalization. She says that while she's nursing him at home, she can babysit Lauren if Susan finds a job.

Susan is sick of going hungry, sick of eating instant noodles morning, noon, and night. She's tired of falling further and further behind on her bills, tired of being a freeloader in her own home. With no cash coming in, the whole family is in hock to Susan's absentee landlord, her great-grandmother, who charges each of her tenants a modest rent to cover the property taxes and supplement her Social Security check. Susan's uncle has been scraping together just enough to pay the utilities with his slim earnings from the occasional side job fixing cars in the backyard. The whole household depends on Susan and Devin's food stamp benefits in order to eat. So as Susan goes about the work of caring for her baby and searching for a job, she is also learning another skill—the art of surviving on virtually nothing.

THE RISE OF $2-A-DAY POVERTY

By 2010, Kathryn Edin had spent more than twenty years canvassing poor communities all over the country, sitting with low-income parents at their kitchen tables or as they went about their work, talking about their economic lives. Beginning in the early 1990s, she and her colleague, Laura Lein, detailed the budgets of hundreds of the nation's welfare recipients.[2] They showed how, despite receiving a few hundred dollars in welfare benefits each month, these families still struggled to survive. Typically, they were able to cover only about three-fifths of their expenses with the cash and in-kind assistance they received from the welfare office. Each month, they had to scramble to bridge the large gap in their budgets. Yet on the whole, Edin and Lein found that by deploying grit and ingenuity, these families were usually able to stave off the most severe forms of material deprivation.

In the summer of 2010, Edin returned to the field to update her work on the very poor. She was struck by how markedly different things appeared from just fifteen years before. In the course of her interviews, she began to encounter many families living in conditions similar to those she would find when she met Susan and Devin Brown in 2012—with no visible means of cash income from any source. These families weren't just poor by American standards. They were the poorest of the poor. Some claimed food stamps, now called SNAP, for the Supplemental Nutrition Assistance Program. A few had a housing subsidy. Most had at least one household member covered by some form of government-funded health insurance. Some received an occasional bag of groceries from a food pantry. But what was so strikingly different from a decade and a half[3] earlier was that there was virtually no cash coming into these homes. Not only were there no earnings, there was no welfare check either. These families didn't just have too little cash to survive on, as was true for the welfare recipients Edin and Lein had met in the early 1990s. They often had no cash at all. The absence of cash permeated every aspect of their lives. It seemed as though not only cash was missing but hope as well.

The question that began to keep Edin up at night was whether something had changed at the very bottom of the bottom of American society. Her observations could have been a fluke. To know for sure, she had to find a survey representative of the U.S. population that asked just the right questions. And it had to have asked them over many years so that she could see whether extreme destitution had been growing, especially since the mid-1990s, when the country's main welfare program, Aid to Families with Dependent Children (AFDC), was replaced by a system of temporary, time-limited aid.

It was entirely a coincidence that in the fall of 2011, Luke Shaefer came to Harvard, where Edin was teaching, for a semester. Shaefer is a leading expert on the Survey of Income and Program Participation (SIPP), the only survey that could answer Edin's question. The SIPP, administered by the U.S. Census Bureau, is based on survey interviews with tens of thousands of American households each year. Census Bureau employees ask detailed questions about every possible source of income, including gifts from family and friends and cash from odd jobs. A key goal of the survey is to get the most accurate accounting possible of the incomes of the poor and the degree to which they participate in government programs. No one claims these data are perfect: people may not want to tell a stranger "from the government" about the intimate details of their finances, especially if they think it could get them in trouble with the law. But the SIPP can tell us more about the economic lives of the poorest Americans than any other source. And because it has asked the same questions over many years, it is the only tool that can reveal if, and how much, the number of the virtually cashless poor has grown in the years since welfare reform.

That fall, during an early morning meeting in her office in Cambridge, Edin shared with Shaefer what she had been seeing on the ground. Shaefer immediately went to work to see if he could detect a trend in the SIPP data that matched Edin's observations. First, though, he needed to determine what income threshold would capture people who were experiencing a level of destitution so deep as to be unthought of in America. Accordingly, he borrowed inspiration from one of the World Bank's metrics of global poverty in the developing world—$2 per person, per day. At the time, the official poverty line for a family of three in the United States worked out to about $16.50 per person, per day over the course of a year. The government's designation of "deep poverty"—set at half the poverty line—equated to about $8.30 per person, per day. As far as Shaefer and Edin could tell, no one had ever looked to see whether any slice of the American poor fell below the even lower threshold of $2 a day for even part of a year. With the SIPP, it was fairly easy to estimate how many American families with children were reporting cash incomes below this very low threshold in any given month[4].

Like any good social scientist, Shaefer tried hard to prove Edin's observations wrong. He wouldn't just focus on family income (as our official poverty measure does). Instead, any cash coming to anyone in the household—related or not—would be included. He would include any government benefits that came in the form of cash. He'd add private pensions. Gifts from family and friends would be counted as well. Even cash from occasional odd jobs would be added in. In short, any dollar that made it into the house—no matter what the source—would be counted toward a family's income. And after he made his initial calculations, he'd do another set of calculations, adding in the value of tax credits plus some of the nation's biggest in-kind assistance programs for the poor, particularly SNAP. SNAP is more like cash than any of the government's noncash programs aimed at helping the poor.

The results of Shaefer's analysis were staggering. In early 2011, 1.5 million households with roughly 3 million children were surviving on cash incomes of no more than $2 per person, per day in any given month. That's about one out of every twenty-five families with children in America. What's more, not only were these figures astoundingly high, but the phenomenon of $2-a-day poverty among households with children had been on the rise since the nation's landmark welfare reform legislation was passed in 1996—and at a distressingly fast pace. As of 2011, the number of families in $2-a-day poverty had more than doubled in just a decade and a half.

It further appeared that the experience of living below the $2-aday threshold didn't discriminate by family type or race. While single-mother families were most at risk of falling into a spell of extreme destitution, more than a third of the households in $2-a-day poverty were headed by a married couple. And although the rate of growth was highest among African Americans and Hispanics, nearly half of the $2-a-day poor were White.

One piece of good news in these findings was that the government safety net was helping at least some households. When Shaefer added in SNAP as if it were cash—a problematic assumption because SNAP cannot legally be converted to cash, so it can't be used to pay the light bill, the rent, or buy a bus pass—the number of families living in $2-a-day poverty fell by about half. This vital in-kind government program was clearly reaching many, though not all, of the poorest of the poor. Even counting SNAP as cash, though, Shaefer found that the increase in the number of families with children living in $2-a-day poverty remained large—up 70 percent in fifteen years. And even after throwing in any tax credits the household could have claimed for the year, plus the cash value of housing subsidies, the data still showed a 50 percent increase.[5] Clearly, the nation was headed in the wrong direction.

Reflecting on these numbers, we, Shaefer and Edin, sought out even more confirmation that what we had found represented a real shift in the circumstances of families at the very bottom. With this in mind, we began to look for other evidence, beyond the SIPP, of the rise of $2-a-day poverty. Reports from the nation's food banks showed a sizable rise in the number of households seeking emergency food assistance since the late 1990s. A look at government data on those receiving SNAP revealed a large increase in the number of families with no other source of income. And reports from the nation's public schools showed that more and more children were facing homelessness. Taken together, these findings seemed to confirm the rise of a new form of poverty that defies every assumption about economic, political, and social progress made over the past three decades.

TRENDS MEET REAL LIVES

Statistics can help identify troubling trends like these, but they can't tell us much about what's going on beneath the numbers. In fact, these statistics led to more questions than answers. What had caused the rise in $2-a-day poverty among households with children? Was the landmark welfare reform of 1996 partly to blame? Were these families completely detached from the world of work? Or were they enmeshed in a low-wage labor market that was itself somehow prompting spells of extreme destitution? How was it even possible to live without cash in modern America? What were families in $2-a-day poverty doing to survive? And were these strategies different from those poor families had been using prior to welfare reform, when Aid to Families with Dependent Children (AFDC) still offered such families a cash cushion against extreme destitution? What was so indispensable about cash—as opposed to in-kind resources such as SNAP—for families trying to survive in twenty-first-century America?

To better understand the lives being lived behind the numbers, we needed to return to where this exploration started—to the homes of people like those Edin had met in 2010. Only families who were themselves living in $2-a-day poverty could tell the story of how they had ended up in such straits. Only their stories could reveal what it actually takes to survive with virtually no cash in the world's most advanced capitalist economy.

In the summer of 2012, we launched in-depth ethnographic studies in locations across the country. If the $2-a-day poor truly constituted more than 4 percent of all households with children—about a fifth of all families living below the poverty line—then it wouldn't exactly be easy to find families in such circumstances. But it shouldn't be impossible either. The first question was where to start the search. We wanted one of our sites to represent the "typical" American city. Another site would be chosen because it represented "old poverty"—a rural locale that had been deeply poor for half a century or more. We also wanted to explore the lives of the $2-a-day poor in a place where widespread poverty was a somewhat more recent phenomenon. With that in mind, we looked for a city that had, until the 1970s, been characterized by widespread affluence but had experienced severe economic decline in the decades since. Finally, we wanted to include a place that had been very poor in prior decades but had recovered in recent years.

With these criteria in mind, we set up field sites in Chicago; in a collection of small, rural hamlets in the Mississippi Delta; in Cleveland; and in a midsize city in the Appalachian region—Johnson City, Tennessee. As we spent time in each locale, we began by reaching out to local nonprofits, especially those with deep roots in the communities they served. We hung flyers in their lobbies, volunteered in their programs, and approached the most destitute of families who walked through their doors. Because many among the

$2-a-day poor are isolated from such sources of aid, we also enlisted the help of trusted community members embedded in neighborhoods where we knew many families were struggling. . . .

In each of these places, we looked for families with children who had spent at least three months living on cash income of less than $2 per person per day. In most cases, these spells of such dire poverty proved to be much longer. We visited with these families over the course of many months—and, in some cases, years—talking with them frequently, sharing meals, and observing their daily lives. As common themes emerged from their stories—such as their surprisingly high level of attachment to the formal labor market and the frequency with which doubling up with family or friends precipitated a spell of $2-a-day poverty—we looked back to the SIPP and to other sources of data to see if we could see them there as well.

In the end, we followed eighteen families. . . . As had been true of those Edin first encountered in the summer of 2010, some of these households received SNAP or lived in subsidized housing. But others weren't getting even those benefits. During the course of our fieldwork, some of these families escaped $2-a-day poverty; others did not. Most escaped only to fall back into extreme destitution again.

Recent public discussions of rising inequality in the United States have largely focused on the biggest winners of the past decade, the top 1 percent. But there is a different inequality at work at the other end of the income scale.

In 1995, Senator Daniel Patrick Moynihan famously predicted that the proposed welfare reform would result in children "sleeping on grates."[6] Most observers think history proved him wrong. But does the rise in the number of the $2-a-day poor represent the (until now unexamined) great failure of welfare reform? Perhaps Moynihan was not so far off after all. Perhaps his only mistake was in assuming that this failure at the very bottom of the economic distribution would be visible and obvious, when in fact, throughout history, American poverty has generally been hidden far from most Americans' view.

America's cash welfare program—the main government program that caught people when they fell—was not merely replaced with the 1996 welfare reform; it was very nearly destroyed. In its place arose a different kind of safety net, one that provides a powerful hand up to some—the working poor—but offers much less to others, those who can't manage to find or keep a job. . . . [W]hat happens when a government safety net that is built on the assumption of fulltime, stable employment at a living wage combines with a low-wage labor market that fails to deliver on any of the above[?] It is this toxic alchemy, we argue, that is spurring the increasing numbers of $2-a-day poor in America. A hidden but growing landscape of survival strategies among those who experience this level of destitution has been the result. At the community level, these strategies can pull families into a web of exploitation and illegality that turns conventional morality upside down.

None of the people . . . [we followed] see a handout from the government—the kind that the old system provided prior to welfare reform—as a solution to their plight. Instead, what they want more than anything else is the chance to work. They would like nothing better than to have a full-time job paying $12 or $13 an hour, a modest dwelling in a safe neighborhood,

and some stability above all else. In the 1990s, we, as a country, began a transformation of the social safety net that serves poor families with children. More aid has been rendered to a group that was previously without much in the way of government assistance—the working poor. Extending the nation's safety net in this way has improved the lives of millions of Americans. But there are simply not enough jobs, much less good jobs, to go around. And for those without work, there is no longer a guarantee of cash assistance.

. . . [T]he transformation of the social safety net is incomplete, with dire consequences. We believe the time has come to finish the job. Doing something more to help these families won't be easy; it will require a commitment by all of us. The government's emphasis on personal responsibility must be matched by bold action to expand access to and improve the quality of jobs. But there will always be circumstances in which work as a primary approach to alleviating poverty won't work. In those cases, we need a system that truly acts as a safety net for families in crisis, catching them when they fall.

NOTES

1. To protect the individuals who are written about in this . . . [reading], the names of people, organizations, places, and some minor details that do not substantively affect the stories have been changed throughout.

2. See Kathryn Edin and Laura Lein, *Making Ends Meet: How Single Mothers Survive Welfare and Low-Wage Work* (New York: Russell Sage Foundation, 1997).

3. H. Luke Shaefer and Kathryn Edin, "Extreme Poverty in the United States, 1996 to 2011" (Policy Brief No. 28, Gerald R. Ford School of Public Policy, University of Michigan, February 2012), http://www.npc.umich.edu/publications/policy_briefs/briefa8/policybriefa8.pdf. See also H. Luke Shaefer and Kathryn Edin, "Rising Extreme Poverty in the United States and the Response of Federal Means-Tested Transfers," *Social Service Review* 87, no. 2 (2013): 250–68.

4. Shaefer and Edin, "Extreme Poverty." See also H. Luke Shaefer, Kathryn Edin, and Elizabeth Talbert, "Understanding the Dynamics of $2-a-Day Poverty in the United States," *RSF: The Russell Sage Foundation Journal of the Social Sciences* (2015): 120–38. Since the publication of these reports, we have updated our baseline estimates through mid-2013, and they remain consistent.

5. Shaefer and Edin, "Rising Extreme Poverty." Note that our longitudinal analysis suggests that SNAP's reach may be greater. See Shaefer, Edin, and Talbert, "Understanding the Dynamics."

6. Ian Fisher, "Moynihan Stands Alone in Welfare Debate," *New York Times*, September 27, 1995, http://www.nytimes.com/i995/09/27/nyregion/moynihan-stands-alone-in-welfare-debate.html.

AMERICANS DEEPEST IN POVERTY LOST MORE GROUND . . .

KRISTEN BIALIK

Although the overall U.S. poverty rate declined and incomes rose rapidly for the second straight year in 2016, many poor Americans fell deeper into poverty, according to a Pew Research Center analysis of U.S. Census Bureau data.[1] The official poverty rate was 12.7 percent [in 2016], close to its pre-Great Recession[2] level (12.5 percent in 2007). This represents 40.6 million people in poverty. But categorizing people as below or above the poverty line is just one way of looking at economic well-being.

The share of the U.S. poor population in severe poverty—defined by the Census Bureau as those with family or individual incomes below half of their poverty threshold—reached its highest point in recent years. It was 45.6 percent in 2016, up from 39.5 percent in 1996. (The share of the total U.S. population in severe poverty declined in 2017 and 2018, alongside the overall poverty rate.)

Poverty thresholds, which the Census Bureau uses to calculate the U.S. poverty rate, vary across families.[3] The Census poverty thresholds in 2016 ranged from around $12,000 for a single-person family to around $25,000 for a family of four, and it rose higher still for larger families. In comparison, the median household income for all households was $59,039 in 2016. For family households only, median household income was $75,062.

---

1 https://www.census.gov/library/publications/2017/demo/p60-259
   .html
2 https://www.federalreservehistory.org/essays/great_recession_
   of_200709
3 https://www.census.gov/topics/income-poverty/poverty/guidance/
   poverty-measures.html

As the share of poor families in severe poverty increased in recent years, these families also saw their incomes fall further below the poverty line. The average family income deficit—that is, the amount a family's income is below its poverty threshold—was $10,505 for all families in poverty in 2016 (excluding individuals living without other family members). After years of gradual increases, it marks a recent high, up roughly $1,000 from [the year] 2000 when the average deficit was $9,509 (after adjusting for inflation). Among poor families, the average income deficit was largest for those led by a woman with no husband present ($11,139), compared with $9,991 for married couples and $9,288 for families led by a man with no wife present.

As the average income deficit increased, the share of poor American families living far below the poverty threshold also grew. In 2016, 28.4 percent of families in poverty had incomes $15,000 or more below their poverty threshold, up from 26.2 percent in 2015. Nearly 2.3 million families had such severe deficits [in 2016].

The Census data show a different trend for American families who were not in poverty in 2016. For the vast majority of these Americans, the average income surplus—the amount a family's income is above its poverty threshold—was at least $15,000. The share of families above poverty with a surplus at least that large has gradually ticked upward in recent years, from around 84 percent in 2010 to 87 percent in 2016.

Married-couple families above the poverty line had the greatest income surplus, with an average of $97,249. The average income surplus was roughly half as large among families led by a woman with no husband ($46,026). Male-led households with no wife had an average surplus of $62,680.

Kristen Bialik, "Americans deepest in poverty lost more ground in 2016." Pew Research Center, October 6, 2017. https://www.pewresearch.org/fact-tank/2017/10/06/americans-deepest-in-poverty-lost-more-ground-in-2016/.

ASHLEY ROCKWELL

8. MAKING BANK ON TRIBAL GAMING? POVERTY AND THE MYTH OF NATIVE AMERICAN PROSPERITY

Like many other racial and ethnic groups, Native Americans experience racism, discrimination, and a host of other social problems that stem from historical and contemporary policies, legislation, and treatment that have had profoundly damaging effects. Many Americans, though, believe in harmful stereotypes about Native Americans which overlook the ways in which these laws, policies, and social trends have contributed to the social problems that many Native Americans face. In this piece, Rockwell debunks stereotypes and discusses the long-lasting impact of damaging policies on Native American communities and individuals. She also describes how Native American organizations are working to alleviate social problems in their communities.

When people find out about my Native American[1] heritage, they often ask me a string of questions. In elementary school, other students would ask me if I could shoot a bow and arrow. After the release of Disney's *Pocahontas*, some of my peers were disappointed to find out I did not have a pet raccoon. As I grew a bit older, the questioners turned to, "Do your parents work at a casino?" (they did not, although some of my relatives did) or "Can you get me the 'good' fireworks?" (the ones that were illegal to buy or use in our town but were available for purchase on the reservation). In college and as an adult, people would ask me if I received a check just for being Native (some tribes distribute a per capita check to their members using the profits from tribal-run businesses such as gaming). My peers insisted that my scholarships and even my entry into college were only the result of my heritage and university affirmative action policies. Overall, I was told that I was luckier than my mostly White peers, implying that my potential access to fireworks, casino employment opportunities, gaming revenues, and scholarships created distinct advantages for me and for my family. While the content of these questions varied over time, the underlying misconceptions and mythology have remained. My presumed luck seemed to erase both the history of oppression and the oppression American Indians continue to experience.

Speaking personally, I am lucky. I did not grow up on the reservation—which means I was insulated from the economic and social issues of living in Indian Country (which I will discuss more fully in this reading). Although we struggled, my father was able to pull us out of poverty by joining the military and using his training and education to secure a well-paying civilian job. This is a strategy used by many Natives and is likely a major reason why a disproportionate number of American Indians serve in the U.S. military (Gover 2017).[2] Those who identify as Native American-only (not multiracial) make up less than 1 percent of the U.S. population, but nearly twice that percentage of active duty military (U.S. Census 2012; U.S. Department of Defense 2010). I attended a predominately White high school where I met people whose parents and siblings had gone to college and could help me during the application process.

Original to *Focus on Social Problems: A Contemporary Reader.*

The advantages I experienced were the result of having opportunities that many Natives do not. I did not have to face directly the numerous social problems my family members have—their experiences run counter to the idea that Native Americans are living prosperous lives off casino profits and are simply handed educational and occupational opportunities.

Life on and off the reservations is much more complicated for vast numbers of American Indians. Native people have the highest poverty rate of any race or ethnic minority group in the United States and face numerous social problems stemming from a history of colonization, decimated population, forced assimilation, forced removal, discrimination, and other structural issues. In this reading, I will explore the causes of this extreme poverty and related social problems that affect the Nation's first peoples.

COLONIZATION AND THE MAKING OF RESERVATIONS

When colonists came to North America, their interactions with the Native people resulted in the deaths of many Natives. Not only did the new arrivals bring diseases that the Natives were not immune to, but there was constant war and fighting for Native lands. With the formation of the United States government, the control of Native populations became even more structured and institutionalized through laws and treaties. Settlers could collect bounties for each Native they killed; the scalps ("redskins") of those killed were removed to present "proof." The Indian Removal Act of 1830, signed by U.S. President Andrew Jackson, forced the indigenous people of the Southeastern United States to relocate further west. The Southeastern Natives including the Choctaw, Creek, and Cherokee were escorted by militia men for a thousand miles toward a new Indian Country (present-day Oklahoma). Those on the trek had very little food and lacked the proper clothing to protect them from the harsh weather encountered along the way. Thousands died from starvation, exposure to the elements, and the rampant diseases that spread in the overcrowded camps. This forced removal would later be termed the "Trail of Tears" to illustrate the extreme hardships the Native people endured.

As settlers moved west, they continued to force more Natives from their land. Reservations were usually the result of treaties with the U.S. government "reserving" a small portion of land for the tribe or group of tribes involved in the treaty. These treaties were often peace treaties that tribal leaders signed while under distress after physical battles for their land. Treaties often included promises of food exchange and provisions for health care, but these policies were rarely implemented. The land that was "reserved" for Natives tended to be land that isolated the Native people, and the land often had fewer natural resources than the land where they used to reside, making it difficult for them to survive due to lack of food and/or different weather conditions. Nomadic tribes that survived on hunting and gathering were often moved to land that could only provide food for them if farmed. This was made even more difficult since tribes were often moved to lands after planting season, so they had no crops to harvest, and "they were made wards by being dependent on the government for farming supplies, sawmills, blacksmith's shops, and the like" (Gidley 1979:42). Many people died fighting to preserve their land, but those who survived faced malnutrition and more health problems living on the scraps of land reserved for them.

The Dawes Allotment Act of 1887 further reduced the size of tribal land. Tribes used to own the land that made up their reservations, but the Dawes Act sought to get rid of communal ownership (Ellinghaus 2017). Due to the complicated and confusing process of proving that one is an American Indian and a descendent of a certain tribe or a certain band in a tribe, many mixed-race people or people of multiple tribes were not allowed to be enrolled as tribal members. Without a tribal membership, they did not receive an allotment of land, often losing the property where they had resided for years (Ellinghaus 2017). The U.S. government broke up tribal land into allotments for tribal families, sometimes giving the "excess" land to White settlers. For some Natives who were allowed land, their property ownership was short-lived. Severe poverty meant many families were forced to sell their land to White settlers who continued to encroach on the reservations. White people began to purchase the Native properties, further diminishing the size of tribal land. Until the Indian Reorganization Act of 1934, tribal members had very little say over how the

U.S. government managed their ever-shrinking amount of land. The Indian Reorganization Act stalled the continued allotment of tribal land and granted many tribes permission to observe their cultural practices. It also pushed for tribal sovereignty that encouraged tribes to form their own tribal governments and maintain their land and businesses.

Beyond allotments, the government has continued to reduce tribal land area in other ways in the modern era, often through construction of state or federal infrastructure projects on tribal land. For example, along the Columbia River, which separates parts of Washington, Oregon, and Idaho, several dams were built to allow for hydroelectric power and a complex irrigation system (Beaty et al. 1999). The building of one of those dams, the Grand Coulee, displaced many Natives from several tribes. Initially, only those individuals who had to relocate from their homes due to the flooding caused by the dam received compensation (Schmidt-Soltau 2006). Not only did the dam flood land and cut off the Columbia River from other areas of land, the dam inhibited spawning salmon from being able to make it back to their birthing sites. For many tribes in the area, including the Colville Confederated Tribes (of which my father is an enrolled member) and the Spokane Tribe, salmon fishing is a way of life and economic livelihood. The dam's interruption of the salmon's spawning run led to a decline in the salmon population, which, in turn, decreased the availability of food and jobs (Ortolano et al. 2000; Schmidt-Soltau 2006). It also reflected a spiritual loss, as salmon fishing is a traditional practice for many tribes—a way to stay connected to tradition and remember ancestors. As my father once explained to me, using the techniques and practices of our ancestors ensures that they are not forgotten. Before construction of the Grand Coulee Dam, the government promised to share the profits of the power generated by the dam with the tribe, but it took over 60 years for any form of payment to be made and only after extensive battles in court. The implementation of the dams represented another form of government interference in Native American livelihood, tradition, independence, and way of life. It is also another example of the U.S. government's unkept promises to Native American people.

AMERICAN INDIAN BOARDING SCHOOLS AND ASSIMILATION POLICY

Beyond getting rid of communal land ownership through the land allotment process, the U.S. government used other methods to forcibly westernize the culture of Native American people. Missionaries and governmental organizations attempted to "civilize" and assimilate the Native people: "While Native Americans were not to be granted formal citizenship of the United States until 1924, they were encouraged at the turn of the century to wear 'citizens' dress, to cut their braids, and to live in fixed houses" as opposed to tipis and pit-houses (Gidley 1979:42). The constitutional right of freedom of religion and worship was not afforded to Natives (Gidley 1979; Irwin 1997). In 1892, Thomas J. Morgan, the Commissioner of Indian Affairs, made it a crime for Natives to take part in many of their cultural traditions, such as certain dances and celebrations, plural marriages, and the uses of medicine men (Gidley 1979; Irwin 1997). In fact, Commissioner Morgan wrote in his "Rules for Indian Courts" that it was a crime for a Native to commit any act that would "prevent Indians from abandoning their barbarous rites and customs" (Gidley 1979:52).

Native children faced the brunt of forced assimilation through Indian Boarding Schools. Initially, religious organizations organized and managed the schools. Then, in 1879, Army officer Richard H. Pratt established the Carlisle Indian School in Pennsylvania (Booth 2009). He converted old military barracks into a school, which he operated in a military style (Lomawaima 1993). Captain Pratt was known for his speech "kill the Indian in him, and save the man" where he argued that one could rid society of the Indians' savagery through education instead of genocide (Lomawaima 1995; Pratt 1892). The government's admiration for the Carlisle School and their goal to "civilize" and assimilate the American Indian population led to the establishment of numerous Federal Indian Boarding Schools throughout the United States (Booth 2009). Government officials traveled to reservations to recruit children for the schools, often taking them coercively or by force from their parents. By 1898, a law was passed giving federal officials legal power to remove children from their homes despite parental objections (Booth 2009). Food and clothing rations were withheld from parents who did not cooperate, and some parents were actually arrested for their refusal to surrender their children. Even Chief Joseph of the Nez Perce, a recognizable and powerful public figure, had food withheld from him and his people for opposing sending their tribal youth to a boarding school (Gidley 1979).

The children were often taken to schools far away from their homes, and in some cases they would not be able to see their family for years. The students learned English and other subjects during the first half of the day and then provided child labor for the school by tending to fields, cooking, and performing other school maintenance tasks (Booth 2009). The school staff severely punished students for the use of Native languages, Native names, and traditional cultural practices. As soon as the children arrived at the boarding schools, their long, traditional hair was cut, they were made to wear Western-style clothes, and they were even given new Anglo names (Booth 2009). The children were told that their bodies, their names, and their traditions were uncivilized and savage (Lomawaima 1993). Some students attempted to secretly speak in their Native language and participate in spiritual practices. To prevent this, school administrators intentionally recruited students from different tribes with different languages, making it harder for the students to communicate with each other in a language other than English (Booth 2009). Homesickness overwhelmed the children, and there were numerous runaway attempts. The children lived in cramped and unsanitary conditions, sometimes sharing the same dirty towel without access to soap (Lomawaima 1995). Malnutrition was common and diseases spread rapidly through the schools. These conditions led to the deaths of many children whose parents were often not notified that their child was sick until after their child had died (Booth 2009; Lomawaima 1995). Death was such a common occurrence that many schools had their own graveyards. At Carlisle Indian School alone, nearly 200 children were buried at the property, with some families only recently gaining access to their family member's remains (Gammage 2016).

My great grandma on my mother's side grew up in a Catholic orphanage for Native children, where she was taught domestic skills such as cooking and sewing. Today, many people would describe how she was treated at the orphanage as child abuse and neglect. Like the boarding schools, the orphanage forced the children to assimilate and abandon their culture. As an adult, my great grandma did not even know to which tribe she belonged. It was not until after she passed away that a family member researching our genealogy determined that she was Ojibwa. The Indian Boarding Schools' organizers believed that teaching Native children a trade would help them become productive members of society (Lomawaima 1993). Girls were taught homemaking skills and how to work as maids for White families, and they taught boys how to farm. Unfortunately, many of these trades were not useful for finding work in Indian Country and resulted in many former students working low-wage, menial jobs as adults. A lack of fertile land and irrigation in Indian Country meant that boys taught how to farm would only be able to work as farmhands for White people rather than work their own farms. Therefore, the skills they acquired from school did not translate into economic prosperity for Native people and their communities.

Transitioning back to life on the reservation after leaving school proved even more difficult, due to loss of their native language and identity. Some former students described feeling they did not belong in either Native or White society (Lomawaima 1993, 1995). The students also had to cope with traumas they had endured while at school. Their trauma-filled childhoods made it difficult for some to be healthy and present parents when they began to have children of their own (Booth 2009; Brave Heart 1999, 2003; Lajimodiere 2012). I grew up thinking that my great grandma and her son (my grandpa) were just cruel and mean, not realizing their demeanor was a result of multigenerational trauma—neither one of them grew up in a loving or supportive household, and both were taught to be ashamed of their Nativeness.

Following the release of the 1928 Meriam Report detailing the unsanitary and inhumane conditions of Indian Boarding Schools, some schools closed and/or shifted their policies (Booth 2009). At the same time, Native children started to be allowed to attend public schools (which they had previously been barred from due to their race). The number of Native children who were forced to attend Indian Boarding Schools began to decrease after the 1930s (Booth 2009). But even through the 1960s, government-run Indian schools continued to punish Native students severely for their cultural practices (Bear 2008). Assimilation policies diminished over time, but punishment for participating in cultural practices did not come to a complete halt. In 1971, police arrested Sun Dancers on the Pine Ridge Reservation for violating an injunction against Sun Dancing (Irwin 1997). It wasn't until 1974, with passage of the Indian Self-Determination and Education Assistance Act, that the United States government authorized a transition from federal control of Indian programs and services to allowing Natives to meaningfully participate in the operation of programs, including educational institutions (Irwin 1997). There are still a handful of Indian Boarding Schools that operate in the United States, but children are no longer forced to attend, and the schools have incorporated classes and extracurricular activities based on Native history and culture (Bear 2008). The forcible removal of Native children to boarding schools or adoption by non-Natives was officially suspended when the Indian Child Welfare Act passed in 1978. The generations of forced relocation, assimilation, and trauma have made it difficult for tribes to prosper. These structural disadvantages and forms of oppression help explain many of the social problems Native Americans currently face.

POVERTY AND UNEMPLOYMENT

Poverty is arguably the most severe social problem affecting Native Americans. American Indians have the highest poverty rate of any racial group in the United States, with 26.2 percent of the Native population living below the poverty line, compared to a national rate of 14 percent (U.S. Census 2017). These poverty rates are often higher within certain reservations. For example, the poverty rate for the Standing Rock Reservation (in North and South Dakota) is 43.2 percent, and even higher for the Pine Ridge Reservation (in South Dakota) at 49.7 percent (Gulledge 2017), meaning that half of the 35,000 reservation residents are impoverished by conservative government

standards (HUD 2015). Both of these reservations face severely cold winters. Low incomes and inadequate housing and electricity make surviving the winter even more difficult. In Pine Ridge, some residents have to wear their winter coats even when they are inside, and a charity was created to distribute firewood for those in need (Gulledge 2017). According to the National Congress of American Indians, "Forty percent of on-reservation housing is considered substandard (compared to 6 percent outside of Indian Country) and nearly one-third of homes on reservations are overcrowded. Less than half of the homes on reservations are connected to public sewer systems, and 16 percent lack indoor plumbing" (NCAI 2016). Lack of proper housing and plumbing is difficult to fix without economic investment in infrastructure on Native land.

Native Americans also face high unemployment rates, making it difficult for them to get out of poverty. The unemployment rate between 2012 and 2016 for Natives throughout the United States averaged 13.7 percent, while the national average was only 8.1 percent (CBPP 2018). Unemployment rates are even higher in poorer reservations and tribal areas; Pine Ridge Indian Reservation suffers an 80 percent unemployment rate (Laughland & Silverstone 2017). Native Americans who live in states with a higher concentration of Natives tend to see higher unemployment rates as well. This discrepancy is most pronounced in Alaska and Arizona. The unemployment rate for Native Americans in Alaska averaged 20.5 percent in 2018 compared to the 7.1 percent unemployment rate for people of other races in Alaska (CBPP 2018). Similarly, approximately 19 percent of Native Americans living in Arizona are unemployed, compared to the 8.4 percent unemployment rate for people of other races in the state (CBPP 2018).

HEALTH AND FOOD ACCESS

High poverty and unemployment rates exacerbate the severe health issues with which many Native Americans must cope. The isolation of many Native Americans deepens and complicates the social problem of poor health by limiting access to healthy food and health care. Compared to other race/ethnic groups in the United States, Native Americans have the highest rate of Type 2 diabetes (IHS 2016), and they are 3.2 times more likely to have diabetes than other racial groups (IHS 2018). Type 2 diabetes can often be regulated or prevented through diet and exercise but maintaining a healthy diet can be difficult for Native Americans, especially for those living in food deserts (places that lack access to affordable and healthy food) and for those who contend with food insecurity. Researchers found that of the 22 American Indian Reservations in Washington State, 15 of the reservations only had convenience stores, with similar selection and food prices you would find at a gas station (O'Connell, Buchwald, & Duncan 2011). Only five contained a supermarket, and two of the reservations had only a grocery store[3] (O'Connell et al. 2011). The Cheyenne River Indian Reservation in South Dakota is larger than Delaware and Rhode Island combined, but it contains neither a grocery store nor a gas station (Friedman 2016). It is not difficult to imagine how hard it would be to attempt to treat or prevent diabetes, malnutrition, and obesity when food access is limited to what you would find at a gas station. The Muckleshoot Indian Tribe's traditional food and medicine program manager, Valerie Segrest, has described the food insecurity problems many Natives face: "It means that you have major challenges to accessing food. It means part of your income is set aside to fund the journey to get food. It means the land you live on does not provide food for you" (Landry 2015).

MENTAL HEALTH AND ADDICTION

Some Natives attempt to escape the stresses and difficulties of their lives by abusing drugs and alcohol. Of people who identify as a single race, Native Americans have the highest rate of drug use (SAMHSA 2018). When asked about their illicit drug use in the past month, 17.9 percent of adult Native Americans indicate they have used illicit drugs compared to the adult national average of 11.5 percent (SAMHSA 2018). Natives are also disproportionally dying from overdoses, as the United States fights an opioid epidemic (CDC 2018; Scott 2017). Alcoholism is another health issue that disproportionately affects Native Americans. The historical trauma that has accumulated over generations due to isolation, assimilation, and poverty has

led some Natives to engage in self-destructive behaviors as well as self-medication through drugs and alcohol to cope with their physical and psychological pain (Bohn 2003; Brave Heart 2003). The rates of substance abuse differ from reservation to reservation and from tribe to tribe. At the Pine Ridge Indian Reservation, two-thirds of the Oglala Lakota adults suffer from alcohol addiction (Laughland & Silverstone 2017). Pine Ridge has attempted to combat alcohol abuse by banning the sale and consumption of alcohol on reservation land. Unfortunately, this tactic has not been successful. The small town of Whiteclay, Nebraska, is located right outside of Pine Ridge and has four liquor stores despite its tiny population of 14 people (Laughland & Silverstone 2017). These liquor stores have sold over 3.5 million cans of beer a year, and overwhelmingly to Native American people (Hammel 2017). Alcohol consumption and its related violence in Whiteclay reached such a level that the state decided to close all of the liquor stores in the town. This decision was upheld by Nebraska's Supreme Court in the summer of 2017 (Hammel 2017; Laughland & Silverstone 2017). Although some in the community have applauded the ruling, others are worried that it will result in an increase of drunk driving as consumers drive even further to access alcohol (Hammel 2017). Rampant alcohol use and limited treatment of alcohol abuse, especially on tribal lands, makes Natives 4.6 times more likely to have chronic liver disease and cirrhosis than other racial groups (IHS 2018). Native Americans are also 6.6 times more likely to die of an alcohol-related death, including accidents that are a result of intoxication (IHS 2018).

In addition to substance abuse, Native Americans face other mental health issues at disproportionately high rates. Native American adults are about two times more likely to have made suicide plans in the past year compared to the national average (2.7 percent versus 1.3 percent) (SAMHSA 2018). Risk of suicide is highest among Native American youth (Leavitt et al. 2018). Natives 10–24 years of age are 2.4 times more likely to have a friend or family member die by suicide than other youth and young adults of different racial groups (Leavitt et al. 2018). At the Pine Ridge Indian Reservation, the youth suicide rate is four times that of the national average of 13.4 per

100,000 (Laughland & Silverstone 2017; NIMH 2018). Health experts and tribal leaders worry that youths' exposure to people taking their own lives will increase the suicide rate among the Native youth (Laughland & Silverstone 2017; Leavitt et al. 2018). In a *Washington Post* article on the "crushing hopelessness" faced by many Native youth, former Chief Judge Theresa M. Pouley of the Tulalip Tribal Court in Washington State noted the disproportionate rates of poverty among Native youth, and explained:

> They graduate high school at a rate 17 percent lower than the national average. Their substance-abuse rates are higher. They're twice as likely as any other race to die before the age of 24. They have a 2.3 percent higher rate of exposure to trauma. They have two times the rate of abuse and neglect. Their experience with post-traumatic stress disorder rivals the rates of returning veterans from Afghanistan. (Horwitz 2014)

Health professional and tribal leaders believe that all of these factors are related to the suicide rate for Native American youth being twice the rate of youth of other races (Alcántara & Gone 2007; Horwitz 2014; Laughland & Silverstone 2017; Leavitt et al. 2018). When I asked my grandma what she thought was the most significant issue faced by those on the reservation, she responded, saying "suicide." She fears that many see it as practical option, due to the high suicide rates. Like other tribal members, my grandma has a personal connection to Native American suicide. The loss of her brother (my great uncle) was truly the culmination of the physical and mental health problems many Natives face that I've described. My uncle was diabetic. He was found dead surrounded by soda cans. It appears that he committed suicide by drinking numerous sugary beverages, and then he purposefully did not use his insulin– suicide by diabetes.

The combination of mental and physical health issues and limited access to emergency services and other forms of health care is also part of the reason American Indians are 2.5 times more likely to die due to unintentional injuries and accidents. Slipping, falling, or getting in a car accident can potentially be fatal for anyone, but having quick and affordable access to emergency health services can help reduce the likelihood of death (IHS 2018).

ACCESS TO HEALTH CARE

There exists a frustrating paradox when it comes to health care access for Native Americans. Since 1787, due to the language in treaties and in the U.S. Constitution, the U.S. government has had a "federal obligation to provide health care to American Indians and Alaska Natives" (Dunbar-Ortiz & Gilio-Whitaker 2016; IHS 2015:1). The U.S. government attempts to provide health care to Natives through Indian Health Services (IHS) (Friedman 2016). Unfortunately, however, IHS is consistently underfunded, and so the health care many Natives have access to is limited and inadequate. The health centers run by IHS offer only a few basic health services, and even getting access to those services is difficult, involving significant travel distances and early morning departures (Friedman 2016). Extensive poverty usually prohibits Natives from going outside this system to access private health care.

My Auntie Phyllis, a Colville tribal elder who resides on the Colville Indian Reservation in rural Washington State, believes that one of biggest hurdles for people on the reservation is just getting to the doctor's office. Compared to other American Indians living on reservations, my aunt is fortunate enough to live on one that has an IHS clinic, but it is still a 45-minute drive from the district where she and many other elders live. Like at other IHS clinics, patients are unable to make appointments ahead of time. She explained the process: "If you have to see the doctor or anything you have to travel all the way to Nespelem [36 miles from my auntie's home] and then you got to be there by 7:30 in the morning and put your name on the list. Sometime between 7:30 and 8:00am they take away the list and what not, and then they start calling people in." If you are lucky enough to have your name called, you may still have to sit in the office and wait all day to be seen. The IHS clinic in Nespelem is only open on weekdays, so for those who work during the week they would have to take an entire day off just to have a chance to see the doctor. My auntie explains further, "those of us who live way over here have to find a way to get way over there, and it's hard." To gain access to medical specialists, tribal members must travel even further (two hours both ways) to reach a town with specialists (IHS n.d.). This is especially problematic for those already facing high poverty rates and who cannot afford the travel costs. Natives with low incomes (like other people with low incomes) could qualify for Medicaid thanks to the Medicaid expansion program. However, those in states like South Dakota, Idaho, Utah, Wisconsin, Wyoming, and Oklahoma (states where 72 federally recognized tribes call home), where politicians have refused to expand Medicaid, have no access (Friedman 2016).

MYTH OF PROSPERITY—MAKING BANK FROM TRIBAL GAMING

Since many of the social issues Natives deal with stem from poverty, some argue that tribes are not doing enough to take care of their own people. A common myth about Native American tribes is that many, if not all, operate successful gaming and casino operations, and that individual tribe members are thriving as a result. The reality of extreme poverty, unemployment, and health issues clash with this idea. A minority of tribes have indeed successfully profited and improved the opportunities, living experiences, health, and wealth of their members through capitalizing on gambling and casinos. There are 573 federally recognized tribes in the United States (BIA 2018) and 459 tribal-run casinos, with some tribes running multiple casinos (Dunbar-Ortiz & Gilio-Whitaker 2016). That means there are many tribes that do not have casinos on their land at all. And even having a casino does not guarantee high revenues for tribes, as evidenced by high poverty and unemployment rates (Evans & Topoleski 2002). Running a casino and actually profiting from gaming are two different things, and only a handful generate significant profits. Thirteen percent of tribal casinos account for 60 percent of all Indian gaming revenue, and that revenue is not distributed across all tribes (Desmond & Emirbayer 2015).

In terms of gaming, the Ho-Chunk Nation has been one of the luckier tribes, as "[I]ndian gambling has allowed the Ho-Chunk to capitalize on what is otherwise the tribe's greatest drawback. Its land holdings are mostly small, scattered in more than a dozen Wisconsin counties. But they include parcels near larger population and visitor centers, such as Madison and the Wisconsin Dells" (Lueders 2014). As mentioned

previously, many tribes were forcibly relocated to isolated areas, which means they lack an adequate population to create and sustain a thriving gaming industry. If tribal land is not located near a big city, it is difficult to get people to visit and spend money on the reservation. For example, compared to tribes located in areas that are more rural, the Puyallup Tribe, which runs Emerald City Casinos in the Tacoma/Seattle area, is thriving economically due to its prime locations. It also takes a large amount of capital to open up a large gaming business, and due to the structural barriers plaguing many tribes, funds and resources are often too limited for such a venture. On the whole, tribal gaming operations (when the tribe can afford to invest in gaming) usually result in a slight improvement in the employment rate for the area around the casino, but "most of this growth in employment is due to growth in non-Native American employment" (Evans & Topoleski 2002:2). For example, the Ho-Chunk Nation is one of the largest employers in the area, providing jobs for a large number of non-Native people. In fact, 72 percent of their employees are not members of the tribe (Lueders 2014).

SOCIAL CHANGE AND THE FUTURE FOR NATIVES

As Toni Stanger-McLaughlin, Director of Tribal Governance at Indigenous Food and Agriculture Initiative, explains, "it's not that poverty is the defining factor of success, it's that [when you are not in poverty] you are not in stress mode, you are not in survival mode. You get to explore more about the world, more about yourself, about education, and just being a human instead of just surviving." There are some tribes and tribal groups that are doing a great job of helping their people from just surviving to thriving. As mentioned previously, the Ho-Chunk Nation has seen great success in their gaming industry, and they have taken profits from gaming and reinvested them in their community. A key goal for the Ho-Chunk is to make their community more sustainable and self-sufficient. To realize this goal, they have created the Ho-Chunk Gardens where they have reintroduced native plant species and are teaching residents how to live off the land (Colson 2011). This has provided people of the Ho-Chunk Nation with food, but also a chance to participate in traditional tribal practices. The Ho-Chunk Nation is also using their profits to fund health and elder care, including a program aimed at reducing the rate of diabetes by paying for tribal members' gym memberships (Lueders 2014). As mentioned earlier, the Ho-Chunk Nation provides economic support for the entire community, employing large numbers of non-Native people (Lueders 2014).

Other tribes are also investing in food sovereignty. Thirty-five percent of Citizen Potawatomi Nation households are food insecure, but the Citizen Potawatomi Nation is fighting food insecurity and limited food access with community gardens throughout the area (CPN 2018). The Quapaw Tribe has numerous greenhouses where they grow the produce that is served in restaurants located on their gaming resort (Eaton 2016). They have even expanded their agricultural operations, operating a cattle company, a beekeeping company, and their own coffee-roasting facility (Eaton 2016). The Winnebago Tribe of Nebraska is also working on becoming self-sustaining; with the densest concentration of solar panels in Nebraska, making them a leader in solar power in the Midwest (Uhlenhuth 2018).

Even on one of the poorest and most remote reservations, the Pine Ridge Indian Reservation—where it would be nearly impossible to have a successful gaming industry—community leaders are working hard to improve living conditions. The Thunder Valley Community Development Corporation has created numerous community gardens and even a geothermal greenhouse, making it possible to grow produce in South Dakota's cold winters (Thunder Valley CDC 2018). Thunder Valley has also created a program that trains young adults in the field of sustainable construction to help reduce unemployment and improve the current housing structures (Thunder Valley CDC 2018).

The misconceptions about Natives and Native American life, as well as the questions I have been asked over the years, demonstrate a lack of knowledge and understanding of the severe social and historical circumstances the indigenous population has endured. Many members of my family have had first-hand experience with these social problems—poverty, poor physical and mental health, lack of access to medical facilities, and unemployment. The competing stereotypes of the Native population living prosperously off casino riches while simultaneously being poor and lazy ignores the complex struggles of Native life. Profits from gaming have greatly improved the quality of life of their member. Unfortunately, opening a casino is not the answer for all tribes. Even though tribal sovereignty can allow tribes to run casinos and other gaming endeavors, it is often not enough to compensate for the history of the discriminatory treatment of American Indians. While there are tribal organizations successfully working to alleviate the effects of these social issues, their ability to do so depends on funding. The future of tribes that do not have access to this type of funding is uncertain.

NOTES

1. I use the terms *Native, Native American,* and *American Indian* interchangeably. My older family members use the term *American Indian* or *Indian* most often, while my younger family members tend to use *Native American* or *Native.* Scholars, activists, and younger people (including myself) are embracing the term *Indigenous* since it encapsulates a similar experience of discrimination and oppression indigenous people have experienced throughout the world. There is a lot of conversation about which terms should be used; to honor those I respect, I use the terminology they use when describing our communities.

2. Despite their service, American Indians and Alaskan Native veterans have the lowest median incomes compared to veterans of other races (U.S. Department of Veterans Affairs 2012).

3. Supermarkets tend to have much larger selection and lower prices compared to grocery stores, while grocery stores tend to have greater selection and better prices than convenience stores.

REFERENCES

Alcántara, Carmela, and Joseph P. Gone. 2007. "Reviewing Suicide in Native American Communities: Situating Risk and Protective Factors within a Transactional–Ecological Framework." *Death Studies* 31(5):457–77.

Bear, Charla. 2008. "American Indian School a Far Cry from the Past." *NPR*, May 13. Retrieved November 26, 2018, from https://www.npr.org/templates/story/story.php?storyId=17645287.

Beaty, Roy E., Henry J. Yuen, Philip A. Meyer, and Michael A. Matylewich. 1999. *Cumulative Impacts on the Peoples of the Nez Perce, Yakama, Umatilla, and Warm Springs Indian Reservations from Construction and Operation of US Army Corps of Engineers' Dams in the Columbia River Basin Upstream of Bonneville Dam, Inclusive. CRITFC Technical Report. 99-02.* Columbia River Inter-Tribal Fish Commission. Retrieved July 8, 2018, from http://www.critfc.org/blog/reports/cumulative-impacts-peoples-nez-perce-yakama-umatilla-warm-springs-indian-reservations-construction-operation-us-army-corps-engineers-dams-columbia-r.

BIA. 2018. "About Us | Indian Affairs." *U.S. Department of the Interior: Bureau of Indian Affairs.* Retrieved July 15, 2018, from https://www.bia.gov/about-us.

Bohn, Diane K. 2003. "Lifetime Physical and Sexual Abuse, Substance Abuse, Depression, and Suicide Attempts among Native American Women." *Issues in Mental Health Nursing* 24(3):333–52.

Booth, Tabatha Toney. 2009. "Cheaper Than Bullets: American Indian Boarding Schools and Assimilation Policy, 1890–1930." Presented at the Images, Imaginations, and Beyond: Proceedings of the Eighth Native American Symposium, November, Southeastern Oklahoma State University.

Brave Heart, Maria Yellow Horse. 1999. "Oyate Ptayela: Rebuilding the Lakota Nation through Addressing Historical Trauma among Lakota Parents." *Journal of Human Behavior in the Social Environment* 2(1-2):109–26.

Brave Heart, Maria Yellow Horse. 2003. "The Historical Trauma Response among Natives and Its Relationship with Substance Abuse: A Lakota Illustration." *Journal of Psychoactive Drugs* 35(1):7–13.

CBPP. 2018. *Harm to American Indians and Alaska Natives From Taking Away Medicaid for Not Meeting Work Requirements. Policy Brief.* Center on Budget and Policy Priorities. Retrieved July 15, 2018, fromhttps://www.cbpp.org/research/health/harm-to-american-indians-and-alaska-natives-from-taking-away-medicaid-for-not.

CDC. 2018. *CDC Provides New Funds to Battle the Opioid Overdose Epidemic. Press Release.* Center for Disease Control. Retrieved November 24, 2018, from https://www.cdc.gov/media/releases/2018/p0919-cdc-opiod-battle-funding.html.

Colson, Cassandra. 2011. "Ho-Chunk Revitalizing Culture through Organic Garden." *La Crosse Tribune.* Retrieved August 6, 2018, from https://lacrossetribune.com/jacksoncochronicle/life-styles/ho-chunk-revitalizing-culture-through-organic-garden/article_f6c691f6-df16-11e0-9cf5-001cc4c002e0.html.

CPN. 2018. "Tribal Culture Aids in Food Sovereignty Efforts Citizen Potawatomi Nation." *Citizen Potawatomi Nation.* Retrieved August 25, 2018, from http://www.potawatomi.org/tribal-culture-aids-in-food-sovereignty-efforts.

Desmond, Matthew, and Mustafa Emirbayer. 2015. *Race in America.* New York: W. W. Norton.

Dunbar-Ortiz, Roxanne, and Dina Gilio-Whitaker. 2016. *"All the Real Indians Died Off": And 20 Other Myths about Native Americans.* Boston: Beacon Press.

Eaton, Kristi. 2016. "Quapaw Tribe Adds Mercantile, Coffee Roasting to Business Ventures." *Indian Country Today.* Retrieved August 6, 2018, from https://newsmaven.io/indiancountrytoday/

archive/quapaw-tribe-adds-mercantile-coffee-roasting-to-business-ventures-bN9DehUVQ EyzHTstWtgEPw.

Ellinghaus, Katherine. 2017. *Blood Will Tell: Native Americans and Assimilation Policy*. Lincoln: University of Nebraska Press.

Evans, William N., and Julie H. Topoleski. 2002. *The Social and Economic Impact of Native American Casinos. Working Paper. 9198*. National Bureau of Economic Research. Retrieved July 15, 2018, from http://www.nber.org/papers/w9198.

Friedman, Misha. 2016. "For Native Americans, Health Care Is a Long, Hard Road Away." *NPR*, April 13. Retrieved from https://www.npr.org/2016/04/13/473264076/for-native-americans-health-care-is-a-long-hard-road-away.

Gammage, Jeff. 2016. "'Those Kids Never Got to Go Home'—Philly." *Philly News*, March 19. Retrieved from https://www.inquirer.com/news/inq/those-kids-never-got-go-home-20160319.html.

Gidley, M. 1979. *With One Sky above Us: Life on an American Indian Reservation at the Turn of the Century*. Seattle: University of Washington Press.

Gover, Kevin. 2017. "American Indians Serve in the U.S. Military in Greater Numbers Than Any Ethnic Group and Have Since the Revolution." *Smithsonian National Museum of the American Indian*. Retrieved from https://www.huffingtonpost.com/national-museum-of-the-american-indian/american-indians-serve-in-the-us-military_b_7417854.html.

Gulledge, Jacqueline. 2017. "American Indians Struggle to Survive Winter in South Dakota." *CNN*, February 13. Retrieved July 15, 2018, from https://www.cnn.com/2017/02/13/health/iyw-american-indian-lakota-charity-one-spirit-firewood-program/index.html.

Hammel, Paul. 2017. "Supreme Court Delivers Victory to Opponents of Whiteclay Beer Sales; 'The Shame of Whiteclay Is Over,' Attorney Says." *Omaha World Herald*, September. Retrieved August 9, 2018, from https://www.omaha.com/news/nebraska/supreme-court-delivers-victory-to-opponents-of-whiteclay-beer-sales/article_653a39aa-a51b-11e7-9823-ef5e85336ab8.html.

Horwitz, Sari. 2014. "The Hard Lives—and High Suicide Rate—of Native American Children on Reservations." *The Washington Post*, March 9. Retrieved October 9, 2018, from https://www.washingtonpost.com/world/national-security/the-hard-lives--and-high-suicide-rate--of-native-american-children/2014/03/09/6e0ad9b2-9f03-11e3-b8d8-94577ff66b28_story.html.

HUD. 2015. *Pine Ridge Promise Zone: Second Round. Promise Zones. 15-049*. U.S. Department of Housing and Urban Development. Retrieved October 9, 2018, from https://www.hud.gov/sites/documents/PROMISEZONE11SD.PDF.

IHS. 2015. *Basis for Health Services. Fact Sheet*. U.S. Department of Health and Human Services: Indian Health Service. Retrieved July 15, 2018, from https://www.ihs.gov/newsroom/includes/themes/responsive2017/display_objects/documents/factsheets/BasisforHealthServices.pdf.

IHS. 2016. *Special Diabetes Program for Indians. Fact Sheet*. U.S. Department of Health and Human Services: Indian Health Service. Retrieved July 15, 2018, from https://www.ihs.gov/newsroom/includes/themes/responsive2017/display_objects/documents/factsheets/Diabetes.pdf.

IHS. 2018. *Indian Health Disparities. Fact Sheet*. U.S. Department of Health and Human Services: Indian Health Service. Retrieved July 15, 2018, from https://www.ihs.gov/newsroom/factsheets/disparities.

IHS. n.d. "Colville Service Unit." *IHS.gov*. Retrieved August 24, 2018, from https://www.ihs.gov/Portland/healthcarefacilities/colville.

Irwin, Lee. 1997. "Freedom, Law, and Prophecy: A Brief History of Native American Religious Resistance." *American Indian Quarterly* 21(1):35–55.

Lajimodiere, Denise. 2012. "A Healing Journey." *Wicazo Sa Review* 27(2):5–19.

Landry, Alysa. 2015. "What Is a Food Desert? Do You Live in One? 23.5 Million in This Country Do." *Indian Country Today*, June 28. Retrieved August 19, 2018, from https://newsmaven.io/indiancountrytoday/archive/what-is-a-food-desert-do-you-live-in-one-23-5-million-in-this-country-do-eCuQcy2Sy0K6EQozR3IsDw.

Laughland, Oliver, and Tom Silverstone. 2017. "Liquid Genocide: Alcohol Destroyed Pine Ridge Reservation – Then They Fought Back." *The Guardian*, September 29. Retrieved August 9, 2018, from http://www.theguardian.com/society/2017/sep/29/pine-ridge-indian-reservation-south-dakota.

Leavitt, Rachel A., Allison Ertl, Kameron Sheats, Emiko Petrosky, Asha Ivey-Stephenson, and Katherine A. Fowler. 2018. *Suicides among American Indian/Alaska Natives—National Violent Death Reporting System, 18 States, 2003–2014*. Volume 67 (8). Centers for Disease Control and Prevention.

Lomawaima, K. Tsianina. 1993. "Domesticity in the Federal Indian Schools: The Power of Authority over Mind and Body." *American Ethnologist* 20(2):227–40.

Lomawaima, K. Tsianina. 1995. *They Called It Prairie Light: The Story of Chilocco Indian School*. Lincoln: University of Nebraska Press.

Lueders, Bill. 2014. "Despite Spawning Conflict, Gambling Has given Tribe New Hope." *La Crosse Tribune*, April 30. Retrieved August 6, 2018, from https://lacrossetribune.com/jacksoncochronicle/news/local/despite-spawning-conflict-gambling-has-given-tribe-new-hope/article_fcfabacb-cb02-57ab-bf66-63abeace6879.html.

NCAI. 2016. *Housing and Infrastructure. Policy Issues and Economic Development and Commerce*. Retrieved October 13, 2018, from http://www.ncai.org/policy-issues/economic-development-commerce/housing-infrastructure.

NIMH. 2018. "National Institute of Mental Health: Suicide." *National Institute of Mental Health*. Retrieved October 9, 2018, from https://www.nimh.nih.gov/health/statistics/suicide.shtml.

O'Connell, Meghan, Dedra S. Buchwald, and Glen E. Duncan. 2011. "Food Access and Cost in American Indian Communities in Washington State." *Journal of the American Dietetic Association* 111(9):1375–79.

Ortolano, Leonard, Katherine Kao Cushing, and Contributing Authors. 2000. *Grand Coulee Dam and the Columbia Basin Project USA. WCD Case Study*. World Commission on Dams.

Pratt, Richard H. 1892. "The Advantages of Mingling Indians with Whites." in *Official Report of the Nineteenth Annual Conference of Charities and Correction*, 4649.

SAMHSA. 2018. *National Survey on Drug Use and Health. Center for Behavioral Health Statistics and Quality Data Review*. Substance Abuse and Mental Health Services Administration.

Schmidt-Soltau, Kai. 2006. *Revised Final Report Addressing Outstanding Social Issues*. United Nations Environment Programme Dams and Development Project. Retrieved August 6, 2018, from http://www.schmidt-soltau.de/PDF/Englisch/2006_Adressing%20Outstanding%20Social%20Issues%20Revised%20Final%20Report.pdf.

Scott, Eugene. 2017. "Native Americans, among the Most Harmed by the Opioid Epidemic, Are Often Left out of Conversation." *Washington Post*, October 30. Retrieved November 24, 2018, from https://www.washingtonpost.com/news/the-fix/wp/2017/10/30/native-americans-among-the-most-harmed-by-the-opioid-epidemic-are-often-left-out-of-conversation.

Thunder Valley CDC. 2018. "The Thunder Valley Community Development Corporation Accomplishments." *Thundervalley.org*. Retrieved August 25, 2018, from http://thundervalley.org/learn-more/accomplishments.

Uhlenhuth, Karen. 2018. "Nebraska Tribe Becomes Solar Power Leader in Midwest." *AP News*. Retrieved August 6, 2018, from https://www.apnews.com/774f18fbd1d24f15879bd4681f91980d.

U.S. Census. 2012. *2010 Census Shows Nearly Half of American Indians and Alaska Natives Report Multiple Races—2010 Census—Newsroom—U.S. Census Bureau.* U.S. Census Bureau Public Information Office. Retrieved October 9, 2018, from https://www.census.gov/newsroom/releases/archives/2010_census/cb12-cn06.html.

U.S. Census. 2017. "FFF: American Indian and Alaska Native Heritage Month: November 2017." Retrieved August 9, 2018, from https://www.census.gov/newsroom/facts-for-features/2017/aian-month.html.

U.S. Department of Defense. 2010. *Demographics 2010: Profile of the Military Community. Demographics Report.* Office of the Deputy Under Secretary of Defense. Retrieved October 9, 2018, from http://download.militaryonesource.mil/12038/MOS/Reports/2010_Demographics_Report.pdf.

U.S. Department of Veterans Affairs. 2012. *American Indian and Alaska Native Servicemembers and Veterans.* Retrieved October 9, 2018, from https://www.va.gov/TRIBALGOVERNMENT/docs/AIAN_Report_FINAL_v2_7.pdf.

ERIC RAVENSCRAFT

9. BEING POOR IS TOO EXPENSIVE

Ravenscraft details the challenges of living in poverty that are often invisible to those who have not experienced it, including costs in terms of time, energy, and money. Based on his experience living in poverty, Ravenscraft describes these challenges, and how small mistakes that more financially secure individuals easily absorb without long-term consequences can result in enormous setbacks for those in poverty.

Some think that being poor is simple. You don't have enough money to buy a lot of stuff, so you're forced to buy less stuff. But that's not really how it works. When you're broke, you can't do all the little things that will improve your budget over the long run. It actually costs *more* to be poor. . . . Worse yet, being poor often comes with hidden, intangible costs that make digging yourself out of poverty even harder.

FOOD CAN BE CHEAP, BUT EATING HEALTHY IS EXPENSIVE

As any college student can tell you, getting food when you're poor isn't that hard. Ramen is under 20 cents a pack. The problem is getting *healthy* food. Ramen consists of 20 percent empty calories and 80 percent salt. If you only ate that for every meal for years, your long-term health would be at serious risk (or so my doctor tells me).

This was the exact situation I found myself in when I was broke.[1] Time was more valuable than my health, and fast food was easier than cooking at home. It wasn't much more expensive either. This led to an unhealthy hierarchy of meals: on a good week, I could buy hot dogs from my local QuikTrip for $2. On a bad week, it was Ramen for days. Two liter bottles of store-brand soda cost less than orange juice or milk, so if I wanted something to drink besides water, that was what I got.

Now, a few years of that diet is already going to be pretty bad. The long-term consequences were worse. Even when I started earning more, the habits stuck. Soda is still a staple of my diet. It's taken a long time to build the habit of making proper, home-cooked meals. It's easy to think that you'll just change your habits once you get more money, but you don't realize just how many bad habits you build.

This is a difficult trap to escape. According to research from the Harvard School of Public Health,[2] healthy meals cost an average of $1.50 more per day (or ~$45 per month) than unhealthy meals. When you have money, that's not a huge deal. However, if you make the federal minimum wage of $7.25 per hour and you work 40 hours per week, that amounts to roughly 3.6 percent of your yearly salary. If you can only get the part-time hours of 32 hours per week (which is more common for minimum wage jobs), it's 4.5 percent of your yearly take-home. Before taxes, by the way.

When $1.50 a day can account for nearly 5 percent of your yearly salary, it's no surprise you choose the $1 soda over the $4 orange juice. Who the hell cares about "long-term health consequences" when you can barely pay rent? You know what has some serious "long-term health consequences"? Getting evicted. I'll pay rent today and worry about heart disease later.

When you're poor, you can't afford to think about the "long run." I knew that it was smart to buy some stuff from big membership stores, but I couldn't even get past the membership fees. I knew that eating gas station hot dogs and ramen was going to kill me some day, but as long as that day wasn't before rent was due, I had to live with it. I probably could've done marginally better if I planned to cook more meals ahead of time but I, like 6.8 million Americans according to the Bureau of Labor Statistics,[3] had to work multiple jobs to get by. I didn't have enough time to be healthy, and I didn't have enough money to save money.

CHEAP CARS COST MORE TO REPAIR, AND PUBLIC TRANSPORTATION IS A TIME SUCK

Having a job doesn't mean much if you can't *get* to your job. Owning a car is expensive even after you've paid off the initial cost. Public transit may be more accommodating to lower-income tiers, but it isn't always available in every city.

Transportation has two major hidden costs when you're poor. First, lots of expensive car repairs are avoidable if you have money to fix them early on. I used to ignore changing my brake pads for months. My car would start making that familiar squealing noise that indicated I didn't have much time left before the brake pads were gone. I hated the noise, but I hated overdrafting on my account more. So, I turned the stereo up a little louder and tried to drive less.

Replacing brake pads can cost an average of $145,[4] depending on your car. If I had to spend $145 to change my brake pads (assuming I even had that much in my account), at best I'd wipe out my food budget for the month. At worst, I wouldn't have enough to pay utilities. So I'd put it off.

On at least one occasion, my brakes got so bad they were grinding down the rotors. In case you've never had this happen, grinding rotors make a terrible, metal-on-metal sound. Replacing a rotor also costs hundreds more[5] than replacing brake pads. Sure, I successfully put off one expense, but when the rotors broke, I was screwed. The longer I waited on basic maintenance, the more expensive the repairs got.

Waiting was often my only option, though. Unlike buying healthy food, there were times I literally didn't *have* the money. Not "I have this money, but I shouldn't spend it." More like, the car repair is $145 and I have $12 in my account. And I still have to drive my car to work. There's no third option.

Public transit is a great option, but a lot of cities don't provide it. If yours does, things still aren't great. With public transit, you face a very different cost: time. What would be a 15-minute drive becomes an hour-long bus ride. Miss a bus and you've lost another 10–15 minutes. When you only have a couple of free hours in the day, that hour on the bus might mean you can't prepare a decent meal or do laundry. This can apply to cars too ("I'll just do that hour-long oil change next week"), but with public transportation, the cost of time really adds up fast.

Unfortunately, transportation isn't exactly optional. If your car breaks down and you don't have money to fix it, you lose out on more wages. Some even lose their jobs. The time costs of public transit can also make it harder to fit in things that help dig yourself out of poverty, like education. Ironically, just getting to work can make it harder to work, if you can't afford all the associated costs that go with it.

YOU NEED TO DRESS NICELY TO MOVE UP, BUT NEW CLOTHES AREN'T A PRIORITY

Despite their necessity, buying new clothes is often seen as one of the most stereotypically frivolous purchases. Why should poor people be shopping for new or nice clothing when they're struggling to make ends meet, right? The problem is, if you don't spend money on clothes, you pay a hefty social cost.

Several years ago, I worked for Walmart. As is the case for most retail employees, I had to buy my own uniform. At the time, we were required to wear dark blue shirts and khaki pants. Since I owned exactly none of either, I had to blow through any clothing budget I had just to be ready for work (before I got my first paycheck, no less). The problem was, I worked outside as a cart-pusher. Navy blue shirts tend to fade in the harsh Georgia sunlight. Plus, my shoes wore through every three months from walking on pavement all day. And not just "they look ratty"—my toes were literally touching burning pavement a few months after getting new shoes.

Needless to say, I looked like crap most of the time. My shirts were faded and my shoes were falling apart, and that was while I was on the clock. The rest of my wardrobe looked even worse. Any money I could spare for clothing usually had to go toward new uniforms. The problem is, if I wanted to get a job somewhere else, the nicest thing I had to wear was my work outfit. It took a long time before I could afford to update my closet with anything even remotely presentable while still keeping up with uniform churn. In the end, I only pulled it off by opening a small line of credit with a clothing retailer. No matter how many people advised against borrowing money when you're broke, I simply couldn't afford the clothing I needed to look presentable to an employer *before* getting the job I was applying for. . . .

Of course, the costs of clothing don't end at social pressures. Merely keeping your clothes clean and presentable can cost time and money, too. If you don't own or have access to a washer and dryer, you need to spend time at a laundromat. Not only does this cost money every single time you clean your clothes, but it takes precious time that could be better spent working, learning a skill, or taking care of your family.

The worst part is how frivolous this all sounds. Frankly, it's demoralizing. As someone who's had to wear crap clothes to work and even crappier clothes on my off days, I know how it feels to be seen differently. You get comments about how you need new clothes. You're reminded, politely and unhelpfully, how your clothes are faded. It's vaguely implied that your failure to buy new shoes isn't a symptom of your low paycheck, but laziness. Why haven't you gone to the store to buy new shoes yet? As if going to the store was the biggest hurdle. . . .

FEES FOR EVERYTHING CAN COMPOUND TO RUIN YOUR BUDGET

Avoiding fees is a life or death survival trait for low-income households. This gets its own category because when you're poor, fees are *everywhere*. Fees for having a bank. Fees for not having a bank. Fees for paying late. Fees for paying with a certain type of card. Fees for not being able to pay a fee. A person can drown in the various fees that disproportionately hurt poor families.

One fee that hurt me a *lot* over the years was overdraft fees. If I charged something to my debit card, and then it turned out I didn't have enough money,

I was charged $35 per transaction. This seems like a no-brainer, right? Just don't spend money you don't have, Eric!

Except that's not how it works when you're broke. You have to obsessively overanalyze every single transaction in your account. Not just how much but when. If you pay the power bill today, but it doesn't clear until next week, then you have to remember that your account is that much emptier than it looks. My credit union in particular had terrible software. . . . The best I could do was to keep a written log of every transaction personally, but if I forgot something or made a math error, I was screwed.

This was made even worse when my credit union would apply transactions in a highest-to-lowest order, rather than chronologically. Say I had $150 in my account, and I accidentally spent $160. One transaction was a $150 power bill, while the rest was four transactions of $2.50 each. Even if the power bill was the last one I paid, I would sometimes find it was taken out of my account first, leaving me with zero dollars. Then, each $2.50 transaction would cost me $35 extra in overdraft fees. If they were charged in the correct order, I would only get one fee, but instead I would be charged $140 in fees. Unfortunately, this happens a lot more often than it should.[6] Sometimes, this was my own fault, but it also occurred when deposits didn't clear when I expected them to, or bills were charged sooner than their due date. A minor mistake for someone with more money destroyed my budget for weeks.

Banks aren't the only ones who charge compounding fees either. Every year, I had to pay to register my car. One particularly bad year, I didn't have spare money to pay registration. I also worked one mile from work, so when it came time to choose between registration or food, I took a risk that I could make it to work without getting pulled over. One week after my registration was due, I got pulled over. I was let off with a warning and told to pay my registration. Another week later (before I'd even earned enough money to pay for registration), I got pulled over again. Since this was the second time for the same offense, I got a citation for nearly $100. This wasn't making it any easier to pay the fine. Eventually, I was finally able to pay it with money I received from relatives on Christmas. Just what I always wanted.

Fees are everywhere when you're poor. Banks may charge a ton of fees for using basic services like checking. A simple traffic ticket can spiral out of control, sometimes even leading to being arrested, plus more fees.[7] Utilities may charge fees if you pay by debit card. If you can't get approval at a bank, payment schemes like pay cards can charge you fees just to use your money.[8] All these fees add up to huge pains that hurt a lot worse when you don't have money. Failing to pay those fees only leads to more fees, which means that, like most areas in life, it costs more to be poor.

With all of these things, there is an element of responsibility. For example, could I have walked to work instead of driving a car with an expired tag? Maybe! Then again, I tried that for a while, got caught in the rain, and my phone was destroyed. . . .

That's what makes being poor so tough. Sure, you can make choices that lighten the load on yourself, but the margin of error is much thinner. Meanwhile, the amount of extra work you have to do just to break even is much higher. You could spend tens of hours each week trying to optimize every dime in your budget, just to have one mistake ruin you for a month.

This is just my experience, but many people had it way worse than I did. At my lowest point, I was fortunate enough to either have people to help out or lucked into receiving a windfall right when I needed it. Others aren't so lucky. When the punishment for making a mistake or having an accident is so harsh, it can make it nearly impossible for even the hardest working people to break out of the cycle of poverty.

NOTES

1. Ravenscraft, Eric. 2013. "The Financial Advice I'm Glad I Ignored When I Was Broke." *Lifehacker*.Retrieved on December 24, 2018, from https://lifehacker.com/the-financial-advice-im-glad-i-ignored-when-i-was-brok-1492198947.

2. Rao, Mayuree, Ashkan Afshin, Gitanjali Singh, and Dariush Mozaffarian. 2013. "Do Healthier Foods and Diet Patterns Cost More than Less Healthy Options? A Systematic Review and Meta-analysis." *BMJ Open*, 13(3). https://bmjopen.bmj.com/content/3/12/e004277 .full?sid=820d6e1a-280e-47a6-b8c5-498bfa4657e3.

3. U.S. Bureau of Labor Statistics. 2015. "Multiple Jobholding over the Past Two Decades." U.S. Department of Labor. Retrieved December 24, 2018, from https://www.bls.gov/opub/mlr/2015/ article/multiple-jobholding-over-the-past-two-decades.htm.

4. "Brake Pad Replacement Cost." Retrieved on December 24, 2018, from https://autoservicecosts. com/brake-pad-replacement-cost.

5. https://repairpal.com/estimator/brake-rotor-replacement-cost.

6. "Brake Rotor Replacement Cost." Retrieved on December 24, 2018, from https://www.forbes. com/sites/halahtouryalai/2013/06/11/yes-banks-are-reordering-your-transactions-and-charging-overdraft-fees/#a0a728b6daa3.

7. https://www.youtube.com/watch?v=0UjpmT5noto&feature=youtu.be.

8. Silver-Greenberg and Stephanie Clifford. 2013. "Paid via Card, Workers Feel Sting of Fees." *The New York Times*, June 30. Retrieved on December 24, 2018, from https://www.nytimes .com/2013/07/01/business/as-pay-cards-replace-paychecks-bank-fees-hurt-workers.html?_r=0.

"I WISH I COULD EAT THAT WELL": MISCONCEPTIONS AND RESENTMENT ABOUT FOOD STAMPS

ARTHUR DELANEY

Janina Riley noticed a woman muttering behind her in the checkout line as she paid for food at a Giant Eagle grocery store in Pittsburgh last April. "I can't believe she's buying that big-ass cake with food stamps," the woman said, according to Riley. Riley, 19, had just used a government-issued debit card to pay for most of her groceries, which included a cake for her son that said "Happy First Birthday Xavier" in a theme from the movie *Cars*. She glared at the woman for a second, then decided to confront her. "I was just like, 'Shut . . . up,'" Riley said. "You don't know what I'm doing with these food stamps."

But many Americans do not want to let people on food stamps eat cake. Cash register resentment of the sort directed at Riley feeds . . . animus toward the Supplemental Nutrition Assistance Program [SNAP]. . . . As SNAP enrollment surged to nearly 50 million in the wake of the Great Recession, the program's annual cost more than doubled to $80 billion. Republicans want[ed] to shrink those numbers. . . . Rep. Louie Gohmert (R-Texas) got to work telling a familiar story, one he said he'd heard many times from broken-hearted and angry constituents. Its protagonist is a hardworking Texan waiting in line at the grocery store. Someone's buying Alaskan king crab legs in front of him, and he's looking at them longingly, dreaming of the day he can afford such a luxury. Then the person buying them whips out his EBT—an Electronic Benefits Transfer card for food stamps. "He looks at the king crab legs and looks at his ground meat and realizes," Gohmert said, "because he does pay income tax . . . he is actually helping pay for the king crab legs when he can't pay for them for himself." And that's how cash register resentment becomes . . . the belief that your own struggles are tangled up in another person's safety net.

Rib-eye steaks and wine

Janina Riley said the situation at Giant Eagle didn't escalate after she confronted the mumbling woman. She figured it wouldn't have started at all if the person had known that she was studying to become a nurse and that she already worked more than 30 hours a week as an aide in a nursing home.

People have to be poor in order to receive nutrition assistance. The maximum gross monthly income for SNAP eligibility in Pennsylvania [in 2013], for instance, is $2,018 for a household of two, and the family can't own assets worth more than $5,500 (though there are several exceptions, like a single car). Most recipients qualify based on their participation in another means-tested

program like Medicaid. At $10 per hour, Riley's wages leave her poor enough to qualify for $124 a month in food stamps. At the Giant Eagle that day, she used her full monthly benefit to pay for part of her cart full of food and roughly $80 of her own money for the rest. "Most people do work. It's just we don't make enough money, that's the problem," Riley said. "The biggest misconception is that people on food stamps sit on their butts all day."

She's part of the 30 percent of SNAP recipients who earn money by working, and the 91 percent whose annual incomes are at or below the poverty line. Most recipients are . . . children, elderly, or disabled. But in the public imagination, hardworking single moms rent a room with king crab welfare queens. It's a gripe going back at least 20 years. In 1993, the *Columbus Dispatch* ran a letter to the editor lamenting a food stamp recipient buying "two bottles of wine, steak and a large bag of king crab legs." The crab complaint has recurred more than a dozen times in newspapers around the country, including this 2007 missive from a reader in the *Myrtle Beach Sun-News*: "After working a typical 12-hour shift, I had to stop by the local grocery store. Standing in line behind an oversized woman with three kids, I noticed the items going through the checkout. She had two 10-pound packs of frozen crab legs and two large packs of rib-eye steaks among a couple of vegetable items totaling up to an excess of $60."

Nutrition assistance is a federal program administered by states at the ground level. State and federal lawmakers have long sought new restrictions on what nutrition assistance can buy. Fancy food stories are often the reason. For instance, Wisconsin state Rep. Dean Kaufert (R-Neenah) cited cash register situations as his rationale for a bill restricting food stamp purchases earlier this year. "Anecdotally, we've all heard the stories about people standing in line behind the person who is buying the tenderloin, the porterhouse and they're using their EBT card to do it, while you and I who are getting by, we're buying ground beef," Kaufert told a local radio station. "That's a small share of those folks. But also I've been at the convenience store many times—the amount of nachos and soda that's being purchased by kids with their parents' EBT card, I think it's time to say no to that."

. . . Junk food and crab legs aren't even the worst of it. "Every day we hear of reports of food stamps being used to pay for beer, cigarettes, cell phone bills, and even cars," Senator Dan Coats (R-Ind.) said on the U.S. Senate floor in February [2013]. "That hardly needs to be mentioned because it is something we

(continued)

have come to understand—there is a lot of misuse of tax dollars." Elizabeth Lower-Basch, an analyst for the Center for Law and Social Policy, noted the secondhand nature of many of the anecdotes. "It's definitely a meme. You hear it a lot," Lower-Basch said. "There's a lot of a-friend-told-me-she-saw type stories. I'm not going to tell you there aren't cases of people making lousy choices, but they are far more visible in the public imagination."

"Plain-out hateful"

Federal law says food stamps can't be used to buy booze, cigarettes, vitamins, or household supplies. But they can buy almost anything else at a supermarket, so long as it isn't served hot for immediate consumption. So what *do* people buy with SNAP? A government survey from the late 1990s found that meats accounted for 34.9 percent of food stamp purchases, grains 19.7 percent, fruits and veggies 19.6 percent, and dairy products 12.5 percent. Soft drinks made up 5.6 percent and sweets 2.5 percent. If the government decides to restrict purchases to "wholesome" food, it won't be easy.

"No clear standards exist for defining individual foods as 'healthy' or 'unhealthy,' and federal dietary guidance focuses on an overall dietary pattern—that is, a total diet approach—that promotes moderation and consumption of a variety of foods without singling out individual foods as 'good' or 'bad,'" the Food Research and Action Center said in a January [2013] report. "Consider the following examples: some candy bars have fewer calories from fat than a serving of cheddar cheese, and soft drinks have less fat and sodium per serving than some granola bars," the report continued. "If the focus for restrictions was foods high in fat and sodium, would candy bars and soft drinks be eligible but cheddar cheese and some granola bars ineligible?" But not even avoiding the most obvious junk food or extravagances will spare an EBT card carrier from cash register resentment.

"You can't win," Lower-Basch said. "When someone's going to think you've got too much sugar, someone else is going to think you've got too much fat. Part of the reason we don't have restrictions is you could never get everyone to agree." While Janina Riley's birthday cake irked one fellow customer, Patrick McCallister's vegetables annoyed another. McCallister said that in 2003 and 2004, he had fallen on hard times after a divorce and used nutrition assistance to feed his three kids. "Especially because my family was on food stamps, I felt like that was a taxpayer-supported program aimed at helping my children do as well as they could in life," McCallister said. "I focused on buying fresh fruits, vegetables, whole-grain bread." McCallister, now 46 and living in Stuart, Florida, had been standing at the Publix supermarket register for several minutes as the cashier sorted through his month's worth of food and his coupons when the confrontation happened.

"This woman comes up behind me," he said. "The food is all tallied up, I pull out the food stamp card, which is very difficult to disguise. In Florida at the time it was a big American flag. The woman remarked, 'I wish I could eat so well. Maybe I should go on food stamps so I could eat that well.'" McCallister, who no longer receives assistance and now works as a reporter for a local newspaper, said he explained he'd taken care to buy good food since he was using taxpayer funds. The lady seemed annoyed by both the quality and perhaps also the quantity of McCallister's food. He said he turned his back as she insulted him. "I felt disappointed in the human race," McCallister said. "I was never happy using food stamps. I don't believe anybody who's shopping with food stamps takes any kind of thrill in standing at the register and pulling out that distinguishable card. . . ."

Feeling poor

Actual food stamp fraud is a real thing. Since Carl Clark of Staten Island, New York, witnessed it firsthand, he thinks of it whenever he hears about nutrition assistance. Clark, 48, said that roughly 10 years ago, he and his ex-wife would habitually take their EBT cards to willing supermarkets and have the cashier ring up $100 worth of fake purchases in exchange for $70 in cash, a payday for customer and cashier both. It's a classic example of SNAP trafficking, a type of fraud the Agriculture Department has long tracked. . . . The government says SNAP fraud has declined dramatically. The trafficking rate is down from 4 cents per dollar of benefits in 1993 to 1 cent from 2006 to 2008, according to the department's latest data.

Buying fancy stuff with food stamps isn't fraud—it's just something that seems unfair to people who think a government safety net should afford poor people modest food only. More broadly, the idea is that the poor should *feel* poor at all times until they're not poor anymore.

Not all poor people see things that way, though. Sara Woods of Knoxville, Tennessee, is not ashamed to say she once bought crab legs with food stamps. In December, she and her husband asked their six kids what they wanted for Christmas dinner. Woods said her husband's good in the kitchen, since he works as a cook in one restaurant and as a sous-chef in another. It was one of the only times he didn't have to work on Christmas Day, and he wanted to cook for his family. Their 15-year-old daughter wanted crab legs. "Everybody could pick one thing, and that was the one thing she wanted," Woods said. She didn't get any guff at the store, but she's familiar with register resentment from when she worked as a cashier in 2004 and 2005. . . .

As for why people make questionable purchases, Woods has a theory from her own experience. "When you get that money, you feel like you can breathe," she said. "I can understand why people would buy things that people think are outrageous. When it comes, you feel like I can buy whatever food I want right now. You never can buy whatever you want. My clothes are hand-me-down, my furniture second-hand. The food is new and mine."

Editor's Note: This rhetoric often includes frustration about dependency and fraud, in particular concerns about providing "handouts" to unemployed adults. In December 2019, the Department of Agriculture under President Trump approved a change to work requirements for food stamp recipients that will remove over 700,000 people from the program. Echoing similar rhetoric about responsibility and dependency, agriculture secretary Sonny Perdue said that the rule was designed to "[give recipients] a helping hand but not allowing it to become an indefinitely giving hand." [Fadulu, Lola. 2019. "Hundreds of Thousands are Losing Access to Food Stamps." The New York Times, December 4. Retrieved on December 7, 2019 from https://www.nytimes.com/2019/12/04/us/politics/food-stamps.html].

MATTHEW DESMOND

10. THE EVICTION ECONOMY

Desmond discusses the lack of affordable housing for low-income individuals and families, and how housing insecurity pushes these families into cycles of eviction, debt, and desperation, while landlords, owners, and other industries (such as payday loan companies) reap the profits. Desmond argues that America has the financial resources to change this situation and improve the living conditions of millions of Americans—we simply choose not to.

I first met Larraine when we both lived in a trailer park on the far South Side of Milwaukee. Fifty-four, with silvering brown hair, Larraine loved mystery novels, "So You Think You Can Dance," and doting on her grandson. Even though she lived in a mobile home park with so many code violations that city inspectors called it an "environmental biohazard," she kept a tidy trailer and used a hand steamer on the curtains. But Larraine spent more than 70 percent of her income on housing—just as one in four of all renting families who live below the poverty line do. After paying the rent, she was left with $5 a day.

Under conditions like these, evictions have become routine. Larraine (whose name has been changed to protect her privacy) was evicted after she borrowed from her rent money to cover part of her gas bill. The eviction movers took her stuff to their storage unit; after Larraine was unable to make payments, they took it to the dump.

Those of us who don't live in trailer parks or inner cities might think low-income families typically benefit from public housing or some other kind of government assistance. But the opposite is true. Three-quarters of families who qualify for housing assistance don't get it because there simply isn't enough to go around. This arrangement would be unthinkable with other social services that cover basic needs. What if food stamps only covered one in four families?

America stands alone among wealthy democracies in the depth and expanse of its poverty. Ask most politicians what we should do about this, and they will answer by calling for more and better jobs. Paul Ryan, the former Republican speaker of the House, thought we needed to do more to "incentivize work." Hillary Clinton, the 2016 Democratic presidential candidate, thought we should raise the minimum wage. But jobs are only part of the solution because poverty is not just a product of joblessness and low wages. It is also a product of exploitation.

Throughout our history, wage gains won by workers through organized protest were quickly absorbed by rising rents. As industrial capitalists tried to put down the strikes, landlords cheered workers on. It is no different today. When incomes rise, the housing market takes its cut, which is why a two-bedroom apartment in the oil boomtown Williston, North Dakota, was going [in 2018] for $2,800 a month and why entire capital-rich cities like San Francisco are becoming unaffordable to the middle class. If rents rise alongside incomes, what progress is made?

Poverty is no accident, an unintended consequence from which no one benefits. Larraine's rent money went to Tobin (also a pseudonym). A second-generation landlord, Tobin was 71, unsmiling and fit. His tenants waited tables at diners or worked as nursing assistants. Some received disability like Larraine did or other forms of welfare, sometimes supplementing their checks by collecting aluminum cans.

Running one of the poorest trailer parks in the city had its challenges, like dealing with mental illness, addiction, and domestic violence. Every so often, tenants wrecked their trailer the night before being evicted. Tobin had a way of dealing with that. He'd pay one of his tenants $20 to clean up the mess, then offer prospective new families the "Handyman Special," a free mobile home as long as they paid "lot rent." Lot rent was the same amount as rent, except the new "owners" would be responsible for maintenance. A family could move their trailer elsewhere, but in reality no one could afford to. When families fell behind in lot rent and were evicted, they inevitably left their trailer behind. Tobin would reclaim it as "abandoned property" and give it to someone else.

Tobin bought the mobile home park, 131 trailers parked on asphalt, for $2.1 million in 1995, paying off the mortgage nine years later. After reviewing Tobin's books and expenses (property taxes, utility bills, missed payments), I estimated that he netted roughly $447,000 a year. Some of Tobin's tenants called him "greedy," but others called him "fair" and "a good man," especially those he had spared from homelessness when they fell on hard times. He bailed tenants out of jail, lent money for funerals, and let some missed payments slide. In a year, he also made 30 times what his tenants getting minimum wage earned.

Landlords like Tobin aren't making money in trailer parks or ghettos in spite of their poverty but because of it. Depressed property values offer lower mortgage payments and tax bills. In poor areas of the cities, rents are lower, too—but not by much. In 2010, the average monthly rent in Milwaukee's poorest neighborhoods was only $50 less than the citywide median.

Landlords renting to poor families can charge slightly reduced rents but, owing to far lower expenses, still command handsome profits. As a landlord with 114 inner-city units once told me, speaking of an affluent suburb near Milwaukee: "In Brookfield, I lost money. But if you do low-income, you get a steady monthly income."

Poor families are stuck. Because they are already at the bottom of the market, they can't get cheaper housing unless they uproot their lives, quit their jobs, and leave the city. Those with eviction records are pushed into substandard private housing in high-crime neighborhoods because many landlords and public housing authorities turn them away. When poor families finally find a new place to rent, they often start off owing their landlord because they simply can't pay the first and last month's rent and a security deposit.

When tenants are behind, protections designed to keep housing safe and decent dissolve. Tenants in arrears tempt eviction if they report housing problems. It's not that low-income renters don't know their rights. They know that exercising those rights could cost them. So many go on paying most of what they have to live with lead paint, exposed wires, and broken plumbing. Saving and stability become wishes, and some days children go hungry because the rent eats first.

Expanding our current housing voucher program to cover all low-income families would rebalance landlords' desire to make a living and tenants' desire to have a home. Eligible families would dedicate 30 percent of their income to rent, allowing them to pursue education, start a savings account, and buy enough food.

When families finally receive housing vouchers after years on the waiting list, the first place many take their freed-up income is to the grocery store. Their children become healthier in the process.

A universal housing voucher program would fundamentally change the face of poverty in the United States. Evictions would plummet, and so would the other social problems they cause, like family and community instability, homelessness, job loss and depression. Suicides attributed to evictions and foreclosures doubled between 2005 and 2010. A universal housing voucher program would help reverse this disturbing trend.

Exploitation is not confined to the housing sector alone. It thrives when it comes to other essentials, like food. Inner-city bodegas take advantage of families' lack of transportation to increase grocery prices, effectively reducing the value of food stamps. The payday lending industry exploits poor people's lack of access to credit by offering high-interest loans and collecting over $7 billion a year in fees.

Most Americans who take out high-interest payday loans do so not to buy luxury items or cover unexpected expenses but to meet regular bills like rent or gas. When James Baldwin observed how "expensive it is to be poor," this is what he meant.

Payday loans are but one of many financial techniques—from overdraft fees to student loans subsidizing for-profit colleges—specifically designed to pull money from the pockets of the poor. This problem generally goes unrecognized by policymakers. But until we confront the fact that people make a lot of money off the poor, our efforts to reduce inequality will always come up short.

We can start with housing, the sturdiest of footholds for economic mobility. A national affordable housing program would be an antipoverty effort, human capital investment, community improvement plan, and public health initiative all rolled into one. It would especially benefit mothers and children, the face of today's eviction epidemic.

This solution is not as expensive as we might think. If we did nothing to make the voucher program more cost-effective—and there is much we could do on this score—expanding housing vouchers to all renting families below the 30th percentile in median income for their area would likely require an additional $22.5 billion a year. The actual figure is likely to be somewhat less, as this estimate does not account for potential savings in the form of reducing homelessness, lowering health care costs, and curbing other costly consequences of the affordable-housing crisis.

We have the money. We've just made choices about how to spend it. In 2008, the year Larraine was evicted, federal expenditures for direct housing assistance totaled more than $40 billion, but homeowner tax benefits exceeded $171 billion, a figure equivalent to the budgets for the Departments of Veterans Affairs, Homeland Security, Justice, and Agriculture combined.

If we are going to spend the bulk of our public dollars on the affluent—at least when it comes to housing—we should own up to that decision and stop repeating the canard about this rich country being unable to afford more. If poverty persists in America, it is not for lack of resources. We lack something else.

SARAH HALPERN-MEEKIN, LAURA TACH, KATHRYN J. EDIN, AND JENNIFER SYKES

11. A HAND UP FOR LOWER-INCOME FAMILIES

The Earned Income Tax Credit (EITC) is a government benefit available to low-income workers with children, which (along with a host of other social benefits) helps to lift millions of kids out of poverty. The authors interviewed and surveyed hundreds of parents to learn about to how the program has helped them and their families by giving them the chance to participate in the small luxuries of life (like buying popcorn at the movies), and generally providing a sense of hope for the future. They discuss how this program has generated and retained widespread popular support (unlike other government benefit programs).

Welfare queens driving Cadillacs. Food stamp kings buying filet mignon. The stereotypes are rife. What if there was a way to support lower-income families without the stigma? There is. And it comes from an unexpected source: the Internal Revenue Service.

First, listen to how Tracy Sherman, a 28-year-old medical coder and single mother of two, described her time on Temporary Assistance for Needy Families (TANF), which provides means-tested cash assistance (known colloquially as "welfare"). Right after her youngest daughter was born, the baby's father, an alcoholic, relapsed, and Tracy turned to TANF, feeling she had no other options. "I didn't feel good as a person. . . . They gave me [cash] plus they gave me food stamps for formula and everything like that. And every time I used it, I felt like crap." Now listen to Tracy's anticipation of her tax refund check, made up largely of government transfers. "I think about [the refund] all year long. . . . It's like, 'Oh, I can't wait until I get my tax money!'" While Tracy said the $800 a month she received from TANF was not "really worth it," the $3,500 she received as a tax refund—a far smaller sum

of money [compared to a year's worth of TANF]—fueled her dreams all year long.

Each year the Earned Income Tax Credit (EITC) and the Child Tax Credit (CTC) lift some five million children above the poverty line. The EITC has been credited with increasing employment, particularly among less-educated single mothers. And that's not all: the EITC has been tied to mothers receiving more prenatal care and being less likely to smoke and drink during pregnancy; in turn, their babies are less likely to be low birthweight or preterm. The benefits for kids continue past infancy, with the children of EITC recipients being more likely to earn higher grades, graduate high school, and enroll in college. . . . All this without the humiliation and shame so many describe experiencing when receiving other means-tested cash and in-kind benefits.

Who qualifies for this program? The EITC is a refundable tax credit available to low-income workers, with its size determined by marital status, number of dependent children, amount of earnings, and job status. For low-income workers without dependent children, only a small refund is available. The vast

Published with permission of SAGE Publications from Halpern-Meekin, S., Tach, L., Sykes, J., & Edin, K. (2016). A Hand Up for Low-Income Families. Contexts, 15(2), 52–57. https://doi.org/10.1177/1536504216648155.

bulk of EITC payments go to parents who work but are still poor. As their incomes rise, so do benefits, with the maximum refund for a single parent of two—$5,548 delivered in one check at tax time—for those earning between $13,870 and $18,110 in 2015.

The average EITC for families with children is about $3,000. In addition, the Child Tax Credit offers up to $1,000 per child, depending on earnings, to those with kids under 17. Many EITC recipient families also benefit from the refundable portion of the CTC, making for quite a substantial refund check at tax time. A single mother of two working full-time at minimum wage can receive the equivalent of more than three months of earnings in her tax refund, pushing her annual income above the poverty line.

To learn more about what role the EITC plays in the lives of working families, we sat in the lobbies of H&R Block tax prep offices and prepared taxes at Volunteer Income Tax Assistance sites in Boston, meeting parents like Tracy as they filed their taxes. After tax time ended, we visited Head Start centers across the metropolitan area to ensure we'd find those parents who filed taxes themselves or used the services of a tax-savvy uncle or friend. Through short surveys with over 300 parents, we learned how much they expected to get back as a tax refund and how they planned to use the money. We then drew a sample for in-depth interviews meant to capture a diversity of Black, White, and Hispanic families and married and unmarried parents; all were EITC recipients who had received at least $1,000 as a tax-time refund. While few were currently receiving TANF benefits, nearly half had done so at some point in the past, and the vast majority was currently receiving some form of government assistance, like SNAP (formerly known as food stamps) or subsidized housing. This allowed us to contrast the tax refund experiences they described with their perceptions of other government assistance programs.

Six months after tax time, we sat down with 115 parents, typically in their homes, to learn about their finances and the role the tax time windfall played in their lives. We solicited details on everything from how much they spent on groceries, to how much they earned braiding hair, to how much an ex handed over in child support each month. And,

perhaps more importantly, we explored what this money meant to parents: the stress of living with debt, the disappointment of not being able to come through for the kids with presents at birthdays or Christmas, and the feelings of jubilation and hope that tax time elicits.

Immersed in research on the stigma recipients often experience when participating in TANF (and its predecessor, Aid to Families with Dependent Children [AFDC]), SNAP, and government housing programs, we were struck by what we heard from EITC-recipient parents. Government assistance could actually be means-tested and socially incorporating, rather than ostracizing. Decades of qualitative research . . . have documented the shame associated with receiving TANF/AFDC, both on the part of the recipients themselves and the public at large. Economist David Ellwood and political scientist Kent Weaver have explained that this is due, in part, to perceptions of such support as inconsistent with the widely shared American values of work, family, and self-reliance.

And while politicians on both sides of the aisle have decried the nation's means-tested cash assistance programs, particularly prior to the 1996 welfare reform, both Republicans, like President Reagan and Speaker Ryan, and Democrats, like Presidents Clinton and Obama, heartily endorsed the EITC. Michael Katz, historian of the American welfare state, noted that the EITC enjoys strong political and popular support because it serves working Americans, lifting up those who are seen as keeping up their end of the social contract. This contrasts with a program like TANF, which targets those who are marginally tied to the labor market. Further, research by political scientists finds that the American public prefers benefit programs that are administered via tax credits over direct spending. Unlike many other forms of government assistance to low-income families, the EITC is in line with these preferences. Although tax refunds do not meet all the needs of low-income workers—and they only assist those who are able to find and keep jobs—this method of delivering financial support offers a blueprint for how social assistance programs can provide a hand up without a perceived slap on the wrist.

In our study, the way parents talked about their tax refunds revealed the connection they saw between these benefits and their work effort. This is an intentional part of the law: When President Clinton oversaw the massive expansion of the EITC in the early 1990s, he noted that it had the power to "make work pay." Like most of us, EITC beneficiaries are fuzzy on the details of the tax code, but they know they get a large refund because they have kids, they work, and they don't earn a lot. The refund, therefore, affirms their core, positive identities as workers and parents. Parents told us their jobs often offered little by way of pay, status, or career mobility; the reward at tax time was, therefore, particularly welcome.

The way parents apply for and receive the EITC is distinct from the process for other means-tested benefits. The words "Overseers of the Public Welfare" are emblazoned above the now-empty home of East Boston's old AFDC office, implying that those making a claim to means-tested cash assistance require monitoring. In contrast, H&R Block's slogan is seen as a welcoming promise: "You've got people!" Unlike applying for TANF, the EITC and CTC application and delivery come through the tax system, which is universally used up and down the income ladder, making it less stigmatizing. Most Americans do not use an Electronic Benefit Transfer card at the supermarket; most Americans do not live in public housing; most Americans do not have to lay bare their lives to a caseworker to get cash welfare; but most Americans do file taxes each year, and most receive a refund check. In fact, Suzanne Mettler's research in *The Submerged State* shows that nearly half of EITC recipients in her survey reported not taking part in any government social programs; this illustrates the disconnect we saw in our qualitative study between EITC receipt and feeling like a proverbial "taker." Unlike so many other government programs, then, assistance via the tax system does not make EITC beneficiaries feel they are marked as anything other than American.

The arrival of the refund check at tax time gave families the opportunity to dig out of debt, pay ahead on bills, and stock up on food. While there are some myths or assumptions that low-income families will blow the lump sum on big-screen TVs or fancy sneakers, we saw that these stereotypes were far from the norm. Tracy explained, "You're thinking of all crazy things that you [could] spend it on. . . . But, I mean, realistically it comes at a good time, at that point where 'Okay, I need to pay bills,' and everything comes in perspective of what is a priority." Like Tracy, respondents in our study spent most tax refund dollars on the mundane necessities of daily life—toilet paper, cleaning supplies, groceries—and getting caught up on bills and paying down debts—credit cards, utility bills, medical debts, student loans. Some saved a part of their refund, mostly to smooth income when the all-too-common "rainy day" arrives. Much of the rest went to durable goods like used cars, furniture, and appliances.

Meanwhile, in the weeks and months following receipt of the EITC, parents in our study described enjoying the small luxury of being able to put items in the shopping cart without an eye on the price comparison between name and store brand. They talked about the relief that came from making real progress digging out from under debt. Among those who put any refund dollars toward debt, the modal parent reduced her debt burden by about half. Some were able to save themselves from eviction, keep the lights from being shut off, get caught up on their student loans, start repairing their credit, and stop the harassing phone calls from creditors. Michelle and Jonah Tavares were a young couple with a baby son; both worked, but making ends meet remained a challenge. Michelle described their thinking when the refund check came: "We had to pay stuff that we knew would get shut off. I mean, you know you have other bills to pay, but you have to think of basic needs for your kid, you know. I have to think about his shelter and stuff. You go and pay your electricity because you want to have light." In short, tax time meant escaping some of the material hardship and easing some of the psychological pressure of living on the financial edge, even if such difficulties would return later in the year.

Parents only spent about one refund dollar in ten on treats, like meals at a sit-down restaurant, vacations, children's toys, and the like. But the chance to indulge in these items and experiences was more than a matter of dollars and cents. Spending on treats made them feel like they were able to fulfill their roles as parents as they wished they could all year round. Tamara Bishop, a 33-year-old assistant preschool teacher, described taking her kids to the movies and letting them buy movie-theater popcorn. What may be a routine rainy-day activity for wealthier families was a special treat for the Bishops. In a consumer culture such as ours, missing out on these little luxuries can make it feel like you're standing on the outside looking in. Extra money in your pocket means you can get off the sidelines and get in the game. Though this increased spending was small in absolute dollars and short-lived, it was symbolically meaningful to parents. As one mother put it, it makes you feel like "real Americans."

Yet another benefit of the refund check comes not in how it is spent, but in the hope it fuels. This massive infusion of cash made the parents we interviewed feel they could dream about a brighter future, one in which a refund check could be turned into a down payment on a home, a nest egg, or even a dream trip to Disney World. Though such dreams rarely come to pass, with more mundane concerns demanding attention, the hope offered by the refund is a benefit in and of itself. Recall Tracy, who enjoyed the flights of fancy anticipating the refund check allowed; while she ultimately spent her refund on necessities, she relished the chance to daydream about a life in which she could buy herself a new laptop. The laptop itself isn't the prize here; rather, the refund's existence buys Tracy a bit of middle-class fantasizing, a welcome break from the penny pinching of her

regular life. Or take, for example, parents' tendency to pay down debt with the refund. They explained that repairing their credit was one way they were moving toward their goal of becoming homeowners. A good credit score would put them in a better position to apply for a mortgage, they said; then, they could save next year's refund check as part of a future down payment.

Unlike TANF or SNAP, government assistance via refundable tax credits tends to fly under the public radar. Yet, while only some 1.8 million families receive TANF benefits, more than 27 million receive the EITC. Recipients perceive neither the social meanings of these tax refunds nor their method of delivery as stigmatizing. The programs' material, psychological, and social consequences are incorporating, making people feel a part of, rather than apart from, mainstream society. The refund fuels dreams of upward mobility and a more comfortable, middle-class life, providing hope for low-income working parents who are often scraping by day-to-day to cover necessities. There are, of course, drawbacks to refundable tax credits: they're of little help to those without jobs or dependent children, for example, nor do they fully address the financial needs of those they serve. Nonetheless, they offer a model for how government assistance can strengthen families financially, psychologically, and socially, with positive consequences for future generations. The refund fuels dreams of upward mobility and a more comfortable, middle-class life, providing hope for low-income working parents who are often scraping by day-to-day to cover necessities.

CHAPTER 4

RACIAL AND ETHNIC INEQUALITY

Despite progress over the last several decades, racial oppression, discrimination, and bias have persisted in the United States. The election of Barack Obama in 2008 and his reelection in 2012 did not, as some alleged, end racial inequality or strife between the races in the United States. Instead, as several authors in this chapter argue, animosity and discord may have actually increased, perhaps evidenced (or exacerbated by) the election of Donald Trump as president in 2016. Understanding the nature of racial and ethnic discrimination is an important part of understanding social problems in our contemporary society, not only because racial bias is a social problem in and of itself, but because race and ethnicity influence how likely people are to experience other social problems such as living in poverty, unequal access to education and health care, and entanglement with the criminal justice system.

Elaine McArdle demonstrates that as overt racial discrimination and bias has decreased over the past few decades, many Americans have begun to rely on a new racial ideology: that of "colorblindness." For those who believe that racial equality has been reached (a common perception among the vast majority of White Americans), institutional- or individual-level racism no longer exists. Thus, they believe one's successes and failures are due exclusively to one's effort and merit. For White Americans, this not only reinforces social values of self-determination and individualism, it also allows them to perceive the playing field as level and to recognize that their own successes are due simply to their own effort rather than to an unearned advantage as the result of race. McArdle traces the history and evolution of this ideology and discusses how political conservatives and liberals alike have used it to support and oppose policies to combat racial discrimination. In a related topic, Dresden Lackey discusses a social location where racial bias has been demonstrated—the retail marketplace. Lackey discusses high-profile incidents of racial profiling in retail spaces, the spread of racial discrimination to online marketplaces such as AirBnb and ridesharing services such as Uber and Lyft, and attempts to counteract profiling and discrimination in retail spaces.

Residential segregation is a form of racial and ethnic discrimination that influences many of the other social problems discussed in this book, since where we live guides many of our social experiences. Solomon Greene, Margery Austin Turner, and Ruth Gourevitch discuss the causes and consequences of racial segregation in neighborhoods, an issue that did not happen "naturally" or through individual choice, but one that has been supported by policies, laws, and practices that denied people of color access to desirable neighborhoods. Structural, institutional, and individual biases have combined to create a persistent level of segregation that contributes to the continued marginalization and unequal treatment of families of color, including access to well-funded public schools and services, and the opportunity to build wealth through homeownership.

While most Americans are aware of the historical existence of Jim Crow laws, many believe that these discriminatory laws were eliminated as part of the civil rights movement of the 1960s. Michelle Alexander argues that the War on Drugs—which started in the 1980s and resulted in the mass incarceration of millions of Americans, in particular poor African Americans—has re-created the racial caste system. Alexander explores the history of the War on Drugs, focusing on how it was designed to target minority communities despite the fact that Whites and people of color use and sell drugs at approximately the same rates. Negative consequences included the exploding prison population, the growth of the for-profit prison industry, and severe individual consequences for those incarcerated, including restriction of future employment, housing discrimination, disenfranchisement, and loss of social safety net benefits. Andrew Cohen expands on this argument by comparing the punitive and harsh response to crack cocaine use by people of color in the 1980s to the government's response to the contemporary heroin "epidemic"—which has impacted White Americans at high rates—with a focus on recovery and treatment rather than incarceration.

Another area where the criminal justice system plays a role in creating and perpetuating racial inequality is in the use of racial profiling as a policing technique. Sharon LaFraniere and Andrew W. Lehren discuss the use of racial profiling at traffic stops—one of the most common ways that people of all races come into contact with police. LaFraniere and Lehren document wide racial disparities in police behaviors that can occur at a traffic stop, beginning with the officer choosing to pull over a driver to the use of force, and argue that these disparities cause further erosion of trust in the police in minority communities. Similarly, Moey Rojas discusses research (based on body camera videos) showing that, independent of the race of the officer, Black motorists are less likely to be spoken to and treated respectfully compared to White drivers. These articles underscore the importance of these seemingly small interactions; not only do they have the potential to increase or decrease trust in the police in minority communities, they increase the chance that a routine interaction will result in violence toward a person of color.

Craig Considine discusses another war—the War on Terror—that has disproportionately impacted minority communities in the United States, particularly Muslim and Arab Americans. Islamophobia in the form of racial profiling at airports, hate crimes, and intolerance of Muslims has increased over time, Considine argues, and affects people based on both their perceived culture and their race, such as when Sikhs are the victims of hate crimes because they are believed to be Muslim. This Islamophobia is the result of the racialization of American Muslims—a blend of cultural and racial bias that has dangerous consequences for many Americans, including potential victimization from hate crimes. Authors from the Southern Poverty Law Center detail the prevalence of hate crimes in the United States, including what motivates offenders, how often hate crimes are prosecuted, and possible policy changes that could lead to a decline in the rates of hate crimes.

Racism is pervasive even in areas of our social life that might seem inconsequential, such as in the names, logos, and chants of our sports teams. In "Tomahawk Chops and 'Red' Skin," Elizabeth S. Cavalier discusses mascots that rely on Native mascots and imagery, the use of which has been the source of much controversy among collegiate and professional sports fans. Applying a sociological perspective to the use of these mascots means we must examine not only how fans, athletes, team owners, and school administrators feel about the continued use of racialized imagery, but also how these symbols permeate our lives and shape our understanding of the culture and history of Native Americans, a group that faces many of the social problems examined in this book.

In the reading "White Fragility," Robin DiAngelo examines the concepts of White privilege and White fragility—specifically, how White Americans are both protected from, and resistant to, difficult conversations about race, racism, and discrimination. A number of circumstances trigger racial stress for White people, such as suggesting that they have a racialized experience, that people of color have different experiences of race and racism than White people, and when White people's colorblind ideology is not allowed to dominate the conversation. This racial stress results in feelings of anger, denial of the existence of racism, and defensiveness. DiAngelo argues that several sociocultural factors create and perpetuate White fragility, including segregation, cultural emphases of individualism and universalism, and the sense that White people have little awareness of the lived experience of people of color, nor do they desire to understand their experience. These observations are reiterated in Amanda Atwell and Amanda M. Jungels's "White Americans' Racial Attitudes and Their Effect on Anti-Discrimination Policies." This reading cites research demonstrating that White and Black Americans have fundamentally different views about the existence of racism. Among these differences are a gap in what racial equality means and whether White Americans experience more discrimination than Black Americans. These views influence support for antidiscrimination policies such as affirmative action and the persistent belief that racism and equality are part of a "zero-sum game" in which White people view racial progress as occurring at their expense. Learning how views about race, racism, discrimination, and bias are created, reinforced, and perpetuated, and understanding the consequences of inaction, are essential to creating a fair, equitable, and antiracist society for all.

SAWSAN SELIM

Sawsan Selim is the Communications Director of the Georgia Chapter of the Council on American Islamic Relations (CAIR).

What is the mission of your organization?

The Georgia Chapter of the Council on American Islamic Relations (CAIR-GA) is a nonprofit organization; CAIR's mission is to enhance the understanding of Islam, encourage dialogue, protect civil liberties, empower American Muslims, and build coalitions that promote justice and mutual understanding.

What does your current position entail?

As Communications Director, I am responsible for managing CAIR-GA's online presence, public relations, and community outreach. This entails managing CAIR-GA's social media handles and website, arranging press conferences and live streams, promoting objectivity of reporting by actively engaging and fostering relationships with the press, and hosting or contributing to community-building events, such as Know Your Rights presentations, self-defense workshops, Islam 101 presentations, and more.

How did you get this position?

During my freshman year of college, I interned with CAIR-GA for a few months. After the 2016 election, the new administration stoked anti-Muslim sentiment with the Muslim travel ban and similar initiatives.

In response, I got involved in planning events geared toward community building. I helped facilitate CAIR-GA's involvement in some of those events, including the Atlanta March for Social Justice and Women (for which I served as Director of Campus Outreach) as well as the Muslim American Society Atlanta Chapter's Annual Family Camp (for which I served as Director for three years). The camp brings hundreds of Muslims throughout Georgia together to unite, learn, grow, and have fun. Due to my role in these large events, I greatly honed my leadership skills, organizing capabilities, and strengthened my network of leaders, professionals, and activists. I was then given the opportunity to intern at a law firm, and eventually, I was hired to work at the law firm long term as a legal assistant. Because it was a boutique law firm, there was a lot of room for me to be creative. At one point, I developed ideas for the marketing plan of the law firm, and my boss liked the ideas so much that he made me head of marketing at the firm. Fast forward to 2019—a leader in my community gave me a call letting me know that CAIR-GA had an opening for a Communications Director and that he thought I would be the perfect match for them. At first, I was hesitant because I really liked my job at the law firm and actually intended on staying there until it was time to go to law school, but I decided to give it a go. When I was being interviewed at CAIR-GA, I immediately felt like I was in my element. The mission, the people—it was where I belonged. A few days later I was notified that I got the job.

How did you first become interested in this type of activism?

When you are Muslim and living in America, your experiences of discrimination generally begin at a very early age. The circumstances surrounding what Muslim children witness and experience make it very difficult to not want to get involved in activism. In my case, shortly following 9/11, my dad's workplace, a major Muslim-owned corporation, was raided by a SWAT team because it was wrongfully "suspected" that it had terroristic ties. I also remember sitting in a car in fear while watching my father run into a grocery store to protect my mother, who wears a hijab, because he saw a KKK member walking into the store. Experiences like these, along with the fact that my parents were, and still are, very active in the community, helped me develop the desire and skill set for activism at a relatively young age.

As an activist in your organization, currently what are your top goals?

At CAIR-GA, we understand that the hate and fear that surrounds Muslims and other minority groups derives from ignorance that is perpetrated, in part, by the media. As a young person and as someone who works in communications, I have seen major movements, social events, and activism, such as the #BlackLivesMatter, #MeToo, and #MuteRKelly movements, come to life through bypassing major news sources during the early stages of development. This is not to say that major news sources are not important or needed—because, in many ways, they are. But it is important to recognize that the movements initially gained traction solely on social media and good-ole-fashioned interpersonal galvanizing. Consequently, when these movements grew large, major news sources were forced to address them and to do so in a way that was aligned with the terms and conditions set by the founders and members of the movements. "Regular"

people can take ownership of the concept of agenda-setting in media, and this has been made easier through social media. That is my goal as Communications Director—to utilize the power of social media, public relations, and community building to promote and mass produce narratives about Muslims that actually come from Muslims themselves, to the point where it no longer becomes acceptable, appropriate, or profitable to misrepresent and marginalize Muslims in the media, through political rhetoric or otherwise.

What strategies do you try to use to enact social change in your area of activism?

I primarily use visual content. We now live in an era that is very much maneuvered and influenced by visual, rather than literary, content. Much of my daily focus is on developing films, photos, art, and graphics that trigger one's emotional intelligence as well as their logical and theoretical frameworks.

What are the major challenges activists in your field face?

Being part of CAIR-GA has a certain danger to it. We get death threats on a regular basis. For our security, our office location is not publicly known or shared (all mail gets sent to a P.O. box). It takes two doors to get into our office and they are locked at all times. I have to be vigilant and aware about where I am and who I am in the presence of, particularly because I wear the hijab.

What would you consider to be your greatest successes as an activist?

Conceptualizing and acting upon the concept of interconnectedness. While my day-to-day interactions and activities are rooted in combating Islamophobia, I know that I will never be free—Muslims will never be free—unless the same freedom is fought for and given to every other category of people. As Director of Campus Outreach for the Atlanta March for Social Justice and Women, I took action on that belief and was able to see, for myself, the beauty of interconnectedness

(*continued*)

and unity. We are all human. We want the same things. And when we come together, share our experiences, and uplift each other, that is where the real "good trouble" takes place. I saw that in the sea of 65,000 people who showed up at the march in Atlanta to fight the good fight—for each other and for themselves.

What are major misconceptions the public has about activism in general and your issue specifically?

There are those who try to discredit what we do by conflating our activism and activist groups with terrorism and deem us as "terrorist-sympathizers." A lot of people don't realize that most of the victims of terrorist groups are Muslim, so it would be counterintuitive to support and actively work toward our own demise, don't you think?

If an individual has little money and time, are there other ways they can contribute?

Be unapologetically yourself and take ownership of your own narrative. Understand your power and never let anyone silence that amazing voice of yours. Actively search for the truth and question those who don't speak it.

What ways can college students enact social change in their daily lives?

A misconception about activism is that it has to be grand—that you have to be at protests, be a part of an organization, be on television, etc. While these are powerful methods, they certainly aren't the only ways to be active. Activism starts with yourself—actively seeking the truth and being aware of, as well as disrupting, the echo chambers that you exist in. Activism develops as you begin to impact people other than yourself—that is, having difficult conversations, researching and challenging authorities (professors, for example) about the information they provide, and generally refusing to passively accept communication or information you are exposed to, no matter how small or large the scale—particularly when it doesn't affect you personally.

ELAINE McARDLE

12. SOCIOLOGISTS ON THE COLORBLIND QUESTION

Americans often argue that they are "colorblind" and that racial discrimination against minority groups is a thing of the past, making America a true meritocracy. But sociological research has shown that discrimination does still exist—it is just hidden and less obvious than discrimination of the past. So why does the colorblind ideology still exist? McArdle discusses the origins and uses of the term and describes how it has been used by those arguing for policies that combat discrimination as well as by those who oppose such policies.

Each May, the city of Myrtle Beach, South Carolina, hosts two separate week-long motorcycle festivals, one at the start of the month, the other around Memorial Day. In most ways the festivals are identical: each attracts more than 200,000 bikers from around the country who gun their cycles down the city's main thoroughfare, proudly displaying their hardware to other cycle enthusiasts and admiring crowds. But there's one striking difference between the events: the bikers who flock to Myrtle Beach for Harley Week are White, those who come for Black Bike Week during Memorial Day are Black.

For Georgia State University sociologist Charles A. "Chip" Gallagher, the twin festivals provided a rare and valuable real-life laboratory for examining racial disparities in modern American society. "For sociologists, it was a perfect natural experiment, which we don't get that often," says Gallagher. "It was, quite literally, two populations that are quite similar coming into the same venue at almost the same time. We can look at the treatment of these two groups, see if it varies, and, if so, why."

Essentially, it provided the opportunity to test whether Myrtle Beach was as colorblind as it claimed to be. That is, whether it treated the bikers as individuals rather than members of the racial groups to which they belonged. The experiment was timely, as sociologists today are increasingly questioning the colorblind ideology and what effects it has on American culture and law. Their interest is due in no small part to the fact that colorblindness is used to support two very different social agendas that are in direct conflict. And there is no arena in which the struggle over the meaning of colorblindness is more consequential than in the nation's courts, where the fate of affirmative action programs and other racially based initiatives hang in the balance. The very different treatment each group received from Myrtle Beach and some local businesses wasn't difficult to measure. Gallagher's challenge was to demonstrate why it happened.

Myrtle Beach, which is about 85 percent White, is heavily dependent on tourism. Harley Week has been held each year since 1940. All week long, White bikers cruise up and down Pacific Boulevard and are

Published with permission of SAGE Publications from McArdle, E. (2008). Sociologists on the Colorblind Question. Contexts, 7(1), 34–37. https://doi.org/10.1525/ctx.2008.7.1.34

enthusiastically embraced with welcome signs, special merchandising, and other displays of appreciation for the tourist dollars that flow in. But during Black Bike Week, the city shut down one lane of traffic on Pacific Boulevard, forcing bikers to wait in queue for their turn to cruise and causing long traffic jams. Myrtle Beach tripled the number of police on duty, ticketed bikers for minor infractions, and even (unsuccessfully) petitioned the governor to send in the National Guard. In contrast to the welcome mat laid out to White bikers by local businesses, 25 restaurants closed their doors over Memorial Day weekend.

In 2003, the National Association for the Advancement of Colored People (NAACP) sued the city of Myrtle Beach and the 25 restaurants, claiming they violated the civil rights of Black bikers by treating them differently because of their race. When two prominent law firms in Washington, D.C., asked for his help as an expert witness in the case, Gallagher warned them what the defendants would claim: that their divergent treatment of the two groups was due to a variety of factors, but race wasn't among them.

Just as Gallagher predicted, the city claimed age differences and increased criminal activity, not race, were the reasons for ramped-up police numbers during Black Bike Week. It alleged the Black bikers were younger, and younger men tend to be involved more in criminal activity. But this allegation weakened when the NAACP showed the average age of the Black bikers was 34 versus 39 for the Whites. Criminal activity peaks in men at age 18 and drops dramatically by age 30, so both groups of bikers had aged out of their peak years for misconduct.

The city also claimed more police were needed because the number of bikers was much higher during Black Bike Week. But it had no hard numbers to back this up, and Gallagher testified that research shows Whites consistently overestimate the size of Black populations by a factor of two to three times. Moreover, the NAACP claimed, the increase in criminal and traffic citations issued during Black Bike Week was the result of the extra police officers on duty, not excessive criminal activity by Blacks. As for more traffic problems during Black Bike Week, this was a direct result of the city's own traffic restrictions, which caused traffic jams that didn't happen during Harley Week, the NAACP argued.

With each of the other factors debunked, the only difference between the two groups was race. "In effect, we were able to control for all the other variables typically used to dismiss charges of racism," Gallagher says. . . . [In 2007], the city settled the cases, agreeing to treat both groups of bikers the same.

The cases were a victory not only for Black bikers but all people of color. And they also supported Gallagher's theories about the current state of race relations and attitudes in the United States. According to national polling, the vast majority of White Americans believe racial minorities no longer face discrimination in schools, housing, jobs, or other arenas, Gallagher notes. They believe the United States has achieved a state of colorblindness, in which a person's race has no meaning other than as a cultural symbol. "White Americans are very invested in the idea of colorblindness," says Gallagher, because it legitimizes their privileged position in society. If the United States has achieved a utopic state where people are no longer judged or disadvantaged by the color of their skin, then someone's fortunes or misfortunes are due entirely to the choices they make. If so, then life circumstances don't control one's fate, self-determination does, a notion deeply engrained in the American ethos, Gallagher notes. "The idea is, you get what you work for. Just like you can choose to be Donald Trump, you can choose to be Condoleezza Rice. And you can choose to be in a ghetto or a barrio. It's a choice, like a smorgasbord," explains Gallagher.

If Whites get an advantage because of the color of their skin, then their dominant status isn't legitimate, an idea that's threatening to them. "Colorblindness lets them see the playing field as being level—because if it isn't level, it means [Whites] have gotten privileges [they] didn't deserve," he says. By embracing the concept of colorblindness, "White America can truly imagine that we're a meritocracy and where you end up reflects individual hard work and bootstrapping." That's why the Myrtle Beach cases were so important, Gallagher says: despite the city's best efforts to prove it was colorblind and that the disparate treatment of Blacks wasn't based on race, the facts proved otherwise.

"Advocates of colorblindness typically do not give the real reasons that they support colorblind social policies," says John Skrentny, a sociologist at the University of California, San Diego. "They will say that colorblindness is important because it preserves meritocracy and equal opportunity, but they also accept all sorts of exceptions to meritocracy—the law gives veterans preferences in civil service jobs, for example, and nepotism is legal."

In 2007 the U.S. Supreme Court struck down two school integration plans—one in Seattle, one in Louisville—that considered students' race during the admissions process in order to maintain diverse student bodies. The court based its decision on an interpretation of colorblindness that holds that racial classifications are unconstitutional except in very narrow circumstances—even when the intention is to redress racial inequities. Writing for the majority, Chief Justice John Roberts said, "The way to stop discrimination on the basis of race is to stop discriminating on the basis of race."

The school cases are the latest in a 20-year series in which the high court has relied on this new interpretation of colorblindness to dismantle programs and initiatives that assist minorities. This trend worries civil rights advocates and continues to garner the interest of social scientists. "What's most interesting about colorblindness is that it both has the ability to fight against inequality [and] can be used to fight against policies designed to reduce inequality. There aren't many ideologies that hold these opposing forces," says Brian Lowery, an associate professor of organizational behavior who studies perceptions of inequality at Stanford University.

In the school cases, both the majority and the dissent relied on *Brown v. the Board of Education*, the seminal case in the fight against racial discrimination, to support their opposing positions, with the majority relying on the notion of colorblindness to support its rejection of the school integration schemes. The majority's use of the term "colorblind" as a weapon against affirmative action is no small irony: it was coined in 1896 by Justice John Marshall Harlan to support civil rights for Blacks. In his solo dissent to *Plessy v. Ferguson*, the landmark case that upheld the policy of "separate but equal" treatment for Blacks and Whites, Harlan—a former slave owner who became a champion of minorities—wrote, "Our Constitution is colorblind, and neither knows nor tolerates classes among citizens. In respect of civil rights,

all citizens are equal before the law." Harlan's word became a rallying point for those supporting racial equality. During the civil rights movement, the term colorblind became essential to the argument that the U.S. Constitution requires all people, regardless of race, receive equal treatment, and overt racism was outlawed.

The civil rights movement focused on glaring examples of racial discrimination. But after that battle ostensibly was won, racism persisted, albeit in more subtle ways. "You still have a lot of racial inequalities but they aren't supported by overt racism. They're justified in more private or covert kinds of ways. Call it 'smiling discrimination,' where there are no names or bad words used, but practices are clear and consistent," says Eduardo Bonilla Silva, a sociologist at Duke University who studies race and ethnicity. Then, 20 years ago, an odd turn of events with enormous social and legal implications took place.

"Sometime in the 1980s, 'colorblind' was essentially hijacked by conservatives, Whites and non-Whites alike, and used for a very different purpose—to advocate for the rights and equal protection of White people," says Victoria Plaut, who studies models of diversity, including colorblindness, at the University of Georgia. If the U.S. Constitution requires the nation be colorblind, this argument goes, then it's illegal to use racial classifications for any purpose, even to address current instances of discrimination.

This interpretation took hold quickly. In the 1990s, the U.S. Supreme Court ruled against the use of racial classification to advance the rights of minorities in numerous cases in the areas of employment, redistricting for voting, and contracts, among others. In 2003, by a slim majority, the high court upheld the University of Michigan Law School's affirmative action program for admissions because race was only one of many factors taken into consideration. But at the same time, the court struck down the admissions scheme in the university's undergraduate program after finding it was more of a quota system where race was the primary factor. The 2007 school cases in Seattle and Louisville . . . seize[d] upon colorblindness to dismantle diversity plans. "That means on the one hand, affirmative action programs, school district plans, and other racially cognizant initiatives are illegal, but on the other, it's very difficult to prove discrimination exists because you don't have anyone owning up to it. So there's no intent to discriminate [unless you have] a smoking gun," says Bonilla Silva.

During the civil rights movement, the smoking guns for change were such things as signs that read: "No Jews, No Blacks." It was easy to use these as concrete evidence of discrimination, Bonilla Silva says. But with discrimination pushed underground today, and surfacing in far more subtle ways, it's much harder to prove. How does a person of color effectively argue to a court that he was discriminated against while shopping because clerks followed him around asking "Can I help you? Can I help you?"

The Supreme Court isn't out on an activist limb in its interpretation of the term colorblind, at least not a limb that's unpopular. Most White Americans share the same definition and believe the use of color or race for any purpose today is wrong, especially since—in their eyes—racial disparities no longer exist. At the same time, racial discrimination is thriving, as the Myrtle Beach cases and other sociologists' work demonstrate.

Devah Pager, a sociologist at Princeton University who studied race, conducted a series of classic audit studies that show just how prevalent discrimination is today. In these field experiments in 2001 and 2004, she had young men pose as job applicants at a variety of employers in Milwaukee and New York City. Their education and workplace qualifications were exactly the same, yet one set of men was White, the other Black. She expected to find a disadvantage in hiring for Black men, but the dramatic results surprised even her.

"The basic finding was that Blacks were half as likely to get a call-back or job offer relative to an equally qualified White applicant," says Pager. But there was an even more disturbing result: Pager found Black men with no criminal history fared no better than a White man just released from prison. "I expected race would be an issue but I didn't think it would rival the effect of a felony conviction," she says. Pager says that many employers believe themselves to be colorblind, looking only for the first person who is well-qualified for a job. But, especially with low-level, entry-level jobs that require few concrete skills or qualifications, employers tend to do a very cursory review of applicants. In those situations, race can unconsciously influence an employer's decision about who seems to be the best candidate. "Those are the ways in which the strength of continuing racial stereotypes undermine our conscious effort to achieve some sort of colorblindness," she says.

Sociologist Katherine Beckett of the University of Washington has studied racial disparities in the enforcement of drug laws in Seattle. She and her research colleagues have compared independent information on drug users against police arrest data and found Blacks are dramatically overrepresented among arrestees. These disparities are impossible to explain by the race-neutral reasons police rely on, including that certain areas in their jurisdictions have higher crime rates or that they are merely responding to increased citizen complaints in a particular area. As Gallagher did in the Myrtle Beach cases, Beckett and her colleagues have demonstrated that these disparities are actually created by different policies and practices, including who's arrested, who's prosecuted, and even where police are patrolling. With regard to arrest rates, cities vary greatly in racial composition, geography, and the use of public space. "Some police departments are less aggressive on arrest, but the disparities are exacerbated at the prosecution or sentencing stage," she says.

"I try to assess the race-neutral explanations for racial disparities, either by looking at the literature or at what officials actually say," she continues. However, her research shows that these colorblind explanations usually fall short. And, for some crimes and in some areas of the law, as Beckett says, "it's nearly impossible to meet the evidentiary standards needed to establish discrimination." Making colorblind ideals and legal standards even more complicated, in Skrentny's view, are new values of diversity and multiculturalism. "Large institutions, including the government, universities, and corporations, want to be racially diverse. A value on diversity is overshadowing a value on colorblindness, in my view, at least in terms of what institutions promote about themselves," he says. But, "Americans don't universally value universalism, so to speak—we vary a lot in what kinds of differences we accept or find appropriate as criteria for preferences or exclusions," he continues. "We give preferences to veterans in civil service jobs and don't decry age categorizations, yet there is great controversy regarding race categorizations."

Meanwhile, the future of race in the legal arena will turn on which interpretation of colorblindness dominates. "If the idea that we can never take race into account is the one that wins, a slew of policies will go away," says Lowery. "On the other hand, if colorblindness means commitment to equality, then certain existing policies will be reinforced." [But] which will prevail?

"My guess is . . . that colorblindness as an aspiration for equality is losing ground," Lowery says. "I think right now colorblindness is a contested idea, in the sense that it's not obvious who's going to win the debate over what it means." Bonilla Silva goes even further. Colorblindness is "Martin Luther King's dream, but not our reality. . . . It's a language dream that provides an image of progress that allows Americans to think we've moved beyond race without really addressing our racial injustices and inequalities." His prediction? "I'm afraid America is becoming meaner and more divided, holding on to colorblind ideas even as the situation of people of color continues to deteriorate. It'll be a schizophrenic America."

RACIALIZED SPACE IN RENTALS AND RIDESHARES

DRESDEN LACKEY

In December of 2017, employees of a Saks Fifth Avenue store in Troy, Michigan, called police on two Black women when they purchased over $6,000 worth of designer goods for Christmas presents (Branigin 2017). Police claimed that Dana Hale and her daughter were being questioned due to suspicion of credit card fraud and a declined credit card, although the credit card was not actually declined. Hale was eventually allowed to leave with the goods. After an internal investigation, Saks claimed their sales personnel training and company-wide procedures already had policies in place that centered on diversity. No company-wide training intervention was made in response to the incident (Kiertzner 2017).

The following spring, Donte Robinson and Rashon Nelson, two young Black men, waited for their friend to arrive at a Philadelphia Starbucks before placing their order. Prior to their friend's arrival, the manager of the Starbucks called police to remove the men for trespassing in the store when they asked to use the restroom. Although witnesses insisted Robinson and Nelson remained calm and explained to the manager and the police that they had intended to place their order once their friend arrived, they were both arrested and spent several hours in police custody prior to being released without charges (Held 2018). Following public outcry, Starbucks later closed nearly 8,000 of its locations for a mandatory employee training day to address racial discrimination with approximately 175,000 of its employees (Feldberg & Kim 2018).

A few days later, police were called to a Nordstrom Rack in Brentwood, Missouri, where three Black teenagers were falsely accused of theft while shopping for their high school prom. Though the teens met with the company co-president and received an apology, the legally agreed upon solution was simply to continue a dialogue with "a common desire to prevent incidents of this nature from happening in the future" (Siegel 2018).

Less than a month later, managers of a Waffle House in Fort Walton Beach, Florida, called police on a Black couple when they questioned a mischarge for orange juice on their receipt. Police handcuffed both customers, claiming they would be jailed if their bill was not paid while the couple insisted that they would happily pay if the mischarged item could be corrected. Once again, no charges were filed (Frej 2018). This was just one of several incidents that involved police being called on Black customers at various Waffle Houses in 2018. Despite the fact that several lawsuits alleging racism have been brought against the restaurant chain in the past twenty years, Waffle House's director of public relations, Pat Warner, denied that race was a relevant factor in these recent incidents (Bates 2018). As a result, several well-known Black community supporters, including the daughter of Martin Luther King Jr., Bernice King, have called for a Waffle House boycott until the restaurant chain mandates corporate training that addresses racial biases company-wide (Suggs 2018).

People of color often find themselves in settings and situations where their everyday behaviors are judged as related to their race. These settings, such as many places of business, are typically overwhelmingly occupied by White people and are

(continued)

Original to *Focus on Social Problems: A Contemporary Reader.*

structured by White influence through predominantly White owners, policymakers, consumers, and sellers (Anderson 2015). In other words, most public spaces are created and maintained by White people, with the understanding that White people belong in that space, while people of color are merely visitors. As visitors, people of color are seen by White onlookers as temporary, not fully belonging, and as tokenized representations of their race, expected to act in racially stereotypical ways (Anderson 2015).

Anderson (2015) describes these settings and situations as "White space," noting that they are approached by Black people and other people of color with caution, seen as figuratively off-limits and perhaps even risky to occupy. For White people, the same spaces are seen as unremarkable, everyday areas to be navigated without incident, judgment, or discomfort based solely on one's perceived race (Anderson 2015). The overwhelming and pervasive nature of White space does not allow people of color to simply avoid it on a daily basis; rather, it must be navigated "as a condition of their existence" (Anderson 2015:11). White space exists in workplaces, schools, neighborhoods, and, as we see above, customer service settings.

These incidents are a few of countless examples that show the inescapable nature of White space in retail settings. Using a public restroom, waiting for a late friend, or purchasing food or drink, when in areas largely occupied by White customers, may not be simple, uneventful tasks for people of color. Instead, seemingly innocent behaviors put Black people (and other people of color) at risk to be questioned, harassed, or arrested for simply "existing while Black" in White space.

In recent years, the growth of online marketplaces has created a retail industry with a paradoxical impact in terms of racial profiling. On one hand, the proliferation of online retailers and the relative anonymity of consumers has allowed non-White customers to forego the risk of racial discrimination they may otherwise experience at brick-and-mortar stores in White space: no salesperson to avoid or confront them, no false accusations of theft or scoffing at purchase choices, and no risk of increased tax or interest rates. On the other hand, some online retailers are able to discern their customers' race and gender based on demographic-exposing user names or profile pictures, and studies suggest that online marketplaces may exacerbate rather than reduce racial bias (Edelman, Luca, & Svirsky 2017). Recent audit studies that looked at two popular online services, short-term property rentals and ridesharing, expand on these effects.

Airbnb: Rental Space or Racialized Space?

Although antidiscrimination laws prevent landlords of rental units from discriminating based on a potential tenant's perceived race, some legal scholars believe that hosts of short-term Airbnb rentals may be bypassing these regulations. Researchers Edelman, Luca, and Svirsky (2017) sought to determine if Airbnb hosts were in fact racially discriminating against potential guests and the subsequent financial impacts of such discrimination. To assess racial discrimination by Airbnb hosts, the researchers collected data on Airbnb properties in Baltimore, Washington, DC, Dallas, St. Louis, and Los Angeles, cities chosen for their diverse geographic locations and similar levels of Airbnb usage (Edelman et al. 2017). The researchers created fake user accounts, identical except for profile user names. Though no photos were used that could potentially signal a guest's race or gender, profile user names were chosen to allow a host to speculate as to race and gender, indicating that the potential renter was an African American man, an African American woman, a White man, or a White woman. For example, hosts could assume that a user named Brad was a White man, and a user named Tamika was a Black woman. A total of 6,400 identical messages were sent out by researchers using these race- and gender-implied names to Airbnb hosts in July 2015, to inquire about the availability of a unit for a specific weekend the following September.

The results showed that racial discrimination against Black customers persists, even in this online market. Potential renters with Black-sounding names received a positive response from hosts indicating they would be willing to rent an available unit to the user roughly 42 percent of the time, compared to a positive response rate of 50 percent for White guests (Edelman et al. 2017). Though you might be thinking a host's own racial characteristics may influence the likelihood of accepting a Black renter, results showed the pervasiveness of anti-Blackness. Black guests were discriminated against by hosts regardless of the hosts' race, gender, age, level of racial diversity in the area in which the rental property was located, price of the rental unit, and whether the hosts allowed the full property to be rented or to be shared with the hosts (Edelman et al. 2017). The society-wide dominance of White space is so pervasive in real-time (offline) marketplace settings that their influence carries over into purportedly race-neutral settings *online*. We see this in how Black customers' status as good or bad houseguests are assumed by Airbnb prior to their stay, based solely on a customer's assumed race, the same way Black customers' intentions to purchase food, designer clothes, or coffee are questioned in real-time (offline) White space. The only time researchers found the racial gap insignificant between hosts renting to Black and White customers was when the hosts had previously rented to Black customers, indicated by a Black user's public review of the property.

Though victims of racial discrimination are generally taking the larger emotional or psychological hit, Airbnb hosts also stand to take a financial loss if their discriminatory behaviors prevent their unit from being booked. Edelman, Luca, and Svirsky's (2017) team later checked to confirm if the September dates they inquired about were eventually booked by other Airbnb users, or if they remained vacant after the host rejected or ignored their inquiries. They found that roughly 25.9 percent of the listings remained unbooked after the hosts rejected or ignored a potential renter. This suggests that hosts who racially discriminate incur a financial cost of approximately $65–$100 per night by rejecting or ignoring Black would-be renters (Edelman et al. 2017).

Rideshares: A Ride to Catch or to be Cancelled?

Similar to the laws preventing landlords from racially discriminating against potential tenants, most major cities mandate that traditional taxi drivers pick up any passenger in need of their services regardless of race or gender (Ge, Knittel, MacKenzie, & Zoepf 2016). However, the increasing popularity of rideshare services like Uber and Lyft may allow discrimination to occur without the overt action of driving past a Black customer waiting for a cab. Ge et al. (2016) sought to assess racial discrimination from rideshare drivers in what the authors consider two liberal-minded cities, Boston and Seattle.

In Seattle, the researchers wanted to assess the quality of customer service received by Black and White passengers using rideshare services (Ge et al. 2016). Using Uber, Lyft, and Flywheel services, they obtained data on 581 rides. Two Black women, two Black men, two White women, and two White men collected data on the number of canceled rides, the amount of time it took their ride to be accepted by a driver, the amount of time it took the driver to arrive, and the amount of time it took for the ride to be completed. Pickup and dropoff locations were the same for all riders. Results showed that Black riders had longer acceptance times prior to the ride compared to White riders. Further, after the ride was accepted by a driver, Black riders waited approximately 30 percent longer to be picked up than White counterparts (Ge et al. 2016).

In Boston, the authors altered the Seattle study's methodology to conduct an audit study. Research assistants who were visually able to pass as either White or Black created two UberX profiles and two Lyft profiles, each with either a Black-sounding name or a White-sounding name, and an identical picture of themselves across their accounts. Racial discrimination was assessed by measuring the amount of time it took for requested rides to be accepted by a driver, the amount of time it took for that driver to arrive at a pickup location, and the amount of time the ride itself took. They also considered how often a driver canceled the pickup after initially accepting it, which was important for collecting data on Uber's services. Uber drivers must accept the ride prior to seeing the photo or name of a customer, and so they must actively cancel a ride requested by a minority customer. In contrast, Lyft drivers are able to see photos of potential customers prior to accepting their ride, which may allow for racial discrimination to occur more discreetly, as drivers who are racially profiling may choose not to accept the customer from the start (Ge et al. 2016). Again, pickup and dropoff locations were the same for all riders.

Although the time it took drivers to pick up customers after they accepted the rides was not significantly different across racial groups in this experiment, researchers found that UberX drivers canceled rides more than twice as often for customers

with traditionally Black-sounding names than those with White-sounding names (Ge et al. 2016). This effect was particularly strong in suburban areas, where Black male passengers faced cancellations more than three times as often as their White male counterparts, indicating the pervasiveness of suburbia as White space. Once again, it is clear that the inescapable nature of White space carries over from offline, real-time interactions to online, app-dependent interactions where non-White customers experience discriminatory treatment prior to even meeting a retailer face to face (Anderson 2015). In White space for White customers, calling a Lyft is mundane, but for customers who are Black and for other people of color, similar everyday behaviors are affected by their race. While the risk of accused theft or fraud may be less salient in ride- and room-share marketplaces than in retail spaces, such studies assessing the experiences of people of color show that White space extends beyond brick-and-mortar retail stores, affecting the quality and timeliness of customer service.

Moving Forward: If We Know Better, Can We Do Better?

Though the exchange of goods and services theoretically benefits both customer and seller, racial profiling allows some sellers to deem Black customers unworthy of their products, whether the product is a rented room, a shared ride, a coffee, or a designer handbag. While many corporations offer diversity training seminars, these programs often fall short of making actual changes in marketplace settings. Petrella and Loggins (2018) argue this is because such programs fail to explain the historical and institutional systems and policies in place that produce White supremacy and racist ideologies, and that without this knowledge and understanding, progress cannot be made. Instead, antiracism courses that address the roots of racial biases and can be tailored to each city would be more effective in dismantling racial profiling (Petralla & Loggins 2018).

While antiracist corporate training may be a solution for employees of Waffle House and Starbucks, such training may not be realistic for Airbnb hosts or rideshare drivers who operate as independent contractors. Instead, Edelman and colleagues (2017) suggest that Airbnb and rideshare developers conceal guest names from hosts or drivers, or offer "Instant Booking" options as traditional hotel websites do, eliminating the need for a seller to accept a customer. In the meantime, Airbnb hosts may opt to use browser plugins such as DebiasYourself[1] to conceal customers' identifying information during the booking process. White space is generally unavoidable for people of color navigating everyday life. While it would be difficult to conceal a person's assumed race in a face-to-face customer service interaction,

---

1   See www.DeBiasYourself.org to obtain more information and to install the browser add-on.

(continued)

such as buying a coffee or a meal, we do have the technology to reduce racial profiling in online marketplaces by concealing names and photos of users requesting a service. Utilizing this technique would create an online space where racial profiling is much less likely, benefiting both customers and sellers in a goods and services exchange. Still, development and usage of such programs do not actually reduce racist ideologies held by people. Rather, it allows them to opt out of the risk that their racial biases will influence their choices about how to treat their potential clients, which is possible in online markets but leaves real-life encounters unexamined. Ultimately, the pervasive ideology of anti-Blackness, the normalization and exclusivity of White space, and the systemic racism that plagues the United States must be addressed outside of marketplace settings in order to be influential within them.

REFERENCES

Anderson, Elijah. 2015. "The White Space." *Sociology of Race and Ethnicity*. 1 (1): 10–21.

Bates, Josiah. 2018. "Black Man Choked, Slammed Against Wall by Officer at Waffle House, Video Shows" *ABC News*, May 11, 2018. Retrieved from https://abcnews.go.com/US/Black-man-choked-slammed-wall-officer-waffle-house/story?id=55094816.

Branigin, Anne. 2017. "Woman Falsely Accused of Fraud After Buying Louis Vuitton at Saks Fifth Avenue." *The Root*, December 26 2017. Retrieved from https://www.theroot.com/woman-falsely-accused-of-fraud-after-buying-louis-vuitt-1821582137.

Edelman, Benjamin, Michael Luca, and Dan Svirsky. 2017. "Racial Discrimination in the Sharing Economy: Evidence from a Field Experiment." *American Economic Journal: Applied Economics* 9(2):1–22.

Feldberg, Alexandra, and Tami Kim. 2018. "Beyond Starbucks: How Racism Shapes Customer Service." *The New York Times*. Retrieved April 20 2018, from https://www.nytimes.com/2018/04/20/opinion/starbucks-racism-customer-service.html.

Frej, Willa. 2018. "Waffle House under Fire after Video Shows Black Customers Handcuffed in Bill Dispute." *Huffington Post*. Retrieved May 15, 2018, from https://www.huffingtonpost.com/entry/boycott-waffle-house-video-handcuff_us_5b238407e4b0d4fc01fd52a2.

Ge, Yanbo, Christopher R. Knittel, Don MacKenzie, and Stephen Zoepf. 2016. "Racial and Gender Discrimination in Transportation Network Companies." Working Paper No. 22776. Retrieved from the National Bureau of Economic Research website: http://www.nber.org/papers/w22778.

Held, Amy. 2018. "Men Arrested at Philadelphia Starbucks Speak Out; Public Commissioner Apologizes," *National Public Radio*. Retrieved April 19, 2018, from https://www.npr.org/sections/thetwo-way/2018/04/19/603917872/they-can-t-be-here-for-us-men-arrested-at-philadelphia-starbucks-speak-out.

Kiertzner, Jim. 2017. "Woman Says She Was Humiliated by Fraud Accusation at Somerset Collection." *WXYZ Detroit*. December 22, 2017. Retrieved from https://www.wxyz.com/news/region/oakland-county/woman-says-she-was-humiliated-by-fraud-accusation-at-somerset-collection.

Patrella, Christopher, and Ameer Hasan Loggins. 2018. "Starbucks Took the Wrong Approach to Anti-Racism Training. Here's the Right One." *New York Magazine*. May 30, 2018. Retrieved from http://nymag.com/daily/intelligencer/2018/05/starbucks-took-the-wrong-approach-to-anti-racism-training.html.

Siegel, Rachel. 2018. "Nordstrom Rack Apologizes After Calling the Police on Three Black Teens Who Were Shopping for Prom." *The Washington Post*. May 9, 2018. Retrieved from https://www.washingtonpost.com/news/business/wp/2018/05/08/nordstrom-rack-called-the-police-on-three-Black-teens-who-were-shopping-for-prom/?utm_term=.467d31edc8df.

Suggs, Ernie. 2018. "Bernice King Calls for Waffle House Boycott after Latest Viral Incident." *myAJC*. May 10, 2018. Retrieved from https://www.myajc.com/news/bernice-king-calls-for-waffle-house-boycott-after-latest-viral-incident/fgVYTmaiijPj1Q8GYk1HHJ.

SOLOMON GREENE, MARGERY AUSTIN TURNER, AND RUTH GOUREVITCH

13. RACIAL RESIDENTIAL SEGREGATION AND NEIGHBORHOOD DISPARITIES

Picking a neighborhood in which to live may feel like an individual decision. Yet, home seekers' personal preferences are not what has driven the United States to become the highly racially segregated society that we are today. Greene, Turner, and Gourevitch discuss the historical causes of racial segregation, contemporary trends in segregation, and long-term consequences for individuals, families, and communities of color when segregation persists.

In 1968, Congress passed the Fair Housing Act in an attempt to end public policies and private discrimination that had created entrenched patterns of racial segregation in cities and regions across the United States. In signing the landmark measure, President Johnson declared, "Now, with this bill, the voice of justice speaks again." While the Fair Housing Act remains a powerful tool to combat segregation, we have a long way to go to ensure the voice of justice is heard. Private practices and public policies that reinforce segregation and limit housing choices continue to lock too many people out of neighborhoods that support their well-being and their children's life chances (Turner et al. 2018). And recent research suggests that regions that are more economically and racially segregated have lower incomes for African American residents and lower levels of upward economic mobility for residents of all races (Acs et al. 2017; Chetty et al. 2014).

This reading focuses on the racial component of residential segregation—primarily drawing on research on Black–White segregation. A typical White person lives in a neighborhood that is 75 percent White and 8 percent African American, while a typical African American person lives in a neighborhood that is only 35 percent White and 45 percent African American (Logan & Stults 2011). What's more, we continue to see people of color overrepresented in high-poverty census tracts. In the United States, a low-income African American person is more than three times more likely to live in a neighborhood with a poverty rate of 40 percent or more than a White person is, and a low-income Latino person is more than twice as likely to live in such a neighborhood (Jargowsky 2015). These statistics show that racial residential segregation and racialized concentrated poverty persist today.

Racially segregated neighborhoods did not come about naturally. They are the physical manifestation of plans, policies, and practices that have systematically denied equal opportunity to people of color. The policies and practices of racial exclusion described in this reading were primarily directed at African Americans but laid the foundation for patterns of segregation among other racial and ethnic groups (Massey & Denton 1987; Charles 2003; Zhang & Logan 2010). Recent research suggests that we are seeing declining segregation across racial and ethnic groups, although

Solomon Greene, Margery Austin Turner, and Ruth Gourevitch, "Racial Residential Segregation and Neighborhood Disparities," U.S. Partnership on Mobility From Poverty and The Urban Institute, August 29th, 2017. Reprinted with permission of the authors.

African Americans remain more highly segregated than any other racial or ethnic group in the United States (Firebaugh & Farrell 2016). This synthesis will outline various factors that have contributed to, and continue to reinforce, this pattern of racial segregation in U.S. metropolitan areas.

HISTORICAL DRIVERS OF RACIAL SEGREGATION IN THE UNITED STATES

Over the 20th century, myriad development policies and practices, primarily directed at African Americans, significantly contributed to racial residential segregation in cities nationwide. In the early 1900s, some cities explicitly used zoning ordinances to racially segregate neighborhoods. Redlining—the practice through which individuals in minority neighborhoods were denied mortgages, and thus homeownership—in the early- and mid-20th century created and reinforced communities segregated by race (Shapiro, Meschede, & Osoro 2013). Redlining maps used by federal agencies and private lenders in the 1930s continue to have a lasting effect on the development of urban neighborhoods through reduced credit access and subsequent disinvestment (Aaronson et al. 2019). Also, beginning in the 1920s, racially restrictive covenants legally prohibited African Americans from owning, leasing, or occupying certain pieces of property, providing a legal framework for the systematic racial segregation of people of color until the late 1940s. Racial covenants were so commonplace that by the end of the 1940s, over 80 percent of both Chicago and Los Angeles carried covenants that banned African American families from living in certain neighborhoods (U.S. Commission on Civil Rights 1973).

In the latter half of the 20th century, new forces emerged that further contributed to the racial segregation of poor people in urban areas. The Federal Highway Act of 1956 demarcated neighborhoods along racial lines, limiting African Americans' access to employment opportunities and often physically separating them from the downtown core (Sanchez, Stolz, & Ma 2003).[1] Highway-oriented transportation policies also helped create "spatial mismatch"—the disparity that prevails when low-skill jobs are located away from the urban core in areas that are difficult to access via public transportation. Public housing, often built in already-distressed communities, limited residential mobility for low-income people of color.[2] Even as attempts were made to desegregate neighborhoods and schools, threats and acts of violence aimed at African American families confined these families to specific neighborhoods and created additional barriers to integration (Smithsimon 2018; Hirsch 1983).

ONGOING DRIVERS OF RESIDENTIAL SEGREGATION IN THE UNITED STATES

By the late 20th century, civil rights legislation—including the Fair Housing Act of 1968—and evolving constitutional jurisprudence prohibited overt forms of discrimination in housing and lifted many formal barriers to residential integration. However, they were quickly replaced by subtler and ostensibly "race-neutral" methods to exclude people of color from predominantly White neighborhoods. Exclusionary zoning policies—such as large lot size requirements and large square footage per dwelling unit mandates—make it difficult for lower-income residents to live in certain communities.[3] Federal and local subsidized housing programs also continue to prioritize building affordable housing in already-distressed neighborhoods, which reinforces the geographic segregation of low-income people of color who are residents. And discrimination by real estate agents and landlords continues to constrain housing choices for people of color, though often in subtle ways that are difficult to detect. Although the incidence of housing discrimination has generally declined since the late 1960s, the 2012 Housing Discrimination Study shows that people of color looking for places to live are still told about fewer homes and apartments than White people (Turner et al. 2013).

The effects of early forms of discrimination have also proved more enduring than formal legal changes would suggest. In "Locked in Segregation," Roithmayr argues that families of color "who live in segregated neighborhoods face the self-reinforcing effects of earlier efforts to exclude them [while] White families enjoy structural advantages, in terms of schooling, job referral networks and other forms of social capital" (2004, 254). Low-income African American homeseekers are unable to gain the capital or feeling of safety to move to White neighborhoods. In addition, neighborhoods that are predominately occupied by people of color often lack the quality services and housing stock necessary to appeal to White home-seekers, who often have other options outside these areas (Cashin 2004). As a result, widening disparities between White and Black neighborhoods can perpetuate segregation, even if the constraints of private discrimination or preferences for segregation are lifted (Greene 2019).

EVIDENCE ON NEIGHBORHOOD PREFERENCES AND CHOICE

Today, African Americans remain more highly segregated than any other racial or ethnic group in the United States, and research on neighborhood preferences highlights the constrained choices that African Americans face in deciding where to live in today's segregated cities (Firebaugh & Farrell 2016). While studies show that the ideal neighborhood for an African American person includes fewer White people than the ideal neighborhood for a White person, few African Americans express a preference for living in a predominantly African American community (Adelman 2005; Harris 2001). As is often mentioned, economic barriers pose great challenges to neighborhood integration. However, research suggests that if households were distributed across neighborhoods based on income only (and not race or ethnicity), then levels of Black–White segregation would significantly decrease (Ellen 2008). This emphasizes the importance of understanding the racial component of residential segregation beyond economic barriers.

In the research surrounding choices and preferences for where individuals live, fear is often highlighted as a force that prevents integration. Fear of hostility from White neighbors after moving into more racially mixed areas has been shown to prevent some African American families from moving out of distressed areas (Krysan & Farley 2002). Further, "White avoidance" of neighborhoods with high concentrations of people of color can stem from the perception that an increase in residents who are people of color will drive down property values, lead to disinvestment, and create neighborhood disorder (Ellen 2008; Krysan 2002). One survey found that White

people with children under the age of 18 are especially unlikely to express a desire to move to areas with large African American populations (Emerson, Chai, & Yancey 2001). Interestingly, African Americans' interest in living in White neighborhoods depends in part on their socioeconomic status: African Americans with higher income levels are more willing to live in integrated settings (Clark 2009).

CURRENT TRENDS IN RACIAL RESIDENTIAL SEGREGATION

Over the past 30 years, racial segregation has been slowly declining, with people of color gradually entering more predominantly White neighborhoods. Nonetheless, segregation levels remain high in most large urban areas, with White individuals typically living in neighborhoods with a low representation of people of color, and African American and Latino people living in neighborhoods with a high proportion of people of color. Black–White segregation remains high in most large U.S. cities, and people of color are more likely to live in high-poverty areas than are White people (Jargowsky 2015; Logan & Stults 2011). Gentrification is also perpetuating the legacy of displacement and segregation in many U.S. cities today. With new, often White, "gentrifiers" moving into neighborhoods primarily occupied by people of color, property values and cost of retail increase, and low-income people of color are thus often unable to stay (Lerman & McKernan 2007).

A heightened understanding of the structural forces that create and perpetuate racial residential segregation continues to emerge with new evidence and research. A relatively recent body of research reveals how violence and policing perpetuate racially concentrated poverty and how segregation, in turn, shapes biased policing. In *The Black Poverty Cycle and How to End It*, Michael Holzman argues that the disproportionately high level of mass incarceration of African Americans in segregated urban neighborhoods is rooted partly in the operations and effects of the criminal justice system, making hyper-incarceration another cause of residential segregation. Between increased police presence in distressed communities, racial profiling, and hyper-incarceration related to drug use, African

Americans are more likely to be sent to jail than people of other races (Holzman 2013). This leads to heightened levels of neighborhood distress and instability, and to the normalization of crime, which perpetuates neighborhood segregation (Turner et al. 2014). On the flip side, entrenched segregation has also created a set of social forces that police have been ill equipped to handle,[4] along with residential patterns in which most White police officers don't live in the neighborhoods or even the cities they serve and patrol.[5]

In an age of globalization and continuing advancements in modern technology, a digital divide between race and income levels diminishes low-income people of color's chances at long-term success. African American and Latino adults are less likely to have access to the Internet than White adults due to a number of factors, including reduced availability of in-home Internet service in lower-income neighborhoods and subsequent reliance on public facilities like libraries for Internet access. This limits their ability to fully partake in society, find economic opportunities, and locate quality services for their families, further confining them to communities of poverty (Campos-Castillo 2015).

More than a century of practices, plans, and policies establishing and enforcing racial residential segregation has created racially segregated enclaves of concentrated poverty in U.S. cities. While the racialization of concentrated poverty has been slowly declining, this reading shows mechanisms through which it continues today and the pressing need to address the racial aspect of concentrated poverty.

IMPLICATIONS

The consequences of persistent racial segregation in the United States have been devastating, not just for people of color, but also for the vitality of major American cities and for the country's long-term prosperity. Segregation of neighborhoods along racial lines has fueled the geographic concentration of poverty and the severe distress of very high-poverty neighborhoods. Living in profoundly poor neighborhoods seriously undermines people's well-being and long-term life chances (Turner & Gourevitch 2017; Greene 2016; Sampson et al. 2002).

A growing body of research convincingly shows that the persistence of residential segregation sustains racial and ethnic inequality by stunting the appreciation of house prices and hence, wealth accumulation among minority homeowners (Traub et al. 2016; Newman & Holupka 2015); undermines school quality and educational attainment (Schwartz 2010); limits employment opportunities and earnings for people of color; and damages the health of children and adults (Brown et al. 2016). These disparities ultimately hurt all of us by depressing property tax revenues, raising the costs of delivering public services, and undermining the competitiveness of the nation's workforce, thereby constraining the vitality and economic performance of urban regions (Leachman et al. 2018; Acs et al. 2017).

Over many decades, public policies built segregated neighborhoods of poverty and distress by simultaneously excluding poor families, especially families of color, from neighborhoods of opportunity and starving neighborhoods with high concentrations of people of color of essential investments. Reversing that legacy requires that today's public policies tackle both the disinvestment and distress plaguing poor neighborhoods and the barriers that exclude people of color from neighborhoods of opportunity (Turner et al. 2018).

NOTES

1. Also, see John Powell, "Race, Place, and Opportunity," *The American Prospect*, September 21, 2008.
2. Sue Popkin, "Public Housing and the Legacy of Segregation," Urban Wire (blog), Urban Institute. August 18, 2013, http://www.urban.org/urban-wire/public-housing-and-legacy-segregation.
3. Elliott Anne Rigsby, "Understanding Exclusionary Zoning and Its Impact on Concentrated Poverty," Commentary, The Century Foundation. June 23, 2016, https://tcf.org/content/facts/understanding-exclusionary-zoning-impact-concentrated-poverty/?agreed=1.

4. Emily Badger, "Baltimore Shows How Historic Segregation Shapes Biased Policing Today," Wonkblog, *Washington Post*. August 10, 2016, https://www.washingtonpost.com/news/wonk/wp/2016/08/10/baltimore-shows-howhistoric-segregation-shapes-biased-policing-today/.
5. Nate Silver, "Most Police Don't Live in the Cities They Serve," FiveThirtyEight. August 20, 2014, http://fivethirtyeight.com/datalab/most-police-dont-live-in-the-cities-they-serve.

REFERENCES

Aaronson, Daniel, Daniel Hartley, and Bhashkar Mazumder. 2019. The Effects of the 1930s HOLC "Redlining" Maps (Working Paper). Chicago: Federal Reserve Bank of Chicago. https://www.chicagofed.org/publications/working-papers/2017/wp2017-12

Acs, Gregory, Rolf Pendall, Mark Treskon, and Amy Khare. 2017. "The Cost of Segregation." Urban Institute. March 27, 2017. https://www.urban.org/research/publication/cost-segregation.

Adelman, Robert M. 2005. "The Roles of Race, Class, and Residential Preferences in the Neighborhood Racial Composition of Middle-Class Blacks and Whites." *Social Science Quarterly* 86 (1): 209–28.

Brown, Elizabeth J., Daniel Polsky, Corentin M. Barbu, Jane W. Seymour, and David Grande. 2016. "Racial Disparities in Geographic Access to Primary Care in Philadelphia." *Health Affairs* 35 (6): 1374–81.

Campos-Castillo, Celeste. 2015. "Revisiting the First-Level Digital Divide in the United States." *Social Science Computer Review* 33 (4): 423–39.

Cashin, Sheryll. 2004. *The Failures of Integration: How Race and Class Undermine America's Dream*. New York: Public Affairs.

Charles, Camille Zubrinsky. 2003. "The Dynamics of Residential Segregation." *Annual Review of Sociology* 29: 167–207.

Chetty, Raj, Nathaniel Hendren, Patrick Kline, and Emmanuel Saez. 2014. "Where Is the Land of Opportunity? The Geography of Intergenerational Mobility in the United States." *Quarterly Journal of Economics* 129 (4): 1553–1623.

Clark, William. 2009. "Changing Residential Preferences across Income, Education, and Age." *Urban Affairs Review* 44 (3): 334–55.

Ellen, Ingrid Gould. 2008. "Continuing Isolation: Segregation in America Today." In *Segregation: The Rising Costs for America*, edited by James H. Carr and Nandinee K. Kutty, 261–77. New York: Routledge.

Emerson, Michael, Karen Chai, and George Yancey. 2001. "Does Race Matter in Residential Segregation? Exploring the Preferences of White Americans." *American Sociological Review* 66 (6): 922–35.

Firebaugh G., and Farrell, C. R. 2016. "Still Large, but Narrowing: The Sizable Decline in Racial Neighborhood Inequality in Metropolitan America, 1980–2010." *Demography* 53(1): 139–164.

Greene, Solomon. 2016. "Can You Tackle Poverty Without Taking on Place?" *Urban Wire*. Retrieved June 28, 2016, from https://www.urban.org/urban-wire/can-you-tackle-poverty-without-taking-place.

Greene, Solomon. 2019. "Sticky Preferences: Racial Exclusion's Staying Power." In *The Dream Revisited: Contemporary Debates about Housing, Segregation and Opportunity*, edited by Ingrid Gould Ellen and Justin Steil, 109–111. New York: Columbia University Press.

Harris, David R. 2001. "Why Are Whites and Blacks Averse to Black Neighbors?" *Social Science Research* 30 (1): 100–16.

Hirsch, Arnold R. 1983. *Making the Second Ghetto: Race and Housing in Chicago 1940–1960*. Chicago: University of Chicago Press.

Holzman, Michael Howard. 2013. *The Black Poverty Cycle and How to End It*. Briarcliff Manor, NY: Chelmsford Press.

Jargowsky, Paul. 2015. *Architecture of Segregation*. New York: Century Foundation.

Krysan, Maria. 2002. "Community Undesirability in Black and White: Examining Racial Residential Preferences through Community Perceptions." *Social Problems* 49(4): 521–43.

Krysan, Maria, and Reynolds Farley. 2002. "The Residential Preferences of Blacks: Do They Explain Persistent Segregation?" *Social Forces* 80(3): 937–80.

Leachman, Michael, Michael Mitchell, Nicholas Johnson, and Erica Williams. 2018. *Advancing Racial Equity with State Tax Policy*. Washington DC: Center on Budget and Policy Priorities.

Lerman, Robert, and Signe-Mary McKernan. 2007. "Promoting Neighborhood Improvement while Protecting Low-Income Families." Washington, DC: Urban Institute.

Logan, John, and Brian Stults. 2011. "The Persistence of Segregation in the Metropolis: New Findings from the 2010 Census." Providence, RI: US2010 Project.

Massey, D. S., and Denton, N. A. 1987. "Trends in the Residential Segregation of Blacks, Hispanics, and Asians: 1970–1980." *American Sociological Review* 52: 802–825.

Newman, Sandra J., and C. Scott Holupka. 2015. "Is Timing Everything? Race, Homeownership and Net Worth in the Tumultuous 2000s." *Real Estate Economics* 44(2): 307–354.

Roithmayr, Daria. 2004. "Locked In Segregation." *Virginia Journal of Social Policy and the Law* 12: 197.

Sampson, Robert, Jeffrey D. Morenoff, and Thomas Gannon-Rowley. 2002. "Assessing Neighborhood Effects: Social Processes and New Directions in Research." *Annual Review of Sociology* 28: 443–78.

Sanchez, Thomas, Rich Stolz, and Jacinta Ma. 2003. "Moving to Equity: Addressing Inequitable Effects of Transportation Policies on Minorities." Cambridge, MA: Harvard University Press.

Schwartz, Heather. 2010. *Housing Policy Is School Policy: Economically Integrative Housing Promotes Academic Success in Montgomery County, Maryland*. New York: Century Foundation.

Shapiro, Thomas, Tatjana Meschede, and Sam Osoro. 2013. "The Roots of the Widening Racial Wealth Gap: Explaining the Black–White Economic Divide." Waltham, MA: Institute on Assets and Social Policy.

Smithsimon, Gregory. 2018. *Cause . . . And How It Doesn't Always Equal Effect*. New York: Melville House.

Traub, Amy, Catherine Ruetschlin, Laura Sullivan, Tatjana Meschede, Lars Dietrich, and Thomas Shapiro. 2016. *The Racial Wealth Gap: Why Policy Matters*. New York: Demos.

Turner, Margery Austin, Peter Edelman, Erika Poethig, and Laudan Aron. 2014. *Tackling Persistent Poverty in Distressed Urban Neighborhoods: History, Principles, and Strategies for Philanthropic Investment*. Washington, DC: Urban Institute.

Turner, Margery Austin, and Ruth Gourevitch. 2017. *How Neighborhoods Affect the Social and Economic Mobility of Their Residents*. Washington, DC: Urban Institute.

Turner, Margery Austin, Solomon Greene, Anthony Iton, and Ruth Gourevitch. 2018. *Opportunity Neighborhoods: Building the Foundation for Economic Mobility in America's Metros*. Washington, DC: Urban Institute.

Turner, Margery Austin, Rob Santos, Diane K. Levy, Doug Wissoker, Claudia Aranda, and Rob Pitingolo. 2013. *Housing Discrimination against Racial and Ethnic Minorities 2012*. Washington, DC: U.S. Department of Housing and Urban Development, Office of Policy Development and Research.

U.S. Commission on Civil Rights. 1973. *Understanding Fair Housing*. Washington, DC: U.S. Government Printing Office.

Zhang, C. and Logan, J. R. 2010. "Global neighborhoods: Paths to Diversity in the Immigrant Metropolis." *American Journal of Sociology* 115: 1069–1109.

ACKNOWLEDGMENTS

This reading was originally prepared for the U.S. Partnership on Mobility from Poverty with funding from the Bill & Melinda Gates Foundation. We are grateful to them and to all our funders.

The views expressed are those of the authors and should not be attributed to organizations represented by the members of the Partnership or to the Urban Institute, its trustees, or its funders.

The authors thank Nisha Patel, Matt Rogers, and Lionel Foster for their helpful guidance. The authors also thank Tony Iton of the California Endowment, Josh Bolten of Business Roundtable, Bill Bynum of the Hope Enterprise Corporation, Raj Chetty of Stanford University, Luis Cortes of Esperanza, Kathy Edin of Johns Hopkins University, Larry Katz of Harvard University, and Juan Salgado of City Colleges of Chicago for their participation in the U.S. Partnership on Mobility from Poverty's Place Learning Group. The authors are responsible for all errors.

MICHELLE ALEXANDER

14. THE NEW JIM CROW

Many people learn about Jim Crow laws in their American history classes, so they believe that the racial caste system that existed prior to the Civil Rights Movement is long gone. But Alexander presents a convincing case that the current trend of mass incarceration of drug offenders—which was developed as part of the War on Drugs and has disproportionately impacted minority communities—is a modern and perhaps more insidious version of Jim Crow.

The subject that I intend to explore today[1] is one that most Americans seem content to ignore. Conversations and debates about race—much less racial caste—are frequently dismissed as yesterday's news, not relevant to the current era. Media pundits and more than a few politicians insist that we, as a nation, have finally "moved beyond race." We have entered into the era of "post-racialism," it is said, the promised land of colorblindness. . . .

This triumphant notion of post-racialism is, in my view, nothing more than fiction—a type of Orwellian doublespeak made no less sinister by virtue of the fact that the people saying it may actually believe it. Racial caste is not dead; it is alive and well in America. The mass incarceration of poor people of color in the United States amounts to a new caste system—one specifically tailored to the political, economic, and social challenges of our time. It is the moral equivalent of Jim Crow.

I am well aware that this kind of claim may be hard for many people to swallow. Particularly if you, yourself, have never spent time in prison or been labeled a felon, the claim may seem downright absurd. I, myself, rejected the notion that something akin to a racial caste system could be functioning in the United States more than a decade ago—something that I now deeply regret.

I first encountered the idea of a new racial caste system in the mid-1990s when I was rushing to catch the bus in Oakland, California and a bright orange poster caught my eye. It screamed in large bold print: THE DRUG WAR IS THE NEW JIM CROW. . . . I sighed and muttered to myself something like, "Yeah, the criminal justice system is racist in many ways, but it really doesn't help to make such absurd comparisons. People will just think you're crazy." I then crossed the street and hopped on the bus. I was headed to my new job, director of the Racial Justice Project for the [American Civil Liberties Union] (ACLU) in Northern California.

When I began my work at the ACLU, I assumed the criminal justice system had problems of racial bias, much in the same way that all major institutions in our society are plagued to some degree with problems associated with conscious and unconscious bias. . . . While at the ACLU, I shifted my focus from employment discrimination to criminal justice reform, and dedicated myself to the task of working with others to identify and eliminate racial bias whenever and wherever it reared its ugly head.

By the time I left the ACLU, I had come to suspect that I was wrong about the criminal justice system. It was not just another institution infected with racial bias, but rather a different beast entirely. The activists who posted the sign on the telephone [pole] . . . were not crazy; nor were the smattering of lawyers and advocates around the country who were beginning to

---

Reprinted from the Ohio State Law Journal, by Permission of Michelle Alexander.

connect the dots between our current system of mass incarceration and earlier forms of social control. Quite belatedly, I came to see that mass incarceration in the United States had, in fact, emerged as a stunningly comprehensive and well-disguised system of racialized social control that functions in a manner strikingly similar to Jim Crow. I state my basic thesis in the introduction to my book, *The New Jim Crow*:

> What has changed since the collapse of Jim Crow has less to do with the basic structure of our society than the language we use to justify it. In the era of color-blindness, it is no longer socially permissible to use race, explicitly, as a justification for discrimination, exclusion, and social contempt. So we don't. Rather than rely on race, we use our criminal justice system to label people of color "criminals" and then engage in all the practices we supposedly left behind. Today it is perfectly legal to discriminate against criminals in nearly all the ways it was once legal to discriminate against African Americans. Once you're labeled a felon, the old forms of discrimination—employment discrimination, housing discrimination, denial of the right to vote, and exclusion from jury service—are suddenly legal. As a criminal, you have scarcely more rights, and arguably less respect, than a Black man living in Alabama at the height of Jim Crow. We have not ended racial caste in America; we have merely redesigned it.[2]

I reached this conclusion reluctantly. . . . But after years of working on issues of racial profiling, police brutality, drug law enforcement in poor communities of color, and attempting to assist people released from prison "re-enter" into a society that never seemed to have much use for them in the first place. . . . I began to awaken to a racial reality that is so obvious to me now that what seems odd in retrospect is that I was blind to it for so long. Here are some facts I uncovered in the course of my work and research that you probably have not heard on the evening news:

- More African American adults are under correctional control today—in prison or jail, on probation or parole—than were enslaved in 1850, a decade before the Civil War began.[3]
- In 2007 more Black men were disenfranchised than in 1870, the year the Fifteenth Amendment was ratified prohibiting laws that explicitly deny

the right to vote on the basis of race.[4] During the Jim Crow era, African Americans continued to be denied access to the ballot through poll taxes and literacy tests. Those laws have been struck down, but today felon disenfranchisement laws accomplish what poll taxes and literacy tests ultimately could not.

- In many large urban areas in the United States, the majority of working-age African American men have criminal records. In fact, it was reported in 2002 that, in the Chicago area, if you take into account prisoners, the figure is nearly 80%.[5]

Those bearing criminal records and cycling in and out of our prisons today are part of a growing undercaste—not class, caste—a group of people, defined largely by race, who are relegated to a permanent second-class status by law. They can be denied the right to vote, automatically excluded from juries, and legally discriminated against in employment, housing, access to education, and public benefits, much as their grandparents and great-grandparents were during the Jim Crow era.

I find that when I tell people that mass incarceration amounts to a New Jim Crow, I am frequently met with shocked disbelief. The standard reply is: "How can you say that a racial caste system exists? Just look at Barack Obama! Just look at Oprah Winfrey! Just look at the Black middle class!" The reaction is understandable. But we ought to question our emotional reflexes. The mere fact that some African Americans have experienced great success in recent years does not mean that something akin to a caste system no longer exists. No caste system in the United States has ever governed all Black people. There have always been "free Blacks" and Black success stories, even during slavery and Jim Crow. During slavery, there were some Black slave owners—not many, but some. And during Jim Crow, there were some Black lawyers and doctors—not many, but some. The unprecedented nature of Black achievement in formerly White domains today certainly suggests that the old Jim Crow is dead, but it does not necessarily mean the end of racial caste. If history is any guide, it may have simply taken a different form.

Any honest observer of American racial history must acknowledge that racism is highly adaptable.

The rules and reasons the legal system employs to en-force status relations of any kind evolve and change as they are challenged.[6] . . . For example, following the collapse of slavery, the system of convict leasing was instituted—a system many historians believe was worse than slavery.[7] After the Civil War, Black men were arrested by the thousands for minor crimes, such as loitering and vagrancy, and sent to prison. They were then leased to plantations. It was our nation's first prison boom. The idea was that prisoners leased to plantations were supposed to earn their freedom. But the catch was they could never earn enough to pay back the plantation owner the cost of their food, clothing and shelter to the owner's satisfaction, and thus they were effectively re-enslaved, sometimes for the rest of their lives. It was a system more brutal in many respects than slavery, because plantation owners had no economic incentive to keep convicts healthy or even alive. They could always get another one.[8]

Today, I believe the criminal justice system has been used once again in a manner that effectively re-creates caste in America. Our criminal justice system functions more like a caste system than a system of crime control. For those who find that claim difficult to swallow, consider the facts. Our prison system has quintupled for reasons that have stunningly little do with crime. In less than 30 years, the U.S. penal popu-lation exploded from around 300,000 to more than 2 million.[9] The United States now has the highest rate of incarceration in the world, dwarfing the rates of nearly every developed country, including highly re-pressive regimes like China and Iran.[10] In fact, if our nation were to return to the incarceration rates of the 1970s—a time, by the way, when civil rights activists thought that imprisonment rates were egregiously high—we would have to release four out of five people who are in prison today.[11] More than a million people employed by the criminal justice system could lose their jobs.[12] That is how enormous and deeply en-trenched the new system has become in a very short period of time.

As staggering as those figures are, they actually ob-scure the severity of the crisis in poor communities of color. . . . The overwhelming majority of the increase in imprisonment has been poor people of color, with the most astonishing rates of incarceration found among Black men. It was estimated several years ago that, in Washington, D.C.—our nation's capital—three out of four young Black men (and nearly all those in the poorest neighborhoods) could expect to serve time in prison.[13] Rates of incarceration nearly as shocking can be found in other communities of color across America.[14]

So what accounts for this vast new system of con-trol? Crime rates? That is the common answer. But no, crime rates have remarkably little to do with skyrock-eting incarceration rates. Crime rates have fluctuated over the past thirty years, and are currently at his-torical lows, but incarceration rates have consistently soared.[15] Most criminologists and sociologists today acknowledge that crime rates and incarceration rates have, for the most part, moved independently of one another.[16] Rates of imprisonment—especially Black imprisonment—have soared regardless of whether crime has been rising or falling in any given commu-nity or the nation as a whole.[17]

So what does explain this vast new system of con-trol, if not crime rates? Ironically, the activists who posted the sign on that telephone pole were right: The War on Drugs. The War on Drugs and the "get tough" movement explain the explosion in incarceration in the United States and the emergence of a vast, new racial undercaste. In fact, drug convictions alone ac-counted for about two-thirds of the increase in the federal system, and more than half of the increase in the state prison population between 1985 and 2000.[18] Drug convictions have increased more than 1000% since the drug war began, an increase that bears no re-lationship to patterns of drug use or sales.[19]

People of all races use and sell drugs at remarkably similar rates, but the enemy in this war has been ra-cially defined.[20] The drug war has been waged almost exclusively in poor communities of color, despite the fact that studies consistently indicate that people of all races use and sell drugs at remarkably similar rates.[21] This evidence defies our basic stereotype of a drug dealer, as a Black kid standing on a street corner, with his pants hanging down.[22] Drug dealing happens in the ghetto, to be sure, but it happens everywhere else in America as well. Illegal drug markets, it turns out—like American society generally—are relatively segre-gated by race.[23] Blacks tend to sell to Blacks, Whites to Whites, Latinos sell to each other. University students sell to each other. People of all races use and sell drugs. A kid in rural Kansas does not drive to the 'hood to get his pot, or meth, or cocaine; he buys it from somebody down the road. In fact, the research suggests that where significant differences by race can be found, White youth are more likely to commit drug crimes than youth of color.[24] But that is not what you would guess when entering our nation's prisons and jails, overflowing as they are with Black and brown drug offenders. In the United States, those who do time for drug crime are overwhelmingly Black and brown.[25] In some states, African Americans constitute 80 to 90% of all drug offenders sent to prison.[26]

I find that many people are willing to concede these racial disparities once they see the data. Even so, they tend to insist that the drug war is motivated by concern over violent crime. They say: just look at our prisons. Nearly half of the people behind bars are violent offenders. . . . The problem with this abbreviated analysis is that violent crime is not responsible for the prison boom. Violent offenders tend to get longer sentences than nonviolent offenders, which is why they comprise such a large share of the prison population. One study suggests that the entire increase in imprisonment can be explained by sentence length, not increases in crime.[27] To get a sense of how large a contribution the drug war has made to mass incarceration, consider this: there are more people in prison today just for drug offenses than were incarcerated in 1980 for all reasons.[28] The reality is that the overwhelming majority of people who are swept into this system are non-violent offenders. In this regard, it is important to keep in mind that most people who are under correctional control are not in prison or jail. As of 2008, there were approximately 2.3 million people in prisons and jails, and a staggering 5.1 million people under "community correctional supervision"—i.e., on probation or parole. . . . [29]

How did this extraordinary system of control, unprecedented in world history, come to pass? Most people insist upon a benign motive. They seem to believe that the War on Drugs was launched in response to rising drug crime and the emergence of crack cocaine in inner city communities. For a long time, I believed that too. But that is not the case. Drug crime was actually declining, not rising, when President Ronald Reagan officially declared the drug war in 1982.[30] President Richard Nixon was the first to coin the term a "war on drugs," but President Reagan turned the rhetorical war into a literal one. From the outset, the war had little to do with drug crime and much to do with racial politics.

The drug war was part of a grand and highly successful Republican Party strategy—often known as the Southern Strategy—of using racially coded political appeals on issues of crime and welfare to attract poor and working class White voters who were resentful of, and threatened by, desegregation, busing, and affirmative action.[31] Poor and working class Whites had their world rocked by the Civil Rights Movement. White elites could send their kids to private schools and give them all of the advantages wealth has to offer. But poor and working class Whites were faced with a social demotion. It was their kids who might be bused across town, and forced to compete for the first time with a new group of people they had long believed to be inferior for decent jobs and educational opportunities.[32] Affirmative action, busing, and desegregation created an understandable feeling of vulnerability, fear, and anxiety among a group already struggling for survival. . . . H. R. Haldeman, President Richard Nixon's former Chief of Staff, reportedly summed up the strategy: "[T]he whole problem is really the Blacks. The key is to devise a system that recognizes this while not appearing to."[33]

A couple years after the drug war was announced, crack cocaine hit the streets of inner-city communities.[34] The Reagan administration seized on this development with glee, hiring staff who were responsible for publicizing inner-city crack babies, crack mothers, the so-called "crack whores," and drug-related violence. The goal was to make inner-city crack abuse and violence a media sensation that, it was hoped, would bolster public support for the drug war and would lead Congress to devote millions of dollars in additional funding to it.[35]

The plan worked like a charm. For more than a decade, Black drug dealers and users became regulars in newspaper stories and saturated the evening TV news—forever changing our conception of who the drug users and dealers are.[36] Once the enemy in the war was racially defined, a wave of punitiveness took over. Congress and state legislatures nationwide devoted billions of dollars to the drug war and passed harsh mandatory minimum sentences for drug crimes—sentences longer than murderers receive in many countries. Many Black politicians joined the "get tough" bandwagon, apparently oblivious to their complicity with the emergence of a system of social control that would, in less than two decades, become unprecedented in world history.[37]

Almost immediately, Democrats began competing with Republicans to prove that they could be even tougher on "them."[38] In President Bill Clinton's boastful words, "I can be nicked on a lot, but no one can say I'm soft on crime."[39] The facts bear him out. Clinton's "'tough on crime' policies resulted in the largest increases in federal and state prison inmates of any president in American history."[40] But Clinton was not satisfied with exploding prison populations. In an effort to appeal to the "White swing voters," he and the so-called "new Democrats" championed legislation banning drug felons from public housing (no matter how minor the offense) and denying them basic public benefits, including food stamps, for life.[41] Discrimination in virtually every aspect of political, economic, and social life is now perfectly legal, once you're labeled a felon.

All of this has been justified on the grounds that getting brutally tough on "them" is the only way to root out violent offenders or drug kingpins. The media images of violence in ghetto communities—particularly when crack first hit the street—led many to believe that the drug war was focused on the most serious offenders. Yet nothing could be further from the truth. Federal funding has flowed to those state and local law enforcement agencies that increase dramatically the volume of drug arrests, not the agencies most successful in bringing down the bosses. What has been rewarded in this war is sheer numbers—the sheer volume of drug arrests.[42] To make matters worse, federal drug forfeiture laws allow state and local law enforcement agencies to keep for their own use 80% of the cash, cars, and homes seized from drug suspects, thus granting law enforcement a direct monetary interest in the profitability of the drug market itself.[43]

The results are predictable. People of color have been rounded up en masse for relatively minor, nonviolent drug offenses. In 2005, for example, four out of five drug arrests were for possession, only one out of five for sales.[44] Most people in state prison for drug offenses have no history of violence or even of significant selling activity.[45] In fact, during the 1990s—the period of the most dramatic expansion of the drug war—nearly 80% of the increase in drug arrests was for marijuana possession, a drug generally considered less harmful than alcohol or tobacco and at least as prevalent in middle-class White communities as in the inner city.[46] In this way, a new racial undercaste has been created in an astonishingly short period of time. Millions of people of color are now saddled with criminal records and legally denied the very rights that were supposedly won in the Civil Rights Movement.

The U.S. Supreme Court, for its part, has mostly turned a blind eye to race discrimination in the criminal justice system. . . . Law enforcement officials are largely free to discriminate on the basis of race today, so long as no one admits it. That's the key. In *McCleskey v. Kemp* and *United States v. Armstrong*, the Supreme Court made clear that only evidence of conscious, intentional racial bias—the sort of bias that is nearly impossible to prove these days in the absence of an admission—is deemed sufficient.[47] . . . [The Supreme Court] has immunized the new caste system from judicial scrutiny for racial bias, much as it once rallied to legitimate and protect slavery and Jim Crow.

In my experience, those who have been incarcerated have little difficulty recognizing the parallels between mass incarceration and Jim Crow. Many former prisoners have told me, "It's slavery on the inside; Jim Crow when you get out." Prisoners are often forced to work for little or no pay. Once released, they are denied basic civil and human rights until they die. They are treated as though they possess an incurable defect, a shameful trait that can never be fully eradicated or redeemed. In the words of one woman who is currently incarcerated:

> When I leave here it will be very difficult for me in the sense that I'm a felon. That I will always be a felon . . . it will affect my job, it will affect my education . . . custody [of my children], it can affect child support, it can affect everywhere—family, friends,

housing. . . . People that are convicted of drug crimes can't even get housing anymore. . . . Yes, I did my prison time. How long are you going to punish me as a result of it?[48]

Willie Johnson, a forty-three year old African American man recently released from prison in Ohio, explained it this way:

My felony conviction has been like a mental punishment, because of all the obstacles. . . . I have had three companies hire me and tell me to come to work the next day. But then the day before they will call me and tell me don't come in—because you have a felony. And that is what is devastating because you think you are about to go to work and they call you and say because of your felony we can't hire [you]. I have run into this at least a dozen times. Two times I got very depressed and sad because I couldn't take care of myself as a man. It was like I wanted to give up—because in society nobody wants to give us a helping hand.[49]

Not surprisingly, for many trapped in the undercaste, the hurt and depression gives way to anger. A Black minister in Waterloo, Mississippi put it this way: "'Felony' is the new N-word. They don't have to call you a nigger anymore. They just say you're a felon. In every ghetto you see alarming numbers of young men with felony convictions. Once you have that felony stamp, your hope of employment, for any kind of integration into society, it begins to fade out. Today's lynching is a felony charge."[50] What is painfully obvious to many trapped within the system, remains largely invisible to those of us who have decent jobs and zoom around on freeways, passing by the virtual and literal prisons in which members of the undercaste live.

None of this is to say, of course, that mass incarceration and Jim Crow are the "same" . . . Just as there were vast differences between slavery and Jim Crow, there are important differences between Jim Crow and mass incarceration. Yet all three (slavery, Jim Crow, and mass incarceration) have operated as tightly networked systems of laws, policies, customs, and institutions that operate collectively to ensure the subordinate status of a group defined largely by race. When we step back and view the system of mass incarceration as a whole, there is a profound sense of deja vu. There is a familiar stigma and shame. There is an elaborate system of control, complete with political disenfranchisement and legalized discrimination in every major realm of economic and social life. And there is the production of racial meaning and racial boundaries. Just consider a few of the rules, laws, and policies that apply to people branded felons today and ask yourself if they remind you of a bygone era:

- Denial of the right to vote. Forty-eight states and the District of Columbia deny prisoners the right to vote. . . . [51] Even after the term of punishment expires, states are free to deny people who have been labeled felons the right to vote for a period of years or their entire lives. In a few states, one in four Black men have been permanently disenfranchised.[52] Nationwide, nearly one in seven Black men are either temporarily or permanently disenfranchised as a result of felon disenfranchisement laws.[53]

- Exclusion from jury service. One hallmark of Jim Crow was the systematic exclusion of Blacks from juries. Today, those labeled felons are automatically excluded from juries, and to make matters worse, people are routinely excluded from juries if they "have had negative experiences with law enforcement."[54] Good luck finding a person of color in a ghetto community today who has not yet had a negative experience with law enforcement. The all-White jury is no longer a thing of the past in many regions of the country, in part, because so many African Americans have been labeled felons and excluded from juries.

- Employment discrimination. Employment discrimination against felons is deemed legal and absolutely routine.[55] Regardless of whether your felony occurred three months ago or thirty-five years ago, for the rest of your life you're required to check that box on employment applications asking the dreaded question: "Have you ever been convicted of a felony?" In one survey, about 70% of employers said they would not hire a drug felon convicted for sales or possession.[56] Most states also deny a wide range of professional licenses to people labeled felons.[57]

- Housing discrimination. Housing discrimination is perfectly legal. Public housing projects as well as private landlords are free to discriminate against criminals. In fact, those labeled felons may be barred from public housing for five years or more and legally discriminated against for the rest of their lives.[58] These laws make it difficult for former prisoners to find shelter, a basic human right.
- Public benefits. Discrimination is legal against those who have been labeled felons in public benefits. In fact, federal law renders drug offenders ineligible for food stamps for the rest of their lives.[59] Fortunately, some states have opted out of the federal ban, but it remains the case that thousands of people, including pregnant women and people with HIV/AIDS, are denied even food stamps, simply because they were once caught with drugs. . . . [60]

What, realistically, do we expect these folks to do? What is this system designed to do? It seems designed to send them right back to prison, which is what in fact happens most of the time. About 70% of released prisoners are rearrested within three years, and the majority of those who return to prison do so within a matter of months, because the barriers to mere survival on the outside are so immense.[61]

Remarkably, as bad as all the formal barriers to political and economic inclusion are, many formerly incarcerated people tell me that is not the worst of it. The worst is the stigma that follows you for the rest of your life. It is not just the denial of the job, but the look that crosses an employer's face when he sees the "box" has been checked. It is not just the denial of public housing, but the shame of being a grown man having to ask your grandma to sleep in her basement at night. The shame associated with criminality can be so intense that people routinely try to "pass." During the Jim Crow era, light-skinned Blacks often tried to pass as White in order to avoid the stigma, shame, and discrimination associated with their race. Today, people labeled criminals lie not only to employers and housing officials, but also to their friends, acquaintances and family members. Children of prisoners lie to friends and relatives saying, "I don't know where my daddy is." Grown men who have been released from prison for years still glance down and look away when asked who they will vote for on election day, ashamed to admit they can't vote. They try to "pass" to avoid the stigma and discrimination associated with the new caste system.

An excellent ethnographic study conducted in Washington, D.C., found that even in neighborhoods hardest hit by mass incarceration—places where nearly every house has a family member behind bars or recently released from prison—people rarely "come out" fully about their own criminal history or that of their loved ones, even when speaking with relatives, friends and neighbors.[62] An eerie silence about this new system of control has befallen us, one rooted for some in shame, and for others in denial.

Yes, denial. There are two major reasons, I believe, that so many of us are in denial about the existence of racial caste in America. The first is traceable to a profound misunderstanding regarding how racial oppression actually works. If someone were to visit the United States from another country (or another planet) and ask: "Is the U.S. criminal justice system some kind of tool of racial control?", most Americans would swiftly deny it. Numerous reasons would leap to mind why that could not possibly be the case. The visitor would be told that crime rates, Black culture, or bad schools were to blame. "The system is not run by a bunch of racists," the apologist would explain. They would say, "It is run by people who are trying to fight crime". . . .

But more than forty-five years ago, Martin Luther King Jr. warned of the danger of precisely this kind of thinking. He insisted that blindness and indifference to racial groups is actually more important than racial hostility to the creation and maintenance of systems of racial control. Those who supported slavery and Jim Crow, he argued, typically were not bad or evil people; they were just blind.[63] Many segregationists were kind to their Black shoe shiners and maids and genuinely wished them well. . . . But, he hastened to add, "They were victims of spiritual and intellectual blindness. They knew not what they did. The whole system of slavery was largely perpetuated by sincere though spiritually ignorant persons."[64] The same is true today. People of good will—and bad—have been unwilling to see Black and brown men, in their humanness, as entitled to the same care, compassion, and concern that would be extended to one's friends, neighbors, or loved ones. After all, who among us would want a loved one struggling with drug abuse to be put in a cage, labeled a felon, and then subjected to a lifetime of discrimination, scorn and social exclusion? Most Americans would not wish that fate on anyone they cared about. But whom do we care about? In America, the answer to that question is still linked to race. Dr. King recognized that it was this indifference to the plight of African Americans that supported the institutions of slavery and Jim Crow. And this callous racial indifference supports mass incarceration today.

Another reason that we remain in deep denial is that we, as a nation, have a false picture of our racial reality. Prisoners are literally erased from the nation's economic picture. Unemployment and poverty statistics do not include people behind bars. In fact, standard reports underestimate the true jobless rates for less educated Black men by as much as 24 percentage points.[65] During the much heralded economic boom of the 1990s—the Clinton years—African American men were the only group to experience a steep increase in real joblessness, a development directly traceable to the increase in the penal population.[66] During the 1990s—the best of times for the rest of America—the true jobless rates for non-college Black men was a staggering 42%.[67]

Affirmative action, though, has put a happy face on this racial reality. Seeing Black people graduate from Harvard and Yale and become CEOs or corporate lawyers—not to mention President of the United States—causes us all to marvel at what a long way we have come. As recent data shows, though, much of Black progress is a myth.[68] In many respects, if you take into account prisoners, African Americans as a group are doing no better than they were when King was assassinated and uprisings swept inner cities across America. And that is with affirmative action! When we pull back the curtain and take a look at what our so-called colorblind society creates without affirmative action, we see a familiar social, political and economic structure—the structure of racial caste. And the entry into this new caste system can be found at the prison gate.

So where do we go from here? What can be done to dismantle this new system of control? . . . What is clear, I think, is that those of us in the civil rights community have allowed a human rights nightmare to occur on our watch. While many of us have been fighting for affirmative action or clinging to the perceived gains of the Civil Rights Movement, millions of people have been rounded up en masse, locked in cages, and then released into a parallel social universe in which they can be discriminated against for the rest of their lives—denied the very rights our parents and grandparents fought for and some died for. The clock has been turned back on racial progress in America, yet scarcely anyone seems to notice.

What is needed, I believe, is a broad based social movement, one that rivals in size, scope, depth, and courage the movement that was begun in the 1960s and left unfinished. It must be a multi-racial, multi-ethnic movement that includes poor and working class Whites—a group that has consistently been pit against poor people of color, triggering the rise of successive new systems of control.

The drug war was born with Black folks in mind, but it is a hungry beast; it has caused incalculable suffering in communities of all colors. . . . If we are going to succeed in bringing this brutal system to an end, we must map the linkages between the suffering of African Americans in the drug war to the experiences of other oppressed and marginalized groups. We must connect the dots. This movement must be multiracial and multi-ethnic, and it must have a keen sense of the racial history and racial dynamics that brought us to this moment in time.

But before this movement can even get underway, a great awakening is required. We must awaken from our colorblind slumber to the realities of race in America. And we must be willing to embrace those labeled criminals—not necessarily their behavior, but them—their humanness. For it has been the refusal and failure to fully acknowledge the humanity and dignity of all persons that has formed the sturdy foundation of all caste systems. It is our task, I firmly believe, to end not just mass incarceration, but the history and cycle of caste in America.

NOTES

1. This article is adapted from two speeches delivered by Professor Michelle Alexander, one at the Zocolo Public Square in Los Angeles on March 17, 2010, and another at an authors symposium sponsored by the National Association of Criminal Defense Lawyers and the Open Society Institute on October 6, 2010.

2. MICHELLE ALEXANDER, THE NEW JIM CROW: MASS INCARCERATION IN THE AGE OF COLORBLINDNESS 2 (2010).

3. One in eleven Black adults was under correctional supervision at year end 2007, or approximately 2.4 million people. PEW CTR. ON THE STATES, PEW CHARITABLE TRUSTS, ONE IN 31: THE LONG REACH OF AMERICAN CORRECTIONS 5 (Mar. 2009), available at http://www.pewcenteronthestates.org/uploadedFiles/PSPP_1in31_report_FINAL_WEB_3-26-09.pdf. According to the 1850 Census, approximately 1.7 million adults (ages 15 and older) were slaves. U.S. CENSUS BUREAU, THE SEVENTH CENSUS OF THE UNITED STATES: 1850 9 (1853), available at http://www2.census.gov/prod2/decennial/documents/1850a-01.pdf; see also University of Virginia Library, Historical Census Browser, UNIVERSITY OF VIRGINIA LIBRARY, http://mapserver.lib.virginia.edu/php/state.php (last visited July 17, 2011).

4. Contribution by Pamela S. Karlan, Forum: Pamela S. Karlan, in GLENN C. LOURY, RACE, INCARCERATION AND AMERICAN VALUES, 41, 42 (2008).

5. PAUL STREET, CHICAGO URBAN LEAGUE, THE VICIOUS CIRCLE: RACE, PRISON, JOBS, AND COMMUNITY IN CHICAGO, ILLINOIS, AND THE NATION 4 (2002).

6. See, e.g., Reva Siegel, Why Equal Protection No Longer Protects: The Evolving Forms of Status-Enforcing Action, 49 STAN. L. REV. 1111, 1113, 1146 (1997) (dubbing the process by which White privilege is maintained, through the rules and rhetoric change, "preservation through transformation").

7. DOUGLAS A. BLACKMON, SLAVERY BY ANOTHER NAME: THE RE-ENSLAVEMENT OF BLACK AMERICANS FROM THE CIVIL WAR TO WORLD WAR II (2008); DAVID M. OSHINSKY, WORSE THAN SLAVERY: PARCHMAN FARM AND THE ORDEAL OF JIM CROW JUSTICE (1996).

8. See id.

9. Key Facts at a Glance: Correctional Populations, BUREAU OF JUSTICE STATISTICS (updated Dec. 16, 2010), available at http://bjs.ojp.usdoj.gov/content/glance/tables/corr2tab.cfm; JOHN IRWIN, ET AL., AMERICA'S ONE MILLION NONVIOLENT PRISONERS, THE JUSTICE POLICY INSTITUTE (1999), available at http://www.hawaii.edu/hivandaids/America_s_One_Million_Nonviolent_Prisoners.pdf; Robert Longley, U.S. Prison Population Tops 2 Million, U.S. GOVERNMENT INFORMATION, http://usgovinfo.about.com/cs/censusstatistic/a/aaprisonpop.htm. https://web.archive.org/web/20140413095835/http://usgovinfo.about.com/cs/censusstatistic/a/aaprisonpop.htm

10. PEW CTR. ON THE STATES, ONE IN 100: BEHIND BARS IN AMERICA 2008, at 5 (Feb. 2008), http://www.pewcenteronthestates.org/uploadedFiles/One%20in%20100.pdf.

11. According to data provided by the Sentencing Project, in 1972, the total rate of incarceration (prison and jail) was approximately 160 per 100,000. See MAUER, supra note 9, at 17. Today, it is about 750 per 100,000. LAUREN E. GLAZE, BUREAU OF JUSTICE STATISTICS, U.S. DEP'T OF JUSTICE, CORRECTIONAL POPULATIONS IN THE UNITED STATES, 2009, at 2 (2010), available at http://bjs.ojp.usdoj.gov/content/pub/pdf/cpus09.pdf. A reduction of 79 percent would be needed to get back to the 160 figure—itself a fairly high number when judged by international standards.

12. According to a report released by the U.S. Department of Justice's Bureau of Statistics in 2006, the U.S. spent a record $185 billion for police protection, detention, judicial, and legal activities in 2003. Adjusting for inflation, these figures reflect a tripling of justice expenditures since 1982. The justice system employed almost 2.4 million people in 2003—58 percent of them at the local level and 31 percent at the state level. If four out of five people were released from prisons, far more than a million people could lose their jobs. KRISTEN A. HUGHES, BUREAU OF JUSTICE STATISTICS, U.S. DEP'T OF JUSTICE, JUSTICE EXPENDITURE AND EMPLOYMENT IN THE UNITED STATES, 2003, at 1 (2006), available at http://bjs.ojp.usdoj.gov/content/pub/pdf/jeeus03.pdf. Updated URL: http://www.bjs.gov/content/pub/pdf/jeeus03.pdf

13. DONALD BRAMAN, DOING TIME ON THE OUTSIDE: INCARCERATION AND FAMILY LIFE IN URBAN AMERICA 3 (2004) (citing D.C. Department of Corrections 2000).

14. ERIC LOTKE & JASON ZIEDENBERG, JUSTICE POLICY INSTITUTE, TIPPING POINT: MARYLAND'S OVERUSE OF INCARCERATION AND THE IMPACT ON COMMUNITY SAFETY 3 (2005) (reporting that in Baltimore the majority of young African American men are currently under correctional supervision). Nationwide, one in three Black men will go to prison during their lifetime. See THOMAS P. BONCSZAR, BUREAU OF JUSTICE STATISTICS, U.S. DEP'T OF JUSTICE, PREVALENCE OF IMPRISONMENT IN THE U.S. POPULATION, 1974–2001 (2003), available at http://bjs.ojp.usdoj.gov/content/pub/pdf/piusp01.pdf. Updated URL: https://bjs.gov/content/pub/pdf/piusp01.pdf

15. BRUCE WESTERN, PUNISHMENT AND INEQUALITY IN AMERICA 30 (2006) (Figure 2.1).

16. See, e.g., MARC MAUER, RACE TO INCARCERATE. 23–35, 92–112 (2d ed. 2006); MICHAEL TONRY, THINKING ABOUT CRIME: SENSE AND SENSIBILITY IN AMERICAN PENAL CULTURE 14 (2004).

17. See, e.g., WESTERN, supra note 16, at 35, 43.

18. MAUER, supra note 17, at 33.

19. MARC MAUER & RYAN S. KING, A 25-YEAR QUAGMIRE: THE WAR ON DRUGS AND ITS IMPACT ON AMERICAN SOCIETY 2, 4 (Sept. 2007), available at http://www.sentencingproject.org/doc/publications/dp_25yearquagmire.pdf.

20. The overwhelming majority of those arrested and incarcerated for drug crimes during the past few decades have been Black and brown. When the War on Drugs gained full steam in the mid-1980s, prison admissions for African Americans "skyrocketed, nearly quadrupling in three years, then increasing steadily until it reached in 2000 a level more than twenty-six times the level in 1983." JEREMY TRAVIS, BUT THEY ALL COME BACK: FACING THE CHALLENGES OF PRISON REENTRY 28 (2002); see, e.g., U.S. DEPT OF HEALTH & HUMAN SERVS., SUBSTANCE ABUSE & MENTAL HEALTH SERVICES ADMINISTRATION, SUMMARY OF FINDINGS FROM THE 2000 NATIONAL HOUSEHOLD SURVEY ON DRUG ABUSE 21 (2001), available at http://oas.samhsa.gov/NHSDA/2kNHSDA/chapter2.htm (reporting that 6.4 percent of Whites, 6.4 percent of Blacks, and 5.3 percent of Hispanics were current illegal drug users in 2000); U.S. DEP'T OF HEALTH AND HUMAN SERVS., SUBSTANCE ABUSE & MENTAL HEALTH SERVS. ADMIN., RESULTS FROM THE 2002 NATIONAL SURVEY ON DRUG USE AND HEALTH: NATIONAL FINDINGS 16 (2003), available at http://oas.samhsa.gov/nsduh/reports.htm#2k2 (revealing nearly identical rates of illegal drug use among Whites and Blacks, only a single percentage point between them); U.S. DEP'T OF HEALTH AND HUMAN SERVS., SUBSTANCE ABUSE & MENTAL HEALTH SERVS. ADMIN., RESULTS FROM THE 2007 NATIONAL SURVEY ON DRUG USE AND HEALTH: NATIONAL FINDINGS 25 (2003), available at http://oas.samhsa.gov/nsduh/reports.htm#2k2 (showing essentially the same findings).

21. See generally supra, note 21.

22. A national survey conducted in 1995 illustrated the profound and pervasive racial stereotypes associated with drug crime. Survey respondents were asked: "Would you close your eyes for a second, envision a drug user, and describe that person to me?" 95 percent of respondents pictured a Black drug user, while only 5 percent imagined all other racial groups combined. Betsy Watson Burston, Dionne Jones, and Pat Robinson-Saunders, Drug Use and African Americans: Myth versus Reality, 40 J. ALCOHOL & DRUG EDUC. 19, 20 (Winter 1995).

23. Researchers have found that drug users are most likely to report using as a main source of drugs someone who is of their own racial or ethnic background. See, e.g., K. JACK RILEY, OFFICE OF NAT'L DRUG CONTROL POLICY, NAT'L INST. OF JUSTICE, CRACK, POWDER COCAINE, AND HEROIN: DRUG PURCHASE AND USE PATTERNS IN SIX U.S. CITIES 1 (1997); Patricia Davis & Pierre Thomas, In Affluent Suburbs, Young Users and Sellers Abound, WASH. POST, Dec. 14, 1997, at A20.

24. The National Household Survey on Drug Abuse reported in 2000 that White youth aged 12–17 were more likely to have used and sold illegal drugs than African American youth. NEELUM ARYA & IAN AUGARTEN, CAMPAIGN FOR YOUTH JUSTICE, CRITICAL CONDITION: AFRICAN-AMERICAN YOUTH IN THE JUSTICE SYSTEM (2003), at table 5, p. 16 and p. 19, available at http://www.campaignforyouthjustice.org/documents/AfricanAmericanBrief.pdf. https://web.archive.org/web/20170420142636/http://www.campaignforyouthjustice.org/documents/AfricanAmericanBrief.pdf.

    Another study published that year revealed that White students use cocaine and heroin at significantly higher rates than Black students, while nearly identical percentages of Black and White students report using marijuana. LLOYD D. JOHNSTON ET AL., NAT'L INST. ON DRUG ABUSE, MONITORING THE FUTURE, NATIONAL SURVEY RESULTS ON DRUG USE, 1975–1999, Vol. 1, SECONDARY SCHO–NATIONAL SURVEY RESULTS ON DRUG USE, 1975–1999, Vol. 1, SECONDARY SCHOOL UNITS 146, 197 (2000), available at http://monitoringthefuture.org/pubs/monographs/mtf-vol1_1999.pdf. More recent studies continue to suggest higher rates of illegal drug use and sales by White youth. See, e.g., HOWARD N. SNYDER & MELISSA SICKMUND, U.S. DEP'T OF JUSTICE, NAT'L CTR. FOR JUVENILE JUSTICE, JUVENILE OFFENDERS AND VICTIMS: 2006 NATIONAL REPORT 81 (2006), available at http://www.ojjdp.gov/ojstatbb/nr2006/downloads/NR2006.pdf (reporting that White youth are more likely than Black youth to engage in illegal drug sales); LLOYD D. JOHNSTON ET AL., NAT'L INST. ON DRUG ABUSE, MONITORING THE FUTURE: NATIONAL SURVEY RESULTS ON DRUG USE, 1975–2006, VOLUME II: COLLEGE STUDENTS & ADULTS AGES 19–45, at 28 (2007), available at http://www.monitoringthefuture.org/pubs/monographs/vol2_2006.pdf (stating "African American 12th graders have consistently shown lower usage rates than White 12th graders for most drugs, both licit and illicit").

25. Although the majority of illegal drug users and dealers nationwide are White, roughly three-fourths of all people imprisoned for drug offenses since the War on Drugs began have been African American or Latino. MARC MAUER & RYAN S. KING, THE SENTENCING PROJECT, SCHOOLS AND PRISONS: FIFTY YEARS AFTER BROWN V. BOARD OF EDUCATION 3 (Apr. 2004). In recent years, rates of Black imprisonment for drug offenses have dipped somewhat—declining approximately 22 percent from their zenith in the mid-1990s—but it remains the case that African Americans are incarcerated at grossly disproportionate rates throughout the United

States. MARC MAUER, THE SENTENCING PROJECT, THE CHANGING RACIAL DYNAMICS OF THE WAR ON DRUGS 5 (2009), available at http://www.sentencingproject.org/doc/dp_raceand-drugs.pdf.

26. HUMAN RIGHTS WATCH, PUNISHMENT AND PREJUDICE: RACIAL DISPARITIES IN THE WAR ON DRUGS, Vol. 12, No. 2, at 19 (May 2000).

27. According to this study, the entire increase in the prison population between 1980 and 2001 can be explained by sentencing policy changes, not increases in crime. MAUER, supra note 17, at 33, 36–38 (citing Warren Young & Mark Brown, Cross national Comparisons of Imprisonment, in CRIME AND JUSTICE: A REVIEW OF RESEARCH, Vol. 27, at 33, 1–49 (Michael Tonry, ed., 1993)).

28. "Unfairness in Federal Cocaine Sentencing: Is It Time to Crack the 100 to 1 Disparity?" Hearing on H.R. 1459, H.R. 1466, H.R. 265, H.R. 2178 and H.R. 18 before the H. Subcomm. on Crime, Terrorism, and Homeland Security of the H. Comm. on the Judiciary, 111th Cong. 2 (2009) (testimony of Marc Mauer, Executive Director, Sentencing Project)."

29. PEW CTR. ON THE STATES, supra note 3, at 4.

30. President Richard Nixon was the first to coin the term a "war on drugs," but the term proved largely rhetorical as he declared illegal drugs "public enemy number one" without proposing dramatic shifts in public policy. President Reagan converted the rhetorical war into a literal one, when he officially announced the War on Drugs in 1982. At the time, less than 2 percent of the American public viewed drugs as the most important issue facing the nation. See KATHERINE BECKETT, MAKING CRIME PAY: LAW AND ORDER IN CONTEMPORARY AMERICAN POLITICS 62, 163 (1997); see also Julian V. Roberts, Public Opinion, Crime, and Criminal Justice, in CRIME AND JUSTICE: A REVIEW OF RESEARCH, Vol. 16, at 99, 129–37 (Michael Tonry ed., 1992).

31. See, e.g., BECKETT, supra note 31, at 31; Vesla M. Weaver, Frontlash: Race and the Development of Punitive Crime Policy, 21 STUD. IN AM. POL. DEV. 230, 233, 237 (Fall 2007). See generally ROBERT PERKINSON, TEXAS TOUGH: THE RISE OF AMERICA'S PRISON EMPIRE (2010) (offering a compelling account of how the backlash against the Civil Rights Movement gave rise to mass incarceration in Texas, and, ultimately, the nation).

32. During the 1950s, the majority of Southern Whites were better off than Southern Blacks, but they were not affluent or well educated by any means; they were semiliterate (with less than twelve years of schooling) and typically quite poor. Only a tiny minority of Whites was affluent and well educated. They stood far apart from the rest of Whites and virtually all Blacks. C. Arnold Anderson, Inequalities in Schooling in the South, 60 AM. J. ON SOCIOLOGY 547, 553, 557 (May 1955); Lani Guinier, From Racial Liberalism to Racial Literacy: Brown v. Board of Education and the Interest Divergence Dilemma, 91 J. AMER. HIST. 92, 103 (June 2004). What lower class Whites did have was what W. E. B. Du Bois described as "the public and psychological wage" paid to White workers, who depended on their status and privileges as Whites to compensate for their low pay and harsh working conditions. W. E. B. DUBOIS, BLACK RECONSTRUCTION IN AMERICA, AN ESSAY TOWARD A HISTORY OF THE PART WHICH BLACK FOLKS PLAYED IN THE ATTEMPT TO RECONSTRUCT DEMOCRACY IN AMERICA, 1860–1880, at 700 (1935). Because the Southern White elite had succeeded in persuading all Whites to think in racial rather than class terms, it is hardly surprising that poor and working class Whites experienced desegregation as a net loss. Derrick A. Bell, Jr., Brown v. Board of Education and the Interest-Convergence Dilemma, 93 HARV. L. REV. 518, 525 (1980).

33. WILLARD M. OLIVER, THE LAW & ORDER PRESIDENCY 126–27 (2003).

34. See Craig Reinarman & Harry G. Levine, The Crack Attack: America's Latest Drug Scare, 1986–1992, in IMAGES OF ISSUES: TYPIFYING CONTEMPORARY SOCIAL PROBLEMS 152 (Joel Best ed., 1995).

35. Id. at 170–71 ("Crack was a godsend to the Right. . . . It could not have appeared at a more politically opportune moment").

36. Id.; DORIS MARIE PROVINE, UNEQUAL UNDER LAW: RACE IN THE WAR ON DRUGS 88 (2007).

37. PROVINE, supra note 38, at 117. Today the Black community is divided in many respects about how best to understand and respond to mass incarceration, with some academics (and celebrities) arguing that poor education and cultural traits explain the millions of Black men rotating in and out of correctional control, and others emphasizing the role of racial bias and structural inequality. See, e.g., DEMICO BOOTHE, WHY ARE SO MANY BLACK MEN IN PRISON? (2007) (emphasizing the discriminatory nature of the prison system); BILL COSBY & ALVIN F. POUSSAINT, COME ON PEOPLE: ON THE PATH FROM VICTIMS TO VICTORS (2007) (arguing that poor education, as well as lack of personal responsibility and discipline, largely explain the status of Black men today). The fact that many African Americans endorse aspects of the current caste system, and insist that the problems of the urban poor can be best explained by their behavior, culture, lack of education, and attitude, does not, in any meaningful way, distinguish mass incarceration from its predecessors. To the contrary, these attitudes and arguments have their roots in the struggles to end slavery and Jim Crow. As numerous scholars have observed, many Black advocates during the Jim Crow era embraced a "politics of respectability" and an "uplift ideology" that led them to distance themselves from the urban poor, and to blame the least educated members of the urban poor for their own condition. See, e.g., KAREN FERGUSON, BLACK POLITICS IN NEW DEAL ATLANTA 5–11 (2002). In fact, some of the most discriminatory federal programs of the New Deal era, including the slum clearance program, received strong support from African American bureaucrats and reformers. Id. At 13.

38. ALEXANDER, supra note 2, at 55–56; BECKETT, supra note 31, at 61.

39. Michael Kramer, The Political Interest Frying Them Isn't the Answer, TIME, Mar. 14, 1994, at 32, available at http://www.time.com/time/magazine/article/0,9171,980318,00.html.

40. Press Release, Justice Policy Institute, Clinton Crime Agenda Ignores Proven Methods for Reducing Crime (Apr. 14. 2008) (on file with the Ohio State Journal of Criminal Law).

41. See ALEXANDER, supra note 2, at 56.

42. See id. at 71–73; see RADLEY BALKO, CATO INST., OVERKILL: THE RISE OF PARAMILITARY POLICE RAIDS IN AMERICA 14–15 (2006).

43. See Eric Blumenson & Eva Nilsen, Policing for Profit: The Drug War's Hidden Economic Agenda, 65 U. CHI. L. REV. 35, 44–45, 51 (1998).

44. MAUER & KING, supra note 20, at 3.

45. Id. at 2.

46. ALEXANDER, supra note 2, at 59; RYAN S. KING & MARC MAUER, THE SENTENCING PROJECT, THE WAR ON MARIJUANA: THE TRANSFORMATION OF THE WAR ON DRUGS IN THE 1990S, at 1 (2005).

47. See United States v. Armstrong, 517 U.S. 456 (1996); McCleskey v. Kemp, 481 U.S. 279 (1987).

48. JEFF MANZA & CHRISTOPHER UGGEN, LOCKED OUT: FELON DISENFRANCHISEMENT AND AMERICAN DEMOCRACY 152 (2006).

49. Interview by Guylando A. M. Moreno with Willie Thompson, in Cincinnati, Ohio (Mar. 2005). See also ALEXANDER, supra note 2, at 158–59.

50. SASHA ABRAMSKY, CONNED: HOW MILLIONS WENT TO PRISON, LOST THE VOTE, AND HELPED SEND GEORGE W. BUSH TO THE WHITE HOUSE 140 (2006).

51. AMERICAN CIVIL LIBERTIES UNION, OUT OF STEP WITH THE WORLD: AN ANALYSIS OF FELONY DISENFRANCHISEMENT IN THE U.S. AND OTHER DEMOCRACIES 3 (2006); THE SENTENCING PROJECT, FELONY DISENFRANCHISEMENT LAWS IN THE UNITED STATES 1 (2011).

52. JAMIE FELLNER & MARC MAUER, THE SENTENCING PROJECT, LOSING THE VOTE: THE IMPACT OF FELONY DISENFRANCHISEMENT LAWS IN THE UNITED STATES 1 (1998), available at http://www.sentencingproject.org/doc/File/FVR/fd_losingthevote.pdf. https://web .archive.org/web/20120914170518/http://www.sentencingproject.org/doc/File/FVR/fd_ losingthevote.pdf

53. Id. These figures may understate the impact of felony disenfranchisement, because they do not take into account the millions of formerly incarcerated people who cannot vote in states that require people convicted of felonies to pay fines or fees before their voting rights can be restored. As legal scholar Pam Karlan has observed, "felony disenfranchisement has decimated the potential Black electorate." LOURY, supra note 4, at 48.

54. See ALEXANDER, supra note 2, at 116–20 (discussing the discriminatory use of preemptory strikes against African American jurors).

55. See DEVAH PAGER, MARKED: RACE, CRIME AND FINDING WORK IN AN ERA OF MASS INCARCERATION 33 (2007); see also LEGAL ACTION CTR., AFTER PRISON: ROADBLOCKS TO REENTRY 10 (2004).

56. EMPLOYERS GRP. RESEARCH SERVS., EMPLOYMENT OF EX-OFFENDERS: A SURVEY OF EMPLOYERS' POLICIES AND PRACTICES 6 (2002); Harry J. Holzer, Steven Raphael & Michael A. Stoll, Will Employers Hire Former Offenders?: Employer Preferences, Background Checks, and Their Determinants, in IMPRISONING AMERICA: THE SOCIAL EFFECTS OF MASS INCARCERATION 205, 209 (Mary Pattillo et al., eds., 2004).

57. LEGAL ACTION CTR., supra note 58, at 10.

58. See HUMAN RIGHTS WATCH, NO SECOND CHANCE: PEOPLE WITH CRIMINAL RECORDS DENIED ACCESS TO PUBLIC HOUSING 33 (2004).

59. See Temporary Assistance for Needy Family Program (TANF), 21 U.S.C. § 862a(a)(2) (2006). See generally Legal Action Center, Opting out of Federal Ban on Food Stamps and TANF, at http://www.lac.org/toolkits/TANF/TANF.htm; Patricia Allard, The Sentencing Project, Life Sentences: Denying Welfare Benefits To Women Convicted Of Drug Offenses (2002), available at http://www.sentencingproject.org/doc/publications/women_lifesentences.pdf. https://web. archive.org/web/20101127140059/http://sentencingproject.org/doc/publications/women_life-sentences.pdf

60. Black Men's Jail Time Hits Entire Communities, NPR TALK OF THE NATION (Aug. 23, 2010), http://www.npr.org/templates/story/story.php?storyId=129379700. 65 RACHEL L. MCLEAN & MICHAEL D. THOMPSON, COUNCIL OF STATE GOV'TS JUSTICE CTR., REPAYING DEBTS 7–8 (2007).

61. See JEREMY TRAVIS, BUT THEY ALL COME BACK: FACING THE CHALLENGES OF PRISONER REENTRY 94 (2005).

62. See BRAMAN, supra note 14, at 219–20.

63. MARTIN LUTHER KING, JR., STRENGTH TO LOVE 45 (Fortress Press 1981) (1963).

64. Id.

65. WESTERN, supra note 16, at 91–92.

66. See Robert W. Fairlie & William A. Sundstrom, The Emergence, Persistence, and Recent Widening of the Racial Unemployment Gap, 52 INDUS. & LAB. REL. REV. 252, 257 Tables 2-3; see also Bruce Western, Black–White Wage Inequality, Employment Rates, and Incarceration, 111 AM.J. SOC. 553, 557 Table 2.

67. WESTERN, supra note 16, at 97.

68. See THE EISENHOWER FOUNDATION, WHAT WE CAN DO TOGETHER: A FORTY YEAR UPDATE OF THE NATIONAL ADVISORY COMMISSION ON CIVIL DISORDERS: PRELIMINARY FINDINGS (2008), available at www.eisenhowerfoundation.org/docs/Kerner%2040%20 Year%20Update,%20Executive%20Summary.pdf.

WHEN HEROIN HITS THE WHITE SUBURBS

ANDREW COHEN

Heroin use and abuse in America has dramatically increased over the past decade. Between 2006 and 2013, federal records reveal[1] that the number of first-time heroin users doubled, from 90,000 to 169,000. Some of those users, no doubt, already are gone. The Centers for Disease Control and Prevention [recently] announced[2] that the rate of deadly heroin overdoses nearly quadrupled between 2002 and 2013.

These troubling figures, and a spate of more recent stories and daunting statistics, have prompted officials across the country to implement bold new policies and practices designed to reduce the harm of heroin use. Although there has been some push to enhance criminal sanctions to combat the heroin surge, much of the institutional reaction to the renewed popularity of the drug has sounded in the realm of medicine, not law.

One public official after another, in states both "red" and "blue," has pressed in recent years to treat increased heroin use as a public safety problem as opposed to a criminal justice matter best left to police, prosecutors, and judges. This is good news. But it forms a vivid contrast with the harsh reaction[s] a generation ago to the sudden rise in the use of crack cocaine, and . . . two generations ago to an earlier heroin epidemic.

What accounts for the differences? Clearly policymakers know more today than they did then about the societal costs of waging a war on drugs, and dispatching low-level, nonviolent drug offenders to prison for decades. The contemporary criminal justice system places more emphasis on treatment and reform than it did, say, during the Reagan years or when New York's draconian "Rockefeller laws" were passed in the 1970s. But there may be another explanation for the less hysterical reaction, one that few policymakers have been willing to acknowledge: race.

Some experts and researchers see in the different responses to these drug epidemics further proof of America's racial divide. Are policymakers going easier today on heroin users (White and often affluent) than their elected predecessors did a generation ago when confronted with crack addicts who were largely Black, disenfranchised, and economically bereft? Can we explain the disparate response to the "Black" heroin epidemic of the 1960s, in which its use and violent crime were commingled in the public consciousness, and the White heroin "epidemic" today, in which its use is considered a disease to be treated or cured, without using race as part of our explanation?

Marc Mauer, the executive director of the Sentencing Project, a group that targets racial disparities in the criminal justice system, has been following this issue closely for decades. He agrees that there is strong historical precedent for comparing the crises through the prism of race:

1   Center for Behavior Health Statistics and Quality. 2013. "Results from the 2013 National Survey on Drug Use and Health: Summary of National Findings." U.S. Department of Health and Human Services. Retrieved on January 29, 2019, from https://www.samhsa.gov/data/sites/default/files/NSDUHresultsPDFWHTML2013/Web/NSDUHresults2013.pdf.

2   Centers for Disease Control and Prevention. 2015. "Today's Heroin Epidemic." Retrieved on January 29, 2019, from http://www.cdc.gov/vitalsigns/heroin/index.html.

Andrew Cohen, "When Heroin Hits the White Suburbs," The Marshall Project, August 12, 2015. Reprinted with permission.

The response to the rise in heroin use follows patterns we've seen over decades of drug scares. When the perception of the user population is primarily people of color, then the response is to demonize and punish. When it's White, then we search for answers. Think of the difference between marijuana attitudes in the "reefer madness" days of the 1930s when the drug was perceived to be used in the "racy" parts of town, and then the 1960s (White) college town explosion in use.

It is now axiomatic that, although the crack epidemic of the 1980s devastated communities of color, the legal and political responses to the crisis compounded the tragedy. Crack was an inner-city drug, a street-corner drug, a drug of gangs and guns that White America largely experienced from a distance. Powder cocaine, the more expensive version of the drug, found its way to more affluent users. The federal Anti-Drug Abuse Act, passed in 1986, imposed mandatory minimum sentences that were far harsher on users of crack cocaine than on those found with the drug in powdered form. The Fair Sentencing Act of 2010 reduced that disparity in sentencing from 100:1 to 18:1, but that remains[3] a striking gap.

Indeed, the harsh, punitive reaction to the crack era was the result of mythology about its use and its users, which later turned out to be false, says Jeffrey Fagan, a Columbia University professor who has long studied the intersection of criminal justice and race. "It was instantly addictive, it created 'super-predators,' you became a sexual deviant, especially if you were a woman, it destroyed maternal instincts," he said. All of that nonsense led to the draconian sentencing laws associated with crack use in the 1980s, Fagan told me. And that, Fagan says, was the sequel to another criminal justice crackdown that had taken place decades earlier. A surge in heroin use among Blacks in the 1960s was blamed for a rise in violent crime and provoked a harsh response.

By contrast to those earlier drug crises, the heroin epidemic of the 21st century is largely a White person's scourge. The Centers for Disease Control and Prevention reports that the cheap, easily accessible drug is attracting affluent suburbanites and women. Nearly 90 percent of the people who tried heroin for the first time in the past decade are White, according to a study published[4] in JAMA Psychiatry in July 2014, and there is no reason to believe the trend has eased since then. According to the researchers, heroin use has changed from an inner-city, minority-centered problem to one that has a more widespread geographical distribution, involving primarily White men and women in their late 20s living outside of large urban areas. The cause for this may be simple. White people addicted to prescription opiates, the sorts of drugs they can conveniently get from a friendly doctor or pharmacist, are finding heroin an obvious (and cheap) substitute now that law enforcement officials have cracked down on those opiates. The hottest fronts in this war now can be seen in rural states like Vermont and in suburban areas that largely missed the ravages of the crack craze.

Politicians on both sides of the aisle clearly are paying attention to what researchers diplomatically call the "changing face of heroin use." According to the Pew Charitable Trusts, [as of 2015], lawmakers in at least 24 states and the District of Columbia have enacted laws . . . that make naloxone, a prescription drug that helps counter the effect of a heroin overdose, more broadly available. . . . Nearly two-dozen states also have passed laws that protect "good Samaritans" who alert doctors or nurses to heroin overdoses.

Such public health responses were not necessarily unthinkable during the crack cocaine wave of the 1980s or the heroin epidemic of the 1960s. But the limited public health measures adopted during those eras were overshadowed by more punitive responses to those crises. Can you imagine the Congress and the White House of 1985 debating a "Recovery Enhancement for Addiction Act" for crack users? Mauer remembers instead the brutal mandatory sentencing laws of that era sweeping toward passage in Congress in near-record time. What accounts for the difference? "I don't think that's only because we are more thoughtful today," Mauer says.

3   Grindler, Gary G. 2010. "Memorandum for All Federal Prosecutors." U.S. Department of Justice, Office of the Deputy Attorney General." Retrieved on January 29, 2019, from http://www.justice.gov/sites/default/files/oip/legacy/2014/07/23/fair-sentencing-act-memo.pdf.

4   Cicero, Theodore J., Matthew S. Ellis, and Surratt, Hilary L. 2014. "The Changing Face of Heroin Use in the United States: A Retrospective Analysis of the Past 50 Years." *JAMA Psychiatry*, 71(7): 821–826.

SHARON LaFRANIERE AND ANDREW W. LEHREN

15. THE DISPROPORTIONATE RISKS OF DRIVING WHILE BLACK

While understanding racial profiling by police is notoriously difficult, research has shown that it simultaneously snares people in the criminal justice system and undermines trust in the police. LaFraniere and Lehren discuss data collected in several North Carolina cities that uncovered racial bias against African American drivers in a wide range of police interactions with citizens (traffic stops, vehicle searches, and the use of force), despite the fact that White drivers were found to be carrying contraband like guns and drugs more often than African Americans. LaFraniere and Lehren describe the continuing efforts by cities to address these disparities and reestablish trust with communities long targeted by police.

Rufus Scales, 26 and Black, was driving his younger brother Devin to his hair-cutting class in the genteel, leafy city [of Greensboro, North Carolina], when they heard the siren's whoop and saw the blue light in the rearview mirror of their Black pickup. Two police officers pulled them over for minor infractions that included expired plates and failing to hang a flag from a load of scrap metal in the pickup's bed. But what happened next was nothing like a routine traffic stop.

Uncertain whether to get out of the car, Rufus Scales said, he reached to restrain his brother from opening the door. A Black officer stunned him with a Taser, he said, and a White officer yanked him from the driver's seat. Temporarily paralyzed by the shock, he said, he fell face down, and the officer dragged him across the asphalt. Rufus Scales emerged from the encounter with four traffic tickets; a charge of assaulting an officer, later dismissed; a chipped tooth; and a split upper lip that required five stitches.

That was May 2013. Today, [even after years have passed], his brother Devin does not leave home without first pocketing a hand-held video camera and a business card with a toll-free number for legal help.

Rufus Scales instinctively turns away if a police car approaches. "Whenever one of them is near, I don't feel comfortable. I don't feel safe," he said.

As most of America now knows, those pervasive doubts about the police mirror those of millions of other African Americans. . . . Turmoil over the deaths of unarmed Blacks after encounters with the police in Ferguson, Missouri, in Baltimore, and elsewhere has sparked a national debate over how much racial bias skews law enforcement behavior, even subconsciously.

Documenting racial profiling in police work is devilishly difficult because a multitude of factors—including elevated violent crime rates in many Black neighborhoods—makes it hard to tease out evidence of bias from other influences. But an analysis by the *New York Times* of tens of thousands of traffic stops and years of arrest data in this racially mixed city of 280,000 uncovered wide racial differences in measure after measure of police conduct. Those same disparities were found across North Carolina, the state that collects the most detailed data on traffic stops. And at least some of them showed up in the six other states that collect comprehensive traffic-stop statistics.

Here in North Carolina's third-largest city, officers pulled over African American drivers for traffic violations at a rate far out of proportion to their share of the local driving population. They used their discretion to search Black drivers or their cars more than twice as often as White motorists—even though they found drugs and weapons significantly more often when the driver was White. Officers were more likely to stop Black drivers for no discernible reason. And they were more likely to use force if the driver was Black, even when they did not encounter physical resistance.

The routine nature of the stops belies their importance. As the public's most common encounter with law enforcement, they largely shape perceptions of the police. Indeed, complaints about traffic-law enforcement are at the root of many accusations that some police departments engage in racial profiling. Since Ferguson erupted in protests in August [2014], three of the deaths of African Americans that have roiled the nation occurred after drivers were pulled over for minor traffic infractions: a broken brake light, a missing front license plate, and failure to signal a lane change (Pérez-Peña 2015). Violence is rare, but routine traffic stops more frequently lead to searches, arrests, and the opening of a trapdoor into the criminal justice system that can have a lifelong impact, especially for those without the financial or other resources to negotiate it.

In Greensboro, which is 41 percent Black, traffic stops help feed the stream of minor charges that draw a mostly African American crowd of defendants to the county courthouse on weekday mornings. National surveys show that Blacks and Whites use marijuana at virtually the same rate, but Black residents here are charged with the sole offense of possession of minor amounts of marijuana five times as often as White residents are. And more than four times as many Blacks as Whites are arrested on the sole charge of resisting, obstructing, or delaying an officer, an offense so borderline that some North Carolina police chiefs discourage its use unless more serious crimes are also involved.

Greensboro police officials said most, if not all, of the racial disparities in their traffic enforcement stemmed from the fact that more African Americans live in neighborhoods with higher crime, where officers patrol more aggressively. Pulling over drivers,

they said, is a standard and effective form of proactive policing. "The way we accomplish our job is through contact, and one of the more common tools we have is stopping cars," Greensboro's police chief, Wayne Scott, who is White, said. Over the years, police officials in cities like New York and Chicago have used much the same argument to justify contentious pedestrian stop-and-frisk campaigns in high-crime areas. Criminals are less likely to frequent crime hot spots, the theory goes, if they know that the police there are especially vigilant.

But increasingly, criminologists and even some police chiefs argue that such tactics needlessly alienate law-abiding citizens and undermine trust in the police. Indeed, in Fayetteville, North Carolina, 100 miles southeast of Greensboro, a new police chief has discouraged officers from stopping motorists for minor infractions. Ronald L. Davis, a former California police chief who now runs the Justice Department's Office of Community Oriented Policing Services, questions whether there are any benefits to intensive traffic enforcement in high-crime neighborhoods. "There is no evidence that just increasing stops reduces crime," he said, pointing to a recent Justice Department review in St. Louis County, which includes Ferguson. The study showed—less convincingly than in Greensboro, because of less-specific data—that the police treated Black motorists more harshly than White ones. "For any chief who faces those racial disparities, they should be of great concern," Mr. Davis said.

Some Greensboro officials are indeed worried. In private meetings with Black community leaders, Mayor Nancy Vaughan, who is White, has asked: "Are we the next Ferguson?" At a recent gathering of hundreds of citizens, she told them, "We need to have this conversation before it's too late."

A NATIONAL UPROAR

A national uproar over racial profiling erupted in the 1990s after New Jersey state troopers were found to have focused on minority drivers for traffic stops in hopes of catching drug couriers. Thousands of local law enforcement departments and more than a dozen state police agencies began collecting traffic-stop information as a result. In the seven states with the most sweeping reporting requirements—Connecticut, Illinois, Maryland, Missouri, Nebraska, North Carolina, and Rhode Island—the data show that police officers are more likely to pull over Black drivers than White ones, given their share of the local driving-age population.

By itself, that proves little because other factors besides race could be in play. Because African Americans are, for example, generally poorer than Whites, they may have more expired vehicle registrations or other automotive lapses that attract officers' attention. More tellingly, many researchers agree, is what happens after a vehicle is pulled over—especially whether officers use their legal discretion to search a car or its occupants and whether those searches uncover illegal contraband. An officer can conduct a "consent search" without any justification if the driver grants permission. A search can also be made without consent if an officer has probable cause to suspect a crime.

In the four states that track the results of consent searches, officers were more likely to conduct them when the driver was Black, even though they consistently found drugs, guns, or other contraband more often if the driver was White. The same pattern held true with probable-cause searches in Illinois and North Carolina, the two states that carefully record them. Searches are not common; officers in North Carolina, for example, conduct them in just one in 40 traffic stops. But they have an outsize impact on police–civilian relations. Surveys show that minorities, especially Blacks, are much less likely than Whites to say officers acted properly at a traffic stop. But far fewer drivers of all races rate the police positively if they are searched.

In most of the states that monitor traffic stops most intensely, officials acknowledge that this close attention has not had a discernible effect. In Missouri, which has collected data for 15 years, Chris Koster, the state attorney general, has said the differences in how Black and White motorists are treated are bigger than ever. Similar racial disparities are revealed in the data that the Nebraska Crime Commission has collected since 2001, but the commission lacks resources to delve into causes or solutions, said the agency's information chief, Michael Overton." Quite honestly, every year I have to pick up my jaw a little bit because the numbers are very, very consistent," he said.

But Rhode Island and Connecticut have each revised practices. After studies in 2003 and 2006 found racially disparate treatment at traffic stops, Rhode Island revamped its law enforcement training regimen. A 2014 study indicated that officers had become more judicious, conducting fewer consent and probable-cause searches of vehicles, but finding contraband more often. "It really seemed to have a good impact," said Jack McDevitt, the lead researcher and director of the Institute on Race and Justice at Northeastern University. "It showed officers can be smarter about searching." Beginning last year, Connecticut measured every law enforcement agency against seven benchmarks, including whether officers stopped minorities more often in the daytime, when a driver's race is easier to detect. In three cities and 2 of 12 state police districts, state officials said, racial differences in the treatment of motorists were unmistakable.

The state is pushing police administrators to explain why. Analysts are also comparing traffic- stop data from officers who patrol similar beats, which some researchers consider the most reliable way to uncover bias, implicit or overt. One change is already in place: Officers now must give every stopped motorist a card explaining how to file a complaint. "Racial profiling is a very real phenomenon, and in some places it is much worse than others," Mike Lawlor, Connecticut's under secretary for criminal justice policy and planning, said. Across the country, the latest outcries over police–minority relations have revived interest in monitoring: [in 2015], California passed a law requiring officers to record both traffic and pedestrian stops.

In North Carolina, mounds of traffic-stop data lay dormant for a decade before academics like Frank R. Baumgartner, a University of North Carolina political science professor, began sifting through the statistics for evidence of bias in 2011. The Southern Coalition for Social Justice, a nonprofit advocacy group based in Durham, has used the patterns of racial disparities to bolster demands for restrictions on searches and other changes. Chief Scott, who . . . [recently] assumed his post, said he was withholding judgment until his own staff analyzed his department's data. "We are not afraid to ask these questions," he said. But so far, he added, "I don't believe there is an underlying, systemic issue" of racial profiling.

ANALYZING THE STOPS

Greensboro has long cherished its reputation as a Southern progressive standout. This was the first Southern city to pledge to integrate its schools after the Supreme Court's 1954 decision in *Brown v. Board of Education*, although it was among the last to actually do so. And when four Black freshmen from North Carolina A&T State University occupied the orange and green stools at Woolworth's Whites-only lunch counter in 1960, Greensboro midwifed a sit-in movement that spread through the South. But this is also where hundreds of National Guardsmen suppressed Black student protesters in 1969 and where, a decade later, five protesters were murdered at an anti-Ku Klux Klan rally conspicuously devoid of police protection. And it was here, in 2009, that 39 minority police officers accused their own department of racial bias in a lawsuit that the city spent nearly $1.3 million fighting before agreeing to settle for $500,000. In a city that is 48 percent White, 75 percent of Greensboro's force of 684 sworn officers remains White.

The Rev. Nelson Johnson, a civil rights leader here since the 1960s, contends that like Greensboro as a whole, the Police Department "has a liberal veneer but a reactionary underbelly." An activist group he heads recently established a citizens' board to hear complaints about the police, arguing that official investigations too often are shams. "This is not about one officer," Mr. Johnson said at a recent meeting about police behavior at the Beloved Community Center. "This is about a culture, a deeply saturated culture that reflects itself in double standards."

The *Times* has analyzed tens of thousands of traffic stops made by hundreds of officers since 2010. Although Blacks made up 39 percent of Greensboro's driving-age population, they constituted 54 percent of the drivers pulled over. While factors like out-of-town drivers can alter the racial composition of a city's motorists, "if the difference is that big, it does give you pause," Dr. McDevitt of Northeastern University said. Most Black Greensboro drivers were stopped for regulatory or equipment violations, infractions that officers have the discretion to ignore. And Black motorists who were stopped were let go with no police action—not even a warning—more often than were Whites.

Criminal justice experts say that raises questions about why they were pulled over at all and can indicate racial profiling.

In the past decade, officers reported using force during traffic stops only about once a month. The vast majority of the subjects were Black, and most had put up resistance. Still, if a motorist was Black, the odds were greater that officers would use force even in cases in which they did not first encounter resistance. Police officials suggested that could be because more Black motorists tried to flee. In an interview, Chief Scott said that, overall, the statistics reflected sound crime-fighting strategies, not bias. They have produced record-low burglary rates, and most citizens welcome the effort, he said.

Deborah Lamm Weisel, an assistant professor of criminal justice at North Carolina Central University in Durham, said the best policing practices "involve officers making proactive contacts with citizens, and traffic stops are the main way they do that." But many criminal justice experts contend that the racial consequences of that strategy far outweigh its benefits—if, indeed, there are any. "This is what people have been complaining about across the nation," said Delores Jones-Brown, a professor at the John Jay College of Criminal Justice in New York. "It means Whites are 'getting away' with very low-level offenses, while people who are poor or people of color are suffering consequences." "It amounts to harassment," she said. "And police cannot demonstrate that it is creating better public safety." To the contrary, she added, it makes minority citizens less likely to help the police prevent and solve crimes.

That critique is ascendant in Fayetteville, about two hours by car from Greensboro. Fayetteville is three-fourths as big but equally diverse: Forty-six percent of its 204,000 residents are White, and 42 percent are Black. More than three years ago, an uproar over reports that Black drivers were disproportionately stopped and searched led to the departure of the police chief and city manager.

The new chief, Harold Medlock, who was appointed in January 2013, is overhauling the department. Like Chief Scott of Greensboro, he deploys more officers in high-crime areas and faces constant demands from citizens to assign even more. But, Chief Medlock said,

"They are not asking for more traffic stops." He said he had told his officers to focus on drivers who speed, drive drunk, or ignore traffic lights and stop signs—the violations that cost lives. Because officers typically cannot see who commits a moving violation like speeding, he said, it also "tends to eliminate the disparity in who is being stopped." Using dashboard videos, Chief Medlock said, the department also pushed out two officers who were accused of singling out Black motorists. At his request, the Justice Department is conducting a review of his department's practices.

Traffic data show the impact of Fayetteville's shift. In the three years before Chief Medlock arrived, slightly more than one-third of the Black motorists who were stopped had committed a moving violation. The police today are still more likely to pull over Blacks than Whites. But so far this year, nearly two-thirds of them were stopped for a moving violation, nearly the same proportion as White motorists. . . .

SEARCHES AND "HITS"

In a certain percentage of traffic stops, the officer's motivation is not to write a traffic ticket but to search for signs of crime. An officer, however, cannot stop a motorist without evidence of a traffic violation or probable cause to suspect a crime. Yet traffic codes are so minutely drawn that virtually every driver will break some rule within a few blocks, experts say. "The traffic code is the best friend of the police officer," said David A. Harris, a University of Pittsburgh law professor who studies police behavior and search-and-seizure law.

When a Greensboro officer pulled over Keith Maryland and Jasmine McRae, who are Black, in Mr. Maryland's burgundy Nissan early one evening in March, even that vast authority was exceeded, claimed Mr. Maryland's lawyer, Graham Holt. In an interview, Mr. Maryland said Officer Christopher Cline had told him that his registration had expired, although it was clearly valid for 15 more days. The officer then said Ms. McRae, sitting in the back seat, "looked like someone" and asked to search her purse. Officers do not have to tell drivers or their passengers that they have the right to refuse, and like the vast majority of people, Ms. McRae agreed. The

officer found a small amount of marijuana and several grams of cocaine and arrested her.

Mr. Holt said the stop was illegal because there was no traffic infraction. And in fact, a police corporal summoned Mr. Maryland to the station the next day and scrawled VOID across the ticket for an expired registration. But the department and a city review board still found that the officer had acted lawfully. And Ms. McRae ended up pleading guilty to a misdemeanor charge of marijuana possession. She was sentenced to probation, incurring hundreds of dollars in fees.

Police officials would call Ms. McRae's search a successful "hit." But most consent searches in Greensboro are not, especially when a stopped vehicle's driver is Black. [Between 2010 and 2015], officers searched Blacks more than twice as often but found contraband only 21 percent of the time, compared with 27 percent of the time with Whites. The same gap prevailed when officers cited probable cause to search without permission. Officers searched Blacks at more than twice the rate of Whites, but found contraband only 52 percent of the time, compared with 62 percent of the time when the driver was White. If those statistics are true, Chief Scott said, "we need to figure out how we can better serve our community in a fairer way."

Fayetteville officials believe that they have an answer. Faced with similar data, the City Council required officers in 2012 to obtain written permission for consent searches—a requirement endorsed [in 2015] by [an Obama administration] . . . task force on policing. Since then, the number of consent searches has plummeted to about one a week. Probable-cause searches dropped by more than half. There is a downside, Chief Medlock acknowledged. Fewer weapons are being confiscated. But because consent searches seldom turned up much contraband anyway, he said, the losses are minimal.

A CATCHALL CHARGE

Carlyle Phillips said he had no trouble with the police when he was growing up in New Jersey. And he has had none in Maryland, where he now lives. But as a student at North Carolina A&T in Greensboro, he said, he had one run-in after another. And he said he saw how routine traffic stops can become a springboard into a criminal justice system that can be hard to escape.

As a college junior in January 2010, Mr. Phillips said, he was pulled over in a predominantly White section of Greensboro for failing to wear his seatbelt—even though, he insisted, he was buckled in. He said he neither used drugs nor had had any with him. But that day, he said, he watched as the officer searching his car planted a plastic bag in it, then claimed it was evidence of drug use. Mr. Phillips was charged with possession of less than half an ounce of marijuana, joining a long list of Greensboro Blacks charged only with that offense since 2009. Five times as many Blacks as Whites were arrested on that charge, despite evidence Whites use marijuana about as often.

Mr. Phillips hired a lawyer, and a judge dismissed the charge. But nine months later, another traffic stop bore more serious consequences. As Mr. Phillips and another Black student, Gian Spells, drove through downtown one night, they said, a police officer pulled alongside, looked at them, then dropped behind, and flashed his lights. "You cut me off," Mr. Spells said Sgt. Thomas Long had told him, according to a complaint the students later filed alleging racial profiling. "Clearly, you've had too much to drink."

Mr. Spells said he had not had any alcohol and asked for a test. Instead, the officer ordered him out of the car—a command within his authority. When Mr. Spells refused, the officer threatened him with pepper spray. Worried he might be framed again, Mr. Phillips said, he raised his hands in the air and told a second officer that he wanted to remain in his seat, only to be threatened with a Taser. The students spent the night in jail, apparently because the officers said they were intoxicated. But they were never charged with drunkenness or reckless driving. They were charged only with resisting, obstructing, or delaying an officer, or R.D.O., in police parlance. Since 2009, the Greensboro police have filed that charge—and no other—against 836 Blacks but only 209 Whites.

A judge eventually dismissed their cases. But in the meantime, Mr. Phillips said, a job offer was thrown into limbo when a background check turned up the pending criminal charge. "That was probably one of the hardest things I had to face," said Mr. Phillips, now 27, who was eventually hired. "Maybe missing out on a great opportunity because some police officer takes offense at something."

The students' complaint of racial profiling was rejected. To this day, Mr. Phillips said, he does not understand why he and his friend were arrested. But Lewis Pitts, a well-known retired civil rights lawyer in Greensboro, sees no mystery. If a Black motorist "does anything but be completely submissive and cower, then you get the classic countercharge by the officer that there was resistance, or disorderly conduct or public intoxication," Mr. Pitts said. "Then they end up in jail." In Fayetteville, Chief Medlock said he had instructed his officers to avoid resisting-an-officer charges unless some more serious offense also occurred. "I tell my folks, if that's all you have, don't charge somebody. Find a way to move them on down the road," he said. Through a police spokeswoman, the Greensboro officers named in this article, all of whom are White, declined to comment. And partly because North Carolina law treats complaints against police officers as confidential personnel matters, accounts like Mr. Phillips's remain one-sided. Two years ago, Greensboro equipped all of its officers with body cameras and required them to film any searches. But those videotapes are confidential, too.

Chief Scott said he believed that if the state allowed the police to share them, at least with the citizens involved in the encounters, it would help dispel suspicions of racial profiling. "I am in favor of more transparency," he said. "Numbers don't say it all." His department is striving hard to improve police practices, he said. It is trying harder to recruit minority officers, discouraging the use of Tasers, bolstering training in unbiased policing practices, he said, and making sure every credible complaint is investigated. By that last measure, police officials point out, most citizens seem satisfied. Greensboro averages about 300,000 calls for police assistance every year. Only 64 people filed complaints in 2014. The department's own investigators deemed that about two-thirds of the allegations were without merit. Most complaints were about rudeness; only five concerned bias.

'I GET A COLD CHILL'

Marie Robinson, 60, and James Fields, 52, are skeptical of that picture. Their run-in with two Greensboro officers ended with them offering an apology. But in fact, they said, they were owed one. Early one afternoon in April 2013, they were sitting in Miss Robinson's Black Honda Accord in front of Mr. Fields's house because Miss Robinson, who has diabetes, had a plunge in her blood sugar level, a recurrent problem that often causes her to lose consciousness. Mr. Fields said he had just brought her some apple juice from his kitchen when Officer Jesse Hillis approached and demanded to know what they were doing.

Mr. Fields said that he had explained, but that the officer had countered: "I think you are a drug dealer and she is a prostitute." Then he ordered him out of the car and pushed him against it, he said. "What is your problem?" Mr. Fields said he had demanded, turning toward the officer. "Why are you stereotyping a Black man?" He ended up face down on the pavement, handcuffed. Miss Robinson said she had staggered faint-headed from the car, only to be thrown back in, hitting her head. "I don't care," she said Officer Justin Kivette had told her. "You don't have a sign on you saying you're diabetic." For more than 90 minutes, Mr. Fields said, the officers refused to summon a paramedic. The two were charged with resisting an officer, although both insist that they offered no resistance. When she asked why she was being charged, Miss Robinson said, one officer pointed to his partner and said, "How about you hit him?" Mr. Fields also was charged with assaulting a public officer.

For eight months while the charges were pending, Mr. Fields was suspended from his job as a department supervisor at the local Walmart. He fell behind in his rent and mowed lawns to make ends meet. Miss Robinson, whose previous brushes with the law consisted of two minor traffic tickets, said the whole experience "kind of took the life out of me." Mayor Vaughan, who is also diabetic, discussed the episode with Miss Robinson at a community meeting. "I felt she was very believable," she said. But police officials apparently did not.

The department not only rejected all allegations in the complaint that she and Mr. Fields filed, they said, but the complaint seemed to backfire. Every night for a month after they filed it, Mr. Fields said, a patrol car parked outside his house. Desperate to reclaim his job, Mr. Fields said, he agreed to write a letter apologizing to both officers. His charges were dismissed, as were those against Miss Robinson, who wrote a similar letter. "I can't tell you how hard it was for me to stand up in court and apologize to them," Mr. Fields said. "I am still very much upset. I almost lost everything I had because two police officers stepped out of line."

"Every time I see a police officer, I get a cold chill," he said. "Even if I needed one, I wouldn't call one." Rufus Scales, who landed in a hospital emergency room after being dragged from his pickup during his 2013 traffic stop, said he shared that sentiment. The steps he and his brother took to deal with it made their latest encounter with the police, in August 2014, a vivid illustration of why that mistrust exists.

One summer afternoon last year, the two men were walking down the residential street where their grandmother lives when a White officer passed them in his cruiser. "Get out of the street, you morons," they said the officer, Travis Cole, had yelled at them, although the street has no sidewalks. When the officer asked for their IDs, Rufus Scales said, he responded with a curse word. Officer Cole then forced him to the ground and handcuffed him, he said. "You can't come out here running your mouth and cursing out in the middle of the street," the officer lectured.

Both men were arrested on charges that they had impeded traffic on the deserted street. Rufus Scales was also charged with being disorderly and drunk, although, he said, he was neither. This encounter differed from the traffic stop in one crucial respect: Devin Scales pulled from his pocket his newly purchased hand-held camera, recorded the episode, and posted the video on Facebook. After the brothers filed a complaint with the police, a prosecutor dropped all the charges. Officer Cole was suspended for two days. The city manager apologized. As Devin Scales wrote in the Facebook posting, which he said had drawn 10,000 "likes": "This wasn't the first time."

"HANDS ON THE WHEEL": DISPARITIES IN RESPECT DURING TRAFFIC STOPS

MOEY ROJAS

The influence of race in police–civilian interactions has been a topic of increased public discourse in recent years, as mobile devices and social media have given communities of color an enhanced capacity to raise awareness about the disproportionate levels of violence they face at the hands of police. For instance, footage of Philando Castile's fatal shooting by police during a traffic stop was viewed over five million times within two days.[1] However, relatively unexplored in the context of extreme examples, such as those that result in civilian deaths, remain the everyday interactions between police and communities of color that occur, for example, during routine traffic stops. As the racial bias that occurs in these situations is normally subtler, it may be somewhat difficult to generalize about the influence of race in these interactions or have enough evidence to demand a concrete policy change. However, the use of officer body cameras has given researchers from the National Academy of Sciences (NAS) a chance to analyze the racial bias that occurs during routine traffic stops. Moreover, their findings have revealed that police are significantly less respectful toward Black members of the communities they patrol than White ones.[2]

The NAS researchers examined 981 stops with 682 Black and 299 White drivers (the number of stops with Black drivers is higher because Black drivers are disproportionately likely to be stopped nationwide)[3]—over 180 hours of body camera footage—in the city of Oakland, California, to perform three connected studies. In the first study, average citizens were given subsets of transcripts of body camera footage of interactions between officers and drivers during routine traffic stops. The participants, or "raters," would then read the transcripts and rate the officers' level of respect (how respectful, polite, friendly, formal, and impartial the officer was during the interaction) on a four-point scale. While raters were not aware of the race of the officer or driver, they were aware of what the driver had said immediately prior to the interaction. For instance, phrases such as "hands on the wheel" and "all right, my man" or use of the driver's first name were ultimately rated as some of the least respectful and least formal forms of interaction, while apologies, gratitude, or use of the driver's last name or another title such as "sir" were all rated as some of the most respectful and most formal. While a concept such as respect can be relatively subjective, the raters were ultimately consistent in their evaluations of officers' language, revealing that people have the capacity to perceive respect reliably.

In the second study, researchers developed computer algorithms that could gauge respectful language (saying thanks, using formal versus informal language, etc.) in the same way the humans in the first study had done. In the third study, the authors used those same computer algorithms to evaluate all 36,000 exchanges between police officers and drivers during the traffic stops made by the Oakland Police Department over a one-month period, to determine if levels of respect varied depending on whether an officer was stopping a White or Black driver.[4]

Ultimately, even when controlling for contextual factors like an officer's race (42 percent White, 23 percent Hispanic, 16 percent Black, 15 percent Asian, 4 percent other), severity of the driver's infraction, stop location, and outcome, researchers ultimately determined language directed toward White drivers was more respectful than language directed toward Black drivers. While White drivers were 57 percent more likely to hear an officer say one of the most respectful phrases in the researchers' model, Black drivers were 61 percent more likely to hear an officer say one of the least respectful utterances. Furthermore, the analysis revealed that officers' varying levels of respect toward White and Black motorists did not vary according to the race of the officer, suggesting that, instead of stemming from a few officers with significant racial biases, racial disparity in officer respect is a systemic issue that occurs within and across races.[5]

While racial disparities in officer respect are not necessarily as pressing an issue as, for instance, officers' excessive

---

1   Bayly, L. (2016, July 9). Police Shootings Test New Era of Violent Social Media Video. Retrieved August 22, 2018, from https://www.nbcnews.com/tech/tech-news/police-shootings-test-new-era-violent-social-media-video-n605366.

2   Voigt, R., Camp, N. P., Prabhakaran, V., Hamilton, W. L., Hetey, R. C., Griffiths, C. M., . . . Eberhardt, J. L. (2017). Language from police body camera footage shows racial disparities in officer respect. *Proceedings of the National Academy of Sciences of the United States of America.* https://doi.org/10.1073/pnas.1702413114

3   Findings. (n.d.). Retrieved August 22, 2018, from https://openpolicing.stanford.edu/findings.

4   Voigt et al., 2017.
5   Voigt et al. 2017.

(*continued*)

Original to *Focus on Social Problems: A Contemporary Reader.*

use of force, the researchers point out that instances like routine traffic stops are much more common, with more than one-quarter of the public coming into contact with the police each year, most frequently as the result of a traffic stop.[6,7] Furthermore, the researchers draw attention to the fact that each interaction with the police is significant; every traffic stop provides an opportunity for the enhancement or erosion of public trust in the police, or even possible violence toward people of color. Furthermore, if a community has diminished trust in their police force. it can negatively affect how they cooperate with police if they need to report a crime.[8] However, large-scale analyses of language offer researchers an opportunity to evaluate police–community interactions, and, hopefully, afford police departments a chance to combat racial disparities in how their officers interact with members of their communities.[9]

6   U.S. Department of Justice Bureau of Justice Statistics. (n.d.). *Police Behavior during Traffic and Street Stops, 2011.*
7   Traffic Stops. (2011). Retrieved 08 8, 2018, from Bureau of Justice Statistics website: https://www.bjs.gov/index.cfm?tid=702&ty=tp.
8   President's Task Force on 21st Century Policing Office of Community Oriented Policing Services. (2015). *Final Report of the President's Task Force on 21st Century Policing.* Washington, DC.
9   Voigt et al., 2017.

CRAIG CONSIDINE

16. THE RACIALIZATION OF ISLAM IN THE UNITED STATES

Islamophobia, Hate Crimes, and "Flying While Brown"

American Muslims and Arab Americans have faced increased hostility since September 11, 2001. Considine argues that the discrimination, bias, and attacks they have faced (known as "Islamophobia") have extended to other groups that are perceived to be Muslim (such as Sikhs) or otherwise "not American." Considine describes contemporary intolerance toward Muslim and Arab Americans, including hate crimes and the consequences of "flying while brown," or racial profiling at airports. Given that American Muslims are a heterogeneous group comprising a wide variety of races, Considine argues that Muslim Americans are being subjected to a form of racism based on both cultural differences and physical appearance, which he refers to as the racialization of Islam.

INTRODUCTION

This [reading] explores the racialization of Islam in the United States and how this discriminatory process is influenced by historic, domestic, and geopolitical trends surrounding American Muslims and people who "look Muslim." In the context of the "War on Terror," the racialization of American Muslims generates local and palpable experiences of exclusion and abuse for both Muslims and non-Muslims. These experiences are captured by the term *Islamophobia*, which is now accepted and designated as a special form of discrimination. . . .

The Council on American-Islamic Relations (CAIR), a civil rights and advocacy organization based in Washington, D.C., is at the forefront of combatting Islamophobia in the United States. In a 2016 report, Nihad Awad, CAIR's Executive Director, stated that fear and hatred of American Muslims have "moved from the fringes of American society to the mainstream" (Council on American-Islamic Relations 2016, p. v).

During the 2016 presidential campaign, candidates of the Republican Party made several controversial comments, including "Islam hates us," "[Muslims are] uncorked animals," and "I would not advocate that we put a Muslim in charge of this nation" (Bradner 2015; Waldman 2015). Another Islamophobic buzzword, the fear of "creeping *sharia*," or Islamic law, has led to legislation designed to vilify or otherwise target Muslims at an institutional level. . . . [As of 2017], at least 32 states across the United States had introduced and debated anti-*sharia* or antiforeign law bills (Rifai 2016). This movement reached its climax in 2011 and 2012, when 78 bills or amendments designed to denigrate Islamic religious practices were introduced in the legislatures of 29 states as well as the U.S. Congress (Saylor 2014). Seventy-three of these bills were introduced by Republicans, while only one bill was introduced by a Democrat (from Alabama). In total, only three anti-*sharia* bills at the state level were bipartisan—in Kansas, South Carolina, and South Dakota (Saylor 2014). . . . According to the Institute for Social Policy

Considine, C. The Racialization of Islam in the United States: Islamophobia, Hate Crimes, and "Flying while Brown". Religions 2017, 8, 165. Republished under Creative Commons license (CC BY 4.0).

145

and Understanding (ISPU), a solution-seeking research institute that tracks Islamophobia in the United States, approximately 80 % of U.S. legislators who sponsor this type of legislation also sponsor bills restricting the rights of other minorities and vulnerable groups in the United States.

Islamophobia is also exacerbated by the Islamophobia industry (Lean 2012). In recent years, anti-Muslim groups and organizations have enjoyed access to at least $205 million to spread fear and hatred of Muslims (Council on American-Islamic Relations 2016, p. v). In 2011, the Center for American Progress (CAP), a public policy research and advocacy organization based in Washington, D.C., found that seven charitable foundations spent $42.6 million between 2001 and 2009 to support the spread of anti-Muslim and anti-Islam rhetoric in the United States (Ali 2011). . . . The culmination of anti-Islam legislation and rhetoric has undoubtedly inspired attacks against Muslims and non-Muslims across the United States. In the last two months of 2015 alone, American Muslims reported 34 violent incidents against their mosques, acts that serve to intimidate Muslim worshippers (Council on American-Islamic Relations 2016, p. v).

In addition to the activities of anti-Muslim groups and organizations, media and entertainment representations of Islam and Muslims are key factors in the rise of Islamophobia across the United States. According to Media Tenor International, a research institute that studies data for nongovernmental organizations (NGOs) and governments, news outlets such as Fox, NBC, and CBS depicted Islam primarily as a source of violence between 2007 and 2013 (Media Tenor International n.d.). In another 2011 report, Media Tenor found that U.S. and European news outlets focused on the Middle East primarily through the context of Muslim militancy (Media Tenor International 2011). The entertainment industry, too, contributes to the racialization of Islam and Muslim, which exacerbates anti-Islam and anti-Muslim sentiments. In a study on news coverage from LexisNexis Academic and CNN for all terrorist attacks in the United States between 2011 and 2015, researchers found that news outlets gave drastically more coverage to attacks by Muslims, particularly foreign-born Muslims—even though these attacks are far less common than other kinds of terrorist attacks (Kearns et al. 2017a). Attacks by Muslim perpetrators received, on average, 449% more coverage than attacks carried out by non-Muslims (Kearns et al. 2017b). Erin Kearns, an author of the study, told National Public Radio (NPR) in June 2017 that when the perpetrator of a terrorist attack is Muslim, "you can expect that attack to receive about four and a half times more media coverage than if the perpetrator was not Muslim." Put another way, as Kearns notes, "a perpetrator who is not Muslim would have to kill on average about seven more people to receive the same amount of coverage as a perpetrator who is Muslim."

The term *racial formation*, as introduced by Omi and Winant (1994), is a useful starting point to explore the ways in which media determine the content and importance of Muslim identities, by which they are then shaped by racial meanings. The reaction of Americans to the genre of action-adventure film, and its increasing use of Arabs and Muslims as villains, shows how Americans' perceptions of Arab and Muslims populations can be shaped and skewed (Wilkins 2008). Jack Shaheen, author of *Reel Bad Arabs: How Hollywood Vilifies People* and *A Is for Arab: Archiving Stereotypes in U.S. Popular Culture*, spent his career analyzing the way that Arabs have been portrayed in American film and television over the last century. In 2006, his book *Reel Bad Arabs* showed that Hollywood depicts Arabs as "brute murderers, sleazy rapists, religious fanatics, oil-rich dimwits and abusers of women."

Shaheen's research documented well over 1,000 films depicting Arabs and subsequently found that 932 films depicted them in a stereotypical or negative light. Only 12 films had a positive depiction. He also cited films that portray Arabs as cold, money-hungry Muslims or inept villainous terrorists who seek to destroy "Western civilization". . . . By reinforcing stereotypes of the Middle East as a place of extremism and Muslims as terrorists, these representations produce support for policies that have dire consequences for Arabs, Muslims, and people who are believed to be Arab and Muslim (Alsultany 2015). These caricatures of Arabs and Muslims also provide a popular "permission to hate," which often unfolds through a synthesis of racial and religious discrimination (Poynting & Mason 2006, p. 367).

Despite the conflation of Arab identity and "radical Muslims," the facts reveal that American Muslims are far from homogeneous. The Pew Research Center estimates that there were about 3.3 million Muslims of all ages living in the United States in 2015 (Mohamed 2016). No single racial or ethnic group makes up for more than 30% of the total Muslim population (Mohamed 2016). Overall, 30% describe themselves as White, 23% as Black, 21% as Asian, 6% as Hispanic, and 19% as other or mixed race (Mohamed 2016). Of those aged 18 and older, more than 6 in 10 (63%) were born abroad, and many are relative newcomers to the United States (Pew Research Center 2011). Approximately one-quarter of all Muslim adults (25%) have arrived in the country since 2000. Despite the high proportion of immigrants in the American Muslim population, the vast majority (81%) report that they are citizens of the United States (Pew Research Center 2011). Recent studies carried out by the Pew Research Center (2007) also reveal that nearly one-quarter of American Muslims say they have converted to Islam; 9 in 10 (91%) converts to Islam were born in the United States, and almost two-thirds (67%) of all converts to Islam came from Protestant churches (Pew Research Center 2007). With this heterogeneity in mind, nearly all Muslim racial or ethnic groups have higher odds of reporting one or more types of perceived discrimination than White Muslims (Zainiddinov 2016). Asian Muslims report the lowest frequency of perceived discrimination than other Muslim racial or ethnic groups (Zainiddinov 2016).

The experiences of European Muslims reveal additional insight into the dynamics of contemporary Islamophobia in Western countries. According to the European Islamophobia Report (2017), Islamophobia has become "a real danger" to the democratic foundations of the European Union. The 2016 EIR [Environmental Implementation Review] country reports, which cover almost all of the European continent, shows that the level of Islamophobia in fields such as education, employment, media, politics, the justice system, and the Internet is on the rise (European Islamophobia Report 2017). In terms of politics, as Hafez (2014 p. 479) notes, "Islamophobia has become a useful tool for right-wing parties to mobilize electors in many European nation-states." This

development, he continues, means that Islamophobia has become a kind of "accepted racism" found not only on the margins of European societies, but also at the center. . . .

METHODOLOGY

. . . Coding of news media stories is one source of examination. Coding in qualitative inquiry is most often used to identify words or short phrases that symbolically assign a summative, salient, essence-capturing, and/or evocative attribute for a portion of language-based or visual data (Saldana 2009, p. 3). The coding process of this research entailed looking through a selected sample of relevant news media coverage and systematically noting its traits as it pertains to the racialization of Islam in the United States (Pew Research Center n.d.). Choosing a sample of articles involved a focus on representativeness and the practical use of the article, specifically in terms of two units of analysis: "race" and "racial profiling."

In terms of the sampling technique, this research can best be described as purposeful sampling. Purposeful sampling is widely used in qualitative research for the identification and selection of information-rich cases for the most effective use of limited resources (Patton 2002). . . . [T]he criterion of importance included terms like race, racism, hate crime, racial profiling, Muslims, and Islamophobia. The selection of the material involved identifying and selecting news articles that are especially pertinent to the role that race played in incidents of anti-Muslim discrimination and violence. Embedded in the . . . sampling strategy is the ability to compare and contrast, to identify similarities and differences across the selected articles. The author framed "news articles" in a broad manner to include print, online news sites, network TV programs, cable TV programs, radio broadcasts, and blogs (Pew Research Center n.d.). In total, 98 articles were examined for initial inclusion in the content analysis. Using the key search words, "racial profiling of Muslims in the United States" and "hate crimes against Muslims in the United States," the news websites were reviewed for further consideration, particularly in light of incidents involving race and racialization. . . . All the news articles examined in the research are considered to be reputable sources and among the largest media outlets in terms of online circulation. . . .

At the first level of coding, the author looked for two categories in the available articles: "race" and "racism." These two categories formed the basic units of the first phase of analysis. Headlines that contained potential information about the representative concepts were examined and noted as a specific Islamophobic incident against Muslims or those perceived to be Muslim. Additional search entries into LexisNexis included "race and hate crimes against Muslims" and "racism and anti-Muslim attacks." After exhausting an online news search of these units of analysis, the research moved to the second level of coding, which focused on locating articles for coverage of specific hate crimes against groups such as Muslims, Arabs, Sikhs, South Asians, and People of Color. The sample of articles examined in the second coding stage relate to concepts such as "looking Muslim," "flying while brown," and "racial profiling" at airports and on planes. Once these stories were identified, the author started to code and relate that coding system to several broad conceptual themes, including Islamophobia, racial profiling, racism and civil rights violations. Islamophobia is the most common word in the cluster of competing phrases that emerged from the coding system. . . . Ultimately, the goal of this study is to reveal how race is a symbolic form of Islamophobia as well as Islamophobic incidents in the United States.

THE INTERSECTIONALITY OF RACE AND ISLAMOPHOBIA

There is a cluster of terms and phrases referring to hostility toward American Muslims. The most widely known term is *Islamophobia*. One of the first uses of Islamophobia in English appears in an article by Said (1985); he initially brought into focus the stigmatized identity of Muslims in his work *Orientalism*, which unpacked the Western perspectives that create dehumanizing representations of the "exotic" and "barbarous" countries of the Middle East, Africa, and Asia (Said 1978). Said (1978) saw many features of Western representations of the "Arab Other" as based on a fear of Muslims. Lurking behind these depictions

is the menace of violent *jihad* and a fear that Muslims (and Arabs) will destroy "Western civilization" and then take over the world (Said 1978, p. 287). These discourses, as Said notes, represent Muslims as systematically different from the "rational, developed, humane, superior" Westerners, while the Muslims and Arabs of the Orient are framed as "aberrant, undeveloped, inferior" (Said 1978, pp. 300–1). The Otherness of Muslims, as Said (1978) points out, is a narrative that judges a Muslim or Muslim group as inferior. This position requires an a priori assertion that the racialized Muslims actually have a core culture or a uniform way of expressing their Islamic beliefs and practices (Modood 2005, pp. 13–14). To assert such a shared cultural inferiority is hardly different from asserting a shared biological inferiority (Dunn et al. 2007, p. 567). . . .

Despite the heterogeneity of the American Muslim population, Muslims in the United States are racialized, meaning they are cast as a potentially threatening Other based on racial characteristics. Racialization, in this light, is a process by which American Muslims are identified and labeled through racial differentiation, such as genetics or skin color, and also through perceived cultural features such as religious symbols, like a beard or head covering. While Muslims are not a "race," they are examined through a racial process that is demarcated by physical features and racial underpinnings. In terms of "War on Terror" discourses, this can be seen "in the dichotomy between the benevolent, deviant masculinity of the 'brown man'" (Khalid 2011, p. 20). . . . Through this racialization, racism surfaces to demonize Muslims as "threats" who need to be handled through racial profiling, coercion, and violence.

. . . Islamophobia [is defined] as the unfounded and close-minded fear and/or hatred of Islam, Muslims or Islamic/Muslim culture. The definition identifies eight components as characteristic of Islamophobia in this sense:

Islam is seen as a monolithic bloc, static and unresponsive to change;

Islam is seen as separate and Other. It does not have values in common with other cultures, is not affected by them, and does not influence them;

Islam is seen as inferior to the West. It is barbaric, irrational, primitive, and sexist;

Islam is seen as violent, aggressive, threatening, supportive of terrorism, and engaged in a *clash of civilizations* (original emphasis);

Islam is seen as a political ideology and is used to acquire political or military advantage;

Criticism of the West by Muslims is rejected out of hand;

Hostility towards Islam is used to justify discriminatory practices towards Muslims and the exclusion of Muslims from mainstream society;

Anti-Muslim hostility is seen as natural or normal. . . . (Runnymede Trust 1997)

The notion that Islamophobia intersects with race is rooted in the idea that race is a social construct rather than a biological fact or reality. Race, a preeminently sociohistorical concept, is given concrete expression by the specific social relations and historical context in which they are embedded (Omi & Winant 1994). In terms of scientific data, experts conclude that there is no single gene or cluster common to various "races" such as Asian, Black, or White. Recent analyses of the human genome have established that human evolution has been recent, copious, and regional, meaning that races or racial identities are fluid rather than static (Wade 2014). As such, the 17th-century concept of defining race based on physical and generic variations is no longer accepted by most sociologists, anthropologists, and biologists. The science of race is now concerned with the social production of race, or what the *American Scientist* (2011) refers to race as "folk taxonomy, not science." While there are geographical differences in human biology, in light of vulnerabilities of particular diseases, we would be remiss to see the differences as meaningfully organized around race. Note carefully that these declarations do not claim that "there is no such thing as race." What scholars mean is that there is no "biological entity [that] warrants the term 'race'" (Brace 2000).

. . . . In the U.S. historical context, racial and religious minority communities have been objectified and exploited as "colored" men and women through racial classifications. This form of discrimination manifested in a direct and personalized prejudice by White Americans against different "races" (Welty 1989).

These "races" are People of Color who were literally prejudged—that is, they were judged before the relevant evidence about their abilities and interests were available to those who would come to judge them (Welty 1989). To reiterate, scholars might refer to "races," but it does not make them coherent biological realities. The approximately 1.8 billion Muslims worldwide do not carry genes for tribalism or violence, nor do they lack genes for freedom or democracy.

Though race and racism appear to be similar, they can be differentiated by a number of factors. Race is a way of classifying human beings based on perceived biological, cultural, and social relationships. Racism, on the other hand, is a way of treating others based on their "race." Racism has been defined as "the coordinated interaction of particular types of stereotypes, prejudices and discrimination" (Jones 1997). Jones further states that racism reflects the discrimination by individuals and institutions in ways that are justified by—and tend to perpetuate—negative beliefs, attitudes, and consequences. Escaping accusations of racism is a common tactic among certain critics of Islam. Those who fall under the umbrella of Islamophobia, for example, might see themselves not as racist or xenophobic, "but as defenders of democracy and human rights against the adherents of a religion they believe is incompatible with both" (Musharbash 2014). Racism and Islamophobia, as Hussain and Bagguley (2012, p. 4) explain, are "analytically distinct," but they also note that these two concepts are "empirically inter-related."

While biological racist discourses have declined, racism derived from perceptions of cultural and religious superiority has emerged as a dominant form of racism worldwide. These kinds of racisms do not even mention the word "race." They are focused on the cultural inferiority/superiority dichotomy of a group of people based on habits, beliefs, behaviors, or values. With increasing frequency, this kind of racism draws links between physical characteristics and perceived social customs, manners and behavior, religious and moral beliefs, as well as cultural practices, language, aesthetic values, and leisure activities (Halstead 1988). Islamophobia has been described as a type of racism that oppresses American Muslims on the grounds that their perceived "Islamic culture" is nefarious and that their "Islamic culture" is antithetical to "American culture." This kind of racism represents intolerance toward cultural and ethnic diversity as a whole, rather than Muslims alone (Welty 1989). Racism, in this context of cultural orientation or imagined cultures, involves prejudice or discrimination against individuals because of their perceived cultural preferences. This kind of "subliminal racism," or "racism without race," lacks a formal system of segregation and other forms of overt racism, but it does suggest a system of inequality, injustice, and racial differentiation (Cole 1997; Gilroy 1987; Hall 1992, pp. 256–58). Islam and American Muslims play a dominant role in these kinds of racist discourses. The contemporary tropes of Muslims as "uncivilized," "barbarian," "primitive," "authoritarian," and "terrorist" depict Islam as an inferior set of beliefs and cultural practices. These tropes are a repetition of older biological racist discourses.

. . . . The [reading] reinforces the racialization framework by arguing that in the United States, American Muslims have become victims of race-based violence through the construction of "visible archetype" of "Muslim identity," utilizing symbolic markers such as name, dress, phenotype, and language (Naber 2008). In the next section, three sets of findings are provided to examine the intersectionality of race and Islamophobia. The first section examines public opinion polls to reveal the extent of anti-Muslim sentiments in the United States. The second and third datasets use a content analysis of news articles that cover hate crimes against Muslims and the racial profiling of "Muslim-looking" people.

ISLAMOPHOBIA, HATE CRIMES, AND "FLYING WHILE BROWN"

A review of recent polls shows that the majority of non-Muslims in the United States have become increasingly hostile toward Muslims, paralleling the developing discourse among politicians and media outlets. The most recent compilation of Islamophobic hate crimes data by the CAIR (2017) shows that, between 2014 and 2016, anti-Muslim bias incidents increased by 65%. In 2016 alone, incidents of Islamophobia rose by 57% (Council on American-Islamic Relations 2017). CAIR's findings were similar

to data collected by the Center for the Study of Hate and Extremism (CSHE) at California State University San Bernardino, which accounted for 20 states and documented a total of 196 incidents in 2015 (Levin 2016b). This number is 29% higher than 2014's total of 154 for the entire nation, as tabulated by the FBI (Levin 2016b). These are levels not seen since the attacks of 9/11, a year that recorded 481 anti-Muslim hate crimes (Levin 2016b). The largest previous increase after 2001 was in 2010, when anti-Muslim hate crimes rose from 107 to 160, an increase of 49.5%, amid the controversy over the "Ground Zero mosque" in New York City (Levin 2016b). Anti-Muslim attacks are not only rising in total numbers, but as a percentage of overall hate crimes (Lichtblau 2016).

Out of all religious groups in the United States, Americans view atheists and Muslims most coldly (Pew Research Center 2014). In 2015, unfavorable attitudes toward American Muslims rose to a high of 67% (Arab American Institute 2015). A YouGov/Huffington Post survey on Americans' views of Muslims show that 55% of those polled had "a somewhat or very unfavorable view" of Islam, while one in four said they were not sure how they viewed the faith (Kaleem 2015). Of the Americans who were surveyed in the YouGov/ Huffington Post poll, only one in 10 said they had ever visited a mosque, and 44% said they would not want to learn more about Islam. In addition to their broadly unfavorable views of Islam, a large percentage (42%) of Americans believe that law enforcement agencies are justified in using racial profiling tactics against Muslims and Arabs (Siddiqui 2014). These trends inevitably contribute to Islamophobic discourse and sentiment. Furthermore, Zogby Analytics, an advocacy group, found the favorability toward Muslims living in the United States was just 27%, compared with 36% in 2010 (Siddiqui 2014). The Zogby poll also found that a growing number of Americans doubt that Muslims or Arabs would be able to perform in a government post without their ethnicity or religion affecting their work (Siddiqui 2014). Finally, anti-Islam and anti-Muslim sentiment is more common among Americans who are 45 and older, those who are Republican, and those who are White (Chalabi 2015). The Americans who voice an unfavorable opinion of Islam may have sympathized with Donald Trump's call for a "total and complete shutdown on Muslims entering the United States" during the 2016 presidential election (Johnson 2015).

While attitudes toward Islam and Muslims should be considered separately, studies suggest that the two overlap considerably, as many people fail to distinguish between the two (Chalabi 2015). According to a poll conducted by Telhami (2015), Americans do differentiate between Muslims and Islam, and they view Islam more unfavorably than they do Muslims. This may have many reasons, but at the core, it is probably easier for Americans to express dislike of an abstract idea (Islam) rather than to appear prejudiced toward people (Muslims) (Telhami 2015). Despite claims that the United States has entered a "post-racial era," racial profiling, a discriminatory practice, occurs every day in cities and towns across the country, when law enforcement and private security target people of color (American Civil Liberties Union n.d.). According to the American Civil Liberties Union (ACLU), this policing tactic is patently illegal because it violates the U.S. Constitution's core promises of equal protection under the law to all, as well as freedom from unreasonable searches and seizures (American Civil Liberties Union n.d.).

HATE CRIMES

A hate crime is understood as "a criminal offense motivated in whole or in part by the actual or perceived group status of another, such as race and ethnicity, religion, disability, sexual orientation, gender and gender identity" (Levin 2016a). According to this definition, an anti-Muslim hate crime constitutes a form of religious hate crime, although these hate crimes can also be understood as a "race hate crime" or as hate that is politically motivated. A persistent difficulty, of course, is that such neat distinctions often break down in the real world (Copsey et al. 2013, p. 6). In reality, the distinction between "religion hate crime" and "race hate crime" can often become blurred, making conceptual and reporting clarity difficult (Copsey et al. 2013, p. 6).

What is more transparent is that hateful rhetoric toward American Muslims has consequences. When a significant number of Americans hold unfavorable views of Islam and Muslims, it can hardly be a surprise, as the Southern Poverty Law Center (SPLC) (2016) points out, that some percentage of them engage in hate crime attacks. Since 9/11, American Muslims, and those living in the United States who are perceived to be Muslims, have faced a spike in racially and religiously motivated hate crimes. A May 2017 report by CAIR showed that hate crimes against Muslims in the United States rose dramatically in 2016, just as they did in 2015 (Pitter 2017).

Key findings in the report highlight how Islamophobic bias has continued its trend toward increasing violence (Council on American-Islamic Relations 2017). In 2016, CAIR recorded a 57% increase in anti-Muslim bias incidents over 2015, which was accompanied by a 44% increase in anti-Muslim hate crimes in the same period. Harassment (a nonviolent or nonthreatening bias incident) was the most frequent type of abuse in 2016, accounting for 18% of the total number of incidents. According to FBI statistics, the number of hate crimes against Muslims, as of 2015, had stabilized at approximately five times the pre-9/11 rate (Ingraham 2015). The number of anti-Muslim hate crimes incidents in the United States is likely higher than the numbers documented in the 2016 CAIR report. American Muslims, the organization wrote, "will often not report incidents such as harassment and bullying since there is a certain level of desensitization." CAIR added that some American Muslims often feel like "nothing can be done" when they are harassed for their faith, feeling that such incidents "have become normal" (Mathias 2017).

What is thought provoking about the prevalence of anti-Muslim hate crimes is that they have not been limited to Muslims. Readers do not need to look far in our time to find people being targeted for "looking Muslim." The case of Cameron Mohammed is notable for being one of the most explicit examples of how the racialization of Islam leads to Islamophobic hate crimes (Goeman 2013). Mohammed, a Florida resident, was shot repeatedly with a pellet gun outside of a Walmart in 2013 (Orlando & Sullivan 2013). The assailant explicitly asked Mohammed if he was in fact a Muslim or from the Middle East; when he answered negatively, the attack did not stop (Goeman 2013). The assailant's remarks to the police after the incident reveal his real motive. When deputies told the assailant that his victim was not Muslim, he told them he did not care, that "they're all the same." In this case, "they" (or "Muslim-looking people") are painted as a monolith. Mohammed's physical appearance, in particular his skin tone, was connected with a social identity (Muslim or Arab). The discrimination that he experienced reinforced a racial identity that was linked to Islam.

Because many U.S. citizens perceive them as threatening and inferior, American Muslims endure regular expressions of hostility in public places, particularly U.S. airports. Selod (2014) interviewed 48 South Asian and Arab Americans about their experiences pre- and post-9/11 in Chicago and the Dallas/Fort Worth area between 2009 and 2012. Her research found that the association of Islam with terror, violence, and the oppression of women contribute to a process of racialized governmentality at airports, which conveys the message that American Muslims are a threat to national security and require careful monitoring and surveillance. This process of racialized governmentality regularly targets Muslims at U.S. airports and has led to many American Muslim men and women being treated with suspicion.

Non-Muslims, too, have been impacted by racial profiling and the racialization of Islam. In May 2016, Guido Menzio, a decorated Ivy League economist from Italy, was removed from an American Airlines flight because his seatmate expressed concerns after seeing him writing math equations in a notebook before the plane's take-off. Menzio, who was described by a passenger as having "dark, curly hair, olive skin and an exotic foreign accent," was taken off the plane for questioning (Danner 2016). Authorities told him he had been suspected of terrorism. Menzio's case is an instance of racial profiling of airline passengers whose skin color, actions, or speech make airline passengers and flight attendants think they are Muslim. His experience highlights the way that internalized racial bias against Islam and Muslims can lead to the perception that U.S. Muslims pose a security treat.

In light of Menzio's experience, Chu (2015) argues that it is hypocritical to say that Islamophobia is a simple consequence of "rational disagreement" with the tenets of Islam rather than xenophobic distrust of people who look different from "normal" Americans.

Chu's point becomes clearer when we see how much of Islamophobia falls on Sikhs. Sikh communities across the United States have been victims of hate crimes perpetrated by Americans. Reports of incidents in the immediate aftermath of 9/11 and concerns that hate crimes would rise prompted the founding of the Sikh Coalition, now the largest Sikh advocacy and civil rights organization in the country (Basu 2016). In the first month after 9/11, the Coalition documented more than 300 cases of violence and discrimination against Sikhs in the United States (Basu 2016). Fifteen years after 9/11, many Sikhs say they feel no safer in the country, primarily because of the continued confusion between Sikhs and Islam (Basu 2016). Ultimately, linking such features of "Muslim-ness" means that people who are not Muslim are also subjected to violence as a result of the racialization of Islam.

Those who attack Sikhs do not appear to care much about such fine distinctions as Sikhism and Islam being two different religions. In September 2001, Balibar Singh Sodhi was shot and killed outside of his Mesa, Arizona, gas station by Frank Roque, a U.S. citizen who told law enforcement he wanted to "kill a Muslim" in retaliation for the attacks on 9/11 (Sikh American Legal Defense and Education Fund 2011). According to one prominent Sikh advocacy group, Sodhi was selected by Roque because he had a beard and wore a turban in accordance with his Sikh faith (Sikh American Legal Defense and Education Fund 2011). Although the Sikh turban signifies commitment to upholding freedom, justice, and dignity for all people, "the physical appearance of a Sikh is often ignorantly conflated with images of foreign [Muslim] terrorists, some of whom also wear turbans and many of whom have received copious publicity in our mainstream media in the post-9/11 environment" (Sikh Coalition 2012). In Roque's case, he confused Sodhi's long beard and turban as a representation of Islam. He then effectively used Sodhi's "race" to categorize and ultimately harm him in the worst way imaginable—murder.

Sodhi's murder is not an isolated case; two other examples alert us to the racialization of Islam and its connection to hate crimes against non-Muslims in the United States. In December 2015, a robber shot an Indian store clerk in Grand Rapids, Iowa. The clerk, a non-Muslim from the Punjab in India, was shot in the face after the assailant called him a "terrorist" (McVicar 2015). Indeed, terms such as "terrorist," "*jihad,*" and "*sharia*" are elements of a widely used Islamophobic lexicon. These components of bias comprise a structure of Muslim-hating that depicts Muslims as the visibly identifiable Other (Singh 2016). In another incident in September 2013, a highly accomplished Sikh doctor was attacked while walking near Central Park in New York City. He had a long beard and wore a turban (Basu 2016). The victim, Prabhjot Singh, heard someone yell: "Terrorist, Osama, get him!" In American public discourse, the name "Osama" is popularly linked to Osama bin Laden, the "terrorist extremist" who allegedly planned the 9/11 attacks. Singh eventually ran from his attacker, but not fast enough. A group of boys and young men on bicycles taunted him using racial slurs (Basu 2016). One pulled his beard and then the attackers punched and kicked him repeatedly (Basu 2016). Singh's attackers conflated religion and race such that religion—in this case Islam—became the inherently "defining criterion" of Muslim identity (Bayoumi 2006, p. 278). Thus, the "visible archetype" became attached to a Sikh, such that religious, ethnic, cultural, and national differences are transformed into racial differences (Naber 2008).

The conflation of Muslims and Sikhs shows how shallow Islamophobia can be—Sikhism does not share Islam's Abrahamic lineage and has no direct connection to Islam, unlike Judaism or Christianity. Sikhs also do not originate from anywhere in the Middle East, but from the Punjab region of India (Chu 2015). Nevertheless, Sikhs are conflated with Muslims for the oversimplified reason that the turban—one of the most common forms of headgear in the world—is associated with the Middle East and ultimately Islam. While turbans are commonplace in many Muslim-majority countries, there is no similar requirement to wear a turban in the Islamic tradition. These hate crimes against Sikhs suggest that one does not actually have to be a Muslim in any theological or cultural sense to be singled out for an Islamophobic assault (Goeman 2013). Rather, what matters is how one expresses their culture, how one looks, and whether those "looks" are conflated in a negative manner with Islam and Muslims.

The data presented on hate crimes against American Muslims and non-Muslims in the United States demonstrate how Islamophobic incidents result from, and contribute to, the idea that "Muslim identity" has racial underpinnings (Samari 2016, p. 1921). Although Sikhs and other "Muslim-looking" people continue to experience hate crimes on account of their identity, the FBI has recently begun to track hate crimes against Sikhs (Sikh Coalition 2015). The Sikh Coalition claims that officially categorizing hate crimes against Sikhs is imperative "because it is impossible to address a problem unless it is being accurately measured" (Sikh Coalition 2012, p. 3). The next section, which examines racial profiling at the institutional level, sheds further light on the idea that race serves as a symbolic form of Islamophobia.

"FLYING WHILE BROWN"

Racial profiling has been defined as "any use of race, religion, ethnicity or national origin by law enforcement agents as a means of deciding who should be investigated" (Leadership Conference Education Fund n.d., p. 11). Under this definition, "racial profiling does not only occur when race is the sole criterion used by a law enforcement agent in determining who to investigate" (Leadership Conference Education Fund n.d., p. 11). Racial profiling heightened with the 2001 Patriot Act and associated legislation, which gave the state new powers to categorize Muslims or "Muslim-like" Americans. The Patriot Act legislation not only contributed to social segregation and differential access to resources (Love 2009), but also effectively "securitized" Muslims such that they became defined as a unique security threat (Hussain & Bagguley 2012). To account for these kinds of institutional security measures, Larsson and Sander (2015, p. 16) use the term *structural* or *institutional Islamophobia*, that is . . . those established laws, customs and practices which systematically reflect and produce inequalities in society between Muslims and non-Muslims. If such inequalities accrue to institutional law, customs, or practices, an institution is Islamophobic whether or not the individuals maintaining those practices have Islamophobic intentions (Richardson 2004, p. 14).

According to this definition, institutional Islamophobia is "distinct from the attitudinal Islamophobia of individuals in being caused by the existence of systematic, pervasive and habitual policies and practices that have the effect of disadvantaging certain racial, religious, or ethnic groups" (Larsson & Sander 2015, p. 16). At the institutional level, programs such as the National Security Entry–Exit Registration System (NSEERS) target Muslims on the basis of their names and national origins rather than religion (Bayoumi 2006). This practice of racial profiling perpetuates "a logic that demands the ability to define what a Muslims looks like from appearance and visual cues" (Rana 2007, p. 149). Because Muslims are often represented as coming from non-White groups, their religious identity becomes linked to their racial identity (Samari 2016, p. 1921). As the author previously highlighted, Islamophobia affects the lives of people with "Muslim-like" appearances in the United States (Samari 2016, p. 1921).

Racial profiling systems in the United States have targeted South Asians, presumably focusing on their perceived racial, ethnic, and religious similarities to the 9/11 hijackers (Chandrasekhar 2003, p. 215). One highly visible and contested manifestation of post–9/11 race-based discrimination has been the widespread increase in airlines' disparate treatment of people of South Asian descent and those individuals who "look Muslim" (Chandrasekhar 2003, p. 216). Since 9/11, airlines have racially profiled "brown, Muslim-like" passengers and subjected them to heightened security screening in the belief that ethnicity or national origin increases passengers' risk of carrying out an act of terrorism (Chandrasekhar 2003, p. 216). In January 2016, for example, an American Airlines attendant kicked four Brooklyn men off a flight for "looking too Muslim"—claiming their appearance made the captain "uneasy" (Carrega-Woodby 2016). Passengers surrounding the men allegedly made racist comments and clutched their children "as if something was going to happen," a lawsuit charges. The four men—two Bangladeshi Muslims, an Arab Muslim, and a Sikh from India—were all ordered off the flight. All of the men have a darker skin complexion; one wears a turban and another has a beard. One man—who communicated by the pseudonym

M. K.—asked the agent if they were thrown off because of their appearance. The agent said their appearance "did not help," according to the lawsuit. Put another way, the detained individuals were "passing" as people who were thought to be Muslim based on a racialized meaning of "Muslim identity." This discriminatory treatment of racial profiling reveals the way that internalized racism against Muslims can lead to the perception that Muslims are a threat (Credo Action n.d.). It also is clear that airline staff may not have adequate skills to protect the rights of passengers who are being racially profiled.

There is a common misperception that all Muslims are the same and all Muslims are Arabs. Muslim, however, does not mean Arab. Moghul (2016) makes this point while discussing a Muslim airline passenger and Iraqi asylee, Khairuldeen Makhzoomi, who was removed from a Southwest Airlines flight because his appearance reportedly set off "alarm bells." According to a Southwest Airlines (2016) statement, Makhzoomi triggered anxiety among other passengers by speaking Arabic. The crew reported the situation to law enforcement agencies to prevent any threat to civil aviation and later requested that Makhzoomi leave the aircraft. Makhzoomi also had a beard and a generically Middle Eastern appearance, which allegedly contributed to the anxiety of the plane's passengers. The willingness to communicate publicly in a language (Arabic) associated with Islam, as well as "looking Muslim," is correlated with being "religiously Muslim" (Moghul 2016). The common thread in these cases of racial profiling seems to be that anyone who does not conform to the standardized appearance of an "American" is made to feel like a criminal. Nor is what happened to these men and others a mere misunderstanding or mistake; it can be viewed as racism based on profiling (Dharas 2016). This kind of racism involves the subordination of People of Color based on institutions that enforce or extend people's personal dislike or mistrust of individuals and groups such as Muslims or those perceived to be Muslims. The implication of these incidents is that Muslims are depicted as "radicalized," or potentially so, and that they present a "security threat" to American society because they "look Muslim."

. . . To be clear, racial profiling on airlines does not attack Islamic theology, but rather Muslim people or people perceived to be Muslim. In this light, racial profiling is not based solely on ideas about Islam, but rather on the color and physical appearance associated with Muslims. It is worth noting that, under current laws, an airline "may not subject a person in air transportation to discrimination on the basis of race, color, national origin, religion, sex, or ancestry" (United States Government 2016). The Department of Transportation is authorized to prevent and seek redress for acts of discrimination (Khan 2016). Given the increasing frequency of, and seemingly arbitrary grounds for, the removal of Muslims and passengers whom others perceive to be Muslim from domestic airlines, it is clear that the Department of Transportation needs to act to counter Islamophobia.

CONCLUSIONS

The findings presented in this [reading] suggest that race is a symbolic form of Islamophobia. According to Allen (2010, p. 189), symbolic forms of Islamophobia are relayed, produced, and constructed before being disseminated through incidents of anti-Muslim discrimination. The incidents examined here suggest that Islamophobia does not belong in the realm of "rational" criticism of Islam or Muslims; it is often discrimination against people who look different to the majority of U.S. citizens. The manifestation of Islamophobia in the United States also often fuses racial and religious bias, largely because the stereotypical Muslim has been constructed as an ominous figure: the bearded, dark-skinned, turban-wearing terrorist guided by perceived archaic religious practices (Singh 2016). The production of Muslims as "visible archetypes" sustains and perpetuates negatively evaluated meanings about Islam and Muslims in the United States. Race, therefore, shapes and determines the perception of Muslims, which then informs and constructs thinking about Islam as "Other" (Allen 2010, p. 190). Racism against Muslims and non-Muslims in the United States, as this [reading] highlights, plays out at the social/interactional as well as institutional level. While anti-Muslim racism often unfolds in everyday interactions between Muslims and non-Muslims, institutionalized power struggles in the United States are key to exacerbating Islamophobia (Allen 2010, p. 188).

Hate crimes against American Muslims and those perceived to be Muslim have created circumstances of second-class citizenship, whereby Muslims and groups linked to Islam see their safety and freedoms limited in the United States. Taking a "colorblind" understanding of Islamophobia—that is, to dismiss the role that race plays in anti-Muslim racism—legitimizes certain racialized practices and maintains inequalities such as racial profiling at airports, police brutality, housing and job discrimination, and voter disenfranchisement (Bonilla-Silva 2013). The Department of Justice (2011) has started to take measures to protect Muslims, as well as members of the Arab, Sikh, and South Asian communities, from threats and violence directed at them because of their race and religion. Identifying the impact that racialization has in hate crimes and institutional racial profiling illuminates a major impediment to building a more pluralist society, one in which people are judged by the content of their character instead of their racial or religious backgrounds. Moreover, following Hopkins (2004, pp. 268–69), improving public understanding of Islam and "Muslim identity," as well as expanding public recognition of American Muslims outside of stereotypical depictions of "Muslim identity," might lead to a decrease in hate crime incidents and racial profiling. Going forward, advocacy groups and organizations could do more to incorporate race and racialized processes in their approach to understanding and combatting Islamophobia. By noting the impact of race and racialization on Islamophobic incidents, these entities can help American Muslims secure their civil rights protections. Whether the term *Islamophobia* captures the endemic suspicion and vilification of Americans Muslims is a promising and important area of inquiry in terms of future research.

In summary, American Muslims can be simultaneously profiled in terms of race and religion. While it might appear that traditional Islamophobic arguments are more likely to come in the form of abuse on the basis of religion, we would be misguided to ignore the role that race plays in incidents where Muslims and non-Muslims are targeted due to stereotypes of "Muslim identity." "Muslim identity," as far as the American context goes, appears to be weighted with racial meaning.

REFERENCES

Ali, Wajahat. 2011. Exposing the Islamophobia Network in America. *The Huffington Post.* August 29. Available online: http://www.huffingtonpost.com/wajahat-ali/exposing-the-islamophobia_b_938777.html (accessed on 8 July 2017).

Allen, Chris. 2010. *Islamophobia.* Farnham, UK: Ashgate.

Alsultany, Evelyn. 2015. Muslims Are Facing a Civil Rights Crisis in America, and It's the Media's Fault. *The Washington Post.* November 11. Available online: https://www.washingtonpost.com/news/in-theory/wp/2015/11/11/muslims-are-facing-a-civil-rights-crisis-in-america/?utm_term=.761f9b9d4bbe (accessed on 8 July 2017).

American Civil Liberties Union. n.d. Racial Profiling. Available online: https://www.aclu.org/issues/racial-justice/race-and-criminal-justice/racial-profiling (accessed on 8 December 2016).

American Scientist. 2011. *Is Race Real?* Available online: http://www.americanscientist.org/issues/pub/2011/4/is-race-real (accessed on 19 November 2016).

Arab American Institute. 2015. American Attitudes towards Arabs and Muslims: 2015. Available online: http://www.aaiusa.org/american_attitudes_toward_arabs_and_muslims_2015 (accessed on 5 November 2016).

Basu, Moni. 2016. 15 years after 9/11, Sikhs still victims of anti-Muslim hate crimes. *CNN.* September 15. Available online: http://www.cnn.com/2016/09/15/us/sikh-hate-crime-victims (accessed on 19 November 2016).

Bayoumi, Moustafa. 2006. Racing Religion. *The New Centennial Review* 6: 267–93.

Bonilla-Silva, Eduardo. 2013. *Racism without Racists: Color-Blind Racism and the Persistence of Racial Inequality in America.* Lanham, MD: Rowman & Littlefield.

Brace, Loring. 2000. Does Race Exist? *Public Broadcasting Service.* November 20. Available online: http://www.pbs.org/wgbh/nova/evolution/does-race-exist.html (accessed on 27 October 2016).

Bradner, Erik. 2015. Ben Carson: U.S. Shouldn't Elect a Muslim President. *CNN.* September 20. Available online: http://www.cnn.com/2015/09/20/politics/ben-carson-muslim-president-2016/ (accessed on 25 November 2016).

Carrega-Woodby, Christina. 2016. Four Brooklyn Men Claim They Were Kicked off Flight for Looking Too Muslim in Lawsuit. *New York Daily News.* January 18. Available online: http://www.nydailynews.com/new-york/lawsuit-claims-flight-ejected-men-muslim-article-1.2499843 (accessed on 22 October 2016).

Chalabi, Mona. 2015. How Anti-Muslim Are Americans? Data Points to Extent of Islamophobia. *The Guardian.* December 8. Available online: https://www.theguardian.com/us-news/2015/dec/08/muslims-us-islam-islamophobia-data-polls (accessed on 19 November 2016).

Chandrasekhar, Charu A. 2003. Flying While Brown: Federal Civil Rights Remedies to Post-9/11 Airline Racial Profiling of South Asians. *Asian American Legal Journal* 10: 215–52.

Chu, Arthur. 2015. Targeting for "Looking Muslim": The Dawkins/Harris Worldview and a Twisted New Hypocrisy Which Feeds Racism. *Salon.* March 12. Available online: http://www.salon.com/2015/03/12/targeted_for_looking_muslim_the_dawkinsharris_worldview_and_a_twisted_new_hypocrisy_which_feeds_racism (accessed on 22 October 2016).

Cole, Jeffrey. 1997. *The New Racism in Europe.* Cambridge: Cambridge University Press.

Copsey, Nigel, Janet Dack, Mark Littler, and Matthew Feldman. 2013. Anti-Muslim Hate Crime and the Far Right. Teeside University. Available online: https://www.tees.ac.uk/docs/DocRepo/Research/Copsey_report3.pdf (accessed on 19 November 2016).

Council on American-Islamic Relations (CAIR). 2016. *Confront Fear: Islamophobia and Its Impact in the United States (2016 Report).* Washington, DC: Council on American-Islamic Relations.

Council on American-Islamic Relations (CAIR). 2017. The Empowerment of Hate: The Civil Rights Implications of Islamophobic Bias in the U.S. 2014–2016. Available online: http://www.islamophobia.org/15-reports/188-the-empowerment-of-hate.html (accessed on 8 July 2017).

Credo Action. n.d. Anti-Muslim Racial Profiling on Planes Must Stop. Available online: http://act.credoaction.com/sign/Stop_Airline_Profiling (accessed on 20 November 2016).

Danner, Chas. 2016. Flight Delayed, Economist Questioned After Doing Math While Looking Middle Eastern. *New York Magazine*. May 7. Available online: http://nymag.com/daily/intelligencer/2016/05/economist-profiled-after-doing-math-on-plane.html (accessed on 24 August 2017).

Department of Justice. 2011. Protect the Civil Rights of American Muslims Outreach and Enforcement Efforts. Available online: https://www.justice.gov/opa/blog/protect-civil-rights-american-muslims-outreach-and-enforcement-efforts (accessed on 8 December 2016).

Dharas, Maryam. 2016. I Was Escorted off a Flight due to Racist Profiling. Britain Must Banish This Bigotry. *The Guardian*. August 25. Available online: https://www.theguardian.com/commentisfree/2016/aug/25/racist-profiling-bigotry-headscarf-flight (accessed on 20 November 2016).

Dunn, Kevin M., Natascha Klocker, and Tanya Salabay. 2007. Contemporary Racism and Islamophobia in Australia: Racializing Religion. *Ethnicities* 7: 564–89.

European Islamophobia Report. 2017. *European Islamophobia Report 2016*. April. Available online: http://www.islamophobiaeurope.com/ (accessed on 8 July 2017).

Gilroy, Paul. 1987. *There Ain't No Black in the Union Jack: The Cultural Politics of Race and Nation*. London: Hutchinson.

Goeman, Stephen. 2013. Islamophobia Is a Racism. *The Huffington Post*. March 12. Available online: http://www.huffingtonpost.com/stephen-goeman/islamophobia-is-a-racism_b_2428792.html (accessed on 11 October 2016).

Hafez, Farid. 2014. Shifting Borders: Islamophobia as Common Ground for Building Pan-European Right-Wing Unity. *Patterns of Prejudice* 48(5):479–99.

Hall, Stuart. 1992. New Ethnicities. In *"Race," Culture and Difference*. Edited by James Donald and Ali Rattansi. Thousand Oaks, CA: Sage, pp. 252–59.

Halstead, Mark. 1988. *Education Justice and Cultural Diversity: An Examination of the Honeyford Affair*. London: London Farmer Press.

Hopkins, Peter E. 2004. Young Muslim men in Scotland: Inclusions and Exclusions. *Children's Geographies* 2: 257–72.

Hussain, Yasmin, and Paul Bagguley. 2012. Securitized Citizens: Islamophobia, Racism and the 7/7 London Bombings. *The Sociological Review* 60: 715–34.

Ingraham, Christopher. 2015. Anti-Muslim Hate Crimes Are Still Five Times More Common Today Than before 9/11. *The Washington Post*. February 11. Available online: https://www.washingtonpost.com/news/wonk/wp/2015/02/11/anti-muslim-hate-crimes-are-still-five-times-more-common-today-than-before-911/ (accessed on 11 October 2016).

Johnson, Jenna. 2015. Trump Calls for "Total and Complete Shutdown of Muslims Entering the United States." *The Washington Post*. December 7. Available online: https://www.washingtonpost.com/news/post-politics/wp/2015/12/07/donald-trump-calls-for-total-and-complete-shutdown-of-muslims-entering-the-united-states/?utm_term=.b45a49448f1d (accessed on 8 December 2016).

Jones, James M. 1997. *Prejudice and Racism*. New York: McGraw-Hill.

Kaleem, Jaweed. 2015. More Than Half of Americans Have Unfavorable View of Islam, Poll Finds. *The Huffington Post*. April 10. Available online: http://www.huffingtonpost.com/2015/04/10/americans-islam-poll_n_7036574.html (accessed on 19 November 2016).

Kearns, Eric M., Allison Betus, and Anthony Lemieux. 2017a. Yes, the Media Do Underreport Some Terrorist Attacks. Just not the Ones Most People Think Of. *The Washington Post*. March 13. Available online: https://www.washingtonpost.com/news/monkey-cage/wp/2017/03/13/yes-the-media-do-underreport-some-terrorist-attacks-just-not-the-ones-most-people-think-of/?utm_term=.88d3b539de96 (accessed on 8 July 2017).

Kearns, Eric M., Allison Betus, and Anthony Lemieux. 2017b. Why Do Some Terrorist Attacks Receive More Media Attention Than Others. *Social Science Research Network*. March 7. Available online: https://papers.ssrn.com/sol3/papers.cfm?abstract_id=2928138 (accessed on 8 July 2017).

Khalid, Maryam. 2011. Gender, Orientalism and Representations of the "Other" in the War on Terror. *Global Change, Peace and Security* 23: 15–29.

Khan, Fatima. 2016. Muslim Advocates and the NAACP Legal Defense Fund Pen Letter to US Department of Transportation Urging Immediate Action to Prevent Profiling of Airline Passengers. *Muslim Advocates*. Available online: https://www.muslimadvocates.org/muslim-advocates-and-the-naacp-legal-defense-fund-pen-letter-to-us-department-of-transportation-urging-immediate-action-to-prevent-profiling-of-airline-passengers/ (accessed on 20 November 2016).

Larsson, Göran, and Åke Sander. 2015. An Urgent Need to Consider How to Define Islamophobia. *Bulletin for the Study of Religion* 44: 13–17.

Leadership Conference Education Fund. n.d. Wrong Then, Wrong Now: Racial Profiling Before & After September 11, 2001. *Civil Rights*. Available online: http://www.civilrights.org/publications/wrong-then/racial_profiling_report.pdf (accessed on 22 October 2016).

Lean, Nathan. 2012. *The Islamophobia Industry: How the Right Manufactures Fear of Muslims*. London: Pluto Press.

Levin, Brian. 2016a. FBI: Hate Crime Went Up 6.8 Percent In 2015; Anti-Muslim Incidents Surge To Second Highest Ever. *The Huffington Post*. November 13. Available online: http://www.huffingtonpost.com/brian-levin-jd/fbi-hate-crime-up-68-in-2_b_12951150.html (accessed on 19 November 2016).

Levin, Brian. 2016b. *Special Status Report: Hate Crime in the United States (20 State Compilation of Official Data)*. San Bernardino: Center for the Study of Hate & Extremism at the California State University, Available online: https://www.documentcloud.org/documents/3110202-SPECIAL-STATUS-REPORT-v5-9-16-16.html (accessed on 8 July 2017).

Lichtblau, Eric. 2016. Hate Crimes against American Muslims Most since Post-9/11 Era. *The New York Times*. September 17. Available online: https://www.nytimes.com/2016/09/18/us/politics/hate-crimes-american-muslims-rise.html (accessed on 8 July 2017).

Love, Erik. 2009. Confronting Islamophobia in the United States: Framing Civil Rights Activism among Middle Eastern Americans. *Patterns of Prejudice* 43: 401–25.

Mathias, C. 2017. 2016 Election Coincided with Horrifying Increase in Anti-Muslim Hate Crimes, Report Finds. *The Huffington Post*. Available online: http://www.huffingtonpost.com/entry/anti-muslim-hate-crimes-2016-council-on-american-islamic-relations_us_5910acf4e4b0d5d9049e96d5 (accessed on 24 August 2017).

McVicar, Brian. 2015. Robber Called Store Clerk "Terrorist" before Shooting Him in Face, Worker Says. *Mlive*. December 14. Available online: http://www.mlive.com/news/grand-rapids/index.ssf/2015/12/robber_called_store_clerk_terr.html (accessed on 11 October 2016).

Media Tenor International. 2011. *A New Era for Arab-Western Relations—Media Analysis*. New York: Media Tenor.

Media Tenor International. n.d. Coverage of American Muslims Gets Worse. *Media Tenor*. Available online: http://us.mediatenor.com/en/library/speeches/260/coverage-of-american-muslims-gets-worse (accessed on 7 July 2017).

Modood, Tariq. 2005. *Multicultural Politics: Racism, Ethnicity and Muslims in Britain*. Minneapolis: University of Minnesota Press, Edinburgh: University of Edinburgh Press.

Moghul, Haroon. 2016. The Unapologetic Racial Profiling of Muslims Has Become America's New Normal. *Quartz*. April 20. Available online: http://qz.com/665317/the-unapologetic-racial-profiling-of-muslims-has-become-americas-new-normal/ (accessed on 20 November 2016).

Mohamed, Besheer. 2016. A New Estimate of the U.S. Muslim Population. *Pew Research Center*. January 6. Available online: http://www.pewresearch.org/fact-tank/2016/01/06/a-new-estimate-of-the-u-s-muslim-population/ (accessed on 5 November 2016).

Musharbash, Yassin. 2014. Islamophobia Is Racism, Pure and Simple. *The Guardian*. December 10. Available online: https://www.theguardian.com/commentisfree/2014/dec/10/islamophobia-racism-dresden-protests-germany-islamisation (accessed on 24 August 2017).

Naber, Nadine. 2008. "Look, Mohammed the Terrorist Is Coming!": Cultural Racism, Nation-Based Racism, and Intersectionality of Oppressions after 9/11. In *Race and Arab Americans Before and After 9/11: From Invisible Citizens to Visible Subjects*. Edited by Amaney Jamal and Nadine Naber. Syracuse, NY: Syracuse University Press, pp. 276–304.

National Public Radio (NPR). 2017. When Is It "Terrorism"? How the Media Cover Attacks by Muslim Perpetrators. *National Public Radio (NPR)*. June 19. Available online: http://www.npr.org/2017/06/19/532963059/when-is-it-terrorism-how-the-media-covers-attacks-by-muslim-perpetrators?utm_campaign=storyshare&utm_source=twitter.com&utm_medium=social (accessed on 8 July 2017).

Omi, Michael, and Howard Winant. 1994. *Racial Formation in the United States: From the 1960s to the 1990s*. New York: Routledge.

Orlando, Alex, and Erin Sullivan. 2013. Victim in Pasco hate crime had gun, decided not to use it. *Tampa Bay Times*. January 4. Available online: http://www.tampabay.com/news/publicsafety/crime/victim-in-pasco-hate-crime-had-gun-decided-not-to-use-it/1268955 (accessed on 11 October 2016).

Patton, Michael Quinn. 2002. *Qualitative Research and Evaluation Methods*. Thousand Oaks, CA: Sage.

Pew Research Center. 2007. Converts to Islam. *The Pew Research Center*. July 21. Available online: http://www.pewresearch.org/fact-tank/2007/07/21/converts-to-islam/ (accessed on 7 July 2017).

Pew Research Center. 2014. How Americans Feel about Religious Groups. *The Pew Forum*. July 16. Available online: http://www.pewforum.org/2014/07/16/how-americans-feel-about-religious-groups/ (accessed on 19 November 2016).

Pew Research Center. 2011. Section 1: A Demographic Portrait of Muslim Americans. *The Pew Research Center*. August 30. Available online: http://www.people-press.org/2011/08/30/section-1-a-demographic-portrait-of-muslim-americans/ (accessed on 5 November 2016).

Pew Research Center. n.d. Human Coding of News Media. *The Pew Research Center*. Available online: http://www.pewresearch.org/methodology/about-content-analysis/human-coding-of-news-media/ (accessed on 7 July 2017).

Pitter, Laura. 2017. Hate Crimes Against Muslims in US Continue to Rise in 2016. *Human Rights Watch*. May 11. Available online: https://www.hrw.org/news/2017/05/11/hate-crimes-against-muslims-us-continue-rise-2016 (accessed on 8 July 2017).

Poynting, Scott, and Victoria Mason. 2006. Tolerance, Freedom, Justice and Peace? Britain, Australia, and anti-Muslim racism since 11 September 2001. *Journal of Intercultural Studies* 27: 61–86.

Rana, Junaid. 2007. The Story of Islamophobia. *Souls* 9: 148–61.

Richardson, Robin, ed. 2004. *Islamophobia, Issues, Challenges and Action: A Report by the Commission on British Muslims and Islamophobia*. Stoke-on-Trent, UK: Trentham Books.

Rifai, Ryan. 2016. Report: Islamophobia Is a Multimillion-Dollar Industry. *Al Jazeera*. June 24. Available online: www.aljazeera.com/indepth/features/2016/06/report-islamophobia-multi-million-dollar-industry-160623144006495.html (accessed on 8 July 2017).

Runnymede Trust 1997. Islamophobia—A Challenge for all of us. Available online: https://www.runnymedetrust.org/companies/17/74/Islamophobia-A-Challenge-for-Us-All.html.

Said, Edward W. 1978. *Orientalism*. New York: Vintage Books.

Said, Edward W. 1985. Orientalism Reconsidered. *Race and Class* 27: 1–15.

Saldana, Johnny. 2009. *The Coding Manual for Qualitative Researchers*. London: Sage Publications.

Samari, Goleen. 2016. Islamophobia and Public Health in the United States. *American Journal of Public Health* 106: 1920–5. [PubMed]

Saylor, Corey. 2014. The U.S. Islamophobia Network: Its Funding and Impact. *Islamophobia Studies Journal 2:* 99–118. Available online: http://crg.berkeley.edu/sites/default/files/Network-CSaylor.pdf (accessed on 8 July 2017)

Selod, Saher. 2014. Citizenship Denied: Racialization of Muslim American Men and Women Post-9/11. *Critical Sociology* 41: 77–95.

Siddiqui, Sabrina. 2014. Americans' Attitudes toward Muslims and Arabs Are Getting Worse, Poll Finds. *The Huffington Post*. July 29. Available online: http://www.huffingtonpost.com/2014/07/29/arab-muslim-poll_n_5628919.html (accessed on 19 November 2016).

Sikh American Legal Defense and Education Fund. 2011. The First 9/11 Backlash Fatality: The Murder of Balbir Singh Sodhi. *Sikh American Legal Defense and Education Fund*. August 30. Available online: http://saldef.org/issues/balbir-singh-sodhi/#.WAuJr5MrKT8 (accessed on 22 October 2016).

Sikh Coalition. 2012. Statement for the Record from the Sikh Coalition. *The Sikh Coalition*. September 19. Available online: http://www.sikhcoalition.org/images/documents/statement fortherecordfromthesikhcoalition.pdf (accessed on 19 November 2016).

Sikh Coalition. 2015. FBI Finally Recognizes Sikhs in New Hate Crime Tracking Program. *The Sikh Coalition*. March 25. Available online: http://www.sikhcoalition.org/advisories/2015/fbi-finally-recognizes-sikhs-in-new-hate-crime-tracking-program (accessed on 19 November 2016).

Singh, Jaideep. 2016. The Death of Islamophobia: The Rise of Islamo-Racism. *Race Files*. February 23. Available online: http://www.racefiles.com/2016/02/23/the-death-of-islamophobia-the-rise-of-islamo-racism (accessed on 11 October 2016).

Southern Poverty Law Center (SPLC). 2016. *A Journalist's Manual: Field Guide to Anti-Muslim Extremists*. October 25. Available online: https://www.splcenter.org/20161025/journalists-manual-field-guide-anti-muslim-extremists (accessed on 8 July 2017).

Southwest Airlines. 2016. Statement Regarding Customer Situation on Flight 4620. *Southwest Airlines*. April 18. Available online: http://swamedia.com/releases/statement-regarding-customer-situation-on-flight-4620?l=enUS&utm_campaign=&utm_content=&utm_medium=&utm_source=&utm_term (accessed on 20 November 2016).

Telhami, Shibley. 2015. What Americans Really Think about Muslims and Islam. *The Brookings Institution*. December 9. Available online: https://www.brookings.edu/blog/markaz/2015/12/09/what-americans-really-think-about-muslims-and-islam (accessed on 8 December 2016).

United States Government. 2016. *49 USC 40127: Prohibitions on Discrimination*; Washington, DC: United States Government. Available online: http://uscode.house.gov/view.xhtml?req=granuleid:USC-prelim-title49-section40127&num=0&edition=prelim (accessed on 20 November 2016).

Wade, Nicholas. 2014. What Science Says about Race and Genetics. *Time*. May 9. Available online: http://time.com/91081/what-science-says-about-race-and-genetics (accessed on 5 December 2016).

Waldman, Paul. 2015. Ben Carson's Anti-Muslim Comments Are at Odds with Traditional American Principles. *The Washington Post*. September 21. Available online: https://www.washingtonpost.com/blogs/plum-line/wp/2015/09/21/ben-carsons-anti-muslim-comments-are-at-odds-with-traditional-american-principles/?utm_term=.b0f4ac89b1d2 (accessed on 25 August 2017).

Welty, Gordon. 1989. *Affirming Affirmative Action: Rejecting the "New" Racism*. Paper presented at the 74th Annual Conference of the Association for the Study of African American Life and History, Dayton, Ohio, 18–21 September 2012; Available online: http://www.wright.edu/~gordon.welty/ASALH_89.pdf (accessed on 5 December 2016).

Wilkins, Karin Gwinn. 2008. *Home/Land/Security: What We Learn about Arab Communities from Action-Adventure Films*. Lanham, MD: Rowman & Littlefield.

Zainiddinov, Hakim. 2016. Racial and Ethnic Differences in Perceptions of Discrimination among Muslims Americans. *Ethnic and Racial Studies* 39: 2701–21.

HATE CRIMES, EXPLAINED

SOUTHERN POVERTY LAW CENTER

Each year, across America, an average of 250,000 people are victimized[1] by hate crimes—criminal expressions of bigotry that terrorize entire communities and fray the social fabric of our country. As defined by the FBI,[2] a hate crime is a violent or property crime—such as murder, arson, assault, or vandalism—that is "motivated in whole or in part by an offender's bias against a race, religion, disability, sexual orientation, ethnicity, gender, or gender identity." Nine out of 10 hate crimes involve violence, and in a quarter of the cases, the offender has a weapon.

The federal government and 45 states—all the states but Arkansas, Georgia, Indiana, South Carolina, and Wyoming—have enacted hate crime laws that enhance penalties for an underlying crime. The laws differ in significant ways. All cover bias based on race, ethnicity, or religion, but many do not include gender, disability, sexual orientation, or gender identity.

The FBI releases a hate crime report each year[3]–typically showing between 5,000 and 6,000 [hate crimes per year]–but it vastly understates the extent of the problem for several reasons. First, in about half the cases, victims never report the crime to police. Second, many of the country's 18,000 law enforcement agencies do a poor job collecting or categorizing hate crime data. Third, agencies are not required[4] to participate in the FBI's Uniform Crime Reporting (UCR) program, which gathers and compiles crime data

from law enforcement to produce the dataset on which the FBI hate crime report is based. In 2016, of the 15,254 agencies that participated, nearly 9 out of 10 reported zero hate crimes. Mississippi agencies reported just seven incidents in the entire state.

The U.S. Justice Department's Bureau of Justice Statistics, however, estimates[5] there have been an average of 250,000 hate crime victimizations each year since 2004. It bases the estimate not on the UCR data collected from law enforcement agencies but rather on its annual National Crime Victimization Survey,[6] which samples nearly 100,000 households.

The targets of hate crime

Of the 8,828 hate crime victims[7] reported to the FBI in 2016 (in 7,175 separate incidents):

- 2,458 were targeted because of anti-Black bias;
- 1,338 because of sexual orientation or gender identity bias;
- 864 because of anti-White bias;
- 1,017 because of anti-Jewish bias;
- 552 because of anti-Hispanic or anti-Latino bias;
- 325 because of anti-Muslim bias;
- 321 because of anti-American Indian or Alaska Native bias.

---

1   https://www.bjs.gov/index.cfm?ty=pbdetail&iid=5967
2   https://www.fbi.gov/investigate/civil-rights/hate-crimes
3   https://www.fbi.gov/news/stories/2017-hate-crime-statistics-released-111318
4   http://www.matthewshepard.org/hate-crimes-reporting/

5   https://www.bjs.gov/index.cfm?ty=pbdetail&iid=5967
6   https://www.bjs.gov/index.cfm?ty=dcdetail&iid=245
7   https://ucr.fbi.gov/hate-crime/2017/tables/table-1.xls

(*continued*)

What motivates hate offenders?

Racial bias is the motivating factor in most hate crimes—about 60 percent, according to the National Institute of Justice. But other factors involving the psychology of the offender have also been the subject of research. In one study[8] widely used by law enforcement, sociologists Jack McDevitt and Jack Levin classified hate offenders as having four main motivations: thrill-seeking, defensive, retaliatory, and mission.

"Thrill-seeking" motivates 66 percent of hate crimes. These offenders are simply looking for excitement; over 90 percent don't know their victims. "Defensive" hate crimes (25 percent) are committed by perpetrators who rationalize their attacks by identifying some sort of threat to themselves, their identities, or their community. In "retaliatory" attacks (8 percent), culprits are acting in response to a real or perceived hate crime either to themselves or to their country. Examples include crimes committed against Muslims after the 2015 San Bernardino terrorist attack. "Mission" hate crimes (1 percent) are committed by offenders who make a career out of hate. They often write at length about their hate and have elaborate, premeditated plans of attack.

Hate crime versus hate speech

Hateful speech—often intended to degrade, intimidate, or incite violence or discrimination against certain groups—is protected by the First Amendment and is not punishable under criminal law. However, racial, anti-Semitic, or anti-LGBT slurs—or other speech that vilifies a targeted group—can be evidence of a hate crime when used by someone during the commission of an underlying crime. In fact, in 99 percent of cases reported to police, hate crime victims cite the language used by the offenders.

Hate crime versus terrorism

Differentiating terrorist attacks from hate crimes[9] is important to understanding motive, addressing the root causes of an offense, and prosecuting the offenders. Hate crimes are motivated at least in part by an offender's personal bias and are sometimes committed by nonpolitical youths simply for the thrill of it. Terrorist attacks, on the other hand, are violent acts inspired primarily by extremist beliefs and intended as political or ideological statements. Rather than target a specific identity—such as Jews or Muslims, as in a hate crime—offenders typically target government installations or groups of civilians related more by proximity than by their individual identity.

Sometimes, a violent crime can be considered both a hate crime and a terrorist attack. An example is the 2015 massacre of nine African Americans at a church in Charleston by White supremacist Dylann Roof. For the most part, though, terrorist attacks are not included in tabulations of hate crimes.

False reporting

Though hate crime reports that turn out to be hoaxes often generate sensational headlines, the phenomenon is relatively rare. The FBI estimates[10] that between 2 and 8 percent of hate crime reports are hoaxes—a tiny number in comparison with the many thousands that the federal government says go unreported (see above). "We do routinely see a very small number of hate crime hoaxes, but we also see hoaxes with respect to arson and auto theft and even reports of sexual assault, yet we don't say the overwhelming number of reports of those crimes are hoaxes, either," Brian Levin, director of the Center on Hate and Extremism at California State University, San Bernardino, told Fox News. Even researchers dedicated to documenting hate crime hoaxes have found relatively few. One website, fakehatecrimes.org, has tallied fewer than 350 since the late 1980s. . . .

Sites and organizations such as *Breitbart News*, once called "the platform for the alt-right," continue to overhype the threat of "fake hate crimes." *Breitbart News*, formerly run by Stephen Bannon, claimed in an article shortly after the election of Donald Trump: "The narrative about a wave of 'hate crimes' inspired by Trump is a deliberate fabrication, meant to tarnish the President-elect." To the contrary, in the first 34 days after the [2016 presidential] election, the Southern Poverty Law Center documented 1,094 bias-related incidents and found that 37 percent of them directly referenced Trump, his campaign slogans, or his notorious comments about sexual assault. Not every incident met the definition of a hate crime, but many did. The FBI later confirmed the sharp uptick in reported hate crimes in the fourth quarter of 2016. Researchers have shown that reported hate crimes following Trump's election made up the second largest surge since the FBI began collecting data in 1992 (trailing only the increase after the 9/11 terror attacks). . . .

Hate crime prosecutions

The issues associated with underreporting of crimes are not the only ones creating obstacles to addressing hate crimes in the United States. The difficulty with prosecution is also an issue. According to the Bureau of Justice Statistics,[11] violent hate crimes are three times *less* likely to result in an arrest than violent crimes not related to bias. In nearly half of reported hate crimes, the victim doesn't know the offender.

Even in states with sufficient hate crime laws and resources, prosecution is difficult. For example, according to the California

---

8   https://jacklevinonviolence.com/articles/HateCrimesencyc
    92206FINAL.pdf
9   https://newrepublic.com/article/134319/orlando-shooting-
    hate-crime-terrorist-act-answer-matters

10 https://www.bostonglobe.com/opinion/2016/12/20/hoaxes-harm-
    real-victims/9iIVKVrHuKpHLYEDXLrQuL/story.html
11 https://www.bjs.gov/content/pub/pdf/hcv0415.pdf?utm_
    source=juststats&utm_medium=email&utm_content=hcv0415_
    report_pdf&utm_campaign=hcv0415&ed2f26df2d9c416fbddddd2
    330a778c6=fvaddfvxvr-fvgjdvmgv

Department of Justice,[12] there were 837 hate incidents in 2015. Of the 189 that were prosecuted, just 59 resulted in a conviction. Hate crimes are difficult to prosecute in part because of the evidence needed to result in a conviction. Prosecutors have to prove the underlying crime beyond a reasonable doubt *and* convince jurors that the offender was motivated by bias. Without hate speech accompanying the crime, it's a difficult hurdle.

When states do not have the necessary resources or authority to prosecute a hate crime, the process is even more arduous. . . . Federal hate crime prosecutions are rare. The DOJ charged just 258 defendants[13] for hate crimes from 2009 to 2016.

Recommendations

The federal government should take a number of actions to combat hate crimes.

The Justice Department, for example, should:

- Incentivize, encourage, and train state and local law enforcement agencies to more comprehensively collect and report hate crime data to the FBI.
- Collect hate crime data from every *federal* law enforcement agency.
- Work with law enforcement organizations to promote and increase funding for the FBI's National Incident-Based Reporting System.

---

12 https://oag.ca.gov/sites/all/files/agweb/pdfs/cjsc/publications/hatecrimes/hc15/hc15.pdf
13 https://www.justice.gov/crt/hate-crime-laws

- Establish a separate working group or task force to address hate violence and bias-motivated incidents.
- Restore funding cuts to key civil rights office budgets.
- To encourage victims to report hate crimes to local law enforcement, rescind federal policies that undermine faith, trust, and relationships with communities of color—such as immigrant communities—and create a strategic plan to rebuild relationships that have been harmed by them.
- Send a clear and consistent message that bias-motivated attacks are unacceptable.
- Aggressively enforce . . . civil and criminal provisions that address hate crimes.
- Promote anti-bias and anti-harassment education, hate crime prevention, and initiatives to combat bullying and cyberbullying.

Congress should:

- Provide funding for states to establish hotlines for reporting and addressing hate crimes; to support training on hate crime data collection and reporting; and to authorize effective rehabilitation services for those convicted of hate crimes.
- Provide funding, for the first time, for grants authorized under the Matthew Shepard and James Byrd Jr. Hate Crimes Prevention Act to promote federal coordination and support for hate crime investigations and prosecutions by state, local, and tribal law enforcement officials.
- Provide funding for the Justice Department's Community Relations Service to hire new professionals to help mediate, train and facilitate in communities with intergroup tensions and in the aftermath of hate crimes.

ELIZABETH S. CAVALIER

17. TOMAHAWK CHOPS AND "RED" SKIN
Cultural Appropriation of Sport Symbols

Cavalier discusses the history and current controversy over the use of Native American mascots in sports. Whereas proponents of team names and mascots claim that these images and mascots are meant to honor Native Americans and represent team strength and pride, opponents argue that they are racially insensitive and damaging to members of Native American communities. Cavalier discusses the changes in public opinion regarding racialized mascots and why this issue should be relevant for us all.

In 1909, the University of Wisconsin–Lacrosse named their athletic team the "Indians" in the first known case of a college team using a Native American mascot (Davis, 1993). By the mid-1990s, Warriors and Indians ranked in the top ten most prevalent college sports team names (Williams, 2007). These team names, ostensibly meant to "honor" Native people, were often accompanied by caricatured imagery that reinforced stereotypes of Native Americans as "screaming savages" (Berg, 2013) and included halftime rituals that mocked sacred Native traditions. Facing a growing shift of public opinion on the issue of Native American mascots, several colleges voluntarily changed their Native American nicknames throughout the 1990s and early 2000s, including the Dartmouth Indians (Big Green), Stanford Indians (Cardinals), St. John's Redmen (Red Storm), and Marquette Warriors (Golden Eagles) (Cummings, 2008). In 2005, the National Collegiate Athletic Association (NCAA) enacted a policy that prohibited NCAA teams from displaying "hostile and abusive" racial, ethnic, or national origin mascots, nicknames, or imagery at any of its championships. Although this policy led to nearly all college sports teams with Native American mascots

changing their nicknames, the mascot issue remains a controversial one in the eyes of alumni, fans, and Native people themselves. And while progress has been made on the collegiate side, both high school and professional sports still struggle with the mascot issue. Although the Native American mascot controversy is not new, there has been a considerable shift in public opinion and media attention in the past several years, resulting in significant developments around the use of racial and ethnic mascots in sport.

RESISTING EFFORTS TO CHANGE

Although the tide of public opinion about Native American mascots in high school, collegiate, and professional sport has changed, resulting in critical op-eds, policy changes, and lawsuits, sport stakeholders and alumni have often resisted efforts to change. In 2013, the Washington Redskins owner Dan Snyder told *USA Today*, "We will never change the name of the team. As a lifelong Redskins fan, and I think that the Redskins fans understand the great tradition and what it's all about and what it means. . . . We'll never change the name. It's that simple. NEVER—you can

Original to *Original to Focus on Social Problems: A Contemporary Reader.*

use caps" (Brady, 2013). In 1999, a hockey alumnus of the University of North Dakota donated $100 million to build a new hockey arena, with the stipulation that the university had to retain the "Fighting Sioux" moniker or he would withdraw his funding (Klugh, 2014).

The story at the high school level is mixed. Although there has been significant public attention and pressure aimed at changing mascot names for college and professional teams, nearly 92 percent of the current team names referencing Native Americans belong to high schools (Munguia, 2014). High schools have faced pressure at the local level to change names, but that pressure has rarely reached the national fervor that accompanies professional and collegiate mascot fights. In 2008 in Natick, Massachusetts, a group that was frustrated by a school board policy that dropped the nickname "Redmen" formed a grassroots protest group called the "Redmen Forever Committee." On their website, they declare the school board policy was "the tyrannical boot of political correctness run amok" and plan to never stop their quest to restore the team name back to the Natick Redmen (Munguia, 2014). In contrast to the approach in Massachusetts, in 2014 both the advisor and the editor-in-chief of the Neshaminy High School newspaper in Langhorne, Pennsylvania, were suspended for refusing to use the mascot name Redskin in the school paper (Mullin, 2014). In a similar trend away from using native mascots, the Oregon Board of Education ordered high schools to ban native mascots or lose public funding in 2012, giving them until 2017 to comply. Fourteen schools fought to add an amendment similar to the NCAA, allowing schools with special permission from tribes to keep their names, but their quest was unanimously rejected in 2016. (Parks, 2016). In 2015, in an effort to offer carrots to schools considering discarding their native mascots, athletic apparel company and global brand Adidas offered "free design resources to [high] schools looking to shelve Native American mascots, nicknames, imagery, or symbolism" (ESPN.com, 2015) including financial support to ensure the cost of changing names was not prohibitive. Adidas was later criticized for creating a program that would benefit the company (through profits and public attention for the brand) more than the schools it was intended to help (Silvy, 2016).

MAKING THE CASE AGAINST NATIVE AMERICAN MASCOTS

Proponents of Native mascots argue that the names, imagery, and logos are meant to honor Native Americans. They suggest that names like Braves and the imagery associated with Chiefs, Indians, and Warriors are complimentary, focusing on an idealized version of Native heritage. To these proponents, those who critique such imagery are being hypersensitive and are only against Native mascots because they are now seen as politically incorrect. They often argue that there are more significant issues to worry about than sports team names and strongly resist any attempts to change team nicknames. However, those who are against the use of Native imagery in sport argue that the rituals mimicked by sports fans (such as war paint and headdresses) are some of the most sacred, hallowed traditions, yet their use promotes caricatures of Native people and lumps disparate tribes into one homogenous group (Cummings, 2008). Logos rely on stereotypical, inaccurate reflections of Native culture, including the "decapitated heads of previously displaced, abused, conscripted, and eliminated people" (Williams, 2007), which have significant effects on contemporary understanding of Native lives. When sports logos and mascots serve as an unquestioned representation of Native people, and especially when it is packaged as "honoring" tribes, it perpetuates a continued misunderstood narrative about the realities of the historical experiences of Native Americans. Additionally, these names and the associated imagery help create and perpetuate a hostile climate on campuses for Native students and are connected to lowered self-esteem and negative self-image for Native people, especially children (Davis, 2002).

Students, fans, and stakeholders often rely on the assumption that Native mascots and imagery are traditional sources of pride for the school or team and that Native people are not offended by such imagery, despite repeated lawsuits, statements, opinion pieces, articles, and testimonies by Native people explicitly discussing how they feel about sport mascots. Some of these assumptions may be based on flawed data. A widely cited 2002 *Sports Illustrated* public opinion poll found that 81 percent of Native American respondents did not feel that high school and college teams should cease the use of Native American mascots, and 83 percent of Native American respondents did not feel that professional teams should stop using such imagery; supporters of the problematic mascots and team names therefore concluded that generally speaking, Native Americans were not offended by Native sport mascots (Price, 2002). However, there has been considerable debate about the methodological accuracy of Price's findings, specifically critiquing the geographical sampling techniques and the false identification with "Indian" heritage claimed by many respondents in the sample (King et al., 2002). In contrast to Price's findings, Laveay et al. (2009) found significant evidence to suggest that American Indians find Indian sport team names, logos, and mascots offensive and were more adamant than the general population that teams that rely on Native American imagery should cease its use. The Oneida Indian Nation created an organization in 2013 called "Change the Mascot," which focuses specifically on ending the use of the name "Redskins" in the NFL. Along with the National Congress of American Indians, they created a powerful video called "Proud to Be" that aired during the 2013 National Basketball Association finals. The video focused on all of the words Native people use to describe themselves and highlighted the one word they do not—Redskin. Although there were major developments in the federal court system about the Washington Redskins in 2014, suggesting this was only recent "outrage," there have been organized protests and lawsuits about the nickname since 1972 (Steinberg, 2014).

COLLEGE SPORTS AND NATIVE MASCOTS

When the NCAA enacted their mascot policy in 2005, they gave teams until 2008 to comply. Prior to 2005, many of the remaining colleges and universities using Native imagery had begun the process to voluntarily change their names, but four schools appealed the NCAA ruling. Three of these teams— the University of Utah Utes, the Central Michigan

University Chippewa, and the Florida State University Seminoles, were granted "special permission" to continue using the nicknames, as long as certain conditions were met. The University of Utah got permission from the local tribe to use the name and collaborated with tribal leaders on an appropriate mascot symbol. Central Michigan dropped their logo and some of their game-day traditions, but kept the name Chippewa in collaboration with the Saginaw Chippewa Tribal Council, while developing specific educational and cultural programs on campus to help foster the relationship between non-Native and Native students. Florida State (FSU) works closely with the Seminole Tribe, actively recruits Seminole students, and offers scholarships for them to attend FSU. However, considerable skepticism exists about the relationship between FSU and the local Seminole tribe—the "permission" by the Seminole tribal leadership happened to coincide with Florida State supporting casino-gambling legislation that would be beneficial to the Seminoles (Laveay et al., 2009). The only school that challenged the NCAA mascot policy and lost was the University of North Dakota Fighting Sioux, who could not gain permission from the local Sioux tribe to keep using the name. After years of legal battles, a two-thirds majority in a 2012 statewide referendum retired the name "Fighting Sioux" for good. They operated as "University of North Dakota Athletics" for a three-year cooling-off period that expired in 2015 (Haga, 2012). In 2015, over 800,000 campus stakeholders voted on a new mascot, deciding upon the "Fighting Hawks." However, the campus leadership has struggled to end the chants and imagery associated with the old Sioux moniker (Springer, 2016).

College sport has seen a tide of change regarding their use of Native American names, mascots, and imagery over the past few decades. Although the NCAA policy officially only prohibits the name, image, and mascot use in post-season play (because these games are more likely to be nationally televised), this policy has, in effect, forced schools into a change regardless. As Cummings and Harper (2009) argue, mascots that are "hostile and abusive" in the postseason should also be considered so in regular season play, and they lament the NCAA policy for not going far enough. However, with the exception of a few schools, most have eradicated the use of Native nicknames, mascots, and the associated imagery.

PROFESSIONAL SPORTS AND STALLED PROGRESS

The near eradication of the use of Native nicknames in college sports stands in contrast to the experience in professional sport. Whereas colleges and universities ostensibly have a mission to foster education and cultural competence and, thus, are under some obligation to ensure they do not perpetuate stereotypical and discriminatory practices, professional franchises are not under the same obligations and have, to this point, strongly resisted any pressure to change their names. Although a professional team has not adopted a Native American nickname since 1963 when the team relocating to Kansas City became the Chiefs (Hylton, 2010), there are still several professional franchises using Native nicknames, including the Cleveland Indians and Atlanta Braves in Major League Baseball, the Chicago Blackhawks in the National Hockey League, and the Kansas City Chiefs and Washington Redskins in the National Football League (NFL). Although some teams have reduced the most explicitly stereotypical imagery in response to public pressure, such as when the Atlanta Braves retired the mascot "Chief Noc-a-Homa" in 1986, practices such as the "Tomahawk Chop" at Braves games or the Warpaint Horse mascot at Kansas City Chiefs games, as well as usage of offensive logos on "throwback" jerseys, remain.

There have been two recent developments regarding mascot use in professional sports. Significant public attention has been paid to the Washington Redskins in the NFL. Despite the defiant pose struck by the owner, Dan Snyder, in 2014 the Trademark Trial and Appeals Board canceled the trademark registration of the name Redskins, deeming it "disparaging" and "offensive" (Vargas, 2014). This served as the first significant legal shift since a lawsuit was first filed against the team in 1992. However, in 2017, the U.S. Supreme Court overruled the decision, finding that canceling the trademark violated the team's First Amendment right to free speech (Shapira and Marimow, 2017). Most recently, the Cleveland Indians in Major League Baseball have agreed with the Commissioner to phase out the use of the "Chief Wahoo" imagery on team jerseys and caps by 2019. "Chief Wahoo" is a caricature of a grinning Native American head with a feather headband, and has been associated with the team since 1938 (Perry, 2018). While it won't be featured on the player's uniforms anymore, the logo will still have a "limited retail presence," by the team, in order to retain control of the trademark. Furthermore, there has been no move towards changing the team name from the Indians.

WHY IT MATTERS: CULTURAL SYMBOLS, NATIVE LIVES

Why do Native American nicknames in sport matter? Nicknames are merely symbols, but cultural symbols matter. As Lindsay (2008) argues, in sport there is a preference for "animals (e.g. Bears, Tigers, Sharks), objects (Bullets, Socks, Maple Leaves), or non-living natural phenomena (Avalanche, Thunder, Lightning, Heat)" (p. 212). When human groups are used, they are most often groups whose "existence has long passed (Buccaneers, Patriots, 49ers, 76ers, Vikings, Packers, Steelers)" (p. 213). Lindsay notes that there is a "striking absence of religious, racial, and ethnic classifications [in sport], except, where the religious, racial, or ethnic group has provided the name to itself (as with Notre Dame's Fighting Irish)" (p. 213). The only group who we see caricaturized in sport against their will are Native Americans.

Native Americans have faced significant historical problems and continue to face considerable contemporary hurdles. As Williams (2007) notes, there was a 74 percent decrease in the population of Native Americans in North America between 1492 and 1800, and they now have the highest poverty, mortality, and unemployment rates and the lowest levels of educational attainment of all racial groups. Williams argues,

In the case of Native mascots, the ability of Corporate America (or universities or other schools) to possess these symbols and cultural markers—and to legally trademark them—constitutes a theft from Native America. In stealing them, the dominant culture robs Native people of the ability to use their culture for themselves, whether for self-determination, profit, or mere survival. Native people have had the whole of their heritage, customs, and imagery stolen, dominated, digested, and regurgitated back to them by the dominant culture; and thus they have no say in how their likeness, traditions, or history is used. Whites continue to "play Indian" without Native permission. (p. 41)

The use of Native mascots matters precisely because sport doesn't matter. When pundits, sports fans, and team owners suggest there are "bigger problems" than Native mascots, they are suggesting that sports are inconsequential, and time would be better spent on "real problems." "Defenders of Native American team names who claim that 'it's no big deal' have it precisely correct: sports names and symbols are trivial—that's the point. The offense of Native American sports names lies precisely in the triviality of them" (Lindsay, 2008, p. 214). Finally, it matters because there is an absence of any other narrative about Native people. Native Americans are "underrepresented throughout the culture, in media, in schools, and in the U.S. political structure" (Laveay et al. 2009). Although they are underrepresented in contemporary social and political life, they very much still exist, unlike the Pirates, Buccaneers, 49ers, and Vikings of the past. As Lindsay (2008) concludes,

> Like 49ers, Native Americans form a part of our past. But unlike 49ers, Native Americans are not only still with us, they are still with us as inheritors of a very different sort of past. Those two facts make their appropriateness for team symbols doubly incomparable. It is one thing to vanquish the historical losers, but it is quite another to strip them of their culture, tradition, history, land (and of course, a goodly number of them), and then in the aftermath, strip them of their dignity. (p. 220)

Imagine another ethnic group receiving the same treatment in sport as Native Americans have. Imagine team names with racial slurs, with negative, inaccurate stereotypical imagery and logo design. Imagine halftime rituals that take sacred, important rituals and mock them or have them mimicked by drunken college students who do not share the ethnic background of the group they are caricaturizing. Imagine opponents of that team creating t-shirts, signs, and chants that mock and disparage the team with ethnic slurs and violent imagery. Imagine this scenario for Hispanics, for African Americans, for Asians, for Germans, for Jews. Would that behavior be acceptable in those cases? Why, then, is it acceptable for Native Americans?

REFERENCES

Berg, 2013. "Braves Pull Back from 'Screaming Savage' Cap after Controversy." *USA Today*, February 11, 2013. Retrieved September 7, 2014. http://www.usatoday.com/story/gameon/2013/02/11/braves-ditch-racist-cap-for-spring-training/1910789/.

Brady, Erik. 2013. "Daniel Snyder Says Redskins Will Never Change Name." *USA Today*, May 10, 2013. Retrieved August 8, 2014. http://www.usatoday.com/story/sports/nfl/redskins/2013/05/09/washington-redskins-daniel-snyder/2148127/.

Cummings, Andre Douglas Pond. 2008. "Progress Realized? The Continuing American Indian Mascot Quandary." *Marquette Sports Law Review* 18(2):309–336.

Cummings, Andre Douglas Pond and Seth E. Harper. 2009. "Wide Right: Why the NCAA's Policy on the American Indian Mascot Issue Misses the Mark." University of Maryland Law Journal of Race, Religion, Class, and Gender 9:135.

Davis, Laurel R. 1993. "Protest against the Use of Native American Nicknames/Logos: A Challenge to Traditional American Identity." *Journal of Sport & Social Issues* 17(1):9–22.

Davis, Laurel R. 2002. "The Problems with Native American Mascots." *Multicultural Education* 9(4):11–14.

Haga, Chuck. 2012. "UND Ties Up Loose Ends as Nickname Is Retired." *Bakken Today*, June 16, 2012. Retrieved August 8, 2014. http://www.bakkentoday.com/event/article/id/238935/publisher_ID/40/.

Hylton, J. Gordon. 2010. "Before the Redskins Were the Redskins: The Use of Native American Team Names in the Formative Era of American Sports, 1857–1933." *North Dakota Law Review* 86(4):879–903.

King, C. Richard, Ellen J. Staurowsky, Lawrence Baca, Laurel R. Davis, and Cornel Pewewardy. 2002. "Of Polls and Race Prejudice: *Sports Illustrated*'s Errant 'Indian Wars.'" *Journal of Sport and Social Issues* 26(2):381–402.

Klugh, Justin. 2014. "'Fighting Sioux' Debate Leaves University of North Dakota Nameless in Frozen Four." Philly.com, April 10, 2014. Retrieved August 8, 2014. http://www.philly.com/philly/sports/colleges/University_of_North_Dakota_goes_nameless_in_Frozen_Four_after_years_of_Fighting_Sioux_debate.html/.

Laveay, Frahser, Coy Callison, and Ann Rodriguez. 2009. "Offensiveness of Native American Names, Mascots, and Logos in Sports: A Survey of Tribal Leaders and the General Population." *International Journal of Sport Communication* 2:81–99.

Lindsay, Peter. 2008. "Representing Redskins: The Ethics of Native American Team Names." *Journal of the Philosophy of Sport* 35:208–224.

Mullin, Benjamin. 2014. "High School Newspaper Editor Suspended for Refusal to Use the Term 'Redskin.'" http://www.poynter.org/news/mediawire/270209/high-school-newspaper-editor-suspended-for-refusal-to-use-the-term-redskin/.

Munguia, Hayley. 2014. "The 2,218 Native American Mascots People Aren't Talking About." *Five Thirty Eight*. September 5, 2014. Retrieved September 7, 2014. http://fivethirtyeight.com/features/the-2128-Native-american-mascots-people-arent-talking-about/.

Parks, Casey. 2016. "Native American Mascots Have to Go, Board of Education Rules." Posted January 22, 2016 on *Oregon Live*. Retrieved February 17, 2019. https://www.oregonlive.com/portland/2015/05/native_american_mascots_have_t.html

Perry, Dayn. 2018. "Indians to Remove Controversial 'Chief Wahoo' logo from Uniforms by 2019." January 29, 2018. *CBSSports.com*. Retrieved February 17, 2019. https://www.cbssports.com/mlb/news/indians-to-remove-controversial-chief-wahoo-logo-from-uniforms-by-2019/

Price, S. L. 2002. "The Indian Wars." *Sports Illustrated* 96(10):66.

ESPN.com Services. 2015. "Adidas Offers to Help Eliminate Native American Mascots." November 5, 2015. Retrieved February 16, 2019. http://www.espn.com/moresports/story/_/id/14057043/adidas-offers-help-eliminate-native-american-mascots

Shapira, Ian and Ann E. Marimow. 2017. "Washington Redskins Win Trademark Fight Over the Team's Name." June 29, 2017. *The Washington Post*. Retrieved February 16, 2019. https://www.washingtonpost.com/local/public-safety/2017/06/29/a26f52f0-5cf6-11e7-9fc6-c7ef4bc58d13_story.html?utm_term=.eb27ea55948f

Silvy, Tyler. 2016. "Will Adidas Follow Through On Promise to Help Schools Transition Away from Native American Mascots?" *Greeley Tribune*, April 3. Retrieved on March 20, 2019 (https://www.greeleytribune.com/news/local/will-adidas-follow-through-on-promise-to-help-schools-transition-away-from-native-american-mascots/).

Springer, Patrick. 2016. "NDSU President Calls for End of 'Hateful' Sioux Chant at Bison Football Games." *Grand Forks Herald* October 17, 2016. Retrieved February 16, 2019. https://www.grandforksherald .com/news/4138709-ndsu-president-calls-end-hateful-sioux-chant-bison-football-games

Steinberg, Dan. 2014. "The Great Redskins Name Debate of . . . 1972?" *The Washington Post*, June 3, 2014. Retrieved August 8, 2014. http://wwwwashingtonpost.com/blogs/dc-sports-bog/wp/2014/ 06/03the-great-redskins-name-debate-of-1972/.

Vargas, Theresa. 2014. "Federal Agency Cancels Redskins Trademark Registration, Says Name Is Disparaging." *The Washington Post*, June 18, 2014. Retrieved August 8, 2014. http://www.washington post.com/local/us-patent-office-cancels-redskins-trademark-registration-says-name-is-disparaging /2014/06/18/e7737bb8-f6ee-8aa9-dad2ec039789_story.html/.

Williams, Dana M. 2007. "No Past, No Respect, and No Power: An Anarchist Evaluation of Native Americans as Sports Nicknames, Logos, and Mascots." *Anarchist Studies* 15(1):31–54.

ROBIN DIANGELO

18. WHITE FRAGILITY

DiAngelo discusses the concept of "White Fragility," the idea that because American Whites are unfamiliar and uncomfortable with discussing and being confronted with racism, when they are forced to engage with it they become defensive, angry, and argumentative. She argues that factors such as racial segregation, universalism, individualism, entitlement to racial comfort, and racial arrogance have positioned White Americans so that they can avoid these conversations entirely, which serves to perpetuate the problem of racial inequality in the United States.

. . . I am a White woman. I am standing beside a Black woman. We are facing a group of White people who are seated in front of us. We are in their workplace and have been hired by their employer to lead them in a dialogue about race. The room is filled with tension and charged with hostility. I have just presented a definition of racism that includes the acknowledgment that Whites hold social and institutional power over people of color. A White man is pounding his fist on the table. His face is red and he is furious. As he pounds he yells, "White people have been discriminated against for 25 years! A White person can't get a job anymore!" I look around the room and see 40 employed people, all White. There are no people of color in this workplace. Something is happening here, and it isn't based in the racial reality of the workplace. I am feeling unnerved by this man's disconnection with that reality, and his lack of sensitivity to the impact this is having on my co-facilitator, the only person of color in the room. Why is this White man so angry? Why is he being so careless about the impact of his anger? Why are all the other White people either sitting in silent agreement with him or tuning out? We have, after all, only articulated a definition of racism.

White people in North America live in a social environment that protects and insulates them from race-based stress.[1] Fine (1997) identifies this insulation when she observes, "how Whiteness accrues privilege and status; gets itself surrounded by protective pillows of resources and/or benefits of the doubt; how Whiteness repels gossip and voyeurism and instead demands dignity" (p. 57). Whites are rarely without these "protective pillows," and when they are, it is usually temporary and by choice. This insulated environment of racial privilege builds White expectations for racial comfort while at the same time lowering the ability to tolerate racial stress.

For many White people, a single required multicultural education course taken in college, or required "cultural competency training" in their workplace, is the only time they may encounter a direct and sustained challenge to their racial understanding. But even in this arena, not all multicultural courses or training programs talk directly about racism, much less address White privilege. It is far more the norm for these courses and programs to use racially coded language such as "urban," "inner city," and "disadvantaged" but to rarely use "White" or "over-advantaged" or "privileged." This racially coded language reproduces racist images and perspectives while it simultaneously reproduces the comfortable illusion that race and its problems are what "they" have, not us. The reasons why the facilitators of these courses and trainings may not directly name the dynamics and beneficiaries of racism range from the lack of a valid analysis

Robin DiAngelo, "White Fragility," International Journal of Critical Pedagogy, Vol 3 (3) (2011) pp 54-70; © 2011 International Journal of Critical Pedagogy.

of racism by White facilitators, personal and economic survival strategies for facilitators of color, and the overall pressure from management to keep the content comfortable and palatable for Whites. However, if and when an educational program does directly address racism and the privileging of Whites, common White responses include anger, withdrawal, emotional incapacitation, guilt, argumentation, and cognitive dissonance (all of which reinforce the pressure on facilitators to avoid directly addressing racism). So-called progressive Whites may not respond with anger but may still insulate themselves via claims that they are beyond the need for engaging with the content because they "already had a class on this" or "already know this." These reactions are often seen in antiracist education endeavors as forms of resistance to the challenge of internalized dominance (Whitehead & Wittig, 2005; Horton & Scott, 2004; McGowan, 2000, O'Donnell, 1998). These reactions do indeed function as resistance, but it may be useful to also conceptualize them as the result of the reduced psychosocial stamina that racial insulation inculcates. I call this lack of racial stamina "White Fragility."

Although mainstream definitions of racism are typically some variation of individual "race prejudice," which anyone of any race can have, Whiteness scholars define racism as encompassing economic, political, social, and cultural structures, actions, and beliefs that systematize and perpetuate an unequal distribution of privileges, resources, and power between White people and people of color (Hilliard, 1992). This unequal distribution benefits Whites and disadvantages people of color overall and as a group. Racism is not fluid in the United States; it does not flow back and forth, one day benefiting Whites and another day (or even era) benefiting people of color. The direction of power between Whites and people of color is historic, traditional, normalized, and deeply embedded in the fabric of U.S. society (Mills, 1999; Feagin, 2006). Whiteness itself refers to the specific dimensions of racism that serve to elevate White people over people of color. This definition counters the dominant representation of racism in mainstream education as isolated in discrete behaviors that some individuals may or may not demonstrate, and it goes beyond naming specific privileges (McIntosh, 1988). Whites are theorized as actively shaped, affected,

defined, and elevated through their racialization and the individual and collective consciousness formed within it (Frankenberg, 1997; Morrison, 1992; Tatum, 1997). . . .

. . . Whiteness is thus conceptualized as a constellation of processes and practices rather than as a discrete entity (i.e., skin color alone). Whiteness is dynamic, relational, and operating at all times and on myriad levels. These processes and practices include basic rights, values, beliefs, perspectives, and experiences purported to be commonly shared by all but which are actually only consistently afforded to White people. Whiteness Studies begin with the premise that racism and White privilege exist in both traditional and modern forms and, rather than work to prove its existence, work to reveal it. This [reading] will explore the dynamics of one aspect of Whiteness and its effects, White Fragility.

TRIGGERS

White Fragility is a state in which even a minimum amount of racial stress becomes intolerable, triggering a range of defensive moves. These moves include the outward display of emotions such as anger, fear, and guilt, and behaviors such as argumentation, silence, and leaving the stress-inducing situation. These behaviors, in turn, function to reinstate White racial equilibrium. Racial stress results from an interruption to what is racially familiar. These interruptions can take a variety of forms and come from a range of sources, including:

- Suggesting that a White person's viewpoint comes from a racialized frame of reference (challenge to objectivity);
- People of color talking directly about their racial perspectives (challenge to White racial codes);
- People of color choosing not to protect the racial feelings of White people in regards to race (challenge to White racial expectations and need/entitlement to racial comfort);
- People of color not being willing to tell their stories or answer questions about their racial experiences (challenge to colonialist relations);
- A fellow White not providing agreement with one's interpretations (challenge to White solidarity);

- Receiving feedback that one's behavior had a racist impact (challenge to White liberalism);
- Suggesting that group membership is significant (challenge to individualism);
- Acknowledging that access is unequal between racial groups (challenge to meritocracy);
- Being presented with a person of color in a position of leadership (challenge to White authority);
- Being presented with information about other racial groups through, for example, movies in which people of color drive the action but are not in stereotypical roles, or multicultural education (challenge to White centrality).

In a White-dominant environment, each of these challenges becomes exceptional. In turn, Whites are often at a loss for how to respond in constructive ways. Whites have not had to build the cognitive or affective skills or develop the stamina that would allow for constructive engagement across racial divides. . . .

Omi and Winant (1986) posit the U.S. racial order as an "unstable equilibrium," kept equilibrated by the state, but still unstable due to continual conflicts of interests and challenges to the racial order (pp. 78–9). . . . When any of the above triggers (challenges in the habitus) occur, the resulting disequilibrium becomes intolerable. Because White Fragility finds its support in and is a function of White privilege, fragility and privilege result in responses that function to restore equilibrium and return the resources "lost" via the challenge—resistance toward the trigger, shutting down and/or tuning out, indulgence in emotional incapacitation such as guilt or "hurt feelings," exiting, or a combination of these responses.

FACTORS THAT INCULCATE WHITE FRAGILITY

SEGREGATION

The first factor leading to White Fragility is the segregated lives that most White people live (Frankenberg, Lee & Orfield, 2003). Even if Whites live in physical proximity to people of color (and this would be exceptional outside of an urban or temporarily mixed-class neighborhood), segregation occurs on multiple levels, including representational and informational.

Because Whites live primarily segregated lives in a White-dominated society, they receive little or no authentic information about racism and are thus unprepared to think about it critically or with complexity. Growing up in segregated environments (schools, workplaces, neighborhoods, media images, and historical perspectives), White interests and perspectives are almost always central. An inability to see or consider significance in the perspectives of people of color results (Collins, 2000).

Further, White people are taught not to feel any loss over the absence of people of color in their lives. In fact, this absence is what defines their schools and neighborhoods as "good"; Whites come to understand that a "good school" or "good neighborhood" is coded language for "White" (Johnson & Shapiro, 2003). The quality of White space, being in large part measured via the absence of people of color (and Blacks in particular), is a profound message indeed, one that is deeply internalized and reinforced daily through normalized discourses about good schools and neighborhoods. This dynamic of gain rather than loss via racial segregation may be the most profound aspect of White racial socialization of all. Yet, while discourses about what makes a space good are tacitly understood as racially coded, this coding is explicitly denied by Whites.

UNIVERSALISM AND INDIVIDUALISM

Whites are taught to see their perspectives as objective and representative of reality (McIntosh, 1988). The belief in objectivity, coupled with positioning White people as outside of culture (and thus the norm for humanity), allows Whites to view themselves as universal humans who can represent all of human experience. This is evidenced through an unracialized identity or location, which functions as a kind of blindness, an inability to think about Whiteness as an identity or as a "state" of being that would or could have an impact on one's life. In this position, Whiteness is not recognized or named by White people, and a universal reference point is assumed. White people are just people. Within this construction, Whites can represent humanity, while people of color, who are never just people but always most particularly Black people, Asian people, and so on, can only represent their own racialized experiences (Dyer, 1997).

The discourse of universalism functions similarly to the discourse of individualism, but instead of declaring that we all need to see each other as individuals (everyone is different), the person declares that we all need to see each other as human beings (everyone is the same). Of course we are all humans, and I do not critique universalism in general, but when applied to racism, universalism functions to deny the significance of race and the advantages of being White. Further, universalism assumes that Whites and people of color have the same realities, the same experiences in the same contexts (i.e., I feel comfortable in this majority White classroom, so you must too), the same responses from others, and it also assumes that the same doors are open to all. Acknowledging racism as a system of privilege conferred on Whites challenges claims to universalism.

At the same time that Whites are taught to see their interests and perspectives as universal, they are also taught to value the individual and to see themselves as individuals rather than as part of a racially socialized group. Individualism erases history and hides the ways in which wealth has been distributed and accumulated over generations to benefit Whites today. It allows Whites to view themselves as unique and original, outside of socialization and unaffected by the relentless racial messages in the culture. Individualism also allows Whites to distance themselves from the actions of their racial group and demand to be granted the benefit of the doubt, as individuals, in all cases. A corollary to this unracialized identity is the ability to recognize Whiteness as something that is significant and that operates in society, but to not see how it relates to one's own life. In this form, a White person recognizes Whiteness as real, but as the individual problem of other "bad" White people (DiAngelo, 2010).

Given the ideology of individualism, Whites often respond defensively when they are linked to other Whites as a group or are "accused" of collectively benefiting from racism, because as individuals, each White person is "different" from any other White person and expects to be seen as such. This narcissism

is not necessarily the result of a consciously held belief that Whites are superior to others (although that may play a role), but a result of the White racial insulation ubiquitous in dominant culture (Dawkins, 2004; Frankenberg, Lee, & Orfield, 2003); a general White inability to see non-White perspectives as significant, except in sporadic and impotent reflexes, which have little or no long-term momentum or political usefulness (Rich, 1979).

Whites invoke these seemingly contradictory discourses—we are either all unique or we are all the same—interchangeably. Both discourses work to deny White privilege and the significance of race. Further, on the cultural level, being an individual or being a human outside of a racial group is a privilege only afforded to White people. In other words, people of color are almost always seen as "having a race" and described in racial terms ("the Black man"), but Whites rarely are ("the man"), allowing Whites to see themselves as objective and non-racialized. In turn, being seen (and seeing ourselves) as individuals outside of race frees Whites from the psychic burden of race in a wholly racialized society. Race and racism become their problems, not ours. Challenging these frameworks becomes a kind of unwelcome shock to the system.

The disavowal of race as an organizing factor, both of individual White consciousness and the institutions of society at large, is necessary to support current structures of capitalism and domination, for without it, the correlation between the distribution of social resources and unearned White privilege would be evident (Flax, 1998). The existence of structural inequality undermines the claim that privilege is simply a reflection of hard work and virtue. Therefore, inequality must be hidden or justified as resulting from lack of effort (Mills, 1999). Individualism accomplishes both of these tasks. . . .

ENTITLEMENT TO RACIAL COMFORT

In the dominant position, Whites are almost always racially comfortable and thus have developed unchallenged expectations to remain so (DiAngelo, 2006b). Whites have not had to build tolerance for racial discomfort, and thus, when racial discomfort arises,

Whites typically respond as if something is "wrong," and they blame the person or event that triggered the discomfort (usually a person of color).

This blame results in a socially sanctioned array of countermoves against the perceived source of the discomfort, including penalization; retaliation; isolation; ostracization; and refusal to continue engagement. White insistence on racial comfort ensures that racism will not be faced. This insistence also functions to punish those who break White codes of comfort. Whites often confuse comfort with safety and state that we don't feel safe when what we really mean is that we don't feel comfortable. This trivializes our history of brutality toward people of color and perverts the reality of that history. Because we don't think complexly about racism, we don't ask ourselves what safety means from a position of societal dominance, or the impact on people of color. . . . [W]e complain about our safety when we are merely *talking* about racism.

RACIAL ARROGANCE

Ideological racism includes strongly positive images of the White self as well as strongly negative images of racial "others" (Feagin, 2000, p. 33). This self-image engenders a self-perpetuating sense of entitlement because many Whites believe their financial and professional successes are the result of their own efforts while ignoring the fact of White privilege. Because most Whites have not been trained to think complexly about racism in schools (Derman-Sparks, Ramsey, & Olsen Edwards, 2006; Sleeter, 1993) or mainstream discourse, and because it benefits White dominance not to do so, we have a very limited understanding of racism. Yet dominance leads to racial arrogance, and in this racial arrogance, Whites have no compunction about debating the knowledge of people who have thought complexly about race. Whites generally feel free to dismiss these informed perspectives rather than have the humility to acknowledge that they are unfamiliar, reflect on them further, or seek more information. This intelligence and expertise are often trivialized and countered with simplistic platitudes (i.e., "People just need to . . . ").

Because of White social, economic, and political power within a White dominant culture, Whites are positioned to legitimize people of color's assertions of racism. Yet Whites are the least likely to see, understand, or be invested in validating those assertions and being honest about their consequences, which leads Whites to claim that they disagree with perspectives that challenge their worldview, when in fact, they don't understand the perspective. Thus, they confuse not understanding with not agreeing. This racial arrogance, coupled with the need for racial comfort, also has Whites insisting that people of color explain White racism in the "right" way. The right way is generally politely and rationally, without any show of emotional upset. . . . [W]hites are usually more receptive to validating White racism if that racism is constructed as residing in individual White people other than themselves.

RACIAL BELONGING

White people enjoy a deeply internalized, largely unconscious sense of racial belonging in U.S. society (DiAngelo, 2006a; McIntosh, 1988). This racial belonging is instilled via the Whiteness embedded in the culture at large. Everywhere we look, we see our own racial image reflected back to us—in our heroes and heroines, in standards of beauty, in our role-models and teachers, in our textbooks and historical memory, in the media, in religious iconography, including the image of God . . . , and so on. In virtually any situation or image deemed valuable in dominant society, Whites belong. Indeed, it is rare for most Whites to experience a sense of not belonging, and such experiences are usually very temporary, easily avoidable situations. Racial belonging becomes deeply internalized and taken for granted. In dominant society, interruption of racial belonging is rare and thus destabilizing and frightening to Whites.

Whites consistently choose and enjoy racial segregation. Living, working, and playing in racial segregation is unremarkable as long as it is not named or made explicitly intentional. For example, in many antiracist endeavors, a common exercise is to separate into caucus groups by race in order to discuss issues specific to your racial group, and without the pressure or stress of other groups' presence. Generally, people of color appreciate this opportunity for racial fellowship, but White people typically become very uncomfortable, agitated, and upset—even though this temporary separation is in the service of addressing racism. Responses include a disorienting sense of themselves as not just people, but most particularly White people; a curious sense of loss about this contrived and temporary separation which they don't feel about the real and ongoing segregation in their daily lives; and anxiety about not knowing what is going on in the groups of color. The irony, again, is that most Whites live in racial segregation every day and, in fact, are the group most likely to intentionally choose that segregation (albeit obscured in racially coded language such as seeking "good schools" and "good neighborhoods"). This segregation is unremarkable until it is named as deliberate —that is, "We are now going to separate by race for a short exercise." I posit that it is the intentionality that is so disquieting—as long as we don't mean to separate, as long as it "just happens" that we live segregated lives, we can maintain a (fragile) identity of racial innocence.

PSYCHIC FREEDOM

Because race is constructed as residing in people of color, Whites don't bear the social burden of race. We move easily through our society without a sense of ourselves as racialized subjects (Dyer, 1997). We see race as operating when people of color are present, but all-White spaces as "pure" spaces—untainted by race vis á vis the absence of the carriers of race (and thereby the racial polluters)—people of color. This perspective is perfectly captured in a familiar White statement, "I was lucky. I grew up in an all-White neighborhood so I didn't learn anything about racism." . . . Because racial segregation is deemed socially valuable while simultaneously unracial and unremarkable, we rarely, if ever, have to think about race and racism, and we receive no penalty for not thinking about it. In fact, Whites are more likely to be penalized (primarily by other Whites) for bringing race up in a social justice context than for ignoring it (however, it is acceptable to bring race up indirectly and in ways that reinforce racist attitudes, i.e. warning other Whites to stay away from certain neighborhoods, etc.). This frees Whites from carrying the psychic burden of race. Race is for

people of color to think about—it is what happens to "them"—they can bring it up if it is an issue for them (although if they do, we can dismiss it as a personal problem, the "race card," or the reason for their problems). This allows Whites to devote much more psychological energy to other issues and prevents us from developing the stamina to sustain attention on an issue as charged and uncomfortable as race.

CONSTANT MESSAGES THAT WE ARE MORE VALUABLE—THROUGH REPRESENTATION IN EVERYTHING

Living in a White-dominant context, we receive constant messages that we are better and more important than people of color. These messages operate on multiple levels and are conveyed in a range of ways. For example: our centrality in history textbooks, historical representations and perspectives; our centrality in media and advertising (for example, a. . . . Vogue magazine cover boldly stated, "The World's Next Top Models," and every woman on the front cover was White); our teachers, role-models, heroes and heroines; everyday discourse on "good" neighborhoods and schools and who is in them; popular TV shows centered around friendship circles that are all White; religious iconography that depicts God, Adam and Eve, and other key figures as White; commentary on news stories about how shocking any crime is that occurs in White suburbs; and the lack of a sense of loss about the absence of people of color in most White people's lives. While one may explicitly reject the notion that one is inherently better than another, one cannot avoid internalizing the message of White superiority, as it is ubiquitous in mainstream culture (Tatum, 1997; Doane, 1997).

What does White Fragility look like?

A large body of research about children and race demonstrates that children start to construct ideas about race very early; a sense of White superiority and knowledge of racial power codes appears to develop as early as preschool (Clark, 1963; Derman-Sparks, Ramsey, & Olsen Edwards, 2006). Marty (1999) states,

As in other Western nations, White children born in the United States inherit the moral predicament of living in a White supremacist society. Raised to experience their racially based advantages as fair and normal, White children receive little if any instruction regarding the predicament they face, let alone any guidance in how to resolve it. Therefore, they experience or learn about racial tension without understanding Euro-Americans' historical responsibility for it and knowing virtually nothing about their contemporary roles in perpetuating it. (p. 51)

At the same time that it is ubiquitous, White superiority also remains unnamed and explicitly denied by most Whites. If White children become adults who explicitly oppose racism, as do many, they often organize their identity around a denial of the racially based privileges they hold that reinforce racist disadvantage for others. What is particularly problematic about this contradiction is that White moral objection to racism increases White resistance to acknowledging complicity with it. In a White supremacist context, White identity in large part rests on a foundation of (superficial) racial toleration and acceptance. Whites who position themselves as liberal often opt to protect what they perceive as their moral reputations, rather than recognize or change their participation in systems of inequity and domination. In so responding, Whites invoke the power to choose when, how, and how much to address or challenge racism. Thus, pointing out White advantage will often trigger patterns of confusion, defensiveness, and righteous indignation. When confronted with a challenge to White racial codes, many White liberals use the speech of self-defense (Van Dijk, 1993) . . . .

Those who lead Whites in discussions of race may find the discourse of self-defense familiar. Via this discourse, Whites position themselves as victimized, slammed, blamed, attacked, and being used as "punching bag[s]" (DiAngelo, 2006b). Whites who describe interactions in this way are responding to the articulation of counternarratives; nothing physically out of the ordinary has ever occurred in any interracial discussion that I am aware of. These self-defense claims work on multiple levels to position the speakers as morally superior while obscuring the true power of their social locations; blame others with less social power for their discomfort; falsely position that discomfort as dangerous; and reinscribe racist imagery. This discourse of victimization also enables Whites

to avoid responsibility for the racial power and privilege they wield. By positioning themselves as victims of antiracist efforts, they cannot be the beneficiaries of White privilege. Claiming that *they* have been treated unfairly via a challenge to their position or an expectation that they listen to the perspectives and experiences of people of color, they are able to demand that more social resources (such as time and attention) be channeled in their direction to help them cope with this mistreatment.

A cogent example of White Fragility occurred recently during a workplace antiracism training I co-facilitated with an interracial team. One of the White participants left the session and went back to her desk, upset at receiving (what appeared to the training team as) sensitive and diplomatic feedback on how some of her statements had impacted several people of color in the room. At break, several other White participants approached us (the trainers) and reported that they had talked to the woman at her desk, and she was very upset that her statements had been challenged. They wanted to alert us to the fact that she literally "might be having a heart-attack." Upon questioning from us, they clarified that they meant this *literally*. These co-workers were sincere in their fear that the young woman might actually physically die as a result of the feedback. Of course, when news of the woman's potentially fatal condition reached the rest of the participant group, all attention was immediately focused back onto her and away from the impact she had had on the people of color. . . .

The language of violence that many Whites use to describe antiracist endeavors is not without significance, as it is another example of the way that White Fragility distorts and perverts reality. By employing terms that connote physical abuse, Whites tap into the classic discourse of people of color (particularly African Americans) as dangerous and violent. This discourse perverts the actual direction of danger that exists between Whites and others. The history of brutal, extensive, institutionalized, and ongoing violence perpetrated by Whites against people of color—slavery, genocide, lynching, whipping, forced sterilization, and medical experimentation to mention a few—becomes profoundly trivialized when Whites claim they don't feel safe or are under attack when in the rare situation of merely talking about race with people of color. The use of this discourse illustrates how fragile and ill equipped most White people are to confront racial tensions, and their subsequent projection of this tension onto people of color (Morrison, 1992). . . .

Bonilla-Silva (2006) documents a manifestation of White Fragility in his study of colorblind White racism. He states, "Because the new racial climate in America forbids the open expression of racially based feelings, views, and positions, when Whites discuss issues that make them uncomfortable, they become almost incomprehensible —I, I, I, I don't mean, you know, but. . . ." (p. 68). Probing forbidden racial issues results in verbal incoherence—digressions, long pauses, repetition, and self-corrections. Bonilla-Silva suggests that this incoherent talk is a function of talking about race in a world that insists race does not matter. This incoherence is one demonstration that many White people are unprepared to engage, even on a preliminary level, in an exploration of their racial perspectives that could lead to a shift in their understanding of racism. . . .

However, an assertion that Whites do not engage with the dynamics of racial discourse is somewhat misleading. White people do notice the racial locations of racial others and discuss this freely among themselves, albeit often in coded ways. Their refusal to directly acknowledge this race talk results in a kind of split consciousness that leads to the incoherence Bonilla-Silva documents above (Feagin, 2000; Flax, 1998; hooks, 1992; Morrison, 1992). This denial also guarantees that the racial misinformation that circulates in the culture and frames their perspectives will be left unexamined. The continual retreat from the discomfort of authentic racial engagement in a culture infused with racial disparity limits the ability to form authentic connections across racial lines, and results in a perpetual cycle that works to hold racism in place.

CONCLUSION

White people often believe that multicultural/antiracist education is only necessary for those who interact with "minorities" or in "diverse" environments. However, the dynamics discussed here suggest that it is critical that all White people build the stamina to sustain conscious and explicit engagement with race. When Whites posit race as nonoperative because there are few, if any, people of color in their immediate environments, Whiteness is reinscribed ever more deeply (Derman-Sparks, & Ramsey, 2006). When Whites only notice "raced others," we reinscribe Whiteness by continuing to posit Whiteness as universal and non-Whiteness as other. Further, if we can't listen to or comprehend the perspectives of people of color, we cannot bridge cross-racial divides. A continual retreat from the discomfort of authentic racial engagement results in a perpetual cycle that works to hold racism in place.

While antiracist efforts ultimately seek to transform institutionalized racism, antiracist education may be most effective by starting at the micro level. The goal is to generate the development of perspectives and skills that enable all people, regardless of racial location, to be active initiators of change. Since all individuals who live within a racist system are enmeshed in its relations, this means that all are responsible for either perpetuating or transforming that system. However, although all individuals play a role in keeping the system active, the responsibility for change is not equally shared. White racism is ultimately a White problem, and the burden for interrupting it belongs to White people (Derman-Sparks & Phillips, 1997; hooks, 1995; Wise, 2003). Conversations about Whiteness might best happen within the context of a larger conversation about racism. . . . Starting with the individual and moving outward to the ultimate framework for racism—Whiteness—allows for the pacing that is necessary for many White people to approach the challenging study of race. In this way, a discourse on Whiteness becomes part of a process rather than an event (Zúñiga, Nagda, & Sevig, 2002).

Many White people have never been given direct or complex information about racism before, and they often cannot explicitly see, feel, or understand it (Trepagnier, 2006; Weber, 2001). People of color are generally much more aware of racism on a personal level, but due to the wider society's silence and denial of it, they often do not have a macro-level framework from which to analyze their experiences (Wing 2003; Bonilla-Silva, 2006). Further, dominant society "assigns" different roles to different groups of color (Smith, 2005), and a critical consciousness about racism varies not only between individuals within groups, but also between groups. For example, many African Americans relate having been "prepared" by parents to live in a racist society, while many Asian heritage people say that racism was never directly discussed in their homes (hooks, 1989; Lee, 1996). . . .

Talking directly about White power and privilege, in addition to providing much needed information and shared definitions, is also in itself a powerful interruption of common (and oppressive) discursive patterns around race. At the same time, White people often need to reflect upon racial information and be allowed to make connections between the information and their own lives. Educators can encourage and support White participants in making their engagement a point of analysis. White Fragility doesn't always manifest in overt ways; silence and withdrawal are also functions of fragility. Who speaks, who doesn't speak, when, for how long, and with what emotional valence are all keys to understanding the relational patterns that hold oppression in place (Gee, 1999; Powell, 1997). Viewing White anger, defensiveness, silence, and withdrawal in response to issues of race through the framework of White Fragility may help frame the problem as an issue of stamina-building and thereby guide our interventions accordingly.

NOTE

1. Although White racial insulation is somewhat mediated by social class (with poor and working-class urban Whites being generally less racially insulated than suburban or rural Whites), the larger social environment insulates and protects Whites as a group through institutions, cultural representations, media, school textbooks, movies, advertising, dominant discourses, etc.

REFERENCES

Bonilla-Silva, E. (2006). *Racism without racists: Color-blind racism and the persistence of racial inequality in the United States* (22nd ed.). New York: Rowman & Littlefield.

Clark, K. B. (1963). *Prejudice and your child*. Boston: Beacon Press.

Dawkins, Casey J. (2004). Recent evidence on the continuing causes of Black-White residential segregation. *Journal of Urban Affairs, 26*(3), 379–400.

Debian, Marty. (1999). White antiracist rhetoric as apologia: Wendell Berry's the hidden wound. In T. K. Nakayama & J. Martin (Eds.), *Whiteness: The communication of social identity* (pp. 51–68). Thousand Oaks, CA: Sage.

Derman-Sparks, L., & Phillips, C. (1997). *Teaching/learning anti-racism: A developmental approach*. New York: Teachers College Press.

Derman-Sparks, L., Ramsey, P., & Olsen Edwards, J. (2006). *What if all the kids are White?: Anti-bias multicultural education with young children and families*. New York: Teachers College Press.

DiAngelo, R. (2006a). My race didn't trump my class: Using oppression to face privilege. *Multicultural Perspectives, 8*(1), 51–56.

DiAngelo, R. (2006b). "I'm leaving!": White fragility in racial dialogue. In B. McMahon & D. Armstrong (Eds.), *Inclusion in urban educational environments: Addressing issues of diversity, equity, and social justice* (pp. 213–240). Centre for Leadership and Diversity. Ontario Institute for Studies in Education of the University of Toronto.

DiAngelo, Robin J. (2010). Why can't we all just be individuals?: Countering the discourse of individualism in anti-racist education. *InterActions: UCLA Journal of Education and Information Studies, 6*(1). Retrieved from http://escholarship.org/uc/item/5fm4h8wm.

Doane, A. W. (1997). White identity and race relations in the 1990s. In G. L. Carter (Ed.), *Perspectives on Current Social Problems* (pp. 151–159). Boston: Allyn and Bacon.

Dyer, R. (1997). *White*. New York: Routledge.

Feagin, J. R. (2000). *Racist America: Roots, Current Realities, and Future Reparations*. New York: Routledge.

Feagin, J. R. (2006). *Systematic Racism: A theory of oppression*. New York: Routledge.

Fine, M. (1997). Witnessing Whiteness. In M. Fine, L. Weis, C. Powell, & L. Wong (Eds.), *Off White: Readings on race, power, and society* (pp. 57–65). New York: Routledge.

Fine, L., Weis, C. Powell, & L. Wong (Eds.). 1997. *Off White: Readings on race, power and society* (pp. vii–xii). New York: Routledge.

Flax, J. (1998). *American dream in Black and White: The Clarence Thomas hearings*. New York: Cornell University Press.

Frankenberg, E., Lee, C., & Orfield, G. (2003). A multiracial society with segregated schools: Are we losing the dream? *The Civil Rights Project*. Retrieved from http://www.civilrightsproject.ucla.edu/research/reseg03/reseg03_full.php.

Frankenberg, R. (1997). Introduction: Local Whitenesses, localizing Whiteness. In R. Frankenberg (Ed.), *Displacing Whiteness: Essays in social and cultural criticism* (pp. 1–33). Durham, NC: Duke University Press.

Gee, J. P. (1999). *An introduction to discourse analysis: Theory and method*. London: Routledge.

Hilliard, A. (1992). Racism: Its origins and how it works. Paper presented at the meeting of the Mid-West Association for the Education of Young Children, Madison, WI.

hooks, b. (1989). *Talking Back: Thinking Feminist, Thinking Black*. Boston: South End Press.

hooks, b. (1992). *Black looks: Race and representation*. Boston: South End Press.

hooks, b. (1995). *Killing rage*. New York: Henry Holt & Company.

Horton, J., & Scott, D. (2004). White students' voices in multicultural teacher education preparation. *Multicultural Education*, 11(4) Retrieved from http://findarticles.com/p/articles/mi_qa3935/is_200407/ai_n9414143.

Johnson, H. B., & Shapiro, T. M. (2003). Good neighborhoods, good schools: race and the "good choices" of White Families. In A. W. Doane & E. Bonilla-Silva (Eds.), *White out: The continuing significance of racism* (pp. 173–187). New York: Routledge.

Lee, T. (1996). *Unraveling the "model-minority" stereotype: Listening to Asian-American youth*. New York: Teachers College Press.

McGowan, J. (2000). Multicultural teaching: African-American faculty classroom teaching experiences in predominantly White colleges and universities. *Multicultural Education*, 8(2), 19–22.

McIntosh, P. (1988). White privilege and male privilege: A personal account of coming to see correspondence through work in women's studies. In M. Anderson & P. Hill Collins (Eds.), *Race, class, and gender: An anthology* (pp. 94–105). Belmont, CA: Wadsworth.

Mills, C. (1999). *The racial contract*. New York: Cornell University Press.

Morrison, T. (1992). *Playing in the dark*. New York: Random House.

O'Donnell, J. (1998). Engaging students' recognition of racial identity. In Chavez, R. C., & O'Donnell, J. (Eds.), *Speaking the unpleasant: The politics of (non) engagement in the multicultural education terrain* (pp. 56–68). Albany: State University of New York Press.

Omi, M., & Winant, H. (1986). Racial Formation in the United States. New York: Routledge.

Powell, L. C. (1997). The achievement (k)not: Whiteness and 'Black underachievement'. In M. Fine, L. Powell, C. Weis, & L. Wong (Eds.), *Off White: Readings on race, power and society* (pp. 3–12). New York: Routledge.

Rich, Adrienne. (1979). Disloyal to Civilization: Feminism, Racism, Gynephobia." In A. Rich (Ed.), *On Lies, Secrets, and Silence: Selected Prose 1966–1978* (p. 306). New York: W. W. Norton & Co.

Sleeter, C. (1993). How White teachers construct race. In C. McCarthy & W. Crichlow (Eds.), *Race identity and representation in education* (pp.157–171). New York: Routledge.

Smith, Andrea (2005). *Conquest: Sexual violence and American Indian genocide*. Cambridge, MA: Southend Press.

Tatum, B. (1997). *"Why are all the Black kids sitting together in the cafeteria?": And other conversations about race*. New York: Basic Books.

Trepagnier, B. (2006). *Silent racism: How well-meaning White people perpetuate the racial divide*. Boulder, CO: Paridigm Publishers.

Van Dijk, T. A. (1993). Principles of critical discourse analysis. *Discourse and Society*, 4(2), 249–283.

Weber, L. (2001). *Understanding race, class, gender, and sexuality: A conceptual framework*. New York: McGraw-Hill.

Whitehead, K. A., & Wittig, M. A. (2005). Discursive management of resistance to a multicultural education programme. *Qualitative Research in Psychology*, 1(3), 267284.

Wing, S. D. (2003). Overcoming our racism: The journey to liberation. San Francisco: Jossey-Bass.

Wise, T. (2003). Whites swim in racial preference. Retrieved from http://www.academic.udayton.edu/race/04needs/affirm20.htm.

Zúñiga, X., Nagda, B., & Sevig, T. (2002). Intergroup dialogues: An educational model for cultivating engagement across differences. *Equity and Excellence in Education*, 6(1), 115–132.

WHITE AMERICANS' RACIAL ATTITUDES AND THEIR EFFECT ON ANTIDISCRIMINATION POLICIES

AMANDA ATWELL AND AMANDA M. JUNGELS

The 2008 and 2012 presidential elections of Barack Obama seemed to signify that the United States was in the process of fulfilling its enduring commitment to ending White supremacy and beginning a new era of racial reconciliation. The fact that a Black man could become president served to support the narrative of a postracial America, where Black people can achieve the highest levels of success through their own merit and determination (Welch & Sigelman, 2011). However, recent attitudinal research suggests that Black and White Americans actually hold competing understandings of how contemporary racial discrimination functions in U.S. society. Considerable portions of White Americans believe that Black Americans do not face a significant amount of discrimination (Norton & Sommers, 2011) and that the remnants of racial inequality in society are generated by Black Americans' inherent inferiority and laziness (Tuch & Hughes, 2011). More recent research conducted in 2016 indicated that White and Black Americans have significantly different views on the reasons African Americans struggle to get ahead in America: 70 percent of Black Americans cited racial discrimination as a major cause, compared to only 36 percent of White Americans (Pew Research 2016). Moreover, this study found that White and Black Americans had very different perceptions about what life is like for Black Americans, which may contribute to their differing opinions. By large margins, Black Americans were more likely than Whites to say that Blacks are treated less fairly than Whites by police (84 percent to 50 percent), in the court system (75 percent to 43 percent), in the workplace (64 percent to 22 percent), and in stores or restaurants (49 percent to 21 percent) (Pew Research 2016).

Over forty-five years ago, Martin Luther King Jr. drew attention to the evolution of this phenomenon (which Tuch and Hughes [2011] refers to as "racial resentment" among White people) and argued that when it comes to White and Black Americans, "There is not even a common language when the term 'equality' is used. Negro and White have a fundamentally different definition" (King, 1968:8). Although White Americans, when surveyed, generally support racial equality as a theoretical concept, they have been especially resistant to support the

(continued)

Original to *Focus on Social Problems: A Contemporary Reader*.

implementation of polices designed to redress centuries of racial oppression against Black Americans. This discrepancy is referred to as the "principle–policy gap" (Tuch & Hughes, 2011). Norton and Sommers (2011) demonstrate that Whites now see racism as a "zero-sum" game where they associate decreases in perceived bias against Black Americans as necessarily increasing bias against White Americans. It is noteworthy that Black respondents did not share these perceptions. Despite an abundance of contradictory empirical evidence, some research now indicates that White Americans believe that they are victims of racism more often than Black Americans (Norton & Sommers, 2011), which suggests that there are stark disparities between documented discrimination and White Americans' individual perceptions of race relations. Similarly, when asked about their personal experiences with discrimination, 71 percent of Black Americans say they have experienced racial discrimination, compared to 30 percent of White Americans who report they have been discriminated against (Pew Research 2016). More tellingly, only 31 percent of Whites say that their race has made it easier for them to succeed in life, demonstrating the invisibility of White privilege to those who benefit from it (DiAngelo 2011; McIntosh 1989).

In effect, White attitudes and "racial resentment," specifically, decrease the likelihood that they will support antidiscrimination policies, such as affirmative action in education and employment. Although affirmative action was originally designed to atone for centuries of enslavement and Jim Crow laws that have historically disadvantaged Black Americans, White Americans now view antidiscrimination policies as a form of "reverse racism" (Norton & Sommers, 2011). These attitudes have trickled all the way up to the Supreme Court, which has increasingly ruled affirmative action policies as injurious to White Americans' right to equal opportunity (Plaut, 2011). It should be no surprise, then, that 82.8 percent of White Americans strongly opposed or opposed hiring and promotion preferences for Black Americans (Tuch & Hughes, 2011).

Plaut (2011:220) succinctly explains how White Americans' view of racism as a zero-sum game impacts public policy decisions: "We are witnessing a shift from the presumption of explicit discrimination against minorities—and the need to legally address that discrimination—to a presumption of discrimination against Whites, intentionally, by the State through unfair preference schemes that advantage racial minorities." Therefore, White Americans have come to associate general, societal-wide affirmative action policies with purposeful discrimination against individual White Americans. In essence, White Americans think that

substantial gains have been made toward racial equality for Black Americans and that this progress has led to an inverse discrimination against White Americans, making it less likely that White Americans will support antidiscrimination policies in the future (Norton & Sommers, 2011). These issues are further complicated by the fact that the United States elected a Black man to the office of the presidency, twice, although without the majority of the White vote (Harvey-Wingfield and Feagin, 2010). Policymakers, educators, and activists will continue to face nuanced challenges in creating a more equitable society, and differing attitudes and opinions about race, racism, and discrimination should be one of many considerations policymakers take into account.

REFERENCES

DiAngelo, Robin. 2011. "White Fragility." *International Journal of Critical Pedagogy* 3(3): 54–70.

Harvey-Wingfield, Adia, and Joe Feagin. 2010. *Yes We Can? White Racial Framing and the 2008 Presidential Campaign.* New York: Routledge.

King, Martin Luther Jr. 1968. *Where Do We Go from Here?: Chaos or Community.* New York: Harper & Row.

McIntosh, Peggy. 1989. "White Privilege: Unpacking the Invisible Knapsack." *The National SEED Project.* Retrieved from https://nationalseedproject.org/white-privilege-unpacking-the-invisible-knapsack on September 23, 2018.

Norton, Michael I., and Samuel R. Sommers. 2011. "Whites See Racism as a Zero-Sum Game That They Are Now Losing." *Perspectives on Psychological Science* 6(3):215–18.

Pew Research Center. 2016. "On Views of Race and Inequality, Blacks and Whites Are Worlds Apart." Retrieved from http://www.pewsocialtrends.org/2016/06/27/on-views-of-race-and-inequality-blacks-and-whites-are-worlds-apart/ on September 23, 2018.

Plaut, Victoria C. 2011. "Law and the Zero-Sum Game of Discrimination: Commentary on Norton and Sommers (2011)." *Perspectives on Psychological Science* 6(3):219–21.

Tuch, Steven A., and Michael Hughes. 2011. "Whites' Racial Policy Attitudes in the Twenty-First Century: The Continuing Significance of Racial Resentment." *The Annals of the American Academy of Political and Social Science* 634(1):134–52.

Welch, Susan, and Lee Sigelman. 2011. "The 'Obama Effect' and White Racial Attitudes." *The Annals of the American Academy of Political and Social Science* 634(1):207–20.

CHAPTER 5

GENDER INEQUALITY

Inequality between the genders and cases of sexism, harassment, and discrimination have received increased attention in the last few years, due to cultural movements such as #MeToo movement and events like the Women's March, momentous moments in women's history (for example, Hillary Clinton's candidacy for president in 2016), and high-profile sexual harassment challenges against Harvey Weinstein, Bill Cosby, and Brett Kavanaugh. Because of these cultural touchstones, more people than ever are aware of the negative effects of what is known as "hostile sexism." In the first reading in this chapter, Melanie Tannenbaum clarifies the difference between hostile and benevolent sexism—which is marked by a positive tone and can even seem to be complimentary. Tannenbaum argues that benevolent sexism can have a pervasively negative effect on women and girls as well as men and boys, and can further entrench rigid perceptions of gender roles. Sexism is also present in a tool that you are likely familiar with as a college student: the end-of-semester evaluations of your instructors. Kiersten Kummerow discusses research that indicates students frequently discuss women faculty members' appearance, personality, and competence in ways they do not for faculty members who are men. When researchers isolated the gender of the instructor in student evaluations, men were consistently rated higher than women even when their performance was the same as that of women instructors and despite the fact that students perform worse in classes taught by men. The underrepresentation of women at the highest levels of academia, together with the negative perceptions of women in positions of leadership and authority, likely contribute to this problem.

The #MeToo movement has been an important one in elevating the issue of harassment and sexism against women, particularly in the workplace, and has highlighted how different generations of women experience and respond to workplace harassment. Anna North discusses recent research showing that even though women across generations experienced sexual harassment at roughly the same rate, women under age 35 were more likely to report incidents of harassment or assault and were more confident that reporting would get the harassment to stop. Older women reported that sexual harassment simply wasn't talked about when they were early in their careers, and in some cases, they were the only woman in their workplace, which reinforced silence and the notion that harassment and assault were problems they had to face on their own. As more people break the silence around their personal experiences of harassment and assault, perhaps there is reason to be optimistic about changing cultural norms around these types of bias.

Focusing on discrimination and sexism toward women is only one part of the gender inequality puzzle. In the reading "Imagining a Better Boyhood," Sarah Rich discusses the restrictive notions of gender expression that men and boys must face. By encouraging women and girls to embrace traditionally masculine gender roles (such as being assertive, strong, and courageous) and not simultaneously encouraging men and boys to take on traditionally feminine roles (such as nurturing, caregiving, and collaboration), we only reinforce the notion that masculinity is preferred and more valuable than femininity. This has long-term consequences for all genders, Rich argues, because it closes off a wide range of human experiences and emotions, and reinforces restrictive notions of what it means to be a man or a woman in today's world. In "Selling Feminism, Consuming Femininity" Amanda M. Gengler builds on our understanding of these restrictive notions in her summary of sociological research on teen magazines such as *Seventeen*. Gengler argues that these magazines reproduce notions of "appropriate" femininity in ways that exploit and commodify modern girls' desire to be independent and empowered.

Finally, Elis Herman and Elroi J. Windsor discuss a form of workplace discrimination that receives comparable little attention: discrimination and bias toward transgender and gender nonconforming people. Transgender and gender nonconforming people face a host of challenges in the workplace, including lack of protections, inconsistent state laws, and high rates of unemployment and mistreatment in the workplace. Legislation proposed by advocacy groups that would protect transgender and gender nonconforming people in the workplace face an uncertain future in a social climate that remains hostile to people who do not fit neatly into the established gender binary.

Gender equality is an issue that all of us face, no matter how we identify, and researchers have documented that we all benefit from increased gender equality. Societies that are more gender-equal have lower poverty rates and food insecurity, less war and conflict, and greater economic development. In fact, societies could experience some relief from a variety of social problems by moving toward gender equity across all social institutions.[1]

---

1   Stacy, Gorman Harmon. 2017. "Why Gender Equality Is Good for the World." In Mindy Stombler and Amanda M. Jungels (Eds.), *Focus on Social Problems: A Contemporary Reader* (pp. 261–66). New York: Oxford University Press.

EMILY MAY

Emily May is the co-founder and executive director of Hollaback!

What is your organization and its mission?

Hollaback! is a movement to end sexual harassment that is powered by a network of local activists around the world. We work together to better understand street harassment, to ignite public conversations, and to develop innovative strategies to ensure equal access to public spaces.

How did you first become interested in this type of activism?

In 2005 a woman named Thao Nguyen was riding the train into work in New York City when she saw a man masturbating across from her. Thao took a picture and brought it to the police, but they didn't do anything. She posted the picture on Flickr, and it quickly went viral and landed on the front cover of the *New York Daily News*. All of a sudden, the whole city was talking about public masturbation, and women citywide were sharing their stories. It seemed like everyone had one.

After that, a group of friends and I (four woman and three men) were talking about street harassment, how pervasive it was, and how frustrating it is that we didn't have a response. Thao inspired us; we thought— what if we post pictures and stories of harassers on a

blog? Hollaback! was born; New Yorkers from all five boroughs were snapping photos and swapping harassment stories.

But then something telling happened. We began to receive posts from outside New York—a lot of them. From outside the United States, even. That's when we knew we had hit a nerve. Now we are in 92 cities, 32 countries, and 18 different languages.

What are your current organizational goals?

We recently published *HOLLA 101: Guide to Street Harassment for Educators and Students* and distributed it to over 200 New York City schools. One of our goals is to train teachers, counselors, and administrators on how to respond to reports of street harassment. We will be working in the schools to provide extensive workshops, safety audits, and assemblies to talk in depth about how middle and high school students experience harassment, and what they want to do about it. We also want to launch and train 75 new leaders from 25 new sites. We currently have a waitlist of people in over 70 cities interested in bringing this movement to their community. We will also launch

HeartMob, our new online harassment bystander platform. Recognizing that online harassment limits free speech, Hollaback! is creating a platform to encourage bystander intervention for online harassment.

What strategies do you use to enact social change?

We use a myriad of strategies to enact social change. We work to inspire international leadership by training over 500 activists from over 80 cities around the world to localize Hollaback! to their community using the Hollaback! digital storytelling platform and on-the-ground resources. We also use digital storytelling, by releasing free iPhone and Droid apps that provide a real-time response to street harassment and illustrate the locations of the harassment on Hollaback!'s publicly available map (resulting in over 8,000 reports of harassment). Incidences are mapped and used to educate policymakers about the prevalence of harassment in their districts and inform research and community based solutions. We also work to engage elected officials. We meet with many legislators each year to discuss community-based solutions to street harassment, including safety audits, trainings, public art projects, and workshop series. We change minds through educational outreach. For example, globally, our site leaders have trained over 2,500 middle and high school students in how to respond to and prevent street harassment. To engage the broad public, we use social media. For example, we've obtained over 1,200 press hits, 40,000 Facebook fans, and 17,000 Twitter followers. A final part of our strategy is performing research. Our site leaders have performed groundbreaking local research in over 38 cities. They use the research to demonstrate the prevalence of street harassment and to engage the community in solutions.

What are the major challenges activists in your field face?

The emerging field of street harassment struggles with a world that isn't ready to accept that street harassment isn't okay—and a funding community that thinks street harassment simply "isn't a big enough problem." I've had the door slammed in my face more times than I care to recount.

I find it helpful to remind myself that if you don't fail from time to time, you're not taking enough risks. That said, failure isn't easy for anyone—especially when the stakes are high, as they are for social entrepreneurs and movement builders.

When failure strikes, remember to take care of yourself: buy a mocha, take a walk, and let it hurt. The next day, you've got to ditch your ego and start learning. Make a list of what worked, what didn't, and figure out how to fix it. Remember that brilliant things often emerge out of failure.

What are major misconceptions the public has about activism in general and your issue specifically?

The one that makes me the craziest is the myth that it is mostly men of color who are doing the harassing. This problem isn't unique to the anti–street harassment movement. Initiatives combating various forms of sexual harassment and assault have continually struggled against the perpetuation of racist stereotypes, and in particular, the construction of men of color as sexual predators. There exist widespread fictions regarding who perpetrators are: the myth of racial minorities, particularly Latino and Black men, as prototypical rapists and as being more prone to violence is quite common. This stems in part from a tragic and violent history in which Black men in the United States were commonly and unjustly accused of assaulting White women and, as such, were "tried" in biased courts and lynched by mobs. Because of the complexity of institutional and socially ingrained prejudices, Hollaback! aims to highlight the interrelations between sexism, racism, and other forms of bias and violence.

Why should students get involved in your line of activism?

There are two reasons to hollaback: for you and for the world.

For you: Hollaback! is all about your right to be you: A person who never has to take it and just keep walking, but one who has a "badass" response when they are messed with. Someone who knows they have the right to define themselves instead of being defined by some creep's point of view. We have a right to be who we are, not who we are told to be. We have a right to define our-selves on our own terms when we walk out the door, whatever that means that day. That hour. That minute.

Street harassment teaches us to be silent, but we aren't listening. We don't put up with harassment in the home, at work, or at school. And now we aren't putting up with it in the street, either. By holla'ing back you are transforming an experience that is lonely and isolating into one that is sharable. You change the power dynamic by flipping the lens off of you and onto the harasser. And you enter a worldwide commu-nity of people who've got your back.

For the world: Stories change the world. Don't be-lieve us? Think about Rodney King,[1] Anita Hill,[2] or Matthew Shepard[3]. These stories didn't just change the world; they shaped policy.

The Internet has given us a new campfire. Each time you hollaback, you are given a king-sized plat-form to tell your story. Thousands will read it and your story will shift their understanding of what ha-rassment means. Some will walk away understanding what it feels like to be in your shoes, others will feel like they are not alone for the first time or that it's not their fault. Your story will redefine safety in your community—it will inspire legislators, the police, and other authorities to take this issue seriously—to ap-proach it with sensitivity, and to create policies that make everyone feel safe. Your story will build an irre-futable case as to why street harassment is not okay—a case strong enough to change the world.

But it all starts with the simplest of gestures: Your hollaback.

What would you consider to be your greatest successes as an activist?

It's been an honor to watch the movement to end street harassment scale so large, include so many young activists globally—from the over 90 organiza-tions that I've seen launch in the past 10 years, to the site leaders we've trained in over 90 cities. It's a whole different landscape than the one we entered into in 2005, in the most beautiful way.

Our sites have collaborated with legislators to pass a resolution against street harassment in the Scottish Parliament, release mobile apps that will make New York City the first city in the world to document street harassment in real time, and presented in front of the United Nations and European Union Parliament.

If an individual has little money and time, are there other ways they can contribute?

Yes, share your story. By doing so, you transform the lonely and isolating experience of street harassment into one that is sharable, and you enter a worldwide community of people who've got your back. Your story will build an irrefutable case as to why street harass-ment is not okay. Some will walk away understanding what it feels like to be in your shoes; others will feel like they are not alone for the first time or that it's not their fault. So far, we've collected over 8,000 stories of harassment from both victims and bystanders who tried to help. Join the conversation today. http://www .ihollaback.org/share.

You could also host a Chalk Walk. Grab some side-walk chalk and a few friends and tell your stories on sidewalks in crowded public areas. It's a way to liter-ally rewrite city streets. It's visceral and unapologeti-cally public.

Finally, you could start a Hollaback site in your community. We'll train you, set you up with a website, and give you access to our supportive global commu-nity of over 400 site leaders around the world.

NOTES

1. Rodney King, an African American man, was beaten by four White Los Angeles police officers after a traffic stop, an assault that was video-taped by a witness and repeatedly aired on television. The acquittal of the officers by an all-White jury is re-garded as the trigger for the 1992 Los Angeles riots as well as the cause of significant reforms of the Los Angeles police department around the issues of excessive force and leadership oversight of offi-cers (Gray, Madison. 2007. "The L.A. Riots: 15 Years After Rodney King." Time Magazine. Accessed from http://content.time. com/time/specials/2007/la_riot/ article/0,28804,1614117_1614084_1614831,00. html. Bliss, Laura. 2015. "LAPD's Police Reforms and the Legacy of Rodney King." The Atlantic City

Lab. Accessed from http://www.citylab.com/politics/2015/05/lapds-police-reforms-and-the-legacy-of-rodney-king/392000/).

2. In 1991, Anita Hill, a law professor at the University of Oklahoma, accused conservative Supreme Court Justice nominee Clarence Thomas of sexual harassment while they worked together at the Equal Employment Opportunity Commission. These accusations, Hill's treatment by the all-male Senate Judiciary Committee, and Thomas's confirmation by a narrow margin, created controversy and inspired abundant media coverage. The case had longterm impacts on American culture, including broader awareness of, and laws about, sexual harassment, as well as the increased representation of women holding elected office after the election cycle of 1992 ("The Year of the Woman"), which many attributed to women's reaction to the poor treatment of Hill (Siegel, Joel. 2011. "Clarence Thomas-Anita Hill Supreme Court Confirmation Hearing 'Empowered Women' and Panel Member Arlen Specter Still Amazed by Reactions." ABC NEWS. Accessed from http://abcnews.go.com/US/clarence-thomas-anita-hill-supreme-court-confirmation-hearing/story?id=14802217. O'Malley, Michael. N.d. "An Outline of the Anita Hill and Clarence Thomas Controversy." Accessed from https://chnm.gmu.edu/courses/122/hill/hillframe.htm).

3. In 1998, Matthew Shepard, a gay 21 year old college student, was attacked and later died after being left to die beside a road in Laramie, Wyoming. His murder, which was characterized as an anti-gay hate crime but could not be prosecuted as such because hate crime legislation did not exist in Wyoming at the time, increased attention regarding state and federal hate crime legislation, as well as the passage of 2009 federal legislation entitled "The Matthew Shepard and James Byrd, Jr. Hate Crimes Prevention Act," which increased federal law enforcement activities, funding, and tracking hate crimes (US Department of Justice. "The Matthew Shepard and James Byrd, Jr., Hate Crimes Prevention Act of 1999." Accessed from http://www.justice.gov/crt/matthew-shepard-and-james-byrd-jr-hate-crimes-prevention-act-2009-0).

MELANIE TANNENBAUM

19. THE PROBLEM WHEN SEXISM JUST SOUNDS SO DARN FRIENDLY

Tannenbaum discusses two different types of sexism: hostile sexism, characterized by negative attitudes toward women, and benevolent sexism, which seems more positive in tone. While hostile sexism may get the most attention, benevolent sexism is perhaps more insidious and harmful because it undermines the perception of women's competence under the guise of seemingly positive or harmless statements. Tannenbaum illustrates that sexism exists in a variety of forms, but that benevolent sexism is particularly difficult to recognize and fight.

Something can't *actually* be sexist if it's really, really nice, right? I mean, if someone compliments me on my looks or my cooking, that's not sexist. That's awesome! I should be thrilled that I'm being noticed for something positive!

Yet there are many comments that, while seemingly complimentary, somehow still feel wrong. These comments may focus on an author's appearance rather than the content of her writing, or mention how surprising it is that she's a woman, being that her field is mostly filled with men. Even though these remarks can sometimes feel good to hear—and no one is denying that this type of comment *can* feel good, especially in the right context—they can also cause a feeling of unease, particularly when one is in the position of trying to draw attention towards her work rather than personal qualities like her gender or appearance.

In social psychology, these seemingly-positive-yet-still-somewhat-unsettling comments and behaviors have a name: *Benevolent Sexism*. Although it is tempting to brush this experience off as an overreaction to compliments or a misunderstanding of benign intent, benevolent sexism is both real and insidiously dangerous.

WHAT IS BENEVOLENT SEXISM?

In 1996, Peter Glick and Susan Fiske wrote a paper on the concept of *ambivalent sexism*, noting that despite common beliefs, there are actually two different kinds of sexist attitudes and behavior. *Hostile sexism* is what most people think of when they picture "sexism"—angry, explicitly negative attitudes towards women. However, the authors note, there is also something called *benevolent sexism*:

> We define *benevolent sexism* as a set of interrelated attitudes toward women that are sexist in terms of viewing women stereotypically and in restricted roles but that are subjectively positive in feeling tone (for the perceiver) and also tend to elicit behaviors typically categorized as prosocial (e.g., helping) or intimacy-seeking (e.g., self-disclosure). (Glick & Fiske, 1996, p. 491)

> [Benevolent sexism is] a subjectively positive orientation of protection, idealization, and affection directed toward women that, like hostile sexism, serves to justify women's subordinate status to men. (Glick et al., 2000, p. 763)

Yes, there's actually an official name for all of those comments and stereotypes that can somehow feel both nice and wrong at the same time, like the belief that women are "delicate flowers" who need to be protected by men, or the notion that women have the special gift of being "more kind and caring" than their male counterparts. It might sound like a compliment, but it still counts as sexism.

For a very recent example of how benevolent sexism might play out in our everyday lives, take a look at this satirical piece,[1] which jokingly rewrites Albert Einstein's obituary. To quote:

> He made sure he shopped for groceries every night on the way home from work, took the garbage out, and hand washed the antimacassars. But to his step-daughters he was just Dad. "He was always there for us," said his step-daughter and first cousin once removed Margo. Albert Einstein, who died on Tuesday, had another life at work, where he sometimes slipped away to peck at projects like showing that atoms really exist. His discovery of something called the photoelectric effect won him a coveted Nobel Prize.

Looks weird, right? Kind of like something you would never actually see in print? Yet the author of rocket scientist Yvonne Brill's obituary didn't hesitate before writing the following[2] about her . . . [in 2013]:

> She made a mean beef stroganoff, followed her husband from job to job, and took eight years off from work to raise three children. "The world's best mom," her son Matthew said. But Yvonne Brill, who died on Wednesday at 88 in Princeton, N.J., was also a brilliant rocket scientist, who in the early 1970s invented a propulsion system to help keep communications satellites from slipping out of their orbits.

In fact, Obituaries editor William McDonald still sees nothing wrong with it. In his words, he's "surprised . . . [because] it never occurred to [him] that this would be read as sexist," and if he had to re-write it again, he still "wouldn't do anything differently."

I want to make one thing perfectly clear. There's not a problem with mentioning Brill's family, friends, and loved ones. It's not a problem to note how wonderfully Brill balanced her domestic and professional lives. Brill was a female scientist during a time when very few women could occupy that role in society, and that means something truly important.

But the problem here is really that if "Yvonne" were "Yvan," the obit would have looked fundamentally different. If we're talking up the importance of work–life balance and familial roles for women but we're not also mentioning those things about men, that's a problem. If a woman's accomplishments must be accompanied by a reassurance that she really was "a good Mom," but a man's accomplishments are allowed to stand on their own, that's a problem. And lest you think that I only care about women, let's not act like this doesn't have a real and dangerous impact on men, too. If a man spends years of his life as a doting father and caring husband, yet his strong devotion to his family is not considered an important fact for his obituary because he's male . . . then yes, that's also a big problem. The fact that so many people don't understand why it might be unnerving that the writer's idea for a good story arc in Brill's obituary was to lead with her role as a wife and mother, and then let the surprise that she was actually a really smart rocket scientist come in later as a shocking twist? That's benevolent sexism.

WHY IS BENEVOLENT SEXISM A PROBLEM?

Admittedly, this research begs an obvious question. If benevolently sexist comments seem like nothing more than compliments, why are they problematic? Is it really "sexism" if the content of the statements seems positive towards women? After all, the obituary noted nothing more than how beloved Brill was as a wife and a mother. Why should anyone be upset by that? Sure, men wouldn't be written about in the same way, but who cares? It's so nice!

Well, for one thing, benevolently sexist statements aren't *all* sunshine and butterflies. They often end up implying that women are weak, sensitive creatures that need to be "protected." While this may seem positive to some, for others—especially women in male-dominated fields—it creates a damaging stereotype. As Glick and Fiske themselves note in their seminal paper:

> We do not consider benevolent sexism a good thing, for despite the positive feelings it may indicate for the perceiver, its underpinnings lie in traditional stereotyping and masculine dominance (e.g., the man as the provider and woman as his dependent), and

its consequences are often damaging. Benevolent sexism is not necessarily experienced as benevolent by the recipient. For example, a man's comment to a female coworker on how "cute" she looks, however well-intentioned, may undermine her feelings of being taken seriously as a professional. (Glick & Fiske, 1996, Pp. 491–492)

In a later paper, Glick and Fiske went on to determine the extent to which 15,000 men and women across 19 different countries endorse both hostile and benevolently sexist statements. First of all, they found that hostile and benevolent sexism tend to correlate highly across nations. So, it is *not* the case that people who endorse hostile sexism don't tend to endorse benevolent sexism, whereas those who endorse benevolent sexism look nothing like the "real" sexists. On the contrary, those who endorsed benevolent sexism were likely to admit that they *also* held explicit, hostile attitudes towards women (although one does not necessarily *have* to endorse these hostile attitudes in order to engage in benevolent sexism).

Secondly, they discovered that benevolent sexism was a significant predictor of nationwide gender inequality, independent of the effects of hostile sexism. In countries where the men were more likely to endorse benevolent sexism, *even when controlling for hostile sexism*, men also lived longer, were more educated, had higher literacy rates, made significantly more money, and actively participated in the political and economic spheres more than their female counterparts. The warm, fuzzy feelings surrounding benevolent sexism come at a cost, and that cost is often actual, objective gender equality.

THE INSIDIOUS NATURE OF BENEVOLENT SEXISM

A . . . paper by Julia Becker and Stephen Wright (2011) details even more of the insidious ways that benevolent sexism might be harmful for both women and social activism. In a series of experiments, women were exposed to statements that either illustrated hostile sexism (e.g., "Women are too easily offended") or benevolent sexism (e.g., "Women have a way of caring that men are not capable of in the same way.") The results are quite discouraging; when the women read

statements illustrating benevolent sexism, they were less willing to engage in anti-sexist collective action, such as signing a petition, participating in a rally, or generally "acting against sexism." Not only that, but this effect was partially mediated by the fact that women who were exposed to benevolent sexism were more likely to think that there are many advantages to being a woman and were also more likely to engage in *system justification*, a process by which people justify the status quo and believe that there are no longer problems facing disadvantaged groups (such as women) in modern day society. Furthermore, women who were exposed to hostile sexism actually displayed the opposite effect—they were *more* likely to intend to engage in collective action, and *more* willing to fight against sexism in their everyday lives.

How might this play out in a day-to-day context? Imagine that there's an anti-female policy being brought to a vote, like a regulation that would make it easier for local businesses to fire pregnant women once they find out that they are expecting. If you are collecting signatures for a petition or trying to gather women to protest this policy and those women were recently exposed to a group of men making comments about the policy in question, it would be significantly easier to gain their support and vote down the policy if the men were commenting that pregnant women *should* be fired because they were dumb for getting pregnant in the first place. However, if they instead happened to mention that women are much more compassionate than men and make better stay-at-home parents as a result, these remarks might actually lead these women to be less likely to fight an objectively sexist policy.

"I MEAN, IS SEXISM REALLY STILL A PROBLEM [TODAY]?"

We often hear people claiming that sexism, racism, or other forms of discrimination that seem to be outdated are "no longer really a problem." Some people legitimately believe this to be true, while others (particularly women and racial minorities) find it ridiculous that others could be so blind to the problems that still exist. So why does this disparity exist? Why is it so difficult for so many people to see that sexism and racism are still alive and thriving?

Maybe the answer lies right here, on the benevolent side of prejudice. While "old fashioned" forms of discrimination may have died down quite a bit (after all, it really isn't quite as socially acceptable in most areas of the world to be as explicitly sexist and/or racist as people have been in the past), more "benevolent" forms of discrimination still very much exist, and they have their own sneaky ways of suppressing equality. Unaffected bystanders (or perpetrators) may construe benevolently sexist sentiments as harmless or even beneficial; in fact, as demonstrated by Becker and Wright, targets may even feel better about themselves after exposure to benevolently sexist statements. This could be, in some ways, even worse than explicit, hostile discrimination; because it hides under the guise of compliments, it's easy to use benevolent sexism to demotivate people against collective action or convince people that there is no longer a need to fight for equality.

However, to those people who *still* may be tempted to argue that benevolent sexism is nothing more than an overreaction to well-intentioned compliments, let me pose this question: What happens when there is a predominant stereotype saying that women are better stay-at-home parents than men because they are inherently more caring, maternal, and compassionate? It seems nice enough, but how does this ideology affect the woman who wants to continue to work full time after having her first child and faces judgment from her colleagues who accuse her of neglecting her child? How does it affect the man who wants to stay at home with his newborn baby, only to discover that his company doesn't offer paternity leave because they assume that women are the better candidates to be staying at home?

At the end of the day, "good intent" is not a panacea. Benevolent sexism may very well seem like harmless flattery to many people, but that doesn't mean it isn't insidiously dangerous.

To conclude, I'll now ask you to think about recent events surrounding Elise Andrew, creator of the wildly popular I F–king Love Science Facebook page. When she shared her personal Twitter account with the page's 4.4 million fans, many commented on the link because they were absolutely SHOCKED . . . about what? Why, of course, about the fact that she is female.

> "I had no idea that IFLS had such a beautiful face!"
> "holy hell, youre a HOTTIE!"
> "you mean you're a girl, AND you're beautiful? wow, i just liked science a lil bit more today ^^" . . .
> "you're a girl!? I always imagined you as a guy; don't know why; well, nice to see to how you look like i guess"
> "What?!!? Gurlz don't like science! LOL Totally thought you were a dude."
> "It's not just being a girl that's the surprise, but being a fit girl! (For any non-Brits, fit, in this context, means hot/bangable/shagtastic/attractive)."

Right. See, that's the thing. Elise felt uncomfortable with this, as did many others out there who saw it—and rightfully so. Yet many people would call her (and others like her) oversensitive for feeling negatively about statements that appear to be compliments. Many thought that Elise should have been happy that others were calling her attractive, or pointing out that it's idiosyncratic for her to be a female who loves science. What Elise (and many others) felt was the benevolently sexist side of things—the side that perpetuates a stereotype that women (especially *attractive* women) don't "do" science, and that the most noteworthy thing to comment on about a female scientist is what she looks like.

Unfortunately, it's very likely that no one walked away from this experience having learned anything. People who could tell that this was offensive were obviously willing to recognize it as such, but people who endorsed those statements just thought they were being nice. Because they weren't calling her incompetent or unworthy, none of them were willing to recognize it as sexism, even when explicitly told that that's what it was—even though, based on research, we know that this sort of behavior has actual, meaningful consequences for society and for gender equality. That right there? That's the *real* problem with benevolent sexism.

NOTES

1. Dusheck, Jennie. 2013. "Guest Post: Family Man Who Invented Relativity and Made Great Chili Dies." *The Last Word on Nothing*, April 1. Retrieved on March 4, 2019 (https://www.lastwordonnothing.com/2013/04/01/guest-post-physicist-dies-made-great-chili/).
2. http://www.newsdiffs.org/diff/192021/192137/www.nytimes.com/2013/03/31/science/space/yvonne-brill-rocket-scientist-dies-at-88.html/.

REFERENCES

Becker, J., & Wright, S. (2011). Yet another Dark Side of Chivalry: Benevolent Sexism Undermines and Hostile Sexism Motivates Collective Action for Social Change. *Journal of Personality and Social Psychology*, 101 (1), 62–77 DOI: 10.1037/a0022615.

Glick, P., & Fiske, S. (1996). The Ambivalent Sexism Inventory: Differentiating Hostile and Benevolent Sexism. *Journal of Personality and Social Psychology*, 70 (3), 491–512 DOI:10.1037//0022-3514.70.3.491.

Glick, P., Fiske, S., Mladinic, A., Saiz, J., Abrams, D., Masser, B., Adetoun, B., Osagie, J., Akande, A., Alao, A., Annetje, B., Willemsen, T., Chipeta, K., Dardenne, B., Dijksterhuis, A., Wigboldus, D., Eckes, T., Six-Materna, I., Expósito, F., Moya, M., Foddy, M., Kim, H., Lameiras, M., Sotelo, M., Mucchi-Faina, A., Romani, M., Sakalli, N., Udegbe, B., Yamamoto, M., Ui, M., Ferreira, M., & López, W. (2000). Beyond Prejudice as Simple Antipathy: Hostile and Benevolent Sexism across Cultures. *Journal of Personality and Social Psychology*, 79 (5), 763–75 DOI:10.1037//0022-3514.79.5.763.

THE FAULT IN OUR SCORES: GENDER AND RACIAL BIAS IN STUDENT EVALUATIONS

KIERSTEN KUMMEROW

Professors are supposed to provide students with useful objective feedback on whether students successfully completed their work, how well they executed their assignments, and whether they were able to demonstrate mastery of the course material. Once the professor has completed their assessment of students, many colleges then turn to students to evaluate the quality of their instructors. The questions universities typically ask on these student evaluations of instructors include things like: "How well did they know the material?", "Did they provide timely feedback?", "Did they connect well with students?", and above all, "Were they effective teachers?" These certainly appear to be objective questions at first glance, and universities use information from these evaluations to help determine which faculty members earn tenure, receive promotions, earn raises, or are rehired. One problem with this system of student evaluation is that, unfortunately, extensive research shows that student evaluations are biased against women professors and professors of color.

Mitchel and Martin (2018) examined reviews on the website RateMyProfessor.com and discovered that students regularly refer to women instructors as "teacher" rather than "professor" (a term that is usually granted to faculty members in higher education who have earned advanced degrees). This pattern is virtually nonexistent for men and is one that undermines women faculty members' authority and their professional achievements. This failure to call women by their appropriate titles is a problem not just in student evaluations. Women physicians are also less likely to be called doctor by their colleagues who are men (Files et al. 2017), and many women report receiving negative pushback when they use their titles on social media (Baird 2018). This lack of respect undermines women's credibility in ways that do not impact their colleagues who are men. It also reinforces the idea that being in a professional field such as medicine or academia is something that is inherently masculine.

Student evaluations are also more likely to discuss women's appearance, personality, and perceived incompetence, and more likely to discuss men's perceived competence or knowledge of the topic (Mitchell & Martin 2018; Schmidt 2015). These differences are fairly large. In the same study of comments on

(*continued*)

Original to *Focus on Social Problems: A Contemporary Reader*.

RateMyProfessor.com, the researchers found that 16 percent of students commented on their woman professor's personality, while only 4 percent commented on their professor's personality when that professor was a man. For example, students were more than twice as likely to write about how entertaining (or not) they found professors who were women as professors who were men (Mitchell & Martin 2018). An earlier study examining reviews at RateMyProfessor.com also found that students commented on women's appearance more frequently than men's appearance. These comments on appearance included positive terms such as "stylish" and "fashionable" as well as negative terms like "frumpy" (Schmidt 2015).

Men are consistently rated higher than women in student evaluations even when the quality of their work is the same (Boring, Ottoboni, & Stark 2016; MacNell, Driscoll, & Hunt 2015; Mitchell & Martin 2018). For example, one study examined two online courses, one taught by a man and one taught by a woman. Even though the online courses used the same format for the class and the same assignments, the woman professor received lower evaluations than the professor who was a man (Mitchell & Martin 2018). The difference between the scores was very revealing; it wasn't just that the woman was scored lower on a few of the items, but that she did not score a higher rating than the man on any of the 23 measures used in the official university evaluation (Mitchell & Martin 2018). Other studies have found similar patterns: students in online classes rated teaching assistants (TAs) that they perceived as men higher than TAs that they perceived as women, even though the students with the TA who was a woman performed better in the class (Boring, Ottoboni & Stark 2016).

Although determining whether the bias is gender-based rather than just discrepancies in individual instructors appears daunting, a number of studies have used several approaches to isolate this variable. One study examined four online discussion groups for the same class. Two of the groups were run by a man and two were run by a woman. Students in one of the groups run by the instructor who was a man were told that the instructor was a woman and vice versa. Though the instructors did not receive evaluations that were statistically different from each other, the man earned lower evaluations from the students who thought he was a woman and the woman instructor earned higher evaluations from students who thought she was a man (MacNell, Driscoll, & Hunt 2015). A similar study found that in an identically administered online class, the instructor who was a man earned significantly higher ratings across almost all categories (Mitchell & Martin 2018). Other studies have found that men also consistently score significantly higher student evaluations even on metrics that have nothing to do with the professor's ability or personality. For example, men earned higher ratings than women on measures of whether they returned assignments promptly even when the assignments were returned after the same amount of time (Boring, Ottoboni, & Stark 2016; Mitchell & Martin 2018).

This pattern of bias persists despite evidence that students do not perform as well in courses headed by men (Boring, Ottoboni, & Stark 2016). In another study that examined TAs, students who had the TA who was a man did substantially worse on a uniform final exam than students who had the TA who was a woman; however, the students rated the man higher in their student evaluations (Boring, Ottoboni, & Stark 2016). Similarly, men get better evaluations even when the students in their class earn lower grades than students in the same course with a woman (Mitchell & Martin 2018). This suggests that students are not just giving higher ratings to professors whom they perceive as "easy" or who give good grades. In other words, women have to work much harder, and still get lower student evaluations than their counterparts who are men.

The bias in student evaluations goes beyond gender; researchers have also documented racial bias. Asian and Latinx professors receive lower evaluations than White professors (DiPietro & Faye 2005), and Black professors tend to receive the lowest evaluations (Reid 2010; Smith & Hawkins 2011). The racial disparities in student evaluations are smaller on concrete items like "the instructor gave presentations which were logically arranged" and larger on items that rely more on student perceptions of the instructor like "overall value of the course" (Smith & Hawkins 2011). These items which rely on general feeling about the quality of the course are more likely to be influenced by unconscious bias on the part of students (Reid 2010). Though there is little research studying the intersections of race and gender on student evaluations, women of color face significant gender and racial bias in other areas of the university, including during general classroom interactions (Pittman 2010) and in university administrative decisions (Turner & González 2011), supporting the likelihood of gender and racialized bias in student evaluations.

So, why is this bias in student evaluations important? Women and people of color are less likely to get tenure (a permanent university appointment that may be granted to a professor after a probationary period at that university) and promotions (De Welde & Stepnick 2015; Perna 2001; Winslow & Davis 2016). Of all women faculty, 27.7 percent are instructors (a nontenure track position), while only 21.5 percent are full professors (the highest ranking faculty position). For comparison, only 12.8 percent of faculty who are men are instructors, while 34 percent are full professors (Hironimus-Wendt & Dedjoe 2015). For women of color, the statistics reveal even more bias; only 16 percent are full professors (Castro 2015). This is at least partially the result of hidden discrimination since student evaluations are presented as objective, even though the evidence shows that they are not. Continuing to use biased evaluations in these types of personnel decisions suggests that university officials are comfortable with the status quo and must be challenged to develop and retain a more diverse faculty. One proposed solution involves simply mathematically correcting for bias since some research shows that women earn, on average, about 0.4 fewer points on a five-point scale (Mitchell & Martin

2018) and Black professors earn, on average, about 0.6 fewer points on a five-point scale (Smith & Hawkins 2011). However, even this solution could be difficult to put in to play because there are many factors which influence the potential bias of evaluations (Boring, Ottoboni, & Stark 2016).

Students can help reduce this bias as well. Now that you are more informed about this phenomenon, you can apply that knowledge to your own evaluations. When you are writing your evaluations, think about your assessments, the language you are using, and whether or not your evaluations contain bias. If you have a professor who is a woman, look at the review and ask yourself, "Would I write this if the professor was a man?" If you have a professor who is a person of color, ask yourself, "Would I write this if the professor was White?" If you wouldn't, reflect on why you are having a different reaction to your professor. Do they not look like what you imagine a professor to be? By examining your initial reactions and understanding where the bias comes from, you can start changing the bias in evaluations.

REFERENCES

Baird, Julia. "Women, Don't Shy from Online Abuse." *The New York Times*, June 30, 2018.

Boring, Anne, Kellie Ottoboni, and Philip Stark. 2016. "Student Evaluations of Teaching (Mostly) Do Not Measure Teaching Effectiveness." *ScienceOpen Research*. doi:10.14293/S2199-1006.1.SOR-EDU.AETBZC.v1.

Castro, Corinne. 2015. "Characteristics and Perceptions of Women of Color Faculty Nationally." In *Disrupting the Culture of Silence: Confronting Gender Inequality and Making Change in Higher Education*, edited by K. De Welde and A. Stepnick, pp. 173–188, VA: Stylus Publishing.

De Welde, Kristine, and Andi Stepnick. 2015. *Disrupting the Culture of Silence: Confronting Gender Inequality and Making Change in Higher Education*. Stylus Publishing.

DiPietro, M. & Faye, A. 2015. *Online student-ratings-of-instruction (SRI) mechanisms for maximal feedback to instructors*. Paper presented at the 30th Annual Meeting of the Professional and Organizational Development Network; Milwaukee, WI.

Files, Julia A., Anita P. Mayer, Marcia G. Ko, Patricia Friedrich, Marjorie Jenkins, Michael J. Bryan, Suneela Vegunta, Christopher M. Wittich, Melissa A. Lyle, Ryan Melikian, Trevor Duston, Yu-Hui H. Chang and Sharonne N. Hayes. 2017. "Speaker Introductions at Internal Medicine Grand Rounds: Forms of Address Reveal Gender Bias." *Journal of Women's Health (15409996)* 26(5):413–19.

Hironimus-Wendt, Robert J., and Doreen A. Dedjoe. 2015. "Glass Ceilings and Gated Communities in Higher Education." In *Disrupting the Culture of Silence: Confronting Gender Inequality and Making Change in Higher Education*, edited by K. De Welde and A. Stepnick. Virginia: Stylus Publishing.

MacNell, Lillian, Adam Driscoll, and Andrea N. Hunt. 2015. "What's in a Name: Exposing Gender Bias in Student Ratings of Teaching." *Innovative Higher Education* 40(4):291–303.

Mitchell, Kristina M. W., and Jonathan Martin. 2018. "Gender Bias in Student Evaluations." *PS: Political Science and Politics* 51(3):648–52.

Perna, Laura W. 2001. "Sex and Race Differences in Faculty Tenure and Promotion." *Research in Higher Education* 42(5):541–67.

Pittman, Chavella T. 2010. "Race and Gender Oppression in the Classroom: The Experiences of Women Faculty of Color with White Male Students." *Teaching Sociology* 38(3):183–96.

Reid, Landon D. 2010. "The Role of Perceived Race and Gender in the Evaluation of College Teaching on Ratemyprofessors. Com." *Journal of Diversity in Higher Education* 3(3):137–52.

Schmidt, Benjamin M. 2015, "Gendered Language in Teacher Reviews". Retrieved July 24, 2018, 2018, from http://benschmidt.org/profGender.

Smith, Bettye P., and Billy Hawkins. 2011. "Examining Student Evaluations of Black College Faculty: Does Race Matter?" *The Journal of Negro Education* (2):149.

Turner, Caroline Sotello Viernes, and Juan Carlos González. 2011. "Faculty Women of Color: The Critical Nexus of Race and Gender." *Journal of Diversity in Higher Education* 4(4):199.

Winslow, Sarah, and Shannon N Davis. 2016. "Gender Inequality across the Academic Life Course." *Sociology Compass* 10(5):404–16.

ANNA NORTH

20. "YOU JUST ACCEPTED IT"

Why Older Women Kept Silent about Sexual Harassment—and Younger Ones are Speaking Out

The #MeToo movement started with Tarana Burke's use of the hashtag in 2006 and was reinvigorated in 2017 following charges of sexual harassment and assault against several high-profile men. Victims of sexual harassment and assault described their own experiences and tagged them #MeToo on social media, in an effort to show solidarity with other victims, to move their experiences out of the shadows, and to highlight the pervasiveness of sexual harassment and assault in and outside of the workplace. North explores how younger and older women experienced similar acts of workplace harassment in different ways.

Shar'Ron Maxx Mahaffey was the sales administration manager for an international electronics company about 20 years ago, when, she says, a vice president at the company developed a crush on her. Mahaffey, now 64, wasn't interested, but she said she knew that if she rejected the VP outright, "everything would've changed" for her at her job. She had gained a lot of authority at the company and worried that it would be taken away if she offended the man. So Mahaffey did what she calls "ducking and dodging": avoiding the VP's advances "without having to say, 'Leave me alone.'" Sometimes that involved physically staying out of his way in the office. "I would have to jump one elevator to the other elevator to outsmart him so we wouldn't end up on the elevator together," Mahaffey recalled.

Mahaffey, who now lives in northern Virginia, was one of about 40 women, ranging in age from their 20s to their late 60s, who participated in a series of focus groups. . . . We wanted to find out how different generations of women think about sexual harassment and assault[1] in the age of #MeToo.[2] We used the findings to develop a nationwide survey,[3] along with Morning Consult, a nonpartisan technology and media company, to measure the attitudes of women of different ages across the country.

One of our key findings in the survey was that women 35 and over were more likely than younger women to say they'd kept silent about sexual harassment they experienced at work. In our focus groups, one possible reason for the difference emerged: Looking back on their lives and careers, older women tended to see sexual misconduct as something they simply had to put up with. As one 50-year-old woman put it, "in the '80s and in the '90s, harassment was accepted. It wasn't talked about." Younger women, meanwhile, were more likely to see sexual harassment at work as something they could change—they described reporting the behavior to authority figures, and sometimes confronting the harassers themselves.

As critiques of the #MeToo movement have rolled in, a media narrative of generational divide has emerged: Some have speculated that younger women define sexual harassment more broadly than older women or that older women have more doubts about #MeToo. Megan McArdle wrote at Bloomberg,[4] for instance, that women in their 40s see a difference between Harvey Weinstein and "guys who press aggressively—embarrassingly, adulterously—for sex," but that "to women in their 20s, it seems that distinction is invisible." But when we looked at a cross section of American women, we found that attitudes toward #MeToo and harassment were generally similar—it was their willingness to report their experiences that was different. . . . Rather than resenting younger women for their willingness to speak out against harassment, older women frequently applauded them. Some felt inspired by their younger counterparts, while others described helping young women come forward. Overall, what we found among older women was a sense of hope that perhaps their daughters and granddaughters would feel more able to speak up than they had.

WOMEN OF DIFFERENT AGES EXPERIENCE HARASSMENT AT SIMILAR RATES—BUT YOUNGER WOMEN ARE MORE LIKELY TO TALK ABOUT IT

In the Vox/Morning Consult survey, younger women were about as likely as older women to say they'd been sexually harassed at work at some point in their careers—29 percent of women between ages 18 and 34 said they'd been harassed, compared with 33 percent of women 35 and over. Where the two groups differed more substantially was in their responses to harassment—53 percent of older women who had been harassed at work said they had never reported it, while 44 percent of younger women said the same.

Older women were about as likely as younger ones to say they'd told a boss or human resources department about harassment—27 percent of women 35 and over had talked to a boss or HR rep about the issue, compared with 29 percent of women 18 to 34. But younger women were more likely to have told colleagues they'd been harassed—25 percent had brought up an incident of harassment with co-workers, compared with 19 percent of older women.

These aren't huge differences; in fact, our survey found few large differences between the two age groups we compared. But they pointed to a pattern we also saw in our focus groups, in which older women said that sexual harassment wasn't talked about when they were younger and that, especially earlier in their careers, they worried they would be retaliated against—or simply ignored—if they reported sexual misconduct at work.

Michelle Blandburg, 66 and now retired after many years of work at a credit union, said a former boss used to ask her questions like, "What bra are you wearing today?" "I just dismissed it," she said. Later, however, she learned he'd been making the same kinds of comments to one of her female co-workers. "But neither one of us thought to or felt we would be believed if we went to HR and complained," Blandburg said. "He's a VP, and here we are, underlings."

A 50-year-old woman, who asked that her name not be used, said harassment wasn't talked about when she worked at an accounting firm at the age of 19 or 20. When partners made suggestive or flirtatious comments, "you just accepted it," she said.

Women in the groups talked about difficulties discussing the issues of sexual harassment, abuse, and assault not just at work but in their families. Laura de la Torre, 69, said she was abused as a child by her uncle. "On my 50th birthday, I gave myself a present of telling my mother and my aunt" about the abuse, she said. Her mother asked her why she'd never said anything before. De la Torre's response: "I couldn't trust you to protect me, to believe me." When she called her aunt (who was not the uncle's wife), de la Torre said, the aunt kept referring to the uncle respectfully as compadre, or "godfather." "I thought, you don't get it, do you?" de la Torre said. "He's not a godfather, he's not a compadre, he's a child molester. And I hung up." Still, "I felt like I had done something for myself," de la Torre said. "I needed to do that for me."

NOT REPORTING TOOK A TOLL

For many women, the feeling that they couldn't talk about harassment or abuse left them forced to deal with the problem alone. De la Torre described the emotional toll of keeping the secret of her uncle's abuse: By age 50, she felt she'd been "dragging this around like this stinking weight behind me all these years."

Mahaffey, meanwhile, described the stress of feeling that she had to "duck and dodge" her way around men's inappropriate behavior. Of her efforts to avoid the VP's advances, she said, "it was exhausting when I got home and I would think about it." She would think, "I've got to go back in there tomorrow," she said, "and then the same thing would happen."

It wasn't just the VP, Mahaffey said. At around the same time she was dealing with his advances, she went on a business trip to Chicago, where a male colleague who lived in the area took her out to dinner and a jazz bar. She assumed he was just being nice, she said. But then he took her to a place where she saw couples walking together and kissing. It turned out to be a popular makeout spot.

She sat there "frozen," she said, thinking, "Oh, God, please don't let him, don't let him, don't let him ask." Eventually, she said, he realized she wasn't going to give him an opening, and he drove away. "I was so scared," she said. "I was just shaking because I knew if he approached me, I would reject him. If I rejected him, I knew everything was going to change between us." If she directly rejected his advances, she'd lose their friendly workplace relationship, she explained, "and I just could not afford to do that."

YOUNGER WOMEN WERE MORE COMFORTABLE SPEAKING OUT ABOUT HARASSMENT

Women under 35 in our focus groups described many of the same kinds of unwelcome experiences with men at work. But in many cases, they also felt comfortable speaking up about those experiences. Angela, 23, who asked that only her first name be used, said that in a previous job, a male co-worker repeatedly asked her inappropriate questions, like whether she'd had sex with anyone since a recent breakup. One day, she confronted him directly. "I was like, 'Dude, shut the fuck up,'" she said. "This is none of your business, I don't like you, you're the scum of the earth. And if you say something to me like this again, we're going to have a problem."

Angela said she felt comfortable confronting her co-worker in part because he wasn't her superior. "I also didn't like my job," she said, "so if he was going to try and do some kind of retaliation, I honestly didn't care."

Samantha Goldstein, 27, said she had experienced—and reported—sexual harassment multiple times in her life. A janitor at her middle school made inappropriate comments to her, she said, offering her money and free food from the cafeteria to try to get her to trust him. She reported him to school officials, and he was fired. As an adult, Goldstein was at a job interview when the male interviewer began brushing his foot against her leg under the table. After the interview, he began texting her. Goldstein didn't get the job, but she reported the man, and he, too, was fired. "I've always been one to be more vocal," Goldstein said, "and never really been fearful of voicing myself."

Not all younger women in the focus groups were confident that they would be believed or supported if they reported harassment at work. One 24-year-old woman, who asked that her name not be used, said there was no HR department where she worked. She said that if she were ever harassed to the degree that she was very uncomfortable, "I would look for a new job because I don't really think there would be much to be done." "I don't want to put myself in the line of fire," she explained.

Meanwhile, some older women said they had reported some of their experiences. Mahaffey did eventually bring up the VP's advances with her company's HR department when she was about to leave the company to move to another city, though she did not file a formal harassment complaint. The HR department ultimately wrote her a favorable letter of recommendation, she said. The VP had already been reassigned to another region for reasons unrelated to harassment; she never heard from him again. But overall, older women were more likely than younger ones to describe sexual harassment as something they had to deal with in silence, on their own.

OLDER WOMEN MAY PLAY A ROLE IN HELPING YOUNGER WOMEN COME FORWARD

When it comes to what might have changed to help younger women feel more comfortable speaking up about harassment than their older counterparts, our survey results offer some hints but no single clear answer.

Younger women were a bit more likely than older ones to believe that if they reported sexual harassment to a boss or HR department, the harassment would stop—37 percent of women ages 18 to 34 were very confident this would happen, compared with 31 percent of women 35 and older. Younger women were also somewhat more confident that their reports would be taken seriously—41 percent were very confident of this, compared with 33 percent of older women.

Though several younger women in the focus groups talked about the possibility of finding another job if they had to leave due to harassment, younger women in the survey were not much more confident about this prospect than their older counterparts—28 percent of women 18 to 34 were very confident they could find a new job quickly, compared with 23 percent of women 35 and older.

In the focus groups, however, older women offered some theories as to why their younger counterparts might be more likely to come forward. Patricia, 64, who asked Vox not to use her last name, noted that women today are less likely to be isolated in male-dominated fields. At the beginning of her career in the space industry, she didn't have female colleagues in her field: "I was the only one, period." Now, said Patricia, who has retired, her old office is "full of women."

The presence of more senior women in workplaces today may help younger women report harassment. The presence of female employees at every level in a company hierarchy can have a major influence on how likely female employees are to be harassed, Frank Dobbin, a sociologist at Harvard University who studies workplace diversity, told Vox. A critical mass of women in positions of power can help junior women report problems. "If there are good examples of women who have succeeded," he explained, "you can talk to them."

Women in senior roles also send the message that the organization values the contributions of women. Patricia, the 64-year-old who worked in the space industry, described playing a protective role for younger women at work. As she rose up in her career, she said,

women began coming to her to talk about problems they were having with men at work. She would "make sure that they had a path forward," sometimes even going to the boss on their behalf to report the issue. "I always was an advocate for them," she said.

Other women over 35 described teaching their daughters that harassment was not something they had to accept. One woman, who asked to remain anonymous, said her teenage daughter had been harassed a few years ago at a summer job. "Her dad and I advocated for her," the woman said, and helped their daughter report the harassment. "I'm teaching my daughter what I wasn't taught," she said.

YOUNGER WOMEN CAN BE A SOURCE OF INSPIRATION FOR OLDER WOMEN—AND #METOO CAN BE A SOURCE OF HOPE

While older women described mentoring and advising younger women, several said they were inspired by younger generations as well. De la Torre spoke of "young kids coming forward" to confront their abusers, "standing there in tears and saying, 'You hurt me.'" She likened young people advocating for the #MeToo movement to those fighting against gun violence. "Our children are teaching us to be strong," she said. De la Torre believes that #MeToo will help future generations feel comfortable reporting harassment. "I really believe that kids are going to feel more empowered and not be fearful," she said.

Some media coverage[5] has suggested that older women are more skeptical than younger women when it comes to the #MeToo movement. Our survey did not find evidence of this. In fact, we found that older women were even more optimistic than younger ones about the possible effects of the movement. [Women over age 35 were more likely than women under age 35 to agree that women would experience lower rates of sexual assault and harassment as the result of the #MeToo movement—55% compared to 47%. In addition, older women were more likely to agree that the #MeToo movement would make men more conscious of inappropriate behavior. Fifty-nine percent of women under age 35 thought this was a likely consequence of the #MeToo movement, compared to 70% of women over age 35].

Among older women in our focus groups, optimism was a common theme. Blandburg said her first reaction to the #MeToo movement was, "At last." Finally, she said, women feel that they "will be believed, that they're not going to be dismissed." Mahaffey described the #MeToo movement as "an awakening of society to the level of sexual harassment of women in every facet of life." "It's empowering for my daughters and granddaughters to know that they'll be heard," she said, "and that they can stand up and do something without fear of retaliation."

NOTES

1. North, Anna. 2017. "What I've Learned Covering Sexual Misconduct This Year." *Vox*, December 27. Retrieved March 4, 2019, from https://www.vox.com/identities/2017/12/27/16803610/sexual-misconduct-harassment-reckoning-metoo.
2. North, Anna, Constance Grady, Laura McGann, and Aja Romano. 2019. "Sexual Harassment and Assault Allegations List." *Vox*. Retrieved on March 4, 2019, from https://www.vox.com/a/sexual-harassment-assault-allegations-list.
3. North, Anna. 2018. "The #MeToo Generation Gap is a Myth." *Vox*, March 20. Retrieved on March 4, 2019, from https://www.vox.com/2018/3/20/17115620/me-too-sexual-harassment-sex-abuse-poll.
4. McArdle, Megan. 2018. "Listen to the 'Bad Feminists.'" *Bloomberg*, January 17. Retrieved on March 4, 2019, from https://www.bloomberg.com/opinion/articles/2018-01-17/listen-to-the-bad-feminists.
5. McArdle, 2018.

SARAH RICH

21. IMAGINING A BETTER BOYHOOD

Rich argues that living in a society that favors qualities typically associated with men—courage, assertiveness, and strength—comes at a cost for both men and women. Whereas women and girls have been increasingly encouraged to take on "masculine" traits and join traditionally male-dominated organizations to increase equality between the sexes, very little effort or work has been done to encourage men and boys to take on character traits traditionally associated with femininity, like caring, cooperation, and empathy. This comes at a real cost to boys and men, who have limited ways in which "real manhood" can be expressed, and it continues to perpetuate cultural values that favor masculinity over femininity.

In hindsight, our son was gearing up to wear a dress to school for quite some time. For months, he wore dresses—or his purple-and-green mermaid costume—on weekends and after school. Then he began wearing them to sleep in lieu of pajamas, changing out of them after breakfast. Finally, one morning, I brought him his clean pants and shirt, and he looked at me and said, "I'm already dressed." He was seated on the couch in a gray cotton sundress covered in doe-eyed unicorns with rainbow manes. He'd slept in it, and in his dreaming hours, I imagine, stood at a podium giving inspirational speeches to an audience composed only of himself. When he'd woken up, he was ready.

He walked the half block to school with a bounce in his step, chest proud. "My friends are going to say dresses aren't for boys," he told me casually over his shoulder. "They might," I agreed. "You can just tell them you are comfortable with yourself and that's all that matters." I thought of all the other things he could tell them. I began to list them, but he was off running across the Blacktop. I scanned the entrance to see whether any parents noticed us as they came and went. I hadn't expected my stomach to churn. I felt proud of him for his self-assuredness, for the way he'd

prepared for this quietly and at his own pace, but I worried about what judgments and conclusions parents and teachers might make. And of course I worried somebody would shame him.

When he walked into his classroom, sure enough, one child immediately remarked, "Why are you wearing a dress? Dresses are for girls." A teacher swiftly and gently shut down the child's commentary and hugged my son tightly. He didn't look troubled, didn't look back at me, so I headed home, tucking a backup T-shirt into his cubby just in case his certainty flagged. In the afternoon, he was still wearing the unicorn dress. He skipped down the sidewalk, reporting that some kids had protested his attire, but he'd assured them that he was comfortable with himself.

With that, the seal was broken. Most days since, he's worn a dress from his small collection, though he also favors a light-blue guayabera—the classic collared button-down worn by men and boys in Cuba and the Philippines. Classmates' objections continued, but with less frequency and conviction. One day when my husband dropped him off, he heard a little girl stand up to a naysayer and shout, "Boys can like beautiful things, too!"

But they can't. Not without someone looking askance. To embrace anything feminine, if you're not biologically female, causes discomfort and confusion, because throughout most of history and in most parts of the world, being a woman has been a disadvantage. Why would a boy, born into all the power of maleness, reach outside his privileged domain? It doesn't compute.

As much as feminism has worked to rebalance the power and privilege between the sexes, the dominant approach to launching young women into positions that garner greater respect, higher status, and better pay still mostly maintains the association between those gains and masculine qualities. Girls' empowerment programs teach assertiveness, strength, and courage—and they must to equip young women for a world that still overwhelmingly favors men. [In 2017], when the Boy Scouts of America announced[1] that they would begin admitting girls into their dens, young women saw a wall come down around a territory that was now theirs to occupy. [*Editor's Note*: The Boy Scouts of America, now rebranded as "Scouts BSA," officially began accepting girls as members on February 1, 2019. Troops remain single-sex for most activities, though girls are now eligible to achieve the rank of Eagle Scout.][2] Parents across the country had argued that girls should have equal access to the activities and pursuits of boys' scouting, saying that Girl Scouts is not a good fit for girls who are "more rough and tumble."[3] But the converse proposition was essentially nonexistent: Not a single article that I could find mentioned the idea that boys might not find Boy Scouts to be a good fit—or, even more unspeakable, that they would want to join the Girl Scouts.

If it's difficult to imagine a boy aspiring to the Girl Scouts' merit badges (oriented far more than the boys' toward friendship, caretaking, and community), what does that say about how American culture regards these traditionally feminine arenas? And what does it say to boys who think joining the Girl Scouts sounds like fun? Even preschool-age boys know they'd be teased or shamed for disclosing such a dream.

While society is chipping away at giving girls broader access to life's possibilities, it isn't presenting boys with a full continuum of how they can be in the world. To carve out a masculine identity requires whittling away everything that falls outside the norms of boyhood. At the earliest ages, it's about external signifiers like favorite colors, TV shows, and clothes. But later, the paring knife cuts away intimate friendships, emotional range, and open communication.

There's research connecting this shedding process to the development, in some adolescent boys, of depression, anxiety, and feelings of isolation. In her 2014 documentary *The Mask You Live In*, the filmmaker Jennifer Siebel Newsom features the voices of dozens of teen boys describing their progression from childhoods rich with friendships to teen years defined by posturing and pressure to prove their manhood. Some of the boys, who present tough exteriors, admit to having suicidal thoughts. The film flashes news clips from the most notable mass shootings of that time—Virginia Tech, Aurora, Sandy Hook—each committed by a young man. "Whether it's homicidal violence or suicidal violence, people resort to such desperate behavior only when they are feeling shamed and humiliated, or feel they would be, if they didn't prove that they were real men," the psychiatrist James Gilligan, who directed Harvard's Center for the Study of Violence, says in the film.

There are so few positive variations on what a "real man" can look like that when the youngest generations show signs of reshaping masculinity, the only word that exists for them is *nonconforming*. The term highlights that nobody knows what to call these variations on maleness. Instead of understanding that children can resist or challenge traditional masculinity from within the bounds of boyhood, it's assumed that they're in a phase, that they need guidance, or that they don't want to be boys.

Numerous parents of gender-nonconforming children report initially trying to stifle their child's tendencies out of a protective instinct, thinking they might forestall bullying if only their child would fit more neatly into the box that's been set up for them. Ultimately, though, most realize that their child is less happy when prevented from gravitating naturally toward their preferences. It's important to note that there are children who do feel they've been born in the wrong body, who long for different anatomy, different pronouns. Trans kids need to be supported and accepted. And, at the same time, not every boy who puts on a dress is communicating a wish to be a girl. Too often gender dysphoria is conflated with the simple possibility that kids, when not steered toward one toy or color, will just like what they like, traditional gender expectations notwithstanding. There is little space given to experimentation and exploration before a child's community seeks to categorize them. Boyhood, as it is popularly imagined, is so narrow and confining that to press against its boundaries is to end up in a different identity altogether.

According to the San Jose State University sociologist Elizabeth Sweet, who studies gender in children's toys throughout the 20th century, American gender categories are more rigid now[4] than at any time in history, at least when it comes to consumer culture. There may be greater recognition in the abstract that gender exists along a spectrum, but for young children (and their parents), consumer products have a huge influence on identity development and presentation. "Toymakers are saying, well, we can sell each family one toy, or if we make separate versions according to gender, we can sell more toys and make families buy multiples for each gender," Sweet told me. The same holds true for clothes, baby gear, school supplies, even snack food. And parents begin gender-coding their children's worlds before those children are even born, sometimes kicked off by "gender reveal" parties, a sort of new version of the baby shower, in which parents-to-be discover the sex of their baby alongside family and friends through a dramatic, colorful display.

There is so much parents can't know when a baby hasn't been born—they can't know the baby's hair color or eye color or whether the baby will be colicky or peaceful, healthy or sick. But they can know their child's anatomy, and with that information they can create a to-do list full of tasks that quell the angst of knowing so little else. They can paint a nursery, buy onesies, pick names. A baby's sex creates a starting point on a cultural road map that the whole family and community can use to direct the child toward defining who they are and who they are not.

Of course today, among a certain set, there's an active rejection of pink for baby girls, whose parents don't want them treated as delicate flowers. But again, the reverse still has no purchase. Exceedingly few parents dress their baby boys in a headband and a dress. Somewhat ironically, those pink-foresaking parents of infant girls often find themselves, three years later, remarking that in spite of shielding their daughters from overly feminized colors, toys, and media, they've still turned out to be princess-obsessed preschoolers. The parents display lighthearted self-consciousness that they couldn't render their girl immune to sparkles. It's unlikely, though, that they shame their girls for their "girliness." They throw up their hands and acquiesce to an Elsa costume. By contrast, boys' parents tend to double down on reinforcing masculinity.

"Most nonconforming adult men, when they talk about their upbringing, say their first bully was their dad," reports Matt Duron, whose wife, Lori Duron, wrote the book *Raising My Rainbow*, about their gender-creative son. Matt, who had a 20-year career as a police officer in Orange County, California, has been a vocal supporter of his son, though in their conservative region, his stance has been attacked. The Durons' son, now 11, gave up dresses years ago, but he still loves makeup and wears his hair long. Classmates bully him, but he finds support from his family and lately, too, at Sephora in his local mall, where male employees demonstrate a different way to be grown men in the world.

The idea of Sephora as a haven for gender-creative suburban American boys is touching and wonderful in its way, but it's bittersweet that alternate models of masculinity are so scarce and relatively unvaried. There are now quite a few books featuring boys who like dresses, but almost all of them follow the same arc: Boy dons dress among friends; boy gets shamed and bullied; boy becomes despondent and hides at home; then, finally, boy returns to friend group and they see his value and embrace him (usually after one last-ditch attempt to reform him through shame). Each time I pick up one of these books to read to my son, I find myself wanting to change the narrative or skip the portions where rejection and suffering show up as inevitable.

"But little kids live in the real world," Ian Hoffman argued when I questioned the trope. Hoffman co-authored the children's book *Jacob's New Dress* with his wife, Sarah. "Would it be nice to have a book with a boy in a dress with no conflict? Yes. Are we there? I don't think so," Hoffman told me. He says that when the book was published in 2014, he and Sarah dreamed that someday it would seem quaint that a boy in a dress was a big deal. Then, just a year ago, their book was banned in North Carolina and cut from a public school unit on bullying and harassment. "The initial first-grade book selection, which focuses on valuing uniqueness and difference, has been replaced due to some concerns about the book," the superintendent of the Charlotte-Mecklenburg Schools system told[5] the *New York Times*. One can imagine that if it had been about a girl who dressed as a firefighter, such extreme measures would not have been taken. There's a word for what's happening here: misogyny. When school officials and parents send a message to children that "boyish" girls are badass but "girlish" boys are embarrassing, they are telling kids that society values and rewards masculinity but not femininity. They are not just keeping individual boys from free self-expression; they are keeping women down too.

It is lopsided to approach gender equality by focusing only on girls' empowerment. If society is to find its way to a post-#MeToo future, parents, teachers, and community members need to build a culture of boyhood that fosters empathy, communication, caretaking, and cooperation. But how? Could there be a space or an organization for boys where they're encouraged to challenge what's expected of them socially, emotionally, and physically? What would the activities be? What would the corresponding catchwords be to the girls' "brave" and "strong" other than "cowardly" and "weak"? It's a societal loss that so many men grow up believing that showing aggression and stifling emotion are the ways to signal manhood. And it's a personal loss to countless little boys who, at best, develop mechanisms for compartmentalizing certain aspects of who they are and, at worst, deny those aspects out of existence.

This fall, our son will start kindergarten, and with kindergarten comes a school uniform. This means pale blue collared shirts for all the kids, paired with navy blue pants, jumpers, or skirts. Currently, there don't seem to be any boys at the school who choose the jumper or skirt, and it remains to be seen whether our son will maintain his penchant for dresses even when the sartorial binary becomes starker—and the dresses more plain.

Whatever he decides is fine with us. My only hope is that if he chooses to stop wearing dresses, it won't be due to feeling that his fullest self-expression no longer has a place. What I want for him, and for all boys, is for the process of becoming men to be expansive, not reductive. I know I'm not alone. More than a century ago, in the October 1902 edition of London's *Cornhill Magazine*, the writer and poet May Byron wrote a piece called "The Little Boy" in which she talked about, among other things, boys' evolving mode of dress as they move through childhood. She tied it then, as I do now, to a mildly tragic departure from a boy's richest relationship with himself:

"Petticoated or kilted, in little sailor suits, and linen smocks, and velvet coats, and miniature reefers, he marches blindly on his destiny," Byron writes. "Soon he will run his dear little head against that blank wall of foregone conclusions which shuts out fairyland from a workaday world."

NOTES

1. Boy Scouts of America, 2017. "The BSA Expands Program to Welcome Girls from Cub Scouts to Highest Rank of Eagle Scots." October 11. Retrieved March 4, 2019, from https://www.scoutingnewsroom.org/press-releases/bsa-expands-programs-welcome-girls-cub-scouts-highest-rank-eagle-scout.
2. Norman, Derek. M. 2019. "Not 'My Grandfather's Boy Scout Troop: It's Now for Girls, Too." *The New York Times*, February 1. https://www.nytimes.com/2019/03/03/nyregion/girls-in-boy-scouts-bsa.html
3. Bosman, Julie, and Niraj Chokshi. 2017. "Boy Scouts Will Accept Girls, in Bid to 'Shape the Next Generation of Leaders.'" *The New York Times*, October 11. Retrieved on March 4, 2019, from https://www.nytimes.com/2017/10/11/us/boy-scouts-girls.html.
4. Sweet, Elizabeth. 2015. "Beyond the Blue and Pink Toy Divide." TEDxUCDavis Talk. Retrieved on March 4, 2019, from https://www.elizabethvsweet.com/tedx-talk.
5. Mele, Christopher. 2017. "North Carolina School System Pulls Book about a Boy in a Dress." *The New York Times*, March 24. Retrieved on March 4, 2019, from https://www.nytimes.com/2017/03/24/us/north-carolina-school-jacobs-new-dress-book.html.

SELLING FEMINISM, CONSUMING FEMININITY

AMANDA M. GENGLER

Many women, even those of us now in our twenties, thirties, forties, and beyond, remember the thrill of coming home from school to the fresh, crisp pages of the latest issue of *Seventeen* . . . [in its 75th year in 2019] hoping for guidance as we struggled to navigate the perils of adolescence. Today's girls consume an even wider range of "teen 'zines," both in print and online, and at increasingly younger ages. Their pages are filled with how-to pieces—how to style your hair in the latest fashion, how to give your lips an enticing shine, even how to kiss correctly. But beyond beauty tips, teen magazines also teach girls, at a basic level, *what it means* to be a girl today.

While we might have hoped traditional ideas about femininity had been relegated to the past along with typewriters and Burma shave, teen magazines are still saturated with them. In their pages, girls should focus on being pretty, pleasing men, and decorating men's spaces. Without the colorful modern layouts and contemporary actresses splayed across their shiny covers, one might mistake the glossies for dusty relics left on the shelf since the 1950s.

Indeed, recent covers offer little more than provocative teases about boys and beauty, such as "Where will you meet your next boyfriend?" or "Is school secretly making you fat?" Pieces that focus on substantive issues—drunk driving, careers, or politics—are rare. The overall message a girl receives, journalist Kate Pierce found in her study of *Seventeen* over time, is that "how she looks is more important than what she thinks, that her main goal in life is to find a man who will take care of her . . . and that her place will be home with the kids and the cooking and the housework."

Sociologist Kelly Massoni also studied *Seventeen*, finding that men held 70 percent of the jobs represented in its pages. Women were disproportionately shown either not working or working in traditionally feminine jobs, with a particular emphasis on modeling and acting careers. Advice on sexuality hasn't evolved much either. Sociologist Laura Carpenter explored the presentation of (almost exclusively hetero-) sexuality in *Seventeen* across the decades, and though she saw greater inclusion of sexual diversity and increased openness to women's sexual agency in recent years, these progressive messages were often presented alongside more traditional ones, with the author or editors emphasizing the latter. Girls might now learn they can "make the first move" or dress in clothing as risqué as fashion

demands, but the subtext is clear: a hip young woman is more concerned with lipstick, boyfriends, and belly-button rings than books, politics, or careers.

So beside how-to features on hair styling, body shaping, and make-up application, there are explicit instructions for interacting with men and boys. While beauticians, personal trainers, actresses, or other women offer advice on beauty, fashion, and exercise, *men* (often adult men in their twenties) advise girls on how to support, entertain, and excite their boyfriends by cheering them on from the sidelines, doing personal favors, making them laugh, and "talking dirty." Despite a new millennium, much remains unchanged.

What *has* changed is the packaging: many of these messages are now couched in feminist language. Advertisers must convince young women that they are in need of constant improvement—largely to get and keep boys' attention—without threatening young women's views of themselves as intelligent, self-directed, and equal. Buzz words like "empowerment," "self-determination," and "independence" are sprinkled liberally across their pages. But this seemingly progressive rhetoric is used to sell products and ideas that keep girls doing gender in appropriately feminine ways, leading them to reproduce, rather than challenge, gender hierarchies. An ad for a depilatory cream, for instance, tells girls that they are "unique, determined, and unstoppable," so they should not "settle . . . for sandpaper skin." Feminist demands for political and economic equality—and the refusal to *settle* for low wages, violence, and second-class citizenship—morph into a refusal to settle for less than silky skin. Pseudo-feminist language allows young women to believe that they can "empower" themselves at the checkout counter by buying the accoutrements of traditional femininity. Girls' potential choice to shun make-up or hair removal disappears, replaced by their choice of an array of beauty products promising to moisturize, soften, and smooth their troubles away.

Everywhere, girls are flooded with messages urging them to see success, as achieved through beauty, just a purchase away. By some estimates, a 10-year-old is likely to spend $300,000 on her hair and face before she reaches 50. In *Beauty and Misogyny*, Sheila Jeffreys catalogs the damage these beauty products, cosmetic treatments, and surgical procedures do to female bodies. Jeffreys argues that beauty practices normalized in Western

(*continued*)

culture—wearing high heels, for example—can injure women physically and socially. These practices are seductive because we learn to take pleasure in them, but they also reinforce the underlying ideology that women's bodies are unattractive when unadorned and must be carefully groomed simply to be presentable.

On top of the advertising that accounts for around half of these texts' content, many articles that *appear* to be editorial—pieces comparing the merits of accessories, fingernail polishes, or facial cleansers, for example—are advertisements in disguise, conveniently including brand names, retail locations, and prices. In her ethnography of teen 'zine consumption in a junior high, Margaret Finders noted that girls often failed to recognize these as marketing, interpreting them as valuable, neutral information instead.

This is not to say that all girls consume teen "zines uncritically. Interviews by sociologists have shown that girls are often critical of airbrushed models and claim to ignore advertisements. Melissa Milkie, for example, found that girls of color were especially skeptical, viewing teen magazines as oriented primarily to White girls and including girls and women of color only when they fit White beauty ideals. For the most part, however, girls' critiques stop at body image, failing to question these texts' nearly exclusive focus on beauty and heterosexual romance. Dawn Curie found that 70 percent of her interviewees were "avid" readers, for whom the reading and sharing of these texts was a significant pastime. These girls spent hours devouring their content and admitted that they turned to the magazines' "real-life" pieces for "practical advice," and used the girls in the magazines as yardsticks by which to measure their own lives and experiences.

Teen girl magazines breathe new life into some very old ideas. Today's successful woman, they proclaim, orients her life around looking beautiful and snagging a man. Seemingly esteem-boosting "grrl power" rhetoric makes this message seem fresh and provides marketers an appealing way to sell even independent-minded girls old-fashioned deference and subordination as "empowerment." Those of us who grew up with these texts can't deny that consuming them, along with the products they push, was often a lot of fun, even a rite of passage. But if feminist goals of equality are to be realized, girls need better options.[1] We can also teach girls to question the basic assumptions embedded in popular media and to become critical consumers (or nonconsumers) of these texts and the culture of beauty and romance they peddle. We might even offer girls the more radical message, learned and lived by earlier generations of feminists, that true empowerment comes not through consumption, but solidarity, critical consciousness, and collective action.

---

1   *New Moon*, newmoon.org, is one attempt to offer an alternative to traditional girls' magazines.

ELIS HERMAN AND ELROI J. WINDSOR

22. TRANSGENDER DISCRIMINATION IN THE WORKPLACE

When considering gender, sexism, and gender discrimination, the perspectives and experiences of those who do not fit easily into the existing gender categories are often disregarded or overlooked. Herman and Windsor discuss the experiences of transgender people at work, focusing on workplace experiences, legal protections, and advocacy organizations that seek equality on behalf of transgender or gender-nonconforming workers.

When studying social issues related to gender, it is critical to examine the experiences of people whose genders do not fit into conventional categories. In this reading, we define key terminology related to transgender experiences and provide an overview of some types of transitions that transgender people may choose in their lives. Then, we consider one social institution that has a tremendous impact on the quality of life for this group: the workplace. For transgender people in the United States, job discrimination, bias, and mistreatment are common problems. Although some legal protections exist that can help mitigate these circumstances, they are currently not widespread. However, issues relevant to trans people are rapidly becoming more and more visible, and organizations that advocate on behalf of transgender people are paving the way for improved opportunities and outcomes.

TERMINOLOGY

Sex and gender terms are often used interchangeably, but it is important to note distinctions when discussing issues that affect gender-nonconforming people. The term "sex" describes internal and external physical characteristics including chromosomes, hormones, genitalia, reproductive organs, and secondary sex characteristics.[1] Although babies are typically assigned a sex of "male" or "female" at birth based on their genitals, variations in sex characteristics complicate these clear-cut categories.[2] Researchers estimate that around 1.7 percent of the world's population (approximately six babies born each day) are intersex. These individuals have sex characteristics that vary from typical medical expectations of maleness and femaleness.[3] Though most intersex babies are born healthy, it is common practice for doctors to perform aesthetic surgeries on intersex infants in order to "normalize" the appearance of their genitals.[4] Groups like the United Nations and Amnesty International have declared these procedures a violation of human rights, and groups like the Intersex Society of North America (now defunct) and InterACT have been working to end genital surgeries on intersex infants in the United States for years.

"Gender" is a general term that describes cultural and social assumptions and expectations associated with women and men. For example, women are expected to be sensitive and nurturing, whereas men are expected be tough and provide for their families. "Gender identity" refers to a person's internal sense of gender. People can use a variety of terms to describe gender identity; woman, man, agender, genderfluid, genderqueer, transgender man or woman, and trans man or woman are just a few of these words. "Cisgender" is used to describe individuals whose

Original to *Focus on Social Problems: A Contemporary Reader*.

gender identities match what was expected based on the sex they were assigned at birth. In other words, cisgender simply means "not transgender."[5] An example would be a person who is assigned female at birth, is raised as a girl, and feels comfortable identifying as a girl and, later in life, a woman. The term "transgender," or "trans," for short, can be used as a broad, inclusive term to describe myriad gender identities and expressions that fall outside of the sex/gender binary or challenge the expectation that there are only two sexes and two genders and that everyone's sex and gender align.[6] Transgender is also a gender identity in itself, and people may choose to identify with that word alone or in conjunction with others. Others refer to themselves simply as "trans."[7]

The words "transgender" and "transsexual" sometimes used to be used interchangeably, though in actuality their meanings have always been nuanced. While "transgender" is an umbrella term under which many experiences fall, the term transsexual was typically used to describe people who transition from one binary sex to the other, often through the use of hormones and surgeries. Because it is associated with binary conceptions of gender, and especially because it is a medicalized term originating from health professions rather than trans communities themselves, it is used less often these days; some even consider the word offensive. Individuals who were assigned female at birth, but identify and live as men, may call themselves transsexual men, but more often might refer to themselves as transgender men, trans men, or FTM (female-to-male). People who were assigned male at birth but live as women may call themselves transsexual women, but more often might refer to themselves as trans women, transgender women, or MTF (male-to-female). Some people who transition do not use the word transsexual at all and prefer to be called "people of transgender/transsexual experience" or simply "women" and "men."[8] People choose the words that best describe their gendered experiences based on complex sociocultural contexts, and the same words may have different meanings from person to person.

The language of gender is ever-changing, and people use new words every day to describe experiences that fall outside of or between the gender binary. Languages around the globe are transforming as people push against binary notions of sex and gender and seek words that more accurately describe how they view themselves and experience the world. The word "genderqueer" has been a popular term used by people whose gendered experiences fall outside of binary expectations. Today, a more popular term is "nonbinary," which also means having a gender that falls outside of the typical sex/gender binary. Like transgender, genderqueer and nonbinary can be used as both umbrella terms and as specific identities. Other nonbinary gender identities include agender (having no gender), neutrois (gender-neutral), bigender (having two gender identities or expressions), gender fluid (moving between genders), and third gender (identifying as a different gender entirely). Some nonbinary people transition using hormones or surgeries; others do not. The range of identity terms and lived experiences within them indicate that there is no single "correct" way to be transgender. "Gender expression" describes how an individual presents their gender to the world through style, behavior, mannerisms, name, and pronouns. Sometimes gender expression is presented as a spectrum, with masculinity at one end and femininity on the other. People may express gender somewhere along that spectrum, or at different points depending on social context. People may also express gender neutrally, or as a blend of masculine and feminine characteristics. A few words commonly used to describe gender expression are "butch" (masculine gender expression), "femme" (feminine gender expression), and "androgynous" (characteristics of femininity and masculinity). Everyone has a sex, gender, gender identity, and gender expression. Some people experience and express these identities in relatively fixed, constant ways throughout their lives; others find their experiences with sex and gender to be more fluid, or less easy to define with available language. Humans "do" gender in indescribably intricate and nuanced ways; thus, there is no single set of definitions that describes either all transgender or all cisgender experiences.

TRANSITIONING ISSUES

Just as the word "transgender" encompasses innumerable identities and expressions, there is also no universal transgender experience. However, because of the institutionalization of binary sex and gender, transgender people often interface with social, medical, and legal institutions in ways that cisgender people do not. These experiences can range from coming out as transgender, to seeking surgeries or hormones, to legally changing name and sex.[9] Although media typically portray transitioning as "getting a sex change," this phrasing is inaccurate and can be considered offensive.[10] For most transgender people, the reality of transitioning, if it is even desired, is a complex and extended process with social, medical, and legal implications.

First, gender is interactional and social. How we dress, style our hair, carry our bodies, and communicate are all pieces of how we convey our genders to the world around us. A trans person may take the first steps to living comfortably by changing the way they look and dress to better reflect their internal sense of gender. Often, trans people decide to go by names and pronouns different from the ones given to them as babies. Many trans people use hormones like estrogen and testosterone to feminize or masculinize their bodies. Some also seek various surgeries to further align their physical characteristics with their genders. Yet many trans people do not use hormones or surgeries for different reasons. Some face barriers to access, such as high costs of care, having preexisting health conditions, or lacking nearby doctors who are skilled in trans health. Others simply do not desire to change their bodies with hormones and surgeries.[11]

For transgender people who choose to medically transition, access to gender-affirming interventions is often heavily regulated. Many surgeons and hormone prescribers require a letter from a mental health professional confirming a diagnosis of "gender dysphoria" before they will approve a patient for gender-related surgeries and hormone therapy. Acquiring this letter can be difficult because therapy is expensive and often not covered by insurance. Many trans people resist the requirement of a diagnosis of gender dysphoria to make decisions regarding their bodies, arguing that gender nonconformity is not a mental illness.[12]

Because sex is so important to social categorization, many transgender people navigate legal and bureaucratic processes to make their lived genders "official." Birth certificates, driver's licenses, and passports are just a few legal documents that bear sex markers. To change sex designations on official documents, individuals must negotiate with different institutions on local, state, and federal levels. For example, to change the sex marker on a passport, an individual must submit a document from a physician certifying "clinical treatment for transition from male to female or female to male" to the U.S. Department of State.[13] Requirements for changing legal sex on driver's licenses and birth certificates vary from state to state. To alter the sex designation on a driver's license, some states require proof of genital surgery, which the majority of trans people in the United States have not had or do not seek.[14] Other states require a court order or letter from a medical professional affirming that the individual lives as his or her professed sex.[15] Forty-seven states and the District of Columbia will change the sex markers on birth certificates when presented with a court order, letter from medical professional, and/or proof of surgery. Many, however, mark new certificates with the word "amended" or leave other evidence that the sex has been altered. Ohio, Tennessee, and Idaho do not change the sex designation on birth certificates under any circumstance.[16] The 2015 US Transgender Survey found that 67 percent of trans people do not possess official identity documentation that reflects their lived genders.[17] This lack of appropriate proof of identity exposes transgender people to heightened discrimination and violence. For example, transgender women who do not possess legal documentation as "female" are commonly incarcerated in prisons for men, which puts them at an increased risk for sexual violence.

The processes that surround altering sex designations on official documents are fraught with complexity and ambiguity. Many trans people live as genders other than those assigned to them at birth, yet never undergo surgeries, so cannot change documentation. Additionally, each government agency requires a separate fee to alter paperwork, and the collective costs pose a barrier for many. The legal processes also fail to account for transgender people who do not identify as men or women. For individuals whose gender identities and expressions fall outside of the gender binary, it is impossible to obtain accurate and consistent identity documents. Outside of the United States, eight countries, including Nepal, India, Pakistan, Bangladesh, Germany, New Zealand, Australia, and Canada provide a third option on legal documents.[18,19] As of 2018, Oregon, Washington, D.C., Maine, California, and Minnesota have begun offering drivers licenses with the third, non-binary gender X, and more US cities and states are likely to follow suit.[20] Some nonbinary and intersex people, however, are hesitant to use these nonbinary sex/gender markers for themselves, for fear that being publically identified as such could put them at increased risk for violence in a culture that still does not accept (and regularly punishes) gender nonconformity.

TRANS AT WORK

The workplace can be a particularly stressful environment for transgender people. In 2015, the National Center for Transgender Equality (NCTE) undertook the largest ever survey of transgender people in the United States, recording responses from almost 28,000 participants. This groundbreaking study expanded on findings from a smaller (n=6,000) 2011 survey, also by NCTE, which found that the workplace experiences of transgender and gender-nonconforming people were shaped by high rates of unemployment, underemployment, and poor working conditions. Still, workplace experiences were not entirely negative, and trans people displayed high rates of resilience.[21]

At work, transgender people must make decisions about whether to disclose their trans status or remain "stealth" to their coworkers. If they are planning to take steps in their transitions, they must consider whether it is safe to do so openly. Overall, the 2015 study found that most transgender people were not out at work. In fact, 53 percent of the people in the study tried to hide their gender identity or gender transition to avoid negative reactions at work. Another 26 percent of trans people delayed their gender transitions because of fears of discrimination. For people who do not conform to expectations and assumptions of masculinity and femininity, coming out to coworkers is not a choice.

Presenting gender outside of the binary often makes being out unavoidable. People who do not "pass" as women or men may disrupt gendered

expectations in the workplace and be subject to greater discomfort and discrimination, as extensive research and both authors of this reading can attest. In spite of the difficulties and dangers being trans at work poses, 68 percent of trans people who were out to coworkers reported receiving supportive responses.[22] Living in their genders also helped to improve their job performances, although half of these people still encountered harassment at work.[23]

Being out as trans can affect trans people's job security. Thirty percent of the people in the 2015 study reported being fired, not hired, or denied promotion for being trans. Another 44 percent reported being underemployed, working in positions where they were overqualified, or working in areas outside of their training and expertise. These numbers are startling, but when compared to the national rates, they become even more troubling. The study demonstrated that transgender people's unemployment rate was *twice as high* as the national unemployment rate. For trans people of color, the unemployment rate was *four times the national average*. These conditions translate into extremely compromised socioeconomic situations for transgender people. Within the sample, 12 percent of people reported living in dire poverty, earning less than $10,000 annually, which is three times the rate of the general population of the United States.[24]

Transgender people also reported high rates of workplace mistreatment. The vast majority of people in the study (77 percent) reported taking actions such as hiding their genders or delaying their transitions to avoid harassment or discrimination.[25] Mistreatment of trans workers included a wide variety of behaviors. Types of mistreatment that occurred more frequently included harassment and having coworkers share inappropriate information about trans workers. One respondent described, "Coworkers would gossip about me as news about my trans status spread through the workplace. I was treated significantly differently once people heard about me being trans. Coworkers felt they had the right to disrespect me because the owners set the tone. I became a spectacle in my own workplace."[26] Hostile workplaces may also target trans workers by imposing restrictive dress codes and bathroom policies. For example, people whose legal sex is "female" may be directed to wear feminine clothing and hairstyles, or they may be required to use the women's restroom, although these people may identify as male and look like men.[27] Other workplace hazards for trans people, although less common, included physical and sexual assault.[28]

Like other aspects of discrimination and bias, the workplace experiences of trans people vary by other demographic factors. NCTE's 2011 survey examined these factors in depth. Overall, trans women were more likely to experience anti-trans bias on the job than trans men, as were people of color, respondents who lived in the southern United States, undocumented immigrants, disabled people, and those whose highest educational level was high school or lower. People who worked in lower-income jobs reported higher rates of harassment. Physical and sexual violence occurred more often among people with lower levels of educational attainment, with undocumented immigrant workers being three times more likely to experience violence at work compared to the rest of the sample.[29]

Given these stark realities, it is not surprising that poor working conditions push some transgender people into working in underground economies where they may sell sex and drugs to survive. Among workers who lost their jobs for being trans in 2015, 37 percent turned to an underground economy. In the sample at large, 20 percent of respondents reported doing sex work, selling drugs, or participating in other criminalized economies at some point in their lives. Black, American Indian, and Latinx[30] workers, as well as undocumented and homeless individuals, were especially likely to have engaged in underground economies. Almost half of trans people who have done sex work report living in poverty currently, and nearly 75 percent report having been sexually assaulted (compared to 44 percent of those who have not done sex work).[31] The negative workplace experiences reported by transgender people have implications beyond employment. When people lose their jobs because of anti-transgender bias, they are at a greater risk for homelessness and incarceration. They are also more likely to experience negative health outcomes such as HIV infection and suicide, as well as tobacco, alcohol, and drug use.[32]

Despite these problems, transgender people exhibit resilience in the face of workplace discrimination.

Among people who lost jobs because of being trans, 58 percent reported being employed at the time of the 2011 NCTE survey. After transitioning, almost 80 percent of both trans women and trans men said that their job situation improved. Of the people who did not lose their jobs because of bias, 86 percent were able to use their preferred bathrooms at work.[33] As one respondent stated, "When I started my transition, the place that I was working was very supportive. My boss had a family member who is transgender. I was treated with respect by everyone."[34]

The experience of Deirdre McCloskey, an economist at the University of Iowa, illustrates an example of a positive experience. When McCloskey announced her transition from male to female in 1995, she anticipated the worst: being denied compensation, being assigned to teach undesirable classes, or, most painfully, being shunned by the colleagues and friends with whom she had worked for decades. McCloskey feared she would be forced to take legal action, which would probably prove unsuccessful. Ultimately, however, McCloskey recalled her coming out to the dean of the College of Business as positive:

> Gary [Fethke, College of Business Dean] sat stunned for a moment. He and I were both economists, conservatives by academic standards, free-market men. Then he spoke as a dean: "Thank God . . . I thought for a moment you were going to confess to converting to socialism!" I laughed, relieved—the dean was going to react like a friend. "And this is great for our affirmative action program—one less man, one more woman!" More laughter, more relief. "And wait a minute—it's even better: as a woman I can cut your salary to 70 cents on the dollar!" Not quite so funny! And then seriously: "That's a strange thing to do." I agreed. And Gary continued: "How can I help?" . . . Gary kept his word, acting as an advocate for me and my strange choice in the administration and the faculty.[35]

McCloskey came out in 1995, before many of today's policies that protect trans people from discrimination at work were in place, but her supervisor's response was positive, nonetheless. But the dean's comments also reveal broader trends in workplace gender inequality. Dean Fethke's jibe about affirmative action exposes a seldom-acknowledged truth about the program. Although affirmative action was meant to increase racial minority representation in the workplace, in practice, the program is most beneficial for White women.[36] Thus, people of color still lose out, despite government initiatives. Fethke's joke about cutting McCloskey's salary also hits a nerve about workplace inequality, given the gender pay gap where women earn about 82 cents for every dollar men make.[37] These realities throw transgender and gender inequalities into sharper focus.

(TRANS)GENDER INEQUALITIES AT WORK

The experiences of trans people like Deirdre McCloskey help to expose broader gender inequalities. Ben Barres, a Stanford University neurobiologist and transgender man, is an outspoken critic of the claim that males are innately more capable in math and science fields than females. Barres believes, instead, that deeply rooted biases and social pressures prevent women from entering and remaining in the sciences. Barres discusses his own experiences working as both a man and a woman in the sciences as evidence that gender inequality persists. Barres recalls that, when working as a woman, his competence in math and science was often questioned; at one time, Barres was even passed over for a fellowship opportunity that was given instead to a less accomplished male peer:

> As a [female] undergrad at the Massachusetts Institute of Technology (MIT), I was the only person in a large class of nearly all men to solve a hard [math] problem, only to be told by the professor that my boyfriend must have solved it for me. I was not given any credit. I am still disappointed about the prestigious fellowship competition I later lost to a male contemporary when I was a PhD student, even though the Harvard dean who had read both applications assured me that my application was much stronger (I had published six high-impact papers whereas my male competitor had published only one). Shortly after I changed sex, a faculty member was heard to say "Ben Barres gave a great seminar today, but then his work is much better than his sister's."[38]

Individuals like Barres and McCloskey who have lived on both sides of the gender binary can provide unique insight into the workings of gender privilege and inequality.

The experiences of transgender people like McCloskey and Barres lend evidence to the reality of workplace inequality for cisgender and transgender people alike. Sociologist Kristen Schilt has conducted some of the only large-scale ethnographic research on trans people's experiences in the workplace. Although this research focuses predominantly on transgender men, her findings shed light on the range of experiences trans people have at work.

Schilt's research, published in 2010, showed that many trans men experience pressure to conform to standards of hegemonic, or dominant, masculinity to be taken seriously in the workplace. Many trans men described feeling hypervigilant about passing as male, particularly early on in their transitions. They also worried that if their employers or coworkers perceived their genders as "in-between" or "ambiguous," they could be at greater risk for mistreatment. One gender-nonconforming respondent, Wayne, recalled being told by a potential employer: "I will hire you only on the condition that you don't ever come in the front [of the restaurant] because you make people uncomfortable."[39] Once Wayne transitioned and began passing as normatively male, his work experiences and opportunities dramatically improved.[40]

In general, transgender men reported that their lives at work got better following their transitions. Many reported that they were treated with more respect and taken more seriously after they transitioned. Some also believed that working as men was a direct reason for promotions, raises, and other economic advantages they would not have had access to prior to transitioning. One respondent, who worked in an office primarily with women, described how his masculine voice granted him undeserved competence at the expense of women: "[In meetings,] everyone will just get quiet and listen to me. But when this [woman expert] speaks, everyone talks over her. And I have no specialization in this area. I don't know anything, yet they are all listening to me."[41] Trans men's financial success and gains in status reflect trends in cisgender workplace inequality.[42]

Not all trans men, however, reported positive changes at work following their transitions. Because hegemonic masculinity is associated with Whiteness, trans men of color often had different experiences than White trans men, which affected them both within and outside of the workplace. One Asian man in Schilt's study described feeling that "people have this impression that Asian guys aren't macho and therefore aren't really male."[43] This emasculated stereotype of Asian men may reduce or negate potential gains at work based on gender alone. Black and Latino men, too, suffered from White-centered ideals of masculinity. Several of Schilt's Black respondents described being stereotyped as aggressive, threatening, and criminal once they moved through the world as men. This racialized hypermasculinity also tainted men's lives at work.[44] Given these factors, it is highly plausible that the positive experiences described earlier by Deirdre McCloskey and Ben Barres were informed by their privileges as White, educated, and upper-middle-class academics.

Workplaces have different strategies for dealing with trans employees. Schilt found that employers' responses fit into four categories: neutralizing challenges to the male/female binary, policing the male/female binary, creating transgender tokens, and incorporating trans men as "one of the guys." Some employers used methods of neutralizing trans workers by forcing them out of the workplace, either through overt means like firing or by creating environments that were so uncomfortable the trans employee chose to leave. Some workplaces, particularly those in conservative areas without nondiscrimination laws, were able to enforce the male/female binary by insisting that trans men work as women to keep their jobs. These employers often cited legal sex and workplace dress code policies to regulate trans employees' genders. Other trans men working in lesbian, gay, bisexual, and transgender (LGBT)-friendly jobs experienced being treated as the token trans person when they were out at work. These individuals described inhabiting an in-between category, where being trans was always or usually treated as their predominant identity. Some workplaces, mostly in the professional sector, chose to incorporate transgender men as "one of the guys." Supervisors in these environments often took steps to ensure that an employee's transition was smooth; some workplaces even held informative sessions about transgender issues. These employers helped make trans men one of the guys by assigning them to stereotypically masculine tasks, incorporating them into men's culture, or "forgetting" that an individual was trans.[45] Although workplaces' strategies for handling trans employees vary, legal recourse can help protect trans people from discriminatory employer reactions.

LEGAL CONSIDERATIONS

Although trans people experience many difficulties in the workplace, they can rely on some legal protections. In the United States, anti-transgender employment discrimination is prohibited on the federal level and in some states through additional legislation. Though the Trump administration has encouraged workplaces to take broader exemptions justifying discrimination on religious grounds and stated that it will no longer consider transgender peoples' discrimination complaints in court, there have been no official changes in federal law as of September 2018.[46]

All workers in the United States are protected by Title VII of the Civil Rights Act, which prohibits discrimination in the workplace based on sex. In 2012, federal courts found that discrimination based on gender identity and expression qualifies as sex discrimination. Therefore, trans workers may file discrimination claims with the Equal Employment Opportunity Commission under Title VII.[47] This victory came after the Transgender Law Center filed a discrimination complaint on behalf of Mia Macy, a transgender woman who was denied a job as a ballistics technician. Macy, a veteran and former police detective, applied for the job as male. Her background expertise made her a highly qualified candidate. But when she disclosed during the hiring process that she was transitioning, she was told funding for the position had been cut. Later, the employer hired someone else for the position. Macy's landmark case set the stage for other trans workers to file suit under Title VII.[48]

In addition, twenty states, plus the District of Columbia and Puerto Rico, offer explicit protection from discrimination in the workplace based on gender identity or expression. However, no statewide legal protections exist for trans people in the southern

United States and most of the Midwest.[49] Some jurisdictions in these regions do provide limited protections to trans workers, such as the cities of Kansas City, Missouri, El Paso, Texas, and Nashville, Tennessee.[50] Ultimately, fewer than half of American workers reside in parts of the country that explicitly protect trans people through statewide nondiscrimination employment laws.[51] Despite the transgender-inclusive interpretation of Title VII, explicitly protecting gender identity and expression at the state level would provide trans people with a more secure foundation in filing discrimination claims.

Advocacy groups like the National Center for Transgender Equality and the Transgender Law Center recommend that Congress pass the Employment Non-Discrimination Act (ENDA), which would include protection from discrimination based on sexual orientation and gender identity.[52] This legislation has been jostled about in Congress since it was first introduced in 1994, when it addressed discrimination based on sexuality orientation only. It was not until 2007 that gender identity was added, albeit with reservation.[53]

TRANSGENDER ACTIVISM AND ADVOCACY

On a broad, policy-based level, national LGBT organizations are working to ensure that transgender people at work are protected under actual legislation, as opposed to the interpretations of Title VII (discussed above). If passed, ENDA would be the only national law that protects LGBT people from employment discrimination.[54] It would expand existing laws that already forbid workplace discrimination based on race, color, religion, and national origin. In addition to lobbying, national organizations provide resources and support around the issue of employment inequality. The Transgender Law Center provides resources about employment discrimination and assistance filing Equal Employment Opportunity Commission (EEOC) claims.[55]

Smaller organizations and support centers are also critical to providing services for trans people regionally. The Trans Employment Program (TEP), based out of the San Francisco LGBT Center, is a community program that helps trans people find jobs and navigate being trans at work. The initiative reaches communities by partnering with other centers and organizations that serve transgender people.[56] In New York City, the Sylvia Rivera Law Project provides legal aid around trans issues, hosts informative trainings for community organizations and launches campaigns related to prisoners' rights, health-care issues, and policy reform.[57] These community organizations help meet the needs of individual people and work for legal reform and protections.

In recent years, advocacy work by well-known transgender people has become more visible. Laverne Cox, an African American trans woman and cast member of the popular television series *Orange Is the New Black*, has lobbied publicly for the acceptance of trans people and has over 3.3 million followers on Instagram. In May 2014, Cox appeared on the cover of *TIME* magazine, and in 2015 became the first trans person to be memorialized in wax at Madame Tussauds (dressed as Dr. Frank-N-Furter of *The Rocky Horror Picture Show*).[58][59] As media platforms like YouTube and Instagram have become more ubiquitous agents of cultural creation and gained traction with teens, in particular, trans experiences are becoming increasingly visible and usual. Miles McKenna is a 23-year-old YouTuber who blogs about his life and transition on the channel MilesChronicles. Miles's channel began as a personal vlog, but has since become one of the most popular trans channels on YouTube, reaching almost 1.2 million subscribers. As of September 2018, McKenna's channel boasts an extraordinary 33,738,478 views. For the first time in history, millions of eyes are fixed on trans people using social media to tell their stories, describe their transitions, and document their exciting (and sometimes even boring) lives. Social media has also offered opportunities for trans folk to disrupt the idea that all trans people are simply "trapped in the wrong body" and seeking medial transition, thus, adding to traditional narratives.[60] The work of national organizations, community partnerships, and individuals continues to propel the issues trans people face into public consciousness, in spite of an increasingly ominous national political climate.

NOTES

1. GLAAD. 2014. "GLAAD Media Reference Guide–Transgender Issues." Retrieved December 19, 2014. http://www.glaad.org/reference/transgender/.
2. Intersex Society of North America. 2008. "How Common Is Intersex?" Retrieved January 11, 2015. http://www.isna.org/faq/frequency/.
3. Blackless, Melanie, Anthony Charuvastra, Amanda Derryck, Anne Fausto-Sterling, Karl Lauzanne, and Ellen Lee. 2000. "How Sexually Dimorphic Are We? Review and Synthesis." *American Journal of Human Biology* 12:151–66.
4. InterACT. 2017. "Intersex 101." Retrieved on September 25, 2018. https://interactadvocates.org/wp-content/uploads/2017/03/INTERSEX101.pdf.
5. GLAAD, 2014.
6. Hill, Mel Reiff, and Jeff Mays. 2011. "The Transgender Umbrella." Pp. 38–39 in *The Gender Book.* Retrieved December 18, 2014. http://issuu.com/thegenderbook/docs/the_gender_book/.
7. "Transgender" is an *adjective* that describes certain gender experiences. For example, one may identify as a transgender woman or man, as a "person of transgender experience," or as just transgender. Although some well-meaning people use it by mistake, the term "transgendered" is neither correct nor accurate. The term cannot be conjugated in the past tense, as in "transgendered," because it is not a verb. It is also inaccurate to use transgender as a noun, as in "John is a transgender." This may be likened to saying "John is a tall." John can be tall, or John can be a tall fellow, but John cannot just be "a tall."
8. GLAAD, 2014.
9. Not all transgender people choose to transition; many simply choose to live as their genders without taking medical or legal steps.
10. "Getting a sex change" is often used more for sensationalism than accuracy. At the best, the phrase is inaccurate. Because sex encompasses a number of physical traits (hormones, reproductive organs, chromosomes, secondary sex characteristics), it is impossible to change it completely in one event. For example, an individual may have her ovaries removed (a hysterectomy), but she can never change her chromosomes. At the worst, describing transitioning as getting a sex change can be offensive. The phrase implies that an individual lives as one gender one moment and then gets a surgery that completely changes the way his or her sex is perceived the next moment. The vast majority of individuals who choose to pursue any sort of surgery already live as their chosen sex. Although transgender surgeries are often referred to as "sex reassignment surgeries," a more accurate description may be "gender-affirming surgeries," because surgical interventions simply help align people's bodies with the genders they feel and live.
11. Grant, Jaime M., Lisa A. Mottet, and Justin Tanis. 2010. *National Transgender Discrimination Survey Report on Health and Health Care.* Washington: National Center for Transgender Equality and the National Gay and Lesbian Task Force. Retrieved December 28, 2014. http://www.thetaskforce.org/downloads/reports/reports/ntds_summary.pdf/.
12. Dreger, Alice. 2013. "Why Gender Dysphoria Should No Longer Be Considered a Mental Disorder." *Pacific Standard,* October 18. Retrieved January 26, 2015. http://www.psmag.com/health-and-behavior/take-gender-identity-disorder-dsm-68308/.
13. U.S. Department of State. 2018. "Change of Sex Marker." Retrieved October 23, 2018. https://travel.state.gov/content/travel/en/passports/apply-renew-passport/change-of-sex-marker.html..
14. Grant et al., 2010.
15. National Center for Transgender Equality. 2013. "Driver's License Policies by State." Retrieved December 28, 2014. http://transequal ity.org/Resources/DL/DL_policies_text.html/.
16. Transgender Law Center. 2017. "State-by-State Overview: Rules for Changing Gender Markers on Birth Certificates." Retrieved September 24, 2018. https://transgenderlawcenter.org/resources/id/state-by-state-overview-changing-gender-markers-on-birth-certificates.
17. James, S. E., J.L. Herman, S. Rankin, M. Keisling, L. Mottet, & M. Anafi. (2016). *The Report of the 2015 U.S.Transgender Survey.* Washington, DC: National Center for Transgender Equality. Retrieved September 24, 2018. https://transequality.org/sites/default/files/docs/usts/USTS-Full-Report-Dec17.pdf.

18. Pasquesoone, Valentine. 2014. "Seven Countries Giving Transgender People Fundamental Rights the U.S. Still Won't." Retrieved February 23, 2015. http://mic.com/articles/87149/7-countries-giving-transgender-people-fundamental-rights-the-u-s-still-won-t/.

19. Sampathkumar, Mythili. 2018. "Canada to Add Third Gender Option to Next Census." Retrieved September 24, 2018. https://www.independent.co.uk/news/world/americas/canada-third-gender-census-lgbtq-rights-spectrum-identity-statistics-a8355031.html.

20. Sopelsa, Brooke. 2018. "Gender 'X': New York City to Add Third Gender Option to Birth Certificates." Retrieved September 24, 2018. https://www.nbcnews.com/feature/nbc-out/gender-x-new-york-city-add-third-gender-option-birth-n909021.

21. James, S. E., J.L. Herman, S. Rankin, M. Keisling, L. Mottet, & M. Anafi. (2016). *The Report of the 2015 U.S. Transgender Survey*. Washington, DC: National Center for Transgender Equality. Retrieved September 24, 2018. https://transequality.org/sites/default/files/docs/usts/USTS-Full-Report-Dec17.pdf.

22. Ibid.

23. Grant, Jaime M., Lisa A. Mottet, Justin Tanis, Jack Harrison, Jody L. Herman, and Mara Keisling. 2011. *Injustice at Every Turn: A Report of the National Transgender Discrimination Survey*. Washington, DC: National Center for Transgender Equality and National Gay and Lesbian Task Force. Retrieved January 8, 2015. http://www.transequality.org/Resources/ntds_full.pdf/.

24. James et al., 2016.

25. Ibid.

26. James et al., 2016. 151.

27. Bender-Baird, Kyla. 2011. *Transgender Employment Experiences: Gendered Perceptions and the Law*. Albany, NY: SUNY Press.

28. Grant et al., 2011.

29. Ibid.

30. The use of "Latinx" is an intentional way to describe Latinos and Latinas to reflect gender-neutral and non-sexist language. The letter "x" allows for a third option that resists language rooted in the gender binary, where the "o" in "Latino" is considered masculine and the "a" in "Latina" is feminine.

31. James et al., 2016.

32. Ibid.

33. Grant et al., 2011.

34. Ibid, 64.

35. McCloskey, Deirdre. 1998. "Happy Endings: Law, Gender, and the University." *The Journal of Gender, Race and Justice* 2(1):78.

36. Goodwin, Michele. 2012. "The Death of Affirmative Action, Part 1." Retrieved January 20, 2015. http://chronicle.com/blogs/brainstorm/the-death-of-affirmative-action-part-i/44860/.

37. Bureau of Labor Statistics. 2013. *Labor Force Statistics from the Current Population Survey*. Retrieved January 26, 2015. http://www.bls.gov/cps/cpsaat39.htm/.

38. Barres, Ben A. 2006. "Does Gender Matter?" *Nature* 442:134.

39. Schilt, Kristen. 2010. *Just One of the Guys? Transgender Men and the Persistence of Gender Inequality*. Chicago: University of Chicago Press, 78.

40. Ibid.

41. Ibid, 71.

42. Ibid.

43. Ibid, 85.

44. Ibid.

45. Ibid.

46. National Center for Transgender Equality. 2017. "Know Your Rights: Employment (General)." Retrieved September 25, 2018. https://transequality.org/know-your-rights/employment-general.

47. Ibid.

48. Transgender Law Center. 2012. "Groundbreaking! Federal Agency Rules Transgender Employees Protected by Sex Discrimination Law." Retrieved December 12, 2014. http://transgenderlawcenter.org/archives/635/.

49. Movement Advancement Project. 2018. "Non-Discrimination Laws." Retrieved September 25, 2018.http://www.lgbtmap.org/equality-maps/non_discrimination_laws.

50. Transgender Law and Policy Institute. 2012. "Non-Discrimination Laws That Include Gender Identity and Expression." Retrieved December 18, 2014. http://transgenderlaw.org/ndlaws/index.htm#maps/.

51. Ibid.

52. National Center for Transgender Equality. 2011. "Discrimination." Retrieved December 18, 2014. http://transequality.org/Issues/discrimination.html/. Transgender Law Center. 2014. "Advocacy." Retrieved December 18, 2014. http://transgenderlawcenter.org/issues/employment/.

53. Human Rights Campaign. 2014. "Employment Non-Discrimination Act: Legislative Timeline." Retrieved December 18, 2014. http://www.hrc.org/resources/entry/employment-non-discrimination-act-legislative-timeline/.

54. Human Rights Campaign. 2014. "Pass ENDA Now." Retrieved January 21, 2015. http://www.hrc.org/campaigns/employment-non-discrimination-act/.

55. Transgender Law Center. "Employment Discrimination." Retrieved January 21, 2015. http://transgenderlawcenter.org/issues/employment/.

56. Transgender Economic Empowerment Initiative. 2008. "About Us." Retrieved January 21, 2015. http://www.teeisf.org/about/.

57. Sylvia Rivera Law Project. 2015. Retrieved January 26, 2015. http://srlp.org/.

58. Steinmetz, Katy. 2014. "Laverne Cox Talks to TIME about the Transgender Movement." Retrieved January 27, 2015. http://time.com/132769/transgender-orange-is-the-new-black-laverne-cox-interview/.

59. Jones, Isabel. 2016. "Laverne Cox Meets Her Rocky Horror Doppelgänger at Madame Tussauds." Retrieved September 24, 2018. https://www.instyle.com/news/laverne-cox-madame-tussauds-rocky-horror.

60. Miller, Jordan F. 2018. "YouTube as a Site of Counternarratives to Transnormativity." *Journal of Homosexuality*: DOI: 10.1080/00918369.2018.1484629.

CHAPTER 6

SOCIAL PROBLEMS RELATED
TO SEXUALITY

Although sexuality can seem like a deeply personal subject, our sexual attitudes and behaviors are both informed by and can, in turn, affect our culture and society. Even in this
seemingly private arena, social problems emerge. Despite cultural assumptions that sexual behavior is driven purely by biology and hormonal urges, sex is actually social. This means that
we learn what behaviors are appropriate, when to do them, with whom, in what context, and
how to do them, through social interaction with others. One arena for sharing best practices is
through formal sex education in the schools. How we choose to educate (or not educate) our
children about sex and sexuality has lasting effects not only on their future reproductive and
sexual knowledge and choices, but also on the public health of the country as a whole. Even
though the majority of Americans favor more comprehensive sex education and the preponderance of evidence supports it as a way to reduce teen pregnancy, sexually transmitted infections (STIs), and riskier sexual behaviors, and to delay first sexual intercourse, state curricula on
sex and sexuality are limited by the interests of a vocal minority that advocates for and funds
"abstinence-only" education. One result is that young Americans have much higher rates of STIs
and teen pregnancy than teens in comparable nations. For example, the Centers for Disease
Control (CDC) reports that young people (those aged 15–24 years) comprise half of all new STI
cases and that one in four sexually active adolescent females today has an STI.[1] Supporting and
funding higher-quality, more inclusive sex education, as described in the reading in this chapter
by Jessica Fields, could ameliorate various social problems in the area of sexuality. Legislation
about sex education—whether it is mandated, whether it is required to be medically accurate,
and what topics must be covered—is decided on a state-by-state basis. Writers at the University
of Southern California Department of Nursing raise concerns about the connection between
vague, biased, or non-existent sex education and the U.S.'s high rates of teen pregnancy and STIs.

---

1   Centers for Disease Control and Prevention. 2017. "Sexually Transmitted Disease Surveillance 2017: Adolescents
    and Young Adults." Retrieved March 4, 2019, from https://www.cdc.gov/std/stats17/adolescents.htm.

The U.S. teen pregnancy rate is one of the highest in the developed world. Sociologists' studies focus on what aspects of our society contribute to these rates, the experiences of teen pregnancy, the stigma associated with teen pregnancy, and which groups are disproportionately experiencing it and why. As explanation, readers may jump to the conclusion that teens in the United States must be more sexually active than teens in other developed countries, but that is not the case. In reality, teens in the United States tend to initiate sexual activity at a similar age and with similar frequency as their counterparts in other developed countries. One reason for our higher pregnancy rates is that teens in the United States use contraception less reliably than teens in comparable countries.[2] Stephanie Mollborn's reading offers a more nuanced understanding of teen pregnancy in the United States, which is experienced differently by race and class. Mollborn calls into question some of the negative consequences of teen pregnancy, while emphasizing the need to support teen parents for best outcomes. A reading in this chapter by Stacy Gorman Harmon offers a partial solution to teen pregnancy: certain types of birth control (long-acting reversible contraception) may be more effective in pregnancy prevention, especially for teens.

When we offer teenagers weak sex education in schools, limiting their knowledge from reputable sources, they may turn to other sources to satisfy their curiosity, namely, pornography. Despite parental attempts to limit their children's access to pornography, teens regularly report easily accessing it. Unfortunately, much of the imagery offers an explicit, yet unrealistic, depiction of sex and sexuality. Teens in the reading by Maggie Jones express their confusion about how to become sexually active through a lens that eroticizes, for example, violence against women. Jones describes innovative ways to counteract the influence of pornography by teaching students about pornographic literacy.

When students consume so much imagery that eroticizes violence, they may begin to "normalize" it. Heather Hlavka demonstrates the ways and the extent to which teenagers, girls in particular, have come to accept gendered violence as just "par for the course." This normalization results in high rates of sexual harassment, sexual coercion, and sexual assault among young women and girls, with most instances going unreported.

Renee M. Shelby's reading focuses on a specific type of sexual coercion and assault, examining the social problem of sex trafficking. Sex trafficking is a criminal activity through which someone uses "force, fraud, or coercion to cause a commercial sex act."[3] Victims may be children or adults, yet traffickers tend to target people with fewer resources and less power in society (people who have experienced other forms of violence or exploitation or who may not be tied in to strong, protective, social networks).[4] Determining what actions and who will be counted as "criminal" in our fight to end it, and the efficacy of strategies to prevent it, continue to evolve.

Sexuality is complicated. Sexual behavior can bring joy and pleasure, as well as harm and pain. How we address sex and sexuality as a society can affect individual lives but also has ramifications for the larger society.

---

2   Holpuch, Amanda. 2016. "US Teenage Birth Rates Fall Again but Still Among Highest in Developed World." *The Guardian*, September 28. Retrieved March 4, 2019, from https://www.theguardian.com/us-news/2016/sep/28/us-teenage-birth-rates-fall-again.

3   Office on Trafficking in Persons. 2017. "Fact Sheet: Human Trafficking." Administration for Children & Families, U.S. Department of Health & Human Services. Retrieved March 4, 2019, from https://www.acf.hhs.gov/otip/resource/fshumantrafficking.

4   Office on Trafficking in Persons. 2017.

ACTIVIST INTERVIEW

HEATHER CORINNA

Heather Corinna is the founder and director of Scarleteen and author of *S.E.X., second edition: The All-You-Need-to-Know Sexuality Guide to Get You through Your Teens and Twenties.*

What is your organization and its mission?

I founded Scarleteen (http://www.scarleteen.com)—a sexuality, sexual health and relationships information, education, and support organization—in 1998. We were one of the very first sex education resources on the web. Most of our work is done online using static content, advice columns. and several one-on-one direct services (using real people, not automated answers or templates). Our mission is to provide adolescents and emerging adults with comprehensive, inclusive, and accessible sexuality information and support.

How did you first become interested in this type of activism?

I was teaching for years before I started teaching at Scarleteen, and to me, teaching well—truly doing what you can to educate and help people learn, not memorize or meet testing ideals—is, all by itself, a lot of what activism is. I also started doing some publishing in adult sexuality, but very quickly, young people began contacting me seeking help and support. It was clear their needs were not being met elsewhere. I wound up leaving my other teaching work within a year of starting Scarleteen, and it quickly became the bulk of what I do.

As an activist in your organization, currently what are your goals?

I want to give young people both the most in-depth, tailored-to-their-expressed-needs information I can and the support that they need to make informed and empowered choices about sex and sexuality. I also want to empower our young volunteers, almost all of whom are under 30 years old. A final goal is to change the cultural conversation about sex, relationships, and young people so that it becomes much more humane and focused on real people and real lives in all their diversity.

What strategies do you use to enact social change?

Talking about sex and sexuality honestly and positively—especially so widely and visibly—strikes me, all by itself, as something with the power for potentially sweeping social change. Treating teens and emerging adults as whole and capable people, and working with them respectfully is also extremely important to us.

What are the major challenges activists in your field face?

The stigma when working in the area of sex remains significant. Working with sex and young people adds

220

another layer to that challenge, and doing so as anything but a White, cisgender, heterosexual, married parent creates additional challenges. So, those of us who are queer or gender nonconforming, of color, not parents, not in the kind of relationships considered to be a moral ideal, or who have been "too" sexual (which usually just means being sexual at all outside of heterosexual norms) have extra challenges. And the more marginalized we are, the more at risk we are doing the work that we do.

Additionally, being involved at a deep and daily level with young people and their struggles and questions about such complex things—and that includes working with abuse and assault—is so rewarding, but also very emotionally hard.

What are major misconceptions the public has about activism in general and your issue specifically?

Well, I do think the idea that activist = fanatic is still prevalent. And it would take volumes to talk about all the misconceptions the public has about sex, sexuality, and sexuality education. But there's an interesting place where both activism in general and sex education activism meet regarding misconceptions, and that's the idea that we (the activists at hand) cannot be trusted, and that there must be some ulterior motive for what we do. But in my experience, it's not at all true of most activists; we're actually quite direct and we mean what we say.

Another misconception is the idea that young people are hurt by being provided sexual information. Of course, it is a total fallacy. In fact, we have so much evidence to the contrary, it's dizzying.

Why should students get involved in your line of activism?

Honestly, I think that peer sex education and peer sexual activism are the most powerful ways to go with this arena. Those of us—like myself—who are older adults, can do our part and have plenty to offer, but are not as powerful as young people speaking for themselves and working together with each other.

What would you consider to be your greatest successes as an activist?

When a young person says—and earnestly means—thank you to me, letting me know I served them well, it truly doesn't get any better than that. And of course, when it happens all the time, it is incredibly rewarding. The fact that there have been so, so many thank you's, from so many diverse youth all over the world tells me, better than anything else can, I'm succeeding in my goals. I've also heard many colleagues and organizations I respect over the years state that Scarleteen and my related work created a model for online education, sex education, and working with youth.

Despite the challenges of never receiving any foundational or institutional funding, staying financially independent has allowed us to truly be and stay radical, in the best meaning of the word, which is a big deal to me because the kind of change we need in the way we approach sexuality education is radical change.

If an individual has little money and time, are there other ways they can contribute?

Absolutely! For one, what we do actually does not cost very much. People are always amazed at how minimal our budget is for the level of service we can provide. So, the idea that this kind of activism has a big price tag is false.

And there are ways to contribute that ask so little. Even things like not getting on board for celebrity or youth shaming around sex (as in, don't retweet or chime in with a slut-shame, or handwring about the sexual irresponsibility of "these kids today") helps a lot, and that actually is just asking someone to do nothing rather than something, to *not* spend even a minute enabling that stuff, rather than spending time doing so. Being an askable, supportive person for youth around sex and sexuality is another major contribution.

JESSICA FIELDS

23. SEXUALITY EDUCATION IN THE UNITED STATES

Shared Cultural Ideas across a Political Divide

Debates over sex education today are usually framed as a fight between abstinence-only and comprehensive sex education. By tracing the history of sex education and examining its content, Fields argues that both types share similar flawed assumptions and messages (e.g., the often gender-, race-, and class-biased messages that frame some kids as sexual victims and others as likely victimizers). Both types ignore the ambiguity and ambivalence characterizing much sex, view sex among youth as inherently dangerous and risky, conflate sexual talk with sexual activity, and regulate youth and their sexuality. Fields calls to move beyond this polarized debate and to allow for a more inclusive and expansive approach to educate youth about sex and sexuality.

INTRODUCTION

In 2009, Barack Obama came through on a promise. His administration eliminated much direct funding for abstinence-only education and instead funded an Office of Adolescent Health (OAH) to administer over $100 million in new support for evidence-based teen pregnancy prevention approaches (Wagoner 2009). OAH funding effectively reversed the second Bush administration's consistent and increasing support for abstinence-only programming.[1] Ironically, the OAH commitment to teen pregnancy prevention also affirms a long-established and conventional approach to sexuality education as a grudging response to vexing social problems. OAH-sponsored teen pregnancy prevention programming might take the form of "comprehensive sexuality education," much to the dismay of those advocating abstinence-only education. Nevertheless, the OAH focus on sexual behaviors—and heterosexual intercourse in particular—threatens to come at the expense of discussing a range of sexual identities, desires, and institutions. The concern with teen pregnancy highlights harmful consequences of heterosexual behaviors for self and society and once again commits education to the conservative aim of promoting the personal and social regulation of young people's sexuality.

Prevailing health- and risk-oriented understandings of youth, sexuality, and education obscure an expansive portrait of youth, sexuality, and learning. Young people learn about sex and sexuality throughout their day-to-day lives, while watching television and movies, listening to music, texting, and surfing the web; at the family dinner table; during religious services; and in their sexual and romantic relationships (see, for example, Best 2000; Brown and Strasburger 2007; Clay 2003; Elliott 2012; Luttrell 2003; Martin 1996; Pascoe 2007; Regnerus 2007; Shapiro 2010; Wilkins 2008). Nevertheless, as a host of researchers (see, for example, Fields 2008; Fine 1988; Fine and McClelland 2006; Irvine 2002; Levine 2002) have pointed out, much contemporary policy making, public debate, and research on sexuality education focuses on the lessons children and youth encounter about sexual danger: Will young people learn what they need to avert risk? Do the lessons themselves put them at risk? Invoking concerns with health and prevention, adults organize policy and instruction for young people around the conventional worry that the sexuality education youth encounter in these institutions and interactions does not help them navigate an increasingly sexualized and dangerous world. Policy and instruction is also motivated by another worry: that sexuality education's lessons are themselves damaging, exacerbating the sexual risks youth and children already face.

Few sites of young people's learning about sex and sexuality have proved more worrisome or contentious in the United States than the school (Fields 2008; Heins 2001; Irvine 2002; Levine 2002; Luker 2006). In school board meetings, state legislatures, and the US Congress, socially conservative advocates and policy makers have insisted that abstaining from sexual activity is the only reliable and safe way of preventing disease and pregnancy and, ultimately, that abstinence is the best choice for all unmarried people. In this argument, "abstinence-only education" is a logical response to concerns over teen pregnancies, HIV and other sexually transmitted infections (STIs), and an overall assault on conventional understandings of gender, family, and sexual expression. Socially liberal educators, advocates, and policy makers have responded to this argument by promoting school-based comprehensive sexuality education, where teachers would emphasize abstinence as one strategy among others—condoms and other contraceptives, for example—that students could adopt to protect their health and well-being. Abstinence-only instruction would emphasize conventional gender and heterosexual expression and identity, including nuclear family structures; comprehensive sexuality education might also include lessons on masturbation; abortion; lesbian, gay, and bisexuality; and gender identity and norms.

Political actors and social movements may take up the cause of abstinence-only or comprehensive sexuality education in part out of concern for children and young people's immediate health and well-being. However, as I discuss below, no matter whether activists and movements advance abstinence-only or comprehensive curricula, the instruction they advocate

promotes or defends against change in cultural ideas regarding gender, sexual expression and identity, and family (Duggan and Hunter 1995; Fields 2008; Irvine 2002; Levine 2002; Luker 2006; Moran 2000; Stein 2006; Zimmerman 2005). Of course, all education participates in, contributes to, and reflects broad cultural ideas (Bourdieu and Passeron 1990). These ideas include values (shared general ideas about what is good and desirable) and more stringent norms (rules and conventions that shape people's sense of what is appropriate and expected in social settings). However, sexuality education has a particular relationship to the broad conflicts over ideas, values, and norms that characterize contemporary US sexual politics. . . .

LASTING STRUGGLES: CONSERVATIVES, LIBERALS, ABSTINENCE-ONLY, AND COMPREHENSIVE SEXUALITY EDUCATION

Sexuality education, the teaching and learning about puberty, sexuality, and relationships that happens in specially designated classrooms in primary and secondary schools, has long been linked to worry about the moral, psychological, and physical well-being of young people. In his history of sexuality education for US adolescents, Jeffrey Moran (2000) argues that public sexuality education emerged in the United States at the turn of the 20th century, as public officials grew concerned that the nation was ill prepared to contend with the sexual temptations associated with increasing urbanization. Over the course of the 20th century, many policy makers and educators came to believe that public health would be well served by what was called "social hygiene," "family life," and "puberty" education in the schools (Moran 2000). However, even as some schools and other public institutions took up the task of teaching children and youth about sexual health and wellbeing, sexuality education remained a primarily private concern in the early 20th century, with parents responsible for their children's upbringing (Kendall 2008).

From the late 1960s to early 1980s, feminism, youth culture, and the gay rights movement wrought significant changes in US sexual values. Though the sexual and gender revolution was neither uninterrupted nor uncontested, a shift was evident.

The liberalization of divorce laws, increased funding for women's and girls' education, widespread availability of contraception, legalized abortion, and new sexual harassment laws allowed women and girls greater freedom and agency in private and public relationships. Same-sex desire and expression became increasingly visible, and lesbian, gay, bisexual, queer, and transgender people made new claims to a right to live free of discrimination. Young people with access to these broad cultural shifts increasingly imagined and pursued sexual and intimate lives that had previously seemed forbidden (Luker 1996).

According to Kristin Luker, the conflict over sexuality education at the turn of the 21st century reflects the ongoing contemporary "culture war" that arose in the wake of the sexual, youth, and civil rights revolutions of the 1960s, "when it seemed as if all of American society might implode" (2006, 68; see also Hunter 1992). In a two-decade study, Luker conducted more than one hundred interviews with adults living in US communities embroiled in sexuality education debates. She argues that sexuality education debates are ultimately "about how men and women relate to each other in all realms of their lives" (2006, 69). She finds also that, like other post-1960s battles, the conflict over sexuality education is caught in a clash between two poles—sexual conservativism and sexual liberalism.

Researchers have critiqued this two-camp account of the sexuality education debate (see, for example, Fields 2008; Fine and McClelland 2006; Irvine 2000, 2006). Abstinence-only and comprehensive sexuality education actually "rely on their opposition" to each other (Lesko 2010, 281), and their shared and interrelated ideas, values, and norms are obscured when educators and policy makers seem to have only two curricular options. In addition, the two-camp account obscures the insistent efforts of grassroots and community-based educators and activists to move beyond the boundaries set forth by a polarized sexuality education debate. Health Initiatives for Youth (http://www.hify.org/), a San Francisco–based multicultural organization that aims to improve the health and well-being of underserved young people, the Population Council's curriculum development guide, *It's All One Curriculum* (2009), and Scarleteen (http://www.scarleteen.com/), an independent website that provides sexuality education and support to young people, are all examples of sexuality education that breaches an apparently clear and unassailable divide between abstinence-only and comprehensive sexuality education.

Despite such efforts, to many onlookers, the contemporary "culture wars" continue to appear as Luker describes it—a contest between conservatives and liberals with two distinct and incompatible visions of gender, sexuality, and family. At one pole of this political spectrum, "sexual conservatives" consider sexuality sacrosanct and thus advocate abstinence-only instruction as part of a larger effort to confine sexual expression to marriage, protect parents' special right to determine the content of children's sexuality education, and preserve sexuality's sacred status in an increasingly secularized, disordered, and permissive world (Luker 2006). Conservative organizations like the John Birch Society lead efforts to challenge instruction they believe promotes promiscuity, immorality, and social degradation and—particularly when housed in public schools—constitutes an assault on the nuclear family and other valued social conventions and formations (Connell and Elliott 2009; Irvine 2002; Moran 2000). "Sexual liberals," the ostensible "other side" of this bifurcated debate, embrace comprehensive sexuality education that challenges social hierarchies and discrimination, affords all young people access to information necessary to responsible and healthy sexual decision making, and thus recognizes sexuality as a natural part of everyone's life. Liberal groups like the Sexuality Education and Information Council of the United States (SIECUS) are among the national leaders in this liberal effort to promote comprehensive sexuality education in the home, school, and community.

For many years, the conservative abstinence-only movement appeared to be winning this two-camp battle. Since the 1980s, the US government has supported educational programs that emphasize chastity, self-discipline, and abstinence as strategies for stemming the problems understood to arise from teen sexual activity. The 1996 Personal Responsibility and Work Opportunity Reconciliation Act, enacted by the Democratic administration of Bill Clinton, increased federal support (and required state grantees to provide matching funds) for "abstinence education." Qualified programs would instruct students in the "social, psychological, and health gains" that come with confining sexual expression to heterosexual marriage and the "harmful psychological and physical effects" of sexual activity and parenting outside marriage (U.S. Department of Health and Human Services 2008).

By 2008, US voters had witnessed an increase in federal funding for abstinence-only education to nearly $200 million, and abstinence-only sentiments increasingly dominated the messages of school-based instruction (Duberstein Lindberg et al. 2006). Despite a persistent failure to convince youth to remain abstinent or to stem disease and unwanted pregnancies among youth (Kirby 2008), abstinence-only education was "beginning to assert a kind of natural cultural authority, in schools and out" (Fine and McClelland 2006, 299). Comprehensive sexuality education advocates who might have otherwise promoted more liberal, progressive, or even radical curriculum and pedagogy were increasingly accountable to the cultural authority of abstinence. The Obama administration's decision to create an Office of Adolescent Health charged with supporting pregnancy prevention is only one example of this accountability.

SHARED COMMITMENTS: THE REGULATION OF SEXUALITY AND YOUTH

The either/or rendering of a debate between a conservative abstinence-only and a liberal comprehensive sexuality education has not held with all policy makers and researchers. Instead, others have argued that the divisions in the battle over school-based abstinence-only and comprehensive sexuality education have not been as absolute as mainstream depictions suggest . . . [T]hough policies and curricula may suggest discrete curricular options, both abstinence-only and comprehensive sexuality educators contribute to the regulation of young people and their sexuality.

This shared commitment rests on a number of cultural values, institutional and interpersonal practices, and social inequalities. As I discuss below, these cultural values are evident in discursive framings that cast children and youth as sexual victims or sexual victimizers; conflate sexual talk and sexual behavior; and assert teaching and learning as predictable and instrumental responses to social crises. These discursive practices contribute to school-based sexuality education remaining,

as Laina Y. Bay-Cheng asserts, "a fundamental force in the very construction and definition of adolescent sexuality" as a site of danger risk, organized around normative heterosexual intercourse, and always entangled with entrenched social inequalities (2003, 62).

CORRUPTIBLE, CORRUPTING, AND CORRUPTED CHILDREN

Sexuality education debates and policy routinely posit young people as categorically less able, less intelligent, and less responsible than their adult counterparts. In the United States, young people's relationships are often denigrated as no more than puppy love, their sexual desires simply signs of raging hormones, and their sexual behaviors transgressions to control. Within this "adultist" framework, young people are at their best when sexually innocent. At their most vulnerable, they are on the verge of succumbing to sexual danger; and, at their most corrupting, they are the source of significant risks to others (Fields 2005; Lesko 2001; Levine 2002; Moran 2000). Consistently, images of the innocent, naïve child and the pubescent teenager undone by hormones point to that general practice that Irvine describes as "making up children" in debates over school-based sexuality education and in broader cultural conflicts over sexual and gender orders (2002, 108–11; see also Angelides 2004; Best 1993; Fields 2005; Kincaid 1997).

Though these adultist images of innocence and corruption are competing and conflicting, they also reflect a shared inclination that Amy Schalet argues is particular to US adults—parents, educators, and policy makers—to "dramatize adolescent sexuality" by highlighting conflict between parents and children, antagonism between girls and boys, and the threat of youth being overwhelmed by new sexual feelings and experiences (2004). Together, these images reflect and buttress ideals of youth as free of sexual experience and knowledge and, in a necessary corollary, youth as reliant upon adults' guidance and protection.

Idealizing and dramatizing images have varying implications for children and youth in the United States. Like other social standards, childhood sexual innocence becomes not only an ideal to which youth are held but also a means of sorting young people into a range of categories: the innocent and the guilty, the vulnerable and the predatory, the pure and the corrupting, those who are "fully participating and valued members of their classrooms and broader communities" and those who are not (Fields and Hirschman 2007, 11). Schalet's sustained comparative analysis demonstrates that Dutch and US youth navigate distinctively normalizing and dramatizing models of youth, gender, and sexuality. Few US girls "are assumed capable of the feelings and relationships that legitimate sexual activity," leaving them vulnerable to charge of "slut" (Schalet 2010, 325). Dutch girls, on the other hand, living within a normalizing paradigm of sexuality, "are assumed to be able to fall in love and form steady sexual relationships"; this assumption defends against an equation of sexual activity with "sluttiness," though the assumption may also "obscure the challenges of negotiating differences" in sexual relationships (Schalet 2010, 325).

In the United States, the dramatizing discourse is a gendered and racialized discourse, and it consistently casts some young people's sexuality as particularly conflictual, antagonistic, and excessive. While White children and youth may find some shelter in the promise of innocence, African American youth cannot count on having access to even this problematic protection in sexuality education debates and classrooms. In an ethnographic study of community responses to abstinence-only legislation, Fields (2008) found that advocates deployed White girls in sexuality education debates as representations of the sexual innocence that sexuality education must protect, while African American girls and boys were routinely "adultified"—cast as "sinister, intentional, fully conscious [and] stripped of any element of childish naiveté" (Ferguson 2001, 83).

Class differences similarly inform sexuality education in insidious ways. Since its emergence at the turn of the 20th century, the category of adolescence has been the purview of White people in the upper and middle classes (Moran 2000; see also Fields 2005). 1996 federal funding for abstinence-only education emerged in the context of welfare reform, where lessons on sexual abstinence contributed to broader conservative efforts to discourage out-of-wedlock pregnancy and thereby, conservatives claimed, to address poverty (Fields 2005; Fineman et al. 2003, Luker 2006). Such policies shape not only formal classroom curriculum but also pedagogical practice:

Fields (2008) found that public school teachers suffered greater scrutiny and less support than private school colleagues. In turn, the least advantaged students received the most restrictive instruction: only the relatively privileged private school students in her study heard in their sexuality education a call to sexual pleasure, agency, and knowledge. The public school students were consistently told that they should mute their desires and equip themselves for a violent sexual world.

Made-up and archetypal children afford both conservative and liberal advocates with foundations for compelling arguments for school-based sexuality education. Images of virgins, pregnant teens, promiscuous girls, predatory boys, suicidal gay students, doomed teens, and confused youth help to clarify and heighten the stakes in debates over curricular goals and social agendas (Connell and Elliott 2009; Fields 2008; Irvine 2002). . . .

CONFLATING SEXUAL TALK AND SEXUAL ACTIVITY

This sense of danger persists in another of the discursive conditions that sexuality education policy makers and advocates navigate—a diminished distinction between sexual speech and sexual activity. Talking with children and youth about sex becomes tantamount to engaging in sexual activity with children and youth: "Sexual speech, modern critics contend, provokes and stimulates. It transforms the so-called natural modesty of children into inflamed desires that may be outside the child's control and thus prompt sexual activity" (Irvine 2000, 62; see also Heins 2001; Irvine 2002). This framing threatens to render sexuality education an indefensible task: a violation of children and youth's sexual innocence and yet another assault on the embattled and idealized child-victim (Best 1993).

The depravity narratives that pervade US debates about sex and sexuality education—in which teachers seduce, corrupt, or otherwise sexually endanger their students—are one sign of this conflation of sexual speech and sexual activity. Through these narratives, classroom talk of even normative heterosexuality comes to constitute an assault that threatens to "persuade, incite, or otherwise arouse youth to later engage in the very acts spoken about" (Irvine 2000, 63); and talk about homosexuality becomes an inherently pred-atory act that initiates children or youth into a host of sexual perversions, including same-sex behaviors and desires (Irvine 2000, 2002; Levine 2002). Such narra-tives rest on a historically available discourse about the corruptible child; they also help to imagine and constitute a world in which the threat of sexual moles-tation looms everywhere, every teacher is potentially a pedophile, and learning happens when "the om-nipotent, all-controlling adult" meets "the powerless, passive child" (Angelides 2004, 160). Sexuality edu-cation, resting as it does on talking with youth about sexuality, threatens to become a crime in which "any teacher is a suspect" (Irvine 2000, 70).

The panic fostered by fears of molestation has sig-nificant implications of sexuality education debates and practice. Some parents become mobilized to resist sexuality education in their children's schools; other parents, along with policy makers and educa-tors, become reluctant to publicly endorse sexuality education that promotes anything other than sexual abstinence, normative family structures, and conven-tional gender expression (Irvine 2002). . . . In this climate, the conflation of sexual speech and sexual acts and the companion panic surrounding sexuality education and the threat of sexual molestation help to naturalize conventional sexual hierarchies in the name of protecting youth. Within this logic, protect-ing youth comes to mean protecting them from sexu-ality education.

TEACHING, LEARNING, KNOWING, AND DOING

The conflation of sexual speech and acts shapes not only public debate but also teaching and learning in the classroom. Looming charges of depravity leave all sexuality education advocates, policy makers, and instructors in a nearly impossible situation: how can they convince parents and community members that their course of instruction does not put young people at risk, let alone that their instruction might ease the risks that young people face? In response, participants in sexuality education debates and policy-making acknowledge that the curriculum they advocate—whether abstinence-only, abstinence-based, or com-prehensive—necessarily includes talk of sex; however,

they argue, that speech is factually sound and medi-cally accurate and thus the logical and rational choice for any adult committed to promoting the health of children and youth (Fields 2008; Fine 1988; Fine and McClelland 2006).

According to Lesko, comprehensive sexuality edu-cation and abstinence-only education build on each other and on a shared cultural moment and, as such, "touch in many ways" (Lesko 2010, 290). In prevail-ing comprehensive models of sexuality education, knowledge is presumed to be "positive and accurate," part of a broad definition of freedom as the product of scientific knowledge and empowerment. Abstinence-only models similarly indulge in this "pan-optimism" (2010, 290), in which knowledge produces desired outcomes—discouraging sexual behavior and promot-ing compliance with gender and sexual norms. Such optimism is possible only with a notion of knowl-edge as stable and decontextualized—a notion that empirical research repeatedly indicates is at odds with meaningful sexuality education. . . . Even with such sensitivity to the context of teaching and learning, a well-designed, theoretically informed curriculum may improve the quality of young people's sexual and emotional lives but have little impact on sexual behav-iors, included unprotected sex, contraceptive use, teen pregnancies, or abortions (Henderson, Wight, Raab, Abraham, Parkes, Scott, and Hart 2007; Wight, Raab, Henderson, Abraham, Buston, Hart, and Scott 2002). The path from knowledge to behavior is far from clear.

This determined pursuit of behavior change through sexuality education mirrors the confi-dence that the language of sexuality, especially when couched in scientific terms, is transparent and neu-tral. A stable, rational, and unambiguous relation-ship between knowledge and behavior is at the heart of sexuality education debates and practice and, in turn, sexuality education research. Both abstinence-only education and comprehensive sexuality educa-tion pursue knowledge as a route to desired behaviors. Mainstream curricular positions continue to try to re-capture an imagined and predictable relationship be-tween knowledge and behavior: teach young people to abstain, and they will; compromise young people with knowledge of sexual behaviors and desires, and they will be endangered; and present information about risk, prevention, and responsible behavior, and you will promote healthy decision-making in youth.

The consequences of dramatizing and idealizing ideas about youth continue inside the sexuality education classroom as sexuality education "socializes children into systems of inequality" (Connell and Elliott 2009, 84). Curriculum and pedagogy that pursue and claim rational and unambiguous knowledge routinely affirm oppressive values and norms about gender, race, and sexuality, even when presenting what appears to be rational, medically accurate information about bodies, diseases and pregnancy prevention, and puberty (Fields 2008; Trudell 1993; Trudell and Whatley 1991; Waxman 2004; Whatley and Trudell 1993). Lessons on menstruation and conception enact gendered norms regarding girls' and women's vulnerability and men's virility (Diorio and Munro 2000; Martin 1991). Youth and families of color appear in textbooks and other instructional material primarily in discussions of risk and disease prevention (Fields 2008; Whatley 1988). Overall, while abstinence-only education may more overtly discourage sexual expression among youth, both abstinence-only and comprehensive instruction persistently assign girls responsibility for managing boys' aggressive desires, maintain heterosexuality's normative status, and suggest that meaningful sexual expression and relationships among youth are unlikely, even rare (Fields 2008).

Much instruction and many curricular materials suggest that boys of all races are potential sexual predators. In a heteronormative sexuality education, this discourse prepares students for antagonistic sexual relationships between men and women. The messages girls receive are no better. Even in sexuality education classrooms formally designated "comprehensive," girls hear little talk from their teachers about female sexual desire. Instead they hear that, as girls and women, they bear the responsibility of deflecting the inevitable, aggressive sexual advances of their male peers (Fields 2008; Fine 1988; Fine and McClelland 2006; Tolman 2002).

Indeed, in practice, comprehensive sexuality education is rarely comprehensive: instructors often shy away from provocative stances on controversial topics, especially lesbian, gay, and bisexuality; and comprehensive educators routinely assert that sexual abstinence is the best choice for youth (Fields 2008; Gilbert 2010; Santelli 2006). Such heteronormative school-based sexuality education systematically denies sexually active young people access to educational resources and adult support that would promote their well-being and health. In addition, those youth who identify as lesbian, gay, bisexual, and queer (LGBQ) contend with sexuality education that emphasizes heterosexual behaviors, desires, and relationships and that, through its refusal to address LGBQ sexuality as anything other than a site of risk and deviance, denies non-conforming youth recognition as fully participating and valued members of their communities who are capable of creating and enjoying meaningful relationships with same-sex partners (Fields 2004; Fields 2008; Gilbert 2006; Russell 2002). . . .

RISKING AMBIGUITY AND AMBIVALENCE

These shared ideas across a seemingly polarized public debate suggest that sexuality education policy and debates are sites of profound conflict and significant ambivalence and ambiguity. While national policy discussions and representations of those discussions often suggest a monolithic abstinence-only agenda, local providers of abstinence-only education are often quite resistant to and ambivalent about funding requirements and streams (Hess 2010). Feminists who strive for a sexuality education that fosters agency and subjectivity among girls and young women and recognizes the importance of intimacy and egalitarianism also grapple with the messiness and difficulty of the sexual relations in which youth and adults are similarly involved (Schalet 2009). And youth themselves navigate significant ambiguity: for example, conflicts between the instrumental lessons of the abstinence-only and abstinence-based sexuality education they encounter in schooling and the more ambiguous messages about sexuality they encounter in popular culture and their everyday lives appear to yield "highly personalized and often contradictory interpretations [of abstinence]" (Sawyer et al. 2007, 51).

Some researchers argue that this ambiguity threatens to undermine young people's well-being. Without a definition of what it means to abstain, adolescents appear to be at risk of stumbling into a world characterized by the dangers of pregnancy and sexual behavior (see, for example, Sawyer et al. 2007). According to this instrumental argument, if "misconceptions and ambiguities" about abstinence are allowed to stand (Goodson et al. 2003, 91), educators and researchers will be unable to offer effective sexuality education, evaluate sexuality education programs, and equip young people to recognize when they are being sexually active and when their behaviors constitute a sexual risk (Haglund, 2003). In response, many social science researchers, like policy makers, have sought an appropriate, clear definition that would help "provide adolescents with the information and decision-making skills to assess and maintain well-being" (Ott et al. 2006, 197).

An alternative lies in the work of researchers who, rather than positing these "highly personalized and often contradictory" definitions as problems to stamp out, approach terms like "abstinence" and their surrounding ambiguity as problems to engage, as conditions of learning and of sexual life. Young people's lack of clarity about abstinence and virginity reflects a broader lack of consensus in our society (Bersamin et al. 2007). Their resistance to clear-cut definitions suggests that young people's experiences of sexuality and of learning about sexuality exceed the normative cultural messages about risk, responsibility, and disease that characterize most abstinence-only and comprehensive sexuality education.

Articulating a vision of education that promotes well-being through a more expansive and less instrumentalist approach to risk, sexuality, and education involves both a rethinking of young people's sexuality as comprising more than risk and an acknowledgement that many of the risks young people face reflect adult-made social conditions (Schaffner 2005). . . .

While such understandings of risk, ambiguity, and ambivalence are not the norm in contemporary sexuality education, some educators and researchers have embraced the approach. . . . In its "Genderpalooza! A Sex & Gender Primer," Scarleteen.com discusses gender not in the conventional binary terms of female and male but instead as

> a [hu]man-made set of concepts and ideas about how men and women are supposed to look, act, relate and interrelate, based on their sex. Gender isn't

anatomical: it's intellectual, psychological and social (and even optional); about identity, roles and status based on ideas about sex and what it means to different people and groups. (http://www.scarleteen.com/article/body/genderpalooza_a_sex_gender_primer)

In its *Young Women's Survival Guide*, Health Initiatives for Youth (HIFY) offers readers a line drawing of "female external genitals" with the caption, "Everyone's vulva is different so don't judge yours by the pictures you see" (2003, 14). And the resource guide, *It's All One Curriculum*, ties values, beliefs, and norms to social contexts and power:

> We often tend to think of our own values and beliefs as "natural." However . . . [s]ocieties enact laws that reflect norms and specify which behaviors are permitted and which are not. Those individuals or groups who have the most power often have the greatest influence in determining both social norms and laws. Some laws, norms, and individual values are concerned with sexuality. (International Sexuality and HIV Curriculum Working Group 2009, 23)

With these lessons, Scarleteen, HIFY, and It's All One Curriculum recognize the ambiguity and ambivalence that characterize young people's and adult's sexual lives, classroom efforts to address those lives, and policy debates about those classroom efforts. Rather than offering the false promise that all risk can be eliminated and avoided, these texts encourage young people to take risks responsibly, to recognize and challenge the ways that social conditions put them and their peers at risk, to think about what might make sexual choices more and less safe, and to contribute to a world that promotes the well-being of all.

CONCLUSIONS

Though abstinence-only and comprehensive sexuality education advocates may offer different responses to the problems routinely associated with teen sexual activity, much of what they offer shares assumptions about youth, sexuality, and learning: that teen sexuality is a site of danger and risk; that such danger and risk is a source of profound worry among adults; and that sexuality education is a necessary, rational, and corrective response to that danger, risk, and worry. Similarly, both abstinence-only and comprehensive sexuality education rest on a particular understanding of education: provide students the requisite knowledge, and they will adopt the behaviors—for example, sexual abstinence or contraceptive use—that teachers advocate.

Such an approach to knowledge casts sexual decision making as wholly rational and denies "affect as a central part of what knowledge does" (Lesko 2010, 282). The affective experiences of learning about sexuality exceed the bounds of rational and predictable knowledge. This excess animates young people's experiences of sexuality and persists in classroom practice. It also pervades local and national sexuality education debates. Consistently, sexuality education evokes a range of fraught social concerns about, for example, which family formations communities will accept and celebrate in their midst; how best to respond to increasing numbers of—and tolerance of—lesbian, gay, and bisexual youth; the relative responsibility of families and schools to provide for young people's sexual well-being and moral character; and how educators,

families, service providers, and other community members will respond to the incidence and risk of teen pregnancies and STIs.

Ambiguity and ambivalence in sexuality education policy and practice represent a call to move beyond the polarized debate between abstinence-only and comprehensive sexuality education and allow instead for an expansive approach to learning and knowing that opens with and sustains questions. Indeed, Jen Gilbert has argued for teaching and learning in which "not knowing and feeling confused [might become] the basis of learning about sexuality" and not something to be corrected (2010, 5). In this vision of sexuality education, the ambivalence, pleasure, worry, and other sexual experiences and associations that are currently interpreted as intruding upon effective teaching, learning, and policy would be recognized and contended with as the cultural conditions in which communities debate sexuality education policy and practice and, ultimately, the stuff of sexuality education itself.

NOTE

1. *Editor's Note*: Despite President Obama's long-standing commitment to directing funding away from abstinence only-until-marriage (AOUM) programs, Congress currently funds these programs at $75 million a year through Title V Sec. 510 of the Social Security Act (up from $50 million a year in 2015) (https://siecus.org/wp-content/uploads/2018/10/AOUM-Funding-Table-FY19-Oct-2018-FINAL.pdf). In addition, fiscal year 2016 brought a new competitive AOUM grant program, SRAE, which has more than doubled its funding since its inception, receiving $25 million in fiscal year 2018 (https://siecus.org/wp-content/uploads/2018/08/A-History-of-AOUM-Funding-Final-Draft.pdf).

REFERENCES

Angelides, Steven. 2004. "Feminism, Child Abuse, and the Erasure of Child Sexuality." *GLQ: A Journal of Lesbian and Gay Studies* 10(2): 141–77.

Bay-Cheng, Laina Y. 2003. "The Trouble of Teen Sex: The Construction of Adolescent Sexuality through School-Based Sexuality Education." *Sex Education: Sexuality, Society and Learning* 3(1): 61–74.

Bersamin, Melina A., Deborah A. Fisher, Samantha Walker, Douglas L. Hill and Joel W. Grube. 2007. "Defining Virginity and Abstinence: Adolescents' Interpretations of Sexual Behaviors." *Journal of Adolescent Health* 41: 182–88.

Best, Amy. 2000. *Prom Night: Youth, Schools and Popular Culture*. New York: Routledge.

Best, Joel. 1993. *Threatened Children: Rhetoric and Concern about Child-Victims*. Chicago: University of Chicago Press.

Bourdieu, Pierre and Jean Claude Passeron. 1990. *Reproduction in Education, Society and Culture*. Trans. Richard Nice. London: Sage Publications.

Brown, Jane D. and Victor C. Strasburger. 2007. "From Calvin Klein to Paris Hilton and MySpace: Adolescents, Sex, and the Media." *Adolescent Sexuality, Adolescent Medicine: State of the Art Reviews* 18(3): 484–507.

Clay, Andreana. 2003. "Keepin' It Real: Black Youth, Hip-Hop Culture, and Black Identity." *American Behavioral Scientist* 46(1): 1346–58.

Connell, Catherine and Sinikka Elliott. 2009. "Beyond the Birds and the Bees: Learning Inequality through Sexuality Education." *American Journal of Sexuality Education* 4: 83–102.

Diorio, Joseph A. and Jennifer A. Munro. 2000. "Doing Harm in the Name of Protection: Menstruation as a Topic for Sex Education." *Gender and Education* 12(3): 347–65.

Duberstein Lindberg, Laura, John S. Santelli and Susheela Singh. 2006. "Changes in Formal Sex Education: 1995–2002." *Perspectives on Sexual and Reproductive Health* 38(4): 182–89.

Duggan, Lisa and Nan D. Hunter. 1995. *Sex Wars: Sexual Dissent and Political Culture*. New York: Routledge.

Elliott, Sinikka. 2012. *Not My Kid: What Parents Believe about the Sex Lives of Their Teenagers*. New York: New York University Press.

Ferguson, Ann Arnett. 2001. *Bad Boys: Public Schools in the Making of Black Masculinity*. Ann Arbor: University of Michigan Press.

Fields, Jessica. 2004. "Same-Sex Marriage, Sodomy Laws, and the Sexual Lives of Young People." *Sexuality Research and Social Policy: Journal of NSRC* 1(3): 11–23.

Fields, Jessica. 2005. "'Children Having Children': Race, Innocence, and Sexuality Education." *Social Problems* 52(4): 549–71.

Fields, Jessica. 2008. *Risky Lessons: Sex Education and Social Inequality*. New Brunswick, NJ: Rutgers University Press.

Fields, Jessica and Celeste Hirschman. 2007. "Citizenship Lessons in Abstinence-Only Sexuality Education." *American Journal of Sexuality Education* 2(2): 3–25.

Fine, Michelle. 1988. "Sexuality, Schooling, and Adolescent Females: The Missing Discourse of Desire." *Harvard Educational Review* 58(1): 29–53.

Fine, Michelle and Sara I. McClelland. 2006. "Sexuality Education and Desire: Still Missing after All These Years." *Harvard Educational Review* 76(3): 297–337.

Fineman, Martha A., Gwendolyn Mink and Anna Marie Smith. 2003. "No Promotion of Marriage in TANF!" *Social Justice* 30(4): 126–34.

Gilbert, Jen. 2006. "'Let Us Say Yes to What or Who Shows Up': Education as Hospitality." *Journal of the Canadian Association of Curriculum Studies* 4(1): 35–44.

Gilbert, Jen. 2010. "Ambivalence Only? Sex Education in the Age of Abstinence." *Sex Education: Sexuality, Society and Learning* 10(3): 233–37.

Goodson, Patricia, Sandy Suther, B. E. Pruitt and Kelly Wilson. 2003. "Defining Abstinence: Views of Directors, Instructors, and Participants in Abstinence-Only-Until-Marriage Programs in Texas." *The Journal of School Health* 73: 91–96.

Haglund, Kristin 2003. "'Sexually Abstinent African American Adolescent Females' Descriptions of Abstinence." *Journal of Nursing Scholarship* 25(3): 231–36.

HealthInitiatives for Youth 2003. *Kickin' Back With the Girls: A Young Woman's Survival Guide*, 22nd ed. San Francisco, CA: Author.

Heins, Marjorie. 2001. *Not in Front of the Children: "Indecency," Censorship, and the Innocence of Youth*. New York: Hill and Wang.

Henderson, Marion, Daniel Wight, Gillian Raab, Charles Abraham, Alison Parkes, Sue Scott and Graham Hart. 2007. "Impact of a Theoretically Based Sex Education Programme (SHARE) Delivered by Teachers on NHS Registered Conceptions and Terminations: Final Results of a Cluster Randomised Trial." *British Medical Journal* 334: 133–36.

Hess, Amie. 2010. "Hold the Sex, Please: The Discursive Politics between National and Local Abstinence Education Providers." *Sex Education: Sexuality, Society and Learning* 10(3): 251–66.

Hunter, James Davison. 1992. *Culture Wars: The Struggle to Define America*. New York: Basic Books.

International Sexuality and HIV Curriculum Working Group 2009. *It's All One Curriculum: Guidelines and Activities for a Unified Approach to Sexuality, Gender, HIV, and Human Rights Education*. New York: The Population Council.

Irvine, Janice M. 2000. "Doing It with Words: Discourse and the Sex Education Culture Wars." *Critical Inquiry* 27(1): 58–76.

Irvine, Janice M. 2002. *Talk about Sex: The Battles over Sex Education in the United States*. Berkeley: University of California Press.

Irvine, Janice M. 2006. "Emotional Scripts of Sex Panics." *Sexuality Research & Social Policy: Journal of NSRC* 3(3): 82–94.

Kendall, NancyXS. 2008. "Sexuality Education in an Abstinence-Only Era: A Comparative Case Study of Two U. S. States." *Sexuality Research and Social Policy: Journal of NSRC* 5(2): 23–44.

Kincaid, James R. 1997. *Erotic Innocence: The Culture of Child Molesting*. Durham, NC: Duke University Press.

Kirby, Douglas. 2008. "The Impact of Abstinence and Comprehensive Sex and STD/HIV Education Programs on Adolescent Sexual Behavior." *Sexuality Research and Social Policy: Journal of NSRC* 5(3): 6–17.

Lesko, Nancy. 2001. *Act Your Age! A Cultural Construction of Adolescence*. New York: Routledge Falmer.

Lesko, Nancy. 2010. "Feeling Abstinent? Feeling Comprehensive? Touching the Affects of Sexuality Curricula." *Sex Education: Sexuality, Society and Learning* 10(3): 281–97.

Levine, Judith. 2002. *Harmful to Minors: The Perils of Protecting Children from Sex*. Minneapolis: University of Minnesota Press.

Luker, Kristin. 1996. *Dubious Conceptions: The Politics of Teen Pregnancy*. Cambridge, MA: Harvard University Press.

Luker, Kristin. 2006. *When Sex Goes to School: Warring Views on Sex—and Sex Education—Since the Sixties*. New York: W. W. Norton.

Luttrell, Wendy. 2003. *Pregnant Bodies, Fertile Minds: Gender, Race, and the Schooling of Pregnant Teens*. New York: Routledge.

Martin, Emily. 1991. "The Egg and the Sperm: How Science Has Constructed a Romance Based on Stereotypical Male–Female Roles." *Signs: Journal of Women in Culture and Society* 16(31): 485–501.

Martin, Karin A. 1996. *Puberty, Sexuality, and the Self: Boys and Girls at Adolescence*. New York: Routledge.

Moran, Jeffrey P. 2000. *Teaching Sex: The Shaping of Adolescence in the 20th Century*. Cambridge, MA: Harvard University Press.

Ott, Mary A., Elizabeth J. Pfeiffer and J. Dennis Fortenberry. 2006. "Perceptions of Sexual Abstinence among High-Risk Early and Middle Adolescents." *Journal of Adolescent Health* 39: 192–98.

Pascoe, C. J. 2007. *Dude, You're a Fag: Masculinity and Sexuality in High School*. Berkeley: University of California Press.

Regnerus, Mark D. 2007. *Forbidden Fruit: Sex & Religion in the Lives of American Teenagers*. New York: Oxford University Press.

Russell, Stephen T. 2002. "Queer in America: Citizenship for Sexual Minority Youth." *Applied Developmental Science* 6(4): 258–63.

Santelli, John S. 2006. "Abstinence-Only Education: Politics, Science, and Ethics." *Social Research* 73(3): 835–58.

Sawyer, Robin G., Donna E. Howard, Jessica Brewster-Gavin, Melissa Jordan and Marla Sherman. 2007. "'We Didn't Have Sex . . . Did We?' College Students' Perceptions of Abstinence." *American Journal of Health Studies* 22(1): 46–55.

Scarleteen.com. 2011. "Genderpalooza! A Sex & Gender Primer." [Online]. Retrieved on 11 October 2011 from: http://www.scarleteen.com/article/body/genderpalooza_a_sex_gender_primer

Schaffner, Laurie. 2005. *So Called Girl-on-Girl Violence is Actually Adult-on-Girl Violence (Great Cities Institute Working Paper No. GCP-05-03)*. Chicago, IL: Author.

Schalet, Amy T. 2004. "Must We Fear Adolescent Sexuality?" *Medscape General Medicine* 6(4): 1–16.

Schalet, Amy T. 2009. "Subjectivity, Intimacy, and the Empowerment Paradigm of Adolescent Sexuality: The Unexplored Room." *Feminist Studies* 35(1): 133–60.

Schalet, Amy T. 2010. "Sexual Subjectivity Revisited: The Significance of Relationships in Dutch and American Girls' Experiences of Sexuality." *Gender & Society* 24: 304.

Shapiro, Eve. 2010. *Gender Circuits: Bodies and Identities in a Technological Age*. New York: Routledge.

Stein, Arlene. 2006. *Shameless: Sexual Dissidence in American Culture*. New York: New York University Press.

Tolman, Deborah L. 2002. *Dilemmas of Desire: Teenage Girls Talk about Sexuality*. Cambridge, MA: Harvard University Press.

Trudell, Bonnie Nelson. 1993. *Doing Sex Education: Gender Politics and Schooling*. New York: Routledge.

Trudell, Bonnie Nelson and Mariamne H. Whatley. 1991. "Sex Respect: A Problematic Public School Sexuality Curriculum." *Journal of Sex Education and Therapy* 17(2): 122–40.

U.S. Department of Health and Human Services. 2008. Health and Human Services Funding for Abstinence Education, Education for Teen Pregnancy and HIV/STD Prevention, and Other Programs that Address Adolescent Sexual Activity. [Online]. Retrieved on 11 October 2011 from: http://aspe.hhs.gov/hsp/08/AbstinenceEducation/report.shtml

Wagoner, James. 2009. "Appropriations Bill Marks Victory for Sexual Health: Advocates Need to Remain Vigilant." Advocates for Youth Blog. [Online]. Retrieved on 11 October 2011 from: http://www.advocatesforyouth.org/blogs-main/advocates-blog/1544-appropriations-bill-marks-victory-for-sexual-health-advocates-need-to-remain-vigilant

Waxman, Henry A. 2004. *The Content of Federally Funded Abstinence-Only Education Programs*. Washington, D.C.: U.S. House of Representatives, Special Investigation Division.

Whatley, Mariamne H. 1988. "Photographic Images of Blacks in Sexuality Texts." *Curriculum Inquiry* 18(2): 83–106.

Whatley, Mariamne H. and Bonnie Nelson Trudell. 1993. "Teen-Aid: Another Problematic School Sexuality Curriculum." *Journal of Sex Education and Therapy* 19(4): 251–71.

Wight, Daniel, Gillian Raab, Marion Henderson, Charles Abraham, Katie Buston, Graham Hart and Sue Scott. 2002. "The Limits of Teacher-Delivered Sex Education: Interim Behavioural Outcomes from a Randomised Trial." *British Medical Journal* 324: 1430–33.

Wilkins, Amy C. 2008. *Wannabes, Goths, and Christians: The Boundaries of Sex, Style, and Status*. Chicago: University of Chicago Press.

Zimmerman, Jonathan. 2005. *Whose America? Culture Wars in the Public Schools*. Cambridge, MA: Harvard University Press.

AMERICA'S SEX EDUCATION: HOW WE ARE FAILING OUR STUDENTS

UNIVERSITY OF SOUTHERN CALIFORNIA, DEPARTMENT OF NURSING

When only 13 states in the nation require sex education to be medically accurate, a lot is left up to interpretation in teenage health literacy. Research published by the Public Library of Science[1] shows that when sex education is comprehensive, students feel more informed, make safer choices, and have healthier outcomes—resulting in fewer unplanned pregnancies and more protection against sexually transmitted diseases and infection. "Sex education is about life skills," said Elizabeth Nash, senior state issues manager at the Guttmacher Institute. "There are so many aspects you take with you for the rest of your life, but you only get it once or twice in school."

Of course, many young students pick up sexual health information from sources other than school—parents, peers, medical professionals, social media, and pop culture. However, public schools are the best opportunity for adolescents to access formal information. So, what happens when that information isn't regulated by the state? Teachers are left to interpret vague legislative guidelines, meaning information might not be accurate or unbiased.

The . . . [information] below compares the legislative policies of all 50 states, including how they mandate specific aspects of sex education like contraception, abstinence, and sexual orientation.

Sex-ed legislation in the United States

Legislation for sex education falls under the jurisdiction of states' rights, creating disparities in what public school students learn in classrooms across the country. The lists below indicate which states require critical components of comprehensive sex education, and whether they mandate sex education at all.[2]

States Where Sex Education Is Mandated

- California
- Delaware
- District of Columbia
- Georgia

- Hawaii
- Iowa
- Kentucky
- Maine
- Maryland
- Minnesota
- Mississippi
- Montana
- Nevada
- New Jersey
- New Mexico
- North Carolina
- North Dakota
- Ohio
- Oregon
- Rhode Island
- South Carolina
- Tennessee: Sex education is required if the pregnancy rate for teen women 15 to 17 years of age is at least 19.5 or higher.
- Utah: This state also prohibits teachers from responding to students' spontaneous questions in ways that conflict with the law's requirements.
- Vermont
- West Virginia

States Where Sex Education Must Be Medically Accurate When Taught

- California
- Colorado
- Hawaii
- Illinois
- Iowa
- Maine
- Michigan: Sex education "shall not be medically inaccurate."
- New Jersey
- North Carolina
- Oregon
- Rhode Island
- Utah
- Washington

States Where Sex Education Must Cover Contraception

- Alabama
- California

1   Stanger-Hall, Kathrin F., and David W. Hall. 2011. "Abstinence-Only Education and Teen Pregnancy Rates: Why We Need Comprehensive Sex Education in the U.S." *PLoS ONE* 6(10).[AU: Pls. add page numbers.—For some reason I am unable to insert comment here. This is an online journal and it cites without page numbers: (Stanger-Hall KF, Hall DW. Abstinence-only education and teen pregnancy rates: why we need comprehensive sex education in the U.S. *PLoS One.* 2011;6(10):e24658. doi:10.1371/journal.pone.0024658)
2   Source: Guttmacher Institute, 2017. https://www.guttmacher.org/state-policy/explore/sex-and-hiv-education

Researched and written by Halah Flynn and Chantal de la Rionda. © 2018 The University of Southern California for its USC Suzanne Dworak-Peck School of Social Work. Reprinted with permission of 2U, Inc.

- Colorado
- Delaware
- District of Columbia
- Hawaii
- Illinois
- Maine
- Maryland
- Mississippi: Localities may include topics such as contraception or STIs only with permission from the State Department of Education.
- New Jersey
- New Mexico
- North Carolina
- Oregon
- Rhode Island
- South Carolina
- Vermont
- Virginia
- Washington
- West Virginia

States Where Sex Education Must Cover Abstinence

- California
- Colorado
- Hawaii
- Kentucky
- Maryland
- Minnesota
- Montana
- New Mexico
- North Dakota
- Vermont
- Virginia
- West Virginia

States Where Sex Education Must Stress Abstinence

- Alabama
- Arizona
- Arkansas
- Delaware
- Florida
- Georgia
- Illinois: Sex education is not mandatory, but health education is required, and it includes medically accurate information on abstinence.
- Indiana
- Louisiana
- Maine
- Massachusetts
- Mississippi
- Missouri

- New Jersey
- North Carolina
- Ohio
- Oklahoma
- Oregon
- Rhode Island
- South Carolina
- Tennessee
- Texas
- Utah
- Washington
- Wisconsin

States Where Sex Education Must Be Inclusive of Sexual Orientation

- California
- Colorado
- Connecticut
- Iowa
- New Jersey
- New Mexico
- Oregon
- Rhode Island
- Washington

States Where Sex Education Must Be Negative Toward Sexual Orientation

- Alabama
- Arizona: If HIV education is taught in Arizona, it cannot "promote" a "homosexual lifestyle" or portray homosexuality in a positive manner.
- Oklahoma: Mandated HIV education in Oklahoma teaches that, among other behaviors, "homosexual activity" is considered to be "responsible for contact with the AIDS virus."
- South Carolina
- Texas

States Without Available Data: Alaska, Kansas, Nebraska, South Dakota, Wyoming

What does comprehensive sex ed look like?

Even when sex education is required, state policies still vary widely regarding the inclusion of critical information. In short, comprehensive sex ed "includes age-appropriate, medically accurate information on a broad set of topics related to sexuality including human development, relationships, decision-making, abstinence, contraception, and disease prevention," according to the Sexuality Information and Education Council of the United States.[3]

USC Suzanne Dworak-Peck School of Social Work Department of Nursing professor Dr. Theresa Granger says that comprehensive sex ed goes beyond the biophysical aspects. "It's about focusing

---

3　https://siecus.org

(continued)

on the emotional, psychosocial and economic impacts of what happens when youth and adolescents engage in sexual intercourse and other sexual practices," she said. Granger said that in order to be comprehensive, sex education programs have to consider the whole student. But many states leave issues like sexual orientation and contraception unaddressed, and some even prohibit public schools from addressing them. "It's hard to get legislators behind comprehensive sex ed," said Nash, who explained that campaigning on controversial and sensitive topics can make lawmakers uncomfortable.

It can take years for policies to change, even in the most progressive states. California is known for pioneering reforms, but it wasn't until 2016 that the state passed a law to mandate comprehensive sex education in public schools. Before the new law went into effect . . . [4] California left sex education as an optional component of health curricula for students in grades 7 through 12. The legislation is part of a nationwide trend—albeit a slow and deliberate one—to transform disjointed sex education laws into comprehensive requirements that lead to better health outcomes for adolescents in public schools, according to Nash, who has tracked sex education policies for over a decade. Other states have a more volatile history with regulating sex education. In 2010, Wisconsin's governor and legislature passed a law mandating comprehensive sex ed. Two years later it was replaced with . . . [the current] abstinence-only policy.[5]

In recent years, states have begun to mandate sex ed to include information about life skills for family communication, avoiding coercion and making healthy decisions. According to Nash, including these skills is part of progressive trends across the country, where states have begun to require discussions of sexual consent, harassment, and sexual orientation. Overall, most trends are slow to change. "Most states will tweak the policies they already have to be more inclusive, or double down on conservative regulations," Nash said.

Health outcomes

The impact of sex education policies becomes clearer when we consider that in 2016, the United States had higher rates of teen pregnancy and sexually transmitted disease than most other industrialized countries. What feels like progress at the state level can be seen as mere catch-up to the policies of other developed nations that require teachers to discuss sex ed as early as kindergarten.[6] Granger said school programs need to work on adapting to current health issues and trends that affect the scope of sexual health literacy. "There are rewards and consequences to our behavior at every age across the lifespan," she said. "We can't always assume that an adolescent will wait to become an adult before making adult decisions."

Teen pregnancy

Although the teen pregnancy rate has hit a historic low in the United States, the nation still holds one of the highest rates in the developed world. These lists show states' disparate birth rates for women ages 15 to 19 in 2015, according to the CDC.[7]

2015 TEEN BIRTH RATES

Births per 1,000 women age 15–19 estimated in each state.

- Alabama 30.1
- Alaska 29.3
- Arizona 26.3
- Arkansas 38
- California: 19 (Estimate based on the number of abortions among all women in the state and the proportion of abortions obtained by women of the same age nationally.)
- Colorado: 19.9
- Connecticut: 10.1
- Delaware: 18.1
- District of Columbia: 25.6
- Florida: 20.8
- Georgia: 25.6
- Hawaii: 20.6
- Idaho: 22.5
- Illinois: 21.1
- Indiana: 26
- Iowa: 18.6
- Kansas: 25.5
- Kentucky: 32.4
- Louisiana: 34.1
- Maine: 15.4
- Maryland: 17 (Estimate based on the number of abortions among all women in the state and the proportion of abortions obtained by women of the same age in neighboring or similar states.)
- Massachusetts: 9.4
- Michigan: 19.4
- Minnesota: 13.7
- Mississippi: 34.8
- Missouri: 25
- Montana: 25.3
- Nebraska: 22
- Nevada: 27.6

4   Adams, Jane Meredith. 2015. "Sex Ed to Become Mandatory in Grades 7–12 in California." *EdSource*. Retrieved February 9, 2019, from https://edsource.org/2015/sex-ed-to-become-mandatory-in-grades-7-12-in-california/88248.

5   Ujifusa, Andrew. 2012. "Walker Signs Abstinence-Only Sex Ed. Bill in Wisconsin." *Education Week—State EdWatch*. Retrieved February 9, 2019, from http://blogs.edweek.org/edweek/state_edwatch/2012/04/walker_signs_abstinence-only_sex_ed_bill.html?cmp=SOC-SHR-FB.

6   de Melker, Saskia. 2015. "The Case for Starting Sex Education in Kindergarten." *PBS NewsHour*. Retrieved February 9, 2019, from https://www.pbs.org/newshour/health/spring-fever.

7   Source: Centers for Disease Control and Prevention, 2015. https://www.cdc.gov/nchs/data/nvsr/nvsr66/nvsr66_01.pdf

- New Hampshire: 10.9 (Estimate based on the number of abortions among all women in the state and the proportion of abortions obtained by women of the same age in neighboring or similar states.)
- New Jersey: 12.1
- New Mexico: 34.6
- New York: 14.6
- North Carolina: 23.6
- North Dakota: 22.2
- Ohio: 23.2
- Oklahoma: 34.8
- Oregon: 19
- Pennsylvania: 17.7
- Rhode Island: 14.3
- South Carolina: 26.2
- South Dakota: 26.4
- Tennessee: 30.5
- Texas: 34.6
- Utah: 17.6
- Vermont: 11.6
- Virginia: 17.1
- Washington: 17.6
- West Virginia: 31.9
- Wisconsin: 16.2
- Wyoming: 29.2 (Estimate based on the number of abortions among all women in the state and the proportion of abortions obtained by women of the same age in neighboring or similar states.)

Even though the United States fell behind other industrialized nations in preventing teen births, its teen pregnancy rates hit an all-time low in 2016, a decade-long trend that has been attributed by many studies to increased education about contraception in public schools. Research published in the *Journal of Adolescent Health*[8] concluded that when sex education included information about contraception, teens had a lower risk of pregnancy than adolescents who received abstinence-only or no sex education. The findings could alleviate a common fear of parents and teachers who worry that students are more likely to increase their sexual activity after receiving comprehensive sex education.

The more teens can access accurate information from a trusted provider, the more prepared they can be when making decisions about their bodies and relationships. Granger said that in her clinical experience, teens will make a decision to engage in sexual activity whether or not they feel adequately informed, leaving health professionals with an opportunity to promote sexual health literacy. "Teens will often reach out for education after they have made their decision," Granger said. "When they reach out, it's important for this education to be accurate and comprehensive, not biased or based on judgment."

Sexually transmitted diseases and infections

People ages 15 to 24 only make up 25 percent of the American population, but they account for 50 percent of all new STDs reported in 2013, which raises concerns from medical professionals about the scope of sex education.[9]

TOTAL STD RATE PER 1,000 CASES

People can report having more than one STD within a year; this data reflects the rate of cases per 1,000 people in specified age group estimated in a state.

- Alabama: 40.388
- Alaska: 36.139
- Arizona: 25.274
- Arkansas: 34.465
- California: 20.683
- Colorado: 21.065
- Connecticut: 20.662
- Delaware: 34.614
- District of Columbia: 42
- Florida: 25.963
- Georgia: 31.347
- Hawaii: 22.959
- Idaho:17.112
- Illinois: 31.336
- Indiana: 26.039
- Iowa: 19.793
- Kansas: 21.67
- Kentucky: 24.424
- Louisiana: 40.515
- Maine: 14.916
- Maryland: 27.75
- Massachusetts: 17.29
- Michigan:28.32
- Minnesota: 20.877
- Missouri: 28.951
- Montana: 20.241
- Nebraska: 21.84
- Nevada: 23.897
- New Hampshire: 12.944
- New Jersey: 19.689

8   Kohler, Pamela K., Lisa E. Manhart, and William E. Lafferty. 2008. "Abstinence-Only and Comprehensive Sex Education and the Initiation of Sexual Activity and Teen Pregnancy | Request PDF." *ResearchGate*. Retrieved February 9, 2019, from https://www. researchgate.net/publication/5505124_Abstinence-Only_and_ Comprehensive_Sex_Education_and_the_Initiation_of_Sexual_ Activity_and_Teen_Pregnancy.

9   Data Source: National Electronic Telecommunications System for Surveillance, Centers for Disease Control and Prevention, 2013. https://www.cdc.gov/std/stats/by-age/15-24-all-stds/default.htm

(*continued*)

- New Mexico: 29.765
- New York: 25.651
- North Carolina: 31.963
- North Dakota: 20.577
- Ohio: 30.583
- Oklahoma: 29.578
- Oregon: 19.3
- Pennsylvania: 26.032
- Rhode Island: 20.014
- South Carolina: 34.17
- South Dakota: 26.481
- Tennessee: 30.013
- Texas: 28.406
- Utah: 11.157
- Vermont: 15.603
- Virginia: 23.954
- Washington: 18.619
- West Virginia: 18.32
- Wisconsin: 24.407
- Wyoming: 18.596

According to the CDC,[10] teens who identify with LGBTQ communities can be at higher risk of contracting STDs, but safeguarding against transmissions becomes difficult when states prohibit teachers from discussing sexual orientation in class. Some states expect that sexual orientation will get discussed at home, but the reality is that many students feel they lack the relationships to comfortably ask parents, teachers, or peers about health information related to orientation. "Teens who are healthy and in supportive relationships involving friends and family will often make much different decisions than those who aren't," said Granger, who has conducted research on the impact of relationships on adolescent development. "Stable, present and meaningful relationships with parents and other family members are all protective factors from a variety of interrelated risky behaviors."

"In some states, teachers are allowed to answer questions from students, even if it focuses on a forbidden topic like STDs or sexual orientation," Nash said. Though this loophole is disappearing in some states like Tennessee, it allows students to stay engaged in discussions that would otherwise exclude them because of focus on heterosexual relationships. "More students are becoming open about their sexual identities and preferences, and schools have to address that," Nash said. But discrepancies persist across communities over the responsibility of providing meaningful sex education.

Having "the talk"

One of the main challenges of mandating comprehensive sex education is considering everyone involved in the process: students,

their classmates, parents, teachers, and legislators. Teachers feel pressure from parents to deliver just the right amount of information, but students tune out[11] when educators fail to address their individual questions.

So whose responsibility is it to make sure young people have the information they need to make healthy choices? In areas where sex ed isn't required, states can assume that parents will educate their children at home, but studies show that adolescents are increasingly more likely to seek information from social media and online communities, which can be more inclusive of gender and sexual minorities, but not consistently reliable for medical accuracy.

Granger said assigning responsibility for "The Talk" is part of the problem that leaves teens uninformed. "One of the weaknesses in our current system is that we're trying to assign primary responsibility and it is too tall of an order for any single entity to try to tackle," she said. When there's a disconnect between the information students get at school and what they can find on the Internet, mixed messaging makes it harder for teens to rely on the people they trust. That's where medical professionals can step in, according to Granger. She currently practices in Washington, one of the few states that allows minors to seek testing and treatment for STDs,[12] as well as contraception, without consent from a parent or guardian. "I do, however, tell patients' parents about the minor's consent to treat law, and the fact that it was designed to help youth seek treatment for communicable disease," Granger said. Though the conversations can be difficult, she said acknowledging the awkwardness can alleviate the tension around discussions of sexual health for parents and their children. "Every practitioner handles this differently," she said. "However, I always try to talk to the parents separately, the child separately, and then the parent and the child together."

Encouraging openness and compassion helps both parents and teens keep communication flowing with honesty, according to Granger, and is something all family nurse practitioners can do with their patients. Sometimes the best place to start can be asking teenage patients to talk about what they already know. "What does having sex mean to you?" Granger recommends asking as a jumping off point to deeper conversations. "People developing these curricula, myself included, need to think about the common goal to help youth maintain a positive sense of self-esteem, work toward healthy life goals and make responsible decisions with their bodies," Granger said. "We all need to do our part. We need to educate teens whenever and wherever they are."

10 Anon. 2019. "Sexual Minority Youth | Disparities | Adolescent and School Health | CDC." Retrieved February 9, 2019, from https://www.cdc.gov/healthyyouth/disparities/smy.htm.

11 Pound, Pandora, Rebecca Langford, and Rona Campbell. 2016. "What Do Young People Think about Their School-Based Sex and Relationship Education? A Qualitative Synthesis of Young People's Views and Experiences." *BMJ Open* 6(9):e011329.

12 https://depts.washington.edu/hcsats/PDF/guidelines/Minors%20Health%20Care%20Rights%20Washington%20State.pdf

STEFANIE MOLLBORN

24. "CHILDREN" HAVING CHILDREN

About one in three girls in the United States will become pregnant as teenagers, with most of them giving birth. These "children" having children have been the focus of media attention and public condemnation, and Mollborn discusses why they are viewed so negatively. Teen pregnancy hasn't always been recognized as a social problem, Mollborn argues, and she examines who these teens are, why rates of teen pregnancy are unequally distributed throughout the population, and the consequences of their pregnancies. Mollborn also offers ways to promote better outcomes for teen moms.

ADRIANA'S STORY

Meet Adriana. She's 17, lives with her parents, and, like about 1 in 6 teen girls in the U.S., she has a child. My research team got to know Adriana and 75 other teen parents through in-depth interviews in the Denver area in 2008–2009. A Latina high school student who looks and acts older than her age, Adriana has a two-year-old son, Marlon. Like the overwhelming majority of teen mothers, Adriana didn't intend to get pregnant: "I would always play with my little baby dolls and stuff, but I wasn't really thinking about, 'Oh, when am I gonna be a mom?' I didn't really care about that stuff. And then actually, to tell you the truth, when I got pregnant, I wasn't really thinking about being a mom yet, either. It just kind of happened."

Similarly, Adriana's boyfriend Michael was like many other young dads: "happy," even "over-excited," about becoming a father. But Adriana said, "Once I found out I was pregnant, I didn't want him to be my boyfriend." Still, he moved in with her family. Later, they lived with Michael's family. In contrast to stereotypes about uninvolved young fathers, it's very common for teen births to occur in the context of a long-term romantic relationship and for the child's father to live with the mom. However, these teen relationships frequently dissolve. Michael and Adriana were together for three years: " . . . after I had my son . . . I told him it was either my own place or I was leaving him. So he got me my own place. We lived there for about a year and a half, and then, like, we would fight all the time. We just realized that we were unhappy together. And last year we just broke up. It's been kind of hard on the baby." She says the breakup is "also a reason, kind of, why I feel awkward about getting pregnant so young, because I didn't really know what love was. I think it would be better if my son had his mom and his dad there together in a relationship, growing up with both parents involved daily. And I think that if I would have waited longer, I would have knew a little more, been a little wiser about who to have a baby with." Marlon saw his father infrequently right after the breakup, but now it's just on weekends at Michael's mother's house.

Marlon now lives with Adriana, her father and stepmother, grandmother, and several siblings. Adriana's father (a fast food worker) and grandmother pay for housing and other bills. Michael provides limited help, but as is typical for teen moms who don't live with their child's father, Adriana is responsible for keeping track of her son's needs and asking Michael for support. Michael's mother helps by providing childcare. Medicaid pays Adriana's medical bills, and the WIC program helped her with buying formula. This reliance on a network of extended family members for considerable support, supplemented by health care and nutritional support from the government (but not by welfare payments), is common. Despite this assistance, Adriana is still in a precarious financial situation. She doesn't often have spending money, because "as long as I don't need something really bad, I don't want to ask for it." Adriana worries about straining her family's resources.

While Adriana's story is certainly personal, it is far from unique. About 1 in 3 girls in the U.S. becomes pregnant before turning 20. About a third of these pregnancies end in abortion, but the majority of the rest become parents. (American girls ages 15–19 are about 3 times as likely as their Canadian peers to have a child, 7 times as likely as Swedes, and almost 9 times as likely as Japanese teens.) Adriana's experience exemplifies many of the larger social realities shaping teen parenthood today. These include historical changes in the typical American life course, shifting attitudes about the "problem" of teen pregnancy, social inequality and the polarized experience of teen parenthood in the U.S., and the many social consequences teen parents face for being "kids having kids."

WHO ARE THE KIDS WHO HAVE KIDS?

Parenting is not evenly distributed among American teenagers. In fact, we might say that teen parenthood is an extremely polarized experience—common in some segments of the population and rare in others.

Teen mothers and fathers overwhelmingly come from lower-income families and neighborhoods, and they are often struggling in school even before the pregnancy. A national study of babies born in 2001 revealed that about half of teen mothers' children live in poverty, and more than half of all children living in poverty have a mother who was once a teenage parent. Teen parenting also varies by race and ethnicity, with Latinos, African Americans, and Native Americans having the highest rates. . . . On the other hand, teen parenthood is relatively rare in high socioeconomic status, Asian American, and White families and neighborhoods.

There's little doubt that contraception (or lack thereof) is an important part of this package. While American teenagers start having sex at similar ages to their peers in many other Western countries, they are much more likely to get pregnant and have children, even though the vast majority of teen pregnancies are unintended. Many researchers attribute this difference to American teens' less consistent contraception patterns. Geography is another intriguing dimension of variation in teen parenthood. White teens in parts of the Southeast are more likely to get pregnant than elsewhere, as are Latina and African American teens in this region. Perhaps counterintuitively, [Southeastern and Southwestern] states with high levels of conservative religious affiliations have some of the highest teen birthrates, and many Evangelical young people are at risk of becoming teen parents.

My recent interviews with college students showed that particularly in low socioeconomic status, conservative religious communities, a negative view of teen parenting is balanced against a "pro-life" social norm that encourages teens not to have an abortion. Teens are told that having the child is the "lesser of two evils." This echoes the Palin family's reaction to daughter Bristol's unwed teen pregnancy, and some of our participants told us it was a recent opinion shift in their communities. In most of the study's higher socioeconomic status, less religious communities, there's no cautiously positive take on teen parenting. Parents actively encourage their children to delay sex, but believe that if they do have sex, they should contracept consistently. Teens who "mess up" by getting themselves or a partner pregnant are not judged as immoral, but as "stupid."

PROBLEMATIC PERCEPTIONS

For many, teen parenthood symbolizes "what's wrong" with America today. Media outlets breathlessly report the details of celebrity pregnancies and create reality shows about teen mothers, then air call-in sessions about the irresponsibility of young people. This simultaneous attention and condemnation is shared by the general public. In a 2004 opinion poll, teen pregnancy was rated by 42 percent as a "very serious problem" in our society, and another 37 percent considered it to be an "important problem."

Why is such a commonplace event viewed so negatively? The fact that teenage pregnancy disproportionately impacts racial minorities and low-income communities is key. Such patterns play into mainstream fears about social disorder and excessive reliance on social services and the welfare state. There is a persistent, racialized public stereotype of the Black or Latina "welfare queen" (even though the vast majority of teenage mothers do not receive welfare benefits).

This interpretation is somewhat confirmed by the fact that the general public's attitudes about teen childbearing are divided along racial lines, too. In a 2005 survey of American adults, for example, I asked people how embarrassed they would be by a hypothetical unwed teen pregnancy in their household. African Americans reported less embarrassment than other racial groups, and people who had attended college reported more embarrassment than those with less education.

Some historical perspective is important here as well. The U.S. has a long history of teen childbearing. . . . Since the start of the Second World War . . . the high point for teen births was in the mid-1950s. Yet teen parenthood did not fully emerge as an important "social problem" until the 1970s. The explanation probably lies in the marital context of teen births.

Back in the 1950s, it was common and socially acceptable for people to get married and immediately become parents in their late teens or early twenties. Technically, this made lots of young people teen parents, but it wasn't considered a problem because they were engaging in a "normal" life course. In contrast, nonmarital births were rare and stigmatized.

Since then, the experience of early adulthood has changed. Many young people now enjoy a longer period of independence before settling into adult roles, and most Americans delay marriage until at least their mid-twenties. At the same time, most have sex before their twentieth birthday, putting them at risk for unintended pregnancy. As it has for all births (4 in 10 births in the U.S. are now nonmarital, compared to 4 in 100 in 1950), the proportion of teen births that are nonmarital has risen dramatically over time: 87 percent of teen births were non-marital in 2008. Sociologist Frank Furstenberg has pointed out that, as nonmarital teen births increased, so did the visibility of teen parenting as a social problem.

These social attitudes and community norms clearly impact young people. In my analysis of a national survey of teenagers in 1995, most teens said they would feel embarrassed if they got (or for boys, got a girl) pregnant. This contradicts the popular idea that teens today think pregnancy is "cool."

Adriana's story illustrates how family and community reactions can shape teen parents' lives. Some of her family members reacted fairly well to her pregnancy, but others did not. Adriana's intelligence and morality were questioned. "My mom was just like, she didn't get mad. She just kind of said that my boyfriend has to take responsibility, 'cause he's the one who got me pregnant. So she kind of was like, 'Oh, well, I guess you're moving in tomorrow and you're gonna pay this bill and this bill and this bill. . . . You're not taking my daughter out of the house.' "Adriana's brother called her "stupid" and wanted "to beat my boyfriend up." But "the only one who really made me feel bad was my grandma," who told her that it was "wrong" for her to get pregnant so young. Adriana said, "I was really close to her. So I took it kind of hard. . . . We really don't talk any more. She talks to my son more than to me."

Adriana also feels socially ostracized. She says, "I really don't have lots of friends." This social isolation is typical and differs sharply from the common stereotype of teen girls encouraging their friends to get pregnant or forming "pregnancy pacts." Out in public, she attracts negative attention: "Sometimes I would be on the bus and people would just stare at me. . . .

[At] prenatal appointments, people were like, 'How old are you? What are you gonna do with a kid this young?' Stuff like that. It looks kind of bad to see a really young girl pregnant, but also, they don't know me, what I do." She's learning to cope, she says. "Now when I look at people, I'm like, 'Whatever. You don't even know me. I'm like, 'I still go to school.' I can throw that in their face. . . . I have something that would possibly hold me back, and I still do it." Like many other teen moms, Adriana has been forced to learn coping skills to negotiate public stigma. Proving skeptical people wrong is one reason why many teen parents told us they wanted to succeed in school.

CONSEQUENCES

The consequences of teen parenthood, for young parents and their children alike, are complicated. For decades, researchers have documented negative outcomes for teen mothers in terms of education, income, mental health, marriage, and more. Teen fathers have lower levels of education and employment than their peers, and, compared to other kids, children of teen parents have compromised development and health starting in early childhood and continuing into adolescence.

In research explaining these consequences, two surprising findings have emerged. First, by comparing teen mothers to natural comparison groups such as their childless twins and sisters and pregnant teens who miscarried, scholars like public health researcher Arline Geronimus and economist V. Joseph Hotz have shown that most of the negative "consequences" of teen childbearing are actually due to experiences in teens' lives from before they got pregnant, such as socioeconomic background and educational achievement. In other words, the experience of teen childbearing itself only moderately worsens these teens' life outcomes.

Second, the negative consequences of teen parenthood are more severe in the short term. In the long term, many teen parents end up with better outcomes than it looked like they would have when they were teens. For example, developmental psychologist Julie Lounds Taylor found in a predominantly White, socioeconomically advantaged sample of 1957 Wisconsin high school graduates that at midlife, former teenage mothers and fathers lagged behind peers with similar characteristics in terms of education, occupational status, marital stability, and physical health. On the other hand, their work involvement, income levels, satisfaction with work and marriage, mental health, and social support were similar. Using more recent data from a national longitudinal study of eighth graders from 1988, I found that 75 percent of teen mothers and 62 percent of fathers finished a high school degree or GED by age 26. However, compared to the typical American, their outcomes were still problematic: both teen moms and dads ended up with two years less education than average by age 26.

Adriana's story is again illustrative. She wasn't on a traditional path to academic success before she got pregnant. As a Latina from a family with low socioeconomic status, she already belonged to a high-risk group, and her academic experiences reflected it. Adriana says, "Before I was a mom, I didn't really go to school. I didn't like school." But once she got pregnant, she thought, "'What am I gonna give my son?' . . . He's gonna have the same life that I had, and then he can follow in my footsteps, and I don't want that. I want him to do some things. . . ." She started attending a school for pregnant teen girls. "Ever since then . . . I've passed all my classes, and now I graduate in December." There are supportive teachers and understanding fellow students. Infant care and other forms of support are available. Adriana now plans to enroll in postsecondary education.

The support context of teen parenthood varies widely. For example, there are racial and ethnic differences in the key people helping teen mothers. My analysis of a national sample of babies born in 2001 found that about 60 percent of Latina and White teen moms were living with their child's father nine months after the birth, compared to just 16 percent of Black teen moms. Instead, nearly 60 percent of Black teen moms were living with other adults, such as a parent. It's not clear which of these situations is most beneficial for teen moms and their children: although as a society we often wish for fathers to be more involved, teen relationships often break up, and instability in mothers' relationships can compromise children's development.

EFFECTIVE SOCIAL SUPPORTS

American teen parenthood is commonplace but polarizing. As our societal safety net shrinks, low-income families' prospects worsen, and education becomes increasingly important for financial success, teen parents face increasingly long odds. Adriana's story helps show how many teen parents are motivated to work hard and make a better life for themselves and their children. Our country has made an important commitment to reducing levels of teen pregnancy, but we also need to find better ways to support teens who are already parents so their families can have a better future.

The federal government has now committed substantial funding for both prevention of teen pregnancies and support for teens who are already parents. Supporting parenting teens is a smart societal investment. First, because most mothers of children living in poverty today were teen moms, targeting these families for intervention would be an effective way to help some of the most marginalized members of our society. This is true regardless of whether the negative outcomes were caused by teen parenthood itself or by factors related to the teen's situation before the pregnancy.

Second, with less financial support available from the government, especially since welfare reform was passed in 1996, teen parents and their children are more dependent on their families for survival. Many low-income families have less money and time than they did in the past, making it harder for them to support teen parents and their children. Research finds that families still provide substantial support, but it often severely strains their budgets and their relationships with the young parents, and many teens' and children's basic needs such as for food and warm clothing are not being met. The current economic crisis has exacerbated this situation.

Finally, as many service providers have long known, the time after a teen birth is a magic moment when societal investments can help nudge young families onto a successful trajectory. Unlike many older parents who can take time out from the labor force and still have attractive options when they re-enter, teens are in a life stage when it is critical for them to invest in education and work. And almost all the teen parents we interviewed were willing to sacrifice to meet their goals. A strong motivation to achieve for their children's sake was common.

Without support from social programs, though, this motivation may not be enough. For example, though Adriana is fully committed to her education and has her family behind her, she has to surmount massive obstacles like transportation and childcare to stay in school. Talking to teen parents like her, it's easy to see how much some short-term support would pay off for her, her son, and our society in the long term.

REDUCING UNINTENDED PREGNANCY: THE ROLE OF LONG-ACTING REVERSIBLE CONTRACEPTIVES

STACY GORMAN HARMON

In the United States, about half of all pregnancies, or 3.4 million annually, are unintended, making the U.S. unintended pregnancy rate the highest among developed countries (Guttmacher Institute, 2013). Unintended and teen pregnancies are a problem because they are associated with greater risk of negative consequences for the families that experience them. For instance, women who have unintended pregnancies are more likely to delay prenatal care and are less likely to breastfeed (D'Angelo et al., 2004; Logan et al., 2007). Among teen parents, both mothers and fathers are more likely to have lower income and educational attainment than their counterparts who delay parenthood (Hoffman & Maynard, 2008; Logan et al., 2007). Children of teens may also be impacted; studies have shown they are more likely to have poorer physical and mental health (Hoffman & Maynard, 2008; Logan et al., 2007).

Low-income women, teens, and all women aged 20 to 24 are especially likely to experience unintended pregnancy, whereas women with higher levels of income and education have the lowest rates of unintended pregnancy (Guttmacher Institute, 2014a). There is also an association between age and

(continued)

Original to *Focus on Social Problems: A Contemporary Reader.*

planned pregnancy; as age increases, unplanned pregnancies decrease (Guttmacher Institute, 2013). Among teens who are sexually active, the rate of unintended pregnancy is twice that of all women (Guttmacher Institute, 2013). Although the teen pregnancy rate between 1990 and 2010 declined by 51 percent (Kost & Henshaw, 2014), in 2010, 615,000 teens still became pregnant in the United States, and 84 percent of these pregnancies were unintended (Kost & Henshaw, 2014). Unlike the specific teen population, among all women of reproductive age (15–44), there has actually been a slight increase in unintended pregnancies since 2001 (Guttmacher Institute, 2013).

Even with the decline among teens, the unintended pregnancy rate is a serious problem for women of all ages. More teens and adult women are using contraceptives than in the past, and it is this behavior, not a decrease in sexual activity, that is largely credited with the most significant reduction in the teen pregnancy rate (Boonstra, 2014). In particular, the use of hormonal contraceptives has increased. Yet many girls and women do not have access to affordable birth control. Researchers and advocates argue that, for this reason, it is essential for publicly funded birth control to be made available to both teens and adult women who otherwise would not have affordable access to it. When birth control is accessible, unplanned pregnancies and abortion rates go down for women of all ages (Guttmacher Institute, 2014a; "Contraceptive Choice Project").

Throughout the United States, publicly funded family planning centers that provide women with contraceptives helped to prevent 2.2 million unintended pregnancies in 2010 (Guttmacher Institute, 2014b). Without these centers, the unintended pregnancy, unintended birth, and abortion rates would have been 66 percent higher (Guttmacher Institute, 2014b). The average woman has about three decades of fertility, so even the cost of less expensive (and often less reliable) methods like condoms can add up (Guttmacher Institute, 2014a). When adult and teen women have education about and access to more reliable forms of contraceptives, they are much more likely to use these methods, ultimately resulting in lower rates of unintended pregnancy (Guttmacher Institute, 2014a; Secura et al. 2014).

Recent studies comparing the effectiveness of contraceptive methods have found that intrauterine devices (IUDs) and implants[1] are the most effective methods of birth control currently available (Hamblin 2014; "Contraceptive Choice Project"). In fact, one study found that they are even more effective than permanent options like tubal ligations or vasectomies (Hamblin, 2014). IUDs and implant birth control methods are known as "long-acting reversible contraceptives" (LARCs). That means they are methods that can be used for longer periods of time without having to be refilled and replaced, like birth control pills

or the patch, but are not permanent or irreversible, like sterilization. A major benefit of these methods is that once they are inserted or implanted, no other action is necessary on the part of the user. In other words, a woman using an IUD or implant for birth control does not have to remember to take a pill every day, to change her birth control patch every week, to buy or carry condoms, or even to go to the doctor's office to get a shot every few months. Instead, for the three to ten years (depending on the IUD or implant), the user has continuous contraceptive coverage until she elects to have the device removed. If a woman using a LARC wants it removed before that time frame is complete, that is always an option.

Despite the ease of use and high effectiveness rates of IUDs and implants, the Guttmacher Institute (2014) reports that fewer than 5 percent of all women ages 15–44 use one of these methods. Instead, the most commonly used methods are the pill, sterilization, and condoms. With the exception of female sterilization,[2] the more commonly used methods also have higher failure rates than IUDs and implants, resulting in unintended pregnancies. So why aren't more women choosing the IUD or implant to prevent pregnancy? Part of the problem[3] might be that these more reliable methods are not as familiar to women seeking birth control. But even for some women who know about IUDs and implants or who learn about them from their health care providers, choosing these methods can be cost prohibitive. Because LARCs are long-lasting methods, they are also more expensive up front than a pack of pills or the patch would be. For patients without insurance or insurance that does not cover LARCs, paying out of pocket would cost several hundred dollars. Although this is a greater expense at the time of purchase, compared to the pill or the patch, it actually works out to be much less expensive over time.

To better understand teens and adult women's contraceptive choices, researchers, doctors, and advocates in St. Louis started the Contraceptive Choice Project. The goals of this research project are "to remove the financial barriers to contraception, promote the most effective methods of birth control, and reduce unintended pregnancy in the St. Louis area" ("Contraceptive Choice Project"). Researchers report some significant findings. Of the 9,256 women who were counseled about all of their contraceptive options and provided their chosen method for free by the project, 75 percent of them chose a LARC ("Contraceptive

---

1   Implants are birth control devices implanted under the skin that release hormones to prevent pregnancy.

2   Tubal ligations (female sterilization) have a failure rate that is comparable to that of implants, but higher than that of some IUDs; male sterilization (vasectomy) has a higher failure rate than both IUDs and implants.

3   Some women may still avoid the IUD because they are familiar with the health risks associated with the first IUD, the Dalkon Shield. The Dalkon Shield was first introduced in the 1960s and then removed from the market in the 1970s after serious complications were reported. Today's IUDs are different from earlier versions and are not associated with the same health risks.

Choice Project"). A year later, when researchers followed up with participants to see how they liked their chosen methods, a greater number of women who had chosen a LARC were still using their method and reported being satisfied with it than women who had chosen a non-LARC, like the pill. Not only did women using LARCs have the highest rates of continued use and satisfaction, but also they had the lowest rates of unintended pregnancies throughout the three years of the study. Participants who had chosen the pill, patch, or ring[4] were 20 times more likely to have an unintended pregnancy in the first year of the study compared to women using LARCs ("Contraceptive Choice Project"). Teens who participated in the study were also more likely to choose LARCs (72 percent), and because they did, the teen pregnancy rate for participants was 34 per 1,000 (Secura et al., 2014). This rate is significantly lower than the 2013 national teen pregnancy rate of 57 per 1,000 (Kost & Henshaw, 2014).[5]

The Contraceptive Choice Project is not the only recent example of women's preference for LARCs and their long-term effects. In Colorado, the Colorado Family Planning Initiative made LARCs available to 30,000 low-income women, funded by an anonymous donor (Sullivan, 2014). Since its implementation in 2009, researchers have made comparisons between the actual pregnancy rates of 15- to 24-year-old women and the expected rates for this age group of Colorado residents. As a result of the program, the number of teens and young women using LARCs has increased and, as a consequence, pregnancy, birth, and abortion rates have declined (Ricketts et al., 2014). In particular, abortion rates declined 34 percent for teens 15 to 19 years old and 18 percent for women 20 to 24 years old (Ricketts et al., 2014).

Making LARCs more affordable is essential to increasing access for many women and ultimately would have a substantial effect on the rate of unintended pregnancies. The Affordable Care Act mandates that health insurance plans cover contraceptives without requiring any copays, deductibles, or other out-of-pocket costs (Healthcare.gov). Although this mandate did not go into effect for most insurance plans until January 2013, researchers are already seeing the cost of birth control declining for many women (Sonfield et al., 2014). This is clearly a major improvement for women's reproductive health care, but despite its benefits, some opponents are challenging it. In June 2014, the Supreme Court struck down the birth control mandate, ruling in

favor of a for-profit company's right to refuse birth control coverage when the refusal is based on religious beliefs (Totenberg, 2014). The craft store chain Hobby Lobby brought the suit because its owners objected to two types of birth control, emergency contraception and IUDs (Totenberg, 2014). This decision is important because it allows employers to opt out of covering any forms of birth control they may oppose on religious grounds. In the Hobby Lobby case, one of the types of birth control it now has the right to refuse coverage of, the IUD, is the same method that many studies have shown to be one of the best ways to decrease unintended pregnancies (Hamblin, 2014; Guttmacher Institute, 2014a; "Contraceptive Choice Project").

When the rate of unintended pregnancy decreases, there are benefits to society at large. Fewer unplanned births mean less money spent on social programs like Women, Infants, and Children (WIC) and Medicaid. Ricketts et al. (2014) found a 23 percent decline in WIC enrollment between 2010 and 2013 in counties that participated in the Colorado Family Planning Initiative. *The Denver Post* (Draper, 2014) reported that for each dollar spent on birth control, there is a $5.68 savings in Medicaid costs. When teenagers are able to avoid unplanned pregnancies, they have a better chance of finishing high school, attending college, and obtaining a higher-paying job, which translates to less money spent on public assistance (Griego, 2014). Reliable contraceptives like LARCs benefit not only individual women but also society as a whole; financial barriers to obtaining all methods should be removed. As the research shows, a majority of women want access to long-acting reversible contraceptives methods, and that access is essential to decreasing unplanned pregnancies and their associated social and financial costs in the United States.

REFERENCES

Boonstra, Heather D. 2014. "What Is Behind the Decline in Teen Pregnancy Rates?" Guttmacher Institute. http://www.guttmacher.org/pubs/gpr/17/3/gpr170315.html.

"Contraceptive Choice Project." N.d. Washington University School of Medicine. http://www.choiceproject.wustl.edu.

D'Angelo, Denise, Brenda Colley Gilbert, Roger W. Rochat, John S. Santelli, and Joan M. Herold. 2004. "Differences between Mistimed and Unwanted Pregnancies among Women Who Have Live Births," *Perspectives on Sexual and Reproductive Health* 36, 5. http://www.guttmacher.org/pubs/journals/3619204.html.

Draper, Electa. 2014. "Colorado Claims Contraceptive Program Caused Big Drop in Teen Birth Rates." *Denver Post.* http://www.denverpost.com/news/ci_26085784/colorado-teen-birth-rates-drop-state-hands-out?ok.

---

4 The ring is a small flexible ring that is placed in the vagina each month, remaining in place for three weeks to prevent pregnancy.

5 It is important to note that the sample in the Choice project is different from the national teenage population in several ways. More than half of the teens in the Choice sample were Black; 97 percent were sexually active at the start of the study, and almost 75 percent reported having had sex in the past 30 days. These two measures of sexual activity are much higher among the Choice project sample than among the larger teen population.

(continued)

Griego, Tina. 2014. "The Simple Policy That Led America's Biggest Drop in Teen Birth Rates." *The Washington Post.* http://www.washingtonpost.com/news/storyline/wp/2014/08/20/the-simple-policy-that-led-americas-biggest-drop-in-teen-pregnancies.

Guttmacher Institute. 2013. "Unintended Pregnancy in the United States." http://www.guttmacher.org/pubs/FB-Unintended-Pregnancy-US.html#14a.

Guttmacher Institute. 2014a. "Contraceptive Use in the United States." http://www.guttmacher.org/pubs/fb_contr_use.html.

Guttmacher Institute. 2014b. "Facts on Publicly Funded Contraceptive Services in the United States." http://www.guttmacher.org/pubs/fb_contraceptive_serv.html/.

Hamblin, James. 2014. "IUDs and Implants are the New Pill." *The Atlantic.* http://m.theatlantic.com/health/archive/2014/10/the-birth-control-shift/380952.

Hoffman, Saul D., and Rebecca A. Maynard. 2008. *Kids Having Kids: Economic Costs and Social Consequences of Teen Pregnancy.* Washington, DC: Urban Institute Press.

Kost, Kathryn, and Stanley Henshaw. 2014. "U.S. Teenage Pregnancies, Births, and Abortions, 2010: National and State Trends by Age, Race and Ethnicity." Guttmacher Institute. http://www.guttmacher.org/pubs/USTPtrends10.pdf.

Logan, Cassandra, Emily Holcombe, Jennifer Manlove, and Suzanne Ryan. 2007. "The Consequences of Unintended Childbearing." http://thenationalcampaign.org/sites/default/files/resource-primary-download/consequences.pdf.

Ricketts, Sue, Greta Klingler, and Renee Schwalberg. 2014. "Game Change in Colorado: Widespread Use of Long-Acting Reversible Contraceptives and Rapid Decline in Births among Young, Low-Income Women." http://www.guttmacher.org/pubs/journals/46e1714.html.

Secura, Gina M., Tessa Madden, Colleen McNicholas, Jennifer Mullersman, Christina M. Buckel, Quihong Zhao, and Jeffrey F. Peipert. 2014. "Provision of No-Cost, Long-Acting Contraception and Teenage Pregnancy." *The New England Journal of Medicine* 371:1316–23.

Sonfield, Adam, Athena Tapales, Rachel K. Jones, & Lawrence B. Finer. 2014. "Impact of the Federal Contraceptive Coverage Guarantee on Out-of-Pocket Payments for Contraceptives: 2014 Update." Guttmacher Institute. http://www.contraceptionjournal.org/article/S0010-7824(14)00687-8/pdf.

Sullivan, Gail. 2014. "How Colorado's Teen Birthrate Dropped 40% in Four Years." http://www.washingtonpost.com/news/morning-mix/wp/2014/08/12/how-colorados-teen-birthrate-dropped-40-in-four-years/.

Totenberg, Nina. 2014. "High Court Allows Some Companies to Opt Out of Contraceptive Mandate". http://www.npr.org/2014/06/30/327064710/high-court-allows-some-companies-to-opt-out-contraceptives-mandate.

MAGGIE JONES

25. WHAT TEENAGERS ARE LEARNING FROM ONLINE PORN

Teens are being exposed to and are specifically seeking out significant amounts of pornography online. Parents underestimate how much their teens are consuming, and as a result of their underestimation and their potential discomfort about the topic, infrequently discuss pornographic content with them. Schools are rarely equipped to pick up the slack. Jones describes a unique pornographic literacy course and the experiences of the kids taking the course, as they navigate early sexual experiences initially through pornographic filters and eventually through a more critical lens encouraged by the curriculum. Despite the fact that they acknowledge that pornography may not be offering accurate depictions of sex, teens admit that they frame their own sexual practices and desires through a pornographic lens. Jones concludes that we, as a society, need to determine the best ways to encourage and share pornographic literacy as part of comprehensive sexuality education.

Drew was 8 years old when he was flipping through TV channels at home and landed on "Girls Gone Wild." A few years later, he came across HBO's late-night soft-core pornography. Then in ninth grade, he found online porn sites on his phone. The videos were good for getting off, he said, but also sources for ideas for future sex positions with future girlfriends. From porn, he learned that guys need to be buff and dominant in bed, doing things like flipping girls over on their stomach during sex. Girls moan a lot and are turned on by pretty much everything a confident guy does. One particular porn scene stuck with him: A woman was bored by a man who approached sex gently but became ecstatic with a far more aggressive guy.

But around 10th grade, it began bothering Drew, an honor-roll student who loves baseball and writing rap lyrics and still confides in his mom, that porn influenced how he thought about girls at school. Were their breasts, he wondered, like the ones in porn? Would girls look at him the way women do in porn when they had sex? Would they give him blow jobs and do the other stuff he saw?

Drew, who asked me to use one of his nicknames, was a junior when I first met him in late 2016, and he told me some of this one Thursday afternoon, as we sat in a small conference room with several other high school boys, eating chips and drinking soda and waiting for an after-school program to begin. Next to Drew was Q., who asked me to identify him by the first initial of his nickname. He was 15, a good student, and a baseball fan, too, and pretty perplexed about how porn translated into real life. Q. hadn't had sex—he liked older, out-of-reach girls, and the last time he had a girlfriend was in sixth grade, and they just fooled around a bit. So he wasn't exactly in a good position to ask girls directly what they liked. But as he told me over several conversations, it wasn't just porn but rough images on Snapchat, Facebook, and other social media that confused him. Like the GIF he saw of a man pushing a woman against a wall with a girl commenting: "I want a guy like this." And the one Drew mentioned of the "pain room" in "Fifty Shades of Grey" with a caption by a girl: "This is awesome!" Watching porn also heightened Q.'s performance anxiety. "You are looking at an adult," he told me. "The guys are built and dominant and have a big penis, and they last a long time." And if you don't do it like the guys in porn, Drew added, "you fear she's not going to like you."

Leaning back in his chair, Drew said some girls acted as if they wanted some thug rather than a smart, sensitive guy. But was it true desire? Was it posturing? Was it what girls thought they were supposed to want? Neither Q. nor Drew knew. A couple of seats away, a sophomore who had been quiet until then added that maybe the girls didn't know either. "I think social media makes girls think they want something," he said, noting he hadn't seen porn more than a handful of times and disliked it. "But I think some of the girls are afraid." "It gets in your head," Q. said. "If this girl wants it, then maybe the majority of girls want it." He'd heard about the importance of consent in sex, but it felt pretty abstract, and it didn't seem as if it would always be realistic in the heat of the moment. Out of nowhere was he supposed to say: Can I pull your hair? Or could he try something and see how a girl responded? He knew that there were certain things—"big things, like sex toys or anal"—that he would not try without asking. "I would just do it," said another boy, in jeans and a sweatshirt. When I asked what he meant, he said anal sex. He assumed that girls like it, because the women in porn do. "I would never do something that looked uncomfortable," Drew said, jumping back into the conversation. "I might say, 'I've seen this in porn—do you want to try it?'"

It was almost 4 p.m., and the boys started to gather their backpacks to head to a class known as Porn Literacy. The course, with the official title The Truth about Pornography: A Pornography-Literacy Curriculum for High School Students Designed to Reduce Sexual and Dating Violence, is a recent addition to Start Strong, a peer-leadership program for teenagers headquartered in Boston's South End and funded by the city's public health agency. About two dozen selected high school students attend every year, most of them Black or Latino, along with a few Asian students, from Boston public high schools, including the city's competitive exam schools and a couple of parochial schools. During most of the year, the teenagers learn about healthy relationships, dating violence and LGBT issues, often through group discussions, role-playing, and other exercises. But for around two hours

each week, for five weeks, the students — sophomores, juniors, and seniors—take part in Porn Literacy, which aims to make them savvier, more critical consumers of porn by examining how gender, sexuality, aggression, consent, race, queer sex, relationships, and body images are portrayed (or, in the case of consent, not portrayed) in porn.

On average, boys are around 13, and girls are around 14, when they first see pornography, says Bryant Paul, an associate professor at Indiana University's Media School and the author of studies on porn content and adolescent and adult viewing habits. In a 2008 University of New Hampshire survey[1], 93 percent of male college students and 62 percent of female students said they saw online porn before they were 18. Many females, in particular, weren't seeking it out. Thirty-five percent of males said they had watched it 10 or more times during adolescence.

Porn Literacy, which began in 2016 and is the focus of a pilot study, was created in part by Emily Rothman, an associate professor at Boston University's School of Public Health who has conducted several studies on dating violence, as well as on porn use by adolescents. She told me that the curriculum isn't designed to scare kids into believing porn is addictive or that it will ruin their lives and relationships and warp their libidos.[2] Instead it is grounded in the reality that most adolescents do see porn, and it takes the approach that teaching them to analyze its messages is far more effective than simply wishing our children could live in a porn-free world.

Imagine that you are a 14-year-old today. A friend might show you a short porn clip on his phone during the bus ride to school or after soccer practice. A pornographic Graphics Interchange Format (GIF) appears on Snapchat. Or you mistype the word "fishing" and end up with a bunch of links to "fisting" videos. Like most 14-year-olds, you haven't had sex, but you're curious, so maybe you start searching and land on one of the many porn sites that work much like YouTube—XVideos.com, Xnxx.com, BongaCams.com—all of them among the 100 most-frequented websites in the world, according to Alexa Top Sites. Or you find Pornhub, the most popular of the group, with 80 million visitors a day and more traffic than Pinterest, Tumblr, or PayPal. The mainstream websites aren't verifying your age, and your phone allows you to watch porn away from the scrutinizing eyes of adults. If you still have parental-control filters, you probably have ways around them. Besides, there's a decent chance your parents don't think you are watching porn. Preliminary analysis of data from a 2016 Indiana University survey of more than 600 pairs of children and their parents reveals a parental naïveté gap: Half as many parents thought their 14- and 18-year-olds had seen porn as had in fact watched it. And depending on the sex act, parents underestimated what their kids saw by as much as 10 times.

What teenagers see on Pornhub depends partly on algorithms and on the clips they've clicked on in the past. Along with stacks of videos on the opening page, there are several dozen categories ("teen," "anal," "blonde," "girl on girl," "ebony," "milf") that can take them to more than six million videos. The clips tend to be short, low on production value, free, and, though Pornhub tries to prevent it, sometimes pirated from paid sites. Many of the heterosexual videos are shot from the male point of view, as if the man were holding the camera while he has sex with a woman whose main job, via oral sex, intercourse, or anal sex is to make him orgasm. Plot lines are thin to nonexistent as the camera zooms in for up-close shots of genitals and penetration that are repetitive, pounding, and—though perhaps not through the eyes of a 14-year-old—banal. (There are alternative narratives in LGBT and feminist porn, and studies show that for gay and bisexual youth, porn can provide affirmation that they are not alone in their sexual desires.)

We don't have many specifics on what kids actually view, in large part because it's extremely difficult to get federal funding for research on children and pornography. A few years ago, frustrated by the dearth of large, recent U.S. studies, Rashida Jones, Jill Bauer, and Ronna Gradus, creators of the 2017 Netflix documentary series "Hot Girls Wanted: Turned On," about technology and porn, paired with several foundations and philanthropists to fund a national survey about porn viewing, sexual attitudes, and behaviors. As part of the survey, led by Debby Herbenick, a professor at the Indiana University School of Public Health and director of the university's Center for Sexual Health Promotion, along with her colleague Bryant Paul,

614 teenagers ages 14 to 18 reported what their experiences were with porn. In preliminary data analysis from the study (Herbenick is submitting an academic paper for publication . . .), of the roughly 300 who did watch porn, one-quarter of the girls and 36 percent of the boys said they had seen videos of men ejaculating on women's faces (known as "facials"), Paul says. Almost one-third of both sexes saw BDSM (bondage, domination, sadism, masochism), and 26 percent of males and 20 percent of females watched videos with double penetration, described in the study as one or more penises or objects in a woman's anus and/or in her vagina. Also, 31 percent of boys said they had seen "gang bangs," or group sex, and "rough oral sex" (a man aggressively thrusting his penis in and out of a mouth); less than half as many girls had.

It's hard to know if, and how, this translates into behavior. While some studies show a small number of teens who watch higher rates of porn engage in earlier sex as well as gender stereotyping and sexual relationships that are less affectionate than their peers, these only indicate correlations, not cause and effect.[3] But surveys do suggest that the kinds of sex some teenagers have may be shifting. The percentage of 18- to 24-year-old women who reported trying anal sex rose to 40 percent in 2009 from 16 percent in 1992, according to the largest survey on American sexual behavior in decades, co-authored by Herbenick and published in *The Journal of Sexual Medicine*. In data from that same survey, 20 percent of 18- to 19-year-old females had tried anal sex and about 6 percent of 14- to 17-year-old females had. And in a 2016 Swedish study of nearly 400 16-year-old girls, the percentage of girls who had tried anal sex doubled if they watched pornography. Like other studies about sex and porn, it only showed a correlation, and girls who are more sexually curious may also be drawn to porn. In addition, some girls may view anal sex as a "safer" alternative to vaginal sex, as there's little risk of pregnancy.

The Indiana University national survey of teenagers asked about other sex behaviors as well. Though the data have not been fully analyzed, preliminary findings suggest that of the teenagers who had had sex, around one-sixth of boys said they had ejaculated on someone's face or choked a sex partner. The survey didn't define choking, but the high school and college-age students I spoke to referred to it as anything from placing a hand gently on a partner's neck to squeezing it.

We don't have longitudinal data on the frequency of ejaculating on a girl's face or choking among American teenagers to know whether either practice is more common now. And as David Finkelhor, director of the Crimes Against Children Research Center at the University of New Hampshire, told me, fewer teenagers have early sex than in the past (in a recent study, 24 percent of American ninth graders had sex; in 1995 about 37 percent had), and arrests of teenagers for sexual assault are also down. But you don't have to believe that porn leads to sexual assault or that it's creating a generation of brutal men to wonder how it helps shape how teenagers talk and think about sex and, by extension, their ideas about masculinity, femininity, intimacy, and power.

Over the year in which I spoke to dozens of older teenagers at Start Strong and around the country, many said that both porn and mainstream media— everything from the TV show "Family Guy" (which references choking and anal sex) to Nicki Minaj's song "Truffle Butter" (with an apparent allusion to anal sex followed by vaginal sex) to the lyrics in Rihanna's "S&M" ("Sticks and Stones May Break My Bones, But Chains and Whips Excite Me")—made anal and rough sex seem almost commonplace. Drew told me he got the sense that girls wanted to be dominated, not only from reading a few pages of "Fifty Shades of Grey" but also from watching the movie *Mr. & Mrs. Smith*, with Brad Pitt and Angelina Jolie. "She's on the table, and she's getting pounded by him. That's all I've seen growing up."

These images confound many teenagers about the kinds of sex they want or think they should have. In part, that's because they aren't always sure what is fake and what is real in porn. Though some told me that porn was fantasy or exaggerated, others said that porn wasn't real only insofar as it wasn't typically two lovers having sex on film. Some of those same teenagers assumed the portrayal of how sex and pleasure worked was largely accurate. That seems to be in keeping with a 2016 survey of 1,001 11- to 16-year-olds in Britain. Of the roughly half who had seen pornography, 53 percent of boys and 39 percent of girls said it was

"realistic."[4] And in the recent Indiana University national survey, only one in six boys and one in four girls believed that women in online porn were not actually experiencing pleasure: As one suburban high school senior boy told me recently, "I've never seen a girl in porn who doesn't look like she's having a good time."

It's not surprising, then, that some adolescents use porn as a how-to guide. In a study that Rothman carried out in 2016 of 72 high schoolers ages 16 and 17, teenagers reported that porn was their primary source for information about sex—more than friends, siblings, schools, or parents. "There's nowhere else to learn about sex," the suburban boy told me. "And porn stars know what they are doing." His words reflect a paradox about sex and pornography in this country. Even as smart phones have made it easier for teenagers to watch porn, sex education in the United States—where abstinence-based sex education remains the norm—is meager. Massachusetts is among 26 states that do not mandate sex ed. And a mere 13 require that the material be medically and scientifically accurate. After some gains by the Obama administration to promote more comprehensive sex ed, which includes pregnancy prevention, discussions of anatomy, birth control, disease prevention, abstinence, and healthy relationships, the Trump administration did not include the program in its proposed 2018 budget and also has requested increased funding for abstinence education. Easy-to-access online porn fills the vacuum, making porn the de facto sex educator for American youth.

One Thursday afternoon, about a dozen teenagers sat in a semicircle of North Face zip-ups, Jordans, combat boots, big hoop earrings and the slumped shoulders of late afternoon. It was the third week of Porn Literacy, and everyone already knew the rules: You don't have to have watched porn to attend; no yucking someone else's yum—no disparaging a student's sexual tastes or sexuality. And avoid sharing personal stories about sex in class. Nicole Daley and Jess Alder, who wrote the curriculum with Emily Rothman and led most of the exercises and discussion, are in their 30s, warm and easygoing. Daley, who until last month was the director of Start Strong, played the slightly more serious favorite-aunt role, while Alder, who runs Start Strong's classes for teenagers, was the goofier, ask-me-anything big sister. Rothman also attended most of the classes, offering information about pornography studies and explaining to them, for example, that there is no scientific evidence that porn is addictive, but that people can become compulsive about it.

In the first class, Daley led an exercise in which the group defined porn terms (BDSM, kink, soft-core, hard-core), so that, as she put it, "everyone is on the same page" and "you can avoid clicking on things you don't want to see." The students also "values voted"— agreeing or disagreeing about whether the legal viewing age of 18 for porn is too high, if working in the porn industry is a good way to make money, and if pornography should be illegal. Later, Daley held up images of a 1940s pinup girl, a Japanese geisha, and Kim Kardashian, to talk about how cultural values about beauty and bodies change over time. In future classes, they would talk about types of intimacy not depicted in porn and nonsexist pickup lines. Finally, Daley would offer a lesson about sexting and sexting laws and the risks of so-called revenge porn (in which, say, a teenager circulates a naked selfie of an ex without consent). And to the teenagers' surprise, they learned that receiving or sending consensual naked photos, even to your boyfriend or girlfriend, can be against the law if the person in the photo is a minor.

Now, in the third week of class, Daley's goal was to undercut porn's allure for teenagers by exposing the underbelly of the business. "When you understand it's not just two people on the screen but an industry," she told me, "it's not as sexy." To that end, Daley started class by detailing a midlevel female performer's salary (taken from the 2008 documentary *The Price of Pleasure*): "Blow job: $300," Daley read from a list. "Anal: $1,000. Double penetration: $1,200. Gang bang: $1,300 for three guys. $100 for each additional guy." "Wow," Drew muttered. "That makes it nasty now." "That's nothing for being penetrated on camera," another boy said.

> Then, as if they had been given a green light to ask about a world that grown-ups rarely acknowledge, they began peppering Daley, Rothman, and Alder with questions. "How much do men get paid?" one girl asked. It is the one of the few professions in which men are paid less, Rothman explained, but they also typically have longer careers. How long do women

stay in their jobs? On average, 6 to 18 months. How do guys get erections if they aren't turned on? Often Viagra, Rothman offered, and sometimes a "fluffer," as an offscreen human stimulator is known. Daley then asked the teenagers to pretend they were contestants on a reality TV show, in which they had to decide if they were willing to participate in certain challenges (your parents might be watching) and for how much money. In one scenario, she said, you would kneel on the ground while someone poured a goopy substance over your face. In another, you'd lick a spoon that had touched fecal matter. The kids debated the fecal matter challenge—most wouldn't to do it for less than $2 million. One wanted to know if the goop smelled. "Can we find out what it is?" asked another. Then Daley explained that each was in fact a simulation of a porn act. The goopy substance was what's called a "baker's dozen," in which 13 men ejaculate on a woman's face, breasts, and mouth. "What?" a girl named Tiffany protested. The second scenario— licking the spoon with fecal matter—was from a porn act known as A.T.M., in which a man puts his penis in a woman's anus and then immediately follows by sticking it in her mouth. "No way," a 15-year-old boy said. "Can't you wash in between?" Nope, Daley said. "We don't question it when we see it in porn, right?" Daley went on. "There's no judgment here, but some of you guys are squeamish about it." "I never knew any of this," Drew said, sounding a bit glum.

Daley went on to detail a 2010 study that coded incidents of aggression in best-selling 2004 and 2005 porn videos. She noted that 88 percent of scenes showed verbal or physical aggression, mostly spanking, slapping, and gagging. (A more recent content analysis of more than 6,000 mainstream online heterosexual porn scenes by Bryant Paul and his colleagues defined aggression specifically as any purposeful action appearing to cause physical or psychological harm to another person and found that 33 percent of scenes met that criteria. In each study, women were on the receiving end of the aggression more than 90 percent of the time.) "Do you think," Daley said, standing in front of the students, "watching porn leads to violence against women? There's no right or wrong here. It's a debate." Kyrah, a 10th-grade feminist with an athlete's compact body and a tendency to speak her opinions, didn't hesitate. "In porn they glamorize calling women a slut or a whore, and younger kids think this is how it is. Or when they have those weird porn scenes and the woman is saying, 'Stop touching me,' and then she ends up enjoying it!" Tiffany, her best friend, snapped her fingers in approval. "Yes and no," one guy interjected. "When a man is choking a woman in porn, people know it is not real, and they aren't supposed to do it because it's violence." He was the same teenager who told me he would just "do" anal sex without asking a girl, because the women in porn like it.

Pornography didn't create the narrative that male pleasure should be first and foremost. But that idea is certainly reinforced by "a male-dominated porn industry shot through a male lens," as Cindy Gallop puts it. Gallop is the creator of an online platform called MakeLoveNotPorn, where users can submit videos of their sexual encounters—which she describes as "real world," consensual sex with "good values"—and pay to watch videos of others. For years, Gallop has been a one-woman laboratory witnessing how easy-to-access mainstream porn influences sex. Now in her 50s, she has spent more than a decade dating 20-something men. She finds them through "cougar" dating sites—where older women connect with younger men—and her main criterion is that they are "nice." Even so, she told me, during sex with these significantly younger nice men, she repeatedly encounters porn memes: facials, "jackhammering" intercourse, more frequent requests for anal sex, and men who seem less focused on female orgasms than men were when she was younger. Gallop takes it upon herself to "re-educate," as she half-jokingly puts it, men raised on porn. Some people, of course, do enjoy these acts. But speaking of teenagers in particular, she told me she worries that hard-core porn leads many girls to think, for example, that "all boys love coming on girls' faces, and all girls love having their faces come on. And therefore, girls feel they must let boys come on their face and pretend to like it."

Though none of the boys I spoke to at Start Strong told me they had ejaculated on a girl's face, Gallop's words reminded me of conversations I had with some older high schoolers in various cities. One senior said that ejaculating on a woman's face was in a majority of porn scenes he had watched and that he had done it with a girlfriend. "I brought it up, or she would say,

'Come on my face.' It was an aspect I liked—and she did, too." Another noted that the act is "talked about a lot" among guys, but said that "a girl's got to be down with it" before he'd ever consider doing it. "There is something that's appealing for guys. The dominance and intimacy and that whole opportunity for eye contact. Guys are obsessed with their come displayed on a girl."

Many girls at Start Strong were decidedly less enthusiastic. One senior told me a boyfriend asked to ejaculate on her face; she said no. And during a conversation I had with three girls, one senior wondered aloud: "What if you don't want a facial?"

"What are you supposed to do? Friends say a boy cleans it with a napkin. A lot of girls my age like facials." But a few moments later, she reversed course. "I actually don't think they like it. They do it because their partner likes it." Next to her, a sophomore added that when older girls talk among themselves, many say it's gross. "But they say you gotta do what you gotta do." And if you don't, the first girl added, "then someone else will."

These are not new power dynamics between girls and boys. In a 2014[5] British study about anal sex and teenagers, girls expressed a similar lack of sexual agency and experienced physical pain. In the survey, of 130 heterosexual teenagers age 16 to 18, teenagers often said they believed porn was a motivating factor for why males wanted anal sex. And among the guys who reported trying it, many said friends encouraged them, or they felt competitive with other guys to do it. At the same time, a majority of girls who had tried anal sex said they didn't actually want to; their partners persuaded or coerced them. Some males took a "try it and see" approach, as researchers called it, attempting to put their finger or penis in a girl's anus and hoping she didn't stop them. Sometimes, one teenager reported, you "just keep going till they just get fed up and let you do it anyway." Both boys and girls blamed the girls for pain they felt during anal sex, and some told researchers the girls needed to "relax" more or "get used to it." Only one girl said she enjoyed it, and only a few boys did. Teenagers may not know that, even while porn makes it seem commonplace, in the 2009 national survey of American sex habits, most men and women who tried anal sex didn't make it a regular part of their sex lives. And in another study, by Indiana University's Debby Herbenick and others in 2015, about 70 percent of women who had anal sex said they experienced pain.

Drew had firsthand experience with what he had seen in porn not translating into actual pleasure. The first time he had sex, he thought he was supposed to exert some physical control over his girlfriend. But the whole thing felt awkward, too rough and not all that fun. And things that looked easy in porn, like sex while taking a shower or mutual oral sex, didn't go so well. At one point during sex, Drew's girlfriend at the time, who was a year older and more experienced, asked him to put his hand around her neck during sex. He did it, without squeezing, and though it didn't exactly bother him, it felt uncomfortable. Drew never asked if she got the idea from porn, but it made him wonder. Had she also picked up other ways of acting? "Like, how do you really know a girl has had a good time?" he said one afternoon, musing aloud while sitting with some friends before Porn Literacy class. "My girlfriend said she had a good time," he went on. "She was moaning. But that's the thing: Is it fake moaning?"

Even if you know porn isn't realistic, it still sets up expectations, one senior told me. In porn, he said, "the clothes are off, and the girl goes down on the guy, he gets hard and he starts having sex with her. It's all very simple and well lit." Before he had sex, porn had supplied his images of oral sex, including scenes in which a woman is on her knees as a man stands over her. At one point, he thought that's how it might go one day when he had sex. But when he talked with his girlfriend, they realized they didn't want to reenact that power dynamic.

I spent a couple of hours on a Wednesday afternoon at Start Strong with a senior girl who took the first Porn Literacy class in the summer of 2016. Looking back over the last several years of middle and high school, A., who asked me to identify her by the first initial of her middle name, said she wished she had had some place—home, school, a community sex ed program—to learn about sex.

Instead, she learned about it from porn. She saw it for the first time by accident, after a group of sixth-grade boys cajoled her to look at tube8.com, which she didn't know was a porn site. She was fascinated. She had never

seen a penis before, "not a drawing of one, nothing." A few years later, she searched online for porn again after listening to girls in the high school locker room talk about masturbation. A.'s parents, whom she describes as conservative about sex, hadn't talked to her about female anatomy or sex, and her school didn't offer any sex education before ninth grade; even then, it focused mostly on the dangers—sexually transmitted infections and diseases and pregnancy.

Aside from some private schools and innovative community programs, relatively few sex ed classes in middle and high school delve in detail into anatomy (female, especially), intimacy, healthy relationships, sexual diversity. Even more rare are discussions of female desire and pleasure. Porn taught A. the basics of masturbation. And porn served as her study guide when she was 16 and was the first among her friends to have sex. She clicked through videos to watch women giving oral sex. She focused on how they moved during sex and listened to how they moaned. She began shaving her vulva ("I've never seen anyone in porn have sex with hair on it"). Porn is "not all bad," said A., who was frank and funny, with a slew of advanced-placement classes on her transcript and a self-assured manner that impresses adults. "I got my sexual ways from porn, and I like the way I am." But what she learned from porn had downsides too. Because she assumed women's pleasure in porn was real, when she first had intercourse and didn't have an orgasm, she figured that was just how it went.

For A., it wasn't enough to know that porn was fake sex. She wanted to understand how real sex worked. Rothman and her team did consult a sex educator while they were writing the Porn Literacy curriculum but decided to include only some basic information about safe sex. It came in the form of a "Porn Jeopardy" game during one class. The teenagers, clustered in teams, chose from four categories: STD/STIs; Birth Control; Teen Violence/Sexual Assault; and Porn on the Brain.

"S.T.I.s/S.T.D.s for $300," one student called out. "Why is lubrication important for sex?" Alder asked. "What's lubrication?" Drew asked. "It's lube," another teenager said, in an attempt to explain.

"Is lubrication only the little tube-y things?" a girl with long Black hair asked. "Or can it be natural?" "I never learned this before," Drew announced to the class after it was mentioned that lubrication decreased friction, increased pleasure, and could reduce the risk of tearing and therefore of STIs and STDs. Drew's only sliver of sex ed was in sixth grade with the school gym teacher, who sweated as he talked about sex, "and it was all about it being bad and we shouldn't do it."

As if to rectify that, Alder offered a quick anatomy lesson, drawing a vulva on the Whiteboard and pointing out the clitoris, the vagina, the urethra. "This is called a vulva," she said. Alder repeated the word slowly and loudly, as if instructing the students in a foreign language. It was both for humor and to normalize a word that some of them may have been hearing for the first time. "This is the clitoris," Alder went on. "This is where women get most pleasure. Most women do not have a G spot. If you want to know how to give a woman pleasure, it's the clitoris."

"Let's move on," Rothman said quietly. Alder had just inched across a line in which anatomy rested on one side and female desire and pleasure on the other. It was a reminder that, as controversial as it is to teach kids about pornography, it can be more taboo to teach them how their bodies work sexually. "The class is about critically analyzing sexually explicit media," Rothman told me later, "not how to have sex. We want to stay in our narrow lane and not be seen as promoting anything parents are uncomfortable with." Daley added: "I wish it were different, but we have to be aware of the limitations of where we are as a society."

Porn education is such new territory that no one knows the best practices, what material should be included, and where to teach it. (Few people are optimistic that it will be taught anytime soon in public schools.) Several years ago, L. Kris Gowen, a sexuality educator and author

of the 2017 book *Sexual Decisions: The Ultimate Teen Guide*, wrote extensive guidelines for teaching teenagers to critique "sexually explicit media" (she avoided the more provocative term *porn literacy*). Even though Oregon, where Gowen lives, has one of the most comprehensive sex ed programs in the country, Gowen said that teachers felt unequipped to talk about porn. And though the guidelines have been circulated at education conferences and made publicly available, Gowen doesn't know of a single educator who has implemented them. In part, she says, people may be waiting for a better sense of what's effective. But also, many schools and teachers are nervous about anything that risks them being "accused of promoting porn."

The most recent sex education guidelines from the World Health Organization's European office note that educators should include discussions about the influence of pornography on sexuality starting with late elementary school and through high school. The guidelines don't, however, provide specific ideas on how to have those conversations. In Britain, nonprofit organizations and a teachers' union, along with members of Parliament, have recommended that schools include discussions about the influence of porn on how children view sex and relationships. Magdalena Mattebo, a researcher at Uppsala University in Sweden who studies pornography and adolescents, would like porn literacy mandated in her country. "We are a little lost in how to handle this," Mattebo told me.

More than 300 schools, youth and community groups, and government agencies in Australia and New Zealand use components of a porn-education resource called "In the Picture" that includes statistics, studies, and exercises primarily for teenagers. It was created by Maree Crabbe, an expert on sexual violence and pornography education, who lives near Melbourne, Australia. As she put it during a U.S. training program for educators and social workers that I attended in 2016: "We want to be positive about sex, positive about masturbation and critical of pornography." One key component of the program is often neglected in porn literacy: providing training to help parents understand and talk about these issues.

Last year, a feminist porn producer, Erika Lust, in consultation with sex educators, created a porn-education website for parents. The Porn Conversation links to research and articles and provides practical tips for parents, including talking to kids about the ways mainstream porn doesn't represent typical bodies or mutually satisfying sex and avoiding accusatory questions about why your kid is watching porn and who showed it to them. "We can't just say, 'I don't like mainstream porn because it's chauvinistic,'" says Lust, whose films feature female- centered pleasure. "We have given our children technology, so we need to teach them how to handle it." But she takes it a step further by suggesting that parents of middle and high schoolers talk to their teenagers about "healthy porn," which she says includes showing female desire and pleasure and being made under fair working conditions. I asked Lust if she would steer her daughters in that direction when they are older (they are 7 and 10). "I would recommend good sites to my daughters at age 15, when I think they are mature enough. We are so curious to find out about sex. People have doubts and insecurities about themselves sexually. 'Is it O.K. that I like that, or this?' I think porn can be a good thing to have as an outlet. I'm not scared by explicit sex per se. I'm afraid of the bad values." . . .

. . . But even if parents decided to help their teenagers find these sites, not only is it illegal to show any kind of porn—good or bad—to anyone under 18, but, really, do teenagers want their parents to do so? And which ones would parents recommend for teenagers? "Unlike organic food, there's no coding system for ethical or feminist porn," Crabbe notes. "They might use condoms and dental dams and still convey the same gender and aggression dynamics." Also, "good porn" isn't typically free or nearly as accessible as the millions of videos streaming on mainstream sites.

Al Vernacchio, a nationally known sexuality educator who teaches progressive sex ed at a private Quaker school outside Philadelphia, believes the better solution is to make porn literacy part of the larger umbrella of comprehensive sex education.

Vernacchio, who is the author of the 2014 book *For Goodness Sex: Changing the Way We Talk to Teens about Sexuality, Values, and Health,* is one of those rare teenage-sex educators who talks directly to his high school students about sexual pleasure and mutuality, along with the ingredients for healthy relationships. The problem with porn "is not just that it often shows misogynistic, unhealthy representations of relationships," Vernacchio says. "You can't learn relationship skills from porn, and if you are looking for pleasure and connection, porn can't teach you how to have those."

Crabbe notes one effective way to get young men to take fewer lessons from porn: "Tell them if you want to be a lazy, selfish lover, look at porn. If you want to be a lover where your partner says, 'That was great,' you won't learn it from porn." And parents should want their teenagers to be generous lovers, Cindy Gallop argues. "Our parents bring us up to have good manners, a work ethic. But nobody brings us up to behave well in bed."

To prepare his students to be comfortable and respectful in sexual situations, Vernacchio shows photos, not just drawings, of genitalia to his high schoolers. "Most people are having sex with real people, not porn stars, and real bodies are highly variable. I would much rather my students have that moment of asking questions or confusion or even laughter in my classroom rather than when they see their partner's naked body for the first time." He, along with Debby Herbenick, who is also the author of the 2012 book *Sex Made Easy:*

Your Awkward Questions Answered for Better, Smarter Amazing Sex, advocate that adolescents should understand that most females don't have orgasms by penetration alone and that clitoral stimulation often requires oral sex, fingers, and sex toys. As she notes: "It's part of human life, and you teach it in smart, sensitive ways." . . .

A., the young woman who said she had never seen an image of a penis until she watched porn, resisted the idea that porn was uniformly bad for teenagers. "At least kids are watching porn and not going out and getting pregnant," she said. But recently, she told me that she'd given up watching it altogether. She disliked looking at women's expressions now, believing that they probably weren't experiencing pleasure and might be in pain. When Drew watched porn, he found himself wondering if women were having sex against their will. As another student said with a sigh: "Nicole and Jess ruined porn for us."

In the months after the class, A. had created a new mission for herself: She was going to always have orgasms during sex. "And I did it!" she told me. It helped that she had been in a relationship with a guy who was open and asked what she liked. But even if Porn Literacy didn't go into as many details about sex as she would have liked, "in this indirect way, the class shows what you deserve and don't deserve," she said. "In porn, the guy cares only about himself. I used to think more about 'Am I doing something right or wrong?'" Porn may neglect women's orgasms, but A. wasn't going to anymore.

Drew, who had once used porn as his main sex educator, was now thinking about sex differently. "Some things need to come to us naturally, not by watching it and seeing what turns you on," he told me. The discussions about anatomy and fake displays of pleasure made him realize that girls didn't always respond as they did in porn and that they didn't all want the same things. And guys didn't either. Maybe that porn clip in which the nice, tender guy didn't excite the girl was wrong. What Drew needed was a girl who was open and honest, as he was, and with whom he could start to figure out how to have good sex. It would take some time and most likely involve some fumbling. But Drew was O.K. with that. He was just starting out.

NOTES

1. Sabina, Chiara, Wolak, Janis, and David Finkelhor. 2008. "The Nature and Dynamics of Internet Pornography Exposure for Youth." *CyberPsychology & Behavior.* 11(6): 1–3.
2. Rothman, E. F., Kaczmarsky, C., Burke, N., Jansen, E., & Baughman, A. 2015. "Without Porn . . . I Wouldn't Know Half the Things I Know Now": A Qualitative Study of Pornography Use Among a Sample of Urban, Low-Income, Black and Hispanic Youth," *The Journal of Sex Research*, 52:7, 736–746, DOI: 10.1080/00224499.2014.960908
3. Jochen, Peter & Patti M. Valkenburg. 2016. "Adolescents and Pornography: A Review of 20 Years of Research," *The Journal of Sex Research*, 53:4–5, 509–531, DOI: 10.1080/00224499.2016.1143441.
4. Martellozzo, E., Monaghan, A, Adler, J. R., Davidson, J, Leyva, R. and Horvath, M. A. H. (2016). "I wasn't sure it was normal to watch it . . ." A quantitative and qualitative examination of the impact of online pornography on the values, attitudes, beliefs and behaviours of children and young people. London: Middlesex University doi:10.6084/m9.figshare.3382393.
5. Marston, Cicely, and R. Lewis. 2014. Anal heterosex among young people and implications for health promotion: A qualitative study in the UK. *BMJ Open, 4(e004996).*

HEATHER R. HLAVKA

26. NORMALIZING SEXUAL VIOLENCE

Young Women Account for Harassment and Abuse

Despite the fact that rates of sexual harassment, coercion, and assault are high among young women and girls, most instances go unreported. Hlavka argues that the cultural ideology surrounding sexuality—that men are the aggressors and women the passive gate-keepers—reinforces and supports this type of violence.

Many regard harassment and violence to be a normal part of everyday life in middle and high schools (Fineran and Bennett 1999), yet most of these crimes go unreported. A 2011 American Association of University Women (AAUW 2011) study found that almost half (48 percent) of the 1,965 students surveyed experienced harassment, but only 9 percent reported the incident to an authority figure. Girls were sexually harassed more than boys (56 percent vs. 40 percent); they were more likely to be pressured for a date, pressured into sexual activity, and verbally harassed (AAUW 2001; Fineran and Bennett 1999).

. . . Data from the Youth Risk Behavior Survey (YRBS) show that almost 20 percent of girls experience physical and sexual violence from dating partners (Silverman et al. 2001), and sexual assault accounts for one-third of preteen victimization (Finkelhor and Ormrod 2000). It is tempting to ask: Why do so few young women formally report their victimization experiences? Assuming that peer sexual harassment and assault is an instrument that creates and maintains gendered and sexed hierarchies (e.g., MacKinnon 1979; Phillips 2000; Tolman et al. 2003), attention instead must turn toward understanding how and why these violent acts are produced, maintained, and normalized in the first place. Despite the considerable body of research that shows high rates of gendered violence among youth, there has been little discussion of its instruments and operations.

This study is concerned with girls' relational experiences of sexuality, harassment and assault, coercion, and consent. With few exceptions, girls' construction of violence has received little attention from victimization scholars and those interested in the gendered power dynamics of adolescent sexual development. The lack of research is clear and a shift in analytical focus toward appraisals of violence is critical. It cannot be assumed that legal definitions of sexual harassment and assault are socially agreed on, understood, or similarly enacted. Research from the vantage point of young women themselves is necessary. How do girls talk about experiences that researchers and the law would label as harassment and rape? In what ways do they account for these experiences? . . .

FEMINIST PERSPECTIVES AND HETERO-RELATIONAL DISCOURSES

Feminist scholarship on compulsory heterosexuality (Connell 1987; Rich 1980; Tolman et al. 2003), heteronormativity (Kitzinger 2005; Martin 2009; Thorne and Luria 1986), and heterogender (Ingraham 1994) consistently finds that traditional gender arrangements, beliefs, and behaviors reinforce women's sexual subordination to men. Heterosexuality is compulsory in that it is an *institution* (Rich 1980) that organizes the conventions by which women and men relate; it is assumed and expected (Jackson 2009) as it is understood as natural and unproblematic (Kitzinger 2005; Schippers 2007). Heteronormative discourses consistently link female sexuality with passivity, vulnerability, and submissiveness, and male sexuality with dominance, aggression, and desire (Butler 1999; Ingraham 1994).

Young people are socialized into a patriarchal culture that normalizes and often encourages male power and aggression, particularly within the context of heterosexual relationships (Fineran and Bennett 1999; Tolman et al. 2003). As men's heterosexual violence is viewed as customary, so too is women's endurance of it (Stanko 1985). For example, Messerschmidt (1986) has argued that "normative heterosexuality" involves a "presumption that men have a special and overwhelming 'urge' or 'drive' toward heterosexual intercourse" . . . normalizing the presumption that men's sexual aggression is simply "boys being boys" (Connell 1987; French 2003; Messerschmidt 2012). Stanko (1985, 73) argued that "women learn, often at a very early age, that their sexuality is not their own and that maleness can at any point intrude into it." Girls are thus expected to endure aggression by men because that is *part* of man. Coupled with the presumption that women are the gatekeepers of male desire (Fine 1988; Tolman 1991), heteronormative discourses have allowed for men's limited accountability for aggressive, harassing, and criminal sexual conduct. . . .

DISCOURSES OF CHILDREN, SEXUALITY, AND SEXUAL ABUSE

. . . Children and youth have largely remained exempt from legal and policy discussions of consent to sexual activity, and little scholarly research has taken up the task, perhaps, in part, because Western cultures today often characterize children as innocent, asexual, ignorant, and in need of protection from adult sexual knowledge and practices (Angelides 2004; Best 1990). Adults have historically worked to police the sexual behavior of young people, particularly of girls (Fine 1988; Gilligan 1982). . . . Youth learn early that they should not talk about sex (Ryan 2000), often extending to sexual violence and harassment (Gilgun 1986; Phillips 2000; Thompson 1995).

. . . Further, feminist theorists argue that "real rape" (Estrich 1987)—or forcible stranger rape—is narrowly defined, largely enforced by law, and reinforced by popular media. Discursively, law and media draw absolutes between healthy heterosexual encounters and dangerous, abusive relationships, creating divisions between what is and what is not violence, between "real rape" and "everyday violence," or what Stanko (1985) termed "little rapes." What counts as sexual violence, then, are the extreme cases "which constrain[s] and construct[s] the framework through which women have to make sense of events" (Kelly and Radford 1990, 41). The struggle to negotiate these tensions has meaningful outcomes, and young people are not exempt. . . .

METHODS

The data for this study include audio-videotaped interviews of youths seen by forensic interviewers for reported cases of sexual abuse between 1995 and 2004. The interviews come from the nonprofit Children's Advocacy Center (CAC) located in an urban Midwest community. The CAC provides investigative interviews and medical examinations for youths who may have been sexually or physically assaulted or witnessed a violent crime. Interviews take place between one forensic interviewer and one child referred to the CAC by law enforcement or Child Protection Services (CPS). Youths were brought to the CAC for an interview because they reported sexual abuse to someone, someone else witnessed or reported the abuse to authorities, or the offender confessed to the abuse.

The forensic interview is based on a semi-structured interview protocol designed to maximize youth's ability to communicate their experiences and conforms to standards set by the American Professional Society on the Abuse of Children (APSAC 2002). Protocol components include first establishing rapport and, next, obtaining details about sexual abuse only if the child first verbally discloses victimization to the interviewer. The two then discuss the circumstances surrounding the abuse using non-suggestive, largely open-ended, questions. So, while the interview is set up to investigate whether or not abuse occurred, youths were consistently allowed to raise and discuss subjects important to them in response to questions such as "What happened? Did you tell anyone? How did they respond? How did you feel about that? Are you worried about anything?" . . .

The study sample included 100 interviews of youths between ages three and 17, stratified disproportionately by gender and age and proportionately by race. Descriptive data were gathered from case files, such as date of the interview, child and offender characteristics when available, pre-interview reports, family background, and CAC investigative assessments. Audiotaped interviews were transcribed verbatim by the author. . . .

The study subsample includes 23 racially diverse young women (13 White girls, six Black girls, and four Latina girls) between 11 and 16 years of age. The reported offenders were known to the girls, either as acquaintances or intimate others (intrafamilial abuse was more common in the larger study sample). Accounts were unpacked as everyday violence, instruments of coercion, and accounts of consent. These categories illuminate the heteronormative cultures within which girls accounted for sexual violence and negotiated what happened, how it happened, and why.

FINDINGS

EVERYDAY VIOLENCE

Objectification, sexual harassment, and abuse appear to be part of the fabric of young women's lives (Orenstein 1994). They had few available safe spaces; girls were harassed and assaulted at parties, in school, on the playground, on buses, and in cars. Young women overwhelmingly depicted boys and men as *natural* sexual aggressors, pointing to one of the main tenets of compulsory heterosexuality. Incorporating

male sexual drive discourse (Phillips 2000), they described men as unable to control their sexual desires. Male power and privilege and female acquiescence were reified in descriptions of "routine" and "normal" sexualized interactions (Fineran and Bennett 1999; French 2003). Assaultive behaviors were often justified, especially when characterized as indiscriminate. For example, Patricia (age 13, White) told the interviewer: "They grab you, touch your butt and try to, like, touch you in the front, and run away, but it's okay, I mean . . . I never think it's a big thing because they do it to everyone." Referring to boys at school, Patricia described unwelcome touching and grabbing as normal, commonplace behaviors.

Compulsory heterosexuality highlights how conventional norms of heterosexual relations produce and often require male dominance and female subordination (Phillips 2000; Tolman et al. 2003). Young women like Patricia described sexually aggressive behaviors as customary: "It just happens," and "They're boys—that's what they do." Similarly, Kelly (age 13, White) told the forensic interviewer about her experiences with 20-year-old Eric:

> [He] would follow me around all the time, tell me I was beautiful and stuff, that he could have me when he wanted to. He did that all the time, like, would touch me and say, "Am I making you wet, do you want me?" when he wanted. I think that's just . . . like, that's what he does, it's just, like, how it goes on and everyone knows it, no one says nothing.

Kelly trivializes her experiences of sexual harassment by a man seven years older, telling the interviewer of this ordinary and allowable "masculine" practice. Her description of ongoing harassment also confounds romance and aggression, because Eric's harassment was fused with courting, compliments, and sexual desire (Phillips 2000).

Girls' characterizations of everyday violence paralleled both their assessments that "boys will be boys" and their understanding of harassment as a normal adolescent rite of passage. Sexual harassment is an instrument that maintains a gendered hierarchy (MacKinnon 1979), and girls described the many ways they protected themselves against expected sexual aggression, at the expense of their own feelings. Carla (age 14, White), for example, cast assault and threats as expected because they were typical. In this passage, she described chronic harassment by a young man as they rode the school bus. He often threatened to "come over to [her] house and rape [her]":

CARLA: Like, on the bus, like when I'll sit, he'll try and sit next to me and then slide his hand under my butt.
INTERVIEWER: Okay, does he say anything?
CARLA: No, he just kinda has this look on his face. And then I'll, like, shove him out of the seat and then he'll get mad.
INTERVIEWER: What happens when he gets mad?
CARLA: He just kinda doesn't talk. He gets, like, his face gets red and he doesn't talk. And he, I guess he feels rejected, but I don't care. He told me . . . he was like, "I'm gonna come over to your house and rape you." And then, I know he's just joking, but that can be a little weird to hear.
INTERVIEWER: Yeah, so when did he tell you that?
CARLA: He tells me it all the time, like the last time I talked to him. He just says that he's gonna come to my house and rape me since I won't do anything with him. And, I mean, I think . . . I'm . . . I know he's joking, it's just hard to, like, why would he say that?

Threats were used for compliance, becoming more persistent and coercive over time. Unsure of whether to take the threats seriously, Carla names her experience "weird" while normalizing the young man's behavior as understandable within a male sexual drive discourse ("I guess he feels rejected"), and trivializes his threats twice, saying, "I know he's just joking." Harassment was dangerously constructed as romance and flirting. These discourses often entitle young men to violate the bodies of young women (Connell 1995; Messerschmidt 2012) . . . .

Given expectations of, and experiences with, male aggression, young women were charged with self-protection by reading and responding to potentially dangerous situations. While some girls attempted to "ignore" the behavior, others had to make additional maneuvers. In her interview, Lana (age 15, White) explained how 18-year-old Mike "tries to bring [girls] downstairs in the [school] basement and, like, try and force 'em to like make out with him and stuff."

She said Mike tried to force her to go downstairs on numerous occasions and he would "get mad when [she'd] say no." In response, Lana altered her behavior by avoiding being alone in the school hallways, at her locker, or in the bathroom. Young women responded to harassment with a barrage of maneuvers, like avoidance and diverting attention. These tactics did not always work, however. In Lana's case, Mike was eventually "able to catch [her] off-guard":

I was going to the bathroom and he wouldn't let me go in. He put his foot in front of [the door], and he's a really strong person, so I didn't really, like, I couldn't open the door. And he said, "I'll let you in if you give me a kiss," and I said, "No." And I was going back to the classroom and he pinned me against the wall and tried to, like, lift up my shirt. And, like, touched me, and then I . . . I got up . . . I started to scream, and I guess someone heard, 'cause then, um, someone started coming. So he got away from me, I just went back in the classroom and forgot about it. I just didn't think it was really anything.

Girls in this study said they did not want to make a "big deal" out of their experiences and rarely reported these incidents to persons in authority. Most questioned whether anyone would care about the behavior; if it was not "rape" it was not serious enough to warrant others' involvement. "Real" assault was narrowly defined and contingent on various conditions that were rarely met (Phillips 2000; Stanko 1985).

Young women constructed classic boundaries between "real rapes" and everyday violence or "little rapes." Terri (age 11, Black) was interviewed at the CAC because she told a friend she was forced to perform oral sex on a 17-year-old neighbor boy: "He forced me, he, uh, he grabbed me tighter, and he said if I didn't do it he was gonna rape me." For Terri, rape was only intercourse, as she candidly explained: "They always say they gonna rape you, if you don't do what they want, they say they'll rape you." Terri's mother also cautioned her about male sexual drives, warning her to expect aggression and to protect herself. Sitting in her apartment stairwell alone that day, Terri assumed responsibility for her own assault. Terri's experience demonstrates that if girls do not acquiesce to the pressure to have sex, they risk being raped. She did not tell her mother, because "I shouldn't have been there, my mom said I should've been home anyway, but I didn't want to get raped so I had to."

INSTRUMENTS OF COERCION

The normalization of violence was intensified in peer groups and assault was often perpetrated by one older man. Peers communicated a specialized sense of sexual acceptability largely based on the perception of women as sexual gatekeepers. Gatekeeping occurred in a variety of ways, including allocation of resources, such as food, alcohol, or a space away from adult others. Janice (age 14, White), for example, told the interviewer that 30-something-year-old Matt touched her and four girlfriends on a regular basis:

> He does, like, touch us, you know? Like, he like rubs my leg, the thigh, but none of us told him, told him to stop, you know? But I . . . I always moved away when he did it. He'd just rub my leg and touch my boobs. And one time when I was over at his house, I asked him for something to eat and he goes, "Not unless I can touch your boobs."

Via access to resources, Matt presented Janice with a "gatekeeping choice" that deflected responsibility. Janice later told the interviewer that Matt had also touched her vagina, commenting, "He does it to everyone, you know, it just happens sometimes," and justified Matt's behavior by placing responsibility on the group: "But none of us told him to stop." Matt's actions were minimized because they were customary and something they "just dealt with."

Sexualized bartering or exchange for in/tangible resources (Orenstein 1994; Thompson 1995; Van Roosmalen 2000) was common. Access or restriction to something was a tactic used by men to coerce young women like Natalie (age 16, Latina) into sexual contact. Natalie was sexually assaulted by Jim, a 37-year-old neighbor. She told the interviewer that Jim allowed Natalie and her friends to "hang out," play basketball in his backyard, and drink beer and vodka. During the interview, Natalie described Jim's sexual touching and kissing as typical male behavior:

> He'd just rub his hand across my butt, and then one time I was sitting there and he—I was, like, laying on

the couch watching TV—and he came home. He was kinda drunk, then he, like, literally just, like, laid *on* me. That's what he . . . well, guys always try to get up on you, like just normal.

Because both were drinking alcohol, Natalie tolerated his actions: "He would be touching my butt, you know, with this hand, going under my butt, under the blanket. I was, like, oh well, but all this . . . nothing like totally big happened."

Overwhelmingly described as "normal stuff" that "guys do" or tolerating what "just happens," young women's sexual desire and consent are largely absent (Martin 1996; Tolman 1994). Sex was understood as something done to them and agency was discursively attributed only to gate-keeping. . . .

ACCOUNTS OF CONSENT

The links between everyday harassment and violence were further reproduced through attributions of blame. Girls criticized each other for not successfully maneuvering men's normalized aggressive behavior. Even when maneuvers "failed," concessions were made. For example, Lily (age 14, Latina) was raped by a 17-year-old school acquaintance in a park as she walked home from school. The offender quickly spread rumors and she was labeled "sexually active" and a "slut" by her classmates: "There's rumors about me already, that aren't even true . . . that I want, that I want to, and I let him do that . . . and it wasn't even true." Cast as promiscuous, she was deemed complicit in her rape. On the rare occasion that rape was reported to an adult or authority figure, young women described feeling suspect. Kiley (age 14, Black) was raped by a 27-year-old family friend at his home. She provided details about the assault, including how he held her down and covered her mouth to muffle her cries:

> I didn't want to but he did, you know, and I don't know, [sex] just happened. I thought he was just a friend and that's it. . . . He was calling me names, he was calling me a "ho" and a "slut" and all this kind of stuff, and that I gave him a lap dance and everything. That I was, I can't . . . I took all my clothes off and that I was, like, asking him for it. That I wanted to be with him, and everyone believed him.

Sexual reputation mattered to girls (Van Roosmalen 2000) and the threat of being labeled a "ho" or a "slut" loomed large. The threat of sexualization and social derogation was often a barrier to rape reporting; it was connected with accusations of exaggeration through which peers decided whether and how to include, label, and ostracize. This finding is consistent with prior studies (Phillips 2000) that find young women are under pressure to manage their sexuality and sexual reputations. This is a confusing endeavor, of course, as girls may gain cultural capital among peers for being desired and pursued but not for sexual agency.

The precarious balancing act of attaining sexual status and avoiding the "slander of the slut" (Schalet 2010) proved powerful. Some girls belittled others' experiences, holding them responsible for their victimizations. Obligated to set limits for sexual behavior (Orenstein 1994), it was girls' duty to be prepared to say "no" (Tolman 1994) and to police each other. When asked about her friend who had reported sexual assault by a mutual acquaintance, Jacki (age 15, White) said, "I don't know why she's making such a big deal out of it anyway. He does it to everyone, so I say, well, 'Just back off,' I say 'No'—so she should if she don't want it, but she probably wants it anyway." Jacki worked to discursively separate herself from her friend as she spoke of sexual desire and exaggeration. . . .

Girls were also aware of double standards and traditional sexual scripts. They claimed "guys get away with everything" and "they can do anything and not get in trouble." This critique stopped short of attributions of sexual responsibility, however; girls self-framed as active subjects by labeling others as passive objects. In this way, the complexities of naming sexual aggression were premised on behavior comparisons. April (age 13, White) reported that her 13-year-old friend "had sex" with Sean, a 22-year-old man. During her interview, she described her friend as passive and naïve:

> I've heard rumors about that he's had sex with girls, and I know Sara has had sex with him, she came out and told me . . . she said that he came over and he was telling her that she was gorgeous and that he loved her and that he wanted to have her baby and all this stuff, and I guess it just happened, and that's

what she said, it just happened, and I was like, "Oh, okay" [laughs], you know, which didn't surprise me, 'cause Sara, she'll be mad at him and then she'll go back to him, like, two days later.

April characterized sexual intercourse ("it") as something men do "to" women. She further interpreted Sean's manipulative tactics ("telling her that she was gorgeous and that he loved her and that he wanted to have her baby") as successful because "it [intercourse] just happened." April said similar ploys did not work on her: "First of all, he asked me, 'Would you. . . would you ever go out with me?' and I said, 'No'. . . and he's like, 'Well, would you ever have sex with me?' and I was like, 'No.'"

Despite April's resistance, Sean put his hands under her shirt, and tried to put her hands in his pants and her head on his penis. April told the interviewer: "I told him to stop and he didn't and he got to, like, right here, you know, he was tryin' to lift up my bra and I was like, 'No, stop!'" Further couched in rumors and reputation, April differentiated herself from Sara: "There's rumors going around saying that Sara had sex with him and so did I and that [she's] a slut and all this stuff." April insisted the rumors about her were untrue because, unlike Sara who let "it just happen," she "said no." As Nelson and Oliver (1998, 573) state, "Under these rules, any girl who permits herself to be persuaded into sexual activity is weak and to blame, as is a girl who voluntarily enters a situation where she can be raped."

CONCLUSION

Research on sexual violence has long asked why victims do not report these incidents. Studies with adults have examined how women account for and "name" their experiences, yet adolescents remain largely outside the scope of this work. Exploring sexual violence via the lens of compulsory heterosexuality highlights the relational dynamics at play in this naming process. . . .

Descriptions of assault here are concerning, having much to do with heteronormativity and compulsory heterosexuality. Sex was "something they [men and boys] do," or "something he wanted," and sexual assault was a "weird" threat, something "they just say," or "something she let happen." When resistance was voiced, as in April's case, it was couched in sexual refusal and used to establish boundaries. In their policing of each other, young women often held themselves and their peers responsible for acting as gatekeepers of men's behaviors; they were responsible for being coerced, for accepting gifts and other resources, for not fending off or resisting men's sexual advances, [or] for miscommunication. . . . The discourses offer insight into how some young women talked about their sexual selves and relationships as they navigated a world ordered by gendered binaries and heterosexual frameworks (Butler 1999).

Importantly, the violence described in this study must be situated both by context and as told within an institutionalized, forensic interview setting. Child crime victims are often positioned as passive in exploitative relationships, in reporting practices, and in criminal justice processes. . . . As the findings demonstrate, girls understand their position in a patriarchal sexual system and therefore might assume authority figures of all types will blame them or perceive them as bad girls who "let it happen." Revealing sexual desire or agency in this setting might be perceived risky in the same way involving law enforcement might be; girls may be viewed as blameworthy for putting themselves in a situation where one can be raped (Nelson and Oliver 1998). The fear of revealing one's use of drugs or alcohol could also influence what and how disclosure is made with interviewers. This might be especially true for minority and socioeconomically disadvantaged youths with little trust of criminal justice authorities (Hlavka 2013). Therefore, conclusions offered here must be tempered not only by class and neighborhood context, but also by how the forensic interview is perceived and interpreted differently by young women depending on race, class, and sexuality. In this study, age, type of offender, and peer groups seemed to affect girls' narratives in important ways, whereas race did not. Also, it is not assumed that all the girls in this study identified as heterosexual, but without a measure of

sexual orientation, the question remains, "How might lesbian or bisexual girls interact with common heteronormative discourses?" . . .

. . . Alternative solutions for the education of young people on sexual relations and abuse are long overdue, and many have called for new sexual paradigms for some time (Fine 1988; Phillips 2000; Tolman 1994; Tolman et al. 2003). The sexual scripts culturally available to girls largely exclude sexual desire and pleasure, representing girls as victims in need of protection against boys' desires (Fine 1988). Placing responsibility on women and girls to "just say no" and excusing boys and men as they "work a 'yes' out" works to erase institutional and structural responsibilities. The lack of safe, supportive space for girls is palpable. We can thus better understand why young women in this study felt they were expected to protect themselves from everyday violence with little help from others, including those in authority positions. The lack of institutional support assumed by girls in this study should be deeply concerning for educators and policy makers. As Stein (1995) has argued, lack of adult interruption or response to sexual harassment and abuse functionally permits and encourages it. It is not enough to establish new policies and practices aimed at increasing reporting; there are larger underlying cultural practices and discourses acting as barriers. By drawing attention to youths' voices, structures of violence, power, and privilege become apparent in their gendered experiences that do not easily translate to law and policy reforms. Sexual education must be gender equity education (Stein et al. 2002), resistant to troubled, heteronormative binaries and cultural constraints that omit discourses of desire, gender, and sexuality. By treating young people as agents and decision makers, we could create spaces where they can work together with adults to appraise experiences of sex, assault, power, coercion, and consent prevalent in their lives.

REFERENCES

AAUW (American Association of University Women). 2001. *Hostile hallways II: Bullying, teasing and sexual harassment in school*. Washington, DC: AAUW.

AAUW (American Association of University Women). 2011. *Crossing the line: Sexual harassment at school*. Washington, DC: Catherine Hill and Holly Kearl.

Angelides, Steven. 2004. Feminism, child sexual abuse, and the erasure of child sexuality. *GLQ: A Journal of Lesbian and Gay Studies* 10:141–77.

APSAC (American Professional Society on the Abuse of Children). 2002. *Investigative interviewing in cases of alleged child abuse*. Chicago: APSAC.

Best, Joel. 1990. *Threatened children: Rhetoric and concern about child victims*. Chicago: University of Chicago Press.

Butler, Judith. 1999. *Gender trouble*. New York: Routledge.

Connell, Raewyn. 1987. *Gender and power*. Cambridge, UK: Polity Press.

Connell, Raewyn. 1995. *Masculinities*. Berkeley: University of California Press.

Estrich, Susan. 1987. *Real rape*. Cambridge, MA: Harvard University Press.

Fine, Michelle. 1988. Sexuality, schooling, and adolescent females: The missing discourse of desire. *Harvard Educational Review* 58:29–53.

Fineran, Susan, and Larry Bennett. 1999. Gender and power issues of peer sexual harassment among teenagers. *Journal of Interpersonal Violence* 14:626–41.

Finkelhor, David, and Richard Ormrod. 2000. *Characteristics of crimes against juveniles*. Washington, DC: U.S. Department of Justice, Office of Justice Programs.

French, Sandra L. 2003. Reflections on healing: Framing strategies utilized by acquaintance rape survivors. *Journal of Applied Communication Research* 31:298–319.

Gilgun, Jane. 1986. Sexually abused girls' knowledge about sexual abuse and sexuality. *Journal of Interpersonal Violence* 1:309–25.

Gilligan, Carol. 1982. *In a different voice*. Cambridge, MA: Harvard University Press.

Hlavka, Heather. 2013. Legal subjectivity among youth victims of sexual abuse. *Law & Social Inquiry*, 39:31–61.

Ingraham, Chrys. 1994. The heterosexual imaginary. *Sociological Theory* 12:203–19.

Jackson, Stevi. 2009. Sexuality, heterosexuality, and gender hierarchy. In *Sex, gender & sexuality*, edited by Abby Ferber, Kimberly Holcomb, and Tre Wentling. New York: Oxford University Press.

Kelly, Liz and Jill Radford. 1990. "Nothing really happened": The invalidation of women's experiences of sexual violence. *Critical Social Policy* 10:39–53.

Kitzinger, Celia. 2005. Heteronormativity in action: Reproducing the heterosexual nuclear family in after-hours medical calls. *Social Problems* 52:477–98.

MacKinnon, Catherine. 1979. *Sexual harassment of working women*. New Haven, CT: Yale University Press.

Martin, Karin. 1996. *Puberty, sexuality, and the self*. New York: Routledge.

Martin, Karin. 2009. Normalizing heterosexuality. *American Sociological Review* 74:190–207.

Messerschmidt, James. 1986. *Capitalism, patriarchy, and crime*. Totowa, NJ: Rowman & Littlefield.

Messerschmidt, James. 2012. *Gender, heterosexuality, and youth violence: The struggle for recognition*. New York: Rowman & Littlefield.

Nelson, Andrea, and Pamela Oliver. 1998. Gender and the construction of consent in child–adult sexual contact: Beyond gender neutrality and male monopoly. *Gender & Society* 12:554–77.

Orenstein, Peggy. 1994. *Schoolgirls: Young women, self-esteem, and the confidence gap*. New York: Doubleday.

Phillips, Lynn M. 2000. *Flirting with danger: Young women's reflections on sexuality and domination*. New York: New York University Press.

Rich, Adrienne. 1980. Compulsory heterosexuality and lesbian existence. *Signs: Journal of Women in Culture and Society* 5:631–60.

Ryan, Gail. 2000. Childhood sexuality: A decade of study. *Child Abuse & Neglect* 24:33–48.

Schalet, Amy. 2010. Sexual subjectivity revisited: The significance of relationships in Dutch and American girls' experiences of sexuality. *Gender & Society* 24:304–29.

Schippers, Mimi. 2007. Recovering the feminine other: Masculinity, femininity, and gender hegemony. *Theory & Society* 36:85–102.

Silverman, Jay, Anita Raj, Lorelei Mucci, and Jeanne Hathaway. 2001. Dating violence against adolescent girls and associated substance use, unhealthy weight control, sexual risk behavior, pregnancy, and suicidality. *Journal of the American Medical Association* 286:572–79.

Stanko, Elizabeth. 1985. *Intimate intrusions: Women's experience of male violence*. London: Routledge and Kegan Paul.

Stein, Nan. 1995. Sexual harassment in K–12 schools: The public performance of gendered violence. *Harvard Educational Review* 65:145–62.

Stein, Nan, Deborah Tolman, Michelle Porche, and Renée Spencer. 2002. Gender safety: A new concept for safer and more equitable schools. *Journal of School Violence* 1:35–50.

Thompson, Sharon. 1995. *Going all the way: Teenage girls' tales of sex, romance, and pregnancy*. New York: Hill and Wang.

Thorne, Barrie, and Zella Luria. 1986. Sexuality and gender in children's daily worlds. *Social Problems* 33:176–90.

Tolman, Deborah. 1991. Adolescent girls, women and sexuality: Discerning dilemmas of desire. In *Women, girls and psychotherapy: Reframing resistance*, edited by C. Gilligan, A. Rogers, and D. Tolman. New York: Haworth.

Tolman, Deborah. 1994. Doing desire: Adolescent girls' struggles for/with sexuality. *Gender & Society* 8:324–42.

Tolman, Deborah, Renée Spencer, Myra Rosen-Reynosa, and Michelle Porche. 2003. Sowing the seeds of violence in heterosexual relationships: Early adolescents narrate compulsory heterosexuality. *Journal of Social Issues* 59:159–78.

Van Roosmalen, Erica. 2000. Forces of patriarchy: Adolescent experiences of sexuality and conceptions of relationships. *Youth & Society* 32:202–27.

RENEE M. SHELBY

27. SEX TRAFFICKING, SOCIAL INEQUALITY, AND OUR EVOLVING LEGAL CONSCIOUSNESS

Sex trafficking is widely acknowledged as a social problem, exploiting those in society with fewer resources and less power. Despite this agreement, determining what actions and who will be counted as "criminal" in our fight to end it has continued to evolve. Shelby discusses the challenges of estimating the breadth and depth of victimization, describes who is more vulnerable to victimization, and then assesses the efficacy of various policies designed to combat sex trafficking.

In 2018, the *New York Post* published a three-part series on sex trafficking in which two teens, Alexis and Shanifa, shared their stories. From the age of 2, Alexis grew up in and out of the foster care system. When she turned 8 years old, her father began to molest her. Her family struggled to pay rent and buy food; her mother sold herself sexually for money in the family apartment, even while Alexis and her siblings were at home. When she turned 14 years old, Alexis gave away a kitten that her family could not care for to a neighborhood man. He turned out to be a pimp. He invited her to a party claiming that entertainer Meek Mill would be there. The man told her to dress sexy because he needed pictures of her to get her on the VIP list. On the way to the party, he drugged her and took her to a motel room where men who had seen her picture on the commercial sex classified site Backpage.com were waiting to have sex with her.[1] The pimp encouraged her to "slide into the loop" (his term for sex work), and she reluctantly agreed, believing she could use the money to help her family. She spent the next two years being sexually trafficked until she found help at a local social service agency.

Shanifa was a junior in high school when she and her family could not afford necessities—from school supplies to underwear. One day, a pimp approached her on social media promising her that he could help her get the money she so desperately needed.[2] After her struggling mom abandoned her, Shanifa became homeless. The pimp promised her money and a new "family" if she got "into the life." But it was a trap. Soon her pimp became violent and escalated his control over her by denying her food, access to showers, and contact with the outside world. Although Shanifa knew the situation was bad, she did not feel she could leave. She recalls the dilemma she struggled with, in which she thought, "I'm getting beat, but I have a place to stay. I'm not always eating, but I have underwear." After she eventually escaped her situation, she described her pimp's combination of abuse and "care taking" as creating a bond similar to Stockholm Syndrome—a psychological condition that causes hostages to develop an alliance with their captors as a survival strategy.

Alexis's and Shanifa's complicated and heartbreaking cases are very familiar to social service providers who work with youth in the juvenile justice system, sex-trafficking survivors, and even adult sex workers seeking outreach. While taking sexual advantage of someone's economic or social inequality is nothing new, with increasing media coverage, sex trafficking is gaining global visibility and entering our "legal consciousness." "Legal consciousness" refers to how people come to understand and agree on the

Original to *Focus on Social Problems: A Contemporary Reader*.

meaning of particular crimes and laws about those crimes. Although the prevalence of sensationalized stereotypes and imagery might suggest our legal consciousness about sex trafficking has stabilized, in fact, the way we think about and address sex trafficking through policy has continued to evolve since the earliest trafficking laws.

Since the mid-2000s, the social problem of sex trafficking has received global attention and an infusion of billions of dollars into local and federal law enforcement offices to combat the problem. While there is no single model of what a sex-trafficking crime looks like, the most widely used definition of sex trafficking is when (1) someone uses force, fraud, or coercion to cause a commercial sex act, or (2) when someone causes a person under the age of 18 to commit a commercial sex act. This definition, which is used around the world, comes from the U.S. Trafficking Victims Protection Act of 2000 (TVPA). Under TVPA, the penalties for sex trafficking are severe. If convicted, offenders could face up to 20 years in prison. If convicted of trafficking a person under the age of 18, the minimum penalty is 10 years and possibly a life sentence, in prison.

EXACTLY HOW MANY PEOPLE EXPERIENCE TRAFFICKING?

There is no doubt that sex trafficking is a severe violation of human rights that affects many people in the United States and across the world. Unfortunately, it is a challenge to estimate precise trafficking estimates because of difficulties in reporting and victim identification. Many research and advocacy organizations, including the World Health Organization and the United Nations, do not even offer hard prevalence estimates because it is not helpful to pretend there is a solid figure.[3,4] Given the frequent coverage of sex trafficking in the media, it may surprise you to learn there are few systems in the United States through which to aggregate or estimate the number of trafficking victims. For example, some data on suspected trafficking incidents are collected through the National Human Trafficking Hotline, which is managed by the nonprofit Polaris and funded through the Department of Health and Human Services. We know that between 2007 and

2017, the hotline received 178,971 calls, webform submissions, and emails about suspected acts of trafficking (including both labor and sex). Hotline contacts resulted in law enforcement opening 40,200 cases; the vast majority of these cases were for sex trafficking.[5,6] However, many local reports about suspected trafficking are not routed through the national hotline but submitted as crime tips to local law enforcement. Although the U.S. federal government collects some information on the number of trafficking arrests through the Uniform Crime Report published by the Federal Bureau of Investigation, many state and local jurisdictions choose not to report this information.[7] The consequence is that no agency can provide a reliable estimate of either the number of cases opened or prosecutions achieved each year.[8]

However, even if we knew precisely how many trafficking cases were opened, it would still not provide an accurate estimate of the actual number of cases. A significant limitation of using "confirmed cases reported to law enforcement" is that it always leads to undercounting crime. Although the legal definition of trafficking seems explicit, the vast majority of trafficking incidents go unidentified and unprosecuted. One reason why is that it is incredibly difficult for prosecutors to prove that "force," "fraud," or "coercion" took place. Recall the experiences of Alexis and Shanifa. Although these men took advantage of the girls' social and economic vulnerabilities, this type of "coercion" is a tough legal standard to prove in court. Similarly, it is often difficult for law enforcement to distinguish sex trafficking from what appears to be consensual adult sex work—especially for sex trafficking that takes place on websites like Backpage.com and in some of the estimated 9,000 illicit massage brothels[9] advertised on websites like RubMaps.com.

Likewise, teachers, doctors, and other community members may not recognize that someone in their neighborhood is sexually exploited, often because those victims do not appear to match the sensationalized imagery of sex trafficking circulated by some well-meaning journalists and advocates. These images, which typically show pictures of bodies bound with rope, chains, or branded with barcodes, do not represent the experiences of most victims studied.[10] These inaccurate images undermine research and efforts to help community members recognize potential victims. Consequently, the Irina Project was created by the University of North Carolina's School of Media and Journalism to hold journalists, researchers, and advocates responsible for images they use and facts they claim with regards to sex trafficking. The Irina Project monitors news coverage to promote responsible sex-trafficking reporting that is skeptical of wild statistical claims, does not blame victims, respects and amplifies the voices of survivors, and recognizes that trafficking is a complex social problem that intersects with social, political, and economic concerns.

The final challenge in measuring rates of sex trafficking is that, similar to other forms of sexual violence, trafficking is highly stigmatizing. Many victims feel hesitant about reporting abuse.[11, 12] This hesitation is often justified, as the United States has very inconsistent laws from state to state protecting victims—especially for victims under the age of 18. According to the legal scholars at the Office for Victims of Crime, as of 2017, states vary widely in whether they classify the sex trafficking of a minor as a form of child abuse and whether prostitution laws apply to minors. Some states do not allow victims of sex trafficking to apply for crime compensation. Some "rape shield laws" that were enacted to reduce the trauma of cross examination do not apply to sex-trafficking victims; and some states do not allow victims to vacate—or void—any criminal charges they accrued while victims.[13] This last issue is especially troubling as law enforcement may arrest victims, especially minor victims, in order to put them in protective custody, leaving them with a criminal record that will negatively impact them for years to come.

Given the high rates of nonreporting and the stigma of trafficking, researchers characterize sex-trafficking survivors as a "hidden population." When a population is "hidden," it means that researchers cannot use conventional sampling methods, like the ones used by the U.S. Census, to create reliable estimates of population demographics, income trends, and employment rates. To help measure crimes that are frequently underreported, the Bureau of Justice Statistics developed the National Crime Victimization Survey (NCVS). This survey is conducted every six months and asks a nationally representative sample of people about their experiences of being victims of crime. The NCVS has been helpful in estimating crimes like rape and intimate partner violence. Unfortunately, the NCVS does not yet ask questions about either sex trafficking or commercial sexual exploitation, making it an even more significant challenge to create generalizable estimates. Despite these limitations, research into the experiences of trafficking survivors has been useful in clarifying how sex trafficking is a crime of social power, who is vulnerable to sex trafficking, and how exploiters take advantage of vulnerabilities.

TRAFFICKING AS A CRIME THAT TAKES ADVANTAGE OF SOCIAL INEQUALITY

Social inequality is produced when the intersecting social prisms of race, gender, and social class pattern people's access to resources in ways that are unequal. While there are many nuances to the micro-level practices of sex trafficking, fundamentally, it is a transactional and commercial crime that exploits social inequality. Although there are known problems with providing hard numbers on trafficking, some existing research by the International Labour Office cautiously estimates there are 4.8 million victims globally—with children under the age of 18 comprising 21 percent of victims.[14] In looking at confirmed cases globally, researchers at the United Nations found a direct relationship between a country's level of economic development and the age of detected victims. In the least economically developed countries, victims are more likely to be younger.[15] Within North America, adults account for 81 percent of confirmed trafficking victims, and people under the age of 18 account for 19 percent of victims.[16] Key factors that can make one vulnerable to sex trafficking include experiencing entrenched and systemic poverty; having few meaningful educational or employment opportunities; being a sexual minority or gender nonconforming person; and living in places with limited social support structures.[17]

As social inequality drives trafficking, "minoritized" communities are at greatest risk for exploitation. The term *minoritized* draws attention to how dominant social power structures place certain groups into subordinate positions.[18] For example, youth who are involved in the child welfare or criminal justice systems; youth with experiences of childhood sexual abuse or rape—especially if these have not been addressed; runaway and homeless youth (including both minors and youth age 18 and over); and lesbian, gay, bisexual, transgender and queer (LGBTQ) individuals are among those most vulnerable for trafficking.[19,20] In 2017, the National Center for Missing and Exploited Children estimated that about one in seven runaway youth were victims of sex trafficking.[21] Many of these youth may be experiencing homelessness because they are fleeing violent or traumatic homes or foster care; many others identify as LGBTQ and are experiencing homelessness because their families outright reject them. Research with women who experienced sex trafficking as part of the sex trade finds that trafficking victims tend to have histories of childhood abuse and neglect, violence, adulthood abuse, and gang involvement.[22] Women and girls are most likely to be victimized because of their lower social status, but men and boys are also trafficked. For the commercial sexual exploitation of youth specifically, there is evidence that the rate of young male victimization is higher than is typically reported. A prevalence and ethnographic study of the commercial sexual exploitation of children (CSEC) in New York estimated there were approximately 3,946 CSEC victims. Approximately 48 percent identified as female, 45 percent identified as male, and 8 percent identified as transgender.[23]

While poverty, discrimination, and inequality are core mechanisms that make a person vulnerable to sex trafficking, individual traffickers use their relative positions of social power to take advantage of these vulnerabilities. The most common tactics include: (1) *intimidation* by using violence as a display of force; (2) *emotional abuse* through humiliation or by convincing victims no one else cares about them; (3) creating *isolation* through confinement or distrust of others; (4) using *minimizing, denying,* and *blaming* to make light of the situation; (5) using *sexual abuse* to normalize sexual violence or using rape as a weapon of control; (6) leveraging positions of *privilege* by deploying gender or nationality stereotypes to suggest superiority and subservience or using certain victims to control other victims; (7) *economic abuse* through debt bondage or controlling money that a victim earns; and

(8) *coercion* and *threats* of physical harm, shame, or reporting someone to the police or immigration.

Many folks tend to think of all traffickers as "pimps." We should use the term *pimp* with extreme caution, as it is deeply connected to racial and gender stereotypes that often do not reflect what "pimping" looks like in practice. In general, traffickers are often the same nationality, ethnicity, or cultural background of the individuals they abuse—as this allows them to build trust based on shared experiences that allow them to better exploit that person's vulnerabilities.[24] Research has consistently shown that, unlike with potential victims, it is difficult to adequately use demographics to identify or predict who might be facilitating sex trafficking. These persons may be independent or gang-involved; they may be family members, business owners, or other prominent community members; or they may even be sex buyers. To further challenge stereotypes, the presence of a traditional "pimp" is not necessary for commercial sexual exploitation to occur, and in many cases, there may be no pimp at all.[25] Increasingly, young people are approached or lured online into trafficking through social media—many times by someone who "grooms" young people by building trust and seeming harmless. However, sometimes that person is a trusted peer who may also be struggling. The New York CSEC study found that "friends" were often cited as the entry point into the commercial sex trade, with 46 percent of girls, 44 percent of boys, and 68 percent of transgender youth reporting they were recruited through peer influence.[26] Some youth who are desperate may "self-traffick" or engage in "survival sex" to obtain needed food, shelter, or clothing.

WHERE DOES TRAFFICKING HAPPEN?

Trafficking is often portrayed as a transnational social problem,[27] with airports serving as hubs through which victims are transported. In 2017, Congress included a requirement in the Federal Aviation Administration reauthorization bill that required airlines to train flight attendants in how to identify human trafficking.[28] Transnational trafficking certainly happens; however, according to the United Nations' 2016 Global Report on Trafficking in Persons report, within North America broadly, 47 percent of identified trafficking is domestic (within countries) and 16 percent involves crossing borders solely within North America (between the United States, Canada, and Mexico).[29] Of the transnational victims in North America, these are most likely to come from East Asia (16 percent) and Central America and the Caribbean (12 percent).[30] Within the United States, many sex-trafficking cases do not involve the transportation of a person across state or national borders;[31] and 63 percent of identified trafficking victims were citizens of the United States, Canada, or Mexico.[32]

Sex trafficking is also frequently thought of as both a problem relegated to the urban core of cities and as something distinct from consensual sex work. However, studies with survivors reveal there are not separate spheres for consensual sex work and sex trafficking.[33] Instead, trafficking takes place alongside sex work that occurs in the streets, in massage brothels, and in hotels and "no-tels" (a term for apartment or neighborhood brothels). The same basic terminology such as "incall" (where the sex buyer comes to the sex provider's home or hotel) and "outcall" (where the sex provider comes to the sex buyer's home or hotel) also applies.

Increasingly, the broader commercial sex marketplace is digital. Insights from the first and second waves of the National Juvenile Online Victimization Study, funded by the Office of Juvenile Justice and Delinquency Prevention, found teen victims of Internet crimes against children increased from 46 percent in 2000 to 66 percent in 2009—likely due to teens' increasing use of the Internet. As well, researchers found that after 2004, over 75 percent of child sexual exploitation victims were advertised online, compared to only 38 percent of victims before 2004.[34] And the National Center for Missing and Exploited Children (NCMEC) recorded an 846 percent increase in reports of child sex trafficking between 2010 and 2015, which they attribute to the convenience of online sex buying and technology-facilitated exploitation.[35] Of all the child sex-trafficking tips reported to NCMEC during this time, approximately 73 percent were related to postings on Backpage.com.[36]

Beyond forums like Backpage.com, trafficking is digitized through online "rub maps" or "john boards."

These types of websites provide user-generated reviews and information about the location of thousands of massage brothels and the women who work there. While some consensual sex work takes place in these brothels, these are also spaces where women "recruited" into trafficking are coerced or defrauded into providing sex for pay. These women are likely to come from China or South Korea, carry massive debts or are under financial pressure, speak little English, and have no more than a high school education.[37] These women may not have control over their passports or are told they will be deported or publicly shamed if they try to leave. In addition to being indebted to their traffickers for international travel expenses, these women are also charged exorbitant fees for rent, food, and "fines" for breaking the business's "rules." Consequently, it is nearly impossible for these women to escape.

WHAT ABOUT THE BUYERS?

Under the law, it is not only pimps who can be charged with trafficking, but also the people who purchase sex with victims. In 2017, prosecutors in Seattle successfully charged a ring of sex buyers who frequented massage brothels and eventually progressed to negotiating the travel and control of internationally trafficked women.[38] While there may be the perception that purchasing sex is a normative masculine behavior, based on longitudinal data taken from the General Social Survey, we know the prevalence of sex buying in the United States has been trending downward since the Vietnam War era—due, in part, to changing social mores about casual sex.[39] Interestingly, findings from a national survey conducted by academic researchers estimate that only about 14 percent of men in the United States have ever paid for sex, while only 1 percent have paid for sex in the past year.[40]

To justify the harsh legal penalties for trafficking outlined in the TVPA, victim advocacy agencies have at times suggested that the men who purchase sex with trafficking victims are fundamentally different from those who buy sex with consenting adults.[41] However, the buyers of consensual sex work and sex trafficking are often one and the same. One reason for this overlap is that sex buyers are often ill equipped to make determinations about whether the transaction is truly "consensual" or even whether the person is an adult. Through dress and makeup, people engaging in sex work or underage trafficking victims may appear older than they truly are. Differences in race between the buyer and the person from whom sex is being purchased may be another reason. Most sex buyers are likely to purchase sex with someone of the same race as they—except for White men—and research demonstrates that White people tend to overestimate the ages of people of color.[42] Researchers have also found sex buyers simply try to remain willfully ignorant of whether they are engaging in consensual sex work.[43] This is exacerbated by the refusal of some sex buyers to believe that power or coercion shapes how people come to enter the commercial sex marketplace. For example, on the popular sex buyer forum USASexGuide.info, one *hobbyist*—the nickname frequent sex buyers give to themselves—claimed, "It's kinda hard to make somebody do something against their free will nowadays."[44] Similarly, a buyer responding to information that trafficked youth are caught up in the sex trade wrote, "It's their fucking fault for [being] under 18 and offering a romantic date night. Their momma wouldn't approve. That's on them. I simply hang out and go out to dinner with my dates."[45]

Some researchers focus on the clients of sex-trafficking victims and sex workers because they are concerned about the potential for violence. One field-based research conducted by the Urban Institute found that 58 percent of trafficked youth who experienced violence in the sex trade experienced abuse from a buyer, including "withholding payments, disagreeing about prices, refusing to wear condoms, and overstepping physical boundaries."[46] The authors noted that "the degree of these altercations covered the full spectrum of violence and ranged from arguments to threats at gunpoint and rape."[47] A similar study of young trafficked and prostituted persons in New York found that buyers posed the most significant threat of violence, including some who kidnapped and held youths hostage.[48] While much more research is needed on the clients of trafficking victims, these are just a few of the studies that reveal people who purchase sex sometimes abuse their positions of power.[49]

CONTROVERSIAL EFFORTS TO STOP TRAFFICKING THROUGH FOSTA

To raise public awareness about the traumas of sex trafficking, some advocates and politicians have invoked sensational language, including terms like "modern-day slavery" and "sexual slavery." As gender studies scholar Jennifer Musto notes, the use of sensational language to help awareness has turned sex trafficking into a highly polemic issue—especially among academic researchers and pro-sex work advocates frustrated with the inaccurate imagery and wide-ranging prevalence statistics.[50] This tension has exploded since the federal government passed FOSTA-SESTA in April 2018.

In April 2018, the Allow States and Victims to Fight Online Sex Trafficking Act (FOSTA) and Stop Enabling Sex Traffickers Act (SESTA) created an exception to Section 230 of the 1996 Communications Decency Act (CDA), which holds third parties responsible if ads for prostitution are posted on their sites. The CDA previously granted protections to websites and Internet forums from being held responsible for the content their users posted and is widely credited with producing the social media-driven Internet of today.[51] The political and social momentum to pass FOSTA-SESTA was largely spurned by accumulating reports that Backpage.com knowingly facilitated the advertisement of minors on its website by editing ads, deleting incriminating words before publishing ads or manually deleting incriminating language that automated filters missed, and coaching users on how to post "clean ads."[52] Previous attempts to hold Backpage accountable had failed because of Section 230 of CDA. In April 2018, its CEO, Carl Lerrer, agreed to testify against Michael Lacey and Jim Larkin with whom he co-founded the website and with whom he laundered over $500 million in revenue since 2004.[53] Part of the government's indictment included seizure of 10 residences, 25 bank accounts, and 35 website domains.[54] Lerrer pled guilty in California, Texas, and Arizona to money laundering, conspiracy to facilitate prostitution, and to the trafficking of 17 teenaged girls.[55] One of these girls, 16-year-old Desiree Robinson, was beaten and stabbed to death in 2016 after responding to an ad placed by her pimp on Backpage.[56] Another teen advertised on the site was forced to perform sex acts at gun point, choked until she had seizures, and gang raped.[57] "Nadia," another teen who advertised on the site, was stabbed to death.[58] And in 2015 yet another girl advertised on the site was murdered by a sex buyer, who subsequently attempted to burn her body afterward. To make matters worse, Backpage had refused her father's requests to remove her images from Backpage after she died.[59]

Although Backpage.com certainly engaged in troubling practices, many critics argue that FOSTA-SESTA was a poor strategy for actually stopping sex trafficking. During the congressional debate over SESTA, Oregon Senator Ron Wyden, who co-authored Section 230 of the CDA, asserted,

> I stand on the Senate floor today in firm agreement with my colleagues that Congress must do more to combat the scourge of sex trafficking. It is a profound and tragic failure of American institutions that trafficking has not only continued to plague this nation — it has increased. Federal law enforcement has failed to root out and prosecute traffickers, even when they're operating in plain sight. So, too, have internet companies failed when it comes to sex traffickers operating on their platforms.
>
> I fear that the legislation before the Senate will be another failure. I fear it will do more to take down ads than take down traffickers. I fear it will send the bad guys beyond the grasp of law enforcement to the shadowy corners of the dark web, where everyday search engines don't go, but where criminals find safe haven for their monstrous acts.[60]

Many sex workers similarly lamented that FOSTA-SESTA was a flawed sex-trafficking intervention that would result in economic and physical harm. They asserted that the bill further conflated sex trafficking with consensual sex work—putting their systems of financial support and safety at risk.[61] Sex workers were explicitly concerned about losing access to review websites that track "bad dates," which allow sex workers to pre-screen potential clients, as well as options to post ads quickly on commercial sex classified websites, like Backpage and the dating section of Craigslist.

Within the first six months after passage of FOSTA-SESTA, its critics seemed to be correct. Because shutting down websites did little to address the demand for commercial sex, the industry moved elsewhere. Digital technology is a normalized facet of modern life, so it is likely that FOSTA-SESTA helped speed the push of trafficking onto encrypted, peer-to-peer platforms, such as Facebook Messenger or WhatsApp. Because these platforms are encrypted, it is impossible for persons outside that trusted peer-to-peer network to monitor conversations or investigate exploitation. From a safety standpoint, some law enforcement and researchers appreciated the visibility of centralized digital forums like Backpage.com because the visibility led to productive tips and investigations of trafficking.[62] While some other commercial sex web forums, like the escorts section of Craigslist, voluntarily shuttered after FOSTA-SESTA, many have remained open. Some of these websites simply ignore the law, while others have made it more difficult for users based in the United States to access the site without using a virtual private network that allows users to manipulate their IP addresses to appear they are in a different country.

What is clear is that FOSTA-SESTA is magnifying the digital divide between those with the economic and technological resources to continue to access commercial sex websites and those without those resources. Many of the websites that remain are high-end escort sites that are costly to post on and require that sex workers adopt the trappings of a high socioeconomic status.[63] Numerous websites have popped up—many of which are financial scams—to fill the gap that Backpage left. Pimps have also swooped in to capitalize on the post–FOSTA-SESTA environment. Laura LeMoon, a sex-trafficking survivor and cofounder of Safe Night Access Project Seattle reported that "[pimps] are taking advantage of the situation sex workers are in. This is why I say FOSTA-SESTA has actually increased trafficking. I've had pimps contacting me. They're leeches. They make money off of [sex workers'] misfortune."[64] Those who are most marginalized, such as sex workers who are LGBTQ+, people of color, and low income, will always absorb the highest costs of the new digital frontier. Unfortunately, since passage of FOSTA-SESTA, law enforcement agencies across the United States have also reported an increase in street prostitution—a space that is more dangerous for both trafficking victims and sex workers because it is tougher to vet clients.[65] Street prostitution is also overwhelmingly pimp-controlled. While FOSTA-SESTA has had many negative consequences, Backpage.com was hardly a model for sex worker empowerment. It charged its users large sums of money to post ads, and it continued to raise its rates after gaining its market monopoly when Craigslist closed its escort section in 2010. Backpage executives made hundreds of millions of dollars off the criminalization of prostitution. Perhaps the closure of the website could be viewed as an opportunity for sex workers to design a safe and more democratic platform—one they have more social and economic control over.

Because sex trafficking is a social problem driven by social inequality, relying solely on criminal justice solutions and Internet policing will ultimately be insufficient to address the problem of sex trafficking. There must be robust community-based interventions to address the inequalities that facilitate sex trafficking. This will entail (1) strengthening educational and intensive one-on-one case management for those vulnerable to sex trafficking; (2) creating meaningful educational and economic opportunities for those vulnerable to sex trafficking as well as sex-trafficking survivors; and (3) improving early intervention systems to help prevent those who are known to be at risk for trafficking from becoming victims. It will also be beneficial to create opportunities for restorative justice programs that seek to center survivors in creating perpetrator accountability, as criminal justice prosecution too often fails to either help survivors or restore their communities. We should also focus on making it easier for victims to have their criminal records related to sex work or trafficking expunged, so they can more easily access economic opportunities. As most sex workers believe sex trafficking is wrong and know the commercial sex market better than anyone, they too are an undertapped resource for helping trafficking victims leave "the life."[66]

Foremost, we should listen to and elevate the voices of those who have experienced trafficking or have been engaged in commercial sex—especially when those voices have diverse or conflicting experiences. Survivor leadership is critical. One such successful program is New York's Girls Educational and Mentoring Services (GEMS). Founded in 1998, GEMS is the nation's leading organization that empowers girls and young women who have been commercially sexually exploited or trafficked domestically. The organization supports survivors in "gaining independence, safety, education, employment, and economic sustainability for themselves and their children."[67] It helps survivors become self-sufficient, empowered self-advocates through their Victim, Survivor, Leader™ program. GEMS also co-wrote the nation's first safe harbor bill that stopped the criminalization of commercially sexually exploited children. The National Survivor Network (NSN) is another program that offers a platform for survivor-led leadership, peer-to-peer mentoring, and empowerment. NSN formed in 2011 to build a national antitrafficking movement, with survivors at the forefront. It has over 200 members from 37 states and three Canadian provinces.[68] In 2017, it launched its peer-to-peer mentoring pilot program to help survivors develop public speaking, presentation, and personal advocacy skills to help survivors achieve their personal and professional goals. It also sends survivor-leaders to Washington, D.C., to meet with members of Congress, the Department of State, the Department of State Bureau of Consular Affairs, the Department of Justice Human Trafficking Prosecution Unit, and the Department of Health and Human Services' Office on Human Trafficking to promote survivor-centered policies and interventions into trafficking. As our understanding and approaches to sex trafficking across the country are still evolving, there are many opportunities to craft more survivor-informed responses.

NOTES

1. Backpage.com was a website that allowed anyone to post advertisements for commercial sex for a fee.
2. Fonrouge, G., Cohen, S., and Gonen, Y. (April 16, 2018). "Sex Trafficking Survivors Reveal How NYC Pimps Prey on the Young and Vulnerable." NYCpost.com. https://nypost.com/2018/04/16/ex-sex-slaves-reveal-how-nyc-pimps-prey-on-the-young-and-vulnerable.

3. UNODC, Global Report on Trafficking in Persons 2016 (United Nations publication, Sales No. E.16.IV.6).

4. Stransky, M., and Finkelhor, D. (2008). *Factsheet: How Many Juveniles Are Involved in Prostitution in the U.S.?* The Crimes Against Children Research Center. Retrieved July 31, 2008, from http://www.unh.edu/ccrc/prostitution/Juvenile_Prostitution_factsheet.pdf.

5. National Human Trafficking Hotline. (2018). *Hotline Statistics.* Available at: https://humantraffickinghotline.org/states [accessed 6 December 2018].

6. National Human Trafficking Hotline. (2018).

7. United States Department of State. (2017). *2017 Trafficking in Persons Report*—United States of America. Available at: https://www.state.gov/documents/organization/271339.pdf [accessed 6 December 2018].

8. United States Department of State. (2018). *2018 Trafficking in Persons Report*—United States of America. Available at: https://www.state.gov/documents/organization/282798.pdf [accessed 26 December 2018].

9. Polaris. (2017). *Human Trafficking in Illicit Massage Businesses.* Washington, DC. Available at: https://polarisproject.org/sites/default/files/Full_Report_Human_Trafficking_in_Illicit_Massage_Businesses.pdf [accessed 8 December 2018].

10. United Nations Global Initiative to Fight Human Trafficking. (2008). *012 Workshop: The Role of the Media in Building Images.* The Vienna Forum to Fight Human Trafficking 13–15 February 2008, Austria Center Vienna Background Paper. https://www.unodc.org/documents/human-trafficking/2008/BP012TheRoleoftheMedia.pdf.

11. National Institute of Justice. (2016). Improving the Investigation and Prosecution of State and Local Human Trafficking Cases." Available at: http://nij.gov/topics/crime/human-trafficking/pages/improving-investigation-and-prosecution-of-human-trafficking-cases.aspx [accessed 6 December 2018].

12. Gerassi, L. (2015). From Exploitation to Industry: Definitions, Risks, and Consequences of Domestic Sexual Exploitation and Sex Work among Women and Girls. *Journal of Human Behavior in the Social Environment, 25*(6), 1–15.

13. Office for Victims of Crime. (2018). *State Laws.* Available at: https://www.ovcttac.gov/taskforceguide/eguide/1-understanding-human-trafficking/14-human-trafficking-laws/state-laws [accessed 26 December 2018].

14. International Labor Office. (2017). "Global Estimates of Modern Slavery: Forced Labour and Forced Marriage." Geneva: ILO Publications. Available at: https://www.ilo.org/wcmsp5/groups/public/@dgreports/@dcomm/documents/publication/wcms_575479.pdf [accessed 6 December 2018]. See page 10.

15. United States Department of State. (2015). *2015 Trafficking in Persons Report*—United States of America. Available at: https://www.state.gov/documents/organization/245365.pdf [accessed 6 December 2018]. See page 25.

16. United States Department of State. (2015). See page 90.

17. Carson, L., & Edwards, K. (2011). Prostitution and Sex Trafficking: What Are the Problems Represented to Be? A Discursive Analysis of Law and Policy in Sweden and Victoria, Australia. *Australian Feminist Law Journal, 34*(1), 63–87.

18. Muñoz, J. E. (2009). *Cruising Utopia: The Then and There of Queer Futurity.* New York: New York University Press.

19. United States Department of State. (2015).

20. National Center for Missing and Exploited Children. (2017). *Child Sex Trafficking Overview.* Available at: http://www.missingkids.org/theissues/trafficking#overview [accessed 6 December 2018].

21. National Center for Missing and Exploited Children. (2017).

22. See Hickle, K., & Roe-Sepowitz, D. (2017). "'Curiosity and a Pimp": Exploring Sex Trafficking Victimization in Experiences of Entering Sex Trade Industry Work among Participants in a Prostitution Diversion Program. *Women and Criminal Justice, 27*(2), 122–38. See also Gerassi, L. (2015). From Exploitation to Industry: Definitions, Risks, and Consequences of Domestic Sexual Exploitation and Sex Work among Women and Girls. *Journal of Human Behavior in the Social Environment, 25*(6), 1–15.

23. Curtis, R., Terry, K., Dank, M., Dombrowski, K. and Khan, B. (2008). *The Commercial Sexual Exploitation of Children in New York City. Volume One: The CSEC Population in New York City: Size, Characteristics, and Needs.* Final report submitted to the National Institute of Justice. New York: Center for Court Innovation and John Jay College of Criminal Justice.

24. See Hughes, D. M., & Denisova, T. A. (2001). The transnational political criminal nexus of trafficking in women from Ukraine. *Trends in Organized Crime, 6*(3–4), 43–67. See also Bales, K., & Lize, S. (2005). "Trafficking in Persons in the United States." Croft Institute for International Studies, University of Mississippi.

25. Curtis et al. (2008).

26. Curtis et al. (2008).

27. McCartney, Scott. (December 13, 2017). "A New Push Against Human Trafficking on Flights." The Wall Street journal.com. Available at: https://www.wsj.com/articles/a-new-push-against-human-trafficking-on-flights-1513178860 [accessed 6 December 2018].

28. H.R.302—FAA Reauthorization Act of 2018. 115th Congress.

29. UNODC, Global Report on Trafficking in Persons 2016 (United Nations publication, Sales No. E.16.IV.6). [accessed 6 December 2018]. See page 94.

30. UNODC, Global Report on Trafficking in Persons 2016. See page xxx.

31. United States Department of State. (2015). See pages 89–97.

32. United States Department of State. (2015). See page 94.

33. See Dank, M., Yahner, J., Madden, K., Banuelos, I., Yu, L., Ritchie, A., and Conner, B. (2015). *Surviving the Streets of New York.* Washington, DC: The Urban Institute. See also Popkin, S. J., Scott, M. M., & Galvez, M. (2016). *Impossible Choices: Teens and Food Insecurity in America. Urban Institute and Feeding America.* Washington, DC: The Urban Institute. Available at: http://www. urban. org/sites/default/files/alfresco/publication-pdfs/2000914-Impossible-Choices-Teens-and-Food-Insecurity-in-America.pdf [accessed 6 December 2018]. See page21. Also Swaner, R., Labriola, M., Rempel, M., Walker, A., & Spadafore, J. (2016). *Youth Involvement in the Sex Trade: A National Study.* New York: Center for Court Involvement.

34. Bouche, V. (2018). *Survivor Insights: The Role of Technology in Domestic Minor Sex Trafficking.* Retrieved from New York, New York: http://27l51l1qnwey246mkc1vzqg0-wpengine.netdna-ssl.com/wp-content/uploads/2018/06/Thorn_Survivor_Insights_061118.pdf [accessed 6 December 2018]. See page 7.

35. Human Trafficking Investigation Hearing. (2015). *United States Senate Subcommittee on Investigations Committee on Homeland Security and Governmental Affairs.* Washington, DC. Available at: https://www.gpo.gov/fdsys/pkg/CHRG-114shrg98445/pdf/CHRG-114shrg98445.pdf [accessed 8 December 2018]. See page 2.

36. Backpage.com was closed by the Department of Justice in April 2018.

37. Polaris. (2017). See page 19.

38. Burleigh, Nina. (21 December 2017). "Tech Pros Bought Sex Trafficking Victims by Using Amazon and Microsoft Work Emails." *Newsweek.* Available at: https://www.newsweek.com/metoo-microsoft-amazon-trafficking-prostitution-sex-silicon-valley-755611 [accessed 8 December 2018].

39. Reyes, E. A. (2 November 2013). "Fewer Men Are Paying for Sex, Survey Suggests." *Los Angeles Times.* Available at: http://articles.latimes.com/2013/nov/02/nation/la-na-paying-for-sex-20131102 [accessed 8 December 2018].

40. Monto, M. A., & Milrod, C. (2014). Ordinary or Peculiar Men? Comparing the Customers of Prostitutes with a Nationally Representative Sample of Men. *International Journal of Offender Therapy and Comparative Criminology, 58*(7), 802–20.

41. Swaner, R., Labriola, M., Rempel, M., Walker, A., & Spadafore, J. (2016). *Youth involvement in the sex trade: A national study.* New York: Center for Court Involvement.

42. Shelby, R., and Trouteaud, A. (2018). *Sex Buyer Momentum.* Working Paper.

43. The Schapiro Group (2010). *Men Who Buy Sex with Adolescent Girls: A Scientific Research Study.* Atlanta, GA: The Schapiro Group.

44. March 9, 2017. USASexGuide.info forum. Retrieved from http://www.usasexguide.info/forum/showthread.php?7463-News-and-Media-Reports.

45. November 27, 2016. USASexGuide.info forum. Retrieved from http://www.usasexguide.info/forum/showthread.php?7463-News-and-Media-Reports.

46. Dank et al. (2015). See page 40.

47. Dank et al. (2015). See page 40.

48. Curtis et al. (2008). Report Submitted to the National Institute of Justice. NIJ 2005-LX-FX-001.

49. Chang, H., & Weng, Y. (2015). Working in the Dark: A Look at the Violence Risk of the Street Prostitution Service. *Journal of Social Service Research, 41*(4), 545–55. Lowman, J. (2000). Violence and the Outlaw Status of (Street) Prostitution in Canada. *Violence Against Women, 6*(9), 987. Monto, M. A. (2004). Female Prostitution, Customers, and Violence. *Violence Against Women, 10*(2), 160–88. Nixon, K., Tutty, L., Downe, P., Gorkoff, K., & Ursel, J. (2002). The Everyday Occurrence: Violence in the Lives of Girls Exploited through Prostitution. *Violence Against Women, 8*(9), 1016–43. Raphael, J., & Shapiro, D. L. (2004). Violence in Indoor and Outdoor Prostitution Venues. *Violence Against Women, 10*(2), 126–39. https://doi.org/10.1177/1077801203260529. Romero-Daza, N., Weeks, M., & Singer, M. (2003). Nobody Gives a Damn If I Live or Die: Violence, Drugs, and Street-Level Prostitution in Inner-City Hartford, Connecticut. *Medical Anthropology, 22*(3), 233–59. Williamson, C., & Folaron, G. (2001). Violence, Risk, and Survival Strategies of street prostitution. *Western Journal of Nursing Research, 23*(5), 463–75. https://doi.org/10.1177/019394590102300505

50. Musto, J. (2009). What's in a Name? Conflations and Contradictions in Contemporary U.S. Discourses on Human Trafficking. *Women's Studies International Forum, 32*(4), 281–87.

51. Lecher, C. (2018). "Sen. Ron Wyden on Breaking Up Facebook, New Neutrality, and the Law that Built the Internet." The Verge.com. (24 July 2018). Available at: https://www.theverge.com/2018/7/24/17606974/oregon-senator-ron-wyden-interview-internet-section-230-net-neutrality [accessed 25 October 2018].

52. U.S. Senate Permanent Subcommittee on Investigations. (2018). *Backpage.com's Knowing Facilitation of Online Sex Trafficking.* Staff Report. Committee on Homeland Security and Governmental Affairs. Washington, DC. Available at: https://www.mccaskill.senate.gov/imo/media/doc/2017.01.10%20Backpage%20Report.pdf [accessed 25 October 2018].

53. Jackman, T. (2018). "Backpage CEO Carl Ferrer Pleads Guilty in Three States, Agrees to Testify Against Other Website Officials." *Washington Post* (13 April 2018). Available at: https://www.washingtonpost.com/news/true-crime/wp/2018/04/13/backpage-ceo-carl-ferrer-pleads-guilty-in-three-states-agrees-to-testify-against-other-website-officials/?noredirect=on&utm_term=.78366a274157 [accessed 26 October 2018].

54. Jackman (2018).
55. Williams, T. (2017). "Backpage's Sex Ads Are Gone. Child Trafficking? Hardly." *New York Times* (11 March 2017). Available at: https://www.nytimes.com/2017/03/11/us/backpage-ads-sex-trafficking.html [accessed 25 October 2018].
56. Jackman, T, & O'Connell, J. (2017). "16-year-old Was Found Beaten, Stabbed to Death after Being Advertised as Prostitute on Backpage." *Washington Post* (11 July 2017). Available at: https://www.washingtonpost.com/local/public-safety/how-a-16-year-old-went-from-backpage-to-prostitution-to-homicide-victim/2017/07/10/72eca33c-5f55-11e7-a4f7-af34fc1d9d39_story.html?utm_term=.1bbef0949dd0 [accessed 26 October 2018].
57. Lynch, S. (2018). "Backpage.com Founders, Others Indicted on Prostitution-Related Charges." Reuters.com. (9 April 2018). Available at: https://www.reuters.com/article/us-usa-justice-backpage/backpage-com-founders-others-indicted-on-prostitution-related-charges-idUSKBN1HG-2ZZ [accessed 26 October 2018].
58. Lynch (2018).
59. Lynch (2018).
60. Wyden, R. (2018). "Floor Remarks: CDA 230 and SESTA." Medium.com. (21 March 2018). Available at: https://medium.com/@RonWyden/floor-remarks-cda-230-and-sesta-32355d669a6e [Accessed 25 October 2018].
61. McCombs, Emily. (May 17, 2018). "This Bill Is Killing Us: 9 Sex Workers on Their Lives in the Wake of FOSTA." HuffingtonPost.com. Retrieved October 25, 2018 from https://www.huffingtonpost.com/entry/sex-workers-sesta-fosta_us_5ad0d7d0e4b0edca2cb964d9.
62. Williams (2017).
63. McCombs (May 17, 2018).
64. Cole, S. (2018). "Pimps Are Preying on Sex Workers Pushed Off the Web Because of FOSTA-SESTA." Motherboard. (30 April 2018). Available at: https://motherboard.vice.com/en_us/article/bjpqvz/fosta-sesta-sex-work-and-trafficking [accessed 26 October 2018].
65. Alptraum, L. (2018). "The Internet Made Sex Work Safer. Now Congress Has Forced It Back in the Shadows." The Verge (1 May 2018). Available at: https://www.theverge.com/2018/5/1/17306486/sex-work-online-fosta-backpage-communications-decency-act [accessed 26 October 2018].
66. Sex Workers Outreach Project. (2018). "Sex Work and Sex Trafficking." SWOPBehindBars.org. Available at: https://swopbehindbars.org/amnesty-international-policy-to-decriminalize-sex-work/the-difference-between-sex-work-and-sex-trafficking [accessed 25 October 2018].
67. Girls Education & Mentoring Services. (2018). "Our Mission." Available at: https://www.gems-girls.org/our-mission/ [accessed 25 October 2018].
68. National Survivor Network. (2017). "2017 Highlights from the National Survivor Network." Available at: https://nationalsurvivornetwork.org [accessed 26 October 2018].

CHAPTER 7

SOCIAL PROBLEMS RELATED TO MEDIA

The consumption of media has become an increasingly important part of Americans' lives. In 2018, the average American adult spent over 11 hours per day interacting with media (including radio, TV, and Internet sources).[1] Social problems related to media present an interesting case from a sociological perspective, as its relationship to social problems is varied and complex. This chapter discusses a wide variety of ways media plays a role in social problems: how it can be the location where social problems occur (such as cyberbullying, harassment, and the rise of online hate groups); the ways that we learn about social problems and social issues (in accurate and inaccurate ways, such as through "fake news" and stereotypes in the media), and how it can be a social problem in and of itself (through the consolidation of sources of information by a few powerful groups).

Given our increased consumption of media, it's important to understand who is generating the messages we receive. The sources of media may seem varied and diverse compared to a few generations ago—think of all the channels, news organizations, and forms of social media we have now—but Desmond Goss argues that in fact, our media landscape has become increasingly homogeneous as media companies have consolidated and monopolized. The effects of this consolidation are far-reaching in terms of the messages, values, and representation of diversity presented in different forms of media, but also for consumers' rights related to pricing, targeted advertising, and equal access to the Internet. Maanvi Singh discusses the value of diversity in media (television shows, in particular), reviewing research indicating that exposure to diverse, multifaceted characters can increase tolerance and temper prejudiced attitudes, whereas consuming media with one-dimensional, restrictive depictions of minority group members can result in less tolerant attitudes.

---

1   Nielsen Company. 2018. "Time Flies: U.S. Adults Now Spend Nearly Half a Day Interacting with Media." Retrieved on March 21, 2019, from https://www.nielsen.com/us/en/insights/news/2018/time-flies-us-adults-now-spend-nearly-half-a-day-interacting-with-media.html.

We learn about social problems—the prevalence, causes, consequences, and the communities most likely to be affected—through the media. But does the media give us an accurate picture of the nature of social problems? Looking through the lens of media coverage of crime, Gary W. Potter and Victor E. Kappeler argue that the media's inaccurate portrayal of crime overemphasizes coverage of uncommon violent crimes that occur between strangers and also offers racially biased depictions of victims and perpetrators. These messages give viewers a false and often racially biased understanding of crime, which raises fear levels and the likelihood of reactionary legislation, policies, and punitive approaches to law enforcement. Applying a sociological perspective means we must not view these messages simply as "entertainment" but instead critically examine their content and its consequences.

Since the 2016 presidential campaign and election, there has been a rise in the presence of fake news stories—conspiracy theories, hoaxes, misinformation, and lies—as well as public figures decrying media coverage they disagree with as "fake news." But how do these stories spread, and why do they have such reach? Robinson Meyer examines research conducted on Twitter posts of fake news which revealed that fake news spreads faster than true news stories. This occurs despite the fact that people spreading true news have a "running start" because they tend to have more followers. Meyer discusses the reasons behind this spread and its possible consequences for an informed democratic citizenry. Alicia Shepard also discusses the rise of fake news, emphasizing that without the traditional "gatekeepers" in the media that existed in previous generations, it is up to the consumer to determine whether the news they are consuming is reliable and believable. To this end, Shepard gives us suggestions for how to determine whether or not the information we are reading is credible.

Alt-right, White supremacist, and White nationalist groups have long used the media to promote racist and anti-Semitic propaganda, but social media networks and websites such as Reddit and 4chan have increasingly become weapons in these racist campaigns, resulting in the increased visibility of hate groups. Jessie Daniels discusses how White supremacist organizations have used the media opportunistically. Through their use of social media, Internet algorithms, and new technology, these organizations promote their ideology and shift political conversations in ways that open the door to White nationalist ideas. As these groups garner more support from wealthy and powerful people, including politicians and other public figures, it's important for us to consider how these forms of media can be used to promote messages that are harmful to less powerful groups and to our democracy. Social media and the Internet can also be used to bully and harass individuals, as Maria Konnivoka discusses. The ubiquity of social media means that it is harder to escape bullying and harassment campaigns and that it can impact adults as often as children and teens. It can also mean that it is harder to identify and intervene when bullying is happening.

Finally, we turn our attention to the ways in which different groups are presented in the media. Nancy Wang Yuen looks at the representation of racial and ethnic minorities on TV and in popular movies, describing both the lack of representation and the stereotypical roles that African American, Latinx, and Asian American actors and actresses are forced to play in order to have careers and win prestigious awards. Stereotypical representations can exacerbate existing racial prejudices and fears, and when viewers are not in regular contact with people in a given group—which happens frequently, given America's level of racial segregation—these stereotypes can begin to stand in for reality in viewers' minds. The consumption of media also has an impact on children, as researchers from Indiana University found. Children compare themselves to what they see on the screen, and for children of color and girls, those images are often negative and result in decreased self-esteem.[2]

2   Indiana University Media Relations. 2012. "Study Finds TV Can Decrease Self-Esteem in Children, Except White Boys." Retrieved on March 21, 2019, from http://newsinfo.iu.edu/news-archive/22445.html.

JOSH GOLIN

Josh Golin is the executive director of the Campaign for a Commercial-Free Childhood.

What organization are you currently working with, and how would you describe its mission?

The Campaign for a Commercial-Free Childhood's (CCFC) mission is to educate the public about commercialism's impact on kids and to advocate for the end of child-targeted marketing.

What are your general duties?

As executive director, I oversee our communications strategy, our advocacy campaigns and policy work, and program to reduce children's screen time. I also am responsible for the financial sustainability of the organization and serve as our primary spokesperson.

How did you first become interested in this type of activism? Who was your inspiration?

My previous work as a teacher made me realize that childhood was being transformed by corporate marketing—and that kids' self-image and habits were being shaped by people who cared nothing about their well-being. My inspiration was Ralph Nader who has been both fearless and tireless in 50 years of

activism. Reading *No Logo* by Naomi Klein was also a transformative experience.

As an activist, what are your current goals?

First, stopping Mattel from releasing Hello Barbie, a doll that records, stores, and analyzes kids' conversations. Second, ending the exploitative practice of McTeachers' Nights, where teachers "work" at a local McDonald's and encourage their students to eat there in hopes of raising much-needed funds for their schools. Third, helping parents and caregivers understand the importance of keeping babies screen-free for their first two years of their lives.

What strategies do you use to enact social change?

Because CCFC is a small organization, we depend on creating campaigns that are interesting to both traditional media and people on social media who can amplify our concerns. We try to generate pressure on corporations so they understand that while engaging in practices that are harmful to children may generate short-term profits, they risk doing long-term damage to their brand.

What are the major challenges activists in your field face?

The biggest challenge is that we're trying to influence the actions of huge multibillion dollar corporations that have budgets that are hundreds or thousands of times bigger than ours, and the power and access that comes along with that money. I combat fatigue by savoring every small victory, by recognizing that things would be considerably worse if we weren't doing the work we were doing, and by spending as much time as possible talking to people who appreciate our work and to other activists.

What are major misconceptions the public has about activism in general and your issue specifically?

I think people tend to think of "activism" as the tactics they are most familiar with, whether it's street demonstrations, social media, etc. But there is no set playbook, and one of the most important things is to think strategically about who you are and what your strengths are and how to best leverage those strengths to bring about change.

Why should students get involved in your line of activism?

Because if corporations completely take over childhood, we will have generations of children who are more concerned about their own material desires than about community or making change in the world. Giving children the time and space to grow up to be critical thinkers is important no matter what your cause or issue is.

What would you consider to be your greatest success as an activist (in your current area of activism)?

We stopped Mattel from releasing Aristotle, the first always-on Amazon Echo type device designed specifically for babies and young children. Mattel designed the device to displace essential parenting functions, like reading bedtime stories and soothing a crying infant. The company hoped to use Aristotle to collect a wealth of data about young children that it could share with its corporate partners. We organized experts in child development and privacy, key lawmakers, and more than 20,000 parents to urge Mattel not to release Aristotle. After a string of bad publicity, Mattel relented and agreed not to release it.

If an individual has little money and time, are there other ways they can contribute?

Yes, we always make our campaigns and resources easy to share with friends and family. Spreading the word to others is a no-cost way to get involved that doesn't take a lot of time.

DESMOND GOSS

28. A MODERN EMPIRE
The Concentration of Media

Spend a day surfing the Internet, watching TV, or listening to the radio and it may feel like your sources of information and entertainment are limitless. But Goss illustrates that this is a ruse and that actually a minute number of companies control the vast amount of content for all types of media. Goss provides historical and structural reasons for increasing consolidation and describes some of the many costs to consumers and to the society. He concludes by pointing to opportunities for change that may already be within reach.

What are your favorite television shows? Do you frequently succumb to the guilty pleasure of reality TV programs like *The Bachelor* or *Love and Hip-Hop*? Are you partial to the heartwarming story-lines of sitcoms like *Black-ish* or *The Big Bang Theory*? Are you drawn to the exciting drama of series like *This Is Us* or *Stranger Things*? Whatever your preference, there seems to be a great diversity in the kinds of programs to which one can "tune in and check out." However, behind the small screen, another world exists. This world is not one of artistry or comedy, nor is it one of drama or thrill. There are no spinning oversized red chairs or cannibalistic zombies. There are no waltzing C-list celebrities, awkward millennials on nude dates, or superheroes-in-waiting. There is only the bottom line: the venerable cultural power of corporate media economy. Beyond the cornucopia of media images on your television, tablet, or computer screen, there are but a few corporations in control.

In the Age of Information, media is everywhere. Billboards, clothing, websites, film, radio, magazines, newspapers, video games, and television all offer mechanisms for the communication of cultural messages. In fact, on average, we spend 70 percent of our day consuming digital media.[1] Clearly, from the mundane to the monumental, media plays a pivotal role in shaping our lived experiences. As such, the power to control media is an immense power indeed. In theory, competition between media enterprises creates a virtual marketplace of ideas that reflect any manner of sociocultural concepts. But as fewer and fewer corporations own more and more media outlets in the United States (and increasingly around the world), the power to control media communication becomes concentrated into the hands of just a few media conglomerates. In 1983, fifty companies owned 90 percent of North American media.[2] Today, nearly the same proportion is owned by just six companies: Comcast (including Universal and Marvel Comics), AT&T (including DC Comics and Cartoon Network), Disney (including ABC and Pixar), Viacom (including MTV and Paramount Pictures), 21st Century Fox (including NatGeo and Fox News), and CBS (including NFL.com and Showtime).[3]

Original to *Focus on Social Problems: A Contemporary Reader*.

THE CONGLOMERATION PROCESS: INTEGRATION AND MERGERS

Media monopolization is not an accident. Underlying this process is an increasing reliance on a consumerist model of media communication where audiences are conceptualized as consumers. This profit-driven model has produced enormous financial gain for corporate media owners. For example, advertising revenue reached an astonishing $309 billion in 2009 during the height of the Great Recession.[4] And, as ownership continues to concentrate among fewer and fewer owners, media communication profits continue to climb. Media conglomeration means more money in fewer hands, as separate companies are consolidated through integration and mergers. Media companies "vertically" integrate by purchasing the companies that supply them goods or to whom they supply. Thus, a cable provider may also possess several television channels, as Time Warner Cable owns HBO, CNN, TBS, and Cartoon Network.[5] "Horizontal" integration, on the other hand, involves purchasing companies that produce similar goods but at lower prices or different qualities. For example, a large movie production enterprise may purchase an independent film company. When companies merge, two or more enterprises become one, and media control that was once dispersed between competitors is now centralized into a single entity, as in the 2000 AOL and Time Warner merger.

No matter the method, the process of corporate conglomeration always has the same result: more money (and power) into fewer hands. Although the deregulatory character of free-market economies may encourage these proceedings, various consumer watchdogs have raised red flags in opposition, though relatively few have had some measure of success. In the landmark Hollywood Antitrust Case of 1948, for example, the U.S. Supreme Court ruled that the "Big Five" movie production studios (Paramount, Loew's/MGM, 20th Century Fox, Warner Bros., and RKO) violated the antitrust law by vertically integrating movie theaters. Prior to this ruling, film production companies were free to restrict access to the films they produced to those theaters under their ownership. As the studios purchased more and more independent theaters, there was more interference from executive bodies into the filmmaking process, less film diversity, and less variety in price. Thus, movie studios had

essentially monopolized the film industry. The Court's decision effectively reversed this trend, thereby marking the beginning of a popular independent film movement and the end of the "Golden Age" of the Big Five's unfettered corporate dominance in the film industry.[6]

Despite limited attempts by the federal government to prevent monopolization, media conglomeration would not be possible without governmental support and scaffolding. The increasing consolidation of media money and power is a product of the cooperative efforts of government and corporate entities concerned with building a society where the needs of free-market capitalism trump the protectionist functions of government intervention. Deregulating industries and privatizing traditionally public organizations are crucial aspects of such neoliberal construction. Incidents like the Hollywood Antitrust Case, which immediately followed the Great Depression, capitalized on the protectionist sentiment that was widespread at the height of the American welfare state. During this era, U.S. citizens saw the advent of federally mandated minimum wages, the Social Security Administration, and the dramatic expansion of labor unions. Similarly, other federal endeavors were undertaken to prevent corporate misconduct and monopolization of markets, such as the creation of the Securities and Exchange Commission, the Federal Trade Commission (FTC), and the Sherman Antitrust Act, under which the above-mentioned film corporates were tried in the Hollywood Antitrust Case.

However, as the conservative turn of the 1970s and 1980s dismantled the welfare state, the power of government regulatory bodies was dramatically diminished—a trend that continues today. For example, in 1980 there were approximately 65 FTC antitrust investigations, whereas in 2009, at the height of the global economic crisis, there were only seven.[7] In 2017, there were 34.[8] The controversial *Citizens United* ruling exemplifies a culmination of neoliberal corporate ideology because the Supreme Court ruled that corporations can no longer be restricted by political campaign finance limits.[9] In essence, corporations, including media enterprises, now have a political incentive to monopolize the market. As long as corporate media continues to grow through integration and mergers, media monopolization could have serious implications for diversity in the media marketplace.

THE EFFECTS OF MEDIA CONCENTRATION BY INDUSTRY

BOOKS

In 1980, only 11 corporations received more than half the revenue from national book sales. By 2009, the number of corporations controlling half the $23.9 billion market had fallen to just five: Bertelsmann (owner of Random House), Pearson, Hachette, News Corp (HarperCollins), and CBS (Simon & Schuster). As a student, you are intimately involved in the corporate concentration of book publishers through the purchase of textbooks. In 2013, the textbook publisher Pearson, the top publisher by revenue, garnered $9.33 billion in sales, almost more than the next two largest publishers combined.[10] Clearly, the textbook industry is booming . . . but at whose expense? Publishers perpetuate high prices by serializing textbooks (adding editions) and bundling them with software packages. The average cost of textbooks for undergraduate students is approximately $1,200 per academic year. One comprehensive survey demonstrated that, with costs this high, some 65 percent of students forgo purchasing one or more required texts, sometimes at the expense of their academic performance.[11]

Moreover, textbooks are at the center of formal education in many contexts, so when so few textbook publishers control so much of the market, there are political implications for curriculum development. Such effects are particularly salient when publishers act as a conduit for state indoctrination. In Hong Kong, for example, government education institutions have implemented a curriculum of "moral and national education" that promotes patriotism while condemning the republican principles of democracy.[12] A major tool in this educational reconstruction is the utilization of textbooks "that promote blind nationalism."[13] (Some of these textbooks are published by Pearson Hong Kong.)[14] In the United States, Texas has frequently been at the center of similar controversies. Conservative politicians, citizens, and lobbies have repeatedly used their influence to encourage governmental education entities to support only those textbooks that espouse conservative ideologies.[15] In the past, these entities have bent to the conservative will about topics like evolution, sex education, war history, the civil rights movement, gay and lesbian culture, gender equality, Islam, Christianity, capitalism, and communism. Importantly, the Texan textbook controversy is not sequestered by state boundary. Texas is the largest purchaser of K–12 textbooks in the country. As such, publishers edit textbooks for Texas schools, which they then market elsewhere around the country. Thus, following the actions of a Texas school board, students in New York may read that the religious figure Moses is also a "founding father" of the United States of America or that chattel slaves were simply "workers."[16]

FILM AND TELEVISION

Despite the Supreme Court's ruling on the Hollywood Antitrust Act of 1948, a few major film companies still produce a vast majority of American movies. In 2017, just six studios (Warner, Disney, Universal, 20th Century Fox, Sony, and Viacom) accounted for nearly half of the revenue from the domestic film market.[17] In the television industry, 3,762 companies control 30 percent of cable television, whereas the remaining 70 percent is controlled by just six corporations (General Electric, News Corp, Disney, Viacom, Time Warner, and CBS).[18] In 2017, four media corporations (CBS, News Corp [Fox], Disney [ABC], and Universal–NBC) acquired 60 percent of all revenue generated from network television advertising.[19] That same year, five broadcast networks (ABC, CBS, NBC, FOX, and the CW) received nearly 50 percent of the multibillion dollar profits of the television advertising industry.[20]

Here, again, corporate control of media markets has consequences for audiences. In 2014, as pricing negotiations between AMC and satellite provider DirecTV stalled, AMC turned to consumers to push DirecTV toward cooperation. During an episode of the popular AMC television series *The Walking Dead*, viewers were presented with an on-screen warning during commercial breaks: "You are at risk of losing AMC and *The Walking Dead*." Losing your favorite television show may be a trite example of the effects of media conglomeration, but the theoretical implications are significant. The control of film and television media in fewer hands means that the content to which we are allowed access is increasingly restricted.

Perhaps the controversy surrounding the Sinclair Broadcast Group provides a more substantive illustration of how media conglomeration can impact cultural ideology. In 2017, the Trump administration overturned a

35-year-old Federal Communications Commission regulation that prevented ownership of both a newspaper and radio or television station in the same local market.[21] This regulation was intended to inhibit any single organization from exerting absolute control over the worldview of U.S. audiences. Now, because of the revocation of this rule, Sinclair is poised to purchase Tribune Media, which would allow access to nearly 70 percent of U.S. households.[22] Importantly, Sinclair chairperson, David Smith, has made large contributions to the Republican Party.

In 2016, Sinclair agreed to provide "fair" coverage of then-candidate Trump in exchange for privileged media access to his campaign.[23] Since Trump's ascendancy to the White House, Sinclair has required its local affiliates to air favorable coverage of his administration, including a now infamous message, broadcast over 193 local stations, where anchors recited verbatim a contrived speech about concern about "one-sided . . . fake stories" informed by "personal bias."[24] Other "must-run" messages have positioned concern over the forced separation of immigrant families at the U.S.–Mexico border as "politically-driven by the liberals"[25] and framed Trump's Democratic challenger, Hillary Clinton, as deceitful ("Why did Hillary Clinton struggle with disclosing her medical diagnosis? Can a president lead with so many questions of transparency and trust?").[26] The impact of these messages on the 2016 presidential election is yet to be determined; the implications, however, are startling.

THE INTERNET

Even newer media are subjected to monopolization. The majority of social media we use is owned by just five corporations: Facebook (which owns Instagram, Light Box, and WhatsApp), Google (which owns YouTube, Blogger, and Android), Twitter (which owns Bluefin), LinkedIn (which owns Pulse and Bizo), and Yahoo (which owns Tumblr, Summly, and Blink!).[27] In 2016 two companies, Google and Yahoo, received 65 percent of the $60 billion generated through Internet advertising revenue.[28] As the two leading search engines, the commercially driven algorithms these corporations use to drive Internet exploration have a potentially profound influence on public knowledge. Companies that manage popular search engines like Google Search and Bing control the flow of Internet information by acting as a filter between raw data and consumers. As such, these companies have an integral role in the process through which we come to know things via the Internet. Moreover, this process has become increasingly tainted by commercialism. Search for virtually anything in these search engines and the top results are almost always paid advertisements for products. Many Internet browsers will also store your search history so that you will be repeatedly reminded of products you are considering purchasing. Search for a pair of Nikes on Zappos but decide not to buy them and you will likely see an ad for those very same shoes tempting you the next time you visit Facebook.

Whatever the industry, reducing the number of companies involved in the production of content increases the potential for limiting diversity in media messages and material. For example, numerous sociologists and other cultural critics have chided the advertising industry for its incessant objectification and oversexualization of women's bodies. Turn on the TV, flip through a magazine, or look over album covers and you're bound to see images where women are reduced to body parts, where their bodies become the product for sale, or where their sole purpose is to serve as background to a male counterpart.[29] Racialized images in the media work in similar ways to support White supremacy and privilege. Media content that features people of color frequently does so while reproducing racist stereotypes. In addition, like women in media, people of color in media often function solely as sidekicks to White characters. A telling example of racialized media is the so-called White savior phenomenon in the film industry. White savior movies typically feature casts made up largely of minorities in some sort of duress. It takes a (White) hero to save them from their dire fate (think Sandra Bullock in *The Blind Side*, Sam Worthington in *Avatar*, Michelle Pfeiffer in *Dangerous Minds*, Clint Eastwood in *Gran Torino*, or Emma Stone in *The Help*).[30] Gender and race ideologies portrayed in media are important because they provide a social discourse—that is, they function as building blocks for social processes in our daily lives. In these cases, the lack of informed diversity that results from media concentration catalyzes the dehumanization and objectification of women and minorities that is necessary for the processes of structural sexism and racism.

Women and people of color are not only misrepresented in media imagery, but also vastly underrepresented in American media. For example, although women compose nearly half of the gaming community, 88 percent of game developers are men. Of the 100 top-grossing films of 2017, women directed only eight of them.[31] Additionally, a study by USC's Media, Diversity, and Social Change Initiative found that of the 1,100 top-grossing films between 2007 and 2017, only 12.1 percent of the speaking roles were for Black actors, 4.8 percent for Asian actors, and 6.2 percent for Latinx actors.[32] A review of more than 150 newspapers and websites by the Institute for Diversity and Ethics in Sports found that the sports journalism community is more than 90 percent male and more than 90 percent White. However, there is evidence to suggest that including women and people of color in the administrative process of media production increases the racial and gender representativeness of media images. For example, in films directed by African Americans, more than half of speaking roles featured Black characters, compared to just 9.9 percent in films with White directors. In 2013, men comprised more than 75 percent of those interviewed for political talk shows,[33] whereas MSNBC's Sunday political news/talk show, the *Melissa Harris-Perry Show* (hosted by an African American woman), featured "a more evenly balanced distribution of solo interviews with White men and women and African American men and women" than any other major Sunday political news/talk show.[34] Clearly, media diversity in any form is good for the numerical representation of minority communities. One way forward may be through pressuring production companies to follow "inclusion riders," which mandate the inclusion of actors of color, women, LGBT actors, and actors with disabilities.[35]

MEDIA FOR THE PEOPLE: ALT MEDIA, NET NEUTRALITY, AND OPEN ACCESS

Like all social institutions, the institution of American media is socially constructed. Therefore, it is open to deconstruction and reconstruction. Although the conglomeration of media may seem a towering monolith, over the past few decades, several alternative models to corporatized media have emerged in various industries. Broadly, alternative

media models work within a more community-oriented structure of ownership, production, and audience relations.[36] Thus, the resulting content is presumably more sociologically informed. Similarly, the issues of "net neutrality" and "open access" offer other possibilities for institutional resistance against media conglomeration. For example, many of us enjoy playing games on our smart phones. Imagine if Verizon decided that all data usage associated with Candy Crush, Angry Birds, and other cellphone games would now be charged double what data usage costs for other applications. Or imagine that Comcast decides that corporations will enjoy faster Internet, whereas individual consumers will be stuck with sluggish access (unless, of course, we pay for the upgrade). Proponents of net neutrality argue that service providers and governments should treat all Internet data as equal, such that service providers cannot overcharge certain data usage for profit and governments cannot block certain Internet platforms in the name of state censorship.[37] Nevertheless, the Federal Communications Commission recently revoked rules that banned "blocking" (discriminating against content by preventing access to websites or apps), "throttling" (discriminating against content by slowing data transmission), and "paid prioritization" (providing faster service to users who can afford to pay for it).[38] As legal challenges of the repeal are pending, net neutrality hangs in the balance.

As a student, the notion of open access may be of particular interest to you. Subscriptions to academic journals can be costly, yet they contain information on the cutting edge of research and theory in the sciences, arts, and humanities. From the efficacy of vaccinations to the consequences of terrorism, academic journals largely inform "what we know" as a society. Proponents of open access argue that this information is too significant to be restricted by publishers concerned primarily with profit-making.[39] Alternative media, net neutrality, and open access each provide a new direction for media, less restricted by capitalistic efforts for industry control through concentration and conglomeration. As the next generation of media consumers and producers, it will be up to you to decide: what is the future of media?

NOTES

1. Heppner, Jake. 2015. "30 Surprising Facts about How We Actually Spend Our Time," *Distractify*, January 6. http://news.distractify.com/dark/trivial-facts/astounding-facts-about-how-we-actually-spend-our-time.

2. Lutz, Ashley. 2012. "These 6 Corporations Control 90% of the Media in America," *Business Insider*, June 14. http://www.businessinsider.com/these-6-corporations-control-90-of-the-media-in-america-2012-6.

3. Rapp, Nicholas, and Aric Jenkins. 2018. "Chart: These 6 Companies Control Much of U.S. Media," *Fortune*, July 24. http://fortune.com/longform/media-company-ownership-consolidation.

4. Johnson, Bradley. 2010. "100 Leading Media Companies," *Advertising Age*, September 27. http://adage.com/article/media/100-leading-media-companies-2010/146004.

5. Time Warner. 2015. "Operating Divisions." Retrieved May 2, 2015, from http://www.timewarner.com/company/operating-divisions.

6. The Society of Independent Motion Picture Producers Research Database. 2005. "The Independent Producers and the Paramount Case, 1938–1949." Retrieved May 2, 2015, from http://www.cobbles.com/simpp_archive/paramountcase_3consent1940.htm.

7. Wright, Josh. 2010. "Monopolization Enforcement at the Antitrust Division by the Numbers," *Truth on the Market: Academic Commentary on Law, Business, Economics and More*, August 2. http://truthonthemarket.com/2010/08/02/monopolization-enforcement-at-the-antitrust-division-by-the-numbers.

8. U.S. Department of Justice. Antitrust Case Filings. Retrieved September 15, 2018, from https://www.justice.gov/atr/antitrust-case-filings?page=2.

9. Cornell University Law School. n.d. "Supreme Court Bulletin: *Citizens United v. Federal Election Commission* (-8-205)." Retrieved May 2, 2015, from http://www.law.cornell.edu/supct/cert/08-205.

10. Publishers Weekly. 2014. "The World's 56 Largest Book Publishers, 2014." Retrieved May 2, 2015, from http://www.publishersweekly.com/pw/by-topic/industry-news/financial-reporting/article/63004-the-world-s-56-largest-book-publishers-2014.html.

11. The Daily Take Team. 2014. "Is the Koch Brothers' Curriculum Coming to Your Child's School?" *Truthout*, December 11. http://truth-out.org/opinion/item/27965-is-the-koch-brothers-curriculum-coming-to-your-child-s-school.

12. The Economist. 2012. "Textbooks Round the World: It Ain't Necessarily So." Retrieved May 2, 2015, from http://www.economist.com/node/21564554.

13. Zhao, Shirley, and Johnny Tam. 2013. "Debate Continues in Hong Kong over Introduction of National Education," *South China Morning Post*, October 8. http://www.scmp.com/news/hong-kong/article/1326760/debate-continues-hong-kong-over-introduction-national-education.

14. The Government of the Hong Kong Special Administrative Region of the People's Republic of China Education Bureau. 2015. "Recommended Textbook List." Retrieved May 2, 2015, from https://cd.edb.gov.hk/rtl/publisherlist.asp/.

15. Associated Press. 2014. "Texas Approves Disputed History Texts for Schools," *The New York Times*, November 22. http://www.nytimes.com/2014/11/23/us/texas-approves-disputed-history-texts-for-schools.html.

16. Schlanger, Zoë. 2015. "Company Behind Texas Textbook Calling Slaves Workers Apologizes: We Made a Mistake," *Newsweek*, October 5. https://www.newsweek.com/company-behind-texas-textbook-calling-slaves-workers-apologizes-we-made-380168.

17. Szalai, George. 2017. "Studio-by-Studio Profitability Ranking: Disney Surges, Sony Sputters," February 2. https://www.hollywoodreporter.com/lists/studio-by-studio-profitability-ranking-disney-surges-sony-sputters-977497/item/walt-disney-studio-profitability-977490.

18. Bennett, Shea. 2014. "Who Owns Social Media? [Infographic]," *Social Times*, September 18. http://www.mediabistro.com/alltwitter/who-owns-social-media_b60182.

19. James, Meg. 2017. "TV Networks Sell a Record $19.7 Billion in Advertising at Surprisingly Strong Upfront Market," *Los Angeles Times*, July 18. http://www.latimes.com/business/hollywood/la-fi-ct-television-upfront-totals-20170718-story.html.

20. Littleton, Cynthia. 2014. "AMC Sounds Alarm about DirecTV Tussle during 'Walking Dead' Episode," *Variety*, November 2. http://variety.com/2014/tv/news/amc-sounds-alarm-about-directv-tussle-during-walking-dead-episode-1201345695.

21. Levitz, Eric. 2017. "Trump's FCC Clears the Way for Big Players to Dominate Local News," *New York*, November 16. http://nymag.com/daily/intelligencer/2017/11/trumps-fcc-clears-the-way-for-consolidation-in-local-news.html.

22. Levitz 2017.

23. Levitz, Eric. 2017. "Trump-Friendly Company Buys Rights to Deliver Local New to 70 Percent of Households," *New York*, May 9. http://nymag.com/daily/intelligencer/2017/05/right-leaning-company-to-deliver-local-news-to-most-of-u.s.html.

24. Levitz, Eric. 2018. "Local News Anchors Are Being Forced to Deliver Pro-Trump Propaganda," *New York*, March 8. http://nymag.com/daily/intelligencer/2018/03/local-news-anchors-now-have-to-read-pro-trump-propaganda.html.

25. Levitz, Eric. 2018. "Sinclair Forced Its Local Stations to Discredit Outrage over Family Separation," *New York*, June 21. http://nymag.com/daily/intelligencer/amp/2018/06/sinclair-broadcasting-group-local-news-stations-attack-critics-of-family-separation-boris-epshteyn.html?__twitter_impression=true.

26. Levitz, Eric. 2017. "Trump-Friendly Company Buys Rights to Deliver Local New to 70 Percent of Households."

27. Bennett, "Who Owns Social Media? [Infographic]."

28. Ingram, Matthew. 2017. "How Google and Facebook Have Taken over the Digital Ad Industry," *Fortune*, January 4. http://fortune.com/2017/01/04/google-facebook-ad-industry.

29. Kilbourne, Jean. 1999. *Killing Us Softly 3*. DVD. New York: Insight Media.

30. Hughey, Matthew W. 2014. *The White Savior Film: Content, Critics, and Consumption*. Philadelphia: Temple University Press.

31. Sun, Rebecca. 2018. "Eight Women Directed a Top 100 Movie in 2017, Study Finds (Exclusive)," *The Hollywood Reporter*, January 4. https://www.hollywoodreporter.com/news/eight-women-directed-a-top-100-movie-2017-study-finds-1071527.

32. Smith, Stacy L., Marc Choueiti, Katherine Pieper, Ariana Case, and Angel Choi. 2018. "Inequality in 1,100 Popular Films: Examining Portrayals of Gender, Race/Ethnicity, LGBT & Disability from 2007–2017." *Annenberg Foundation*. Retrieved September 16, 2018, from http://assets.uscannenberg.org/docs/inequality-in-1100-popular-films.pdf.

33. Klos, Diana Mitsu. 2014. "The Status of Women in the U.S. Media 2013." Women's Media Center. Retrieved May 2. 2015, from http://wmc.3cdn.net/51113ed5df3e0d0b79_zzzm6go0b.pdf.

34. Media Matters. 2013. "Report: The Sunday Morning Shows Are Still White, Conservative, and Male." Retrieved May 2, 2015, from http://mediamatters.org/research/2013/07/10/report-the-sunday-morning-shows-are-still-white/194820.

35. Desta, Yohana. 2018. "Hollywood's Diversity Fail: There's Been 'No Meaningful Change' in 10 Years," *Vanity Fair*, July 31. https://www.vanityfair.com/hollywood/2018/07/usc-annenberg-study-hollywood-inclusion-riders.

36. Leung, Dennis, and Lee Francis. 2014. "Cultivating an Active Online Counterpublic Examining Usage and Political Impact of Internet Alternative Media." *The International Journal of Press and Politics* 4(1):340–59.

37. American Civil Liberties Union. 2015. "What Is New Neutrality?" Retrieved May 2, 2015, from https://www.aclu.org/net-neutrality/.

38. Collins, Keith. 2018. "Net Neutrality Hass Officially Been Repealed. Here's How That Could Affect You," *The New York Times,* June 11. https://www.nytimes.com/2018/06/11/technology/net-neutrality-repeal.html.

39 Curry, Stephen. 2012. "Science Must Be Liberated from the Paywalls of Publishers," *The Guardian,* April 10. http://www.theguardian.com/commentisfree/2012/apr/10/science-open-access-publishing.

HOW SHOWS LIKE *WILL & GRACE* AND *BLACK-ISH* CAN CHANGE YOUR BRAIN

MAANVI SINGH

Will Smith from *The Fresh Prince of Bel-Air* was my first American friend. Ours was an unlikely friendship: a shy Indian kid, fresh off the boat, with big glasses and a thick accent, and a high school b-ball player from West Philadelphia, chillin' out maxin' and relaxin' all cool. And yet, I was with Will all the way, unnerved when he accidentally gave Carlton speed, shaken when he got shot in Season 5, and deeply embarrassed every time he wiped out in front of Veronica.

Psychologists say it's not uncommon to think of fictional characters as your friends. They call these attachments parasocial relationships, and a growing body of research suggests there may be more to these connections than we realize. It turns out that, as we grow emotionally attached to characters who are part of a minority group, our prejudices tend to recede.

It was rare to encounter Black people where I lived in Mumbai. When my family moved to the States, we settled in a neighborhood of mostly White and Asian families. The Banks family on *Fresh Prince* was the first African American family I felt like I "got to know." Of course, these were highly stylized, focus-group-tested, fictional characters. But could it be that watching a show like *Fresh Prince* helped mold my broader worldviews?

That's the sort of thing Edward Schiappa, a media studies researcher at MIT, wanted to figure out. He looked into whether shows that prominently feature gay men could lower prejudice toward LGBTQ people. He and his colleagues surveyed people[1] who watched *Will & Grace,* measuring whether or not they agreed with statements like "Sex between two men is just plain wrong" and "Lesbians are sick." Sure enough, Schiappa found that those who watched the show most often were least prejudiced toward the queer community.

But how do we know the show was really behind the responses? What if *Will & Grace* simply attracts viewers who were already open-minded about sexuality? To test that premise, Schiappa and his colleagues rounded up 175 college students and assessed their attitudes toward the LGBTQ community. Then, the researchers had all the students watch a season of *Six Feet Under* over the course of five weeks. When the researchers surveyed the students afterward, the students felt more positive toward gay men. Another study on the effect of watching *Queer Eye for the Straight Guy* yielded similar results. "At this point, it's a pretty unequivocal finding that TV can affect how people feel and think about others," Schiappa says.

What's more, these findings square with the way people overcome prejudice in the real world. Psychologists have consistently found[2] that the most effective way to rid people from majority groups of bigoted ideas about, say, Black people, immigrants, or queer folks, is to have them interact with people from those groups. They call it the intergroup contact theory[3]: When majority and minority groups mingle—under the right circumstances—negative feelings about each other tend to dissipate. "What happens when you're exposed to a wide variety of people in a certain minority group is that your ideas about that group get more complicated," says Schiappa.

So does this mean we can eradicate racism and homophobia through a series of strategic dinner parties? Not quite. Back in 1954, psychologist Gordon Allport found[4] that the intergroup contact theory holds true only when everyone in a social situation feels safe, comfortable, and respected. In the real world, if we were to round up a few proud homophobes and lock them in a room with a bunch of queer folks, it would probably look something like, well, MTV's *The Real World.*

In the first season of that show, which debuted in 1992, the producers brought together a disparate group of 20-somethings and encouraged sparks to fly. Julie, the Southern belle, offends

1 Schiappa, Edward, Peter B. Gregg, and Dean E. Hewes. 2006. "Can One TV Show Make a Difference? *Will & Grace* and the Parasocial Contact Hypothesis." *Journal of Homosexuality,* 51(4): 15–37.

2 Pettigrew, Thomas F. 1998."Intergroup Contact Theory." *Annual Review of Psychology* 49: 65–85.

3 Allport, Gordon W. 1979. *The Nature of Prejudice,* 25th Anniversary Edition. Reading, MA: Addison-Wesley. Retrieved on March 21, 2019, from http://faculty.washington.edu/caporaso/courses/203/readings/allport_Nature_of_prejudice.pdf.

4 Allport, *The Nature of Prejudice.*

Heather, a Black rapper, by joking about how she could be a drug dealer. Eric, the White dude with boy-band hair, has a blowout[5] with Kevin, who's Black, after Eric insists that White privilege isn't a thing. None of this was accidental; as the intro to each episode says, the goal is—say it with me now—"to find out what happens when people stop being polite, and start getting real."

"People can feel immediately put off or threatened when they meet someone they don't normally interact with," Schiappa says. "And that can sometimes even increase prejudice." In the *real* real world, most people tend to hang out with others who look and think like them. Last year, a big survey by the Public Religion Research Institute[6] found that most White Americans have just one Black friend, one Latino friend, and one Asian friend—overall, 91 percent of their friends are White. And the social circles of African Americans were 80 percent Black. "It's not easy to get different types of people to just organically become friends," Schiappa says. So how do you get the benefits of intergroup contact theory in a socially segregated world? That's where television and my good friend the Fresh Prince come in.

Media researchers say it counts for something that on TV, we can meet all sorts of people who may be nothing like us: a cancer-stricken chemistry teacher desperate to pay his medical bills [AMC's *Breaking Bad*], a 10-year-old Chinese kid who loves hip-hop [ABC's *Fresh Off the Boat*], a Black woman with a high-powered political career [ABC's *Scandal*], or a couple of gay men raising a daughter they adopted from Vietnam [ABC's *Modern Family*]. "When I really get into a TV show, I start to feel like I know the characters," says Bradley Bond, an assistant professor of communications studies at the University of San Diego. "These characters almost become my friends."

And Bond says it's easy to connect with them precisely because they live inside your TV screen. "You meet these characters in the safety of your own home," he explains. The TV screen offers a sense of separation and security that can help people lower their defenses and connect with people they might try to avoid in real life. And as Schiappa's research has shown, that connection can lead to boosts in people's ability to empathize with people they might not otherwise relate to.

Of course, just because television can encourage acceptance and open-mindedness doesn't mean it always works out that way. "It's not enough to just have a diversity of characters portrayed on TV," says Srividya Ramasubramanian, an associate professor of communications at Texas A&M University. "How the minority characters are portrayed really matters." Often when minority characters are portrayed on-screen, she says, they're in demeaning roles. *The Big Bang Theory* is one of Ramasubramanian's favorite shows, but she bristles at the character of Raj, an Indian astrophysicist, who has a thick accent, overbearing parents, and zero game.

In her work, Ramasubramanian has found that those sorts of one-dimensional representations can actually reinforce prejudice. In a 2011 study published in *Communications Research*, she polled a bunch of college kids on whether they admired or disliked a bunch of widely recognized TV characters and personalities, some White, some Black. In the results, David Palmer from *24* and Oprah were widely admired. Flavor Flav and *The Apprentice*'s Omarosa were widely disliked. Then, Ramasubramanian rounded up a different group, composed of 450 young Caucasian people. She showed some of them pictures of the admired characters and some of the disliked characters. Then, she put the pictures away and gave everyone in that group a survey measuring how likely they were to associate the words "lazy," "criminal," and "uneducated" with Black people. It turns out that being exposed to the lesser-liked Black characters made people more likely to associate negative stereotypes with Black people and less likely to support affirmative action policies.

As researchers begin to understand more about how TV can both advance and regress our ideas about race and sexuality, the challenge, Ramasubramanian says, is to convince mainstream TV networks that a diverse set of well-rounded characters can make for popular—and profitable—entertainment. She says highly rated shows like *Black-ish*, *Orange Is the New Black*, *Scandal*, and *Fresh Off the Boat* are a start.[7] But there's still work to be done. . . .

Winning over network bigwigs is the challenge, says Brad Bond, the social psychologist at the University of San Diego. "The media industry has become more concerned with what we refer to as social responsibility," he says, but as NPR's Linda Holmes recently pointed out,[8] that has yet to translate to widespread diversity on-screen or in writer's rooms. "Our discipline is still trying to figure out how not to just preach to the choir," Bond says, and "translate the research into actual change."

5   Ossad, Jordana. 2014. "The Most Iconic Moments from 'Real World's' First 10 Seasons. *MTV.com*. Retrieved on March 21, 2019, from http://www.mtv.com/news/2016306/real-world-iconic-moments-part-1.

6   Cox, Daniel, Juhem Navarro-Rivera, Robert P. Jones. 2016. "Race, Religion, and Political Affiliation of Americans' Core Social Networks." Public Religion Research Institute. Retrieved on March 21, 2019, from https://www.prri.org/research/poll-race-religion-politics-americans-social-networks.

7   Kissel, Rick. 2015. "Wednesday Ratings: 'Black-ish' Hits 2015 High as ABC Wins Night." *Variety*, April 2. Retrieved on March 21, 2019, from https://variety.com/2015/tv/news/wednesday-ratings-black-ish-hits-2015-high-as-abc-wins-night-1201465227;   Maglio, Tony. 2015. "Ratings: 'Scandal' Returns Up Double Digits, but ABC Can't Top CBS." *The Wrap*, April 17. Retrieved on March 21, 2019, from https://www.thewrap.com/ratings-scandal-returns-up-double-digits-but-abc-cant-top-cbs; Collins, Scott. 2013. "Netflix and 'Orange Is the New Black': We Know Its Ratings (Maybe)." *Los Angeles Times*, July 22. Retrieved on March 21, 2019, from https://www.latimes.com/entertainment/tv/showtracker/la-et-st-netflix-orange-is-the-new-black-we-know-its-ratings-maybe-20130722-story.html.

8   Holmes, Linda. 2015. "Television 2015: Hammering on the Door of Diversity." *National Public Radio*, August 21. Retrieved on March 21, 2019, from https://www.npr.org/2015/08/21/433214404/television-2015-hammering-on-the-door-of-diversity.

GARY W. POTTER AND VICTOR E. KAPPELER

29. CONSTRUCTING CRIME

Potter and Kappeler argue that consumers of media develop an inaccurate picture of crime in the United States. Most Americans will never be victims of a crime, yet they fear they are in imminent danger of being victimized. According to Potter and Kappeler, media representations of crime focus on violent stranger crime and rare types of crimes (e.g., those where wealthy White women are victims). Potter and Kappeler demonstrate how media portrayals of crime flame racial tensions through selective coverage and that media consumption may actually contribute to decreased accuracy in knowledge about crime, deflecting our attention from serious crime issues in our culture.

There is probably no issue that invokes greater emotion and more consistently influences public opinion than crime. Whether the issue is drug-related crime, violent crime, juvenile crime, child abductions, serial killers, youth gangs, or crime against the elderly, a public consensus exists that crime is rampant, dangerous, and threatening to explode. The dangers of crime are seen as immediate, omnipresent, and almost inescapable. For more than three decades in the United States, the fear of crime has been so real that one can almost reach out and touch it. Politicians, law enforcement executives, the private crime industry, and the media cater to the public mood. Their increasingly draconian responses—in the form of more police, more arrests, longer sentences, more prisons, and more executions—affirm public fears, and that fear grows unabated. Each new crime story, each new crime movie, each new governmental pronouncement on crime increases the public thirst for more crime control, less personal freedom, and greater intervention by the state.

In contrast to seemingly tangible public fear, crime facts are far more difficult to assess. The emotional reaction to crime makes the public policy issue of control intensely sensitive. The issue responds to manipulation and pandering so predictably that advertisers and public relations experts would be envious of the responses elicited. Why are crime facts so difficult to determine but crime fear so easy to manipulate? Through what process do rumors, gossip, urban legends, and apocryphal stories become public "common sense"? Through what mechanisms do isolated and rare incidents weave a tapestry of fear, panic, and hysteria? More importantly, who benefits from the construction of this labyrinth? . . . A careful look at crime and crime-related issues can help us see beyond the web of public fear. Public opinion and crime facts demonstrate no congruence. The reality of crime in the United States has been blanketed by a constructed reality. The policies and programs emanating from that constructed reality do far more damage than good to public safety and crime control.

CRIME KNOWLEDGE

What does the public really know about crime and how do they know it? The most reliable crime data available clearly demonstrate that the vast majority of people living in the United States will never be victims of crime. In fact, over 90 percent of the U.S. population has no direct experience with crime at all (Kappeler & Potter, 2005). Yet the public remains convinced of imminent danger—changing their personal habits and lives to accommodate fears and voting for politicians who promise solutions to the conjured problem. What is the basis for these opinions, fears, and impressions?

In addition to their own experiences, people interpret and internalize the experiences of others. They hear—often second-, third-, or fourth-hand—about crime incidents involving neighbors, relatives, friends, and friends of friends. This process of socialization carries crime "facts" and crime-related experiences from one person to many others like a virus. Crime is a topic of conversation, both public and private. Strong opinions and reactions amplify and extend the content of actual experiences. Lost in the retelling is the relatively isolated aspect of the incidents . . .

For centuries, the only means of disseminating knowledge from one person to another was oral communication. Reaching larger audiences was a slow, repetitive process limited by time and place. The printing press and public education were important revolutions that allowed written messages from one person to reach many readers. Newer technologies today have created a maelstrom of information. The mass media can disseminate messages literally with the speed of light and sound. Publishers produce thousands of books about crime—some fictional, some true, some simply crude "pot-boilers." Movies make crime a central theme. Producers know that movies like *The Clearing, Kill Bill, Memento, Pulp Fiction, Natural Born Killers*, and *The Usual Suspects* attract large audiences. Television programs also use crime and violence to attract attention. Police programs have been a staple of television programming from *Dragnet* to *CSI*. The creator of the *Law & Order* series, Dick Wolf, comments:

> Crime is a constantly renewable resource. Every day people continue to kill each other in bizarre and unfathomable ways. Even if murder goes down by double digits, there are still thousands of people killed in this country every year and killers who warrant prosecution. (Smith, 2006, p. 16)

Because of the public's fixation on crime, the television industry constructed a new type of programming in 1989—a hybrid between entertainment and crime news called reality TV. By the end of 1993, there were seven national programs fitting this profile. Two survived until the mid 2010s . . . and continued to attract viewers: *America's Most Wanted* and *Unsolved Mysteries*. In 2006 the web site for *America's Most Wanted* advertised its hotline (1-800-CRIME-TV) for tips from viewers and proclaimed, "You have helped catch 876 fugitives to date." There is also an AMW case tracker that tells viewers there are 1,185 open cases. You . . . could select the type of crime from a drop-down list, including terrorism, or you can click on an area on the map of the United States and look at crimes by region. Other features of the web site included: "In the Line of Duty," which claims more than 1,600 law enforcement officers—"an average of one death every 53 hours"—died on the job during the past 10 years and an advertisement for a "fun safety DVD for kids" (AMW, 2006). In 2006 the portal to the web site for *Unsolved Mysteries* flashed "missing," "lost love," "homicide," and "fugitive" before showing the title of the program and a button to click to enter the site, where the viewer is told this is one of television's first interactive series (*Unsolved Mysteries*, 2006).

According to research, the mass media are the basic sources of information on crime, criminals, crime control policies, and the criminal justice system for most people (Barak, 1994; Ericson, Baranek, & Chan, 1989; Graber, 1980; Warr, 1995). Crime themes are a mother lode for the media; crime attracts viewers. More viewers mean greater newspaper and magazine circulations, larger television audiences, and consequently larger advertising fees (Barkan, 1997). The local news and reality crime shows focus on dramatic themes to attract viewers: police "hot pursuits"; violent crimes (particularly strange and heinous crimes with innocent and unsuspecting victims); and crime alleged to be committed by social deviants like drug addicts, pedophiles, prostitutes, and terrorists.

THE PORTRAYAL OF CRIME IN THE MASS MEDIA

Crime rates have decreased every year since 1991, and victimization surveys indicate that serious crime has been on a perpetual decline since the early 1970s

(Kappeler & Potter, 2005). The media, however, provide a distorted view of how much crime there is in society. The media create a wholly inaccurate image of a society in which violent crime is rampant and in which crime is constantly and immutably on the increase. In addition, media coverage of crime seriously distorts public perception of the types of crime being committed and the frequency with which violent crimes occur. The media have a preoccupation with violent crime. Researchers have demonstrated a consistent and strong bias in the news toward murder, sexual crimes, gangs and violence, and drug-related violence (Beirne & Messerschmidt, 1995; Livingston, 1996).

One study looked at local television news programs in 13 major cities and found that crime far outdistanced all other topics in local newscasts, even weather and sports. Commercial advertisements and crime stories dominated the average 30-minute newscast in the study. Crime made up 20 percent of all local TV stories, followed by weather at 11 percent and accidents and disasters at 9 percent (*Public Health Reports*, 1998). The media not only overreport crime, but they also focus on the least common crimes, crimes of violence (Lundman, 2003). Another focus is random violence committed by strangers, despite the fact that violence overwhelmingly occurs among friends and intimates (Feld, 2003).

The less common a crime is, the more coverage it will generate. For example, crimes against small children and wealthy White women are featured in most crime reporting despite the fact that these groups have the lowest victimization rates of any social groups in the United States (Feld, 2003). Sensational and rare crimes that dovetail conveniently into news themes with moralistic messages are particularly popular. Over the years the media have created crime scares by formulating news themes around issues of "White-slavery" in the prostitution industry; sexual psychopaths running rampant in major cities; satanists engaged in mass murder, child sacrifice, and ritualistic child abuse; serial killers roaming the countryside; and many others. As Philip Jenkins (1996) comments:

> If we relied solely on the evidence of the mass media, we might well believe that every few years, a particular form of immoral or criminal behavior becomes so dangerous as almost to threaten the foundations of

society.... These panics are important in their own right for what they reveal about social concerns and prejudices—often based on xenophobia and anti-immigrant prejudice. (pp. 67–70)

Mass murders by satanic cults, the predations of roaming serial killers, and organized child abuse in day-care centers are so rare as to be total aberrations. The media choose to ignore common, everyday, typical crime. White-collar crimes such as price-fixing, illegal disposal of toxic waste, and unsafe work conditions get little coverage, so the public tends not to view these activities as "real crime."

Crime reports in the media inflame racial tensions and fears through biased and selective coverage. Crime stories on television news programs and in newspapers focus on crimes by African-American and Hispanic offenders, creating a wildly exaggerated view of their involvement in street crime and violent crime (Dorfman & Schiraldi, 2001; Lundman, 2003). The media also distort the race of victims in three important ways. First, newspapers carry a vastly inflated number of stories about White victims when compared to NCVS [National Crime Victimization Survey] statistics on victimization. Second, stories featuring White victims are longer and more detailed than stories about African-American victims. Finally, despite the fact that violent crime is overwhelmingly intraracial, newspapers focus on stories involving White victims and African-American offenders (Lundman, 2003).

When a story deals with an African-American or Hispanic offender, the focus is usually on interracial crime as evidenced by accompanying photographs of the offender being taken into police custody or a mug shot of the offender (Chiricos & Eschholz, 2002; Feld, 2003). The impact of this racial profiling by the media is stunning. One study found that 60 percent of the people interviewed recalled an offender being shown in a television news story about crime when no offender images were included. Of those who saw the phantom offender, 70 percent were certain the offender was African American (Gilliam & Iyengar, 2000).

The media are also guilty of bias by age in the depiction of crime and violent crime. Both television and newspaper coverage of crime portrays young people as offenders in violent incidents (Dorfman &

Schiraldi, 2001). In fact, the research shows that 68 percent of all television news stories on violent crime highlight youthful offenders, and 55 percent of all stories about young people highlight violence. The reality is that less than 4 percent of all arrests of youths are for violent crime, and less than 16 percent of all crime is committed by young people (FBI, 2005).

The many distortions about crime, types of crime, race, and demographics found in media reporting help explain public ignorance about crime, the criminal justice system, and crime control policy in the United States (Cullen, Fisher, & Applegate, 2000). A study of 500 students taking introductory criminal justice classes found that they estimated the annual number of homicides in the United States at about 250,000 (Vandiver & Giacopassi, 1997, p. 141). In 1997, there were slightly more than 18,208 murders; in 2004 there were 16,137. Similarly a Gallup Poll in 2002 found that 62 percent of the U.S. public thought crime was higher than in 2001, despite a steady ten year drop in crime rates (Maguire & Pastore, 2004).[1]

MEDIA ATTENTION AND CITIZEN FEAR OF CRIME

With such heavy exposure to crime themes in both news and entertainment programming, it would appear to be common sense that more media exposure should be directly related to a greater fear of crime. However, unlike media analysts and news anchors, social scientists are constrained by their craft to be more circumspect in their claims. A correlation between media exposure and concerns about crime is easy to demonstrate, but correlation is a long way from causation. Direct relationships are not easy to prove. For example, it is difficult to demonstrate whether greater media exposure causes fear of crime or whether fear of crime causes greater media exposure because people are staying home watching crime on television. As we pointed out earlier, people are exposed to information other than that provided by the media that may influence their viewpoints (i.e., rumors, gossip, urban legends). In addition, media research is difficult, complex, and subject to many pitfalls. For example, how does one measure the impact of the media? Is viewing time a measure? Do column inches constitute

an index? Does the quality and the impact of language and content take precedence? (Miethe & Lee, 1984; Skogan & Maxfield, 1981; Surette, 1998).

Despite the need for caution and the constraints of science, much evidence indicates that the media do influence the level of fear of crime and contribute to the persistence of crime as a major national issue. George Gerbner, a leading media researcher at the Annenberg School of Communications at the University of Pennsylvania, developed cultivation theory—the "mean world" syndrome—to describe the impact of the media. Gerbner argues that research demonstrates that heavy viewers of television violence, whether in entertainment or news mediums, increasingly develop the feeling that they are living in a state of siege. Gerbner's research shows that heavy television viewers: (1) seriously overestimate the probability that they will be victims of violence; (2) believe their own neighborhoods to be unsafe; (3) rank fear of crime as one of their most compelling personal problems; (4) assume crime rates are going up regardless of whether they really are; (5) support punitive anti-crime measures; and (6) are more likely to buy guns and anti-crime safety devices (Gerbner, 1994). Other research demonstrates that "heavy viewers . . . exhibit an exaggerated fear of victimization and a perception that people cannot be trusted" (Carlson, 1995, p. 190).

It is difficult to gauge the impact of the media on fear of crime. One thing, however, is clear from the research: the more you watch television news, the more fearful you are of crime. People who watch more television news and more television crime dramas express dramatically higher rates of fear about crime than those who watch fewer broadcasts (Eschholz, Chiricos, & Gertz, 2003). A study in Philadelphia found that people who watched the television news four times a week were 40 percent more likely to be very worried about crime than those who did not watch the news (Bunch, 1999).

In addition to increasing public fear, media crime coverage has other effects on public perceptions and views of crime. Heavy coverage shapes perceptions and directs much public discourse on the crime issue. For example, the media regularly and falsely direct attention to crimes allegedly committed by young, poor, urban males, who are often members of minority groups (Reiman, 2004). Media coverage directs people's attention to specific crimes and helps to shape those crimes as social problems (i.e., drug use, gangs). Media coverage limits discourse on crime control options to present policies—suggesting that the only options are more laws, more police, longer sentences, and more prisons (Kappeler & Potter, 2005). The impact of media coverage is readily apparent in the creation of crime scares and moral panics.

MORAL PANICS

The concept of a moral panic was developed by Stanley Cohen (1980). A moral panic occurs when a group or type of activity is perceived as a threat to the stability and well-being of society. The media provide copious details and information (not necessarily accurate); this is followed by attention from law enforcement officials, politicians, and editorial writers who begin to comment on the panic. "Experts" then join the fray and try to explain the panic and offer policy options for dealing with it.

Moral panics direct public attention toward the activity or group and organize public fear for the well-being of society. The attention amplifies the behavior of the groups under scrutiny. . . .

. . . In 1922, future Supreme Court Justice Felix Frankfurter and legal scholar Roscoe Pound took the media to task for creating crime scares. Frankfurter and Pound noted that newspapers in Cleveland had dramatically increased their coverage of crime stories during 1919, even though crimes reported to the police had increased only slightly. They charged that the press was needlessly alarming the public and that the effect was a dangerous tendency for the public to pressure police to ignore due process rights and constitutional protections in their pursuit of criminals (Frankfurter & Pound, 1922).

The "sex fiend" panic of the 1930s and 1940s resulted in the passage of sexual psychopath laws in 28 states. One analysis of the development of these laws reveals a key role played by the media (McCaghy & Capron, 1997). Sex fiend panics typically began with the commission of a sex crime, particularly a crime against a child, accompanied by heavy mass media coverage. This panic included estimates, without any basis

in fact, that thousands of sex fiends were at large in the community. These "sex crime waves" were not related to any increase in the actual numbers of reported sex crimes; the panic was artificially induced by media coverage of particularly salacious cases (see Sutherland, 1950). The media advocated such solutions as castration, the outlawing of pornography, and life imprisonment for sex offenders. Special sexual psychopath laws were passed that allowed indeterminate confinement for any offender, whether a child molester or an exhibitionist or a fornicator, until the state deemed them to be cured. In some states, the original offense didn't even have to be a sex offense—it could be robbery or arson, as long as a psychiatrist could identify sexual dysfunctions in the accused. . . .

In the 1980s the same kind of moral panic surfaced with regard to the use of crack (a smokable form of cocaine hydrochloride). Craig Reinarman and Harry Levine (1989) carefully researched the media's creation of a drug scare surrounding crack. Reinarman and Levine define a "drug scare" as a historical period in which all manner of social difficulties (such as crime, health problems, the failure of the education system) are blamed on a chemical substance. "Drug scares" are not new. Problems of opiate addiction at the turn of the century were blamed on Chinese immigrants; African Americans were portrayed as "cocaine fiends" during the 1920s; violent behavior resulting from marijuana consumption was linked to Mexican farm laborers in the 1920s and 1930s. The construction of the crack scare was similar in that it linked the use of crack-cocaine to inner-city Blacks, Hispanics, and youths. In the 1970s, when the use of expensive cocaine hydrochloride was concentrated among affluent Whites, both the media and the state focused on heroin, seen as a drug of the inner-city poor. Only when cocaine became available in an inexpensive form, crack, did the scapegoating common to drug scares begin.

The media hype began in 1986, following the spread of crack into poor and working class neighborhoods. *Time* and *Newsweek* ran five cover stories each on crack during 1986. The three major television networks quickly joined the feeding frenzy. NBC did 400 news stories on crack between June and December 1986; in July 1986, all three networks ran 74 drug stories on their nightly newscasts. These stories contained highly inflated estimates of crack use and warnings about the dangers of the drug.

Those news stories were particularly troubling precisely because they were entirely incorrect. Research from the National Institute of Drug Abuse [NIDA] showed that the use of all forms of cocaine by youth and young adults had reached its peak four years earlier and had been declining ever since. Every indicator showed that at the height of the media frenzy crack use was relatively rare (Walker, 1998). Surveys of high school students demonstrated that experimentation with cocaine and cocaine products had been decreasing steadily since 1980. In fact, the government's own statistics showed that 96 percent of young people in the United States had never even tried crack. If there had been an epidemic, it was long over.

Officially produced data strongly refuted other claims about crack use. The media reports claimed that crack and cocaine were highly addictive and that crack, in particular, was so addictive that one experience with the drug could addict a user for life. However, NIDA estimates showed that of the 22 million people who had used cocaine and cocaine-products, very few of them ever became addicted. In fact, very few of them ever escalated to daily use. NIDA's own estimates indicated that fewer than 3 percent of cocaine users would ever become "problem" users (Kappeler & Potter, 2005). The health dangers of cocaine and crack were also widely exaggerated; few users ever required medical treatment because of using the drug.

The impact of the crack scare was tangible and immediate. New laws were passed increasing mandatory sentences for crack use and sales. Ironically, these laws resulted in a situation where someone arrested for crack faced the prospect of a prison sentence three to eight times longer than a sentence for cocaine hydrochloride, the substance needed to produce crack. The drug laws for crack inverted the typical ratio—wholesalers receive less severe sanctions than retailers and users. . . .

CRIME MYTHOLOGY

False beliefs about crime abound in U.S. society and play a disproportionate role in the formulation of government and law enforcement policies. The crime that does exist is not predominantly violent, and violent crime is not as common or debilitating as the media would lead us to believe. The media, the state, and criminal justice officials create and perpetuate crime myths.

Crime myths focus on unpopular, minority, and deviant groups in society. Drug problems have consistently been laid squarely at the feet of immigrant groups, minority groups, and inner-city residents, wholly displacing the reality of drug use. Problems of opiate addiction in the late 1800s and early 1900s were blamed on immigrant Chinese workers, while the actual problem resulted from the overuse of over-the-counter elixirs by White, middle-aged, rural, Protestant women. The reputed cocaine epidemic of the 1980s was blamed on the irresponsible and hedonistic lifestyles of inner-city minorities, while the facts were that cocaine was primarily a drug of choice of affluent, suburban Whites. Law enforcement agencies and the media have combined their efforts to tie serial murder, child abduction, ritualistic child abuse, and child sacrifice and murder to the activities of unpopular religious groups and sexual minorities.

Crime myths come in many forms. For example, in the mid-1970s the media reported that children had been murdered as the result of the poisoning of their Halloween candy. However, careful investigation revealed something quite different from a wave of poisoning by strangers. There had been only two incidents: one child died from ingesting heroin he found in his uncle's house; the other child was poisoned by his father, who put cyanide in the boy's candy. As with most crime myths, the truth was ignored while tales of mythical savagery circulated (Best & Horiuchi, 1985). To this day local television stations run cautionary stories before each Halloween.

In the early 1980s the media and the government helped create a panic over the issue of child abduction. It was estimated that somewhere between 1.5 and 2.5 million children were abducted from their homes every year; of that number, 50,000 would never be heard from again, presumably the victims of homicides. Pictures of "missing children" appeared on milk cartons, billboards, in newspapers, and on television. Children and parents were cautioned against contacts with strangers. The police in one town even wanted to etch identification numbers on school children's teeth so their bodies would be easier to identify (Dunn, 1994). The child abduction "epidemic" never existed. About 95 percent of those missing children were runaways (most of whom were home within 48 hours) or children abducted by a parent in a custody dispute. The fact is there are no more than 50 to 150 child abductions by strangers each year in the United States (Kappeler & Potter, 2005).

From 1983 to 1985 official estimates and media hype fueled a serial killer panic. Using FBI estimates of unsolved and motiveless homicides, media sources falsely reported that roughly 20 percent of all homicides, or about 4,000 murders a year, were the handiwork of serial killers. The media fed the myth with shocking and untrue confessions from Henry Lee Lucas, Ted Bundy, and others. Congress funded the Violent Criminal Apprehension Program and a behavioral sciences center for the FBI. When the data was subjected to careful analysis, scholars determined that at most there were 50 or 60 serial killer victims a year and that serial killers could account for no more than two percent of all homicides (Jenkins, 1996). Serial murder remains an extremely uncommon event.

The media play a vital role in the construction of crime mythology. Through selective interviewing the media can, and often do, fit isolated and rare incidents into what Fishman calls "news themes" (Fishman, 1978). For example, reporting the details of a crime involving an elderly victim and then interviewing a police official in charge of a special unit targeting crimes against the elderly creates a news theme—and can eventually create both a "crime wave" and a "crime myth." The use of value-laden language also contributes heavily to crime mythology. Youth gang members "prey" upon unsuspecting victims; serial killers "stalk"; child abductors "lurk" in the shadows; organized criminals are "mafiosi." Such language is common in crime news and substantially changes both the content and the context of crime stories. The media also frequently present misleading data. . . . Uncritical reproduction of officially produced statistics often organizes stories into news themes and deflects alternative interpretations of the data.

Crime myths are not just curiosities or examples of sloppy work by journalists. They have tangible and serious policy implications. Spurred by crime mythology,

politicians clamor for ever tougher sanctions against criminals. Crime myths divert attention away from the social and cultural forces that cause crime and toward individual pathologies; they reinforce stereotypes of minorities, poor people, and people who are "different."

DIVERTING ATTENTION FROM SERIOUS SOCIAL PROBLEMS

There is a corollary harm to directing our attention to certain kinds of criminality. Exaggerating the incidence and importance of violent crime, for example, deflects our attention from other serious issues . . .

The media pay little substantive attention to corporate crime and other forms of White-collar crime. Since the public is far more likely to be seriously harmed by corporate criminals than by violent criminals, this is a major disservice. In addition, ignoring such offenses encourages corporate crime by removing one of the primary modes of deterring that behavior—publicity. The media's neglect of White-collar crime stems from several sources, including: the risk of libel suits; social relationships between media executives and business executives; a pro-business orientation in the media; and the difficulty of adequately investigating and reporting on White-collar crime. In addition, corporations own the major newspapers, television networks, and television stations. Finally, media revenue comes primarily from advertising purchased by corporations.

The processes through which the media amplify and exaggerate crime and focus our attention on disadvantaged and relatively powerless groups in society are also used to deflect and diffuse concern over other types of crime. A case in point is the media's treatment of crimes against women, particularly rape and wife battering. The media frequently distort rape coverage by referring to "careless" behavior by the victim or provocative actions or clothing. The fact is that rape is a crime of violence, and the behavior of the perpetrator should be the focus. The media further distort the rape issue by giving primary coverage to stranger rapes, failing to emphasize the far more common case in which rape is committed by acquaintances, relatives, and "friends." Stories about non-stranger rape frequently repeat and reflect police skepticism about such cases. Acquaintance rape stories often emphasize cases of false reporting, a very rare occurrence.

Similarly, the media distort the issue of battering in a variety of ways. First, battering is a relatively uncovered story in a crime-saturated news environment. When battering is reported, it is treated as a bizarre spectacle and news stories make use of euphemistic or evasive language (i.e., marital disputes, domestic disturbance, spouse abuse). Such language obscures the gendered nature of battering and implies the woman may be at fault. Stories on battering often raise the question of why the woman didn't leave her batterer, ignoring the fact that many do try to leave and that many have good reasons not to leave. Battering stories often project a clear implication that women are responsible for their own victimization. In addition, the media frequently overplay the extremely rare occurrences of women abusing their husbands. Rather than focusing on the common crime of spouse battering, media sources often focus on cases where governors have released women from prison who were convicted of murdering abusive husbands. The story often reports that the woman was not living with her husband when she killed him, implying that the danger to the woman had passed. The story usually fails to report that this is precisely the most dangerous time for battered women. News stories frequently imply that pardons and releases encourage battered women to commit acts of violence against their abusers (Barkan, 1997; Devitt, 1992; Devitt & Downey, 1992; Kamen & Rhodes, 1992).

In a particularly egregious example of gender bias, media coverage of school shootings in the 1990s failed to point out that all the offenders were males and a majority of the victims were females (Danner & Carmody, 2001).

MAKING SENSE OF MEDIA REPRESENTATIONS OF CRIME

Three fundamental questions for analyzing how the media approach crime issues are: What functions do the media serve?; How do they accomplish those tasks?; and Who benefits from media actions? As one of society's dominant institutions, the media share certain characteristics with other dominant institutions, like the state, corporations, the law enforcement community, and the military . . .

The media operate in the same ideological arena as do the educational system, religious institutions, and the family. Ideology is a means of organizing impressions, thoughts, knowledge, and observations to interpret the world around us. The media most frequently voice and, because of their ability to reach such an extensive audience, amplify the views and interests of groups with the greatest political, economic, and social power. Journalists and other media professionals are trained, educated, and socialized to internalize the values and norms of the dominant, mainstream culture. As a result, the media interpret or mediate news, information, and complex issues in a way that is usually consistent with the dominant culture and with the interests of powerful groups. The audience is, of course, free to interpret reports and stories by subjecting them to rigorous analysis, but people generally lack the time, resources, and information to construct alternative definitions and frameworks—in addition to having been socialized in the very same environment that influenced the stories.

The mass media are part of the culture industry that produces tangible products. In general, but not exclusively, the products they produce will reflect the ideas, conceptions, theories, and views of those with power in society. There have been notable examples of investigative reporters whose efforts, for example, have focused attention on abuses in the juvenile justice system in Chicago, forced the San Francisco police department to change how it tracks officers who abuse force, or exonerated inmates on death row (Coen, 2005; Headden, 2006; Worden, 2006). The media more frequently, however, present viewpoints that are consistent with those held by powerful groups. They present those viewpoints as the "obvious" or "natural" perspectives; alternative views, if presented at all, are clearly labeled as deviant, different, or dangerous. The mass media tend to avoid unpopular and unconventional ideas. They repeat widely held views that do not offend audiences, advertisers, or owners.

We discussed media reliance on the portrayal of violence in both news and entertainment programming. These portrayals are not just attention grabbing; they serve other purposes as well. They provide legitimacy to the criminal justice system and the police. They build support for more draconian laws and for more state intervention into people's daily activities. They warn us about people who are different, outsiders, and the dangers of defying social conventions. In other words, they reinforce, they amplify, and they extend the existing state of affairs that makes up the dominant culture and the current distribution of power (Althusser, 1971; Alvarado & Boyd-Barrett, 1992; Hall, 1980; Hall, Critcher, Jefferson, Clarke, & Roberts, 1978; Stevenson, 1995).

Of course, the media are only one half of the equation. The audience is the other half. Are audiences passive individuals who absorb ideological propaganda from newspapers, television, movies, and magazines? Of course not. People rely on other experiences and interactions. Social identities are determined by interactions with all kinds of institutions: the family, the school, the state, language, and the media. However, people generally find their sense of identity and their understanding of the reality around them as a result of social identities molded by those institutions—all of which are "ideological state apparatuses" (Althusser, 1971; Lapley & Westlake, 1988). The media have the capacity to concentrate those definitions and interactions in a way that convinces people that the media are presenting an accurate reflection of everyday lives.

Can audiences resist the power of media representations and definitions? Yes. We have seen that some crime scares and moral panics never get off the ground. Ideological state apparatuses are not always successful in defining people's roles and consciousness. While the mass media relay certain ideological images, the audience—if it has the ability, the resources, and the inclination—can remold, adapt, and integrate those messages into an entirely different system of meaning (Althusser, 1971; Berger, 1991; Hall, 1980; Hall et al., 1978; McQuail, 1994),

Mass media (movies, television, news organizations) form a culture industry in modern capitalist societies. They sell their products. The shape and content of those products will be influenced by the economic interests of the organization producing the products. Businesses operating in the culture industry must cater to the needs of advertisers. News shows are set up in standardized formats that cater to the demands of advertising. News must be fitted into the air time and column inches left over after paid advertising is accounted for. As a result, a standard format with news, weather, and sports segments has evolved around the needs of advertisers. They are unlikely to sponsor programs that attack their interests.

Media businesses must maximize their audiences. They do this in several ways. First, they include heavy doses of sex and violence. Second, they appeal to noncontroversial, mainstream views—trying to achieve a nonoffensive middle-ground on most issues. Finally, they treat the news as light entertainment, something not requiring a great deal of thought or attention on the part of the reader or viewer. In the process, they reduce the danger of alternative interpretations of a story by the audience.

In general we can safely say that: (1) ownership and economic control of the media are important factors in determining the content of media messages and (2) the media are a powerful influence in shaping public consciousness. The media are something of an irresistible force in modern society. The media are instrumental but not the only players in defining the terms through which we think about the world around us (Marcuse, 1991; Strinati, 1995). Stuart Hall points out that there is a "preferred reading" of the media's message that buttresses the dominant political, economic, and social relations in society. However, it is not the only interpretation. Some audiences "negotiate" that message and transform it slightly. Others read that message from a very different perspective and create "oppositional" meanings that are in direct conflict with the views of the powerful.

That is how we should interpret crime news. We must ask questions: Where did that information come from? Who supplied it? Do they have a vested interest in how we react to that information? We must begin to deconstruct the taken-for-granted "common sense" messages of the media.

NOTE

1. This trend has continued, with homicide rates currently at levels not seen since the mid 1960s (Cooper and Smith, 2011).

REFERENCES

Althusser, L. (1971). Ideology and ideological state apparatuses. In L. Althusser (Ed.), *Lenin and philosophy and other essays*. London: New Left Books.

Alvarado, M., & Boyd-Barrett, O. (Eds.). (1992). *Media education: An introduction*. London: BFI/Open University.

America's Most Wanted. Accessed February 15, 2006 from http://www.amw.com/.

Barak, G. (1994). Media, society, and criminology. In G. Barak (Ed.), *Media, process, and the social construction of crime* (pp. 3–45). New York: Garland Publishing.

Barkan, S. F. (1997). *Criminology: A sociological understanding*. Englewood Cliffs, NJ: Prentice-Hall.

Beirne, P., & Messerschmidt, J. (1995). *Criminology* (22nd ed.). Ft. Worth: Harcourt Brace Jovanovich.

Berger, A. (1991). *Media analysts' techniques* (Rev. ed.). Newbury Park, CA: Sage.

Best, J., & Horiuchi, G. (1985). The razor and the apple: The social construction of urban legends. *Social Problems*, 32, 488–99.

Bunch, W. (1999). Survey: Crime fear is linked to TV news. *Philadelphia Daily News*, March 16, p. Al.

Carlson, J. (1995). *Prime time enforcement*. New York: Praeger.

Chiricos, T., & Eschholz, S. (2002). The racial and ethnic: Typification of crime and the criminal typification of race and ethnicity in local television news. *Journal of Research in Crime and Delinquency*, 39, 400–20.

Coen, J. (2005, September 5). Report leads to changes in defense for juveniles. *Chicago Tribune*, sec. 4, p. 1.

Cohen, S. (1980). *Folk devils and moral panics: The creation of the mods and rockers*. New York: St. Martin's Press.

Cooper, A., & Smith, E. 2011. *Homicide Trends in the United States, 1980–2008*. Bureau of Justice Statistics. NCJ 236018. Washington, DC: U.S. Department of Justice. http://www.bjs.gov/index.cfm?ty=pbdetail&iid=2221.

Cullen, F., Fisher, B., & Applegate, B. (2000). Public opinion about punishment and corrections. *Crime and Justice: A Review of Research*, 27, 1–79.

Danner, M., & Carmody, D. (2001). Missing gender in cases of infamous school violence: Investigating research and media explanation. *Justice Quarterly*, 18, 87–114.

Devitt, T. (1992). Media circus at Palm Beach rape trial. *Extra!* (Publication of FAIR, Fairness and Accuracy in Reporting). Special issue, 9–10, 24.

Devitt, T., & Downey, J. (1992). Battered women take a beating from the press. *Extra!* (Publication of FAIR, Fairness and Accuracy in Reporting). Special issue, 14–16.

Dorfman, L., & Schiraldi, V. (2001). *Off balance: Youth, race and crime in the news*. Washington, DC: Building Blocks for Youth.

Dunn, K. (1994, April 10). Crime and embellishment. *Los Angeles Times Magazine*, p. 24.

Ericson, R., Baranek, P., & Chan, J. (1989). *Negotiating control: A study of news sources*. Toronto: University of Toronto Press.

Eschholz, S., Chiricos, T., & Gertz, M. (2003). Television and fear of crime: Program types, audience traits, and the mediating effect of perceived neighborhood racial composition. *Social Problems*, 50, 395–415.

Federal Bureau of Investigation. (2005). *Crime in the United States, 2004: Uniform crime reports*. Washington, DC: U.S. Department of Justice.

Feld, B. (2003). The politics of race and juvenile justice: The "due process revolution" and the conservative reaction. *Justice Quarterly*, 20, 765–800.

Fishman, M. (1978). Crime waves as ideology. In G.W. Potter & V.E. Kappeler (Eds.) (2006). *Constructing Crime: Perspectives on Making News and Social Problems* (22nd ed., pp. 42–58). Long Grove, IL: Waveland Press, Inc.

Frankfurter, F., & Pound, R. (1922). *Criminal justice in Cleveland*. Cleveland: The Cleveland Foundation.

Gerbner, G. (1994, July). Television violence: The art of asking the wrong question. *Currents in Modern Thought*, 385–97.

Gilliam, F., & Iyengar, S. (2000). Prime suspects: The influence of local television news on the viewing public. *American Journal of Political Science*, 44, 560–73.

Graber, D. (1980). *Crime news and the public*. New York: Praeger.

Hall, S. (1980). Encoding/decoding. In Centre for Contemporary Cultural Studies (Ed.), *Culture, media, language*. London: Hutchinson.

Hall, S., Critcher, C., Jefferson, T., Clarke, J., & Roberts, B. (1978). *Policing the crisis*. London: Macmillan.

Headden, S. (2006, February 20). A tempest over police shootings. *U.S. News & World Report*, 140, 18.

Jenkins, P. (1988). Myth and murder: The serial killer panic of 1983–5. *Criminal Justice Research Bulletin*, 3, 11, 1–7.

Jenkins, P. (1996). *Moral panic: Changing concepts of the child molester in modern America*. New Haven, CT: Yale University Press.

Kamen, P., & Rhodes, S. (1992). Reporting on acquaintance rape. *Extra!* (Publication of FAIR, Fairness and Accuracy in Reporting). *Special issue*, 11.

Kappeler, V., & Potter, G. (2005). *The mythology of crime and criminal justice* (44th ed.). Long Grove, IL: Waveland Press.

Lapley, R., & Westlake, M. (1988). *Film theory: An introduction*. Manchester, England: Manchester University Press.

Livingston, J. (1996). *Crime & criminology* (22nd ed.). Englewood Cliffs, NJ: Prentice-Hall.

Lundman, R. (2003). The newsworthiness and selection bias in news about murder: Comparative and relative effects of novelty and race and gender typifications in newspaper coverage of homicide. *Sociological Forum*, 18, 257–86.

Maguire, K., & Pastore, A. (Eds.). (2004). Sourcebook of criminal justice statistics. [Online]. Available: http://www.albany.edu/sourcebook.

Marcuse, H. (1991). *One-dimensional man* (Rev. ed.). Boston: Beacon.

McCaghy, C., & Capron, T. (1997). *Deviant behavior: Crime, conflict and interest groups* (4th ed.). New York: Macmillan.

McQuail, D. (1994). *Mass communication theory* (33rd ed.). London: Sage.

Miethe, T., & Lee, G. (1984). Fear of crime among older people: A reassessment of the predictive power of crime-related factors, *Sociological Quarterly*, 25, 397–415.

Public Health Reports. (1998). Health ranks fifth on local TV news. *Public Health Reports*, 113, 296–97.

Reiman, J. (2004). *The rich get richer and the poor get prison* (77th ed.). Boston: Allyn and Bacon.

Reinarman, C., & Levine, H. (1989). Crack in context: Politics and media in the making of a drug scare. *Contemporary Drug Problems*, 16, 535–77.

Skogan, W., & Maxfield, M. (1981). *Coping with crime: Individual and neighborhood reactions*. Beverly Hills, CA: Sage.

Smith, S. (2006, February 12). Police TV shows are all the rage, and here's why. *Chicago Tribune*, sec. 7, pp. 1, 16.

Stevenson, N. (1995). *Understanding media cultures: Social theory and mass communication*. London: Sage.

Strinati, D. (1995). *An introduction to theories of popular culture*. London: Routledge.

Surette, R. (1998). *Media, crime, and criminal justice: Images and realities* (22nd ed.). Pacific Grove, CA: Brooks/Cole.

Sutherland, E. (1950). The diffusion of sexual psychopath laws. *American Journal of Sociology*, 56, 142–48.

Unsolved Mysteries. Accessed February 15, 2006 from http://www.unsolved.com/.

Vandiver, M., & Giacopassi, D. (1997). One million and counting: Students' estimates of the annual number of homicides occurring in the U.S. *Journal of Research in Crime and Delinquency*, 18, 91–131.

Walker, S. (1998). *Sense and nonsense about crime and drugs: A policy guide* (44th ed.). Belmont, CA: Wadsworth.

Warr, M. (1995). Public perceptions of crime and punishment. In J. Sheley (Ed.), *Criminology: A contemporary handbook* (pp. 15–31). Belmont, CA: Wadsworth.

Worden, R. (2006). *Wilkie Collins's "The dead alive": The novel, the case, and wrongful convictions*. Evanston: Northwestern University Press.

30. THE GRIM CONCLUSIONS OF THE LARGEST-EVER STUDY OF FAKE NEWS

You are probably familiar with the phrase "fake news," and you have probably been exposed to some if you spend any time on social media. But have you ever wondered how and why fake news stories are able to spread so quickly? Meyer discusses research that found that fake news stories have much greater depth, reach, and speed in their spread than accurate ones. This can have real consequences for our democracy and in the ability of our citizens to be informed, Meyer argues, especially since there is no clear solution to the problem of fake news.

"Falsehood flies, and the Truth comes limping after it," Jonathan Swift once wrote. It was hyperbole three centuries ago. But it is a factual description of social media, according to an ambitious and first-of-its-kind study[1] published . . . [in 2018]. The massive new study analyzes every major contested news story in English across the span of Twitter's existence—some 126,000 stories, tweeted by 3 million users, over more than 10 years—and finds that the truth simply cannot compete with hoax and rumor. By every common metric, falsehood consistently dominates the truth on Twitter, the study finds: Fake news and false rumors reach more people, penetrate deeper into the social network, and spread much faster than accurate stories. "It seems to be pretty clear [from our study] that false information outperforms true information," said Soroush Vosoughi, a data scientist at MIT who has studied fake news since 2013 and who led this study. "And that is not just because of bots. It might have something to do with human nature."

The study has already prompted alarm from social scientists. "We must redesign our information ecosystem in the twenty-first century," write a group of 16 political scientists and legal scholars in an essay also published[2] . . . in *Science*. They call for a new drive of interdisciplinary research "to reduce the spread of fake news and to address the underlying pathologies it has revealed." "How can we create a news ecosystem . . . that values and promotes truth?" they ask.

The new study suggests that it will not be easy. Though Vosoughi and his colleagues only focus on Twitter—the study was conducted using exclusive data that the company made available to MIT—their work has implications for Facebook, YouTube, and every major social network. Any platform that regularly amplifies engaging or provocative content runs the risk of amplifying fake news along with it.

Though the study is written in the clinical language of statistics, it offers a methodical indictment of the accuracy of information that spreads on these platforms. A false story is much more likely to go viral than a real story, the authors find. A false story reaches 1,500 people six times quicker, on average, than a true story does. And while false stories outperform the truth on every subject—including business, terrorism and war, science and technology, and entertainment—fake news about politics regularly does best.

Twitter users seem almost to *prefer* sharing falsehoods. Even when the researchers controlled for every difference between the accounts originating rumors—like whether that person had more followers or was verified—falsehoods were still 70 percent more likely to get retweeted than accurate news. And blame for this problem cannot be laid with our robotic brethren. From 2006 to 2016, Twitter bots amplified true stories as much as they amplified false ones, the study found. Fake news prospers, the authors write, "because humans, not robots, are more likely to spread it."

Political scientists and social media researchers largely praised the study, saying it gave the broadest and most rigorous look so far into the scale of the fake news problem on social networks, though some disputed its findings about bots and questioned its definition of news. "This is a really interesting and impressive study, and the results around how demonstrably untrue assertions spread faster and wider than demonstrable true ones do, within the sample, seem very robust, consistent, and well supported," said Rasmus Kleis Nielsen, a professor of political communication at the University of Oxford, in an email . . .

What makes this study different? In the past, researchers have looked into the problem of falsehoods spreading online. They've often focused on rumors around singular events. . . . This new paper takes a far grander scale, looking at nearly the entire lifespan of Twitter: every piece of controversial news that propagated on the service from September 2006 to December 2016. But to do that, Vosoughi and his colleagues had to answer a more preliminary question first: *What is truth? And how do we know?* It's a question that can have life-or-death consequences. "[Fake news] has become a white-hot political and, really, cultural topic, but the trigger for us was personal events that hit Boston five years ago," said Deb Roy, a media scientist at MIT and one of the authors of the new study.

On April 15, 2013, two bombs exploded near the route of the Boston Marathon, killing three people and injuring hundreds more. Almost immediately, wild conspiracy theories about the bombings took over Twitter and other social media platforms. The mess

of information only grew more intense on April 19, when the governor of Massachusetts asked millions of people to remain in their homes as police conducted a huge manhunt. "I was on lockdown with my wife and kids in our house in Belmont for two days, and Soroush was on lockdown in Cambridge," Roy told me. Stuck inside, Twitter became their lifeline to the outside world. "We heard a lot of things that were not true, and we heard a lot of things that did turn out to be true" using the service, he said.

The ordeal soon ended. But when the two men reunited on campus, they agreed that it seemed silly for Vosoughi—then a PhD student focused on social media—to research anything but what they had just lived through. Roy, his adviser, blessed the project. He made a truth machine: an algorithm that could sort through torrents of tweets and pull out the facts most likely to be accurate from them. It focused on three attributes of a given tweet: the properties of its author (were they verified?), the kind of language it used (was it sophisticated?), and how a given tweet propagated through the network. "The model that Soroush developed was able to predict accuracy with a far-above-chance performance," said Roy. He earned his PhD in 2015.

After that, the two men—and Sinan Aral, a professor of management at MIT—turned to examining how falsehoods move across Twitter as a whole. But they were back not only at the "what is truth?" question, but its more pertinent twin: How does *the computer* know what truth is? They opted to turn to the ultimate arbiter of fact online: the third-party fact-checking sites. By scraping and analyzing six different fact-checking sites—including *Snopes*, *Politifact*, and FactCheck.org—they generated a list of tens of thousands of online rumors that had spread between 2006 and 2016 on Twitter. Then they searched Twitter for these rumors, using a proprietary search engine owned by the social network called Gnip.

Ultimately, they found about 126,000 tweets, which, together, had been retweeted more than 4.5 million times. Some linked to "fake" stories hosted on other websites. Some started rumors themselves, either in the text of a tweet or in an attached image. (The team used a special program that could search for words contained within static tweet images.) And some contained true information or linked to it elsewhere. Then they ran a series of analyses, comparing the popularity of the fake rumors with the popularity of the real news. What they found astounded them.

. . . Vosoughi gave me an example: There are lots of ways for a tweet to get 10,000 retweets, he said. If a celebrity sends Tweet A, and they have a couple million followers, maybe 10,000 people will see Tweet A in their timeline and decide to retweet it. Tweet A was broadcast, creating a big but shallow pattern. Meanwhile, someone without many followers sends Tweet B. It goes out to their 20 followers—but one of those people sees it and retweets it, and then one of *their* followers sees it and retweets it too, on and on until tens of thousands of people have seen and shared Tweet B. Tweet A and Tweet B both have the same size audience, but Tweet B has more "depth," to use Vosoughi's term. It chained together retweets, going viral in a way that Tweet A never did. "It could reach 1,000 retweets, but it has a very different shape," he said.

Here's the thing: Fake news dominates *according to both metrics*. It consistently reaches a larger audience, *and* it tunnels much deeper into social networks than real news does. The authors found that accurate news wasn't able to chain together more than 10 retweets. Fake news could put together a retweet chain 19 links long—and do it 10 times as fast as accurate news put together its measly 10 retweets.

These results proved robust even when they were checked by humans, not bots. Separate from the main inquiry, a group of undergraduate students fact-checked a random selection of roughly 13,000 English-language tweets from the same period. They found that false information outperformed true information in ways "nearly identical" to the main dataset, according to the study.

What does this look like in real life? Take two examples from the . . . presidential election [in 2016]. In August 2015, a rumor circulated on social media that Donald Trump had let a sick child use his plane to get urgent medical care. *Snopes* confirmed almost all of the tale as true.[3] But according to the team's estimates, only about 1,300 people shared or retweeted the story. In February 2016, a rumor developed that Trump's elderly cousin had recently died and that he had opposed the magnate's presidential bid in his obituary. "As a proud bearer of the Trump name, I implore you all, please

don't let that walking mucus bag become president," the obituary reportedly said. But *Snopes* could not find evidence of the cousin, or his obituary, and rejected the story as false.[4] Nonetheless, roughly 38,000 Twitter users shared the story. And it put together a retweet chain three times as long as the sick child story managed. A false story alleging the boxer Floyd Mayweather had worn a Muslim head scarf[5] to a Trump rally also reached an audience more than 10 times the size of the sick child story.

Why does falsehood do so well? The MIT team settled on two hypotheses. First, fake news seems to be more "novel" than real news. Falsehoods are often notably different from all the tweets that have appeared in a user's timeline 60 days prior to their retweeting them, the team found. Second, fake news evokes much more emotion than the average tweet. The researchers created a database of the words that Twitter users used to reply to the 126,000 contested tweets, then analyzed it with a state-of-the-art sentiment-analysis tool.[6] Fake tweets tended to elicit words associated with surprise and disgust, while accurate tweets summoned words associated with sadness and trust, they found.

The team wanted to answer one more question: Were Twitter bots helping to spread misinformation? After using two different bot-detection algorithms on their sample of three million Twitter users, they found that the automated bots were spreading false news— but they were retweeting it at the same rate that they retweeted accurate information. "The massive differences in how true and false news spreads on Twitter cannot be explained by the presence of bots," Aral told me. But some political scientists cautioned that this should not be used to disprove the role of Russian bots in seeding disinformation. . . . "It can both be the case that (1) over the whole 10-year data set, bots don't favor false propaganda and (2) in a recent subset of cases, botnets have been strategically deployed to spread the reach of false propaganda claims," said Dave Karpf, a political scientist at George Washington University, in an email. . . . Vosoughi agrees that his paper does not determine whether the use of botnets changed around the 2016 election. "We did not study the change in the role of bots across time," he told me in an email. "This is an interesting question and one that we will probably look at in future work."

Some political scientists also questioned the study's definition of "news." By turning to the fact-checking sites, the study blurs together a wide range of false information: outright lies, urban legends, hoaxes, spoofs, falsehoods, *and* "fake news." It does not just look at fake news by itself—that is, articles or videos that look like news content and which appear to have gone through a journalistic process, but which are actually made up. Therefore, the study may undercount "noncontested news": accurate news that is widely understood to be true. For many years, the most retweeted post in Twitter's history celebrated Obama's reelection as president.[7] But as his victory was not a widely disputed fact, *Snopes* and other fact-checking sites never confirmed it.

The study also elides *content* and *news*. "All our audience research suggests a vast majority of users see news as clearly distinct from content more broadly," Nielsen, the Oxford professor, said in an email. "Saying that untrue content, including rumors, spread faster than true statements on Twitter is a bit different from saying false news and true news spread at different rates." But many researchers told me that simply understanding *why* false rumors travel so far, so fast, was as important as knowing that they do so in the first place. "The key takeaway is really that content that *arouses strong emotions* spreads further, faster, more deeply, and more broadly on Twitter," said Rebekah Tromble, the political scientist, in an email. . . . "False information online is often really novel and frequently negative," said Brendan Nyhan, [a] Dartmouth professor [of government] . . .

Nyhan lauded Twitter for making its data available to researchers and called on other major platforms, like Facebook, to do the same. "In terms of research, the platforms are the whole ballgame. We have so much to learn but we're so constrained in what we can study without platform partnership and collaboration," he said. "These companies now exercise a great deal of power and influence over the news that people get in our democracy. The amount of power that platforms now hold means they have to face a great deal of scrutiny and transparency," he said. "We can study Twitter all day, but only about 12 percent of Americans are on it. It's important for journalists and academics, but it's not how most people get their news." . . .

. . . Tromble, the political science professor, said that the findings would likely apply to Facebook, too. "Earlier this year, Facebook announced that it would restructure its News Feed to favor 'meaningful interaction,'" she told me. "It became clear that they would

gauge 'meaningful interaction' based on the number of comments and replies to comments a post receives. But, as this study shows, that only further incentivizes creating posts full of disinformation and other content likely to garner strong emotional reactions," she added. "Putting my conservative scientist hat on, I'm not comfortable saying how this applies to other social networks. We only studied Twitter here," said Sinan Aral, one of the researchers. "But my intuition is that these findings are broadly applicable to social-media platforms in general. You could run this exact same study if you worked with Facebook's data."

Yet these do not encompass the most depressing finding of the study. When they began their research, the MIT team expected that users who shared the most fake news would basically be crowd-pleasers. They assumed they would find a group of people who obsessively use Twitter in a partisan or sensationalist way, accumulating more fans and followers than their more fact-based peers. In fact, the team found that the opposite is true. Users who share accurate information have more followers, and send more tweets, than fake news sharers. These fact-guided users have also been on Twitter for longer, and they are more likely to be verified. In short, the most trustworthy users can boast every obvious structural advantage that Twitter, either as a company or a community, can bestow on its best users. The truth has a running start, in other words—but inaccuracies, somehow, still win the race. "Falsehood diffused further and faster than the truth *despite* these differences [between accounts], not because of them," write the authors.

This finding should dispirit every user who turns to social media to find or distribute accurate information. It suggests that no matter how adroitly people *plan* to use Twitter—no matter how meticulously they curate their feed or follow reliable sources—they can still get snookered by a falsehood in the heat of the moment.

It suggests—to me, at least, a Twitter user since 2007 . . .—that social media platforms do not encourage the kind of behavior that anchors a democratic government. On platforms where every user is at once a reader, a writer, and a publisher, falsehoods are too seductive not to succeed: The thrill of novelty is too alluring, the titillation of disgust too difficult to transcend. After a long and aggravating day, even the most staid users might find themselves lunging for the politically advantageous rumor. Amid an anxious election season, even the most public-minded users might subvert their higher interest to win an argument.

It is unclear which interventions, if any, could reverse this tendency toward falsehood. "We don't know enough to say what works and what doesn't," Aral told me. There is little evidence that people change their opinion because they see a fact-checking site reject one of their beliefs, for instance. Labeling fake news as such, on a social network or search engine, may do little to deter it as well. In short, social media seems to systematically amplify falsehood at the expense of the truth, and no one—neither experts nor politicians nor tech companies—knows how to reverse that trend. It is a dangerous moment for any system of government premised on a common public reality.

NOTES

1. Vosoughi, Soroush, Deb Roy, and Sinan Aral. 2018. "The Spread of True and False News Online," *Science*, 359 (6380): 1146–51.
2. Lazer, David M. J., et al. 2018. "The Science of Fake News." *Science*, 359 (6380): 1094–96.
3. Snopes Staff. 2015. "Donald Trump's Jet Carried a Critically Ill 3-Year-Old Jewish Boy from California to New York for Medical Treatment." *Snopes.com*. Retrieved on March 21, 2019, from https://www.snopes.com/fact-check/trump-flies-sick-boy.
4. Evon, Dan. 2016. "Is This Donald Trump's Cousin's Obituary?" *Snopes.com*. Retrieved on March 20, 2019 from https://www.snopes.com/fact-check/trumps-cousins-obituary.
5. Evon, Dan. 2016. "Floyd Mayweather Wore Hijab to Donald Trump Rally." *Snopes.com*. Retrieved on March 20, 2019, from https://www.snopes.com/fact-check/floyd-mayweather-muslim-headwear.
6. http://saifmohammad.com/WebPages/NRC-Canada-Sentiment.htm
7. https://twitter.com/barackobama/status/266031293945503744?lang=en

---

A SAVVY NEWS CONSUMER'S GUIDE: HOW NOT TO GET DUPED

ALICIA SHEPARD

Well news fans, to mix metaphors, the ball is now squarely in your court.

"Fake news" is everywhere. For instance:

- Millions voted illegally for Hillary Clinton.[1]
- Protesters were paid to disrupt Trump rallies.[2]
- Pope Francis endorsed Donald Trump.[3]

And one that turned up just days before the [2016 presidential] election: Clinton was behind the murder–suicide of an FBI agent involved in her private email debacle.[4] That's just a partial list of "stories." All unequivocally false. And [in 2016], a "fake news" story with real-life consequences: a 28-year-old man fired an assault rifle inside a DC pizzeria[5] . . . after reading an outlandish story linking the restaurant and (why not?) Clinton to a child sex-trafficking ring.

1 Seipel, Arnie. 2016. "Trump Makes Unfounded Claims That 'Millions' Voted Illegally for Clinton." *National Public Radio*, November 27. Retrieved on March 20, 2019, from https://www.npr.org/2016/11/27/503506026/trump-makes-unfounded-claim-that-millions-voted-illegally-for-clinton.

2 Maheshwari, Sapna. 2016. "How Fake News Goes Viral: A Case Study." *The New York Times*. Retrieved on March 20, 2019, from https://www.nytimes.com/2016/11/20/business/media/how-fake-news-spreads.html.

3 Snopes.com. n.d. "Pope Francis Shocks World, Endorses Donald Trump for President." Retrieved on March 20, 2019, from https://www.snopes.com/fact-check/pope-francis-donald-trump-endorsement.

4 National Public Radio. 2016. "Finding the Fake News King." Retrieved on March 20, 2019, from https://www.npr.org/sections/money/2016/12/02/504155809/episode-739-finding-the-fake-news-king.

5 Siddiqui, Faiz, and Susan Svriuga. 2016. "N.C. Man Told Police He Went to D.C. Pizzeria with Gun to Investigate Conspiracy Theory." *The Washington Post*, December 5. Retrieved on March 20, 2019, from https://www.washingtonpost.com/news/local/wp/2016/12/04/d-c-police-respond-to-report-of-a-man-with-a-gun-at-comet-ping-pong-restaurant/?utm_term=.07d54dab467e.

There is nothing new about "fake news." What is different today are the vast social media networks that allow all information—minor or major—to zip around the Internet in nanoseconds without regard to truth or importance. The proliferation of news consumption on social media means Americans are dealing with a firehose of information with little curation or verification. By age 18, according to a 2015 study by the Media Insight Project,[6] 88 percent of Millennials get news regularly from Facebook and other social media. According to the Pew Research Center,[7] nearly half of all adults get their news from Facebook, which is currently struggling with how to handle the thorny issue[8] of vetting fake news without violating First Amendment rights. All of this means that when it comes to determining fact from fake and understanding how one's own biases affect how news is accessed, processed, and shared, the onus in today's unfiltered media world is irrevocably on the news consumer.

The days when the mainstream news media were trusted gatekeepers who only published or aired deeply reported stories are *long* over. Each of us must act as our own editor, adopting the skills and taking the time (yes) to determine the real deal. One of the key newsroom axioms to adopt: "If your mother says she loves you, check it out."[9] In other words, the more you are inclined to believe something, the more you should be skeptical.

The failure to do this is why, no matter how rigorously mainstream news outlets fact-check false stories . . . it often doesn't matter. Liberals and conservatives believe what they want to believe no matter how far-fetched. It's known as confirmation bias.[10] People search out information that confirms or reinforces what they already think. All too often, they are not open to information that should cause them to question those beliefs. Research shows that when people are confronted with information that contradicts what they believe, our capacity to reason often shuts down! . . . In fact, Americans have gotten more entrenched in their beliefs[11] and their unwillingness to absorb information that contradicts or complicates their beliefs.

Philo Wasburn, a Purdue University sociology professor who co-wrote a book on media bias, knows this well. He told me . . . that research going back to the 1960s shows how difficult, if not impossible, it is to change people's central core beliefs. "When people are really committed to some ideological position, especially with politics, even if you present them with empirical evidence that supports the opposite of what they believe, they will reject it," said Wasburn. "Core beliefs are very, very resistant to change."

There already are efforts underway to educate the next generation on how to navigate news. The News Literacy Project[12] is a nonprofit dedicated to educating students in middle and high school on how to accurately sniff out the truth. The Center for News Literacy[13] at Stony Brook University works around the world providing tools to develop smarter news consumers. The need for such education is clear. A recent Stanford University study[14] found that 82 percent of middle schoolers did not know the difference between a real news story and an ad that clearly stated it was "sponsored content," basically unedited advertising. . . . "Students need to be able to understand newsworthiness, sourcing, documentation, fundamental fairness and the aspiration of minimizing bias in a dispassionate search for truth," wrote . . . [Alan Miller, a Pulitzer Prize-winning journalist]. "They also need to be familiar with concepts of transparency and accountability."

After a presidential election in which "fake news" played such a prominent role, the need for news literacy has never been greater. "The nature of the [2016] presidential campaign combined with the recent disclosures of the prevalence and power of 'fake news' have underscored the urgency of teaching news literacy to the next generation," said Miller. . . .

While baby boomers now miss the days when CBS's Walter Cronkite was the most trusted man in America, the problem with "fake news" isn't going away any time soon. Buzzfeed, which has been a leader in unmasking fake news . . . released a study [in 2016][15] showing that most Americans who see "fake news" believe it. As long as money can be made and people can be fooled, "fake news" designed to confuse and raise doubts will

6   American Press Institute. 2015. "How Millennials Get News: Inside the Habits of America's First Digital Generation." Retrieved on March 20, 2019, from https://www.americanpressinstitute.org/publications/reports/survey-research/millennials-news.

7   NiemanLab. 2016. "Nearly Half of U.S. Adults Get News on Facebook, Pew Says." Retrieved on March 20, 2019, from http://www.niemanlab.org/2016/05/pew-report-44-percent-of-u-s-adults-get-news-on-facebook.

8   Lee, Timothy B. 2016. "Facebook's Fake News Problem." *Vox*, November 16. Retrieved on March 20, 2019, from https://www.vox.com/new-money/2016/11/16/13637310/facebook-fake-news-explained.

9   Scanlan, Chip. 2003. "If Your Mother Says She Loves You, Check It Out: A Reporter's Cautionary Tale." Poytner.org. Retrieved on March 20, 2019, from https://www.poynter.org/reporting-editing/2003/if-your-mother-says-she-loves-you-a-reporters-cautionary-tale/.

10 Koerth-Baker, Maggie. 2013. "Why Rational People Buy into Conspiracy Theories." *The New York Times*, May 21. Retrieved on March 21, 2019, from https://www.nytimes.com/2013/05/26/magazine/why-rational-people-buy-into-conspiracy-theories.html.

11 Pew Research Center. 2016. "A Wider Ideological Gap Between More and Less Educated Adults." Retrieved on March 21, 2019, from https://www.people-press.org/2016/04/26/a-wider-ideological-gap-between-more-and-less-educated-adults/#partisan-divides-have-widened-on-many-political-value.

12 https://newslit.org

13 http://www.centerfornewsliteracy.org

14 Wineburg, Sam, et al. 2016. "Evaluating Information: The Cornerstone of Civic Online Reasoning." *Stanford Digital Repository*. Retrieved on March 21, 2019, from https://purl.stanford.edu/fv751yt5934.

15 Silverman, Craig, and Jeremy Singer-Vine. 2016. "Most Americans Who See Fake News Believe It, New Survey Says." *BuzzfeedNews*, December 6. Retrieved on March 21, 2019, from https://www.buzzfeednews.com/article/craigsilverman/fake-news-survey.

(continued)

flourish. One perpetrator of "fake news" told NPR[16] that he earned between $10,000 and $30,000 a month making stuff up to feed voracious partisan appetites. . . .

So What Can You Do?

Slow down. Don't reflexively pass on something. Start by *always* employing critical thinking skills. Be skeptical, not cynical. Expect to be fooled. Be vigilant. Don't make sweeping generalizations. Examine news stories on a case-by-case basis. A savvy news consumer's responsibility is to learn how to discern credible information from opinion, sponsored content, "fake news," viral rumors, clickbait, doctored videos or images, and plain old political propaganda. Here are some tips on how:

1. Consider the source.
   - Is it a site you are familiar with? If not, check the URL. Watch out for URLs with .co added to what looks like a mainstream news site . . .
   - Also watch for sites that end in "lo" like Newslo. "These sites take pieces of accurate information and then packag[e] that information with other false or misleading 'facts' (sometimes for the purposes of satire or comedy)," according to Merrimack College Professor Melissa Zimdars,[17] who has made a specialty of studying "fake news."
   - Read the "About Us" section. Does it seem credible? It, too, may be made up.
   - Is there a way to contact the news organization?
   - Does it have a link to its editorial standards?
   - How credible does the website look? Is it screaming ALL-CAPS? Are there distracting gizmos for you to click on and win $10,000? Exit, immediately.
2. Read beyond the headlines.
   Too often we read an outrageous headline that confirms our biases and quickly pass it on. Don't. Read deeper into the story and ask:
   - How many sources are there? Is there documentation or links to back up the claim? Could you independently verify the contents? In most mainstream media stories, people are quoted by name, title, and where they work (although sometimes they are quoted anonymously), and there are links to reports or court documents.
   - Search the names of people, places, or titles in a story. For example, the false story about Clinton being behind an FBI agent's murder–suicide, said it took place in

Walkerville, Maryland. There is no such place[18]. There is a Walkersville. Tricky.
   - Check out a far-fetched quote by copying and pasting it into a search engine. Anyone else have that [news story or headline]?
   - Check out the author's name. Search it or click on it. Has he or she written anything else? Is it credible?
   - Is there any context included in the story? Does it seem fair? Are there opposing points of view?
   - Drill down to find out who is behind the site—especially if it's a contentious issue.
3. Check the date.
   Too many times, a story is recycled with a new, exaggerated headline. You'd be surprised how many times people die. . . . I got an email that famous journalist Helen Thomas had died. I started to forward it, but something didn't seem right. Why? She had died three years ago.
4. Double check suspicious photos.
   This is fairly easy to do by right-clicking on an image and then doing a Google search [or use a Reverse Image search] . . .
5. Check your biases.
   Know your own biases. Try taking Harvard University's Project Implicit[19] bias test.
6. Learn from a wide variety of sources.
   - If you lean left, . . . read the *Wall Street Journal* editorial page, *Weekly Standard*, *National Review*, and *Reason* magazine. Be aware and skeptical of what's being said on Alex Jones, Rush Limbaugh, and Breitbart.
   - If you lean right, tune in to Rachel Maddow on MSNBC. Pay attention to Amy Goodman's Democracy Now! While the left doesn't appear to have as many well-established (and popular) conspiracy-theory, faux-news peddlers, the same goes for what you might hear on the other side. Be skeptical: If it sounds too good to be true, it bears checking out.
   - Or watch more middle-of-the-road news on PBS's *NewsHour* [or] listen to NPR.
   - Check out Media Matters, which monitors conservative media and the Media Research Center, which monitors the mainstream media.
   - If you walk away with one useful piece of information, always ask this question: *How do you know that?*
   - Do it all with a healthy skepticism. Every story you agree with isn't necessarily so. Every story you disagree with is not necessarily biased either. Be open to views you don't agree with.
   - Verify, verify, verify. And keep honing your skills.

16 Sydell, Laura. 2016. "We Tracked Down a Fake-News Creator in the Suburbs. Here's What We Learned." *National Public Radio*, November 23. Retrieved on March 21, 2019, from https://www.npr.org/sections/alltechconsidered/2016/11/23/503146770/npr-finds-the-head-of-a-covert-fake-news-operation-in-the-suburbs.

17 Zimbars, Melissa. 2016. "False, Misleading, Clickbait-y and Satirical 'News' Sources." https://docs.google.com/document/d/10eA5-mCZLSS4MQY5QGb5ewC3VAL6pLkT53V_81ZyitM/preview

18 Mikkelson, David. N.d. "FBI Agent Suspected in Hillary Email Leaks Found Dead in Apparent Murder." *Snopes.com*. Retrieved on March 21, 2019 from https://www.snopes.com/fact-check/fbi-agent-murder-suicide/

19 https://implicit.harvard.edu/implicit

JESSIE DANIELS

31. THE ALGORITHMIC RISE OF THE "ALT-RIGHT"

The rise of the "alt-right," organizations and individuals that promote racist White supremacist and White nationalist viewpoints and agendas, has depended largely on access to websites like Reddit and 4chan, as well as social media sites like Twitter. Daniels argues that the contemporary alt-right movement is a continuation of White supremacist media propaganda that has existed throughout American history, but that current White supremacist movements have taken advantage of the democratization of social media where there are no gatekeepers to spread their messages. This rising threat of White supremacy and White nationalism represents a great threat not only to less powerful groups and people in our society, but to our democracy in general.

On a late summer evening in 2017, members of the far-right descended on Charlottesville, Virginia, with tiki-torches held up in defense of Confederate general Robert E. Lee's statue in what was dubbed a "Unite the Right" rally, which had been organized mostly online. The next day, August 13, White nationalists rallied again and violently clashed with counter protestors. One drove his car into a multiracial crowd, killing one and seriously injuring 19 others. As it has turned out, the events in Charlottesville were a watershed moment in the algorithmic rise of White nationalism in the United States.

White nationalism has gone "from being a conversation you could hold in a bathroom, to the front parlor," according to William H. Regnery II. A multimillionaire, Regnery has spent a significant sum of his inherited wealth pushing his "race realist" agenda via a publishing house and the National Policy Institute, a think-tank. When his protégé and grantee, Richard Spencer, coined the new term *alt-right* in 2008, few took notice. Back then, Jared Taylor, publisher of the White nationalist site American Renaissance, said he thought of his own efforts as "just making a racket,"

but now he sees himself as part of an ascendant social movement, with Spencer in a lead role. He, along with Jason Kessler, helped organize the rally in Charlottesville.

"I think Tuesday was the most important day in the White nationalist movement," Derek Black told a *New York Times* reporter. Black, a former White nationalist, was referring to the Tuesday following the Charlottesville rally, when [President Donald Trump] . . . repeated White nationalist talking points defending the statues of America's founding slaveholders. In that *New York Times* interview, Black went on to describe his shock, "Tuesday just took my breath away. I was sitting in a coffee shop and I thought the news from this was done when I read that he had come back and he said there were good people in the White nationalist rally and he salvaged their message." It's certainly not the first time that a sitting president has openly heralded White supremacy from the Oval Office, but it is the first time that the ideology of White supremacy from both extreme and mainstream sources has been spread through the algorithms of search engines and social media platforms.

There are two strands of conventional wisdom unfolding in popular accounts of the rise of the alt-right. One says that what's really happening can be attributed to a crisis in White identity: the alt-right is simply a manifestation of the angry White male who has status anxiety about his declining social power. Others contend that the alt-right is an unfortunate eddy in the vast ocean of Internet culture. Related to this thesis is the idea that polarization, exacerbated by filter bubbles, has facilitated the spread of Internet memes and fake news promulgated by the alt-right. While the first explanation tends to ignore the influence of the Internet, the second dismisses the importance of White nationalism. I contend that we have to understand both at the same time.

For the better part of 20 years, I have been working with emerging technology and studying White supremacy in various forms of media. In the 1990s, I examined hundreds of printed newsletters from extremist groups and found that many of their talking points resonated with mainstream popular culture and politicians, like Pat Buchanan and Bill Clinton. After that, I left academia for a while and worked in the tech industry, where I produced online coverage of events like the 2000 presidential recount. When I returned to academic research, I did a follow-up study tracking how some of the groups I'd studied in print had—or had not—made it on to the Internet. I spent time at places like Stormfront, the White nationalist portal launched in the mid-1990s, and found that some groups had gained a much more nefarious presence than in their print-only days. And, I interviewed young people about how they made sense of White supremacy they encountered online. About the time I finished my second book in 2008, social media platforms and their algorithms began to change the way White nationalists used the Internet. Now I look at the current ascendance of the alt-right from a dual vantage point, informed both my research into White supremacy and my experience in the tech industry.

The rise of the alt-right is both a continuation of a centuries-old dimension of racism in the United States and part of an emerging media ecosystem powered by algorithms. White supremacy has been a feature of the political landscape in the United States since the start; vigilante White supremacist movements have been a constant since just after the Confederacy lost its battle to continue slavery. The ideology of the contemporary alt-right is entirely consistent with earlier manifestations of extremist White supremacy, with only slightly modifications in style and emphasis. This incarnation is much less steeped in Christian symbolism (few crosses, burning or otherwise), yet trades heavily in anti-Semitism. Even the Islamophobia among the alt-right has more to do with the racialization of people who follow Islam and the long history of connecting Whiteness to citizenship in the United States than it does with beliefs about Christendom. Movement members aim to establish a White ethno-state, consistent with every other extremist, White nationalist movement and more than a few mainstream politicians.

This iteration is newly enabled by algorithms, which do several things. Algorithms deliver search results for those who seek confirmation for racist notions and connect newcomers to like-minded racists, as when Dylann Roof [the White supremacist perpetrator of the Charleston Emanuel AME Church shooting in June 2015, which killed nine African American parishioners] searched for "Black on White crime" and Google provided racist websites and a community of others to confirm and grow his hatred. Algorithms speed up the spread of White supremacist ideology, as when memes like "Pepe the Frog" travel from 4chan or Reddit to mainstream news sites. And algorithms, aided by cable news networks, amplify and systematically move White supremacist talking points into the mainstream of political discourse. Like always, White nationalists are being "innovation opportunists," finding openings in the latest technologies to spread their message. To understand how all this works, it's necessary to think about several things at once: how race is embedded in the Internet at the same time that it is ignored, how White supremacy operates now, and the ways these interact.

BUILDING RACE INTO THE "RACELESS" INTERNET

The rise of the alt-right would not be possible without the infrastructure built by the tech industry, and yet, the industry likes to imagine itself as creating a "raceless" Internet. In a 1997 ad from a now-defunct telecom company, the Internet was touted as a "place where we can communicate mind-to-mind, where there is no race, no gender, no infirmities . . . only minds." Then the narration poses the question, "Is this utopia?" as the word is typed out. "No, the Internet." In many ways, the ad reflected what was then a rather obscure document, written by John Perry Barlow in 1996. Barlow . . . wrote A Declaration of the Independence of Cyberspace,[1] a manifesto-style manuscript in which he conceives of the Internet as a "place," much like the imaginary American frontier in a Hollywood Western, that should remain free from control by "governments of the industrial world," those "weary giants of flesh and steel." He ends with a grand hope of building "a civilization of the Mind in Cyberspace. May it be more humane and fair than the world your governments have made before."

While the giddy notion of a "mind-to-mind" utopia online may seem quaint by the standards of today's "don't-read-the-comments" Internet, Barlow's view remains, more than 20 years later, foundational in Silicon Valley. And it informs thinking in the tech industry when it comes to the alt-right. When several tech companies kicked alt-right users off their platforms after Charlottesville, they were met with a vigorous backlash from many in the industry. Matthew Prince, CEO and co-founder of Cloudflare, who reluctantly banned the virulently racist site, *The Daily Stormer*, from his service, fretted about the decision. "As [an] internet user, I think it's pretty dangerous if my moral, political or economic whims play some role in deciding who can and cannot be online," he said. The Electronic Frontier Foundation issued a statement that read, in part, "we believe that no one—not the government and not private commercial enterprises—should decide who gets to speak and who doesn't," closely echoing Barlow's manifesto.

. . . Critical writing about the Internet has followed, demonstrating the myriad ways race is built into digital technologies. The DOS commands of "master" disk and "slave" disk prompt, Anna Everett points out, reinscribe the master/slave narrative into the level of code. Recent concerns about digital surveillance technologies draw much from pre-digital

technologies developed to control enslaved peoples, Simone Browne has explained. Racial categories are coded into dropdown menus and the visual culture of nearly every platform, Lisa Nakamura observes. The nearly ubiquitous White hand-pointer acts as a kind of avatar that, in turn, becomes "attached" to depictions of White people in advertisements, the default "universal" Internet user at the keyboard that becomes part of the collective imagination, Michele White notes. Ideas about race are inextricably linked with the development of tech products, such as "Blackbird" (a web browser) or "Ms. Dewey" (a search tool), André Brock and Miriam Sweeney have written. The $13 billion digital video gaming industry has race coded into its interfaces and has enabled the alt-right, Kishonna Gray observes. The algorithms of search engines and their autocomplete features often suggest racism to users and direct them to White supremacist sites, Safiya Noble documents. And it goes on. Yet despite all this evidence that race is coded into these platforms, the ideology of colorblindness in technology—both in the industry and in popular understandings of technology—serves a key mechanism enabling White nationalists to exploit technological innovations. By ignoring race in the design process and eschewing discussion of it after products are launched, the tech industry has left an opening for White nationalists—and they are always looking for opportunities to push their ideology.

WHITE NATIONALISTS AS INNOVATION OPPORTUNISTS

The filmmaker D. W. Griffith is recognized as a cinematic visionary who helped launch an art form and an industry. His signature film, *Birth of a Nation* (1915), is also widely regarded as "disgustingly racist." Indeed, White supremacists seized upon it (and the emerging film technology) when it was released. At the film's premiere, members of the Klan paraded outside the theater, celebrating its depiction of their group's rise as a sign of Southern White society's recovery from the humiliation of defeat in the Civil War. When Griffith screened the film at the White House for Woodrow Wilson, who is quoted in the film, the president declared *Birth of a Nation* "history writ with lightning."

Capitalizing on this new technology, the KKK created film companies and produced their own feature films with titles like *The Toll of Justice* (1923) and *The Traitor Within* (1924), screening them at outdoor events, churches, and schools. By the middle of the 1920s, the Klan had an estimated five million members. This growth was aided by White supremacists' recognition of the opportunity to use the new technology of motion pictures to spread their message.

Almost a century later, another generation saw that same potential in digital technologies. "I believe that the Internet will begin a chain reaction of racial enlightenment that will shake the world by the speed of its intellectual conquest," wrote former KKK Grand Wizard David Duke on his website in 1998. . . . [Duke] was one who made the transition from the print-only era to the digital era. Duke joined forces with Don Black, another former KKK Grand Wizard, who shared a belief in new technologies for "racial enlightenment." Together, they helped the movement ditch Klan robes as the *costume de rigueur* of White supremacy and trade them for high-speed modems. Don Black created Stormfront in 1996. The site hosted a podcast created by Duke and pushed to more than 300,000 registered users at the site. Don Black's son recalled in a recent interview that they were a family of early adopters, always looking for the next technological innovations that they could exploit for the White nationalist movement:

> Pioneering White nationalism on the web was my dad's goal. That was what drove him from the early '90s, from [the] beginning of the web. We had the latest computers, we were the first people in the neighborhood to have broadband because we had to keep Stormfront running, and so technology and connecting people on the website, long before social media.

Part of what I observed in the shift of the White supremacist movement from print to digital is that they were very good, prescient even, at understanding how to exploit emerging technologies to further their ideological goals.

A few years after he launched Stormfront, Don Black created another, possibly even more pernicious site. In 1999, he registered the domain name martinlutherking.org, and set up a site that appears to be a tribute to Dr. King. But it is what I call a "cloaked site," a sort of precursor to today's "fake news." Cloaked sites are a form of propaganda, intentionally disguising authorship in order to conceal a political agenda. I originally discovered this one through a student's online search during a class; I easily figured out the source by scrolling all the way to the bottom of the page where it clearly says "Hosted by Stormfront." But such sites can be deceptive: the URL is misleading and most of us, around 85 percent, never scroll all the way to the bottom of a page. . . . So we see that White nationalists, as early adopters, are constantly looking for the vulnerabilities in new technologies as spots into which their ideology can be inserted. In the mid-1990s, it was domain name registration. The fact that a site with clunky design can be deceptive is due in large part to the web address. One young participant in my study said, "it says, martin luther king dot org, so that means they must be dedicated to that." To him, the "dot org" suffix on the domain name indicated that a nonprofit group "dedicated to Dr. King" was behind the URL.

White supremacists like Don Black understood that the paradigm shift in media distribution from the old broadcast model of "one-to-many" to Internet's "many-to-many" model was an opening. The kind of propaganda at the site about Dr. King works well in this "many-to-many" sharing environment in which there are no gatekeepers. The goal in this instance is to call into question the hard-won moral, cultural, and political victories of the civil rights movement by undermining Dr. King's personal reputation. Other cloaked sites suggest that slavery "wasn't that bad." This strategy, shifting the range of the acceptable ideas to discuss, is known as moving the "Overton window." White nationalists of the alt-right are using the "raceless" approach of platforms and the technological innovation of algorithms to push the Overton window.

The anything-goes approach to racist speech on platforms like Twitter, 4chan, and Reddit means that White nationalists now have many places beyond Stormfront to congregate online. These platforms have been adept in spreading White nationalist symbols and ideas, themselves accelerated and amplified by algorithms. Take "Pepe the Frog," an innocuous cartoon character that so thoroughly changed meaning that, in September 2016, the Anti-Defamation League added the character to its database of online hate symbols. This transformation began on 4chan, moved to Twitter, and, by August 2016, it had made it into a speech by presidential candidate Hillary Clinton.

"Turning Pepe into a White nationalist icon was one of our original goals," an anonymous White supremacist on Twitter told a reporter for the *Daily Beast* in 2016. The move to remake Pepe began on /r9k/, a 4chan board where a wide variety of users, including hackers, tech guys (and they were mostly guys), libertarians, and White supremacists who migrated from Stormfront gathered online. The content at 4chan is eclectic, or, as one writer put it, "a jumble of content, hosting anything from pictures of cute kittens to wildly disturbing images and language." It's also one of the most popular websites ever, with 20 million unique visitors a month, according to founder Christopher "Moot" Poole. "We basically mixed Pepe in with Nazi propaganda, etc. We built that association [on 4chan]," a White nationalist who goes by @JaredTSwift said. Once a journalist mentioned the connection on Twitter, White nationalists counted it as a victory—and it was: the mention of the 4chan meme by a "normie" on Twitter was a prank with a big attention payoff.

"In a sense, we've managed to push White nationalism into a very mainstream position," @JaredTSwift said. "Now, we've pushed the Overton window," referring to the range of ideas tolerated in public discourse. Twitter is the key platform for shaping that discourse. "People have adopted our rhetoric, sometimes without even realizing it. We're setting up for a massive cultural shift," @JaredTSwift said. Among White supremacists, the thinking goes: if today we can get "normies" talking about Pepe the Frog, then tomorrow we can get them to ask the other questions on our agenda: "Are Jews people?" or "What about Black on White crime?" And, when they have a sitting president who will retweet accounts that use #whitegenocide hashtags and defend them after a deadly rally, it is fair to say that White supremacists are succeeding at using media and technology to take their message mainstream.

NETWORKED WHITE RAGE

CNN commentator Van Jones dubbed the 2016 election a "Whitelash," a very real political backlash by White voters. Across all income levels, White voters (including 53 percent of White women) preferred the candidate who had retweeted #whitegenocide over the one warning against the alt-right. For many, the uprising of the Black Lives Matter movement coupled with the putative insult of a Black man in the White House were such a threat to personal and national identity that it provoked what Carol Anderson identifies as White Rage.

In the span of U.S. racial history, the first election of President Barack Obama was heralded as a high point for so-called American race relations. His second term was the apotheosis of this symbolic progress. Some even suggested we were now "postracial." But the post-Obama era proves the lie that we were ever postracial, and it may, when we have the clarity of hindsight, mark the end of an era. If one charts a course from the civil rights movement, taking 1954 (*Brown v. Board of Education*) as a rough starting point and the rise of the Black Lives Matter movement and the close of Obama's second term as the end point, we might see this as a five-decades-long "Second Reconstruction" culminating in the 2016 presidential election.

Taking the long view makes the rise of the alt-right look less like a unique eruption and more like a continuation of our national story of systemic racism. Historian Rayford Logan made the persuasive argument that retrenchment and the brutal reassertion of White supremacy through Jim Crow laws and the systematic violence of lynching was the White response to "too much" progress by those just a generation from slavery. He called this period, 1877–1920, the "nadir of American race relations." And the rise of the alt-right may signal the start of a second nadir, itself a reaction to the progress of Black Americans. The difference this time is that the "Whitelash" is algorithmically amplified, sped up, and circulated through networks to other White ethnonationalist movements around the world, ignored all the while by a tech industry that "doesn't see race" in the tools it creates.

MEDIA, TECHNOLOGY, AND WHITE NATIONALISM

Today, there is a new technological and media paradigm emerging, and no one is sure what we will call it. Some refer to it as "the outrage industry," and others refer to "the mediated construction of reality." With great respect for these contributions, neither term quite captures the scope of what we are witnessing, especially when it comes to the alt-right. We are certainly no longer in the era of "one-to-many" broadcast distribution, but the power of algorithms and cable news networks to amplify social media conversations suggests that we are no longer in a "peer-to-peer" model either. And very little of our scholarship has caught up in trying to explain the role that "dark money" plays in driving all of this. For example, Rebekah Mercer (daughter of hedge fund billionaire and libertarian Robert Mercer), has been called the "First Lady of the Alt-Right" for her $10 million underwriting of *Breitbart News*, helmed for most of its existence by former White House senior advisor Steve Bannon, who called it the "platform of the alt-right." White nationalists have clearly sighted this emerging media paradigm and are seizing—and being provided with millions to help them take hold of—opportunities to exploit these innovations with alacrity. For their part, the tech industry has done shockingly little to stop White nationalists, blinded by their unwillingness to see how the platforms they build are suited for speeding us along to the next genocide.

The second nadir, if that's what this is, is disorienting because of the swirl of competing articulations of racism across a distracting media ecosystem. Yet, the view that circulates in popular understandings of the alt-right and of tech culture by mostly White liberal writers, scholars, and journalists is one in which racism is a "bug" rather than a "feature" of the system. They report with alarm that there's racism on the Internet (or, in the last election), as if this is a revelation, or they "journey" into the heart of the racist right, as if it isn't everywhere in plain sight. Or they write with a kind of shock mixed with reassurance that alt-right proponents live next door, have gone to college, gotten a proper haircut, look like hipsters, or, sometimes, put on a suit and tie. Our understanding of the algorithmic rise of the alt-right must do better than these quick, hot takes.

If we're to stop the next Charlottesville or the next Emanuel AME Church massacre, we have to recognize that the algorithms of search engines and social media platforms facilitated these hate crimes. To grasp the 21st-century world around us involves parsing different inflections of contemporary racism: the overt and ideologically committed White nationalists commingle with the tech industry, run by boy-kings steeped in cyberlibertarian notions of freedom, racelessness, and an ethos in which the only evil is restricting the flow of information on the Internet (and, thereby, their profits). In the wake of Charleston and Charlottesville, it is becoming harder and harder to sell the idea of an Internet "where there is no race . . . only minds." Yet, here we are, locked in this iron cage.

NOTE

1. https://www.eff.org/cyberspace-independence

HOW THE INTERNET HAS CHANGED BULLYING

MARIA KONNIKOVA

This summer, *American Psychologist*, the official journal of the American Psychological Association, released a special issue[1] on the topic of bullying and victimization. Bullying is, presumably, as old as humanity, but research into it is relatively young: in 1997, when Susan Swearer, one of the issue's two editors, first started studying the problem, she was one of the first researchers in the United States to do so. Back then, only four states had official statutes against bullying behavior, and the only existing

1   "School Bullying and Victimization." 2015. *American Psychologist*, 70(4). https://www.apa.org/pubs/journals/special/4017005

longitudinal work had come out of Scandinavia, in the seventies. After Columbine, however, the landscape changed. The popular narrative at the time held that the shooters, Eric Harris and Dylan Klebold, had been bullied, and that idea—which has since been challenged[2]—prompted a nationwide conversation about bullying, which researchers around the country began studying in earnest. This special issue marks one of the first attempts to systematically review what we've learned in the last two decades—and, especially, to explore whether and how the Internet has changed the bullying landscape.

In some ways, bullying research has affirmed what we already know. Bullying is the result of an unequal power dynamic—the strong attacking the weak. It can happen in different ways: through physical violence, verbal abuse (in person or online), or the management of relationships (spreading rumors, humiliation, and exclusion). It is usually prolonged (most bullies are repeat offenders) and widespread (a bully targets multiple victims). Longitudinal work shows that bullies and victims can switch places: there is an entire category of bully-victims—people who are victims in one set of circumstances and perpetrators in another. Finally, emerging research demonstrates[3] that bullying follows us throughout life. Workplace and professional bullying is just as common as childhood bullying; often, it's just less obvious. (At work—one hopes—people don't steal your bicycle or give you a wedgie.)

To date, no one has systematically studied how different bullying settings affect bullying behavior—whether bullying in the Northeast differs from bullying in the Midwest, or whether bullying in certain cultures, neighborhoods, or professions comes with its own characteristics. What Swearer has noticed, however, in her nearly two decades of bullying research is a persistent—and seemingly fundamental—environmental distinction between urban and rural bullying. In urban and even midsized city environments, anonymity is possible. Even if you're bullied in school, you can have a supportive friend group at your local pickup basketball game. And there are multiple schools and multiple neighborhoods, which means you can float from one to the other, leaving bullying behind you in the process.

By contrast, in rural settings, "There aren't options," Swearer said, when we spoke earlier this month. "It's impossible to get away." The next school may be a hundred miles distant, so you are stuck where you are. What's more, everyone knows everyone. The problems of reporting a bully—or, if you are a bully, of becoming less of one—become much more intractable because your reputation surrounds you, and behavioral patterns are harder to escape. "Your world becomes an isolated and small place," Swearer says. Isolation itself, she points out, can lead to a sense of helplessness and lack of control—feelings that are associated with some of the worst, most persistent psychological problems in any population, including bullying.

In some ways, when it comes to bullying, the Internet has made the world more rural. Before the Internet, bullying ended when you withdrew from whatever environment you were in. But now, the bullying dynamic is harder to contain and harder to ignore. If you're harassed on your Facebook page, all of your social circles know about it; as long as you have access to the network, a ceaseless stream of notifications leaves you vulnerable to victimhood. Bullying may not have become more prevalent—in fact, a recent review of international data[4] suggests that its incidence has declined by as much as 10 percent around the world. But getting away from it has become more difficult.

The inescapability of "cyberbullying" has huge consequences not just for children but also for adults. While workplace bullying is still a new field of study, adults seem to experience bullying just as much as kids do.[5] A 2012 study[6] from the University of Nottingham and the University of Sheffield, in the UK, found that eight out of 10 of the 320 adults surveyed across three different universities had been victims of cyberbullying in the last six months; about a quarter reported feeling humiliated or ignored, or being the subject of online gossip, at least once a week. The effects of adult bullying can be just as severe, if not more so, than those of childhood bullying. While students can go to their teachers if they're being bullied, if you report your boss, you could be out of a job. And adult victims of cyberbullying tend to suffer higher levels of mental strain and lower job satisfaction than those subjected to more traditional forms of bullying. An undermining colleague can be put out of mind at the end of the day. But someone who persecutes you over e-mail, social networks, or anonymous comments is far more difficult to avoid and dismiss.

2   Cullen, Dave. 2004. "The Depressive and the Psychopath." *Slate.com*, April 20. Retrieved on March 21, 2019, from https://slate.com/news-and-politics/2004/04/at-last-we-know-why-the-columbine-killers-did-it.html.

3   Laschinger, Heather, K. Spence, and Amanda Nosko. 2013. "Exposure to Workplace Bullying and Post-Traumatic Stress Symptomology: The Role of Protective Psychological Resources." *Journal of Nursing Management* 23(2): 252–262.

4   Rigby, Ken, and Peter K. Smith. 2011. "Is School Bullying Really on the Rise?" *School Psychology of Education*, 14(4): 441–55.

5   Einarsen, Ståle, and Anders Skogstad. 1996. "Bullying at Work: Epidemiological Findings in Public and Private Organizations." *European Journal of Work and Organizational Psychology* 5(2): 185–201.

6   Sprigg, C., Axtell, C., Farley, S., and Coyne, I., 2012. "Punched from the Screen: Workplace Cyberbullying." *Economic and Social Research Council Festival of Social Science*, Sheffield, UK, 3.

(continued)

Many forms of adult bullying are uncomfortably close to the sorts of shaming behaviors outlined by Jon Ronson in his recent book, *So You've Been Publicly Shamed.* . . . Ronson documents the rise of cyberbrigades which unite in virtual outrage, on Twitter, Reddit, or elsewhere online, to disparage someone's words or behavior. Participants often feel that their abusive actions flow from justified outrage—but all bullies think that their behavior is justified. "We know from moral disengagement work that all bullies feel morally justified in their actions," Swearer pointed out. Ask people why they bully, and they rarely say, "Because I can." They say, "Because I need to." Bullies believe they are teaching someone a lesson; they claim that their victims, through their own actions or faults, are asking for it, and that they need to be called out and corrected. "They say it's retaliatory. 'I just retaliated,'" Swearer said. "They build narratives of their behaviors." Many of the bullies Swearer has dealt with don't seem to have realized that what they did was bullying: they demonstrate "a lack of insight and self-awareness." Instead, they see themselves as righteous crusaders.

In children, it's possible to instill self-awareness about bullying through schoolwide interventions. Catherine Bradshaw, a psychologist and associate dean at the University of Virginia who studies bullying prevention, has found[7] that the most effective approaches are multilayered and include training, behavior-modification guidelines, and systems for detailed data collection (more, in other words, than a stray assembly or distributed book). Unfortunately, the equivalent for adults can be hard to find. Many adult bullies hide behind the idea that bullying happens only among children. They conceive of themselves as adults who know better and are offering their hard-earned wisdom to others. The Internet makes that sort of certainty easier to attain: looking at their screens, adult bullies rarely see the impact of their words and actions. Instead, they comfortably bask in self-righteous glory. The UK study from 2012 found that online bystanders, too, are disengaged. Observing the actions of cyberbullies, they were less concerned than when they watched in-person bullying.

In short, the picture that's emerged suggests that the Internet has made bullying both harder to escape and harder to identify. It has also, perhaps, made bullies out of some of us who would otherwise not be. We are immersed in an online world in which consequences often go unseen—and that has made it easier to deceive ourselves about what we are doing. The first step to preventing bullying among adults, therefore, might be simple: introspection.

---

7   Bradshaw, Catherine. 2015. "Translating Research to Practice in Bullying Prevention." *American Psychologist*, 70(4): 322–332.

NANCY WANG YUEN

32. REEL INEQUALITY

Hollywood Actors and Racism

When you sit down to watch a movie or TV show, do you think about the race of the actors and actresses, and whether or not they are representative of the diverse audiences that consume media? Yuen argues that Hollywood is an industry steeped in racial bias and discrimination, a trend that has continued for decades. The exclusion of people of color from TV and film, and the restrictive, stereotypical roles they do receive, have wide-reaching consequences not just for the actors and actresses (who miss out on roles, income, and acclaim), but on our larger society.

#OscarsSoWhite . . . Again I will not be attending the Oscar ceremony this coming February. We cannot support it. . . . How is it possible for the second consecutive year all 20 contenders under the actor category are White? And let's not even get into the other branches. 40 White actors in 2 years and no flava at all. We can't act?! WTF!!

—Spike Lee [2016]

In 2016, for the second consecutive year, the Academy of Motion Picture Arts and Sciences nominated White actors for all acting awards. This revived the hashtag #OscarsSoWhite, pulling back the curtain on Hollywood's enduring race problem.[1] Despite showing talent, resilience, and bankability, why do actors of color continue to lag [behind] White actors in numbers and prominence? At the epicenter is the industry's racial and gender homogeneity,

epitomized by the Academy's corps of invited-only members. With a 93 percent White and 76 percent male membership,[2] the Academy has come under pressure to diversify. In protest, Spike Lee and Jada Pinkett Smith both announced they would not attend the Oscars ceremony.[3] The Academy's president, Cheryl Boone Isaacs, responded quickly with promises of change. Several (White) Academy members defended the status quo. Oscar nominee Charlotte Rampling called the protest "racist to Whites" and suggested that perhaps "Black actors did not deserve to make the final list."[4] Similarly, double-Oscar-winner Michael Caine said, "In the end, you can't vote for an actor because he's Black. You can't say, 'I'm going to vote for him. He's not very good, but he's Black.'"[5] Cries of reverse racism and blaming actors of color for their own marginalization are commonplace in Hollywood. These arguments falsely assume an equal playing field while dismissing institutional racial biases that privilege White actors for roles and recognition.

Hollywood's systemic exclusion of actors of color is evident in the Academy's abysmal record of nominating and awarding actors of color. [As of 2016], in Oscar's 88-year history, actors of color had received only 6.2 percent of total acting nominations and won only 7.8 percent of total acting awards.[6]. . . The only woman of color to ever win a best actress award was African American actor Halle Berry in 2002 for her performance in *Monster's Ball*. Fifty-nine years have passed since the last (and only) Asian female actor won an acting Oscar (Miyoshi Umeki, 1957 best supporting actress for her performance in *Sayonara*) and 25 years since a Latina took home an acting Oscar (Mercedes Ruehl, 1991 best supporting actress for her performance in *The Fisher King*). No acting Oscar has gone to an actor of Asian, Latina/o, or indigenous descent for the past 15 years. By deeming only White actors worth honoring, the Academy reproduces Hollywood's structural racial bias. [*Editor's Note*: The 2019 Oscars were a somewhat mixed bag for racial diversity and inclusion. African American actress Regina King won Best Supporting Actress for her role in *If Beale Street Could Talk*, African American actor Mashershala Ali won Best Supporting Actor for *The Green Book*, and African American director Spike Lee won Best Adapted Screenplay for his film *BlacKkKlansman*. In addition, two African American women were the first-ever African American winners in their roles: *Black Panther*'s costume designer Ruth Carter won for Best Costume Design and production designer Hannah Beachler won for Best Production Design. The Best Picture Oscar, though, was awarded to the film *Green Book*, a film whose approach to racism "follows the same White-centering narrative as previous winners such as *Driving Miss Daisy*, *The Help*, and *The Blind Side*."[7]]

Though public pressures have prompted the Academy to implement immediate changes to diversify its membership,[8] the impact on future nominations remains uncertain. This is because the Academy's diversity problem is not just numerical but also ideological. The Academy constrains actors of color by granting Oscars to a narrow set of stereotyped roles.

David Oyelowo describes how Black actors "have been celebrated more for when we are subservient . . . not just in the Academy, but in life generally. We have been slaves, we have been domestic servants, we have been criminals, we have been all of those things. But we have been leaders, we have been kings, we have been those who changed the world."[9] Hattie McDaniel, the first African American actor to win an Academy Award (best supporting actress in 1940), played house slave Mammy in *Gone with the Wind* (1939). More than 70 years later, Academy Award winners of color still play servile roles. Octavia Spencer won the 2012 best supporting actress award for playing a maid in *The Help*, and Lupita Nyong'o won the 2014 best supporting actress award for playing a slave in *12 Years a Slave*. Producer Ice Cube, in discussing *Straight Outta Compton*'s 2016 Oscar snubs, joked, "Maybe we should've put a slave in *Straight Outta Compton*. I think that's where we messed up . . . just one random slave for the Academy members to recognize us as a real, Black movie."[10]

Though actors of color have played leaders, they rarely win Oscars for such roles. Denzel Washington won the best actor Oscar for playing a corrupt cop in *Training Day* (2001), but not for his widely lauded performance of the title character in *Malcom X* (1992). Another noteworthy performance, David Oyelowo's critically acclaimed portrayal of Martin Luther King Jr. in *Selma* (2014), did not even garner a nomination. By honoring actors of color for playing slaves, maids, and criminals rather than civil rights leaders, the Academy denies them the full breadth of accolades afforded to White actors. The Academy may or may not intentionally vote for roles that keep people of color "in their place," but its record reveals a pattern of bias. Consequently, the Academy will have to diversify more than just members' numbers, but their hearts and minds as well.

#OscarsSoWhite is a symptom of Hollywood's larger race problem. The exclusion and stereotyping of actors of color extend far beyond the Academy Awards. Even though people of color made up 37.4 percent of the U.S. population in 2013, actors of color played only 6.5 percent of lead roles in broadcast television shows and 16.7 percent of lead roles in films.[11] Furthermore, Hollywood tends to view actors of color—from the Oscar contenders to the average working actor—through a racist lens, reducing them to tokens and caricatures. Hiro,[12] a veteran Japanese American working actor in his late sixties, told me that Hollywood never sees him beyond his race. When he was a guest star on a television show, the White male director continually referred to him as an "Asian actor in this part," but described another White male guest star as a "good killer" and "gushed" about his "wonderful [acting] moments." For White actors, race is a privilege rather than a reduction. From *Iron Man* to *Mad Men*, White men access a dazzling array of lead roles in nearly every genre and medium. In my interviews, several White male actors confessed to having a racial advantage. Roane, a White male actor in his mid-twenties, said, "I'm very lucky. There are a lot of roles for young, White kids. I've got buddies who are Puerto Rican or African American, and they have a hard time finding work."

This [reading] is about how actors of color experience racism in the Hollywood industry, which I define as the system of major and minor film and television studios along with the production companies they fund.[13] Although the current Hollywood industry is less centralized than the earliest studio system, racial barriers continue to persist, even if they have diminished somewhat over the years. Roles have increased for actors of color, but most groups have yet to achieve U.S. population parity. Even as more actors of color star in their own shows and films, most continue to play supporting and bit parts. From talent agent offices to film sets, actors of color still face stereotypes that bar them from reaching their full artistic potential. The persistent exclusion and stereotyping of actors of color for the past century demonstrate how far we are from a postracial society; that is, a society in which racism no longer exists. At the same time, actors of color demonstrate resilience as they creatively challenge stereotypes in their auditions and performances. A growing number of performers of color create original Web series, some of which cross over into mainstream Hollywood. So while Hollywood still represents race in problematic ways, actors of color are performing countertakes informed by their own identities and experiences. Taking readers behind the

scenes, this [reading] reveals how actors of color suffer and survive in spite of the odds.

EFFECTS OF MEDIA STEREOTYPES

Growing up as an immigrant kid in Southern California, just miles from the Hollywood industry, I watched hours of television for amusement. This continues to be the norm today. In 2015, the average U.S. resident consumed "traditional and digital media for over 1.7 trillion hours, an average of approximately 15 and-a-half hours per person per day."[14] In the same year, children (eight- to 12-year-olds) consumed an average of six hours of media a day, and teens consumed nine hours.[15] This mindboggling amount of media consumption shapes how we see the world we live in. Even though my neighborhood was racially and ethnically diverse when I was growing up, the world looked completely White on television. I absorbed a very narrow vision of U.S. culture. All throughout my childhood, I did not see myself represented in film and television beyond the occasional cringeworthy Asian nerd or massage parlor worker. In the film and television worlds, only White lives mattered, and the rest of us were either marginalized or demonized. In college, where I learned that race is not biological but socially constructed, I also saw how Hollywood dramatized racial differences as natural and fixed. Far from neutral, mass media institutions such as Hollywood are major transmitters of racist ideologies. Antonio Gramsci theorized that society's elites use the mass media to maintain "hegemony," or the dominance one social group holds over others.[16] Hollywood's dominant narratives of Whites as heroes and actors of color as sidekicks or villains legitimate and reproduce the racial hierarchies existent in U.S. society.

Though they are largely fictional, on-screen images can shape our views of reality. I witnessed this firsthand when I went to see *Skyfall* (2012), a James Bond film. Preview after preview of action films featured White male protagonists shooting and killing people, yet it was the preview for *Django Unchained* (2012) that elicited an extreme audience reaction. In one scene, Django (played by Jamie Foxx), a Black slave-turned-bounty-hunter, says, "Kill White folks, and they pay you for it—what's not to like?" This statement caused two middle-aged White women sitting in my row to groan loudly, as one of them griped, "That's what's wrong with our urban areas!" Even though we were about to watch a violent James Bond film and had just sat through brutal violence enacted by Tom Cruise, Bruce Willis, and Arnold Schwarzenegger, none of those previews elicited critique. The lack of Black heroes in film and television, coupled with the preponderance of White heroes and Black villains, demonizes Black male violence and legitimizes White male violence. Furthermore, this extrapolation of a fictional Django to "our urban areas" demonstrates how audiences fail to distinguish between fiction and reality in racial stereotypes. Through countless reiterations in popular media, racial stereotypes can become *real* in the minds of audiences.[17]

Popular media can have a negative impact on Whites' perceptions of people of color. One study found that nonverbal racial biases in facial expressions and body language, as represented on popular television shows, influence White viewers' racial biases.[18] Furthermore, a lack of contact between racial groups can lead to greater reliance on media stereotypes when formulating ideas about people outside one's race.[19] Studies show that audiences substitute stereotypes they see on screen for reality when they have not had any direct interactions with particular racial groups.[20] For instance, Latino stereotypes in the media can lead audiences negatively to associate immigration with increased unemployment and crime.[21] Film and television can also exacerbate preexisting racist fears. For example, people who perceive that they live in a neighborhood with a high percentage of Blacks are more likely than those who do not hold that perception to fear crime after watching scripted crime dramas.[22]

Given that Whites greatly overestimate the share of crimes committed by Blacks,[23] media stereotypes can aggravate such misperceptions and can be used to justify violence against people of color. Darren Wilson—the White police officer who shot and killed Michael Brown, an unarmed Black man, in Ferguson, Missouri—characterized Brown as a "demon" and a "hulk." Journalists pointed out that Wilson's descriptors came from the "Black brute" racial stereotype, a "stock figure of White supremacist rhetoric in the

lynching era of the late nineteenth and early twentieth centuries,"[24] as popularized in Hollywood films.[25] Furthermore, the media's tendency to fuel racial misperceptions can contribute to the disparate punishment of people of color.[26] Film and television can also cultivate existent fears of foreign threat. In 2014, a journalist critiqued the popular cable television show *Homeland* as perpetuating Middle Eastern stereotypes used to "justify actions in the real world—U.S. wars, covert operations and drone strikes; CIA detention and torture; racist policing, domestic surveillance and militarized borders."[27] Racism, when packaged as entertainment, can skew the way viewers understand and categorize people.

In addition to aggravating racial tensions, the erasure and negative portrayals of people of color can adversely affect how people of color see themselves. Prolonged television exposure predicts a decrease in self-esteem for all girls and for Black boys, and an increase in self-esteem for White boys.[28] These differences correlate with the racial and gender biases in Hollywood, which casts only White men as heroes, while erasing or subordinating other groups as villains, sidekicks, and sexual objects. Studies also show how media images of Native American mascots lower the self-esteem and affect the moods of Native American adolescents and young adults, who have the highest suicide rates in the United States.[29] The ubiquity of racist imagery can have cumulative effects on society. We cannot dismiss the media's differential portrayals of racial groups as mere entertainment if we are to take seriously their impact on our youth.

A BRIEF HISTORY OF HOLLYWOOD'S RACISM

Racism, in the form of job exclusion and racially stereotyped roles, has defined the Hollywood film industry since its birth in the early 1900s. The first characters of color were portrayed as morally and intellectually deficient by White actors in Blackface, brownface, and yellowface—makeup used to portray characters of a different race. The practice of White actors playing characters of color came from minstrel shows, popularized in the United States in the 1830s and 1840s.[30] The early performers were mainly Irish and Jewish immigrants, who did not share equal status with earlier

European immigrants (mainly of Anglo-Saxon origin) to the United States.[31] Through their performances, the Irish and Jewish minstrels "Whitened themselves" by promoting White ethnic behaviors as acceptable, while denouncing behaviors by Blacks, Native Americans, and Chinese as abnormal and criminal.[32] Minstrelsy on stage and screen was a widespread form of entertainment and helped the Irish and Jews assimilate into White culture and status.[33] In fact, Jewish studio magnates in the 1920s and 1930s purposefully "presented a Hollywood version of Jewishness that was just as White and equally 'American,'" focusing on virtues of hard work, sacrifice, and family values.[34] Many White ethnic actors achieved stardom (and assimilation) in the 1940s and 1950s by dropping their ethnic names: Doris Kapplehoff became Doris Day and Dino Crocetti became Dean Martin.[35] In contrast, Hollywood's systemic discrimination prevented actors of color from achieving stardom. James Shigeta, a Japanese American actor whose work in Hollywood began in the late 1950s, recalled a musical film producer telling him, "If you were White, you'd be a hell of a big star."[36] Although race can change over time for some groups (as demonstrated by the "Whitening" of the Irish and Jews), the majority of African Americans, Asian Americans, Latinx, and Native Americans continue to experience race (and racism) as paramount over other identifiers.[37]

Hollywood's early films drew on the legacy of minstrelsy, presenting people of color as comedic buffoons or lecherous villains. From the Blackface portrayals of African Americans as fools, rapists, and schemers in D. W. Griffith's *The Birth of a Nation* (1915) to the yellowface performances of Asians as diabolical, inscrutable, and exotic foreigners, Hollywood has a rich history of casting White actors to mock people of color. The brownface portrayals of Latinx [people] as *banditos* (or violent and immoral criminals), starting with the silent "greaser" films in the 1910s,[38] became so egregious that the Mexican government banned such films in early 1922.[39] The Mexican government lifted the ban on November 6, 1922, after the Motion Picture Producers and Distributors of America (MPPDA)[40] agreed to stop making films offensive to Mexico or any other Latin American country. However, the Hollywood studios got around this agreement

by inventing fake Latin American countries, such as Orinomo and San Benito, to recycle the same offensive stereotypes.[41] When actors of color did appear on screen in the twentieth century, they were mainly background characters, stereotypes, and occasional foils to White leads. Roles for women of color were extremely rare and were played mostly by White women. Luise Rainer played the lead Chinese female character in *The Good Earth* (1937), Katharine Hepburn played the lead Chinese female character in *Dragon Seed* (1944), and Natalie Wood played the lead Puerto Rican female character in *West Side Story* (1961).[42] The few notable exceptions were all men of color: Sessue Hayakawa (Japanese American) and Ramón Novarro (Mexican American) were matinee idols in the 1910s and 1920s, and Anthony Quinn (Oscar-winning Mexican American) and Sidney Poitier (Oscar-winning African American) were film stars in the 1950s and 1960s.[43] Despite achieving rare stardom, these actors of color still faced stereotyped roles.

Institutionally, Hollywood excluded actors of color from equal employment access through its production codes. From 1930 to 1956, Hollywood formally barred actors of color from most film leads through an anti-miscegenation clause that banned depictions of interracial relationships.[44] This clause was part of Hollywood's self-imposed censorship regulations (called the Motion Picture Production Code, or Hays code) and mirrored anti-miscegenation laws that criminalized marriage and intimate relationships between White persons and any persons of color. Because actors of color were not allowed to star in a relationship with a White actor (even if the White actor was playing a character of color), they were systematically excluded from lead roles. The Hays code prevented Chinese American actor Anna May Wong from being cast as O-lan, the Chinese female lead in *The Good Earth* (1937), opposite a White actor cast to play the Chinese male lead [Paul Muni].[45] Instead, as mentioned earlier, Luise Rainer (a White actor) was cast to play O-lan—winning a best actress Oscar for her performance. Given the scarcity of stories about people of color, the casting of White actors as leads of color prevented actors of color from achieving stardom. [*Editor's Note*: The trend of "Whitewashing" Asian roles has continued through the 2000s. In 2018, author Kevin Kwan revealed that when a Hollywood producer originally offered to make his best-selling novel *Crazy Rich Asians* into a movie, the deal was contingent on rewriting the main character from an "American-born Chinese woman" to be a White woman. The movie was eventually made with an all-Asian cast.[46]]

Throughout the years, Hollywood also bypassed equal employment laws. In March 1969, the Equal Employment Opportunity Commission (EEOC) held a one-day hearing in Hollywood to address the "clear evidence of a pattern or practice of discrimination in violation of Title VII of the Civil Rights Act of 1964" in the film industry.[47] They presented evidence that people of color were excluded from nearly all jobs in Hollywood except the lowest paying and lowest-skill jobs.[48] In response, the Justice Department prepared lawsuits against six of the seven major motion picture studios, the Association of Motion Picture and Television Producers (AMPTP), and the International Alliance of Theatrical State Employees (IATSE) to address the "gross underutilization" of racial minority workers in major positions of talent and production.[49] However, the film studios successfully lobbied and campaigned against this intervention, solidifying White domination in the industry to this day.

Hollywood producers also use the protection of the First Amendment to bypass nondiscriminatory hiring laws. Requests for particular racial and gender categories in casting notices (or job advertisements for actors) should violate Title VII of the Civil Rights Act of 1964, which protects minorities from discrimination. However, producers can hire actors based on specific racial, gender, and age categories by simply claiming that the categories serve the story they want to tell. . . . In fact, no court has ever made a formal judgment or decision about an actor's claim of race or gender discrimination in job advertisements.[50]

With a history of exclusion and no legal protection, actors of color continue to face stunted opportunities in mainstream film and television. For example, in 1999, no actor of color had a lead role on any of the 26 new shows premiering on the major broadcast television networks.[51] More than a decade later, change has been minimal. Despite an increased number of broadcast television shows featuring actors of color in the 2014–2015 prime-time season, the overall season still saw White actors playing show regulars at a rate nearly 10 percent greater than their percentage of the U.S. population.[52] Even though people of color comprised 37.4 percent of the U.S. population and purchased 44 percent of domestically sold tickets in 2014,[53] actors of color played only a quarter of the speaking characters in the top 100 films.[54] These discrepancies demonstrate systemic barriers that prevent actors of color from accessing the same opportunities as White actors.

Exacerbating these low numbers is the continued casting of Whites as characters of color, which reduces the number of leads for actors of color. White actors played the Latino leads in films such as *Casa de Mi Padre* (2012) and *Argo* (2012), the African American leads in *A Mighty Heart* (2007) and *Stuck* (2007), the Asian leads in *Aloha* (2015) and *Ghost in the Shell* (2017), Native American characters in films such as *Pan* (2015) and *The Lone Ranger* (2013), and the Egyptian leads in *Exodus: Gods and Kings* (2014).[55] . . . Even when critiqued, Hollywood executives and directors defend such castings. In response to criticisms of *Exodus*'s casting, media mogul Rupert Murdoch tweeted, "Since when are Egyptians not White? All I know are."[56] Similarly, when asked why he cast himself (a White male) and not a Latino to play the Latino lead (based on real-life CIA officer, Tony Mendez) in *Argo* (2012), Ben Affleck answered, "Tony does not have, I don't know what you would say, a Latin/Spanish accent," and "You wouldn't necessarily select him out of a line of 10 people and go, 'This guy's Latino.'"[57] Affleck basically stated that Latino actors should only play accented roles. This is part of a larger industry perception that actors of color are only fit to play a limited, often stereotyped set of roles. Hollywood continues to cast White actors to portray the range of humanity, while barring qualified actors of color from portraying people of color.

In an ideal Hollywood industry, all actors can play all ethnicities equally. After all, acting is pretending to be someone else. However, Hollywood is not an equal playing field when actors of color remain invisible or sidelined to a select few shows while White actors enjoy the privilege of portraying every role under the sun—even characters of color. Film and television shows continue to exclude talented actors of color based solely on their race. Case in point, acclaimed Black British actor Idris Elba, despite being a fan favorite to play the next James Bond, has met resistance from Roger Moore (former Bond actor), who said Bond should be "English-English,"[58] and from Anthony Horowitz (the author commissioned by Ian Fleming's estate to write the next James Bond novel), who said Elba was "too 'street' for Bond."[59] These racially coded comments demonstrate the double standard actors of color face when playing crossover characters. Until Hollywood provides actors of color proportionate access to all roles (especially leads), White actors should not play characters of color. For example, White actors should not play Latina/o leads, given that none of the top ten films or network television shows in 2013 cast a single Latina/o actor in a lead role.[60] With Latinos making up 17 percent of the U.S. population, their invisibility in Hollywood is a gross misrepresentation of the American landscape. In that same year, the Academy awarded the best picture Oscar to *Argo* (in which White actor Ben Affleck plays the Latino lead) but no acting Oscar to an actor of color. When the types of roles are unlimited for White actors, their chances of winning awards increase. This is in great contrast with actors of color, who struggle to find lead roles that showcase their talent.

THE INDUSTRY TODAY

Today, Hollywood is one of the biggest entertainment and media industries in the world, with its $449 billion profits exceeding those of professional sports ($23 billion), the alcohol industry ($227 billion), and the gambling industry ($37 billion).[61] Such large sums of money also bring great risk. If a film flops, a studio can lose hundreds of millions of dollars. Consequently, Hollywood relies heavily on past hits, formulas, and big-name actors. This institutional risk aversion goes hand in hand with racial bias. Within this system, actors of color are often caught in a vicious cycle wherein they have few opportunities to become bankable stars, making them financial risks, which in turn limits their role prospects and prominence . . .

There are approximately 63,230 professional actors working in the United States.[62] The average member of the actors' union earns $52,000 a year,[63] while 95 percent make less than $100,000 annually.[64] The actors I interviewed exemplify the average member.[65] They call themselves "working," "middle-class," and "journeyman" actors. These working actors have modest and often unstable income streams. . . . Not only do working actors make up the majority of the talent pool, but working actors also populate the supporting and background roles, most of which are one-dimensional. Furthermore, they have to audition for all of their work rather than being offered roles by studios. Dick, a 45-year-old White male actor, describes the different expectations directors have for "stars" versus working actors: "The stars have the luxury of actually being able to experiment and try stuff and have that creative relationship with the director. But, with workhorses like myself, they want us to do what they paid us to do and for us not to be a headache or a question mark." Hollywood expects little to no deviance in performances from working actors. But those expectations differ for White actors and actors of color. . . .

Professional actors are an ideal group for studying racism in Hollywood. . . . Furthermore, acting has long been used as a framework to understand the process by which people create and perform social roles in everyday life.[66] . . . Professional actors of color are self-consciously aware of racial stereotyping because they are literally asked to perform and embody stereotyped traits. As they intentionally take on false roles, actors are highly aware of the tension between role playing and their "true" identities . . . Though they are limited in power, working actors of color see themselves as activists—challenging Hollywood's racism one costume or one accent at a time. Moreover, they can turn to digital media spaces, such as YouTube, to create and star in original shows. . . . Professional actors' experiences shed light on how people of color experience discrimination but manage to preserve their identities within racially biased environments. Although actors' stories of racism demonstrate how far we are from a postracial society, their attempts to subvert and challenge stereotypes reveal their resilience and creativity . . .

NOTES

1. Tre'vell Anderson, "#OscarsSoWhite Creator on Oscar Noms: 'Don't Tell Me That People of Color, Women Cannot Fill Seats,'" *Los Angeles Times*, January 14, 2016, from http://www.latimes.com/entertainment/envelope/la-et-mn-april-reign-oscars-so-white-diversity-20160114-story.html.

2. John Horn and Doug Smith, "Diversity Efforts Slow to Change the Face of Oscar Voters," *Los Angeles Times*, December 21, 2013, from http://www.latimes.com/entertainment/movies/moviesnow/la-et-mn-diversity-oscar-academy-members-20131221-story.html.

3. David Ng, "Spike Lee and Jada Pinkett Smith to Boycott Oscars; Academy Responds," *Los Angeles Times*, January 18, 2016, from http://www.latimes.com/ entertainment/movies/la-et-spike-lee-to-boycott-oscars-html- 20160118-htmlstory.html.

4. Ben Child, "Oscars 2016: Charlotte Rampling Says Diversity Row Is 'Racist to White People,'" *Guardian*, January 22, 2016, from http://www.theguardian.com/film/2016/jan/22/oscars-2016-charlotte-rampling-diversity-row-racist-to-white-people.

5. Yesha Callahan, "#OscarsSoWhite: Michael Caine Thinks Blacks Should Be Patient; Charlotte Rampling Says Diversity Complaints Are Racist against Whites," *The Root*, January 22, 2016, from http://www.theroot.com/blogs/the_grapevine/2016/01/_oscarssowhite_michael_caine_thinks_blacks_should_be_patient_charlotte_rampling.html.

6. Data from Academy of Motion Picture Arts and Sciences, "The Official Academy Awards® Database," from http://awardsdatabase.oscars.org/ampas_awards/BasicSearchInput.jsp; Susan King, "Oscar Diversity: It's Been 54 Years since a Latina Took Home an Academy Award," Los Angeles Times, January 21, 2016, from http://www.latimes.com/entertainment/movies/la-et-mn-oscar-diversity-asian-latino-indigenous-nominees-winners-20160120-story.html; Ana Maria Benedetti, "A Look Back at the Lack of Latinos in Oscar History," Huffpost Latino Voices, February 20, 2015, from http://www.huffingtonpost.com/2015/02/20/latino-oscar-history_n_6723284.html.

7. Pollard, Alexandra. 2019. "Four Years after #OscarsSoWhite, the 91st Academy Awards Headed Toward Redemption but Fell at the Final Hurdle." *The Independent*, February 25. Retrieved on March 20, 2019, from https://www.independent.co.uk/arts-entertainment/films/features/oscars-2019-oscarssowhite-green-book-bohemian-rhapsody-black-panther-olivia-colman-spike-lee-a8795331.html.

8. Janice Min, "#OscarsSoWhite: Academy Chiefs Reveal Behind-the- Scenes Drama That Led to Historic Change (Exclusive)," *Hollywood Reporter*, January 27, 2016, from http://www.hollywoodreporter.com/features/oscarssowhite-academy-chiefs-reveal-behind-859693.

9. Scott Feinberg, "'Selma' Star David Oyelowo Says Academy Favors 'Subservient' Black Roles," *Hollywood Reporter*, February 2, 2015, from http://www.hollywoodreporter.com/race/selma-star-david-oyelowo-says-769032.

10. Ice Cube, *The Angie Martinez Show*, Power 105.1, January 20, 2016, from http://www.power1051fm.com/articles/trending-104655/watch-ice-cube-blames-oscar-nomination-14294665.

11. U.S. Population (2014 estimate): U.S. Census, "State and County Quickfacts," http://quickfacts.census.gov/qfd/states/00000.html; lead roles in broadcast television shows (2012–2013) and lead roles in film (2011–2013): Darnell Hunt and Ana-Christina Ramon, "2015 Hollywood Diversity Report: Flipping the Script" (Los Angeles: Ralph J. Bunche Center for African American Studies at UCLA, 2015), 9, 13.

12. I use first-name pseudonyms and no surnames for all of my interviewees.

13. After consulting with industry insiders, I use "Hollywood" and "Hollywood industry" to mean the current system of major and minor studios (i.e., majors such as Universal, Disney, and Warner Bros., and minors such as Lionsgate, Summit, and the Weinstein Company), as well as the production companies that are funded and/or distributed in some way by those studios (i.e., Legendary, New Regency, and Amblin). Furthermore, even though funding comes from both international and domestic sources, as long as the primary funding or distribution is funneled through the studios or Hollywood institutions (and not independent sources), the practices of these studios are generalizable to the rest.

14. James E. Short, "How Much Media? 2013 Report on American Consumers," Los Angeles: Institute for Communications Technology Management, Marshall School of Business, University of Southern California, October 2013.

15. Vicky Rideout, "The Common Sense Census: Media Use by Tweens and Teens," San Francisco: Common Sense Media, 2015, 13.

16. Antonio Gramsci, *Selections from Cultural Writings* (Cambridge, MA: Harvard University Press, 1978); James Lull, *Media Communications and Culture: A Global Approach* (New York: Columbia University Press, 1995).

17. Michael Omi, "In Living Color: Race and American Culture," in *Signs of Life in the USA: Readings on Popular Culture for Writers*, ed. S. Maasik and J. Solomon (Boston: Bedford Books, 1997), 500.

18. Max Weisbuch et al., "The Subtle Transmission of Race Bias via Televised Nonverbal Behavior," *Science* 326 (December 18, 2009): 1711.

19. Qingwen Dong and Arthur Phillip Murrillo, "The Impact of Television Viewing on Young Adults' Stereotypes towards Hispanic Americans," *Human Communication* 19, no. 1 (2007); Robert M. Entman and Andrew Rojecki, *The Black Image in the White Mind: Media and Race in America*, Studies in Communication, Media, and Public Opinion (Chicago: University of Chicago Press, 2000).

20. Joe R. Feagin, *Racist America: Roots, Current Realities, and Future Reparations* (New York: Routledge, 2000), 141–42.

21. Jeffrey M. Timberlake et al., "Who 'They' Are Matters: Immigrant Stereotypes and Assessments of the Impact of Immigration," *Social Science Quarterly* 56, no. 2 (2015): 267–99.

22. Sarah Eschholz et al., "Television and Fear of Crime: Program Types, Audience Traits, and the Mediating Effect of Perceived Neighborhood Racial Composition," *Social Problems* 50, no. 3 (2003): 395–415.

23. Ana Swanson, "Whites Greatly Overestimate the Share of Crimes Committed by Black People," *Washington Post*, December 1, 2014, from https://www.washingtonpost.com/news/wonk/wp/2014/12/01/whites-greatly-overestimate-the-share-of-crimes-committed-by-black-people.

24. Jamelle Bouie, "Michael Brown Wasn't a Superhuman Demon: But Darren Wilson's Racial Prejudice Told Him Otherwise," *Slate*, November 26, 2014, from http://www.slate.com/articles/news_and_politics/politics/2014/11/darren_wilson_s_racial_portrayal_of_michael_brown_as_a_superhuman_demon.single.html; Frederica Boswell, "In Darren Wilson's Testimony, Familiar Themes about Black Men," National Public Radio (November 26, 2014)

25. Donald Bogle, *Toms, Coons, Mulattoes, Mammies, and Bucks: An Interpretive History of Blacks in American Films* (New York: Continuum, 2001), 10.

26. Nazgol Ghandnoosh, "Race and Punishment: Racial Perceptions of Crime and Support for Punitive Policies" (Washington, DC: The Sentencing Project, 2014), from http://sentencingproject.org/doc/publications/rd_Race_and_Punishment.pdf.

27. Laura Durkay, "'Homeland' Is the Most Bigoted Show on Television," *Washington Post*, October 2, 2014, from https://www.washingtonpost.com/posteverything/wp/2014/10/02/homeland-is-the-most-bigoted-show-on-television.

28. N. Martins and K. Harrison, "Racial and Gender Differences in the Relationship between Children's Television Use and Self-Esteem: A Longitudinal Panel Study," *Communication Research* 39, no. 3 (2011): 338.

29. Michael A. Friedman, "The Harmful Psychological Effects of the Washington Football Mascot," 2013. From http://www.changethemascot.org/wp-content/uploads/2013/10/DrFriedmanReport.pdf.

30. "Blackface Minstrelsy," Public Broadcasting System, from http://www.pbs.org/wgbh/amex/foster/sfeature/sf_minstrelsy_1.html.

31. Noel Ignatiev, *How the Irish Became White* (New York: Routledge, 1995); David R. Roediger, *The Wages of Whiteness: Race and the Making of the American Working Class*, rev. ed., Haymarket Series (London: Verso, 1999); Michael Rogin, *Blackface, White Noise: Jewish Immigrants in the Hollywood Melting Pot* (Berkeley: University of California Press, 1996).

32. Robert G. Lee, *Orientals: Asian Americans in Popular Culture* (Philadelphia: Temple University Press, 1999), 34–35.

33. Lee, *Orientals.*

34. Karen Brodkin, *How Jews Became White Folks and What That Says about Race in America* (New Brunswick, NJ: Rutgers University Press, 1998), 156.

35. Stanley Lieberson, *A Piece of the Pie: Blacks and White Immigrants since 1880* (Berkeley: University of California Press, 1980), 32–33.

36. Quoted in Nancy Wang Yuen, "Actors, Asian American," in *Asian American Society: An Encyclopedia*, ed. Mary Yu Danico (Thousand Oaks, CA: Sage, 2014), 18.

37. Feagin, *Racist America;* Lieberson, *A Piece of the Pie;* Michael Omiand Howard Winant, *Racial Formation in the United States: From the 1960s to the 1980s* (New York: Routledge & Kegan Paul, 1986); Mia Tuan, *Forever Foreigners or Honorary Whites?: The Asian Ethnic Experience Today* (New Brunswick, NJ: Rutgers University Press, 1998); Mary C. Waters, *Ethnic Options: Choosing Identities in America* (Berkeley: University of California Press, 1990).

38. Charles Ramírez Berg, *Latino Images in Film: Stereotypes, Subversion, Resistance* (Austin: University of Texas Press, 2002), 68. *Greaser* is a "derogatory American English slang for native Mexican or Latin American, first attested 1849, so called from appearance." Definition from *Dictionary.com. Online Etymology Dictionary.* Douglas Harper, Historian. http://www.dictionary.com/browse/greaser.

39. Clint C. Wilson, Félix Gutiérrez, and Lena M. Chao, *Racism, Sexism, and the Media: Multicultural Issues into the New Communications Age*, 4th ed. (Thousand Oaks, CA: Sage, 2013), 77.

40. The Motion Picture Producers and Distributors of America (MPPDA) was the trade association for the major companies in the motion picture industry during the 1920s and 1930s.

41. Laura Serna, "'As a Mexican I Feel It's My Duty:' Citizenship, Censorship, and the Campaign against Derogatory Films in Mexico, 1922–1930," *The Americas* 63, no. 2 (October 2006): 232.

42. Meredith Simons, "100 Times a White Actor Played Someone Who Wasn't White," *Washington Post*, January 28, 2016, from https://www.washingtonpost.com/posteverything/wp/2016/01/28/100-times-a-white-actor-played-someone-who-wasnt-white.

43. Info from http://www.IMDB.com.

44. Susan Courtney, *Hollywood Fantasies of Miscegenation: Spectacular Narratives of Gender and Race, 1903–1967* (Princeton, NJ: Princeton University Press, 2005), 115–16.

45. Timothy P. Fong, Valerie Soe, and Allan Aquino, "Portrayals in Film and Television," in *Encyclopedia of Asian American Issues Today*, ed. Edith W. Chen and Grace J. Yoo (Westport, CT: Greenwood Press, 2009), 644.

46. Stefansky, Emma. 2017. "Hollywood Tried to Make *Crazy Rich Asians* about a White Woman." *Vanity Fair*, November 4. Retrieved on March 20, 2019, from https://www.vanityfair.com/hollywood/2017/11/hollywood-tried-to-make-crazy-rich-asians-about-a-white-woman.

47. Eithne Quinn, "Closing Doors: Hollywood, Affirmative Action, and the Revitalization of Conservative Racial Politics," *Journal of American History* 99, no. 2 (2012): 466.

48. Quinn, "Closing Doors," 470.

49. Quinn, "Closing Doors," 466.

50. As of 2007, according to Russell Robinson, "Casting and Caste-ing: Reconciling Artistic Freedom and Antidiscrimination Norms," *California Law Review* 95, no. 1 (February 2007): 73.

51. Greg Braxton, "A White, White World on TV's Fall Schedule," *Los Angeles Times*, May 28, 1999, from http://articles.latimes.com/1999/may/28/ news/mn-41995.

52. Author's analysis of the 2014–2015 prime-time season on broadcast television, based on regular cast listings on the network's own websites, reveals that Whites occupied 72 percent of all regular roles, nearly 10 percent above their 2013 U.S. Census percentage of 62.6 percent.

53. Motion Picture Association of America, "Theatrical Market Statistics 2014" (Washington, DC: Author, 2015), 12. From http://www.mpaa.org/wp-con-tent/uploads/2015/03/MPAA-Theatrical-Market-Statistics-2014.pdf.

54. Stacey Smith, Marc Choueiti, and Katherine Pieper, "Race/Ethnicity in 600 Popular Films: Examining on Screen Portrayals and Behind the Camera Diversity," in *Media, Diversity, and Social Change Initiative* (Los Angeles: University of Southern California Annenberg School for Communication and Journalism, 2014), 1.

55. Simons, "100 Times a White Actor Played Someone Who Wasn't White."

56. Ryan Gajewski, "Rupert Murdoch Defends 'Exodus' Cast: 'Since When Are Egyptians Not White?'" *Hollywood Reporter*, November 29, 2014, from http://www.hollywoodreporter.com/news/rupert-murdoch-defends-exodus-cast-752805.

57. Ruben Navarrette Jr., "Latino Should Have Played Lead in 'Argo,'" *CNN.com* (2013), from http://www.cnn.com/2013/01/09/opinion/navarrette-argo-affleck-latino/index.html.

58. Ben Child, "Roger Moore Denies Racist Comments about Idris Elba Playing James Bond," *Guardian*, March 30, 2015, http://www.theguardian.com/film/2015/mar/30/roger-moore-denies-racist-comments-about-idris-elba-playing-james-bond.

59. Eliza Berman, "James Bond Author Apologizes for Calling Idris Elba 'Too Street' to Play 007," *Time*, September 1, 2015, from http://time.com/ 4018556/anthony-horowitz-idris-elba-james-bond.

60. Frances Negron-Muntaner et al., "The Latino Media Gap: A Report on the State of Latinos in U.S. Media" (New York: Center for the Study of Ethnicity and Race, Columbia University, 2014).

61. McKinsey & Company, "Global Media Report 2014: Global Industry Overview" (2014). Plunkett Research, "Introduction to the Sports Indus- try," Plunkette Research, Ltd., from http://www.plunkettresearch.com/sports-recreation-leisure-market-research/industry-trends; David Hunkar, "The World's Five Biggest Alcohol Companies by Market Cap," Seeking Alpha, http://seekingalpha.com/article/198673-the-world-s-five-biggest-alcohol-companies-by-market-cap; American Gaming Association, "State of the States: The Aga Survey of Casino Entertainment" (Washington, DC: Author, 2013).

62. U.S. Department of Labor, "Occupational Employment and Wages—May 2013," in *Bureau of Labor Statistics* (U.S. Department of Labor, 2014).

63. THR Staff, "Hollywood Salaries Revealed, from Movie Stars to Agents (and Even Their Assistants)," *Hollywood Reporter*, October 2, 2014, from http://www.hollywoodreporter.com/news/hollywood-salaries-revealed-movie-stars-737321.

64. Jonathan Handel, "Dues for Middle-Class SAG Actors, Most Dual Cardholders Would Decrease in Merger (Analysis)," *Hollywood Reporter*, March 3, 2012, from http://www.hollywoodreporter.com/news/sag-aftra-merger-dues-decrease-296663.

65. See appendix B of *Reel Inequality: Hollywood Actors and Racism* for details on the interview participants and methods.

66. Erving Goffman, *The Presentation of Self in Everyday Life* (New York: Doubleday Anchor, 1959); Arlie Russell Hochschild, *The Managed Heart: Commercialization of Human Feeling* (Berkeley: University of California Press, 1983); Richard Sennett, *The Fall of Public Man* (New York: Norton, 1974), 107–22.

CHAPTER 8

SOCIAL PROBLEMS RELATED
TO EDUCATION

Education is often touted as the solution to many social problems—higher educated individuals tend to earn more income, have lower rates of unemployment, and have better health outcomes than those with lower levels of education.[1] Higher educated individuals also pass some benefits of education to their children—there is a strong relationship between parents' educational attainment and their children's academic success.[2] At the same time, many of our social problems are replicated in the education system, including race, gender, and class inequalities. Our education system is not equal-access, equally high-quality, or inclusive for all students, which can reproduce many social inequalities. Readings in this chapter discuss inequalities and social problems in the education system, and examine ways in which policymakers, educators, parents, and students can create positive change in our education system.

Many Americans assume that after segregated schools were prohibited in *Brown v Board of Education* in 1954 many of the issues of inequality in schools were eliminated. As Linda Darling-Hammond discusses, extreme inequalities in the education system persist, in particular for students of color. These inequalities have continued in large part because of the way public schools are funded—through property taxes—which replicates inequalities between upper-, middle-, and lower-income neighborhoods through unequal access to resources, well-maintained facilities and equipment, and experienced teachers. This funding structure amplifies the advantages that wealthier children have in place when they enter the school environment, and it leaves many lower-income students and students of color behind. Public education is a public good—an institution we all contribute to, which benefits all

---

1   Schanzenbach, Diane Whitmore, Lauren Bauer, and Audrey Breitwieser. 2017. "Eight Economic Facts on Higher Education." The Hamilton Project, The Brookings Institute. Retrieved on March 19, 2019, from https://www.brookings.edu/wpcontent/uploads/2017/04/thp_20170426_eight_economic_facts_higher_education.pdf.
2   Egalite, Anna J. 2016. "How Family Background Influences Student Achievement." *Education Next*, 16(2): 70–79.

citizens, even if we don't directly benefit ourselves. A cultural shift that prioritizes individual over collective benefits has led to the neglect of the public good in favor of profit maximization; this shift could threaten our democracy and our values of fairness, equity, and justice.[3]

Unequal access to quality education and funding for schooling is a major reproducer of inequality, but there are other factors that impact academic outcomes for students. For example, students enter school with very different skill levels, parents engage in different levels of advocacy on behalf of their children, and home environments differ. Moreover, in a typical year, kids spend just 25 percent of their waking hours in school. Given this statistic, how can we know how much the school environment alone actually matters for a child's educational achievement? Douglas B. Downey and Benjamin G. Gibbs argue that it is as important to take the social context outside of schools into consideration when developing educational policies and programs to solve educational inequalities. Access to the Internet outside of school and in one's home—and whether or not smart phones alone offer enough Internet access for children to complete schoolwork and study—is one example of how out-of-school context matters for kids' educational attainment, as discussed in a reading by Alina Selyukh.

Inequalities in the education system and in educational outcomes start early in our educational careers—as early as preschool. Jeneen Interlandi discusses the challenges of educating preschool-aged children—a job typically seen as low-skill and so typically not paid well—and how increased knowledge about how, when, and what types of intellectual stimulation children need have changed our perception of early childhood educators and the need for high-quality early education for all children. As more and more cities and states begin to require higher education of preschool teachers—an expectation many of the educators did not anticipate when they entered the field—Interlandi asks how we can support both the students and their teachers on their educational journeys. Another unexpected change in the educational landscape that teachers did not anticipate is the rise in violence in schools—namely, school shootings. Ashley Lamb-Sinclair discusses how the tragic ubiquity of school shootings has increased calls for active-shooter training, the presence of law enforcement, and the arming of teachers to protect the nation's children—often at the cost of the mental health of teachers and their students.

While some are calling for a greater law enforcement presence in elementary, middle, and high schools, other activists are calling for less. The presence of "school resource officers," often hired to prevent school-based violence, has become a tool for enforcing strict discipline standards in school. As Mimi Kirk details, the persistence of implicit bias against students of color—in particular, against male students—results in broad disciplinary infractions like "insubordination" which can often result in suspension, expulsion, and arrest. These punishments increase students' contact with the criminal justice system and can have negative impacts on their education. And because they happen disproportionately across race, class, and gender lines, they reproduce inequalities that are present in the larger society.

---

3   Hannah-Jones, Nikole. 2017. "Have We Lost Sight of the Promise of Public Schools?" *The New York Times*. February 21.

Indeed, Yolanda Young discusses research indicating that as early as preschool, implicit racial bias leads teachers to observe Black students more closely and to indicate their behavior as problematic, opening up access to a school-to-prison pipeline that can have severe long-term consequences for students.

Inequalities run through the entire education experience, even for students in higher education. The rising cost of education means that not only is educational attainment out of reach for an increasing number of Americans, but those who are able to enroll in college often face additional financial stressors, such as food and housing instability. Katharine Broton and Sara Goldrick-Rab explain that, while students across all types of institutions of higher education struggle financially, students from families on the lower end of the income spectrum are more likely to report food insecurity and hunger as college students. Broton and Goldrick-Rab argue that food and housing insecurity threaten students' abilities to complete school, and that colleges and universities need to do more to support students and reduce the stigma of financial difficulty.

Finally, Bailey A. Brown discusses another social problem related to education: rising student loan debt. At the same time as higher education is promoted as a solution to individual problems and societal issues, the cost of a college education has ballooned. Students are leaving college with higher debt loads than at any other time in American history, negatively impacting their career outcomes, financial stability, and wealth-generating opportunities in the future. As with the other educational problems discussed in this chapter, this burden does not land equally on all Americans: students from low-income families, first-generation college students, and students of color are more likely to have the most severe debt burden, and so are most likely to be negatively impacted by the "investment" in higher education. By examining the ways in which the education system replicates and creates social inequality, we can have a better understanding of how, or whether, education is a path out of the problems.

JESSE HAGOPIAN

Jesse Hagopian teaches ethnic studies and history and is the co-adviser to the Black Student Union at Garfield High School in Seattle, Washington. He is a founding member of Social Equity Educators, co-editor of *Teaching for Black Lives*, and editor *of More Than a Score: The New Uprising Against High-Stakes Testing*. He also serves as the Director of the Black Education Matters Student Activist Award.

What is the mission of Social Equity Educators?

Social Equity Educators (SEE) emerged in 2008 from the struggle to stop school closures in the Seattle area. When the Great Recession was in full swing, many public schools in our area were slated for closure. We knew we needed an organization to push our union to fight these sorts of issues. We organized a grassroots movement of students, parents, and teachers and were successful in keeping some of those schools off of the chopping block, though some were still closed. We grew from a handful of teachers at the beginning to a large formal organization that focuses on defending our schools from corporate education reform and fighting against institutional racism and other forms of oppression. We want to strengthen our teachers' unions by organizing the power of labor, together with parents, students, and the wider community, to fight to defend and transform public education and to produce a socially just society. We believe that unions should go far beyond specific contractual disputes and partner with various social justice movements. For example, what if educators went on strike until all the migrant families were reunited at the border?

What was your role?

I have been on the Steering Committee of SEE for a long time. We've run candidates for office in the union, organized conferences, and participated at various rallies and protests supporting more funding for the public schools. We became well known for helping to spread a boycott against a high-stakes standardized test called "the MAP test" from Garfield High School in Seattle to several other schools. One of the most powerful actions of SEE was to support the educators at John Muir Elementary School who wore Black Lives Matter shirts to school. With the support of SEE, Black Lives Matter at School became a day of action observed by some 3,000 educators around Seattle in 2016.

What motivated the MAP test boycott?

The boycott was motivated by the complete uselessness of the MAP test as a pedagogical tool. It was not properly aligned to our curriculum, and yet it was taking over schools. It was wasting weeks of classroom and instructional time; it wasn't culturally or linguistically appropriate for our English-language learners, and it just wasn't giving any useful feedback for teachers. And because it was computer-administered, it was taking over our computer labs and libraries and taking those resources away from students.

My fellow educators and I actually know what quality assessment looks like, and we were already using far superior assessments in our classrooms. This test and punish model really was demoralizing. We agreed that we needed to push back against a corporate education reform model that believes in reducing the process of teaching and learning down to a single test score, which they then use to label schools as "failing" and to bust up teachers' unions by tying employment to this model of testing. We felt we didn't need to pull kids out of class and waste instructional time anymore, so we took a unanimous vote not to administer the exam. The teachers were threatened with a ten-day suspension, without pay. But because of the unanimous vote of the Parent–Teacher–Student Association (PTSA) and Student Government, the teachers had the confidence not to back down and continue with their struggle. Letters of solidarity poured in from all over the country—literally thousands of signatures came flooding into Garfield High School. Ever since, we've been in an ongoing "Education Spring" with record numbers of people engaged in resisting high-stakes testing in U.S. history.

At the end of that year, the Superintendent announced that the MAP test would no longer be mandatory for high schools in Seattle. We have not had the MAP test since, which really showed the power of solidarity.

What inspired you to become an education activist?

I began teaching in Washington, DC, in a school that was 100 percent African American, and I would pass the White House on the way to my school. My classroom had a hole in the ceiling and when it rained, my classroom literally flooded. I got to school one morning, and the first project I had ever assigned, one where students were to write about a figure in American history that they admired, was ruined. That was the same year No Child Left Behind was implemented. I saw the federal government blaming teachers, shaming schools, and focusing on standardized test scores, while at the same time they were unwilling to provide

the basic resources that our kids needed. They were leaving our schools racially segregated and isolated. I realized it was going to have to be those of us in the classroom who would have to have to fight back.

What are your future activism goals?

I would like to continue participation in the Black Lives Matter at School movement. What started in Seattle in 2016 inspired teachers around the country to conduct similar actions. Educators in Philadelphia even took our day of action and expanded it into a week of action that has now become a national uprising for racial justice in the schools. We currently have a national BLM at School coalition with thousands of educators around the United States who wear Black Lives Matter shirts to school and teach lessons about structural racism, intersectional Black identities, Black history and antiracist movements. Our coalition has four demands: End "zero tolerance" discipline and implement restorative justice; hire more Black teachers; mandate Black history and ethnic studies in the K–12 curriculum; and fund counselors, not cops. We won't stop building this movement until public education fulfills its promise to unlock the potential of every student and all the structures of institutional racism are brought down.

What types of strategies do you use to enact social change?

Most important is building relationships among colleagues, parents, community members, and leaders of various organizations. Within those relationships we need to educate leaders, activists, and the general public about how high-stakes testing is ruining public education. Corporate stakeholders are trying to reduce the intellectual process of teaching and learning to a number—training a whole generation of children that wisdom is the ability to eliminate wrong answer choices rather than to collaborate on a project to solve a problem or to be creative and imaginative. Finally, you need to organize and plan actions, big and small. Whether it is a forum, or a public film showing, a boycott, or a strike, you have to take action. It's not enough just to educate. You need to agitate.

What are the major challenges you face in your activist efforts?

One of the major challenges is the threat that comes from those in power. Those in power stand to make a lot of money from high-stakes standardized testing, such as directly profiting from sales of the tests (like the multibillion dollar corporation, Pearson). Others who stand to benefit are the privatizers who want to be able to label schools as "failing" so that they can shut them down and open up private charter schools. There's a lot of money to be made off high-stakes testing, and that's why the threats against those of us engaged in this work are getting more and more severe. The superintendent of the Seattle school district threatened the teachers of Seattle with a ten-day suspension without pay if they engaged in boycotts. But threats can be overcome with solidarity, which we saw in action during the MAP test boycott. The real challenge is how to build solidarity among diverse communities and get parents, students, and teachers to see that they have the same interest in the struggle. That kind of solidarity is only possible if our movement directly challenges institutional racism and shows educators of color that this movement will support their most pressing needs.

What would you consider to be your greatest success as an activist?

The MAP test boycott is the clearest example of the power of solidarity. It inspired people around the country and the world, and it was a decisive victory. It has also been amazing to see the development of educators joining the struggle for racial justice and Black students organizing walkouts against police brutality. And there has been an immense power of solidarity in educators building the Black Lives Matter at School movement.

Why should students get involved in educational activism?

We face immense challenges in our world: mass incarceration, a national epidemic of sexual assault and violence against women, historic levels of income inequality, xenophobic attacks on immigrants, and so much more. And perhaps no threat is bigger than climate change, which threatens the future of humanity to survive on the planet in the not too distant future. If we're going to continue to survive as a human race on this planet, we have to redefine education, assessment, and learning as being more than filling in a bubble on a test. Implementing critical thinking and problem solving in education is actually the fight for us to survive on this planet, as those skills will help us to solve the other challenges we face as a nation and as global citizens. It is worth the sacrifices this work entails to be part of that struggle.

What can students do with limited time and money?

Students can stay connected with others doing this work around the country, whether it's following the work of other activists online or attending conferences. *Rethinking Schools* magazine, for example, is a resource that continually inspires me. And I would recommend that you join two of the biggest movements to defend and transform public education: The opt-out movement, and the Black Lives Matter at School movement. When movements against corporate education reform join with antiracist struggles, we will have the power to build a school system that truly affirms the lives of every student.

LINDA DARLING-HAMMOND

33. INEQUALITY AND SCHOOL RESOURCES

What It Will Take to Close the Opportunity Gap

Darling-Hammond discusses the major factors that contribute to inequalities in educational outcomes, including high levels of child poverty, the unequal allocation of school resources, the re-segregation of schools, and the lack of high-quality teachers and curriculum in low-income and minority schools. These inequities create formidable barriers to students' academic success and have long-term consequences for individual students, entire communities, and our country as a whole.

Enormous energy is devoted in the United States to discussions of the achievement gap.[1] Much less attention, however, is paid to the opportunity gap, the cumulative differences in access to key educational resources that support learning at home and at school: expert teachers, personalized attention, high-quality curriculum opportunities, good educational materials, and plentiful information resources. Systemic inequalities in all of these resources, compounded over generations, have created what Gloria Ladson-Billings has called an "educational debt" owed to those who have been denied access to quality education for hundreds of years[2]. . . .

Institutionally sanctioned discrimination in access to education is as old as the United States itself. From the time that southern states made it illegal to teach an enslaved person to read, through Emancipation and Jim Crow, and well into the twentieth century, African Americans faced de facto and de jure exclusion from public schools, as did Native Americans and, frequently, Mexican Americans.[3] Even in the North,

problems of exclusion, segregation, and lack of resources were severe. In 1857, for example, a group of African American leaders protested to a New York State investigating committee that the New York City board of education spent sixteen dollars per White child and only one cent per Black child for school buildings. While Black students occupied schools described as "dark and cheerless" in neighborhoods "full of vice and filth," White students were taught in "splendid, almost palatial edifices, with manifold comforts, conveniences, and elegancies."[4]

The *Williams v. California* case, a class action lawsuit filed in 2000 on behalf of California's low-income students of color, demonstrated that wide disparities still exist almost 150 years later. The plaintiffs' complaint included many descriptions of schools like this middle school in San Francisco:

At Luther Burbank, students cannot take textbooks home for homework in any core subject because their teachers have enough textbooks for use in class only. . . . For homework, students must take home photocopied pages, with no accompanying text for guidance or reference, when and if their teachers have enough paper to use to make homework copies. . . . Luther Burbank is infested with vermin and roaches, and students routinely see mice in their classrooms. One dead rodent has remained, decomposing, in a corner in the gymnasium since the beginning of the school year. The school library is rarely open, has no librarian, and has not recently been updated. The latest version of the encyclopedia in the library was published in approximately 1988. Luther Burbank classrooms do not have computers. Computer instruction and research skills are not, therefore, part of Luther Burbank students' regular instruction. The school no longer offers any art classes for budgetary reasons. . . . Two of the three bathrooms at Luther Burbank are locked all day, every day. . . . Students have urinated or defecated on themselves at school because they could not get into an unlocked bathroom. . . . When the bathrooms are not locked, they often lack toilet paper, soap, and paper towels, and the toilets frequently are clogged and overflowing. . . . Ceiling tiles are missing and cracked in the school gym, and school children are afraid to play games in the gym because they worry that more ceiling tiles will fall on them during their games. . . . The school has no air conditioning. On hot days classroom temperatures climb into the 90s. The school heating system does not work well. In winter, children often wear coats, hats, and gloves during class to keep warm. . . . Eleven of the 35 teachers at Luther Burbank have not yet obtained regular, nonemergency teaching credentials, and 17 of the 35 teachers only began teaching at Luther Burbank this school year.[5]

These inequities are in part a function of how public education in the United States is funded. In most states, education costs are supported primarily by local property taxes, along with state grants-in-aid that are somewhat equalizing but typically insufficient to close the gaps caused by differences in local property values. Rich districts can spend more even when poorer districts tax themselves at proportionally higher rates. In most states there is at least a three-to-one ratio between per pupil spending in the richest and poorest districts.[6]

Disparities also exist among states, with per pupil expenditures in 2008 ranging from nearly $18,000 in Vermont to just over $6,000 in Utah.[7] The federal government has no policies that compensate adequately for these disparities. In fact, the largest federal education program, Title I of the Elementary and Secondary Education Act, which is intended to redress the effects of poverty on children's learning, allocates funds in part based on levels of state per pupil spending, reinforcing rather than ameliorating these wealth-based inequalities.[8]

Funding disparities might not undermine equal educational opportunity if the differentials were due to pupils' needs (such as special education, acquisition of English, or other learning requirements), or if they reflected differences in the cost of living. But differentials do not tend to favor the districts serving the highest-need students, and they persist after differences in the cost of living and pupil needs are taken into account. In California, for example, high-poverty districts spent, on average, $259 less per pupil than low-poverty districts, and high-minority districts spent $499 less than low-minority districts. In higher-spending New York, these differentials were even greater: $2,927 and $2,636, respectively.[9]

EXPLAINING INEQUALITY

Many great schools in this country offer students opportunities to learn in empowering and engaging ways, and more of them are open to a wider range of children than was once the case. The fact that de jure segregation is no longer legal and that some students of color can now attend good schools leads many Americans to assume that inequality has been eliminated from public education. Yet, precisely because de facto segregation currently cordons off poor communities of color from the rest of society, most policy makers, reporters, editorial writers, and concerned citizens don't know how the "other half" experiences school. . . . School segregation remains pervasive throughout the United States. The assumption that equal educational opportunity now exists reinforces beliefs that the causes of continued low levels of achievement on the part of students of color must be intrinsic to them, their families, or their communities. Educational outcomes for students of color are, however, at least as much a function of their unequal access to key educational resources, both inside and outside of school, as they are a function of race, class, or culture.[10]

Four major resource-linked factors. . . account for unequal and inadequate educational outcomes in the United States:

- The high level of childhood poverty coupled with the low level of social supports for low-income children's health and welfare, including their early learning opportunities
- The unequal allocation of school resources, which is made politically easier by the increasing resegregation of schools
- Inadequate systems for providing high-quality teachers and teaching to all children in all communities
- Rationing of high-quality curriculum through tracking and interschool disparities.

Together, . . . all these factors generate opportunity-to-learn barriers that can sabotage success.

POVERTY AND SOCIAL SUPPORTS

The United States not only has the highest poverty rates for children among industrialized nations but also provides fewer social supports for their well-being and fewer resources for their education.[11] . . .[in 2013], about one out of four US children live[d] in poverty, more than twice the rate of most European nations. Child poverty in America has risen since the early 1970s, when the War on Poverty improved the lives of many children.[12] This country has a much weaker safety net for children than other industrialized countries have, where universal health care, housing subsidies, and high-quality child care are the norm. In other developed countries, schools can focus primarily on providing education, rather than also having to provide breakfasts and lunches, help families find housing and health care, or deal with constant mobility due to factors such as evictions. US schools must also often address the effects of untreated physical and mental illness and the large gaps in children's readiness that exist when they enter school.

The devastating effects of these conditions were brought home poignantly in a. . . Congressional briefing by John Deasy, then superintendent of the Prince

Georges County Public Schools, an urban district bordering on Washington, DC, who described a nine-year-old child in his district, living within sight of the Capitol building, who had recently died of sepsis from an infected cavity that had gone untreated because the child lacked dental insurance.[13] Disparate access to health care, including maternal prenatal care, contributes to a child mortality rate that is far higher in the United States than in any other wealthy country.[14]

Another contributing factor is unequal access to learning opportunities before children enter school. Many children do not have the kinds of experiences at home or in a preschool that allow them to develop the communication and interaction skills, motor skills, social–emotional skills, and cognitive skills that are required for them to be independent learners when they start school, which undermines their academic success in both the short and the longer run. . . .

Nobel prize–winning economist James Heckman points out that "compared to 50 years ago, a greater fraction of American children is being born into disadvantaged families where investments in children are smaller than in advantaged families."[15] The inadequacy of early education and health care negatively affects school success and adult outcomes. Yet, he argues, there is convincing evidence that if interventions occur early enough, they can significantly improve children's health, welfare, and learning.

Although prekindergarten enrollment has been growing recently, low-income children continue to participate in early education at much lower rates than children from higher-income families. In 2000, although 65 percent of children ages three to five whose parents earned $50,000 or more were enrolled in prekindergarten, only 44 percent of children the same ages with family incomes below $15,000 were enrolled. Publicly funded programs, which are the primary source of child care for low-income families, can serve only a minority of those who are entitled to participate.[16] By contrast, in most European countries, publicly supported child care and early education are widely available. In high-achieving Finland, for example, all children have the right to government-subsidized day care until they go to school at the age of seven, and 75 percent are enrolled. Parents also receive subsidies to stay home with their children if they so choose. In addition, over 96 percent of children attend tuition-free preschool at the age of six.[17] These kinds of policies eliminate the achievement gap that otherwise is created before school even begins.

RESEGREGATION AND UNEQUAL SCHOOLING

Beyond the large and growing inequalities that exist among families, profound inequalities in resource allocations to schools have been reinforced by increasing resegregation. Although desegregation has enabled many students of color to attend schools they could never before have accessed, many others have been left behind. Progress was made steadily only for about a decade after the passage of the 1964 Civil Rights Act. Segregation began to increase again in the 1980s, when desegregation policies were largely abandoned by the federal government, and courts were asked to end judicial oversight of desegregating districts.[18]

By 2000, 72 percent of the nation's Black students attended predominantly minority schools, up significantly from the low point of 63 percent in 1980. More than one-third of African American and Latino students (37 and 38 percent, respectively) attended schools with a minority enrollment of 90 percent to 100 percent.[19] At the turn of the twenty-first century, the level of segregation in US schools stood almost exactly where it had been 30 years earlier, as the ground gained during the 1970s was lost in a giant ideological tug-of-war.

The situation threatens to become worse as a result of the US Supreme Court's 2007 decision in conjoined cases brought by parents from Jefferson County, Kentucky, and Seattle, Washington. Both districts had placed race-based constraints on their school choice plans, as a way to avoid additional segregation. The court ruled that local school authorities could no longer routinely use individuals' race as a basis for decision making in school assignments.[20] More than 550 scholars signed a social science amicus brief offered by the Civil Rights Project at Harvard.

The. . . Civil Rights Project briefs summarized an extensive body of research showing the educational and community benefits of integrated schools for both White and minority students, documenting the persisting inequalities of segregated minority schools,

and examining evidence that schools will resegregate in the absence of race-conscious policies. The Civil Rights Project's statement concluded that

> more often than not, segregated minority schools offer profoundly unequal educational opportunities. This inequality is manifested in many ways, including fewer qualified, experienced teachers, greater instability caused by rapid turnover of faculty, fewer educational resources, and limited exposure to peers who can positively influence academic learning. No doubt as a result of these disparities, measures of educational outcomes, such as scores on standardized achievement tests and high school graduation rates, are lower in schools with high percentages of non-White students.[21]

Part of the problem is that segregated minority schools are almost always schools with high concentrations of poverty.[22] A number of studies have found that concentrated poverty has an independent influence on student achievement beyond the individual student's own socioeconomic status, confirming the 1966 Coleman Report finding that "the social composition of [a school's] student body is more highly related to student achievement, independent of the student's own social background, than is any school factor."[23]

The phrase "concentrated poverty" is shorthand for a constellation of mutually reinforcing socioeconomic inequalities that affect schooling. These schools typically have less qualified and less experienced teachers and fewer learning resources, lower levels of peer group support and competition, more limited curricula taught at less challenging levels, more serious health and safety problems, much more student and family mobility, and many other factors that seriously affect academic achievement.[24]

High levels of segregation produce linguistic isolation in schools with many native Spanish speakers and few fluent native speakers of English. The lack of opportunity for ongoing conversation with native English speakers impedes students' acquisition of academic English required for success in high school and college.[25] Furthermore, economic segregation reinforces disparities in educational quality. The social capital and clout brought by higher-income parents typically result in higher levels of services from the central administration and greater accountability for performance from schools.

Deepening segregation is closely tied to dwindling resources. Black and Hispanic students are increasingly concentrated in central city public schools, many of which have become majority minority over the past decade while their funding has fallen further behind that of their suburbs. . . . In 2005, students of color made up 71 percent of those served by the 100 largest school districts in the country.[26] By the late 1990s, in cities across the nation, a group of schools had emerged that might be characterized as "apartheid schools," serving exclusively students of color in low-income communities. Whether in Compton, California, or Chicago, Illinois, these schools have crumbling, overcrowded buildings, poor libraries and few materials, old and dilapidated texts so scarce that students must share them in class and cannot take them home for homework, and a revolving-door teaching force with little professional expertise.

These conditions arose as taxpayer revolts pulled the bottom out from under state education funding, and the distribution of funds became more unequal.[27] The extent to which many urban and some rural schools serving high proportions of low-income students of color could be abandoned without major outcry was in part a function of their intense segregation. Indeed, this public indifference to deprivation was one of the reasons civil rights advocates sought desegregation in the first place. Their long struggle to end segregation was not motivated purely by a desire to have minority children sit next to White children. Instead, there was strong evidence that the "equal" part of the "separate but equal" principle enunciated by the Supreme Court in its 1896 *Plessy v. Ferguson* decision had never been honored and that predominantly White schools offered better opportunities on many levels—more resources, higher rates of graduation and college attendance, more demanding courses, and better facilities and equipment.

Furthermore, there was a belief that these schools, once integrated, would continue to be advantaged by the greater public commitment occasioned by the more affluent people they serve. This belief seems borne out by the rapid deterioration of resegregated schools in cities that were turning Black and brown during the 1980s and 1990s, where the conditions of severe resource impoverishment came to resemble those in underdeveloped nations.[28]

The differences in resources that typically exist between city and suburban schools can strongly influence school outcomes. For example, an experimental study of African American high school youth randomly placed in public housing in the Chicago suburbs rather than in the city found that, compared to their urban peers who started with equivalent income and academic attainment, the students who attended better-funded, largely White suburban schools with higher quality teachers and curriculum had better educational outcomes. They were substantially more likely to have the opportunity to take challenging courses, receive additional academic help, graduate on time, attend college, and secure good jobs.[29]

Finally, not only do urban districts receive fewer resources than their suburban neighbors, but schools with high concentrations of low-income and minority students typically receive fewer resources than other schools within these districts.[30] This disparity occurs for at least two reasons: upper-income parents lobby more effectively for academic programs, computers, libraries, and other supports and tolerate less neglect when it comes to building maintenance and physical amenities. Also, more-affluent schools generally secure more experienced and better educated teachers as schools with better conditions can attract a wider array of applicants.

UNEQUAL ACCESS TO QUALIFIED TEACHERS

More important than the contrasts between up-to-date and dilapidated buildings or even between overflowing libraries and empty shelves are the differences in the teachers children encounter. In the United States, teachers are the most inequitably distributed school resource. . . . This inequity is strongly linked to resources; financially struggling schools have a very difficult time hiring and retaining experienced, well-trained teachers.

Although federal policies such as service scholarships ended the shortage of teachers by the late 1970s, the cancellation of these policies in the 1980s led to increasing numbers of underqualified teachers being hired in many cities when teacher demand began to increase while resources were declining. In 1990, for example, the Los Angeles Unified School District settled a lawsuit brought by students in predominantly minority schools because their schools were not only more crowded and less well funded than other schools but also disproportionately staffed by inexperienced and unprepared teachers hired on emergency credentials.[31] The practice of lowering or waiving credentialing standards to fill classrooms in high-minority, low-income schools—a practice that is unheard of in high-achieving nations and in other professions—became commonplace in many US states during this period, especially those with large minority and immigrant populations such as California, Texas, Florida, and New York.

A decade later, the entire California system was subjected to legal challenge, as disparities in access to well-qualified teachers had grown even worse. In 2001, for example, students in California's most intensely minority schools were more than five times as likely to have uncertified teachers than those in predominantly White schools. As standards were lowered and nearly half of the state's new teachers entered without training, virtually all of them were assigned to teach in high-need schools. In the 20 percent of schools serving almost exclusively students of color, more than one-fifth of teachers were uncertified, and in some schools they comprised the majority of the teaching force. . . .[32]

A 1999 episode of the Merrow Report[33] illustrates how debilitating these policies had become for a group of students in Oakland—although the segment could as easily have been about schools in Philadelphia, Los Angeles, Chicago, Newark, Atlanta, or New York City. Zooming into a portable classroom in a middle school comprising entirely of American and Latino students, Merrow interviewed students in an eighth-grade math class that had been without a regular math teacher for most of the year, asking: "How many math teachers have you had this year?" One young man with a good memory started to count: "Let's see, there is Mr. Berry, Miss Gaines, Mr. Lee, Mr. Dijon, Mr. Franklin. . . . Coach Brown was one of our substitutes one day." A studious-looking girl chimed in: "We had Miss Nakasako; we had Miss Gaines; we had Miss Elmore; we had this

other man named. . . he had like curly hair. His name was Mr. umm. . . ." Merrow remarked: "So you've had so many teachers you can't remember all their names?" The children nodded in agreement.

A few miles away at Oakland High School, a ninth-grade science class had had nothing but substitutes and spent the entire year without a certified science teacher. Merrow asked what it was like having so many teachers. Students' frustration was evident as they answered. Said one boy: "It's just weird. It's like we have to get used to a new teacher every couple of weeks or so." Another added, "I'm feeling shorthanded, because this is the third year. . . ever since I got into junior high school, I haven't had a science teacher. . . . [I've had] substitutes all three years." When Merrow asked: "Have you learned much science this year?" the students shook their heads no. One particular Black student, laying his hand on the book in front of him as though it were a life raft, shook his head sadly and answered: "Not really. We haven't had the chance to."

The reporter went on to interview several fully certified science teachers who had applied to teach in the district and had not gotten a call back from the personnel office. Here, as in some other underresourced urban districts, instead of teachers with preparation and experience, uncredentialed teachers and temporary staff were hired to save money. In recent years, Oakland's new leadership has worked heroically to change these practices and to seek out and hire teachers who will become better prepared and stay in the district. Yet the district, like many others in the state, still struggles with the inadequate funding and low salaries that make staffing its schools an uphill climb.

Similar inequalities have been documented in lawsuits challenging school funding in other states, including Massachusetts, New Jersey, New York, South Carolina, and Texas. In Massachusetts in 2002, students in predominantly minority schools were five times more likely to have uncertified teachers than those in the quartile of schools serving the fewest students of color.[34] In South Carolina and Texas they were four times more likely.[35]

By every measure of qualifications—certification, subject matter background, pedagogical training, selectivity of college attended, test scores, or experience—less qualified teachers are found in schools serving greater numbers of low-income and minority students.[36] As noted by Kati Haycock, president of The Education Trust, these statistics on differentials in credentials and experience, as shocking as they are, actually *understate* the degree of the problem:

> For one thing, these effects are additive. The fact that only 25% of the teachers in a school are uncertified doesn't mean that the other 75% are fine. More often, they are either brand new, assigned to teach out of field, or low-performers on the licensure exam. . . . There are, in other words, significant numbers of schools that are essentially dumping grounds for unqualified teachers—just as they are dumping grounds for the children they serve.[37]

THE INFLUENCE OF TEACHER QUALITY ON STUDENT ACHIEVEMENT

All of these aspects of teacher quality matter. Studies at the state, district, school, and individual level have found that teachers' academic background, preparation for teaching, and certification status as well as their experience, significantly affect their students' achievement.[38] Similar patterns appear around the world. For example, the most significant predictors of mathematics achievement across 46 nations include teacher certification, a major in mathematics or mathematics education, and at least three years of teaching experience.[39]

Teachers' qualifications can have very large effects. For example, a recent study of high school students in North Carolina found that students' achievement was significantly higher if they were taught by a teacher who was certified in the field he or she taught, was fully prepared upon entry, had higher scores on the teacher licensing test, graduated from a competitive college, had taught for more than two years, or was National Board Certified.[40] While each of these traits made teachers more effective, the combined influence of having a teacher with most of these qualifications was larger than the effects of race and parent education combined. That is, the difference between the effect of having a very well-qualified teacher rather than one who was poorly qualified was larger than the average difference in achievement between a typical White student with college-educated parents and a typical Black student with high-school-educated parents. The achievement gap would be significantly reduced if low-income minority students were routinely assigned highly qualified teachers rather than the poorly qualified teachers they most often encounter. . . .

The good news is that when New York City raised salaries as the result of a school finance lawsuit and adopted policies to distribute teachers more equitably, improvements in these qualifications reduced achievement disparities between the schools serving the poorest and most affluent student bodies by one-fourth within only a few years.[41] Persistence in solving this problem could make a major difference in the opportunities available to students. Indeed, because of public attention to these disparities and to the importance of teacher quality,[42] Congress included a provision in the No Child Left Behind Act of 2002 that states should ensure that all students have access to "highly qualified teachers," defined as teachers with full certification and demonstrated competence in the subject matter fields they teach. This provision was historic, especially because the students targeted by federal legislation—those who are low-income, low-achieving, new English language learners, or identified with special education needs—have in many communities been the least likely to be served by experienced and well-prepared teachers.[43]

At the same time, reflecting a key Bush administration agenda, the law encouraged states to expand alternative certification programs, and regulations developed by the US Department of Education (DOE) allow candidates who have just begun, but not yet completed, such a program to be counted as "highly qualified" classroom teachers. These regulations led parents of low-income, minority students taught by such teachers in California to sue the DOE.[44] They claimed that the rule sanctioned inadequate teaching for their children and masked the fact that they were being underserved, reducing the pressure on policy makers to create incentives that would give their children access to fully prepared teachers. . . .

The problems created by underprepared teachers have effects on schools as a whole. A teacher in a California school with a revolving door of underprepared teachers explained the consequences for students and other teachers:

> Teachers who had not been through [preparation] programs had more concerns about classroom management and about effective methods for delivering instruction to the student population at our school than teachers who had been through credential programs. It was a topic that was discussed at the lunch table. . . the fact we had a class that had so many substitutes and had an uncredentialed teacher who was not able to handle the situation and ended up not returning, and that the kids were going to struggle and the teachers who received them the next year would probably have a difficult time with those students because of what they had been through.[45]

Student achievement declines as the proportion of inexperienced, underprepared, or uncertified increases within a school.[46] The high turnover rates of underprepared, inexperienced teachers, which disproportionately affect low-income, high-minority schools, drain financial and human resources.[47] Most important, the constant staff churn consigns a large share of children in high-need schools to a parade of relatively ineffective teachers, leading to higher rates of remediation, grade retention, and dropping out. These longer-term costs are borne by society as well as by individual students. Without additional resources, schools serving the nation's most vulnerable students are ill-prepared to create the working environments and compensation packages needed to attract and retain experienced, well-trained teachers.

LACK OF ACCESS TO HIGH-QUALITY CURRICULUM

In addition to being taught by less expert teachers than their White counterparts, students of color face stark differences in courses, curriculum programs, materials and equipment, as well as in the human environment in which they attend school. High-quality instruction, which is shaped by all these factors and supported by tangible resources, matters greatly for student achievement. For example, when sociologist Robert Dreeben studied reading instruction for 300 Black and White first graders across seven schools in the Chicago area, he found that differences in reading achievement were almost entirely explained, not by socioeconomic status or race, but by the quality of curriculum and teaching the students received:

> Our evidence shows that the level of learning responds strongly to the quality of instruction: having and using enough time, covering a substantial amount of rich curricular material, and matching instruction appropriately to the ability levels of groups. . . . When Black and White children of comparable ability experience the same instruction, they do about equally well, and this is true when the instruction is excellent in quality and when it is inadequate.[48]

Yet the quality of instruction received by African American students was, on average, much lower than that received by White students, creating a racial gap in aggregate achievement at the end of first grade. In fact, the highest ability group in Dreeben's sample at the start of the study was in a school in a low-income African American neighborhood. These students attended a school that was unable to provide the quality instruction they deserved, and they learned less during first grade than their White counterparts.

In a variety of subtle and not-so-subtle ways, US schools allocate different learning opportunities to different students. Sorting often begins as early as kindergarten or first grade, with decisions about which students are placed in remedial or "gifted and talented" programs. Affluent and poor schools differ sharply in what is offered. Wealthy districts often offer foreign languages early in elementary school, while poor districts offer few such courses even at the high school level; richer districts typically provide extensive music and art programs, project-based science, and elaborate technology supports, while poor districts often have none of these and often offer stripped down drill-and-practice approaches to reading and math rather than teaching for higher-order applications.[49]

For reasons of both resources and expectations, schools serving African American, Latino, and Native American students are "bottom heavy"—that is, they offer fewer academic and college preparatory courses and more remedial and vocational courses that train students for low-status occupations, such as cosmetology and sewing.[50] For example, in 2005 only 30 percent of highly segregated schools serving African

American and Latino students in California had a sufficient number of the state-required college preparatory courses to accommodate all their students. These schools, serving more than 90 percent students of color, constitute a quarter of all schools in the state. Furthermore, in a large majority of these highly segregated schools more than one-fifth of the college-preparatory courses they did offer were taught by underqualified teachers.[51] As a result of these conditions, very few African American and Latino high school graduates had taken and passed both the courses and the tests required to be eligible for admission to the state university system.[52]

Tracking is another well-established mechanism used to differentiate access to knowledge. . . . In racially mixed schools, the tracks are generally color-coded: honors or advanced courses are reserved primarily for White students, while the lower tracks are disproportionately filled with students of color. Unequal access to high-level courses and challenging curriculum explains much of the difference in achievement between minority students and White students.

Little has changed since Jonathan Kozol eloquently described two decades ago how, within ostensibly integrated schools in New York City, minority children were disproportionately assigned to special education classes that occupy small, cramped corners and split classrooms, while gifted and talented classes, which were exclusively composed of White and Asian students, enjoyed spaces filled with books and computers and learned logical reasoning and problem solving.[53] School pathways locking in inequality can be found in most districts today, as high-quality education is rationed to the privileged few. Furthermore, race and ethnicity are associated with placement in higher or lower tracks independently of students' achievement levels.[54] In addition to inequitable access to knowledge, cross-school segregation and within-school tracking reduce the extent to which different kinds of students have the opportunity to interact with one another and gain access to multiple perspectives. . . .

FUNDING EQUITABLE EDUCATION

Ultimately, the proof is in the pudding. A number of states that have raised and equalized funding as part of systemic reforms have raised student achievement and reduced the opportunity gap.[55] Consider Massachusetts. For the past decade, Massachusetts has led all states in student achievement on the National Assessment of Educational Progress. The meteoric rise began in 1992 with a court decision in *Hancock v. Driscoll* requiring an overhaul of school funding. The school finance formula adopted in 1993 as part of Massachusetts' Education Reform Act led to substantially greater investments in needier schools by equalizing funding and local effort simultaneously and adding funding increments based on the proportions of low-income students and English language learners in a district.

This progressive funding approach was accompanied by new statewide learning standards, curriculum frameworks, and assessments; expanded learning time in core content areas; technology investments; and stronger licensing requirements for teachers. The next year Massachusetts adopted a plan for professional development that provided dedicated funding to districts, led to intensive summer institutes in math and science, and set up continuing education requirements for certification, as well as a new set of standards and expectations for local educator evaluation. The Attracting Excellence to Teaching Program subsidized preparation for qualified entrants to the profession.

In addition, the state quintupled its funding for local early childhood programs, created a Commission on Early Childhood Education to develop a statewide plan, established model preschool programs, and awarded hundreds of Community Partnerships for Children grants to expand access to early education for children in need. By the year 2000, Massachusetts had underwritten these reforms with more than $2 billion in new state dollars for its public schools, greatly expanding the state share of funding and enhancing equity.

Economist Jonathan Guryan found that increased educational funding for historically low-spending districts led to improved student achievement in all subject areas, especially for traditionally low-scoring students.[56] By 2002, the state had dramatically improved overall achievement and sharply reduced its achievement gap. Massachusetts demonstrates how investments, wisely spent in concert with a systemic approach to reform, can make a difference in educational outcomes.

New Jersey provides another, more recent, case. For many years, the state spent about half as much on the education of low-income, minority students in cities like Camden, Trenton, Newark, and Paterson as it did in wealthy districts. After 30 years of litigation and nine court decisions finding the New Jersey school finance system unconstitutional, the state finally agreed to make a major infusion of funding to the 28 highest-need districts to bring them into parity with the per-pupil expenditures in the state's successful suburban districts. The new funding, which began in 1998, was spent to implement a new state curriculum linked to the state standards; support whole school reform; ensure early childhood education for three- and four-year-olds as well as full-day kindergarten; educate preschool teachers; reduce class sizes; invest in technology; ensure adequate facilities; and support health, social services, alternative, and summer school programs to help students catch up. In addition, an early literacy program provided reading coaches and professional development for teachers in kindergarten through third grade.[57]

New Jersey launched a set of new teacher education programs focused on preparing teachers for effective teaching in high-need urban districts, using school–university partnerships to provide both intensive field experiences for teacher candidates and professional learning opportunities for veteran teachers. It developed extensive professional development supports for teaching content area standards and for supporting English language learners and other special needs students, with dedicated funding and assistance in high-needs schools to model effective practices.[58] Gradually, the districts that had become dysfunctional during the lean years began to gain ground.

By 2007, New Jersey had substantially increased its standing on national reading and math assessments, ranking among the top five states in all subject areas and grade levels on the NAEP and first in writing. It was also one of four states that made the most progress nationally in closing performance gaps between White, Black, and Hispanic students in fourth- and eighth-grade reading and math.[59] By 2007, although parity had not yet been achieved, Hispanic and Black students scored between 5 and 10 points above their peers nationwide, depending on the test.[60] The state also reduced the achievement gap for students with disabilities and for socioeconomically disadvantaged students.

Clearly, money well spent does make a difference. Equalizing access to resources creates the possibility that all students will receive what should be their birthright: a genuine opportunity to learn.

NOTES

1. This reading draws in part on Linda Darling-Hammond, *The Flat World and Education: How America's Commitment to Equity Will Determine Our Future* (New York: Teachers College Press, 2010), and Linda Darling-Hammond, "Inequality and the Right to Learn: Access to Qualified Teachers in California's Public Schools," *Teachers College Record*, 106(10) (October 2004), 1936–1966.
2. Ladson-Billings, 2006.
3. Tyack, 1974, 109–25; Kluger, 1976; Meier, Stewart, & England, 1989; Schofield, 1995.
4. Quoted in Tyack, 1974, 119.
5. *Williams et al. v. State of California*, Superior Court of the State of California for the County of San Francisco, 2001, Complaint, 569–66.
6. Darling-Hammond, 2010.
7. Baker, Sciarra, & Farrie, 2010.
8. Liu, 2008.
9. Education Trust, 2006.
10. See Rothstein, 2013, and Darling-Hammond, 2010.

11. Bell, Bernstein, & Greenberg, 2008.
12. DeNavas-Walt, Proctor, & Lee, 2005; U.S. Bureau of the Census, 2006.
13. Darling-Hammond, 2010.
14. UNICEF, 2001, 3.
15. Heckman 2008, 49.
16. Children's Defense Fund, 2001.
17. Sahlberg, 2011.
18. Rumberger & Palardy, 2005; see also Orfield, 2013.
19. Orfield, G., 2001.
20. *Parents Involved in Community Schools v. Seattle School District No. 1*, 551 U.S. 701 (2007).
21. Civil Rights Project (2006), amicus brief filed in *Parents Involved in Community Education v. Seattle School District No. 1*, pg. 3.
22. Orfield, 2001.
23. 1966 Coleman Report, p. 325. For a recent review of this evidence, see Kahlenberg, 2001.
24. Schofield, 1995; Anyon, 1997; Dawkins & Braddock, 1994; Natriello, McDill, & Pallas, 1990.
25. Lee, 2004; Horn, 2002; See also the discussion in Gándara, 2013.
26. Garofano, Sable, & Hoffman, 2008.
27. Resnick, 1995.
28. Darling-Hammond, 2010.
29. Kaufman and Rosenbaum, 1992.
30. Education Trust, 2006.
31. Darling-Hammond, 2004.
32. Shields et al., 2001.
33. John Merrow Reports are available from Learning Matters at http://learningmatters.tv/.
34. Darling-Hammond, 2004.
35. Analyses of teacher distribution data were conducted by the author.
36. NCES, 1997; Lankford, Loeb, & Wyckoff, 2002.
37. Haycock, 2000, 11.
38. These findings are documented in Betts, Rueben, & Dannenberg, 2000; Boyd et al., 2006; Clotfelter, Ladd, & Vigdor, 2007; Darling-Hammond, 2000; Darling-Hammond, Holtzman, Gatlin, & Heilig, 2005; . . . .; Fetler, 1999; Goldhaber & Brewer, 2000; Goe, 2002; Hawk, Coble, & Swanson, 1985; Monk, 1994; Strauss and Sawyer, 1986.
39. Akiba, LeTendre, & Scribner, 2007.
40. Clotfelter, Ladd, & Vigdor, 2007.
41. Boyd et al., 2006.
42. NCTAF, 1996.
43. Ibid.
44. *Renee v. Duncan*, 623 F. 3d 787 (2010). The court ruling favored the plaintiffs, but Congress subsequently wrote the department's regulations into law, for a time period that currently extends until June 2013. This means that, until that time, teachers-in-training will be considered "highly qualified."
45. Darling-Hammond, 2003, 128.
46. Betts, Rueben, & Dannenberg, 2000; Darling-Hammond, 2000; Fetler, 1999; Fuller, 2000; Goe, 2002; Strauss & Sawyer, 1986.
47. Shields, Humphrey, Wechsler, et al., 2001.
48. Dreeben, 1987, 34.

49. Kozol, 2005; Darling-Hammond, 2010.
50. College Board, 1985; Pelavin & Kane, 1990; Oakes, 2005.
51. Oakes et al., 2006.
52. California Postsecondary Education Commission, 2007.
53. Kozol, 1992.
54. Oakes, 1993, 2005; Welner, 2001.
55. Darling-Hammond, 2010.
56. Guryan, 2001.
57. Assistant Commissioner Jay Doolan and State Assessment Director, Timothy Peters, Presentation to the New Jersey State Board of Education, *NAEP* 2007: *Reading and Mathematics, Grades 4 and 8*, October 17, 2007.
58. See "New Jersey's Plan for Meeting the Highly Qualified Teacher Goals," submitted July 7, 2006, to the US Department of Education, http://liberty.state.nj.us/education/data/hqt/06/plan.pdf.
59. NCES, *Top Four States in Closing Achievement Gap*. Retrieved on August 2, 2008, from http://www.fldoe.org/asp/naep/pdf/Top-4-states.pdf.
60. NCES, 2007.

REFERENCES

Akiba, M., LeTendre, G. K., & Scribner, J. P. (2007). Teacher quality, opportunity gap, and national achievement in 46 countries. *Educational Researcher*, 36(7), 369–387.

Anyon, J. (1997). *Ghetto schooling: A political economy of urban educational reform*. New York: Teachers College Press.

Baker, B. D., Sciarra, D., & Farrie, D. (2010). *Is school funding fair? A national report card*. Newark, NJ: Education Law Center.

Bell, K., Bernstein, J., & Greenberg, M. (2008). Lessons for the United States from other advanced economies in tackling child poverty. In *Big ideas for children: Investing in our nation's future*, ed. First Focus, 81–92. Washington, DC: First Focus.

Betts, J. R., Rueben, K. S., Danenberg, A. (2000). *Equal resources, equal outcomes? The distribution of school resources and student achievement in California*. San Francisco: Public Policy Institute of California.

Boyd, D., Grossman, P., Lankford, H., Loeb, S., and Wyckoff, J. (2006). How changes in entry requirements alter the teacher workforce and affect student achievement. *Education Finance & Policy*, 1, 176–216.

California Postsecondary Education Commission. (2007). *College-going rates: A performance measure in California's higher education accountability framework* (Commission Report No. 07–04). Sacramento, CA: Author.

Children's Defense Fund. (2001). Children's Defense Fund calculations, based on data from U.S. Bureau of the Census. June.

Clotfelter, C. T., Ladd, H. F., & Vigdor, J. L. (2007). Teacher credentials and student achievement: Longitudinal analysis with student fixed effects. *Economics of Education Review*, 26(6), 673–682.

College Board. (1985). *Equality and excellence: The educational status of Black Americans*. New York: College Entrance Examination Board.

Darling-Hammond, L. (2000). Teacher quality and student achievement: A review of state policy evidence. *Educational Policy Analysis Archives*, 8(1). Retrieved from http://epaa.asu.edu/epaa/v8n1.

Darling-Hammond, L. (2003). Access to quality teaching: An analysis of inequality in California's public schools. *Santa Clara Law Review*, 43, 101–239.

Darling-Hammond, L. (2004). Inequality and the right to learn: Access to qualified teachers in California's public schools. *Teachers College Record, 106*(10), 1936–1966.

Darling-Hammond, L. (2007). A Marshall Plan for teaching: What it will really take to leave no child behind. *Education Week.* Retrieved from http://www.edweek.org/ew/articles/2007/01/10/18hammond.h26.html.

Darling-Hammond, L. (2010). *The flat world and education: How America's commitment to equity will determine our future.* New York: Teachers College Press.

Darling-Hammond, L., Holtzman, D., Gatlin, S. J., & Heilig, J. V. (2005). Does teacher preparation matter? Evidence about teacher certification, Teach for America, *and teacher effectiveness. Education Policy Analysis Archives, 13*(42). Retrieved from http://epaa.asu.edu/epaa/v13n42/.

Dawkins, M. P., & Braddock J. H. (1994). The continuing significance of desegregation: School racial composition and African American inclusion in American society. *Journal of Negro Education, 63*(3), 394–405.

DeNavas-Walt, C., Proctor, B. D., & Lee, C. H. (2005). Income, poverty, and health insurance coverage in the United States: 2005. In *Current Population Reports.* Washington, DC: US Department of Commerce.

Dreeben, R. (1987). Closing the divide: What teachers and administrators can do to help Black students reach their reading potential. *American Educator, 11*(4), 28–35.

Education Trust. (2006). Funding gaps 2006. Retrieved from http://www.edtrust.org/sites/edtrust.civications.net/files/publications/files/FundingGap2006.pdf.

Fetler, M. (1999). High school staff characteristics and mathematics test results. *Education Policy Analysis Archives, 7* (March 24). Retrieved from http://epaa.asu.edu.

Fuller, B., ed. (2000). *Inside charter schools: The paradox of radical decentralization.* Cambridge, MA: Harvard University. Press.

Gándara, P. (2013). Meeting the needs of language minorities. In *Closing the opportunity gap: What America must do to give every child an even chance,* ed. P. Carter and K. Welner, 156–168. New York: Oxford University Press.

Garofano, A., Sable, J., & Hoffman, L. (2008). *Characteristics of the 100 largest public elementary and secondary school districts in the United States: 2004–05.* US Department of Education, National Center for Education Statistics. Washington, DC: US Government Printing Office.

Goe, L. (2002). Legislating equity: The distribution of emergency permit teachers in California. *Educational Policy Analysis Archives online, 10*(42). Retrieved from http://epaa.asu.edu/epaa/v10n42/.

Goldhaber, D. D. & Brewer, D. J. (2000). Does teacher certification matter? High school certification status and student achievement. *Educational Evaluation and Policy Analysis, 22,* 129–145.

Guryan, J. (2001). *Does money matter? Regression-discontinuity estimates from education finance reform in Massachusetts.* NBER Working Paper 8269. Cambridge, MA.

Hawk, P., Coble, C. R., and Swanson, M. (1985). Certification: It does matter. *Journal of Teacher Education, 36*(3), 13–15.

Haycock, K. (2000). No more settling for less. *Thinking K-16, 4*(1), 3–8, 10–12. Washington, DC: Education Trust.

Heckman, J. J. (2008). The case for investing in disadvantaged young children. In *Big ideas for children: Investing in our nation's future,* ed. First Focus, 49–66. Washington, DC: First Focus.

Horn, C. (2002). *The intersection of race, class and English learner status.* Working Paper. Prepared for National Research Council.

Kahlenberg, R. D. (2001). *All together now: Creating middle class schools through public school choice.* Washington, DC: Brookings Institution Press.

Kaufman, J. E., & Rosenbaum, J. E. (1992). Education and employment of low-income Black youth in White suburbs. *Educational Evaluation and Policy Analysis, 14*(3), 229–240.

Kluger, R. (1976). *Simple justice.* NY: Vintage.

Kozol, J. (1992). *Savage inequalities: Children in America's schools.* New York: Harper Perennial.

Kozol, J. (2005). *The shame of the nation: The restoration of apartheid schooling in America.* New York: Crown Books.

Ladson-Billings, G. (2006). From the achievement gap to the education debt: Understanding achievement in U.S. schools. *Educational Researcher 35*(7), 3–12.

Lankford, H., Loeb, S., & Wyckoff, J. (2002). Teacher sorting and the plight of urban schools: A descriptive analysis. *Education Evaluation and Policy Analysis, 24*(1), 37–62.

Lee, C. (2004). *Racial segregation and educational outcomes in metropolitan Boston.* Cambridge, MA: The Civil Rights Project at Harvard University.

Liu, G. (2008). Improving Title 1 funding equity across states, districts, and schools, *Iowa Law Review, 93,* 973–1013.

Meier, K. J., Stewart, J. Jr., & England, R. E. (1989). *Race, class and education: The politics of second-generation discrimination.* Madison: University of Wisconsin Press.

Monk, D. H. (1994). Subject matter preparation of secondary mathematics and science teachers and student achievement. *Economics of Education Review, 13*(2), 125–145.

National Center for Education Statistics (NCES) (1997). *America's teachers: Profile of a profession, 1993–94.* Washington, DC: US Department of Education.

National Commission on Teaching and America's Future (NCTAF). (1996). *What matters most: Teaching for America's future.* New York: Author.

NCES, *Top Four States in Closing Achievement Gap.* Retrieved on August 2, 2008, from http://www.fldoe.org/asp/naep/pdf/Top-4-states.pdf.

Natriello, G., McDill, E. L., & Pallas, A. M. (1990). *Schooling disadvantaged children: Racing against catastrophe.* New York: Teachers College Press.

Oakes, J. (1993). *Ability grouping, tracking, and within-school segregation in the San Jose Unified School District.* Los Angeles: University of California, Los Angeles.

Oakes, J. (2005) *Keeping track: How schools structure inequality,* 2nd ed. New Haven, CT: Yale University Press.

Oakes, J., Rogers, J., Silver, D., Valladares, S., Terriquez, V., McDonough, P., Renée, M., & Lipton, M. (2006). *Removing the roadblocks: Fair college opportunities for all California students.* Los Angeles: University of California/All Campus Consortium for Research Diversity and UCLA Institute for Democracy, Education, and Access.

Orfield, G. (2001). *Schools more separate: Consequences of a decade of resegregation,* Cambridge, MA: Civil Rights Project. Harvard University.

Orfield, G. (2013). Housing segregation produces unequal schools: Causes and solutions. In *Closing the opportunity gap: What America must do to give every child an even chance,* ed. P. Carter and K. Welner, 40–60. New York: Oxford University Press.

Pelavin, S. H., & Kane, M. (1990). *Changing the odds: Factors increasing access to college.* New York: College Entrance Examination Board.

Resnick, L. (1995). From aptitude to effort: A new foundation for our schools. *Daedalus, 124*(4), 55–62.

Rothstein, R. (2013). Why children from lower socioeconomic classes, on average, have lower academic achievement than middle-class children. In *Closing the opportunity gap: What America must do to give every child an even chance,* ed. P. Carter and K. Welner, 61–76. New York: Oxford University Press.

Rumberger, R. W., & Palardy, G. J. (2005). Does resegregation matter? The impact of social composition on academic achievement in Southern high schools. In *School resegregation: Must the South turn back?* ed. John Charles Boger & Gary Orfield, 127–147. Chapel Hill: University of North Carolina Press.

Sahlberg, P. (2011). *Finnish lessons: What can the world learn from educational change in Finland?* New York: Teachers College Press.

Schofield, J. (1995). Review of research on school desegregation's impact on elementary and secondary school students. In *Handbook of research on multicultural education*, ed. J. A. Banks & C. A. M. Banks, 799–812. New York: Simon & Schuster/Macmillan.

Shields, P. M., Humphrey, D. C., Wechsler, M. E., Riel, L. M., Tiffany-Morales, J., Woodworth, K., Youg, V. M., & Price, T. (2001). *The status of the teaching profession 2001*. Santa Cruz, CA: Center for the Future of Teaching and Learning.

Strauss, R. P., & Sawyer, E. A. (1986). Some new evidence on teacher and student competencies. *Economics of Education Review, 5*(1), 41–48.

Tyack, D. (1974). *The one best system: A history of American urban education*. Cambridge, MA: Harvard University Press.

U.S. Bureau of the Census (2006). *Poverty status of people, by age, race, and Hispanic origin: 1959–2006*. Washington, DC: US Department of Commerce.

UNICEF (2001). *A league table of child deaths by injury in rich nations: Innocenti report card 2*. Florence: UNICEF, Innocenti Research Centre.

Welner, K. G. (2001). *Legal rights, local wrongs: When community control collides with educational equity*. Albany, New York: State University of New York Press.

DOUGLAS B. DOWNEY AND BENJAMIN G. GIBBS

34. HOW SCHOOLS REALLY MATTER

Although the authors acknowledge structural inequalities across schools and their role in reproducing educational inequality, Downey and Gibbs focus on factors outside of the school environment (such as home environment, access to educational resources, and parents' ability to assist children with homework) that contribute to inequality. Downey and Gibbs take a "contextual approach" to understanding education gaps and conclude by discussing policies that may help to close them.

There's an old joke about a man on a street corner, down on his hands and knees searching for his lost wallet. A passerby stops to help, asking, "So you lost it right around here?" "Oh no," the man replies, "I lost the wallet several blocks ago. I'm just looking on this street corner because this is where the lighting is good."

It's tempting to look for the source of a problem in places where the lighting is good even if we're not in the right place. When we hear about high dropout rates; persistent Black/White gaps in test scores; low American reading, math, and science scores; dramatic differences in resources among schools; and even growing childhood obesity, it's sort of easy to ascribe these negative outcomes to schools. In fact, this is the "traditional" story we hear about American schools.

THE TRADITIONAL TALE OF SCHOOLS

The tendency to view schools as the source of so many problems is especially true when we consider equality of opportunity, an important American value. There are many good reasons to believe that schools are the primary engines of inequality. First, children attending schools with lots of high-income children tend to perform better on standardized tests than kids at schools

with lots of low-income children. Second, there are clear resource differences between these schools, rooted in the fact that, in most states, local tax revenues constitute a significant portion of the school's budget. For example, Ohio's local taxes constitute about half of a school's budget (state taxes constitute 43 percent and federal taxes about seven percent). As a result of the heavy emphasis on local taxes, some schools are able to spend substantially more money per student than others. This means schools located in areas with expensive houses and successful businesses can spend more on new textbooks, teacher pay, recreational facilities, extracurricular activities, and help for students with special needs. Third, in high-resource schools, teachers encounter fewer children with behavioral problems and more parents engaged in their children's education, factors that can attract and retain better teachers. Based on these patterns, it seems obvious that if we want to improve the quality of life for the disadvantaged in the U.S., the best place to start is schools.

But this traditional story has developed largely without understanding the way in which children's academic outcomes are shaped by many factors outside of schools. Simply look at the amount of time children spend outside of school. If we focus on the nine-month academic year only, the proportion of time children spend in school is about *one-third*. And if we include the non-school summer, children spend just one-quarter of their waking hours in school each year. Now if we also include the years before kindergarten—which certainly affect children—we find that the typical 18-year-old American has spent just 13 percent of his or her waking hours in school. For most of us, it's surprising to learn that such a large percentage of children's time is spent outside of school, but it's important to keep in mind if we're serious about understanding how schools really matter.

A contextual perspective reminds us to look at the rest of kids' lives. For instance, not every student comes to school with the same economic, social, or cultural resources. Even with the same educational opportunities, some students benefit from home environments that prepare them for school work and so they are better able to take advantage of education.

Moving away from the traditional, narrow view of schools that forgets the importance of children's time outside the classroom, we endorse adopting a contextualized (or impact) view of schools. This new emphasis can really change how we think about what schools can—and can't—do for our kids.

PIANOS AND PARENTS

Imagine that we want to compare the effectiveness of two piano instructors who will both teach 10-week piano classes for beginners. We flip a coin and assign one instructor to place A and the other to place B. Our goal is complicated, however, by the fact that in place B, due to cost, almost no students come from a home with a piano, whereas in place A, whose parents have more disposable income, most students have a piano at home. As a result, place A's students have already had some practice time on a piano, whereas place B's students have had little to none. In addition, while both instructors teach a session once a week, place A's students practice on their own several times a week, whereas in place B—where few have pianos at home—students have a much harder time finding a way to practice.

Obviously, if we just compared the piano students' skills at the end of the 10-week program we couldn't accurately assess the quality of the two instructors— the two groups' skills differed before the lessons began. And if we compared how much the students' skills improved during the instructional period, it would still be hard to know which instructor was more effective because place A's students practiced more often than place B's students did. Given that these two instructors face different challenges, is there a way to evaluate them fairly? Can we isolate how the piano teachers really mattered?

This is the quandary we have when trying to understand how schools (or teachers) matter for children's lives; the same kinds of complicating factors are at work. First, children begin schooling with very different levels of academic skills. For example, the Black/White gap in math and reading skills is roughly a standard deviation at the end of high school, but half of this gap is evident at the beginning of kindergarten, before schools have had a chance to matter. And the differences in skills between high- and low-socioeconomic status (SES) students at the start of kindergarten are even larger. Obviously, these variations aren't a consequence of differences in school quality, but of the different kinds of students schools serve.

Thinking contextually, some home environments complement what occurs at school as parents help with homework, communicate with teachers, reinforce school concepts, provide a safe and stable environment for study, and attend to children's medical needs (by, for instance, providing consistent visits to doctors and dentists). In her book *Home Advantage*, sociologist Annette Lareau gives a poignant description of just how important parents can be, getting involved in their child's coursework and with their teachers in ways that promote academic success and instilling in their children a kind of academic entitlement. She wrote that these parents "made an effort to integrate educational goals into family life including teaching children new words when driving by billboards, having children practice penmanship and vocabulary by writing out shopping lists, practicing mathematics during baking projects, and practicing vocabulary during breakfast time." Interacting with instructors, the upper-middle class parents Lareau observed requested specific classroom teachers or asked that their child be placed in school programs for the gifted, for speech therapy, or with the learning resource center. In contrast, low-SES parents tended to have less time for involvement with their children's schoolwork, leaving educational experiences in the hands of the "experts." Much like having a piano at home, these contexts of advantage and disadvantage play a critical role in shaping how children gain academic skills during their school years.

BRINGING IN CONTEXT

By using a contextual perspective, sociologists have contributed considerably to our understanding of how schools matter. One of the most influential studies was the 1966 Coleman Report, a massive analysis of American schools that was commissioned by the Federal Department of Education. James Coleman, the lead author of the report, directed the collection of data from 4,000 schools and more than 645,000 American school children in the early 1960s. The researchers were interested in why some children had high math and reading skills and others did not. They measured many characteristics of schools (including school curriculum, facilities, teacher qualities, and student body characteristics) and many characteristics of children's home lives (like parents' SES—education, income, and occupation level) to see which were more closely related to academic skills. Surprisingly, school characteristics were only weakly related to academic skills. It turned out that differences between schools in terms of quality played only a small role in understanding the variation in students' academic skills while home life (parents' SES showed the strongest relationship) mattered much more. Skeptics of this conclusion, such as sociologist Christopher Jencks, re-evaluated Coleman's conclusion with new data, but ended up finding similar patterns.

Of course, one limitation of this approach is that it depends heavily on whether Coleman and Jencks were measuring the right things about schools. Maybe they were missing what really mattered. While they were measuring per pupil expenditures, teacher/student ratios, and racial composition, they missed critical factors like teacher quality. If they failed to measure a lot of important things about schools, then their conclusions that schools play only a minor role in explaining inequality of skills might be wrong.

SEASONAL COMPARISON RESEARCH

What researchers need is a way to untangle the role of school and non-school influences. Observing student learning during the school year tells us little about how schools matter because students are exposed to both school and non-school environments. When we compare annually-collected test scores, for example, it becomes very difficult to know why some students fall behind and some get ahead. Sociologist Barbara Heyns pointed out that during the summer children are influenced by non-school factors only. The best way to understand how schools matter, she reasoned, was to observe how things change between the non-school period (summer) and the school period. This strategy works like a natural experiment, separating the "treatment" from the treated. Knowing what happens to group-level differences in achievement by race, class, or gender when school is in session (the treatment) compared to when it is not (the control) is a good way to know if schools make educational gaps bigger or smaller.

This important insight led Heyns to collect a different kind of data. She evaluated fifth, sixth, and seventh grade students at the beginning and end of the academic years in Atlanta. By testing them both in the fall and spring, she was able to tell how much they learned during the summer, when school was out. This study design allowed her to uncover a provocative pattern—high- and low-SES students gained academic skills at about the same rate during the nine-month academic year. Gaps in skills developed during the summers. Although schools did not close achievement gaps between groups, these results bolstered Coleman and Jencks's initial conclusions that schools were not the primary reason for group-level inequalities. Heyns's provocative findings were replicated by sociologists Doris Entwisle and Karl Alexander in Baltimore and, more recently, by myself with colleagues at Ohio State. With nationally representative data, we found that low- and high-SES children learned math and reading at similar rates during the nine-month kindergarten and first grade periods, but that gaps in skills grew quickly during the summer in between, when school was out.

Taken together, the overall pattern from this seasonal research supports Coleman's conclusion:

schools are not the source of inequality. The seasonal approach to understanding schools gives us a much more accurate understanding of how schools influence inequality. This research consistently produces an unconventional conclusion—if we lived in a world with no schools at all, inequality would be much worse. In other words, when it comes to inequality, schools are more part of the solution than the problem.

This contextual way of thinking about schools and inequality is difficult to reconcile, however, with the "traditional" story—that wide variations in school quality are the engine of inequality. By adopting a more contextual perspective on schools, we can understand this counterintuitive claim: despite the fact that some schools have more resources than others, schools end up being an equalizing force. The key is that the inequalities that exist outside of school are considerably larger than the ones students experience in school.

SCHOOLS, CONTEXT, AND POLICY

At the beginning of this [reading], we pointed out that it's natural to look to schools for the source of many of our kids' problems—they're the corner with the best "lighting." The often-unexplored terrain *outside* of schools, though, remains shadowy and seemingly inaccessible. This doesn't need to be the case. And, though extending the light beyond schools reveals that group-level inequality would be much worse if not for schools, it doesn't mean that schools are off the hook. In fact, using school impact as a guide, many "successful" schools in the traditional view are revealed as low-impact—good students don't always signal good instructors. In these schools, children pass proficiency exams, but since they started off in a better position, it's arguable that the schools didn't actually serve their students.

Clearly, when we employ a contextual perspective, we think about school policy, child development, and social problems in a new light. A contextual approach to schools promotes sensible policy, efficiently targeted resources, and reasonable assessment tools that recognize that some schools and teachers face very different challenges than others.

For example, a tremendous amount of energy and money is directed toward developing accountability systems for schools. But recall the analogy of the two piano instructors. It's difficult to determine which instructor is best, given that place A has students that start with more skills and practice more outside of instruction. Now suppose that we knew one more piece of information: how fast each group of piano players gained skills when not taking lessons. Suddenly, we could compare the rate of improvement outside of instruction with the rate observed during the instructional period. We could see how much instruction mattered.

This "impact" view has recently been applied to schools. In 2008, with fellow sociologists Paul T. von Hippel and Melanie Hughes, I constructed impact measures by taking a school's average difference between its students' first-grade learning rate and the learning rate observed in the summer prior to first grade. The key finding was that not all the schools deemed as "failing" under traditional criteria were really failing. Indeed, three out of four schools had been incorrectly evaluated. That's not to say that there were no variations in school quality, but many schools did much better than expected when we took a contextual approach to measurement. And some did much worse. If impact evaluations are more accurate, then teachers serving disadvantaged children are doing a better job than previously thought and current methods of school evaluation are producing substantial errors.

With its contextual orientation, seasonal research has also provided insights into other ways that schools matter. For example, researchers have considered whether "summer setback" can be avoided by modifying the school year so that there is no long gap in school exposure. Von Hippel has compared math and reading learning in schools with year-long calendars versus those with traditional school-year/summer break calendars. In both conditions, children attended school for about 180 days a year, but the timing of those days was spread more evenly in year-round schools. It turned out that, once a calendar year was up, both groups had learned about the same. The policy lesson is that increasing school exposure is probably more important than fiddling with how school days are distributed across the year.

Given that school exposure appears critical, many have viewed summer school (restricted to academically struggling children) as an attractive option for reducing inequality. It turns out, though, that children attending summer school gain fewer academic skills than we would expect. This may be because the academic programs in the summer are of lower quality, but it may also be because the kinds of students who typically attend summer school are also the kind who would typically suffer a "summer setback" without it. Viewed in this light, just treading water or maintaining the same academic skills during the summer could be viewed as a positive outcome.

And in other research employing seasonal comparisons, researchers have shown that children gain body mass index (BMI) three times faster during the summer than during the school year. Obviously, schools shouldn't abandon attempts to improve the

quality of lunches or the schooling environment, but research suggests that attention should be paid to non-school factors as the primary sources of childhood obesity.

In the end, looking at schools through a contextual lens provides exciting insights. When we forget how other aspects of children's lives figure into their development, we create a distorted view of schools. The contextual perspective corrects this error and produces a more accurate understanding of how schools really matter. It suggests that if we are serious about improving American children's school performance, we will need to take a broader view of education policy. In addition to school reform, we must also aim to improve children's lives where they spend the vast majority of their time—with their families and in their neighborhoods.

HOW LIMITED INTERNET ACCESS CAN SUBTRACT FROM KIDS' EDUCATION

ALINA SELYUKH

Can a kid succeed in school with only a mobile device for Internet access at home? Lorena Uribe doesn't have to think about that one: "Absolutely not," she says. When her old computer broke down several years ago, she and her teenage daughter found themselves in a bind for about five months: homework to do and no computer or broadband access at home. "I would take her to the mall and have her sit in Panera so she could use the Wi-Fi on her iPad from school," Uribe says. Now, the Internet connection at their home near San Diego is a cord in the wall, attached to a desktop that they bought through a discount program at school. Uribe says sometimes Web pages take a while to load and it can get annoying—but it works. "You have Internet; you have a computer. What more do you really, really need?" she says.

Researchers from Rutgers University and the Joan Ganz Cooney Center at Sesame Workshop collected dozens of stories like Uribe's for a new study[1] focused specifically on lower-income

families with school-age children. They surveyed nearly 1,200 parents with kids between six and 13 years of age, whose income is below the national median for families with children. They found that even among the poorest households, nine in 10 families do have some access to the Internet, but in many cases that means dial-up or a mobile data plan.

"Our data is one of the first, if not the first time that we can really comprehensively look at whether or not having mobile-only access—meaning that you don't have it through a computer or a desktop—whether or not it's equivalent. And what our findings show is that it is not," says co-author Vikki Katz. The study puts in a new light the important progress that smart phones brought to many disconnected households.

As early as 2013, the U.S. Census Bureau reported that phones were reducing[2] historic Internet use disparities among different racial and ethnic groups. Similarly, smart phones

---

1   Rideout, Victoria, and Vikki Katz. 2014. "Opportunity for All? Technology and Learning in Lower-Income Families." The Joan Ganz Cooney Center at Sesame Workshop. Retrieved on March 19, 2019, from http://digitalequityforlearning.org/wp-content/uploads/2015/12/jgcc_opportunityforall.pdf.

2   Stiles, Matt. 2013. "Census: Smartphones Bridging Digital Divide." National Public Radio, June 10. Retrieved on March 19, 2019, from https://www.npr.org/sections/codeswitch/2013/06/10/190415432/census-smartphones-bridging-digital-divide.

became the gateway to the Internet for many less wealthy Americans, and surveys like Pew[3] still find people with lower incomes to be more heavily dependent on their smart phones for Web access. What that has produced, however, is a quarter of lower-income families with kids in school having only a mobile device for Internet access. Among families living below the poverty level, the proportion rises to a third. And it's highest at 41 percent among immigrant Hispanic families in particular.

Can you do homework on a phone?

For children, that means they're less likely to use the Internet on a daily basis, according to the study. And that charts a far harder road for a kid to become a digitally savvy student and worker. Katz says that also makes it hard for children to explore topics and ideas that interest them personally—what educators sometimes call interest-driven learning—which can prevent them from cementing, say, an interest in a musical instrument or developing another expertise. "These are important factors in thinking about how the homework gap is much broader than just homework," she says.

And even for regular homework, limited technology at home can be a setback. "It could be, in a general term, a question of what is the homework that's being asked of the child," says Ernesto Villanueva, an executive director and former teacher and principal at Chula Vista Elementary School District in San Diego County. "And now we find . . . we are in a place where we want students to be creative, to be artistic, to demonstrate the skill sets that aren't only about reading something or watching a video but also doing something with that."

In that sense, it can be a matter of a small screen and lack of a keyboard, making even a tablet an upgrade as a device. (And it's important to note that a "mobile device" in the Rutgers/Cooney study did account for tablets as well.) But if there's no Wi-Fi at home, a tablet would have to rely on a mobile data plan, posing its own challenges like data caps, weak connections, or shared access with multiple family members. "If we're asking kids to go home and watch a video and Mom and Dad are on a measured plan, well that's going to pose a problem," Villanueva says, "because Mom can't have you watch three of those high-intensity videos and then she no longer has access for the rest of the month."

Discount internet programs don't reach

As expected, the main reason lower-income families reported a lack of high-quality Internet access at home was cost. "It's not that they don't understand the importance of this for their kids' education," says Katz's co-author Victoria Rideout. "It's not that they don't desire it. It's not that they don't feel confident using the Internet. It's that they don't have the financial resources to be as connected as they want to be."

Various Internet service providers do have discount programs targeted at low-income Americans . . . but the study found they weren't reaching many of the families surveyed. Of the families who would generally be eligible by income level, only six percent said they've ever signed up for such discount programs, according to the report. Why aren't more families using the programs? "There's a few problems, but one of them is that they presume that these families are still on the 'wrong' side of a digital divide, meaning that they have little to no technology in their homes," says Katz. "And we can see from [the survey] and from the interviews, that that's not true."

For instance, some of the programs only offer wired Ethernet connections, which are restricting for a household with several children; or only accept homes that have not had any Internet service for several months, which means eligible families who previously signed up for a higher-cost service have to go without Internet to qualify for the discounted service.

Some shifts are starting to happen . . . The Federal Communications Commission . . . [voted] to begin restructuring its old telephone subsidy called Lifeline to also cover broadband[4]. [*Editor's Note*: The Lifeline Modernization Order, issued in 2016, subsidizes broadband for consumers who meet the requirement, offering $9.25 per month in support.[5]] And digital equity experts say the most important thing will be changing the way we think about the issue: no longer will the question be whether there's access, but rather what the quality is.

3   Smith, Aaron. 2015. "U.S. Smartphone Use in 2015." Pew Research Center. Retrieved on March 19, 2019, from http://www.pewinternet.org/2015/04/01/us-smartphone-use-in-2015.

4   Naylor, Brian. 2015. "FCC Chairman Wants to Help Low-Income Americans Afford Broadband." *National Public Radio*, May 28. Retrieved on March 19, 2019 from https://www.npr.org/sections/thetwo-way/2015/05/28/410351224/fcc-chairman-wants-to-help-low-income-americans-afford-broadband.

5   Lifeline Program for Low-Income Consumers. 2019. Federal Communications Commission. Retrieved on March 19, 2019, from https://www.fcc.gov/general/lifeline-program-low-income-consumers.

JENEEN INTERLANDI

35. WHY ARE OUR MOST IMPORTANT TEACHERS PAID THE LEAST?

Inequalities in the educational system are documentable as early as preschool. Because caring for and educating young children is often seen as low-skill work that doesn't require an advanced degree, early childhood educators are poorly compensated and often experience many of the social problems discussed in this book, including poverty and poor health. Interlandi discusses recent research in the field of developmental psychology that indicates the importance of high-quality educational experiences in early childhood, in particular for children from lower-income families and neighborhoods, and describes increasing calls for preschool educators to have college degrees and training (and to be compensated for their investments). Interlandi asks how we can support these teachers as workers and individuals, while simultaneously increasing positive educational outcomes for young children.

One snowy February morning at the Arbors Kids preschool branch in downtown Springfield, Massachusetts, 38-year-old Kejo Kelly crouched low over a large, faded carpet and locked eyes with a blond-haired boy of three. It was circle time, and Kelly was trying to get each of her 13 tiny students to articulate a feeling. "Good morning, good morning, and how do you do?" she sang softly to the little boy. "Jamal's silly! Amir's happy! And how about you?" Kelly's classroom was known for what one visiting specialist called its "singsonginess." The good-morning bit was standard fare, but Kelly also sang her own impromptu ditties throughout the day. She'd found that a good melody could cajole even her most obstinate students into completing dreaded tasks: There was a song about washing hands, and one about cleaning up messes, and another about how shouting and running were for outside only.

Most children squealed with delight when their turn came to name a feeling: They offered up happys and sillys with abandon. Even the more bashful ones, who had to be prompted, were visibly thrilled by Kelly's attention, which seemed to beat out a limited toy-dinosaur collection as the class's chief attraction. But not the blond-haired boy. During the opening exercise, in which each child got a turn to dance in the center of the circle to a song of his choosing, he neither picked a song nor danced to the one Kelly offered. Instead, he flung himself at her feet and writhed like a fish out of water, then went completely still in a belligerent game of possum. Now, at least, Kelly had made eye contact. "How are you today?" she asked, holding both of his hands in hers as she spoke. "Are you happy? Angry? Sad? Or silly?"

If any of her students—or "little friends," as she called them—had sung her song back to her just then, Kelly would have answered that she was stressed. Three teachers had called out from work that morning, including the assistant teacher assigned to Kelly's room. Massachusetts state law prohibits the child-to-teacher ratio in full-day preschool classrooms from exceeding 10 to 1, so normally, Kelly had 13 students and one co-teacher. But staff shortages were a common occurrence at Springfield Arbors, where teachers earned

$10 an hour on average and staff turnover was high. In practice, there was a lot of juggling: On any given day, students and teachers shuffled from one room to another, combining some classes and breaking others up in an effort to keep each room within the permissible ratio. That day, Kelly would absorb six additional students and one co-teacher from another classroom.

The extra little ones didn't trouble her as much as the prospect of being stuck late again. She was supposed to be off by 4 p.m., but most of her kids didn't leave until 5:30, and the teacher who was scheduled to stay late was among those who were out. Of the teachers who were present, all either had children of their own to fetch from day care or night classes to get to at the community college. Kelly had neither. Her own kids were 17 and 20, and she had long since forgone higher education in favor of working.

But none of that concerned the blond boy, who was blinking and smiling at her. Kelly kept her own eyes locked on his even as another student—a little girl with a devilish grin and a long dark ponytail—leapt onto Kelly's back and began tugging at her hairnet. "How are you?" Kelly asked the boy again. "Can you tell me a feeling?"

The ponytailed girl was hardly the only one threatening to break the moment open. Someone was crying. Someone else was throwing toys not meant to be thrown and jumping on toys not meant to be jumped on. Someone smelled like poop and needed to be taken into the bathroom and guided through the basics of toilet use. And several someones were demanding things of Kelly specifically—that she hug them, or carry them round the room on her shoulders, or play a special game with just them. The children were ravenous for their teacher. And for each moment that she focused exclusively on the little blond boy, she risked losing the rest of her class to an irrevocable anarchy.

To an outsider, it was tough to say which of the children's behaviors were normal for three- and four-year-olds and which were signs of bigger issues. Increasingly, classrooms like the one over which Kelly presides are being eyed by social scientists and policymakers as both the place where problems emerge and the safety net that stands the best chance of addressing them. Preschool is often thought of as mere

babysitting. But a growing body of research suggests that when done right, it can be much more than that. An effective early-education program can level the playing field for low-income Black and Hispanic students relative to their White or wealthier counterparts, so much so that gaps in language comprehension and numeracy can often disappear by the start of kindergarten. And according to at least two longitudinal studies, the very best programs can produce effects that reach far beyond those early years, increasing the rates of high school completion and college attendance among participants and reducing the incidence of teenage parenthood, welfare dependence, and arrests.

The community Kelly taught in was low income by all the standard metrics. Many of her students came from single-parent households—some from teenage mothers, at least one from foster care—and nearly all of them qualified for state-funded child care vouchers. Programs like Springfield Arbors that accepted such vouchers received about $35 a day for each child, enough to cover basics like food and art supplies but not enough to pay for on-site behavioral specialists or occupational therapists. The school did make referrals. By Massachusetts law, all three- and four-year-olds are eligible to receive special-needs services at the local public school; there is even a free shuttle to shepherd them back and forth. But the waiting list for those services can be long, and in the winter of 2016, few parents at the school bothered to put their children's names on it.

So Kelly kept her own fractured vigil—taking note of which students couldn't control their emotions, or sit still for the life of them, or engage with others in a meaningful way—and giving those students whatever extra attention could be spared. She sometimes imagined the classroom as a bubble, inside which her students were temporarily spared from the hazards of everyday life. Her job, as she saw it, was to hold that bubble open for the ones who couldn't always hold it open themselves. "Come on, my friend," she said now to the little blond boy. "Talk to me."

The idea that we can deliberately influence the cognitive and social development of very young children is a fairly new one. In the early twentieth century, some doctors considered intellectual stimulation so detrimental to infants that they routinely advised young mothers to avoid it. At the beginning of the 1960s, the prevailing wisdom was only slightly less dire. Trying to stimulate a very young mind wasn't considered dangerous so much as pointless, because zero- to four-year-olds were "concrete thinkers," incapable of theorizing or abstraction.

But such thinking began to shift with two seminal preschool experiments: the HighScope Perry Preschool Study, which began in 1962 in Ypsilanti, Michigan, and the Carolina Abecedarian Project, which began in 1972 in and around Chapel Hill, North Carolina. Perry provided free half-day classes and weekly home visits to 58 Black children living in a high-poverty district near Detroit. Abecedarian provided 57 children of a similar cohort with full weekday care for their first five years of life, including not only preschool but also health care and social services. Both programs employed highly trained teachers and kept student-to-teacher ratios low. The Perry study also used a curriculum rooted in "active participatory learning," in which cognitive and social skills are developed through educational games that the children themselves initiate and direct.

The short-term results of these interventions were mixed. Some of the preschoolers, for example, were more aggressive at the end of the programs than they had been at the start, even if this difference disappeared by second grade. Decades later, however, when researchers went back, they found a surprise. At age 21, the Abecedarian children were half as likely to have been teenage parents and 2.5 times more likely to have enrolled in college than the control group, who did not attend preschool. At 40, the Perry children had higher median incomes than their control-group peers; they were less likely to be on welfare and less likely to have been arrested. Those results were not uniform. For example, while Perry seemed to reduce arrests and increase high school graduation rates, Abecedarian had no impact on either. But the findings still caused a stir among social scientists and educators: Both programs appeared to have affected the children in ways that could still be seen in adulthood.

In the decades since those results were published, the biological and social sciences have radically altered our understanding of early-childhood development. We now know that infants and toddlers have the capacity for complex thought. According to a recent report from the Institute of Medicine, they can understand other people's intentions, reason about cause, and effect and intuit the more basic aspects of addition and subtraction. We also know that the earliest years are a period of intense and rapid neural development—MRI studies suggest that 80 percent of all neural connections form by age three—and that a child's ability to capitalize on these years is directly related to her environment. Social scientists have shown that, owing to a shortage of books and toddler-friendly conversation, children from families on welfare understand roughly one-third the number of words that their middle-class peers do by the start of kindergarten.

Scientists and educators have begun to build on this new understanding, creating pedagogy and designing curriculums around the needs of our earliest learners. But one crucial question remains unanswered: What actually works? What are the defining features of an excellent preschool education? "There is no empirically based definition of 'high-quality preschool,'" says Mark Lipsey, a social scientist at Vanderbilt University. "We throw the phrase around a lot, but we don't actually know what it means."

Part of the problem is that the benefits of a preschool education tend to manifest unevenly. Developmental gains made by the start of kindergarten can be enough to close racial achievement gaps, but those gains often evaporate by third or fourth grade, a phenomenon that education researchers call the fade-out effect. And so far, the longer-term rebounds found in Perry and Abecedarian—in which children who attend good preschools fare better in adulthood than their peers who attend no such program—have been difficult to parse or replicate. In 2017, a group of prominent early-education researchers published a consensus statement declaring that preschool classrooms were a "Black box" and that much more research was needed before anyone could say with certainty which ingredients were essential to improving long-term developmental trajectories.

Amid that uncertainty, though, at least two things seem clear: Children in low-income and minority neighborhoods stand to gain (or lose) the most from whatever preschool system we ultimately establish. And the one-on-one exchanges between students and teachers—what developmental psychologists call "process quality"—may well be the key to success or failure. In other words, if preschool classrooms really are crackling with the kind of raw power that can change the course of a life, that power most likely resides in the ability of teachers like Kelly to connect with students like the little blond boy.

But if teachers are crucial to high-quality preschool, they are also its most neglected component. Even as investment in early-childhood education soars, teachers like Kelly continue to earn as little as $28,500 a year on average, a valuation that puts them on par with file clerks and switchboard operators, but well below K–12 teachers, who, according to the most recent national survey, earn roughly $53,100 a year. According to a recent briefing from the Economic Policy Institute, a majority of preschool teachers are low-income women of color with no more than a high school diploma. Only 15 percent of them receive employer-sponsored health insurance, and depending on which state they are in, nearly half belong to families that rely on public assistance. "Teaching preschoolers is every bit as complicated and important as teaching any of the K–12 grades, if not more so," says Marcy Whitebook, a director of the Center for the Study of Child Care Employment at the University of California, Berkeley. "But we still treat preschool teachers like babysitters. We want them to ameliorate poverty even as they live in it themselves."

The solution to this paradox seems obvious: Hold preschool teachers to the same standards as their K–12 counterparts, and pay them a salary commensurate with that training. But that proposition is rife with intractable questions. Who will pay the higher salaries? How will current teachers rise to meet the new credential requirements? And if they can't or won't, who will take their place? At the heart of those questions is this one: What, exactly, makes a good preschool teacher?

Springfield Arbors preschool consists of one long hallway on the ground floor of an assisted-living facility, with several classrooms strung along either side. The surrounding neighborhood, known as Six Corners, is home to a high school (the same one that Kelly attended), a community college, and a steady beat of drug- and gang-related violence. Six Corners children live on the down side of what's known in education circles as the achievement gap. According to analysis done by the Massachusetts-based nonprofit Strategies for Children, between 12 and 14 percent of third graders in some Six Corners schools read at or above grade level, compared with between 37 and 43 percent in nearby Forest Park, a neighborhood known for its well-preserved Victorian homes and as the birthplace of Dr. Seuss, the city's most famous native son.

Kelly came to preschool teaching about a decade ago, when the local caterer she was working for abruptly shut down. For a single mother with a high school diploma, the options in Springfield were limited: Home health aides, retail salespeople, and food-service workers all made about the same salary. Receptionists and secretaries made more, but those jobs required office experience, and the work itself sounded dull. Kelly wanted a job helping people. She had only ever worked in food service, but when she found a local preschool with an opening in the kitchen, she saw a chance to pivot.

She started by making herself known in the classroom, lingering to help out when she delivered lunches, introducing herself to parents in the hallway, befriending the teachers and asking them about their work. When an assistant teacher spot opened up, she jumped on it. She considered it a promotion, even though the teacher's salary ($9 an hour) was actually $1 an hour less than what she made as a school cook. For the first year, she split her time between the kitchen and the classroom while she earned her Child Development Associate certification, or CDA, which required her to complete a nine-month course that met for four hours every Saturday at the local YMCA.

At first she thought that credential would help her carve a path to some greater edification: a higher degree, maybe, and a higher wage along with it. But those dreams were quickly jettisoned. In 2011, just as she was completing her first class at the community college, an electrical fire tore through the three-family home that Kelly and her two children shared with her grandmother, mother, aunt, and cousin. Her relatives' apartments weren't damaged much, but Kelly and her children lost nearly all their possessions. Worse, the fire seemed to usher in a newly dark chapter in her life.

In 2012, her younger brother died in a horrific car accident; a year later, her cousin was shot and killed, and her aunt died. Her daughter's boyfriend—the father of her newborn grandson—was also killed, in another shooting. Somewhere in the middle of those heartaches, the preschool she worked at closed, and Kelly moved on to Springfield Arbors.

The CDA taught her the basics of lesson planning, class structure, and family engagement, but her real training came through trial and error. Kelly's classroom was often chaotic, but parents quickly learned that they could come to her with concerns, even after their children had aged out of her classroom. One mother asked her to step in as foster parent during a particularly tough time. Others hired her to babysit when they picked up night shifts at one job or another, so that Kelly might welcome a given child at eight in the morning and not return him to his mother until well after 10 or 11 at night. The work was exhausting, but she found she had a knack for it—an instinct for what her students needed, an ability to relate to them and, when all else failed, a willingness to keep trying.

One early-spring afternoon, when a rainstorm kept the children indoors during what would normally be playtime, Kelly tried arranging a field trip to the basement hallway—the only substitute playground at Springfield Arbors. But when too many of them fell into tantrum mode at the same time, she changed tack and set up the portable chalkboard at the front of the room. It did not take long for one, then three, then a dozen of the children to notice her chalking letters and gather around. The letter of the week was "D," and she had been teaching the students what words it was used in and showing them how to write and pronounce it. "Down, over, over," she said in a long, slow drawl, as she drew first the spine and then the hump of the letter. She was speaking to one little boy specifically, and when she was done, she handed the chalk to him and held his hand as he repeated her movements. Then she removed her hand and nodded at him to try on his own.

At first, the class was enthralled by this demonstration. But then one little boy started screaming. Grandma, an elderly volunteer who sometimes came for an hour or two and mostly sat in back of the room on a small couch, grabbed the boy's arm and yanked

him to her side. "Cut it out," she said. "Come sit!" The boy yanked his arm back, flopped onto the floor, and wailed. Kelly kept her focus on the students at the Blackboard. Eventually the screamer ran back over to the circle and forced another little boy off his seat, which made the other boy cry, which distracted the rest of the class and set half of them wandering off, before anyone had made a full D.

When nap time came, it seemed impossible that any one of the tiny, furious bodies twirling through the room could be stilled long enough to let sleep come, let alone all of them at once. But the sleeping mats were soon laid out across the room, and the children took their cue, except for the little blond boy, who wouldn't lie still. One of Kelly's colleagues sat on the floor near him, urging him to calm himself. "Relax your body," she said over and over, patting his back. But it was no use, so she traded spots with Kelly. Kelly leaned over the little blond boy and made eye contact with him and allowed him to grab at her hands with his. This seemed to do the trick. When he settled in just enough to release his grip, she took her cell phone out and played soft music, just for him, which clinched the deal.

By the time all the children fell asleep, Kelly was sitting cross-legged on the floor with four little ones unfurled like flower petals around her. She was rubbing each of their backs in turn with one hand—rub, rub, pat, next; rub, rub, pat, next—while rocking a fifth in her other arm. Her classroom had a total of 19 students just then, and in order for her to grab lunch, the school's cook had to be summoned to sit with the sleeping children. She pulled a pack of noodles from her coat pocket and tiptoed toward the door. "It's a ramen week," she whispered. "I just spent a fortune on household stuff yesterday, and my son has two basketball games this week." The high school charged $5 admission to each game, and Kelly rarely missed one, even when it meant skimping on meals. She returned a few minutes later with a bowl of steaming noodles and two co-teachers. As the children snoozed, the three women slipped into a whispered chat. . . . One teacher, Miss RJ, was summoned to the office: The nurse at her own children's school was calling to say that both of them were sick. But Springfield Arbors was still short-staffed. So Miss RJ was stuck there, and her own children were stuck with someone else.

In the United States, the care of children who have not yet aged into public school has long run on two tracks, separated mostly by household income. The upper- and middle-income track was designed specifically to engage and nourish young minds at their ripest juncture. The low-income track originated in the social-welfare system; its programs were created not just for children but also for their mothers, who needed to work. As such, they tend to be larger and staffed by teachers with high school diplomas. They also tend to be chronically underfunded.

The last half-century is littered with attempts to merge these two tracks—that is, to make the day cares of the poor more like the preschools of the middle class and wealthy. But those efforts have long been plagued by a deep cultural ambivalence toward both charity and working mothers. When Head Start, the nation's first public preschool, began in 1965 as part of the War on Poverty, its goals were twofold: to provide underprivileged preschoolers the tools they needed to keep up with their better-off peers; and to offer an economic boost for their mothers, some of whom were recruited and trained to work at the centers as educators. The program was part of what would come to be known as the country's biggest peacetime mobilization of human resources, but enthusiasm for it was short-lived. Amid concerns about "family weakening" in the 1970s and "welfare queens" in the 1980s, funding for early education stalled. Today Head Start serves less than one-third of the nation's eligible students. As part of a wave of reforms about a decade ago, Head Start began requiring half of its lead teachers to hold bachelor's degrees. It's too soon to tell what impact this has had on teaching and learning, but one unintended consequence is that it's harder for teachers like Kelly to find work at the centers.

Head Start is not the only program to raise credentialing requirements for preschool teachers. In 1998, as a result of a lawsuit filed by the Education Law Center, an advocacy group for New Jersey public school children, the New Jersey Supreme Court ordered 31 low-income school districts to provide high-quality preschool for all three- and four-year-olds. Among other things, the court's definition of "high quality" included full-day programs staffed by college-educated teachers who earned salaries equal to those of their K-12 counterparts. The resulting program—known as the Abbott preschool program, after the lawsuit that led to the mandate—represents one of the first efforts among education reformers to replicate the models of Perry and Abecedarian and bring them to scale.

One recent morning in a brightly colored classroom at Egenolf, an Abbott preschool in Elizabeth, New Jersey, a three-year-old girl with soft brown pigtails and a White shirt examined a row of water bottles, each of which had a pine cone submerged in a different liquid, and dictated observations to her teacher, Yamila Lopez Hevia. The cone in the "cold water" bottle was closing up. The one in warm water was closing, too—but more slowly. "And what do we think is going on?" Lopez asked. "Why might that happen?" After a brief pause, the girl pulled up two big words, each of which she had heard from Lopez. The pine cones, she explained, were *a-dap-ting* to their *en-viron-ment*.

It was the crowning moment to a much larger project that began when the children noticed that it was getting colder out and that the leaves were changing color. Lopez led them through a dialogue about how trees and other plants get ready for winter. From there, they turned their attention to what animals do. Lopez took the class to a local park, where they noticed squirrels collecting nuts and looked for birds who might be getting ready to migrate. In the end, they circled back to themselves, discussing sweaters and warm coats and winter boots. "We introduced some big concepts," Lopez told me when I visited her class recently. "And it all started with that one simple question: 'What do you see happening around you?'" The technique was called scaffolding, and it was a key tenet of current preschool pedagogy, which Lopez learned as a student teacher.

According to that pedagogy, preschoolers discover the world around them through trial, error, and experimentation. They learn by doing things more than by thinking about them. The techniques that educators and developmental psychologists have devised for cultivating this natural tendency are decidedly Socratic. Rather than standing at a Blackboard chalking letters or leading a large group in song, they assert, teachers like Kelly and Lopez should pay close attention to what the children themselves are interested in, or puzzled by, and respond to that. Any given moment is ripe with the opportunity to teach in this way, but doing it well requires a suite of disparate skills. A squirrel collecting nuts for the winter might hold a biology lesson; but to offer that lesson, a teacher needs to recognize the moment as it occurs. She also needs a grounding in that discipline and a clear sense of where the student in question sits on the developmental spectrum.

"The bottom line is really individualized intentional teaching," says Steven Barnett, co-director of the National Institute for Early Education Research at Rutgers University. "And there's specialized knowledge that preschool teachers need that's different even from what kindergarten and first-grade teachers need." For example, he says, preschoolers are apt to reverse letters. "It really helps to understand why they do that, if you want to help them get it right," he says. "It's not an isolated thing. Like, let's take my sippy cup. My whole life up to now, my sippy cup is a sippy cup no matter what way I hold it — upside down, sideways, whatever. But now you give me this thing called a *d*. And I put it down one way and it's a *b*. And another way and you tell me it's a *p*. What's with that?"

Barnett and others say that the ability to guide preschoolers through this stage of development takes a college degree. Teachers who don't have rich vocabularies or grounding in math and science can't impart those things to their students, he says. In a 2015 report, the Institute of Medicine agreed. The report argued that holding preschool teachers to lower standards than public school teachers has fed the perception that the work itself is low-skill and in turn has helped justify policies that keep preschool teachers' wages down and prevent them from growing professionally. But teachers themselves have been divided over the prospect of new job requirements. Many of them migrated to the field precisely because it did not require a higher degree. College—navigating financial aid, carving out the hours for class and homework—takes time and money and know-how. And for those who have been doing the job for years or even decades, the suggestion that they need additional training can feel like an insult.

Abbott addressed these issues head-on. It provided intensive college-admissions counseling, including help with financial-aid forms and scheduling. It also covered tuition for teachers in the program and nudged the college programs to bring their classes to the preschools. "We had the college professors go into the Newark schools and hold their classes there so that the teachers didn't have to travel," Barnett says. "We also paid for substitutes when the teachers needed to go to classes during the day, because we knew that not everybody could do this at night school." The process was neither cheap nor easy nor fast, he adds. Many teachers struggled through remedial courses and community college before making their way into bachelor's degree programs. All told, it costs $14,000 per child per year, more than twice the national average.

Those figures have made Abbott a lightning rod in the debate over public preschool in general and teacher credentials in particular. Critics say that the program is far too expensive given how little it may affect student outcomes in the long term (Abbott studies show fade-out effects, albeit less significant ones than in many other preschool studies). But proponents argue that it's unfair to judge the success or value of such programs by performance in the middle school or high school years—in part because there may be rebound effects later on. And in any case, the program works demonstrably well in achieving its primary objective: preparing children for elementary school. It has also helped stabilize the preschool workforce. Because Abbott teachers earn solid middle-class salaries—between $55,000 and $57,000 per year on average—staff turnover is less of a problem, which in turn means that classrooms are less chaotic.

This latter benefit underscores all the others: A successful preschool teacher needs to make her students feel safe and help them understand their emotions and regulate their own behavior. Children can't concentrate long enough to absorb new ideas or develop new skills if every slight sets them off crying or swinging at other children, or if they feel constantly threatened or mistrustful of their surroundings. And teachers who earn poverty-level wages can't be expected to create consistent and reassuring classrooms. "Security is an essential foundation for early learning," says Whitebook of U.C. Berkeley. "An older kid might be able to learn about math or history from a teacher they don't like. But a young child, a preschool-aged child, is going to have a very hard time learning anything from an adult whom they feel averse to. For very young children especially, you have to meet them where they are, both literally and figuratively, and you have to make them feel safe in that space."

Little of what experts like Barnett and Whitebook espouse would surprise Kelly, who in the time I spent in her classroom seemed always to be on bended knee, talking one child or another through their tears, gently but firmly explaining the reality of other people's feelings or helping them understand the relationships between their physical behavior and its consequences. One day, I watched her spend a full 15 minutes on a small boy in bright orange shorts who had gotten in the habit of tearing through the room at full speed. In the course of a morning, he had knocked two little girls to the ground and destroyed a block city that two other children were building. The assistant teacher had threatened him with suspension from class, to no avail. Kelly, applying the same squat-down/direct-eye-contact treatment that she used on the blond-haired boy, led him through a string of questions:

"What happens when we run?" "We go fast!"
"What else happens?" "We . . . hit things?"
"Why do we hit things when we run fast, but not when we walk?" "Because . . . it takes longer to stop!"

From there they discussed how barreling into a person might make that person feel. Eventually, the boy concluded that it was best to save fast running for outside, where there was more space. It was as good a lesson in physics and feelings as any four-year-old was likely to get, in any school. . . .

If there was a shortcoming to Kelly's work, it was that her skills were almost always deployed to resolve a crisis or defuse tension, and rarely to nurture some budding curiosity. Kelly didn't doubt the vastness of her students' inner mental worlds; nor did she discount the importance of meeting them where they were or of treating them with frankness and intelligence. In fact, she seemed to grasp those principles intuitively. What she lacked was the support she needed to build on her natural talents or cultivate her own ambitions.

One such ambition was taking more of a leadership role at the center. In April 2016, she was

unofficially promoted from lead teacher to assistant director—an office job that came with a small raise. But then in June, two teachers quit and another was fired, and she was sent back to the classroom. "I feel like I can't move forward," she told me at the time. "I keep picking up slack for all these other people moving forward with their careers, and their lives. And I'm stuck."

That feeling had become more pronounced lately, owing to a string of incidents outside the classroom. First was the robbery: When she and her daughter stopped at the bank one evening after work, they were held at gunpoint by a man in a ski mask demanding all the money behind the counter. The entire episode passed in 15 minutes. But while Kelly's daughter compartmentalized it quickly, Kelly replayed it in her head for weeks, enumerating to herself all the ways that trouble had nearly missed them: She did not normally stop at that branch but had taken a different route home to run an errand. They had been about to leave; Kelly's hands were on the door when the gunman came through it from the other side, thrusting his weapon in her face. He was never caught, but the Springfield Police Department sent the Kelly household a pamphlet on how to deal with the aftermath of a robbery.

Then, as summer approached, Kelly received a summons asking her to testify in a murder trial. The actual killing took place in 2013, on her brother's birthday. It was the first of his birthdays since his death, and Kelly and her sister were sitting up in her sister's kitchen, weathering the internal storm that such anniversaries tend to bring, when they heard shots. Kelly looked down from the second-story window to find a gaggle of teenagers, including her nephew, scrambling for cover. She grabbed every glass object she could get her hands on—plates, vases, dishes—and hurled them out the window at the gunman, ducking in between throws to protect herself.

When the shooting stopped, she and her sister ran out to the street, where they found one boy down. Kelly gave him CPR and even got him back to breathing for a few minutes, but he died before the ambulance arrived. In addition to reminding her of that day, the court summons had the effect of putting her children on edge; there had already been more than one shooting in their neighborhood that summer, and it was never good to be the only person standing between an accused killer and a possible life sentence. Kelly prided herself on setting those worries aside when she was at work. But with each fresh calamity, she felt the walls of her own bubble closing in.

One late afternoon, as fall tipped into winter, a squirrel perched itself on the ledge just outside Kelly's classroom window and caught the attention of a small boy with milk-chocolate skin and big, round eyes. He pointed at the animal, silently but with gusto. When Kelly walked by, he tugged at the leg of her pants. She scooped him up, rested him on her hip and, for a brief moment, watched with him as the creature scurried up and down a tree at the playground's edge. "Yes," she said. "That's a squirrel." The boy continued to point, but it was late in the day, and Kelly was tired and distracted, so the conversation ended there.

. . . In the last decade or so, the percentage of children served by state programs has doubled; 43 states and the District of Columbia now have public preschool programs of one kind or another. But that recent progress is now being tempered by federal indifference: [As of 2018], the Secretary of Education Betsy DeVos, has yet to appoint a director of the Office of Early Learning, established under the Obama administration to help facilitate the integration of preschool into the public education system; and President Trump has eliminated preschool funding increases from his proposed budget. What's more, experts are still divided over what credentials early childhood educators should have. . . .

The other argument is that increasing credential requirements without first raising wages places too much of a burden on already-overtaxed teachers. Mary Alice McCarthy, director of the Center on Education and Skills at the New America foundation, has proffered a different approach: apprenticeships. Like many human-service jobs, she says, teaching is best taught through "iterative interactions," where a person with experience helps a newcomer identify and respond to challenges. And the structure of an apprenticeship may be better suited to teachers who need to work full time while they learn. "You can't say the goal is to level the playing field for low-income kids," McCarthy says, "and then cut low-income teachers who have been doing this work forever out of the equation."

Amy O'Leary, a former preschool teacher and current campaign director for Strategies for Children, agrees: "The existing preschool workforce is much more diverse than the elementary workforce, and we want to preserve that," she says. "If you hire only those teachers who have the means to do it on their own, you displace the existing ones, who often come from the communities they teach in and have their own specialized knowledge of what it is to live in neighborhoods like Six Corners."

A Philadelphia-area community college, a union, and a number of local preschools joined forces to make the first attempts at training preschool teachers in this way. The program pairs apprentice teachers with mentors as they progress through a structured curriculum while working in the classroom full time. They get four wage increases over a two-year period, so that by the time they complete the program, which grants them both an associate degree and a journeyman card, they are already earning $2 to $3 more an hour. "That's a life-changing increase," McCarthy says.

It's also classroom-changing. The program is still in its infancy, but I spoke with apprentices, teachers, and center directors who say that improvements in classroom dynamics and staff turnover, not to mention actual teaching, are already apparent. "I feel like I've learned more about how their little brains work, and also about the best ways to reach them," says Briana Gonsiewski, an apprentice at Spin preschool in Philadelphia, who taught for 10 years before joining the program in 2017. "Before, I did not see playing on the ground as something structural. Now I get how they are really learning all the time, and I can start to see how to tap into that."

It will take a few years more to say how the apprentice program stacks up against programs like Abbott, or even like Springfield Arbors, and if the teacher training affects student outcomes in any measurable way. And then individual communities will have to decide if the gains are worth the price. "We have to come to terms with the fact that this is going to cost a lot more money," O'Leary says. "And to accept that, I think we still have to shed a lot of prejudices about working mothers and the working poor, and what it means to help them." In the meantime, with limited funds, policymakers and educators are caught between competing imperatives: Use the money they have to expand access so that as many students as possible receive some form of early education, or use it to improve quality in specific places like Six Corners, where both the need and potential payoff are greatest.

Investing in teacher education, as Abbott or the apprenticeship programs do, means choosing the latter, and that's a tough sell to taxpayers who need child care themselves. "Politicians are understandably reluctant to tell parents who need to work and who are on the waiting list for subsidies, 'Well, we're not going to expand access this year, because we are putting that money into quality,'" Barnett says. "It's true that the lowest-income areas stand to benefit the most from good preschools. But it's not just the very poor that are struggling. The story of inequality is increasingly that the very rich are leaving everyone else behind."

For now, Kelly and hers were making do. Her son was accepted at six of the ten colleges he applied to.

He had qualified for some scholarship money, which would help bring his tuition down, but Kelly was scrambling to come up with the rest. She had found a second job working nights and weekends at Kohl's, and was cutting corners where she could. One such economy was her car: a 2001 Buick Park Avenue, bought from a friend for $700. The engine was solid, but the gas meter was busted, so that you had to pay very close attention to the amount of driving you did relative to the amount of money you had put in the tank, or you'd end up stranded. Kelly learned this the hard way one evening. After a day filled with staff shortages and screaming children, she was heading through Six Corners toward home when the car sputtered to a stop. Both snow and darkness were falling fast, but there was a gas station just two miles up the road. Kelly called her daughter to say she'd be home late. Then she fished a plastic container from the trunk, hunched her back against the cold, and set out for the long walk by herself.

TEACHING WHILE AFRAID

ASHLEY LAMB-SINCLAIR

This is where things are today: The notion that teachers should be armed in order to protect students from shooters is a serious proposal now under debate. During . . . [a] White House listening session with students, teachers, and parents affected by school shootings, President Trump suggested[1] that allowing teachers with military training or other training experience to bring guns to school could help mitigate the effects of future attacks. School districts across the country, including some in Georgia[2] and

Florida,[3] are considering proposals to arm teachers, and legislation is being considered in several states. [*Editor's Note:* In 2018, Florida passed a "school guardian" law that allows some administrators to be trained to carry weapons. Despite the fact that the majority of the state's counties have not opted into the program, the program has spent nearly $2 million on firearm supplies such as weapons and ammunition, and an additional $3 million to pay the salaries of the trainers.[4] Georgia's legislators approved a law

1   Taylor, Jessica. 2018. "Trump Backs Arming Teachers during Emotional White House Listening Session." *National Public Radio*, February 21. Retrieved on March 19, 2019, from https://www.npr.org/2018/02/21/587775635/trump-backs-arming-teachers-during-emotional-white-house-listening-session.

2   Fultz, Natalie. 2018. "North Georgia School District Discusses Arming Teaches in Classroom." *Fox 5 Atlanta*, February 20. Retrieved on March 19, 2019, from http://www.fox5atlanta.com/news/north-georgia-school-district-discusses-arming-teachers-in-classroom.

3   Sandoval, Erik, and Vanessa Araiza. 2018. "Lake County School District Considers Arming Teachers with Guns." *ClickOrlando.com*, February 22. Retrieved on March 19, 2019, from https://www.clickorlando.com/news/lake-county-schools-considers-arming-teachers-with-guns.

4   Ceballos, Ana. 2019. "$2 Million for Florida School 'Guardian' Program Goes to Gun Equipment." *Orlando Sentinel*, February 13. Retrieved on March 19, 2019, from https://www.orlandosentinel.com/news/politics/political-pulse/os-ne-school-guardian-guns-20190213-story.html.

in 2012 allowing school systems to arm teachers, and several school districts have proposals under consideration by administrators, with one district having already approved such a plan.[5] The idea was met with backlash from many educators, parents, and administrators. "I don't think teachers should be armed," said Scott Israel, the sheriff in Broward County where the Florida shooting took place, at a CNN town hall. "I think teachers should teach." How are teachers themselves coping with all of this?

Educators across the country field incidents of school violence day in and day out. The exact number of school shootings in the United States is a point of contention[6], but since 2014 there have been five[7] school shootings on average per month, as well as countless other incidents of school violence of all sorts. For teachers, school violence imposes tough demands—not only that they may have to put their lives on the line should a shooting happen in their school, but the more quotidian reality of providing emotional support for children who are terrified of the prospect of such a thing occurring.

I reached out to fellow educators around the country to better understand how they think about their role as teachers in an era of school shootings. In these conversations, what I came to understand is that being a teacher today means working in a climate of intense fear—both their own and that of their students. Like me, many of my colleagues have experienced a violent act in their schools or know of an educator who has. To say the least, it's not what they thought they were signing up for. "When going through college to become a teacher, even after the Heath High School shooting in Paducah [Kentucky in 1997], it never crossed my mind that I would need or ever receive active-shooter training," said a Kentucky teacher, Staci Clark Hughes. "I never thought I would have to worry about turning a broom handle into a weapon of defense or how to lock my classroom door within seconds. I never thought I would need to know what a discharged weapon sounded like in a school hallway. . . . We did not go to college for this."

Schools are trying to bring teachers up to speed with active-shooter training and drills—protocols that can simultaneously assuage and exacerbate fears. Many teachers told me that the school-violence training they had received was disorganized and insufficient. Some shared that they had been encouraged to stock their rooms with canned goods to throw at potential attackers should they enter the classroom, or to search their rooms for potential barricades to block the door should an active shooter enter the building. One teacher, Ryan Kaiser, the 2016 Maryland Teacher of the Year, told me he considered bringing in a bucket of rocks, just in case, but still felt helpless because his doors didn't automatically lock. And because his door opened outward, he would be unable to barricade the door.

Even so, the teachers I spoke with generally felt that active-shooter training had improved since Columbine, a time period during which 32 states[8] have passed laws requiring schools to conduct lockdown drills. By 2015, nearly 95 percent of schools were conducting drills, according to the National Center for Education Statistics. Many teachers discussed the plans they've made on their own and with students, independent of school instruction. Some teachers spend time searching their classrooms for potential protective weapons, places to hide, and escape routes. An art teacher told me she had a pile of box cutters in her storage closet that she told her students was there just in case. Many teachers regularly check and double-check the locks on their classroom doors and storage closets, to ensure they can hide in these rooms if needed. A couple of teachers noted that they were considering their placement in the building—whether they were close to the front door, near a potential escape exit, or close to communal areas. Tiffany Hursh Gruen, a Kentucky teacher, told me that the silence in her school building when class is in session is striking to her now, post-Columbine[9]—doors are locked and learning takes place in closed spaces. "There was a time in my career when we encouraged teachers to keep their doors open, let the learning spill out, fill the halls with the sounds of excited exploration," she said. "Now, it's silence."

Teachers also reported that students tended to make their own safety plans as well. One teacher told me that a student told him she had even searched online for a bullet-proof vest but was discouraged when she discovered that the least expensive one she could find was $500. Another Kentucky teacher, Tanya Boyle, told me, "Several students told me this week that if a shooter was in the building, they would want to be with me." She continued, "This seemed odd, considering that I would struggle to help them because my mobility is so poor. They then told me that they wanted to be with me because I have a big closet that is perfect for hiding." Christine Porter Marsh, the 2016 Arizona

5   Broady, Arlinda Smith. 2018. "Armed Teachers Become a Reality in Georgia." *Atlanta Journal-Constitution*, May 4. Retrieved on March 19, 2019, from https://www.ajc.com/news/local-education/armed-teachers-become-reality-georgia/z0S3TawrlJodR42r6nOL6K.

6   Fattal, Isabel. 2018. "Another School Shooting—But Who's Counting?" *The Atlantic*, February 14. Retrieved on March 19, 2019, from https://www.theatlantic.com/education/archive/2018/02/another-school-shootingbut-whos-counting/553412.

7   Patel, Jugal K. 2018. "After Sandy Hook, More than 400 People Have Been Shot in over 200 School Shootings." *The New York Times*, February 15. Retrieved on March 19, 2019, from https://www.nytimes.com/interactive/2018/02/15/us/school-shootings-sandy-hook-parkland.html.

8   Campbell, Alexia Fernández. 2018. "After Parkland, A Push for More School Shooting Drills." *Vox*, March 14. Retrieved on March 19, 2019, from https://www.vox.com/policy-and-politics/2018/2/16/17016382/school-shooting-drills-training.

9   Sutter, John D. 2009. "Columbine Massacre Changed School Security." *CNN*, April 20. Retrieved on March 19, 2019, from http://www.cnn.com/2009/LIVING/04/20/columbine.school.safety/index.html.

Teacher of the Year, shared with me that her classroom had a wall of windows, and students in her classroom latched on to this detail after. . . . [the] attack in Parkland, Florida. Marsh said the rule had always been to lock the doors and keep them locked at all times because no active shooter had ever entered a locked door before, but Nikolas Cruz shot through windows, rendering their old code of safety useless.

The concerns on teachers' minds go well beyond the specific physical risk of school shootings. Many teachers are thinking about the need for social and emotional learning and mental health supports in schools; the need for more kindness, empathy, and dialogue within classrooms and outside them; and how family dynamics affect young people. They're frustrated with standardized testing and its impact on the time and energy teachers could be putting into addressing these other student needs, and with the lack of training of all kinds—active-shooter training, but also mental health training—for the country's teachers. They're concerned about the lack of time, follow-through, and communication on the part of counselors and other school personnel when violent incidents do occur.

Some teachers wondered about their ability to protect students, and—heartbreakingly—some wondered if they have students in their classes from whom they and the rest of their students might have to be protected. Many teachers were skeptical of the idea of arming teachers, the solution that's most quickly making headlines[10] and even reaching legislative chambers. . . . Instead, many conversations among teachers on social media focused on what teachers saw as longer-term solutions, such as finding ways to increase mental health support and for more expansive safety training in schools. Some teachers recommended more metal detectors or trained armed guards rather than armed teachers. Teachers also seemed concerned about the question of which teachers should be armed and which should not—who would decide? And if teachers are focused on the gun in their room that they might someday have to use, will they lose track of

their main purpose—teaching? Many already feel overwhelmed with the emotional burden they are being asked to carry; adding a weapon to this load feels unthinkable to some. But there are those teachers who said they would protect their students no matter what, and some[11] argue that carrying a weapon would enable them to better do this.

The new reality of choosing to become a teacher is that one can die while teaching children. This is not a reality that most teachers think about when they walk into their first classrooms—or their thirtieth. Some teachers are worried about what they actually would be willing to do.[12] Many have contemplated whether they would take a bullet for their students, as the Parkland assistant football coach Aaron Feis reportedly did.[13] But most of the teachers I spoke with believe that they signed up for teaching because they want to help kids—and they view saving students' lives as part of that job. "As a kindergarten teacher I would have no hesitation to lay my life down for one of my students," said Patrice McCrary, a well-known Kentucky teacher. "My family struggles knowing that statement is true. . . . I am an inducted member of the National Teacher Hall of Fame. Not far from the Hall of Fame is a Fallen Educators monument. Seeing the list of names on the monument is heart wrenching." She added that "most sobering of all is the fact there are empty spaces left for future additions. As of this week, three more names will be added."

10 Associated Press. 2016. "Colorado School District Will Allow Teachers to Carry Guns." *Associated Press*, December 15. Retrieved on March 19, 2019, from https://nypost.com/2016/12/15/colorado-school-district-will-allow-teachers-to-carry-guns.

11 Gunter, Joel. 2018. "After Another Deadly School Shooting, Is It Time for US Teachers to Carry Guns?" *BBC*, February 15. Retrieved on March 19, 2019, from https://www.bbc.com/news/world-us-canada-42804741).

12 Turkewitz, Julie. 2018. "School Shootings Put Teachers in New Role as Human Shields." *The New York Times*, February 19. Retrieved on March 19, 2019, from https://www.nytimes.com/2018/02/19/us/teachers-school-shootings.html?smid=fb-nytimes&smtyp=cur&referrer=http%253A%252F%252Fm.facebook.com).

13 Chuck, Elizabeth, and Associated Press. 2018. "Parkland School Shooting: Football Coach Aaron Feis Died Shielding Students." *NBC News*, February 15. Retrieved on March 19, 2019, from https://www.nbcnews.com/news/us-news/parkland-school-shooting-hero-football-coach-aaron-feis-died-shielding-n848311.

MIMI KIRK

36. STAUNCHING THE SCHOOL-TO-PRISON PIPELINE

Just as education is connected to future income, negative educational experiences, such as suspensions and expulsions, can create connections to the criminal justice system. Kirk discusses the "school-to-prison pipeline," wherein punishments for broadly defined and/or relatively minor offenses such as "defiance" can result in interactions with the criminal justice system for even very young students. Because of race and gender biases, these punishments are not meted out equally; students of color, those from impoverished families, and those with disabilities are more likely to be affected and to suffer the negative consequences of suspension and expulsion, such as repeating grades and dropping out of school.

In 2014, when Kalyb Primm Wiley was seven years old, 50 pounds, and not even four feet tall, he was handcuffed by his school's law enforcement officer after he cried and yelled in his Kansas City, Missouri, classroom. Kalyb, who is hearing impaired and was teased regularly about it, was reacting to a bullying incident. When the officer took Kalyb out of class and he tried to walk away, the officer handcuffed Kalyb and led him to the principal's office. Kalyb's father said[1] his son was left cuffed in a chair until he arrived. Kalyb was traumatized, and his mother homeschooled him for the next two years. . . . the ACLU filed a suit[2] against Kansas City Public Schools, as well as the officer and principal involved, accusing them of violating Kalyb's constitutional rights by "unlawfully restraining" him.

The past 20 years have seen a surge in severe school punishments, including suspensions, arrests, and referrals to juvenile court. Suspensions start as early as pre-kindergarten, and all punishments disproportionately involve students of color and students with a disability—raising the likelihood that these students will embark on a path to prison, dubbed the "school-to-prison pipeline." As a . . . report from the ACLU in Missouri[3] notes, "Students who come in contact with law enforcement and the criminal justice system because of their in-school behaviors have a greater likelihood of continued interaction with the criminal justice system." The unequal punishment of students of color is mirrored in the prison system: While people of color make up 37 percent of the country's population, they comprise 67 percent of the prison population.[4]

The ACLU report and another study published . . .[5] by the Legal Aid Justice Center in Virginia show that despite efforts by school administrators, policymakers, parents, and others to correct school discipline injustices, more must be done.[6] In Missouri, for instance, Black students are 4.5 times more likely to be suspended than White students— more than the already high national average of around four times more likely. And during Virginia's 2015–2016 school year, Black male students with disabilities were almost 20 times more likely to be suspended than White female students without disabilities.

HOW DID WE GET HERE?

Over the past decades, schools have increasingly adopted zero-tolerance policies and ascribed to the "broken-windows" theory of policing made popular in the 1990s. This model punishes people for peccadillos like vandalism to supposedly create an orderly atmosphere and deter more serious crime. In schools, punishment is often meted out for small infractions, such as the possession of a cell phone, minor insubordination, or inappropriate language, all classified under vague terms like "disruptive behavior" or "disorderly conduct."

More and more schools[7] have hired officers like the one who handcuffed Kalyb—called School Resource Officers, or SROs—with the stated goal of protecting students from school violence (hiring of SROs increased after the Columbine massacre of 1999). However, these officers often help enforce strict discipline standards. The Justice Policy Institute found,[8] for instance, that schools with SROs had five times as many arrests for "disorderly conduct" compared to schools without these officers.

In 1973, suspensions were relatively rare[9]: less than three percent of Hispanic students, around three percent of White students, and six percent of Black students were suspended. This rate has more than doubled for Hispanic and Black students since—but not for White students. The latest figures[10] from the National Center for Education Statistics show that in 2012, around four percent of White students were suspended, while figures for Hispanic students and Black students were six percent and 15 percent, respectively. Twelve percent of students with disabilities were suspended.

Research is clear that suspensions have far-reaching negative effects. Students who are suspended just once are more likely to ultimately repeat a grade[11] or drop out of school,[12] and to later be in contact with a county's juvenile probation department. A comprehensive study conducted in Texas[13] showed that 31 percent of students who were suspended or expelled from school repeated their grade, versus five percent of other students.

While it's difficult to prove causality—the suspended students may have had troubles later regardless of the discipline they received—the Texas study revealed[14] that students who had been suspended or expelled were twice as likely to drop out of school compared with students with similar characteristics at similar schools who were not suspended or expelled.

WHAT CAN WE DO?

In light of such grim statistics, many are working to stem the school-to-prison pipeline—and there's no lack of ideas about how to do it. Strategies include those for parents (know your child's rights at school), school administrators (train teachers and SROs so they understand a student's needs if they have a disability or have experienced trauma), and state policymakers (eliminate or limit the length of suspensions). Sara Baker, Legislative Policy Director at the ACLU of Missouri, says that the vague language states and schools use as grounds for punishment, such as "defiance," is particularly harmful. Because such terms are open to broad interpretation, they often result in punishment for small offenses. Amy Woolard of Virginia's Legal Aid Justice Center adds, "These are the kinds of violations where we see a great deal of disparities based on race and disability—one student's coping mechanism of walking away to 'cool down' is another student's 'defiance' charge." Woolard's center has been pushing for schools to describe prohibited conduct with specificity.

The Virginia Center and Missouri ACLU also call for local governments and school districts to direct resources into alternatives to suspension and expulsion, including "restorative practices." This technique brings those involved in an incident—students, teachers, parents—together to discuss how the incident impacted the people involved, the school, and the community. The goal is for students to talk through their problems and make amends, instead of receiving detention, suspension, or worse.

Sharonica Hardin-Bartley, the superintendent of St. Louis's University City district, is a proponent of restorative justice. In the 16 months she's been on the job, she has hired a restorative practices coordinator and has arranged training in the technique for students, counselors, and teachers. Hardin-Bartley notes that her schools still suspend students for violations such as drugs and weapons, but have started to use these practices for lesser offenses. "It's a lot different than saying, 'You did something wrong and now you're out of school,'" she says.

Hardin-Bartley is also creating more relaxed environments in her schools. She's encouraging classroom seating beyond the usual desks and chairs, such as bean bags and yoga balls, as well as setting aside quiet areas with soft furniture where students can decompress. Hardin-Bartley has also started yoga classes in some of her district's elementary schools. "These are de-escalation strategies," she says. "We're shifting the question aimed at students from, 'What's wrong with you?' to 'What happened to you?' We're considering the 'why' behind some of the behaviors we see."

Erica Meiners, a professor at Northeastern Illinois University and the author of *For the Children? Protecting Innocence in a Carceral State*, says that the problem is larger than schools themselves. "It's a wider issue of how our communities and culture have constructed ideas of children and childhood," she says. "Certain children in our culture get to be children, and others don't." Meiners points to the abundance of research demonstrating that U.S. society doesn't see Black children as children[15] but as "thuggish" and "predatory"— sometimes with lethal results. This tendency was clear in the way some officials[16] and observers[17] portrayed Tamir Rice, the 12-year-old boy holding a toy gun who police shot to death on a Cleveland playground in 2014. "He's menacing. . . . He's a 12-year-old in an adult body," Steve Loomis, the head of Cleveland's police union, said in 2015.[18]

For Meiners, one strategy is to transform the harm that caused such a situation in the first place. This can mean redirecting resources, such as working to block the creation of more policing institutions—she cites the nearly $100 million police academy slated to be built in Chicago[19]—and using the money for school counselors or art, music, and sports in impoverished schools—gentler ways to "discipline" kids usually reserved for Whiter, wealthier students.

While Meiners says that using restorative practices and dismantling punitive disciplinary policies are important, they are "first steps." "We need a wider discussion of how we have naturalized logics and practices of carcerality in our communities and classrooms," she says. "Looking at childhood—who benefits from this category, who doesn't, and why—can also help us understand how and why queer youth, Black and Latino youth, and disabled youth routinely experience the highest rates of school disciplinary action."

NOTES

1. Bergen, Katy. 2016. "Bullied Child, 7, Handcuffed for Crying, Suit Says." *Miami Herald*, September 9. Retrieved on March 19, 2019, from https://www.miamiherald.com/news/nation-world/national/article100767257.html.

2. Bergen, Katy. 2016. "ACLU Sues KC Schools, Saying Bullied Child, 7, Was Handcuffed for Crying." *The Kansas City Star*, September 8. Retrieved on March 19, 2019, from https://www.kansascity.com/news/local/article100679792.html.

3. ACLU of Missouri. 2017. "From School to Prison: Missouri's Pipeline of Injustice." Retrieved on March 19, 2019, from https://www.aclu-mo.org/en/publications/school-prison-missouris-pipeline-injustice.

4. The Sentencing Project. 2017. "Criminal Justice Facts." Retrieved on March 19, 2019, from https://www.sentencingproject.org/criminal-justice-facts.

5. Woolard, Amy. 2017. "Suspended Progress 2017." Legal Aid and Justice Center. Retrieved on March 19, 2019, from https://www.justice4all.org/wp-content/uploads/2016/04/Suspended-Progress-2017.pdf.

6. Eldeib, Duaa. 2017. "For Some Youths, 'Minor' Offenses Lead to Major Sentences in Adult Prison." *ProPublica Illinois*. Retrieved on March 19, 2019, from https://www.propublica.org/article/illinois-youths-adult-prison?utm_source=pardot&utm_medium=email&utm_campaign=majorinvestigations.

7. Justice Policy Institute. 2017. "Education under Arrest: The Case Against Police in Schools." Retrieved on March 19, 2019, from http://www.justicepolicy.org/uploads/justicepolicy/documents/educationunderarrest_fullreport.pdf.

8. Nelson, Libby, and Dara Lind. 2015. "The School to Prison Pipeline, Explained." *Justice Policy Institute*. Retrieved on March 19, 2019, from http://www.justicepolicy.org/news/8775.

9. Losen, Daniel J., and Russell J. Skiba. N.d. "Suspended Education: Urban Middle Schools in Crisis." Southern Poverty Law Center. Retrieved on March 19, 2019, from https://www.splcenter.org/sites/default/files/d6_legacy_files/downloads/publication/Suspended_Education.pdf.

10. Snyder, Thomas D., Cristobal de Brey, and Sally A. Dillow. 2016. "Digest of Education Statistics." National Center for Education Statistics, U.S. Department of Education. Retrieved on March 19, 2019, from https://nces.ed.gov/pubs2016/2016014.pdf.

11. Fabelo, Tony, Michael D. Thomspon, Martha Plotkin, Dottie Carmichael, Mine P. Marchbanks III, and Eric A. Booth. 2011. "Breaking Schools' Rules: A Statewide Study of How School Discipline Relates to Students' Success and Juvenile Justice Involvement." Council of State Governments Justice Center and the Public Policy Research Institute at Texas A&M University. Retrieved on March 19, 2019, from https://csgjusticecenter.org/wp-content/uploads/2012/08/Breaking_Schools_Rules_Report_Final.pdf.

12. Blafanz, Roberty, Vaughan Byrnes, and Joanne Fox. 2012. "Sent Home and Put Off-Track: The Antecedents, Disproportionalities, and Consequences of Being Suspended in the Ninth Grade." Center for Civil Rights Remedies and the Research-to-Practice Collaborative, National Conference on Race and Gender Disparities in Discipline. Retrieved on March 19, 2019, from http://www.sese.org/wp-content/uploads/2013/08/Sent-Home-and-Put-Off-Track.pdf.

13. Fabelo et al., 2011.

14. Nelson and Lind, 2015.

15. Southerland, Vincent M. 2015. "Youth Matters: The Need to Treat Children Like Children." *Journal of Civil Rights and Economic Development*, 27(4): 2013-2015.

16. Willgress, Lydia. 2016 "'Act Like a Thug and You'll Be Treated Like One': Miami Police Union Chief Claims Officers Were Right to Shoot 12-Year-Old Tamir Rice." *Daily Mail*, January 1. Retrieved on March 19, 2019, from https://www.dailymail.co.uk/news/article-3381001/Act-like-thug-ll-treated-like-one-Miami-police-union-chief-claims-officers-right-shoot-12-year-old-Tamir-Rice.html.

17. Letter to the Editor. 2015. "Tamir Rice Was Hardly an 'Innocent Little Boy.'" *Cleveland.com*. Retrieved on March 19, 2019, from http://blog.cleveland.com/letters/2015/11/innocent_little_boy.html.

18. Stahl, Jeremy. 2016. "Cleveland Police Union Boss Says Awful Thing about Tamir Rice Again." *Slate.com*, April 25. Retrieved on March 19, 2019, from https://slate.com/news-and-politics/2016/04/steve-loomis-says-awful-thing-about-tamir-rice-again.html.

19. Cherone, Heather. 2017. "New Police Training Center Advances; Protesters Want Funds Spent Elsewhere." *DNAInfo Chicago*. Retrieved on March 19, 2019, from https://www.dnainfo.com/chicago/20170920/garfield-park/new-police-training-center-advances-as-anti-police-groups-rally-against-it.

TEACHERS' IMPLICIT BIAS STARTS IN PRESCHOOL

YOLANDA YOUNG

If anyone ever doubted that Black children are not treated equally in the classroom, the research released . . . [in 2016] surely proved them wrong. In June, studies stated that Black students are nearly four times as likely to be suspended[1] as White students, and nearly twice as likely to be expelled. In September, we heard that Black preschoolers are 3.6 times[2] more likely to receive one or more out-of-school suspensions. And . . . new research[3] from the Yale Child Study Center finally pointed to clues as to why these disparities may exist: implicit bias.

Implicit biases take the form of subtle, sometimes subconscious stereotypes held by White teachers, which had been shown to result in lower expectations and rates of gifted program referrals for Black students.[4] Yale's study revealed these biases are directed at much younger children than previously thought and are present in Black and White teachers' behaviors.

Researchers led by Yale professor Walter Gilliam showed 135 educators videos of children in a classroom setting. Each video had a Black boy and girl, and a White boy and girl. The teachers were told the following:

We are interested in learning about how teachers detect challenging behavior in the classroom. Sometimes this involves seeing behavior before it becomes problematic. The video segments you are about to view are of preschoolers engaging in various activities. Some clips may or may not contain challenging behaviors. Your job is to press the enter key on the external keypad every time you see a behavior that could become a potential challenge.

While the teachers were asked to detect "challenging behavior," no such behavior existed in any of the videos. Yet when asked which children required the most attention, 42 percent of the teachers identified the Black boy.

The participants' conscious appraisal of whom they believed required the most attention closely mirrored the independent results of an eye-tracking technology used by the research team, which noted that preschool teachers "show a tendency to more closely observe Black students, and especially boys, when challenging behaviors are expected."

Allison R. Brown, executive director of the Communities for Just Schools Fund, an organization which seeks to combat the "school-to-prison pipeline," found the report heartbreaking but not surprising. "Black bodies are policed in the streets and in the classroom. . . . [Research] demonstrates that Black boys are viewed as four and five years older[5] than they are. Research demonstrates that racial disparities in school discipline exist in the most subjective of categories—'willful defiance,' 'insubordination,' 'disrespect.'" Those racial disparities decrease significantly for the most objective of categories: possession of alcohol on campus, possession of drugs with intent to distribute, [and] possession of a loaded weapon. Brown worries that the study supports what headlines suggest to her: Black people are seen as less than human, less deserving of dignity and respect.

The study's findings suggested an underpinning of Brown's anxiety but found that it wasn't limited to Black people. Researchers noted that when teachers were also given information about the disruptive child's home life and family stressors, teachers only reacted more empathetically if the teacher and student were of the same race. Otherwise, teachers rated the students more severely. The report suspects this is because teachers felt powerless to improve the student's situation. "These findings suggest that teachers need support in understanding family struggles as they may relate to child behaviors, especially when the teacher and child are of different races," Gilliam, the lead researcher, said. . . .

To solve this dilemma, Gilliam recommends anti-bias training programs and suggests consulting the work done . . . on racial literacy and racial climate in schools. Gilliam offers reasons to be hopeful. He reminds us that educators, who are paid very little, pursue teaching because they love young children. To the parents of Black children, he offers this advice: "Don't wait until you are worried about whether biases may impact the relationship between your child and his or her teachers. Be proactive. Get to know your child's teachers, director and staff. In all of my years of studying this issue, I've never seen a case where a child was expelled or suspended from a child care or preschool setting when the parents and teachers knew and liked each other. Not once."

1 Felton, Ryan. 2016. "Black Students in US Nearly Four Times as Likely to Be Suspended as White Students." *The Guardian*, June 8. Retrieved on March 19, 2019, from https://www.theguardian.com/education/2016/jun/08/us-education-survey-race-student-suspensions-absenteeism.

2 Prakash, Nidhi. 2016. "For Black Kids, the School-to-Prison Pipeline Opens the Second They Start Preschool." *Splinter*, June 8. Retrieved on March 19, 2019, from https://splinternews.com/for-black-kids-the-school-to-prison-pipeline-opens-the-1793857336.

3 Gilliam, Walter S., Angela N. Maupin, Chin R. Reyes, Maria Accavitti, and Frederic Shic. 2016. "Do Early Educators' Implicit Bias Regarding Sex and Race Relate to Behavior Expectations and Recommendations of Preschool Expulsions and Suspensions?" Yale University Child Study Center. Retrieved on March 19, 2019, from https://medicine.yale.edu/childstudy/zigler/publications/Preschool%20Implicit%20Bias%20Policy%20Brief_final_9_26_276766_5379_v1.pdf.

4 2016. "New Study Reveals Race of Students Triggers Alarming Bias in Teacher Expectations." American University School of Public Affairs. Retrieved on March 19, 2019, from https://www.american.edu/spa/news/race-bias-in-teacher-expectations-03302016.cfm.

5 Goff, Phillp Atiba, Matthew Christian Jackson, Brooke Allison Lewis Di Leone, Carmen Marie Culotta, and Natalie Ann DiTomasso. 2014. "The Essence of Innocence: Consequences of Dehumanizing Black Children." *Journal of Personality and Social Psychology*, 106(4): 526–45.

KATHARINE BROTON AND SARA GOLDRICK-RAB

37. THE DARK SIDE OF COLLEGE (UN)AFFORDABILITY

Food and Housing Insecurity in Higher Education

With the cost of higher education rising, many students struggle to afford not only college, but also the daily necessities of life such as food and housing. Housing and food insecurity can, in turn, impact the likelihood that these students will successfully complete their education. Broton and Goldrick-Rab discuss the economic challenges that students face when enrolling in college, as well as the ways college and university administers and community organizations can support students who struggle financially.

Most Americans agree that the current high price of college attendance renders it unaffordable, even for middle-class families with students enrolled in the public sector. Costs have risen and subsidies have declined, while real wages for earners outside of the top five percent have fallen. Despite massive public investments in financial aid, students from families earning an average of just $20,000 a year are now required to pay at least $8,000 for one year of community college and more than $12,000 a year at a public university (Goldrick-Rab & Kendall, 2014). That "net price" is what these students face after all grants (including the Pell and state and institutional grants) are subtracted from the cost of attending college. This price has gone up substantially over time, particularly since the Great Recession, and it is often impossible to cover the cost entirely with federal loans (Goldrick-Rab, 2016).

What happens when economically insecure people enroll in college, partly enticed by offers of financial aid, and then face prices that are beyond their reach? Since 2008, researchers at the Wisconsin HOPE Lab have posed this question in studies conducted in Wisconsin and across the nation. The answer, we have learned, is that even though they often work, a growing number of low-income students also experience food and housing insecurity. These material hardships affect learning and the effort that can be devoted to school. They compromise students' chances for degree completion and affect the institutions in which the students enroll (Broton, Frank, & Goldrick-Rab, 2014; Goldrick-Rab, 2016). While higher education has focused on helping the poor attend college—succeeding in placing almost 10 million Pell Grant recipients into colleges and universities—it has inadequately addressed the conditions of poverty confronting students as they pursue degrees.

DOING WITHOUT

When people lack a minimal level of basic goods such as food and shelter, they are said to confront "material hardship." Available data suggest that the incidence of food and housing insecurity is now greater among college students than it is in the general population (Broton, Frank, & Goldrick-Rab, 2014). Although prevalence rates vary across colleges, even students attending Ivy League universities with full financial-aid packages report going without food and struggling with hunger (Jack, 2015).

A New York University student reports,

> I live on $2 to $5 dollars a day. That means two meals a day, and incredibly unhealthy food. I'm hungry all the time. Being so hungry while you're trying to work two jobs to pay your rent and still keep up with your coursework is practically impossible—and more common than you would ever think at a university like this. (NYU Faculty Against the Sexton Plan, 2015)

Approximately half of all Pell Grant recipients are from families living below the official poverty line. In addition, evidence from a study by the Wisconsin HOPE Lab indicates that one in four Pell grantees grew up in families where at least sometimes there was not enough food to eat at home (Goldrick-Rab, 2016). That study followed 3,000 students from low-income families who enrolled in a public two- or four-year college or university in the state of Wisconsin shortly after graduating from high school.[1]

When we surveyed students during their first semester of college, nearly 90 percent indicated that they were upset or worried about not having enough money to pay for the things they needed in order to attend college; 78 percent stated that they were having difficulty paying their bills.

To make ends meet, students:

- cut back on social activities (80 percent)
- changed their food shopping or eating habits (71 percent)
- cut back or stopped driving (48 percent)
- borrowed money or used credit cards more (39 percent)
- increased the amount of time spent working (38 percent)
- postponed medical or dental care (24 percent)
- put off paying bills (24 percent)
- reduced utility usage (23 percent)
- went without a computer (19 percent)
- did not buy all required books or supplies (15 percent)

When we followed up with these same students a year later, 27 percent reported that in the past month, they did not have enough money to buy food, ate less than they felt they should, or cut the size of their meals. Seven percent had recently gone without eating for an entire day (Goldrick-Rab, 2016). Unsurprisingly, students who reported that they had grown up in food-insecure households were more likely to report experiences of hunger in college than were other Pell grantees (Mai, 2014).

The results of our study are not unique. An earlier survey at the University of Hawaii, for example, reported that 21 percent of students had reduced their food intake due to resource limitations in the prior year. An additional 24 percent reported anxiety about their food supply due to a lack of money (Chaparro, Zaghloul, Holck, & Dobbs, 2009). A recent survey of more than 4,000 undergraduates at 10 community colleges across seven states indicates that approximately half of students are food insecure, including 20 percent who had gone hungry in the last month (Goldrick-Rab, Broton, & Eisenberg, 2015).

Across these studies, the risk of food insecurity is unevenly distributed. At the City University of New York, for instance, 39 percent of students had experienced food insecurity in the prior year, but those at an increased risk include (Freudenberg et al., 2011):

- students with fair or poor health (56 percent incidence rate)
- those with incomes under $20,000 (55 percent)
- Hispanic students (48 percent)
- Black students (42 percent)
- financially independent students (46 percent)
- students who work 20 or more hours per week (44 percent)

Young adults are especially at risk for housing insecurity because they often lack a rental history, enough savings for a security deposit, or someone who can act as a guarantor (Joint Center for Housing Studies of Harvard University, 2011; Dworsky et al., 2012; Wilder Research, 2008). According to the Free Application for Federal Student Aid (FAFSA), 58,000 college students are homeless, although this is certainly an underestimate due to the reporting requirements and concerns about stigma (NAEHCY, 2014). In our Wisconsin HOPE Lab study, one-quarter of two-year college students indicated that they were unable to pay utility bills, and an additional 24 percent couldn't pay rent within the past year. Four-year college students were half as likely to report trouble paying rent and utilities. Results from a survey of undergraduates attending 10 community colleges indicates that half of students are housing insecure, including 13 percent who were homeless in the past year (Goldrick-Rab, Broton, & Eisenberg, 2015). Similarly, 42 percent of students at the City University of New York are housing insecure (Tsui et al., 2011). In both studies, students who experienced food insecurity were at greater risk of housing insecurity, and vice versa.

HURTING CHANCES OF COLLEGE COMPLETION

Material hardship seems to inhibit educational attainment. While there have not been studies (yet) measuring the impact of food and housing insecurity on college attainment, research from K–12 education and descriptive work in higher education is clear. For example, one study found that college students who report struggling to get enough food to eat are 22 percent less likely to earn a 3.5–4.0 GPA rather than a 2.0–2.49 GPA, after controlling for other background factors (Maroto, Snelling, & Linck, 2015). Madeline Pumariega, now chancellor of the Florida University System, explained why Miami Dade College had taken steps to alleviate food insecurity in an interview we did when she was president of the college's Wolfson campus (Goldrick-Rab, Broton, & Gates, 2013):

> When a student is hungry, he does not feel safe, and it is hard to help him synthesize material. We have to meet students' basic needs in order for them to fully concentrate on assimilating the information in a class in a way that they can apply it, learn, and take it forward.

. . . It can be very difficult to focus on school when you are unsure where you will sleep at night. In 2008, for example, we met "Anne," a student in the Wisconsin Scholars Longitudinal Study. Anne went to college in Milwaukee to obtain the skills to find a good job and a better life for herself and her mother. She had grown up in public housing as her mother cycled on and off assistance from the state, struggling to hold a job

while coping with lupus, a chronic disease. Anne had attended one of the city's better high schools, where she completed an International Baccalaureate program, before enrolling in the public four-year college. She was adjusting well to college life. Then the manager of the apartment building where she lived with her mother informed her that, by enrolling in school full time, she had violated the terms of the family's subsidized housing. Anne did not know what policy dictated this situation but thought it might have to do with perceptions of undergraduate behavior. In fact, Anne may have run up against her local public housing authority's definition of eligibility, which deprioritized full-time students.

If the idea of this policy was to prevent people from taking advantage of public housing, it made little sense in Anne's case. She was not a student seeking a new, inexpensive place to live for a few years but rather a long-term resident who had lived in the building for years and who had very few assets of her own—and little ability to make significant money without a college degree. Anne could see no recourse, so she switched to taking classes part-time. Her college academic advisor issued a letter for her to give to her landlord, proving she had done this. Yet it seems that no one at Anne's school, including her advisor or financial-aid counselor, called the housing authority in an effort to clarify the situation or intervene. Such a call may have allowed Anne to maintain full-time status but, as a part-time student, Anne received much less grant aid and was concerned about the extra time it would take to earn a degree. She spoke with her advisor about her concerns on several occasions; she did not know whom else to turn to. There did not seem to be any support at her college for this type of problem.

Anne had few options. If she worked, her income could disqualify her—and her mother—from receiving the housing subsidy, which they needed to make ends meet. A year later, Anne's mom was hospitalized, and Anne was struggling to juggle all of her responsibilities. Around this same time, the apartment manager reappeared, telling her that she could now enroll full time. Anne did not trust this information and did not go through with the paperwork and hassle to switch again. Anne's feelings of confusion and distrust were neither uncommon nor unusual, but they had significant implications. For each additional semester she stayed in school, the costs mounted and the odds of completing a degree diminished.

The last time we saw Anne was at the start of her third year of college. She was trying to work a little but not too much, since she needed money to pay the bills but did not want to make too much and be disqualified from her housing or her financial aid. She seemed on track with school. Subsequent administrative records indicate that she remained continuously enrolled until spring 2014. But then she left, without a degree in hand.

INSTITUTIONAL PRACTICES

We have met with administrators, faculty, and staff in colleges across the nation who are working to directly support students who are struggling to meet their basic needs. Our research suggests that the most strategic college leaders take a local approach. They investigate the specific needs of their students and draw on the strengths of the college and community to help meet those challenges.

Students and staff can readily point to policies that create bottlenecks and break points for food-and housing-insecure people. For example, the start of the school year can be especially stressful for students of limited financial means. Full tuition and fees are typically due at the same time that students need to buy school supplies and possibly put down a security deposit for housing accommodations. A lack of savings or a delay in financial-aid disbursement means that students are unable to make ends meet. The repercussions, such as being dropped from class rosters or losing an apartment, can be devastating (Rivera, 2015).

Several colleges have adapted their policies or put low-cost programs in place to address these concerns. For instance, one college implemented an interest-free short-term loan program for students who expect to receive financial aid but who have a delayed payment, so that the late timing of the aid does not derail the students' educational plans. The financial-aid office administers the program to streamline the process and ensure that the program poses a low financial risk to the college. Similarly, another college implemented an interest-free book-loan program, regardless of financial-aid status. Officials at this college recognized that many students work their way through school and do not have the lump sum needed at the beginning of the term but could manage smaller monthly payments.

Other schools we visited chose to change the rules regarding due dates or the consequences of late payment. For example, one college shifted the due date for fees by several weeks to allow students more time to work and earn money in order to make the payment. Another institution pushed back the date on which a student is dropped from class rosters for non-payment. Some colleges have hired individuals with backgrounds in social work or who have prior work experiences with individuals whose basic needs are not being met to fill critical student-service positions on campus. In these examples, college leaders and their teams reviewed and adapted policies or procedures to better serve students from low-income and poor families while maintaining the financial health and integrity of their institutions.

College leaders also turn to their communities to create partnerships that support poor college students. One of the more common arrangements is for a local food bank or pantry to serve students on campus. According to the College and University Food Bank Alliance (CUFBA), some pantries operate out of a closet one day a week, while others supply upwards of 50,000 pounds of food per year, with regular distributions. One college we visited coordinates with the college's culinary arts program to provide healthy-cooking demonstrations in partnership with the food bank. Students emphasize the importance of co-locating community services, such as a food bank, on campus. This reduces not only time and transportation costs but the stigma associated with accessing these supports. Students report an increased sense of belonging and integration with the college when officials advertise poverty-alleviation supports as just another student support service—along with academic advising, tutoring, or free flu shots—rather than as a supplemental service for marginalized students.

In addition to food pantries, some colleges work with their school cafeterias and food vendors to support students who are food insecure. At some colleges, this means that the administration purchases discounted meal vouchers, which it then distributes to students via different programs or services. In other cases, student organizations work with food vendors to save surplus edible food that would otherwise be thrown out each night. Although these food-rescue programs often look beyond the local college when deciding where to donate recovered food, more are realizing that the leftover food could be distributed to college students in need (Environmental Protection Agency, 2014). Finally, some students and college officials are encouraging on-campus food vendors to accept food stamps or Supplemental Nutrition Assistance Program (SNAP) benefits (Song, 2015). Again, the students we talked with described feelings of alienation when the college cafeteria or food vendor refused to accept their food stamps.

Many of the colleges we visited provide free on-campus tax-preparation services to students. . . . In comparison to food and shelter, this may not seem like a particularly pressing need for college students. But free tax-preparation services save students hundreds of dollars that many spend on professional filing fees. They also ensure that students receive all eligible higher education credits and exemptions for low-income families (e.g., Earned Income Tax Credit). These services encourage early filing of the FAFSA because completed tax documents are a required part of the application. Colleges that offer tax and FAFSA preparation services in tandem promote timely completion of the FAFSA. This increases the odds that eligible low-income students will receive all of their grant aid, as states often run out of need-based financial aid before all eligible students receive support (e.g., Cohen, 2012). Several colleges we visited collaborate with the Volunteer Income Tax Assistance program. This is an Internal Revenue Service (IRS) initiative that offers free tax-preparation services for low-income individuals and provides the service on campus. Other colleges rely on local partnerships or trained business students to become certified tax preparers.

GETTING HELP

The IRS program is not the only partnership that some colleges have established with nonprofit organizations. CUFBA, for example, was formed to help more

than 200 institutions coordinate food pantries on campus to help meet the demand for nutritionally adequate food. Other colleges have partnered with nonprofit organizations such as Single Stop or the Center for Working Families, which draw on existing social safety-net resources to help students attain financial stability and move up the economic ladder by providing comprehensive supports that promote degree attainment.

Single Stop originated as a community-based organization helping low-income individuals and families access food pantries, shelters, health centers, and job-training sites. In 2009, Single Stop launched its Community College Initiative and began providing similar poverty-alleviation supports to students and their families on college campuses. The organization works with colleges to create a one-stop campus center with resources from the college and community, where students who are struggling to make ends meet can go for support. Using proprietary technology, students are screened to determine their eligibility for federal, state, and local public benefits such as food stamps or health insurance. On average, we estimate that eligible students receive an additional $5,400 in cash and non-cash benefits—an amount nearly equivalent to the maximum Pell Grant (Goldrick-Rab, Broton, & Gates, 2013). In addition to these case-management services, Single Stop provides free financial counseling and legal and tax-preparation services. The multipronged intervention is based on the idea that the combination of cash and noncash benefits obtained in a timely and efficient manner, along with additional information and counseling support, can substantially improve retention and graduation rates. Preliminary evidence suggests that the program is working; with a credential in hand, students are much better positioned to obtain a good job and a more secure financial future (Single Stop, 2015).

The Center for Working Families, supported by the Annie E. Casey Foundation, takes a similar approach in collaborating with community colleges. It provides students with a coordinated set of services, including employment and career-advancement services, income and work supports (e.g., public benefits and tax-preparation assistance), and financial services and asset-building supports. Like Single Stop, the program continues to expand, and preliminary results are positive. A greater proportion of community college students served by the Center for Working Families persist in college (80–85 percent) compared to the overall college persistence rate (66–70 percent) (Liston & Donnan, 2012).

Both of these organizations do more than serve students. They also change the institutional culture of the college by reimagining the role of student services. In this new vision, comprehensive supports, including those helping students access the existing public safety net, are the norm.

A ROLE FOR FEDERAL AND STATE POLICY

At the federal level, educational and social policies have not caught up to the challenge. The current social safety net typically excludes college students with financial need from receiving support. This is true even though receipt of public benefits promotes academic progress. And it's true even though a college education is one of the most effective ways to reduce material hardship and future reliance on social benefits (Price et al., 2014). This makes it harder to reach national educational and economic goals (Goldrick-Rab, Broton, & Eisenberg, 2015). Advocates for change are working to remedy problems such as work requirements for food stamps, which make it difficult for undergraduates to receive that support while in school, or financial-aid questions that require students to "prove" that they are homeless in order to render them eligible for additional support.

While many young people rely on the National Free and Reduced Price Lunch Program during elementary and secondary school, upon transitioning to college they find themselves facing high prices with no such support. This has led Professor Wick Sloane (2013) of Bunker Hill Community College to write letters to federal officials asking for help. To quote from one of those letters:

> One peanut butter sandwich per school day for each of the nine million students on a Pell grant. How many of these are the same students who were eligible for free and reduced lunch in high school? No one knows and no one is counting. How many are from households on food stamps? No one's asking, either. Why not, then, 45 million peanut butter sandwiches at colleges each week? Until we come up with a better idea.

In recent testimony to the National Commission on Hunger, we echoed his calls and formalized a request for federal action to extend that program to the nation's community colleges (Broton & Goldrick-Rab, 2015).

Meeting students' housing needs may be even more difficult than providing food or tax assistance. Federal housing assistance is not an entitlement program. Scholars estimate that just one-quarter of families who need housing support actually receive it (Broton & Goldrick-Rab, 2014). Moreover, college students' eligibility for housing assistance is restricted (HUD, 2015a). The Tacoma Community College Housing Assistance Program provides one model for colleges seeking ways to help support housing-insecure students. In partnership with the local housing authority, the community college provides Housing Choice Vouchers to full-time students who maintain a 2.0 GPA and are homeless or at serious risk of homelessness. Many of the students are part of a workforce-development program and must participate in support services. Results after one year are preliminary but promising. Of the 22 students to receive a housing voucher, 21 (95 percent) remained enrolled in college. In comparison, 24 percent (35 out of 146) of eligible participants who were on the waiting list persisted in college (Tacoma Housing Authority, 2015).

The architects of this program emphasize a triple bottom line, saying, "This project is an effort to spend a housing dollar not just to house someone and their family but to get other things done: help them succeed in school and promote the success of schools that serve low-income students" (HUD 2015a, p. 7). Currently, officials from the federal Department of Housing and Urban Development are working with colleges and universities to determine better ways to support college students (HUD, 2015b).

THE MOST CRITICAL STEPS: GETTING INFORMED AND GETTING HELP

Higher education leaders vary in their knowledge and skills regarding direct poverty-alleviation initiatives. Many of the leaders we interviewed explained that the higher education programs that trained them to be deans or chancellors had actually prepared them to be leaders of twentieth-century colleges rather than innovators who respond to the challenges faced by twenty-first century college students. But these college leaders argue that helping students meet their basic needs not only is the right thing to do morally but also has instrumental purposes by helping colleges retain and graduate more students. Moreover, those who earn a college credential improve their economic prospects, which is good for the community and society. As one college president said:

> If students do not have a safe place to live, food to eat, or a way to get to school, they cannot do their best in the classroom. There are these moments where you are going to continue in college or life is going to get in the way. . . . It is not like they dropped their iPod or phone in the toilet. It is real. There are students that are studying under candlelight because they have not paid their utility bill, and they are still trying to persist. If we do not address some of those issues, they get in the way of the education process.

So at the core of our work is this educational mission. (Broton et al., 2014)

Advocacy groups, including the American Council on Education, have called attention to the high rate of food insecurity on college campuses. They are working with their members to share best practices and promote state- and federal-level policy changes (Nellum, 2015). Students across the nation are organizing and demanding that their basic needs be met. Proposals for tuition-free and debt-free college underscore the economic pressures faced by American families today and the opportunity for higher education to promote a basic standard of living (e.g., The White House, 2015). A truly affordable college system would go a long way in reducing the poverty experiences of college students. Coordination with the social safety net would bring about even greater opportunities for all Americans to pursue a higher education, regardless of economic background.

NOTE

1. See www.wihopelab.com for details.

REFERENCES

Broton, K., Frank, V., and Goldrick-Rab, S. (2014). Safety, security, and college attainment: An investigation of undergraduates' basic needs and institutional response. Madison, WI: Wisconsin HOPE Lab.

Broton, K., and Goldrick-Rab, S. (2014). The problem of college students without reliable housing. Cambridge, MA: Scholars Strategy Network Policy Brief.

Broton, K., and Goldrick-Rab, S. (2015). Public testimony on hunger in higher education. Submitted to the National Hunger Commission. Madison, WI: Wisconsin HOPE Lab.

Chaparro, M. P., Zaghloul, S. S., Holck, P., and Dobbs, J. (2009). "Food insecurity prevalence among college students at the University of Hawai'i at Manoa." *Public Health Nutrition*, 12(11), 2097–2103.

Coalition for University Food Bank Alliances. (2015). Retrieved from www.cufba.org.

Cohen, J. (2012, March 21). "State runs out of financial aid for college students." *Chicago Tribune*.

Dworsky, A., Dillman, K-N., Dion, M. R., Coffee-Borden, B-D., and Rosenau, M. (2012). *Housing for youth aging out of foster care: A review of the literature and program typology*. Washington, DC: Mathematica Policy Research.

Environmental Protection Agency. (2014). Feed families, not landfills. Retrieved from http://www.epa.gov/wastes/conserve/foodwaste/fd-donate.htm.

Freudenberg, N., Manzo, L., Jones, H., Kwan, A., Tsui, E., and Gagnon, M. (2011). *Food insecurity at CUNY: Results from a survey of CUNY undergraduate students*. New York: Healthy CUNY Initiative, City University of New York.

Goldrick-Rab, S. (2016). *Paying the price: College costs, financial aid, and the betrayal of the American dream*. Chicago: University of Chicago Press.

Goldrick-Rab, S., Broton, K., and Eisenberg, D. (2015). *Hungry to learn: Addressing food and housing insecurity among undergraduates*. Madison, WI: Wisconsin HOPE Lab.

Goldrick-Rab, S., Broton, K., and Gates, C. (2013). *Clearing the path to a brighter future: Addressing barriers to community college access and success.* Washington, DC: Association of Community College Trustees and Single Stop USA.

Goldrick-Rab, S., and Kendall, N. (2014). *F2CO. Redefining college affordability: Securing America's future with a free two year college option.* Indianapolis, IN: Lumina Foundation.

Housing and Urban Development. (2015a, February). *Barriers to success: Housing insecurity for U.S. college students.* Washington, DC: Office of Policy Development and Research.

Housing and Urban Development. (2015b, September 6). *Community college student housing insecurity.* Washington, DC: Office of Policy Development and Research Expert Convening.

Jack, A. A. (2015, April 24). *"I, too, am hungry": An examination of structural exclusion at an elite university.* Invited presentation at the University of Wisconsin–Madison.

Joint Center for Housing Studies. (2011). *America's rental housing: Meeting challenges, building on opportunities.* Cambridge, MA: President and Fellows of Harvard College.

Liston, C., and Donnan, R. (2012). *Center for Working Families at Community Colleges: Clearing the financial barriers to student success.* Durham, NC: MDC.

Mai, M. (2014). *Hunger in higher education: Food insecurity among Wisconsin low-income undergraduates.* Unpublished master's thesis, Department of Educational Policy Studies. University of Wisconsin–Madison.

Maroto, M. E., Snelling, A., and Linck, H. (2015). "Food insecurity among community college students: Prevalence and association with grade point average." *Community College Journal of Research and Practice,* 39(6), 515–526.

National Association for the Education of Homeless Children and Youth. (2014). *Financial aid for unaccompanied homeless youth: A survey report.* Washington, DC: National Association of Student Financial Aid Administrators.

Nellum, C. (2015, June 29). "Fighting food insecurity on campus." *Higher Education Today.* Retrieved from www.higheredtoday.org.

NYU Faculty Against the Sexton Plan. (2015). The art of the gouge. Retrieved from http://nyufasp. com/the-art-of-the-gouge-how-nyu-squeezes-billions-from-our-students-and-where-that-money-goes-2.

Price, D., Long, M., Quast, S., McMaken, J., and Kioukis, G. (2014). *Public benefits and community colleges: Lessons from the benefits access for college completion evaluation.* Philadelphia, PA: OMG Center for Collaborative Learning.

Rivera, C. (2015, August 3). "Some college students on financial aid don't get it in time to pay fees." *Los Angeles Times.*

Single Stop. (2015). Retrieved from www.singlestopusa.org.

Sloane, W. (2013, December 20). "Lunch for 9 million?" *Inside Higher Ed.* Retrieved from https://www.insidehighered.com/views/2013/12/20/higher-ed-reform-45-million-peanut-butter-sandwiches-essay.

Song, J. (2015, August 3). "Rise in college food banks linked to the economy and campus demographics." *Los Angeles Times.*

Tacoma Housing Authority. (2015, September 11). Tacoma Community College Housing Assistance Program: A summary. Retrieved from www.tacomahousing.net.

The White House. (2015, January 9). *White House unveils America's College Promise proposal: Tuition-free community college for responsible students.* Press Release.

Tsui, E., Freudenberg, N., Manzo, L., Jones, H., Kwan, A., and Gagnon, M. (2011). *Housing instability at CUNY: Results from a survey of CUNY undergraduate students.* New York: Healthy CUNY Initiative, City University of New York.

Wilder Research. (2008). *Overview of young and young adult homelessness in Minnesota: Facts and analysis of data from the 2006 statewide study.* St. Paul, MN: Author.

BAILEY A. BROWN

38. DOES INVESTING IN KNOWLEDGE STILL PAY THE BEST INTEREST?

As a college student, you are likely well aware that the cost of higher education has increased over the past few decades. Brown examines why the cost of college has increased, the uneven impact of student loan debt, and the implications of the rising costs for individuals as well as the larger society. Brown questions whether higher education is worth pursuing, given the higher costs.

Everyone knows that college is expensive and that costs are increasing every year. But just how costly is college becoming and to what end? Is pursuing college through the use of student loans still worth the economic burden? Or to paraphrase Benjamin Franklin: does the investment in knowledge still pay the best interest?

For many Americans, the current cost of college is virtually unaffordable without access to a student loan.[1] Over the last decade, prices for undergraduate tuition, fees, room, and board have increased by 20 percent, after adjustment for inflation.[2] Grant aid and tax benefits have failed to keep pace, resulting in students paying more to attend college.[3] To cover the difference, students may amass thousands of dollars in loans to finance their education. Over the course of several decades, student loan debt in the United States has ballooned to $1.5 trillion, and it impacts 43 million Americans.[4]

In 2016, students on average graduated with $32,731 in student loans.[5] Despite public loan forgiveness programs and lower interest rates for federal loans, few students are able to repay their loans in 10 years or less. Based on data from the U.S. Department of Education, only half of students were able to pay off their federal student loans even 20 years after beginning college in the mid-1990s.[6] The inability to repay student loans and the accumulation of debt has

increased over the last several decades. This substantial growth is not surprising, given the rise in postsecondary enrollment, increasing costs of college tuition, and expanding inequality in the wake of the Great Recession.[7] To date, student loan debt has reached $1.5 trillion, surpassing almost all other forms of household debt held in the United States.[8]

It is clear that student loan debt has severe and long-lasting financial consequences. Failure to repay student loans can damage a borrower's credit, lead to wage garnishment, and even hinder a borrower's ability to purchase a home or find employment. Even for borrowers who steadily pay off their student loans, having high debt-to-income ratios can make it difficult to be approved for mortgages, car loans, or credit cards. While higher education may be one of the most powerful avenues for upward economic mobility, growing student loan debt is also a tremendous barrier to future economic stability for borrowers. So, how did the rise in student debt develop? And what happens when young Americans graduate from college with tens of thousands of dollars in debt?

THE RISE IN STUDENT DEBT

When grants, scholarships, and savings are not enough to cover the cost of tuition, prospective college students turn to student loans to make up the difference.

Original to *Focus on Social Problems*

Student loans were first offered to high school students in 1958 under the National Defense Education Act to bolster America's ability to compete with other countries, particularly the Soviet Union. The Higher Education Act followed seven years later and would guarantee "Educational Opportunity Grants" for students with demonstrated financial need. This led to the formation of the Federal Family Education Loan Program, which soon allowed banks and other financial institutions to provide student loans.[9] Later, the Free Application for Federal Student Aid (FAFSA) was adopted to allow students to apply directly to the government for financial assistance. Despite the 2007 adoption of Income-Based Repayment (IBR) plans and the Public Service Loan Forgiveness (PSLF) Program, both of which were meant to make student loan repayment more affordable, student loan debt surpassed $1 trillion just five years later.

As student loan debt has ballooned over time, it is crucial to understand this crisis relative to past generations. Young college students now enter the workforce with unprecedented levels of student debt and are much more likely to be burdened with student debt than their parents or grandparents. Average student debt for 25- to 34-year-olds more than tripled from 1989 to 2016, after adjusting for inflation.[10] Compared to past generations, young Americans also face increasing economic vulnerability. Rising economic inequality since the 1980s and declining social and economic mobility that followed the Great Recession have added greater precarity to future employment outcomes. Post-recession borrowers, in fact, have experienced the most difficulty repaying loans. Students who graduated during and after the 2008 recession entered a weaker job market and struggled to find high-paying employment following graduation. The combined impact of increasing postsecondary enrollment, higher borrowing rates due to rising costs of education and lower incomes, and long-term economic instability have all contributed to the current $1.5 trillion student debt.

THE CHANGING HIGHER EDUCATION LANDSCAPE

The increase in student loan volume is also tied to the changing composition and structure of U.S. higher education. Three critical changes have shifted the higher education landscape: the backgrounds of students attending universities, the rise in for-profit colleges, and national and state funding policies.

First, the historical selection criteria that once excluded racial and ethnic minorities have shifted. Today's more inclusive admissions policies have led to diversity gains in colleges and dramatically changed the student populations at universities.[11] Since 1976, the percentage of college students who identify as Hispanic, Asian/Pacific Islander, and Black has increased by over 20 percent.[12] However, higher proportions of minority, low-income, and first-generation students experience greater hardship financing college and repaying student loans.[13] These shifts have happened as economic inequality has continued to rise since the 1980s, leading to declining social and economic mobility for many Americans. As more minority, low-income, and first-generation students borrow for postsecondary enrollment in this current economic climate, student debt continues to rise.

In addition to the changing student composition at U.S. colleges, state support for public institutions has also waned. In recent years, major flagship universities across several states have scaled back funding for programming and teaching. Compared to before the recession, over 45 U.S. states are now spending less per pupil for higher education.[14] Free-market advocates argue that this divestment more appropriately shifts the cost burden to families and individual degree earners rather than society at large.[15] State and local tax cuts, however, require students to take on a larger share of higher education costs. This is particularly detrimental considering that state universities provide students who cannot afford more expensive private tuition with access to an affordable college option.

These shifts in state funding may also make for-profit colleges more appealing to students seeking options that appear to be low-cost. Since 1990, enrollment in for-profit colleges has increased by over 600 percent.[16] The dramatic growth of for-profit colleges has also altered the structure of higher education. This change has been so profound that sociologists have called for-profit institutions a form of "disruptive innovation."[17] For-profit colleges fracture the traditional structure of higher education by selling education as a marketable good. However, in order to operate, for-profit institutions must aggressively increase enrollment and drive revenue, often at the expense of students.[18] As a result, students in the growing number of for-profit schools struggle substantially with student debt. Default rates for student loans are substantially higher at for-profit institutions compared to other higher education institutions. Students at for-profit institutions also experience lower economic returns than those from public and nonprofit colleges.[19]

For-profit institutional recruitment and enrollment strategies partially fuel this inequality. Recent research has found that for-profit colleges aggressively target veterans, low-income individuals, and racial and ethnic minorities with promises of educational opportunity, with little mention of the high risks involved in pursing higher education at a for-profit institution.[20] Overall loan repayment, default rates, and total borrowing rates have been substantially shaped by these structural changes to U.S. higher education. The changing composition of student bodies, rollbacks in state funding, and the growth of for-profit schools have been instrumental in shaping student loan debt over the last several decades.

THE UNEVEN IMPACT OF STUDENT LOAN DEBT

While the compounding nature of structural changes to U.S. higher education impacts students across education institutions, student debt is still unevenly experienced. Students experience different debt repayment challenges depending on their socioeconomic background, the type of institution they attend, and their ability to finish their degree. Because of these factors, student debt further exploits students who are already in vulnerable situations. While student loan debt is a pressing concern for 43 million Americans, the impact of this debt is unequal. Student debt is most severe for students whose parents often have the least amount of wealth or assets to help finance a college degree.[21] This particularly impacts first-generation students and students from low-income and minority backgrounds who may owe more in student loans and may experience greater challenges repaying loans in comparison to other groups.[22] Borrowing for postsecondary

enrollment may pave the way for college access for these students, but difficulties with student loan repayments can hinder their future financial well-being.

Hierarchies in college selectivity today also create sharp differences in outcomes for students from different backgrounds and for students graduating from private, public, and for-profit institutions.[23] The uneven rise in student debt over the last two decades—particularly for students attending less selective degree programs—sheds light on the inequality that persists across higher education institutions. Compared to students at the most selective public and private institutions, students in for-profit programs experience greater debt repayment challenges as these degrees hold less value on the job market.[24] The long-standing dominance of elite and affluent students at the most selective colleges better positions these students in the employment marketplace following college. Their higher earning potential and access to cultural and social capital[25] through these prestigious universities can widen long-term wealth gaps at the same time as it improves their overall individual financial well-being.

STUDENT DEBT AND CAREER OUTCOMES

Rising student debt is also related to employment and career outcomes following college. With the looming pressure to repay student loans after graduation, students may be pushed toward careers that promise greater earning potential (for example, business or computer science), which can result in some career fields and academic subjects being privileged above others. The burden of student loans requires a dependable income and significantly alters how recent graduates make employment decisions.[26] This can dissuade students—especially the less well-off—from pursing public service or education careers or studying the liberal arts, as these majors and career paths offer lower returns. Recent data suggests that students whose parents make less money have less latitude in the academic tracks they can feasibly pursue.[27] Students from lower-earning families may turn to majors oriented toward business and science that are less risky and offer a potentially greater financial return, whereas students from higher-earning families can afford to pursue the liberal arts and humanities.[28]

These educational choices and constraints can have long-term impacts on society. If fewer people pursue careers in the public service and majors in liberal arts decline, then this can threaten our ability to see multiple viewpoints, think critically, and grapple with challenging social issues.[29] In times of economic uncertainty and political polarization, the ability to see beyond one perspective is critical. Deeply concerning, however, is the way rising tuition costs and student loans can potentially narrow the set of majors and career options available to college students. By constraining college opportunities, student debt can perpetuate inequality and impact students' long-term economic well-being and personal and professional fulfillment.[30]

THE FUTURE OF STUDENT DEBT

With student loan debt now affecting 40 million Americans, what can be done to improve the financial well-being of recent graduates? Even more importantly, what are the broader consequences of student debt? Current findings paint a mixed picture of the future of student loan debt. On one hand, student debt is expected to rise over the next several years as borrowing rates continue to increase. The expansion of debt is expected to remain steady as college tuition continues to rise, even after controlling for inflation.[31] If college is increasingly unaffordable for low- and middle-income families and states continue to decrease funding for public universities, we can expect to see a growth in borrowing rates over the next few decades. This rise will have long-term consequences for young people, considering that higher debt balances dampen homeownership rates.[32]

On the other hand, a closer look at loan default rates shows decreases in the past five years—an indication that there may be optimistic repayment findings in the years to come.[33] In terms of economic mobility and well-being, a college degree still brings substantial returns, particularly for students from low-income backgrounds. Homeownership rates are higher for those with a college education, and for those in the bottom 20 percent, having a college degree makes a person more than three times more likely to rise from the bottom household income brackets.[34] These comparative trends in economic mobility, however, have yet to account for the way the rise in student debt will impact upward mobility and stability for future generations.

The future of student loans will require interventions on multiple fronts, but it is unclear whether these combined efforts will make a substantial difference in student debt for future generations. Federal refinancing options like Income Based Repayment plans and the Public Service Loan Forgiveness (PSLF) program are only somewhat promising. The PSLF program, for instance, is intended to forgive student loans for those working in public service careers, but many who qualify are delayed, denied, or deferred access.[35] Thus, relief through the program is limited.

There is recent hope that financial education and career counseling in high school and college can help students become better informed about student loans. Research finds that students receiving financial education in high school are more likely to take out federal loans rather than private loans and are less likely to have credit card balances.[36] This suggests that broad statewide policies and even the institutional participation of universities may assist students who struggle with complicated financial and career decisions.

Regardless of whether or not the future of student loan debt is slightly brighter than in the past decade, the current volume of debt is still a pressing concern. This raises important questions about how rising student loan debt shapes access to college, and given this rise, whether a college degree still guarantees economic prosperity. Higher education is foundational to the narrative of upward social mobility, but as student debt continues to grow, fewer and fewer students may see the promise of social mobility realized.

NOTES

1. College Board. 2019. "Trends in Student Aid 2019." Retrieved December 6, 2019 from https://research.collegeboard.org/trends/student-aid.
2. College Board. 2019. "Trends in College Pricing 2019" Retrieved December 7, 2019 from https://research.collegeboard.org/trends/college-pricing.

3. U.S. Department of Education, National Center for Education Statistics (2017). Repayment of Student Loans as of 2015 Among 1995–96 and 2003–04 First-Time Beginning Students: First Look (NCES 2018-410).

4. Cilluffo, Anthony. 2019. "5 Facts about student loans." Pew Research Center. Retrieved December 7, 2019 https://www.pewresearch.org/fact-tank/2019/08/13/facts-about-student-loans/.

5. Board of Governors of the Federal Reserve System. 2017. "Report on the Economic Well-Being of U.S. Households in 2016- May 2017." Retrieved June 14, 2017 https://www.federalreserve.gov/publications/2017-economic-well-being-of-us-households-in-2016-education-debt-loans.htm.

6. Woo, Jennie H., Alexander H. Bentz, Stephen Lew, Erin Dunlop Velez, Nichole Smith. 2017. "Repayment of Student Loans as of 2015 Among 1995-96 and 2003-04 First-Time Beginning Students." U.S. Department of Education: National Center for Education Statistics. Retrieved December 7, 2019 from https://nces.ed.gov/pubs2018/2018410.pdf.

7. Velez, Erin Dunlop, Jennie H. Woo. 2017. "The Debt Burden of Bachelor's Degree Recipients." U.S. Department of Education: National Center for Education Statistics. Retrieved December 7, 2019 from https://nces.ed.gov/pubs2017/2017436.pdf.

8. Federal Reserve Bank of NY. "Quarterly Report on Household Debt and Credit." Retrieved December 7, 2019 from https://www.newyorkfed.org/microeconomics/topics/student-debt.

9. Federal Student Aid. 2003. FSA Handbook: Direct Loan and FFEL Programs. Retrieved December 8, 2019 from https://ifap.ed.gov/sfahandbooks/0304FSAHbkVol8.html.

10. Peter G. Peterson Foundation. 2018. "Student Debt Continues to Rise." Retrieved December 8, 2019 from https://www.pgpf.org/blog/2018/07/the-facts-about-student-debt.

11. Alon, Sigal. 2015. *Race, Class, and Affirmative Action*. Russell Sage Foundation.

12. U.S. Department of Education, National Center for Education Statistics. (2019). *Digest of Education Statistics, 2017* (NCES 2018-070), Chapter 3.

13. Scott-Clayton, Judith. 2018. "The looming student loan default crisis is worse than we thought." Brookings: Evidence Speaks Reports. Retrieved December 8, 2019 from https://www.brookings.edu/research/the-looming-student-loan-default-crisis-is-worse-than-we-thought/.

14. Mitchell, Michael, Michael Leachman, Kathleen Masterson. 2016. "Funding Down, Tuition Up." Center on Budget and Policy Priorities. Retrieved December 8, 2019 from https://www.cbpp.org/research/state-budget-and-tax/funding-down-tuition-up.

15. Deruy, Emily. 2016. "The Politics of Higher Education." The Atlantic. Retrieved on December 9, 2019 from https://www.theatlantic.com/education/archive/2016/09/the-politics-of-higher-education/498551/.

16. Beaver, William. 2017. "The Rise and Fall of For-Profit Higher Education." American Association of University Professors" Retrieved December 8, 2019 from https://www.aaup.org/article/rise-and-fall-profit-higher-education#.XeyWtDJKgmo.

17. Michael W. Kirst & Mitchell L. Stevens (eds.). *Remaking College: The Changing Ecology of Higher Education*. Stanford University Press.

18. David Deming, Claudia Goldin, and Lawrence Katz. 2013, Spring. "For-Profit Colleges." *The Future of Children*, 23(1), Postsecondary Education in the United States.

19. Deming et al., 2013.

20. Cottom, Tressie McMillan. 2017. *Lower Ed: The Troubling Rise of For-Profit Colleges in the New Economy*. The New Press.

21. Addo, F., Houle, J., and Simon, D. 2016. "Young, Black and (Still) in the Red: Parental Wealth, Race, and Student Loan Debt." *Race and Social Problems*, 8: 64–76.

22. Bohanan, Mariah. 2017. "Black and Low-income Students Struggle the Most to Pay Off Student Loan Debt." Insight into Diversity. Retrieved December 8, 2019 from https://www.insightintodiversity.com/black-and-low-income-students-are-least-likely-to-pay-off-student-loan-debt-report-reveals/

23. Karabel, Jerome. 2005. *The chosen: The hidden history of admission and exclusion at Harvard, Yale, and Princeton*. Boston, MA: Houghton Mifflin.

24. Board of Governors of the Federal Reserve System. 2017. "Report on the Economic Well-Being of U.S. Households in 2016, May 2017" Retrieved June 14, 2017 from https://www.federalreserve.gov/publications/2017-economic-well-being-of-us-households-in-2016-education-debt-loans.htm.

25. Ann L. Mullen. 2010. *Degrees of Inequality: Culture, Class and Gender in American Higher Education*. The Johns Hopkins University Press.

26. Konczal. Mike. 2015. "The Surprising New Effort to Tackle the Student-Debt Crisis." *Rolling Stone*. Retrieved December 8, 2019 from https://www.rollingstone.com/politics/politics-news/the-surprising-new-effort-to-tackle-the-student-debt-crisis-52272/.

27. Pinsker. 2015. "Rich Kids Study English" The Atlantic. Retrieved December 9, 2019 from https://www.theatlantic.com/business/archive/2015/07/college-major-rich-families-liberal-arts/397439/.

28. Rothstein, Jesse & Rouse, Cecilia Elena. 2011. "Constrained after college: Student loans and early-career occupational choices," *Journal of Public Economics*, Elsevier, vol. 95(1-2), pages 149–163, February.

29. Dix. Willard. 2016. "A Liberal Arts Degree is More Important than Ever." *Forbes*. Retrieved December 9, 2019 from https://www.forbes.com/sites/willarddix/2016/11/16/a-liberal-arts-degree-is-more-important-than-ever/#61488168339f.

30. Anders. Georgie 2017. "The Unexpected Value of the Liberal Arts." *The Atlantic*. Retrieved December 9, 2019 from https://www.theatlantic.com/education/archive/2017/08/the-unexpected-value-of-the-liberal-arts/535482/.

31. College Board. 2019. "Trends in College Pricing 2019." Retrieved December 7, 2019 from https://research.collegeboard.org/trends/college-pricing).

32. Brown, M., and Caldwell, S. 2013. Young Student Loan Borrowers Retreat from Housing and Auto Markets. *Liberty Street Economics*, April 17. Retrieved December 9, 2019 from http://libertystreeteconomics.newyorkfed.org/2013/04/youngstudent-loan-borrowers-retreat-fromhousing-and-auto-markets.html.

33. Federal Reserve Bank of New York. 2017. "2017 Press Briefing: Household Borrowing, Student Debt Trends and Homeownership." Retrieved December 9, 2019 from https://www.newyorkfed.org/press/pressbriefings/household-borrowing-student-loans-homeownership.

34. The Pew Charitable Trusts. 2012. "Pursuing the American Dream: Economic Mobility Across Generations." Retrieved Dec. 8, 2019 from https://www.pewtrusts.org/~/media/legacy/uploadedfiles/pcs_assets/2012/pursuingamericandreampdf.pdf.

35. Dickler, Jessica and Annie Nova. 2019. "This Fix to Public Service Loan Forgiveness Hasn't Helped Very Much." *CNBC: Personal Finance*. Retrieved December 8, 2019 from https://www.cnbc.com/2019/09/05/this-fix-to-public-service-loan-forgiveness-hasnt-helped-very-much.html.

36. National Endowment for Financial Education. 2018. "Better Borrowing: How State-Mandated Financial Education Drives College Financing Behavior." Retrieved December 8, 2019 from https://www.nefe.org/images/research/Effects-of-K-12-Financial-Education-Mandates/Better-Borrowing-Report-MSU-Executive-Summary.pdf.

CHAPTER 9

SOCIAL PROBLEMS RELATED TO FAMILIES

Families in the United States face a multitude of social problems. While your experience in your own family may feel quite unique and individualized, families operate within the context of economic, political, and legal environments. Not all families thrive in our capitalist economy, where rising inequality, changes in the structure of the economy, the decline in real wages, an unlivable minimum wage, and the rising costs of education contribute to family struggles.

Households headed by one woman are a family form in the United States that faces disproportionate suffering. With a poverty rate of 26 percent,[1] these households face unique challenges. In the reading "Families Facing Untenable Choices," Lisa Dodson and Wendy Luttrell demonstrate, through the experiences of these mothers, that their lives are a series of problematic choices of whether to prioritize their work (and be good workers) or prioritize motherhood (and be good parents). Policies in the workplace and cultural expectations of mothering (such as being present in the educational setting) conflict, setting single mothers up to fail in both realms. In poor families with children, the struggle is all-encompassing; even necessities are unaffordable. Few would argue against diapers being a necessity, and Jennifer Randles exposes the "diaper dilemma" that poor families face, pointing to policy changes being enacted that model solutions.

Given the financial and social challenges poor families face (in particular, those headed by mothers alone), some Americans question why they choose to have children at all, particularly outside of the context of marriage. Politicians frequently push policies to incentivize marriage, given that poverty rates are lower in two-parent families than in those headed by women. But marriage often only improves poor mothers' financial situations marginally (and only if they stay with their partner, as they can end up worse off than before if they divorce). Poor mothers tend to marry poor or low-income partners and often lose access to

---

1   Fontenot, Kayla, Jessica Semega, and Melissa Kollar, U.S. Census Bureau, Current Population Reports, P60-263, Income and Poverty in the United States: 2017, U.S. Government Printing Office, Washington, DC, 2018.

reliable benefits in the process. Based on their interviews with poor single mothers, Kathryn J. Edin and Maria Kefalas learned that poor single mothers are having children outside of marriage because, like middle-class women, they value marriage as a lifelong commitment and want to marry men with careers and financial stability, or to at least be financially stable on their own in case the marriage fails. In search of eligible partners and their own financial stability, poor single women delay or forgo marriage altogether. Edin and Kefalas conclude that the answer is not to push marriage, but to provide poor women access to quality jobs that will enable their financial independence; they argue that if we do not do so, poor women will continue to have children outside of marriage as they wait for rather elusive financially stable marriage partners.

Even when women with children do move into the paid labor force, the challenges that families face do not end. Kirstin Ralston-Coley demonstrates how employers discriminate against working mothers, threatening the economic survival of some families. Discrimination and bias against mothers in the workplace and an absence of workplace structures and policies that support parents in general contribute to what researchers call the "motherhood penalty" where women with children earn lower wages than child-free women and men, as well as working fathers. Households with both adults working face often tense negotiations about how to share in the responsibility of maintaining and running a household. As Wendy Klein, Carolina Izquierdo, and Thomas N. Bradbury point out, much of the responsibility for child care and household chores falls on women, even when they work longer hours and have higher salaries than their husbands.

LGBT families and families with mixed immigration statuses are family types that face additional stressors and discrimination as a result of the current legal and sociopolitical environment. In "Love Wins?" Amanda K. Baumle and D'Lane R. Compton explain how, despite the legalization of same-sex marriage, LGBT families continue to experience a lack of protection and distrust in the continued existence of their marital rights. Brooke Jarvis documents the experience of families where a parent is an undocumented immigrant as parental deportations increase, breaking up families. Fear of family breakup and the actual separation of parents from children have devastating consequences, as Omolara T. Uwemedimo, Ana C. Monterrey, and Julie M. Linton discuss.

And, sadly, sometimes families can be a site of social problems in and of themselves. One in four women and one in nine men experience domestic violence.[3] As Tim Stelloh discusses in "Fighting Back," some innovative programs have been designed to help victims escape violent relationships, though the future of these programs—and the lives that they may save—are often at the mercy of politicians and lawmakers.

---

2   Anon. 2019. "National Statistics Domestic Violence Fact Sheet." Retrieved from https://www.speakcdn.com/assets/2497/domestic_violence2.pdf.

3   Anon. 2019. "National Statistics Domestic Violence Fact Sheet." Retrieved from https://www.speakcdn.com/assets/2497/domestic_violence2.pdf.

ANA HERNÁNDEZ

Ana Vidina Hernández is program coordinator for Girasol, a Texas-based organization that supports immigrant children and families.

What is the mission of your organization?

Girasol strives to help Texas immigrant children and families to heal from trauma through support, education, and connection. Girasol is housed in the Texas Institute for Child and Family Wellbeing within the Steve Hicks School of Social Work at the University of Texas at Austin. Girasol works to create a community of trauma-informed professionals ensuring access to integrated systems of support and resources for the wellbeing of all immigrant families. We do so by training professionals about trauma and migration, providing opportunities for social work students to work with families in detention and at the border, and facilitating increased access to information about services and resources accessible to the immigrant community.

How did you first become interested in this type of activism?

My father is an immigrant, my godparents were immigrants, and many of my friends are immigrants. My parents were engaged in activism both as organizers and musicians. Much of their work was centered on supporting communities impacted by dictatorships in Latin America in the 1970s and 1980s. As a young child, I attended benefit concerts, protests, and community events regularly. This instilled a desire to fight for social justice at an early age.

As an undergraduate student, I became involved in my university's chapter of Amnesty International and with University Leadership Initiative, an organization run by and for undocumented students. I pursued a joint Master's in Social Work and Latin American Studies as an opportunity to obtain degrees in fields that would enable me to engage in this work in my professional life. I remain actively engaged in conversations around human rights on and off campus, organizing events and fundraisers, and working with community organizations.

As an activist in your organization, currently what are your top goals?

As an activist, my goals are always focused on access and impact. Access in the sense of increasing space for *who* can have access to academia, nonprofits, and organizing spaces. This means considering how organizations view race, ethnicity, sexual orientation, gender identity, different abilities, etc. As a social worker engaging specifically with the immigrant community, this also means thinking about barriers to accessing

(continued)

resources, employment, and health and mental health care. One of my primary goals is to break down those barriers, find innovative strategies that ensure people can thrive, and maintain a social justice lens as central to our program's work both internally and externally.

I strongly believe that attention to accessibility is vital to increasing our impact. We cannot be truly impactful if we do not hold an intersectional perspective in our work and broaden our understanding of health, productivity, and well-being. By training social work students and providing them with opportunities to engage in meaningful community-based work, I know that we broaden our impact both immediately and in the future.

What strategies do you try to use to enact social change in your area of activism?

The primary strategies I use to enact social change are education, advocacy, providing direct services, and creating sustainable community partnerships. At Girasol we provide trainings to lawyers on trauma-informed interviewing and trainings to service providers on working with mixed-status families. Since immigrant families have oftentimes experienced violence or other potentially traumatic or stressful events, it is important for service providers to understand how to best support and problem-solve for these families by finding ways to help calm them and to understand their potential cultural differences. Our goal is that they are able to do this while taking into consideration the barriers that undocumented status may place on access to resources and the fear their clients may have as a result of U.S. immigration policies. Through this education, we are able to impact the work of many more professionals who will touch lives in our immigrant communities. We also provide training and education to social work students specifically for working with immigrant women and families in detention or in shelters along the border. Through this work, we are ensuring that the next generation of social workers who have volunteered with our program will be better able to support future clients who may have experienced trauma along their migration journey or in detention.

Through the resource website we created, Navegando Austin (Navigating Austin), we are providing education about safe services for community members and educating service providers about how they can safely provide referrals to undocumented clients who may be wary of accessing resources. As advocates at Girasol, we facilitate the changes needed in spaces at agencies to be mindful of the mental health needs of immigrants who have experienced trauma. We advocate for resources to include additional languages and to publicly state their requirements for services. We saw the importance of this type of information following ICE (Immigration and Customs Enforcement) raids in Austin, Texas, in the spring of 2017. Many families in our community were afraid to take their children to school or even leave their homes. Families we spoke with were afraid that by accessing medical, educational, or other resources, they might be reported to ICE. In vetting local community resources to ensure that Navegando Austin only lists those that do not have restrictions based on citizenship (i.e., they will not make people reveal their immigration status) and do have bilingual staff, we are working to make sure that families can feel an increased sense of safety when seeking support.

Additionally, we support our social work volunteers who work in interdisciplinary teams with law students to assist immigrant women and children in navigating the legal system while detained. We also help orient migrant families at bus stations after they are detained in *hieleras* and *perreras*. When immigrants arrive at the U.S.–Mexico border to seek asylum, they either ask for asylum at an entry point or when they are apprehended by CBP (Customs and Border Patrol) after crossing the border and are asked if they are afraid to return to their country. While it is hard to generalize, they are usually detained first at centers at the border called the *hieleras* and *perreras*. Hielera translates to "ice box" and perrera translates to "dog cage." The centers have been given these informal names because the hieleras, concrete holding cells, are kept at extremely cold temperatures and the perreras often have metal fencing throughout. From what we have seen, individuals and families are kept in these centers for one to three days in each. Then, they are either released to sponsors (relatives, friends, or organizations who are willing to vouch for them and house them) or sent to an additional detention center. Individual adults can be held for a few months or a few years, depending on their legal situations. Human Rights Watch and the Detention Watch Network have released several reports on the poor conditions of detention centers, including medical issues left untreated, migrant deaths, and barriers to accessing nonprofit legal services seeking to support individuals and families in detention.

Undocumented immigrants are not required to have legal representation like others in the United States, which can make it extremely difficult for them to understand the legal process and to be released from detention sooner. Generally speaking, unaccompanied minors are detained in shelters through the Office of Refugee Resettlement (ORR), while families and individuals are most often detained in privately run for-profit prisons throughout the United States that are overseen by ICE. There are several instances throughout this process during which families may be separated. The first is at the border, where adults can be separated from one another when detained in the hieleras or perreras. Within these facilities, there have also been reports of children being separated from their families inside by metal fencing. We have also met mothers detained with their children who have been separated from the father, who was sent to a different center. In these cases, the family members are not informed of the location of their relatives. Depending on the outcome of their cases, families may also be separated if any of the members are deported as a result of an immigration official deeming their claim as being not credible.

As our program primarily works at the intersection of mental health and immigration, we focus on the detrimental impact of detention and family separation on the mental health of immigrants seeking asylum in the United States. We work to help families understand the system that they are navigating and advocate for increased mental health supports, in particular because they have often experienced trauma in their home countries as part of why they are seeking asylum in the first place. Most of the people we have spoken with have been victims of sexual assault, domestic violence, gang violence, extortion, or threats to their life. To then be detained in the country that you came to for safety and protection can add an additional layer of trauma that needs to be addressed. We could not do any of this work without creating sustainable partnerships with community organizations engaged in immigrant rights work. We collaborate with legal agencies, organizers, mental health agencies, and other nonprofits working to support immigrants, which helps us to have a large impact, despite being a small program.

What are the major challenges activists in your field face?

In the current field of immigration work, one of the major challenges is the fact that the landscape is constantly shifting. Detention centers frequently change their policies and numbers of detained individuals with no notice. They place barriers to entry and tend to have little transparency with those detained and the service providers attempting to support them. For example, these centers are often placed in rural areas hours away from major cities where there are nonprofits to provide resources and legal supports to immigrants. They have prison-like restrictions that can prevent lawyers from accessing their clients in detention, and generally mean that undocumented family members have no visitation rights without being potentially detained themselves. As the majority of detention centers are operated by private prison corporations, such as CCA (Core Civic) and GEO Group, they tend to have fewer federal regulations and are not required to make their medical and other records public. As a result, it can be difficult to investigate and administer consequences for the numerous allegations of sexual assaults, medical emergencies, and even deaths in immigrant detention centers around the country. Similarly, immigration law constantly changes with different court cases, decisions, and class-action lawsuits. Policies around border entry for asylum seekers have also shifted immensely in the last couple of years. It can feel difficult to create systems of support when you have to work within the bounds of institutions and laws that are constantly in motion.

Another challenge in the field of immigration is the heightened focus on the issue over the last few years. It is hard to turn on the television or radio, or to read news headlines without hearing something about immigration. As a social worker in this role specifically, I think a lot about what self-care and communal care can and should look like. When there is a

(continued)

constant barrage of information about your issue area, it can feel as though you never get a break from the intensity of it. Knowing how and when to lean on others for support is another essential part of sustaining myself in this work. Engaging in creativity and working to create beauty out of the chaos through exercises and activities with coworkers and clients has been an important way for me to shift the negative energy that can come from constant anti-immigrant rhetoric and facing barriers to supporting my community.

What would you consider to be your greatest successes as an activist?

I am very proud of everything we have accomplished with Girasol. We have trained over 100 lawyers and service providers, facilitated opportunities for over 60 social work students and professionals to volunteer to support immigrants, and directly served over 700 immigrants in the state of Texas. As someone who has always cared about having a direct impact, I am grateful for the opportunity to have created a program that touches so many lives.

We are often navigating systems and spaces that can be cold, dispassionate, and unjust. I have worked hard to integrate everything I have learned about mental health and healing into my work through creativity and finding joy in human connection. Every time we are able to exchange a smile with someone in detention and let them know that we care, that is a success. Every time we bring our creativity to making an art piece with the people we work with, a self-care activity, or even a beautiful logo for our organization, we are turning something dark and oppressive into something light and beautiful. I believe that our success is always rooted in our connections with others, our ability to create new ideas and projects, and the prioritizing of well-being on every level. Approaching activism, organizing, and social work in this way is part of how I stay grounded in this difficult work.

What are major misconceptions the public has about activism in general and your issue specifically?

Given the ways in which history textbooks have been edited with particular biases in this country, many people do not recognize the fact that most systemic change has come from activism that has worked both outside and inside of institutions. Without protests to raise awareness, civil disobedience to bring issues to the forefront, and boycotts to shine a light on injustices, many of the regulations and acts we value today would not exist. It often takes a combination of working on many levels to be impactful. Movies often make it look like activism can be done solely from the phone or computer, or that it happens overnight with one large rally. In reality, organizing is long-term, hard work, and made up of many small accomplishments and setbacks on a daily basis that in the end amount to larger movement on issues.

Misconceptions around immigration can also be harmful. This includes the idea that some immigrants need or deserve the opportunities more (for example, there is a belief that migrating for work is not as traumatic as migrating for safety) or that undocumented immigrants are "criminals" because they broke a law by entering without documentation or overstaying visas. Every day on the news right now we see stories about how detention will work as a deterrent to immigration. In reality, criminalizing migration is a choice that has the effect of dehumanizing people. There is no evidence to support the notion that immigrant detention has ever deterred migrants from coming to the United States. I have heard women in detention explain that with the choice of death or detention, they would choose detention every time. Wouldn't it be a better world if they didn't have to choose between such horrific options?

Why should students get involved in your line of activism?

I feel strongly about advocating for the importance of the intersection of mental health and immigration. There is a need for organizers, social workers, and activists to work to support the well-being of immigrants. Individuals often experience grief and loss of people and places, poor treatment in many receiving countries, and don't have the supports needed to heal. You can do this in many capacities—you don't have to be a mental health professional to care about incorporating a recognition of trauma into your work. We need people from all backgrounds and all walks of life to ensure that this work is being done by those impacted, by those with particular skill sets, and by those who can see the bigger picture of systemic change. Immigrant individuals, families, and communities bring many strengths to this country, and no matter your background, there are ways for you to get involved fighting the injustices in our immigration laws, detention systems, and barriers to resource access.

We need innovative solutions and new energy in this area of activism. As undergraduate students, you have immense potential to choose paths that integrate your newfound knowledge with your own experiences in powerful ways. Immigration may be an issue at the forefront of the national conversation now, but it has always involved the separation of families, deaths at the border or in detention, and exploitative work environments. You don't have to be a full-time activist to be involved in working toward immigrant rights and increased awareness about the importance of mental health. You can think critically about any work space and how it can integrate these two issues to provide better services. Whether you want to be a lawyer, a doctor, a social worker, a small business owner, a community organizer, or in any other profession, there is a space for you in the immigrant rights movement.

If an individual has little money and time, are there other ways they can contribute to the work you are doing?

You don't have to make activism or working in the field of immigration your full-time job to have an impact. One way that you can become involved is by receiving and sharing updates and alerts from organizations that support immigrant communities. They often have opportunities to call senators or representatives about legislation or preventing deportations, share information about ICE raids in your community, or sign petitions that support immigrant rights. You can also contribute by sharing social media posts of organizations working at the border which often need donations for supplies they provide to asylum seekers released from detention. Being mindful of the language you use and your own conversations with others is something that you can do every day that will make a big difference. Both in terms of mental health and in terms of immigration, words such as "crazy," "illegal," and "alien" can reinforce harmful stigmas that exist in the United States

and around the world. You can make a difference by shifting your vocabulary *and* the way you think about others. Everyone has had an experience in which they felt misunderstood, alone, stereotyped, or mistreated. Think about the difference it makes to hear someone use language validating your ethnicity, gender identity, sexual orientation, abilities, size, religion, spirituality, or any other important part of your identity. These may seem like small steps, but they have a large impact.

What ways can college students enact social change in their daily lives?

There are many other ways that you can enact change in your daily life in addition to working to better understand your own implicit biases and the ways in which you, as everyone else, have been socialized in particular ways. You can apply a critical lens to your own thoughts and behavior *as well as* consider ways to work toward larger change on your campus. As college students who pay tuition to your universities, you hold a lot of power in negotiating positive change at your own institutions of higher education. Notice what the racial make-up of your school is and ask critical questions about inequities. Ask what your campus policy is on supporting noncitizen students and work with others to demand increased protections, resources on campus, and even a "dream center." Dream centers, such as those created at the University of California, Berkeley and the University of Texas at San Antonio, are generally spaces on a university campus with paid staff dedicated to supporting the well-being of immigrant students on campus through resources, scholarships, and even legal assistance. Be the student in your class to speak out against injustice and support other students who do. You may be surprised at how many people on your campus will be your allies when you take a stand. Always remember, we can't make change alone. Addressing systemwide inequities can feel like a massive challenge, but students around the country have successfully advocated for rights for undocumented students, wage increases, cutting ties with corporations that utilize sweatshops, and many more initiatives. I encourage you to find what you're passionate about, know your skills and limitations, prioritize your own well-being, and never be afraid to use your voice for change.

LISA DODSON AND WENDY LUTTRELL

39. FAMILIES FACING UNTENABLE CHOICES

Dodson and Luttrell discuss the strains on low-wage mothers and their children and how the norms of social institutions demand "untenable choices" from these families. The authors discuss how the emphasis on work as part of welfare reform has created additional problems for low-income women and their children and how middle-class ideologies about "good mothering" create stigma against low-income working mothers.

It is 9:00 a.m. and six-year-old Antonio stands in the doorway of his school's main office. He and his brother Cesar live in a public housing complex around the corner from the school in an urban district that serves working poor families of color, mostly immigrants. Miss Corey, the school secretary, greets him with a smile, asking, "Did you just get here?" Antonio nods his head yes. "Your mother didn't wake you up this morning?" Antonio rocks back and forth. "Did your brother already go to his classroom?" Antonio grins from ear to ear and nods his head yes. "Go ahead on, I won't write you up." Before Antonio's out the door, Miss Corey remarks, "He's covering for his mother. It is a tough home situation, so tough. His mom has two jobs and works double shifts every other weekend. His older brother is in third grade and has been getting himself to school since kindergarten, and now he's responsible for getting Antonio to school, too. They are late all the time."

Miss Corey is sympathetic to the boys' single mom who works tirelessly to provide for her children, and so she reluctantly stretches school rules to accommodate the situation. She feels it isn't fair to punish the boys because of their mother's work demands. A single mom herself, Miss Corey explains that, were it not for the fact that her own children are on an "early school schedule" that allows her to drop them off on her way to work, she doesn't know how she would manage. Miss Corey is grateful for her job; even though she "pinches pennies at the end of each month," she has health insurance, paid sick days, vacation days, and, if need be, she can always get someone to "cover" for her in the office if one of her children gets sick at school. In contrast, Antonio's mom couldn't be reached when he got a fever. "We called her employer (she works at a nursing home across town) but they didn't give her the message, and the poor child sat in the nurse's office all day. It breaks my heart."

Antonio's mom and Miss Corey are part of an important and expansive group within the labor force: working mothers. According to the Bureau of Labor Statistics, in 2008, seven out of ten mothers were employed.[1] Based on the growth of the service, retail, and carework job sectors, many mothers—disproportionately women of color, immigrants, and single women—are working in low paying, demanding jobs.

For decades, sociologists have studied women's increased labor force participation, focusing on women's lost career opportunity related to family care needs. Arlie Hochschild famously coined the term "second shift" for women's juggling of family care with work demands. The gendered division of household labor that Hochschild reported years ago continues largely unaltered, with women responsible for family care whether they provide it themselves or organize and schedule others to do so. In light of this second shift, sociologist Pam Stone describes how some professional women may feel compelled to "opt out" of high-powered professions to take care of family needs.

Our focus is the dynamic of the second—or more accurately, *multiple*—shifts faced by low wage mothers with few (if any) opting-out choices. Service, retail, and care work jobs pay $8-$12 per hour, so workers are hard-pressed to cover their basics: rent, food, transportation, heat, healthcare, and utilities. Further, these kinds of jobs are more likely to encroach on routine family time, before and after school, or in the evenings and on weekends. The work often involves irregular schedules and unpredictable hours, leaving little flexibility to take care of everyday family life, and employment in these sectors offers few benefits or career ladders that might mean sacrifice today, but bring better times tomorrow. Perhaps most startlingly, taking one of these jobs can also mean taking immediate losses. Economist Randy Albelda calls this the "cliff effect" of post-welfare policy: even the smallest wage increase can result in steep losses in essential public benefits such as housing, healthcare, and food stamps.

What are the particular conditions—material and social—that moms and children face in the real world of low wage work and family? Across the scholarship on low-income families, we find three themes that stand out. First, research points out how inflexible and often unpredictable work schedules undermine mothers' abilities to provide family care. While higher earnings could offset some of this dilemma, a "market solution" is out of reach for these families. The second theme is the stigma faced by low-income mothers and children when they don't meet the middle class norms of work and school in order to put family care first. Finally, we explore a theme infused throughout low-income work/family scholarship: how the norms of major social institutions (employment and education) operate according to rules that demand untenable choices from mothers and children. This angle on the work and family dilemma tends to be ignored or, if highlighted, used as evidence of personal irresponsibility and failed families. Recognizing the true conditions

facing tens of millions of families is crucial for reformulating work, family, and educational policy.

INFLEXIBILITY AT WORK

In 2004, Norma described her job loss this way: "My company is a big corporation, and there are no exceptions. . . . I had attendance problems because of my son's illness. . .but I went ahead. . . . I pushed it and made a choice for family. No matter what it took, I was going to be there sacrificing a risk of attendance problems. So I had no flexibility with work at my employment . . ." For Norma, "pushing it" meant taking two extra days off until her son, who had been gravely ill, was in stable condition. She lost her job for "abusing" the company's sick day policy.

Research on work schedules in retail, service, and care work jobs reveals a wide spectrum of inflexibilities. Schedules may change with little notice, overtime work may suddenly become mandatory, and productivity (often involving direct contact with customers) may be constantly monitored. The face-to-face nature of much of the retail, personal care, and service labor markets makes small accommodations like breaks, adjustments to start and stop time, or phone calls all but impossible. Work and family scholars Julie Henly and Elaine Waxman, researching retail workers, reported that employees may learn of their work schedule with only a few days' notice. They wrote, for these workers, "Everything is open. Nothing is consistent." Just as Norma described, employees find almost no room for negotiation, regardless of the gravity of a family need.

In the past, the rigidity and unpredictability of these jobs led many mothers who had no savings, family money, or higher-earning spouse to turn to welfare if their children needed more intensive care. But by the late 1990s, the policy for low-income moms became "work first." Mothers had to negotiate family care based on the hard terms set by the low-wage labor market.

Deborah spoke of how she once used welfare to navigate family and job demands, believing children "should be with someone who's about raising them." By 2002, new welfare regulations meant Deborah saw no choice but to take a low-wage job, even though her childcare arrangements were "sub par."

This is a hidden layer of risk that arises when inflexible work is coupled with insufficient income to buy good childcare. According to the National Center for Children in Poverty, only eight percent of infant/toddler care and 24 percent of preschool care is considered high quality. Thus, like many parents, Deborah could find no affordable and decent childcare so she left them in "self care," which is to say, on their own. But she says, "I'm always afraid. I'm afraid they will say something at school [about her absence] and I'm afraid that something will happen to them." Deborah isn't alone. Federal research reveals that [in 2011] only 17 percent of eligible children receive publicly subsidized childcare. Many parents, then, are living with twin fears: they're terrified by both the possibility of harm that could come to children left alone and the possibility that they'll face investigation by state children's services for child neglect.

Tayisha discovered something else that plagues other parents: childcare cheap enough for her budget can be substandard. Cleaning out her daughter Amy's bag she found ". . .all these notes in the bottom of her backpack. She hated it [the after school program]. These kids were picking on her, and the teacher told her she had to work it out. So she would write me notes about being shoved around, spat at. . ." Trying to handle the abuse on her own, Amy had apparently written down what was happening to her, but didn't pass along the notes in order to protect her mother. Coming upon these frequent, painful, but hidden moments in her daughter's life led Tayisha to quit her job. She had little else to fall back on and nothing in the bank. But Tayisha said, "I don't care what. . .I am not going to have her be in a situation like that." Tayisha knew that her job supervisor regarded the abrupt quit a confirmation of her poor work ethic.

Pointedly, the growing demand for all kinds of care work draws low wage mothers' caring labor out of the family and into the labor market. Antonio's mom and so many others like her face this paradox. One nurse's aide said the supervisors in her nursing home workplace "kind of make you feel like 'We're first and your family's second.'"

Inflexible, family-unfriendly, low-paid jobs create a minefield of bad options for millions of families. Yet, it gets worse because mothers and children find that the strategies they design to try to handle these tough conditions can lead to multiple layers of stigma. Studying workplace discrimination, legal scholar Joan

Williams notes, "professional women who request a flexible schedule find themselves labeled as uncommitted. Low-wage mothers, for whom no flexibility is available, find themselves stigmatized as irresponsible workers when they need time off in order to be responsible mothers."

STIGMA

"They (teachers) see it as we aren't being responsible if we don't attend [meetings] and all that."

Low-wage working mothers find that while they are. . .[faced with] inflexible work demands, they must also contend with the contemporary standards of "good mothering." Numerous sociological studies have documented class differences in the meaning of good mothering. Poverty researchers Kathryn Edin and Maria Kefalas have written, "Ask a middle-class woman if she's a good mother, and she'll likely reply, 'Ask me in twenty years,' for then she will know her daughter's score on the SAT, the list of college acceptances she has garnered, and where her career trajectory has led. . . . Ask a poor woman whether she's a good mother, and she'll likely point to how clean and well-fed her children are, or how she stands by them through whatever problems come their way."

Middle-class working moms are operating in the world of *hurried* childhood, aimed at creating early academic and social wins. The standard for them requires countless extracurricular activities and skill enhancement to give children a competitive edge throughout life. Family sociologist Annette Lareau describes the demands that this intense schedule places on both children and parents, primarily mothers. By contrast, low-income moms are operating in the world of *adultified* childhood, in which children join the "heavy lifting" in the service of family survival. In these conditions, "girls' family labor" has long been a critical, if largely ignored, alternative source of family work. Family and poverty scholar Linda Burton's work on youth in low income families explores how the *adultification* of children is a critical family coping strategy, yet is out of sync with contemporary expectations of intense and early achievement for future success.

This is the world that Antonio, Cesar, and their mother inhabit. They know their "out of sync" care strategies are stigmatized. Low-income school children, perhaps very involved in family care that pulls them out of school, can easily run into conflict with authorities, attitudes, and regulations in their schools. Indeed, a U.S. Department of Education survey of dropout rates indicates that shouldering family responsibilities plays a major role in kids' decisions to leave school. Importantly, low-income youth recognize the stigma that surrounds their families' ways of getting by; they're attuned to social judgment. Sociologist. . . Barrie Thorne has documented that children hear adult talk at home and at school, and they learn how to listen for and read signs of anxiety and stigma. Antonio heard the sympathetic Miss Corey describe how he was "covering for his mother." Her words were a kindness, but one tinged with implications of maternal deficiency. Very early in their lives, children sense the public scrutiny that their working poor mothers face and will attempt to protect them (as Amy did when she hid the notes that would upset her mother). Or children may actively duplicate the stigmatized family ethic, treating the immediate care needs of siblings, parents, even extended family as immediate priority. Yet, just as job supervisors regard mothers engaging in such behavior as "abusing" the system, teachers and school authorities may regard children as uncooperative with school rules and uninterested in getting an education.

Mothers may also find themselves regarded as uncommitted to their children's education by those pointing to their lack of parental participation in school activities. Focusing on the hidden work of mothers, researchers Alison Griffith and Dorothy Smith argue that unequal educational opportunities are built into the contemporary institution of schooling that expects "mothering for schooling," or maternal involvement, to be integral to children's progress. No-show mothers (and their kids) are known by school authorities. Studying urban schools, Michelle Fine quotes a mother who recognizes this attitude, "Society says you're supposed to know what your children are doing at all time. It's not so. I take two hours to travel to work, two hours to travel back and I'm on my feet 10 hours a day."

We heard the same story in our research. For example, Atlanta, a mother of three in Denver, described a 19-hour day. First she gets one child off to school, and then "I get back and get my older daughters off to their school. So then I can do. . . any extra jobs [under the table manicuring] and then pick her up and later her sisters can watch her and then I go to work at 5:00 p.m. I do cleaning office buildings at this point; it starts late so I can spend a little time before." She works until midnight. "I don't even think about ever getting sick."

Cultural critic Joan Morgan describes the "strong Black-woman" image (which extends its cultural reach to ethnic minority, immigrant, and even working class White women) as one that celebrates a capacity to endure hardship and pain. It's true that, in the face of such challenges, Atlanta took pride in her child-rearing accomplishments and her older daughters took pride in their skills as substitutes when their mother needed them. Yet, these are hardly recognized as essential capabilities or remarkable achievements in most work and family and schooling discourse. In fact, these caring strategies may even be turned into their opposite, treated as signs of negligent parenting and inappropriately adultified children, stigmatizing both mothers and children.

UNTENABLE CHOICES

"Don't expect 'them' to get it cause 'they' don't. . . and they don't matter. . . in the end you got to choose."

Mothers and children, trying to manage inflexible work and school demands, without sufficient income to purchase help, face untenable choices. Mothers are pulled to spend more time at work to meet supervisors' expectations and to bring in more sorely needed income. They may turn to children to manage daily household needs and younger children's care. But, in the intensified world of high stakes schooling and extracurricular engagement, siphoning off young people's time and attention to provide family care can cost them dearly. Youngsters are aware of the stakes; they hear talk about achievement and failure all the time and are constantly advised to focus on scoring and winning. In both work and school cultures, the focus on individual effort and personal gain is primary. Yet, in a context in which keeping a family intact may depend on practices that include consciously putting self aside for family needs, mothers and children who put care first may find themselves viewed as deficient, even deviant.

The sociologist Judith Hennessey describes a "moral hierarchy" that guides low-income mothers as they try to manage their choices; mothers commonly say, "children come first." In our research, this language of priority comes up often. We believe that this assertion of primacy of caring for others reflects extreme work, family, and education conditions. It is, ultimately, about survival. Social theorist Patricia Hill Collins, describing how women of color approach family care, asserts, "Without women's motherwork, communities would not survive." Choosing children (and in the children's case, sometimes choosing family care) "first" can be seen as an assertion of the family's right to continue to even be a family tomorrow.

The interplay of low pay, inflexible work, and school design, coupled with social stigma, create untold hardship for millions of low-income families. These forces also set the stage for the people who live in and care for these families to question the priorities of major social institutions. Reflecting this, in a low-income mothers' group discussion in 2005, we heard a woman offer advice: "It's yours to take care of, and that means your kids come first. That's it, there's no other way. Don't expect 'them' to get it cause 'they' don't. . . and they don't matter. . . in the end you got to choose." All the other mothers nodded as if they knew who "they" were.

PRIVATE TROUBLES, COLLECTIVE RESPONSIBILITIES

Echoes of the private troubles these difficult care choices create, the structural barriers that must be overcome, and a call for "them" to "get it" are heard from wage-poor, working mothers throughout sociological literature. If "they" are government entities, responsible for the good of the people, establishing a sustainable wage and also providing subsidies to reach it would make a significant difference. If "they" are employers, whose market success rests on the larger society, investing in families by providing work flexibility would go a long way to support that society. If "they" are public education leaders who oversee the route to social mobility, then integrating the real conditions of low-income youth into school policies and practices would help provide equity. But, for now, none of these powerful social institutions demonstrates a commitment to address the real conditions facing low-wage families.

Taking care of family remains a private enterprise in the U.S. Antonio's mother must rely on working multiple shifts, self-care by Antonio and his brother, and self-styled flexibilities, while other families can purchase services to take care of family needs. Yet, the focus on private strategies for untenable choices, some stigmatized and others affirmed, diverts us from the collective responsibility we share for the care of all families.

NOTE

1. *Editor's note*: This rate has remained stable since 2008, with slightly over 70 percent of women with children participating in the labor force in 2017. (Bureau of Labor Statistics, 2019. "Employment Characteristics of Families." Retrieved on March 9, 2019 [https://www.bls.gov/news.release/pdf/famee.pdf]).

THE DIAPER DILEMMA

JENNIFER RANDLES

Just before he left office, Barack Obama proposed a $10 million federal initiative to test potential projects aimed at increasing the access of low-income families to diapers. The funding was never administered. States have tried, too: in September 2016, by a vote of 54 to 12, the California Assembly passed the first state-level diaper assistance bill. It would have provided $50 monthly diaper vouchers to cover the 120,000 children receiving state welfare aid, but the governor, Jerry Brown, vetoed it, citing the bill's $120 million price tag. He subsequently vetoed another bill, one that would have eliminated state sales taxes on diapers, which the California Assembly had deemed "medically necessary" and therefore qualified for a tax exemption.

The problem these bills aimed to remedy, diaper need, is a common and often hidden consequence of American poverty. One in three mothers in the United States experience diaper need—the lack of sufficient diapers to keep an infant dry, comfortable, and healthy—and 45 percent of infants and toddlers under the age of three live in low-income families whose budgets are impossibly tight. All together, diaper need affects over five million U.S. children, and disproportionately those who are Black and Latinx, those from immigrant families, and those whose parents lack a high school diploma or experience unemployment.

Diaper need can lead to several problems for children, including infections and rashes, irritability, and trouble securing child care. Severe cases of diaper dermatitis ("diaper rash") can require emergency room visits and hospitalization. For parents, diaper need creates stress, guilt, and anxiety. Diaper need can also interfere with children's educational opportunities and parents' abilities to work, as most child care centers require parents to bring at least a week's worth of diapers at a time. If they cannot fully provide diapers, alongside other needs, including milk and medicine, parents are left feeling inadequate. As one mother studied by psychologist C. Cybele Raver and colleagues explained, "It's the same thing as not being able to put food in their mouth. It's more of a need than a want." Yet diapers are still not conceptualized as a need in U.S. social policy.

Diaper Gaps

The average cost of disposable diapers is $18 a week, or $936 annually, per child. This is over six percent of a year-round, full-time federal minimum wage salary ($15,080). Though existing federal and state policies do not cover all eligible families, there are currently public programs that address every other essential need young children have, including food, housing, health care, and education. But diapers are not an "allowable expense"

for Women, Infants, and Children (WIC) or the Supplemental Nutrition Assistance Program (SNAP). California's food stamp program categorizes diapers as "invalid purchases" alongside cigarettes and alcohol. Parents can use Temporary Assistance for Needy Families (TANF) or welfare cash aid for this expense, but if they do, the benefits do not usually stretch enough to cover other basic needs. In 2016, the average monthly TANF benefit for a single-parent family of three ranged from $170 in Mississippi to $923 in Alaska. The average monthly diaper bill would use up between eight and over 40 percent of a family's cash aid check—and only one in four U.S. families in poverty receives any TANF benefits at all. Early Head Start programs provide diapers and formula, but here, too, only a fraction of low-income children are enrolled, and the program does not offer diapers for evenings and weekends.

Cloth diapers are not a viable alternative for most low-income families because they cannot afford in-home washers and dryers (assuming they have homes); it is illegal to wash reusable diapers in most public laundry facilities; and daycare centers require disposables. This leaves many parents struggling to devise "diaper-stretching" strategies, including: borrowing from friends and family, creating makeshift diapers from plastic bags and paper towels, reusing diapers by hanging wet ones to dry or scraping feces from dirty diapers, or toilet training children much earlier than recommended. Poor parents also lack access to diaper cost-cutting strategies that more affluent parents take for granted, such as subscription services and bulk purchasing. Diapers can cost up to twice as much at the local markets and drug stores that are closer to where low-income parents live, and parents in poverty rarely have access to transportation to get to big box stores or the space needed to store diapers even if they could purchase in bulk. All this means that poor parents often end up spending *more* on diapers than higher-income families do.

Diaper need is a huge *need*, and it has negative health, social, and economic consequences for low-income families. So why are policymakers willing to ignore this issue? They seem willing to assume that, contrary to readily available data, all parents can make childbearing and diapering choices unconstrained by economic need.

Needs, Wants, and Public Policy

In addition to the efforts noted earlier, in November 2015, federal lawmakers introduced the Hygiene Assistance for Families of Infants and Toddlers Act. If passed, the law would have funded

(*continued*)

state-based pilot programs to test innovative approaches to providing diapers or diaper vouchers, such as integrating diaper distribution programs with other need-based government services. The bill would have amended the federal Social Security Act to recognize that "access to a reliable supply of clean diapers is a medical necessity for the health and welfare of infants and toddlers, their families, and child care and health care providers." The bill explicitly acknowledged that diapers are necessary for children's access to safe, quality child care and parents' abilities to work and fully care for their children. It further recognized that parents need diapers in order to comply with the requirements of other means-tested programs. For example, parents need to supply diapers to child care providers so that they can work in order to meet the requirements of receiving TANF cash aid. The Hygiene Act bill never got past the Subcommittee on Human Resources.

What about the California diaper bill that Governor Brown vetoed . . . [in 2016]? California Assemblyperson Lorena Gonzalez Fletcher's persistence paid off. She reintroduced a revised bill that passed both the State Assembly and Senate by a wide margin in October 2017. Brown immediately signed the bill, AB480: Diaper Assistance for CalWORKS Families, which will provide a $30 monthly diaper voucher for the state's welfare-to-work program participants. As the country's first statewide public diaper program, it . . . [went] into effect in April 2018 and perhaps will be a model for other states considering diaper legislation. Not all families who experience diaper need will be eligible for the vouchers, nor will it cover eligible families' full needs, but it is a start.

Families across the country are also able to reach out for help from nonprofit diaper banks, which work much like food banks and often partner with family agencies. Founded in 2011,

the National Diaper Bank Network (NDBN) consists of over 300 diaper banks and is the largest national organization advocating on behalf of policy solutions for diaper need. The NDBN has contracted with national diaper manufacturers to allow community organizations to purchase their products for distribution at a substantial discount. Though nonprofit and market-based solutions—such as founding diaper banks and creating more efficient packaging and diapers without licensed cartoons that drive up production expenses—have significantly reduced the costs of diapers, community organizations still struggle to meet families' full needs.

Together, diaper need and the policy vacuum surrounding it represent a distinct cultural and economic problem. It is also an important case in how some services and resources get framed as "needs," while others are conceptualized as "wants," unworthy of a policy remedy. The notion that diaper need is not worthy of political intervention rests on the assumptions that disposable diapers are a luxury and that poor parents can simply choose reusable options that presumably cost less, last longer, and have a smaller environmental impact. Many policymakers have ignored this issue because they erroneously assume that disadvantaged parents make choices about diapering within middle-class circumstances—or that they should have never chosen to have children at all. Some lawmakers object to diaper legislation because they believe it supports low-income parents' choices to have children they cannot afford. This critique echoes racist and classist "welfare queen" stereotypes and exhortations that people in poverty should simply choose not to have babies. This misguided political culture of choice harms poor families by discounting how access to an array of diapering options is a form of privilege and how access to any diapers at all is, in fact, a crucial family need.

KATHRYN J. EDIN AND MARIA KEFALAS

40. UNMARRIED WITH CHILDREN

Many Americans wonder why poor young women choose to have children outside of marriage, despite the potential economic and social consequences. Based on their interviews with poor single mothers, Edin and Kefalas argue that many impoverished young women who become single mothers choose to remain single not because marriage has declined in value, but because they revere it and believe that a failed marriage is a more significant stigma than an out-of-wedlock birth. The authors conclude that until poor young women have access to jobs that will allow them to be financially independent, they will continue to have children first, while waiting for potentially stable marital partners.

Jen Burke, a White tenth-grade dropout who is 17 years old, lives with her stepmother, her sister, and her 16-month old son in a cramped but tidy row home in Philadelphia's beleaguered Kensington neighborhood. She is broke, on welfare, and struggling to complete her GED. Wouldn't she and her son have been better off if she had finished high school, found a job, and married her son's father first?

In 1950, when Jen's grandmother came of age, only one in 20 American children was born to an unmarried mother. Today, that rate is one in three—and they are usually born to those least likely to be able to support a child on their own. In our book, *Promises I Can Keep: Why Poor Women Put Motherhood before Marriage*, we discuss the lives of 162 White, African American, and Puerto Rican low-income single mothers living in eight destitute neighborhoods across Philadelphia and its poorest industrial suburb, Camden. We spent five years chatting over kitchen tables and on front stoops, giving mothers like Jen the opportunity to speak to the question so many affluent Americans ask about them: Why do they have children while still young and unmarried when they will face such an uphill struggle to support them?

ROMANCE AT LIGHTNING SPEED

Jen started having sex with her 20-year-old boyfriend Rick just before her 15th birthday. A month and a half later, she was pregnant. "I didn't want to get pregnant," she claims. "*He* wanted me to get pregnant." "As soon as he met me, he wanted to have a kid with me," she explains. Though Jen's college-bound suburban peers would be appalled by such a declaration, on the streets of Jen's neighborhood, it is something of a badge of honor. "All those other girls he was with, he didn't want to have a baby with any of them," Jen boasts. "I asked him, 'Why did you choose me to have a kid when you could have a kid with any one of them?' He was like, 'I want to have a kid with *you*.'" Looking back, Jen says she now believes that the reason "he wanted me to have a kid that early is so that I didn't leave him."

In inner-city neighborhoods like Kensington, where childbearing within marriage has become rare, romantic relationships like Jen and Rick's proceed at lightning speed. A young man's avowal, "I want to have a baby by you," is often part of the courtship ritual from the beginning. This is more than idle talk, as their first child is typically conceived within a year from the time a couple begins "kicking it." Yet while poor couples' pillow talk often revolves around dreams of shared children, the news of a pregnancy—the first indelible sign of the huge changes to come—puts these still-new relationships into overdrive. Suddenly, the would-be mother begins to scrutinize her mate as never before, wondering whether he can "get himself together"—find a job, settle down, and become a family man—in time.

Jen began pestering Rick to get a real job instead of picking up day-labor jobs at nearby construction sites. She also wanted him to stop hanging out with his ne'er-do-well friends, who had been getting him into serious trouble for more than a decade. Most of all, she wanted Rick to shed what she calls his "kiddie mentality"—his habit of spending money on alcohol and drugs rather than recognizing his growing financial obligations at home.

Rick did not try to deny paternity, as many would-be fathers do. Nor did he abandon or mistreat Jen, at least intentionally. But Rick, who had been in and out of juvenile detention since he was eight years old for everything from stealing cars to selling drugs, proved unable to stay away from his unsavory friends. At the beginning of her seventh month of pregnancy, an escapade that began as a drunken lark landed Rick in jail on a carjacking charge. Jen moved back home with her stepmother, applied for welfare, and spent the last two-and-a-half months of her pregnancy without Rick.

Rick sent penitent letters from jail. "I thought he changed by the letters he wrote me. I thought he changed a lot," she says. "He used to tell me that he loved me when he was in jail. . . . It was always gonna be me and him and the baby when he got out." Thus, when Rick's alleged victim failed to appear to testify and he was released just days before Colin's birth, the couple's reunion was a happy one. Often, the magic moment of childbirth calms the troubled waters of such relationships. New parents typically make amends and resolve to stay together for the sake of their child. When surveyed just after a child's birth, eight in ten unmarried parents say they are still together, and most plan to stay together and raise the child.

Promoting marriage among the poor has become the new war on poverty. . . . And it is true that the correlation between marital status and child poverty is strong. But poor single mothers already believe in marriage. Jen insists that she will walk down the aisle one day, though she admits it might not be with Rick. And demographers still project that more than seven in ten women who had a child outside of marriage will eventually wed someone. First, though, Jen wants to get a good job, finish school, and get her son out of Kensington.

Most poor, unmarried mothers and fathers readily admit that bearing children while poor and unmarried is not the ideal way to do things. Jen believes the best time to become a mother is "after you're out of school and you got a job, at least, when you're like 21. . . . When you're ready to have kids, you should have everything ready, have your house, have a job, so when that baby comes, the baby can have its own room." Yet given their already limited economic prospects, the poor have little motivation to time their births as precisely as their middle-class counterparts do. The dreams of young people like Jen and Rick center on children at a time of life when their more affluent peers plan for college and careers. Poor girls coming of age in the inner city value children highly, anticipate them eagerly, and believe strongly that they are up to the job of mothering—even in difficult circumstances. Jen, for example, tells us, "People outside the neighborhood, they're like, 'You're 15! You're pregnant?' I'm like, it's not none of their business. I'm gonna be able to take care of my kid. They have nothing to worry about." Jen says she has concluded that "some people. . . are better at having kids at a younger age. . . . I think it's better for some people to have kids younger."

WHEN I BECOME A MOM

When we asked mothers like Jen what their lives would be like if they had not had children, we expected them to express regret over foregone opportunities for school and careers. Instead, most believe their children "saved" them. They describe their lives as spinning out of control before becoming pregnant—struggles with parents and peers, "wild," risky behavior, depression, and school failure. Jen speaks to this poignantly. "I was just real bad. I hung with a real bad crowd. I was doing pills. I was really depressed. . . . I was drinking. That was before I was pregnant." "I think," she reflects, "if I never had a baby or anything. . . I would still be doing the things I was doing. I would probably still be doing drugs. I'd probably still be drinking." Jen admits that when she first became pregnant, she was angry that she "couldn't be out no more. Couldn't be out with my friends. Couldn't do nothing." Now, though, she says, "I'm glad I have a son. . . because I would still be doing all that stuff."

Children offer poor youth like Jen a compelling sense of purpose. Jen paints a before-and-after picture of her life that was common among the mothers we interviewed. "Before, I didn't have nobody to take care of. I didn't have nothing left to go home for. . . . Now I have my son to take care of. I have him to go home for. . . . I don't have to go buy weed or drugs with my money. I could buy my son stuff with my money!. . . I have something to look up to now." Children also are a crucial source of relational intimacy, a self-made community of care. After a nasty fight with Rick, Jen recalls, "I was crying. My son came in the room. He was hugging me. He's 16 months and he was hugging me with his little arms. He was really cute and happy, so I got happy. That's one of the good things. When you're sad, the baby's always gonna be there for you no matter what." Lately she has been thinking a lot about what her life was like back then, before the baby. "I thought about the stuff before I became a mom, what my life was like back then. I used to see pictures of me, and I would hide in every picture. This baby did so much for me. My son did a lot for me. He helped me a lot. I'm thankful that I had my baby."

Around the time of the birth, most unmarried parents claim they plan to get married eventually. Rick did not propose marriage when Jen's first child was born, but when she conceived a second time, at 17, Rick informed his dad, "It's time for me to get married. It's time for me to straighten up. This is the one I wanna be with. I had a baby with her, I'm gonna have another baby with her." Yet despite their intentions, few of these couples actually marry. Indeed, most break up well before their child enters preschool.

I'D LIKE TO GET MARRIED, BUT . . .

The sharp decline in marriage in impoverished urban areas has led some to charge that the poor have abandoned the marriage norm. Yet we found few who had given up on the idea of marriage. But like their elite counterparts, disadvantaged women set a high

financial bar for marriage. For the poor, marriage has become an elusive goal—one they feel ought to be reserved for those who can support a "White picket fence" lifestyle: a mortgage on a modest row home, a car and some furniture, some savings in the bank, and enough money left over to pay for a "decent" wedding. Jen's views on marriage provide a perfect case in point. "If I was gonna get married, I would want to be married like my Aunt Nancy and my Uncle Pat. They live in the mountains. She has a job. My Uncle Pat is a state trooper; he has lots of money. They live in the [Poconos]. It's real nice out there. Her kids go to Catholic school. . . . That's the kind of life I would want to have. If I get married, I would have a life like [theirs]." She adds, "And I would wanna have a big wedding, a real nice wedding."

Unlike the women of their mothers' and grandmothers' generations, young women like Jen are not merely content to rely on a man's earnings. Instead, they insist on being economically "set" in their own right before taking marriage vows. This is partly because they want a partnership of equals, and they believe money buys say-so in a relationship. Jen explains, "I'm not gonna just get into marrying him and not have my own house! Not have a job! I still wanna do a lot of things before I get married. He [already] tells me I can't do nothing. I can't go out. What's gonna happen when I marry him? He's gonna say he owns me!"

Economic independence is also insurance against a marriage gone bad. Jen explains, "I want to have everything ready, in case something goes wrong. . . . If we got a divorce, that would be my house. I bought that house, he can't kick me out or he can't take my kids from me." "That's what I want in case that ever happens. I know a lot of people that happened to. I don't want it to happen to me." These statements reveal that despite her desire to marry, Rick's role in the family's future is provisional at best. "We get along, but we fight a lot. If he's there, he's there, but if he's not, that's why I want a job. . . a job with computers. . . so I could afford my kids, could afford the house. . . . I don't want to be living off him. I want my kids to be living off me."

Why is Jen, who describes Rick as "the love of my life," so insistent on planning an exit strategy before she is willing to take the vows she firmly believes ought to last "forever?" If love is so sure, why does mistrust seem so palpable and strong? In relationships among poor couples like Jen and Rick, mistrust is often spawned by chronic violence and infidelity, drug and alcohol abuse, criminal activity, and the threat of imprisonment. In these tarnished corners of urban America, the stigma of a failed marriage is far worse than an out-of-wedlock birth. New mothers like Jen feel they must test the relationship over three, four, even five years' time. This is the only way, they believe, to ensure that their marriages will last.

Trust has been an enormous issue in Jen's relationship with Rick. "My son was born December 23rd, and [Rick] started cheating on me again . . . in March. He started cheating on me with some girl—Amanda. . . . Then it was another girl, another girl, another girl after. I didn't wanna believe it. My friends would come up to me and be like, 'Oh yeah, your boyfriend's cheating on you with this person.' I wouldn't believe it. . . . I would see him with them. He used to have hickies. He used to make up some excuse that he was drunk—that was always his excuse for everything." Things finally came to a head when Rick got another girl pregnant. "For a while, I forgave him for everything. Now, I don't forgive him for nothing." Now we begin to understand the source of Jen's hesitancy. "He wants me to marry him, [but] I'm not really sure. . . . If I can't trust him, I can't marry him, 'cause we would get a divorce. If you're gonna get married, you're supposed to be faithful!" she insists. To Jen and her peers, the worst thing that could happen is "to get married just to get divorced."

Given the economic challenges and often perilously low quality of the romantic relationships among unmarried parents, poor women may be right to be cautious about marriage. Five years after we first spoke with her, we met with Jen again. We learned that Jen's second pregnancy ended in a miscarriage. We also learned that Rick was out of the picture—apparently for good. "You know that bar [down the street?] It happened in that bar. . . . They were in the bar, and this guy was like badmouthing [Rick's friend] Mikey, talking stuff to him or whatever. So Rick had to go get involved in it and start with this guy. . . . Then he goes outside and fights the guy [and] the guy dies of head trauma. They were all on drugs, they were all drinking, and things just got out of control, and that's what happened. He got fourteen to thirty years."

THESE ARE CARDS I DEALT MYSELF

Jen stuck with Rick for the first two and a half years of his prison sentence, but when another girl's name replaced her own on the visitors' list, Jen decided she was finished with him once and for all. Readers might be asking what Jen ever saw in a man like Rick. But Jen and Rick operate in a partner market where the better-off men go to the better-off women. The only way for someone like Jen to forge a satisfying relationship with a man is to find a diamond in the rough or improve her own economic position so that she can realistically compete for more upwardly mobile partners, which is what Jen is trying to do now. "There's this kid, Donny, he works at my job. He works on C shift. He's a supervisor! He's funny, three years older, and he's not a geek or anything, but he's not a real preppy good boy either. But he's not [a player like Rick] and them. He has a job, you know, so that's good. He doesn't do drugs or anything. And he asked my dad if he could take me out!"

These days, there is a new air of determination, even pride, about Jen. The aimless high school dropout pulls ten-hour shifts entering data at a warehouse distribution center Monday through Thursday. She has held the job for three years, and her aptitude and hard work have earned her a series of raises. Her current salary is higher than anyone in her household commands—$10.25 per hour, and she now gets two weeks of paid vacation, four personal days, 60 hours of sick time, and medical benefits. She has saved up the necessary $400 in tuition for a high school completion program that offers evening and weekend classes. Now all that stands between her and a diploma is a passing grade in mathematics, her least favorite subject. "My plan is to start college in January. [This month] I take my math test. . . so I can get my diploma," she confides.

Jen clearly sees how her life has improved since Rick's dramatic exit from the scene. "That's when I really started [to get better] because I didn't have to worry about what *he* was doing, didn't have to worry about him cheating on me, all this stuff. [It was] then I realized that I had to do what I had to do to take care of my son. . . . When he was there, I think that my whole life revolved around him, you know, so I always messed up somehow because I was so busy worrying about what *he* was doing. Like I would leave the [GED] programs I was in just to go home and see what he was doing. My mind was never concentrating." Now, she says, "a lot of people in my family look up to me now, because all my sisters dropped out from school, you know, nobody went back to school. I went back to school, you know?. . . I went back to school, and I plan to go to college, and a lot of people look up to me for that, you know? So that makes me happy. . . because five years ago nobody looked up to me. I was just like everybody else."

Yet the journey has not been easy. "Being a young mom, being 15, it's hard, hard, hard, you know." She says, "I have no life. . . . I work from 6:30 in the morning until 5:00 at night. I leave here at 5:30 in the morning. I don't get home until about 6:00 at night." Yet she measures her worth as a mother by the fact that she has managed to provide for her son largely on her own. "I don't depend on nobody. I might live with my dad and them, but I don't depend on them, you know." She continues, "There [used to] be days when I'd be so stressed out, like, 'I can't do this!' And I would just cry and cry and cry. . . . Then I look at Colin, and he'll be sleeping, and I'll just look at him and think I don't have no [reason to feel sorry for myself]. The cards I have I've dealt myself so I have to deal with it now. I'm older. I can't change anything. He's my responsibility—he's nobody else's but mine—so I have to deal with that."

Becoming a mother transformed Jen's point of view on just about everything. She says, "I thought hanging on the corner drinking, getting high—I thought that was a good life, and I thought I could live that way for eternity, like sitting out with my friends. But it's not as fun once you have your own kid. . . . I think it changes [you]. I think, 'Would I want Colin to do that? Would I want my son to be like that. . .?' It was fun to me but it's not fun anymore. Half the people I hung with are either. . . . Some have died from drug overdoses, some are in jail, and some people are just out there living the same life that they always lived, and they don't look really good. They look really bad." In the end, Jen

believes, Colin's birth has brought far more good into her life than bad. "I know I could have waited [to have a child], but in a way I think Colin's the best thing that could have happened to me. . . . So I think I had my son for a purpose because I think Colin changed my life. He *saved* my life, really. My whole life revolves around Colin!"

PROMISES I CAN KEEP

There are unique themes in Jen's story—most fathers are only one or two, not five years older than the mothers of their children, and few fathers have as many glaring problems as Rick—but we heard most of these themes repeatedly in the stories of the 161 other poor, single mothers we came to know. Notably, poor women do not reject marriage; they revere it. Indeed, it is the conviction that marriage is forever that makes them think that divorce is worse than having a baby outside of marriage. Their children, far from being liabilities, provide crucial social–psychological resources—a strong sense of purpose and a profound source of intimacy. Jen and the other mothers we came to know are coming of age in an America that is profoundly unequal—where the gap between rich and poor continues to grow. This economic reality has convinced them that they have little to lose and, perhaps, something to gain by a seemingly "ill-timed" birth.

The lesson one draws from stories like Jen's is quite simple: Until poor young women have more access to jobs that lead to financial independence—until there is reason to hope for the rewarding life pathways that their privileged peers pursue—the poor will continue to have children far sooner than most Americans think they should, while still deferring marriage. Marital standards have risen for all Americans, and the poor want the same things that everyone now wants out of marriage. The poor want to marry too, but they insist on marrying well. This, in their view, is the only way to avoid an almost certain divorce. Like Jen, they are simply not willing to make promises they are not sure they can keep.

KIRSTIN RALSTON-COLEY

41. DOES IT PAY TO HAVE KIDS? NOT FOR WORKING MOMS

Much of the research about gender inequality in the workplace focuses on discrimination faced by women, but little focuses on the experiences of working women with children. The "motherhood penalty," or the fact that women with children earn less than child-free men and women as well as working fathers, is a major obstacle that working mothers face. Ralston-Coley discusses the factors that contribute to the existence of this penalty, including the gendered division of labor within families and the role of discrimination and bias against mothers in the workplace. Ralston-Coley argues that until attitudes about gendered expectations for mothers and fathers change and until there are more supportive workplace policies for parents, the motherhood penalty will likely persist.

Since the turn of the past century, women have made great strides in labor force participation. According to the Bureau of Labor Statistics (BLS, 2011), the percentage of women working in the paid labor force, full time, year round, has increased from just over 40 percent in 1970 to 47 percent in 2017, down from a high of 58 percent in 2011. Additionally, women own close to 10 million businesses, with over $1 trillion in receipts annually. Although these statistics show an increase in the labor force participation of women in the past four decades, the numbers are even more impressive for working mothers. In 1975, just over 47 percent of mothers with children under eighteen years of age were working at least part-time. By 2017, this number had jumped to almost 71 percent with 75 percent of these women working full time (U.S. Bureau of Labor Statistics, 2017). Additionally, while in 1960 just four percent of married women with children earned more than their husbands or partners, by 2018, four in 10 families have mothers who are the primary breadwinners (Pew Research Center, 2018). You've come a long way, Mom! Well, not quite.

Unfortunately, although mothers are increasing their labor force participation and their contribution to the family income, the wages for working mothers continue to be significantly less than the wages of child-free working women, child-free working men, and working fathers. In 2001, researchers Budig and England estimated full-time working mothers earned between five and seven percent less *per child* than women without children. For a mother of two, this works out to roughly 10 to 14 percent less per paycheck than working women without children. When this wage gap is coupled with the significant gender wage gap (82 cents earned by a full-time, year-round working woman for every dollar earned by a man in 2017), it is no surprise that mothers, in particular, are disproportionately represented at the bottom of the earnings distribution of workers. In fact, Glass (2004) argues the low wages earned by mothers are what account for the majority of the gender wage gap as a whole.

What's the reason for this significant wage gap for working mothers? The short answer: the motherhood penalty. The motherhood penalty is the negative impact on wages that is experienced by working women who are also mothers. It has been well documented in the United States and even, to a much

Original to *Focus on Social Problems: A Contemporary Reader*.

smaller extent, in the family-friendly country of Sweden, with its sixteen months of paid parental leave shared between mothers and fathers (Budig and England, 2001; Harkness and Waldfogel, 2003; SCB, 2012). The motherhood penalty seems to persist across all earning levels but appears most significant for low-wage workers and workers toward the bottom of the earnings distribution (Budig and Hodges, 2010). Unfortunately, it seems the women who "can least afford it pay the largest proportionate penalty for motherhood" (Budig and Hodges, 2010:725). This motherhood penalty is explained, in large part, by two perspectives on parenting and work: (1) research that focuses on the gendered division of labor and how it negatively impacts a working mother's wages and (2) research that focuses on actual discrimination experienced by the working mother for simply being a mother.

GENDERED DIVISION OF LABOR PERSPECTIVE

The body of research on the gendered division of labor and its negative impact on working mother's wages examines the effect of society's (and the workplace's) traditional notions of gender where mothers and fathers were believed to be experts in separate "spheres." This is an extension of gender roles expected of men and women (and boys and girls) in general. A mother's sphere of expertise was believed to be within a family's private life, such as with childcare and the management of the home. A father's sphere of expertise was within public life, such as the workforce or politics. This belief in separate spheres starts with how children are socialized to fit into these roles and how their parents reinforce them. A study from the University of Michigan's Institute of Social Research (2007) asked children to keep track of their time using time diaries and found that school-age girls do two more hours of chores at home per week than boys their own age, and boys spend even *less* time doing chores when they have a sister in the home. Yet, although school-age girls are doing more chores inside the home, they are actually being paid less allowance, on average, than boys for said chores, according to the same study. This disparity in allowance was also found in a 2018 survey

by the mobile app BusyKid. BusyKid allows kids to earn and track their allowance. After analysis, BusyKid (2018) reported that boys between the age of five and seven years old made 50 percent more than girls in the same age group. Thus, the gender wage gap starts early and continues, albeit in more complicated ways, in the sphere of paid work in the labor force. Approaching the issue of the wage gap for working mothers from the division of labor perspective largely focuses on the work decisions of mothers and fathers when dealing with childcare.

Some researchers who focus on the gendered division of labor perspective have found that a portion of the motherhood penalty is explained by the actual loss of employment time resulting from pregnancy, childbirth, and childcare later in the home (Cohen and Bianchi, 1999). As a result, working mothers, especially hourly workers who may not be eligible for paid maternity leave, lose wages because they are not actually working for some length of time because of things like labor and recovery. Only 13 percent of full-time employees are eligible for paid leave and these employees are more likely to be highly educated, higher-earning males (U.S. Bureau of Labor Statistics, 2013). Over time, this loss of wages impacts lifetime earnings for mothers. The Center for American Progress (2016) calculated the potential losses for a 26 year old, working mother with an annual income $35,520 if she takes a year off to care for a child. Over a mother's lifetime of earnings in the workforce, the Center calculates this loss to be nearly $125,000 due to a combination of lost wages, lost wage grow, and retirement benefits. Although it affects low-wage earners more significantly, research suggests that even high wage–earning mothers experience a loss in opportunities and seniority because of missed work (Budig and England, 2001; Budig and Hodges, 2010). It seems easy to say, "You miss work, therefore you miss opportunities." Unfortunately, the reality is far more unfair when we consider that historically women have been considered the go-to parent for childcare. According to researchers at the Kaiser Family Foundation (Ranji and Salganicoff, 2014), only three percent of fathers report being the parent who usually leaves work to take care of a sick child.

Other division-of-labor research focuses on the types of jobs working mothers take to maintain their primary caretaker status. For example, Budig and England (2001) found that working mothers may choose more flexible occupations or leave full-time work altogether, opting for part-time work, so their time away from home is minimized or is adaptable to the needs of the family. Unfortunately, most part-time or flexible jobs are more unstable, offer fewer work-related benefits (like retirement or health insurance), and pay less per hour than full-time jobs. As a result, working mothers in these types of jobs will have lower earnings over time as well. Some might argue this is a choice mothers make, but with skyrocketing childcare costs it might not be much of a choice. In most of the United States, monthly childcare for two children can be more expensive than a mortgage or rent (Child Care Aware, 2013). When mothers are the lower wage earners in married households (often making less than the cost of childcare per month), many will choose to maximize the higher wage earner's income and opt out of working altogether. Of course, having a "choice" to take a part-time job or leave work altogether means there is most likely another paycheck coming into the household. For the nearly 29 percent of mothers in the full-time workforce who are also single, there is no choice, and reduced paychecks resulting from labor, delivery, parenting, and childcare are a stinging fact of life.

DISCRIMINATION IN THE WORKPLACE

Research into the role of the gendered division of labor explains some portion of the motherhood penalty, especially as it relates to some of the decisions mothers and fathers make when it comes to having and taking care of their children. However, it doesn't account for the reality that women also experience outright discrimination for simply being mothers. One study suggests working mothers might face significant discrimination even in the job application process. Correll et al. (2007) conducted an experimental study and asked participants to evaluate two potential applicants who were equally qualified in education and experience for a mid-level marketing position. The only difference between the applicants was the inclusion of outside activities that might be relevant. The fictitious mother was listed as being a "Parent–Teacher

Association Coordinator," whereas the other applicant was listed as being involved in "fundraising" for her neighborhood association. In this particular study, the mother was significantly less likely to be recommended for the position. In addition, if recommended for the position, the suggested starting salary for the mothers was $11,000 less than the starting salary for the applicants without children. In a similar follow-up study with actual employers, Correll et al. (2007) found employers, when presented with a fictional pair of equally qualified candidates, *never* chose to contact the mother for an interview over the applicant without children. Although using a candidate's marital status against them in hiring decisions is illegal, employers can get around this by asking questions like "Can you travel?" or "Do you have other responsibilities that might prevent you from working overtime, if needed?"

Why would employers devalue working mothers? Since mothers are assumed to be experts in the family's private sphere, it is most likely presumed they will either be bad workers (because they will always be prioritizing their families) or they will be bad mothers (by not prioritizing their families). Thus, employers may be assuming that a working mother is going to fail somewhere and it will most likely be her job, given traditional gender expectations.

In addition, mothers who prioritize their family often lose a portion of their wages because of a lack of family-friendly work policies. As mentioned previously, the Kaiser Family Foundation (2013) found that only three percent of working fathers are usually the parent who takes off work when a child is sick, compared to 39 percent of working mothers. When mothers do not have backup childcare options and/or when mothers are paid by the hour, this can have significant economic ramifications. According to data cited by Ranji and Salganicoff (2014), as many as one-fifth of school-age children miss a week or more of school during the school year for which mothers might be required to miss work. These most likely unpaid, missed days of work directly translate to lower paychecks.

Unfortunately, even working mothers who prioritize their careers over family cannot escape discrimination. Benard and Correll (2010) found that on the job, women with children face additional discrimination through lower performance evaluations and are viewed as less likeable or selfish compared to other workers. In terms of career advancement, these qualities impacted mothers negatively because they were less likely to be offered promotions. This type of discrimination is not based on job performance, but on the woman's violation of gender expectations, much like the violations of separate spheres discussed previously. The expectation is that mothers *should* prioritize family over work. Thus, even when a mother is seen as a competent and committed employee, she is still penalized for violating the gendered division of labor that necessitates putting family first.

WHAT ABOUT FATHERS?

It might be easy to assume this is merely a parenthood penalty and perhaps fathers, too, experience similar discrimination in the workplace. In April 2014, Daniel Murphy, second baseman for the New York Mets, was eviscerated by talk radio hosts for missing two games to be with his wife during and after the birth of their first child. Although this instance probably did not result in lost wages for Mr. Murphy, some research does suggest fathers who violate gender norms by taking employer-approved paternity leave experience negative evaluations. In an experimental study, Allen and Russell (1999) found that men who took employer-approved paternity leave were less likely to be considered for promotions than men who did not take paternity leave. Later, Wayne and Cordeiro (2003) asked undergraduate students to read a fictitious personnel file and rate the employees on compliance to work expectations. They found that fathers who took leave were rated lower in competence than mothers who took leave, especially by male students in the study.

Although these two studies suggest fathers might experience a fatherhood penalty, the bulk of research (and more recent research) on parental wage penalties suggests that most fathers actually experience "fatherhood benefits" in terms of positive evaluations and higher salaries. Correll et al. (2007) found that unlike mothers, who are seen as less committed employees than women without children, fathers were actually perceived as *more* committed than men without children. As a result, fathers were recommended for

higher starting salaries than the men without children. Using data collected from 1979 to 2014, Budig (2014) found that women's earnings decreased four percent for each child and men's earnings increased by more than six percent for each child. The gap was consistent when controlling for education, income earned by a spouse, and number of hours worked. Some evidence suggests that even in academia, a seemingly egalitarian and progressive landscape, a father is far more likely to achieve the status of full professor than a mother with similar experience, work output, marital status, and background (Garmendia, 2011). One notable exception is sociology departments, where women with children are just as likely to have "ideal" careers (defined as being in a tenured position with high scholarly productivity) as the fathers and men without children (Spalter-Roth and Van Vooren, 2012). However, fathers, for the most part, have an advantage that mothers do not. The expectation of fathers to be the breadwinner is confirmed and *rewarded* in the workplace, whereas the expectation of mothers to be the primary caretaker is confirmed and *penalized*.

FUTURE OF THE MOTHERHOOD PENALTY

In August 2014, Ipshita Pal and Jane Waldfogel released a paper for Columbia University that suggests the motherhood penalty has remained consistent since at least 1977. Despite the significant gains working mothers have made in labor force participation, they continue to experience the most significant penalty for being in the labor force—more than three decades of persistent wage penalties for mothers compared to child-free women, child-free men, and fathers (Pal and Waldfogel, 2014).

Not all the news is bad. Some recent research suggests attitudes are changing regarding gender expectations of mothers (and fathers) in the workforce and other research suggests discrimination toward mothers in the workforce might become less prevalent in the future. Coleman and Franuik (2011) found that undergraduates rated parents (both mothers and fathers) who took some form of parental leave more favorably in competence and overall impression than parents who stayed at home permanently or parents who took no leave. Although this study focused on attitudes toward parents and not just mothers or fathers, the results are in direct contrast to the previously mentioned findings of Wayne and Cordeiro from 2003. Although this may be a cohort effect, given that younger generations are more likely to hold more gender egalitarian attitudes, it is a sign of potential progress. This generation's attitudes have empirical support. A study from January 2014 suggests that working mothers (and fathers) with two or more children are actually slightly more productive than their peers with fewer or no children (Krapf et al., 2014). The authors speculate this may be because parents use their time more efficiently than their childless coworkers. Although this may not translate into less discrimination for working mothers at the moment, there may come a time when working mothers are seen as less of a liability simply because they are mothers. Legislation passed in December 2017 suggests there is a changing attitude towards parents in the workforce, too. According the Congressional Research Service (2018), in December 2017, Congress passed H.R. 1 (P.L. 115-97), which included tax incentives to employers to offer paid family and medical leave voluntarily to employees. Fathers, too, are seeing a positive change in attitudes towards paternity leave, at least in California. According to the Department of Labor, California's paid family policy that provides equal access to paid parental leave for both mothers and fathers has had a significant impact on fathers. The Department of Labor Statistics (2009) reports that California's program has more than doubled the odds that a new father will take parental leave.

Changing perceptions of gender roles in the workforce combined with decreasing discrimination toward working mothers may be the key to weakening (or even ending) the motherhood penalty. The evidence for this argument may already be seen in countries like Sweden, with its public policy push toward more egalitarian views and family-friendly policies. Swedes, it seems, have realized that mothers leaving the workforce (or even switching to part-time work) has not been beneficial to the country as a whole. In fact, Swedish fathers are encouraged to take some portion of parental leave and parents, combined, can take up to sixteen months of paid leave. Yes, *paid* leave, earning 90 percent of their wages! Additionally, tax breaks are in place to help with the cost of childcare for all working parents, regardless of marital status (SCB, 2012).

Perhaps the recent Swedish baby boom is a testament to how well these policies are working for the Swedes! Research in the United States suggests these policies are actually beneficial to the economy and the businesses that choose to offer paid leave. The parental leave policy in California mentioned previously has saved employers more than $85 million a year by implementing these paid leave programs. Employees took the paid leave and ultimately returned to work. This saved their employers from the time-consuming and costly hiring and training process involved with finding replacements (Applebaum and Milkman, 2011).

It might seem that working mothers are united in their view of the gender expectations for mothers and the effects of discrimination on mothers as problematic, but recent discussions in academia and in the business world suggest otherwise. Sheryl Sandberg, Chief Operating Officer of Facebook, and Nell Scovell, TV and magazine writer, collaborated on the book *Lean In: Women, Work, and the Will to Lead* (2013). While on the surface this book seemed to be a playbook for how women (and mothers) can be successful in the fast-paced, long hour, male dominated world of business, the reality of the arguments presented in this book are far more complicated. In response, many academic and critical cultural observers responded swiftly and harshly. Most observers see the "Lean In Movement" promoted by the book as a way to both condemn women who speak out against gender discrimination in their workplaces and simultaneously promotes an 'every woman for herself' mentality. Susan Faludi, Pulitzer Prize winning journalist, suggests that Sandberg's and Scovell's arguments are simply a corporate manual for how ambitious, White women should keep their heads down and focus on their own success (Faludi, 2013). Acclaimed author and social activist bell hooks, too, responded to the book by saying it was a form of "faux feminism." hooks points out how the book ignores social structures and social institutions that perpetuate discrimination based upon race, social class, and sexuality. In addition, hooks argues that Sandberg and Scovell have a position in society that already puts them way ahead of other women. Both Faludi and hooks argue the "Lean In Movement" promotes individual success and makes no recommendations for structural change that would help all women (Faludi, 2013; hooks 2013). Recently, former first lady Michelle Obama weighed in on the "Lean In Movement," too, at a recent tour stop for her book *Becoming*. When asked about balancing it all, work and family life, Obama responded with "I tell women that whole 'you can have it all' — mmm, nope, not at the same time, that's a lie." For someone who seemingly balanced one of the highest profile family in the United States, her honesty speaks volumes.

The evidence reported here suggests maintaining the status quo in the United States will continue to perpetuate the motherhood penalty, as it has for approximately four decades, and will continue to create the largest wage gap for the mothers who can't afford it. Changing gender attitudes alone are not enough, especially given that gender attitudes have already changed during those same four decades. Changing gender attitudes coupled with workplace policies that truly give all parents an alternative to either opting out of work or settling for lower-wage jobs might be a good place to start. In February 2015, the Council of Economic Advisers at the Federal Reserve Bank reported that although women's labor force participation in the United States had been on track with that of women in Canada, the United Kingdom, Germany, France, and Japan for decades, it was now falling behind (Federal Reserve Bank, 2015). What is different about these other countries? They recognize the benefit of working mothers and have made it easier for them to continue working by offering workplace benefits like childcare and paid leave. In the United States, until we significantly change the way we see mothers and acknowledge the value (and growing necessity) of their careers, the motherhood penalty will most likely persist. President Barack Obama called for such action in his January 2015 State of the Union Address by stressing the necessity of women working in our economy today and arguing that programs like affordable childcare are not only a woman's issue, but also a "national economic priority" for us all.

REFERENCES

Allen, Tammy D., and Joyce E. A. Russell. 1999. "Parental Leave of Absence: Some Not So Family-Friendly Implications." *Journal of Applied Social Psychology* 29(1): 166–191.

Applebaum, Eileen, and Ruth Milkman. 2011. *Leaves That Pay: Employer and Worker Experiences with Paid Family Leave in California.* Washington, DC: Center for Economic and Policy Research.

Child Care Aware. 2013. Cost of Care Survey Report 2013. http://www.childcareaware.org/.

Benard, Stephen, and Shelley J. Correll. 2010. "Normative Discrimination and the Motherhood Penalty." *Gender & Society* 24:616–646.

Budig, Michelle. 2014. *The Fatherhood Bonus and the Motherhood Penalty: Parenthood and the Gender Gap in Pay.* Washington, DC: Third Way.

Budig, Michelle, and Paula England. 2001. "The Wage Penalty for Motherhood." *American Sociological Review* 66:204–225.

Budig, Michelle, and Melissa Hodges. 2010. "Differences in Disadvantage: Variation in the Motherhood Penalty across White Women's Earnings Distribution." *American Sociological Review* 75:705–728.

BusyKid. 2018. Gender Pay Gap Starts With Kids in America. https://busykid.com/2018/06/29/gender-pay-gap-starts-with-kids-in-america/.

Center for American Progress. 2016. Calculating the Hidden Cost of Interrupting a Career for Child Care. https://www.americanprogress.org/issues/early-childhood/reports/2016/06/21/139731/calculating-the-hidden-cost-of-interrupting-a-career-for-child-care/.

Cohen, Philip N., and Suzanne M. Bianchi. 1999. "Marriage, Children, and Women's Employment: What Do We Know?" *Monthly Labor Review* 122(12):22–31.

Coleman, Jill M., and Renae Franiuk. 2011. "Perceptions of Mothers and Fathers Who Take Temporary Work Leave." *Sex Roles* 64(5):311–323.

Congressional Research Service. 2018. "Paid Family Leave in the United States." https://fas.org/sgp/crs/misc/R44835.pdf.

Correll, Shelley J., Stephen Benard, and In Paik. 2007. "Getting a Job: Is There a Motherhood Penalty?" *American Journal of Sociology* 112:1297–1338.

Faludi, Susan. 2013. "Facebook Feminism, Like It or Not." *The Baffler* 23: August 2013. https://the-baffler.com/salvos/facebook-feminism-like-it-or-not.

Federal Reserve Bank. 2015. Activity Rate for Global Female Workers Aged 25–54. http://research.stlouisfed.org/fred2/series/LRAC25FEJPM156S/.

Garmendia, Cristina. 2011. White Paper on the Position of Women in Science in Spain. http://www.idi.mineco.gob.es/stfls/MICINN/Ministerio/FICHEROS/UMYC/WhitePaper_Interactive.pdf/.

Glass, Jennifer. 2004. "Blessing or Curse? Work–Family Policies and Mothers' Wage Growth over Time." *Work and Occupations* 31:367–394.

Harkness, Susan, and Jane Waldfogel. 2003. "The Family Gap in Pay: Evidence from Seven Industrialized Countries." *Research in Labor Economics* 22:369–414.

hooks, bell. 2013. "Dig Deep: Beyond Lean In." *The Feminist Wire*. https://www.thefeministwire.com/2013/10/17973/.

Krapf, Matthias, Heinrich Urpsrung, and Christian Zimmerman. 2014. "Parenthood and Productivity of Highly Skilled Labor: Evidence from the Groves of Academe." *Working Paper Series*. St. Louis: Federal Reserve Bank.

Pal, Ipshita, and J. Waldfogel. 2014. "Re-Visiting the Family Gap in Pay in the United States." Paper presented for Columbia University, New York.

Pew Research Center. 2013. Social and Demographic Trends. http://www.pewsocialtrends.org/.

Pew Research Center. 2018. "Facts about U.S. Moms". http://www.pewresearch.org/fact-tank/2018/05/10/facts-about-u-s-mothers/.

Ranji, Usha, and Alina Salganicoff. 2014. "*Data Note: Balancing on Shaky Ground: Women, Work, and Family Health.*" Menlo Park, CA: Kaiser Family Foundation. http://kff.org/womens-health-policy/issue-brief/data-note-balancing-on-shaky-ground-women-work-and-family-health/.

Sandberg, Sheryl. 2013. *Lean in: Women, Work, and the Will to Lead*. New York, NY, US: Alfred A. Knopf.

SCB. 2012. Official Statistics of Sweden. http://www.scb.se/en_/.

Spalter-Roth, Roberta, and Nicole Van Vooren. 2012. "Mothers in Pursuit of Ideal Careers." Washington DC: American Sociological Association.

U.S. Bureau of Labor Statistics. 2011. "Women in the Labor Force: A Databook." Washington, DC: U.S. Government Printing Office. http://www.bls.gov/cps/wlf-databook-2012.pdf/.

U.S. Bureau of Labor Statistics. 2013. "Paid Leave in Private Industry Over the Past 20 Years." *Beyond the Numbers* 2(18). http://www.bls.gov/opub/btn/volume-2/paid-leave-in-private-industry-over-the-past-20-years.htm.

U.S. Bureau of Labor Statistics. 2017. "Highlights of Women's Earnings in 2017." *U.S. Government Printing Office*. https://www.bls.gov/opub/reports/womens-earnings/2017/home.htm.

U.S. Department of Labor Statistics. 2009. "California's Paid Family Leave Law." https://www.dol.gov/wb/resources/california_paid_family_leave_law.pdf.

University of Michigan, Institute for Social Research. 2007. "Time, Money, and Who Does the Laundry." Research Update. January 2007: Number 4.

Wayne, Julie H., and Bryanne L. Cordeiro. 2003. "Who Is a Good Organizational Citizen? Social Perception of Male and Female Employees Who Use Family Leave." *Sex Roles* 49:233–246.

WENDY KLEIN, CAROLINA IZQUIERDO, AND THOMAS N. BRADBURY

42. THE DIFFERENCE BETWEEN A HAPPY MARRIAGE AND A MISERABLE ONE

Chores

It is common today for both members of a couple to work in the paid labor force. Thus, partners are likely to have to negotiate a successful distribution of household chores that may look different from that of couples in the past. Klein, Izquierdo, and Bradbury share the results of their research on division of household responsibilities regarding who does the most of each kind of household labor, how working couples perceive their division of chores, and interactional patterns that working couples used around chores. The ways that working couples divided labor and interacted around this division led to more or less conflict in families, affecting the quality of their relationships.

In the United States, ambiguity in division of household responsibilities between working couples often results in ongoing negotiations, resentment, and tension. According to a 2007 Pew Research Poll,[1] sharing household chores was in the top three highest-ranking issues associated with a successful marriage—third only to faithfulness and good sex. In this poll, 62 percent of adults said that sharing household chores is very important to marital success. There were no differences of opinion reported between men and women, between older adults and younger adults, or between married people and singles.

Mirroring trends in industrialized nations around the world, men's participation in housework in U.S. families has nearly doubled in the past 40 years, and their amount of time spent on child care has tripled. Yet in the United States women still perform the majority of household tasks, and most of the couples in our study reported having no clear models for achieving a mutually satisfying arrangement.

Determining who was responsible for various household tasks was a particularly contentious process for couples who tended to bicker about housework on a regular basis. Other couples, however, appeared to carry out tasks separately or in collaboration without much tension or discussion. Studying how couples divide their many household chores is important on its own terms, as the results of the Pew Poll suggest. More importantly, close examination of how husbands and wives collaborate on or fail to coordinate their household activities allows us to contemplate more encompassing phenomena such as gender roles, issues of power, respect, intimacy, and attempts to broker an equitable or fair partnership. What are couples' perceptions of their roles in the division of labor in the home? How do spouses coordinate and enact different patterns of household labor? How do family systems operate to sustain particular distributions of labor?

WORKING COUPLES AND THE DIVISION OF LABOR AT HOME

Among couples we studied, on average, men worked longer hours outside the home, yet even in families where women worked equivalent or longer hours and earned higher salaries, they still took on more household responsibilities. When our data were merged with the Chicago Sloan Study of 500 working families, we learned that men spent 18 percent of their time doing housework and took on 33 percent of household tasks, whereas women spent 22 percent of their time on housework and carried out 67 percent of household tasks. Women performed over twice the number of tasks and assumed the burden of "mental labor" or "invisible work," that is, planning and coordination of tasks. Moreover, leisure was most frequent for fathers (30 percent) and children (39 percent) and least frequent for mothers (22 percent).

In our study, we categorized household work into three activities: (1) household maintenance (e.g., organizing objects and managing storage issues); (2) household chores (e.g., meal preparation, cleaning, outdoor work); and (3) child care (e.g., bathing, dressing, grooming, feeding, putting to bed). While men spent slightly more of their time on household maintenance tasks (4 vs. 3 percent), women spent more time on chores (26 vs. 14 percent) and child care (9.1 vs. 5.6 percent, respectively). Women on average spent 39 percent of their time on these activities, compared to 23 percent for men. Women prepared 91 percent of weekday and 81 percent of weekend dinners, even though fathers were present at 80 percent of weekday and 88 percent of weekend dinners. Overall, women spent much more of their time cooking, cleaning, and taking care of children, compared to their husbands. Women also spent more time multitasking, often juggling meal preparation with cleaning tasks and child care.

Although our quantitative findings replicate the well-documented disparity in the division of labor between men and women, we also found that the nuanced ways couples interact with one another about and during these tasks were linked to the couples' relationship satisfaction and sense of well-being. More than constituting a series of simple instrumental tasks, household work represents a complex set of interpersonal exchanges that enable family members to achieve (or fail to achieve) solidarity and cohesiveness.

COUPLES' PERCEPTIONS OF THEIR ROLES AT HOME

While watching television on a Saturday morning, John kicks back in a lounge chair as his wife, Susannah,

sits on the couch folding laundry and talks on the telephone to arrange a play date for their eight-year-old son. At one point, their one-year-old daughter cries for Susannah's attention, and she puts down the clothes to pick her up. Hanging up the telephone, she goes into the kitchen to start preparing a meal. Previously in an interview, Susannah described how she holds down a full-time job while also handling most of the household work and the child care—even when John is home:

> Personally, I don't have a life. My life is my family because whatever their needs are they always come first before mine and I can honestly say that. He— and I think it's great—he does his golfing, he does his bike riding, and it doesn't take a long time and he needs that. I don't get that yet. I don't have that yet. I don't have the time or the luxury. That for me is like a huge luxury that I don't see happening in any time in the near future.

According to Susannah, while her husband has time to pursue his own interests, she views herself as the only member of the family who must continually sacrifice her well-being for the needs of others. Having time for oneself is equated with "having a life," and not only does this mother feel that she has neither, but she does not foresee any changes on the horizon. The strong sense of being burdened that Susannah expressed was not unusual among the women in our study.

Although working women's feelings of being overwhelmed is well documented, in some cases men are also often highly stressed by managing everyday household decisions and prioritizing the needs of family members. Travis, the father of two boys ages two and a half and eight, laments the constant demand of "managing someone else's needs," specifically, being unable to fulfill the "demands" of his wife, which often comes at the expense of his own health. He talks about his concerns as he spontaneously interviews himself in front of a video camera, which we provided to him for conducting a self-guided home tour:

> You'll notice when I'm walking around the house that, um, there's basically very little respite for me. It's all about, um, managing someone else's needs most of the time, and admittedly, I'm not as strong and caring of my own needs, but I see that my own

physical health is being compromised by not doing that, so, um, I'm starting to do more of that, which of course leads to aggravation from my demanding wife, um, by not paying attention to her and not fulfilling her needs.

So I think my house kind of represents, um, work. And my workplace kind of represents rest in a certain way.

This perspective on the workplace as a sanctuary reflects the phenomenon discussed by sociologist Arlie Russell Hochschild, who found that for working parents one's job offered a less stressful environment than life at home.

Travis and his wife, Alice, discussed their perspectives on their domestic lives in an interview. Alice explained that she and Travis have different orientations to handling household tasks: she recognizes that she is an "accomplisher" who can be "domineering" and less "easygoing" than Travis. Alice then elaborated on the consequences of these differences:

> I have to, like, I manage the household, and, like, I delegate what needs to be done, 'cause basically I'm the one in charge of seeing that—everything needs to get done. That's how I look at it. Anyway, so that's a real source of tension between both of us, I think. It's not like the trust thing. It's just that—that, um, it wouldn't be like Travis would walk into the room and go, gee, my underwear's on the floor; I guess I'd better pick it up. It'll be, like, Travis, pick up your underwear off the floor. I mean, it's like, basically for me, it's like having three kids in the house. Sorry, no offense. I love you very much.

From Alice's perspective, the need to push Travis stems from her belief that it is the only way to make sure that chores will get done. Alice and Travis expressed having divergent needs and expectations of what is necessary for running a household successfully. They have different ideas about how to organize their everyday lives, and they debate these approaches throughout the interview.

TRAVIS: I mean, she's no—she's not a saint in terms of keeping the place clean and, uh, fixing stuff or—she doesn't fix anything.
ALICE: No, but I cook meals. I just can't do it all. I don't. But I made you dinner tonight.

TRAVIS: That's good.
ALICE: There you go. I'm no saint, but I just can't do everything. I can't buy all the groceries, cook the dinner—
TRAVIS: I know, but just for the—don't you think that there's—you know that little board we have on the refrigerator?
ALICE: Mm hmm.
TRAVIS: Why don't you use that and, like, say, like, um, write me notes?
ALICE: I don't want to.
TRAVIS: Number one, dishwasher. Number two, rain gutter.
ALICE: To be honest with you, I don't want to have to tell you to do stuff. I want you to figure out that the—that the dishwasher needs to be—that you need to figure it out that the dishwasher needs to be—
TRAVIS: I did. Did you ask me to fix the dishwasher, or did I?
ALICE: No, you ordered a part, and then six months went by and we don't know what happened to it. I don't want to be, like, micromanaging you. Anyway, that's a whole other story.

Alice's frustration is evident in the content of her utterances and in her demeanor during the interview. Her tone of voice is tense and defiant as she expresses her exasperation. In the first several lines, she emphasizes that she "can't do it all," repeating the words *can't* and *don't want to* throughout the excerpt. During this exchange, it becomes clear that Alice does not wish to constantly remind Travis what to do around the house.

Perhaps as a way to distance himself from the nagging he experiences, Travis suggests that Alice post notes on the refrigerator, listing tasks that need to be done. She responds that she would prefer that he "figure it out," indicating, once again, her desire for him to take initiative without her constant input, or as she refers to it, "micromanaging," an approach that does not work for either of them. For Travis, Alice's micromanaging is problematic because it does not occur only when something needs to be done; it permeates almost every moment of his waking life. He comments on his wife's continual negative appraisals and states that there is a great deal of "punitive language coming my direction."

Several findings stand out from the above excerpts. First, the burden spouses experience managing household responsibilities interferes with individual well-being and expressions of intimacy. Spouses spontaneously mention the struggles they experience in their relationship over the allocation and completion of chores, and when they reflect on the division of labor in their families they sometimes couch their arrangement in terms of trust (e.g., Does my partner trust me to do what I am expected to do?) and authority and subordination (e.g., I want my partner to recognize what to do and do it vs. I want my partner to prompt me when tasks need attention).

Housework appears to be far more than the mere completion of tasks needed to keep the family running smoothly. It also colors individuals' daily experiences and appears to affect how couples characterize their partnership.

INTERACTIONAL PATTERNS BETWEEN COUPLES

While several of the spouses in our sample expressed frustration regarding household division of labor, some couples seemed to be particularly skilled at smoothly accomplishing domestic tasks. A study of the couples preparing dinner together revealed a variety of interactional styles, including (1) "silent collaboration," in which both partners worked in the same space and went about the task at hand; (2) "one partner as expert," in which one spouse was considered an expert or authority in a particular task, either humorously or with genuine respect; (3) "coordinating together," in which partners verbally organized the activity in concert; and (4) "collaborating apart," in which partners carried out their share of the labor in separate locations.

When coordinating together, couples displayed how they related to and treated one another in the midst of carrying out domestic tasks. In the following example, one couple collaborates harmoniously as they unwind after work one evening. As the dinner preparation begins, Adam has just put on a jazz CD and offers his wife, Cheryl, something to drink (he uses her nickname, "Sweeps").

ADAM: Sweeps, you want any wine?
CHERYL: Sure.
ADAM: I bought you zinfandel that you *love*.

Adam displays his attentiveness to his wife as he uses a term of endearment and pours her a glass of wine. This couple often made dinner together, alternating who took the lead. At one point while Adam is out on the patio barbecuing chicken, Cheryl comes out to offer to help.

CHERYL: Adam, what do you want me to do? Rice? Salad?
ADAM: I'm doing rice already.
CHERYL: Okay, You got broccoli?
ADAM: I have mixed vegetables steamed.
CHERYL: You want that paper out here, or can I bring it in?
ADAM: Yeah, that's all done, I'm done with all that.
CHERYL: Okay.

In these exchanges we see that each spouse is trying to anticipate each other's needs regarding the task at hand, as well as attending to other features of the setting and concurrent activities. Adam opens a bottle of his wife's favorite wine and turns on music they enjoy; Cheryl asks about helping with the food preparation and checks with her husband on where he would prefer her to put the newspaper he had been reading.

When couples coordinate together, however, there is also the potential for counter-collaborative communication, which may produce tension and lead to conflict. In the following example, David is preparing dinner, which is particularly challenging for him since he only recently began to take on cooking responsibilities. He attempts to appease his wife, Julie's, numerous queries, demands, and requests, which target him repeatedly throughout the dinner-making activity.

DAVID: I'm making such a mess.
JULIE: You always make a mess, David.
DAVID: I know.
JULIE: It's like you don't know how to cook.
JULIE: (This is going)—look at what you've done!
DAVID: (*laughs*)

When David acknowledges that he is "making such a mess," Julie confirms and generalizes his assessment to all the occasions on which he takes on meal preparation. Her next comment, "It's like you don't know how to cook," is a further critique of his poor performance. David calmly accepts her condemnation and even finds his performance humorous. Instead of joining her husband in laughing about the situation, Julie continues to adopt a critical supervisory role.

JULIE: First of all, you don't do this *on* the stove. You do it over on the counter. Ugh. You're going to have to clean up, too. So sorry to inform you.
DAVID: I know that. I'll clean it up.

As Julie watches over and evaluates her husband's actions, her tone is authoritative and her imperatives are unmitigated. She makes no attempt to soften her stance or to couch her talk as suggestions rather than orders. She does not respond to David's humor and instead maintains a monitoring role in the interaction. This pattern of participation also surfaces on a subsequent evening in the couple's kitchen.

David fields Julie's interrogations and comments without hesitation, and he appears to be doing his best to meet her expectations of how the meal should be prepared. He attempts to inject humor into the situation on more than one occasion. Julie continues to monitor the activity and notes that the researchers are videotaping his missteps. She then refers to a news story about police videotaping interviews with suspected criminals. David's manner then shifts. He makes no more attempts at humor and self-deprecation; instead, his tone becomes curt and his words more adversarial.

JULIE: You know what, I heard this morning on NPR that police departments are going to start taping their interviews with um ((*pause*)) you know, suspects.
DAVID: You don't say.
JULIE: Well, they haven't been doing it before.
DAVID: Genius idea. Yeah.
JULIE: You know what? I don't need your sarcasm.
DAVID: Yeah you do.

David's response to Julie's comment is received as antagonistic. David criticizes the idea behind the news story she is relaying rather than anything about Julie personally, yet she chooses to defend the idea and appears to feel slighted personally by his comment. Her annoyance is apparent in her hostile response ("I don't need your sarcasm"). We can only speculate about the longer-term implications these exchanges have for future conversations between these spouses, yet psychological analyses of family interaction would suggest that David might respond more negatively to Julie's incursions

(by avoiding her more or criticizing her), perhaps leading her to escalate her requests even further.

While working women often complain that men engage less in accomplishing multiple and simultaneous family-related tasks, men express dissatisfaction about consistently being "nagged" by their wives, giving rise to the "henpecked" husband. Several studies have identified a pattern called *demand–withdraw* as a reliable marker of maladaptive communication and future relationship distress. In this pattern, "one member (the demander) criticizes, nags, and makes a demand on the other, while the partner (the withdrawer) avoids confrontation, withdraws, and becomes defensive." Withdrawing responses can take many forms and can serve specific functions, including avoiding intimacy, avoiding conflict, and angry withdrawal.

The tension that arises in everyday interactions concerning household management can influence the quality and nature of communication between couples as they broach other domains of discussion. As some psychological studies note, humor and positive affect in marital interactions foreshadows marital success and can neutralize the effects of poor communication skills. Interactional patterns of conflict in marriage are complex and are often the symptom of underlying tension concerning other issues related to professional work status and differing rights, obligations, and expectations. For example, in the excerpt above David was temporarily unemployed and seeking work, which may have contributed to Julie's frustration, to David's willingness to adopt a subordinate and subservient role, and to the apparent tension in their interactions.

PARTNERSHIP AND SHARED UNDERSTANDINGS

The couples in our study who lacked clarity on *what, when,* and *how* household tasks and responsibilities would be carried out often said that they felt drained and rushed and had difficulty communicating their dissatisfaction in their lives. Spouses who appeared to have a clear and respectful understanding of one another's roles and tasks, in contrast, did not spend as much time negotiating responsibilities; their daily lives seemed to flow more smoothly. For example, in one family, the couple emphasized the importance of establishing a mutual perspective on managing household chores.

INTERVIEWER: How do you divide the chores between you two?

RAYA: He does outside chores, and I do inside chores; that's very clear.

INTERVIEWER: That's how it works?

RAYA: Yeah, very clear distinction. We both have professions, we both are strong minded so we make it clear—this is what you do, this is what I do, and I don't go out and do, you know, his outside chores and he doesn't do the inside chores.

SAM: Like, like, you know, groceries, most of the times I do it. If it's things like—we need to get for the house I do it; things of that nature, but the thing—the way that we do it is if she does it, I don't interfere; if I do it, she doesn't interfere, so you know one person.

(*pause*)

INTERVIEWER: Like, for example, for cooking.

SAM: Then she does it.

INTERVIEWER: And you know that.

SAM: I know that it's clear, it's very clear.

Above Raya explains the need for clarity. "Outside chores" for this couple does not refer to the typical inside/outside distinction of the woman taking on the housework while the husband mows the lawn. The "outside" chores include doing all the shopping and often shepherding the children to various activities. What we ended up observing, however, was that each spouse frequently assisted the other with whatever needed to be done in each domain. On the weekend, for example, Sam cooked a rice and vegetable dish for lunch. The following morning, it was Raya who took the boys to their soccer games. While they appeared to have a clear division of labor, the underlying principle expressed through their actions was that they were a team, working together to keep their lives running smoothly. The frequent use of the second-person plural "we" by both parties indicates the management of the household as a joint project.

In the interview above, Sam's realization that interference is a potential problem—one that can be avoided by a clear and consensual division of labor—is a critical insight. Couples that established a shared understanding of

their respective responsibilities were less likely to monitor and critique each other's behavior. These spouses were also more likely to spontaneously chip in when their partners were sick, away, or otherwise unavailable to carry out a task. These findings upend conventional wisdom about the value of communication between working partners: the *absence* of communication in certain domains may be an indicator of a healthy and efficient partnership in which spouses display mutual respect.

Couples are composed of individuals who coordinate their behaviors in relation to one another. In working families—where both adults work outside the home and raise school-aged children—the challenge of coordinating behaviors to meet family needs is especially great. The emotional tone of family life pivots to a significant degree on the extent to which family members negotiate and enact effective strategies for contending with the numerous tasks encountered in their daily lives. More generally, observing family members as they go about their everyday routines reveals important insights into family dynamics and communication. Although we have noted some salient exceptions here, our global impression is that expectations and roles are not yet clear and that satisfying domestic routines for many working couples have yet to be established.

Among the couples we studied, mutually shared understandings of responsibilities minimized the need for spouses to evaluate and manage one another's task-related behaviors. These understandings enabled partners to fulfill their household duties with the knowledge that established boundaries would be not be crossed. Demands were few, disengagement in the face of demands was unnecessary, and partners were more likely to feel respected for the contributions they made. Conflict was more prevalent when couples had not worked out a clear division of labor in the home and had to renegotiate responsibilities from one day to the next.

Ambiguous models appeared to provide ample opportunity for partners to express displeasure toward one another as they completed their chores, such that various attempts at controlling these exchanges—for example, through requests and avoidance of these requests—revealed the ongoing and occasionally tense negotiation of power and influence between partners.

NOTE

1. Pew Research Center. 2007. "Modern Marriage." Retrieved on March 9, 2019 (http://www.pewsocialtrends.org/2007/07/18/modern-marriage/#fnref-542-1).

AMANDA K. BAUMLE AND D'LANE R. COMPTON

43. LOVE WINS?

Despite the legalization of same-sex marriage, lesbian, gay, bisexual, and transgender (LGBT) couples continue to face a variety of legal obstacles and, based on the current and historical legal and sociopolitical context, may feel distrust of the protective aspect and permanence of marriage equality. Baumle and Compton interviewed 137 LGBT parents, analyzing how parents perceived and experienced the current legal protections for their families. They explain how marriage, in and of itself, may not be the ultimate protective solution for LGBT family rights.

In June 2015, the U.S. Supreme Court rendered its decision in favor of marriage equality, prompting widespread declarations of victory for LGBT couples. The immediate claims of "Love Wins" were quickly followed by a sense of "mission accomplished," powerfully driven home by the shuttering of the grassroots organization, Marriage Equality, in May 2016. Activists have shifted their focus toward other areas of inequality, including discrimination in employment and housing and against the transgender population. In many respects, this transition is both unsurprising and warranted. Access to legal marriage has been a game-changer for LGBT families. Marriage provides easier access to establishing paternity through opportunities such as joint adoption, the marital presumption of paternity in some jurisdictions, and recognition of a legal stepparent. Legal marriage also removes the necessity of consulting with attorneys to draft documents that mimic many of the legal rights of marriage, including rights to make decisions for their child or partner. On a broader scale, the Court's decision has ripple effects that legitimate LGBT families and their legal rights, meaning that favorable outcomes are more likely even when family issues arise outside of legal marriage. Despite these important shifts, treating marriage equality as the catch-all solution for legal obstacles faced by LGBT families is problematic.

Interactions with the law are determined by more than simply the law on the books. Prior experiences with the law and the legal and sociopolitical environment shape the degree of trust people place in the law and legal institutions, including their willingness to engage with the legal system.

In the years leading up to national marriage equality, we interviewed 137 parents across the United States to explore when and how LGBT individuals use the law on behalf of their families. Our sample included men, women, and transgender individuals who became parents through insemination, prior heterosexual relationships, adoption, marriage, and other approaches. We sampled across states we . . . [assessed as] legally positive, legally negative, and legally neutral based on laws and judicial precedents that directly affected LGBT families, including marriage, adoption, second parent adoption, foster, and surrogacy laws. States with protective laws on these topics were coded as positive, and those with laws impinging on rights for LGBT families were coded as negative. States without statutes or judicial precedent on these issues were classified as legally neutral, though these states typically had negative sociopolitical environments. Approximately a third of our sample came from each of these types of legal contexts, with approximately one-third from states that offered same-sex marriage.

We found that a history of LGBT conflict with the legal system has produced, for many, an enduring distrust of the law within their family lives. For some, this distrust manifests in continuing to seek added legal protections outside of marriage. Many of our parents recognized that while marriage may have secured a spousal relationship, it did not necessarily secure parenting rights, particularly for a nonbiological parent. Indeed, one profound impact of marriage equality may be that it provides a false sense of security to some parents about their rights, including their right to make medical or education decisions for their child and their right to custody or visitation. For others, distrust of the law contributes to a rejection of legal relationship recognition as counter to their personal or political interests. Overall, our research indicates that, regardless of whether or not individuals marry, legal issues persist for LGBT families and their children in this post-equality era. . . .

SKEPTICISM ABOUT MARRIAGE

One consequence of the historical conflict between the legal system and LGBT families is the creation of skepticism about the capacity of the law to resolve family issues. This lack of confidence was a common response by our participants to the acquisition of legal rights for their families. For example, Hannah, a partnered White lesbian, lived in a legally neutral state that was sociopolitically hostile. Unlike LGBT individuals in some states, Hannah was able to complete a second-parent adoption of the child that she and her partner, Beth, had together. Despite her legal status as an adoptive parent, Hannah continued to feel nervous about her relationship to her child. She explained: "Honestly, I'm grateful that we live in a state that has second-parent adoption. . . . I feel, though, that if push kind of came to shove, whereby Beth and I separated or something happened, that I could very well lose [our child] or have reduced rights. And this is just the perception that I feel like, even though I am legally the second parent, that because of the state that we live in, the climate that we live in, that my rights could be easily undermined or challenged or extinguished." For Hannah, the availability and use of a legal right was insufficient to create a feeling of security about her

parent–child relationship, to overcome the experience of years of hostility directed toward same-sex couples within her jurisdiction.

This cynicism about the law was echoed by participants across sociopolitical and legal contexts, including those living in states where same-sex marriage was permitted. The idea that legal rights can be easily removed reflects an awareness of the history of antagonism directed toward LGBT families through legislation and by legal actors. Post marriage equality, these fears are reinforced by conflicting messages from the Trump administration regarding LGBT rights, including leaks of potential executive orders that broaden exceptions to marriage and antidiscrimination laws based on religious freedom and the nomination of a conservative justice to the Supreme Court. In addition, support for legal actors, such as county clerks, who refuse to issue marriage licenses or honor legal marriages drives home the tenuous nature of fledgling legal rights—after all, laws and practices often differ. In this environment, it is unsurprising that some LGBT parents would hesitate to rely on marriage as the solution to their family's legal needs.

For many of our participants, distrust about the stability of LGBT-friendly legal decisions resulted in proactive measures to shore up their legal status. In particular, many married couples discussed their decision for the nonbiological parent to complete a second-parent adoption of children born after their marriage. Although the marital presumption of paternity would provide parental rights for a nonbiological parent in a heterosexual relationship, some remained nervous about whether this presumption would translate to same-sex couples.

For example, Johanna is a married White lesbian who resides in a legally neutral state that is sociopolitically hostile to LGBT individuals. As a nonbiological parent, she described her desire to obtain second-parent adoption as based, in part, on a lack of confidence in marriage for conveying parental rights, saying: "I think everybody sort of thinks that their relationship is strong—well, I don't know about everybody, but most people who get married think it is going to be for a long time. And I felt that way, but I still felt that . . . having it legalized would protect me." Her statement that second-parent adoption offered her protection reflects the belief that marriage is insufficient to create an incontrovertible parental right.

Judges have frequently treated nonbiological parents as "not real parents," and there was a great deal of fear voiced by our participants about a biological parent having a superior claim over a child in the event of dissolution. Although legal marriage might provide a foundation for arguing parental rights, nonbiological parents are often unwilling to rely on marriage when it comes to something as important as establishing a legal relationship with their child. Given recent legal decisions that have refused to apply the marital presumption of paternity to same-sex marriages, these fears are not unfounded. It is unsurprising, then, that LGBT individuals continue to feel the need to seek out extra protection outside of marriage for themselves and their families.

For some individuals in our study, having the names of both parents on the birth certificate was viewed as establishing a superior parental claim over a child for the nonbiological parent. Some of our parents viewed this document as more practically important than a marriage certificate for demonstrating family relationships because it is often requested or required for many aspects of family life, including for school enrollments, social security, or passports. Despite the fact that birth certificates are administrative documents that carry less legal weight than adoption or marriage, our participants often treated them as a less contestable form of generating parental rights. After marriage equality, there have been challenges by LGBT individuals to change birth certificate forms and procedures in order to include both partners. In addition, same-sex couples who had children prior to marriage equality have petitioned to retroactively include their partner on the birth certificate. These practices emphasize the suspicion that some LGBT individuals feel about parental rights conferred through marriage and the desire to shore up their legal relationship with their children.

REJECTION OF MARRIAGE

Despite this distrust, some of the legal issues experienced by LGBT parents *can* be resolved through marriage. This assumes, however, both the availability of a partner and a willingness to marry. As voiced by some of our couples, fear of backlash from marriage and rejection of a heteronormative institution can lead LGBT couples to forego the marriage option. This produces challenges if individuals choose to establish marriage-like legal rights through contract or equity principles, and also leaves some individuals without legal parental rights.

Given that employment discrimination based on sexual orientation or gender identity is not prohibited across all states, LGBT individuals who are not open about their sexuality at work expose themselves to termination if they marry. Some of our participants residing in legally negative jurisdictions raised concerns regarding employer backlash related to marriage, and others who chose to marry expressed fear that their marriage would be discovered.

For example, Julia, is a married White lesbian who resides in a legally negative state. She was active in the military when she and her partner married in another state. She was concerned about marrying while "Don't Ask, Don't Tell" was in effect, but explained that they felt they could keep their marriage a secret: "I wanted to change my last name, too, because she has a very unique last name, but I knew I probably couldn't do it then because I didn't know if the military would be able to find out about it or not. But I knew the marriage itself, more than likely, they wouldn't, unless there was some reason for them to go researching, which they probably wouldn't." Although married, the couple was unable to take advantage of many employee marital benefits out of concern that their marriage could result in expulsion from the military. While law and policy has changed surrounding sexuality and military service, LGBT individuals residing in states without employment protection face similar apprehension about the potential fallout of marriage from their employers. These concerns can result in the decision not to marry among those otherwise inclined to do so.

In addition to avoiding marriage over fears of being fired, some LGBT individuals would prefer not to marry. Many of our participants living in jurisdictions with access to marriage indicated that they were strongly opposed to marriage and would prefer to obtain legal or social recognition through other means. Others married despite these sentiments, usually voicing a sense that there were some social benefits of marriage that could not be re-created through other legal mechanisms. Janis and Laura, a White lesbian couple living in a legally positive state, were resistant to marriage, but Janis explained that their political opposition to marriage dwindled when they considered the security that it could bring to their children: "[W]hen gay marriage became legal, we felt that we didn't particularly want to participate in an institution that was normative and hegemonic. . . . Once I was pregnant, we thought—these little girls are going to someday ask us if we're married and they're going to be pretty young when they do that and they're not going to understand our queer critique of the institution of marriage at that age. And what they're really going to be asking is, do you love each other, are you going to stay together? And we want to just be able to say yes, in a way that they would understand."

This story, echoed by other participants in legally positive states, demonstrates that the decision to make use of an available legal right is not always a simple one. For LGBT individuals who have experienced exclusion from legal marriage, the choice to suddenly embrace an institution that they perceive as flawed, discriminatory, and symbolic of gender inequality is often difficult to reconcile. Although some couples begrudgingly choose to marry in order to acquire legal and social benefits for themselves and their children, others do not. They either continue to rely on contractual agreements that mimic, but cannot replicate, legal marital rights, or they forego legal protections altogether.

With the availability of marriage, some worry that LGBT individuals will be *expected* to marry if they wish to obtain legal parental rights; failure to do so could indicate an overt decision not to parent. Indeed, one of our couples residing in a legally positive state described a situation where a judge required them to marry prior to completing a second-parent adoption. Maxine and Allison, a White queer-lesbian couple, had not planned to marry, but chose to do so after their judge indicated that he would not approve Maxine's second-parent adoption of their child unless they were married. As Allison explained, "I'm really curious about what would have happened if we

had had a more experienced lawyer and if we would have tried to fight it. But again, Maxine was very uncomfortable with not having done the adoption so we just did whatever we needed to do to make it go faster. But if I had the time and the money to make political statements, I'm pretty curious about what would have happened."

For couples who would prefer not to marry, the notion that the availability of marriage creates an expectation or requirement for marriage in order to acquire parental rights is fundamentally problematic. Indeed, some recent decisions surrounding parental rights suggest that judges might consider whether a couple takes advantage of legal marriage as evidence of intent to parent a child.

LEGAL CONSCIOUSNESS IN FLUX

Despite the huge gains experienced by LGBT families following marriage equality, changes in formal law do not immediately translate into changes in how people understand or use the law. Changing the legal experiences of LGBT families cannot be accomplished in a single sweeping gesture, but must evolve as part of an interactive process involving formal law, legal actors, individual desires, and the context in which individuals are nested.

This is made evident by our parents' distrust of the permanence of legal rights once they are acquired, which often led to bolstering their legal claims by combining legal and administrative approaches. Lack of confidence in the law is a product of a history of legal attacks on LGBT individuals and their families, and is particularly experienced in states that are more sociopolitically negative toward LGBT individuals. These attacks have persisted post-marriage equality in judges' decisions regarding issues such as the marital presumption of paternity, proposed religious freedom laws that enable discrimination against LGBT individuals, and politicians' calls to reverse the Supreme Court's marriage decision. Consequently, the notion that LGBT individuals would fully embrace marriage equality as the resolution of family legal matters is not realistic. Shifts in legal consciousness will be more gradual and will be responsive to the way that this new legal reality unfolds in the coming years.

In addition, many of our participants emphasized that the marital institution is not fully embraced by all members of the LGBT community. Treating marriage as the primary goal for equality ignores this fact and, as raised by several parents, instead might mandate a heteronormative outcome for LGBT families. The focus on marriage also ignores the legal challenges faced by single LGBT parents. Given that the same-sex marriage debate made salient the tie between marriage and hundreds of legal rights and social privileges, there remains the possibility that evolving LGBT legal consciousness will include a push to reconsider our privileging of the marital institution. The path forward from marriage will reflect the many ways that legal consciousness is affected by events and interactions among actors, further demonstrating it as dynamic and always in flux.

BROOKE JARVIS

44. "WILL THEY TAKE ME, TOO?"

Millions of American children live in "mixed-status" families, where a parent is an undocumented immigrant. As parental deportations increase, families must decide whether to uproot their American children and take them back to a country foreign to them (and possibly unsafe or without educational and financial opportunities that they have here) or to break families up, leaving children in the United States (sometimes with no parents remaining to care for them). In this reading, Jarvis takes us into the lives of some of these families, sharing their levels of desperation (such as signing power of attorney over to citizen strangers) and the psychological and physical impact that parental deportations and the immigration policies that drive them have on children.

Because she didn't know what to tell her children, she tried not to tell them anything. When they asked where their father was, she gave flimsy excuses: Yes, he came home last night, but he left while you were still asleep. He's working late, he's working early, he just stepped out, he'll be back soon. "You just missed him," she found herself repeating.

The strategy worked, for a few days at least, with the youngest three. They were all under five and were used to the world going about its strange business without them. But then there was Kelly. She was eight and sharp-eyed, a good student who preferred English to Spanish and wanted to someday be a doctor, or maybe a gymnast, and who had watched a presidential candidate on television say he wanted to send people back to Mexico, where both of her parents grew up.

Kelly came home from school one day in October last year and demanded to know where her father was. Because his construction job started so early in the morning, Javier was usually the first home. That was part of how he and Kelly's mother, T., fell in love. They boarded in the same house more than a decade ago, when she was 19 and freshly arrived in South Florida, having followed her sister from their small village in southern Mexico. T., who is being identified by her first initial to shield her identity, quit school after sixth grade. She helped her parents plant corn and beans but dreamed of something better for herself and her infant son; she decided to leave him in her mother's care and support him from afar. Javier was from the same region, and because he finished work early, he cooked for her while she was still out in the Florida sun. The food was delicious and tasted like home. Soon they were a couple, and then Kelly was born, and her father, who fainted with anxiety in the birthing room, adored her, and she adored him back.

"He's late from work," T. told her daughter.

But Kelly wasn't having it. Before heading to school that morning, she saw uniformed men come to the door and ask her mother for her father's passport; she heard her mother on the phone, asking what had happened, what to do. "Don't lie to me," Kelly said, and started to cry. "Where did they take him? What did he do?"

By now T. knew. One of her first phone calls was to an immigrant advocate and former refugee named Nora Sándigo, who, in this poor area south of Miami, was the most powerful person in many people's worlds: She knew lawyers, county commissioners, even members of Congress. After T. called her, Sándigo quickly discovered that Javier had been detained by the Department of Homeland Security. T. didn't tell Kelly the details she had learned from Sándigo, or from Javier, when he was finally able to make a brief call. That they arrested him just a few yards away from their home, as he stood waiting for his ride to work. That now he was on the edge of the Everglades, in a gray-and-tan detention center adjacent to a state prison, a half-hour's drive away, a distance that, for T., had suddenly become unbridgeable. "He was arrested," she told Kelly, simply. "We have no papers to be here, like you do."

"Will they take me, too?" Kelly asked. She didn't know what papers her mother was talking about, what this thing was that she had and her parents didn't.

T. didn't tell her daughter the other reason she called Sándigo. Across South Florida, T. knew, undocumented parents of citizen children were preparing for possible deportation by signing power-of-attorney forms that allowed Sándigo to step in should their own parenthood be interrupted by a surprise visit from Immigration and Customs Enforcement, or ICE. If they were taken away, at least Norita, as they called her, could provide stability while the family sorted out what to do; she could also sign forms on their children's behalf at school, or at the hospital, or in federal court.

Sándigo's responsibilities extended to many hundreds of children and were growing all the time. Parents, some of whom had never met her in person, were desperate for any solution. Her qualifications were simple. She was compassionate. She was willing. And, like their children, she was a United States citizen.

For years, T. never felt the need for such an extreme contingency plan. Now she was thinking of adding her own children to Sándigo's list. "Imagine if they detained me too," she said after Javier was gone. She couldn't envision taking her American children with her to Mexico, where she "wouldn't be able to give them education, shoes, clothes," and where they would be separated from their friends and lives and ambitions, from the only home they had ever known. But what would happen if they stayed behind, with no parents left to care for them?

There's a common misconception that having a citizen child—a so-called anchor baby—allows undocumented parents to gain legal status in the United States. In fact, parents of citizen children are deported annually by the tens of thousands, according to ICE's own reports to Congress. Randy Capps, a demographer with the Migration Policy Institute, estimates that as many as a quarter of the people deported from the United States interior (who are counted separately from those deported at a border) are the parents of American children. Though immigration law prioritizes family connections, including legal status for the family members of Americans who petition on their behalf, children are the exception. They cannot, by law, petition for anyone until they turn 21—by which time, of course, they won't need their parents nearly as much.

Families like Kelly's are known as "mixed status"— a reminder that the way we talk about immigration, with clear lines of legality separating groups of people, is often a fantasy. The reality is a world of families with separate legal statuses but intertwined fates. More than four million American children are estimated to have a parent in the country illegally. If deported, those parents face a difficult choice: Take their children to a country they do not know, whose language they may not speak, and one that lacks the security and opportunities they have in the United States; or leave them behind, dividing the family. Courts have regularly responded to the argument that a parent's deportation will deny a child, as one lawyer put it, "the right which she has as an American citizen to continue to reside in the United States," with the counterargument that such children are not, in fact, deprived because they retain the right to stay in their country and the right to live with their parents—just not both at the same time. "That's what I call a choiceless choice," says David B. Thronson, a professor at the Michigan State University College of Law, who helped found the Immigration Law Clinic.

But it's a choice that's familiar to millions of families, including Sándigo's. "I lived that," she said one day when I met her at her office in the suburbs of Miami, a one-story stucco house that serves as the headquarters of the Nora Sándigo Children Foundation. When she was 16, her parents sent her away from Nicaragua to escape the violence of its civil war; her family, she says, was targeted for opposing the Sandinistas.

"I feel like I am one of those kids," she continued, "because I came with the same problem. I had my father and mother, but I was an orphan without them. Separate from their parents, they become orphans, like me." She remembers sobbing as she watched the country of her birth recede from the plane window.

When she left Nicaragua, Sándigo went to Venezuela, then France, "trying to get something legal," and in 1988 finally ended up in the United States, where the organization that helped her settle here offered her a job working with other refugees from Central America and advocating for their asylum. The Nicaraguan Adjustment and Central American Relief Act was passed in 1997. In Miami, she helped other immigrants with paperwork and resettlement matters, like looking for apartments or jobs. She also started a business of small nursing homes, which, along with a plant nursery, helps cover her foundation's bills. She never went back to Nicaragua, not even when her father was dying. He told her to stay in the United States and be safe. It was her country now, he said.

As Sándigo's reputation grew, it became common for strangers in Miami's immigrant communities to seek her out, asking for help; the requests opened Sándigo's eyes to the depth of people's need. She remembers bringing six towels to a woman with five children, who was shocked at the abundance: "So many!" One call, in 2006, was for a new kind of assistance: A Peruvian woman, whom Sándigo had never met, was being held in a detention center, and she wanted to give Sándigo power of attorney to make decisions about her children's care. (Unlike full legal guardianship, which is conferred by a court, power-of-attorney forms don't involve a transfer of parental rights.) Others in the center had warned her that if she didn't do something, she might lose her children to the child welfare system. Sándigo doesn't know why the woman thought of her, but she felt honored, and obligated, by her trust: "When she called, she had the papers signed and notarized already in my name."

The Peruvian woman's children never called on Sándigo, but word of what she had done got out. In 2009, a brother and sister, ages nine and 11, showed up at Sándigo's door with their uncle; their mother, they said, was in detention, and they weren't going to eat until she was released. Sándigo remembers the

oldest, Cecia, now a student at Georgetown University, saying, "We'll stay with you," to which she replied, "But this is an office, baby." Still, she made a place for them. Jerryann, one of Sándigo's two biological daughters, recalled: "You were like, 'Oh, they're going to stay the night.' And then one night became forever." The children moved in — they ended up staying for six years—the case attracted a lot of publicity and soon there was a steady stream of requests. "That gave the perception to the people, probably, that I was accepting the power of attorney from everyone in the same situation," Sándigo said.

Many of the people who contacted Sándigo wanted only a temporary backup, a documented adult whom their kids could call in the moment of crisis to avoid ending up in the child-welfare system. According to an ICE spokeswoman, "ICE is committed to ensuring that the agency's immigration-enforcement activities, including detention and removal, do not unnecessarily disrupt the parental rights of alien parents and legal guardians of minor children." But navigating the immigration and child-welfare systems simultaneously can be difficult. Emily Butera, a senior policy adviser at the Women's Refugee Commission, told me that many parents have come to believe that they will lose their rights automatically: "We've started explicitly saying to people, 'Your children are not the property of the U.S. government.'"

Other parents planned for their children to stay with their undocumented friends or relatives but wanted Sándigo to sign papers or fill official roles that they couldn't. Still others hoped that their children would live with her, maybe for the remainder of their childhoods—something Sándigo wasn't promising and worried that people assumed she was. But still, she never said no. When people came to her looking for help, Sándigo found it impossible to deny them. The numbers grew into the dozens, and then to the hundreds. "We never planned this," Sándigo said one day. "It was planned by nobody. It just came."

After the election of President Trump, who proposed a border wall and tighter enforcement of immigration law, more families than ever began asking for Sándigo's help. Some parents wanted her to be their child's backup guardian, while others simply wanted advice or help understanding what they called *la carta poder*—the power letter. "Hello Señora," one message read in unpunctuated, hurried Spanish. "I live in North Carolina and I live in fear and stress what do I do I have three children and I don't go out and my husband does what can we do." Sándigo, now 52, tried to keep up with all the new requests for help and advice but shook her head at how often she failed. Several times, I saw her taking two calls at once, a cell phone held to each ear.

In April, a volunteer updated Sándigo's spreadsheet of names and, before she had finished, showed Sándigo a number that made her quail. "We are now at 1,089!" she gasped—more than a thousand kids who might call her at any moment to say that their parents were gone and they needed help figuring out what to do. "I don't want to say that," Sándigo said. "It's too much! Too many kids, in the last few months with Mr. Trump. The increase is incredible." The latest count is 1,252.

Sándigo's office is decorated with American and Nicaraguan flags and pictures of her—in neat makeup, her long auburn hair worn loose—meeting various politicians. Beyond the public spaces are two emergency bedrooms, their shelves filled with picture books and SAT prep guides, and a hallway stacked with beans and rice and diapers and condensed milk.

The filing cabinets in her office are filled with photos and birth certificates and power-of-attorney letters. She opened one drawer of one cabinet and began flipping through folders of families, some of whom she still knew and some she'd never met and had only heard from once, in the form of a packet of documents and a note asking for help in case something happened. "If they call me," she said, "I will go immediately." Responsibilities looked back at her: a toddler asleep on a Looney Tunes pillow; an 11-year-old girl in a headband sitting up rod-straight; a chubby boy in a yellow baseball uniform. She pointed to a name in a folder marked "Ramírez," with a Post-it note on the outside: *madre deportada* (2007)." The boy, she said, stayed in the country with his father. He was now an adult and a professional, and after 10 years his mother was able to return.

The chance that many of these children would need her help all at once seemed higher now. In the past, it was unusual for ICE to deport both parents of a child—fathers were more commonly deported—but the immigrants Sándigo knew feared that the rules were changing. The same month that ICE reported that its arrest of noncriminals had doubled under the new administration, a mother of four with no criminal record—someone who in previous years wouldn't have been a priority for enforcement—was deported from Ohio. Sándigo saw the possible future of her charges. She estimates that perhaps a third of the children on her list have already had at least one parent deported. What if there were a sudden wave of children who needed her?

"That could happen anytime," Sándigo's husband, Reymundo Otero, told her one day. "It's for real, you know." Sándigo did know. "I don't have enough time or resources even for the first hundred kids," Sándigo said. "Even for the first 10!"

It was dark when Sándigo pulled up to a small house where Kelly's mother and seven other parents were waiting under a carport with their children. She was running late, as usual; she'd had to wait at the office for a donor. Kelly's mother told her that a number of parents, who got up early to work before the sun became too hot, had already left.

Sándigo began pulling donated clothes out of her minivan. With Sándigo was one of her wards, 16-year-old Ritibh, who was helping unload groceries. He was born in Washington State, but his parents were deported to India when he was nine. They were caught, he said, at a checkpoint while driving him to Disneyland. Though he had moved to India with them, he dreamed of finishing high school in the United States and going to the Naval Academy, so he contacted Sándigo on Facebook and asked her to take him in. He was sure she'd say no, that her famous helpfulness must be a scam. He had now been living with her for nearly eight months, and they had developed an easy rapport; he likes to help with family-support work, which often keeps them up late into the night. That evening, fueled by sugary coffee, they had rushed through a discount grocery store, piling cart after cart with staples. At the checkout, Ritibh practiced his Spanish with the cashier, listing what they had bought: 50 cucumbers, 20 bags of onions, six 20-packs of chicken legs, 20 gallons of milk, 20 loaves of bread and so on. "And one bag of hot Cheetos for myself," he added.

Ritibh kicked a soccer ball with some of the kids as Sándigo caught up with their parents. She wasn't sure, when I asked her, which of the parents had actually entrusted her with their children's care; she would have to check her files. It didn't really matter, she said. The power-of-attorney forms were about the future, and most days it was all she could do to focus on more pressing needs. Kelly's mother confided that she'd been fired from her job the week before, after reporting her supervisor to the police for physical assault. She didn't know how she was going to take care of the kids. . . .

Ever since her husband was detained, T. explained, Kelly had had no energy, no desire to eat. Before, she loved school and did her homework without being asked. But after the detention, she lay motionless on the couch. She didn't want to sleep; when she did sleep, she couldn't make herself get up. Within a week, her teacher called T. to ask what was wrong, saying that Kelly was "not the same student." She was always distracted, either staring at her fingernails or chewing on them. "It's like she's not there," the teacher said. When T. tried to make Kelly eat, she would cry and refuse. She had lost five pounds—a lot when you're supposed to be growing and you weigh only 45 pounds to begin with.

T. was sure Kelly was sick. She took her to a pediatrician, but there was nothing physically wrong. "Why have you changed so much?" she begged her child one day as they sat at the round wooden table squeezed between the couch and the kitchen, which she'd painted teal and pink in an effort at cheerfulness. "Did something happen to you? Was it at school? Trust me, tell me."

"I want my dad," Kelly answered. "I need him with me. Why did they take him?"

T. hadn't considered that her husband's absence alone could change her daughter so profoundly. It was hard on everyone, of course; even the younger kids had caught on enough to say, "*Mami*, they're going to take you too!" whenever they saw a police car. T. couldn't visit Javier in detention—"I couldn't go and put myself in the mouth of the wolf!"—but his children, as citizens, went twice with family friends. When T. asked them how it went, Kelly refused to say a word. Ana, who was five and the next oldest, said: "Kelly cried, my little sister cried, I cried a little. He's wearing orange pants and a shirt. My *papi* cried, too." When it was time to go, the woman who accompanied them had to drag the girls away.

Luis H. Zayas, a psychologist and the dean of the University of Texas at Austin School of Social Work, has examined many citizen children of undocumented parents, whom he refers to as "forgotten citizens," a new generation of American exiles and orphans. The first to arouse his interest in the issue hadn't spoken at school in some 15 months, so great was her fear of revealing her parents' status. He calls what he sees "psychological erosion": clinical levels of depression, separation anxiety, and low self-esteem. As Joanna Dreby, a sociologist at the University at Albany, writes, even "the threat of deportability" can be devastating, plunging children into a state of constant dread and hypervigilance.

T. herself was afraid. Driving was a huge risk given that she had no license and that a misdemeanor could get her deported ("If you go out to work, you risk everything," she said), but she began taking Kelly across the county twice a week to see a psychologist. She didn't know what else to do for her daughter. "For her—her world, I don't know, it ended."

By the time Ritibh and Sándigo finished handing out supplies, it was 11 p.m., but Sándigo didn't go to sleep. Late nights and early mornings are her time for writing, for trying to think strategically. For years, she had been pushing the county to provide crisis housing for kids she calls "the orphans of immigration," and a Miami-Dade County commissioner recently agreed to help. Sándigo was now trying to raise money for a dorm-style building, but she worried that it wouldn't be ready quickly enough. To speed things up, she was looking into trailers. If it came to it, she said, there was always her own house and office. "Maybe we will be sleeping like, how do you say, *perros calientes*?" Like hot dogs.

Before Trump was elected, Sándigo dreamed of a political solution for her young charges that went far beyond housing. In April 2016, she took some of them, including T. and her daughters, to Washington to advocate for an Obama order known as Deferred Action for Parents of Americans (DAPA), a kind of sister action to Deferred Action for Childhood Arrivals

(DACA) that would have allowed parents to apply for work permits and temporary protection from deportation in order to care for their kids. Thanks to a lawsuit and a split Supreme Court, DAPA never went into effect, and this June the Trump administration officially rescinded it.

In U.S. family law, "the best interests of the child" is a widely accepted standard. Judges are required to use it in every state when deciding custody cases, and dozens of states explicitly list the maintenance of family unity or family emotional ties as primary components of "best interests." Immigration law is the exception. Children affected by their parents' immigration cases "have no opportunity for their best interests to be considered," writes Bridgette A. Carr, founding director of the University of Michigan Law School's Human Trafficking Clinic. The closest option, before 1996, was that immigrants living in the United States for at least seven years could petition to cancel their removal on the grounds that it would cause "extreme hardship" for themselves, their children, or other qualifying relatives. Acceptable reasons included war in the home country or serious medical needs. Hardships like being separated from your parents or having to leave your country usually didn't count, explains Thronson, of the Immigration Law Clinic, because "that always happens in deportation — that's just your starting point."

In the immigration overhaul of the mid-1990s, Congress made the standard even harder to meet, changing "extreme hardship" to "exceptional and extremely unusual hardship" and imposing a limit of 4,000 cases a year. Alfonso Oviedo-Reyes, a lawyer who works with Sándigo, says he's lucky if one client qualifies a year. "They should have said a nearly impossible hardship," he said. "No one can withstand it!"

"Generally speaking, under the law," says Donald L. Schlemmer, an attorney specializing in immigration law, "if there's some kind of wrong, there should be some kind of remedy—or at least you should have your day in court." But the Illegal Immigration Reform and Immigrant Responsibility Act, the same 1996 law that raised the standard for deportation relief, made it much more difficult to use class-action lawsuits to challenge immigration policies. When Sándigo tried

filing a lawsuit in federal circuit court in 2007, on which Schlemmer worked, they were told that only the Supreme Court had jurisdiction to hear such cases; when she brought the case to the Supreme Court, the clerk replied with a letter explaining that there was no jurisdiction there either. Oviedo-Reyes says that letter is their chance: proof that citizen children, unconstitutionally, have nowhere to go for redress.

Since Trump's election, Sándigo has been combing through her list of children to see which would be good candidates for a class-action lawsuit—something that might lead to the kind of law that helped the Central American refugees she worked with. . . . Valerie was counting on being reunited with her parents through DAPA. When it failed, she says, "all my hopes went down. I just started to cry. It was bad." Like other children in her situation, she has only one legal avenue: wait until she's not a child anymore, and then, when she has fewer needs but more rights, try to sponsor her parents for green cards. To get her parents back, Valerie says, "I have to wait until I'm 21."

On a Sunday in June, T. took her children to Sándigo's office to sign papers. Some were permission forms; Sándigo was about to take the kids on another advocacy trip to Washington. The other papers were power-of-attorney forms. T. had decided she was ready to sign. A notary arrived, and T. sat down next to him at Sándigo's desk. *"Tu nombre y appellido?"* he asked her, and she spelled her name. . . .

Kelly was more animated than she had been a few months before. The psychologist had played games with her and explained, as Kelly put it: "I need to get better so I can have more energy. I need to eat food so I can't be dead." But what helped the most, T. thought, was when Javier was released from detention to return to Mexico. From there, he could at least talk to her on the phone every day. Still, things were hardly back to normal; Kelly had just failed the school year. She looked over at her mother signing the papers. "Each day I get sadder and sadder," she said quietly. "But I don't want to tell my mom because she could get worried about me." The notary stamped the paper that showed how worried her mother already was. *"Quién falta?"* he asked, looking around. "Who's next?"

Another family stepped forward: a couple and their three American sons, ages three, 10, and 11. . . . The family took their turn with the notary, then stuck around to eat cake and sing "Happy Birthday" to Matthew, who was turning 15 that day, far from his parents. "It's already my second birthday without them," he said. He misses them the most, he said, when he scores a goal at a soccer game. "He sees friends with their parents, all the social media posts with parents," explained Valerie, in braces and pastel-blue fingernail polish. "Sometimes he asks me, 'Why can't we be with them?' And I'm like, 'I don't know, you're asking the wrong person.'" Valerie's phone rang; it was their mother, asking how the birthday was going. Valerie estimated it was the 10th call of the day from her. During the school year, the first ring always comes at 6 a.m., a long-distance version of the wake-ups that used to happen in person.

Two days later, nine adults and 36 children gathered at Sándigo's house to pack into three rented vans for the 18-hour drive to Washington. T. tried to find space under a seat for a stroller—she was bringing all four daughters—while Sándigo stood in front of local news cameras, speaking in Spanish. "How can they be American citizens if in their own country they're treated so harshly?" she asked.

Kelly wandered into the frame, and Sándigo pointed to her: "Her father was deported," she said.

"It's very hard." Kelly noticed the cameras turning to her and darted away. "We hope they'll listen to these American children," T.'s sister told Telemundo. Finally, space was found for all the diaper bags and suitcases and gallons of frozen milk. The kids lined up for a group photo around an American flag. The plan was to drive through the night, a challenge with so few licensable drivers among the adults. The vans pulled out past a small lineup of news cameras. A few minutes later, they were back. Sándigo had gotten a call from the only English-language station to respond to her news release: The cameraman was running late. Sándigo agreed to redo the exit scene. "For us, the English news is the most important," she said. Its viewers were the ones whom she most wanted to hear from the children, their fellow citizens.

Kelly and the others dutifully spilled out of the van into the sunshine. Valerie, in her native, teenage English, told the new camera the same things she'd told the others in Spanish: about missing her parents, about how hard it was. She was proud that she'd finally learned to talk about them without crying. Then the children all climbed back inside for another try at reaching their nation's capital. The cameraman stood in the empty street for a long time, watching them disappear.

TIM STELLOH

45. FIGHTING BACK

Despite the development of a successful movement to support victims of domestic violence, the number of domestic violence homicides remains high. Police officers often discount the risk that male partners and ex-partners pose to women, and many strategies used by law enforcement to intervene in domestic violence cases are inadequate. Stelloh examines Maryland's success reducing their domestic violence homicide rate by 40 percent, largely by training officers to use a particular set of screening questions called the "lethality screen." The screen allows officers to effectively assess the risk of homicide, allowing them to act more effectively and to communicate this increased risk to the victim.

Jo'Anna Bird arrived at her family's two-story, wood-frame house at about 11 p.m. on a winter night three years ago. The house sits on a quiet street in one of the poorer corners of one of America's richest counties: New Cassel, in Nassau, on Western Long Island. Bird, 24, was a mother of two who often wore her long brown hair in a ponytail. She had worked as a school bus monitor, a medical assistant, a Walmart cashier, a supervisor at BJ's Wholesale Club, and she now hoped to be a corrections officer. She had come to stay with her mother and stepfather because the possessiveness of her ex-boyfriend—the father of her young son—had evolved into something much more frightening, and she did not want to be alone.

Leonardo Valdez-Cruz, known to most as "Pito," waited for Bird that night behind a row of hedges in the front yard. After she parked, he appeared and said he wanted to talk. Bird refused, went into the house, and locked the front door. "We assumed he left. We all went to bed," says Sharon Dorsett, Bird's mother. "The next thing we heard was her screaming." Valdez-Cruz had broken in through the basement and tried to smother Bird, who was lying on a couch in the living room watching television, Dorsett told me. When he dashed to the kitchen and grabbed a steak knife,

Bird ran to her nephew's room. Bird's stepfather told Valdez-Cruz to leave, which he did. A short time later, Valdez-Cruz tried climbing in through a bedroom window, but Bird's nephew threatened to stab the intruder with a fork. Next, Valdez-Cruz tried squeezing in the bathroom window, but he couldn't fit, although his baseball cap toppled into the tub. Bird's stepfather called the police.

The two officers arrived sometime after midnight. As the family crowded into the living room to explain what had happened, Valdez-Cruz returned to the house and casually knocked on the front door. One of the officers let him in. Bird had two protection orders against Valdez-Cruz, but the police did not arrest him. "They said, 'Pito, get out of here, go take a walk somewhere,'" Dorsett says. It was a response that was by now familiar to Bird. "He's going to kill me," Dorsett recalls her daughter saying. "I'm going to die."

A couple of months later, on the afternoon of March 19, 2009, Jo'Anna Bird's body was in the back of a Nassau County Police ambulance. Her outstretched hand dangled off the side of a stretcher; her blood-streaked face tilted to the left. A gland ballooned from her neck, which had been sliced from ear to ear. As the investigator filming the area moved from the ambulance into Bird's spartan two-bedroom apartment, the evidence of a brutal struggle and its aftermath was everywhere: a clump of hair in the front yard; pools of blood in the stairwell; a knocked-out screen in the window. Bird had been tortured and left bleeding to death inside her apartment. According to the autopsy, she had suffered blunt force trauma to the torso and head, and her trachea, esophagus, and jugular had been perforated.

By the following year, Valdez-Cruz had been convicted of Bird's murder and given a life sentence. Dorsett believed her daughter's death had been preventable, so she sued Nassau County in federal court. Her case cast the police department and other government officials as completely ineffective. Even as Bird lay dying, Dorsett's lawsuit claimed, police officers who had been called to her apartment did nothing; one dismissed the call as "the Pito thing again." Eventually, Nassau County settled with Dorsett for $7.7 million. The police commissioner said that seven officers were found to have improperly handled Bird's calls. But, earlier this year, after reading a secret internal affairs report detailing Bird's death, a member of the legislature told a local TV station that 22 officers "ought to be ashamed to look at themselves in the mirror every morning when they get up to shave—much less be wearing the badge."

In recent decades, one of the great grassroots movements of the twentieth century built a raft of protections designed to help abused women. These included a sprawling network of community shelters, gun restrictions for abusers, protection orders, and the nation's first federal anti-domestic violence legislation, the Violence against Women Act (VAWA). Yet, despite this sustained effort—and even as overall homicides have plummeted nationwide—victims of domestic violence like Jo'Anna Bird are today killed in basically the same numbers as they were about 15 years ago. Between 40 and 50 percent of female homicide victims are killed by their husbands, boyfriends, and exes. And, for about half of these victims, police had been alerted to previous incidents of abuse.

There is, however, one exception to this grim trend: Maryland. Since 2007, domestic violence homicides in the state have fallen by a stunning 40 percent. What is Maryland doing that other states are not? The

answer appears to lie with a former high school nurse, an ex-Washington, D.C., police lieutenant, and their ground-breaking efforts to protect the most vulnerable victims of abuse.

In a recent afternoon, Jacquelyn Campbell, a professor of nursing at Johns Hopkins University, stood at the foot of a large, sloped lecture hall at Quinnipiac University's law school, just outside New Haven, Connecticut. Peering down at her were more than 150 police officers, advocates, lawyers, and social workers. Campbell, who is 65, and has wavy, reddish-brown hair, spends much of her time traveling the country, explaining tools to help predict domestic violence—tools which she has spent much of her career developing. In her personable, matter-of-fact manner, she moved through a PowerPoint presentation, illuminating numbers and graphs with harrowing anecdotes. At one point, she recalled the response of a man from Baltimore who admitted to police that he had strangled his wife to death. "You have to understand: I didn't mean to kill her," the man said, according to Campbell. "I've done this a bunch of times before and she never died."

Campbell has been researching domestic violence since the late 1970s, when she was pursuing a master's degree in nursing at Wright State University in Dayton, Ohio. A former high school nurse, she had moved into community health work and wanted to know why so many young Black women in the area were being murdered. For her thesis, Campbell spent a year digging through case files with the local homicide unit. She was shocked to find that most of the women had been killed by their husbands, boyfriends, and exes. In one case, police had been called to a home 54 times before the woman was killed. Then, her research took on a personal significance: The mother of Campbell's own goddaughter was stabbed to death by her boyfriend, a charming man whom Campbell had never suspected of abuse. "It was one of those incredibly horrible tragic things that made me all the more committed to doing something about it," she says.

Back then, there was little awareness of domestic violence. There was no such thing as a protection order or a mandatory arrest. It was the era of "The Burning Bed," the infamous case of Francine Hughes, a Michigan housewife who, after suffering years of abuse, waited until her husband was asleep one night, then doused him with gasoline and set him ablaze. At the time, nearly as many men died from domestic violence as women—about 2,100 women and 1,600 men in 1976, according to Campbell, who provided the statistics for this story. (Campbell uses Department of Justice and FBI statistics on domestic violence homicides, but includes women murdered by their ex-boyfriends, a category often left out of final reports.) About three-quarters of the men were, like Hughes's husband, both victim and abuser.

In 1980, Campbell moved to Detroit, where she began teaching at Wayne State University and volunteering at a shelter. When women would tell her their stories, she was reminded of the homicides she had studied in Dayton. These women had been choked and raped, punched while they were pregnant, threatened with murder. Campbell gave the women calendars so they could mark the days that they had been abused. And she developed a 15-item questionnaire, which she called a "danger assessment," that nurses, advocates, and others who dealt with abused women could use to determine if someone was high-risk.

A few years after moving to Johns Hopkins in 1993, Campbell and a team of researchers began studying domestic violence murders in Maryland. Their work, which was published in 2002, sought to identify the key indicators that predicted whether a case of domestic violence was likely to become a domestic homicide. The study produced some surprisingly precise findings. If a man had a history of hitting his partner, that in itself was a predictor of murder. But certain kinds of behavior came with even higher chances of death. For instance, if a man choked his partner, she was five times more likely to be killed by him at some point. If he was unemployed, he was four times more likely to kill her. The researchers also found that only four percent of homicide victims had ever sought help from a shelter; in a follow-up study, they found that a stay in a safehouse decreased the risk of violent re-assault by 60 percent. Their findings offered new ways to measure risk. "It also informed the system about which cases needed heightened scrutiny," says Campbell.

After Campbell's work was published, she was contacted by David Sargent, a former lieutenant in the Metropolitan Police Department in Washington, D.C. Sargent is the law enforcement coordinator with the Maryland Network against Domestic Violence, and, during the '90s, he had developed a training course for police officers to help them respond to domestic abuse calls. But that seemed to have little effect on intimate partner murders, and the "referral"—the standard police approach of giving victims a shelter hotline phone number—seemed too passive to do much good.

Indeed, it was clear that the prevailing methods of dealing with domestic violence were inadequate. There had been a slight dip in domestic violence murders in the '90s following the passage of VAWA (which funded anti-domestic violence training and services) and the Brady Law (which required gun dealers to run background checks). But, since then, the number of women killed each year by their partners and exes has hovered around 1,600—that is, only about 500 fewer deaths per year than in 1976. For men, however, domestic homicides have declined from about 1,600 to 600. In other words, all the increased protections for women, the infrastructure of shelters and hotlines, had done a better job of protecting abusers rather than their victims.

In 2003, Sargent, Campbell, and 15 other academics, lawyers, and law enforcement officials met at the Maryland Network's offices in Bowie. There, they began the first of two years of discussions on how to translate Campbell's danger assessment into an easy-to-use field tool for first-responders. At one point, Michael Cogan, a prosecutor from Anne Arundel County, told the group, "If we do this, this is going to represent a paradigm shift in the way we work with victims."

By the end of 2005, the group had developed a series of questions that they called "the screen." The first three questions concerned the most important predictors of future homicide: Has the abuser used a weapon against you? Has he threatened to kill you? Do you think he might kill you? If the woman answered yes to any of those questions, she "screened in." If she answered no, but yes to four of the remaining eight questions, again, she was in. Among these were other, less obvious indicators of fatal violence:

Has he ever tried to kill himself? Does she have a child that he knows isn't his?

The officer would then present her with an assessment: Others in your circumstances have been killed; help is available if you want it. If the woman agreed, an officer would dial the local shelter from a police cell phone (to prevent the abuser from finding out about the call) and hand it over.

The screen's first taker was the Sheriff's Office in Kent County, a rural, lightly populated region on Maryland's Eastern Shore. "They don't have drug problems. They don't have gang problems," Sargent told me. "They do have domestic violence. And, when they have homicides, they're domestic violence homicides."

Today, the screen is used by nearly all of the state's police departments. More than 3,000 women have sought help with everything from filing protection orders to counseling. Proponents are careful to say it is not the only solution to stopping domestic violence murders and that it is impossible to determine precisely why Maryland's domestic homicide rate has fallen. Still, Juley Fulcher, director of policy programs at Break the Cycle, an anti-domestic violence organization, told me that Maryland's 40 percent drop in intimate partner murders is "incredible." Scott Shepardson, a veteran officer in Frederick, Maryland, observed that, for years, he had watched victims of repeated abuse fill out incident forms seemingly out of routine, paying little attention to the injuries they were describing. "They're so used to it," Shepardson says. The process of answering the screening questions enabled them to see the seriousness of the violence in a new light. "It's changed to, 'Oh my God—he *did* try to kill me.'"

Christine considered herself a well-informed, responsible adult. She had a degree in psychology and had bought a house when she was 24. Two years later, she got married. The abuse wasn't that bad at first. But as it got worse, it became harder to leave. Christine and her husband had a son and a daughter. They lived in a nice home in a quiet neighborhood. "By that time, you're in it," says Christine, whose name I've changed to protect her identity.

Once, while she was eating at the dinner table, her husband jammed her bean burrito from Taco Bell into her mouth and up her nose, then held it there. "It was suffocation by burrito," she says. (Christine called the police; he disputed her claims and was not arrested.) In a petition to the court, she wrote, "He has stalked me, threatened to cap my ass, knock my teeth in, kill me, rape me, etc." After her husband moved out for a brief time, Christine told me that he called her and said he was going to slice her throat and watch her bleed. She called the police and sought a protection order. However, he was not arrested and the order was denied for insufficient evidence.

One Friday night two years ago, Christine was outside talking to a neighbor, enjoying a beer. This didn't sit right with her husband, who left for a bar, she told me. Later that night, after he stumbled into the house, Christine heard what sounded like a dresser drawer being emptied—the rustling of papers, the clinking of drill bits and coins. She panicked. "It clicked in my head what he was doing," she recalls. "He was searching for bullets."

Christine is about five and a half feet tall and 130 pounds. Her husband is over six feet and pushing 270. Though Christine didn't have much of a plan, she raced upstairs—all she knew was that she needed to "make it stop," she says. There, in the bedroom, they struggled for his loaded .357 revolver. Christine grabbed the gun, trying to jerk it free. "Somehow, I got between him and it," she says. "I got it in my hand and spun." She doubled over on the bed, with him on top of her, still hanging on. Christine eventually wrestled the revolver away and things calmed down for a few hours. But the next morning, as she was preparing to go to a softball match with their daughter, he threw her over the living room couch, then pushed her into the bathroom. Christine called the police.

After the officers arrived, they asked her questions that she doesn't remember. They put her on the phone with someone at the local shelter, but today, most of the details of that conversation escape her, too. By Monday, she had a lawyer and an advocate who had been provided by the shelter. She was at the courthouse seeking a protection order—something she thought she would never do again.

Over the next year and a half, her advocate was there if she had to go to the sheriff's office, if she had to go to court, or if she panicked about her husband. The protection order came through. Then came the next step: divorce. "There were many times when she wanted to give up," her advocate told me. "I said, 'No.' I said, 'It's not worth it.'" By October of last year, it was over: Christine and her husband were legally divorced. "If that police officer hadn't handed me that phone," she told me, "I probably would have washed it under the best that I could."

The lethality screen has now been adopted by law enforcement agencies in 14 states, from Barre City, Vermont, to Kansas City, Missouri. Nurses use it in emergency rooms, as do case workers from children's services departments. Since the Washington D.C. police department introduced a variation of the screen in 2009, domestic violence homicides have been cut in half, according to Elisabeth Olds, co-executive director at SAFE, an advocacy group. As for other states, there has been no equivalent of the 40 percent decline in homicides that occurred in Maryland, Sargent told me, but it is too soon to expect such dramatic results. In 2008, a Harvard competition named the Lethality Assessment Program one of the country's 50 best innovations in government.

Yet, as simple as the screen is, it requires increased funding. Training police to use the questionnaire is financially negligible, Sargent told me—the process takes less than an hour. But, if the screen leads to more victims seeking legal help, counseling, or refuge, that means greater costs for the places that provide those services.

When the Kansas City Police Department introduced the screen in 2009, a local shelter, the Rose Brooks Center, had anticipated less than a half-dozen new calls every week to its hotline. "From day one, we were getting four to six [more] calls a day," says Susan Miller, the center's CEO. The number of people staying at the shelter rose from about 70 nightly to an average of 90; cots were added to conference rooms and offices. In the first year that the screen was in use, the center turned away 2,300 people seeking shelter. In 2011, it turned away 4,178. At the same time, the center has seen cutbacks in state and federal funding and has launched a $2 million emergency fund-raising drive to build a new wing containing 25 additional beds.

The future of the lethality assessment is now caught up, like so much else, in the ongoing ideological war over government spending. Every five years, VAWA—which acts, among other things, as a funding mechanism for domestic violence shelters and training programs—must be reauthorized, a process that allows lawmakers to refocus how the money is spent based on new developments in the field. . . . For high-risk women, [funding for] such a program could mean the difference between life and death—between ending up like Jo'Anna Bird or ending up like Christine. [*Editor's Note*: VAWA was last renewed in 2013, after a political battle because "some Republicans took issue with provisions that offered new protections for Native women and lesbian, gay, bisexual, and transgender people" (Gathright 2018). VAWA expired in December 2018 due to the government shutdown over President Trump's demands to fund a border wall. Activists would like to see VAWA permanently reauthorized.[1]]

These days, Christine is trying her best to create some semblance of normality. She has a few key rules that she follows to keep herself safe. She only answers phone calls from numbers she recognizes. She tries to avoid places her ex might be. But, in the six months since her divorce was finalized, she has found something she hasn't known in a long time: "Relief," she wrote to me in a text message. "With the ability to breathe." [*Editor's Note*: In April 2018, the Department of Justice's Office on Violence Against Women significantly changed the definition of domestic violence. The new Trump administration discarded the broader definition used during the Obama administration that included behaviors that "encompass the dynamics of power and control. . ." including emotional, psychological, or economic abuse. and stated that only behaviors that constitute a misdemeanor or a felony may be called "domestic violence." This change fails to acknowledge how domestic violence often begins with emotional abuse and escalates to violence, which advocates say may negatively impact awareness of this cycle.[2]].

NOTES

1. Gathright, Jenny. 2018. "Violence Against Women Act Expires Because of Government Shutdown." *National Public Radio*, December 24. Retrieved on March 11, 2019 (https://www.npr.org/2018/12/24/679838115/violence-against-women-act-expires-because-of-government-shutdown).

2. Nanasi, Natalie. 2019. "The Trump Administration Quietly Changed the Definition of Domestic Violence and We Have No Idea What For." *Slate.com*, January 21. Retrieved on March 11, 2019 (https://slate.com/news-and-politics/2019/01/trump-domestic-violence-definition-change.html).

CHAPTER 10

SOCIAL PROBLEMS RELATED TO HEALTH AND THE HEALTH CARE SYSTEM

It can be challenging to see health problems as social problems, since they impact individual people and are often attributed to individuals' good and bad choices. But when viewed through a sociological lens, issues related to health—our access to health care, the likelihood that we will experience a health crisis or addiction in our lives, and our general level of health and disease—are shaped by our social environment and institutions, and not just our individual choices.

In "They've Got a Pill for That: The Medicalization of Society," Stephanie Medley-Rath outlines the ways in which behaviors that used to be defined as normal are increasingly falling under the purview of medical professionals, to be treated and managed through the lens of a "medical problem." This process begins with claims makers—for example, pharmaceutical companies advertising directly to consumers—positioning a condition as a medical problem that is in need of intervention, including testing, diagnosis, and treatment. The problem, Medley-Rath points out, is that medicalization results in the narrowing of what is considered "normal," can have serious harmful side effects for patients, is economically and psychologically costly, and focuses attention on treatment of the individual rather than of harmful social conditions that may have created the problem in the first place. It is important to consider these costs to individuals and society whenever we seek a medical answer to a problem.

One consequence of medicalization is that we increase our interactions with the medical system; this comes at a steep economic price. As Elisabeth Rosenthal points out, the United States is one of the most expensive health care systems in the world, regardless of whether you compare the U.S. system to private or national health care systems in other countries. This isn't necessarily because of special drugs or procedures that are exorbitantly expensive, but the high price of routine, everyday procedures like colonoscopies. By examining the case of the colonoscopy—a routine procedure once conducted in a doctor's office that has transitioned to one that is now typically performed at a surgical center, attended by anesthesiologists—Rosenthal demonstrates that the rising costs of American health care do not necessarily result in better care or health outcomes, but do yield enormous profits for the health care industry.

One area of the health care industry where profit is concentrated is in hands of large pharmaceutical corporations. Nicknamed "Big Pharma," large pharmaceutical companies have sizeable control over the medical industry and our individual lives, in part because of their ability to set prices on medications and the incredible profits they generate (and its accompanying power). Rose Weitz warns us that Big Pharma's quest for immense profit puts patients at risk, as medicines may not be properly tested or may be unaffordable for patients. One example of Big Pharma prioritizing profit over safety can be seen in the role Purdue Pharma played in the current opioid crisis. In an effort to sell more OxyContin, Purdue Pharma marketed heavily to physicians, increasing prescriptions, all while downplaying the risks of addiction and potential abuse. Purdue Pharma generated billions of dollars while hundreds of thousands of people were dying from opioid overdoses.[1] Recent research demonstrates that counties that had heavier direct-to-physician marketing of opioids had higher overdose mortality rates a year later.[2] In "The Addicts Next Door," Margaret Talbot demonstrates the effect of the opioid crisis on the lives of a group of West Virginians, residents of a state disproportionately suffering from the crisis.

The opioid crisis is considered unique in that it disproportionately affects White Americans, possibly because of their access to prescription medications and also bias among physicians who do not take the pain of people of color as seriously.[3] Readings in this chapter explore the ways in which systems of oppression can intersect, resulting in unequal access to medical care and treatment, looking specifically at the cases of African American women, low-income White women, and immigrants. Linda Villarosa documents the high infant and maternal mortality rates of Black women, with Black infants more than two times as likely to die as White infants, and Black mothers more than three to four times as likely to die as White mothers from pregnancy-related causes. She explores the efficacy of different interventions, including innovative doula programs. While race and gender play a role in health disparities, social class contributes as well. Monica Potts explores why life expectancy for poor, undereducated White women has dropped dramatically. Potts discusses cultural and structural issues as well as less tangible factors that may be contributing to their early

1   Meier, Barry. 2019. "Sacklers Directed Efforts to Mislead Public about OxyContin, Court Filing Claims." *The New York Times*, January 15; Walters, Joanna. 2019. "Sackler Family behind OxyContin Made $4bn Amid Opioid Crisis, Filings Claim." *The Guardian*, February 1.

2   Hadland, Scott E., Ariadne Rivera-Aguirre, Brandon D. L. Marshall, and Magdalena Cerdá. 2019. "Association of Pharmaceutical Industry Marketing of Opioid Products with Mortality from Opioid-Related Overdoses." *JAMA Network Open*2(1):e186007.

3   National Public Radio. 2017. "Why Is the Opioid Epidemic Overwhelmingly White?" *NPR.Org*. Retrieved March 20, 2019, from https://www.npr.org/2017/11/04/562137082/why-is-the-opioid-epidemic-overwhelmingly-white.

deaths. Lack of access to medical care, racism, sexism, and desperation associated with poverty, and the impact of stigmatization of one's identity may all contribute to health disparities. Brittany N. Morey describes how xenophobia and resulting stigmatization affect the health of our immigrant population. In combination with lack of access, she describes how recent anti-immigrant sentiment risks harming their immigrants' psychological and physical health. Otis Webb Brawley's and Paul Goldberg's "How We Do Harm" explains how race and social class affect the health of patients, focusing, in particular, on women's experiences of and risk for breast cancer.

We all interact with the for-profit health care and medical system at some point in our lives. With increased medical intervention, it is important to develop a critical lens to view its role and question why medical care in the United States is so much more expensive, but lower in quality, than medical care in other Western nations and why disempowered populations suffer from poor care in this system.

ACTIVIST INTERVIEW

ELBA L. SAAVEDRA

Elba L. Saavedra, PhD, is the director of the Comadre a Comadre program, University of New Mexico, College of Education, Department of Health, Exercise & Sports Sciences, Health Education program.

What are the history and mission of the Comadre a Comadre [Friend to Friend] program?

I co-created the Comadre a Comadre program along with six Hispanic/Latina breast cancer survivors in 2003. Our mission is to empower the lives of Hispanic/Latina women and their loved ones through advocacy, education, information, resources, and support about breast health and breast cancer. In the Hispanic/Latina community, a *comadre* is a close and supportive female friend; this bond can be as strong as family. The Comadre program integrates traditional Hispanic/Latino cultural values such as the importance of family and spirituality as part of a community-based culturally and linguistically competent intervention. We offer patient navigation, peer support, and case management to assist Hispanic/Latina woman who have been diagnosed with breast cancer, need free or low-cost mammograms, or need assistance with medical appointments. We do this through a racially and ethnically diverse network of breast cancer survivors who are culturally and linguistically competent to provide support to women and their loved ones during a time of great stress. The Comadre program is rooted in the principles of *community-based participatory research*

methodology. We emphasize shared decision-making processes, seeking input from peer survivors, staff, and students alike.

What are your main duties as a program director?

My duties as director involve a variety of administrative functions overseeing the day-to-day activities of the Comadre program. This includes monitoring our program's implementation, goals, and objectives and ensuring that we are accomplishing them in a timely fashion. I also prepare grant applications and conduct analysis on data collected through the program. I use the analysis to write reports on program outcomes to our funding sponsors. I also oversee staff meetings and volunteer training, and I provide mentorship for student interns who conduct their practicum with our Comadre Program.

Why is there a need to reach out to Latinas, in particular?

As an ethnic group, Hispanic/Latina women have lower rates of mammography utilization. When they receive abnormal screening results or discover breast abnormalities on their own, their follow-up care is more likely to be delayed, negatively affecting their health outcomes. Hispanic women are also more likely to be diagnosed with the types of tumors that are more difficult to treat. Yet even when their age, stage of cancer, and tumor characteristics are similar, Hispanic women are still more likely to die from breast cancer compared to non-Hispanic White women. What contributes to these disparities in outcomes? Researchers point to differences in access to health care (both prevention and treatment). Intervention programs, like ours, that follow patients throughout treatment in order to enhance communication between the surgeon, oncologist, and patient have been shown to reduce disparities in breast cancer care.[1]

How did you first become interested in advocating for underserved populations in the area of health?

I arrived from Puerto Rico when I was five years old, speaking only Spanish and later becoming the interpreter for my parents. Six years later, I experienced the devastating loss of my father to medical negligence at a local county hospital. Still etched in my mind is the horror I felt watching my mother grabbing the physician's necktie and shaking him, yelling, "You killed my husband!" in her broken English as he broke the news to her. The death of my father changed my life forever, as I came to realize the role that injustice would play in my life. I was awakened to the realities of our lives as Puerto Ricans in New York and in the United States.

Later, at 17 years old, I became involved in community activism, wanting to change the living conditions in my South Bronx, New York City, neighborhood. I took part in beautification projects (like cleaning up a dilapidated empty lot, where children played amidst broken glass, adorning a nearby wall with a freshly painted mural) and tenant and block organizing (helping push slumlords to make housing repairs). At 19 years old, I moved away from home and worked at a shoe factory where I encountered poor safety practices. I led efforts to unionize workers at the factory. These experiences drove me to be an agent of change, seeking improvements especially in the area of health care access to good patient care for Hispanic/Latinas with breast cancer.

I know first-hand what it feels like to be overwhelmed with decisions about treatment. I also know first-hand the importance of advocacy. For this reason, Comadre a Comadre's mission is deeply personal. Not only did I experience the devastating loss of my father through medical negligence, perhaps due to lack of medical interpretation, but I would myself later become a caregiver and patient advocate to my mother, my brother, and my sister—all of whom were diagnosed with cancer.

Who was your inspiration?

My mother was a tremendous role model for self-advocacy. She supported our involvement for change, though she often feared what was to become of us. Suddenly widowed at the age of 50, she continued to provide for my siblings and me through her hard work.

What strategies do you find are most successful in enacting social change?

Change needs to come from within the community, or in the case of the work I do, the change or program or intervention must truly be derived from the survivors themselves. I try to "make change *with*" and not "do change *to*." The specific strategies also need to be derived or flow from a collective process. Strategies include:

1. Pay attention to what has been done before to enact that change—what can be learned from what has come before? Do we reinvent the wheel or enhance?
2. Build partnerships and collaborate with others from the start.
3. Acknowledge that power imbalances exist and that in order to build trust, egos need to be left at the door. This involves establishing ground rules so that everyone has an equal voice and feels safe using it. As members of communities of color who have been marginalized, this is absolutely critical. A place must be made at the table for all who are participating.
4. Strive to be inclusive of other issues. While efforts may require that you stay somewhat focused on

(continued)

one driving issue, people experience a host of related issues to which activists should be attentive.

Change is most gratifying and empowering when it is imbued with a collective voice. I grew up listening to my mother recite her favorite *"dicho"* [saying]: *"en la union esta la fuerza"*—"in unity there is strength." I live by that dicho!

What are the major challenges activists and advocates in your field face?

One of the challenges is the lack of experience among advocacy groups or community-based groups to commit to working together in a collaborative manner. This includes a willingness to share resources among groups and to be aware that we are stronger when we are united than when we stand alone.

What are major misconceptions the public has about activism in general and in your area of advocacy, specifically?

Misconceptions that exist have to do with relegating activism to the act of "one" individual instead of the strengths of a cohesive group or coalition. In my area of advocacy, health-care system change, a misconception that patients and families and health advocates may have is that they can't enact change from within. But health care administrators can be open to change, and when patients and their families are given that place at the table, they are well positioned to enact change within the health care system.

What would you consider to be your greatest successes as an activist (in your current area of activism)?

It has been most rewarding, as an activist, to witness the growth of our program over the past 10 years. Breast cancer survivors in our program have moved beyond the role of "passive patients" to both actively influencing their own health care and changing the realities of care for other women with breast cancer. Survivors in our program now serve as role models and supporters for the community of women experiencing the same health challenges. The peer survivors teach other women about breast health, they serve on advisory councils, they provide input on research, and they have become leaders in their community. For me, my personal success has been my commitment to assisting my own family, as the only college graduate, and despite all the financial hardships I faced. I became that "voice" for my own family members as they interfaced with the health care system. Finally, I am most proud of my own "self-advocacy"—reaching the highest level of educational attainment by earning my doctorate. With that I kept my promise to my father—to become educated in this country.

Why should students get involved in the work that you do?

Students who intern and volunteer with our Comadre Program learn a lot about community engagement and especially advocacy in the health care system. They learn about the challenges that people face and how structural barriers make change challenging to accomplish. Students become sensitized to the social determinants of health. They see how food and housing insecurity and inadequate transportation—even not having enough gasoline—become seemingly insurmountable barriers to treatment completion. When students work shoulder to shoulder with peer survivors or community health care workers, observing factors such as low literacy, lack of health literacy, absence of language interpretation, and limited medical insurance for immigrant patients with cancer, they learn how to develop effective strategies for change.

NOTE

1. American Cancer Society. Cancer Facts and Figures for Hispanics/Latinos 2012–2014. Atlanta: American Cancer Society, 2012.

STEPHANIE MEDLEY-RATH

46. THEY'VE GOT A PILL FOR THAT

The Medicalization of Society

If you consume social media or watch TV you know that there are pharmaceutical solutions to many ailments. Although seemingly inconsequential, Medley-Rath argues that this is evidence of the medicalization of society, or the interpretation of behavior through the lens of medicine. Medicalization can lead to increased medical intervention into our daily lives (in the form of more doctors' visits, prescriptions, and unnecessary tests), with possible negative outcomes for the patient and larger society. Medley-Rath argues that although demedicalization can be challenging, there are routes that individuals and the society can take to reduce the medicalization of our culture.

INTRODUCTION

Medicalization refers to how we interpret social behavior through the lens of medicine, regardless of medical necessity. Medicalization has some benefits, such as promoting access to resources (e.g., insurance coverage, school accommodations), reducing social stigma by locating blame in a person's physiology rather than a personal failing (e.g., mental illness explained by a chemical imbalance of the brain), and promoting harm reduction (e.g., needle-exchange programs for heroin users). Moreover, medicalization gives an explanation and treatment options for people who are suffering—that is, providing relief by acknowledging their complaints. Yet, many people argue that medicalization is, instead, a social problem. Social problems are phenomena that at least some people (i.e., claims makers) argue are harmful to the well-being of society. Opponents of medicalization argue that the boundaries of what is a medical matter are expanding so that more challenges of everyday life are treated medically. Further, medicalization occurs through increasing levels of medical intervention regardless of increasing levels of medical need.

Medicalization achieves social problem status when medical intervention occurs regardless of medical need and causes harm to members of society. Critics of medicalization point out that there are several harmful consequences of medicalization, including narrowing the boundaries of what is considered "normal," increased medical interventions without benefit and sometimes with serious side effects, and recommending individual over structural solutions for large-scale problems. In this reading, we will explore how medicalization works using examples such as erectile dysfunction and attention deficit hyperactivity disorder (ADHD). Keep in mind that it is beyond the scope of this reading to assess the validity of a medical designation for any condition considered.

CLAIMS-MAKING

For a social phenomenon or complaint to become medicalized, someone must claim that medical intervention is necessary—primarily through using medicalized language to describe the complaint. These claims makers (Best, 2013) or agents of medicalization (Conrad and Leiter, 2004) include doctors, patients, pharmaceutical companies, social movement organizations, and potential patients, among others.

Claims-making is used to promote conditions as legitimate medical problems. For instance,

Original to *Focus on Social Problems: A Contemporary Reader*.

pharmaceutical companies advertise diseases and conditions directly to consumers. This advertising encourages potential patients to ask their doctor about the promoted drug to treat their problems and complaints (see Conrad, 2007). In 1997, the Food and Drug Administration (FDA) weakened guidelines about direct-to-consumer advertising so that pharmaceutical companies could begin advertising directly to consumers.

Direct-to-consumer advertising led to the runaway success of Viagra, which the FDA approved for erectile dysfunction treatment in 1998. Viagra was originally intended to treat angina (chest pains associated with heart disease) yet produced erections as an unintended side effect. The discovery of the side effect led to Pfizer Pharmaceuticals redefining erectile dysfunction from an individual psychological issue or a symptom of aging to a medical condition that a pill (i.e., Viagra) would fix (Loe, 2004). Pfizer Pharmaceuticals began marketing this newly defined medical condition and its fix to Americans through direct-to-consumer advertising, targeting men who suffered from erectile dysfunction because of age, prostate cancer, or other medical conditions. The advertising for erectile dysfunction drugs quickly shifted to marketing the pill to younger men who did not meet the original diagnostic criteria (a concept called diagnostic expansion). For example, in the early 2000s, thirty-seven-year-old professional baseball player Raphael Palmeiro starred in an advertising campaign for Viagra. When asked about it, he said that while he had used Viagra, he did not need the pill (Moore, 2002). Viagra patients now include men who are not suffering from erectile dysfunction but instead are seeking improved sexual performance more generally (Conrad and Leiter, 2004, 2008; Loe, 2004).

Medicalization rarely happens because of one claims maker's persistence. The medicalization of erectile dysfunction occurred through the collaboration of pharmaceutical companies marketing directly to consumers, potential patients asking their doctors about accessing the drugs, doctors writing prescriptions, and the willingness of insurance companies to pay for treatment (see Frances, 2013; Watters, 2010). Prescriptions for Viagra (and other erectile dysfunction drugs) are declining in the United States because of the limited coverage provided by insurance for these drugs (James, 2011; see also Le et al., 2017). Claims-making by one group (e.g., pharmaceutical companies) may be challenged by other groups (e.g., insurance companies) as the case of diagnostic expansion of erectile dysfunction shows.

REDEFINING NORMAL

When diagnostic expansion occurs, people (i.e., potential patients, doctors, among others) consider a narrower range of behaviors and conditions as "normal." According to Conrad (2007), the diagnostic criteria are expanded in such a way that more people (previously thought "healthy" or "normal") are inevitably diagnosed with medical conditions.

Consider the example of idiopathic short stature (ISS), which illustrates how normal changes. ISS diagnosis is based on a person's height falling at least two standard deviations below the mean for a child's age and sex without the presence of disease (e.g., Turner Syndrome) (Cohen et al., 2008). Children who are part of the shortest 1.2 percent of children with ISS can be treated with synthetic human growth hormones (Conrad, 2007). Treatment for ISS is motivated by the perceived "psychological and social advantages that height increase might bring to children" (Murano, 2017:249). As more children receive treatment for ISS, the entire population of children gets taller, on average, and the statistical cutoff point for diagnosis moves upward—meaning what counts as "too short" changes, and those kids previously considered normal become regarded as too short and may be offered treatment (some of which includes possible harmful side effects). In general, as the boundaries of normality further constrict, there is more pressure for people to conform to a narrower range of acceptability, thereby decreasing "diversity in society" (Conrad, 2007:95). Pharmaceutical companies have become successful at "turning difference into illness" (Frances, 2013:280) and then proposing treatments. However, it is not just the fault of pharmaceutical companies. Consumers perpetuate this vicious cycle as well when they seek medical intervention to achieve normalcy.

Perhaps the most troubling aspect of the narrowing of normal is that American medical interpretations of mental disorders are inappropriately applied cross-culturally (Watters, 2010). For example, in the Middle East, signs of happiness and sadness differ, and mental illness has long been addressed with traditional and religious healers along with broader family support (Sayar and Kose, 2012). Sayar and Kose (2012) caution against applying Western models of psychiatric care cross-culturally because both the meaning and the treatment of mental illness vary across cultures. Critics (see Watters, 2010) contend that pushing the same medical model globally runs the risk of decreasing the diversity among humanity, as well as exporting potentially harmful overreliance on medicine to solve problems.

WHAT'S THE HARM?

The market for antidepressants has grown overseas and in the United States, with increasing numbers of youth diagnosed, for example, with bipolar disorder (Moreno et al., 2007). Zito and colleagues (2003:17) found that between 1987 and 1996, the use of psychotropic medications among youth "increased 2- to 3-fold." In the U.S., about six percent of adolescents use psychotropic drugs (Jonas, Gu, and Albertorio-Diaz, 2013). Although these prescriptions undoubtedly help some patients, they are not without consequences. Since 2004, selective serotonin reuptake inhibitors or SSRIs (i.e., antidepressants) have included a "Black box" warning when prescribed to patients age 25 and younger because they produce a higher risk of suicidal thinking and behavior among this age group (National Institute of Mental Health, n.d.). Research suggests that the Black box warning contributed to a decline in the number of SSRI prescriptions for children (Mitchell et al., 2014). Further, Sharpe (2012) points out that prescribing antidepressants during this time of life coincides with and may affect teens' developing sense of self and identity. As these teenagers reach adulthood, they may be less willing to try living without antidepressants, even if their symptoms have declined, because they have little idea what that might mean. The antidepressant becomes the safer bet even if it is not the cause of declining depressive symptoms (see Whitaker, 2010).

Medicalization has harmful side effects and is economically costly (Conrad et al., 2010; Hinshaw and Scheffler, 2014b). For example, annual cancer screenings treat people like potential patients, yet research shows that the costs and risks of some of these screenings outweigh the benefits (Brawley, 2012a). High rates of false positives result in invasive follow-up testing and treatment, costing both time and money and putting healthy people at risk. This, in part, explains the rationale for the U.S. Preventive Services Task Force's 2009 statement recommending fewer mammograms for women and to base their use on individual risk factors (see Pace and Keating, 2014). One in five breast cancers is over-diagnosed (i.e., will never cause disease or death) but is treated with surgery or radiation, with possible serious side effects (Jin, 2014). Welch and Fisher (2017:2209) note that "[e]xcessive testing of low-risk people produces real harm, leading to treatments that have no benefit (because there is nothing to fix) but can nonetheless result in medication side effects, surgical complications, and occasionally even death." Most troubling is that a false positive can cause undue emotional distress because the person now comes to identify incorrectly as a cancer patient.

In addition to the emotional and physical costs of overdiagnosis and false positives, Kale and colleagues (2011) have found that approximately $6.8 billion is spent each year on unnecessary medical services. These services account for 2.7 percent of Medicare spending (Schwartz et al., 2014). A study conducted in the state of Washington finds that more than one third of the 47 medical tests or services examined were unnecessary (e.g., annual cervical cancer testing or electrocardiograms instead of testing as indicated) (Allen, 2018). Physicians concur that about 20 percent of medical care (e.g., prescriptions, procedures) is unnecessary (Lyu et al., 2017). Further, the side effects of one medical intervention can lead to more medical interventions. For instance, the pharmaceutical company Eli Lilly developed Zyprexa to treat manic episodes caused by SSRIs such as Prozac (another Eli Lilly product), which treats depression (Whitaker, 2010).

Medicalization is big business. In 2017, $8.4 billion worth of industry payments were made to physicians and teaching hospitals (Center for Medicare & Medicaid Services, 2017). A majority of doctors (84 percent as of 2009) have financial ties with a drug or medical device company (Ornstein et al., 2014). Moreover, these payments influence physicians' recommendations for treatments. For example, there is a positive correlation between physician payments from industry and prescribing rates of name-brand prescription drugs (Ornstein, Tigas, and Jones, 2016).

The pharmaceutical industry has higher profit margins—ranging from 10 to 43 percent in 2013—than other industries (Anderson, 2014). A substantial amount of money stands to be made through the medicalization of more conditions, especially those with the best potential for profit. Pedrique and colleagues (2013) found that from 2000 to 2011 only four percent of new therapeutic products were to treat (low-profit) neglected diseases, such as malaria and Ebola. A gap in research and disease burden also exists. Disease burden refers to the economic (i.e., lost productivity, cost of healthcare) and biomedical (i.e., morbidity, mortality) impact of disease on a society (NCCID 2016). For example, the disease burden for "infectious diseases and neonatal disorders in Sub-Saharan Africa and South Asia" is high (meaning there are major economic costs as well as high mortality and morbidity rates) with little research devoted to these problems or regions of the world (Atal et al., 2018:123). The medicalization of high-profit conditions and behaviors comes at the cost of neglecting research on treating, preventing, and curing deadly diseases around the world.

Proponents of medicalization claim that increased medical intervention reduces stigma among sufferers. Direct-to-consumer advertising is argued as having an educational benefit by emphasizing the causes and symptoms of a condition, which is theorized to reduce stigma and to educate the population. However, research has shown that understanding the biological underpinnings of a disease or condition does not reduce stigma. Payton and Thoits (2011) found that the introduction of direct-to-consumer advertising did not reduce the stigma of having a mental illness for which pharmaceutical treatments were heavily advertised (i.e., depression) compared to a mental illness that was not advertised (i.e., schizophrenia). In other words, exposure to a medical explanation of depression did nothing, comparatively, to reduce the stigma associated with the illness.

MEDICALIZATION, SOCIAL CONTROL, AND INDIVIDUALIZED SOLUTIONS

In addition to the costs of medicalization, it is important to understand how medicalization expands the reach of medical social control as increasing amounts of authority are given to medical experts (Conrad, 1979, 1992, 2007). Conrad (1979:2) writes, "medical social control of deviant behavior is usually a variant of medical intervention that seeks to eliminate, modify, isolate or regulate behavior, socially defined as deviant, with medical means and in the name of health." Medicalizing a behavior or complaint suggests that it exists within the individual rather than in the social structure (Conrad, 2007). Critics of medicalization contend that ADHD is an example of medicalizing the problem behaviors of students, rather than a medical condition with a known etiology (see Saul, 2014). In the case of ADHD, the problem of a child who does not behave as expected in the classroom now belongs to the physician rather than the teacher or parent. The child's problem behavior and a teacher's classroom management are then controlled by medical means (i.e., pharmaceutical drugs).

ADHD diagnosis rates have increased from 6.1 percent in 1997 to 10.1 percent in 2016 among U.S. children and adolescents (Xu et al., 2018). Between six and 11 percent of U.S. children and adolescents are estimated to have ever had an ADHD diagnosis (Center for Disease Control and Prevention, 2018; Danielson et al., 2018; Visser et al., 2014). Even defining ADHD as a diagnosis is misleading because it is more accurately a constellation of symptoms (Saul, 2014) and parents and teachers do not consistently agree on the presence or absence of ADHD symptoms (Murray et al., 2007). Increasing ADHD rates may have more to do with structural issues than an increase in true cases of ADHD because an ADHD diagnosis is both biologically and socially determined (Bowden, 2013).

An ADHD diagnosis may be treating biological symptoms, or it may be making a student fit better into the expectations of school, making the medication use an enhancement rather than treatment of a medical condition (see Conrad, 2007). Some children are prescribed ADHD medications only during the school week and not at home (Hruska, 2012), suggesting that environment plays a major role. Doctors admit to prescribing ADHD drugs to "boost academic performance," rather than because of medical need (Schwartz, 2012). Poorer children in underfunded schools are prescribed drugs to treat ADHD instead of adequately funding schools to help these students succeed academically (Schwartz, 2012; see also Hinshaw and Scheffler, 2014a).

Even more disturbing is that ADHD diagnosis rates correlate with the implementation of education policies that penalize schools for not meeting standardized testing goals (e.g., No Child Left Behind) (Hinshaw and Scheffler, 2014b; see also Hinshaw 2018). No Child Left Behind was signed into law in 2002. Since then, sales of stimulants used to treat ADHD have quintupled (Schwartz, 2013). This suggests that untreated ADHD is thought to be correlated with poor standardized test scores and that treating ADHD may improve those scores. If this is the case, then there is a perception that the social problem of "failing schools" is at least partially caused by children's medical conditions rather than problems within the institution. The problems in schools and classrooms can then be solved through the medical treatment of individual students rather than through adequate funding and support for educational institutions and the people they serve.

IS DEMEDICALIZATION POSSIBLE?

An ever-growing number of medical solutions exist for complaints of everyday living (e.g., erectile dysfunction) and social problems (e.g., rising educational expectations without a corresponding increase in government funding for education). Medicalization, however, is not inevitable. Once a complaint is medicalized, it can be demedicalized; that is, it is "no longer defined in medical terms, and the involvement of medical personnel is no longer deemed appropriate" (Conrad, 2007:97).

Physicians and their professional organizations (e.g., the American Medical Association), as well as other health-care workers, have long promoted preventative medicine via annual exams and screenings regardless of our feeling of illness (Frances, 2013). The increasing sophistication of technology has encouraged us to put a great deal of trust in its ability to prevent disease, and we rely on this technology to manage risk (Sulik, 2011). Most of us have been socialized to imagine ourselves as potential patients and are reminded of this during reoccurring physicals or screenings, such as Pap tests or colonoscopies.

The Pap test screens for cervical cancer—a disease that was once the deadliest form of cancer for women (Brawley, 2012b). Few women look forward to their annual Pap test because of its invasiveness (cells are scraped from the cervix) and the potentially alarming result of a cancer diagnosis. But is there such a thing as too much screening? In the case of cervical cancer screening, the answer seems to be "yes." Brawley (2012b) states that women under age twenty-one, for example, should not be screened:

> Many sexually active women under 21 will develop a human papillomavirus infection, or HPV, which can lead to pre-cancerous lesions. And when doctors see those lesions on a Pap test, they want to treat them. Yet nearly all of those lesions will disappear on their own without residual effects. And those that do not are easily treated years later. Treating them as soon as they're spotted can lead to cervical incompetence and miscarriage down the road.

In other words, most lesions are nothing to worry about, but overtreatment can cause harm. Today, the U.S. Preventative Services Task Force (2018) recommends that women aged 21-29 have a Pap smear every three years and that women aged 30-65 may opt for a Pap smear every three to five years or an HPV test every five years. Although revised cancer screening recommendations do not end medical social control, they do suggest the possibility of demedicalization. Moreover, the case of Pap tests shows how medicalization and demedicalization can happen simultaneously (Halfmann, 2011). The Pap test's role as a cancer screening tool is more prominent, while the reduced frequency of its use suggests partial demedicalization of women's bodies.

The model case of demedicalization is homosexuality (Conrad, 2007). Homosexuality was initially medicalized to protect gays and lesbians from punitive legal sanctions (Conrad and Angell, 2004). Medical treatment for homosexuality included electroshock aversion therapy, psychoanalysis, and hormone treatment (Smith et al., 2004). Medicalizing homosexuality reduced the harm directed to gays and lesbians by the legal system but introduced new (and reinforced existing) harms by the mental health community. For example, mental health professionals have used conversion therapy under the premise that a person can change his or her sexual orientation. In 1973, homosexuality was declassified as a mental illness in the *DSM-II*. Today, the American Psychological Association condemns the practice of conversion or reparative therapy because it is harmful and unscientific (APA Task Force on Appropriate Therapeutic Responses to Sexual Orientation, 2009). Complete demedicalization may be possible and certainly desirable for some complaints, whereas partial demedicalization may be more appropriate for other features of our lives (e.g., cancer prevention).

CONCLUSION

Medicalization is both a positive and a negative force in our lives. Medicalization means that an individual can gain access to resources used to treat or manage complaints, along with having socially acceptable language to explain the complaint. Moreover, medicalization promotes harm reduction caused by the complaint. Despite this, many people consider medicalization itself a social problem. A complaint that is medicalized may not be a medical matter, thereby expanding medical social control. The medical solution may provide few, if any, benefits (e.g., reducing stigma), with high emotional and financial costs and even physical harm. Medicalization narrows what is accepted as normal human variation.

The tendency to medicalize social phenomena should be viewed with a critical eye. The costs of medicalizing an issue should be carefully weighed against any benefits of medicalization. In particular, we should ask the following questions: (1) is medicalization necessary? (2) does medicalization further narrow what it means to be normal? (3) do the benefits of the treatment outweigh any harms of the treatment? and (4) are there changes that could be made at the structural level that could replace the need of medicalizing at the individual level? As the quest for profit and quick fixes encourages more aspects of everyday life to become medicalized, it is important to remember that it is not inevitable and demedicalization is possible.

REFERENCES

Allen, Marshall. 2018. "Unnecessary Medical Care Is More Common Than You Think." *ProPublica*, February 1. Retrieved September 25, 2018, from https://www.propublica.org/article/unnecessary-medical-care-is-more-common-than-you-think.

Anderson, Richard. 2014. "Pharmaceutical Industry Gets High on Fat Profits." *BBC News*, November 6. Retrieved March 19, 2015. http://www.bbc.com/news/business-28212223/.

APA Task Force on Appropriate Therapeutic Responses to Sexual Orientation. 2009. Report of the Task Force on Appropriate Therapeutic Responses to Sexual Orientation. Washington, DC: American Psychological Association. Retrieved June 23, 2014. http://www.apa.org/pi/lgbt/resources/therapeutic-response.pdf/.

Atal, Ignacio, Ludovic Trinquart, Philippe Ravaud, and Raphaël Porcher. 2018. A Mapping of 115,000 Randomized Trials Revealed a Mismatch Between Research Effort and Health Needs in Non–High-Income Regions. *Journal of Clinical Epidemiology* 98:123–32. doi:10.1016/j.jclinepi.2018.01.006.

Best, Joel. 2013. *Social Problems*. 22nd ed. New York: W. W. Norton.

Bowden, Gregory. 2013. "The Merit of Sociological Accounts of Disorder: The Attention-Deficit Hyperactivity Disorder Case." *Health* 18(4):422–38.

Brawley, Otis. 2012a. "Value of Mass Prostate Cancer Screenings Questioned." *CNN*, March 14. Retrieved June 3, 2014. http://www.cnn.com/2012/03/14/health/brawley-prostate-cancer-screenings/.

Brawley, Otis. 2012b. "No More Annual Pap Smear: New Cervical Cancer Screening Guidelines." *CNN*, March 15. Retrieved April 25, 2014. http://www.cnn.com/2012/03/14/health/brawley-cervical-cancer-screenings/index.html/.

Center for Disease Control and Prevention. 2018. "Attention-Deficit/Hyperactivity Disorder(ADHD): Data & Statistics." March 20. Retrieved September 25, 2018 https://www.cdc.gov/ncbddd/adhd/data.html.

Center for Medicare & Medicaid Services. 2017. "Open Payments Program Year 2017 Fact Sheet." Retrieved September 25, 2018 https://www.cms.gov/OpenPayments/Downloads/2017-fact-sheet.pdf.

Cohen, Pinchas, Alan D. Rogol, Cheri L. Deal, Paul Saenger, Edward O. Reiter, Judith L. Ross, Steven D. Chernausek, Martin O. Savage, and Jan M. Wit, 2007 ISS Consensus Workshop participants. 2008. "Consensus Statement on the Diagnosis and Treatment of Children with Idiopathic Short Stature: A Summary of the Growth Hormone Research Society, the Lawson Wilkins Pediatric Endocrine Society, and the European Society for Paediatric Endocrinology Workshop." *The Journal of Clinical Endocrinology & Metabolism* 93(11):4210–17. doi: 10.1210/jc.2008-0509.

Conrad, Peter. 1979. "Types of Medical Social Control." *Sociology of Health and Illness* 1(1):1–11.

Conrad, Peter. 1992. "Medicalization and Social Control." *Annual Review of Sociology* 18:209–32.

Conrad, Peter. 2007. *The Medicalization of Society: On the Transformation of Human Conditions into Treatable Disorders*. Baltimore: Johns Hopkins University Press.

Conrad, Peter, and Alison Angell. 2004. "Homosexuality and Remedicalization." *Society* 41(5):32–39.

Conrad, Peter, and Valerie Leiter. 2004. "Medicalization, Markets and Consumers." *Journal of Health and Social Behavior* 45:158–76.

Conrad, Peter, and Valerie Leiter. 2008. "From Lydia Pinkham to Queen Levitra: Direct-to-Consumer Advertising and Medicalisation." *Sociology of Health & Illness* 30(6):825–38.

Conrad, Peter, Thomas Mackie, and Ateev Mehrotra. 2010. "Estimating the Costs of Medicalization." *Social Science & Medicine* 70(12):1943–47.

Danielson, Melissa L., Rebecca H. Bitsko, Reem M. Ghandour, Joseph R. Holbrook, Michael D. Kogan, and Stephen J. Blumberg. 2018. "Prevalence of Parent-Reported ADHD Diagnosis and Associated Treatment among U.S. Children and Adolescents, 2016." *Journal of Clinical Child & Adolescent Psychology* 47(2):199–12. doi:10.1080/15374416.2017.1417860

Frances, Allen. 2013. *Saving Normal: An Insider's Revolt against Out-of-Control Psychiatric Diagnosis, DSM-5, Big Pharma, and the Medicalization of Ordinary Life*. New York: Morrow.

Halfmann, Drew. 2011. "Recognizing Medicalization and Demedicalization: Discourses, Practices, and Identities." *Health: An Interdisciplinary Journal for the Social Study of Health, Illness and Medicine* 16(2):186–07. doi:10.1177/1363459311403947.

Hinshaw, Stephen P., and Richard M. Scheffler. 2014a. "Expand Pre-K, Not A.D.H.D." *New York Times*, February 23. Retrieved April 28, 2014. http://www.nytimes.com/2014/02/24/opinion/expand-pre-k-not-adhd.html/.

Hinshaw, Stephen P., and Richard M. Scheffler. 2014b. *The ADHD Explosion: Myths, Medication, Money, and Today's Push for Performance*. New York: Oxford University Press.

Hinshaw, Stephen P. 2018. "Attention Deficit Hyperactivity Disorder (ADHD): Controversy, Developmental Mechanisms, and Multiple Levels of Analysis." *Annual Review of Clinical Psychology* 14(1):291–16. doi:10.1146/annurev-clinpsy-050817-084917.

Hruska, Bronwen. 2012. "Raising the Ritalin Generation." *The New York Times*, August 18th. http://www.nytimes.com/2012/08/19/opinion/sunday/raising-the-ritalin-generation.html.

James, Susan Donaldson. 2011. "Honeymoon with Viagra® Could Be Over, Say Doctors." *ABC News*, June 9. Retrieved February 11, 2015. http://abcnews.go.com/Health/Viagra-prescription-sales-sexual-expectations/story?id=13794726/.

Jin, Jill. 2014. "Breast Cancer Screening: Benefits and Harms." *Journal of the American Medical Association* 312(23):2585.

Jonas, Bruce S., Qiuping Gu, and Juan R. Albertorio-Diaz. 2013. "Psychotropic Medication Use Among Adolescents: United States, 2005-2010." U.S. Department of Health and Human Services. Retrieved September 25, 2018 https://www.cdc.gov/nchs/pressroom/calendar/2013_schedule.htm#Dec.

Kale, Minal, Tara F. Bishop, Alex D. Federman, and Salomeh Keyhani. 2011. "'Top 5' Lists Top $5 Billion FREE." *Archives of Internal Medicine* 171(20):1858–59.

Le, Brian, Sarah McAchran, David Paolone, Dan Gralnek, Daniel Williams IV, and Wade Bushman. 2017. "Assessing the Variability in Insurance Coverage Transparency for Male Sexual Health Conditions in the United States." *Urology*, 102:126–29. doi:10.1016/j.urology.2016.12.031.

Loe, Meika. 2004. *The Rise of Viagra®: How the Little Blue Pill Changed Sex in America*. New York: New York University Press.

Lyu, Heather, Tim Xu, Daniel Brotman, Brandan Mayer-Blackwell, Michol Cooper, Michael Daniel, Elizabeth C. Wick, Vikas Saini, Shannon Brownlee, and Martin A. Makary. 2017. "Overtreatment in the United States." *Plos One* 12(9):1–11. doi:10.1371/journal.pone.0181970.

Mitchell, Ann M., Marilyn A. Davies, Christine Cassesse, and Ryan Curran. 2014. "Antidepressant Use in Children, Adolescents, and Young Adults: 10 Years after the Food and Drug Administration Black Box Warning." *The Journal of Nurse Practitioners* 10(3):149–56.

Moore, Jim. 2002. "Hard Topic, Easy Money; Palmeiro Cashes in on Viagra." *Seattle Post-Intelligencer*, August 1. Retrieved March 19, 2015. http://www.seattlepi.com/news/article/Hard-topic-easy-money-Palmeiro-cashes-in-on-1092712.php/.

Moreno, Carmen, Gonzalo Laje, Carlos Blanco, Huiping Jiang, Andrew B. Schmidt, and Mark Oflson. 2007. "National Trends in the Outpatient Diagnosis and Treatment of Bipolar Disorder in Youth." *Archives of General Psychology* 64(9):1032–39.

Murano, Maria Cristina. 2017. "Medicalising Short Children with Growth Hormone? Ethical Considerations of the Underlying Sociocultural Aspects." *Medicine, Health Care and Philosophy* 21(2):243–53. doi:10.1007/s11019-017-9798-6.

Murray, Desiree W., Scott H. Kollins, Kristina K. Hardy, Howard B. Abikoff, James M. Swanson, Charles Cunningham, Benedetto Vitiello, Mark A. Riddle, Mark Davies, Laurence L. Greenhill, James T. McCracken, James J. McGough, Kelly Posner, Anne M. Skrobala, Tim Wigal, Sharon Wigal, Jaswinder K. Ghuman, and Shirley Z. Chuang. 2007. "Parent versus Teacher Ratings of Attention-Deficit/Hyperactivity Disorder Symptoms in the Preschoolers with Attention-Deficit/Hyperactivity Disorder Treatment Study (PATS)." *Journal of Child and Adolescent Psychopharmacology* 17(5):605–19.

National Collaborating Centre for Infectious Diseases. 2016. "Influenza: More than Just Numbers: Exploring the Concept of 'Burden of Disease.'" Retrieved November 2, 2018. https://nccid.ca/wp-content/uploads/sites/2/2016/07/ExploringBoD_E.pdf.

National Institute of Mental Health. n.d. "Antidepressant Medications for Children and Adolescents: Information for Parents and Caregivers." Retrieved February 19, 2015. http://web.archive.org/web/20150404214159/http://www.nimh.nih.gov/health/topics/child-and-adolescent-mental-health/antidepressant-medications-for-children-and-adolescents-information-for-parents-and-caregivers.shtml/.

Ornstein, Charles, Eric Sagara, and Ryann Grochowski Jones. 2014. "What We've Learned From Four Years of Diving into Dollars for Docs." *Pro-Publica*. http://www.propublica.org/article/what-weve-learned-from-four-years-of-diving-into-dollars-for-docs.

Ornstein, Charles, Mike Tigas, and Ryann Grochowski Jones. 2016. "Now There's Proof: Docs Who Get Company Cash Tend to Prescribe More Brand-Name Meds." *ProPublica*, March 17. Retrieved September 25, 2018 https://www.propublica.org/article/doctors-who-take-company-cash-tend-to-prescribe-more-brand-name-drugs.

Pace, Lydia E., and Nancy L. Keating. 2014. "A Systematic Assessment of Benefits and Risks to Guide Breast Cancer Screening Decisions." *JAMA: The Journal of the American Medical Association* 311(13):1327–35.

Payton, Andrew R., and Peggy A. Thoits. 2011. "Medicalization, Direct-to-Consumer Advertising, and Mental Illness Stigma." *Society and Mental Health* 1(1):55–70.

Pedrique, Belen, Nathalie Strub-Wourgaft, Claudette Some, Piero Olliaro, Patrice Trouiller, Nathan Ford, Benard Pécoul, and Jean-Hervé Bradol. 2013. "The Drug and Vaccine Landscape for Neglected Diseases (2000–11): A Systematic Assessment." *The Lancet* 1:e371–79.

Saul, Richard. 2014. *ADHD Does Not Exist: The Truth about Attention Deficit and Hyperactivity Disorder*. New York: Harper Wave.

Sayar, Kemal, and Samet Kose. 2012. "Psychopathology and Depression in the Middle East." *Journal of Mood Disorders* 2(1):21–27.

Schwartz, Aaron L., Bruce E. Landon, Adam G. Elshaug, Michael E. Chernew, and Michael McWilliams. 2014. "Measuring Low-Value Care in Medicare." *JAMA Internal Medicine* 1101.

Schwartz, Alan. 2012. "Attention Disorder or Not, Pills to Help in School." *New York Times,* October 9. Retrieved April 28, 2014. http://www.nytimes.com/2012/10/09/health/attention-disorder-or-not-children-prescribed-pills-to-help-in-school.html?/.

Schwartz, Alan. 2013. "The Selling of Attention Deficit Disorder." *New York Times*, December 14. Retrieved March 19, 2015. http://www.nytimes.com/2013/12/15/health/the-selling-of-attention-deficit-disorder.html/.

Sharpe, Katherine. 2012. *Coming of Age on Zoloft: How Antidepressants Cheered Us Up, Let Us Down, and Changed Who We Are*. New York: Harper Perennial.

Smith, Glenn, Annie Bartlett, and Michael King. 2004. "Treatments of Homosexuality in Britain Since the 1950s—An Oral History: The Experience of Patients." *British Medical Journal* 328:429. Retrieved June 23, 2014. http://www.bmj.com/content/328/7437/427/.

Sulik, Gayle A. 2011. "'Our Diagnoses, Our Selves': The Rise of the Technoscientific Illness Identity." *Sociology Compass* 5(6):463–77.

U.S. Preventative Services Task Force. 2018. "Screening for Cervical Cancer: U.S. Preventative Services Task Force Recommendation Statement." *JAMA* 320(7):674–86. 10.1001/jama.2018.10897.

Visser, Susanna N., Melissa L. Danielson, Rebecca H. Bitsko, Joseph R. Holbrook, Michael D. Kogan, Reem M. Ghandour, Ruth Perou, and Stephen J. Blumberg. 2014. "Trends in the Parent-Report of Health Care Provider-Diagnosed and Medicated Attention-Deficit/Hyperactivity Disorder: United States, 2003–2011." *Journal of the American Academy of Child & Adolescent Psychiatry* 53(1):34–46.e2. doi:10.1016/j.jaac.2013.09.001.

Watters, Ethan. 2010. *Crazy Like Us: The Globalization of the American Psyche*. New York: Free Press.

Welch, H. Gilbert, and Elliot S. Fisher. 2017. "Income and Cancer Overdiagnosis – When Too Much Care Is Harmful." *The New England Journal of Medicine* 376(23):2208–09. doi: 10.1056/NEJMp1615069.

Whitaker, Robert. 2010. *Anatomy of an Epidemic: Magic Bullets, Psychiatric Drugs, and the Astonishing Rise of Mental Illness in America*. New York: Broadway Books.

Xu, Guifeng, Lane Strathearn, Buyun Liu, Binrang Yang, and Wei Bao. 2018. "Twenty-Year Trends in Diagnosed Attention-Deficit/Hyperactivity Disorder among U.S. Children and Adolescents, 1997–2016." *JAMA Network Open* 1(4):1–9. doi:10.1001/jamanetworkopen.2018.1471.

Zito, Julie Magno, Daniel J. Safer, Susan DosReis, James F. Gardner, Laurence Magder, Karen Soeken, Myde Boles, Frances Lynch, and Mark A. Riddle. 2003. "Psychotropic Practice Patterns for Youth: A 10-Year Perspective." *Archives of Pediatric Adolescent Medicine* 157(1):17–25.

ELISABETH ROSENTHAL

47. PAYING TILL IT HURTS

The $2.7 Trillion Medical Bill

Why are medical costs so high in the United States? Using colonoscopies as a case study, Rosenthal explores how inflated price tags for regular procedures are a significant contributor to rising medical costs. The increasing medicalization of these procedures along with attempts from multiple parties to maximize revenue and obscure pricing policies, mask both procedural costs and whether procedures are even medically necessary. Despite what we spend, our health outcomes are no better (and are sometimes worse) than those in other countries where costs are lower.

Deirdre Yapalater's recent colonoscopy at a surgical center near her home here on Long Island went smoothly: she was whisked from pre-op to an operating room where a gastroenterologist, assisted by an anesthesiologist and a nurse, performed the routine cancer screening procedure in less than an hour. The test, which found nothing worrisome, racked up what is likely her most expensive medical bill of the year: $6,385.

That is fairly typical: in Keene, N.H., Matt Meyer's colonoscopy was billed at $7,563.56. Maggie Christ of Chappaqua, N.Y., received $9,142.84 in bills for the procedure. In Durham, N.C., the charges for Curtiss Devereux came to $19,438, which included a polyp removal. While their insurers negotiated down the price, the final tab for each test was more than $3,500. "Could that be right?" said Ms. Yapalater, stunned by charges on the statement on her dining room table. Although her insurer covered the procedure and she paid nothing, her health care costs still bite: Her premium payments jumped 10 percent last year, and rising co-payments and deductibles are straining the finances of her middle-class family, with its mission-style house in the suburbs and two S.U.V.'s parked

outside. "You keep thinking it's free," she said. "We call it free, but of course it's not."

In many other developed countries, a basic colonoscopy costs just a few hundred dollars and certainly well under $1,000. That chasm in price helps explain why the United States is far and away the world leader in medical spending, even though numerous studies have concluded that Americans do not get better care. Whether directly from their wallets or through insurance policies, Americans pay more for almost every interaction with the medical system. They are typically prescribed more expensive procedures and tests than people in other countries, no matter if those nations operate a private or national health system. A list of drug, scan and procedure prices compiled by the International Federation of Health Plans, a global network of health insurers, found that the United States came out the most costly in all 21 categories—and often by a huge margin.

Americans pay, on average, about four times as much for a hip replacement as patients in Switzerland or France and more than three times as much for a Caesarean section as those in New Zealand or Britain. The average price for Nasonex, a common nasal spray for allergies, is $108 in the United States compared with $21 in Spain. The costs of hospital stays here are about triple those in other developed countries, even though they last no longer, according to a recent report by the Commonwealth Fund, a foundation that studies health policy. While the United States medical system is famous for drugs costing hundreds of thousands of dollars and heroic care at the end of life, it turns out that a more significant factor in the nation's $2.7 trillion annual health care bill may not be the use of extraordinary services, but the high price tag of ordinary ones. "The U.S. just pays providers of health care much more for everything," said Tom Sackville, chief executive of the health plans federation and a former British health minister.

Colonoscopies offer a compelling case study. They are the most expensive screening test that healthy Americans routinely undergo—and often cost more than childbirth or an appendectomy in most other developed countries. Their numbers have increased many fold over the last 15 years, with data from the Centers for Disease Control and Prevention suggesting that more than 10 million people get them each year, adding up to more than $10 billion in annual costs. Largely an office procedure when widespread screening was first recommended, colonoscopies have moved into surgery centers—which were created as a step down from costly hospital care but are now often a lucrative step up from doctors' examining rooms—where they are billed like a quasi operation. They are often prescribed and performed more frequently than medical guidelines recommend.

The high price paid for colonoscopies mostly results not from top-notch patient care, according to interviews with health care experts and economists, but from business plans seeking to maximize revenue; haggling between hospitals and insurers that have no relation to the actual costs of performing the procedure; and lobbying, marketing and turf battles among specialists that increase patient fees. While several cheaper and less invasive tests to screen for colon cancer are recommended as equally effective by the federal government's expert panel on preventive care—and are commonly used in other countries— colonoscopy has become the go-to procedure in the United States. "We've defaulted to by far the most

expensive option, without much if any data to support it," said Dr. H. Gilbert Welch, a professor of medicine at the Dartmouth Institute for Health Policy and Clinical Practice.

. . .Hospitals, drug companies, device makers, physicians and other providers can benefit by charging inflated prices, favoring the most costly treatment options and curbing competition that could give patients more, and cheaper, choices. And almost every interaction can be an opportunity to send multiple, often opaque bills with long lists of charges: $100 for the ice pack applied for 10 minutes after a physical therapy session, or $30,000 for the artificial joint implanted in surgery.

The United States spends about 18 percent of its gross domestic product on health care, nearly twice as much as most other developed countries. The Congressional Budget Office has said that if medical costs continue to grow unabated, "total spending on health care would eventually account for all of the country's economic output." And it identified federal spending on government health programs as a primary cause of long-term budget deficits. While the rise in health care spending in the United States has slowed in the past four years—to about four percent annually from about eight percent—it is still expected to rise faster than the gross domestic product. Aging baby boomers and tens of millions of patients newly insured under the Affordable Care Act are likely to add to the burden.

With health insurance premiums eating up ever more of her flat paycheck, Ms. Yapalater, a customer relations specialist for a small Long Island company, recently decided to forgo physical therapy for an injury sustained during Hurricane Sandy because of high out-of-pocket expenses. She refused a dermatology medication prescribed for her daughter when the pharmacist said the co-payment was $130. "I said, 'That's impossible, I have insurance,'" Ms. Yapalater recalled. "I called the dermatologist and asked for something cheaper, even if it's not as good." The more than $35,000 annually that Ms. Yapalater and her employer collectively pay in premiums—her share is $15,000— for her family's Oxford Freedom Plan would be more than sufficient to cover their medical needs in most other countries. She and her husband, Jeff, 63, a sales and marketing consultant, have three children in their 20s with good jobs. Everyone in the family exercises, and none has had a serious illness.

Like the Yapalaters, many other Americans have habits or traits that arguably could put the nation at the low end of the medical cost spectrum. Patients in the United States make fewer doctors' visits and have fewer hospital stays than citizens of many other developed countries, according to the Commonwealth Fund report. People in Japan get more CT scans. People in Germany, Switzerland and Britain have more frequent hip replacements. The American population is younger and has fewer smokers than those in most other developed countries. Pushing costs in the other direction, though, is that the United States has relatively high rates of obesity and limited access to routine care for the poor.

A major factor behind the high costs is that the United States, unique among industrialized nations, does not generally regulate or intervene in medical pricing, aside from setting payment rates for Medicare and Medicaid, the government programs for older people and the poor. Many other countries deliver health care on a private fee-for-service basis, as does much of the American health care system, but they set rates as if health care were a public utility or negotiate fees with providers and insurers nationwide, for example. "In the U.S., we like to consider health care a free market," said Dr. David Blumenthal, president of the Commonwealth Fund and a former adviser to President Obama. "But it is a very weird market, riddled with market failures."

Consider this:

Consumers, the patients, do not see prices until after a service is provided, if they see them at all. And there is little quality data on hospitals and doctors to help determine good value, aside from surveys conducted by popular Web sites and magazines. Patients with insurance pay a tiny fraction of the bill, providing scant disincentive for spending.

Even doctors often do not know the costs of the tests and procedures they prescribe. When Dr. Michael Collins, an internist in East Hartford, Conn., called the hospital that he is affiliated with to price lab tests and a colonoscopy, he could not get an answer. "It's impossible for me to think about cost,"

he said. "If you go to the supermarket and there are no prices, how can you make intelligent decisions?" Instead, payments are often determined in countless negotiations between a doctor, hospital or pharmacy, and an insurer, with the result often depending on their relative negotiating power. Insurers have limited incentive to bargain forcefully, since they can raise premiums to cover costs. "It all comes down to market share, and very rarely is anyone looking out for the patient," said Dr. Jeffrey Rice, the chief executive of Healthcare Blue Book, which tracks commercial insurance payments. "People think it's like other purchases: that if you pay more you get a better car. But in medicine, it's not like that."

A MARKET IS BORN

As the cases of bottled water and energy drinks stacked in the corner of the Yapalaters' dining room attest, the family is cost conscious—especially since a photography business long owned by the family succumbed eight years ago in the shift to digital imaging. They moved out of Manhattan. They rent out their summer home on Fire Island. They have put off restoring the wallpaper in their dining room. And yet, Ms. Yapalater recalled, she did not ask her doctors about the cost of her colonoscopy because it was covered by insurance and because "if a doctor says you need it, you don't ask." In many other countries, price lists of common procedures are publicly available in every clinic and office. Here, it can be nearly impossible to find out.

Until the last decade or so, colonoscopies were mostly performed in doctors' office suites and only on patients at high risk for colon cancer, or to seek a diagnosis for intestinal bleeding. But several highly publicized studies by gastroenterologists in 2000 and 2001 found that a colonoscopy detected early cancers and precancerous growths in healthy people. They did not directly compare screening colonoscopies with far less invasive and cheaper screening methods, including annual tests for blood in the stool or a sigmoidoscopy, which looks at the lower colon where most cancers occur, every five years. "The idea wasn't to say these growths would have been missed by the other methods, but people extrapolated to that," said Dr. Douglas

Robertson, of the Department of Veterans Affairs, which is beginning a large trial to compare the tests.

Experts agree that screening for colon cancer is crucial, and a colonoscopy is intuitively appealing because it looks directly at the entire colon and doctors can remove potentially precancerous lesions that might not yet be prone to bleeding. But studies have not clearly shown that a colonoscopy prevents colon cancer or death better than the other screening methods. Indeed, some recent papers suggest that it does not, in part because early lesions may be hard to see in some parts of the colon. But in 2000, the American College of Gastroenterology anointed colonoscopy as "the preferred strategy" for colon cancer prevention—and America followed.

Katie Couric, who lost her husband to colorectal cancer, had a colonoscopy on television that year, giving rise to what medical journals called the "Katie Couric effect": prompting patients to demand the test. Gastroenterology groups successfully lobbied Congress to have the procedure covered by Medicare for cancer screening every 10 years, effectively meaning that commercial insurance plans would also have to provide coverage. Though Medicare negotiates for what are considered frugal prices, its database shows that it paid an average of $531 for a colonoscopy in 2011. But that does not include the payments to anesthesiologists, which could substantially increase the cost. "As long as it's deemed medically necessary," said Jonathan Blum, the deputy administrator at the Centers for Medicare and Medicaid Services, "we have to pay for it."

If the American health care system were a true market, the increased volume of colonoscopies—numbers rose 50 percent from 2003 to 2009 for those with commercial insurance—might have brought down the costs because of economies of scale and more competition. Instead, it became a new business opportunity.

PROFITS CLIMB

Just as with real estate, location matters in medicine. Although many procedures can be performed in either a doctor's office or a separate surgery center, prices generally skyrocket at the special centers, as do profits. That is because insurers will pay an additional "facility fee" to ambulatory surgery centers and hospitals that is intended to cover their higher costs. And anesthesia, more monitoring, a wristband and sometimes preoperative testing, along with their extra costs, are more likely to be added on.

. . .Ms. Yapalater, a trim woman who looks far younger than her 64 years, had two prior colonoscopies in doctor's offices (one turned up a polyp that required a five-year follow-up instead of the usual 10 years). But for her routine colonoscopy this January, Ms. Yapalater was referred to Dr. Felice Mirsky of Gastroenterology Associates, a group practice in Garden City, N.Y., that performs the procedures at an ambulatory surgery center called the Long Island Center for Digestive Health. The doctors in the gastroenterology practice, which is just down the hall, are owners of the center. "It was very fancy, with nurses and ORs," Ms. Yapalater said. "It felt like you were in a hospital."

That explains the fees. "If you work as a 'facility,' you can charge a lot more for the same procedure," said Dr. Soeren Mattke, a senior scientist at the RAND Corporation. The bills to Ms. Yapalater's insurer reflected these charges: $1,075 for the gastroenterologist, $2,400 for the anesthesia—and $2,910 for the facility fee. When popularized in the 1980s, outpatient surgical centers were hailed as a cost-saving innovation because they cut down on expensive hospital stays for minor operations like knee arthroscopy. But the cost savings have been offset as procedures once done in a doctor's office have filled up the centers, and bills have multiplied.

It is a lucrative migration. The Long Island center was set up with the help of a company based in Pennsylvania called Physicians Endoscopy. On its Web site, the business tells prospective physician partners that they can look forward to "distributions averaging over $1.4 million a year to all owners," "typically 100 percent return on capital investment within 18 months" and "a return on investment of 500 percent to 2,000 percent over the initial seven years." Dr. Leonard Stein, the senior partner in Gastroenterology Associates and medical director of the surgery center, declined to discuss patient fees or the center's profits, citing privacy issues. But he said the center contracted with insurance companies in the area to minimize patients' out-of-pocket costs.

In 2009, the last year[1] for which such statistics are available, gastroenterologists performed more procedures in ambulatory surgery centers than specialists in any other field. Once they bought into a center, studies show, the number of procedures they performed rose 27 percent. The specialists earn an average of $433,000 a year, among the highest paid doctors, according to Merritt Hawkins & Associates, a medical staffing firm. Hospitals and doctors say that critics should not take the high "rack rates" in bills as reflective of the cost of health care because insurers usually pay less. But those rates are the starting point for negotiations with Medicare and private insurers. Those without insurance or with high-deductible plans have little weight to reduce the charges and often face the highest bills. Nassau Anesthesia Associates—the group practice that handled Ms. Yapalater's sedation—has sued dozens of patients for nonpayment, including Larry Chin, a businessman from Hicksville, N.Y., who said in court that he was then unemployed and uninsured. He was billed $8,675 for anesthesia during cardiac surgery. For the same service, the anesthesia group accepted $6,970 from United Healthcare, $5,208.01 from Blue Cross and Blue Shield, $1,605.29 from Medicare and $797.50 from Medicaid. A judge ruled that Mr. Chin should pay $4,252.11.

Ms. Yapalater's insurer paid $1,568 of the $2,400 anesthesiologist's charge for her colonoscopy, but many medical experts question why anesthesiologists are involved at all. Colonoscopies do not require general anesthesia—a deep sleep that suppresses breathing and often requires a breathing tube. Instead, they require only "moderate sedation," generally with a Valium-like drug or a low dose of propofol, an intravenous medicine that takes effect quickly and wears off within minutes. In other countries, such sedative mixes are administered in offices and hospitals by a wide range of doctors and nurses for countless minor procedures, including colonoscopies. Nonetheless, between 2003 and 2009, the use of an anesthesiologist for colonoscopies in the United States doubled, according to a RAND Corporation study published last year. Payments to anesthesiologists for colonoscopies per patient quadrupled during that period, the researchers found, estimating that ending the practice

for healthy patients could save $1.1 billion a year because "studies have shown no benefit" for them, Dr. Mattke said.

But turf battles and lobbying have helped keep anesthesiologists in the room. When propofol won the approval of the Food and Drug Administration in 1989 as an anesthesia drug, it carried a label advising that it "should be administered only by those who are trained in the administration of general anesthesia" because of concerns that too high a dose could depress breathing and blood pressure to a point requiring resuscitation. Since 2005, the American College of Gastroenterology has repeatedly pressed the F.D.A. to remove or amend the restriction, arguing that gastroenterologists and their nurses are able to safely administer the drug in lower doses as a sedative. But the American Society of Anesthesiologists has aggressively lobbied for keeping the advisory, which so far the F.D.A. has done. A Food and Drug Administration spokeswoman said that the label did not necessarily require an anesthesiologist and that it was safe for the others to administer propofol if they had appropriate training. But many gastroenterologists fear lawsuits if something goes wrong. If anything, that concern has grown since Michael Jackson died in 2009 after being given propofol, along with at least two other sedatives, without close monitoring.

"TOO MUCH FOR TOO LITTLE"

The Department of Veterans Affairs, which performs about a quarter-million colonoscopies annually, does not routinely use an anesthesiologist for screening colonoscopies. In Austria, where colonoscopies are also used widely for cancer screening, the procedure is performed, with sedation, in the office by a doctor and a nurse and "is very safe that way," said Dr. Monika Ferlitsch, a gastroenterologist and professor at the Medical University of Vienna, who directs the national program on quality assurance. But she noted that gastroenterologists in Austria do have their financial concerns. They are complaining to the government and insurers that they cannot afford to do the 30-minute procedure, with prep time, maintenance of equipment and anesthesia, for the current approved rate—between $200 and $300, all included. "I think the cheapest colonoscopy in the U.S. is about $950," Dr. Ferlitsch said. "We'd love to get half of that."

Dr. Cesare Hassan, an Italian gastroenterologist who is the chairman of the Guidelines Committee of the European Society of Gastrointestinal Endoscopy, noted that studies in Europe had estimated that the procedure cost about $400 to $800 to perform, including biopsies and sedation. "The U.S. is paying way too much for too little—it leads to opportunistic colonoscopies," done for profit rather than health, he said.

. . .And some large employers have begun fighting back on costs. Three years ago, Safeway realized that it was paying between $848 and $5,984 for a colonoscopy in California and could find no link to the quality of service at those extremes. So the company established an all-inclusive "reference price" it was willing to pay, which it said was set at a level high enough to give employees access to a range of high-quality options. Above that price, employees would have to pay the difference. Safeway chose $1,250, one-third the amount paid for Ms. Yapalater's procedure—and found plenty of doctors willing to accept the price.

Still, the United States health care industry is nimble at protecting profits. When Aetna tried in 2007 to disallow payment for anesthesiologists delivering propofol during colonoscopies, the insurer backed down after a barrage of attacks from anesthesiologists and endoscopy groups. With Medicare contemplating lowering facility fees for ambulatory surgery centers, experts worry that physician-owners will sell the centers to hospitals, where fees remain higher.

And then there is aggressive marketing. People who do not have insurance or who are covered by Medicaid typically get far less colon cancer screening than they need. But those with insurance are appealing targets. Nineteen months after Matt Meyer, who owns a saddle-fitting company near Keene, N.H., had his first colonoscopy, he received a certified letter from his gastroenterologist. It began, "Our records show that you are due for a repeat colonoscopy," and it advised him to schedule an appointment or "allow us to note your reason for not scheduling." Although his prior test had found a polyp, medical guidelines do not recommend such frequent screening. "I have great doctors, but the economics is daunting," Mr. Meyer said in an interview. "A computer-generated letter telling me to come in for a procedure that costs more than $5,000? It was the weirdest thing."

NOTE

1. *Editor's note*: The latest CDC report, published in 2017 (based on 2010 data), offered consistent data (https://www.cdc.gov/nchs/data/nhsr/nhsr102.pdf).

ROSE WEITZ

48. BIG PHARMA COMES OF AGE

The pharmaceutical industry is the most profitable industry in the United States. Following major legal changes in the 1980s that were deemed "business-friendly," such as direct marketing to consumers and doctors, profits rose dramatically. Weitz demonstrates that this enhanced profitability is accompanied by significant expenses, usually borne by patients, whose prescription drugs may no longer be adequately researched or who may pay excessively high prices for their medicines. Compromises to safety and integrity are made in the name of profit, Weitz argues, and health-care consumers suffer as a result.

BIG PHARMA COMES OF AGE

The pharmaceutical industry is an enormous—and enormously profitable—enterprise. Indeed, it has been the most profitable industry in the United States since the early 1980s (Angell, 2004). Although the pharmaceutical industry routinely argues that their high profits merely reflect the high cost of researching and developing new drugs, such work accounts for only 14% of their budgets. In contrast, marketing accounts for about 50% (Angell, 2004). Largely because of this marketing, American citizens now spend a total of about $230 billion per year—10% of all U.S. health care expenses—on prescription drugs, *not* including drugs purchased by doctors, nursing homes, hospitals, and other institutions (Centers for Medicare & Medicaid Services, 2010). Americans are buying *more* drugs, buying more *expensive* drugs, and seeing the *prices* of popular drugs rise more often than ever before. (The price of the popular antihistamine Claritin, for example, rose 13 times in five years.)

The pharmaceutical industry has not always been this profitable. Profits only began soaring in the early 1980s after a series of legal changes reflecting both the increasingly "business-friendly" atmosphere in the federal government and the increased influence of the pharmaceutical industry lobby—now the biggest spending lobby in Washington. First, new laws allowed researchers funded by federal agencies (including university professors and researchers working for small biotech companies) to patent their discoveries and then license those patents to pharmaceutical companies. This change dramatically reduced pharmaceutical companies' research costs—while giving these researchers a vested interest in emphasizing the benefits of new drugs. Second, new laws almost doubled the life of drug patents. As long as a drug is under patent, the company owning that patent has the sole right to sell that drug. As a result, it can set the drug's price as high as the market will bear. In addition, companies can now extend their patents by developing "me-too" drugs, which differ only slightly from existing drugs; these drugs now account for about 75% of all new drugs (Angell, 2004). Third, the pharmaceutical industry won the right to market drugs direct to consumers. Direct-to-consumer advertising—a $4.3 billion business in 2009—has proven highly effective

(Centers for Medicare & Medicaid Services, 2010b). According to a nationally representative survey conducted in 2008 for the nonprofit Kaiser Family Foundation, almost one-third of American adults have asked their doctors about drugs they've seen advertised, and 82% of those who asked for a prescription received one (Appleby, 2008).

Passage of the Medicare drug benefit program, which went into effect in 2008, has increased pharmaceutical profits even more. The pharmaceutical industry was heavily involved in the drafting and passage of this program, under which Medicare recipients can choose to buy supplemental insurance to cover some of their prescription drug costs (Abramson, 2004; Angell, 2004). However, most Medicare recipients who participate in the drug program now pay more in premiums and in *deductibles* (required minimum amounts individuals must pay out of pocket before their insurance coverage kicks in) than they save by enrolling in the program.

DEVELOPING NEW DRUGS

Much of the recent rise in health care costs in the United States comes from the shift to new drugs. Whenever a new drug is developed, the crucial question for health care providers and patients is whether its benefits outweigh its dangers. For this reason, it is crucial that any new drug be extensively tested to determine whether it works better than already available drugs (which almost certainly are cheaper), whether it works differently in different populations (does it help men as well as women? persons with both early- and late-stage disease?), what dosages are appropriate, and what side effects are likely. But because pharmaceutical companies earn their profits by selling drugs, they have a vested interest in overstating benefits and understating dangers. And increasingly, these companies are both willing and able to manipulate the data available to outside researchers, doctors, federal regulators, and consumers (Abramson, 2004; Angell, 2004). For example, because scientific testing is typically designed to be accurate 95% of the time, manufacturers know that if they test a drug enough times, they will eventually hit the other 5% and obtain data that inaccurately suggest a drug works in some population. . . .

In the past, university-based drug researchers provided at least a partial check on the drug research process by bringing a more objective eye to their research. Since 1980, however, pharmaceutical industry funding for research by university-based scientists has skyrocketed (Lemmens, 2004). That funding comes in many forms, from research grants, to stock options, to all-expenses-paid conferences in Hawaii. Moreover, as other federal funding for universities declined over the past quarter century, university administrators came to expect their faculty to seek pharmaceutical funding. Importantly, when the pharmaceutical industry funds university-based research, it often retains the rights to the research results and so can keep university researchers from publishing any data suggesting that a particular drug is ineffective or dangerous (Angell, 2004; Lemmens, 2004).

At the same time that the pharmaceutical industry has increased its funding to university-based researchers, it has even more dramatically increased funding to *commercial* research organizations (Lemmens, 2004). These organizations are paid not only to conduct research but also to promote it. To keep on the good side of the companies that fund them, these research organizations must make drugs look as effective and safe as possible by, for example, selecting research subjects who are least likely to experience side effects, studying drugs' effects only briefly before side effects can appear, underestimating the severity of any side effects that do appear, and choosing not to publish any studies suggesting that a drug harms or doesn't help.

Doctors, medical researchers, sociologists, and others have raised concerns about the impact of bias on research publications (Bodenheimer, 2000). Researchers have found that medical journal articles written by individuals who received pharmaceutical industry funding are four to five times more likely to recommend the tested drug than are articles written by those without such funding (Abramson, 2004:97). Similarly, researchers have found that research studies suggesting a drug is effective are several times more likely to be submitted and accepted for publication than are those that suggest it is ineffective (Hadler, 2008; Turner et al., 2008). Concern about such biases led the *New England Journal of Medicine* (one of the top two medical journals in the United States) to forbid authors from publishing articles on drugs in which they had financial interests. The policy, however, was dropped quickly because it proved virtually impossible to find authors who did *not* have financial conflicts (Lemmens, 2004).

Even more astonishing than pharmaceutical industry funding of university-based researchers is the growing practice of paying such researchers to sign their names to articles written by industry employees (Elliott, 2004). For example, between 1988 and 2000, 96 articles were published in medical journals on the popular antidepressant Zoloft. Just over half of these were written by pharmaceutical industry employees but published under the names of university-based researchers. Moreover, these ghost-written articles were *more* likely than other articles to be published in prestigious medical journals (Elliott, 2004).

REGULATING DRUGS

In the United States, ensuring the safety of pharmaceutical drugs falls to the Food and Drug Administration (FDA). But during the same time period that the profits and power of the pharmaceutical industry grew, the FDA's power and funding declined as part of a broader public and political movement away from "big government." These two changes are not unrelated: The pharmaceutical industry now routinely provides funding of various sorts to staff members at government advisory agencies, doctors who serve on FDA advisory panels, and legislators who support reducing the FDA's powers (Lemmens, 2004).

Under current regulations, the FDA must make its decisions based primarily on data reported to it by the pharmaceutical industry. Yet the industry is required to report only a small fraction of the research it conducts. For example, the company that produced the antidepressant Paxil had considerable data indicating that, among teenagers, Paxil did *not* reduce depression but *could* lead to suicide. To avoid making this information public, the company submitted to the FDA only its data from studies on adults (Lemmens, 2004). Similarly, drug companies need only demonstrate that new drugs

work better than *placebos*, not that they work better than existing (cheaper) drugs. For example, because of intensive marketing campaigns, new antipsychotic drugs such as Zyprexa have largely replaced older, cheaper drugs even though the new drugs work little better than placebos and carry life-threatening risks (Wilson, 2010).

MARKETING DRUGS

Once the pharmaceutical industry develops a drug and gets FDA approval, the next step is to market the drug. One of the most important limitations to the FDA's power is that, once it approves a drug for a single use in a single population, doctors legally can prescribe it for *any* purpose to *any* population. For example, doctors increasingly are prescribing Botox injections to treat migraines even though the FDA has not approved its use for that purpose.

Drug marketing has two major audiences, doctors and the public. Marketing to doctors begins during medical school as students quickly learn that pharmaceutical companies provide a ready source not only of drug samples and information but also of pens, notepads, lunches, and all-expense-paid "educational" conferences at major resorts. After graduation, the pharmaceutical industry continues to serve as doctors' main source of information about drugs. The *Physicians' Desk Reference* (or *PDR*), the main reference doctors turn to for drug information, is solely composed of drug descriptions written by drug manufacturers. In addition, the pharmaceutical industry spends $6,000 to $11,000 (depending on medical specialty) per doctor per year to send salespeople to doctors' offices on top of the money it spends advertising drugs to doctors in other ways. Most doctors meet with pharmaceutical salespeople at least four times per month and believe their behavior is unaffected by these salespeople. Yet doctors who meet with drug salespeople prescribe promoted drugs more often than do other doctors, even when the promoted drugs are more costly and less effective than the alternatives (Angell, 2004; Shapiro, 2004). In addition, the pharmaceutical companies now surreptitiously provide much of the "continuing education courses" doctors must take each year by paying for-profit firms to teach the courses and to arrange with universities to accredit the courses (Angell, 2004).

In recent years, and as noted earlier, marketing directly to consumers has become as important as marketing to doctors. To the companies, such advertising is simply an extension of normal business practices, no different from any other form of advertising. Moreover, they argue, advertising to consumers is a public service because it can encourage consumers to seek medical care for problems they otherwise might have ignored. Finally, companies have argued that these advertisements pose no health risks because consumers still must get prescriptions before they can purchase drugs, thus leaving the final decisions in doctors' hands. Those who oppose such advertisements, on the other hand, argue that the advertisements are frequently misleading, encourage consumers to pressure their doctors into prescribing the drugs, and encourage both doctors and patients to treat normal human conditions (such as baldness) with pharmaceutical drugs (Angell, 2004; Hadler, 2008).

MARKETING DISEASES

As this suggests, the pharmaceutical industry sells not only drugs but also diseases to doctors and the public alike. In some cases, drug companies have encouraged doctors and the public to define disease *risks* (such as high blood pressure) as *diseases* (such as hypertensive disease). In other cases . . . drug companies have defined symptoms into new diseases.

One example of this is the newly defined illness *pseudobulbar affect*, or PBA. PBA refers to uncontrollable laughing or crying unrelated to individuals' emotional state and can be caused by various disabling neurological conditions (such as head trauma, stroke, and Lou Gehrig's disease). The concept of PBA was developed by Avanir Pharmaceuticals, which markets the drug Neurodex as a treatment for it (Pollack, 2005). Although Neurodex seems to help some patients, its side effects are serious enough that at least one-quarter of users—all of whom already have serious health problems and must take numerous other medications—soon stop taking it.

To convince doctors that uncontrollable laughing and crying is a disease in itself, Avanir has advertised in medical journals and sponsored continuing education courses, conferences, and a PBA newsletter. Avanir also has marketed the concept of PBA directly to consumers through its PBA website and through educational grants it has given to advocacy groups for those living with stroke, multiple sclerosis, and other diseases (Pollack, 2005).

REFERENCES

Abramson, John. 2004. *Overdosed America: The Broken Promise of American Medicine*. New York: Harper Collins.

Angell, Marcia. 2004. *The Truth about the Drug Companies: How They Deceive Us and What to Do About It*. New York: Random House.

Appleby, Julie. 2008. "Survey: Many Request Drugs Advertised on TV." *Arizona Republic* March 4:A12.

Bodenheimer, Thomas. 2000. "Uneasy Alliance: Clinical Investigators and the Pharmaceutical Industry." *New England Journal of Medicine* 342:1539–43.

Centers for Medicare & Medicaid Services. 2010. *National Health Expenditure Accounts, Historical*. http://www.cms.gov/NationalHealthExpend-Data/, accessed November 2010.

Centers for Medicare & Medicaid Services. 2010b. *National Health Expenditure Accounts, Historical*. http://www.cms.gov/NationalHealthExpend-Data/, accessed November 2010.

Elliott, Carl. 2004. "Pharma Goes to the Laundry: Public Relations and the Subject of Medical Education." *Hastings Center Review* 34:18–23.

Hadler, Nortin M. 2008. *Worried Sick*. Chapel Hill, NC: University of North Carolina Press.

Lemmens, Trudo. 2004. "Piercing the Veil of Corporate Secrecy about Clinical Trials." *Hastings Center Review* 34:14–18.

Pollack, Andrew. 2005. "Marketing a Disease, and also a Drug to Treat It." *New York Times* May 9:C1+.

Shapiro, Dan. 2004. "Drug Companies Get Too Close for Med School's Comfort." *New York Times* January 20:D7+.

Turner, Erick H., Annette M. Matthews, Eftihia Linardatos, Robert A. Tell, and Robert Rosenthal. 2008. "Selective Publication of Antidepressant Trials and Its Influence on Apparent Efficacy." *New England Journal of Medicine* 358:252–60.

Wilson, Duff. 2010. "Side Effects May Include Law Suits." *New York Times* October 3:BY 1+.

49. THE ADDICTS NEXT DOOR

Michael Barrett and Jenna Mulligan, who work as emergency paramedics in Berkeley County, West Virginia, recently got a call that sent them to the youth softball field in a tiny town called Hedgesville. It was the first practice of the season for the girls' Little League team, and dusk was descending. Barrett and Mulligan drove past a clubhouse with a blue-and-yellow sign that read "Home of the Lady Eagles" and stopped near a scrubby set of bleachers, where parents had gathered to watch their daughters bat and field.

Two of the parents were lying on the ground, unconscious, several yards apart. As Barrett later recalled, the couple's 13-year-old daughter was sitting behind a chain link backstop with her teammates, who were hugging and comforting her. The couple's younger children, aged 10 and 7, were running back and forth between their parents, screaming, "Wake up! Wake up!" When Barrett and Mulligan knelt down to administer Narcan, a drug that reverses heroin overdoses, some of the other parents got angry. "You know, saying, 'This is bullcrap,'" Barrett told me. "'Why's my kid gotta see this? Just let 'em lay there.'" After a few minutes, the man and woman began to groan as they revived. Adults ushered the younger children away. From the other side of the backstop, the older kids asked Barrett if the parents had overdosed. "I was, like, 'I'm not gonna say.' But the kids aren't stupid. They know people don't just pass out for no reason." During the chaos, someone made a call to Child Protective Services.

At this stage of the American opioid epidemic, many addicts are collapsing in public—in gas stations, in restaurant bathrooms, in the aisles of big-box stores. Brian Costello, a former Army medic who is the director of the Berkeley County Emergency Medical Services, believes that more overdoses are occurring in this way because users figure that somebody will find them before they die. "To people who don't have that addiction, that sounds crazy," he said. "But, from a health care provider's standpoint, you say to yourself, 'No, this is survival to them.' They're struggling with using but not wanting to die."

A month after the incident, the couple from the softball field, Angel Dawn Holt, who is 35, and her boyfriend, Christopher Schildt, who is 33, were arraigned on felony charges of child neglect. A local newspaper, the Martinsburg *Journal*, ran an article about the charges, noting that the couple's children, who had been "crying when law enforcement arrived," had been "turned over to their grandfather."

West Virginia has the highest overdose death rate in the country, and heroin has flooded into the state's Eastern Panhandle, which includes Hedgesville and the larger town of Martinsburg. Like the vast majority of residents there, nearly all the addicts are White, were born in the area, and have modest incomes. Some locals view them with empathy, others as community embarrassments. Many people in the Panhandle have embraced the idea of addiction as a disease, but a vocal cohort dismisses that view as sentimental claptrap disseminated by urban liberals.

These tensions were evident in the online comments that soon amassed beneath the *Journal* article. A waitress named Sandy wrote, "Omgsh, How sad!! Shouldnt be able to have there kids back! Seems the heroin was more important to them, than watchn

---

there kids have fun play ball, and have there parents proud of them!!" Another comment came from a woman named Valerie, who wrote, "Stop giving them Narcan! At the tax payers expense." Such dismissals were countered by a reader named Diana: "I'm sure the parents didn't get up that morning and say hey let's scar the kids for life. I'm sure they wished they could sit through the kids practice without having to get high. The only way to understand it is to have lived it. The children need to be in a safe home and the adults need help. They are sick, i know from the outside it looks like a choice but its not. Shaming and judging will not help anyone."

One day, Angel Holt started posting her own comments. "I don't neglect," she wrote. "Had a bad judgment I love my kids and my kids love me there honor roll students my oldest son is about to graduate they play sports and have a ruff over there head that I own and food, and things they just want I messed up give me a chance to prove my self I don't have to prove shit to none of u just my children n they know who I am and who I'm not."

A few weeks later, I spoke to Holt on the phone. "Where it happened was really horrible," she said. "I can't sit here and say different." But, she said, it had been almost impossible to find help for her addiction. On the day of the softball practice, she had ingested a small portion of a package of heroin that she and Schildt had just bought, figuring it wasn't enough to lay her out flat. She had promised her daughter that she'd be at practice and she really wanted to come through. But the heroin had a strange purple tint—it must have been cut with something nasty, she wasn't sure what. She started feeling weird, and passed out. She knew that she shouldn't have touched heroin that was so obviously adulterated. But, she added, "if you're an addict, and if you have the stuff, you do it."

In Berkeley County, which has a population of 114,000, when someone under 60 dies and the cause of death isn't mentioned in the paper, people just assume that it was an overdose. It's becoming the default explanation when an ambulance stops outside a neighbor's house and the best guess for why someone is sitting in his car on the side of the road in the middle of a sunny afternoon. On January 18, county officials started using a new app to record overdoses. According

to this data, during the next two and a half months emergency medical personnel responded to 145 overdoses, 18 of which were fatal. This is almost certainly an underestimate, since not all overdoses prompt 911 calls. Last year, the county's annual budget for emergency medication was $27,000. Narcan, which costs $50 a dose, consumed two-thirds of that allotment. The medication was administered 223 times in 2014 and 403 times in 2016.

One Thursday in March, a few weeks before Michael Barrett responded to Angel Holt's overdose, I rode with him in his paramedic vehicle, a specially equipped SUV. He had started his day as he often does, with bacon and eggs at the Olde Country Diner in Martinsburg. Barrett, who is 33, with a russet-colored beard and mustache, works two 24-hour shifts a week, starting at 7 A.M. The diner shares a strip mall with the EMT station, and, if he has to leave on a call before he can finish eating, the servers know to box up his food in a hurry. Barrett's father and his uncles were volunteer firemen in the area, and, growing up, he often accompanied them in the fire truck. As they'd pull people from crumpled cars or burning buildings, he'd say to himself, "Man, they *doing* stuff—they're awesome." When Barrett became a paramedic, in his 20s, he knew that he could make a lot more money "going down the road," as people around there say, referring to Baltimore or Washington, D.C. But he liked it when older colleagues told him, "I used to hold you at the fire department when you were a baby."

Barrett's first overdose call of the day came at 8 A.M., for a 20-year-old woman. Several family members were present at the home, and while Barrett and his colleagues worked on the young woman, the family members cried and blamed one another and themselves for not watching her more closely. The woman was given Narcan, but she was too far gone; she died after arriving at the hospital.

We stopped by a local fire station, where the men and women on duty talked about all the OD calls they took each week. Sometimes they knew the person from high school or were related to the person. Barrett said that, in such cases you tended "to get more angry at them—you're, like, 'Man, you got a *kid*, what the hell's wrong with you?'"

Barrett sometimes had to return several times in one day to the same house—once, a father, a mother, and a teenage daughter overdosed on heroin in succession. Such stories seemed like a dark twist on the small-town generational solidarity he so appreciated; as Barrett put it, even if one family member wanted to get clean, it would be next to impossible unless the others did, too. He was used to OD. calls by now, except for the ones in which kids were present. He once arrived at a home to find a 7-year-old and a 5-year-old following the instructions of a 911 operator and performing CPR on their parents. (The parents survived.)

Around three o'clock, the dispatcher reported that a man in Hedgesville was slumped over the steering wheel of a jeep. By the time we got there, the man, who appeared to be in his early 30s, had been helped out of his vehicle and into an ambulance. A skinny young sheriff's deputy on the scene showed us a half-filled syringe: the contents resembled clean sand, which suggested pure heroin. That was a good thing— these days, the narcotic is often cut with synthetic opioids such as fentanyl, which is fifty times as powerful as heroin.

The man had floppy brown hair and a handsome face; he was wearing jeans, work boots, and a Black windbreaker. He'd been revived with oxygen—he hadn't needed Narcan—but as he sat in the ambulance, his eyes were only partly opened, the pupils constricted to pinpoints. Barrett asked him, "Did you take a half syringe? 'Cause there's half a syringe left." The man looked up briefly and said, "Yeah? I was trying to take it all." He said that he was sorry—he'd been clean for a month. Then he mumbled something about having a headache. "Well, sure you do," another paramedic said. "You weren't breathing there for a while. Your brain didn't have any oxygen."

I looked over and noticed that the man's jeep was still sitting in the middle of a sloping street, doors flung open, as though it had been dropped by a cyclone. A woman surveying the scene, with her arms folded across her chest, introduced herself to me as Ethel. She had been driving behind the man when he lost consciousness. "I just rolled up, saw he was slumped over the wheel," she said. "I knew what it was right away." She beeped her horn, but he didn't

move. She called 911 and stayed until the first responders showed up, "in case he started to roll forward, and maybe I could stop traffic—and to make sure he was OK." I asked if the man's jeep had been running during this time. "Oh, yeah," said Ethel, looking over to check on a young kid in the backseat of her own car. "He just happened to stop with his foot on the brake." Barrett shared some protocol: whenever he came across people passed out in a car, he put the transmission in park and took their keys, in case they abruptly revived. He'd heard of people driving off with EMT personnel halfway inside.

The sky was a dazzling blue; fluffy White clouds scudded overhead. The man took a sobriety test, wobbling across the tidy lawn of a Methodist church. "That guy's still high as a kite," somebody said.

We were driving away from Hedgesville when the third overdose call of the day came, for a 29-year-old male. Inside a nicely kept house in a modern subdivision, the man was lying unconscious on the bathroom floor, taking intermittent gasps. He was pale, though not yet the blue-tinged gray that people turn when they've been breathing poorly for a while. Opioid overdoses usually kill people by inhibiting respiration: breathing slows and starts to sound labored, then stops altogether. Barrett began preparing a Narcan dose. Generally, the goal was to get people breathing well again, not necessarily to wake them completely. A full dose of Narcan is 2 milligrams, and in Berkeley County the medics administer 0.4 milligrams at a time, so as not to snatch patients' high away too abruptly: you didn't want them to go into instant withdrawal, feel terribly sick, and become belligerent. Barrett crouched next to the man and started an IV. A minute later, the man sat up, looking bewildered and resentful. He vomited. Barrett said, "Couple more minutes and you would have died, buddy."

"Thank you," the man said.

"You're welcome—but now you need to go to the hospital."

The man's girlfriend was standing nearby, her hair in a loose bun. She responded calmly to questions: "Yeah, he does heroin"; "Yeah, he just ate." The family dog was snuffling at the front door, and one of the sheriff's deputies asked if he could let it outside. The girlfriend said, "Sure." Brian Costello had told me that family members sometimes seemed unfazed by these EMT visits: "That's the scary part—that it's becoming the norm." The man stood up, and then, swaying in the doorway, vomited a second time.

"We're gonna take him to the hospital," Barrett told the girlfriend. "He could stop breathing again."

As we drove away, Barrett predicted that the man would check himself out of the hospital as soon as he could; most of the OD patients he saw refused further treatment. "It's kind of hard to feel good about it," Barrett said of the intervention. "Though he did say, 'Thanks for waking me up.' Well, that's our job. But do you feel like you're really making a difference? Ninety-nine percent of the time, no." The next week, Barrett's crew was called back to the same house repeatedly. The man overdosed three times; his girlfriend, once.

It was getting dark, and Barrett stopped at a convenience store for a snack—chocolate milk and a beef stick. That evening, he dealt with one more OD. A young woman had passed out in her car in the parking lot of a 7-Eleven, with her little girl squirming in a car seat. An older woman who happened on the scene had taken the girl, a 4-year-old, into the store and bought her some hot chocolate and Skittles. After the young woman received Narcan, Barrett told her that she could have killed her daughter, and she started sobbing. Meanwhile, several guys in the parking lot were becoming agitated. They had given the woman CPR, but someone had called 911 and suggested that they had supplied her with the heroin. The men were Black and everybody else—the overdosing woman, the older woman, the cops, the ambulance crew—was White. The men were told to remain at the scene while the cops did background checks. Barrett attempted to defuse the tension by saying, "Hey, you guys gave her CPR? Thanks. We really appreciate that." The criminal checks turned up nothing; there was no reason to suspect that the men were anything but Good Samaritans. The cops let the men go, the young woman went to the ER, and the little girl was retrieved by her father.

Heroin is an alluringly cheap alternative to prescription pain medication. In 1996, Purdue Pharma introduced OxyContin, marketing it as a safer form of opiate—the class of painkillers derived from the poppy plant. (The term "opioids" encompasses synthetic versions of opiates as well.) Opiates such as morphine block pain but also produce a dreamy euphoria, and over time they cause physical cravings. OxyContin was sold in time-release capsules that leveled out the high and supposedly diminished the risk of addiction, but people soon discovered that the capsules could be crushed into powder and then injected or snorted. Between 2000 and 2014, the number of overdose deaths in the United States jumped by 137 percent.

Some parts of the country were inundated with opiates. According to the Charleston *Gazette-Mail*, between 2007 and 2012 drug wholesalers shipped to West Virginia 780 million pills of hydrocodone (the generic name for Vicodin) and oxycodone (the generic name for OxyContin). That was enough to give each resident 433 pills. The state has a disproportionate number of people whose jobs—coal mining, for instance—can result in chronic physical pain. It also has high levels of poverty and joblessness—sources of psychic pain. Mental health services, meanwhile, are scant, as they are in many rural areas of the country. Chess Yellott, a retired family practitioner in Martinsburg, told me that he often saw people self-medicate to mute depression, anxiety, and posttraumatic stress from sexual assault or childhood abuse. "Those things are treatable, and upper-middle-class parents generally get their kids treated," he said. "But in families with a lot of chaos and money problems, kids don't get help."

In 2010, Purdue introduced a reformulated capsule that is harder to crush or dissolve. The Centers for Disease Control and Prevention (CDC) subsequently issued new guidelines stipulating that doctors should not routinely treat chronic pain with opioids and instead should try approaches such as exercise and behavioral therapy. The number of prescriptions for opioids began to drop.

But when prescription opioids became scarcer, their street price went up. Drug cartels sensed an opportunity and began pouring heroin into rural America. Daniel Ciccarone, a professor at the UC-San Francisco School of Medicine, studies the heroin market. He said of the cartels, "They're multinational, savvy, borderless entities. They worked very hard to move high-quality heroin into places like rural Vermont." They also kept the price low. In West Virginia, many addicts told me, an oxycodone pill now sells for about $80; a dose of heroin can be bought for about $10.

A recent paper from the National Bureau of Economic Research concludes that "following the OxyContin reformulation in 2010, abuse of prescription opioid medications and overdose deaths decreased for the first time since 1990. However, this drop coincided with an unprecedented rise in heroin overdoses." According to the CDC, three out of four new heroin users report having first abused opioid pills.

"The Changing Face of Heroin Use in the United States," a 2014 study led by Theodore Cicero of Washington University in St. Louis, looked at some 3,000 heroin addicts in substance-abuse programs. Half of those who began using heroin before 1980 were White; nearly 90 percent of those who began using in the past decade were White. This demographic shift may be connected to racially charged prescribing patterns. A 2012 study by a University of Pennsylvania researcher found that Black patients were 34 percent less likely than White patients to be prescribed opioids for such chronic conditions as back pain and migraines, and 14 percent less likely to receive such prescriptions after surgery or traumatic injury.

But a larger factor, it seems, was the despair of White people in struggling small towns. Judith Feinberg, a professor at West Virginia University who studies drug addiction, described opioids as "the ultimate escape drugs." She told me, "Boredom and a sense of uselessness and inadequacy—these are human failings that lead you to just want to withdraw. On heroin, you curl up in a corner and blank out the world. It's an extremely seductive drug for dead-end towns because it makes the world's problems go away. Much more so than coke or meth, where you want to run around and *do* things, you get aggressive, razzed and jazzed."

Peter Callahan, a psychotherapist in Martinsburg, said that heroin "is a very tough drug to get off of, because, while it was meant to numb *physical* pain, it numbs emotional pain as well—quickly and intensely." In tight-knit Appalachian towns, heroin has become a social contagion. Nearly everyone I met in Martinsburg had ties to someone—a child, a sibling, a girlfriend, an in-law, an old high school coach—who has struggled with opioids. As Callahan put it, "If the lady next door is using, and so are other neighbors,

and people in your family are, too, the odds are good that you're going to join in."

In 2015, Berkeley County created a new position, recovery-services coordinator, to connect residents with rehab. But there is a chronic shortage of beds in the state for addicts who want help. Kevin Knowles, who was appointed to the job, told me, "If they have private insurance, I can hook them right up. If they're on Medicaid—and 95 percent of the people I work with are—it's going to be a long wait for them. Weeks, months." He said, "The number of beds would have to increase by a factor of three or four to make any impact."

West Virginia has an overdose death rate of 41.5 per 100,000 people. (New Hampshire has the second-highest rate: 34.3 per 100,000.) This year, for the sixth straight year, West Virginia's indigent burial fund, which helps families who can't afford a funeral pay for one, ran out of money. Fred Kitchen, the president of the West Virginia Funeral Directors Association, told me that, in the funeral business, "we know the reason for that was the increase in overdose deaths." He added, "Families take out second mortgages, cash in 401(k)s, and go broke to try and save a son or daughter, who then overdoses and dies." Without the help of the burial fund, funeral directors must either give away caskets, plots, and cremation services—and risk going out of business—or, Kitchen said, look "mothers, fathers, husbands, wives, and children in the eye while they're saying, 'You have nothing to help us?'"

Martinsburg, which has a population of 17,000, is a hilly town filled with brick and clapboard row houses. It was founded in 1778, by Adam Stephen, a Revolutionary War general. The town became a depot for the B & O Railroad and grew into an industrial center dominated by woolen mills. Interwoven, established in the 1890s, was the first electric-powered textile plant in the United States. The company became the largest men's-sock manufacturer in the world. At its height, it employed 3,000 people in Martinsburg, and commissioned sumptuous advertising illustrations of handsome men in snappy socks by the likes of Norman Rockwell. The Interwoven factory whistle could be heard all over town, summoning workers every morning at a quarter to seven. In 1971, when the mill closed, an editorial in the Martinsburg *Journal* mourned the passing of "what was once this community's greatest pride." In 2004, the last woolen mill in town, Royce Hosiery, ceased operations.

It would be simplistic to trace the town's opioid epidemic directly to the erosion of industrial jobs. Nevertheless, many residents I met brought up this history, as part of a larger story of lost purpose that has made the town vulnerable to the opioid onslaught. In 2012, Macy's opened a distribution center in the Martinsburg area, but, Knowles said, the company has found it difficult to hire longtime residents because so many fail the required drug test. (The void has been filled, only partially, by people from neighboring states.) Knowles wonders if Procter & Gamble, which is opening a manufacturing plant in the area this fall, will have a similar problem.

The Eastern Panhandle is one of the wealthier parts of a poor state. (The most destitute counties depend on coal mining.) Berkeley County is close enough to Washington and Baltimore that many residents commute for work. Nevertheless, Martinsburg feels isolated. Several people I met there expressed surprise, or sympathy, when I told them that I live in D.C. or politely said that they'd like to visit the capital one of these days. Like every other county in West Virginia, Berkeley County voted for Donald Trump.

Michael Chalmers is the publisher of an Eastern Panhandle newspaper, the *Observer*, which is based in Shepherdstown, a picturesque college town near the Maryland border. Chalmers, who is 42, grew up in Martinsburg, and in 2014 he lost his younger brother, Jason, to an overdose. I asked him why he thought that Martinsburg was struggling so much with drugs. "In my opinion, the desperation in the Panhandle, and places like it, is a *social* vacancy," he said. "People don't feel they have a purpose." There was a "shame element in small-town culture." Many drug addicts, he explained, are "trying to escape the reality that this place doesn't give them anything." He added, "That's really hard to live with—when you look around and you see that seven out of ten of your friends from high school are still here, and nobody makes more than $36,000 a year, and everybody's just bitching about bills and watching these crazy shows on reality TV and not *doing anything*."

Queen Street, Martinsburg's main thoroughfare, has a bunch of thrift and antique shops, some of them no longer in business, their big, dusty display windows scattered with random items—a gum-ball machine and a gramophone, a couple of naked mannequins. It's not as if nobody's trying. The Chamber of Commerce hosts events to attract people downtown, and at Christmas there are snowmen painted by school kids. People always seemed to be eating burgers at the Blue White Grill. But as I walked along Queen Street one February afternoon, an older man in a cardigan stopped and asked me, "What in the world are they going to do with all these empty buildings?"

The Interwoven mill, derelict and grand, still dominates the center of town. One corner of it has been turned into a restaurant, but the rest sits empty. Lately, there's been talk of an ambitious renovation. A police officer named Andrew Garcia has a plan, called Martinsburg Renew, which would turn most of the mill into a rehab facility. One chilly, gray day, Todd Funkhouser, who runs the Berkeley County Historical Society, showed me around. "Martinsburg is an industrial town," he said. "That's its identity. But what's the industry now? Maybe it will be drug rehab."

In the past several months, I have returned to Martinsburg many times and spoken to a number of people struggling with addiction. But in some ways I learned the most about the crisis from residents who were not themselves drug users, but whose lives had been irrevocably altered by others' addiction. Looking through the microcosm of one town at a nationwide epidemic, I wanted to know how it had blown people off course and how they were responding.

Lori Swadley is a portrait and wedding photographer in Martinsburg. When I came across her website while researching local businesses, I could see she seemed to be in demand all over the area, and her photographs were lovely: her brides glowed in golden hour light, her high school seniors looked polished and confident. But what caught my attention was a side project she had been pursuing, called 52 Addicts—a series of portraits that called attention to the drug epidemic in and around Martinsburg. It was clear that Swadley had a full life: her husband, Jon, worked with her in the photography business, and they had three small children, Juniper, Bastian, and Bodhi. Her website noted that she loved fashion and gardening, and it included this message: "I'm happy that you've stumbled upon our little slice of heaven!" The 52 Addicts series seemed like a surprising project for someone so busy and cheerful. . . .

We met one day at Mugs & Muffins, a cozy coffee shop on Queen Street. Swadley is 39, tall and slender, and she looked elegant in jeans, a charcoal-colored turtleneck, and knee-high boots. She and her husband had moved to Martinsburg in 2010, she told me, looking for an affordable place to raise children close to where she had grown up, in the Shenandoah Valley of Virginia. Soon after they arrived, they settled into a subdivision outside of town, and Swadley started reading the Martinsburg *Journal* online. She told me, "I'd see these stories about addiction—whether it was somebody who'd passed away, and the family wanted to tell their story, or it was the overdose statistics, or whatever." Many of the stories were written by the same reporter, Jenni Vincent. "She was very persistent, and—I don't know what the word for it is—very *in your face*," Swadley said. "You could tell she wanted the problem to be known. Because at that time it seemed like everybody else wanted to hide it. And, to me, that seemed like the worst thing you could do."

Swadley told me she had thirteen friends who had died of opioid overdoses. I said that seemed like an extraordinarily high number, especially for someone who was not herself a drug user. She agreed, but there it was. All thirteen were young men—Swadley had met most of them when she was in her early 20s, and she had been kind of an overgrown tomboy then, at ease with guys who treated her like a fun sister. She had been photographing a wedding for some mutual friends the first time she heard about one of the guys dying. A group of Swadley's buddies were sitting around a bonfire at the end of the day, when she happened to mention, laughing at the memory, the wacky horror film she and a guy named Jeremy had made together in high school. Somebody said Jeremy had died not long before, from a heroin overdose. Swadley felt like she'd been punched in the gut. She stood up and vomited, and then, driving home, ended up wrecking her car.

At the time, Swadley was hanging out with her old crowd in bars and restaurants every weekend. One by one, the group dwindled. Many of them—"the preppy

boys, the hippie boys"—eventually got into heroin, she said. They tried to help one another, but "we were in our 20s—we had no clue." She'd call rehab places on friends' behalf and have to tell them that the price was staggering, and that in any case it might be six months before they could be admitted. As the overdoses piled up, she was appalled to realize that sometimes she had trouble keeping track of which of her friends were dead.

The funerals had a peculiar aspect. "The parents didn't want anyone to know how it had happened, and they tried to keep the friends out," she said. At the services for one of them—a sweet, goofy guy with shaggy blond hair—Swadley and her friends got close enough to the casket to see that his hair had been shorn, so that "he looked clean-cut." She went on, "It was clear that his mother didn't want us there. It was understandable—she didn't know if any of us had been supplying him."

One day Swadley decided that she needed to write down all thirteen names before she forgot one. And in January, 2016, she started on another quest to see and remember: she would photograph addicts in recovery. In her introduction to the series, on Instagram, she wrote about her friends who had died and about the lack of drug treatment. She found the culture of denial enraging.

For the first few portraits, Swadley reached out to her subjects, but soon people started coming to her. She took their pictures, asked them about their lives, and told their stories in a paragraph or so. There are now two dozen images in the series.

In one of the portraits, an ER nurse hugs her daughter, Hope, from whom she'd been estranged. They had reconnected at the hospital, when the nurse saw Hope's name listed as an overdose patient in the emergency room. Swadley photographed a Martinsburg woman named Crystal, who'd been hit by a car one night when she was walking to her dealer's house; Crystal was now off drugs, but she was confined to a wheelchair. A woman named Tiffany posed holding a snapshot of her younger sister, Tabby. Both women had started on pills—Tabby had developed a problem after a gallbladder operation left her with a thirty-day supply of meds—and then she got addicted to heroin. Tiffany had received treatment, but

Tabby had fatally overdosed while she was waiting for a rehab bed. Swadley took the portrait in a park where Tiffany had once begged Tabby to stop using. When I called Tiffany, she told me that she had recently lost a second sister to heroin.

Swadley hopes that her photographs will someday be displayed all around town—in coffee shops, restaurants, the library. She wants a public reckoning with the stories she's collected. "The whole point of this project is to show naysayers out there that people do recover," she said. "They are good people. I want to show people they deserve a chance. I want it in people's faces, so they see that it could be their neighbor, or their best friend."

During one of our conversations, Swadley told me about a local effort against heroin addiction, called the Hope Dealer Project. It was run by three women: Tina Stride, who had a 26-year-old son in recovery; Tara Mayson, whose close friend had gone through periods of addiction; and Lisa Melcher, whose son-in-law had died of an overdose and whose 32-year-old daughter, Christina, was struggling to overcome heroin addiction. All three had known addicts who wanted to get clean but had no place to go. Last fall, like carpool moms with a harrowing new mission, they had begun driving people to detox facilities all over the state— any place that could take them, sometimes as far as five hours away. The few with private insurance could get rehab anywhere in the country, and the Hope Dealer women were prepared to suggest options. But most people in town had Medicaid or no insurance at all, and such addicts had to receive treatment somewhere in the state. Currently, the detox facility closest to Martinsburg is about two hours away.

Stride works full time at the General Services Administration, in Washington but spends up to 24 hours a week giving rides to drug users. The other two focus on reaching out to people in addiction and families. Stride noted, "I have to talk to the addict, or the client—that's what we try to call them—all the way to that detox center. Because they're sick. And we pass hospitals all the way, and they're begging, 'Just take me there—they can help me!' But they really can't, the hospitals."

When Stride and her client arrive at a detox facility, nurses are waiting at the door. At that point, Stride said, "they're, like, 'What do you mean, you're *leaving* me?'" She went on, "They're scared because now it's reality. They know they're not going to get their dope or their pills. For them to walk in those doors, that takes a lot. They're heroes to me."

After five to ten days in detox, patients are released. "When our clients get clean and the drugs are out of their system, they believe they're OK," Stride said. "And they're not. That's just getting the poison out of their bodies. So we try to explain to them, 'No, you need to go through rehab, and learn *why* you are using, and learn how to fight it.' Some will do it. Some won't. And then our issue becomes how we're going to find them a bed in rehab. If beds are all full, a lot of times they come back here to Martinsburg, because they have nowhere else to go." Stride tries to keep those clients under constant watch. "That addict brain is telling them, 'You know what you need, and it's right here—go get it.'"

Stride usually drives clients to a detox center immediately after picking them up. But there was one time when she had to put a stranger up overnight at her home because a bed wasn't available for the woman until the morning. "All I said was 'Please, don't rob me,'" Stride recalled. "I'm here to help you. But I guess if you *are* gonna rob me there's not a whole lot I can do about it.' This young lady had to go through the night—she was so sick, she didn't sleep. I tried to stay up, but I knew I had to drive four hours to the detox place, and four hours back. So I slept some. We were up at 4 A.M., and at the detox place at eight. And she's doing good now—she calls me to touch base sometimes."

The Hope Dealer women and I met near an apartment complex that Melcher manages and drank McDonald's mochas that she had brought for all of us. Melcher, who is 53, with abundant blond ringlets and a warm, husky voice, told me that she loved flower arranging and refinishing old furniture—activities that would be occupying her days more often if there weren't a heroin crisis. Stride, who is 47, wore her hair in a ponytail and had curly bangs; Mayson, who is 46, had long, sparkly nails.

At one point, Stride said, "Please don't think I'm rude," as she picked up her phone to read a text.

"He's in!" she cried. "He made it!"

The women cheered.

They had spent the previous day working on behalf of a woman and her 21-year-old son, who is addicted to heroin. He had private insurance, so they had signed him up for a drug rehab program in New Hampshire. "We had a plane ticket ready, and they were ready to go to the airport," Stride said. "I left them, and then the mother called me and said, 'My son's lips are blue—he's overdosed. What do I do?'" Stride became teary. "And I said, 'Call 911. I'm coming right back over.'"

Stride went on, "So he was in the hospital, and then his mom reached out to me late last night and said, 'He's been released.' First question I asked is 'Where is he?', because we're afraid he's going to run. And she said, 'Instead of putting him on a plane, can we drive him? Because I want to know he makes it.' And I said, 'Yes, you can.' So they are driving eight hours to take him to his detox. Detox was good to go—so we know for the next seven to ten days he's safe." After that, the man was set to go to Florida, to attend a thirty-day program that Stride respected.

Melcher said, "Praise God, he made it," and the women all nodded.

Mayson, who works at the Department of Veterans Affairs and has two adult children, said that the Hope Dealer women had become like sisters. When one of them has a hard day, she can count on one of the others to tell her to rest and recharge—or, as Melcher often says, to "*breeeathe.*"

As mothers, they felt that they had a particular ability to communicate with women who needed help with their addicted children. Stride said, "I remember when I first found out my son was an addict. I was devastated. I didn't know who to turn to, who I could trust. And I worked and worked to find my son a place, and that's rough. Hearing 'No' or 'We can't take him today, but we can take him a week from today.' 'No, you need to take him *now*. My son's gonna *die*.' So now, when moms reach out to us, we're, like, 'We've got this!'"

Melcher said, "When you're in that space? Oh, my gosh, you can hardly breathe, you're a cryin' mess."

Stride nodded and said, "So when we come in and say, 'Mom, we're gonna take care of your child,' I don't care if that child is 50 years old—you see a relief."

On May 21, I got an e-mail from Melcher, telling me that Christina, her daughter, had fatally overdosed on heroin. Christina, she said, had completed rehab several times and had been clean for 90 days before relapsing. Melcher refused to hide the fact that Christina had "lost her battle with addiction," but added, "When a child passes away, the last thing a mother wants to say is that the child was an addict." Melcher plans to continue her volunteer work, in honor of Christina's "beautiful but tortured life."

John Aldis doesn't look like a maverick. He's 71, White-haired and pink-cheeked, with a neat mustache, half-rimmed spectacles, and a penchant for sweater vests and bow ties. You could imagine him playing the Stage Manager in a production of "Our Town." But two years ago Aldis became the first doctor in West Virginia to offer free public classes to teach anybody—not just first responders and health professionals—how to reverse overdoses with Narcan.

Aldis is a family practitioner with a background in public health and tropical medicine. His mother taught nursing, and his father was an obstetrician. "We never made it through the second feature at the drive-in," Aldis recalled. "He would always be summoned over the loudspeaker to attend a birth." There was no question in Aldis's mind that he would become a doctor, too. He spent most of his career in Asia and Africa, as a U.S. Navy physician and as a medical officer with the State Department. He retired in 2001. He and his wife, Pheny, a medical technologist, bought the house where he'd lived as a small child, in Shepherdstown. They filled it with art and antiques, acquired two Jack Russell terriers, and prepared for a quiet life enlivened by visits from their two daughters and the grandkids.

But Aldis soon became aware of the opioid epidemic in the Eastern Panhandle—several people he'd hired to work on his house were "good fellows" as he described them who were also addicted to drugs. "When I started to see it, I could not look away," he told me. He took a job at the New Life Clinic, in Martinsburg, where he could prescribe Suboxone, one of the long-term treatments for opioid addiction. He found it enormously frustrating that addicts were often urged to quit heroin cold turkey or to stop taking Suboxone (or methadone or naltrexone, the other drugs used, with considerable success, to treat addiction and counteract withdrawal symptoms). In his view, this was wholly unrealistic. Most addicts needed what is known as medication-assisted treatment for a long time, if not the rest of their lives. He found the work at the clinic the most satisfying he'd done since graduating from medical school, 46 years earlier. Patients struggled, and many of them failed, but when one of them told him, "Doc, I talked to my mom for the first time in three years yesterday," that was, Aldis said, "just the greatest thing."

Aldis is generally a forbearing man, but he can be dismissive of people who don't share his sense of urgency. As he wrote to me in an e-mail, "The lack of understanding of medication-assisted treatment among otherwise reasonably intelligent people at all levels of our community is astounding and (for me) completely unacceptable."

In 2015, West Virginia University's Injury Control Research Center, along with several state and county agencies, started investigating ways to make naloxone—the generic name for Narcan—more widely available, in the hope of saving people in the throes of an overdose. Aldis attended a talk on the subject by the center's deputy director, Herb Linn, and afterward he approached him and urged, "Let's not study this anymore. Let's just start a program." Linn recalls, "I told him, 'Just do it! You could actually prescribe it to your patients.'"

Aldis taught his first class on administering Narcan on September 3, 2015, at the New Life Clinic. Nine days later, a woman who'd attended the class used Narcan to revive a pregnant woman who had overdosed at a motel where they were both living. During the next few weeks, Aldis heard of five more people saved by people who'd attended the class.

In his seminars, Aldis addresses why addicts' lives are worth saving. One might assume that was self-evident, but at this point in the opioid epidemic, some West Virginians feel too exhausted and resentful to help. People like Lori Swadley and the Hope Dealer women and John Aldis must combat an attitude that some people I spoke with summed up as "Leave 'em lie, let 'em die." Some frustrated locals worry that making Narcan easily available could foster complacency about overdoses because they could be handled more discreetly.

William Poe, a paramedic, told me, "The thing about Narcan is that it kind of makes it OK to overdose because then you can keep it in your house and keep it private. And a lot of times *we're* the wakeup call. I remember one time, we had a kid who had OD'd, and we had him in the ambulance. A call came over the radio—someone about his age had just died from an overdose. And the kid was, like, 'I'm so glad you guys brought me back.'" It was humiliating when an ambulance showed up at your house and carted you out, pale and retching, but it also might push you to change. Then again, Poe mused, when most of your neighbors—not to mention your mom and your grandma—already knew that you used heroin, shaming might not be as much of a thing.

This past winter, I watched Aldis teach two classes in Berkeley Springs, an Eastern Panhandle town, at a storefront church between a convenience store and a pawnshop. The bare trees on the ridge above us were outlined like Black lace against the twilight. Inside, a few dozen people, mostly women, sipped coffee from Styrofoam cups in an unadorned room with a low ceiling, tan carpeting, and rows of tan chairs.

Aldis touched briefly on what an overdose looks like but acknowledged that the attendees probably already knew. ("Oh, Lord, yes," a woman behind me muttered.) He demonstrated how to spray Narcan up a patient's nose—take-home kits come in atomizer form—and announced that at the end of class he'd be writing prescriptions, which those in attendance could get filled at a pharmacy. If they had Medicaid or private insurance, the kit would cost only a few dollars; if they didn't, it could cost anywhere from $125 to $300. At the first meeting I attended, in November, a few women began to cry when they heard that. At the second, in January, Aldis had some good news: the state had agreed to provide 180 free kits.

Aldis told me that he'd like to see Narcan "inundating the community." It carried no potential for abuse, and couldn't harm you if someone gave it to you, mistaking some other medical emergency for an overdose. "They ought to be selling this stuff next to the peanut butter in the Walmart," he liked to say. And free supplies of Narcan should be everywhere, like fire extinguishers: "kitchen cabinets, your purse, schools, gyms, shopping malls, motels."

Melody Stotler, who ran a local organization for recovering addicts, had been the one to invite Aldis to speak that evening. She said to the class, "Unfortunately, there are people in this community who don't understand addiction, who don't think Narcan should be out there."

"They say we're enablers," Aldis put in. "Somebody who has a heart attack—are we enabling them by giving them CPR? 'But their cholesterol's too high! We shouldn't have saved his life!'" People laughed ruefully.

Aldis introduced Kathy Williams, a former patient of his and the mother of two little girls. She had twice saved people with Narcan. One time, while she was driving, she spotted a car on the side of the road, and a man lying on his back next to it. The other time, a neighbor in her apartment complex knocked on her door and said that a guy was overdosing in the parking lot. "So I grabbed my Narcan kit, and I ran out there," she recalled. She saw a woman tending to the man. "What had happened was that these two had stopped at Kmart. She went in to pick up her layaways, and when she came out, he had just done shooting up and said, 'Please take me home.' Well, he was overdosing from Kmart all the way. By the time I got there, he was in the back of the car, completely blue, and I had another guy help me pull him out—a neighbor, 'cause where I live, I been there almost 30 years now, and I know everybody. A couple people saw me running, and they started running, too, because they said, 'Kathy's running—something must be going on.' We gave him two doses of Narcan, and, by the time the EMT got there. his eyes were just starting to flicker, and I really thought we were too late." The man began to stir.

A woman named Tara, who was at the January meeting with her teenage stepdaughter, told me that she had revived a guy who lived in the trailer park where she did some babysitting. He'd refused to go to the hospital, even though he was "puking like he was possessed." I asked Tara—who was 30 and had a soft, kind face—if the man had said anything to her after she saved him. "Every day, the next four days after that, he thanked me every time," she told me. "He also

said it was stupid and he'd never do that again, which wasn't true because he was arrested for driving under the influence of heroin a few weeks ago. Nodded out in the McDonald's parking lot. Someone called the police."

Tara wasn't judging. She got it. She was a recovering addict herself—seven years now, and studying to be a medical assistant.

Jason Chalmers loved his children, that's for sure. He crawled around on all fours, pretending to be a pony, to amuse his daughter, Jacey, and her younger brother, Liam. He submitted to Jacey whenever she wanted to cover his face with makeup. When Jacey was 6 months old, Jason wrote a letter to his grandparents in which he described the "absolute, overwhelming" love that he felt for his daughter. "It's not for or about me any more," he wrote. "That's probably for the best because I never did well with myself. She deserves a father who's going to love her unconditionally, and so help me God, I'm going to do it. Maybe she's the answer to why I'm still here."

Liam was born in 2009. His mother, Angie, had an opioid problem and had taken Suboxone to combat it during her pregnancy. She told me that she also "might have used" heroin "a couple of times." At the hospital, Jason felt that something was amiss with his son. His mother, Christine Chalmers, recalled, "He says, 'Mom, this baby is in withdrawal. They can't release him—he's in terrible pain. If we take him home, he's going to scream and scream and scream, and we won't have anything to help him.'" So we called the doctor and, by golly, they checked him over, and he was in total withdrawal. He was on morphine for two solid weeks in the hospital."

Jason, who grew up in Martinsburg, was addicted to heroin for most of his life, a fact that puzzled his family almost as deeply as it saddened them. He grew up in an attractive, wooded development on a country road, with horses and dogs, and a kindhearted mother. His grandparents lived in the development, too, and Jason and his two siblings waited for the school bus together on a wooden bench that a neighbor had carved for them.

There were scraps of an explanation here and there. Jason's parents had divorced when he was 8, and he was a shy, anxious kid. When he was 25, he was given a diagnosis of obsessive-compulsive disorder. His older brother, Michael—the publisher of the Shepherdstown *Observer*—told me, "If you gave us a bag of Reese's peanut-butter cups when we were kids, Jason would eat fifty of them. I'd eat five. I would've *liked* to eat fifty, but I was, like, 'Nah, I'll eat five.'" Maybe, Michael suggested, this was evidence that Jason had a genetic predisposition for addiction. But who knew, really?

In high school, Jason was "smart, good-looking, and athletic," Michael recalled, but he became the "king of the stoners." He barely got his diploma. It was the beginning of a self-destructive pattern. Jason did things while he was on drugs, or trying to get drugs, that walloped him with shame; to mute those terrible feelings, at least for a while, he'd get high again. He got into using heroin, then into selling it. A friend's father was a dealer, and Jason went to work for him, driving up to New York to procure drugs and driving back to Martinsburg to sell them. He introduced heroin to a girlfriend—a good student who had a scholarship to an excellent university. She dropped out, overdosed, and died. He got a tattoo of the girlfriend's initials next to a dove, a tattoo of Jesus, and a tattoo that represented his addiction: a desperate-looking demon with a gaping mouth. He went to jail dozens of times (for drug possession, credit-card theft) and had a series of nearly fatal overdoses. In 2002, he stole his grandfather's checkbook and emptied his bank account. Christine urged her father to press charges, both because she felt that Jason had to be held responsible and because she felt safest—and could actually sleep through a night—when he was behind bars. He lied to her and stole from her, and after using heroin, he would pass out on her deck, in her garage, at the end of her driveway.

Jason did not go to college, and he could not keep a job for long; he worked for a few weeks at a minimart but got fired when the background check on him came in. He'd get clean in jail and write abject letters of apology to his family. Then he'd return to Martinsburg and start hanging out again with his addict friends. Michael moved to Chicago to start a career as an advertising copywriter, and their sister, Antonia, got married, bought a house, and went to work for the school system. Jason, now in his 30s, was stuck—walking everywhere because he couldn't get a driver's license and showing up at his mother's house in the middle of the night to beg for milk and cereal.

In 2008, Jason wrote to his grandparents, "If I was a gambling man, which if you look at my track record my whole life has been a gamble, I'd have to say there's not enough time left in the world to make good on the pain I've caused." He observed, "Damaged people can be dangerous because they know they can survive, but for some reason they don't know quite how to live."

Christine Chalmers had struggled financially to raise three children as a single mother. But in 2002, when Jason was 26, she was doing well as a real estate agent, and she sent Jason to a month-long rehab program in Colorado that cost $10,000. She recalled, "I went after a couple of weeks, for parents' weekend, and you know what? It was so worth it. He'd been on heroin for ten years at this point, and it was the first time in all that time I saw him like my boy. He says, 'It's like a new world, Mom—I can see things, I can smell things, I can feel things.'" She paused. "I thought, You know what? If I never have anything else, he had a month, and I had a weekend, and he was my boy."

On April 28, 2014, Jason fatally overdosed. He was 37. His death did not come as a surprise: he had started telling Christine that the worst part of overdosing was waking up.

After an overdose death, an autopsy is usually performed. Because of the epidemic, coroners in West Virginia are often backed up. It took two weeks before Jason's body was returned to the Chalmers family. Afterward, Christine thought about how consumed she had been by her attempts to save Jason and, later, [by her efforts] to protect his children from him. One day, Michael and Antonia had been cleaning up Jason's apartment, and they brought over to Christine the contents of his kitchen cabinet. Christine told me, "There were a couple of cans of peas. And I had never served peas—I didn't like them. I said, 'I didn't know Jason liked peas!' There's your boy, your baby, and you never knew he liked peas. Such a simple thing. But I started crying, because I thought, What did we know about him as a *person*?"

When the man who sold Jason his final dose of heroin went on trial, Christine testified. "But, you know, from that point on I have felt terrible about it," she said. "The guy got 10 years. And in some sense his life was saved, because he would have ended up the same as Jase. But when I look at him I know he'd just done the same things Jason did. I mean, who knows who Jase sold to? Who knows who lived or died because he sold to them?"

Christine, who is now 64, and works full time as a secretary in the Berkeley County government, has found herself raising Jacey, who is in the third grade. (Liam lives with his mother, in another state.) One of the biggest collateral effects of the opioid crisis is the growing number of children being raised by people other than their parents or being placed in foster care. In West Virginia, the number of children removed from parental care because of drug abuse rose from 970 in 2006 to 2,171 in 2016. Shawn Valentine, a program director for a nonprofit that helps children navigate foster care in West Virginia, says that, although the goal is to reunite children with their parents, this happens in "less than 25 percent of the cases we are involved in." A major reason is that parents often can't get access to recovery programs or medication-assisted treatment because of waiting lists and financial obstacles.

Valentine said, "I had a 6-year-old once tell me that he had to hold the stretchy thing on his mom's arm. What would happen if he just didn't want to do that? He told me, 'Well, she would smack my head down, so that powdery stuff got all over my face.'"

Christine and Jacey live in Martinsburg, in a pretty bungalow with a porch swing and a glider, and a front door with bright-yellow trim. Down the street, there's a couple with five adopted children whose parents were addicted to opioids. Across the street, a woman named Melissa lives with her elderly father and her youngest sister's two little boys. Their mother was addicted to heroin and lost custody of the kids two years ago. At the time, Melissa, who is a medical technician at a nursing home, was working and living in Maryland—she is divorced, and her own children are grown. She rushed home to Martinsburg to care for her nephews, whom I'll call Cody and Aiden.

One afternoon, I sat talking with Melissa and Christine on Christine's front porch, while Jacey and the boys ran around in a ragged, laughing pack. Christine served some brownies that she had baked.

Melissa recalled that, when her sister lost custody, her nephews' caseworker told her that Aiden, who was then a toddler, would be quickly adopted but that 8-year-old Cody, who bore more obvious signs of trauma and could be difficult to manage, would probably languish in foster care. Melissa said that she couldn't stand to see them separated. "I was, like, 'What choice do I have?'" she said.

Christine patted her on the knee. "Good girl," she said.

Jacey kept a close eye on Aiden, who kept wandering over to the neighbor's yard, where there was a new Chihuahua puppy.

Christine said, "The sad thing about it is there are so many of these kids."

"Yes!" Melissa said. "Aiden's pre-K teacher told me 40 percent of the kids in her class are being raised by somebody other than a parent."

"That means 40 percent have been found out," Christine said. "Who knows what's going on with the other parents?"

Jacey is a bright, curious kid, with pearly pink glasses and a sprinkling of freckles. The first time I met her, she catalogued her accomplishments in gymnastics. "I can do a handstand, a round-off, I'm working on my back handspring," she said. "I can do a front flip. I want to try a back flip, but it's kinda hard. I still have a lot more ahead of me."

Christine has been honest with Jacey about Jason's addiction, in the hope that it will keep her from ending up on a similar path. But in any case, it would be hard to keep the truth from Jacey: she remembers finding her father's needles, and she remembers him getting high. He often dropped into a state of suspended animation—still standing, bent over at the waist, head dangling near his knees. Jacey told me that she and Liam used to think it was a game: "It was, like, he's dead, but he's also alive. You could tap on him and talk to him—he'd just be snoring there. But you could also feel that he was breathing. We would put our hands up to his nose, and we could feel the air coming in and out."

Last fall, Jacey won a statewide poster-making contest, called "Kids Kick Opioids," that was sponsored by the West Virginia attorney general's office. Jacey's poster—one of 2,000 entries—included a photograph of Jason in a backward baseball cap and baggy shorts, holding a grinning Liam on one hip and Jacey on the other. She had written a little passage about how much she missed him after he'd "died from taking drugs," and how she wanted to "hug and kiss him every day." She wrote, "It is very sad when kids don't have their daddy to play with."

Christine said of the poster, "I think Jason would have wanted it. Jason wanted so badly for people not to follow him."

One day when I was visiting, Jacey lay on the porch floor, drawing a rainbow with some colored pencils. Christine was telling me she thought that it was wrong to send opioid addicts to prison.

Jacey piped up. "Yeah, but they should take them away from their home town. Also, get them help."

"Yes," Christine said. "Long-term help. A month is not enough."

"But take them away from, say, Martinsburg," Jacey said, looking down at her rainbow. "Maybe take them across the world."

Recently, Martinsburg has begun to treat the heroin crisis more openly as a public health problem. The police chief, a Chicago transplant named Maurice Richards, had devised a progressive-sounding plan called the Martinsburg Initiative, which would direct support services toward children who appeared to be at risk for addiction because their families were struggling socially or emotionally. In December, Tina Stride and several other local citizens stood up at a zoning meeting to proclaim the need for a detox center. They took issue with residents who testified that such a center would bring more addicts and more heroin to their neighborhoods. "I'm here to say that's already here," a woman in favor of the proposal said. "It's in your neighbor's house, in the bathroom at Wendy's, in our schools." She added, "We're talking about making America great again? Well, it starts here."

That night, the Board of Zoning Appeals voted to allow a detox center, run by Peter Callahan, the psychotherapist, to occupy an unused commercial building in town. People in the hearing room cheered and cried and hugged one another. The facility will have only sixteen beds and won't be ready for patients until December, but the Hope Dealer women were thrilled about it. Now they wouldn't have to drive halfway across the state every time an addict called them up.

John Aldis, who was sitting next to me during the vote, breathed a sigh of relief. He said later, "It's like that Winston Churchill quote: 'This is not the end. It is not even the beginning of the end. But it is, perhaps, the end of the beginning.'"

This spring, Berkeley County started its first needle-exchange program, and other efforts are being made to help addicts survive. The new app that first responders are using to document overdoses allows them to input how many times a patient is given Narcan; when multiple doses are required, it can often mean the heroin was adulterated with potent synthetics, such as fentanyl. The data can help the health department and law enforcement track dangerous batches of drugs and warn addicts.

Some Martinsburg residents who had been skeptical of medication-assisted treatment told me that they were coming around to the idea. A few cited the Surgeon General's report on substance abuse, released in November, which encouraged the expansion of such treatment, noting that studies have repeatedly demonstrated its efficacy in "reducing illicit drug use and overdose deaths." In Berkeley County, it felt like a turning point, though the Trump Administration was likely to resist such approaches. Tom Price, the new Secretary of Health and Human Services, had dismissed medication-assisted treatment as "substituting one opioid for another." It was also unclear how most addicts would pay for treatment if the Affordable Care Act were to be repealed.

Martinsburg residents, meanwhile, tried to take heart from small breakthroughs. Angel Holt, the mother who'd overdosed at the softball practice, told me that she and her boyfriend had stayed clean since that day, and she was hoping to regain custody of her children. She'd been moved by the kindness of an older couple, Karen and Ed Schildt, who lived in Thurmont, Maryland. A year earlier, the Schildts had lost their 25-year-old son, Chris, to a heroin overdose. They were deeply religious, and when they heard what happened to Angel Holt and Christopher Schildt, they decided to reach out to them. The fact that their son had the same name as Holt's boyfriend surely meant that God had put the couple in their path. Karen texted words of encouragement to Holt almost daily.

In February, I spent an afternoon with Shawn Valentine, the nonprofit program director whom I'd talked to about foster care and the opioid crisis. Valentine introduced me to Shelby, her 25-year-old daughter. Shelby had become addicted to opioids at the age of 21. She'd been depressed, living at home again after a brief stint in Florida, arguing with her mom a lot, waitressing at a Waffle House, falling asleep in the college classes she was trying to keep up with. Her co-workers always seemed to know how to get their hands on pills somewhere or other, often from a guy who hung out behind the Food Lion. When the meds got too expensive, but she couldn't seem to do without them anymore, Shelby turned to heroin.

Shelby, Valentine, and I were sitting in Valentine's kitchen, along with Shelby's 15-year-old brother, Patrick, a sweet kid who was listening closely to her. Shelby said, "People don't realize what the brain goes through when you're addicted—it's like a mental shutdown. Everything is gray. You have these blinders on." As she described it, the constant hunt for heroin imposed a kind of order on life's confounding open-endedness. Addiction told you what every day was for, when otherwise you might not have known.

For close to a year, Shelby had been in a program that required her to place a dissolvable strip of Suboxone on her tongue every day, and she also attended group and individual therapy. (The word "assisted" in "medication-assisted treatment" indicates the primacy of the need for recovering addicts to undertake therapy as well, to figure out how to restructure their lives and maybe what got them into opioids to begin with.) Shelby said that Suboxone helped curb her craving for heroin, without sedating her. "There are triggers," she said. "But the urge to run a hundred yards down the street and try to find my ex-dealer and pay him, then shove a used rig in my arm real quick? That's gone."

She can now be relied upon not to pilfer the kinds of treasured possessions she once took and sold for drug money: her little brother's video-game console, her mom's four-leaf-clover necklace. When every day was about getting ahold of heroin, she couldn't be bothered to wash or comb her long, auburn hair hardly at all; her mother once spent four hours trying to untangle it, strand by snarled strand. Now her hair is silky and soft.

Valentine told me that, if Shelby had to be on Suboxone all her life, "I'm absolutely on board with that." She turned to Shelby. "Whatever it takes for you to be a healthy, productive human being."

Recently, Shelby's mother had made a big concession that felt sort of like hope in action. She'd told Shelby, "OK, I'll let you take the truck without me, to take your brother to the movies." Shelby recalled, "I was almost, like, 'Pinch me, wake me up—this can't be true.' Because without her truck there's no working. That's how she makes her living. She said, 'Here's a piece of trust. Don't throw it away.'"

Shelby and her brother drove to the mall and saw a horror movie. It was a pretty dumb one, they agreed, but it didn't matter—Shelby had made it to the mall and back, trust intact. They headed down the long road home in the dark, and the moment they got inside, Shelby put the keys to the truck in her mother's hand.

Margaret Talbot has lightly revised the essay that appears in this volume from the version that appeared in the New Yorker *on June 5, 2017.*

LINDA VILLAROSA

50. WHY AMERICA'S BLACK MOTHERS AND BABIES ARE IN A LIFE-OR-DEATH CRISIS

Despite medical advances resulting in a decline in infant mortality since the beginning of the last century, progress in this area has halted, and the United States now has one of the highest rates among comparable wealthy countries. Researchers point to the race gap, with Black mothers bearing the brunt of the crisis and tragedy associated with infant mortality. While disproportionate levels of poverty and associated lack of access to quality medical care play a role, researchers have found that the race gap is maintained across class lines, pointing to the role that discrimination itself (structural and interactional) play in this crisis.

When Simone Landrum felt tired and both nauseated and ravenous at the same time in the spring of 2016, she recognized the signs of pregnancy. Her beloved grandmother died earlier that year, and Landrum felt a sense of divine order when her doctor confirmed on Muma's birthday that she was carrying a girl. She decided she would name her daughter Harmony. "I pictured myself teaching my daughter to sing," says Landrum, now 23, who lives in New Orleans. "It was something I thought we could do together."

But Landrum, who was the mother of two young sons, noticed something different about this pregnancy as it progressed. The trouble began with constant headaches and sensitivity to light; Landrum described the pain as "shocking." It would have been reasonable to guess that the crippling headaches had something to do with stress: Her relationship with her boyfriend, the baby's father, had become increasingly contentious and eventually physically violent. Three months into her pregnancy, he became angry at her for wanting to hang out with friends and threw her to the ground outside their apartment. She scrambled to her feet, ran inside, and called the police. He continued to pursue her, so she grabbed a knife. "Back up—I have a baby," she screamed. After the police arrived, he was arrested and charged with multiple offenses, including battery. He was released on bond pending a trial that would not be held until the next year. Though she had broken up with him several times, Landrum took him back, out of love and also out of fear that she couldn't support herself, her sons, and the child she was carrying on the paycheck from her waitress gig at a restaurant in the French Quarter.

As her January due date grew closer, Landrum noticed that her hands, her feet, and even her face were swollen, and she had to quit her job because she felt so ill. But her doctor, whom several friends had recommended and who accepted Medicaid, brushed aside her complaints. He recommended Tylenol for the headaches. "I am not a person who likes to take medicine, but I was always popping Tylenol," Landrum says. "When I told him my head still hurt, he said to take more."

At a prenatal appointment a few days before her baby shower in November, Landrum reported that the headache had intensified and that she felt achy and tired. A handwritten note from the appointment, sandwiched into a printed file of Landrum's electronic medical records that she later obtained, shows an elevated blood pressure reading of 143/86. A top number of 140 or more or a bottom number higher than 90, especially combined with headaches, swelling, and fatigue, points to the possibility of pre-eclampsia: dangerously high blood pressure during pregnancy.

High blood pressure and cardiovascular disease are two of the leading causes of maternal death, according to the Centers for Disease Control and Prevention (CDC), and hypertensive disorders in pregnancy, including preeclampsia, have been on the rise over the past two decades, increasing 72 percent from 1993 to 2014. A Department of Health and Human Services report [issued in 2018] found that preeclampsia and eclampsia (seizures that develop after preeclampsia) are 60 percent more common in African American women and also more severe. Landrum's medical records note that she received printed educational material about preeclampsia during a prenatal visit. But Landrum would comprehend the details about the disorder only months later, doing online research on her own.

When Landrum complained about how she was feeling more forcefully at the appointment, she recalls, her doctor told her to lie down—and calm down. She says that he also warned her that he was planning to go out of town and told her that he could deliver the baby by C-section that day if she wished, six weeks before her early-January due date. Landrum says it seemed like an ultimatum, centered on his schedule and convenience. So she took a deep breath and lay on her back for 40 minutes until her blood pressure dropped within normal range. Aside from the handwritten note, Landrum's medical records don't mention the hypertensive episode, the headaches, or the swelling, and she says that was the last time the doctor or anyone from his office spoke to her. "It was like he threw me away," Landrum says angrily.

Four days later, Landrum could no longer deny that something was very wrong. She was suffering from severe back pain and felt bone-tired, unable to get out of bed. That evening, she packed a bag and asked her boyfriend to take her sons to her stepfather's house and then drive her to the hospital. In the car on the way to drop off the boys, she felt wetness between her legs and assumed her water had broken. But when she looked at the seat, she saw blood. At her stepfather's house, she called 911. Before she got into the ambulance, Landrum pulled her sons close. "Mommy loves you," she told them, willing them to stay calm. "I have to go away, but when I come back I will have your sister."

By the time she was lying on a gurney in the emergency room of Touro Infirmary, a hospital in the Uptown section of New Orleans, the splash of blood had turned into a steady stream. "I could feel it draining out of me, like if you get a jug of milk and pour it onto the floor," she recalls. Elevated blood pressure—Landrum's medical records show a reading of 160/100 that day—had caused an abruption: the separation of the placenta from her uterine wall.

With doctors and nurses hovering over her, everything became both hazy and chaotic. When a nurse moved a monitor across her belly, Landrum couldn't hear a heartbeat. "I kept saying: 'Is she OK? Is she all right?'" Landrum recalls. "Nobody said a word. I have never heard a room so silent in my life." She remembers that the emergency room doctor dropped his head. Then he looked into her eyes. "He told me my baby was dead inside of me. I was like: What just happened? Is this a dream? And then I turned my head to the side and threw up."

Sedated but conscious, Landrum felt her mind growing foggy. "I was just so tired," she says. "I felt like giving up." Then she pictured the faces of her two young sons. "I thought, Who's going to take care of them if I'm gone?" That's the last thing she recalls clearly. When she became more alert sometime later, a nurse told her that she had almost bled to death and had required a half dozen units of transfused blood and platelets to survive. "The nurse told me: 'You know, you been sick. You are very lucky to be alive,'" Landrum remembers. "She said it more than once."

A few hours later, a nurse brought Harmony, who had been delivered stillborn via C-section, to her. Wrapped in a hospital blanket, her hair thick and Black, the baby looked peaceful, as if she were dozing. "She was so beautiful—she reminded me of a doll," Landrum says. "I know I was still sedated, but as I held her, I kept looking at her, thinking, Why doesn't she wake up? I tried to feel love, but after a while I got more and more angry. I thought, Why is God doing this to me?"

The hardest part was going to pick up her sons empty-handed and telling them that their sister had died. "I felt like I failed them," Landrum says, choking up. "I felt like someone had taken something from me, but also from them."

In 1850, when the death of a baby was simply a fact of life, and babies died so often that parents avoided naming their children before their first birthdays, the United States began keeping records of infant mortality by race. That year, the reported Black infant-mortality rate was 340 per 1,000; the White rate was 217 per 1,000. This Black–White divide in infant mortality has been a source of both concern and debate for over a century. . . .

From 1915 through the 1990s, amid vast improvements in hygiene, nutrition, living conditions, and health care, the number of babies of all races who died in the first year of life dropped by over 90 percent — a decrease unparalleled by reductions in other causes of death. But that national decline in infant mortality has since slowed. In 1960, the United States was ranked 12th among developed countries in infant mortality. Since then, with its rate largely driven by the deaths of Black babies, the United States has fallen behind and now ranks 32nd out of the 35 wealthiest nations. Low birthweight is a key factor in infant death, and a new report released in March [2018] by the Robert Wood Johnson Foundation and the University of Wisconsin suggests that the number of low-birthweight babies born in the United States—also driven by the data for Black babies—has inched up for the first time in a decade.

Black infants in America are now more than twice as likely to die as White infants—11.3 per 1,000 Black babies, compared with 4.9 per 1,000 White babies, according to the most recent government data — a racial disparity that is actually wider than in 1850, 15 years before the end of slavery, when most Black women were considered chattel. In one year, that racial gap adds up to more than 4,000 lost Black babies. Education and income offer little protection. In fact, a Black woman with an advanced degree is more likely to lose her baby than a White woman with less than an eighth-grade education.

This tragedy of Black infant mortality is intimately intertwined with another tragedy: a crisis of death and near death in Black mothers themselves. The United States is one of only 13 countries in the world where the rate of maternal mortality—the death of a woman related to pregnancy or childbirth up to a year after the end of pregnancy—is now worse than it was 25 years ago. Each year, an estimated 700 to 900 maternal deaths occur in the United States. In addition, the CDC reports more than 50,000 potentially preventable near-deaths, like Landrum's, per year—a number that rose nearly 200 percent from 1993 to 2014, the last year for which statistics are available. Black women are three to four times as likely to die from pregnancy-related causes as their White counterparts, according to the CDC—a disproportionate rate that is higher than that of Mexico, where nearly half the population lives in poverty—and as with infants, the high numbers for Black women drive the national numbers. . . .

The crisis of maternal death and near-death also persists for Black women across class lines. In 2018, the tennis star Serena Williams shared in *Vogue* the story of the birth of her first child and in further detail in a Facebook post. The day after delivering her daughter, Alexis Olympia, via C-section in September, Williams experienced a pulmonary embolism, the sudden blockage of an artery in the lung by a blood clot. Although she had a history of this disorder and was gasping for breath, she says medical personnel initially ignored her concerns. Although Williams should have been able to count on the most attentive health care in the world, her medical team seems to have been unprepared to monitor her for complications after her Cesarean, including blood clots, one of the most common side effects of C-sections. Even after she received treatment, her problems continued; coughing, triggered by the embolism, caused her C-section wound to rupture. When she returned to surgery, physicians discovered a large hematoma, or collection of blood, in her abdomen, which required more surgery. Williams, 36, spent the first six weeks of her baby's life bedridden.

The reasons for the Black–White divide in both infant and maternal mortality have been debated by researchers and doctors for more than two decades. But recently there has been growing acceptance of what has largely been, for the medical establishment, a shocking idea: For Black women in America, an inescapable atmosphere of societal and systemic racism can create a kind of toxic physiological stress, resulting in conditions—including hypertension and preeclampsia—that lead directly to higher rates of infant and maternal death. And that societal racism is further expressed in a pervasive, longstanding racial bias in health care—including the dismissal of legitimate concerns and symptoms— that can help explain poor birth outcomes even in the case of Black women with the most advantages.

"Actual institutional and structural racism has a big bearing on our patients' lives, and it's our responsibility to talk about that more than just saying that it's a problem," says Dr. Sanithia L. Williams, an African American OB-GYN in the Bay Area and a fellow with the nonprofit organization Physicians for Reproductive Health. "That has been the missing piece, I think, for a long time in medicine."

After Harmony's death, Landrum's life grew more chaotic. Her boyfriend blamed her for what happened to their baby and grew more abusive. Around Christmas 2016, in a rage, he attacked her, choking her so hard that she urinated on herself. "He said to me, 'Do you want to die in front of your kids?'" Landrum said, her hands shaking with the memory.

Then he tore off her clothes and sexually assaulted her. She called the police, who arrested him and charged him with second-degree rape. Landrum got a restraining order, but the district attorney eventually declined to prosecute. She also sought the assistance of the New Orleans Family Justice Center, an organization that provides advocacy and support for survivors of domestic violence and sexual assault. Counselors secreted her and her sons to a safe house, before moving them to a more permanent home early [in 2017].

Landrum had a brief relationship with another man and found out in March 2017 that she was pregnant again and due in December. "I'm not going to lie; though I had a lot going on, I wanted to give my boys back the sister they had lost," Landrum said, looking down at her lap. "They don't forget. Every night they always say their prayers, like: 'Goodnight, Harmony. Goodnight, God. We love you, sister.'" She paused and took a breath. "But I was also afraid, because of what happened to me before."

Early last fall, Landrum's case manager at the Family Justice Center, Mary Ann Bartkowicz, attended a workshop conducted by Latona Giwa, the 31-year-old co-founder of the Birthmark Doula Collective. The group's 12 racially diverse birth doulas, ages 26 to 46, work as professional companions during pregnancy and childbirth and for six weeks after the baby is born, serving about 400 clients across New Orleans each year, ranging from wealthy women who live in the upscale Garden District to women from the Katrina-ravaged Lower Ninth Ward and other communities of color who are referred through clinics, school counselors, and social-service organizations. Birthmark offers pro bono services to these women in need.

Right away, the case manager thought of her young, pregnant client. Losing her baby, nearly bleeding to death, and fleeing an abusive partner were only the latest in a cascade of harrowing life events that Landrum had lived through since childhood. She was 10 when Hurricane Katrina devastated New Orleans in 2005. She and her family first fled to a hotel and then walked more than a mile through the rising water to the Superdome, where thousands of evacuees were already packed in with little food, water, or space. She remembers passing Charity Hospital, where she was born. "The water was getting deeper and deeper, and by the end, I was on my tippy-toes, and the water was starting to go right by my mouth," Landrum recalls. "When I saw the hospital, honestly I thought, I'm going to die where I was born." Landrum wasn't sure what doulas were, but once Bartkowicz explained their role as a source of support and information, she requested the service. Latona Giwa would be her doula.

Giwa, the daughter of a White mother and a Nigerian immigrant father, took her first doula training while she was still a student at Grinnell College in Iowa. She moved to New Orleans for a fellowship in community organizing before getting a degree in nursing. After working as a labor and delivery nurse and then as a visiting nurse for Medicaid clients in St. Bernard Parish, an area of southeast New Orleans where every structure was damaged by Katrina floodwaters, she devoted herself to doula work and childbirth education. She founded Birthmark in 2011 with Dana Keren, another doula who was motivated to provide services for women in New Orleans who most needed support during pregnancy but couldn't afford it.

"Being a labor and delivery nurse in the United States means seeing patients come in acute medical need, because we haven't been practicing preventive and supportive care all along," Giwa says. Louisiana ranks 44th out of all 50 states in maternal mortality; Black mothers in the state die at 3.5 times the rate of White mothers. Among the 1,500 clients the Birthmark doulas have served since the collective's founding seven years ago, 10 infant deaths have occurred, including late-term miscarriage and stillbirth, which is lower than the overall rate for both Louisiana and the United States, as well as the rates for Black infants. No mothers have died.

A scientific examination of 26 studies of nearly 16,000 subjects first conducted in 2003 and updated last year by Cochrane, a nonprofit network of independent researchers, found that pregnant women who received the continuous support that doulas provide were 39 percent less likely to have C-sections. In general, women with continuous support tended to have babies who were healthier at birth. Though empirical research has not yet linked doula support with decreased maternal and infant mortality, there are promising anecdotal reports. Last year, the American College of Obstetricians and Gynecologists released a statement noting that "evidence suggests that, in addition to regular nursing care, continuous one-to-one emotional support provided by support personnel, such as a doula, is associated with improved outcomes for women in labor."

In early November, the air was thick with humidity as Giwa pulled up to Landrum's house, half of a woodframe duplex, for their second meeting. Landrum opened the door, happy to see the smiling, fresh-faced Giwa, who at first glance looked younger than her 23-year-old client. Giwa would continue to meet with Landrum weekly until her December 22 due date, would be with her during labor and delivery, and would make six postpartum home visits to assure that both mother and baby son remained healthy. Landrum led Giwa through her living room, which was empty except for a tangle of disconnected cable cords. She had left most of her belongings behind— including her dog and the children's new Christmas toys—when she fled from her abusive boyfriend, and she still couldn't afford to replace all her furniture.

They sat at the kitchen table, where Giwa asked about Landrum's last doctor visit, prodding her for details. Landrum reassured her that her blood pressure and weight, as well as the baby's size and position, were all on target. "Have you been getting rid of things that are stressful?" Giwa asked, handing her a tin of lavender balm, homemade from herbs in her garden. "I'm trying not to be worried, but sometimes. . . . " Landrum said haltingly, looking down at the table as her hair, tipped orange at the ends, brushed her shoulders. "I feel like my heart is so anxious."

Taking crayons from her bag, Giwa suggested that they write affirmations on sheets of White paper for Landrum to post around her home, to see and remind her of the good in her life. Landrum took a purple crayon, her favorite color, and scribbled in tight, tiny letters. But even as she wrote the affirmations, she began to recite a litany of fears: bleeding again when she goes into labor, coming home empty-handed, dying, and leaving her sons motherless. Giwa leaned across the table, speaking evenly. "I know that it was a tragedy and a huge loss with Harmony, but don't forget that you survived, you made it, you came home to your sons," she said. Landrum stopped writing and looked at Giwa.

"If it's OK, why don't I write down something you told me when we talked last time?" Giwa asked. Landrum nodded. "I know God has his arms wrapped around me and my son," Giwa wrote in large purple letters, outlining "God" and "arms" in red, as Landrum watched. She took out another sheet of paper and wrote, "Harmony is here with us, protecting us." After the period, she drew two purple butterflies.

Landrum's eyes locked on the butterflies. "Every day, I see a butterfly, and I think that's her. I really do," she said, finally smiling, her large, dark eyes crinkling into half moons. "I like that a lot, because I think that's something that I can look at and be like, Girl, you going to be OK."

With this pregnancy, Landrum was focused on making sure everything went right. She had switched to a new doctor, a woman who specialized in high-risk pregnancies and accepted Medicaid, and she would deliver this baby at a different hospital. Now she asked Giwa to review the birth plan one more time.

"On November 30, I go on call, and that means this phone is always on me," Giwa said, holding up her iPhone.

"What if. . . . " Landrum began tentatively.

"I'm keeping a backup doula informed of everything," Giwa said. "Just in case." "I think everything's going to be OK this time," Landrum said. But it sounded like a question.

When the Black–White disparity in infant mortality first became the subject of study, discussion, and media attention more than two decades ago, the high rate of infant death for Black women was widely believed by almost everyone, including doctors and public health experts, to affect only poor, less educated women—who do experience the highest numbers of infant deaths. This led inevitably to blaming the mother. Was she eating badly, smoking, drinking, using drugs, overweight, not taking prenatal vitamins or getting enough rest, afraid to be proactive during prenatal visits, skipping them altogether, too young, unmarried? . . .

In 1992, I was a journalism fellow at the Harvard T.H. Chan School of Public Health. One day a professor of health policy, Dr. Robert Blendon, who knew I was the health editor of *Essence*, said, "I thought you'd be interested in this." He handed me the latest issue of the *New England Journal of Medicine*, which contained what is now considered the watershed study on race, class, and infant mortality. The study, conducted by four researchers at the CDC—Kenneth Schoendorf, Carol Hogue, Joel Kleinman, and Diane Rowley—mined a database of close to a million previously unavailable linked birth and death certificates and found that infants born to college-educated Black parents were twice as likely to die as infants born to similarly educated White parents. In 72 percent of the cases, low birthweight was to blame. I was so surprised and skeptical that I peppered him with the kinds of questions about medical research that he encouraged us to ask in his course. Mainly I wanted to know *why*. "No one knows," he told me, "but this might have something to do with stress."

Though I wouldn't learn of her work until years later, Dr. Arline Geronimus, a professor in the Department of Health Behavior and Health Education at the University of Michigan School of Public Health, first linked stress and Black infant mortality with her theory of "weathering." She believed that a kind of toxic stress triggered the premature deterioration of the bodies of African American women as a consequence of repeated exposure to a climate of discrimination and insults. The weathering of the mother's body, she theorized, could lead to poor pregnancy outcomes, including the death of her infant.

After graduating from the Harvard School of Public Health, Geronimus landed at Michigan in 1987, where she continued her research. That year, in a report published in the journal *Population and Development Review*, she noted that Black women in their mid-20s experienced higher rates of infant death than teenage girls did—presumably because they were older and stress had more time to affect their bodies. For White mothers, the opposite proved true: Teenagers had the highest risk of infant mortality, and women in their mid-20s the lowest.

Geronimus's work contradicted the widely accepted belief that Black teenage girls (assumed to be careless, poor, and uneducated) were to blame for the high rate of Black infant mortality. The backlash was swift. Politicians, media commentators and even other scientists accused her of promoting teenage pregnancy. She was attacked by colleagues and even received anonymous death threats at her office in Ann Arbor and at home. "At that time, which is now 25 or so years ago, there were more calls to complain about me to the University of Michigan, to say I should be fired, than had happened to anybody in the history of the university," recalls Geronimus, who in 1992 went on to publish what is now considered her seminal study on weathering and Black women and infants in the journal *Ethnicity and Disease*.

By the late 1990s, other researchers were trying to chip away at the mystery of the Black–White gap in infant mortality. Poverty on its own had been disproved to explain infant mortality, and a study of more than 1,000 women in New York and Chicago, published in the *American Journal of Public Health* in 1997, found that Black women were less likely to drink and smoke during pregnancy and that even when they had access to prenatal care, their babies were often born small.

Experts wondered if the high rates of infant death in Black women, understood to be related to small, preterm babies, had a genetic component. Were Black women passing along a defect that was affecting their offspring? But science has refuted that theory too: A 1997 study published by two Chicago neonatologists, Richard David and James Collins, in the *New England Journal of Medicine* found that babies born to new immigrants from impoverished West African nations weighed more than their Black American-born counterparts and were similar in size to White babies[1]. In other words, they were more likely to be born full term, which lowers the risk of death. In 2002, the same researchers made a further discovery: The daughters of African and Caribbean immigrants who grew up in the United States went on to have babies who were smaller than their mothers had been at birth, while the grandchildren of White European women actually weighed more than their mothers had at birth. It took just one generation for the American Black–White disparity to manifest. . . .

Though it seemed radical 25 years ago, few in the field now dispute that the Black–White disparity in the deaths of babies is related not to the genetics of race but to the lived experience of race in this country. In 2007, David and Collins published an even more thorough examination of race and infant mortality in the *American Journal of Public Health*, again dispelling the notion of some sort of gene that would predispose Black women to preterm birth or low birth weight[2]. To make sure the message of the research was crystal clear, David, a professor of pediatrics at the University of Illinois, Chicago, stated his hypothesis in media-friendly but blunt-force terms in interviews: "For Black women," he said, "something about growing up in America seems to be bad for your baby's birth weight."

On a December morning three days before her due date, Landrum went to the hospital for her last ultrasound before the birth. Because of the stillbirth the previous year, her doctor did not want to let the pregnancy go past 40 weeks, to avoid the complications that can come with post-term delivery, so an induction had been scheduled in 48 hours. . . .

Now, lying on the table, Landrum looked out the window, smiling as the sound of her baby's heartbeat filled the room. A few minutes later, the technician returned and looked at the monitor. The baby's heart rate appeared less like little mountains than chicken scratching. He was also either not moving consistently or not breathing properly. A nurse left the room to call Landrum's doctor to get her opinion. The nurse returned in 20 minutes and gave Landrum the news that the baby would be induced not in two days but now. "We don't want to wait; we're going to get him out today," she said to Landrum.

"I'm very anxious," Landrum told Giwa on the phone as she walked to labor and delivery, a few floors up in the same hospital, "but I'm ready." An hour later, Giwa arrived, wearing purple scrubs, her cloth bag filled with snacks, lavender lotion, and clary sage oil. She made sure the crayon-drawn affirmations were taped on the wall within Landrum's line of vision, then settled into a chair next to the bed, low-key but watchful. . . .

A medical resident, who was White, like all of the staff who would attend Landrum throughout her labor and delivery, walked into the room with paperwork. Right away, she asked Landrum briskly, "Have you had any children before?"

She hadn't read the chart.

"Yes, I've had three babies, but one died," Landrum explained warily, for the third time since she had arrived at the hospital that day. Her voice was flat. "I had a stillbirth."

"The demise was last year?" the resident asked without looking up to see Landrum stiffen at the word "demise."

"May I speak to you outside," Giwa said to the nurse caring for Landrum. In the hall, she asked her to please make a note in Landrum's chart about the stillbirth. "Each time she has to go over what happened, it brings her mind back to a place of fear and anxiety and loss," Giwa said later. "This is really serious. She's having a high-risk delivery, and I would hope that her care team would thoroughly review her chart before walking into her room."

One of the most important roles that doulas play is as advocate in the medical system for their clients. "At the point a woman is most vulnerable, she has another set of ears and another voice to help get through some of the potentially traumatic decisions that have to be made," says Dána-Ain Davis, the director of the Center for the Study of Women and Society at the City University of New York, the author of a forthcoming book on pregnancy, race, and premature birth and a Black woman who is a doula herself. Doulas, she adds, "are a critical piece of the puzzle in the crisis of premature birth, infant and maternal mortality in Black women."

Over the next 10 hours, Giwa left Landrum's side only briefly. About five hours in, Landrum requested an epidural. The anesthesiologist required all visitors to leave the room while it was administered. When Giwa returned about a half-hour later, Landrum was angry and agitated, clenching her fists and talking much faster than usual. She had mistakenly been given a spinal dose of anesthesia—generally reserved for C-sections performed in the operating room—rather than the epidural dose usually used in vaginal childbirth. Now she had no feeling at all in her legs and a splitting headache. When she questioned the incorrect dose of anesthesia, Landrum told Giwa, one nurse said, "You ask a lot of questions, don't you?" and winked at another nurse in the room and then rolled her eyes.

As Landrum loudly complained about what occurred, her blood pressure shot up, while the baby's heart rate dropped. Giwa glanced nervously at the monitor, the blinking lights reflecting off her face. "What happened was wrong," she said to Landrum, lowering her voice to a whisper. "But for the sake of the baby, it's time to let it go."

She asked Landrum to close her eyes and imagine the color of her stress. "Red," Landrum snapped, before finally laying her head onto the pillow.

"What color is really soothing and relaxing?" Giwa asked, massaging her hand with lotion.

"Lavender," Landrum replied, taking a deep breath. Over the next 10 minutes, Landrum's blood pressure dropped within normal range as the baby's heart rate stabilized.

At 1 a.m., a team of three young female residents bustled into the room; the labor and delivery nurse followed them, flipping on the overhead light. They were accompanied by an older man Landrum had never seen. He briefly introduced himself as the attending physician before plunging his hand between Landrum's legs to feel for the baby. Landrum had been told that her OB-GYN might not deliver her infant, but a nurse had reassured her earlier in the day that if her doctor was not available, her doctor's husband, also an OB-GYN, would cover for her. This doctor, however, was not the husband, and no one explained

the switch. Giwa raised an eyebrow. The Listening to Mothers Survey III, a national sampling of 2,400 women who gave birth in 2011 and 2012, found that more than a quarter of Black women meet their birth attendants for the first time during childbirth, compared with 18 percent of White women.

"He's ready," the doctor said, snapping off his gloves. "It's time to push."

One resident stepped forward and took his place, putting her hand into Landrum's vagina, feeling for the baby. Landrum gripped the side of the bed and closed her eyes, grimacing. "You're a rock star," Giwa said. The nurse, standing at her side, told Landrum: "Push! Now. You can do it." After about 20 minutes of pushing, the baby's head appeared. "This is it," the nurse told her. "You can do this," Giwa whispered on her other side.

Landrum bore down and pushed again. "You're doing amazing," Giwa said, not taking her eyes away from Landrum. The attending physician left the room to put on a clean gown. Landrum breathed in, closed her eyes, and pushed. More of the infant's head appeared, a slick cluster of Black curls. The senior resident motioned to the third and most junior of the women, standing at her shoulder, and told her, "Here's your chance." The young resident took the baby's head and eased the slippery infant out. Landrum was oblivious to the procession of young residents taking turns between her legs or the fact that the attending physician wasn't in the room at all.

She was sobbing, shaking, laughing—all at the same time—flooded with the kind of hysterical relief a woman feels when a baby leaves her body and emerges into the world.

The resident lay the infant, purple, wrinkled, and still as a stone, on Landrum's bare chest. "Is he all right? Is he OK?" Landrum asked, panicking as she looked down at the motionless baby. A second later, his tiny arms and legs tensed, and he opened his mouth and let out a definitive cry.

"He's perfect," Giwa told her, touching her shoulder.

"I did it," Landrum said, looking up at Giwa and laying her hands on the baby's back, still coated with blood and amniotic fluid. She had decided to name him Kingston Blessed Landrum.

"Yes," Giwa said, finally allowing herself a wide smile. "You did."

In 1995, a pregnant African American doctoral student had a preterm birth after her water broke unexpectedly at 34 weeks. Her baby was on a ventilator for 48 hours and a feeding tube for six days during his 10-day stay in the neonatal intensive-care unit.

The woman was part of a team of female researchers from Boston and Howard universities working on the Black Women's Health Study, an ongoing examination, funded by the National Institutes of Health, of conditions like preterm birth that affect Black women disproportionately. The team had started the study after they noticed that most large, long-term medical investigations of women overwhelmingly comprised White women. The Black Women's Health Study researchers, except for two Black women, were also all White.

What happened to the doctoral student altered the course of the study. "We're thinking, "Here's a middle-class, well-educated Black woman having a preterm birth when no one else in our group had a preterm birth," says Dr. Julie Palmer, associate director of the Slone Epidemiology Center at Boston University and a principal investigator of the continuing study of 59,000 subjects. "That's when I became aware that the race difference in preterm birth has got to be something different, that it really cuts across class. People had already done some studies showing the health effects of racism, so we wanted to ask about that as soon as possible."

In 1997, the study investigators added several yes-or-no questions about everyday race-related insults: I receive poorer service than others; people act as if I am not intelligent; people act as if I am dishonest; people act as if they are better than me; people act as if they are afraid of me. They also included a set of questions about more significant discrimination: I have been treated unfairly because of my race at my job, in housing, or by the police. The findings showed higher levels of preterm birth among women who reported the greatest experiences of racism.

The bone-deep accumulation of traumatizing life experiences and persistent insults that the study pinpointed is not the sort of "lean in" stress relieved by meditation and "me time." When a person is faced

with a threat, the brain responds to the stress by releasing a flood of hormones, which allow the body to adapt and respond to the challenge. When stress is sustained, long-term exposure to stress hormones can lead to wear and tear on the cardiovascular, metabolic, and immune systems, making the body vulnerable to illness and even early death.

Although Arline Geronimus's early research had focused on birth outcomes mainly in disadvantaged teenagers and young women, she went on to apply her weathering theory across class lines. In 2006, she and her colleagues used government data, blood tests, and questionnaires to measure the effects of stress associated with weathering on the systems of the body. Even when controlling for income and education, African American women had the highest allostatic load scores—an algorithmic measurement of stress-associated body chemicals and their cumulative effect on the body's systems—higher than White women and Black men. Writing in the *American Journal of Public Health*, Geronimus and her colleagues concluded that "persistent racial differences in health may be influenced by the stress of living in a race-conscious society. These effects may be felt particularly by Black women because of [the] double jeopardy of gender and racial discrimination."

People of color, particularly Black people, are treated differently the moment they enter the health care system. In 2002, the groundbreaking report "Unequal Treatment: Confronting Racial and Ethnic Disparities in Health Care," published by a division of the National Academy of Sciences, took an exhaustive plunge into 100 previous studies, careful to decouple class from race, by comparing subjects with similar income and insurance coverage. The researchers found that people of color were less likely to be given appropriate medications for heart disease, or to undergo coronary bypass surgery, and received kidney dialysis and transplants less frequently than White people, which resulted in higher death rates. Black people were 3.6 times as likely as White people to have their legs and feet amputated as a result of diabetes, even when all other factors were equal. One study analyzed in the report found that cesarean sections were 40 percent more likely among Black women compared with White women. "Some of us on the committee were surprised and shocked at the extent of the evidence," noted the chairman of the panel of physicians and scientists who compiled the research.

In 2016, a study by researchers at the University of Virginia examined why African American patients receive inadequate treatment for pain not only compared with White patients but also relative to World Health Organization guidelines. The study found that White medical students and residents often believed incorrect and sometimes "fantastical" biological fallacies about racial differences in patients. For example, many thought, falsely, that Blacks have less sensitive nerve endings than Whites, that Black people's blood coagulates more quickly, and that Black skin is thicker than White. For these assumptions, researchers blamed not individual prejudice but deeply ingrained unconscious stereotypes about people of color, as well as physicians' difficulty in empathizing with patients whose experiences differ from their own. In specific research regarding childbirth, the Listening to Mothers Survey III found that one in five Black and Hispanic women reported poor treatment from hospital staff because of race, ethnicity, cultural background, or language, compared with eight percent of White mothers. . . .

Two days after the birth of Landrum's baby, she had moved out of labor and delivery and into a hospital room, with the butterfly-decorated, crayon-drawn affirmations taped above her bed. She'd had a few hours of sleep and felt rested and cheerful in a peach-colored jumpsuit she brought from home, with baby Kingston, who had weighed in at a healthy six pounds 13 ounces, napping in a plastic crib next to her bed. But over the next hours, Landrum's mood worsened. When Giwa walked into her room after leaving for a few hours to change and nap, Landrum once again angrily recounted the mishap with the epidural and complained about the nurses and even the hospital food. Finally, Giwa put her hand on Landrum's arm and asked, "Simone, where are the boys?"

Landrum stopped, and her entire body sagged. She told Giwa that her sons were staying on the other side of town with her godmother, whom she called Nanny. But with children of her own, Nanny was unable to make the 40-minute drive to bring Landrum's sons to the hospital to see their mama and meet their brother.

"After they lost their sister, it's really important that they see Kingston," Landrum said.

"I understand," Giwa said, stroking her shoulder. "You need the boys to see their brother, to know that he is alive, that this is all real." Landrum nodded. She made several phone calls from her hospital bed but could find no one to get the boys, so she left to drive across town and pick them up. It took Giwa's attentive eyes, and the months of building trust and a relationship with Landrum, to recognize a problem that couldn't be addressed medically but one that could have emotional and physical consequences.

The doula consumer market has been largely driven by and tailored for White women, but the kind of support Giwa was providing to Landrum was actually originated by Black women, the granny midwives of the South. Inspired by that historic legacy and by increasingly visible reproductive-justice activism, dozens of doula groups like Birthmark in New Orleans have emerged or expanded in the past several years in Brooklyn, Los Angeles, Atlanta, Dallas, Memphis, Miami, Washington, and many other cities, providing services to women of color, often free or on a sliding scale.

The By My Side Birth Support Program in New York City, administered by the city's Department of Health, offers free doula services during pregnancy, labor and delivery, and postpartum for mothers in central and eastern Brooklyn's predominantly Black and brown neighborhoods where maternal and infant mortality are highest. A team of 12 doulas has served more than 800 families since 2010, and an analysis of the program shows that from 2010 to 2015, mothers receiving doula support had half as many preterm births and low-birthweight babies as other women in the same community. . . .

"It is really hard for American health care professionals to get their heads around that when you have an organized community-based team that connects technical clinical issues with a deep, embedded set of relationships, you can make real breakthroughs," says Dr. Prabhjot Singh, the director of the Arnhold Institute for Global Health at the Icahn School of Medicine at Mount Sinai, who studies community health worker models and how they can be used in the United States. "In the U.S., doulas can't do it by themselves, but based on work that's taken place globally, they can help reduce infant and maternal deaths using what is essentially a very simple solution." . . .

On a cool, sunny afternoon in March, Landrum led me into her living room, which now held a used couch—a gift from a congregant of her church, where she is an active member. . . . [S]he told me that the new baby had motivated her to put her life in order. She had been doing hair and makeup for church members and friends out of her house to earn money to buy a car. She had applied to Delgado Community College to study to be an ultrasound technician. . . .

Latona Giwa continued to care for Landrum for two months after Kingston's birth. The CDC measures American maternal mortality not just by deaths that occur in pregnancy or childbirth, or in the immediate days afterward, but rather by all deaths during pregnancy and the year after the end of pregnancy— suggesting the need for continued care and monitoring, especially for women who are most at risk of complications.

It was Giwa who drove Landrum and the baby home from the hospital, moving her own 2-year-old daughter's car seat from the back of her Honda and replacing it with a backward-facing infant seat, when Landrum had no other ride. It was Giwa who ushered the new mother into her home and then surprised her by taking a bag of groceries and a tray of homemade lasagna, still warm, from the back of the car. And it was Giwa who asked her, six weeks after childbirth, if she had talked to her doctor about getting a contraceptive implant to avoid pregnancy. When Landrum told her that her doctor had never called her about a checkup, Giwa was livid. "High-risk patients with complicated maternal histories often have an appointment two weeks after they've been discharged," she said later, after insisting that Landrum call to make an

appointment. "Her life is hectic; she's at home with three children. Luckily she's fine, but at minimum someone should've called to check on her."

For Giwa's work with Landrum, from October to February, she earned just $600. Like the other Birthmark doulas, Giwa can't make ends meet doing just doula work; she is employed as a lactation consultant for new mothers both privately and at a "latch clinic" in a New Orleans office of the federal Women, Infants and Children Food and Nutrition Service that supports low-income pregnant and postpartum women.

"We need to recognize that there is actual medical benefit to having doula support—and make the argument that insurance should pay for it," says Sanithia Williams, the Bay Area OB-GYN. "It is a job. People do have to be paid for that work." Insurance would mean some standardization; Williams notes that many programs securing public funding or grants to provide doula support to lower-income women can't match the kind of money that private doulas can command. These programs often have "all Black women who are doulas," she says. "Yes, it's fantastic that these women are training to be doulas and supporting other Black women—but they're not making as much as these other doulas." If, she asks, "doula support is important and can have this beneficial outcome for women, especially Black women, how can we actually move forward to make that more accessible to everybody?". . . .

Kingston stirred when he heard his mother's voice. He lifted his head briefly and looked into Landrum's face. Their eyes met, his still slightly crossed with new-baby nearsightedness. Landrum paused long enough to stroke his head and kiss his damp cheek. The baby sighed. Then he burrowed his head back into the warmth and safety of his mother's chest.

NOTES

1. David, Richard J., and James W. Collins Jr. 1997. "Differing birth weight among infants of US-born Blacks, African-born Blacks, and US-born Whites." *New England Journal of Medicine* 337(17): 1209–1214.
2. David, Richard, and James Collins Jr. 2007. "Disparities in infant mortality: what's genetics got to do with it?." *American journal of public health* 97(7): 1191–1197.

MONICA POTTS

51. WHAT'S KILLING POOR WHITE WOMEN?

Potts follows the life history of a poor rural woman, attempting to understand why life expectancy for poor, undereducated White women has dropped dramatically in the past two decades. Potts discusses cultural factors (e.g., traditional gender norms), structural issues (e.g., poverty and unemployment), and less tangible factors (e.g., feelings of desperation) that may be contributing to their early deaths.

On the night of May 23, 2012, which turned out to be the last of her life, Crystal Wilson baby-sat her infant granddaughter, Kelly. It was how she would have preferred to spend every night. Crystal had joined Facebook the previous year, and the picture of her daughter cradling the newborn in the hospital bed substituted for a picture of herself. Crystal's entire wall was a catalog of visits from her nieces, nephews, cousins' kids, and, more recently, the days she baby-sat Kelly. She was a mother hen, people said of Crystal. She'd wanted a house full of children, but she'd only had one.

The picture the family chose for her obituary shows Crystal and her husband holding the infant. Crystal leans in from the side, with dark, curly hair, an unsmiling round face, and Black eyebrows knit together. She was 38 and bore an unhealthy heft, more than 200 pounds. Crystal had been to the doctor, who told her she was overweight and diabetic. She was waiting to get medicine, but few in her family knew it, and no one thought she was near death.

Crystal's 17-year-old daughter, Megan, split her time between her parents' house in Cave City, Arkansas, and that of her boyfriend, Corey, in nearby Evening Shade. Megan made sure that each set of grandparents could spend time with the baby. The night before Crystal's death, Megan and Corey were moving with his parents to a five-acre patch near Crystal. Megan and Corey were running late, so they didn't pick the baby up until 11 P.M. Crystal seemed fine. "You couldn't tell she was sick," Megan says. "She never felt sick." They went back home, and Megan got a text from her mom around midnight. "She said she loved me, give Kelly kisses, and give Corey hugs and tell him to take care of her girls and she'd see me in the morning. I was supposed to drop Kelly off at ten o'clock and finish moving."

Instead, at around 9:30 the next morning, when Megan was getting ready to leave, Corey's grandfather called and said Crystal was dead. Megan didn't believe him. If one of her parents passed, it had to be her dad. "I thought it was my dad that died because he was always the unhealthy one." Megan left Kelly with her mother-in-law and raced with Corey and his dad in the truck, hazards on, laying on the horn, and pulled into the dirt driveway outside her parents' tan-and-brown single-wide trailer. "Daddy was sitting there in the recliner crying," Megan says. "It was Momma gone, not him." Crystal had died in her bed early in the morning.

Just after 10 A.M., nearly every relative Crystal had was in the rutted driveway in front of the trailer. Crystal was the last of six children and considered the baby of the family. She was the third sibling to die. Her brother Terry, the "Big Man," who hosted all the holiday dinners and coached the family softball team, had died three months earlier at age 47, and her sister Laura, whom everybody called Pete, died at age 45 in 2004. The police—dozens, it seemed, from the county and from the town—had arrived and blocked off the bedroom where she lay and were interviewing people to figure out what had killed her.

The coroner arrived and pronounced Crystal dead at 11:40. Her body was rolled out on a gurney and shipped to the state lab in Little Rock. One of the officers, Gerald Traw, later told me an autopsy is routine when someone dies without a doctor present. "We like to know why somebody died," he says.

Everything about Crystal's life was ordinary, except for her death. She is one of a demographic—White women who don't graduate from high school—whose life expectancy has declined dramatically over the past 18 years. These women can now expect to die five years earlier than the generation before them. It is an unheard-of drop for a wealthy country in the age of modern medicine. Throughout history, technological and scientific innovation have put death off longer and longer, but the benefits of those advances have not been shared equally, especially across the race and class divides that characterize twenty-first century America. Lack of access to education, medical care, good wages, and healthy food isn't just leaving the worst-off Americans behind. It's killing them.

The journal *Health Affairs* reported the five-year drop last August. The article's lead author, Jay Olshansky, who studies human longevity at the University of Illinois at Chicago, with a team of researchers looked at death rates for different groups from 1990 to 2008. White men without high-school diplomas had lost three years of life expectancy, but it was the decline for women like Crystal that made the study news. Previous studies had shown that the least-educated Whites began dying younger in the 2000s, but only by about a year. Olshansky and his colleagues did something the other studies hadn't: They isolated high-school dropouts and measured their outcomes

instead of lumping them in with high-school graduates who did not go to college.

The last time researchers found a change of this magnitude, Russian men had lost seven years after the fall of the Soviet Union, when they began drinking more and taking on other risky behaviors. Although women generally outlive men in the U.S., such a large decline in the average age of death, from almost 79 to a little more than 73, suggests that an increasing number of women are dying in their twenties, thirties, and forties. "We actually don't know the exact reasons why it's happened," Olshansky says. "I wish we did."

Most Americans, including high-school dropouts of other races, are gaining life expectancy, just at different speeds. Absent a war, genocide, pandemic, or massive governmental collapse, drops in life expectancy are rare. "If you look at the history of longevity in the United States, there have been no dramatic negative or positive shocks," Olshansky says. "With the exception of the 1918 influenza pandemic, everything has been relatively steady, slow changes. This is a five-year drop in an 18-year time period. That's dramatic."

Researchers had known education was linked to longer life since the 1960s, but it was difficult to tell whether it was a proxy for other important factors—like coming from a wealthy family or earning a high income as an adult. In 1999, a Columbia economics graduate student named Adriana Lleras-Muney decided to figure out if education was the principal cause. She found that each additional year of schooling added about a year of life. Subsequent studies suggested the link was less direct. Education is strongly associated with a longer life, but that doesn't mean that every year of education is an elixir. "It is the biggest association, but it is also the thing that we measure about people the best," Lleras-Muney says. "It is one of those things that we can collect data on. There could be other things that matter a lot more, but they're just very difficult to measure."

As is often the case when researchers encounter something fuzzy, they start suggesting causes that sound decidedly unscientific. Their best guess is that staying in school teaches people to delay gratification. The more educated among us are better at forgoing pleasurable and possibly risky behavior because we've learned to look ahead to the future. That connection isn't new, however, and it wouldn't explain why the least-educated Whites like Crystal are dying so much younger today than the same group was two decades ago.

Cave City gives itself the low-stakes title of "Home of the World's Sweetest Watermelons." Beneath the ground, the Crystal River carves out the caverns that lend the town its name. Above it, 1,900 people live in single-wides in neighborhoods dotted with fenced lawns or along spindly red-dirt trails off the main highway. In this part of Arkansas, the Ozark Plateau flattens to meet the Mississippi embayment, and the hills give way to rice paddies. About 17,000 people live in Sharp County, a long string of small towns with Cave City at the bottom and the Missouri border at the top. Most of the residents are White—96 percent—with a median household income of $29,590. Nearly a quarter live in poverty, and Crystal was among them; for most of her married life, she relied on income from her husband's disability checks.

For work, people drive to the college town of Batesville, about 20 minutes south, which has a chicken-processing plant that periodically threatens to close and an industrial bakery with 12-hour shifts that make it hard for a mother to raise children. Less than 13 percent of county residents have a bachelor's degree. Society is divided into opposites: Godly folk go to church and sinners chase the devil, students go to college and dropouts seek hard labor, and men call the shots and women cook for them.

Crystal's parents, Junior and Martha Justice, had moved to the area when her three oldest siblings were still toddlers. . . . Junior farmed, which fed his family and brought in a little money. He found a piece of land on a country road called Antioch and bought a prefabricated home from the Jim Walters company. It was on this land they had their next three children. Crystal, born July 6, 1973, was the sixth and youngest.

Their life was old-school country. They raised chickens and goats and grew their own vegetables. The house was small, with only three bedrooms. Crystal's closest sibling, Terry, was seven years older. Linda was a full 15 years older than Crystal, which made her more like a second mom than a sister. When Crystal was two, Linda's twin sister, Pete, began having children and, fleeing a string of abusive relationships,

turned over custody to her parents. Having four slightly younger nieces and nephews in the house gave Crystal playmates her own age.

It was Linda, the doting older sister and aunt, who would take all the kids to Dogpatch, a creaky little Ozarks amusement park based on the comic strip, with actors playing Daisy Mae and Li'l Abner. Linda keeps Polaroids of Crystal from that time. They show her with long, curly blond hair and often half-clothed, happy, covered in clay and mud. "Grandpa used to call her his little Shirley Temple," says Crystal's niece, Lori.

When Crystal was starting out in elementary school, the family moved to a trailer to be closer to town. . . . Crystal was well behaved in school, and teachers would ask Lori, only two years behind, "Why aren't you like her, she was so quiet and shy?" Crystal loved basketball and, especially, softball, which she played in summer clubs even as an adult. As she got older, her hair darkened and she became stocky and muscular. She played ball like a bulldozer and was aggressive on the field and mouthy off. The whole family would play and bicker and joke. Crystal would smack people across the butt with the bat if they weren't moving fast enough.

"It wasn't until we got in high school that I realized she was struggling so bad in school," Lori says. "I was in the seventh grade, and she was in the ninth, and I wasn't really smart myself. But I could help her do some of her work." In 1988, Junior died from lung cancer at age 55. Both he and Martha were smokers. The next year Crystal met Carl Wilson, whom everybody called Possum. He was related to a cousin through marriage and, at 28, was 12 years her senior. They kept their relationship secret for a few months. "He came up to see her at the school," Lori says. "So I pretty much put two and two together. I was the one that told my grandmother." Lori thought that would put an end to it; instead, Martha let them marry. According to Linda, Martha had one admonition for Possum: "Momma said, 'As long as you take care of her and don't hit her, you have my permission.' He done what he could do for her. They was mates."

Possum moved in with the family in the trailer. He and Crystal had one room, Martha another, and the four nephews and nieces shared two bunk beds in the third. Crystal dropped out in the tenth grade because she had married. That was the way things were. None of Crystal's siblings finished high school. Instead, they became adults when they were teenagers. Crystal would spend the rest of her years as a housewife to a husband who soon became ill and as a mother to a daughter who would grow up as fast as she did.

Researchers have long known that high-school dropouts like Crystal are unlikely to live as long as people who have gone to college. But why would they be slipping behind the generation before them? James Jackson, a public-health researcher at the University of Michigan, believes it's because life became more difficult for the least-educated in the 1990s and 2000s. Broad-scale shifts in society increasingly isolate those who don't finish high school from good jobs, marriageable partners, and healthier communities. "Hope is lowered. If you drop out of school, say, in the last 20 years or so, you just had less hope for ever making it and being anything," Jackson says. "The opportunities available to you are very different than what they were 20 or 30 years ago. What kind of job are you going to get if you drop out at 16? No job."

. . .Jennifer Karas Montez of the Harvard University Center for Population and Development Studies co-authored the first paper investigating why White women without high-school diplomas might be dying. Most research has looked at which diseases are the cause of death, but Montez and her co-author wanted to tease out quality of life: economic indicators like employment and income, whether women were married and how educated their spouses were, and health behaviors like smoking and alcohol abuse. It is well known that smoking shortens life; in fact, smoking led to the early deaths of both of Crystal's parents and her sister and brother. Crystal, though, never smoked or drank. But the researchers discovered something else that was driving women like her to early graves: Whether the women had a job mattered, and it mattered more than income or other signs of financial stability, like homeownership. In fact, smoking and employment were the only two factors of any significance.

At first, Montez and her co-author suspected that women who are already unhealthy are less able to work and so are already more likely to die. When they investigated that hypothesis, however, it didn't hold up. Jobs themselves contributed something to health. But what? It could be, the authors suggested, that work connects women to friends and other social networks they otherwise wouldn't have. Even more squishy sounding, Montez wrote that jobs might give women a "sense of purpose."

Better-educated women are the most likely to work and to achieve parity with men: Seventy-two percent are in the workforce, compared with 81 percent of their male counterparts. Women without high-school diplomas are the least likely to work. Only about a third are in the workforce, compared to about half of their male counterparts. If they do find work, women are more likely than men to have minimum-wage jobs. They account for most workers in the largest low-paying occupations—child-care providers, housecleaners, food servers. Even if they do have minimum-wage jobs, this group of women is more likely to leave the labor force to take care of young children because child care is prohibitively expensive.

Montez's joblessness study, however, raised more questions. Would any job do? What does giving women a "sense of purpose" mean? And why would joblessness hit White women harder than other groups? Overall, men lost more jobs during the Great Recession. Why are women losing years at a faster rate?

. . . Crystal wanted to start a family as soon as she was married but couldn't. Her first three pregnancies, in the early '90s, ended in miscarriages. The first two occurred so late she gave the babies names, Justin and Crystal; the last was a set of twins. None of her relatives knew if she ever went to a doctor to find out why she miscarried. "I just thought maybe it was one of those things, you know, some people can have them and carry them and some can't," Lori says. Megan said her mother had had "female cancer," a catchall phrase for cervical cancer and the infections and dysplasia leading up to it.

When Lori's son was born, Crystal teased her about stealing him. She was always volunteering to baby-sit the kids in the family. When Crystal finally got pregnant with Megan, no one was sure she would make it, least of all Crystal and Possum. "They ended up just praying for me," Megan says. She was born July 20, 1994, and became the center of Crystal's world.

By the time Megan was born, Crystal and Possum were living in their own trailer but were struggling financially. Possum had worked the first four years of their marriage at the chicken-processing plant before quitting for good because of health problems. An accident on an oil rig when he was a teenager had left him with a plate in his skull. Chicken-processing plants are tough places to work, and besides, he qualified for disability. Crystal spent her life taking him to specialists—he was covered by Medicaid—but the problems piled up. He had a congenital heart condition and a bad back. A young-old man.

When Megan was 12, Crystal worked for a brief spell as a housekeeper at a nursing home in Cave City, where Linda and Lori worked. Mostly, though, she stayed home to take care of Possum and Megan. Babysitting brought in small amounts of cash, but she and Possum relied on disability, which was about $1,000 a month. Outside of a brief trip to Texas after Megan was born to show her off to Possum's family, and a trip to a small town near St. Louis to visit a niece after one of the trailers they lived in burned down, Crystal passed her entire life in Cave City.

Crystal spent what money she had on Megan. She gave her any new toy she wanted and, later, name-brand clothes, a four-wheeler, a laptop, and a phone. When Megan started playing softball, Crystal spent money on shoes, gloves, and club fees. "Crystal was a super mom," says Steve Green, the school superintendent and Megan's softball coach. "They didn't have a lot of revenue, but they put everything they had into Megan." Crystal and Possum made it to every practice and every game, even if it meant driving for an hour, deep into the mountains. They brought snacks and sports drinks for Megan's teammates. Crystal would watch her nieces, nephews, and cousins' kids play, and she still played for her family team in Batesville. Crystal went with Linda to a missionary Baptist church near the family road in Antioch, but she and Possum weren't every-Sunday Christians—it was the softball field her spring weekends revolved around. But when Terry was diagnosed with cancer in 2009, the family stopped playing, and Crystal lost her favorite activity.

When her relatives look back, they think Crystal was probably lonely. Her mother had died three years after Megan was born. Although she and Possum had a Ford Contour, Crystal seldom drove, relying on relatives to come by to take her to the grocery store. It was a chance to visit. When Linda's daughter took her truck-driver husband to pick up his 18-wheeler for his next haul, Crystal would always want to go with them. She would call her family members throughout the day, gossiping. She didn't stir up trouble, but she reveled in drama. Crystal would often go to Linda's for homemade biscuits and gravy for breakfast, and she'd ask Linda to buy her liter bottles of Dr Pepper whenever she ran out. She was addicted to Dr Pepper. Sometimes, relatives paid for Possum's medicine; Linda's daughter remembers paying as much as $64 in one visit. Crystal's nieces and nephews had gotten older and started their own families, and now she relied on them as much as she had her older siblings.

Another mystery emerged from the lifespan study: Black women without a high-school diploma are now outliving their White counterparts. As a group, Blacks are more likely to die young, because the factors that determine wellbeing—income, education, access to health care—tend to be worse for Blacks. Yet Blacks on the whole are closing the life-expectancy gap with Whites. In a country where racism still plays a significant role in all that contributes to a healthier, longer life, what could be affecting Whites more than Blacks?

One theory is that low-income White women smoke and drink and abuse prescription drugs like OxyContin and street drugs like meth more than Black women. Despite Crystal's weight and diabetes, those problems are more common among Black women and usually kill more slowly. Meth and alcohol kill quickly. It could be that White women, as a group, are better at killing themselves.

Still, why would White women be more likely to engage in risky behaviors? Another theory is that the kind of place people live in, who is around them, and what those neighbors are doing play a central role. Health is also a matter of place and time. . . . Two researchers from the University of Wisconsin reported that women in nearly half of 3,140 counties in the

United States saw their death rates rise during the same time period that Olshansky studied. The researchers colored the counties with an increase in female mortality a bright red, and the red splashed over Appalachia, down through Kentucky and Tennessee, north of the Cotton Belt, and across the Ozarks—the parts of the South where poor White people live. Location seemed to matter more than other indicators, like drug use, which has been waning. The Wisconsin researchers recommended more studies examining "cultural, political, or religious factors."

Something less tangible, it seems, is shaping the lives of White women in the South, beyond what science can measure. Surely these forces weigh on Black women, too, but perhaps they are more likely to have stronger networks of other women. Perhaps after centuries of slavery and Jim Crow, Black women are more likely to feel like they're on an upward trajectory. Perhaps they have more control relative to the men in their communities. In low-income White communities of the South, it is still women who are responsible for the home and for raising children, but increasingly they are also raising their husbands. A husband is a burden and an occasional heartache rather than a helpmate, but one women are told they cannot do without. More and more, data show that poor women are working the hardest and earning the most in their families but can't take the credit for being the breadwinners. Women do the emotional work for their families, while men reap the most benefits from marriage. The rural South is a place that often wants to remain unchanged from the 1950s and 1960s, and its women are now dying as if they lived in that era, too.

Crystal's world was getting smaller and smaller and more sedentary. Everyone was worried about Possum, but Crystal's own health was bad. She'd had a cystic ovary removed when Megan was 13, and about a year before her death she had a hysterectomy. The surgery was necessary after Crystal had started hemorrhaging, which was brought on by another miscarriage—something her family didn't know about until the autopsy. It's unclear when she learned she was a diabetic. Megan thinks her mom might have heard it for the first time when she was pregnant with her, but Crystal never had regular medical care because she didn't qualify for Medicaid as Possum did.

Megan started spending more time away from her mom in the tenth grade, when Corey and his family moved to town. Crystal consented to their high-school romance, though she warned Corey that if he ever hit her daughter, she'd put him in the ground herself. Within a year of going out with Corey, Megan was pregnant. She swears she didn't know it until she was seven and a half months along, when Corey's mother made her take a pregnancy test. They had a short time to prepare for Kelly's birth in February 2012, but Crystal was happy about the new baby. It was a way for her to have another child. But after Kelly's birth, Crystal and Megan argued; Megan was worried her mother would spoil Kelly. Because Corey's father worked, his family had a bit more money, and they bought more baby clothes than Crystal could, which only made her feel worse.

In the final months of her life, Crystal complained of chest aches, but when she went to the emergency room, the doctors assured her it wasn't a heart attack. She said that she felt like she had the flu or allergies. In hindsight, it was after Terry's death—he died a week after Kelly was born—when Crystal really began to suffer. He had been the linchpin of the family, and now they were breaking apart. After he died, Crystal would call Linda's daughter and say, "I wish God would have took me instead of Terry." Crystal posted regularly about Terry on her Facebook page. Crystal had stopped coming to Linda's for breakfast, too, because Possum was growing sicker and had started falling when he tried to walk on his own. He was diagnosed with cancer about a week before Crystal's death. "I couldn't help but wonder if maybe some of it might have been attributed to her system just being drug down from having to take care of Carl and Megan," says Steve Green, the school superintendent. "Just everyday stress."

The night before she died, Crystal made herself a peanut-butter-and-jelly sandwich for dinner. After Megan took Kelly home, she went to bed and fell asleep, but Possum said she woke up at 1 A.M., said she was thirsty, and went to the kitchen. She was a fitful sleeper, and she returned to bed. When Crystal wasn't up before him the next morning, it struck Possum as odd, but he let her sleep. Crystal usually called her relatives around 6 or 7 A.M. to see what their plans were for the day. They wondered if something was wrong when their phones didn't beep. Finally, Possum sent in his brother, who'd been staying with them, to wake Crystal up; they were always going after each other, and he thought the teasing would spur her out of bed.

Crystal's funeral was small, mostly attended by family, and held at the funeral home in Cave City. They buried her in a tiny graveyard next to a little White chapel on Antioch Road, near the land where Crystal was born. Megan went to stay with Corey's family, and they offered to buy Possum a prefabricated barn so he could come live near them, but there was no need. He spent most of the next four weeks in and out of the hospital, until he died of massive heart failure on June 22. Possum was buried right beside Crystal. Both graves are marked with temporary notices. Linda has promised Megan she will help buy tombstones.

The medical examiner's investigation into Crystal's death was closed because it was determined she died of natural causes. The police report lists no official cause. With untreated, unmanaged diabetes, her blood would have been thick and sticky—the damage would have been building for years—and it could have caused cardiac arrest or a stroke. Linda has her own explanation: "Her heart exploded." And, in a way, it had.

After her mom's death, Megan was 17, hitched, and living on the same land where Crystal had given birth to her. Was it going to be the same life over again? At school, a number of administrators and teachers stepped in to make sure Megan felt supported; one of them was the technology coordinator for the Cave City schools, Julie Johnson. With big gray eyes and a neat gray bob, she seems younger than 46. When I visited the school this spring, Julie showed me a picture of Megan with Kelly, Corey, and his family that Megan copied and gave to her. They became close last winter when Julie walked into one of Megan's classrooms and the teacher asked, "Have you congratulated Megan?" Julie turned to her and said, "What have you done, sister?" Megan told her that she'd given birth only a week before but that she'd wanted to come back to school. Julie said, "Dang, you're tough!"

Julie has seen a lot of teen mothers. Arkansas ranks number one in the country in teenage births.

About a month before Megan gave birth to Kelly, another young woman from the school had gotten married and had a baby, then died mysteriously. Nobody knew what had caused it, and the girl, Bethany, was in the back of Julie's mind when she saw Megan. "I've been in education for 25 years. I kind of got a good eye and sensed where she was coming from. And I was troubled because, as I kept thinking, OK, if a teacher here at school has a baby, they have a big shower for her, and if somebody at church has a baby, they have a shower for her, but if you have a child as a child, we don't do anything."

She prayed on what to do, and prayed some more. It led her to start the Bethany Project, a donation program that would give Megan and other young mothers baby clothes, school supplies, and community support. Megan was only in the spring of her junior year when she had Kelly. Megan told Julie she'd promised her mother she'd stay in school—Megan told me Crystal wanted her to have a good job so she could take care of Kelly and spoil her rotten—and Julie thinks Megan's mother-in-law helped her uphold her promise. "Corey's mother, I think she would have fought the devil to make sure those two finished school." They did. Megan and Corey finished school on May 3 of this year, were married eight days later on May 11, and then graduated on May 18, just a few days shy of the anniversary of Crystal's death. Megan found a job at Wendy's and plans to enroll in the community college in Batesville. Finishing college would give her the best chance to escape her mother's fate.

Julie knows a lot of young women who will never break the cycle. She has her own thoughts about what might be dragging down their life expectancy. "Desperation," she says. "You look at the poverty level in this county—I love this place. It's where I'm from. I don't want you to think I'm being negative about it." But she gestures toward the highway and notes how little is there: a few convenience stores, a grocery, and a nursing home. You have to drive north to the county seat in Ash Flat for a Walmart, or you can negotiate traffic in Batesville, where you might get a job at the chicken plant or a fast-food restaurant. "If you are a woman, and you are a poorly educated woman, opportunities for you are next to nothing. You get married and you have kids. You can't necessarily provide as well as you'd like to for those kids. Oftentimes, the way things are, you're better off if you're not working. You get more help. You get better care for your kids if you're not working. It's a horrible cycle.

"You don't even hear about women's lib, because that's come and gone. But you hear about glass ceilings, and I think girls, most especially girls, have to be taught that just because they're girls doesn't mean they can't do something. That they are just as smart, that they are just as valuable as males. And we have to teach boys that girls can be that way, too. They all need the love, nurturing, and support from somebody from their family or who's not their family. Somebody who's willing to step up. There has to be something to inspire kids to want more, to want better. And they have to realize that they're going to have to work hard to get it. I don't know how you do that.

"It's just horrible, you know? I don't know if 'horrible' is the right word." Julie puts her face into her hands. "The desperation of the times. I don't know anything about anything, but that's what kills them."

BRITTANY N. MOREY

52. MECHANISMS BY WHICH ANTI-IMMIGRANT STIGMA EXACERBATES RACIAL/ETHNIC HEALTH DISPARITIES

Anti-immigrant sentiment has been on the rise since the 2016 presidential campaign. Morey argues that the change in the sociopolitical climate stigmatizes immigrants and risks harming their psychological and physical health. She discusses the ways that immigration policy and the social stigmas, lack of access to care, and added stressors that result from such policies can affect public health.

Anti-immigrant rhetoric and political actions gained prominence and public support before, during, and after the 2016 presidential election. This anti-immigrant political environment threatens to increase health disparities among undocumented persons, immigrant groups, and people of color.

I discuss the mechanisms by which anti-immigrant stigma exacerbates racial/ethnic health disparities through increasing multilevel discrimination and stress, deportation and detention, and policies that limit health resources. I argue that the anti-immigrant sociopolitical context is a social determinant of health that affects mostly communities of color, both immigrants and nonimmigrants.

Public health has a moral obligation to consider how immigration policy is health policy and to be prepared to respond to worsening health disparities as a result of anti-immigrant racism.

> Before I built a wall I'd ask to know What I was walling in or walling out, And to whom I was like to give offence.
>
> —ROBERT FROST, *"Mending Wall" (1914)*

"Build the wall!" has been the most prominent slogan of the current U.S. president and was echoed repeatedly during campaign rallies by his supporters. This chant signifies more than mere agreement with the president's premier policy to build a giant wall along the U.S.-Mexico border. Underlying this rhetoric is a strongly held anti-immigrant sentiment that seeks to exclude and stigmatize people in U.S. society who are from other countries. Even more nefarious, anti-immigrant speech and politics are coded in a way that denigrates and criminalizes people of color more generally, who do not fit in with some Americans' views of who should be considered "true" Americans—namely, non-Hispanic White Americans.

Xenophobic attitudes have become popularized by unfounded claims made throughout the presidential campaign that immigrants fuel crime, terrorism, and economic instability. In keeping with anti-immigrant rhetoric that infused his campaign, President Trump has now responded with action by signing numerous executive orders that discourage immigration and limit immigrants' rights. Anti-immigration rhetoric and policies, whether intentionally or unintentionally, will

Brittany N. Morey, "Mechanisms by Which Anti-Immigrant Stigma Exacerbates Racial/Ethnic Health Disparities," American Journal of Public Health, 108(4) April 2018: 460–463. Reprinted with permission.

not only harm the health of immigrant groups living and seeking to live in the United States but also exacerbate racial health disparities among U.S. citizens.

Since 1978, the American Public Health Association has issued multiple policy statements opposing anti-immigrant policies that exacerbate health disparities and violate principles of social justice.[1-3] Although anti-immigrant racism is nothing new in U.S. history, the current administration's blatant "tough on immigration" stance coinciding with thinly veiled racist remarks has created an urgent need for public health to commit itself fully to a strong response that protects health and promotes justice.

Immigration policy is also health policy. When immigration policy responds to the worst sentiments of anti-immigrant bias with punitive action, disparity-inducing health consequences follow. When this happens, the vision of Healthy People 2020 of "a society in which all people live long, healthy lives" is compromised. We must recognize how the xenophobic and racist underpinnings of the current anti-immigrant environment contribute to widening health disparities.

ANTI-IMMIGRANT ENVIRONMENT CONTRIBUTE TO WIDENING HEALTH DISPARITIES

Anti-immigrant policies and rhetoric are the direct result of societal stigmatization of immigrants. When anti-immigrant stigma increases, three interrelated social and political processes manifest to harm health: multilevel discrimination and stress, deportation and detention, and policies that limit health resources. I provide evidence concerning the health effects of each of these processes to support my contention that anti-immigrant policies will increase health disparities. These policies lead to premature death among people of color and do nothing to keep Americans safe.

Stigma is defined as the presence of labeling, stereotyping, separation, status loss, and discrimination that occurs in situations in which power differentials are prominent.[4] By this definition, immigrants experience stigma because they are constantly being labeled "foreigners" or "outsiders" and stereotyped as undocumented or criminals. This separates them and gives

them a lower status than that of White Americans in a society where they have less political power. Stigma can occur on multiple levels to affect health disparities, including the individual (e.g., perceived deportation threat), interpersonal (e.g., anti-immigrant discrimination), and structural (e.g., immigration policy).

Anti-immigrant stigma has spillover effects on broader populations of people of color. This is because undocumented and citizenship statuses cannot be determined by visually assessing a person; these statuses are concealable. Therefore, inasmuch as people in the dominant group falsely conflate being undocumented with being an immigrant and being an immigrant with being non-White, populations that include all racial/ethnic minorities who might be suspected of being an immigrant are likely to be the victims of stigma against immigrant and undocumented persons, regardless of their actual legal or citizenship status. Because of this background, anyone who is a visible racial/ethnic or religious minority (e.g., Arabs, Asians, Blacks, Latinos, Muslims, Sikhs) may be subject to anti-immigrant stigma. According to intersectionality theory, the interaction of multiple stigmatized identities—including immigration status, skin color, gender expression, sexual orientation, and religion—may further incite marginalization.

MULTILEVEL DISCRIMINATION AND STRESS

Increased stigmatization of immigrants leads to greater discrimination directed against people of color. There is extensive literature linking personal experiences of discrimination with poor health. Since the November 2016 election, people who hold anti-immigrant views have felt emboldened, leading to disturbing reports of hate crimes against people perceived to be immigrants.[5] One fatal example occurred in February 2017, when Srinivas Kuchibhotla, an Indian man living in Kansas, was shot and killed by a White male screaming, "Get out of my country!"[6]

These more extreme cases of violence against people of color suspected of being immigrants and other forms of visible interpersonal discrimination are only the tip of the iceberg. Simply living in a country where experiencing this type of discrimination is a possibility increases the vigilance of people of color who fear they might be subject to such anti-immigrant hate, even if they have not personally been a victim of discriminatory violence. Stress caused by the threat of a sociopolitical environment that specifically aims to exclude and disenfranchise entire population groups can accumulate over time to cause greater "wear and tear" on their bodies, leading to higher levels of chronic disease, risky health behaviors, and premature mortality.[7]

In this discriminatory environment, children in kindergarten through 12th grade may be especially susceptible, as reports of bullying and harassment of students of color in school have spiked since the 2016 presidential election.[5] Research has highlighted how children of Mexican immigrants are aware of the sociopolitical stigma against them, leading to internalized racism and low self-esteem.[8] These children express fears of familial separation and shame of their immigrant background, regardless of their legal status, revealing that even children's incomplete understanding of an anti-immigrant environment can have devastating effects.

Beyond individuals' experiences and perceptions, discrimination and stress can occur at multiple ecological levels to affect the health of communities.[9] One study examined the effect of an immigration raid in Washtenaw County, Michigan, that resulted in the detainment and deportation of several people in the county's Latino population.[10] Researchers found that after controlling for demographics, including nativity, people surveyed after the raid reported higher levels of immigration enforcement stress and lower self-rated health than did those surveyed before the raid. Another study found that infants born to Latina mothers following a major federal immigration raid in Postville, Iowa, had a 24 percent greater risk of low birthweight after than before the raid.[11] These changes in birthweight were observed among both U.S.-born and foreign-born Latina mothers and were not observed among non-Latina White mothers, revealing the racialized nature of immigration enforcement as a community stressor. Furthermore, anti-immigrant prejudice at the community level has been found to be associated with higher risk of mortality among U.S.-born "other race" respondents, which was composed largely of Asians and Hispanics.[12] These studies show that community-level stress and discrimination against immigrants can have widespread detrimental effects on the health of racial/ethnic minorities.

DEPORTATION AND DETENTION

Anti-immigrant stigma also leads to worsened health by separating immigrants from the rest of U.S. society through deportation and detention.[9] To be clear, the number of people being deported from the United States was high long before the last election cycle. However, the Obama administration's deportation efforts were focused mainly on people recently detained while crossing the border and undocumented immigrants who had committed violent crimes. Since President Trump took office in January 2017, the number of arrests immigration officials have made has increased to more than 30 percent higher than in the same period in 2016,[13] with priorities for deportation broadening to include a greater percentage of people whose only crime is not having documentation status. Currently, 11.3 million undocumented persons living in the United States, the vast majority of whom have been peaceably living and working in the United States for a decade or more,[14] are under the constant threat of deportation and detention.

Deportation and detention have immediate effects on health. People who are deported face violence, crime, oppression, and poverty in the places they are sent. Factors contributing to their initial immigration to the United States, including persecution, are likely to be worsened on their return. Their mental and physical health may be endangered as a result of being cut off from health-promoting social and economic support in the United States. However, few studies have been able to track the health effects of deportation once people are forced to leave the United States.

There have been several reports of the poor conditions of immigrant detention centers around the country, including excessive use of physical restraints, inadequate access to health care, lack of opportunities for nutrition and exercise, and physical and verbal abuse by detention center officers,[15] which in the most extreme cases have resulted in death. Since 2003, 172 people have died in immigration detention centers—many of them owned by private prison companies with little government oversight.[16] The inhumane treatment received at these centers, some of which hold children and families, has prompted advocates to label benign-sounding detention centers what they truly resemble: immigrant prisons.

The children and other family members who are left behind also feel the profound effects of deportation and detainment. The sudden removal of one or multiple caregivers has left children stranded at school or at home and has forced some into the foster care system and others into single-parent households. Such an event is clearly traumatizing to children of undocumented parents, 80 percent of whom are legal U.S. citizens.[17] In the short term, children with a deported parent are significantly more likely to display mental health problems than are those whose parents were not deported or were in the process of deportation.[18] In the longer term, the loss of a caregiver or income earner often leaves families in direr financial situations, leading to housing instability, homelessness, unsupervised care, and food insecurity.[17]

The mere threat of immigration enforcement can indirectly affect health by fostering fear and mistrust of law enforcement among immigrant groups. Although undocumented immigrants and their families fear that any interaction with law enforcement may lead to their apprehension, legal immigrants and U.S.-born people of color also fear harassment by law enforcement because of racial profiling.[19] Increased immigration enforcement has been shown to restrict Latinos' access to transportation, employment, nutrition, physical activity, and health care.[20,21] Evidence shows that in the wake of the 2016 presidential election, reports of interpersonal violence, including sexual assault and domestic violence among Latino residents, dropped dramatically in several cities across the nation.[22] These statistics suggest that Latinos are unwilling to report interpersonal crimes to law enforcement out of fear, raising concerns that populations with large numbers of immigrants are suffering from unaddressed interpersonal violence in the wake of the current anti-immigrant sociopolitical environment.

POLICIES THAT LIMIT HEALTH RESOURCES

In an increasingly anti-immigrant environment, it has become more likely that anti-immigrant policies are being proposed and passed, resulting in the worsening of health disparities through further limiting health resources. "Health resources" refer not only to health care and health insurance but also to jobs, education, wealth, social capital, and social services, which have been shown to fundamentally support health.

In the United States, undocumented immigrants are completely ineligible to receive the vast majority of federally funded safety net benefits, including Social Security—although they pay an estimated $12 billion per year into Social Security through payroll taxes.[23] Many undocumented immigrants are forced to work illegally in precarious situations where they are subject to exploitation and abuse from employers. Undocumented immigrants face barriers to higher education because they are barred from receiving federal education benefits and must often pay higher rates to attend public colleges or universities. Furthermore, undocumented immigrants are ineligible for non-emergency Medicaid benefits and are prohibited from purchasing coverage or receiving subsidies through the Affordable Care Act. Because undocumented immigrants are more likely to have a low income and do not qualify for most government-funded health plans, they are more likely to rely on emergency care or community clinics or to forgo care altogether.

Legal immigrants also face restrictions to receiving health resources. Federal law requires a five-year waiting period before legal immigrants can qualify to receive federal benefits. Research has shown that when legal immigrants are eligible to receive public benefits, few take advantage of the government programs out of fear of being considered a ward of the state and thereby jeopardizing obtaining full citizenship status in the future.[24] Contrary to the belief that immigrants overuse public benefits, lower percentages of poor immigrants than similarly poor U.S.-born natives use public benefits; when they do, they cost the government less per beneficiary, reducing costs.[25]

Policies that limit health resources for immigrants can also affect U.S. citizens. Studies have found that in states with more anti-immigrant laws, Latino

Americans experience more barriers to accessing health care and higher rates of poor mental health days.[26,27] These studies demonstrate how anti-immigration policies act as forms of structural racism against people of color to negatively affect health.[9]

Conversely, policies that increase immigrants' access to health resources may lessen health disparities. One study of the effects of the Deferred Action for Childhood Arrivals (DACA) program, the U.S. policy that provided renewable work permits and deferred deportation for undocumented young adults, found significant mental health benefits in the form of decreased psychological distress among those eligible, compared with those ineligible, for the program.[28] In addition, the DACA program contributed to well-being by increasing access to important health resources for undocumented Asian and Pacific Islander young adults.[29] These studies demonstrate the importance of increasing undocumented immigrants' access to health resources to address disparities. Unfortunately, President Trump ended the DACA program [in 2017] without replacing it with a long-term policy fix, causing even more uncertainty for the future of undocumented immigrants.

CONCLUSIONS

I have provided a critical perspective for understanding how an anti-immigrant sociopolitical environment worsens racial/ethnic health disparities by stigmatizing people on the basis of their country of birth and the color of their skin. Public health must first recognize that anti-immigrant policies are forms of structural racism that are antithetical to valuing health for all. In the effort to eliminate health disparities, I encourage public health to proactively work against anti-immigrant racism in our organizations, communities, and nation as a whole.

More research is needed to highlight the multilevel effects of anti-immigrant rhetoric and policies on communities and individuals as well as the intersectionality of immigration status, race, and other aspects of stigmatized identity. Public health has a moral duty to protect the health of all by breaking down the walls formed by an anti-immigrant political environment.

ACKNOWLEDGMENTS

This commentary was supported by the Chancellor's Postdoctoral Fellowship Program at the University of California, Riverside.

Special thanks go to Bruce G. Link, PhD, and to Gilbert C. Gee, PhD, for their feedback on previous versions of this article. I also thank the anonymous reviewers for their thoughtful comments and suggestions.

Note. The contents of this commentary are solely the responsibility of the author and do not necessarily represent the official views of the University of California.

HUMAN PARTICIPANT PROTECTION

Because no human participants were involved, no institutional review board approval was required.

NOTES

1. American Public Health Association. *Public Health Consideration Related to Un-documented Persons.* Washington, DC; 1978. APHA Policy Statement no. 7833.
2. American Public Health Association. *Public Health Impact of US Immigration Policy.* Washington, DC; 2010. APHA Policy Statement no. LB-10-02.
3. American Public Health Association. *Ensuring Access to Health Services for Undocumented Immigrants. Washington, DC; 1994, APHA Policy Statement no. 9401.*
4. Link BG, Phelan JC. Conceptualizing stigma. *Annu Rev Soviol.* 2001;27:363–385.
5. *Ten Days After: Harassment and Intimidation in the Aftermath of the Election.* Washington, DC: Southern Poverty Law Center; 2016.

6. Berman M, Schmidt S. He yelled "Get out of my country," witnesses say, and then shot 2 men from India, killing one. Available at: https://www.washingtonpost.com/news/morningmix/wp/2017/02/24/get-out-of-mycountry-kansan-reportedly-yelled-before-shooting-2-men-from-indiakilling-one. Accessed August 31, 2017.

7. Williams DR, Medlock MM. Health effects of dramatic societal events—ramifications of the recent presidential election. *N Engl J Med.* 2017;376(23):2295–2299.

8. Ayón C. Talking to Latino children about race, inequality, and discrimination: raising families in an anti-immigrant political environment. *J Soc Social Work Res.* 2016;7(3):449–477.

9. Gee GC, Ford CL. Structural racism and health inequities. *Du Bois Rev.* 2011; 8(1):115–132.

10. Lopez WD, Kruger DJ, Delva J, et al. Health implications of an immigration raid: findings from a Latino community in the midwestern United States. *J Immigr Minor Health.* 2017;19(3):702-708.

11. Novak NL, Geronimus AT, Martinez-Cardoso AM. Change in birth outcomes among infants born to Latina mothers after a major immigration raid. *Int J Epidemiol.* 2017;46(3):839–849.

12. Morey BN, Gee GC, Muennig P, Hatzenbuehler ML. Community-level prejudice and mortality among immigrant groups. *Soc Sci Med.* 2017;199:561-66.

13. Sacchetti M. ICE immigration arrests of noncriminals double under Trump. 2017. Available at: https://www.washingtonpost.com/local/immigration-arrests-of-noncriminals-double-under-trump/2017/04/16/98a2f1e2-2096-11e7-be2a-3a1fb24d4671_story.html?utm_term=.8136a3f2f9e2. Accessed August 31, 2017.

14. Krogstad JM, Passel JS, Cohn DV. 5 Facts about illegal immigration in the U.S. 2017. Available at: https://www.pewresearch.org/fact-tank/2019/06/12/5-facts-about-illegal-immigration-in-the-u-s/. Accessed August 31, 2017.

15. Amnesty International. *Jailed Without Justice: Immigration Detention in the USA.* New York: Amnesty International; 2011.

16. US Immigration and Customs Enforcement. List of deaths in ICE custody: Data from: 10/01/2003 to 06/05/2017. 2017. Available at: https://www.ice.gov/doclib/foia/reports/detaineedeaths-2003-2017.pdf. Accessed September 11, 2017.

17. Capps R, Koball H, Campetella A, Perreira K, Hooker S, Pedroza JM. *Implications of Immigration Enforcement Activities for the Well-Being of Children in Immigrant Families: A Review of the Literature.* Washington, DC: Urban Institute and Migration Policy Institute; 2015.

18. Allen B, Cisneros EM, Tellez A. The children left behind: The impact of parental deportation on mental health. *J Child Fam Stud.* 2015;24(2):386–392.

19. Dreby J. The burden of deportation on children in Mexican immigrant families. *J Marriage Fam.* 2012;74(4):829–845.

20. Hardy LJ, Getrich CM, Quezada JC, Guay A, Michalowski RJ, Henley E. A call for further research on the impact of state-level immigration policies on public health. *Am J Public Health.* 2012;102(7):1250–1254.

21. Hacker K, Chu J, Leung C, et al. The impact of immigration and customs enforcement on immigrant health: perceptions of immigrants in Everett, Massachusetts, USA. *Soc Sci Med.* 2011; 73(4):586–594.

22. Medina J. Too scared to report sexual abuse. The fear: deportation. 2017. Available at: https://www.nytimes.com/2017/04/30/us/immigrants-deportation-sexual-abuse.html. Accessed August 31, 2017.

23. Gross SW, Wade A, Skirvin JP, Morris M, Bye KM, Huston D. *Effects of Unauthorized Immigration on the Actuarial Status of Social Security Trust Funds.* Baltimore, MD: Social Security Administration; 2013.

24. Hagan J, Rodriguez N, Capps R, Kabiri N. The effects of recent welfare and immigration reforms on immigrants' access to health care. *Int Migr Rev*, 2003; 37(2):444-463.

25. Ku L, Bruen B. Poor immigrants use public benefits at a lower rate than poor native-born citizens. 2013. Available at: https://www.cato.org/publications/economic-development-bulletin/poor-immigrants-use-public-benefits-lower-rate-poor. Accessed August 31, 2017.

26. White K, Yeager VA, Menachemi N, Scarinci IC. Impact of Alabama's immigration law on access to health care among Latina immigrants and children: implications for national reform. *Am J Public Health*. 2014;104(3):397–405.

27. Hatzenbuehler ML, Prins SJ, Flake M, et al. Immigration policies and mental health morbidity among Latinos: a state-level analysis. *Soc Sci Med*. 2017;174:169–178.

28. Venkataramani AS, Shah SJ, O'Brien R, Kawachi I, Tsai AC. Health consequences of the US Deferred Action for Childhood Arrivals (DACA) immigration programme: a quasi-experimental study. *Lancet Public Health*. 2017;2(4):e175–e181.

29. Sudhinaraset M, To TM, Ling I, Melo J, Chavarin J. The influence of Deferred Action for Childhood Arrivals on undocumented Asian and Pacific Islander young adults: through a social determinants of health lens. *J Adolesc Health*. 2017; 60(6):741–746.

OTIS WEBB BRAWLEY AND PAUL GOLDBERG

53. HOW WE DO HARM

With the tragic story of one of his patients framing his analysis, Brawley discusses racial and class disparities in the health-care system and how the current organization of the system harms patients.

She walks through the emergency-room doors sometime in the early morning. In a plastic bag, she carries an object wrapped in a moist towel. She is not bleeding. She is not in shock. Her vital signs are okay. There is no reason to think that she will collapse on the spot. Since she is not truly an emergency patient, she is triaged to the back of the line, and other folks, those in immediate distress, get in for treatment ahead of her. She waits on a gurney in a cavernous, green hallway. The "chief complaint" on her chart at Grady Memorial Hospital, in downtown Atlanta, might have set off a wave of nausea at a hospital in a White suburb or almost any place in the civilized world. It reads, "My breast has fallen off. Can you reattach it?" She waits for at least four hours—likely, five or six. The triage nurse doesn't seek to determine the whereabouts of the breast. Obviously, the breast is in the bag.

I am making rounds on the tenth floor when I get a page from Tammie Quest in the Emergency Department. At Grady, we take care of patients who can't pay, patients no one wants. They come to us with their bleeding wounds, their run-amok diabetes, their end-stage tumors, their drama. You deal with this wreckage for a while and you develop a coping mechanism. You detach. That's why many doctors, nurses, and social workers here come off as if they have departed for a less turbulent planet. Tammie is not like

that. She emotes, and I like having her as the queen of ER—an experienced Black woman who gives a shit. When Dr. Quest pages me, I know it isn't because she needs a social interaction. It has to be something serious. "We are wanted in the ER," I tell my team. The cancer team today consists of a fellow, a resident, two medical students, and yours truly, in a flowing White coat, as the attending physician. I lead the way down the hall. Having grown up Catholic, I can't help thinking of the med students and young doctors as altar boys following a priest.

I am a medical oncologist, the kind of doctor who gives chemotherapy. My other interests are epidemiology and biostatistics. I am someone you might ask whether a drug works, whether you should get a cancer screening test, and whether a White man's cancer differs from a Black man's cancer. You can also ask me if we are winning the "war" on the cluster of diseases we call cancer. As chief medical officer of the American Cancer Society [ACS]—a position I have held since 2007—I often end up quoted in the newspapers, and I am on television a lot. In addition to my academic, journalistic, and public-policy roles, I have been taking care of cancer patients at Grady for nearly a decade, first as the founding director of the cancer center, and now as chief doctor at the ACS.

My retinue behind me, I keep up a fast pace, this side of a jog. Bill Bernstein, the fellow, is the most

---

senior of the group. Bill is a Newton, Massachusetts, suburbanite, still boyish. He is having trouble adjusting to the South, to Atlanta, to its inner city. He is trying, but it's hard to miss that Black people and poor people perplex him. Contact with so much despair makes him awkward. But he has a good heart, a surfeit of common sense—and he is smart. Whatever we teach him at Grady will make him a better doctor wherever he ends up. Grady suffers from what the administration here calls a "vertical transportation problem." Our elevators are slow at best, broken at worst. We head for the stairs, rushing down to the first floor, then through long, green hallways into the ER.

Grady is a monument to racism. Racism is built into it, as is poverty, as is despair. Shaped like a capital letter *H*, Grady is essentially two hospitals with a hallway—a crossover—in the middle to keep things separate but equal for sixteen stories. In the 1950s and '60s, White patients were wheeled into the front section, which faces the city. Blacks went to the back of the *H*. This structure—built in 1953—was actually an improvement over the previous incarnation. The Big *H*—the current Grady—replaced two separate buildings—the Whites got a brick building, the Blacks a run-down wood-frame structure. Older Atlantans continue to refer to the place in a chilling plural, the Gradys.

You end up at Grady for four main reasons. It could happen because you have no insurance and are denied care at a private hospital, or because you are unconscious when you arrive by ambulance. When your lights are out, you are in no position to ask to be taken to a cleaner, better-lit, suburban palace of medicine. A third, small contingent are older Black folks with insurance, who could go anywhere but have retained a dim memory of Grady as the only Atlanta hospital that accepted us. The fourth category, injured cops and firemen, know that we see a lot of shock and trauma and are good at it. We are their ER of choice.

Today, our 950-bed behemoth stands for another form of segregation: poor versus rich, separate but with no pretense of equality. Grady is Atlanta's safety-net hospital. It is also the largest hospital in the United States. The ER, arguably the principal entry point to Grady, was built in the center of the hospital, filling in some of the *H* on the first floor. To build

it, Grady administrators got some federal funds in time for the 1996 Summer Olympics. This fueled financial machinations, which led to criminal charges, which led to prison terms. (In retrospect, the bulk of the money was put to good use. Many of the victims of the Olympic Park bombing came through our ER.) The hallways here are incredibly crowded, even by the standards of inner-city hospitals. Patients are triaged into three color-coded lines—surgery, internal medicine, obstetrics—and placed on gurneys two-deep, leaving almost no room for staff to squeeze through.

You might see a homeless woman drifting in and out of consciousness next to a Georgia Tech student bloodied from being pistol-whipped in an armed robbery, next to a fifty-seven-year-old suburban secretary terrified by a sudden loss of vision, next to a twenty-eight-year-old hooker writhing in pain that shoots up from her lower abdomen, next to a conventioneer who Blacked out briefly in a cylindrical tower of a downtown hotel, next to a fourteen-year-old slum dweller who struggles for breath as his asthma attack subsides. When I first arrived in Atlanta and all of this was new to me, I took my wife, Yolanda, through the Grady ER on a Friday night. "Oh, the humanity," she said. Yolanda, a lawyer with the U.S. Securities and Exchange Commission, feels happier above the Mason–Dixon Line.

. . . Elsewhere, patients might trust us doctors, admire us, even bow to our robes, our honorifics, and the all-caps abbreviations that follow our names. Here, not so much. A place called Tuskegee is about two hours away from here. It's where government doctors staged a medical experiment in the thirties: they watched Black men die of syphilis, withholding treatment even after effective drugs were invented. Tuskegee is not an abstraction in these parts. It's a physical place, as palpable as a big, deep wound, and eighty-plus years don't mean a thing. Tuskegee is a huge, flashing CAUTION sign in the consciousness of Southern Black folks. It explains why they don't trust doctors much and why good docs such as Tammie have to fight so hard to earn their elementary trust. Like me, Tammie is a member of the medical-school faculty at Emory University, and, like me, she has several academic interests. One of these interests is end-of-life care for cancer patients: controlling the symptoms when someone with advanced cancer shows up in your ER.

Seeing us approach, she walks toward us and hands me a wooden clipboard with the Grady forms. I look at her face, gauging the mixture of sadness, moral outrage, and fatigue. She says something like "This patient *needs* someone who cares," and disappears. I glance at the chief complaint. "Holy shit," I say to Bill Bernstein and, more so, to myself.

I introduce myself to a trim, middle-aged, Black woman, not unattractive, wearing a blue examination gown conspicuously stamped GRADY. (At Grady, things such as gowns, infusion pumps, and money tend to vanish.) From the moment Tammie paged me, I knew that the situation had to be more than a run-of-the-mill emergency. This patient clearly is not about to die on the examination table. She doesn't need emergency treatment. Before anything, she needs somebody to talk to. She needs attention, both medical and human.

The patient, Edna Riggs, is fifty-three. She works for the phone company and lives on the southeast side of Atlanta. Sitting on an exam table, she looks placid. When she extends her hand, it feels limp. She makes fleeting eye contact. This is depression, maybe. Shame does the same thing, as does a sense of doom. *Fatalism* is the word doctors have repurposed to describe this last form of alienation.

In medicine, we speak a language of our own, and Edna's physical problem has a name in doctorese: automastectomy. It's a fancy way of saying that the patient's breast has fallen off by itself. An automastectomy can occur when a tumor grows so big and so deep that it cuts off the blood supply from the chest to the breast. Denied oxygen, breast tissue dies and the breast starts to detach from the chest wall. At places such as Grady, automastectomies are seen a couple of times a year, often enough to be taken in stride.

This case is different from others I have seen only because Edna Riggs has wrapped her detached breast in a moist, light-blue towel and brought it with her for reattachment. I can't help wondering why the towel is moist. Some deliberateness has gone into the breast's care. I cringe at the thought that Edna has kept that package next to her on the gurney in the ER for hours. In the exam gown, Edna's chest looks surprisingly normal. I ask how long she has had a "breast problem." She first felt something in her breast when her

son was in second grade, she replies. It has grown over the years. She speaks correct English, not the language of the streets. She sounds like someone who has had schooling, a person who reads. Her hair is clean and combed, she is dressed neatly. What grade is her son in now? Eleventh. I don't react, not visibly. She has known she had a problem for nine years—why did she do nothing? I ask Edna's permission to examine her. She nods. I ask her to lie down, my entourage gathering around.

I help her remove her right arm from the gown, trying to respect her modesty and preserve as much dignity as possible. I undrape the right breast, or the place where the right breast had been. The chest wall is now rugged. I see yellowish, fibrous tissue and dry blood. There is the unforgettable smell of anaerobic bacteria. The wound is infected. I reach for examination gloves. I palpate her chest wall and feel under her armpit, looking for evidence of enlarged nodes. After examining the breast wall, I look in the towel. Her amputated breast could fit on her chest as if it were a puzzle piece.

I am not looking forward to Edna's repeating her request to reattach the breast. If she asks directly, I will have to say that this is not possible and explain why not. My preference is to move slowly, to let her adjust, to make her comfortable with me, with receiving medical care for her condition. I fear that she will get up, leave, and never return. Fortunately, Edna doesn't repeat her request. Perhaps the magnitude of the problem confronting her is starting to sink in, Edna's breast cancer has been growing for at least nine years. It's unheard-of that cancer such as this would be anything but metastatic. The disease has to have disseminated to her bones, lungs, brain, liver. I feel a wave of frustration and anger.

Another day at Grady Memorial Hospital. Here I sit, talking with a patient whom we would probably have cured nine years earlier, and today I will have to tell her that she has a terminal disease. The rest is logistics. I arrange for the pathology and radiology to get confirmation. We always get pathologic confirmation of cancer, even when we are almost certain that it is cancer. An old medical saying goes: "When you hear hoofbeats, think horses, not zebras." This saying has an important corollary: "You don't want to be bit on the ass by a zebra." There is a remote possibility that Edna's automastectomy was caused by leprosy or some unusual infectious disease. It's cheap and easy to get verification that it's cancer.

I ask Bill Bernstein to talk with Edna, to take a full history, to perform a full examination. The objective is to rule out neurologic problems from spread of the disease to the brain or spine, to look for other evidence of problems caused by the disease. If you take me aside and ask why I'm withdrawing from the scene, I will say that I am trying to awaken Bill's compassion. But it is something else as well, something about me. I am afraid of growing callous. I acknowledge this readily, as a means of staving it off. I am trying to avoid accepting the unnecessary loss of yet another life. In the case of Edna Riggs, the abstract, scholarly term *health disparities* acquires a very real smell of a rotting breast. I take my leave and, with the resident, start arranging tests to confirm the diagnosis and get Edna ready for treatment. We will fight, even though we are going to lose. Metastatic breast cancer always wins. We have drugs to decrease pain and even make most people live longer, but we can beat breast cancer only when it's caught early.

We admit Edna Riggs into the hospital, to get the tests done and to start antibiotic treatment of the infected wound. We could have done the workup without admitting her, but I fear that she will leave the system as abruptly as she entered. Psychological and emotional support are legitimate reasons for admittance, though most insurance companies and Medicaid would disagree. As she starts to trust me, Edna tells me how frightened she was when she found a lump in her breast. Right away, she knew it was breast cancer, and in her experience, everyone who got breast cancer died quickly, painfully. Insurance problems kept her away from the doctor, as did the fear of dying. She knew she would die after going to the doctor. Several of her friends had.

Early on, Edna had some insurance, which didn't do her any good. Her employer wouldn't let her take just two or three hours of sick leave to go to the doctor. If she needed to take sick leave, she had to take it in increments of one day. This guaranteed that an employee would exhaust all the leave quickly. If Edna had been fired for taking time off after exhausting her

sick leave, her three kids, too, would have lost support and insurance. Acknowledging the physical problem and facing the consequences became increasingly difficult. Edna tells me that she feared the disease, but she also feared the system. Would the doctors scold her? Would they experiment on her? Would they give her drugs that caused nausea, vomiting, hair loss? Would the hospital kill her?

Edna's decision to stay out of the medical system was about fear: fear of breast cancer, fear of the medical profession, fear of losing the roof over her kids' heads. Fear intensified after her employer started to require copayments from workers who wanted to be insured. This extra $3,000 a year made health insurance too expensive to keep. Payment for medical services and sick-leave policies determine the quality of care we receive. Several years ago, my research team at the American Cancer Society published data showing that people diagnosed with cancer who had no insurance or were insured through Medicaid were 1.6 times more likely to die in five years as those with private insurance. In breast cancer, patients with private insurance were more likely to be diagnosed with Stage I breast cancer than those who had no insurance or were receiving Medicaid. In colon cancer, too, the chances of catching the disease at an earlier, treatable stage were lower in the uninsured and Medicaid populations. Even when the disease was found early, an uninsured patient did worse than one with insurance. For example, an insured patient with Stage II colon cancer had better odds of being alive five years after diagnosis than an uninsured patient with what should be highly curable Stage I cancer . . . .

ACS epidemiologists estimate that the lack of insurance annually costs eight thousand Americans their lives due to inability to receive cancer treatment. Even controlling cancer pain is no small challenge if you are poor. Uninsured patients cannot afford pain medicines. The social programs that give them medication heavily ration pain meds. Even if you have insurance that will pay for your treatment, you may still not be able to afford to receive it.

I have seen poor breast-cancer patients choose mastectomy (surgical removal of the entire breast) over a lumpectomy (removal of the tumor) because of employer sick-leave policies. A woman who chooses a lumpectomy must also receive radiation, which has to be given daily, Monday through Friday, for six to eight weeks. The treatment requires fifteen minutes in the clinic, but it's done only during business hours. Unfortunately, this less disfiguring treatment is hardly an option for a woman who knows that longer postoperative treatment will cause her to lose her job . . . .

Patients most likely to have the worst outcomes are defined in a couple of ways. Poverty is the biggest driver, followed by race . . . . Much of the problem is that poor people don't get care that would be likely to help them. The reasons for this are complex. Perhaps they can't get care, or don't know where care is available, or they haven't been offered insurance or steady access to care by their jobs or social services.

Here is the problem: Poor Americans consume too little health care, especially preventive health care. Other Americans—often rich Americans—consume too much health care, often unwisely, and sometimes to their detriment. The American health-care system combines famine with gluttony. We could improve dismal health outcomes on both ends of the socioeconomic spectrum if we were simply faithful to science, if we provided and practiced care that we know to be effective.

Early on, Edna ignored her tumor. She accomplished this easily during her busy days, but not when she was alone at night. The disease progressed relentlessly. The lump grew. Then the tumor broke through the skin, causing a gaping wound, which became infected. The odor caused problems at work. Edna tried to conceal it with body powder and cologne, which worked at first. Her kids started trying to get her to come in and get help several months earlier, after a powerful, relentless stench finally set in.

Since Edna couldn't pay for private insurance and have enough money left over to provide for her family, she had to come to Grady. Officially, Grady treats any resident of the two counties that support it: Fulton and DeKalb. When I arrived in Atlanta in 2001, the hospital was lax in enforcing the residency requirement. It ended up being the hospital for poor people in many surrounding counties, even though only Fulton and DeKalb taxpayers paid. As costs grew, Grady was forced to require proof of residency.

Our doctors are good, but free care comes at the cost of time lost waiting for appointments, waiting for tests. You can spend an entire day waiting for a service that a private doctor's office provides in fifteen minutes or less. People like Edna, who need every day's earnings and who can easily be jettisoned from their jobs, can afford time away from work even less than professionals, who may have some savings and job security. So people like Edna wait until it's impossible to wait any longer; they come to see us when it's too late.

Why do Black women end up with more aggressive breast cancer? Is this due to some biological characteristic that correlates with race, perhaps even determined by it? Can there be such a thing as White breast cancer and Black breast cancer? Could these be different diseases? You have to synthesize a pile of statistical data and medical literature to get insight into these problems, but it's worth the effort: You end up with extraordinarily valuable insights into the epidemiology and biology of cancer. More than that, you gain insight into economic structures in our society and, ultimately, something very big: the meaning of race.

At a glance, breast cancer in a Black woman like Edna appears to differ from breast cancer in an average White woman. If you plot breast cancer on a spectrum from the worst prognosis to the best, a higher proportion of Black women would wind up on the worst end. One of the most ominous varieties of breast cancer is called triple-negative, because it is immune to three commonly used treatments . . . all we can do is resort to desperate measures: harsher chemotherapies, which we know are frequently of little or no use. About 30 percent of breast cancer in Black women is triple-negative disease, compared to 18 percent in White women. This disparity could appear to suggest a biological difference, but in fact it's rooted in cultural, historical, and societal divides. To understand this, we have to look at the potential causes of breast cancer in White and Black women.

To start with, let's consider the incidence of better-prognosis cancer among White women. Instead of asking why Black women are more likely to get more virulent breast cancer, let's ask why White women are more likely to develop the disease that has a better prognosis. The answer can be gleaned in part from the incidence statistics. For the past three decades—or for as long as we have had a national registry—the incidence of breast cancer has been higher in White women than in Black women. In 2000, the National Cancer Institute's Surveillance, Epidemiology, and End Results registry reported that during the previous year, Blacks had an age-adjusted incidence rate of 125 per 100,000 women. In the past twenty years, the Black incidence rate has bounced between the low of 105 per 100,000 in 1989 to the high point of 126 in 2008. In 2000, White women had an incidence rate of 143 per 100,000. The breast cancer incidence rate in Whites had risen from the 1970s, peaked at 147 per 100,000 in 1999, and has fallen to 129 per 100,000 in 2008. The incidence rates were substantially apart over the past couple of decades, but have now nearly evened out. Was this occurring because White women were using mammography more and were therefore more likely to get diagnosed? Not quite. The proportion of women getting mammography screening is roughly the same among Whites and Blacks. (I suspect that the proportion getting high-quality mammography is greater among Whites than Blacks, but this difference has not been adequately studied.)

The delay of pregnancy and childbirth is a more plausible explanation. White women tend to have children later in life than Black women. Professional women, regardless of their race, go to college, establish their careers, and then have kids. Delaying childbirth past the age of thirty clearly increases the risk of breast cancer. To be specific, it increases the risk of estrogen-receptor-positive breast cancer, which has a better prognosis. Also, White women have been more likely to use postmenopausal hormone-replacement therapy (HRT). Doctors prescribed HRT because it made sense logically. Without definitive data on the therapy's biological effect, doctors were, in effect, staging a decades-long societal experiment.

By 2003, 35 percent of postmenopausal White American women had taken this therapy at some time. For cultural and socioeconomic reasons, Black women tended not to take HRT. Fewer than five percent of postmenopausal Black women took HRT. This is important, because HRT is associated with better prognosis breast cancer. In 2003, an analysis from

the well-designed study called the Women's Health Initiative showed that HRT was correlated with an increased risk of breast cancer. It was actually correlated with an increased risk of estrogen-receptor-positive, better prognosis breast cancer. The societal experiment was over. The analysis led to a drop in the use of HRT, which likely accounts for the drop in breast cancer in White women from 147 per 100,000 in 1999 to 129 per 100,000 in 2008.

Let's return to the disparity in triple-negative breast cancer by race: 30 percent in Black breast cancer patients, and 18 percent in White patients. There is no difference in the proportion of Black and White women with progesterone-positive or HER2-positive disease. So if we are to focus on the 12 percent disparity, we must look exclusively at the racial difference in the prevalence of the estrogen receptor. Does *this* suggest that skin color stands for some biological difference? Not really.

Because of dietary differences that are caused by culture and socioeconomic status, a Black girl in the United States accumulates weight much faster than a White girl. In the 1960s, the Centers for Disease Control and Prevention compared the start of menstruation by age. The study showed that the average age of menarche for White American girls was 12.8 years. For Black American girls, it was 12.4 years. This is a bigger difference than it might seem. It means that 53 percent of Black girls have started menstruating by their thirteenth birthday, compared to 43 percent of White girls. [Just the simple number of uninterrupted menstrual cycles increases the risk of breast cancer later in life].

Body mass index, a calculation based on weight and height, correlates with early nutrition status, which has a lot to do with age at first menstruation. Poor Americans have diets higher in calories and reach the weight of one hundred pounds faster . . . . The reason for this rapid weight gain in Black girls has nothing to do with race, but reflects a high caloric intake and a diet rich in carbohydrates, a socioeconomic determinant of health. It's not about race. It's at least in part about the sort of food that is available in poor areas of inner cities.

The area of Detroit where I grew up and the areas of Atlanta where my patients come from are known as produce deserts. Grocery stores there carry all the chips, sodas, and mentholated cigarettes you may desire, but if you want a head of lettuce, you are out of luck. You observe the same problems among poor Whites, yet you don't see them among wealthy, well-educated Blacks . . . . This extrapolation produces a deeply disturbing picture: the Black–White gap in the onset of menstruation and body weight has dramatically widened, which means that the disease disparities will widen also.

Edna has Stage IV breast cancer. Disease has spread all over her body. Had she come to see me early in the course of her disease, it would have cost about $30,000 to cure her. She could have remained a taxpayer. Her kids could have had a mother. Now, the cure is not an option. Still, we'll fight. We will give her breast-cancer chemotherapy that will cost more than $150,000, even though the chances are she will still die in less than two years. If you are a caring doctor, you realize she is just fifty-three, with kids and folks who love her, and your motivation is akin to a philosophy of Wayne Gretzky: "You miss every shot you don't take."

Every time I start chemo for metastatic disease I think of a patient named Sandra, a lively, young Black woman whom I have treated for six years. She had brain metastases when I first met her. She has had active disease ever since, and even the doctor who sent her to me reminds me every time he sees me that he is amazed that she is alive, functional, and enjoying life.

Yes, sometimes cancer drugs give us "long-term survival," in the dispassionate language of those of us who study outcomes. But for every Sandra, we get fifty patients with metastatic disease who "don't do well." They live a median eighteen months, which means that half are living and half are dead a year and a half after diagnosis.

We try three treatments and contain Edna's disease for a while. She dies at age fifty-five, about twenty months after walking into the ER.

NOTES

1. A history of Grady Memorial Hospital can be found in Jerry Gentry, *Grady Baby: A Year in the Life of Atlanta's Grady Hospital* (Jackson: University Press of Mississippi, 1999).
2. Discussion of the Grady mission with some historical perspective is found in A. G. Yancey Sr., "Medical Education in Atlanta and Health Care of Black, Minority and Low-Income People," *Journal of the National Medical Association* 80 (April 1988):476–76.
3. The Tuskegee Syphilis Study and rumors about it are mentioned as reason why African-Americans are often suspicious of medicine. The facts of the trial are frequently inaccurately conveyed even in the news media. Factual accounts have been written, such as S. M. Baker, O. W. Brawley, and L. S. Marks, "Effects of untreated syphilis in the Negro male, 1932 to 1972: A closure comes to the Tuskegee study, 2004," *Urology* 65 (2005). James H. Jones, *Bad Blood: The Tuskegee Syphilis Experiment* (1981; repr., New York: Free Press, 1993), is a history of "The Study of Untreated Syphilis in the Negro Male" (this is the official name of the Tuskegee Syphilis Study). Jones's book also mentions many of the atrocities that humans have perpetrated upon vulnerable humans and called research.
4. *Medical Apartheid* by Harriet Washington is a superb history and ethical analysis. She painstakingly researched and documented numerous medical abuses over the past two centuries, including abuses within the past decade. Many of these abuses have been long talked about in the African American oral history tradition. Washington was able to find proof of alarming truths. These findings justify distrust of the American medical profession.
5. The literature on the fears that African-Americans have of the American medical system is portrayed in Rebecca Skloot, *The Immortal Life of Henrietta Lacks* (New York: Crown Publishers, 2010).

6. A number of patterns-of-care studies demonstrate that the poor as a group do not receive as high a quality of medical care as the middle class and have worse health-care outcomes; S. A. Fedewa, S. B. Edge, A. K. Stewart, M. T. Halpern, N. M. Marlow, and E. M. Ward, "Race and ethnicity are associated with delays in breast cancer treatment (2003–2006)," *Journal of Health Care for the Poor and Underserved* 22, no. 1 (2001); 128–41; A. S. Robbins, A. L. Pavluck, S. A. Fedewa, A. Y. Chen, and E. M. Ward, "Insurance status, comorbidity level, and survival among colorectal cancer patients age 18 to 64 years in the National Cancer Data Base from 2003 to 2005," *Journal of Clinical Oncology* 27, no. 22 (August 1, 2009); 3627–33 (epub, May 26, 2009); and E. Ward, H. Halpern, N. Schrag, V. Cokkinides, C. DeSantis, P. Bandi, R. Siegel, A. Stewart, and A. Jemal, "Association of insurance with cancer care utilization and outcomes," *CA: A Cancer Journal for Clinicians*, 58, no. 1 (January–February 2008: 9–31 (epub, December 20, 2007).

7. The NCI defines the medically underserved as "individuals who lack access to primary and specialty care either because they are socioeconomically disadvantaged and they may live in areas with high poverty rates or because they reside in rural areas": http://deais.nci.nih.gov/glossary/terms?alpha=M&currentPage=1.

8. Trends in breast cancer by race and ethnicity: C. Smigal, A. Jemal, E. Ward, V. Cokkinides, R. Smith, H. L. Howe, and M. Thun, "Update 2006," *CA: A Cancer Journal for Clinicians* 56, no. 3 (May–June 2006): 168–83.

9. A higher proportion of the African-American breast cancer population has triple negative disease compared to the population of White women with breast cancer. Triple negative breast cancer is the most serious type of breast cancer. Other forms of the disease are more aggressive, but targeted therapies can slow the progression of the disease. This is explained in L. A. Carey, E. C. Dees, L. Sawyer, et al., "The triple negative paradox: Primary tumor chemosensitivity of breast cancer subtypes," Clinical Cancer Research 13, no. 8 (April 15, 2007): 2329–34; and K. M. O'Brien, S. R. Cole, C. K. Tse, C. M. Perou, L. A. Carey, W. D. Foulkes, L. G. Dressler, J. Geradts, and R. C. Millikan, "Intrinsic breast tumor subtypes, race, and long-term survival in the Carolina Breast Cancer Study," *Clinical Cancer Research* 16, no. 24 (December 15, 2010): 6100–6110.

10. U.S. breast cancer rates by race are provided by the National Cancer Institute Cancer Statistics Review at https://seer.cancer.gov.

11. The effect of postmenopausal hormone replacement therapy (HRT or HT) was studied in the Women's Health Initiative, a study sponsored by the National Institutes of Health.

12. The decline in breast cancer incidence was documented in M. Ravdin, K. A. Cronin, N. Howlader, C. D. Berg, R. T. Chlebowski, E. J. Feuer, B. K. Edwards, and D. A. Berry, "The decrease in breast cancer incidence in 2003 in the United States," *New England Journal of Medicine* 356, no. 16 (April 19, 2007); and Million Women Study Collaborators, "Patterns of use of hormone replacement therapy in one million women in Britain, 1996–2000," *BJOG* 109, no. 12 (December 2002): 1319–30.

13. Public law 103-43, signed in 1993 by President William Clinton, mandated the Long Island Breast Cancer Study. A good description of the study is found in M. D. Gammon, A. I. Neugut, R. M. Santella, et al., "The Long Island Breast Cancer Study Project: Description of a multi-institutional collaboration to identify environmental risk factors for breast cancer," *Breast Cancer Research and Treatment* 74, no. 3 (June 2002): 235–54.

14. The correlation between weight gain in childhood and earlier age of menarche is discussed in S. E. Anderson, G. E. Dallal, and A. Must, "Relative weight and race influence average age at menarche: Results from two nationally representative surveys of US girls studied 25 years apart," *Pediatrics* 111, no. 4 (pt. 1) (April 2003): 844–50.

15. The relation between age at menarche and race and its relationship to disease in adulthood is discussed in D. S. Freedman, L. K. Khan, M. K. Serdula, W. H. Dietz, S. R. Srinivasan, and G. S. Berenson, "Relation of age at menarche to race, time period, and anthropometric dimensions: The Bogalusa Heart Study," *Pediatrics* 110, no. 4 (October 2002): e43.

16. Population trends in breast cancer in Scotland can tell us a lot about breast cancer in the United States: S. B. Brown, D. J. Hole, and T. G. Cooke, "Breast cancer incidence trends in deprived and affluent Scottish women," *Breast Cancer Research and Treatment* 103, no. (June 2007):233–38 (epub, October 11, 2006); U. Macleod, S. Ross, C. Twelves, W. D. George, C. Gillis, and G. C. Watt, "Primary and secondary care management of women with early breast cancer from affluent and deprived areas: Retrospective review of hospital and general practice records," *BMJ* 320, no. 7247 (May 27, 2000): 1442–45; C. S. Thomson, D. J. Hole, C. J. Twelves, D. H. Brewster, and R. J. Black, "Prognostic factors in women with breast cancer: Distribution by socioeconomic status and effect on differences in survival," *Journal of Epidemiology and Community Health* 55 (2001): 308–15; N. H. Gordon, "Socioeconomic factors and breast cancer in Black and White Americans," *Cancer and Metastasis Reviews* 22 (2003): 55–65; B. K. Dunn, T. Agurs-Collins, D. Browne, R. Lubet, and K. A. Johnson, "Health disparities in breast cancer: Biology meets socioeconomic status," *American Journal of Public Health* 100, no. S1 (April 1, 2010): S132–39 (epub, February 10, 2010); and N. Krieger, J. T. Chen, and P. D. Waterman, "Decline in US breast cancer rates after the Women's Health Initiative: Socioeconomic and racial/ethnic differentials," *American Journal of Public Health* 100, no. 6 (June 2010): 972.

CHAPTER 11

SOCIAL PROBLEMS RELATED TO CRIME AND THE CRIMINAL JUSTICE SYSTEM

Many social problems texts address crime by examining crime rates, victim and offender characteristics, and theories about why crime occurs. Although the selected readings in this chapter touch on these issues, we focus more deeply on the ways in which the criminal justice system intersects with other systems of inequality, including wealth and poverty, racial inequality, and gender discrimination. We begin with a reading by Tristan Bridges and Tara Leigh Tober that examines an issue that is a matter of concern for many people—mass shootings—and the role that gender and culture play in this type of gun violence. Our nation has been rocked repeatedly by mass shootings: Marjory Stoneman Douglas High School in Parkland, Florida; Tree of Life Synagogue in Philadelphia, Pennsylvania; Santa Fe High School in Santa Fe, Texas; and *The Capital* Newspaper, in Annapolis, Maryland. Many of us have become numbed from the repeated violence and threats of violence, and "active shooter drills" in all levels of schooling have become normalized. The violence itself harms our society and citizens, but even preparing for potential violence has its consequences. Petula Dvorak invites us to consider the psychic damage we are doing to our children by both failing to protect them and normalizing such drills. Understanding why these events are increasing and what is uniquely American about them will help us address them.

Miriam Konrad and Angie Luvara address issues of wealth and income inequality in relation to the criminal justice system, including how the most powerful members of our society are able to use their resources to shape the legal system to focus on crimes of the poor rather than their own misdeeds and how the criminal justice system perpetuates racial and class-based inequality through mass incarceration and its myriad consequences. Erin Thomas documents race-based inequality in her reading on the death penalty, Amanda Atwell and Amanda M. Jungles demonstrate how the prison industrial complex reproduces inequality by race and class as corporations profit handily from incarceration, and Heather Ann Thompson discusses the political ramifications of mass incarceration.

One high-profile area where the criminal justice system perpetuates inequality is through policing. Police tactics continue to face scrutiny as incidents are caught on camera and are covered by media, and as activists, journalists, and researchers work to document race-based

516

patterns in police interactions, especially those involving deadly force. Rory Kramer, Brianna Remster, and Camille Z. Charles provide evidence that racial bias in policing exists and is linked to varied forms of racism.

Media may draw our attention to overlooked social issues, such as the racial bias in policing discussed above, but their attention may also result in exaggerated concern. Our media environment and politicians' deliberate attempts to stoke fear in their constituents result in an American public that overestimates crime and also potentially mischaracterizes its perpetrators. Watoii Rabii takes on the myth that immigrants increase crime rates, a fallacy spread by politicians that is not borne out by the evidence. Another misconception is that Americans believe that crime rates have been regularly increasing since the early 1990s, despite the fact that both violent crime and property crime have declined significantly during that same time period.[1]

Our beliefs about crime—how often it happens, whether we are likely to be victims of it, and who the likely perpetrators are—influence our interactions with others in society as well as our views on law enforcement policies. Ronald Weitzer examines factors that influence attitudes toward police; provides ample evidence of inequalities in our criminal justice system in terms of surveillance, stops, searches, arrests, convictions, sentencing, and incarceration; and discusses the opportunities and potential for reform in law enforcement practices. Brentin Mock outlines the connection between other forms of institutional racism and police violence against people of color. Taken together, the readings in this chapter offer nuanced analyses of the causes and consequences of these inequities that remain a part of our democratic society.

---

1   Gramlich, John. 2019. "5 Facts about Crime in the U.S." Pew Research Center. Retrieved March 20, 2019, from https://www.pewresearch.org/fact-tank/2019/01/03/5-facts-about-crime-in-the-u-s.

NICOLE D. PORTER

Nicole D. Porter is Director of Advocacy for The Sentencing Project.

What is The Sentencing Project's mission, and as director of advocacy, what do you do?

The Sentencing Project works to achieve a fair and effective U.S. criminal justice system by promoting reforms in sentencing policy, addressing unjust racial disparities and practices in the criminal justice system, and advocating for alternatives to incarceration.

As director of advocacy I work with state and local organizations and individuals on state and local policy reform and on advocacy campaigns that align with the Sentencing Project's mission. For example, I supported campaigns to address ending life without parole as a sentencing option in Missouri and California. The number of people serving life sentences in U.S. prisons is at an all-time high. As of 2016, there were more than 206,000 sentenced to life imprisonment in the United States. That's more than the number of people in prison in 1970.

How did you first become interested in this type of activism?

I grew up in a political family and have always been interested in politics and in critiquing the unfinished project of American democracy. I became interested in

criminal justice advocacy when my twin brother was incarcerated, and I realized many of the young men I had grown up with had criminal records and had cycled in and out of jail as young adults.

As an activist in your organization, currently what are your top goals?

I want to reduce the number of people in prison and under criminal justice supervision, eliminate racial disparity and inequality in the criminal justice system, and promote a broader concept of public safety that does not rely on arrests or sentencing people to prison. I support solutions that address underlying issues that lead to contact with law enforcement, such as advocating for living-wage employment and access to high-quality education. In communities with high rates of incarceration, these solutions will help prevent contact with the criminal justice system.

What strategies do you use to enact social change?

I use research, communications, and advocacy. To raise public awareness about inequities I write policy reports and produce materials for members of the general public, policymakers, and the media. This usually involves a lot of research about laws and policies. For example, in order to address the problem of mass incarceration, I researched the laws and practices that trigger automatic prison sentences (otherwise known as mandatory minimum sentences), lengthen prison terms, and impose collateral consequences long after a conviction (such as being barred from public assistance or subsidized housing even after being released from prison), and then I advocated to reform those laws. I have also worked to change policies known to have a racially disparate impact on sentencing (such as the disparity between sentences for crack and powder cocaine possession).

Working as a policy advocate means engaging directly with the process to change laws and practices. Changing laws involves engaging with lawmakers at the state and federal level around policy reforms known to have an impact, based on our research. Engagement involves visiting with lawmakers, working to write and introduce legislation, and identifying constituent contacts who will also serve as activists and advocates for us (for example, citizens, leadership from different faith communities, and law enforcement officials whose opinions legislators may value).

What would you consider to be your greatest successes as an activist?

I have helped change the law in several states including Texas, Missouri, and California. While at the Texas American Civil Liberties Union (ACLU), I organized campaigns to address in-prison sexual assault and expand voting rights to persons with felony convictions. While at The Sentencing Project I supported efforts in Missouri to modify that state's crack-powder sentencing disparity and the federal lifetime ban on food stamps for persons with felony drug convictions.

I also contributed to a national narrative that critiques mass incarceration. It involves advancing sentencing reform arguments by assessing which policies or practices are most easily addressed and changed, how to change the political calculus related to sentencing reform, and determining which mechanisms are most likely to raise people's consciousness about these issues. These mechanisms include media strategies like press conferences and opinion editorials,

organizing around policy goals to change laws and practices, and mobilizing diverse coalitions of people who may have the power to emphasize changes in public awareness about mass incarceration. I measure this success through media reports that reinforce the approach that my colleagues and I contribute to, as well as the fact that this narrative has been mainstreamed in recent years.

What are the major challenges activists in your field face?

We often lack the capacity and the resources to scale an advocacy infrastructure to the magnitude of need, especially when there are many people impacted nationwide, as there are with issues related to the criminal justice system. And, despite decades of research documenting that our current approach to public safety does not deter crime and exacerbates inequality and racial disparity, there is still a lack of political will to enact policy change that we must fight against. Another challenge is the American culture of punitiveness and retribution that reinforces excessive sentencing practices for not only the incarcerated, but also for civil sanctions that people with criminal records face. All of these challenges can create fatigue among advocates, but we combat this by working with other allies and finding short-term ways to build momentum and deepen the critique. We stay energized by being self-aware and reflective about what's possible and what remains to be done.

What are major misconceptions the public has about activism in general and your issue specifically?

I am not sure about "major misconceptions." I do think that activists can be marginalized and discredited when they are perceived as too radical, even though radical analyses are, indeed, relevant to social policy.

Why should students get involved in your line of activism?

Students can help shift attitudes and beliefs about public safety and punitiveness, creating more political will to change the system. Student-led campaigns can also help change the law by bringing more awareness to the issues, both to the general population as well as to their elected and local law enforcement officials.

If an individual has little money and time, are there other ways they can contribute?

Engage directly with elected officials or other targets over demands to change law, policy, or practice. Be curious and critical about social policy. Participate in discussions and efforts to improve any social condition by working with civic groups and engaging in activism you are interested in.

TRISTAN BRIDGES AND TARA LEIGH TOBER

54. MASS SHOOTINGS, MASCULINITY, AND GUN VIOLENCE AS SOCIAL PROBLEMS

Mass shootings have become more frequent in the United States, and more and more attention has been paid to preventing them, such as increasing gun control as well as challenging and changing gun culture. Bridges and Tober discuss an underexamined facet that almost all mass shootings in the United States share: men were the perpetrators. They discuss explanations for this phenomenon, arguing that masculinity, violence, and aggression have been intrinsically linked in American culture, resulting in higher rates of these sorts of crimes compared to other countries around the world. As U.S. culture has changed and privileged groups (such as young White men) perceive they are losing some of their power, a sense of aggrieved entitlement may cause them to lash out.

On April 20, 1999, Eric Harris and Dylan Klebold went to their school in Littlefield, CO in Black trench coats and a collection of guns rivaling action movies like *The Matrix*. They killed 12 students, injured an additional 21 people and ushered in a new age of school shootings in the U.S. At the end of the massacre at Columbine High School, both shooters turned their own weapons on themselves and each pulled the trigger. In 2007, an undergraduate student at Virginia Tech, Seung-Hui Cho, committed a similar act, walking around campus dressed for combat. He took pictures of himself before the attack wielding the guns he later turned on professors, staff and classmates as though posing for an action movie poster.

In Newtown, Connecticut in 2012, Adam Lanza shot and killed his mother early on December 12 before driving to Sandy Hook Elementary school. Using a semi-automatic rifle, he shot his way into the building, ultimately killing 20 children and 6 adults. Like Harris and Klebold, Lanza turned a gun on himself at the end of his attack. That same year, James Eagan Holmes walked into a movie theatre showing *The Dark Knight* in Aurora, Colorado with a pistol, shotgun, and rifle. He opened fire on moviegoers while the film was playing, killing 12 and injuring an additional 70 people.

On October 1, 2017, Stephen Paddock broke the glass of his two windows in his 32nd floor hotel room in Las Vegas, Nevada. His room looked down on a music festival below. In the days leading up to the attack, Paddock stockpiled a large arsenal of weapons including (among others) fourteen AR-15 rifles. At 10:05pm, Paddock shot at the crowd, killing 58 people and leaving an additional 851 injured. This event was among the deadliest mass shootings in recent history.

Less than a year later, on Valentine's Day, 2018, Nikolas Cruz was dropped off near Marjory Stoneman Douglas High School in Parkland, Florida with a backpack and duffel bag. Cruz quietly entered one of the buildings, pulled a fire alarm, and waited with the semi-automatic rifle and magazines he'd brought to school, firing indiscriminately at students and teachers as they exited classrooms. Seventeen people were killed and an additional seventeen were injured.

Following Cruz's attack, students at school took to the streets and began starting a social movement opposing gun violence and with the goal of impacting gun legislation in this country. Still today, these

Original to *Focus on Social Problems: A Contemporary Reader*.

students have inserted themselves into the national dialogue about gun control. And the shootings continue. Sadly, as we were writing this reading, another school shooting happened at Santa Fe High School in Texas on May 18, 2018. 10 people were killed and at least an additional thirteen were wounded.

Following all of these attacks, people have called on politicians to enact stricter gun control legislation, to reduce both the number and type of guns allowed in U.S. households. And gun control is a vital part of the problem of mass shootings in the United States. But mass shootings are about more than guns. Mass shootings are statistically rare, but they happen more in the United States than anywhere else in the world. Though they are rare, mass shootings are significant in a cultural sense as they leave indelible wounds in the social fabric, evoking collective feelings of fear, helplessness, anger, and heartache. And the people who commit them share more in common with the shooters above than U.S. citizenship. Indeed, the single most patterned fact about mass shooters is gender—these violent acts are overwhelmingly carried out by *men*.

Any explanation of mass shootings has two separate questions to answer. Why are men so overwhelmingly more likely to commit mass shootings than women? And why is it that American men commit these crimes more than people in any other society in the world?

We argue that we cannot hope to understand mass shootings in the U.S. if we ignore their connection with American masculinity (Bridges and Tober 2016). And to fully appreciate this, we first explain what we mean when we say that mass shootings happen more in the United States than in any other society in the world. Next, we examine the relationship between gun control and gun violence by differentiating between "gun control" and what scholars refer to as "gun culture." And finally, we offer a two-part explanation for mass shootings in the U.S.—a *social psychological explanation* to understand why men turn to this type of violence so much more frequently than women and a *cultural explanation* to clarify what it is about American masculinity that causes the U.S. to stand out internationally when it comes to this particular type of gun violence. When combined, these explanations offer us a fuller, more nuanced understanding of the nature and causes of mass shooting as a social problem.

WHAT ARE MASS SHOOTINGS AND ARE THEY MORE COMMON IN THE U.S.?

How many mass shootings occurred in the United States last year? And how does that number compare with other societies around the world? These sound like easy questions to answer. It ought to simply be a matter of counting them. Yet, they are challenging to answer for two separate reasons: one related to how we define a "mass shooting" in the first place and the other to finding reliable sources of data. And as it turns out, neither of these issues have easy solutions.

People tend to rely on either broad or restrictive definitions of mass shootings to reinforce their particular stance on gun control. But, after the 2012 school shooting at Sandy Hook Elementary, the U.S. Congress defined "mass killings" as incidents in which three or more homicides took place in a single incident. Frederic Lemieux (2014) examined rates of mass shootings between 1983 and 2012 in a collection of 25 separate nations. Lemieux defines mass shootings as incidents involving one or more shooters in which four of more people are killed in one public location. In that period, United States experienced 78 mass shootings; the country with the next highest frequency was Germany, with 7 mass shootings in the same period. And if we compare the number of mass shootings by nation in Lemieux's sample with the number of guns per 100 people in each society, you can see a relationship between the number of guns and the number of mass shootings (see Figure 1).

Each of the data points in Figure 1 represents a different country in Lemieux's (2014) sample. There does appear to be a correlation between more guns and more mass shootings. But there are two other things worth noticing. For instance, just consider the number of nations in this sample that have approximately 30 guns per 100 people: Austria (30.4), Canada (30.8), France (31.2), Germany (30.3), Iceland (30.3), Norway (31.3), and Sweden (31.6). They don't all have the same rate of mass shootings over the period of 30 years. Iceland had zero; Norway had one; and Sweden had two. But France had six, and Germany had seven. These are small numbers, but even here, the range is large enough to suggest that the ratio of guns per people is not the *only* factor influencing mass shootings.

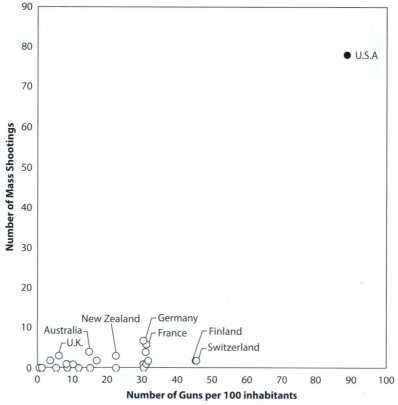

FIGURE 1

Source: Lemieux, Frederic. 2014. "Effect of Gun Culture and Firearm Laws on Gun Violence and Mass Shootings in the United States: A Multi-Level Quantitative Analysis." International Journal of Criminal Justice Sciences 9(1): 74–93.

It is also worth noting just how much of an outlier the U.S. is when put in international perspective. Sure, we have roughly twice as many guns per capita as the other societies with high numbers of guns owned per inhabitant. But the number of mass shootings the U.S. has experienced makes us an extreme outlier in these data. Indeed, Lankford's (2016) international research comes to a similar conclusion with a different sample—nations with high rates of firearm ownership are more at risk of public mass shootings.

A common argument is that the United States simply has more *people* than the other nations included in Lemieux's (2014) sample, and thus more mass shootings. With a population of almost 320 million in 2013, the odds that a rare event like a mass shooting would occur are just higher. Figure 2 charts the number of mass shootings by society against the number of

mass shootings per 1,000,000 people in the population (as of 2013) in each of the nations that Lemieux (2014) studied. Here, we can see from the Black bars that the U.S. has a much higher number of mass shootings than the other nations, but our *rate* of mass shootings per 1 million people (the dots associated with the axis on the right of the figure) puts us *below* the rates of other nations— New Zealand and Finland in particular.

Sometimes, those opposed to gun control legislation will rely on figures like Figure 2 to suggest that mass shootings in the U.S. are not the problem they are sometimes made to appear. After all, these are rare events. And with a population large enough, you are bound to experience *some*.

The problem with looking at the *rate* of mass shootings as opposed to the *number* of mass shootings is that these are rare events – particularly with restrictive

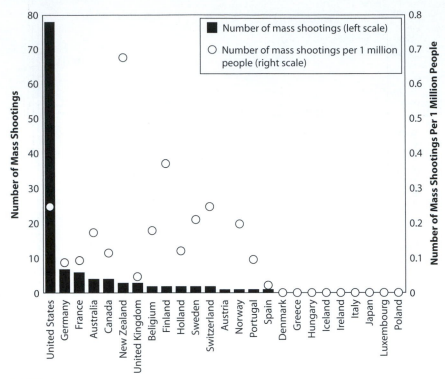

FIGURE 2
Source: Lemieux, Frederic. 2014. "Effect of Gun Culture and Firearm Laws on Gun
Violence and Mass Shootings in the United States: A Multi-Level Quantitative Analysis."
International Journal of Criminal Justice Sciences 9(1): 74–93. 2013 Population estimates
from The World Bank, IBRD. IDA. Available at: https://data.worldbank.org

definitions that often exclude things like gang violence,
multiple shooters, spree shootings (happening in multiple locations), and more. Small sample sizes make
is difficult to analyze data like these statistically. New
Zealand tops the list of mass shootings per 1 million
people in Figure 2, but they only experienced 3 mass
shootings over the 30 years analyzed. The second highest rate in the sample is Finland, with 2.

In statistics, as we examine larger populations,
they tend to move toward some basic average (something statisticians call "regression toward the mean").
Smaller populations are more erratic and more susceptible to random fluctuations. This is why 1 or even
2 mass shootings in a country with a small population can propel the group to the top of the list for the
rate of mass shootings. In medical research, populations with less that a certain baseline number of incidents of a particular injury or disease are considered

unreliable—in these cases, it is not possible to statistically distinguish random fluctuations from some
kind of meaningful change in the *rate* of disease. Thus,
claiming that Figure 2 is a more accurate representation of the problem of mass shootings than Figure 1
is inaccurate—and sometimes deceptive. It ignores the
fact that the United States experienced 1.9 times as
many mass shootings in the period analyzed as all of
the other nations in the sample combined.

Defining mass shootings as Lemieux (2014) does is
restrictive and likely to produce conservative estimates
(Bridges, Tober, and Wheeler 2015). For instance, the
shooting on Virginia Tech's campus in 2007 fails to
qualify—it happened in more than one building on
campus (so, it did not happen in "one location").
Many datasets of mass shootings rely on different
definitions—and different definitions produce different samples. So, while we know that mass shootings

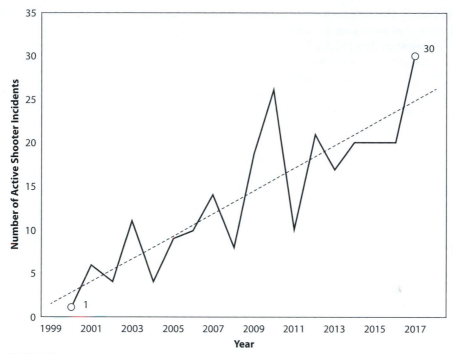

FIGURE 3

Source: Blair, J. Pete, and Schweit, Katherine W. 2014. "A Study of Active Shooter Incidents, 2000-2013. " Texas State University and Federal Bureau of Investigation, U.S. Department of Justice, Washington D.C. 2014. Schweit, Katherine W. 2016. "Active Shooter Incidents in the United States in 2014 and 2015. "Federal Bureau of Investigation, U.S. Department of Justice, Washington D.C. 2016. Active Shooter Incidents in the United States in 2016 and 2017, the Advanced Law Enforcement Rapid Response Training (ALERRT) Center at Texas State University and Federal Bureau of Investigation, U.S. Department of Justice, Washington D.C. 2018.

happen more in the U.S. than elsewhere, a more difficult question is whether or not they are occurring more frequently today in the U.S. than they used to occur. In other words, are mass shootings on the rise?

In 2013, President Barack Obama signed the "Investigative Assistance for Violent Crimes Act" into law which granted the attorney general the authority to study mass killings (and attempted mass killings) with guns in the U.S. And this resulted in a series of studies by the FBI of what they started calling "active shooter incidents" in which an individual (or, in some cases, individuals) is/are engaged in killing or attempting to kill people. These are not all mass shooting incidents, but incidents like mass shootings in which authorities have the opportunity to intervene to possibly change the outcome and save lives. Figure 3 shows the frequency of active shooter incidents between 2000 and 2017 from three separate FBI reports

along with a trendline indicating the overall direction of change represented by the sample.

Thus, despite being rare events, mass shootings happen more often in the United States than anywhere else in the world. And, as the FBI and Follman, et al. (2014) found, the rate of occurrence of mass shootings in the U.S. has been *increasing* in recent years—they happen more than they used to.

GUN CONTROL VS. "GUN CULTURE"

Mass shootings are a social problem with more than a single cause. An important element is the ability to acquire a gun. And the vast majority of guns used in mass shootings in the U.S. were obtained legally. But guns are only one piece of a larger problem when it comes to mass shootings.

Those advocating for fewer gun restrictions and who oppose gun control legislation often point to

Switzerland and Israel. They rely on these two cases to make the argument that more guns do not necessarily lead to more gun violence (e.g., Klein 2012). Indeed, you can see Switzerland among the nations included in Lemieux's (2014) sample illustrated in Figure 1. It's an outlier— lots of guns, but a low number of mass shootings. In Switzerland, military service is compulsory for men; in Israel military service is virtually universal. Because of broad military service, large numbers of Swiss and Israelis have access to guns. Yet, the homicide rate in the United States is more than four times the rate in either Switzerland or Israel (United Nations Office on Drugs and Crime 2018).

Additionally, Janet Rosenbaum's (2012) research shows that Switzerland and Israel are not the "gun utopias" they are sometimes presented to be. For instance, both nations have more strict gun laws than the U.S. For example, owning a gun is not an individual "right" in Israel or Switzerland; you must have a reason to possess a gun. And in Israel, the government rejects around 4 out of every 10 applications submitted for gun permits. Both nations also have strict laws about *where* guns can be, requiring gun owners to leave firearms on military bases (in Israel) or in gun depots (in Switzerland). Both rules severely limit access to firearms among off- duty soldiers and other people who own firearms. So, for instance, as a rule in both Israel and Switzerland, guns are not generally found in households (Rosenbaum 2012).

Like Switzerland and Israel, another nation with high rates of gun ownership but low rates of gun violence is Canada. According to the Small Arms Survey (2011), the United States rate of guns per 100 residents is higher than anywhere else in the world at 89. The nation with the closest rate of gun ownership is Yemen with 55. Canada has about 31 guns per 100 residents, enough to situate Canada among the top 15 nations by rates of gun ownership. Yet rates of firearm homicide are dramatically lower in Canada—0.61 per 100,000 people as of 2016. That rate is almost 8 times smaller than the U.S. the same year, though in Canada it qualifies as the highest homicide by firearms rate since 2005 (Statistics Canada, 2017).

But why the large disparities in gun violence between nations that all have lots of guns? It is for this reason that scholars studying guns differentiate between things like rates of gun ownership and gun

control legislation on the one hand, and what they refer to as "gun culture" on the other. Sociologist Jennifer Carlson (2015a, 2015b) argues that the meanings surrounding guns are very different in the U.S. and Canada and argues that the gun *culture* in each society cannot be reduced to rates of gun *ownership*. One fact that supports Carlson's argument relates to the primary type of gun owned in each society. In Canada, for example, gun owners are more likely to own long guns as opposed to handguns. Long guns are more often used for hunting, while handguns are generally used for other purposes, like target shootings and self-defense.

A Congressional Research Service report states that as of 2009, the estimated total number of firearms available to civilians in the United States was 310 million (comprising 114 million handguns, 110 million rifles, and 86 million shotguns) (Krouse 2012). To help put that figure in perspective, consider that 310 million guns represents a number higher than the population of the United States in 2009 (306.8 million)—a society with more guns that people. These facts suggest a unique *gun culture* in the United States, and one that is dramatically different from other nations that might also have high rates of gun ownership (Carlson 2015a).

But what is the relationship between gun culture and mass shootings? The slogan that the National Rifle Association (NRA) uses to oppose gun legislation in the U.S. is "Guns don't kill people, people kill people." And this is true. In Switzerland, Israel, and Canada, there are lots of guns, but not a lot of gun-related homicides. The NRA leans on this logic when claiming that it is *people* (and not *guns*) that are responsible for gun violence. We suggest, however, that the slogan would be more accurate if it read: "Guns don't kill people, *men* with guns kill people." But we can do better still. It's not just men with guns; it's *American* men with guns. This is why we argue that the problem of mass shootings is about more than guns, men, and American culture; it's about the relationship between all three.

A SOCIAL PSYCHOLOGICAL EXPLANATION

In a famous essay on the relationship between masculinity and homophobia, Michael Kimmel writes "I have a standing bet with a friend that I can walk onto any playground in America where 6-year-old boys are happily playing and by asking one question, I can provoke a fight. That question is simple: 'Who's a sissy around here?'" (1994: 131). Here, Kimmel provides a simple explanation of a more general social process that social psychologists refer to as "social identity threat." The general idea behind the theory of *social identity threat* is that when a person perceives some elements of their identity that they care about to be called into question, they respond in a patterned way: they attempt to over-demonstrate qualities associated with that identity. Kimmel's bet is premised on this understanding. By forcing a situation in which some boy's gender identity will be called into question, Kimmel assumes he can count on that boy to overcompensate by responding with violence to challenge the accusation. There are certainly other ways the boy might respond. But if we can agree that violence is an available (and possibly predictable) response, then this provides evidence that violence and masculinity are connected.

The research on social identity threat is primarily experimental, meaning that people come in to labs, receive different sorts of stimuli, and their responses are measured against others who are subjected to different stimuli. Experimentally "threatening" men's gender identities is the subject of a small body of scholarship testing what Willer et al. (2013) refer to as the "masculine overcompensation thesis"—the idea that men will respond to "masculinity threats" by *over-* demonstrating masculinity. So, the question is: do men whose masculinity has been threatened respond differently from men who have not experienced masculinity threat? And we now have a large body of research showing that the answer to this question is absolutely "Yes." To consider how this relates to mass shootings and violence, we have to consider *how* men respond to masculinity threat.

Christin Munsch and Robb Willer (2012) studied masculinity threat in assessing the ways that college men make sense of sexual interactions in which men are forcing or coercing women into sexual interactions. Munsch and Willer (2012) had men read scenarios involving sexual coercion or force by men against women and found that men whose masculinity had been threatened were *less* likely to identify sexual coercion as sexually coercive and more likely to blame the women victimized in the scenario. Willer et al. (2013) subjected the masculinity overcompensation

thesis to a larger number of outcomes. They discovered men whose masculinity had been threatened were more supportive of violence and war, more likely to agree with statements about the "inherent superiority of males," more likely to be supportive of sexual prejudice toward gay men, more likely to identify as Republican, and even more likely to say that they wanted to purchase a sport utility vehicle.

This body of social psychological research is important in making sense of mass shootings as many of the men who participate in mass shootings have experiences they perceive as threatening to their gender identities. Indeed, as Kimmel and Mahler (2003) discovered in a review of school shootings between 1982 and 2001, nearly all of the incidents were boys who perceived themselves as being targeted and bullied. And the most common type of bullying they discovered was "gay baiting"—none of the shooters in their sample identified as gay, but virtually all of them had been teased for being "gay." More recent work also suggests that gender-specific bullying, and homophobic bullying specifically has become part of the profile for those boys and young men identified as "at risk" of becoming school shooters (Reuter-Rice 2008). And research shows that homophobic bullying is an endemic feature of American high school for many boys and young men (e.g., Pascoe 2007).

A simplistic reading of men who commit mass shootings is that they are *outliers*—social outcasts who react very differently from "the rest of us." But the shooters are *not* outliers in an important sense—they are men who perceive their gender identities to have been threatened and respond by overcompensating. Masculinity threat research is important because it helps us identify what men understand as "masculine" in the first place. If we experimentally threaten men's masculinity, what do they turn to when they overcompensate for their perceived loss? This body of scholarship has identified a collection of behaviors to which men turn: dominance over women, sexual prejudice, support for sexual violence and violence more generally.

Messerschmidt's (1999) research with young boys is supportive of this notion as well. He defines "masculinity resources" as the collection of behaviors through which boys and men enact masculinity. He found that violence is understood as *the* resource boys and young men turn to in a crisis. This understanding of mass shootings as violent gendered behavior helps explain why crimes like mass shootings are so overwhelmingly committed by men—these crimes are enactments of masculinity.

This body of social psychological scholarship answers an important question about mass shootings: why they are so overwhelmingly committed by men. But it does not help us answer a separate question: why *American* men? That question requires a cultural explanation.

A CULTURAL EXPLANATION

Boys and men in the U.S. are teased, endure homophobic and other kinds of bullying and emasculation, and sometimes feel that their gender identities are being "threatened." But boys and men in other nations experience these things as well. So, why is it that mass shootings are so much more common in the U.S. if—as we discussed above—it is not only a question of gun control? To answer this question requires a *cultural explanation*—one that attends to the unique role that American culture plays in influencing boys and young men to turn to this type of violence so much more often than men anywhere else. To address this necessitates shifting our attention away from the individual characteristics of the shooters themselves to investigate the sociocultural contexts in which violent masculinities are produced and valorized (e.g., Carlson 2015a; Tonso 2009; Kimmel 2013, 2018).

Upward mobility remains a popular characterization of American society—"the land of opportunity." But opportunities for *some* are made possible by systemically and structurally denying those same opportunities to *others*. This has been true throughout American history, and White men have long benefitted as recipients of these privileges. Over the course of the 20th and 21st centuries, however, social movements of various kinds have worked to identify, question, and chip away at these inequalities. Though young, straight, class-advantaged, White men today continue to benefit from racial, gender, sexual, and class inequality, they also work alongside women, racial and sexual minorities in ways less true of their parents and grandparents. Today, these men have to compete with women, people of color, and more because of the gradual erosion of some of the privileges that historically worked in their interest.

Kimmel argues that one of the outcomes associated with moves toward equal rights has been the production of a new emotional framework for White American men living in this age of decline—something Kimmel (2013, 2018) calls "aggrieved entitlement." Aggrieved entitlement refers to the "gendered sense of entitlement thwarted by larger economic and political shifts" (2018: 15) White men in the U.S. experience.

Aggrieved entitlement is a gendered political psychology that authorizes violence by entitling boys and men to exact revenge on others when they perceive their masculinity to have been threatened or otherwise inaccessible. But it is important to note that, for Kimmel (2013), aggrieved entitlement does not only or always lead to mass shootings. More commonly, it leads to racist and sexist sentiments toward women and racial minorities. Rather, as Kimmel understands it, mass shootings are simply an extremely violent example of a much larger sociocultural issue.

Michael Kimmel (2013) suggests that the relationship between violence and masculinity is particularly acute among a group he labels "angry White men." When this group acts out, they turn to violence, and when they kill, access to guns and mental health are often quick to be blamed. These explanations are not simply problematic because they are wrong; they are dangerous because they focus attention *only* on individuals rather than the societies in which they live. In 2014, *The New York Times'* editorial board collaborated on an essay on what we know about school shootings, noting that rates of "severe mental illness [are] roughly stable around the world . . . while gun violence varies." And research on gun violence in the U.S. corroborates this as only a tiny fraction of gun deaths in the U.S. can be attributed to mental health issues (Swanson et al. 2015). Simply put, explanations that put the focus on individuals are inadequate explanations for *social* problem.

Indeed, Pascoe's (2007) research on the lives of high school boys discovered that many of the struggles that put boys "at risk" of becoming school shooters are incredibly common. While Kimmel and Mahler (2003) found that school shooters were incredibly likely to have been teased for being "gay" at school, Pascoe (2007) shows that that experience is not unique to the shooters. It's part of the drinking water in American high schools. Kimmel's (2013, 2018) research on angry White men builds on this suggestion in Pascoe's research, suggesting that many American men (White men in particular) perceive themselves as being denied social positions and status in social hierarchies that they feel are rightfully theirs. Indeed, Tonso (2009) found that many young men in the U.S. experience a sense of shame and humiliation that stems, in part, from their perceived loss of privilege—an experience acutely experienced in small social networks, like schools.

In Jennifer Carlson's (2015a, 2015b) study of American gun owners, she found many men talked about a very specific kind of "nostalgic longing for a particular version of America" (2015b: 390). Some invoked it by name, referring to it as "Mayberry" or "Mayberry America." They were relying on a fictional town in North Carolina from *The Andy Griffith Show*—a 1960s era family sitcom representing a family in a small community of suburban single-family homes, safety and security. Though historian Stephanie Coontz (1992) has shown that this image of mid–century American family life has always been more fiction than fact, "Mayberry" represents a symbolic image of some of what has been lost to many American men. In an age of economic decline, the men in Carlson's study are living through the evaporation of the manufacturing economy in the U.S. While previous generations of men might have been able to "do" gender by economically providing for their households, this is less possible for many men today. And the men in Carlson's study use guns to mourn this social, cultural, and economic transition—a cultural process Carlson (2015a) refers to as "mourning Mayberry."

Indeed, in Yamane's (2017) history of U.S. gun culture, he argues that at the end of the turn of the 21st century, U.S. gun culture shifted from a culture of recreation to one of armed self- defense and citizenship. And scholarship on gun owners like Carlson's reflect this shift (e.g., Carlson 2015a, 2015b; Stroud 2012). In Stroud's (2012) analysis of *who* was applying for concealed carry licenses, she found that the vast majority of applicants were White men. And racial anxiety was a primary motivation cited by the White men in Stroud's study.

In Carlson's (2015a) research, she shows how the large swathes of men unable to access a "breadwinner" model of masculinity led to a rise of what she terms "protector masculinity"—a model of manhood

in which guns provide evidence of gendered status. In support of this, Mencken and Froese (2017) discovered that White men who have experienced economic setbacks or who experience a great deal of anxiety about their economic futures are the group of gun owners *most* attached to their guns. As they write, "White men in economic distress find comfort in guns as a means to reestablish a sense of individual power and moral certitude in the face of changing times" (2017: 22). And the most recent data on gun ownership in the U.S. shows that White people are more likely to own guns than are any other racial group—men much more so than women (Parker et al. 2017).

This is the sociocultural landscape of the relationship between masculinities and guns today in the United States. And this *cultural explanation* builds on our *social psychological explanation* by helping to make sense of why boys and men in the U.S. are so much more likely to engage in mass shootings.

CONCLUSION

School shootings are such a problem in the U.S. that American schools conduct "active shooter drills" the way Cold War era American children endured "duck and cover" drills in case of nuclear explosion. These drills are responses to larger cultural problems. Indeed, there are so many mass shootings in the United States that they are classified by type—often place. So, we have school shootings, workplace shootings, church shootings, nightclub shootings, mall shootings, and more.

The scale of mass shootings is a social and cultural problem unique to the United States. Rates of gun ownership and access are an important piece of this problem. But when we zoom out from the gun itself to the people wielding the gun and back again to the gun culture within which that action is understood, gender becomes impossible to ignore. Mass shootings are enactments of masculinity. But men only rely on guns this way when violence has been culturally masculinized in the first place. Men otherwise unable to access a gendered sense of status in their social hierarchies only turn to guns and violence as *resources* to accomplish masculinity in societies in which violence is understood as "proof" of masculinity. It is essential to consider the multiple cultural causes of mass shootings if we hope to reduce the destruction they create.

REFERENCES

Bridges, Tristan, Tara Leigh Tober, and Nicole Wheeler. 2015. "What Constitutes a Mass Shooting and Why You Should Care." *Feminist Reflections (blog)*, December 17. Available online at: https://thesocietypages.org/feminist/2015/12/17/what-constitutes-a-mass-shooting-and-why-you-should-care/.

Bridges, Tristan and Tara Leigh Tober. 2016. "Mass Shootings and Masculinity." Pp. 507–12 in *Focus on Social Problems: A Contemporary Reader*, edited by Mindy Stombler and Amanda Jungels. New York: Oxford University Press.

Carlson, Jennifer. 2015a. *Citizen-Protectors: The Everyday Politics of Guns in an Age of Decline*. New York: Oxford University Press.

Carlson, Jennifer. 2015b. "Mourning Mayberry: Guns, Masculinity, and Socioeconomic Decline." *Gender & Society* 29(3): 386–409.

Coontz, Stephanie. 1992. *The Way We Never Were: American Families and the Nostalgia Trap*. New York: Basic Books.

Department of Justice. Bureau of Justice Statistics. 2013. Firearm Violence, 1993-2011 [Data File]. Retrieved March 19, 2015 from Global Study on Homicide. (2013, January 1). Retrieved March 19, 2014, from http://www.unodc.org/documents/gsh/pdfs/2014_GLOBAL_HOMICIDE_BOOK_web.pdf.

Editorial Board, *New York Times*. (2014, Dec. 3). "Mental Illness and Guns at Newtown." Retrieved March 13, 2015, from http://www.nytimes.com/2014/12/04/opinion/mental-illness-and-guns-at-newtown.html?_r=0.

Follman, Mark, Gavin Aronson, and Deanna Pan. (2014, May 24). "A Guide to Mass Shootings in America." *Mother Jones*. Retrieved March 13, 2015, from http://www.motherjones.com/politics/2012/07/mass-shootings-map.

Global Study on Homicide. (2013). Retrieved March 19, 2014, from http://www.unodc.org/documents/gsh/pdfs/2014_GLOBAL_HOMICIDE_BOOK_web.pdf.

Government of Canada. Statistics Canada. 2014. Firearms and Violent Crime in Canada, 2012 [Data File]. Retrieved March 19th, 2015 from http://www.statcan.gc.ca/pub/85-002-x/2014001/article/11925-eng.htm#a1.

Kimmel, Michael. 1994. "Masculinity as Homophobia." In *Theorizing Masculinities*, edited by Harry Brod and Michael Kaufman, 119–41. Thousand Oaks, CA: Sage.

Kimmel, Michael. and Matthew Mahler. 2003. "Adolescent Masculinity, Homophobia, and Violence: Random School Shootings, 1982-2001." *American Behavioral Scientist* 46(1): 1439–58.

Kimmel, Michael. 2013. *Angry White Men: American Masculinity at the End of an Era*. New York: Nation Books.

Kimmel, Michael. 2018. *Healing from Hate: How Young Men Get Into—and Out of—Violent Extremism*. Berkeley: University of California Press.

Klein, Ezra. (2012, December 14). Mythbusting: Israel and Switzerland are not Gun-Toting Utopias. *The Washington Post*. Retrieved March 13, 2015, from http://www.washingtonpost.com/blogs/wonkblog/wp/2012/12/14/mythbusting-israel-and-switzerland-are-not-gun-toting-utopias/.

Krouse, William J. (2012, November 14). "Gun Control Legislation." *Federation of American Scientists*. Retrieved March 23, 2015 from http://fas.org/sgp/crs/misc/RL32842.pdf.

Lankford, Adam. 2016. "Public Mass Shooters and Firearms: A Cross-National Study of 171 Countries." *Violence and Victims* 31(2): 187–99.

Lemieux, Frederic. 2014. "Effect of Gun Culture and Firearm Laws on Gun Violent and Mass Shootings in the United States: A Multi-Level Quantitative Analysis." *International Journal of Criminal Justice Sciences* 9(1): 74–93.

Mencken, F. Carson and Paul Froese. 2017. "Gun Culture in Action." *Social Problems.* Messerschmidt, James W. 1999. *Nine Lives: Adolescent Masculinities, the Body, and Violence.* Boulder: Westview Press.

Munsch, Christin, and Robb Willer. 2012. "The Role of Gender Identity Threat in Perceptions of Date Rape and Sexual Coercion." *Violence against Women* 18: 1125–46.

Newman, Katherine, Cybelle Fox, Wendy Roth, Jal Mehta, and David Harding. 2004. *Rampage: The Social Roots of School Shootings.* New York: Basic Books.

Parker, Kim, Juliana Menasce Horowitz, Ruth Igielnik, Baxter Oliphant, and Anna Brown. 2017. "The Demographics of Gun Ownership." *Pew Research Center | Social & Demographic Trends,* June 22. Retrieved May 18, 2018, from http://www.pewsocialtrends.org/2017/06/22/the-demographics-of-gun-ownership/.

Pascoe, C.J. 2007. *Dude, You're a Fag: Masculinity and Sexuality in High School.* Berkeley, CA: University of California Press.

Reuter-Rice, Karin. 2008. "Male Adolescent Bullying and the School Shooter." *The Journal of Nursing* 24(6): 350–59.

Rosenbaum, Janet. 2012. "Gun Utopias? Firearm Access and Ownership in Israel and Switzerland." *Journal of Public Health Policy* 33(1): 46–58.

Tonso, Karen. 2009. "Violent Masculinities as Tropes for School Shooters: The Montreal Massacre, the Columbine Attack, and Rethinking Schools." *American Behavioral Scientist* 52(9): 1266–85.

Stroud, Angela. 2012. "Good Guys with Guns: Hegemonic Masculinity and Concealed Handguns." *Gender & Society* 26(2): 216–38.

Swanson, Jeffrey, E. Elizabeth McGinty, Seena Fazel, and Vickie Mays. 2015. "Mental Illness and reduction of Gun Violence and Suicide: Brining Epidemiological Research to Policy." *Annals of Epidemiology* 25(5): 366–76.

Small Arms Survey. (2011, September). "Estimating Civilian Owned Firearms." *Research Notes: Armed Actors* 9. Available online at: http://www.smallarmssurvey.org/fileadmin/docs/H-Research_Notes/SAS-Research-Note-9.pdf.

Statistics Canada. (2017, November 22). "Homicide in Canada, 2016." Available online at: https://www.statcan.gc.ca/daily-quotidien/171122/dq171122b-eng.pdf.

United Nations Office on Drugs and Crime. (2018, May). *UNODC Statistics.* Available online at: https://data.unodc.org/.

Willer, Robb, Christabel L. Rogalin, Bridget Conlon, and Michael T. Wojnowicz. 2013. "Overdoing Gender: A Test of the Masculine Overcompensation Thesis." *American Journal of Sociology* 118(4): 980–1022.

Yamane, David. 2017. "The Sociology of U.S. Gun Culture." *Sociology Compass* 11: 1–10.

MILLIONS OF KIDS HAVEN'T LIVED THROUGH A SCHOOL SHOOTING BUT FEAR THAT THEY WILL

PETULA DVORAK

Turned out to be nothing, the full-alert police swarm on a Maryland middle school, and the kids sheltering in place most of . . . [that] morning. But the threat that gun = shooter = massacre is not make-believe. "As a mom, you can't tell them, 'Oh, this is never going to happen here,'" said Kathleen Isaacson, whose eighth-grader was in class at Silver Spring International Middle School

(*continued*)

when the school received a report of a gun. "Because that would be a big, fat lie. It has happened. Kids have seen that these things happen." At Silver Spring International, Isaacson's child and about 1,000 others knew what to do: They hunkered down in their locked classrooms. . . . [The next day], the target was nearby Albert Einstein High School, where a bomb threat led to a lockdown for 1,700 students. A helicopter circled as bomb-sniffing dogs arrived with their handlers to investigate.

This is the awful, unnerving reality with which our children are growing up. There have been a rash of threats across the country[1] since a gunman with an AR-15 semiautomatic rifle walked into Marjory Stoneman Douglas High School in Parkland, Fla., on Valentine's Day and slaughtered 17 people. Ordinarily, according to the Educator's School Safety Network,[2] about 10 threats or violent incidents are reported each day in American schools. Since Parkland, the network, which has been tracking these incidents for years, said reports have increased sevenfold. The network is recording about 70 incidents every day—673 since the Parkland shooting.

Active-shooter drills are part of our kids' education. They learn to hide in closets and stay silent while an imaginary gunman prowls the halls. Some elementary schools tell their students to pretend they are hiding from a deadly tiger. Millions of kids have not lived through a school shooting but are filled with fear that they will. . . . [Some] will dismiss the idea that the drills themselves are traumatizing: "Come on, we faced down nuclear annihilation when we did duck-and-cover drills as kids! They'll be fine!" . . . [But] the threat of nuclear annihilation was coming from an enemy an ocean away. No school was ever blown up. Today, kids expect the worst because they've seen it again and again.

In Silver Spring, the students weren't even told about the gun threat. They figured it out after reading social media and seeing reports, and some texted goodbye messages to frantic parents. Some sat stone-faced at dinner that night. Isaacson's eighth-grader even asked her mom to stay in her room while she fell asleep . . . [that] night, a return to toddler years. Other parents told Isaacson that their kids did the same. My son's school hasn't had a lockdown, but it recently conducted an intense active-shooter drill. The next weekend, my son ducked for cover

in the laundry room when he heard a loud noise outside. That night, he slept on the floor of our bedroom. He's 11.

Last week, someone tweeted, "2/22/18 I am coming and no one can stop me be prepared . . .," and then, "Fairfax high school is some [expletives] i hate that damn school so much," then explained, using more foul language, that he was suspended and "I have been planning this for months now and now I am going to act. Better watch out fairfax. . . ." Alarmed folks collected his tweets[3] and told police, while parents debated online whether to send their children to school. Police added security at the school that day and investigated the threat.

It has become routine. And yes, go ahead, Gen Xers—remind us how someone called in a bomb threat every time midterms came around. But were schools actually blown up? No, not since the one in Bath Township, Michigan, in 1927, where 45 people were killed.[4] Horrible, but it hasn't happened again in 90 years. The shootings are different. They're real, and they're relentless. More than 150,000 students attending at least 170 primary or secondary schools have experienced a shooting on campus since the Columbine High School massacre in 1999, according to an ongoing and conservative *Washington Post* analysis that does not include after-school assaults, accidents and suicides that involve guns.[5]

So our nation runs kids through regular active-shooter drills, and we're talking about arming teachers and fortifying school buildings with metal detectors, moats, smoke cannons and bulletproof glass. What about parks, health clinics, movie theaters and shopping malls? Is the Cinnabon cashier at the mall[6] or the ticket taker at the multiplex going to have to carry a weapon? Our nation will not be safe unless we get to the heart of the problem. We all know what that is: guns.

1   Eltagouri, Marwa, J. Freedom du Lac, and Lindsay Bever. 2018. "Copycat Threats and Rumors of 'Florida Pt 2' Put Schools on High Alert after Shooting Rampage." *Washington Post*. Retrieved January 30, 2019, from https://www.washingtonpost.com/news/education/wp/2018/02/15/threats-hoaxes-anxiety-and-arrests-an-uneasiness-in-schools-after-florida-shooting.

2   Anon. n.d. "The Educator's School Safety Network." *The Educator's School Safety Network*. Retrieved January 30, 2019, from http://eschoolsafety.org.

3   https://twitter.com/LandenRulez34/status/966421901005545473

4   Vargas, Theresa. 2017. "Virginia Tech Was Not the Worst School Massacre in U.S. History. This Was." *Washington Post*. Retrieved January 30, 2019, from https://www.washingtonpost.com/news/retropolis/wp/2017/04/16/virginia-tech-was-not-the-worst-school-massacre-in-u-s-history-this-was.

5   Cox, John Woodrow and Steven Rich. 2018. "Analysis | No, There Haven't Been 18 School Shootings in 2018. That Number Is Flat Wrong." *Washington Post*. Retrieved January 30, 2019, from https://www.washingtonpost.com/local/no-there-havent-been-18-school-shooting-in-2018-that-number-is-flat-wrong/2018/02/15/65b6cf72-1264-11e8-8ea1-c1d91fcec3fe_story.html.

6   Dvorak, Petula. 2014. "A Mall Shooting Rips Away Our Collective Security Blanket." *Washington Post*. Retrieved January 30, 2019, from https://www.washingtonpost.com/local/a-mall-shooting-rips-away-our-collective-security-blanket/2014/01/27/d63b9a38-879f-11e3-a5bd-844629433ba3_story.html.

MIRIAM KONRAD AND ANGIE LUVARA

55. CRIMES OF THE POWERFUL
Crafting Criminality

When you envision a criminal, what comes to mind? Konrad and Luvara call attention to a type of crime that is often underestimated in terms of its costs to individuals and society: crimes of the powerful (White-collar crime, corporate crime, and large-scale violations that are damaging and serious, but not necessarily illegal). Konrad and Luvara define and quantify, for example, the costs and consequences of White-collar crime compared to street crime and describe the great disparities in punishment for these types of crimes. They illustrate that the most powerful people in society get to define what "counts" as a crime and that their definitions serve their own interests.

The best way to rob a bank is to own one.

—WILLIAM CRAWFORD, 1989[1]

INTRODUCTION

It is increasingly common knowledge that the wealthy generally compound their wealth while the poor remain poor. A 2011 study using IRS tax data confirmed that between 1987 and 2009, the rich became permanently richer and the poor permanently poorer as a result of frozen wages, the shift away from manufacturing, and a tax system that strongly favors the wealthy (DeBacker et al., 2011). The wealth gap has continued to widen since 2009, and additional tax cuts passed in 2017 promise to make this already dire situation even worse (Alvaredo et al., 2017). Even the average American recognizes this process, with a substantial majority of Americans (65 percent) reporting they "believed the income gap between the rich and poor had widened over the last decade" (Drake 2013:1). The explanations for this gap, however, are not so widely agreed on and views seem to break down fairly consistently by political party affiliation. According to a Pew Research study, 68 percent

of Democrats believe that the poor remain poor largely because of factors beyond their control (in sociological terms, because of structural factors), whereas 48 percent of Republicans believe it is because of lack of personal effort. Similarly, 71 percent of Republicans believed the rich to be hard working, versus 22 percent of Democrats (Pew Research Center 2018). This chasm in perceptions of the rich and the poor has consequences that go far beyond mere purchasing power.

The perceptions regarding the causes of the gap also play into determining people's life chances because those perceptions are key in determining poverty policies. For instance, if the ability to fail or succeed is largely viewed through the lens of personal responsibility, then it follows that social services would be limited and highly contingent on recipients' individual attributes. If, in contrast, well-being is recognized as being deeply dependent on social markers like race, class, and gender, policy would favor liberal welfare and social justice components. One of the arenas in which the divide has significant impact is in the criminal justice system (CJS), which is what shall be explored herein.

Original to *Focus on Social Problems: A Contemporary Reader*.

By definition, that which is criminal is anything that is against the law. It follows then that anyone who breaks the law is a criminal. When one is in a position to make the laws, it is easy to understand how those laws might be made in the interest of maintaining the balance of power, exonerating one's own group at the expense of another set of social actors. Since those with the most resources tend to make the laws, it is little wonder that those with fewer resources are increasingly marginalized, pathologized, and even criminalized.

One of the ways this plays out is the difference in perception and treatment of White-collar crime and street crime. Let us begin with definitional matters. According to Braithwaite (1985), as early as 1916 Willem Bonger spoke of "crime in the streets" versus "crime in the suites" (2). Braithwaite further notes that early scholars and social commentators, known as muckrakers, were also investigating the concept:

> In journalistic exposes and fictionalized accounts, these writers laid bare the occupational safety abuses of mining magnates, the flagrant disregard for consumer health of the meat packing industry, the corporate bribery of legislatures, and many other abuses. The muckrakers were responsible for some of the important statutes, like the U.S. Federal Food, Drug, and Cosmetic Act of 1906, which criminalized many forms of corporate misconduct (1985:2).

It was Edwin Sutherland, however, who first coined the term White-collar crime in 1939, and it has since come into popular usage. In *Crime and the American Dream* (2007), Messner and Rosenfeld define White-collar crime as "crimes committed by persons against the organization for which they work (embezzlement, for example) or on behalf of those organizations (for instance, price fixing)" (28). Although there is no universal definition, this one incorporates much of what most people think of when the term is invoked.

Also important (and extremely difficult to measure) is just how costly White-collar crime is to society. The FBI (U.S. Department of Justice, 2017) estimates that White-collar crime costs over $500 billion annually, while other researchers estimate costs of anywhere from $200 billion (Reiman, 2001:120) up to $1.7 trillion (Helmkamp, Townsend, and Sundra 1997:11). Not only is it extremely costly by any measure, but also (counterintuitively and somewhat invisibly) it is far

costlier than street crime. Rosoff et al. (2003) inform us that the cost of White-collar crime is about fourteen times the estimated annual cost of robbery, burglary, assault, and other street crimes combined (53).[2]

Despite the greater costs and potentially deeper and broader harms to society, it is generally street crime that is feared by the common person, not crime in the suites. When most people think about crime, we tend to think about violence, and when we think about violence, we think about direct brutality: assault, battery, rape, murder. These images are frightening, palpable, and easily conjured in our own minds and reinforced constantly by media imagery. We are much less likely to have the same kinds of visceral reactions to the often hidden violence of White-collar crimes. Although we are not as attuned to their brutality, such criminality in fact often harms larger numbers of people at once and cuts just as deeply as any blade—for example, entire communities with severe birth defects (such as Kettlemen City, California [Griswold 2016] or Millsboro, Delaware [Lauria 2018]) and high cancer rates (such as Oakdale, Minnesota [Fellner 2018] or Pompton Lakes, New Jersey [O'Neill and Fallon 2018]) from illegal corporate waste disposal. The reasons that we are less likely to see these harms are manifold and, as alluded to above, have much to do with the power to define, the power to punish, and the power to escape punishment. All of these powers will be illuminated through the examples and discussion that follow, as will the ways in which such crimes devastate, destroy, and demolish people's lives.

BANKS, BAILOUTS, AND BAMBOOZLING

The recent financial crises in the United States were caused by the reckless actions of wealthy individuals and corporations. However, these individuals and corporations did not bear the brunt of the financial burden caused by these crises—the American people did. Beyond that, the American people were also left with the responsibility of undoing the damage done so that the country could work toward recovery. The devastation caused by these reckless actions can clearly be identified as White-collar or corporate crime (a term meant to emphasize culpability of corporations rather than simply individuals who might work in corporate settings and thus distinguishes itself from common understandings of White-collar crime). Simon (2008:86) tells us "according to a 2003 estimate, corporate crime, which includes antitrust, advertising law, [and] pollution law violations, cost American consumers an estimated *$3 trillion. The amount taken in bank robberies that year was 6,000 times less.* This figure is 40 times more than estimated losses from street crime."

A few of the most glaring instances in the past several decades deserve to be noted. First, the savings and loan crisis of the 1980s and 1990s was estimated to have cost taxpayers some $341 billion. This loss was caused by reckless investment, irresponsible speculation, and in many cases unmitigated fraud. Although there were many indictments and some executives even did prison time, many argue that the punishments were not commensurate with the harm done (Wilentz, 2009). Some argue that the punishments have gotten weaker rather than stronger since that crisis, which many believed could have acted as a wake-up call. For example, between 2001 and 2004, Enron (an energy, commodities, and service company based in Houston, Texas) was responsible for the loss of approximately $63 billion by its employees and shareholders (Messner and Rosenfeld, 2007:1). This disaster, too, was the result of far more than simple mismanagement. For instance:

> Enron officials refused to permit employees to withdraw their savings from the company's retirement plan at the same time company executives were cashing in their Enron stock holdings for millions. By the time employees were finally allowed to sell the stock in their 401K retirement accounts, Enron stock prices had plummeted (29).

The chief executive officer of Enron, Jeffrey Skilling, was sentenced to twenty-four years in prison, a harsh penalty compared to most meted out for White-collar crime. In June 2013, however, an appeal resulted in ten years being shaved off this sentence. In the end, Skilling served 12 years of his initial 24-year sentence in a minimum-security prison and was released from prison in 2018 (Gibson 2018). In both these cases, the taxpayers paid handsomely for the squandering of the nation's resources by conglomerates, and the businesses and their executives received little in the way of punishment.

The 2008 bank failure that resulted in the Great Recession, from which we have yet to fully recover (DePillis 2017; Soergel 2017), is an even more dramatic instance of mismanagement, corruption, and gross negligence. The fallout from this recession was widespread. Some 8.7 million jobs were lost between 2007 and 2010 (Center on Budget and Policy Priorities, 2014). High unemployment rates led to severe middle-class slippage for many individuals and families, with many seeking government assistance in the form of food stamps and other relief programs. There was a 76 percent increase on the Supplemental Nutrition Assistance Program rosters between 2007 and 2012 (Zedlewski et al., 2012). Many lost lifetime savings and their homes. According to a Mortgage Banker's Association report released in 2010, more than 1.2 million homes were lost between 2005 and 2008. Of course, the burden of the recession was not distributed equally. White households lost less wealth in the recession and have been steadily recovering those losses since 2010 (Asante-Muhammad et al. 2017). On the other hand, Black and Latino households lost all the wealth they had gained since the 1980s in the Great Recession, and have never recovered those losses (Asante-Muhammad et al. 2017).

The bankers escaped punishment, and were even rewarded through a hefty bailout. The formal title of the bailout was the Troubled Asset Relief Program (TARP). Funded by the American people, this relief to banks was agreed on by both Republican and Democratic leadership. William M. Isaac (2010) explains:

> The purpose of the TARP, as peddled to Congress by then Treasury Secretary Henry Paulson, was for taxpayers to purchase $700 billion of "toxic assets" from large financial institutions. Paulson theorized this would relieve firms of the burden of carrying the toxic assets and inspire them to lend again. . . Two weeks after the TARP was enacted, Paulson abandoned the toxic asset plan and announced that the money would instead be used to shore up the capital of banks.

Although many agree that TARP did help to avert a greater crisis, there are other measures by which it cannot be said to have fared as well. In a 2011 op-ed piece in the *New York Times*, Neil Barofsky, special inspector general for TARP, spoke strongly of its failure to meet its stated goals. He noted that in his role he could only make recommendations to the Treasury Department, not implement them. Although the goal of preserving and even increasing the riches of banks was well achieved, Barofsky declared the parallel goal of helping millions of homeowners save their homes "a colossal failure" (2011:3).

It is difficult to accurately estimate because of myriad complicating factors, but the most conservative estimates claim the bailout cost $48 billion in taxpayer money (Yip, 2011). One of many complicating factors, it appears, is that the funds being paid back to taxpayers are being paid back with other taxpayer money, and thus the estimate would be much higher (de Rugy, 2012). Yet, despite this greater harm and enormous cost, "studies of punishment in corporate crime cases reveal that only about two percent of corporate crime cases result in imprisonment" (de Rugy, 2012:86).

PEOPLE AS PAWNS FOR PROFIT

Some sociological criminologists argue the terms "White-collar crime" and "corporate crime" simply are not broad enough to reflect immoral and unjust behaviors by those with the bulk of the power in society. They recommend "crimes of the powerful" to reference large-scale human rights violations, environmental (in)justices, unsafe working conditions, and much more. Critical criminologists often prefer this term, as Carrabine et al. (2009) note:

> The application of the term "crime" here is a signal about what indeed may not be legally "criminal" but arguably should be, given its far-reaching seriousness. This is a tradition that has continued in critical criminology and does not mean that writers are ignorant of the law when they refer to . . . the "crimes" of the powerful . . . but rather that they are drawing attention to biases in the law-making and criminal justice systems (247).

The term employs the word "crimes" as a reminder that those with power use that power to decide what a crime is and who is criminal, and implies that many of their acts would be considered criminal if the legal definitions were constructed fairly.

Some notable crimes of the powerful include the blatant and willful use of citizens as guinea pigs. For instance:

From 1946 to 1963, between 250,000 and 300,000 soldiers and civilians were exposed to radiation during 192 nuclear bomb tests. Among the tests conducted by the Army was one that assessed the resultant psychological effects on soldiers who observed an atomic blast four times the size of the bomb dropped on Hiroshima from a distance of two miles (Simon, 2008:260).

The unwitting participants suffered many negative consequences, including far higher incidences of leukemia and other cancers than the average citizen, yet rather than take responsibility for these acts and criminalizing them as they surely should have, the government instead chose to condone and conceal them (Simon, 2008:261).

> Between the 1940s and 1970s various radiation studies were performed on human subjects, some with prior knowledge and some without. The incarcerated were often ideal candidates for such experimentation. For example, ". . . from 1963 to 1971, x-rays were applied to the testes of 131 inmates at Oregon and Washington state prisons" (Simon, 2008:261).

In 1978, regulations were passed to limit the use of prison inmates in research, at which point companies transitioned to exploiting students and the poor with the promise of small but very needed stipends in return for participation in these potentially harmful studies (Wiegand 2007). Websites and blogs encourage those who need to make quick cash to seek out paid clinical trials in their area (Zackowicz 2014; Mutton 2018). It is important to note that these clinical trials are not always safe. Initially healthy participants in the U.S., France, and England have experienced organ failure, future susceptibility to cancer and auto-immune diseases, and death during these trials (Matharu 2016). Some formerly incarcerated individuals participate in these studies routinely for income because they have trouble finding stable employment due to their legal history (Bichell 2016). Thus, the use of prison inmates in research has not been *restricted* as much as *rescheduled*—instead of participating in research during their incarceration, formerly incarcerated individuals now often participate in research after their release.

Less obvious but equally heinous is the promotion and sale of unsafe products, ranging from toxic toys for children to carcinogenic chemicals in our consumables. The United States Consumer Product Safety Commission estimates that over 13 million people visited an emergency room as a result of injuries sustained from incidents connected with consumer safety (NEISS 2017). Perhaps the most infamous of the unsafe product cases occur in the automobile industry. A prime example of this is the story of the Ford Pinto, a hot seller in the 1970s. From its introduction to the market, the Pinto had a serious flaw. It had a "fuel system that ruptured easily in rear-end collisions" (Simon, 2008:120). Although the company was well aware of this issue, style and speed of production considerations overrode concerns about human suffering and even fatalities. Ford calculated that it would cost a mere $11 per vehicle to make each one safe, but determined this was more than they were willing to pay. Simon notes,

> Ford reasoned that 180 burn deaths, 180 serious burn injuries, and 2,100 burned vehicles would cost $49.5 million (each death was figured at $200,000). But doing a recall of all Pintos and making each $11 repair would amount to $137 million. . . . In addition to the decision to leave the Pinto alone, Ford lobbied in Washington to convince government regulatory agencies and Congress that auto accidents are caused not by cars but by 1) people and 2) highway conditions (2008:121).

Simon (2008) goes on to assert that this kind of reasoning is akin to suggesting that if you carry money on your person, you are inviting robbery, therefore making you, not the robber, culpable for the crime.

It would be nice to believe that the automobile industry has outgrown such indiscretions, but unfortunately evidence says otherwise. In June 2014, General Motors admitted to errant neglect on the part of some of its employees regarding a faulty ignition switch dating back to at least 2002 (Hirsch, 2014). The admission resulted in fifteen employees being fired and much scrambling to shift the blame and find a scapegoat. By their own spokesperson's admission, the faulty part was responsible for at least thirteen deaths and many more injuries. This switch was initially chosen over a safer one strictly because it was cheaper to manufacture. The long-overdue confession and subsequent disciplining of some employees is cold comfort for the surviving family members of victims.

In addition to the woeful neglect involved in the creation and failure to improve products found to be unsafe, there are the myriad preventable "accidents" that take place in the workplace as a result of dangerous working conditions and the illnesses caused by exposure to hazardous chemicals on the job. On the job accidents annually cause 2.9 million injuries (Bureau of Labor Statistics 2017). Exposure to hazardous chemicals causes worker illness as well. For example, the CDC estimates that over 13 million workers in the United States are exposed to toxic chemicals that can be absorbed through the skin, making occupational skin disease (OSD) the second most common type of occupational disease in the U.S. (Centers for Disease Control and Prevention, 2018). The most common form of OSD, contact dermatitis, costs us over $1 billion annually (Centers for Disease Control and Prevention, 2018). The vast majority cannot be blamed on worker carelessness because the companies responsible for the conditions (as was the case with Ford and the Pinto) are often not only aware of the issues, but also go the extra mile to make sure that they do not come to light. For example, in 2017 Michael Grabell exposed the unsafe and exploitative conditions at a Case Farms chicken plant in Ohio— documented in Occupational Safety and Health Administration (OSHA) reports for over 25 years— that caused workers to incur many injuries, including debilitating carpel tunnel as well as the loss of fingers and limbs. The company continues to operate some of the most dangerous workplaces in America, merely paying fines for the OSHA violations that keep their employees in danger rather than addressing the hazardous conditions (Grabell 2017).

Both the scope and the heinousness of these legal, semi-legal, and illegal acts that constitute crimes of the powerful make them worthy of more attention from the press, the CJS, and the general public. In terms of the sheer numbers, even if we compare only the 100,000 deaths from exposure to toxic chemicals to the nearly 17,800 deaths from homicide in the United States in 2015, according to the Centers for Disease Control and Prevention (2017), we can see that the deaths occurring from crimes of the powerful are considerably higher. We might likewise compare the aforementioned 3.3 million injuries from job accidents to the 800,000 nonfatal aggravated assaults each year (Bureau of Justice Statistics, 2017). Thus, it becomes clear that many more people are maimed or killed by corporate neglect and dangerous practices than by direct, one-on-one brutality.

GREEN CRIMES AND RACISM

Beyond these workplace and manufacturing hazards, environmental devastation is so pervasive and so destructive that a whole new branch of criminology has sprung up around it called green criminology. Green criminology examines such things as air pollution, deforestation, water pollution, resource depletion, species decline, and animal abuse (Carrabine et al., 2009:385–391).

> As with so many crimes, environmental crimes and harms have a strong link to inequalities. Indeed, we can speak of *environmental racism* as a pattern by which environmental hazards are perceived to be greatest in proximity to poor people, and especially those belonging to [racial] minorities (Carrabine et al., 2009:405).

This environmental racism plays out at both the macro and the micro levels. At the global level, developing countries are used as large-scale dumping sites. Unhealthy and unwanted waste from more developed nations is often banned for burial in those countries unless companies are willing to use costly and time-consuming treatment and burial methods. Annually, 400 million tons of toxic waste are produced by the most developed nations, with 60 percent of that coming from the United States (Simon, 2008:180). Increasingly, this toxic waste is made up of "e-waste"—TVs, phones, computers, and other toxic electronic components that companies often claim to recycle but instead discard. The U.S. alone generated 10 million tons of e-waste in 2012, most of which gets discarded in developing countries in Asia and Africa (Vidal 2013). Such waste is often shipped to countries with weaker laws (and/or weaker enforcement) for a fee. The receiving country gains some financial profit but at great health and safety costs to its citizenry. For example, "Guinea-Bissau, which has a gross national product of $150 million, will make $150 to $600 million over a five-year period in a deal to accept toxic waste from three

European nations" (Simon, 2008:180). Although these waste products have been found to cause cancer and birth defects, the biggest problem is that this activity is legal. While the governments of these nation states are engaging in such exchanges willingly, it is the average citizen that is paying the cost in health and quality-of-life losses. The only recourse left for these victims is to try to bring public attention to the issue (Simon, 2008:181).

Of course, not all the toxic waste produced here in the U.S. is disposed of in other countries. A report by Environment America found that over 206 million pounds of toxic chemicals were dumped into waterways in the U.S. in 2012 alone (Kirth and Vinyard 2012). Even more disturbingly, in 2017 and 2018 the Trump administration rolled back over 75 policies designed to protect our environment from corporate toxic waste (Popovich, Albeck-Ripka, and Pierre-Louis 2018), which experts estimate will result in an additional 80,000 extra deaths per decade and cause respiratory problems for over one million people (Cutler and Dominici 2018). It is important to note that, at the local level in the United States, it is communities of color that often bear the brunt of toxic waste disposal. In *Dumping in Dixie* (2000), Robert Bullard reminds us that

> the problem of polluted Black communities is not a new phenomenon. Historically, toxic dumping and the location of locally unwanted land uses (LULUs) have followed the "path of least resistance," meaning that Black and poor communities have been disproportionally burdened with these types of externalities (3).

Bullard cites many examples of poor communities of color that are plagued by these problems, not the least of which is Ascension Parish in Louisiana, just south of Baton Rouge. The situation is so intense here that it is often referred to as a "toxic sacrifice zone," in which

> eighteen petrochemical plants are crammed into a nine and a half square mile area. Companies such as BASF, Vulcan, Triad, CF Industries, Liquid Airbonic, Bordon Chemical, Shell, Uniroyal, Rubicon, Ciba-Geigy, and others discharge 196 million pounds of pollutants annually into the water and air. Discharges include the carcinogens vinyl chloride and benzene,

mercury (which is harmful to the nervous system), chloroform, toluene, and carbon tetrachloride (which can cause birth defects) (Bullard, 2000:106).

Cunningham (2017) argues that toxic sacrifice zones are common across the southern United States, operating as dumping grounds for the rest of the nation's toxic waste.

Despite the ubiquitous and atrocious nature of these acts, all outward signs would indicate that street crime is the real threat. The media reinforce this view and so does the CJS, which is designed in such a way as to, in the words of Jeffrey Reiman (2001), "weed out the wealthy" and funnel the poor into prison (113-114). He notes,

> *For the same criminal behavior*, the poor are more likely to be arrested; if arrested, they are more likely to be charged; if charged, more likely to be convicted; if convicted, more likely to be sentenced to prison; and if sentenced, more likely to be given longer prison terms than members of the middle and upper classes (Reiman, 2001:110).

The notion of the "typical criminal," brought to us courtesy of the media and reinforced by CJS policies and procedures, has not only class implications but also racial ones. The stereotypical association of Blackness with criminality results in absurd levels of incarceration of Black people—especially those whom are poor—for largely nonviolent crimes. As noted by Michelle Alexander in *The New Jim Crow*,

> More African American adults are under correctional control today—in prison or jail, on probation or parole—than were enslaved in 1850, a decade before the Civil War began.. . . Thousands of Blacks have disappeared into prisons and jails, locked away for drug crimes that are largely ignored when committed by Whites (2012:180).

The U.S. Bureau of Justice Statistics (2014) tells us that 37 percent of the total prison and jail population in 2013 was Black, whereas only about 13.5 percent of the U.S. population was Black. Additionally, only seven percent of sentenced prisoners in federal prisons as of September 2013 were incarcerated for violent crimes (Bureau of Justice Statistics, 2014). Much of the overincarceration of nonviolent offenders has been

actualized through the infamously ineffective "War on Drugs," which has been the site of much CJS activity over the past several decades, from the unprecedentedly high incarcerations rates, to the brutality at the Mexican/American border, to the increasing numbers of women in prison, and more. Many argue that outdated and counterproductive drug laws such as those prohibiting the use of marijuana significantly contribute to this incarceration orgy. However, states that have legalized recreational marijuana use still produce racial disparities in arrest rates. In Colorado, marijuana arrest rates for White people declined from pre-legalization rates by 53 percent, compared to a decline of only 33 percent for Latinx people and 25 percent for Black people (Drug Policy Alliance 2018). Similar patterns have been found in Washington, D.C. and Alaska post-decriminalization (Drug Policy Alliance 2018), suggesting that marijuana legalization alone will not eliminate racially disproportionate drug arrest and incarceration rates.

AFFLUENZA

Another manifestation of the double standard regarding who and what is considered criminal comes to light in the so-called "Affluenza defense." This is controversial (there were unsuccessful efforts to ban its use in California in 2014 [Steinmetz 2014], for instance) yet illustrative (Abcarian, 2014). Ethan Couch, a sixteen-year-old boy in Texas, killed four pedestrians while driving under the influence of alcohol and received only probation as a consequence. The argument his attorney proffered was that Couch could not be held fully accountable for his actions because his upper-class upbringing did not afford him the opportunity to fully comprehend the distinction between right and wrong. He was so shielded from the harsh realities of life, the argument went, that he simply did not comprehend the basic concept of personal responsibility. The attorney called this condition "affluenza" (Associated Press, 2013). It could be seen as an ironic twist that the term is being employed in this fashion. When it was coined by de Graaf et al. in the book entitled *Affluenza: The All-Consuming Epidemic* (2005), the authors were attempting to expose a society sinking rapidly and pervasively into greed, self-absorption, and entitlement. Their scathing and insightful social commentary was never intended to be used as a defense or an excuse for criminal or negligent behavior resulting in the deaths of other human beings. We need only imagine for a moment the reverse defense being offered to appreciate the totality and absurdity of the hypocrisy. What if a defense attorney suggested that her client could not be held accountable for his actions that resulted in the death of four people because of poverty and lack of access to the better things in life? Such a defense would likely be met with derision and incredulity. To remove this statement from the purely speculative, the same judge (Jean Boyd) who sentenced Ethan Couch to an extremely expensive and comfortable rehabilitation facility and probation gave a different sentence to another young boy. In 2012, a fourteen-year-old boy punched someone whose head hit the pavement; as a result, the victim died two days later. Judge Boyd sentenced the young Black boy (who was not wealthy) to ten years in prison (Sterbenz, 2013).

To add insult to injury, yet another collateral consequence of being poor and in the CJS is that one is increasingly asked now to pay (in dollars as well as in time and energy) for one's own punishment. Joe Shapiro, in a May 18, 2014, National Public Radio report, speaks of this phenomenon. In one example he explains, "in Georgia, I met a man who stole a can of beer, and as a condition of his release, the court said 'Wear this leg monitor.' But those things are expensive and it was $12 a day for him. He was homeless" (Shapiro, 2014:1). Shapiro tells us that forty-nine states charge for those electronic monitors, forty-three states charge at least administrative fees for a public defender (which by definition is supposed to be a free service), forty-two states charge for room and board while in jail or prison, and forty-four states charge a fee for probation and parole supervision (2014:2). The list goes on, with some states allowing charges for juries, court-ordered drug treatment, arrest warrants, and more, with incarceration of those who cannot afford these fees. Across the nation, over 600 jurisdictions have enlisted offender-funded private companies to control their probation departments (Friedlin 2017). These private probation companies operate solely off the costs charged to their probationers—without the use of any tax dollars—and often generate large profits (like the private probation company operating in Greenwood, Mississippi—a town of 15,000 with an average income of $14,000—that turned an average profit of $48,000 per month [Phippen 2015]).

CONCLUSION

It is clear, then, at both the macro and the micro levels, that wealth buys power and influence, both in terms of defining what is criminal and in terms of escaping punishment even when the acts of the wealthy are eventually defined as illegal. In *Class, Status and Party*, the eminent sociologist Max Weber defined power as the ability to exercise one's own will, even in the face of resistance from others (Grusky and Szelenyi, 2011:56). He goes on to expound on the variety of ways in which this power may be exercised, including (but not limited to) bribery, force, subtle coercion, charisma, and media influence (Grusky and Szelenyi, 2011:67). The wealthy have the wherewithal to employ these methods to maintain and increase their power as well as to set the terms of crime and punishment.

As demonstrated in this short piece and as quoted at the outset, the best way to rob a bank is indeed to own one. In *The Divide: American Injustice in the Age of the Wealth Gap*, Matt Taibbi (2014) further explicates the ideological underpinnings that facilitate this heist. He notes,

> legally, there is absolutely no difference between a woman on welfare who falsely declares that her boyfriend no longer lives in the home and a bank that uses a robo-signer[3] to cook up a document swearing that he has kept regular records of your credit card account. But morally and politically, they're worlds apart (383).

He goes on to explain that in the case of the woman on welfare, her behavior is met with media-induced public scorn and moral outrage because she "committed the political crime of being needy and an eyesore," whereas the bankers commit the comparable acts over and over again with not only lack of condemnation but also actual accolades (Taibbi 2014:384). Taibbi argues that "the system is not disgusted by the organized, mechanized search for profit. It's more like it's impressed by it" (2014:384).

As long as money buys influence, as long as the abuse of power is rewarded with increased power, as long as poverty is criminalized and the poor are demonized, that is how long crimes of the powerful will be viewed as benign or even laudable and survival tactics of the impoverished will be made illegal and punished. Justice is a commodity that is sold to the highest bidder. It is abundantly clear that wealth trumps poverty when it comes to exoneration from culpability both at the macro and at the micro levels. Not only do corporations get away with crimes because they can hide behind a shield of respectability, legitimacy, and job creation, but also even individuals can now claim freedom from guilt based on ignorance bred from wealth and innocence derived from prosperity.

NOTES

1. Taibbi, 2014.
2. The cost of street crime is measured by combining costs to the victim (e.g., financial loss, medical bills) and costs to the larger society, including police protection, legal and judicial fees, and incarceration (McCollister et al., 2010).
3. A robo-signer is an employee of a mortgage servicing company that signs foreclosure documents without reviewing them. Rather than actually reviewing the individual details of each case, robo-signers assume the paperwork to be correct and sign it automatically, like robots (http://www.investopedia.com/terms/r/robo-signer.asp/).

REFERENCES

Abcarian, Robin. 2014. "Groundbreaking California Measure Would Outlaw 'Affluenza' Defense." *Los Angeles Times*. January 15, 2014. http://www.comm/local/abcarian/la-me-groundbreaking-california-law-would-outlaw-affluenza-defense-2014/.

Alexander, Michelle. 2012. *The New Jim Crow*. New York: New Press.

Alvaredo, Facundo, Lucas Chancel, Thomas Piketty, Emmanuel Saez, and Gabriel Zucman. 2017. "World Inequality Report." *World Inequality Lab*.

Asante-Muhammad, Dedrick, Chuck Collins, Josh Hoxie, and Emanuel Nieves. 2017. "The Road to Zero Wealth: How the Racial Wealth Divide is Hollowing Out America's Middle Class." *The Institute for Policy Studies*.

Associated Press. "Teen Who Killed Four Drunk Driving Gets Probation on 'Affluenza' Defense." 2013, December 13. *The Washington Times*. http://www.washingtontimes.com/news/2013/dec/13/teen-who-killed-four-drunk-driving-gets-probation-/?page=all/.

Barofsky, Neil. 2011. "Where the Bailout Went Wrong." *New York Times*. March 29, 2011. http://www.nytimes.com/2011/03/30/opinion/30barofsky.html?_r=0/.

Bichell, RaeEllen. 2016. "Professional 'Guinea Pigs' Can Make a Living Testing Drugs. *National Public Radio*, May 8. https://www.npr.org/sections/health-shots/2016/05/08/476797735/professional-guinea-pigs-can-make-a-living-testing-drugs.

Braithwaite, John. 1985. "White Collar Crime." *Annual Reviews Inc.* 11:1–25.

Bullard, Robert. 2000. *Dumping in Dixie: Race, Class, and Environmental Quality*, 33rd ed. Boulder, CO: Westview Press.

Bureau of Justice Statistics. 2017. https://ucr.fbi.gov/crime-in-the-u.s/2016/crime-in-the-u.s.-2016/topic-pages/aggravated-assault.

Bureau of Labor Statistics. 2017. https://www.bls.gov/news.release/pdf/osh.pdf.

Carrabine, Eamonn, Pam Cox, Maggy Lee, Ken Plummer, and Nigel South. 2009. *Criminology: A Sociological Introduction*, 22nd ed. London: Routledge Press.

Center on Budget and Policy Priorities Report. 2014, June 10. "Chart Book: The Legacy of the Great Recession." http://www.cbpp.org/cms/index.cfm?fa=view&id=3252/.

Centers for Disease Control and Prevention. 2017. "FastStats: Assault or Homicide." http://www.cdc.gov/nchs/fastats/homicide.htm/.

Centers for Disease Control and Prevention. 2018. "Skin Exposures and Effects." https://www.cdc.gov/niosh/topics/skin/default.html.

Cunningham, Anne. 2017. *Environmental Racism and Classism*. New York. Greenhaven Publishing.

Cutler, David, and Francesca Dominici. 2018. "A Breath of Bad Air: Trump Environmental Agenda May Lead to 80,000 Extra Deaths Per Decade." *Journal of the American Medical Association Forum*. https://newsatjama.jama.com/2018/05/10/jama-forum-a-breath-of-bad-air-trump-environmental-agenda-may-lead-to-80%E2%80%85000-extra-deaths-per-decade/.

De Rugy, Veronique. 2012. "The Real Cost of TARP." *National Review Online*. March 14, 2012. http://www.nationalreview.com/corner/293408/real-cost-tarp-veronique-de-rugy/.

DeBacker, Jason, Bradley Heim, Vasia Panousi, and Ivan Vidangos. 2011. "Rising Inequality: Transitory or Permanent? New Evidence from a U.S. Panel of Household Income 1987–2006." http://www.federalreserve.gov/pubs/feds/2011/201160/201160abs.html/.

DePillis, Lydia. 2017. "10 Years After the Recession Began, Have Americans Recovered?" *CNN Business*, December 1. https://money.cnn.com/2017/12/01/news/economy/recession-anniversary/index.html.

Drake, Bruce. 2013. "Americans See Growing Gap Between Rich and Poor." *Pew Research Center*, December 5. https://www.pewresearch.org/fact-tank/2013/12/05/americans-see-growing-gap-between-rich-and-poor/.

Drug Policy Alliance. 2018. "From Prohibition to Progress: A Status Report on Marijuana Legalization." http://www.drugpolicy.org/sites/default/files/dpa_marijuana_legalization_report_feb14_2018_0.pdf.

Fellner, Carrie. 2018. "Toxic Secrets: The Town that 3M Built—Where Kids are Dying of Cancer." *The Sydney Morning-Herald*, June 15. https://www.smh.com.au/world/north-america/toxic-secrets-the-town-that-3m-built-where-kids-are-dying-of-cancer-20180613-p4zl83.html.

Friedlin, Akiva. 2017. "The Poor Shouldn't Pay for Punishment." *Slate*, April 19. https://slate.com/news-and-politics/2017/04/georgias-pay-only-system-funded-government-at-the-expense-of-the-poor.html.

Gibson, Kate. 2018. "Former Enron CEO Jeffrey Skilling Released From Prison." *CBS News Money Watch*, August 30. https://www.cbsnews.com/news/former-enron-ceo-jeffrey-skilling-released-from-prison/.

de Graaf, John, David Wann, and Thomas H. Naylor. 2005. *Affluenza: How Overconsumption Is Killing Us and How to Fight Back*. San Francisco, CA: Berrett-Koehler Publishers, Inc.

Grabell, Michael. 2017. "Exploitation and Abuse at the Chicken Plant." *New Yorker*, May 8. https://www.newyorker.com/magazine/2017/05/08/exploitation-and-abuse-at-the-chicken-plant.

Griswold, Lewis. 2016. "Environmentalists, State Settle Differences Over Hazardous Waste Site." *Fresno Bee*, September 5. https://www.fresnobee.com/news/local/article100013267.html.

Grusky, David B. and Szonja Szelényi. 2011. *The Inequality Reader: Contemporary and Foundational Readings in Race, Class, and Gender*, 22nd Edition. Boulder, CO: Westview Press.

Helmkamp, James C., Kitty J. Townsend, and Jenny A. Sundra. 1997. "How Much Does White Collar Crime Cost?" National White Collar Crime Center.

Hirsch, Jerry. 2014. "GM Inquiry into Defective Ignition Switch Draws Fire." *Los Angeles Times*, June 5. http://www.latimes.com/business/autos/la-fi-gm-recal-findings-20140606-story.html#page=1/.

Isaac, William M. 2010. "Was TARP Worth It?" *Forbes*, October 1. https://www.forbes.com/sites/billisaac/2010/10/01/was-tarp-worth-it/#7a12d51750f3.

Kirth, Rob, and Kelley Vinyard. 2012. "Wasting Our Waterways 2012: Toxic Industrial Pollution and the Unfulfilled Promise of the Clean Water Act." Environment America Research and Policy Center.

Lauria, Maddy. 2018. "Lawyers Threaten Federal Lawsuit to Hold Delaware Chicken Plant Accountable for Pollution." *Delaware News-Journal*, March 28. https://www.delawareonline.com/story/news/local/2018/03/28/lawyers-threaten-federal-lawsuit-hold-delaware-chicken-plant-accountable-pollution/447524002/.

Matharu, Hardeep. 2016. "The Troubled History of Clinical Drug Trials." *The Independent*, January 15. https://www.independent.co.uk/life-style/health-and-families/health-news/the-drug-trials-that-went-wrong-a6814696.html.

McCollister, Kathyn, Michael French, and Hai Fang. 2010. "The Cost of Crime to Society: New Crime-Specific Estimates for Policy and Program Evaluation." *Drug and Alcohol Dependence* 108:98–109.

Messner, Steven F., and Richard Rosenfeld. 2007. *Crime and the American Dream*, 44th ed. Belmont, CA: Wadsworth Press.

Mortgage Bankers Association Press Release. 2010, April 7. "MBA: An Estimated 1.2 Million Households Were Lost during Recession." http://www.mbaa.org/NewsandMedia/PressCenter/72490.htm/.

Mutton, Ashleigh. 2018. "How to Make Money From Drug Trials." *Save the Student*, August 17. https://www.savethestudent.org/make-money/get-paid-for-drug-trials.html.

National Electronic Injury Surveillance System (NEISS). 2017. "NEISS Data Highlights – 2017."

O'Neill, James M., and Scott Fallon. 2018. "Toxic Secrets: N.J. Community Faces High Rates of Cancer, Rare Illnesses." *North Jersey News*, February 19. https://www.northjersey.com/story/news/watchdog/2018/02/14/dupont-pompton-lakes-pollution-cancer-home-values/931861001/.

Pew Research Center. 2018. "2018 Midterm Voters: Issues and Political Values." Pew Research Center.

Phippen, J. Weston. 2015. "The For-Profit Probation Maze." *The Atlantic*, December 16. https://www.theatlantic.com/politics/archive/2015/12/the-for-profit-probation-maze/433656/.

Popovitch, Nadja, Livia Albeck-Ripka, and Kendra Pierre-Louis. 2018. "76 Environmental Rules on the Way Out Under Trump." *New York Times*, July 6.

Reiman, Jefferey. 2001. *The Rich Get Richer and the Poor Get Prison: Ideology, Class, and Criminal Justice*, 66th ed. Boston: Allyn & Bacon.

Rosoff, Stephen M., Henry N. Pontell, and Robert H. Tilman. 2003. *Looting America: Greed, Corruption, Villains and Victims*. Upper Saddle River, NJ: Prentice Hall.

Shapiro, Joe. 2014. "Court User Fees Bill Defendants for Their Punishment." *National Public Radio*. http://www.npr.org/2014/05/18/313618296/court-user-fees-bill-defendants-for-their-punishment/.

Simon, David R. 2008. *Elite Deviance*, 99th ed. Boston: Pearson.

Soergel, Andrew. 2017. "Study: 3 in 10 Americans Haven't Recovered From Great Recession." *U.S. News*, July 13. https://www.usnews.com/news/economy/articles/2017-07-13/study-3-in-10-americans-havent-recovered-from-great-recession.

Steinmetz, Katy. 2014. "California Bill Banning 'Affluenza' Defense is Nixed." *Time*, April 22. http://time.com/72227/affluenza-bill-gets-killed/.

Sterbenz, Christina. 2013. "Judge in Affluenza Case Sentenced a Black Teen to Ten Years for Killing a Guy with a Single Punch." *Business Insider*. http://www.businessinsider.com/judge-jen-boyd-black-teen-prison-2013-12/.

Taibbi, Matt. 2014. *The Divide: American Injustice in the Age of the Wealth Gap*. New York: Spiegel & Grau.

United States Department of Justice, Federal Bureau of Investigation. 2017. "Crime in the United States, 2016."

United States Bureau of Justice Statistics. 2014. "Prisoners in 2013." Retrieved from https://www.bjs.gov/content/pub/pdf/p13.pdf.

Vidal, John. 2013. "Toxic E-Waste Dumped in Poor Nations, Says United Nations." *The Guardian*, December 14. https://www.theguardian.com/global-development/2013/dec/14/toxic-ewaste-illegal-dumping-developing-countries.

Wiegand, Timothy J. 2007. "Captive Subjects: Pharmaceutical Testing and Prisoners." *Journal of Medical Toxicology*, 3(1): 37-39.

Wilentz, Sean. 2009. *The Age of Reagan: A History 1974–2008*. New York: Harper Perennial.

Yip, Jonathan. 2011. "The Bank Bailout in Perspective." *Harvard Political Review*. http://harvardpolitics.com/arusa/the-bank-bailout-in-perspective/.

Zakowicz, Halina. 2014. "Get Paid to Participate in Clinical Trials: 7 Places to Find Opportunities." *The Penny Hoarder*, July 31. http://web.archive.org/web/20170921043812/https://www.thepennyhoarder.com/make-money/side-gigs/participating-clinical-trials-can-earn-serious-cash/.

Zedlewski, Sheila, Elaine Waxman, and Craig Gundersen. 2012. "SNAP's Role in the Great Recession and Beyond." *Urban Institute*. http://www.urban.org/UploadedPDF/412613-SNAPs-Role-in-the-Great-Recession-and-Beyondpdf/.

INEQUALITY IN LIFE AND DEATH: THE DEATH PENALTY IN THE UNITED STATES

ERIN THOMAS

Warren McCleskey, a Black man, was accused of committing an armed robbery that resulted in the death of the White police officer responding to the scene. The jury trying his case—made up of one Black person and 11 White people—found McCleskey guilty of murder, and the court sentenced him to death. For more than a decade, his lawyers fought the death penalty sentence. They provided evidence that Georgia courts had condemned to death the defendants who killed White victims at a rate four times that of the defendants who killed Black victims. Despite that argument, in 1987 the Supreme Court ruled the evidence was insufficient to prove discriminatory sentencing. Instead, they argued, McCleskey's lawyers needed to prove explicit racist intent on the part of the judge, prosecutors, or jury. They were unable to do so, and in 1991 McCleskey was put to death in Georgia's electric chair.

The United States has the highest incarceration rate in the world. One in 38 persons in the United States was under correctional supervision in 2016, and although Black Americans make up only about 13.6 percent of the general U.S. population, they comprise 36 percent of the prison population (Kaeble et al., 2016; U.S. Department of Justice, 2014). Black Americans are similarly overrepresented on death row: 42 percent of the death row population in the United States is Black (NAACP, 2016; Ford, 2014). Although most other industrialized nations have outlawed the death penalty, the United States retains capital punishment as a legal form of punishment in the majority of states, for the federal government, and within the military codes of justice.

This most serious of punishments has a long history of being unequally dispensed. From 1930 to 1967, 54 percent of the executions that took place nationwide involved non-White offenders (U.S. Department of Justice, 1980). This percentage indicates a serious overrepresentation of racial minorities among those executed. Considering the racial antagonisms that characterized this era, these unjust numbers are potentially unsurprising. However, research suggests that inequality in death sentencing and execution continues today.

One of the most consistent findings that researchers have identified in studies of racial discrimination in the death penalty is substantial evidence that offenders who kill White people are more likely to receive the death penalty than offenders who kill non-White people (Baldus & Woodworth, 1998; Baldus et al., 1998; Johnson et al., 2011; Pierce, Radelet, & Sharp, 2017).

Original to *Focus on Social Problems: A Contemporary Reader*.

A study conducted in Durham County, North Carolina, concluded that prosecutors are about 43 percent more likely to seek the death penalty in cases in which the victim is White and the defendant is Black compared to cases in which both the victim and the defendant are Black (Unah, 2009). Researchers at Stanford University have also analyzed photos of defendants and found that those whose appearance was perceived as more stereotypically Black (darker skin, broader nose, larger lips, etc.) were more likely to receive a death sentence than defendants whose appearance was perceived as less stereotypically Black (Eberhardt et al., 2006).

Similarly, Katherine Beckett and Heather Evans (2014; 2016) looked at trial reports pertaining to aggravated murder in Washington State's Supreme Court between 1981 and 2014 to assess if race of the defendant impacted sentencing. Beckett and Evans found that prosecutors in Washington State did not seek the death penalty for Black defendants more than White defendants. However, because capital punishment cases go to a jury for sentencing and jurors may have either conscious or unconscious bias against Black defendants, Black defendants were four times as likely to receive the death penalty death when sentenced. The results of their study led the Washington State Supreme Court to conclude that the "death penalty is invalid because it is imposed in an arbitrary and racially biased manner . . ." and the death penalty was subsequently disallowed in Washington State (Clarridge & Kamb, 2018). [*Editor's Note*: In May 2019, New Hampshire became the 21st state to abolish the death penalty, overriding a veto by the state's governor.]

This miscarriage of justice not only takes the lives of the sentenced individuals, but also has serious economic costs. Phillip Cook (2009) of Duke University analyzed death penalty–related state expenditures for North Carolina and found that the state spent 11 million more per year because of the costs of appeals and high security associated with death row imprisonment, than it would have had the death penalty been outlawed. John Roman and colleagues (2008), similarly found that an average capital-eligible case in which prosecutors did not seek the death penalty will cost approximately $1.1 million over the lifetime of the case. A capital-eligible case in which prosecutors unsuccessfully sought the death penalty will cost $1.8 million, and a capital-eligible case resulting in a death sentence will cost approximately $3 million.

Despite the cost and severity of capital punishment, research on the impact of the death penalty on curbing crime is mixed or inconclusive. The vast majority of the evidence indicates that, at best, use of the death penalty is not correlated with a decline in crime rates (Donohue & Wolfers, 2006; Kovandzic et al., 2009; Peterson & Bailey, 1988). In addition, 88 percent of American criminologists do not believe the death penalty serves as a deterrent to homicide (Radelet & Lacock, 2009).

Capital punishment is also fraught with the potential for other forms of human error. Since 1973, more than 140 people have been released from death row because they were found to be innocent of the crimes for which they were sentenced to death. In a 2014 study that analyzed the 7,482 death sentences that were handed down between 1973 and 2004, the authors concluded that more than four percent of inmates sentenced to the death penalty are likely to be innocent (Gross et al., 2014). Considering this error rate, it is likely that several dozen of the 1,320 individuals who have been executed since 1977 were innocent. Even incarcerated individuals who later had their convictions overturned and were released do not always receive compensation for time served and their wrongful conviction. Although some states provide a set amount of compensation for each year that an innocent individual was incarcerated, many states offer no promise of compensation (Emanuel, 2014). By incarcerating innocent people—often without just compensation—and operating in a racially discriminatory manner, the criminal justice system strays from the American ideals of equal protection under the law.

A few organizations are stepping in to attempt to provide remedies. For example, the Innocence Project is an organization that helps assist prisoners who believe they can prove their innocence through appeals. The organization has dedicated itself to using DNA testing to exonerate wrongfully convicted individuals and to reform the criminal justice system to prevent further wrongful convictions. The Innocence Project also belongs to the Innocence Network, a group of organizations that aim to provide voluntary and unpaid legal and investigative services to the wrongfully convicted. Many of the clients who seek out the assistance of the Innocence Project have run out of other legal options, are poor, and have been forgotten in prison.

In 2000, one of these falsely accused inmates, Kennedy Brewer, wrote to the Innocence Project and said,

> Back in 1992, I was accused of killing a three-year-old child, something I know I didn't do. I've been on death row in Mississippi for five years, and I know if I can get someone to look into my case, carefully, I know they will easily see they have the wrong person locked up. . . . I don't want to lose my life for something I know I didn't do.

With the help of the Innocence Project, Kennedy Brewer was exonerated in 2008 after serving a total of 15 years behind bars for a crime that DNA testing proved he did not commit. Brewer's case is not isolated. You can visit the National Registry of Exonerations (2018) to learn more about similar cases and the factors that contribute to wrongful convictions.

Considerable changes in policy are needed to ensure that the color of one's skin does not influence the sentence and execution one receives. Potential policy interventions include requiring "super due process" for all capital punishment cases—where the defendant in a capital case is allowed more leeway than standard due process would grant and can present evidence unique to the defendant. Other interventions include exempting individuals who are suffering from serious mental illness or intellectual disabilities from being sentenced to death, giving robust access to postconviction DNA testing, ensuring that all evidence in a case is retained for use in future appeals, repealing the use of capital punishment all together and replacing it with life without parole, permitting the use of statistical evidence to demonstrate when decisions are based on race, and passing laws that compensate innocent people for the harm experienced for wrongful conviction (Innocence Project, 2018; National Conference of State Legislators, 2018).

REFERENCES

Baldus, David C., and George Woodworth. 1998. "Race Discrimination and the Death Penalty: An Empirical Overview." In James R. Acker, Robert M. Bohn, and Charles S. Lanier (eds.), *America's Experiment with Capital Punishment: Reflections on the Past, Present, and Future of the Ultimate Penal Sanction*, pp. 385–415. Durham, NC: Carolina Academic Press.

Baldus, David C., George Woodworth, David Zuckerman, Neil Alan Weiner, and Barbara Broftitt. 1998. "Racial Discrimination and the Death Penalty in the Post-Furman Era: An Empirical and Legal Overview, with Recent Findings from Philadelphia." *Cornell Law Review* 83:1643–1770.

Beckett, Katherine, and Heather Evan. 2016. Race, Death, and Justice: Capital Sentencing in Washington State, 1981-2014. *Columbia Journal of Race and Law*, 6, 77.

Beckett, Katherine, and Heather Evans. 2014. The Role of Race in Washington State Capital Sentencing, 1981–2014. *Report. University of Washington*. http://web.archive.org/web/20150922033431/https://lsj.Washington.edu/.publications/katherine-beckett-and-heather-evans-2014-role-race-washington-state-capital-sentencing.

Clarridge, Christine and Lewis Kamb. 2018. "Death Penalty Struck Down by Washington Supreme Court, Taking 8 Men Off Death Row." *The Seattle Times*. Retrieved October 30, 2018, from https://www.seattletimes.com/seattle-news/death-penalty-opponents-cheer-washington-supreme-court-ruling-that-struck-punishment-down.

Cook, Philip J. 2009. "Potential Savings from Abolition of the Death Penalty in North Carolina." *American Law and Economics Review*, 11(2): 1–32.

Donohue, John J., and Justin Wolfers. 2006. "Uses and Abuses of Empirical Evidence in the Death Penalty Debate." *Stanford Law Review* 58:791–846.

Eberhardt, Jennifer L., Paul G. Davies, Valerie J. Purdie-Vaughns, and Sheri Lynn Johnson. 2006. "Looking Deathworthy. Perceived Stereotypicality of Black Defendants Predicts Capital-Sentencing Outcomes." *Psychological Science* 17(5):383–86.

Emanuel, Gabrielle. 2014. "When Innocent People Go to Prison, States Pay." Retrieved June 2014, from https://www.npr.org/sections/money/2014/06/16/320356084/when-innocent-people-go-to-prison-states-pay.

Ford, Matt. 2014. "Racism and the Execution Chamber." Retrieved June 2014, from http://m.theatlantic.com/politics/archive/2014/06/race-and-the-death-penalty/373081.

Gross, Samuel., Barbara O'Brien, Chen Hu, and Edward Kennedy. 2014. "Rate of False Conviction of Criminal Defendants Who Are Sentenced to Death." *Proceedings of the National Academy of Sciences of the United States of America* 111(20):7230–35.

Innocence Project. 2018. "Policy Reform." Retrieved November 2018 from https://www.innocenceproject.org/policy.

Johnson, Sheri. L., Blume, John. H., Eisenberg, Theodore., and Hans, Valarie. P. 2011. "The Delaware Death Penalty: An Empirical Study." *Iowa Law Review* 97, 1925.

Kaeble, Danielle, Glaze, Lauren, Tsoutis, Anastasios, and Minton, Todd. 2016. "Correctional Populations in the United States, 2014." *Bureau of Justice Statistics*, 1–19.

Kovandzic, T., L. Vieraitis, and D. Paquette Boots. 2009. "Does the Death Penalty Save Lives? New Evidence from State Panel Data, 1977 to 2006." *Criminology and Public Policy* 8(4):803–43.

NAACP. 2016. "Death row, USA. A Quarterly Report by the Capital Punishment Project of the NAACP Legal Defense and Education Fund, Inc. Summer." https://files.deathpenaltyinfo.org/legacy/documents/DRUSA_Summer_2016.pdf.

National Conference of State Legislators. 2018. "States and Capital Punishment." Retrieved October 2018 from http://www.ncsl.org/research/civil-and-criminal-justice/death-penalty.aspx.

National Registry of Exonerations. 2018. Retrieved October 2018 from https://www.law.umich.edu/special/exoneration.

Peterson, Ruth, and William Bailey. 1988. "Murder and Capital Punishment in the Evolving Context of the Post-Furman Era." *Social Forces* 66(3):774–807.

Pierce, Glen L., Radelet, Michael L., & Sharp, Susan (2017). "Race and Death Sentencing for Oklahoma Homicides Committed between 1990 and 2012." *Journal of Criminal Law and Criminology*, 107, 733.

Radelet, Michael, and Traci Lacock, "Do Executions Lower Homicide Rates? The Views of Leading Criminologists." *Journal of Criminal Law and Criminology* 489 (2009).

Roman, J., Chalfin, A., Sundquist, A., Knight, C., Darmenov, A., and Center, J. P. 2008. "The Cost of the Death Penalty in Maryland." Abell Foundation.

Unah, Isaac. 2009. "Choosing Those Who Will Die: The Effect of Race, Gender, and Law in Prosecutorial Decisions to Seek the Death Penalty in Durham County, North Carolina." *Michigan Journal of Race and Law* 15:135–81.

U.S. Department of Justice. 1980. *"Capital Punishment, 1979."* Washington, DC: U.S. Government Printing Office.

U.S. Department of Justice. 2014. "Jail Inmates at Midyear 2013—Statistical Tables." Retrieved June 2013. http://www.bjs.gov/content/pub/pdf/jim13st.pdf.

AMANDA ATWELL AND AMANDA M. JUNGELS

56. FOR-PROFIT JUSTICE

How the Private Prison Industry and the Criminal Justice System Benefit from Mass Incarceration

Although scholars and activists have long demonstrated biases in the criminal justice system by social class, Atwell and Jungels highlight a relatively new trend in criminal justice that serves to exacerbate these biases: the privatization of prison facilities, services, and goods. Atwell and Jungels show how the relationship between the private corporations (which seek to profit from crime and punishment) and government (which ostensibly seeks to administer punishment in a just way) disproportionately disadvantages vulnerable populations and contributes to increasing prison populations around the country. They question whether profits act as an incentive to bring people into the system, where they serve as a commodity, reducing any inherent fairness in the system.

Mass incarceration and the use of prisons to redress social and economic problems have become ubiquitous features of contemporary U.S. society. Although popular crime and drama television shows help to normalize high incarceration rates, the United States is quite the anomaly when it comes to the criminal justice system. The United States imprisons approximately 860 people per 100,000 citizens over age 18, or 2.1 million individuals. The U.S. incarceration rate, and the total number of people incarcerated, is higher than any other country in the world including China (with a prison population of 1.6 million) and more than four times higher than Western Europe (Gramlich, 2018). Put another way, the United States imprisons one-fifth of the world's prisoners, yet represents only five percent of the world's total population (Liptak, 2008b; Lee, 2015). The United States is also the only country that actively sentences youth to life in prison without the possibility of parole (The Sentencing Project, 2018b; Southerland and Kent Levy, 2017). Since the 1980s, states across the country have been contracting with private corporations that operate on a for-profit basis to house, feed, and care for the exploding prison population (Cheung, 2004; Shapiro, 2011). As of 2016, private state and federal prisons housed over 128,000 people, or nearly 10 percent of the total state and prison population, and since 2000, the number of prisoners incarcerated in private prisons has increased 47 percent (The Sentencing Project, 2018c). In this reading, we trace the origins of mass incarceration in the United States (or "prison boom") to the war on drugs (coined by President Nixon and intensified by President Reagan) and analyze the subsequent privatization of prison facilities, services, and goods as an exploitative partnership between the state and private corporations.

PRIVATE PRISONS AND THE WAR ON DRUGS

The 1980s marked the decade in which the government began to deregulate its responses to mental health issues (like drug addiction) while simultaneously implementing private prisons across the country for the first time. In fact, the first private prison contract was

Original to *Focus on Social Problems: A Contemporary Reader*.

awarded to the Corrections Corporation of America by the state of Tennessee in 1984 (Cheung, 2004). The incentive to imprison rather than to rehabilitate drug users was fueled by federal initiatives such as the "war on drugs," which has helped the U.S. prison rate to more than quadruple since 1980 (Klein and Soltas, 2013). Since the official launch of the war on drugs in 1982, the United States has experienced a 500 percent overall surge in its incarceration rate, and the length of sentences has simultaneously increased (The Sentencing Project, 2018a). This trend is evidenced, in particular, by drug conviction sentences. For example, in 1986 the average time spent behind bars for a drug conviction was 22 months, or almost two years; by 2004 this figure jumped to an average of 62 months, or over five years (The Sentencing Project, 2018a). One need only to look at the Clinton and Obama presidential administrations to know that the war on drugs has truly been a bipartisan effort, championed by Democrats and Republicans alike. Currently, more than half of those in prison are serving time for drug convictions. In 1980 there were 40,900 people incarcerated for drug offenses and by 2016 that number had skyrocketed to nearly half a million (450,345) (The Sentencing Project, 2018a). While diligently filling prisons, the war on drugs does not seem to have curbed Americans' appetite for drugs. According to the White House Office of National Drug Control Policy, drug use remains a relatively stable (though consistently increasing) feature of U.S. society; in 1985, 34.4 percent of those polled reported illegal drug use at least once during their lifetime, and by 2001 that number had increased to 41.7 percent of those polled (Lloyd, 2002). By 2017, 57 percent of Americans aged 18 to 25 and 51.3 percent of those over age 26 had used illegal drugs in their lifetimes (National Institute on Drug Abuse, 2018).

American Civil Liberties Union (ACLU) staff attorney David Shapiro (2011) and Amy Cheung (2004) of the Sentencing Project argue that the relatively recent trend of private prison expansion further exacerbates the preexisting moral failings of the criminal justice system by financially incentivizing mass incarceration. In other words, when arresting and imprisoning people are profitable enterprises, high incarceration rates become a self-fulfilling prophecy. As states across the country have faced an exploding prison population

along with rapidly increasing crime-control and law enforcement costs over the past thirty years, legislatures turned to the private sector in an attempt to defray some of their financial burden and, in some cases, even generate income. The burgeoning private prison industry is composed of multiple layers of shareholders and stakeholders who have a vested interest in maintaining or increasing incarceration rates because their profits are dependent on keeping prison beds full (or meeting "occupancy requirements"), regardless of actual crime rates (Cheung, 2004; Shapiro, 2011; Kroll, 2013). In fact, the private prison incarceration rate increased by 1,600 percent between 1990 and 2009 (Shapiro, 2011), reaping huge profits for two of the largest private prison companies, CoreCivic (previously named Corrections Corporation of America as mentioned above, but renamed in 2016) and the GEO Group. In 2012, CoreCivic reported revenue of $1.7 billion (Takei, 2013). During the same year, the chief executive officer from CoreCivic took home $3.7 million and that of the GEO Group took home $5.7 million (Lee, 2012). By 2017, CoreCivic and GEO Group generated combined revenues of over $4 billion (Urban Justice Center, 2018). Private prison corporations profit not only from their contracts with states, but also from unmet occupancy requirements (i.e., states are required to pay for unfilled beds). These quotas create an incentive for the state to maintain and increase arrest rates to avoid financial penalties, regardless of crime rates (Kirkham, 2013).

COSTS OF PRIVATIZATION

The economic burden of operating prisons in the era of mass incarceration increasingly falls on taxpayers, although the private prison model has been adopted to help defray the costs of incarceration to states. More than half (forty-one of sixty-two) of the private prison contracts across the country require that prison beds remain 90 to 100 percent full or the state will face a financial penalty, which ultimately must be paid by the taxpayers (Kirkham, 2013). The taxpayers of the state of Arizona had to pay the private prison company Management and Training Corporation $3 million in fees because the state failed to maintain the 97 percent occupancy requirement (Hall and Diehm, 2013). In states such as Arizona, the cost of operating a private prison cost the taxpayers $3.5 million more than the cost to operate a state-run facility (Shen, 2012). It is not just large corrections corporations that benefit from the private prison model—increasingly, small companies and businesses have been shown to profit as well, a profit that comes at taxpayers' expense. The Corrections Accountability Project found that over 3,100 corporations benefit from the exploding incarceration rates, including companies that provide health care, food, commissary supplies, financial services, and transportation to prisons (Urban Justice Center, 2018). In fact, over half of the $80 billion spent annually on incarceration in the United States goes to these vendors (Urban Justice Center, 2018).

Analyzing the racial makeup of private prisons reveals another layer of inequality that is difficult to ignore. In 2013, approximately 130,000 people were held in for-profit prisons run by corporations such as CoreCivic, the vast majority of whom were people of color (Wade, 2013a, Quandt, 2014). Although the increasingly popular trend of privatizing the criminal justice system may seem like a common-sense, efficient way to handle social problems in our society, the consequences that result from these systems being privatized are disastrous and far reaching. Although illegal drug use remains slightly higher among White Americans (Knafo, 2013), men and women of color are disproportionately targeted for arrest and convicted of drug crimes. In 2010, for example, Black people were 3.7 times as likely as White people to be arrested for marijuana possession (Ghandnoosh, 2015). Similarly, in 2009, 79 percent of those convicted in crack cocaine cases were Black (Kurtzleben, 2010). According to the Bureau of Justice Statistics, Black women are arrested at a rate three times higher than White women and two times higher than Latina women. These stark numbers reveal that people of color are disproportionately represented in the profitable private prison industry (Wade, 2013a; Quandt, 2014).

PRIVATIZATION OF YOUTH AND IMMIGRANT DETENTION FACILITIES

Privatization is also a particularly prominent feature of detention centers for youths and immigrants. Forty percent of all juvenile offenders are committed to private facilities, which have been found to be rife with corruption and dangerous conditions ranging from unsanitary food to cases of sexual abuse by prison staff against the youth prisoners (Kirkham, 2013). Research demonstrates that people of color (Wade, 2013a), youth (Kirkham, 2013), immigrants (National Network for Immigrant and Refugee Rights, 2010), and the poor (Liptak, 2008a) are particularly vulnerable to exploitation by the private prison industry. The public–private partnership between government and prison corporations is also clearly evident in recent anti-immigration backlash. A statement from the National Network for Immigrant and Refugee Rights (2010) explains that "Arizona's controversial immigration law SB1070[1] was developed by lawmakers in collaboration with corporations that build private jails to incarcerate immigrants; these companies stand to earn considerable profits from the growing trend of detaining immigrants for enforcement and deterrence."

Private corporations are responsible for running nine out of ten of the largest immigration detention centers in the U.S. (Harlan, 2016). As of 2017, ICE reported detaining over 39,000 immigrants per day, about 71 percent of whom were housed in privately run detention facilities (Cullen, 2018). This is a dramatic increase from two decades earlier, when fewer than 8,000 people were held in detention per day (Takei, 2016), and the Trump administration estimated in 2017 that it would need to double the daily capacity to house 80,000 migrants (Sainato, 2017). Immigration advocates were hopeful that President Obama would deprivatize many privately-run immigrant detention centers after his administration in 2009 stopped using a notorious family detention center run by CoreCivic in Taylor, Texas. The American Civil Liberties Union filed a lawsuit on behalf of detained women and children in this Texas facility, alleging that children were required to wear prison uniforms, received little education, were allowed to play for only one hour a day, and were disciplined by guards by threatening to remove children from their parents (Harlan, 2016; American Civil Liberties Union, 2007).

Prior to 2014, asylum-seekers were rarely detained in facilities; instead, they were allowed to settle where they liked, and were required to report to court when required. Studies show that almost all detainees who are released to await trial, but who receive some form of monitoring (such as ankle monitors) will appear for their court date (Hylton, 2015). In 2014, however, the Obama administration responded to fears of increased numbers of asylum-seekers by instituting an "aggressive deterrence strategy" by dramatically increasing the rates of detention for families (Harlan, 2016). In accordance with this change in policy, in 2014, the Obama administration and Immigration and Customs Enforcement (ICE) officials granted CoreCivic a four-year, $1 billion no-bid contract to build and run a detention facility for women and children seeking asylum in Dilley, Texas (Harlan, 2016). This contract was renewed for an additional five years in October 2016. Unlike in other contracts ICE holds with private companies running immigrant detention facilities, this contract does not adjust payouts to CoreCivic in response to the number of immigrants being housed; instead, CoreCivic is paid in full regardless of the level of occupancy (Harlan, 2016). Because CoreCivic is required to have full staffing and services no matter the level of occupancy, the contract is less cost-effective when less than full; when full, the government spends $285 a day, per person, and when it's half-full (or even less), as it was for significant portions of 2016, the government pays significantly more per day (Harlan, 2016). Critics of ICE argue that more cost-effective alternatives, such as ankle-monitors, could be used at mere dollars a day (Harlan, 2016). The Dilley facility shows how a policy change representing a crack-down on immigration can "bolster a private sector that benefits from a get-tough stance" (Harlan, 2016).

In 2016, concurrent with its increased use of private detention facilities for immigrants and asylum seekers, the Obama administration issued a decision that it would phase out the use of private prisons to house federal inmates, citing a decline in the overall number of federal inmates, as well as significant safety and security problems at the facilities (Savage, 2016). This policy change was overturned by the Trump administration shortly after the change in administration (Lichtblau, 2017). That policy change, coupled with the Trump administration's "zero-tolerance" policy on illegal immigration, has led to over 100 percent increases in stock prices for CoreCivic and GEO Group, as well as dramatic increases in profits (Richardson, 2018; Sainato, 2017). GEO Group donated $225,000 to a Trump Super PAC during the 2016 election cycle, and both GEO Group and CoreCivic donated $250,000 to the Trump Inaugural Committee (Richardson, 2018). The GEO Group alone spent over $1.3 million on lobbying efforts in the six months year of Trump's presidency, and received over $770 million in government contracts in the same time period (Sainato, 2017). In 2017, GEO Group held its annual leadership conference at a golf resort owned by President Trump (Sainato, 2017).

PRIORITIZING PRISONS OVER EDUCATION

The current state of mass incarceration also poses troubling implications for people and institutions that are, at least theoretically, beyond the scope of the criminal justice system. In addition to the private prison subsidies that burden taxpayers, the restructuring of state and local government budgets that accompany private prison expansion tend to prioritize the funding of incarceration over education. According to a report by the U.S. Department of Education (2016), state and local government spending on prisons and jails has increased three times as fast as spending on K-12 education. In every state in the U.S., spending growth on corrections was higher than for education, and in most states the rate of growth on corrections spending was more than 100 percentage points higher than for education (U.S. Department of Education, 2016). Across the nation, states utilize more public funds for housing prisoners than for educating public school students. For instance, the state of Georgia spends an average of $10,805 per public school student annually, compared to an average of $21,039 per inmate (Klein, 2014). This disparity is even greater in states like California, which spends an average of $11,420 per public school student each year, compared to an average of $44,421 per inmate annually (Klein, 2014).

WHO ELSE PROFITS?

In addition to the profit gained from arresting, booking, and housing prisoners, some of America's most iconic companies (Nordstrom, Eddie Bauer, Motorola, Microsoft, Victoria's Secret, Compaq, IBM, Boeing, AT&T, Texas Instruments, Revlon, Macy's, Target stores, Nortel, Hewlett Packard, Intel,

Honeywell, etc.) contract with prison factories such as UNICOR that employ prisoners in both state and private facilities to manufacture some of our most coveted consumer items for pennies an hour (Seandel, 2013; Wade, 2013b). In fact, UNICOR is the country's largest prison factory corporation, operating 110 factories across 79 federal prisons, with the Department of Defense representing the company's most profitable contract (Seandel, 2013). It is estimated that prisoners working for UNICOR manufacture all military identification tags, helmets, ammunition belts, and bulletproof vests, among other national defense equipment (Seandel, 2013). Furthermore, trading private prison stock has become profitable for those on Wall Street, with corporations such as Allstate, American Express, General Electric, Goldman Sachs & Co., and Merrill Lynch investing millions annually in the top private prison corporations (Silverstein, 2000; Pelaez, 2014). Even the Gates Foundation, the world's largest private foundation that awards grants for initiatives based in education, health, and world population, invested $2.2 million in the GEO Group (Park, 2014; Brunner, 2018).

Moreover, companies such as the Dial Corporation also bid to win contracts for their products to be used or sold within prisons, whereas companies like AT&T charge exorbitant rates for phone calls made from prison, sometimes resulting in phone bills up to $20,000 for family and friends of prisoners (Martin, 2013). Reporting for *The New York Times*, Clifford and Silver-Greenberg (2014) found that business arrangements between state detention centers and private companies are a common feature of the criminal justice system in nearly every state. Private companies such as JPay and Global Tel-Link control phone, Internet, and money order services in prisons across the country, where prisoners are beyond the reach of consumer protection laws and are viewed as business opportunities, and prisons are regarded as money-making ventures rather than as places for rehabilitation or retribution (Clifford and Silver-Greenberg, 2014). Telephone calls commonly start at $3.15, sending an email outside of prison walls costs $0.33 or more, and transferring money to prisoners for their commissary needs begins at $4.95 (Clifford and Silver-Greenberg, 2014). States profit from these

partnerships as well. For instance, in Baldwin County, Alabama, 84 percent of the gross revenue from all telephone calls made in jail is given back to the Sheriff's Department (Clifford and Silver-Greenberg, 2014). Of course, attaching high fees to the most basic services places the heaviest burden on prisoners who are poor, as well as their families, who struggle to find the resources to remain connected to them.

THE COSTS OF BEING ECONOMICALLY DISADVANTAGED

The privatization of justice even begins prior to imprisonment and is a core feature of the commercial bail bond system. Although private prisons clearly exacerbate the financial troubles that prisoners and their families must cope with, the bail bond industry presents incarcerated individuals with unique challenges. In exchange for a fee or some type of collateral, a bondsperson agrees to post bail. Even if the defendant is found "not guilty" at trial, he or she still has to pay bail and the various fees the bondsperson decides to charge (Eligon, 2011). In most countries outside of the United States, paying someone else's bail in exchange for a fee is illegal (Liptak, 2008a), but for the vast majority of poor and middle-class defendants, posting bail through a bondsperson means the difference between temporary freedom or remaining jailed until trial. In one Texas town, judges and bondspeople were found to be colluding to ensure high bails for defendants and high profits for the local bail bond owners (Liptak, 2008b). This system disproportionately harms those without assets, most likely working-class and poor individuals, because collateral, often in the form of property, such as a house or vehicle, is required to cover the bond fees. Although our criminal justice system is founded on ideals of fairness and assumed innocence, the current structure of the system seems stacked against those without means—at every stage in the process. These unequal relationships challenge the core ideals of democracy in this nation, particularly that citizenship guarantees liberty and justice for all.

Other problems related to wealth and poverty abound in the criminal justice system. In a recent NPR special series, "Guilty and Charged," investigative reporter Joseph Shapiro (2014) found that states across the nation are passing on court operating costs to those convicted of misdemeanor and felony charges. In addition to receiving the sentence commensurate with the crime they committed, defendants are burdened with an average fee of $2,500 (the cost associated with operating the court), because legislators fear the political backlash that could ensue from raising taxes to cover these costs. Defendants who cannot afford their court fees are typically given a longer prison sentence than those who are able to pay the fees up front because the inability to pay these types of fees is increasingly becoming criminalized (Shapiro, 2014). In certain cases, judges have been willing to extend a payment plan for offenders who cannot pay the full amount; however, one missed payment can result directly in jail time because this infraction is considered a violation of probation. Although some of the money collected from the fees is dispersed to victims' advocacy groups, forty-three states charge an administrative fee for court-appointed attorneys (also known as public defenders) that are typically conceived of as being a free service for indigent defendants (Shapiro, 2014). However, the incentive for states to continue charging defendants the cost of running the court system remains high because states like Michigan bring in an average $345 million a year in revenue from fees.[2]

Similarly, a recent Human Rights Watch (2014) report titled "Profiting from Probation: America's 'Offender-Funded' Probation Industry" detailed an increasingly common practice of state courts requiring people found guilty of misdemeanor crimes to pay their probation fees to private companies. It also detailed the existence of a practice known as "pay only probation," wherein people are sentenced to probation in order to supervise the payment of their court costs and fees, rather than the traditional use as an alternative to a jail sentence (Human Rights Watch, 2018a). In addition to collecting debt owed to the court, private probation companies charge a monthly "supervision" fee, so those who take longer to pay off their debt, most often the poor, pay disproportionately more than those who have the ability to pay their fees up front (Human Rights Watch, 2014). Those who cannot afford to keep up with payments face going

into debt, vehicle repossession, abusive threats, and potential jail time (Human Rights Watch, 2014).

Private probation companies have a clear financial incentive to see more people convicted of minor crimes and misdemeanors sentenced to probation, and to keep those individuals on probation for as long as possible (Human Rights Watch, 2018a). Some companies also offer services related to the rehabilitation of persons on probation (e.g., alcohol/drug rehabilitation, anger management classes, and electronic monitoring), the costs of which are passed directly to the probationer (Human Rights Watch, 2018a). In one such case, Cindy Rodriguez, a 53-year old woman from Tennessee living in poverty and surviving on disability payments totaling $753 a month, was arrested for the first time in her life for shoplifting. Her public defender advised her to plead guilty and accept probation, but Ms. Rodriguez quickly found herself unable to pay the court costs, fines, and the associated probation fees imposed by the private company that supervised her probation:

> Rodriguez was placed on probation for 11 months and 29 days under the supervision of Providence Community Corrections, Inc. (PCC), a private company that had contracted with the Rutherford County government to supervise misdemeanor probationers. Rodriguez's lawyer told her probation was nothing to worry about, that she would just have to visit her probation officer once a week and pay her fees and fines. When she informed the judge about her stark financial situation and disability payments, he told her to do the best that she could. She owed the court $578 for the fine and associated fees, and on top of that she would have to pay PCC a $35-45 monthly supervision fee. PCC also conducted random drug tests, though she was not charged with a drug-related offense, for which she would pay approximately $20 a test. The costs of probation ruined her life (Human Rights Watch, 2018a).

For Ms. Rodriguez, the additional fees associated with her privatized probation nearly doubled her overall costs, a common occurrence for privatized probationers. In Florida, a $750 fine for driving under the influence can end up costing more than $2,495 when adding in court costs (an additional $635) and probation fees ($1,080). In Tennessee, an $250 fine for simple drug possession can result in an additional $946 in court costs and $1,035 in probation fees, totaling $2,231, nearly ten times the original fine (Human Rights Watch, 2018b). In a troubling development, private prison companies such as GEO Group have become more involved in the electronic monitoring and tracking (or "e-monitoring") of people on probation, racking up more than $200 million in revenue from e-monitoring alone (Alexander, 2018). As Alexander (2018: 2) points out:

> Companies that earned millions on contracts to run or serve prisons have, in an era of prison restructuring, begun to shift their business model to add electronic surveillance and monitoring of the same population. Even if old-fashioned prisons fade away, the profit margins of these companies will widen so long as growing numbers of people find themselves subject to perpetual criminalization, surveillance, monitoring and control.

Charging defendants for the cost of operating the court system—and then punishing those who cannot pay—challenges one of the basic tenants of the criminal justice system, that all people should be treated equally before the law. At each stage of the incarceration process, from posting bail, to the trial and sentencing court hearings, to prison facilities and the corporations that invest in and operate within them, the privatization of the criminal justice system contributes greatly to the exploitation of our society's most marginalized communities.

OPPORTUNITIES FOR REFORM

Reform advocates such as ACLU staff attorney David Shapiro (2011), along with organizations such as the National Public Service Council to Abolish Private Prisons, the Anti-Recidivism Coalition, and the National Association for the Advancement of Colored People, recommend abolishing the practice of privatizing prisons and prison services while simultaneously investing in an effort to reduce the number of people targeted for imprisonment each year. Considering that the nationwide private prison population is disproportionately representative of marginalized communities, such as youth, people of color, immigrants, and

the poor, coalitions among activist groups may be particularly successful at creating viable solutions to mass incarceration. A comparative example of prison phone calls from two different states provides some insight into the effect that deprivatizing prison services may have for those burdened with rising costs. In Kentucky, where the state has a contract with a private company, a fifteen-minute phone call costs $5.70; in New York, where the state does not accept commissions from telephone service providers, a fifteen-minute phone call costs just $0.64 (Human Rights Defense Center, 2018). In September 2018, New York City became the first major city to make all calls from local jails free, and the state of Texas reduced the costs of interstate calls from $0.26 to $0.06, making a 15-minute call $0.90, rather than $3.90 (Lecher, 2018). In general, evidence suggests that defendants and prisoners are at greater risk for exploitation and violence when the state attempts to defer the costs associated with operating the criminal justice system by striking deals to contract with private corporations whose central motive is profit, rather than the rehabilitation of its inmates. Investing in rehabilitation rather than incarceration may reduce recidivism and subsequently reduce the rising costs of running the world's busiest court and prison system.

Considering the pervasive nature of the private prison industry, the simultaneous implementation of several reform strategies may be necessary to effectively reduce the harm caused by the privatization of the criminal justice system. For instance, in 2013 Californians voted to amend their three-strikes law that previously mandated that individuals convicted of their third felony charge would be sentenced from twenty-five years to life in prison, no matter the severity of the crime. The amendments to this law now allow for nonviolent third-time offenders to be treated as if they were second-time offenders, potentially cutting the time spent behind bars in half (Laird, 2013). As of April 2014, over 1,500 non-violent prisoners have been released after being allowed to petition the court for a resentencing hearing and nearly 2,500 more inmates are waiting to have their cases reviewed (Stanford Law School, 2014), though in 2017 the California Supreme Court ruled that judges had "broad authority" to decline to reduce the sentences of "three-strike" inmates (Dolan, 2017). The recidivism rate for prisoners released under the amended law is less than two percent, significantly lower than the average recidivism rate (30 percent) (Stanford Law School, 2014) Moreover, between 2012 and 2014, the change in the three-strikes law has saved the state of California over $30 million dollars, and if the law was fully implemented (i.e., by reducing the sentence of every eligible prisoner), California would save an addition $750 million dollars over the next 10 years (Stanford Law School, 2014).

Additionally, Alaska, California, Colorado, Maine, Massachusetts, Oregon, Vermont, Washington, Washington D.C., have legalized recreational marijuana, and an additional 13 states have removed jail time for individuals possessing small amounts of marijuana, creating the potential to further reduce the number of people funneled through the criminal justice system each year (Marijuana Policy Project, 2018). Efforts to reform marijuana laws are part of a greater mission to end the war on drugs and thus have direct implications for lessening the private sector's grip on the criminal justice system. Experts from a range of disciplines, including Nobel Prize–winning economists of the London School of Economics' IDEAS Center, have realized the widespread negative outcomes that these draconian practices have caused and advocate a swift end to this endless war (Ferner, 2014). Overall, any effort aimed at reducing the current state of mass incarceration is likely to negatively impact the private prison industry and improve the life chances of some of those caught in the profit-driven criminal justice system.

NOTES

1. SB1070 has been described as the country's toughest and most comprehensive law aimed at criminalizing and deporting "illegal" immigrants (Archibold, 2010). According to this law, failing to maintain immigration documentation at all times is a crime and, as such, police officers have the right to detain anyone suspected of being in the country illegally (Archibold, 2010).

2. One of the most egregious examples of local governments criminalizing and exploiting their most marginalized citizens for profit is found in the case of Ferguson, Missouri, which has been described as a site of contemporary racial apartheid (Kristof, 2014). Following the September 2014 tragic murder of Michael Brown, an unarmed Black teenager shot to death by a police officer, the U.S. Department of Justice (2015) issued a six-month investigation into the local criminal justice system of Ferguson and found practices that indeed confirm the presence of a deeply pervasive system of racialized social control. According to a summary of their report, the official Investigation of the Ferguson Police Department (U.S. Department of Justice, 2015:i) conducted by the Department of Justice's Civil Rights Division found that "Ferguson law enforcement efforts are focused on generating revenue" and, more specifically, that "Ferguson law enforcement practices violate the law and undermine community trust, especially among African Americans."

REFERENCES

Alexander, Michelle. 2018. "The Newest Jim Crow." *The New York Times*, November 8. Retrieved from https://www.nytimes.com/2018/11/08/opinion/sunday/criminal-justice-reforms-race-technology .html?action=click&module=Opinion&pgtype=Homepage.

American Civil Liberties Union. 2007. ACLU Challenges Prison-Like Conditions at Hutto Detention Center. Retrieved from https://www.aclu.org/aclu-challenges-prison-conditions-hutto-detention-center.

Archibold, Randall C. 2010. "Arizona Enacts Stringent Law on Immigration." *The New York Times*, April 23. Retrieved from https://www.nytimes.com/2010/04/24/us/politics/24immig.html.

Brunner, Jim. 2018. "Senator Patty Murray Got Campaign Money from Company Running Tacoma Center Where Undocumented Immigrants are Held." *The Seattle Times*, June 22. Retrieved from https://www.seattletimes.com/seattle-news/politics/sen-patty-murray-received-donations-from-private-immigration-prison-firms/.

Cheung, Amy. 2004. "Prison Privatization and the Use of Incarceration." *The Sentencing Project*. Retrieved from https://www.privateci.org/private_pics/inc_prisonprivatization%5B1%5D.pdf.

Clifford, Stephanie, and Jessica Silver-Greenberg. 2014. "In Prisons, Sky-High Phone Rates and Money Transfer Fees." *The New York Times*, June 26. Retrieved from http://www.nytimes.com/2014/06/27/business/in-prisons-sky-high-phone-rates-and-money-transfer-fees.html.

Cullen, Tara Tidwell. 2018. "ICE Released Its Most Comprehensive Immigration Detention Data Yet. It's Alarming." National Immigrant Justice Center. Retrieved from https://immigrantjustice.org/staff/blog/ice-released-its-most-comprehensive-immigration-detention-data-yet.

Dolan, Maura. 2017. "California Supreme Court Makes it Harder for Three-Strike Prisoners to Get Sentence Reductions." *Los Angeles Times*, July 3. Retrieved from http://www.latimes.com/local/lanow/la-me-ln-three-strikes-court-20170703-story.html.

Eligon, John. 2011. "For Poor, Bail System Can Be an Obstacle to Freedom." *The New York Times*, January 9. Retrieved from http://www.nytimes.com/2011/01/10/nyregion/10bailbonds.html.

Ferner, Matt. 2014. "End the War on Drugs, Say Nobel Prize–Winning Economists." *Huffington Post*, May 6. Retrieved from http://www.huffingtonpost.com/2014/05/06/end-drug-war_n_5275078.html/.

Ghandnoosh, Nazgol. 2015. "Black Lives Matter: Eliminating Racial Inequity in the Criminal Justice System." *The Sentencing Project*. Retrieved from http://sentencingproject.org/wp-content/uploads/2015/11/Black-Lives-Matter.pdf.

Hall, Katy, and Diehm, Jan. 2013. "One Disturbing Reason for Our Exploding Prison Population (INFOGRAPHIC)." *Huffington Post*, September 19. Retrieved from http://www.huffingtonpost.com/2013/09/19/private-prisons_n_3955686.html.

Harlan, Chico. 2016. "Inside the Administration's $1 Billion Deal to Detain Central American Asylum Seekers." *The Washington Post*, August 14. Retrieved from https://www.washingtonpost.com/business/economy/inside-the-administrations-1-billion-deal-to-detain-central-american-asylum-seekers/2016/08/14/e47f1960-5819-11e6-9aee-8075993d73a2_story.html?utm_term=.8a2b25f726c4.

Human Rights Defense Center. 2018. "Prison Phone Justice." Retrieved from https://www.prison-phonejustice.org.

Human Rights Watch. 2014. "Profiting from Probation: America's 'Offender-Funded' Probation Industry." Retrieved from https://www.hrw.org/report/2014/02/05/profiting-probation/americas-offender-funded-probation-industry.

Human Rights Watch. 2018a. "Set Up to Fail: The Impact of Offender-Funded Private Probation on the Poor." Retrieved from https://www.hrw.org/report/2018/02/20/set-fail/impact-offender-funded-private-probation-poor.

Human Rights Watch. 2018b. "U.S.: Private Probation Harming the Poor." *Human Rights Watch*, February 20. Retrieved from https://www.hrw.org/news/2018/02/20/us-private-probation-harming-poor.

Hylton, Wil S. 2015. "The Shame of America's Family Detention Camps." *The New York Times*, February 4. Retrieved from https://www.nytimes.com/2015/02/08/magazine/the-shame-of-americas-family-detention-camps.html.

Gramlich. John. 2018. "America's Incarceration Rate is at a Two-Decade Low." Pew Research Center, May 2. Retrieved from http://www.pewresearch.org/fact-tank/2018/05/02/americas-incarceration-rate-is-at-a-two-decade-low/.

Kirkham, Chris. 2013. "Prison Quotas Push Lawmakers to Fill Beds, Derail Reform." *Huffington Post*, September 19. Retrieved from http://www.huffingtonpost.com/2013/09/19/private-prison-quotas_n_3953483.html.

Klein, Ezra, and Evan Soltas. 2013. "Wonkbook: 11 Facts about America's Prison Population." *Washington Post*, August 13. Retrieved from http://www.washingtonpost.com/blogs/wonkblog/wp/2013/08/13/wonkbook-11-facts-about-americas-prison-population.

Klein, Rebecca. 2014. "States Are Prioritizing Prisons over Education, Budgets Show." *Huffington Post*, October 30. Retrieved from http://www.huffingtonpost.com/2014/10/30/state-spending-prison-and-education_n_6072318.html.

Knafo, Saki. 2013. "When It Comes to Illegal Drug Use, White America Does the Crime, Black America Gets the Time." *Huffington Post*, September 17. Retrieved from http://www.huffington-post.com/2013/09/17/racial-disparity-drug-use_n_3941346.html/.

Kristof, Nicholas. 2014. "When Whites Just Don't Get It: After Ferguson, Race Deserves More Attention, Not Less." *The New York Times*, August 30. Retrieved from http://www.nytimes.com/2014/08/31/opinion/sunday/nicholas-kristof-after-ferguson-race-deserves-more-attention-not-less.html.

Kroll, Andy. 2013. "This Is How Private Prison Companies Make Millions Even When Crime Rates Fall." *Mother Jones*, September 19. Retrieved from http://www.motherjones.com/mojo/2013/09/private-prisons-occupancy-quota-cca-crime.

Kurtzleben, Danielle. 2010. "Data Show Racial Disparity in Crack Sentencing." *US News*, August 3. Retrieved from http://www.usnews.com/news/articles/2010/08/03/data-show-racial-disparity-in-crack-sentencing.

Laird, Lorelei. 2013. "California Begins to Release Prisoners after Reforming Its Three-Strikes Law." *American Bar Association Journal*, December 1. Retrieved from http://www.abajournal.com/magazine/article/california_begins_to_release_prisoners_after_reforming_its_three-strikes_la.

Lecher, Colin. 2018. "Texas and New York City are Slashing Inmate Phone Call Rates." *The Verge*, September 1. Retrieved from https://www.theverge.com/2018/9/1/17800338/texas-new-york-prison-jail-phone-rates.

Lee, Michelle Ye Hee. 2015. "Does the United States Really Have 5 Percent of the World's Population and One Quarter of the World's Prisoners?" *The Washington Post*, April 30. Retrieved from https://www.washingtonpost.com/news/fact-checker/wp/2015/04/30/does-the-united-states-really-have-five-percent-of-worlds-population-and-one-quarter-of-the-worlds-prisoners/?utm_term=.0c123beb7a71.

Lee, Suevon. 2012. "By the Numbers: America's Growing For-Profit Detention Industry." *Huffington Post*, June 21. Retrieved from http://www.huffingtonpost.com/2012/06/21/for-profit-prisons_n_1613696.html.

Lichtblau, Eric. 2017. "Justice Department Keeps For-Profit Prisons, Scrapping an Obama Plan." *The New York Times*, February 23. Retrieved from https://www.nytimes.com/2017/02/23/us/politics/justice-department-private-prisons.html.

Liptak, Adam. 2008a. "Illegal Globally, Bail for Profit Remains in U.S." *The New York Times*, January 29. Retrieved from http://www.nytimes.com/2008/01/29/us/29bail.html?pagewanted=all.

Liptak, Adam. 2008b. "U.S. Prison Population Dwarfs That of Other Nations." *The New York Times*, April 23. Retrieved from http://www.nytimes.com/2008/04/23/world/americas/23iht-23prison.12253738.html?pagewanted=all.

Lloyd, Jennifer. 2002. "Drug Use Trends." White *House Office of National Drug Control Policy*. Retrieved from https://www.ncjrs.gov/App/Publications/abstract.aspx?ID=190780/.

Marijuana Policy Project. 2018. "State Policy." Retrieved from https://www.mpp.org/states/.

Martin, Jonathan. 2013. "AT&T to Pay Washington Prisoners' Families $45 Million in Telephone Class Action Settlement." *Seattle Times*, February 3. Retrieved from http://blogs.seattletimes.com/opinionnw/2013/02/03/att-to-pay-washington-prisoners-families-45-million-in-telephone-class-action-settlement/.

National Institute on Drug Abuse. 2018. "National Survey of Drug Use and Health." Retrieved from https://www.drugabuse.gov/national-survey-drug-use-health.

National Network for Immigrant and Refugee Rights. 2010. *Injustice for All: The Rise of the U.S. Immigration Policing Regime*. Human Rights Immigrant Community Action Network, an initiative of the National Network for Immigrant and Refugee Rights. Retrieved from http://www.nnirr.org/~nnirrorg/drupal/sites/default/files/injustice_for_all_executive_summary.pdf.

Park, Alex. 2014. "Is the Gates Foundation Still Investing in Private Prisons?" *Mother Jones*, December 8. Retrieved from http://www.motherjones.com/politics/2014/12/gates-foundation-still-investing-private-prisons.

Pelaez, Vicky. 2014. "The Prison Industry in the United States: Big Business or a New Form of Slavery?" Global Research Centre for Research on Globalization. Retrieved from http://www.globalresearch.ca/the-prison-industry-in-the-united-states-big-business-or-a-new-form-of-slavery/8289/.

Quandt, Katie Rose. 2014. "Why There's an Even Larger Racial Disparity in Private Prisons Than in Public Ones." *Mother Jones*, February 17. Retrieved from http://www.motherjones.com/mojo/2014/01/even-larger-racial-disparity-private-prisons-public-prisons.

Richardson, Davis. 2018. "Private Prison Stocks are Soaring Amid the Trump Administration's Immigration Crisis." *The Observer*, June 20. Retrieved from https://observer.com/2018/06/private-prison-stocks-soar-amid-immigration-crisis/.

Sainato, Michael. 2017. "Private Prison Industry Lobbying, Profits Soar Under Trump Administration." *The Observer*, October 27. Retrieved from https://observer.com/2017/10/geo-group-private-prison-industry-profits-soar-under-trump/.

Savage, Charlie. 2016. "U.S. to Phase Out Use of Private Prisons for Federal Inmates." *The New York Times*, August 18. Retrieved from https://www.nytimes.com/2016/08/19/us/us-to-phase-out-use-of-private-prisons-for-federal-inmates.html?module=inline.

Seandel, Caitlin. 2013. "Prison Labor: Three Strikes and You're Hired." Ella Baker Center for *Human Rights*. Retrieved from http://ellabakercenter.org/blog/2013/06/prison-labor-is-the-new-slave-labor.

Shapiro, David. 2011. "Banking on Bondage: Private Prisons and Mass Incarceration." *American Civil Liberties Union*. Retrieved from https://www.aclu.org/files/assets/bankingonbondage_20111102.pdf.

Shapiro, Joseph. 2014. "Special Series: Guilty and Charged." *National Public Radio*. Retrieved from http://www.npr.org/series/313986316/guilty-and-charged.

Shen, Aviva. 2012. "Private Prisons Cost Arizona $3.5 Million More per Year Than State-Run Prisons." *Think Progress*. Retrieved from http://thinkprogress.org/justice/2012/08/06/641971/private-prisons-cost-arizona-35-million-more-per-year-than-state-run-prisons

Silverstein, Ken. 2000. "US: America's Private Gulag." *CorpWatch*. Retrieved from https://corpwatch.org/article/us-americas-private-gulag.

Southerland, Vincent M. and Jody Kent Lavy. 2017. "Why are We Sentencing Children to Life in Prison Without Parole?" *Newsweek*, August 10. Retrieved from https://www.newsweek.com/why-are-we-sentencing-children-life-prison-without-parole-649162.

Stanford Law School. 2014. "Proposition 36 Progress Report: April 2014." Stanford Law School Three Strikes Project, with the NAACP Legal Defense and Education Fund. Retrieved from https://law.stanford.edu/wp-content/uploads/sites/default/files/child-page/595365/doc/slspublic/ThreeStrikesReport.pdf.

Takei, Carl. 2013. "Happy Birthday to the Corrections Corporation of America? Thirty Years of Banking on Bondage Leaves Little to Celebrate." *American Civil Liberties Union.* Retrieved from https://www.aclu.org/blog/happy-birthday-corrections-corporation-america-thirty-years-banking-bondage-leaves-little?redirect=blog/speakeasy/happy-birthday-corrections-corporation-america-thirty-years-banking-bondage-leaves.

Takei, Carl. 2016. "The Government's Out-of-Control Detention Practices Could Bail Out the Private Prison Industry." *American Civil Liberties Union.* Retrieved from https://www.aclu.org/blog/immigrants-rights/immigrants-rights-and-detention/governments-out-control-detention-practices.

The Sentencing Project. 2018a. "Fact Sheet: Trends in U.S. Corrections." https://www.sentencingproject.org/wp-content/uploads/2016/01/Trends-in-US-Corrections.pdf.

The Sentencing Project. 2018b. "Juvenile Life without Parole: An Overview." https://www.sentencingproject.org/publications/juvenile-life-without-parole/.

The Sentencing Project. 2018c. "Fact Sheet: Private Prisons in the United States." Retrieved from https://www.sentencingproject.org/publications/private-prisons-united-states/.

Urban Justice Center. 2018. "The Prison Industrial Complex: Mapping Private Sector Players." *Corrections Accountability Project.* Retrieved from https://static1.squarespace.com/static/58e127cb1b10e31ed45b20f4/t/5ade0281f950b7ab293c86a6/1524499083424/The+Prison+Industrial+Complex+-+Mapping+Private+Sector+Players+%28April+2018%29.pdf.

U.S. Department of Education. 2016. "State and Local Expenditures on Corrections and Education." Retrieved from https://www2.ed.gov/rschstat/eval/other/expenditures-corrections-education/brief.pdf.

U.S. Department of Justice, Civil Rights Division. 2015. "Investigation of the Ferguson Police Department." Retrieved from http://www.justice.gov/sites/default/files/opa/press-releases/attachments/2015/03/04/ferguson_police_department_report.pdf.

Wade, Lisa. 2013a. "Race, Rehabilitation, and the Private Prison Industry." *The Society Pages.* Retrieved from http://thesocietypages.org/socimages/2013/01/25/race-rehabilitation-and-the-private-prison-industry.

Wade, Lisa. 2013b. "Prison Labor and Taxpayer Dollars." *The Society Pages.* Retrieved from http://thesocietypages.org/socimages/2013/04/04/prison-labor-and-taxpayer-dollars.

HOW PRISONS CHANGE THE BALANCE OF POWER IN AMERICA

HEATHER ANN THOMPSON

What has it really cost the United States to build the world's most massive prison system? To answer this question, some[1] point to the nearly two million people who are now locked up in an American prison—overwhelmingly this nation's poorest, most mentally ill, and least-educated citizens—and ponder the moral costs. Others[2] have pointed to the enormous expense of having

---

[1] CBS News. 2012. "The Cost of a Nation of Incarceration." *CBSNews.* http://www.cbsnews.com/8301-3445_162-57418495/the-cost-of-a-nation-of-incarceration/?pageNum=2.

[2] Henrichson, Christian and Ruth Delaney. 2012. http://www.vera.org/pubs/price-prisons-what-incarceration-costs-taxpayers.

---

more than seven million Americans under some form of correctional supervision and argued that the system is not economically sustainable. Still others[3] highlight the high price that our nation's already most-fragile communities, in particular, have paid for the rise of such an enormous carceral state. A few[4] have also asked Americans to consider what it means for the future of our society that our system of punishment is so deeply racialized.[1]

With so many powerful arguments being made against our current criminal justice system, why then does it persist? Why haven't the American people, particularly those who are most negatively affected by this most unsettling and unsavory state of affairs, undone the policies that have led us here? The answer, in part, stems from the fact that locking up unprecedented numbers of citizens over the last forty years has *itself* made the prison system highly resistant to reform through the democratic process. To an extent that few Americans have yet appreciated, record rates of incarceration have, in fact, undermined our American democracy, both by impacting who gets to vote and how votes are counted.

The unsettling story of how this came to be actually begins in 1865, when the abolition of slavery led to bitter constitutional battles[5] over who would and would not be included in our polity. To fully understand it, though, we must look more closely than we yet have at the year 1965, a century later—a moment when, on the one hand, politicians were pressured into opening the franchise by passing the most comprehensive Voting Rights Act to date, but on the other hand, were also beginning a devastatingly ambitious War on Crime.

From voting rights to the war on crime

The Voting Rights Act of 1965 gave the federal government a number of meaningful tools with which it could monitor state elections and make sure that states with a particularly grim history of discriminatory voting practices would make no voting policy without its approval. The act had been intended to combat the intimidation and legal maneuvers—such as passage of poll taxes, literacy requirements, and so-called "Grandfather clauses"—that had left only five percent of Black Americans, by the 1940s, able to vote, despite passage of the 14th and 15th amendments after the Civil War.

But the very same year that Lyndon Johnson signed the Voting Rights Act of 1965, he also signed another act into law: the Law Enforcement Administration Act (LEAA), a piece of legislation that, well before crime rates across America hit record highs, created the bureaucracy and provided the funding that would enable a historically and internationally unparalleled war on crime.

So, at the *very same moment* that the American Civil Rights Movement had succeeded in newly empowering African Americans in the political sphere by securing passage of the Voting Rights Act of 1965, America's White politicians decided to begin a massive new war on crime that would eventually undercut myriad gains of the Civil Rights Movement—*particularly* those promised by the Voting Rights Act itself.

From the war on crime to mass incarceration

Thanks to LEAA and America's post-1965 commitment to the War on Crime, and more specifically, thanks to the dramatic escalation of policing in cities across the nation as well as the legal changes wrought by an ever-intensifying War on Drugs, between 1970 and 2010 more people ended up in prison in this country than anywhere else in the world. At no other point in this nation's recorded past had the economic, social, and political institutions of a country become so bound up with the practice of punishment. . . .

The nation's decision to embark on a massive War on Crime in the mid-1960s has had a profound impact on the way that American history evolved over the course of the later twentieth and into the twenty-first centuries. As we now know from countless studies, such staggering rates of incarceration have proven both socially devastating[6] and economically destructive for wide swaths of this country—particularly those areas of America inhabited by people of color.[7] This nation's incarceration rate was hardly color blind. Eventually one in nine young Black men were locked up in America and, by 2010, Black women and girls too were being locked up at a record rate.

Diluting our democracy

So how did this overwhelmingly racialized mass incarceration end up mattering to our very democracy? How is it that this act of locking up so many Americans, particularly Americans of color, *itself* distorted our political process and made it almost

3   Orson, Diane. 2012. "Million-Dollar Blocks' Map Incarceration Costs." *National Public Radio.* http://www.npr.org/2012/10/02/162149431/million-dollar-blocks-map-incarcerations-costs.

4   The Huffington Post. 2011. "Lisa Ling's 'Our America' Looks at Mass Incarceration of Black Men." *The Huffington Post.* http://www.huffingtonpost.com/2011/11/17/lisa-lings-our-america-ex_n_1099668.html.

5   Holloway, Pippa. 2013. *Living in Infamy: Felon Disenfranchisement and the History of American Citizenship.* Oxford University Press.

6   Clear, Todd R. *Imprisoning Communities: How Mass Incarceration Makes Disadvantaged Neighborhoods Worse.* Oxford University Press.

7   Alexander, Michelle. 2012. *The New Jim Crow: Mass Incarceration in the Age of Colorblindness.* The New Press.

(continued)

impossible for those most affected by mass incarceration to eliminate the policies that have undergirded it at the ballot box? The answer lies back in the 1870s and in a little-known caveat to the 14th Amendment.

Ratifying the 14th Amendment was one of Congress's first efforts to broaden the franchise after the Civil War. A key worry among northern politicians, however, was that since White southerners could no longer rely on the notorious "three-fifths" rule to pad their own political power, they would now try to inflate their census population for the purposes of representation by counting African Americans as citizens while denying them access to the ballot.

So, to prevent any power grab on the part of ex-Confederates, Congress decided to add so-called Section 2 to the 14th Amendment. Firstly, it stipulated that any state that "denied" the vote "to any of the male inhabitants of such state, being twenty-one years of age, and citizens of the United States" would have its representation downsized in proportion to the number of individuals being disenfranchised. Secondly, Section 2 allowed for the disenfranchisement of otherwise eligible citizens—without affecting representation—if they had participated "in rebellion, or other crime." The idea here was to keep those who had committed crimes against the Union and those who might still be in rebellion against the Union from wielding political power in the wake of the Civil War.

This latter provision of Section 2, however, proved damaging to Black freedom—political and otherwise. Almost overnight, White southerners began policing African Americans[8] with new zeal and charging them with "crimes" that had never before been on the books. Within a decade of the Civil War, thousands of African Americans found themselves leased out and locked up on prison plantations and in penitentiaries.

Southern Whites, of course, profited from these new laws politically as well as economically. By making so many Blacks into convicts, Whites could deny them the right to vote under Section 2 without undermining their state's census population for the purposes of political representation. And, because of another clause of another Amendment, the 13th, which allowed the continuation of slavery for those who had committed a crime, these same White southerners were able to force thousands of newly imprisoned Black southerners to work for free[9] under the convict lease system.[10]

Fast-forward 100 years when, in the wake of the Civil Rights movement, another War on Crime began that also, almost overnight, led to the mass imprisonment of this nation's

African American citizens. In 1974, as the number of imprisoned Americans was rising precipitously and when states once again began to disfranchise individuals with criminal convictions, the U.S. Supreme Court was asked in a landmark case, *Richardson v. Ramirez*, to rule explicitly on the issue of whether it was constitutional under the 14th Amendment to disfranchise those serving, or who have served, time in prison. The court did the same thing that many southern states did after the Civil War—it interpreted Section A of the 14th amendment very, very differently than it was intended to be interpreted. It, too, decided that disenfranchisement would be permitted when a citizen was convicted of *any* crime, without regard to whether such crimes might be thought of as ideologically analogous to rebellion or were more likely to affect African Americans than others.

Notably, Justice Thurgood Marshall dissented vigorously in this case. The purpose of Section 2, he argued, was clearly to enfranchise, not disenfranchise, former slaves and their descendants. Marshall's fellow members of the bench, though, felt that their decision would not have any discriminatory effect because the nation already had the Voting Rights Act of 1965 to handle this issue.

And yet, the negative impact of *Richardson v. Ramirez* on African American voting was vast and immediate. By the year 2000, 1.8 million African Americans had been barred from the polls because so many felon disfranchisement laws had been passed in states across the country after 1974. Not only were their votes not counted in that year's hotly contested presidential election, but by the next presidential election a full ten states, according to The Sentencing Project, had "African American disenfranchisement rates above 15 percent,"[11] which clearly affected the outcome of that contest as well.

By 2006, 48 out of 50 states had passed disfranchisement laws and, with more than 47 million Americans (one-quarter of the adult population) having criminal records by that year, the nation's political process had been fundamentally altered. By 2011, 23.3 percent of African Americans in Florida, 18.3 percent of the Black population of Wyoming, and 20.4 percent of African Americans in Virginia were barred from the ballot.

According to sociologists Jeff Manza and Christopher Uggen, not only did African Americans pay a high price for the disfranchisement policies that accompanied the nation's War on Crime, but so did liberal voters in general. According to their research,[12] such policies "affected the outcome of seven U.S. Senate races from 1970 to 1998. . .[and] in each case the Democratic

8   Blackmon, Douglas A. 2008. *Slavery by Another Name: The Re-Enslavement of Black People in America from the Civil War to World War II*. Doubleday. http://www.slaverybyanothername.com/.

9   Curtin, Mary Ellen. 2000. *Black Prisoners and Their World, 1865–1900*. University of Virginia Press.

10 Lichtenstein, Alex. 1996. *Twice the Work of Free Labor: The Political Economy of Convict Labor in the New South*.

11 FairPlan2020. 2008. "Felon Disenfranchisement by State." http://www.fairvote2020.org/2008/03/felon-disenfranchisement-by-state.html.

12 Manza, Jeff, Christopher Uggen. 2006. *Locked Out: Felon Disenfranchisement and American Democracy*. Oxford University Press.

candidate would have won rather than the Republican victor" and these outcomes likely "prevented Democratic control of the Senate from 1986 to 2000" as well.

Distorting our democracy

Disfranchising thousands of voters is only part of the story of how mass incarceration has distorted American democracy. Today, just as it did more than a hundred years earlier, the way the Census calculates resident population also plays a subtle but significant role. As ex-Confederates knew well, prisoners would be counted as residents of a given county, even if they could not themselves vote: High numbers of prisoners could easily translate to greater political power for those who put them behind bars.

With the advent of mass incarceration, and as the number of people imprisoned not only rose dramatically, but also began moving urbanites of color into overwhelmingly White rural counties that housed prisons, the political process was again distorted. In short, thanks to this process that we now call "prison-gerrymandering," overwhelmingly White and Republican areas of the United States that built prisons as the War on Crime escalated got more political power, whereas areas of country where policing was particularly concentrated and aggressive, areas in which levels of incarceration were, as a result, staggering, lost political power.

Consider research by the Prison Policy Initiative[13] showing how voters across the country gain political power from housing a penal facility. In Powhatan County, Virginia[14] 41 percent of the 5th Board of Supervisors District that was drawn after the 2000 Census were actually people in prison and in both the First and Third Supervisory Districts of Nottoway County, approximately one-quarter of their population comes from large prisons within the county. In the case of Southampton County, such prison-based gerrymandering means that votes of those citizens who live there are worth almost more than twice as much as votes cast in other districts that have the required number of actual residents.

In Michigan[15] as well, mass incarceration has meant distorted democracy. A full four state senate districts drawn after the 2000 Census (17, 19, 33 and 37), and a full five house districts (65, 70, 92, 107 and 110) meet federal minimum population requirements only because they claim prisoners as constituents.

Similarly in Pennsylvania,[16] no fewer than eight state legislative districts would comply with the federal "one person, one vote" civil rights standard if nonvoting state and federal prisoners in those districts were not counted as district residents.

Why we should care

As Americans go to the polls . . . to vote on criminal justice issues that directly affect our lives—ranging from proposals to decriminalize marijuana, to roll back three strikes laws, to fund more prison construction—the massive carceral state that we are trying to shape at the ballot box has already distorted our democracy. Americans' power to even rethink, let alone undo, the policies and practices that have led to mass incarceration via the franchise has been severely compromised—in no small part due to the fact that the parties that benefitted the most from the rise of this enormous carceral state are now empowered, seemingly in perpetuity, by its sheer size and scope.

There are, of course, other ways to dismantle the carceral state. Indeed, history shows us that we ended the brutal convict leasing system of the Post–Civil War era not by going to the polls but by grassroots and legal activism. Nevertheless, we should all be concerned about the ways mass incarceration has eroded our democracy. Even if we don't care about the record rate of imprisonment in this country—despite its myriad ugly consequences, its unsustainable cost, and its particularly devastating fallout on communities of color—when the principle of "one person, one vote" no longer has real meaning in a society, and when political power is no longer attained via its people but rather through a manipulation of their laws, we must all question the future of our nation.

[*Editor's note*: In 2018 voters in Florida approved a constitutional amendment restoring the right to vote to individuals who had been convicted of a felony, following the completion of serving their sentence. In the same year on the federal level, Congress passed The FIRST STEP Act, reducing the severity of the "three strikes" rule (for three or more convictions) from a life sentence to 25 years in prison, shortening mandatory minimum sentences for nonviolent drug offenses, and allowing judges more discretion when sentencing nonviolent drug offenders. This law is aimed at reducing mass incarceration.[17]

13 Prison Policy Initiative. http://www.prisonpolicy.org/.
14 Prison Policy Initiative. 2010. "Fixing Prison-Based Gerrymandering after the 201 Census: Virginia." http://www.prisonersofthecensus.org/50states/VA.html.
15 Prison Policy Initiative. 2010. "Fixing Prison-Based Gerrymandering after the 201 Census: Michigan." http://www.prisonersofthecensus.org/50states/MI.html.
16 Prison Policy Initiative. 2010. "Fixing Prison-Based Gerrymandering after the 201 Census: Pennsylvania." http://www.prisonersofthecensus.org/50states/PA.html.
17 Sullivan, Dan. 2018. "Text - S.756 - 115th Congress (2017-2018): First Step Act of 2018." Retrieved January 30, 2019 (https://www.congress.gov/bill/115th-congress/senate-bill/756/text).

RORY KRAMER, BRIANNA REMSTER, AND CAMILLE Z. CHARLES

57. BLACK LIVES AND POLICE TACTICS MATTER

Kramer, Remster, and Charles use data to test the arguments of the Black Lives Matter movement and the counterclaims of All Lives Matter/Blue Lives Matter responses, examining whether or not Black people are more likely to experience violence at the hands of police. After discussing challenges with existing datasets that can be used to test these arguments, they analyze data on pedestrian stops conducted by New York City police officers. The authors document extensive disparities in police violence by race, even when controlling for other possible explanatory variables, and then test whether policy and training affected these disparities.

Do police provide a public good or do they perpetuate racial inequality? Like most institutions, they do both. Nonetheless, thanks to the tragic deaths of Michael Brown, Eric Garner, Rekia Boyd, Tamir Rice, and hundreds of others, this blunt question remains at the heart of political debate. Social movements like Black Lives Matter (BLM) and Say Her Name, focused on civilian deaths at the hands of . . . [police], have changed the national discourse around what . . . [police officers] should be doing—and how they should do it.

Of course, social movements inspire responses. Two slogans in particular are indicative of negative reactions to BLM: "All Lives Matter" and "Blue Lives Matter." The first assumes that BLM suggests that Black lives matter more than others, while the latter asserts that critiques of the police, such as those lodged by BLM, have created a backlash—sometimes called the "Ferguson effect" in reference to Mike Brown's death in Missouri—that feeds mistrust and hampers policing, incites violence against police officers, and makes everyone less safe. If the core divide between Black Lives Matter and All/Blue Lives Matter is whether Black people are more likely to experience violence at the hands of police than other Americans, then we need to know the answer.

As sociologists of race and crime, we were surprised to discover that there have been few systematic analyses of disparities in police use of force. Among those, none examines the specific intersectional claims made by activists on both "sides" of the issue. One big reason is a lack of good data—government data and crowd-sourced data like that produced by the newspaper *The Guardian's* project, "The Counted,"[1] consider only deaths or shootings at the hands of the police. Without a comparison group (such as nonfatal police encounters) and without adjusting for competing explanations for variations in victimization, it is hard to draw any meaningful conclusions. Fortunately, there is an alternative data source: the New York Police Department (NYPD) records all investigatory civilian stops, regardless of whether or not they involve the use of force. We harness these citywide data to investigate whether police use more force against Black individuals (particularly Black youth) than White and whether and how gender factors into this equation.

STUDYING POLICE ENCOUNTERS

Despite sustained outrage over police use of force on Black bodies, research has lagged. For instance, just because "The Counted" finds that Black people were more likely than Whites to be killed by police in 2016, it does not necessarily mean that police are racially biased. Perhaps the most common justification police offer for the overrepresentation of Black victims in use-of-force incidents is that it follows from racial disparities in crime rates. In this scenario, if police use of force is random across civilian interactions, but Blacks commit more crime, any racial disparities in shootings could very well be the result of Blacks' greater contact with police. It's a simple, if stereotypical and damaging, narrative, and it shows why it is imperative that any estimates of disparities in police violence adjust for crime rates by race.

Further, in each of the most infamous recent deaths in connection with law enforcement, there have been other aspects of the interaction that proponents of All Lives Matter or Blue Lives Matter wield as their explanations for why the situation ended in violence. In Missouri, Officer Darren Wilson described Michael Brown as being so physically large that his body alone was construed as a deadly weapon; New York City's Eric Garner was accused of being noncompliant as Officer Daniel Panteleo attempted to handcuff Garner; thus Panteleo had to use what would become a fatal chokehold; and Freddie Gray was stopped, beaten, and arrested in a high-crime, high-poverty, and predominantly Black neighborhood—just the kind of neighborhood the Blue Lives Matter folks insist are particularly dangerous to police.

Importantly, any explanation is post hoc; it may be true, it may be false. After all, North Charleston police officer Michael Slager insisted that Walter Scott had been threatening his life, but video evidence shows Scott being shot while running away. If even after adjusting for all of these potential explanations, including any civilian behavior that inspired the stop, where and when the stop occurred, local crime rates, and neighborhood poverty and racial demographics, we still find evidence of disparities in police violence, then BLM's critiques of over-policing and overuse of force against Black Americans would gain powerful empirical support.

We are not the first to use police records to study BLM critiques, but data limitations prevent most from accounting for more than one or two competing explanations. As an exception, economist Roland Fryer made quite a media splash when he found no evidence of racial bias in police shootings (though he did find evidence of bias in lesser forms of police violence). But in his analyses, Fryer compared police shootings to police encounters in which the officer could have been justified in shooting but did not (such as when a civilian is resisting arrest).

Sociologists know, however, that such arrests are themselves racialized: officers are more likely to perceive people of color as aggressive or noncompliant compared with Whites and, as such, are more likely to arrest them on such a charge. In short, Fryer obscured racial bias in shootings by using a biased comparison group in that part of his project. The question remains: are there racial disparities in police use of force, even after we consider justifications?

DATA STRIKES BACK

As part of a 1999 settlement agreement in *Daniels et al. v. City of New York*, New York City agreed to make public detailed data on all civilian stops executed by NYPD officers under its highly contested stop-and-frisk policy. These reports, based on officers' own reports, are the best available data for studying racial disparities in policing. In fact, their release contributed to a federal judge's 2013 ruling that New York City's stop-and-frisk policy was racially discriminatory. Thereafter, the NYPD dramatically reduced the number of its civilian stops and revised training and policies toward more civil, less confrontational community interactions. The changes mean we can now see whether police tactics and training matter in reducing disparities in police violence. Or, to be a bit more wonky, can organizational change reduce victimization inequalities in police officers' use of force?

With data from 3.3 million NYPD investigative pedestrian stops conducted between 2007 and 2014, supplemented by U.S. Census and crime data provided by the New York City Division of Criminal Justice Services, we directly tested whether policy and training changes affected associations between race, stops, and violence. In addition, BLM makes intersectional claims that Black children (like 12-year-old Tamir Rice who was shot to death by Cleveland police) are more likely to experience police force than are White children and that Black women (like Korryn Gaines, a Maryland mother shot by police after earlier violent interactions) are more likely than White women to endure the experience. Since deaths at the hands of police are rare (in 2013, NYPD shot and killed a total of eight people), we examined incidents in which police pointed a firearm at a civilian, which occurred in less than one percent of all stops (police are trained to draw their guns only when prepared to use lethal force). To broaden our lens as much as possible, we then considered any use of force by police, ranging from "hands on suspect" to "pointing firearm at suspect." We then adjusted our estimates for every justification for police use of force put forward to date.

TARGETING YOUNG BLACK BODIES

We find gaping inequalities in police violence. Black people are more likely than Whites to be subject to police violence—regardless of whether they are doing anything illegal, the time of day, their height, their age, their gender, their behavior during the stop, police justification for the stop, neighborhood socioeconomic and racial characteristics, the precinct's stop rate, or local arrest rates broken down by race. In fact, the majority of stops in which police used force against Black individuals did not lead to arrest or the discovery of any contraband.

Even as scholars well versed in racial disparities in criminal justice contacts, we were surprised by the sheer number of young Black children in our data. On average, more than seven Black children aged 10–13 were stopped by police in New York City each day between 2007 and 2014 (approximately 20,000 stops). More Black teens experienced police violence during a stop than did Whites of all ages combined. When we add controls, including teens' behavior during police stops, when and where they were stopped, and whether or not they were arrested, the racial disparity in police violence persisted. We have long known that young Blacks are more likely to be stopped, but our results show that this disparity extends to police

violence. . . . Overall, and at any age, Black individuals stopped by police are more likely to experience force (including an officer drawing and/or pointing a gun). The racial gap is largest among youth: stops of Black youth are more likely than those of White youth to include force, though the effect shrinks, albeit only slightly, with age. Although we don't know for sure why the likelihood of experiencing police violence declines with age, it may be that Black men have simply had more time to learn how to navigate police encounters and decrease the likelihood of enduring police violence. Importantly, these results hold even after adjusting for police justifications and a host of variables in stops.

. . . Consistent with work by social psychologists, such as Philip Goff, who has shown that Black youth are perceived as older and more threatening than White youth of the same physical size and age, we find bias. . . . Black youth are 41 percent more likely to be victims of any police use of force than comparable White youth. Sadly, the patterns are similar when we predict stops in which officers pull their guns and are prepared to shoot—Black youth are more than 50 percent more likely than White youth in similar stops to find themselves staring down the barrel of a gun. So Tamir Rice and Tyre King, aged 12 and 13, are not tragic outliers, but important examples of a systematic pattern of racial inequality in police violence.

We also tested the Say Her Name activists' critique that Black women are more likely than White women to experience police violence and that such violence is especially unlikely to be covered in debates about police violence. We have shown predicted probabilities for girls ages 10–17, but the findings hold across all age groups in our sample. Although women overall experience fewer stops than men, Black women are more likely to experience police use of force—including having a gun drawn on them—during a stop than White women, even after accounting for alternative explanations. And Black girls' predicted probability is about the same as White boys' (15 to 14 percent, respectively). Within race, gender is not associated with a difference in police drawing guns during a stop (see above); in other words, it's about as likely that a Black woman or a Black man will have a gun drawn on them, and the same holds for Whites. Taken together, we find that gender influences whether force is used with adults, but it does not affect whether police draw and/or aim their guns at children.

POLICE TACTICS MATTER

The history of policing is intimately linked to the history of racial subjugation. Even though today's police officers and those in leadership roles are more diverse than they were even a few decades ago, police—and citizens—have not escaped the institution's legacy of racially disparate violence. Not only do police stop people at different rates according to their race, age, and gender, but they also behave differently during otherwise similar interactions.

There is scant evidence to support stop-and-frisk as a crime-fighting strategy in New York City. As Mayor Bill De Blasio tweeted, "We've reduced stop-and-frisk by 97 percent in New York City and crime is down significantly. Not everyone knows that." Moreover, we find that when the NYPD reduced the use of stop-and-frisk and instituted changes in officer training in late 2013—due in part to the policy being ruled unconstitutional—police used force less frequently in all stops. Still, the racial disparity in who is subjected to force did not shrink. . . . The racial disparity in police violence of any type grew after the NYPD's 2013 reform. This is because use of force declined more dramatically for Whites than Blacks, widening the violence gap even as violence, overall, decreased in police interactions. In better news, there are hundreds of thousands fewer stops made by New York City cops, the rate of force has declined for both Black and White civilians, and, perhaps most importantly, the 2013 reforms shrank racial inequities in police gun violence. But that race is no longer a significant predictor of whether a NYPD officer will draw a firearm in a citizen interaction owes to a change in how and how often NYPD officers stop civilians, rather than to any "disappearance" of racial inequality in policing and use of force.

Given these findings, there is no good reason for any police department to pursue stop-and-frisk. There is growing evidence that it sours public perceptions of police, especially in communities of color, which have been treated violently by powerful institutions since the very birth of the country.

WHAT NOW?

Conversations need to shift from *whether* there are racial disparities in policing to what can be done to reduce or eliminate racial disparities in policing. Our findings suggest that policy changes such as New York City's discontinuation of stop-and-frisk practices and the revision of police training courses are promising avenues, at least with regard to disparities in gun use and in reducing the sheer quantity of force used. Because police force is not restricted to investigatory pedestrian stops, police training and policy also deserve a much broader reconceptualization; currently, officer training modules prioritize weapons training over de-escalation techniques. However, law enforcement agencies like those in Sanford, Florida (where Trayvon Martin was killed) are beginning to incorporate implicit bias training programs (to help counter cops' sense of Black civilians, particularly young, Black males, as threatening), while others have adapted their training and policies to emphasize de-escalation tactics. These steps are vital in reducing force as a primary tool of policing. Holding police departments and individual officers accountable for disparities in civilian interactions is also critical in improving police–civilian relations. After all, when people don't trust the police, they don't call the police; communities and crime victims suffer when they are unable to use law enforcement to enforce the laws meant to protect them.

Although many good proposals have been put forward with an eye toward reducing inequalities in police violence, at a basic level, we need better data to understand the problem we want to solve. The FBI, the agency tasked with overseeing systematic data collection, began its work with federal agencies in 2017, but we do not yet know when state and local departments will be phased in, which local agencies will agree to share their data (the FBI has said all data collection will be voluntary), nor even the level of detail the FBI will require on each incident. Further, the FBI has announced that information will only be gathered on officer-involved deaths or instances involving "serious bodily injury." So rather than understanding inequalities, this data collection effort is geared toward obtaining accurate incident counts. As our analysis demonstrates, for public oversight to be effective and to reduce racial inequality, data must consider all police contacts. Unfortunately, then Attorney General Jeff Sessions [President Trump's first attorney general, who resigned in late 2018] disbanded the National Commission on Forensic Science and questioned the value of consent decrees focused on fixing systemic racial biases in local police forces. Therefore, we are not optimistic about the role of the federal government in obtaining, releasing, and responding to data on racial disparities in police use of force in the near future. . . .

NOTE

1. Anon. n.d. "The Counted: People Killed by Police in the U.S." *Theguardian.com*. Retrieved February 4, 2019, from https://www.theguardian.com/us-news/ng-interactive/2015/jun/01/the-counted-police-killings-us-database.

THE TRAGIC FICTION OF IMMIGRANT THREAT

WATOII RABII

Despite being a nation of immigrants, Americans have a long history of holding anti-immigrant stances, with policies to match these sentiments. While our anti-immigration stances have remained constant, the focus of our anti-immigrant legislation, and the groups that they target, have changed over time. In the late nineteenth and early twentieth centuries, White Anglo-Saxon Protestants (WASPs) perceived immigrants from southern, central, and eastern European countries as threats (Keating & Fischer-Baum 2018). Asian immigrants were perceived as threats dating from as early as the mid-nineteenth century through the mid-twentieth century (Hing 1993; Bolash-Goza 2015). During the twentieth century and more recently, White citizens have also perceived immigrants from Mexico and other Latin American countries and predominantly Muslim countries as threats (Chavez 2008, Keating & Fischer-Baum 2018). While some researchers attribute this perception to fear of cultural change on the part of native-born Americans (called the racial threat hypothesis), more often we hear about the perceived threats of job competition[1] and criminality, despite the fact that research has demonstrated that these fears are unfounded. While job concerns have not faded into the background, the persistent and deeply damaging myth that immigrants have criminal tendencies and that high concentrations of immigrants increase crime rates in neighborhoods and cities has been reinvigorated.

Donald Trump's comments about immigrants during his campaign and presidency rely upon and bolster the myth of immigrant criminality. During his address announcing his 2016 presidential campaign, Trump stated that, "When Mexico sends its people, they're not sending their best. . . . They're sending people that have lots of problems, and they're bringing those problems with [sic] us. They're bringing drugs. They're bringing crime. They're rapists. And some, I assume, are good people" (Reilly, 2016). These were remarks that he has reiterated throughout his presidency, using often violent and dehumanizing rhetoric (Scott, 2019). Despite the longevity and prevalence of the belief in immigrant criminality, it continues to lack empirical support (Sampson 2008; Nielsen & Martinez 2011; Martinez and Stowell 2012; Bersani 2014). Sociologists and criminologists have generally found that immigrants do not contribute to increasing crime rates in the United States. Some scholars have even found that crime rates decrease as immigrant concentration increases (Lee, Martinez, & Rosenfield 2001; Stumpf 2006; Desmond & Kubrin 2009; Akins, Rumbaut, Stansfield 2009; Ousey & Kubrin 2014). Recently, Adelman et al. (2017) contributed to this line of research by demonstrating, once again, that the notion of the criminal immigrant is a myth.

In their study, Adelman et al. (2017) analyzed the relationship between immigration and crime rates in American metropolitan areas between 1970 and 2010. Specifically, the authors examined the impact of the size of an immigrant population on crime rates in 200 metropolitan areas in the United States. Although there are other explanations for the decreases in crime experienced by these areas in the last thirty years, Adelman et al. (2017) show that, on average, as immigration increases in metropolitan areas, rates of violent and property crime actually

---

1 The myth that immigrants threaten the economy and American workers' jobs is a powerful one. However, research indicates that immigration does not reduce employment rates for native-born workers, that even with improved benefits and higher wages, employers have little to no success attracting native-born employees to work in some of the fields in which immigrants are concentrated (Costa, Cooper, and Shierholz 2014).

Original to *Focus on Social Problems: A Contemporary Reader*.

decrease. The authors conclude, "It appears, then, that for the latter part of the 20th century and early part of the 21st, the presence of immigrants consistently helped to decrease violent and property crime in U.S. metropolitan areas" (2017:69). The implications of these findings are at odds with the idea that immigrants, generally, are criminals. As a whole, this study supports the larger literature about the relationship between immigration and crime.

Other scholars have examined the relationship between immigration and crime and reached similar conclusions. For example, MacDonald, Hipp, and Gill (2013) combined crime data from the Los Angeles Police Department and U.S. Census data to investigate the impact of the foreign-born population on crime. They found that neighborhoods with large immigrant populations experienced reductions in crime. Similarly, Akins, Rumbaut, and Stansfield (2009) showed that there was no relationship between immigration and homicide at the community level. Nielsen and Martinez (2011) demonstrated that in Miami, immigrants were less likely to be arrested for robbery and aggravated assault than the native-born population. And using data from the National Neighborhood Crime Study, Gostjev (2018) found that neighborhoods that have greater ethnic diversity and a high immigrant concentration have lower violent crime rates.

Although there have always been individual immigrants who have committed crimes, the relationship at a macro level does not support the myth that immigrants are criminals. The perpetuation of this myth is based on racism, nativism, and xenophobia rather than empirical data. A common way these false beliefs are perpetuated is through the media (Jhally & Lewis 1992; Asultany 2008; Harris-Perry 2011; Kopacz & Lawton 2011; Golash-Boza 2015). For decades, print and visual media have portrayed immigrants as contributing to and perpetuating social problems (Chavez 2008; Massey & Sanchez 2010; Esses, Medianu, & Lawson 2013; Menjívar 2016). These platforms have stoked and exacerbated fears that immigrants would change the cultural landscape, commit crimes, and steal jobs. These persistent notions, combined with the power of modern media and politicians' rhetoric, can contribute to moral panics, where fears of exaggerated threats to a society are stoked (Cohen 1972; Foner 2014; Golash-Boza 2015; Schramm & Tibbetts 2014). Some researchers have indicated that native-born populations' fear of immigrants has less to do with economic and criminal concerns, and more to do with fear of cultural change (Norris 2018).[2]

The consequences of these moral panics have been devastating for immigrants (Golash-Boza 2015; Healy & O'Brien 2014; Lee 2002; Lindsay 1998; Spiro 2009). Deportation, Jim Crow laws, repatriation, mass incarceration, internment, sterilization, exclusionary immigration policies, and scapegoating are examples of how native-born populations have responded to perceptions of cultural, criminal, and occupational threat (Franklin & Moss 2000; Hing 1993; Ngai 2004; Pfeiffer 2004).

Another disturbing consequence for immigrants is the recent increase in harassment, profiling, and hate crimes. In the post-September 11 and post-2016 election world, this continues to be especially pronounced for Latino and Muslim immigrants (Alsultany 2012; Chavez 2008; Love 2017). Rates of hate crimes have increased every year since 2014, the year with the lowest-ever reported rates of hate crimes (Levin, Nolan, & Reitzel 2018). In the state of California alone, anti-Hispanic hate crimes have more than doubled since 2016 (Hinojosa 2018). Hate crimes targeting Muslims doubled between the years of 2014 and 2016 (Cohen 2017). Hate crimes can include violent attacks, damage to property (e.g., graffiti), or verbal assaults, such as when a Mexican man was attacked and told to "Go back to your country" (Paul & Bever 2018) and Muslim college students at a McDonald's were attacked by a man who said, "You don't deserve American food" (Flynn 2018). The myth of the criminal immigrant has led to moral panics, discriminatory policies, and racial terrorism over the course of the nation's history, despite the fact that it is just that: a myth.

REFERENCES

Adelman, Robert M., Lesley Williams Reid, Gail Markle, Saskia Weiss, and Charles Jaret. 2017. "Urban Crime Rates and the Changing Face of Immigration: Evidence across Four Decades." *Journal of Ethnicity in Criminal Justice* 15(1):52–77.

Akins, Scott, Rumbaut, Rubén G., and Richard Stansfield. 2009. "Immigration, Economic Disadvantage, and Homicide: A Community-Level Analysis of Austin, Texas." *Homicide Studies* 13(3):307–14.

Alsultany, Evelyn. "The prime time plight of the Arab Muslim American after 9/11." *Race and Arab Americans Before and After* 9.11 (2008): 204-228.

Alsultany, Evelyn. 2012. *Arabs and Muslims in the Media: Race and Representation after 9/11.* New York: New York University Press.

Bersani, Bianca E. 2014. "An Examination of First and Second Generation Immigrant Offending Trajectories." *Justice Quarterly* 31(2): 315-343.

Chavez, Leo. 2008. *The Latino Threat: Constructing Immigrants, Citizens, and the Nation.* Stanford, CA: Stanford University Press.

---

2   These fears were stoked, for example, during the 2016 presidential campaign when a Latino representative from Latinos for Trump stated during a televised interview on MSNBC, "My culture is a very dominant culture, and it's imposing and it's causing problems. If you don't do something about it, you're going to have taco trucks on every corner" (Chokshi 2016). President Trump has spoken generally about immigration's impact on the dominant culture (in the context of Europe) as problematic, arguing that it is "changing the culture" and "a very negative thing. . . ." (Hinojosa 2018).

Chokshi, Niraj. 2016. "'Taco Trucks on Every Corner': Trump Supporter's Anti-Immigration Warning." *The New York Times*, September 2. Retrieved on September 29, 2018, from https://www.nytimes.com/2016/09/03/us/politics/taco-trucks-on-every-corner-trump-supporters-anti-immigration-warning.html.

Cohen, Richard. 2017. "Hate Crimes Rise for Second Straight Year; Anti-Muslim Violence Soars and President Trump's Xenophobic Rhetoric." Southern Poverty Law Center, November 13. Retrieved on September 29, 2018, from https://www.splcenter.org/news/2017/11/13/hate-crimes-rise-second-straight-year-anti-muslim-violence-soars-amid-president-trumps.

Cohen, Stanley. 1972. *Folk Devils and Moral Panics: The Creation of the Mods and Rockers*. London: MacGibbon and Kee.

Costa, Daniel, David Cooper, and Heidi Shierholz. 2014. "Facts about Immigration and the U.S. Economy." *Economic Policy Institute*, August 12. Retrieved from https://www.epi.org/publication/immigration-facts/.

Desmond, Scott A., and Charis E. Kubrin. 2009. "The power of place: Immigrant communities and adolescent violence." *The Sociological Quarterly* 50(4): 581607.

Esses, Victoria. M., Stelian Medianu, and Andrea S. Lawson. 2013. "Uncertainty, Threat, and the Role of the Media in Promoting the Dehumanization of Immigrants and Refugees." *Journal of Social Issues*, 69(3): 518–36.

Flynn, Meagan. 2018. "'You Don't Deserve American Food!': Muslim Students Attacked at McDonald's, Police Say." *The Washington Post*, May 25. Retrieved September 6, 2018, from https://www.washingtonpost.com/news/morning-mix/wp/2018/05/25/you-dont-deserve-american-food-man-attacked-muslims-at-mcdonalds-police-say/?utm_term=.c4cff18e0b47.

Foner, Eric. 2014. *Give Me Liberty. An American History*. New York: W. W. Norton.

Franklin, John H., and Alfred A. Moss. 2000. *From Slavery to Freedom: A History of African Americans*. Boston: McGraw-Hill.

Golash-Boza, Tanya Maria. 2015. *Race and Racisms: A Critical Approach*. New York: Oxford University Press.

Gostjev, Feodor. 2018. "United We Stand? The Role of Ethnic Heterogeneity in the Immigration and Violent Crime Relationship at the Neighborhood Level. *Sociology of Race and Ethnicity* 3(3):398–416.

Healy, Joseph, and Eileen O'Brien. 2014. *Race, Ethnicity, Gender, and Class: The Sociology of Group Conflict and Change*. New York: Sage.

Hing, Bill O. 1993. *Making and Remaking Asian America through Immigration Policy, 1850–1990*. Stanford, CA: Stanford University Press.

Hinojosa, Maria. 2018. "Hate Crimes against Latinos Increase in California." *National Public Radio*

July 15. Retrieved on September 29, 2018, from https://www.npr.org/2018/07/15/629212976/hate-crimes-against-latinos-increase-in-california.

Jhally, Sut, and Justin M. Lewis. 1992. *Enlightened Racism: The Cosby Show, Audiences, and the Myth of the American Dream*. Boulder, CO: Avalon Publishing.

Keating, Dan, and Reuben Fischer-Baum. 2018. "How U.S. Immigration Has Changed." *The Washington Post*, January 12. Retrieved on September 29, 2018, from https://www.washingtonpost.com/graphics/2018/national/immigration-waves/?utm_term=.a790b2ff570b.

Kopacz, Maria, and Bessie Lee Lawton. 2011. "The YouTube Indian: Portrayals of Native Americans on a Viral Video Site." *New Media and Society* 12(2):330–49.

Lee, Erika. 2002. "The Chinese Exclusion Example: Race, Immigration, and American Gatekeeping, 1882–1924." *Journal of American Ethnic History* 21(3):36–62.

Lee, Matthew T., Ramiro Martinez, and Richard Rosenfeld. 2001. "Does immigration increase homicide? Negative evidence from three border cities." *The Sociological Quarterly* 42(4): 559-580.

Levin, Brian, James J. Nolan, and John David Reitzel. 2018. "New Data Shows US Hate Crimes Continued to Rise in 2017." *The Conversation*, June 26. Retrieved on September 29, 2018, from https://theconversation.com/new-data-shows-us-hate-crimes-continued-to-rise-in-2017-97989.

Lindsay, Matthew. 1998. "Reproducing a Fit Citizenry: Dependency, Eugenics, and the Law of Marriage in the United States, 1869–1920." *Law and Social Inquiry* 23(3):541–85.

Love, Erik. 2017. *Islamophobia and Racism in America*. New York: New York University Press.

MacDonald, John M., John R. Hipp, and Charlotte Gill. 2013. "The Effects of Immigrant Concentration Changes in Neighborhood Crime Rates." *Journal of Quantitative Criminology* 29(2): 191–215.

Martinez Jr., Ramiro and Jacob I. Stowell. 2012. "Extending Immigration and Crime Studies: National Implications and Local Settings." *The Annals of the American Academy of Political and Social Science*, 641(1): 174-191.

Massey, Douglas, and Magalay Sanchez. 2010. *Brokered Boundaries: Creating Immigrant Identity in Anti-Immigrant Times*. New York: Russell Sage Foundation.

Menjívar, Cecilia. 2016. "Immigrant Criminalization in Law and the Media: Effects on Latino Immigrant Workers' Identities in Arizona." *American Behavioral Scientist*, 60(5–6): 597–616.

Ngai, Mae. 2004. *Impossible Subjects: Illegal Aliens and the Making of Modern America*. Princeton, NJ: Princeton University Press.

Nielsen, Amie L., and Ramiro Martinez, Jr. 2011. "Nationality, Immigrant Groups, and Arrest: Examining the Diversity of Arrestees for Urban Violent Crime." *Journal of Contemporary Criminal Justice*, 27(3):342–60.

Norris, Michele. 2018. "As America Changes, Some Anxious Whites Feel Left Behind." *National Geographic.* Retrieved on September 29, 2018, from https://www.nationalgeographic.com/magazine/2018/04/race-rising-anxiety-white-america.

Ousey, Graham C., and Charis E. Kubrin. 2014. "Immigration and the Changing Nature of Homicide in U.S. Cities, 1980–2010." *Journal of Quantitative Criminology*, 30(3):453–83.

Paul, Deana, and Lindsey Bever. 2018. "Woman Arrested in Assault of 91-year-old Mexican Man Who Was Told to 'Go Back to Your Country.'" *The Washington Post*, July 11. Retrieved September 6, 2018, from https://www.washingtonpost.com/news/post-nation/wp/2018/07/11/woman-arrested-in-assault-of-91-year-old-mexican-man-who-was-told-to-go-back-to-your-country/?utm_term=.8e810aaa3e7f.

Perry, Melissa V. 2011. *Sister Citizen: Shame, Stereotypes, and Black Women in America.* New Haven, CT: Yale University Press.

Pfeiffer, Michael J. 2004. *Rough Justice: Lynching and American Society, 1874–1947.* Urbana: University of Illinois.

Reilly, Katie. 2016. "Here Are All the Times Donald Trump Insulted Mexico." *Time Magazine*, August 31. Retrieved from https://time.com/4473972/donald-trumpmexico-meeting-insult/.

Sampson, Robert J. 2008. "Rethinking Crime and Immigration." *Contexts* 7(1): 2833.

Schramm, Pamela, and Stephen J. Tibbetts. 2014. *Introduction Criminology: Why Do They Do It?* Thousand Oaks, CA: Sage.

Scott, Eugene. 2019. "Trump's Most Insulting—and Violent—Language is Often Reserved for Immigrants." *The Washington Post* October 2. Retrieved from https://www.washingtonpost.com/politics/2019/10/02/trumps-most-insulting-violent-language-is-often-reserved-immigrants/.

Spiro, Johnathon P. 2009. *Defending the Master Race: Conservation, Eugenics, and the Legacy of Madison Grant.* Burlington, VT: University of Vermont Press.

Stumpf, Juliet. 2006. "The Immigration Crisis: Immigrants, Crime, and Sovereign Power." *American University Law Review*, 56(2): 367–420.

CHAPTER 12

SOCIAL PROBLEMS RELATED TO THE ECONOMY AND WORK

With the unemployment rate at a low four percent,[1] most Americans seeking jobs will find one. But what is the quality of the working conditions, benefits, and wages of the available jobs? How stable are they? And do all of us have the same access to high-quality positions? This chapter focuses on work and economic problems that connect closely to many of the other social problems we have discussed, as one's ability to earn a living wage is essential for success in all other areas of social life. This chapter begins by challenging the assumption that jobs, in and of themselves, are the solution to the incredibly high poverty rates discussed earlier. Matthew Desmond finds that many of the jobs that are available today to poor people eligible to work do not provide a living wage, enough hours, or benefits. Nor do they offer the flexibility many workers, particularly women raising children on their own, need to support themselves or their families or even to pull themselves out of poverty. Thus, while low unemployment rates can signal the health of the economy and the availability of employment opportunities, these rates can mask the decreasing *quality* of available jobs.

When well-paying jobs with excellent benefits are not available, workers increasingly turn to the "gig economy" which offers flexibility (like setting your own hours) but no benefits, protections, or job security. Whether it is driving an Uber or Lyft, delivering food for DoorDash, putting together IKEA furniture for a client through TaskRabbit, or delivering packages, gig workers typically struggle financially. Yet gig work has been increasing and is expected to continue to do so.[2] Alana Semuels, a reporter who accepted a job delivering packages through Amazon "Flex," where workers deliver Amazon packages using their own vehicles, shares some of the pros and cons of the transition to work in the gig economy. The expansion of the gig economy is but one major economic shift currently occurring. Our economy is also globalizing, with production frequently shifting overseas, resulting in the loss of manufacturing jobs in the United States. Despite the focus on job loss caused by

---

1   U.S. Census Bureau, Current Population Survey, 1961 to 2018 Annual Social and Economic Supplements (https://data.bls.gov/timeseries/lns14000000).

2   Muhammed, Abdullahi. 2018. "4 Reasons Why the Gig Economy Will Only Keep Growing in Numbers." *Forbes*. Retrieved March 19, 2019, from https://www.forbes.com/sites/abdullahimuhammed/2018/06/28/4-reasons-why-the-gig-economy-will-only-keep-growing-in-numbers.

globalization, Claire Cain Miller argues that it is automation that is most responsible for the loss of relatively good jobs and that we should expect to lose even more blue-collar jobs, and White-collar jobs as well, as a result of increased automation.

One sector of the economy where some of the lowest paying and toughest jobs are concentrated is in the area of food production. Often, it is the most disempowered workers who cannot find other jobs and must therefore settle for dangerous, degrading, and low-paying work. Michael Grabell offers detailed information about the vulnerability of immigrant workers in poultry production in the United States. Immigrant workers, some of whom are unable to return to dangerous home countries and who may be undocumented, are particularly easy for the industry to exploit. As a report from the Food Chain Workers Alliance and Solidarity Research Collective illustrates, food workers are exploited up and down the food chain, from productive lines to harvest workers to frontline service positions in fast-food restaurants. Given the number of people who work in the food chain, we should note how low wages and poor working conditions have long-term impacts not only on those workers, some of whom are already vulnerable, but also on the nation as a whole.

Even when jobs pay relatively well, varied forms of discrimination serve to keep different groups of people at the bottom rungs of the economic ladder. For example, women in the workforce face unique challenges, one of which is experiencing a wage gap when compared to men (currently, it is around 79 to 81 cents to the dollar[3]). Anastasia Prokos helps explain the gender wage gap by demonstrating how it is partly a result of gender segregation of jobs and occupations, creating a structural form of discrimination against women. While the gender wage gap is persistent, we know that not all women experience it identically. Adia Harvey Wingfield describes how the gender wage gap varies by race, with Black and Latina women earning significantly less than White women. Wingfield notes that race and gender, while both affecting women of color, are not simply additive, but rather combine in an intersectional way to create a unique discriminatory position. She discusses how race and gender act in conjunction with one another and how social change on this front will require recognition of these processes.

Workplace discrimination affects people of color in the United States even when employers may try to fight race-based discrimination by trying to ignore difference. Carmen Nobel describes how employer attempts to be "colorblind" in their hiring and promotion practices may actually backfire and serve to reinforce racial inequities. While many Americans would like to believe that employers and managers don't behave in racially biased or discriminatory ways (and thus believe hiring policies should not be race-conscious), Erin Thomas describes how researchers continue to document clear racial bias in hiring decisions. Researchers mailed fictitious resumes to employers in which levels of education and experience were the same, but the names on the forms were either "Black-" or "White"-sounding, and they were able to capture clear patterns of racial discrimination in hiring. These discriminatory behaviors don't just impact one person looking for a job; because of the importance of the economy and workforce to the functioning of our society, they have much broader consequences for families, communities, and the nation as a whole. It is important to acknowledge that there is much work to be done to make work more equitable and to reward workers fairly for their labor in the changing economy.

---

3 Fontenot, Kayla, Jessica Semega, and Melissa Kollar, U.S. Census Bureau, Current Population Reports, P60-263, Income and Poverty in the United States: 2017, U.S. Government Printing Office, Washington, DC, 2018. (https://www.census.gov/content/dam/Census/library/visualizations/2018/demo/p60-263/figure2.pdf).

ACTIVIST INTERVIEW

AI-JEN POO

Ai-jen Poo is the director of the National Domestic Workers Alliance and co-director of the Caring across Generations campaign.

What is your organization and its mission?

The National Domestic Workers Alliance fights for the rights, recognition, and dignity of over two million nannies, house cleaners, and care workers who support our families, care for our aging loved ones, and ensure that people living with disabilities can live independently.

How did you first become interested in this type of activism? What/who was your inspiration?

My mother has long been an inspiration to me. As an immigrant to the United States, she learned English, worked and went to school, and she raised my sister and me. I remember her dropping me off at daycare, heading to work or school, picking me up, making dinner, cleaning the house, and ironing clothes. She did this every day without taking a break—I don't think that she saw a break as an option. It was assumed that she would be primarily responsible for taking care of the household and her children, in addition to her work outside of the home. As a young person, I became aware that we live in a world that relies upon women's work, yet does little to value, recognize, or

support that work. So I joined a women's organization in high school and never looked back.

As an activist in your organization, currently what are your top goals?

Our first goal is to expand economic opportunity for women at the bottom of the economy, beginning with domestic workers and care workers, many of whom are women of color. For over 75 years, domestic workers have faced exclusion from the most basic workplace protections from minimum wage to freedom from sexual harassment. Domestic workers care for the most precious elements of our lives—our families and our homes—and yet are among the most vulnerable workers in our economy today. Our goal is to transform these jobs from poverty wage jobs in the shadows of our economy into twenty-first century living wage jobs, with real pathways to opportunity and security. We can do that by winning innovative legislation and organizing, while experimenting with private-sector strategies that aggregate our collective power.

Second, we are in the midst of a significant demographic shift in America. The Baby Boom generation is reaching retirement age at a rate of 10,000 people per day, and people are living longer than ever as a result of advances in health care and technology. By the year 2030, more than 20 percent of our population will be over the age of 65, and by the year 2050, 27 million of us will need care or assistance just to meet our basic needs. The need for care is growing, and we have no plan in place to support the care that's needed. Our goal is to create a new approach to caregiving in America that makes care, especially good care at home, more affordable and accessible, and elevates the quality of care jobs.

Our third goal is to seize upon the unprecedented levels of political activism among women, to transform the political power of women of color and low-income women. In states like Georgia, women of color have been in motion at the grassroots level, driving electoral strategy, knocking on doors, winning campaigns, and challenging the status quo. As some of the most reliable progressive voters, we need to invest in Black women and women of color as voters, organizers, and candidates.

What strategies do you use to enact social change?

We believe in organizing, which involves bringing domestic workers and the people who are connected to them together to increase our power, visibility, and ability to achieve our goals. We believe that the experiences of domestic workers should inform the development of public policy and help shape the future of our democracy and economy. To that end, we seek to change policy. We work with employers to promote fair standards in domestic employment relationships, and through the power of storytelling, we seek to change the way domestic workers and the work they do are viewed and valued. We believe that in organizing for basic human dignity, there's no such thing as an unlikely ally, so we actively seek to build partnerships to promote the dignity and value of caregiving and domestic work.

What are the major challenges activists in your field face?

Our workforce is dispersed and isolated in unmarked homes around the country—any home could be a workplace. In the current political climate, many domestic workers are fearful of losing their jobs or being targeted or discriminated against on the basis of their immigration status, so engaging in activism poses a challenge. They are also working long, unpredictable hours with many family and economic responsibilities. In that context, our organizers must be extremely creative under challenging conditions, with few resources and little capacity. The process of making change is often extremely slow—passing legislation takes years, and building political power goes beyond the election cycle. Cultural change can take longer. The way we combat burnout is to support one another as a movement, to ensure that no one feels alone, and provide safe spaces for healing and personal transformation. Our leadership program supports the need for workers and organizers in our movement to step away from the work and reflect upon what they each require to bring the best of who they are to the work and to sustain over time. We create a community of support for personal goal setting and healing of the individuals within our movement. And we set bold, inspiring goals that people want to work toward year after year.

What are major misconceptions the public has about activism in general and your issue specifically?

Many think that domestic work is marginal within our economy and only affects a small group of people. All of us will, at some point in our lives, need care. Home care is one of the fastest growing occupations in the nation because of the tremendous need on the part of all American families for caregiving support. By 2030, care jobs will be among the largest occupations in the entire workforce. And, the conditions that define domestic work—long and unpredictable hours, lack of training or job security, no benefits, isolation— have come to define reality for more and more of the American workforce. As a majority women of color and immigrant workforce, what happens to domestic workers in our economy and democracy impacts all communities they are part of.

We are all connected and in many ways interdependent in this economy. This is a moment to turn toward one another, see the connections between us as a source of strength to make change, find common ground, and address the severe inequality in our economy together because it's unsustainable for everyone. And when we put the workers who have been the least visible and most vulnerable at the center of our solutions, we can ensure that no one will be left behind.

Why should students get involved in your line of activism?

Domestic workers experience the world at the intersection of gender, race, class, and immigration. When we create better policies and systems in our society for domestic workers, we are helping to create a more sustainable, inclusive economy and democracy for everyone. For example, if the caregiving workforce has the ability to care for their families, work, and retire with dignity, we can be sure we have achieved a new level of recognition of the work that goes into family care. By placing domestic workers at the center of our collective vision for the future, we can and must have the kinds of conversations about exclusion that will help us avoid past errors, learning from and leading with the solutions and perspectives of those least visible in our current reality.

What would you consider to be your greatest successes as an activist?

My greatest success is a collective achievement of thousands of women who have together created a national platform for care workers and domestic workers to shape the future of our democracy and economy. Over the last decade, the National Domestic Workers Alliance has harnessed the power of domestic workers to enact innovative policy change, such as our signature Domestic Workers Bill of Rights, in eight states and one city. We brought more than 2 million home care workers under the protection of federal minimum wage and overtime laws, and launched Alia, the first benefits platform for housecleaners. As our movement grows, we place domestic workers at the center of some of the key historical and cultural moments of our time from the fight against family separation at the border to the #MeToo movement. And we are changing dominant cultural narratives across all institutions, including Hollywood, through efforts like the Roma social impact campaign, which utilized the power of an Oscar-winning film to spark national conversations about the right of domestic workers.

Every day, I wake up feeling fortunate to be part of a movement that gives voice and visibility to the courage and power of working women, particularly women of color, who have shaped this country in profound ways, and yet whose leadership is still undervalued and under-recognized in society at large.

If an individual has little money and time, are there other ways they can contribute?

We encourage people to contribute their unique skills and talents toward building the movement in the way that feels appropriate to them. Change can start at home, with initiating a conversation about the kind of caregiving relationships you want in your home, and developing a plan with your loved ones for your future caregiving needs. We encourage people to get involved through joining our online community at www.domesticworkers.org or www.caringacross.org, and we encourage people to vote their values. We need people to engage in the civic process at every level, and to help us change the culture and politics of our country to reflect the values of opportunity, equity, dignity, and interdependence.

What ways can students enact social change in their daily lives?

Students should get out and experience campaigns and movements for social change at every opportunity—from joining a rally, naming injustice and inequity around them, studying past movements for change, seeking out mentors in the community that have been engaged in social change work, joining a student organization or a community organization, or interning at a social justice organization in the summertime. Campaigns for change are containers for tremendous learning and transformation; it's always a good time to get out there and get proactive about creating the world in which we want to live.

MATTHEW DESMOND

58. AMERICANS WANT TO BELIEVE JOBS ARE THE SOLUTION TO POVERTY. THEY'RE NOT.

Historic and current governmental policies and programs assume that work will solve the social problem of poverty. Desmond describes how the current economic structure is replete with low-wage, low-mobility, unstable jobs with poor benefits. Along with work requirements to receive government assistance, the lack of jobs adequate to support a family results in a large group of Americans who are part of the "working poor." Desmond concludes that despite the fact that poor people have a desire to work, simply moving them into the available jobs in our current labor market will not solve our poverty problem.

Vanessa Solivan and her three children fled their last place in June 2015, after a young man was shot and killed around the corner. They found a floor to sleep on in Vanessa's parents' home on North Clinton Avenue in East Trenton. It wasn't a safer neighborhood, but it was a known one. Vanessa took only what she could cram into her station wagon, a 2004 Chrysler Pacifica, letting the bed bugs have the rest.

At her childhood home, Vanessa began caring for her ailing father. He had been a functional crack addict for most of her life, working as a landscaper in the warmer months and collecting unemployment when business slowed down. "It was something you got used to seeing," Vanessa said about her father's drug habit. "My dad was a junkie, but he never left us." Vanessa, 33, has Black hair that is usually pulled into a bun and wire-framed glasses that slide down her nose; a shy smile peeks out when she feels proud of herself. Vanessa's father died a year after Vanessa moved in. The family erected a shrine to him in the living room, a faded, large photo of a younger man surrounded by silk flowers and slowly sinking balloons. Vanessa's mother, Zaida, is 62 and from Puerto Rico, as was her husband. She uses a walker to get around.

Her husband's death left her with little income, and Vanessa was often broke herself. Her health failing, Zaida could take only so much of Vanessa's children, Taliya, 17, Shamal, 14, and Tatiyana, 12. When things got too loud or one of her grandchildren gave her lip, she would ask Vanessa to take her children somewhere else.

If Vanessa had the money, or if a local nonprofit did, she would book a motel room. She liked the Red Roof Inn, which she saw as "more civilized" than many of the other motels she had stayed in. It looked like a highway motel: two stories with doors that opened to the outside. The last time the family checked in, the kids carried their homework up to the room as Vanessa followed with small grocery bags from the food pantry, passing two men sipping Modelos and apologizing for their loud music. Inside their room, Vanessa placed her insulin in the minifridge as her children chose beds, where they would sleep two to a mattress. Then she slid into a small chair, saying, "Y'all don't know how tired Mommy is." After a quiet moment, Vanessa reached over and rubbed Shamal's back, telling him, "I wish we had a nice place like this." Then her eye spotted a roach feeling its way over the stucco wall. "Op!

Not too nice," Vanessa said, grinning. With a flick, she sent the bug flying toward Taliya, who squealed and jerked back. Laughter burst from the room. When Vanessa couldn't get a motel, the family spent the night in the Chrysler. The back of the station wagon held the essentials: pillows and blankets, combs and toothbrushes, extra clothes, jackets, and nonperishable food. But there were also wrinkled photos of her kids. One showed Taliya at her eighth-grade graduation in a cream dress holding flowers. Another showed all three children at a quinceañera—Shamal kneeling in front, with a powder blue clip-on bow tie framing his baby face, and Tatiyana tucked in back with a deep-dimpled smile.

So that the kids wouldn't run away out of anger or shame, Vanessa learned to park off Route 1, in crevices of the city that were so still and abandoned that no one dared crack a door until daybreak. Come morning, Vanessa would drive to her mother's home so the kids could get ready for school and she could get ready for work. In May, Vanessa finally secured a spot in public housing. But for almost three years, she had belonged to the "working homeless," a now-necessary phrase in today's low-wage/high-rent society. She is a home health aide, the same job her mother had until her knees and back gave out. Her work uniform is Betty Boop scrubs, sneakers, and an ID badge that hangs on a red Bayada Home Healthcare lanyard. Vanessa works steady hours and likes her job, even the tougher bits like bathing the infirm or hoisting someone out of bed with a Hoyer lift. "I get to help people," she said, "and be around older people and learn a lot of stuff from them." Her rate fluctuates: She gets $10 an hour for one client, $14 for another. It doesn't have to do with the nature of the work—"Sometimes the hardest ones can be the cheapest ones," Vanessa said—but with reimbursement rates, which differ according to the client's health care coverage. After juggling the kids and managing her diabetes, Vanessa is able to work 20 to 30 hours a week, which earns her around $1,200 a month. And that's when things go well.

These days, we're told that the American economy is strong. Unemployment is down, the Dow Jones industrial average is north of 25,000 and millions of jobs are going unfilled. But for people like Vanessa, the question is not, Can I land a job? (The answer is almost certainly, Yes, you can.) Instead the question is, What kinds of jobs are available to people without much education? By and large, the answer is: jobs that do not pay enough to live on.

In recent decades, the nation's tremendous economic growth has not led to broad social uplift. Economists call it the "productivity-pay gap"—the fact that over the last 40 years, the economy has expanded and corporate profits have risen, but real wages have remained flat for workers without a college education. Since 1973, American productivity has increased by 77 percent, while hourly pay has grown by only 12 percent. If the federal minimum wage tracked productivity, it would be more than $20 an hour, not today's poverty wage of $7.25.

American workers are being shut out of the profits they are helping to generate. The decline of unions is a big reason. During the twentieth century, inequality in America decreased when unionization increased, but economic transformations and political attacks have crippled organized labor, emboldening corporate interests and disempowering the rank and file. This imbalanced economy explains why America's poverty rate has remained consistent over the past several decades, even as per capita welfare spending has increased. It's not that safety-net programs don't help; on the contrary, they lift millions of families above the poverty line each year. But one of the most effective antipoverty solutions is a decent-paying job, and those have become scarce for people like Vanessa. Today, 41.7 million laborers—nearly a third of the American workforce—earn less than $12 an hour, and almost none of their employers offer health insurance.

The Bureau of Labor Statistics defines a "working poor" person as someone below the poverty line who spent at least half the year either working or looking for employment. In 2016, there were roughly 7.6 million Americans who fell into this category. Most working poor people are over 35, while fewer than five in 100 are between the ages of 16 and 19. In other words, the working poor are not primarily teenagers bagging groceries or scooping ice cream in paper hats. They are adults—and often parents—wiping down hotel showers and toilets, taking food orders and bussing tables, eviscerating chickens at meat-processing plants, minding children at 24-hour daycare centers, picking berries, emptying trash cans, stacking grocery shelves at midnight, driving taxis and Ubers, answering customer-service hotlines, smoothing hot asphalt on freeways, teaching community college students as adjunct professors and, yes, bagging groceries and scooping ice cream in paper hats.

America prides itself on being the country of economic mobility, a place where your station in life is limited only by your ambition and grit. But changes in the labor market have shrunk the already slim odds of launching yourself from the mailroom to the boardroom. For one, the job market has bifurcated, increasing the distance between good and bad jobs. Working harder and longer will not translate into a promotion if employers pull up the ladders and offer supervisory positions exclusively to people with college degrees. Because large companies now farm out many positions to independent contractors, those who buff the floors at Microsoft or wash the sheets at the Sheraton typically are not employed by Microsoft or Sheraton, thwarting any hope of advancing within the company. Plus, working harder and longer often isn't even an option for those at the mercy of an unpredictable schedule. Nearly 40 percent of full-time hourly workers know their work schedules just a week or less in advance. And if you give it your all in a job you can land with a high school diploma (or less), that job might not exist for very long: Half of all new positions are eliminated within the first year. According to the labor sociologist Arne Kalleberg (2011:39), permanent terminations have become "a basic component of employers' restructuring strategies."[1]

Home health care has emerged as an archetypal job in this new, low-pay service economy. Demand for home health care has surged as the population has aged, but according to the latest data from the Bureau of Labor Statistics, the 2017 median annual income for home health aides in the United States was just $23,130. Half of these workers depend on public assistance to make ends meet. Vanessa formed a rapport with several of her clients, to whom she confided that she was homeless. One replied, "Oh, Vanessa, I wish I could do something for you." When Vanessa told her supervisor about her situation, he asked if she wanted time off. "No!" Vanessa said. She needed the money and had been picking up fill-in shifts. The supervisor

was prepared for the moment; he'd been there before. He reached into a drawer and gave her a $50 gas card to Shell and a $100 grocery card to ShopRite. Vanessa was grateful for the help. She thought Bayada was a generous and sympathetic employer, but her rate hadn't changed much in the three years she had worked there. Vanessa earned $9,815.75 in 2015, $12,763.94 in 2016 and $10,446.81 last year.

To afford basic necessities, the federal government estimates that Vanessa's family would need to bring in $29,420 a year. Vanessa is not even close—and she is one of the lucky ones, at least among the poor. The nation's safety net now strongly favors the employed, with benefits like the earned-income tax credit, a once-a-year cash boost that applies only to people who work. Last year, Vanessa received a tax return of around $5,000, which included earned-income and child tax credits. They helped raise her income but not above the poverty line. If the working poor are doing better than the nonworking poor, which is the case, it's not so much because of their jobs per se, but because their employment status provides them access to desperately needed government help. This has caused growing inequality below the poverty line, with the working poor receiving much more social aid than the abandoned nonworking poor or the precariously employed, who are plunged into destitution. . . .

Vanessa received some help last year, when her youngest child, Tatiyana, was approved for Supplemental Security Income because of a learning disability. Vanessa began receiving a monthly $766 disability check. But when the Mercer County Board of Social Services learned of this additional money, it sent Vanessa a letter announcing that her Supplemental Nutrition Assistance Program benefits would be reduced to $234 from $544. Food was a constant struggle, and this news didn't help. A 2013 study by Oxfam America found that two-thirds of working poor people worry about being able to afford enough food. When Vanessa stayed at a hotel, her food options were limited to what she could heat in the microwave; when she slept in her car, the family had to settle for grab-and-go options, which tend to be more expensive. Sometimes Vanessa stopped by a bodega and ordered four chicken-and-rice dishes for $15. Sometimes her kids went to school hungry. "I just didn't have nothing," Vanessa told me one morning. For dinner, she planned to stop by a food pantry, hoping they still had the mac-and-cheese that Shamal liked.

In America, if you work hard, you will succeed. So those who do not succeed have not worked hard. It's an idea found deep in the marrow of the nation. William Byrd, an eighteenth-century Virginia planter, wrote of poor men who were "intolerable lazy" and "Sloathful in everything but getting of Children." Thomas Jefferson advocated confinement in poorhouses for vagabonds who "waste their time in idle and dissolute courses." Leap into the twentieth century, and there's Barry Goldwater saying that Americans with little education exhibit "low intelligence or low ambition" and Ronald Reagan disparaging "welfare queens." In 2004, Bill O'Reilly said of poor people: "You gotta look people in the eye and tell 'em they're irresponsible and lazy," and then continued, "Because that's what poverty is, ladies and gentlemen."

Americans often assume that the poor do not work. According to a 2016 survey conducted by the American Enterprise Institute, nearly two-thirds of respondents did not think most poor people held a steady job; in reality, that year a majority of nondisabled working-age adults were part of the labor force. Slightly over one-third of respondents in the survey believed that most welfare recipients would prefer to stay on welfare rather than earn a living. These sorts of assumptions about the poor are an American phenomenon. A 2013 study by the sociologist Ofer Sharone found that unemployed workers in the United States blame themselves, while unemployed workers in Israel blame the hiring system[2]. When Americans see a homeless man cocooned in blankets, we often wonder how he failed. When the French see the same man, they wonder how the state failed him.

If you believe that people are poor because they are not working, then the solution is not to make work pay but to make the poor work—to force them to clock in somewhere, anywhere, and log as many hours as they can. But consider Vanessa. Her story is emblematic of a larger problem: the fact that millions of Americans work with little hope of finding security and comfort. In recent decades, America has witnessed the rise of bad jobs offering low pay, no benefits, and little certainty. When it comes to poverty, a willingness to work is not the problem, and work itself is no longer the solution.

Until the late eighteenth century, poverty in the West was considered not only durable but desirable for economic growth. Mercantilism, the dominant economic theory of the early modern period, held that hunger incentivized work and kept wages low. Wards of public charity were jailed and required to work to eat. In the current era, politicians and their publics have continued to demand toil and sweat from the poor. In the 1980s, conservatives wanted to attach work requirements to food stamps. In the 1990s, they wanted to impose work requirements on subsidized-housing programs. Both proposals failed, but the impulse has endured.

Advocates of work requirements scored a landmark victory with welfare reform in the mid-1990s. Proposed by House Republicans, led by Speaker Newt Gingrich, and signed into law by President Bill Clinton, welfare reform affixed work requirements and time limits to cash assistance.

Caseloads fell to 4.5 million in 2011 from 12.3 million in 1996. Did "welfare to work" in fact work? Was it a major success in reducing poverty and sowing prosperity? Hardly. As Kathryn Edin and Laura Lein showed in their landmark book, *Making Ends Meet*, single mothers pushed into the low-wage labor market earned more money than they did on welfare, but they also incurred more expenses, like transportation and child care, which nullified modest income gains. Most troubling, without guaranteed cash assistance for the most needy, extreme poverty in America surged. The number of Americans living on only $2 or less per person per day has more than doubled since welfare reform. Roughly three million children—which exceeds the population of Chicago—now suffer under these conditions. Most of those children live with an adult who held a job sometime during the year.

A top priority for the Trump administration . . . [has been] expanding work requirements for some of the nation's biggest safety-net programs. In . . . [2018], the federal government announced that it would let states require that Medicaid recipients work. A dozen states have formally applied for a federal waiver to affix work requirements to their Medicaid programs. Four have been approved. . . . Arkansas became the first to implement newly approved work requirements. If all states instated Medicaid work requirements similar to that of Arkansas, as many as four million Americans could lose their health insurance.

. . . [In 2018] President Trump issued an executive order mandating that federal agencies review welfare programs, from the Supplemental Nutrition Assistance Program (SNAP) to housing assistance, and propose new standards. Although SNAP already has work requirements, . . . the House passed a draft farm bill that would deny able-bodied adults SNAP benefits for an entire year if they did not work or engage in work-related activities (like job training) for at least 20 hours a week during a single month. Falling short a second time could get you barred for three years. The Senate's farm bill, a bipartisan effort, removed these rules and stringent penalties, [and set]. . .up a showdown with the House, whose version Trump. . .endorsed. The Congressional Budget Office estimates that work requirements could deny 1.2 million people a benefit that they use to eat. Work requirements affixed to other programs make similar demands. Kentucky's proposed Medicaid requirements are satisfied only after 80 hours of work or work-related training each month. In a low-wage labor market characterized by fluctuating hours, tenuous employment and involuntary part-time work, a large share of vulnerable workers fall short of these requirements. Nationally representative data from the Survey of Income and Program Participation show that among workers who qualify for Medicaid, almost 50 percent logged fewer than 80 hours in at least one month.

In [2018], the White House Council of Economic Advisers issued a report enthusiastically endorsing work requirements for the nation's largest welfare programs. The council favored "negative incentives," tying aid to labor-market effort, and dismissed "positive incentives," like tax benefits for low-income workers, because the former is cheaper. The council also claimed that America's welfare policies have brought about a "decline in self-sufficiency."

Is that true? Researchers set out to study welfare dependency in the 1980s and 1990s, when this issue dominated public debate. They didn't find much evidence of it. Most people started using cash welfare

after a divorce or separation and didn't stay long on the dole, even if they returned to welfare periodically. One study found that 90 percent of young women on welfare stopped relying on it within two years of starting the program, but most of them returned to welfare sometime down the road. Even at its peak, welfare did not function as a dependency trap for a majority of recipients; rather, it was something people relied on when they were between jobs or after a family crisis. A 1988 review in *Science* concluded that "the welfare system does not foster reliance on welfare so much as it acts as insurance against temporary misfortune[3]" (Duncan, Hill & Hoffman, 1998: 239).

Today as then, the able-bodied, poor, and idle adult remains a rare creature. According to the Brookings Institution, in 2016 one-third of those living in poverty were children, 11 percent were elderly, and 24 percent were working-age adults (18 to 64) in the labor force, working or seeking work. The majority of working-age poor people connected to the labor market were part-time workers. Most couldn't take on many more hours either because of caregiver responsibilities, as with Vanessa, or because their employer didn't offer this option, rendering them involuntary part-time workers. Among the remaining working-age adults, 12 percent were out of the labor force owing to a disability (including some enrolled in federal programs that limit work), 15 percent were either students or caregivers, and three percent were early retirees. That leaves two percent of poor people who did not fit into one of these categories. That is, among the poor, two in 100 are working-age adults disconnected from the labor market for unknown reasons. The nonworking poor person getting something for nothing is a lot like the cheat committing voter fraud: pariahs who loom far larger in the American imagination than in real life. . . .

Shamal and Tatiyana's father had recently moved back to Trenton, "carrying a sack like a hobo," Vanessa remembered. Other than erratic child-support payments and a single trip to Chuck E. Cheese's, he doesn't play much of a role in his children's lives. Taliya's father went to prison when she was one. He was released when she was eight and was killed a few months later, shot in the chest. Sometimes Vanessa's three kids teased one another about their fathers.

"Your dad is dead," Tatiyana would say. "Yeah? Your dad's around, but he don't give a crap about you," Taliya would shoot back. Other times, though, the siblings offered soft reassurances that their fathers' absence wasn't their fault. "I don't have time for him," Tatiyana said once, as if it were her choice. "I have time for my real friends." Taliya looked at her baby sister and replied: "Watch. When you're doing good, he gonna start coming around."

If Vanessa clocked more hours, it would be difficult to keep up with all the ways she manages her family: doing the laundry, arranging dentist appointments, counseling the children about sex, studying their deep mysteries to extract their gifts and troubles. Yet our political leaders tend to refuse to view child care as work. During the early days of welfare reform, some local authorities thought up useless jobs for single mothers receiving the benefit. In one outrageous case, recipients were made to sort small plastic toys into different colors, only to have their supervisor end the day by mixing everything up, so the work could start anew the next morning. This was thought more important than keeping children safe and fed.

Caring for a sick or dying parent doesn't count either. Vanessa spooned *arroz con gandules* into her ailing father's mouth, refilled his medications, and emptied his bedpan. But only when she does these things for virtual strangers, as a Bayada employee, does she "work" and therefore become worthy of concern. As Evelyn Nakano Glenn argues in her 2010 book, *Forced to Care*,[4] industrialization caused American families to become increasingly reliant on wages, which had the effect of reducing tasks that usually fell to women (homemaking, cooking, child care) to "moral and spiritual vocations." "In contrast to men's paid labor," Glenn[5] writes, "women's unpaid caring was simultaneously priceless and worthless—that is, not monetized." She[6] continues: "To add insult to injury, because they could not live up to the ideal of full-time motherhood, poor women of color were seen as deficient mothers and caregivers."

Vanessa attributed her own academic setbacks—a good student in middle school, she began cutting class and courting trouble in high school—to the fact that her parents were checked out. At a critical juncture when Vanessa needed guidance and discipline, her father was using drugs and her mother seemed always to be at work. She didn't want to make the same mistake with her kids. Vanessa's life revolved around a small routine: drop the kids off at school; work; try finding an apartment that rents for less than $1,000 a month; pick the kids up; feed them; sleep. She didn't spend her money on extras, including cigarettes and alcohol. She was trying to save "the little money that I got," she told me, "so when we do get a place, I can get the kids washcloths and towels."

We might think that the existence of millions of working poor Americans like Vanessa would cause us to question the notion that indolence and poverty go hand in hand. But no. While other inequality-justifying myths have withered under the force of collective rebuke, we cling to this devastatingly effective formula. Most of us lack a confident account for increasing political polarization, rising prescription drug costs, urban sprawl, or any number of social ills. But ask us why the poor are poor, and we have a response quick at the ready, grasping for this palliative of explanation. We have to, or else the national shame would be too much to bear. How can a country with such a high poverty rate—higher than those in Latvia, Greece, Poland, Ireland, and all other member countries of the Organization for Economic Cooperation and Development—lay claim to being the greatest on earth? Vanessa's presence is a judgment. But rather than hold itself accountable, America reverses roles by blaming the poor for their own miseries.

Here is the blueprint. First, valorize work as the ticket out of poverty, and debase caregiving as not work. Look at a single mother without a formal job, and say she is not working; spot one working part time and demand she work more. Transform love into laziness. Next, force the poor to log more hours in a labor market that treats them as expendables. Rest assured that you can pay them little and deny them sick time and health insurance because the American taxpayer will step in, subsidizing programs like the earned-income tax credit and food stamps on which your work force will rely. Watch welfare spending increase while the poverty rate stagnates because, well, you are hoarding profits. When that happens, skirt responsibility by blaming the safety net itself. From there, politicians will invent new ways of denying families relief, like slapping unrealistic work requirements on aid for the poor. . . .

Because liberals have allowed conservatives to set the terms of the poverty debate, they find themselves arguing about radical solutions that imagine either a fully employed nation (like a jobs guarantee) or a post-work society (like a universal basic income). Neither plan has the faintest hope of being actually implemented nationwide anytime soon, which means neither is any good to Vanessa and millions like her. When so much attention is spent on far-off, utopian solutions, we neglect the importance of the poverty fixes we already have. Safety-net programs that help families confront food insecurity, housing unaffordability, and unemployment spells lift tens of millions of people above the poverty line each year. By itself, SNAP annually pulls over eight million people out of poverty. According to a 2015 study, without federal tax benefits and transfers, the number of Americans living in deep poverty (half below the poverty threshold) would jump from five percent to almost 19 percent. Effective social-mobility programs should be championed, expanded, and stripped of draconian work requirements.

While Washington continues to require more of vulnerable workers, it has required little from employers in the form of living wages or job security, creating a labor market in which the biggest disincentive to work is not welfare but the lousy jobs that are available. Judging from the current state of the nation's

poverty agenda, it appears that most people creating federal and state policy don't know many people like Vanessa. "Half of the people in City Hall don't even live in Trenton," Vanessa once told me, flustered. "They don't even know what goes on here." Meanwhile, this is the richest Congress on record, with one in 13 members belonging to the top 1 percent. From such a high perch, poverty appears a smaller problem, something less gutting, and work appears a bigger solution, something more gratifying. But when we shrink the problem, the solution shrinks with it; when small solutions are applied to a huge problem, they don't work; and when weak antipoverty initiatives don't work, many throw up their hands and argue that we should stop tossing money at the problem altogether. Cheap solutions only cheapen the problem. . . .

We need a new language for talking about poverty. "Nobody who works should be poor," we say. That's not good enough. Nobody in America should be poor, period. No single mother struggling to raise children on her own; no formerly incarcerated man who has served his time; no young heroin user struggling with addiction and pain; no retired bus driver whose pension was squandered; nobody. And if we respect hard work, then we should reward it, instead of deploying this value to shame the poor and justify our unconscionable and growing inequality. "I've worked hard to get where I am," you might say. Well, sure. But Vanessa has worked hard to get where she is, too.

NOTES

1. Kalleberg, A. L. 2011. "Good Jobs, Bad Jobs: The Rise of Polarized and Precarious Employment Systems in the United States, 1970s–2000s." United States: Russell Sage Foundation.

2. Sharone, O. 2013. *Flawed system/flawed self: Job searching and unemployment experiences.* Chicago: University of Chicago Press.

3. Duncan, Greg J., Martha S. Hill, and Saul D. Hoffman. 1988. "Welfare dependence within and across generations." *Science* 239(4839): 467–471.

4. Glenn, Evelyn Nakano. 2010. *Forced to Care: Coercion and Caregiving in America.* Cambridge, MA: Harvard University Press.

5. Glenn, 2010: 35.

6. Glenn, 2010: 37.

ALANA SEMUELS

59. I DELIVERED PACKAGES FOR AMAZON AND IT WAS A NIGHTMARE

Increasingly, workers are turning to jobs in the "gig economy" for both sole or supplemental income. While jobs in the gig economy offer some flexibility as to when you work, workers may be at risk of lower overall wages (especially when considering expenses incurred on the job) and lack of protections like health insurance. Semuels describes her own experience working for Amazon Flex.

I'm sure I looked comical as I staggered down a downtown San Francisco street on a recent weekday, arms full of packages—as I dropped one and bent down to pick it up, another fell, and as I tried to rein that one in, another toppled.

Yet it wasn't funny, not really. There I was, wearing a bright-yellow safety vest and working for Amazon Flex, a program in which the e-commerce giant pays regular people to deliver packages from their own vehicles for $18 to $25 an hour, before expenses. I was racing to make the deliveries before I got a ticket—there are few places for drivers without commercial vehicles to park in downtown San Francisco during the day—and also battling a growing rage as I lugged parcels to offices of tech companies that offered free food and impressive salaries to their employees, who seemed to spend their days ordering stuff online. Technology was allowing these people a good life, but it was just making me stressed and cranky. "NOT. A. GOOD. DEAL," I scrawled in my notebook, after having walked down nine flights of stairs, sick of waiting for a freight elevator that may or may not have been broken, and returned to my car for another armful of packages.

Welcome to the future of package delivery. As people shop more online, companies like Amazon are turning to independent contractors—essentially anyone with a car—to drop parcels at homes and businesses. Flex is necessary because Amazon is growing so quickly—the company shipped five billion Prime items last year—that it can't just rely on FedEx, UPS, and the Postal Service. Flex takes care of "last-mile" deliveries, the most complicated part of getting goods from where they're made to your doorstep. It also allows Amazon to meet increases in demand during the holiday season, Prime Day, and other busy times of the year, a spokeswoman told me in an email.

But Flex operates year-round, not just during the holiday season, which suggests there's another reason for it: It's cheap. As the larger trucking industry has discovered[1] over the past decade, using independent contractors rather than unionized drivers saves money because so many expenses are borne by the drivers rather than the company.

Amazon has rolled out Flex in more than 50 cities, including New York; Indianapolis, Indiana; and Memphis, Tennessee. The company doesn't share information about how many drivers it has, but one Seattle economist calculated that 11,262 individuals drove for Flex in California between October 2016 and March 2017, based on information Amazon shared with him to help the company defend a lawsuit about Flex drivers.

On the surface, these jobs, like many others in the gig economy, seem like a good deal. But Flex workers get no health insurance or pension and are not guaranteed a certain number of hours or shifts a week.

They are not covered by basic labor protections like minimum wage and overtime pay, and they don't get unemployment benefits if they suddenly can't work anymore. And when workers calculate how much they're pulling in on a daily basis, they often don't account for the expenses that they'll incur doing these jobs. "A lot of these gig-type services essentially rely on people not doing the math on what it actually costs you," Sucharita Kodali, a Forrester analyst who covers e-commerce, told me.

One Amazon Flex driver in Cleveland, Chris Miller, 63, told me that though he makes $18 an hour, he spends about 40 cents per mile he drives on expenses like gas and car repairs. He bought his car, used, with 40,000 miles on it. It now has 140,000, after driving for Flex for seven months, and Uber and Lyft before that. That means he's incurred about $40,000 in expenses—things he didn't think about initially, like changing the oil more frequently and replacing headlights and tail lights. He made slightly less than $10 an hour driving for Uber, he told me, once he factored in these expenses; Flex pays a bit better.

Miller's wife has a full-time job with benefits, so his Flex earnings are helpful for paying off his family's credit-card bills. But "if I were trying to make this work as a single guy on my own, it would be tough to do that," he said. His costs might actually be lower than what most drivers spend: The standard mileage rates for use of a car for business purposes, according to the IRS, were 54.5 cents a mile[2] in 2018.

I became an Amazon Flex independent contractor by downloading an app, going through a background check, and watching 19 videos that explained in great detail the process of delivering packages. (I did not get paid for the time it took to watch these videos, nor was there any guarantee that I would be approved as a driver once I watched the videos.) The videos covered topics like what to do if customers decide they don't want their order anymore ("Isn't this customer nuts?!," Amazon asks) and how to deliver alcohol (asking customers how old they are, it turns out, is not an acceptable form of checking ID). Because the videos were followed by quizzes, I actually had to pay attention.

After I was finally approved as a driver, a process that took weeks, I signed up for a shift. Flex drivers get work by opening the app and clicking on available shifts; current Flex drivers told me that newbies get offered the best hours and rates. My first shift was from 11:00 a.m. to 2:30 p.m. on a Tuesday, delivering packages from an Amazon logistics center in South San Francisco, about 30 minutes from my apartment. Different shifts offer varying rates; my three-and-a-half-hour block was going to net me $70, according to the app, though of course I had to pay for my own fuel and tolls. The app would tell me where to pick up the packages, where to drop them off, and what route to take, so the task seemed pretty easy. I anticipated a few leisurely hours driving between houses in a sleepy San Francisco suburb, listening to an audiobook as I dropped packages on doorsteps, smelling the lavender and sagebrush that grace many front lawns here.

My first hint that the afternoon was not going to be the bucolic day I had imagined came when I drove into the Amazon warehouse to pick up the packages. I was handed a yellow safety vest to wear inside the warehouse so other drivers could see me, "compliments of Amazon," a man told me, and was directed to a parking spot where a cart of packages awaited. I began loading them into my trunk, but paused when I saw the addresses printed on them. I was assigned 43 packages but only two addresses: two office buildings on Market Street, the main thoroughfare in downtown San Francisco. This meant driving into downtown San Francisco in the middle of a workday, stashing my car somewhere and walking between floors and offices in the two buildings.

"Where am I supposed to park?" I asked the two men who were guiding traffic in the warehouse, as I loaded giant boxes and slim White Prime envelopes into my overstuffed car. They both shrugged. "Lots of people just get tickets," one told me.

I was still feeling optimistic as I headed through 30 minutes of traffic to downtown San Francisco. I saw container ships on the horizon of the Bay as I drove up Highway 101, and for a moment, I felt like an integral part of a global delivery chain that brought these packages from China, across the sea, to the port, over the roads, into the backseat of my car, and now to the people eagerly awaiting them.

By some measures, delivering packages is one of the few "good" jobs left in America for people without college degrees. The Teamsters represent roughly 260,000 UPS workers, who make around $36 an hour.[3] The American Postal Workers Union represents around 156,000 clerks and support workers, who make, on average, $75,500 annually, according to the union. The National Association of Letter Carriers, which did not respond to requests for comment, represents the actual Postal Service delivery workers.

Yet these union jobs are under pressure. "These are good jobs, and they can get much worse really fast," Steve Viscelli, a sociologist at the University of Pennsylvania who writes about the trucking industry, told me. The Teamsters recently gave workers the go-ahead[4] to call a strike amid ongoing contract negotiations, although the two sides said . . . they'd reached a tentative deal. The American Postal Workers Union is about to begin[5] contract negotiations too. Workers are pushing back over weekend deliveries and the lower pay and benefits given to part-time workers. UPS now has a second tier of part-time workers who make as little as $10 an hour; the Postal Service has added workers it calls city carrier assistants who make less than regular mail carriers.

And then, of course, there's Flex. If the delivery workforce continues to shift toward nonunionized workers and independent contractors, the industry could go from one where workers can support a family to one where they are making less than minimum wage. That's what happened in the long-haul trucking industry, according to Viscelli. The average long-haul trucker today makes about $40,000,[6] down from the equivalent of $100,000 in 1980.

"There's been a whole movement to try to contain costs and undercut labor costs by classifying drivers as independent contractors so companies don't have to worry about wage laws," says Shannon Liss-Riordan, an attorney who has filed numerous lawsuits against tech companies for misclassifying workers as independent contractors. Amazon Flex employees sometimes make below the minimum wage in the city where they live—including in Seattle, where the minimum wage is $15 an hour—and they do not receive time-and-a-half for the hours they work over 40 hours a week, according to a lawsuit Liss-Riordan filed on behalf of Flex workers in U.S. District Court in Washington State. (Amazon said it does not comment on pending litigation.)

For some people, being an independent contractor is one of the best parts of driving for Flex. Jeremy Brown, a 36-year-old Flex driver in Milwaukee, told me that he likes the freedom of being his own boss. If he wakes up in the morning and doesn't feel like driving for Flex, he can go back to sleep, or spend his time leading the music worship service at his church, or homeschooling his kids. He makes enough money— around $120 a day, when he factors in expenses— from Flex that his family relies on it for the bulk of their income.

Brown often finishes his two-hour shifts in a shorter time than Amazon has estimated they will take. But if it takes a Flex driver longer to complete their deliveries than Amazon has calculated it will, they don't get paid for the extra time. (An Amazon spokeswoman told me that "the vast majority" of blocks are completed within or in less than the estimated time.) If the driver gets into a car accident, the driver, not Amazon, is responsible for medical and insurance costs. If a driver gets a speeding ticket, the driver pays. (UPS and FedEx usually pay[7] their trucks' tickets, but Amazon explicitly says in the contract Flex drivers sign that drivers are responsible for fees and fines.)

Because of the way Flex works, drivers rarely know when blocks of time will become available, and don't know when they'll be working or how much they'll be making on any given day. Brown likes to work two shifts delivering groceries for Amazon, from 4:30 to 6:30 a.m. and 6:30 to 8:30 a.m., but the morning we talked, no 4:30 shifts were available. He sometimes wakes up at 3 a.m. and does what Flex workers call the "sip and tap," sitting at home and drinking coffee while refreshing the app, hoping new blocks come up. He does not get paid for the hour he spends tapping. Twice in the last year, he's been barred from seeing new blocks for seven days because Amazon accused him of using a bot to grab blocks—he says he just taps the app so frequently Amazon assumes he's cheating. When he is barred from seeing blocks, he has no recourse but to repeatedly email Amazon, which has never led to his suspension being lifted. Amazon also does not break down how much he receives in tips and how much he receives in pay from the company— for all he knows, people are tipping him $20 and

Amazon is paying him less than minimum wage. And he doesn't have a boss he can ask what's going on.

Kelly Cheeseman, an Amazon spokeswoman, told me that Flex is a great opportunity for people to be their own boss and set their own schedule. If workers prefer to be full-time employees, rather than independent contractors, the company has a "wide variety" of full- and part-time opportunities, she said. (Of course, many of the full-time jobs are physically challenging[8] as well. Chris Miller, the Cleveland worker, told me that he preferred working as a contractor to working as an employee for Amazon, which is infamous for high levels of stress[9] and pressure among employees.)

Cheeseman said that most Flex workers are doing the job as a side gig to make money when they're in school or raising kids. But Nikolay Akunts, a driver who administers a Facebook group for Flex workers in the San Francisco Bay Area, told me that 70 to 80 percent of the drivers in the group are doing so full-time. (Akunts drives for Flex in Sunnyvale, California, from 4:30 to 8:30 a.m. and then goes to his full-time job at a software company.)

Even people who work for Flex full-time know they can't always depend on the app to make money. Akunts said that people often get "deactivated," which means they receive a message telling them they can no longer drive for Flex. Sometimes, the workers don't know why they've been terminated and their contract annulled, he told me. It can take as long as a month to get reinstated. Akunts, who likes working for Flex and makes a lot of money doing so, told me that he's one of the only drivers left after three years delivering packages in Sunnyvale who hasn't been deactivated or quit. "Amazon keeps you on a high standard," Akhunts said. If someone ordered a grocery delivery but doesn't answer the phone, Akunts keeps trying—the customer might be in the shower or on the other line, he said. This dedication to the customer, he said, is what Amazon expects from its workers.

When I arrived at the Market Street address where the first batch of packages was supposed to be delivered, I swiped "I've arrived" on the Flex app. The app informed me that I should actually be delivering the packages at the freight elevator on Ellis Street, in the back of the building—a two-minute walk, but a traffic-choked 10-minute drive, away. Once I arrived there, I discovered there was nowhere to park legally. I was already nearly an hour into my shift and hadn't delivered a package yet, so I parked at a red parking meter reserved for trucks with six wheels or more from 7 a.m. to 6 p.m. and started to make trips to the building, my arms full of parcels.

I tried to move quickly so that I wasn't leaving my car unattended for very long, but after walking in circles through the building, I reemerged onto Ellis Street and encountered a parking enforcement officer about to write me a ticket. I explained my difficulty: that I was delivering for Amazon, but there was nowhere to park, since I didn't have commercial plates. What was I supposed to do? My only option, since I was driving a personal car, he said, was to park in a garage, or deliver the packages at night. But lots of people risk it and park illegally in meters, he told me—the number of parking citations issued in the first three months of the year for people parking illegally at red and yellow meters grew 29 percent from 2016, according to data provided to me by the city. I eventually convinced him not to give me a ticket, which would have cost $110 and wiped out my earnings for the day, but even as he pulled away, he warned me that another officer could be coming by soon and wouldn't hesitate to write me one. Later, when I returned to the warehouse, I encountered a few Flex drivers who had two people in the car, presumably so one could drive and watch out for traffic enforcement officers while the other hopped out to deliver packages.

Parking headaches weren't the only problem. One of the packages I had to deliver was a huge box weighing more than 30 pounds. Because of the limited parking, I ended up walking two blocks with it, resting every 100 steps or so. At one point, a friendly police officer tried to lift it for kicks and groaned audibly. The security guard at the front door of the office building chastised me for carrying the box, and told me that I should be using a dolly to transport it. (None of the 19 videos I had to watch to be a Flex driver recommended bringing a delivery cart or a dolly.) Had I injured myself carrying the package, I would not have been able to receive workers' compensation or paid medical time off. I also would have been responsible for my own medical care. Brown, the Milwaukee Amazon Flex driver, is the sole provider for his family and uses BadgerCare, the Wisconsin health-insurance program for low-income residents, for his family's health insurance.

And then there was the fact that the Flex technology itself was difficult to use. Flex workers are supposed to scan each package before they deliver it, but the app wouldn't accept my scans. When I called support, unsure of what to do, I received a recorded messaging saying support was experiencing technical difficulties but would be up again soon. Then I got a message on my phone telling me the current average wait time for support was "less than 114,767 minutes." I ended up just handing the packages to people in the offices without scanning them, hoping that someone, somewhere, was tracking where they went. (Amazon says it is constantly taking driver feedback into consideration to improve Flex.)

Two of the small offices I was supposed to deliver packages to were locked, and there was no information about where to leave the deliveries. When I finally reached support and asked what to do with those undeliverable packages, I was told I could either drive them back to the warehouse in South San Francisco, 35 minutes away through worsening traffic, or keep trying to deliver them until the recipients returned. When I tried to use the app to call the recipients, it directed me to the wrong phone numbers; I eventually called a phone number printed on an office door and left a message. But there was no efficient way to register my problems with Amazon—I was on my own.

All my frustration really hit when I went to the second office building on Market Street, home to a few big tech companies. One of them took up multiple floors, smelled strongly of pizza, and had dog leashes and kibble near the front door.

Young workers milled around with laptops and lattes, talking about weekend plans. They were benefiting from the technology boom, sharing in the prosperity that comes with a company's rapid growth. Technology was making their jobs better—they worked in offices that provided free food and drinks, and they received good salaries, benefits, and stock options. They could click a button and use Amazon to get whatever they wanted delivered to their offices—I brought 16 packages for 13 people to one office; one was so light I was sure it was a pack of gum, another felt like a bug-spray container.

Until then, I had been, like them, blithely ordering things on Amazon so I wouldn't have to wait in line at a store or go searching for a particular product (even though I knew, from talking to warehouse workers,[10] that many of the jobs that get those packages to my door aren't good ones). But now, technology was enabling Amazon to hire me to deliver these packages with no benefits or perks. If one of these workers put the wrong address on the package, they would get a refund, while I was scurrying around trying to figure out what they meant when they listed their address as "fifth floor" and there was no fifth floor. How could these two different types of jobs exist in the same economy?

Gig-economy jobs like this one are becoming more and more common. The number of "nonemployer firms" in the ground-transportation sector—essentially freelancers providing rides through various platforms—grew 69 percent from 2010 to 2014, the most recent year for which there is data available, according to a Brookings analysis[11] of Census Bureau and Moody's data. Big cities like San Francisco, Boston, and Denver led the growth, according to Mark Muro, a senior fellow and policy director at the Metropolitan Policy Program at Brookings. Regular payroll employment in ground-transportation companies grew at a much slower rate, Brookings found.

People are worried that automation is going to create a "job apocalypse," but there will likely be thousands more driving and delivery jobs in upcoming years, according to Viscelli. Technology has allowed people to outsource the things they don't want to do; they can now have someone else go grocery shopping for them, pick up their takeout, bring them packages in under two hours so they don't have to go to a store. "We're going to take the billion hours Americans spend driving to stores and taking things off shelves, and we're going to turn it into jobs," Viscelli said. "The fundamental question is really what the quality of these jobs is going to be."

This shift could create even more congestion in cities as hundreds of small passenger cars flood the streets. It also could fundamentally change people's relationship with their employers—think of people like Chris Miller, the Ohio Flex driver, who for years was a full-time employee at various radio stations, and now is on his own. "It concerns me that this could be the way of the world," he told me.

There are efforts to make some of the people who drive for Flex employees rather than independent contractors, a move that worker advocates say could go a long way in improving the quality of these jobs. The lawsuit filed by Shannon Liss-Riordan in Washington State, for example, argues that Flex drivers are employees, not independent contractors, because they receive unpaid training about how to interact with customers and handle deliveries, they must follow Amazon's instructions about where to make deliveries, and they can be terminated if they don't follow the company's policies. Liss-Riordan filed the lawsuit on behalf of five plaintiffs but is hoping to add more.

The California Supreme Court ruled[12] in . . . [2018] that businesses must use an "ABC" standard when deciding how to classify workers. The standard, already in use in Massachusetts and New Jersey, means a worker is an independent contractor only if the work is done without direction and control from the employer, outside the course of the employer's usual business, and is done by someone who has his or her own independent business doing that kind of work. This may make it harder for employers to classify workers as contractors—but still, it will be hard for Amazon Flex workers in California to change their classification. They will have to file a formal complaint or take the matter to court, assuming Amazon and other gig-economy companies do not reclassify them on their own.

Liss-Riordan says one of the biggest obstacles in getting workers to take legal action over their classification is that many Flex workers agree, upon signing up to deliver packages, to resolve disputes with Amazon through arbitration. Companies can now use arbitration clauses to prevent workers from joining together to file class-action lawsuits, because of a . . . [recent] Supreme Court ruling.[13] (A new lawsuit[14] . . . in front of the Supreme Court argues that transportation workers are exempt from that rule.) Looking back through the many things I'd agreed to when signing up for Flex, I found that I, too, was governed by a binding arbitration agreement. The only way to opt out of this arbitration agreement would have been to inform Amazon I did not want to be covered by it within 14 days of signing the agreement.

For me, being an independent contractor meant that the job was lonely, with no colleagues to share stories with and no boss to ask about the many confusing aspects of being a first-day driver. (Flex drivers complained to me that even when they do contact support with a complaint, they often receive back a form letter, making them feel like they are working for a robot rather than a company that employs actual humans.) Many drivers take to Facebook to share stories and tips, but I only found those pages much later. My only interactions, aside from the parking enforcement officer, were with the people receiving the packages, who often said a distracted "thank you" as they tore open their packages, and with receptionists, who would nod me to mail rooms overflowing with brown boxes.

Being an independent contractor also meant that the job was hard to leave behind, even when I was done for the day. A few hours after I'd finished my shift, I received a call on my cell phone from a woman to whom I'd tried to deliver a package earlier that day. There had been no instructions about where to leave the package, but she told me she had frequently asked Amazon to leave her packages with another office. As she began chastising me—and Amazon—for my failures, I told her I wasn't responsible anymore and hung up the phone. Even weeks after I'd stopped driving for Flex, I kept getting new notifications from Amazon, telling me that increased rates were available, tempting me to log back in and make a few extra bucks, making me feel guilty for not opening the app, even though I have another job. And I didn't even have to put up with the early, unpaid hours of the "sip and tap" drivers who depended on Flex for work that they never knew for sure was coming the next day.

Flex was not a good deal for me. My shift lasted slightly longer than the three and a half hours Amazon had told me it would, because I had to return two undeliverable packages to the South San Francisco warehouse. On my traffic-choked drive there, I passed a billboard showing a man who had made millions through Bitcoin sitting on a beach.

My tech-economy experience was far less lucrative. In total, I drove about 40 miles (not counting the 26 miles I had to drive between the warehouse and my apartment). I was paid $70, but had $20 in expenses, based on the IRS mileage standards. I had narrowly avoided a $110 parking ticket, which felt like a win, but my earnings, added up, were $13.33 an hour. That's less than San Francisco's $14 minimum wage. I eagerly awaited my paycheck, which was supposed to be deposited into my bank account the Friday after my shift. It never came. Something had gone wrong with the way I entered my bank account number into the app, and when I wrote to support to report this, I received a form letter back that said I was emailing Amazon from the wrong email address. I'm still corresponding with Amazon to figure out exactly how to get paid—more time spent trying to eke out a meager wage in the gig economy.

NOTES

1. Uhler, Andy. 2015. "Truckers: Contractors or Employees?" Retrieved March 13, 2019, from http://www.marketplace.org/2016/06/02/world/truck-drivers-want-be-classified-employees.

2. https://www.irs.gov/newsroom/standard-mileage-rates-for-2018-up-from-rates-for-2017.

3. CNN Wire. 2018. "UPS, Teamsters May Be Headed toward America's Biggest Labor Strike in Decades." *KTLA*. Retrieved March 13, 2019, from https://ktla.com/2018/06/05/ups-teamsters-may-be-headed-toward-americas-biggest-labor-strike-in-decades.

4. Gibson, Kate. 2018. "Teamsters: 260,000 UPS Workers Ready to Strike for Better Contract." Retrieved March 13, 2019, from https://www.cbsnews.com/news/teamsters-ups-strike-authorization-vote-new-contract-july-31-deadline-2018-0607.

5. Zimmerman, Vance. 2017. "2018 Contract Negotiations - Preparations Underway." *APWU*. Retrieved March 13, 2019, from http://www.apwu.org/news/deptdiv-news-article/2018-contract-negotiations-preparations-underway.

6. Viscelli, Steve. 2016. "How One of America's Steadiest Jobs Turned into One of Its Most Grueling." *The Atlantic*. Retrieved March 13, 2019, from https://www.theatlantic.com/business/archive/2016/05/truck-stop/481926.

7. Zaleski, Andrew. 2017. "The Flip Side of the Retail Meltdown: The Delivery Truck Siege." *CityLab*. Retrieved March 13, 2019, from https://www.citylab.com/transportation/2017/04/cities-seek-deliverance-from-the-e-commerce-boom/523671.

8. Semuels, Alana. 2018. "What Amazon Does to Poor Cities." *The Atlantic*, February 1. https://www.theatlantic.com/business/archive/2018/02/amazon-warehouses-poor-cities/552020/.

9. Kantor, Jodi, and David Streitfeld. 2015. "Inside Amazon: Wrestling Big Ideas in a Bruising Workplace." *The New York Times*, August 15.

10. Semuels, 2018.

11. Hathaway, Ian, and Mark Muro. 2017. "Ridesharing Hits Hyper-Growth." *Brookings*. Retrieved March 13, 2019, from https://www.brookings.edu/blog/the-avenue/2017/06/01/ridesharing-hits-hyper-growth.

12. Dolan, Maura, and Andrew Khouri. 2018. "California's Top Court Makes It More Difficult for Employers to Classify Workers as Independent Contractors." *Latimes.Com*. Retrieved March 13, 2019, from https://www.latimes.com/local/lanow/la-me-ln-independent-contract-20180430-story.html.

13. Liptak, Adam. 2018. "Supreme Court Upholds Workplace Arbitration Contracts Barring Class Actions." *The New York Times*, May 21.

14. Estreicher, Samuel, and Holly H. Weiss. 2018. "SCOTUS to Decide If the Federal Arbitration Act Exemption for Transportation Workers Extends to Independent Truckers." *New York Law Journal*. Retrieved March 13, 2019, from https://www.law.com/newyorklawjournal/2018/03/16/scotus-to-decide-if-the-federal-arbitration-act-exemption-for-transportation-workers-extends-to-independent-truckers.

THE LONG-TERM JOBS KILLER IS NOT CHINA. IT'S AUTOMATION

CLAIRE CAIN MILLER

The first job that Sherry Johnson, 56, lost to automation was at the local newspaper in Marietta, Georgia, where she fed paper into the printing machines and laid out pages. Later, she watched machines learn to do her jobs on a factory floor making breathing machines, and in inventory and filing.

"It actually kind of ticked me off because it's like, How are we supposed to make a living?" she said. She took a computer class at Goodwill, but it was too little too late. "The 20- and 30-year-olds are more up to date on that stuff than we are because we didn't have that when we were growing up," said Ms. Johnson, who is now on disability and lives in a housing project in Jefferson City, Tennessee. Donald J. Trump told workers like Ms. Johnson that he would bring back their jobs by clamping down on trade, offshoring, and immigration. But economists say the bigger threat to their jobs has been something else: automation. "Over the long haul, clearly automation's been much more important—it's not even close," said Lawrence Katz, an economics professor at Harvard who studies labor and technological change.

No candidate talked much about automation on the [2016 presidential] campaign trail. Technology is not as convenient a villain as China or Mexico; there is no clear way to stop it, and many of the technology companies are in the United States and benefit the country in many ways. Mr. Trump told a group of tech company leaders . . . "We want you to keep going with the incredible innovation. Anything we can do to help this go along, we're going to be there for you."[1] Andrew F. Puzder, Mr. Trump's pick for labor secretary and chief executive of CKE Restaurants, extolled the virtues of robot employees over the human kind in an interview with Business Insider. . . . "They're always polite, they always upsell, they never take a vacation, they never show up late, there's never a slip-and-fall, or an age, sex or race discrimination case," he said.[2]

Globalization is clearly responsible for some of the job losses, particularly trade with China during the 2000s, which led to the rapid loss of 2 million to 2.4 million net jobs, according to research by economists, including Daron Acemoglu and David

Autor of MIT.[3] People who work in parts of the country most affected by imports generally have greater unemployment and reduced income for the rest of their lives, Mr. Autor found in a paper published in . . . [2016].[4] Still, over time, automation has had a far bigger effect than globalization and would have eventually eliminated those jobs anyway, he said in an interview. "Some of it is globalization, but a lot of it is we require many fewer workers to do the same amount of work," he said. "Workers are basically supervisors of machines."

When Greg Hayes, the chief executive of United Technologies, agreed to invest $16 million in one of its Carrier factories as part of a Trump deal to keep some jobs in Indiana instead of moving them to Mexico, he said the money would go toward automation. "What that ultimately means is there will be fewer jobs," he said on CNBC.[5] Take the steel industry. It lost 400,000 people, 75 percent of its workforce, between 1962 and 2005. But its shipments did not decline, according to a study[6] published in the *American Economic Review* last year. The reason was a new technology called the minimill. Its effect remained strong even after controlling for management practices; job losses in the Midwest; international trade; and unionization rates, found the authors of the study, Allan Collard-Wexler of Duke and Jan De Loecker of Princeton. Another analysis,[7] from Ball State University, attributed roughly 13 percent of manufacturing job losses to trade and the rest to enhanced productivity because of automation. Apparel making was hit hardest by trade, it said, and computer and electronics manufacturing was hit hardest by technological advances.

3   Acemoglu, Daron, David Autor, David Dorn, Gordon H. Hanson, and Brendan Price. 2016. "Import Competition and the Great US Employment Sag of the 2000s." *Journal of Labor Economics* 34(S1): S141–98.

4   Autor, David H., David Dorn, and Gordon H. Hanson. 2016. "The China Shock: Learning from Labor-Market Adjustment to Large Changes in Trade." *Annual Review of Economics* 8(1):205–40.

5   CNBC. 2016. "CNBC Transcript: United Technologies Chairman & CEO Greg Hayes on CNBC's 'Mad Money w/ Jim Cramer' Today." Retrieved March 17, 2019, from https://www.cnbc.com/2016/12/05/cnbc-transcript-united-technologies-chairman-ceo-greg-hayes-on-cnbcs-mad-money-w-jim-cramer-today.html.

6   Collard-Wexler, Allan, and Jan De Loecker. 2015. "Reallocation and Technology: Evidence from the US Steel Industry." *The American Economic Review* 105(1):131–71.

7   Hicks, Michael J., and Srikant Devaraj. 2015. *The Myth and Reality of Manufacturing in America*. Center for Business and Economic Research: Ball State University.

1   Streitfeld, David. 2016. "'I'm Here to Help,' Trump Tells Tech Executives at Meeting." *The New York Times*, December 14.

2   Taylor, Kate. 2016. "Fast-Food CEO Says He's Investing in Machines Because the Government Is Making It Difficult to Afford Employees." *Business Insider*. Retrieved March 17, 2019, from https://www.businessinsider.com/carls-jr-wants-open-automated-location-2016-3.

Over time, automation has generally had a happy ending: As it has displaced jobs, it has created new ones. But some experts are beginning to worry that this time could be different.[8] Even as the economy has improved, jobs and wages for a large segment of workers—particularly men without college degrees doing manual labor—have not recovered. Even in the best case, automation leaves the first generation of workers it displaces in a lurch because they usually don't have the skills to do new and more complex tasks, Mr. Acemoglu found in a paper published in . . . [2016].

Robert Stilwell, 35, of Evansville, Indiana, is one of them. He did not graduate from high school and worked in factories building parts for tools and cars, wrapping them up and loading them onto trucks. After he was laid off, he got a job as a convenience store cashier, which pays a lot less. "I used to have a really good job, and I liked the people I worked with—until it got overtaken by a machine, and then I was let go," he said.

Dennis Kriebel's last job was as a supervisor at an aluminum extrusion factory, where he had spent a decade punching out parts for cars and tractors. Then, about five years ago, he lost it to a robot. "Everything we did, you could program a robot to do it," said Kriebel, who is 55 and lives in Youngstown, Ohio, the town about which Bruce Springsteen sang, "Seven hundred tons of metal a day / Now sir you tell me the world's changed." Since then, Kriebel has barely been scraping by doing odd jobs. Many of the new jobs at factories require technical skills, but he doesn't own a computer and doesn't want to.

Labor economists say there are ways to ease the transition for workers whose jobs have been displaced by robots. They include retraining programs, stronger unions, more public-sector jobs, a higher minimum wage, a bigger earned-income tax credit and, for the next generation of workers, more college degrees. The White House . . . released a report on automation and the economy that called for better education from early childhood through adult job transitions and for updating the social safety net with tools like wage insurance. Few are policies that Mr. Trump has said he will pursue. "Just allowing the private market to automate without any support is a recipe for blaming immigrants and trade and other things, even when it's the long impact of technology," said Lawrence Katz, who was the Labor Department's chief economist under President Clinton.

The changes are not just affecting manual labor: Computers are rapidly learning to do some White-collar and service-sector work, too. Existing technology could automate 45 percent of activities people are paid to do, according to a . . . report by McKinsey.[9] Work that requires creativity, management of people, or caregiving is least at risk.

Ms. Johnson in Tennessee said that both her favorite and highest-paying job, at $8.65 an hour, was at an animal shelter, caring for puppies. It was also the least likely to be done by a machine, she said: "I would hope a computer couldn't do that, unless they like changing dirty papers and giving them love and attention."

8   Miller, Claire Cain. 2014. "As Robots Grow Smarter, American Workers Struggle to Keep Up." *The New York Times*, December 15.

9   Chui, Michael, James Manyika, and Mehdi Miremadi. 2016. "Where Machines Could Replace Humans—and Where They Can't (Yet)| McKinsey." Retrieved March 17, 2019, from https://www.mckinsey.com/business-functions/digital-mckinsey/our-insights/where-machines-could-replace-humans-and-where-they-cant-yet.

MICHAEL GRABELL

60. EXPLOITATION AND ABUSE
AT THE CHICKEN PLANT

Agricultural industries have long relied on immigrants (documented and undocumented) to fill jobs that U.S. citizens have declined. Grabell researched employment at the Case Farms chicken plants, documenting the exploitation and abuse of vulnerable workers, in particular undocumented workers escaping violence in their home countries. He found that workers enduring terrible working conditions have little protection and recourse and that many suffer long-term injuries as a result of their work at the plants.

By late afternoon, the smell from the Case Farms chicken plant in Canton, Ohio, is like a pungent fog, drifting over a highway lined with dollar stores and auto-parts shops. When the stink is at its ripest, it means that the day's 180,000 chickens have been slaughtered, drained of blood, stripped of feathers, and carved into pieces—and it's time for workers like Osiel López Pérez to clean up. On April 7, 2015, Osiel put on bulky rubber boots and a White hard hat, and trained a pressurized hose on the plant's stainless-steel machines, blasting off the leftover grease, meat, and blood.

A Guatemalan immigrant, Osiel was just weeks past his seventeenth birthday, too young by law to work in a factory. A year earlier, after gang members shot his mother and tried to kidnap his sisters, he left his home in the mountainous village of Tectitán and sought asylum in the United States. He got the job at Case Farms with a driver's license that said his name was Francisco Sepulveda, age 28. The photograph on the ID was that of his older brother, who looked nothing like him, but nobody asked any questions.

Osiel sanitized the liver-giblet chiller, a tublike contraption that cools chicken innards by cycling them through a near-freezing bath, then looked for a ladder, so that he could turn off the water valve above the machine. As usual, he said, there weren't enough ladders to go around, so he did as a supervisor had

shown him: he climbed up the machine, onto the edge of the tank, and reached for the valve. His foot slipped; the machine automatically kicked on. Its paddles grabbed his left leg, pulling and twisting until it snapped at the knee and rotating it a 180 degrees, so that his toes rested on his pelvis. The machine "literally ripped off his left leg," medical reports said, leaving it hanging by a frayed ligament and a 5-inch flap of skin. Osiel was rushed to Mercy Medical Center, where surgeons amputated his lower leg.

Back at the plant, Osiel's supervisors hurriedly demanded workers' identification papers. Technically, Osiel worked for Case Farms' closely affiliated sanitation contractor, and suddenly the bosses seemed to care about immigration status. Within days, Osiel and several others—all underage and undocumented—were fired.

Though Case Farms isn't a household name, you've probably eaten its chicken. Each year, it produces nearly a billion pounds for customers such as Kentucky Fried Chicken, Popeyes, and Taco Bell. Boar's Head sells its chicken as deli meat in supermarkets. Since 2011, the U.S. government has purchased nearly 17 million dollars' worth of Case Farms chicken, mostly for the federal school-lunch program.

Case Farms plants are among the most dangerous workplaces in America. In 2015 alone, federal

Reprinted with permission of ProPublica. This story was co-published with The New Yorker.

workplace-safety inspectors fined the company nearly $2 million, and in the past seven years it has been cited for 240 violations. That's more than any other company in the poultry industry except Tyson Foods, which has more than 30 times as many employees. David Michaels, the former head of the Occupational Safety and Health Administration (OSHA), called Case Farms "an outrageously dangerous place to work." Four years before Osiel lost his leg, Michaels's inspectors had seen Case Farms employees standing on top of machines to sanitize them and warned the company that someone would get hurt. Just a week before Osiel's accident, an inspector noted in a report that Case Farms had repeatedly taken advantage of loopholes in the law and given the agency false information. "The company has a 25-year track record of failing to comply with federal workplace-safety standards," Michaels said.

Case Farms has built its business by recruiting some of the world's most vulnerable immigrants, who endure harsh and at times illegal conditions that few Americans would put up with. When these workers have fought for higher pay and better conditions, the company has used their immigration status to get rid of vocal workers, avoid paying for injuries, and quash dissent. Thirty years ago, Congress passed an immigration law mandating fines and even jail time for employers who hire unauthorized workers, but trivial penalties and weak enforcement have allowed employers to evade responsibility. Under President Obama, Immigration and Customs Enforcement agreed not to investigate workers during labor disputes. Advocates worry that President Trump, whose administration has targeted unauthorized immigrants, will scrap those agreements, emboldening employers to simply call ICE anytime workers complain.

. . . [When]President [Trump] stirs up fears about Latino immigrants and refugees, he ignores the role that companies, particularly in the poultry and meatpacking industry, have played in bringing those immigrants to the Midwest and the Southeast. The newcomers' arrival in small, mostly White cities experiencing industrial decline in turn helped foment the economic and ethnic anxieties that brought Trump to office. Osiel ended up in Ohio by following a generation of indigenous Guatemalans, who

have been the backbone of Case Farms' workforce since 1989, when a manager drove a van down to the orange groves and tomato fields around Indiantown, Florida, and came back with the company's first load of Mayan refugees. . . .

Just before the presidential election in November 2016, I toured Case Farms' chicken plant in Canton with several managers. After putting on hairnets and butcher coats, we walked into a vast, refrigerated factory that is kept at 45 degrees in order to prevent bacterial growth. The sound of machines drowned out everything except shouting. Thousands of raw chickens whizzed by on overhead shackles, slid into chutes, and were mechanically sawed into thighs and drumsticks. A bird, I learned, could go from clucking to nuggets in less than three hours, and be in your bucket or burrito by lunchtime the next day.

Poultry processing begins in the chicken houses of contracted farmers. At night, when the chickens are sleeping, crews of chicken catchers round them up, grabbing four in each hand and caging them as the birds peck and scratch and defecate. Workers told me that they are paid around $2.25 for every thousand chickens. Two crews of nine catchers can bring in about 75,000 chickens a night. At the plant, the birds are dumped into a chute that leads to the "live hang" area, a room bathed in Black light, which keeps the birds calm. Every two seconds, employees grab a chicken and hang it upside down by its feet. "This piece here is called a breast rub," Chester Hawk, the plant's burly maintenance manager, told me, pointing to a plastic pad. "It's rubbing their breast, and it's giving them a calming sensation. You can see the bird coming toward the stunner. He's very calm." The birds are stunned by an electric pulse before entering the "kill room," where a razor slits their throats as they pass. The room looks like the set of a horror movie: blood splatters everywhere and pools on the floor. One worker, known as the "backup killer," stands in the middle, poking chickens with his knife and slicing their necks if they're still alive.

The headless chickens are sent to the "defeathering room," a sweltering space with a barnlike smell. Here the dead birds are scalded with hot water before mechanical fingers pluck their feathers. In 2014, an animal-welfare group said that Case Farms had the "worst chicken plants for animal cruelty" after it found that two of the company's plants had more federal humane-handling violations than any other chicken plant in the country. Inspectors reported that dozens of birds were scalded alive or frozen to their cages.

Next, the chickens enter the "evisceration department," where they begin to look less like animals and more like meat. One overhead line has nothing but chicken feet. The floors are slick with water and blood, and a fast-moving wastewater canal, which workers call "the river," runs through the plant. Mechanical claws extract the birds' insides, and a line of hooks carry away the "gut pack"—the livers, gizzards, and hearts, with the intestines dangling like limp spaghetti.

On the refrigerated side of the plant, there's a long table called the "deboning line." After being chilled, then sawed in half by a mechanical blade, the chickens, minus legs and thighs, end up here. At this point, the workers take over. Two workers grab the chickens and place them on steel cones, as if they were winter hats with earflaps. The chickens then move to stations where dozens of cutters, wearing aprons and hairnets and armed with knives, stand shoulder to shoulder, each performing a rapid series of cuts—slicing wings, removing breasts, and pulling out the pink meat for chicken tenders. Case Farms managers said that the lines in Canton run about 35 birds a minute, but workers at other Case Farms plants told me that their lines run as fast as 45 birds a minute. In 2015, meat, poultry, and fish cutters, repeating similar motions more than 15,000 times a day, experienced carpal-tunnel syndrome at nearly 20 times the rate of workers in other industries. The combination of speed, sharp blades, and close quarters is dangerous: since 2010, more than 750 processing workers have suffered amputations. Case Farms says it allows bathroom breaks at reasonable intervals, but workers in North Carolina told me that they must wait so long that some of them wear diapers. One woman told me that the company disciplined her for leaving the line to use the bathroom, even though she was seven months pregnant.[1]

Case Farms was founded in 1986, when Tom Shelton, a longtime poultry executive, bought a family-owned operation called Case Egg & Poultry, whose plant was in Winesburg, Ohio. In the world of larger-than-life chicken tycoons, like Bo Pilgrim—who

built a grandiose mansion in rural Texas nicknamed Cluckingham Palace—Shelton, with a neat mustache, a corporate hair style, and a mild manner, stood out. The son of a farmer, Shelton majored in poultry technology at North Carolina State, where he was the president of the poultry club and participated in national competitions in which teams of aspiring poultrymen graded chicken carcasses for quality and defects. Perdue Farms hired him right out of college, and he quickly rose through the ranks, attending Harvard Business School's Advanced Management Program before becoming Perdue's president, at the age of 43.

In 1986, the year that Shelton resigned from Perdue and started Case Farms, he gave a keynote address at the International Poultry Trade Show. It was a time of change: new mass-market products such as nuggets, fingers, and buffalo wings—along with health concerns over red meat—had made chicken a staple of American diets. With more women working, families no longer had time to cut up whole chickens. To meet the growing demand, Shelton told the audience, poultry plants would have to become more automated, and they would also need lots of labor. Shelton was the kind of manager who could recite the details involved in every step of production, from the density of breeding cages to the number of birds processed per man-hour. He set about maximizing line speeds at Case Farms, buying additional family-owned operations and implementing modern factory practices. Today, the company's four plants—Morganton and Dudley, in North Carolina, and Canton and Winesburg, in Ohio—employ more than 3,000 people.

Winesburg, the home of Shelton's first plant, is a small community in the middle of Amish country. Even today, it's not uncommon for drivers to yield for horse-drawn buggies or to see women in long dresses and bonnets carrying goods home from Whitmer's General Store. Before Shelton bought the plant, it had employed mostly young Amish women and Mennonites. But, as the company expanded, it stopped recognizing Amish holidays and began hiring outside the insular community. "The Amish fathers found the urban newcomers objectionable because of such things as coarse slogans on T-shirts, vulgarity in conversations, and 'necking' in the parking lot," the company said later, in federal court filings. The Amish workers left Case Farms, and, almost immediately, the company had trouble finding people who were willing to work under its poor conditions for little more than minimum wage. It turned first to the residents of nearby Rust Belt cities, which had fallen on hard times following the collapse of the steel and rubber industries. Turnover was high. About 25 to 30 of its 500 employees left every week.

Scrambling to find workers in the late 1980s and early 1990s, Case Farms sent recruiters across the country to hire Latino workers. Many of the new arrivals found the conditions intolerable. In one instance, the recruiters hired dozens of migrant farmworkers from border towns in Texas, offering them bus tickets to Ohio and housing once there. When workers arrived, they encountered a situation that a federal judge later called "wretched and loathsome." They were packed in small houses with about 20 other people. Although it was the middle of winter, the houses had no heat, furniture, or blankets. One worker said that his house had no water, so he flushed the toilet with melted snow. They slept on the floor, where cockroaches crawled over them. At dawn, they rode to the plant in a dilapidated van whose seating consisted of wooden planks resting on cinder blocks. Exhaust fumes seeped in through holes in the floor. The Texas farmworkers quit, but by then Case Farms had found a new solution to its labor problems.

One spring night in 1989, a Case Farms human resources manager named Norman Beecher got behind the wheel of a large passenger van and headed south. He had gotten a tip about a Catholic church in Florida that was helping refugees from the Guatemalan civil war. Thousands of Mayans had been living in Indiantown after fleeing a campaign of violence carried out by the Guatemalan military. More than 200,000 people, most of them Mayan, were killed or forcibly disappeared in the conflict. A report commissioned by the United Nations described instances of soldiers beating children "against walls or throwing them alive into pits," and covering people "in petrol and burning them alive." In 1981, in a village of Aguacatán, where many Case Farms workers come from, soldiers rounded up and shot 22 men. They then split their skulls and ate their brains, dumping the bodies into a ravine.

Through the years, the United States had supported Guatemala's dictators with money, weapons, intelligence, and training. Amid the worst of the violence, President Reagan, after meeting with General Efraín Ríos Montt, told the press that he believed the regime had "been getting a bum rap." The administration viewed the Guatemalan refugees as economic migrants and communist sympathizers—threats to national security. Only a handful received asylum. The Mayans who made it to Florida had limited options.

Beecher arrived at the church in time for Sunday Mass and set himself up in its office. He had no trouble recruiting parishioners to return with him to the Case Farms plant in Morganton, in the foothills of the Blue Ridge Mountains. Those first Guatemalans worked so hard, Beecher told the labor historian Leon Fink in his book, *The Maya of Morganton*, that supervisors kept asking for more, prompting a return trip. Soon vans were running regularly between Indiantown and Morganton, bringing in new recruits. "I didn't want [Mexicans]," Beecher, who died in 2014, told Fink. "Mexicans will go back home at Christmastime. You're going to lose them for six weeks. And in the poultry business you can't afford that. You just can't do it. But Guatemalans can't go back home. They're here as political refugees. If they go back home, they get shot." Shelton approved hiring the immigrants, Beecher said, and when the plant was fully staffed and production had doubled "he was tickled to death."

Evodia González Dimas could feel the pain in her left arm getting worse. For eight hours a day, she stood at a cutting table at the Case Farms Morganton plant, using a knife or scissors to remove fat and bones from chicken legs every two to three seconds. She wore a chainmail glove on her noncutting hand to protect it from accidental stabs by her knife or by the blades of her co-workers. The glove weighed about as much as a softball but grew heavier as grease and fat got caught in the steel mesh. By 2006, the pain and swelling were routinely driving González to the plant's first-aid station. A nursing assistant would give her pain relievers and send her back to the line. She could no longer lift a gallon of milk and had trouble making a fist. At night, after putting her children to bed, she'd rub soothing lotion on her swollen wrist and forearm.

One Friday in September 2006, González was called to Case Farms' human resources office. The director told her that the company had received a letter from the Social Security Administration informing it that the Social Security number she had provided wasn't valid. González, one of the few Mexicans at the plant, told me that the director sold her a new permanent-resident card, with the name Claudia Zamora, for $500 and helped her fill out a new application. (The human resources director denied selling her the ID). She was assigned to the same job, with the same supervisor. And Case Farms paid her more than it did new hires, noting in her file that she "had previous poultry experience."

Around that time, Case Farms workers began complaining that their yellow latex gloves ripped easily, soaking their hands with cold chicken juice. Only after pieces of rubber began appearing in packages of chicken did Case Farms buy more expensive, better-quality gloves. It passed the extra expense along to its employees, charging workers, who were making between $7 and $8 an hour, 50 cents a pair if they used more than three pairs during a shift.

The morning the policy took effect, in October 2006, there were grumbles throughout the plant's locker rooms. As workers began cutting chickens, the line abruptly stopped. One woman yelled that if they stuck together they could force the company to change the policy. When they refused to go back to work, managers called the police, and officers escorted workers off the premises.

More than 250 workers left the plant, gathering at a Catholic church nearby. González and another woman agreed to speak to a local newspaper reporter. Quoted as Claudia Zamora, González said, "Workers at Case Farms are routinely told to ignore notes from doctors about work restrictions when they've been injured on the job." OSHA later found that Case Farms often made workers wait months to see a doctor, flouted restrictions, and fired injured workers who couldn't do their job.

Returning to the factory on the Monday after the walkout, González brought a note from the local medical clinic prescribing "light work or no work" for a week. She gave it to the safety manager, who asked her to fill out a report stating when the pain began. When

she wrote "2003," he was baffled. According to personnel records, "Zamora" had worked there for only a month. The human resources director who had hired González as Zamora summoned her to the office; she had been sent a copy of the newspaper article quoting González. The pain couldn't be related to work at Case Farms, the director told González. After all, she was a new employee. González didn't understand. "I'm not new," she said, her voice rising. "You know how many years I've been working here." "Claudia, you're a probationary employee," the director replied. "I don't have a job for you."

González challenged her firing before the National Labor Relations Board (NLRB), a federal body created to protect workers' rights to organize. The NLRB judge wrote, "In my opinion, [Case Farms] knew exactly what was going on with respect to her employment status." The company, he said, "took advantage of the situation." The board eventually ruled that González had been illegally fired for protesting working conditions. But the victory was largely symbolic. In 2002, the Supreme Court had ruled, in a 5–4 decision, that undocumented workers had the right to complain about labor violations, but that companies had no obligation to rehire them or to pay back wages. In the dissent, Justice Stephen Breyer predicted that the Court's decision would incentivize employers to hire undocumented workers "with a wink and a nod," knowing that "they can violate the labor laws at least once with impunity." Case Farms had broken the law, but there was nothing González could do about it. The doctor told her that she needed surgery for carpal-tunnel syndrome, but she never got it. A decade later, her hand is limp, and her anger still fresh. "This hand," she told me, sitting in her living room, "I try not to use it at all."

What happened to González was part of Case Farms' decades-long strategy to beat back worker unrest with creative uses of immigration law. The year that Case Farms was founded, Congress passed the Immigration Reform and Control Act, which made it illegal to "knowingly" hire undocumented immigrants. But employers aren't required to be document experts, which makes it hard to penalize them. The requirement that workers fill out an I-9 form, however, declaring under penalty of perjury that they're authorized to work, makes it easy for employers to re-taliate against workers.

In 1993, around 100 Case Farms employees re-fused to work in protest against low pay, lack of bath-room breaks, and payroll deductions for aprons and gloves. In response, Case Farms had 52 of them ar-rested for trespassing. In 1995, more than 200 work-ers walked out of the plant and, after striking for four days, voted to unionize. Three weeks after the protest, Case Farms requested documents from more than 100 employees whose work permits had expired or were about to expire. Case Farms refused to negotiate with the union for three years, appealing the election results all the way to the Supreme Court. After the company lost the case, it reduced the workweek to four days in an effort to put pressure on the employees.

Eventually, the union pulled out.

Case Farms followed the same playbook in 2007, when workers at the Winesburg plant complained about faster line speeds and a procedure that re-quired them to cut three wings at a time by stacking the wings and running them through a spinning saw. Occasionally, the wings broke, and bones got caught in workers' gloves, dragging their fingers through the saw. One day, a Guatemalan immigrant named Juan Ixcoy refused to cut the wings that way. As word spread through the plant, workers stopped the lines and gath-ered in the cafeteria. Ixcoy, who is now 42, became a leader in a new fight to unionize. "They saw that I didn't have fear," he told me.

In July 2008, more than 150 workers went on strike. For nine months, through the depths of the re-cession, they picketed in a cornfield across the street from the plant. In the winter, they bundled up in snowsuits and protested from a shed made of ply-wood and bales of hay. According to the NLRB, when the workers walked out again, in 2010, a manager told an employee that he would take out the strike leaders "one at a time." A short time later, Ixcoy was fired for insubordination after an argument with a manager on the plant floor prompted some workers to bang their knives and yell "Strike!" A judge with the NLRB found that Ixcoy had been unlawfully fired for his union ac-tivity and ordered that he be reinstated. After Ixcoy re-turned to work, however, the union received a letter saying that it had come to the company's attention

that nine of its employees might not be legally autho-rized to work in the United States. Seven were on the union organizing committee, including Ixcoy. All were fired.

The company's sudden discovery that the union organizers were undocumented was hard to credit. Ixcoy had first been hired in 1999, as Elmer Noel Rosado. After a few years, a Case Farms manager told him that the company had received notice that there was another person, in California, working under the same ID "The manager, he told me if you can buy another paper you're welcome to come back," Ixcoy said. So he bought another ID for $1,000 and returned to Case Farms under the name Omar Carrion Rivera. Current and former workers at Case Farms' four plants said that the company had an unspoken policy of allowing them to come back with a new ID. An em-ployee in Dudley told me that he had worked at the plant under four different names. Case Farms execu-tives had to have known that many of their employees were unauthorized. On at least three occasions, scores of workers fled their plants, fearing immigration raids. Ixcoy eventually received a special visa for crime vic-tims because of the workplace abuses he had suffered. "Ixcoy lived in an atmosphere of fear created by super-visors at Case Farms," the Labor Department wrote in his visa application. "He feared for his own safety, that if he complained or cooperated with authorities, he would be arrested or deported."

In the past few years, Tom Shelton has cast himself as the genial proprietor of a winery that he runs on his 40-acre estate on Maryland's Eastern Shore. . . .Shelton never responded to my calls or letters. A Case Farms public relations person said he declined to be inter-viewed and, instead, arranged for me to meet with the company's vice-chairman, Mike Popowycz, and other managers in a conference room in Winesburg. Popowycz is the son of Ukrainian immigrants, who came to America after World War II. His father was a steelworker, and his mother worked nights in a thread mill. "I know what these people go through every day," he said. "I can see the struggles that they go through because those are the struggles my parents went through."

Popowycz, who is the chairman of the indus-try's trade group, the National Chicken Council, said that Case Farms had made some safety mistakes but was working hard to correct them. He defended the company on every question I had. Case Farms, he said, treated its workers well and never refused to let them use the bathroom. Fees for replacement equipment discouraged workers from throwing things away. As for unions, the company didn't need someone to stand between it and its employees. "Our goal is to prove that we're not the company that OSHA has basically said we are," he told me.

Popowycz seemed unaware of many of the specific incidents I cited. He was almost like a parent hearing of his teenager's delinquency: he hoped supervisors didn't do that, but, if they did, it was wrong. Case Farms operates under a decentralized management system, which Shelton instituted early on. Every Monday at 8 a.m., Shelton hosts a conference call from Maryland, but many decisions are left to local managers. "We want the people at the locations to manage their business as if it's their own," Popowycz said.

I found it hard to believe that Shelton, who is known to ask questions about a $10,000 equipment expense, wouldn't be aware of workplace disputes costing tens of thousands of dollars in legal fees. I contacted 60 former Case Farms managers, supervisors, and human resources representatives. Most declined to comment or didn't return my calls, but I spoke to eight of them. Many agreed that Shelton gave them a good deal of autonomy, and they denied that there was pressure to produce chickens faster and more cheaply. "When I was there, any problems that we saw, we took care of it," Andy Cilona, a human resources director in Winesburg in the 1990s, told me. But two said that promotions went to those who pushed employees hardest, which led some supervisors to treat workers harshly.

Popowycz acknowledged that some human resources supervisors had sold fake IDs; when the company found out, it fired them. He insisted that Case Farms complied with immigration laws. It was one of the first companies in Ohio to report Social Security numbers to immigration in the 1990s. Case Farms also periodically audits its personnel records, and when it receives letters from the authorities about discrepancies in workers' IDs it investigates. But the company has never used immigration status to retaliate against

injured or vocal workers, Popowycz said; any firings that occurred after protests were coincidental. "At the end of the day, we need labor in our plants; we're not looking to get rid of these folks," Popowycz said. "Do we do everything right? We hope we do."

. . . I traveled to several villages in the Guatemalan state of Huehuetenango in the hope of finding former Case Farms workers. After passing through the market town of Aguacatán, where women in White-and-red *huipiles* sell everything from garlic to geese, I headed 45 minutes up a mountain to the village of Chex, where I found a cargo truck that had careened over the side of a road. Dozens of men came from the nearby fields and helped brace the truck with branches and ropes. I asked the men if any of them had worked for Case Farms. "I worked there for a year, around 1999 to 2000," one man said. "2003," another added. "Six months. It's killer work." "Eleven years," said another. Two said that they had been among the first Guatemalans to work in Winesburg.

Former Case Farms workers turned up everywhere—the hotel clerk in Aguacatán, members of the local church, a hitchhiker I picked up on the way to another village. One man in Chex had been a chicken catcher in Winesburg, but years of overuse had left his elbow swollen and in chronic pain. Unaware that Case Farms is supposed to pay for workplace injuries, he told me that he had returned to Guatemala to heal and had spent thousands of dollars seeing doctors. Now his arm lay frozen at his side.

The village where Osiel grew up, Tectitán, is at the top of another mountain five hours west, reachable by a winding red-dirt road. It's so isolated that it has its own language, Tektiteko. Like Chex, Tectitán has a long history of sending residents north to work at Case Farms. By the time Osiel was a teenager, a man watching a soccer match could make fun of the Guatemalan team's goalie on Facebook by saying that he "couldn't even grab the chickens at Case Farms."

I met Osiel at Centro San Jose, a social-welfare agency and legal clinic operated from an old redbrick Lutheran church on the edge of downtown Canton. For the past few years, Centro San Jose has been swamped by hundreds of unaccompanied minors fleeing gang violence in Guatemala. Osiel was wearing a blue knit hat with a pompom, a White compression shirt, sweatpants with patches, and blue sneakers. He told me that he left Guatemala on his sixteenth birthday, after his mother's murder and, two weeks later, was in the custody of border-patrol agents in Arizona. He moved in with an uncle in Canton and befriended some other teenagers from Tectitán who were working nights at Case Farms. He worked at the plant for eight months, earning $9 an hour before the accident.

Osiel said that, on the night of the accident, after passing out in the machine, he awoke in the hospital. "The nurses told me that I lost my leg," he recalled. "I couldn't believe it. I didn't feel any pain. And then, hours later, I tried to touch it. I didn't have anything there. I started crying." Today, he lives with two of his brothers in a weathered gable-front house next to a vacant lot. He is still getting used to the prosthesis, and hobbles when he walks. "I never thought that something like this could happen to me," he said. "They told me that they couldn't do anything for my leg to get better. They told me that everything was going to be OK."

The Labor Department, in addition to finding numerous safety violations, fined Cal-Clean, Case Farms' sanitation contractor, $63,000 for employing four child laborers, including Osiel. The fines and the citations against Case Farms have continued to accumulate. Last September, OSHA determined that the company's line speeds and work flow were so hazardous to workers' hands and arms that it should "investigate and change immediately" nearly all the positions on the line. As the company fights the fines, it finds new ways to keep labor costs down. For a time, after the Guatemalan workers began to organize, Case Farms recruited Burmese refugees. Then it turned to ethnic Nepalis expelled from Bhutan, who today make up nearly 35 percent of the company's employees in Ohio. "It's an industry that targets the most vulnerable group of workers and brings them in," Debbie Berkowitz, OSHA's former senior policy adviser, told me. "And when one group gets too powerful and stands up for their rights, they figure out who's even more vulnerable and move them in."

Recently, Case Farms has found a more captive workforce. One blazing morning last summer in Morganton, an old yellow school bus arrived at Case Farms and passed through the plant's gates, pulling up to the employee entrance. Dozens of inmates from the local prison filed off, ready to work at the plant. Even their days may be numbered, however. During the tour in Canton, Popowycz and other Case Farms managers showed me something they were excited about, something that would help solve their labor problems and also reduce injuries: in a corner of the plant was a shiny new machine called an "automatic deboner." It would soon replace 70 percent of the workers on the line.

NOTE

1. *Editor's Note*: Oxfam America's 2016 report, "No Relief: Denial of Bathroom Breaks in the Poultry Industry" confirms that across the poultry processing industry, an industry that is making record profits, workers are denied bathroom breaks. Supervisors mock worker requests, telling them not to drink or eat as much, and they even threaten workers with punishment and firing. Workers who do get breaks must rush across slippery factory floors soaked in blood and fat, quickly remove their protective gear, take about a minute to use the restroom, and then redon their gear in time to make it back to the production line. Workers are forced to wear diapers or risk urinating or defecating on themselves when replacements do not arrive to the production line in time to relieve them. Many say they reduce their intake of liquids and food to prevent the need to use the bathroom, resulting in dehydration. Pregnant and menstruating workers are hit particularly hard. Oxfam is working across the industry to document and seek change for this dehumanizing work condition.

61. NO PIECE OF THE PIE

Food Workers in the United States

As we roll our shopping carts along the aisles of our grocery stores, most Americans rarely consider the process of food production and the workers along the food chain. The Food Chain Workers Alliance and Solidarity Research Cooperative direct our attention to the poor working conditions (including high rates of injuries) and low wages of the workers who produce, process, distribute, and sell our food. This reading documents the high rate at which our food system workers are reliant on social safety net programs, including programs, ironically, that help families of food workers who are facing food insecurity and hunger.

INTRODUCTION

The 21.5 million workers in the food system make up the largest employment sector in the United States with over one out of seven workers in the United States working along the food chain. . . . Food-related industries are the third largest contributor to U.S. gross output after manufacturing and the financial sector, generating approximately $3.5 trillion, or more than 11 percent of the annual total.[1] The average household spends approximately 10 percent of its yearly pretax income—over $7,000—on food expenses.[2]

Human labor is a central component at every step of the chain, which includes production, processing, distribution, retail, and service. Food workers include laborers in fields and fisheries (production), bakers and slaughterhouse workers (processing), drivers and warehouse workers (distribution), grocery store cashiers and stockers (retail), and restaurant servers, cooks, dishwashers, and street vendors (service). While some of these workers routinely interact with consumers, many of them—and their job site conditions—remain hidden, whether in remote agricultural fields, behind the closed doors of processing facilities, or in

the back of restaurants and retail stores. The vast majority of these are low-wage jobs. . . .

THE CONTEXT OF THE FOOD SYSTEM

RACISM

The modern food system is inseparable from the legacy of slavery and the twentieth-century inheritance of racism and oppression. The latter includes the use of indentured laborers from Asia, impoverished Black sharecroppers in the South, and small farmers driven from their homes during the Dust Bowl. New Deal legislation in the 1930s introduced a host of important labor regulations and protections, including the right to organize unions. However, jobs that were dominated by Black workers such as agricultural and domestic work were intentionally left out of the laws. During World War II, Mexican laborers were brought to U.S. fields to work under the bracero program, described by Department of Labor official Lee Williams as a system of "legalized slavery."[3] This program set the stage for the contemporary reliance on undocumented immigrants in farm work.

Food Chain Workers Alliance and Solidarity Research Cooperative. November 2016. No Piece of the Pie: U.S. Food Workers in 2016. Los Angeles, CA: Food Chain Workers Alliance.

SEXISM

The relegation of women to lesser economic and social roles in the United States is reflected in the organization of labor in the food system. Historically, women's work has been devalued due to patriarchal systems that view their labor as less valuable than that of men.[4] While women perform the majority of food-related work both in the home and in the food system, they are less likely to be decision makers, to hold positions of authority, or to be paid fairly for their work. Culturally, women experience a complicated relationship with food at the personal level due to social norms. Women are the unpaid and often undervalued food workers in the home.[5] While both women and people of color are the lowest paid workers in the food system, gender is more significant than race in terms of its impact on low wages for agricultural, production, retail, and service work.[6] In the restaurant industry, both White women and women of color are segregated by job function and earn the lowest wages overall.[7] The barriers to advancement can include sexual discrimination, a lack of training or social networks, and few options for child care.[8]

CONSOLIDATION

The various sectors of the industrial food system are often dominated by a handful of large corporations. Concentration is considerable in meat processing and in food retail, for example, where there have recently been sweeping consolidations as companies struggle to compete with corporate giants.[9] These businesses argue that consolidation will increase efficiency, lower prices, and improve customer service. In reality, consolidation gives a small number of companies enormous control over how food is produced, transported, and sold, while exerting downward pressure on wages and undermining unionization.

A striking example is Walmart, the largest grocery store chain and corporation in the world. When Walmart demands that suppliers keep costs low, companies along the food chain must respond in order to remain in business. This often results in a domino effect of depressed wages, lower unionization rates, and poor working conditions throughout the food system.[10] Walmart's employment practices also set the tone for many competing businesses in the retail sector, as its low wages help keep costs low and exert pressure on their competition. These low wages come at a price for society, however: research demonstrates that taxpayers subsidize Walmart through programs such as health insurance, public housing, and food assistance provided to their employees to the tune of $900,000 to $1.7 million for every store per year.[11]

GOVERNMENT INTERVENTION

U.S. labor laws have historically facilitated cheap labor and oppressive conditions within the food system, although the lack of regulations is often equally damaging.[12] Even when labor protections exist, enforcement can be weak or absent.[13] The government intervenes in food production more directly through major subsidies of agricultural goods, especially corn and soy. Large, profitable farms receive over 70 percent of subsidy payments, which encourages further consolidation of farms into large-scale agribusiness.[14] In short, government policies incentivize an industrial food system that is highly consolidated and emboldened to produce cheap, processed foods.

METHODS

The findings in this report come from an analysis of national data from the U.S. Bureau of Labor Statistics and the U.S. Census Bureau as well as current discussions in academic and policy literature. Research for this report also included original in-depth interviews with 20 food workers across all five sectors of the food chain from member organizations of the Food Chain Workers Alliance. . . .

RESULTS

. . . The data in this report reveal a food system that continues to grow in terms of employment and yet is beset by stagnant wages, poor working conditions, lack of benefits, health and safety issues, and mistreatment at work. While the median wages for all workers have risen in the past four years, wages in all five major food industries remain below the national median. . . . Moreover, since 2003, the economy has seen a 19 percent increase in labor productivity, while food system wages have remained stagnant in comparison.[15]

Practices like temporary labor contracting have spread from farms to other sectors of the food system, including warehouses, logistics, food manufacturing, processing, and food service. . . . Without significant changes to workplace conditions, treatment, and wages, workers in the food system will have few opportunities for upward mobility. . . .

EMPLOYMENT IN THE FOOD CHAIN IS ROBUST AND GROWING

. . . With such a large percentage of U.S. workers employed in the food chain, the wages and conditions have a major impact on overall workplace trends as well as the economy in general. This is especially true because employment in the food chain has been growing at a rate more than double that of all other industries over the past 14 years. In the four years that passed after the 2012 publication of *The Hands That Feed Us*, the economy as a whole was recovering from high levels of unemployment due to the Great Recession [of 2008]. All industries except for the food chain lost six percent of total employment during the recession. The food system, on the other hand, lost only 1.5 percent of total employment and recovered much more quickly. . . .

DESPITE GROWTH, FOOD SYSTEM EMPLOYERS PAY LOWEST HOURLY MEDIAN WAGE TO FRONTLINE WORKERS

The working people who comprise the food chain have felt little of the economic recovery in their lives. Given the rebounding employment numbers post-recession, one might assume that wage gains for frontline workers would have followed suit. Yet wages in the food system remain much lower than the median wage across the economy. Even during the Great Recession, median U.S. hourly wages increased from 2007 to 2009. However, median hourly earnings for food workers dipped below $10 even before the downturn officially began in 2007. . . . Wages did not recover to their pre-downturn levels until 2015, six years after the recession ended. In addition, while the United States as a whole enjoyed a four percent boost in median household income in 2016, food system incomes only rose by two percent.[16] . . . With more than half of all food system workers making less than $10 per hour, pay

is far below the 2015 U.S. livable wage of $15.12 per hour, before taxes.[17] In contrast to these low wages, in government, the highest-paying U.S. industry, median pay is $48,000 per year and $18 per hour.[18] A comparable rank-and-file worker in construction would earn nearly double the typical food worker's earnings, bringing in $30,000 per year and $17 per hour. . . .

FOOD CHAIN WORKERS RELY ON PUBLIC ASSISTANCE AND ARE FOOD INSECURE

Low pay has consequences. Frontline food workers are struggling to make ends meet. In 2010, 11 percent of food system workers were on food stamps—now known as the Supplemental Nutrition Assistance Program, an important indicator of economic insecurity—compared to six percent of workers in other industries. . . . By 2016, 13 percent of food workers, equal to nearly 2.8 million people, were on food stamps, compared with six percent across other industries. Food workers therefore use food stamps at 2.2 times the rate of all other industries, a tremendous increase from 1.8 times the rate of all other industries in 2010. This reveals that there is a growing gap between the percentage of food workers living in poverty and workers in other industries. Looking closely at 2016, food workers relied on public assistance programs for basic needs at a greater rate than the general population. . . . Employers are shifting what should be their costs—living wages—onto taxpayers by paying such low wages that food workers are forced to use public assistance programs. [*Editor's note*: While CEOs and corporations are making record profits, taxpayers shoulder the burden of providing a safety net for their underpaid employees.]

More than 15 million households (13 percent) in the United States lacked food security in 2015 and experienced difficulty securing enough food for all their family members due to limited resources.[19] The irony for workers in the food chain, who make it possible for us to eat, is that 4.3 million, or almost 20 percent, lacked food security in 2014. . . . Looking at households supported by a food chain worker, more than 2.5 million experienced low food security in 2014 (previously referred to by the U.S. Department of Agriculture as *food insecurity without hunger*), while over

1.7 million were very low in food security (previously labeled *food insecurity with hunger*).[20] Households who experience food insecurity reported reductions in the quality, variety, or desirability of their diets. However, those with very low food security also didn't have money for food and reduced their intake. Food insecurity increased for workers in the food system during the Great Recession. . . .

MOST FOOD CHAIN WORKERS ARE IN FRONTLINE POSITIONS WITH FEW OPPORTUNITIES AT THE TOP

Labor in the food chain can be represented by a pyramid, with over 16 million, or 82 percent, of all food chain workers concentrated on the bottom rungs as frontline workers. This means that for every one job as a chief executive officer in the food industry, there are 1,465 frontline workers. . . . In 2015, 0.06 percent of those employed in the food system worked as CEOs, and fewer than 10 percent were managers and supervisors, offering little room for workers to advance to top positions. Sectors in the food chain vary in their ratios of workers to CEOs. Food service has the greatest number of frontline workers per CEO, with almost 4,000 rank-and-file workers to one CEO. With close to 2,000 frontline workers for every CEO, food retail comes in second. In food production, there are more than 1,200 workers for every CEO. Processing and distribution have slightly higher rates of CEOs to workers, with more than 500 workers per CEO in these sectors.

FRONTLINE FOOD WORKERS ARE RACIALLY DIVERSE AND EDUCATED, BUT WHITE MEN ARE IN LEADERSHIP

Food chain workers are diverse in terms of race, ethnicity, and education. Racial and ethnic diversity in the food chain reflects the broader demographic trend predicted by the Pew Research Center that by 2055 the nation will not have one single racial or ethnic majority.[21] In 2014, almost 40 percent of food workers were people of color. . . . This is nearly 10 percentage points higher than the private industry racial makeup as a whole.[22] The largest non-White segment were Latinos, who comprised 23 percent of the food chain. A little over 20 percent of food workers were born outside of

the United States. In addition, close to 8 percent of food chain workers were age 65 or older in 2014.[23] We expect that this trend will continue based on estimates by the U.S. Census that the population over 65 will double by the year 2050.

The food system is composed of an educated labor force. In 2014, over 37 percent of food chain workers had attained a high school degree, while over 30 percent also had some college education. An additional 12 percent of food workers held a bachelor's or graduate-level degree. This pattern of diversity did not hold among food chain leadership. More than 72 percent of the chief executive officers in food industries were White men, . . . compared with cross-industry estimates that 62 percent of total private-sector executives are White men. Fewer than 15 percent were White women. Latino men composed five percent of CEOs; Black men and Latina females comprised less than two percent. Other population groups, such as Black and Asian women as well as Natives of either gender, were one percent or less of food CEOs. . . .

SIGNIFICANT WAGE DIFFERENCES BY GENDER AND RACE/ETHNICITY EXIST IN THE FOOD CHAIN

The patterns of inequality in the food system that keep women and people of color in frontline positions also produce significant wage gaps. For every dollar earned by White men, Latin men earned 76 cents and Black men 60 cents. White women earned less than half of their White male counterparts at 47 cents to every dollar. Women of color earned 42 and 45 cents, respectively, to every dollar paid to a White man. Within Asian communities, males earned 81 cents and females earned 58 cents for each dollar earned by White men. Native peoples, both men and women, suffered the largest wage gap compared to White men, earning 44 and 36 cents, respectively, to every dollar. The Census reported that households maintained by a foreign-born worker were among the lowest paid.[24] In addition, the Census found that Asian households overall enjoyed the highest median income, $77,166, in 2015. For Asians employed in the food chain, however, wages for both men and women were below those earned by White men.

RATES OF INJURY AND ILLNESS AT WORK HAVE RISEN SINCE 2010

The official data on the job injuries recorded by the U.S. Health and Occupational Safety Administration (OSHA) reveal that food system workers are hurt or injured at higher rates than other workers. While the average rate of injuries for private industries was 3.2 cases per 100 workers in 2014, for agricultural and food manufacturing workers, these numbers jump to 5.5 and 5.1.[25] Nonetheless, the standards OSHA uses for counting workplace injuries have been criticized as too narrow, leading to potentially serious problems of undercounting.[26] Direct surveys of workers indicate that the rates of injury can be much higher. For example, upwards of 72 percent of poultry workers in Alabama, 42 percent of food processing workers in New York City, and 57 percent of all food workers have reported suffering an injury or health problem on the job in these samples.[27] Even with problems of undercounting, when we looked more closely at food chain industries with particularly high rates of injuries, like animal and crop production, we found that rates of injuries have risen since 2010, despite overall improvement across private industry. . . . Additionally, high injury rates are an example of how general improvement across the economy does not reach frontline food workers.

UNION MEMBERSHIP AND DENSITY HAVE DECLINED

Unions help ensure higher wages and better conditions for workers. As with many sectors of the economy, there has been a dramatic decrease in unionization in the food system over the past 30 years. While food production and service have always had low union membership, the food processing, distribution, and retail sectors have seen large declines in union density over this time. . . . Unions represented 16.4 million wage and salary workers in the United States in 2015.[28] This included 14.8 million members of trade unions as well as 1.6 million workers who were not affiliated with unions but held jobs that were covered by a union contract. The union membership rate across all industries in 2015 was 11 percent, almost half of the 18 percent membership rate in 1985. Food chain sectors had a lower union membership rate at six percent, or 1.1 million workers. . . . Almost seven percent, or 1.2 million workers, were covered by a union contract regardless of membership. . . .

RECOMMENDATIONS

Significant changes are necessary in order to address issues of poor wages and working conditions across the food system. Raising minimum wages and mandating benefits will ensure that workers have the capacity to feed their families, protect their own personal health, and produce our food in fair working conditions. Strengthening and enforcing labor regulations will help to raise standards for all workers by not allowing bad actors to undercut honest employers. Both policymakers and consumers can take steps to improve job conditions across the food system. . . .

NOTES

1. Solidarity Research Collective (SRC) Analysis of Gross Output by Industry, 2015. U.S. Bureau of Economic Analysis.
2. SRC Analysis of Consumer Expenditures—2015. U.S. Bureau of Labor Statistics.
3. Bauer, Mary. 2013. *Close to Slavery: Guestworker Programs in the United States*. Montgomery, AL: The Southern Poverty Law Center. https://www.splcenter.org/20130218/ close-slavery-guestworker-programs-united-states.
4. Jaffe, Joann, and Michael Gertler. June 2006. "Victual Vicissitudes: Consumer Deskilling and the (Gendered) Transformation of Food Systems." *Agriculture and Human Values* 23, no. 2: 143–62.
5. Allen, Patricia, and Carolyn Sachs. 2007. "Women and Food Chains: The Gendered Politics of Food." *International Journal of Sociology of Agriculture and Food* 15, no 1: 1–23.

6. Restaurant Opportunities Center United. 2015. *Ending Jim Crow in America's Restaurants: Racial and Gender Occupational Segregation in the Restaurant Industry.* New York: ROC United.

7. Restaurant Opportunities Center United. 2015.

8. Restaurant Opportunities Centers United. 2013. *The Third Shift: Child Care Needs and Access for Working Mothers in Restaurants.* New York: ROC United. http://rocunited.org/the-third-shift.

9. Davis, David. 2013. "Price and Promotion Effects of Supermarket Mergers." South Dakota State University Working Paper Number 12009; DePhillips, Lydia. "Supermarkets Are Merging Again." 2016. *The Washington Post*, July 28. Accessed July 24, 2016. https://www.washingtonpost.com/news/wonk/wp/2013/07/28/supermarkets-are-merging-again-what-does-that-mean-for-your-grocery-bill.

10. The Food Chain Workers Alliance. 2015. *Walmart at the Crossroads.* Los Angeles: The Food Chain Workers Alliance.

11. U.S. House Committee on Education and the Work Force. 2012. *The Low Wage Drag on Our Economy.* Washington, DC: U.S. House of Representatives.

12. Rodman, Sarah, Colleen Barry, Megan Clayton, Shannon Frattaroli, Roni Neff, and Lainie Rutkow. 2016. "Agricultural Exceptionalism at the State Level: Characterization of Wage and Hour Laws for U.S. Farmworkers." *Journal of Agriculture, Food Systems, and Community Development*: 1–22.

13. Galvin, Daniel J. 2016. "Deterring Wage Theft: Alt-Labor, State Politics, and the Policy Determinants of Minimum Wage Compliance." *Perspectives on Politics* 14, no. 2: 324–50.

14. Seawell, Joshua. 2009. *Corporate Consolidation in Agriculture Fact Sheet.* Washington, DC: Taxpayers for Common. Accessed July 24, 2016, from http://www.taxpayer.net/library/ article/ corporate-consolidation-in-agriculture-fact-sheet.

15. U.S. Bureau of Labor Statistics, Labor Productivity and Costs 2016, Major Sector Productivity and Costs database.

16. SRC analysis of CPS ASEC, 2014–2016.

17. Glasmeier, Amy. 2016. "New Living Wage Calculator 2016." Cambridge: Massachusetts Institute of Technology. http://livingwage.mit.edu/articles/18-new-2015-living-wage-data.

18. SRC analysis of wage and salary workers, CPS ASEC and ORGs 2016.

19. Coleman-Jensen, Alisha, et al. 2016. *Household Food Security in the United States in 2015.* Economic Research Service U.S. Department of Agriculture, September. www.ers.usda.gov/media/2137657/err215_summary.pdf.

20. "Definitions of Food Security." 2016. U.S. Department of Agriculture, September 6. http://www.ers.usda.gov/topics/food-nutrition-assistance/food-security-in-the-us/definitions-of-food-security.aspx.

21. Ortman, J. M., et al. 2014. "An Aging Nation: The Older Population in the United States." Current Population Reports, U.S. Census, May. http://www.census.gov/content/dam/ Census/library/publications/2014/demo/p25-1140.pdf.

22. "Labor Force Statistics from the Current Population Survey." 2015. "Employed Persons by Detailed Occupation, Sex, Race, and Hispanic or Latino Ethnicity." http://www.bls.gov/cps/cpsaat11.htm.

23. Cohn, D., and A. Caumont. 2016. "10 Demographic Trends That Are Shaping the U.S. and the World." FactTank, Pew Research Center, March 31. http://www.pewresearch. org/fact-tank/2016/03/31/10-demographic-trends-that-are-shaping-the-u-s-and-the-world.

24. Proctor, B. D., et al. 2016. "Income and Poverty in the United States: 2015." U.S. Census, September 15. http://www.census.gov/content/dam/Census/library/publications/2016/ demo/p60-256.pdf.

25. Proctor, B. D., et al. 2016. "Income and Poverty in the United States: 2015." U.S. Census, September 15. http://www.census.gov/content/dam/Census/library/publications/2016/demo/ p60-256.pdf.

26. Ruser, John W. 2008. "Examining Evidence on Whether BLS Undercounts Workplace Injuries and Illnesses." *Monthly Labor Review*. Washington, DC: U.S. Bureau of Labor Statistics, August: 20–30. http://www.bls.gov/opub/mlr/2008/08/art2full.pdf.

27. Fritzche, Tom. 2012. *Unsafe at These Speeds*. Montgomery, AL: The Southern Poverty Law Center. /www.splcenter.org/20130228/unsafe-these-speeds; Brandworkers and Community Development Project at the Urban Justice Center. 2014. *Feeding New York*. New York: The Urban Justice Center; The Food Chain Workers Alliance. 2012.

28. "Union Members 2015." 2016. U.S. Bureau of Labor Statistics, January 28. http://www.bls.gov/ news.release/union2.nr0.htm.

ANASTASIA PROKOS

62. GENDER SEGREGATION AT WORK

You may have noticed that women and men are often separated into different types of occupations, a phenomenon known as "gender segregation." Prokos examines the historical and social factors that have contributed to the existence of gender segregation in the workplace and the factors that perpetuate it, including gender socialization, employer biases, and discrimination. Prokos concludes by discussing the consequences of gender segregation and possible solutions to the problem.

INTRODUCTION

Take one look around a typical business or office the next time you need to make a major purchase, take out a loan from a bank, or fill out student aid paperwork. Although you will often see women and men working together to get things done, a closer look might reveal that women and men are often doing different tasks in the same place of business. For example, in a bank the tellers might all be mostly women, whereas men primarily act as the mortgage specialists and supervisors. That is probably no surprise to most people who pay close attention to the world of work. Yet many of us may take this aspect of life for granted and may even think it is somehow part of the natural order of things. Sociologists, of course, delve deeper. We ask questions about how universal the gendered division of labor is (or is not), why women and men tend to do particular kinds of work, and what happens when people try to move beyond commonly accepted career paths. Also, what are the consequences for women's and men's work lives?

The work that both women and men do has changed dramatically in the past century. In fact, many occupations are organized quite differently from in the past or have disappeared altogether. Another major shift has been in the gender composition of occupations and jobs; today women and men are more likely to have similar occupations and jobs than they were 50 to 100 years ago. Yet even with these remarkable transformations in employment patterns, women and men in the contemporary United States continue to be concentrated in different occupations, jobs, and industries.

The gender segregation of work, when women and men work in different occupations, jobs, or in different workplaces, is a striking feature of the U.S. labor force.[1] In 2017, 217 of 536 specific occupations were dominated by men (defined as 75 percent or more men), and 48 percent of all men worked in those occupations. Only 75 of the 536 specific occupations were dominated by women (with 75 percent or more women), and 43 percent of all women were employed in those occupations. Some occupations, like emergency management directors, brokerage clerks, and locksmiths, are extremely dominated by men, with virtually no women in the occupation (or at least none sampled in the March 2017 Current Population Survey). In contrast, occupations like dental hygienists and preschool and kindergarten teachers are notoriously dominated by women, with few men in them. This article delves deeper into these trends, explaining where they came from, why they persist, and their consequences.

The explanations for gender segregation in employment were obvious in the not-so-distant past: women were simply barred from many types of

Original to *Focus on Social Problems: A Contemporary Reader*.

employment, and "women's work" was so low in pay that most men had no compelling reason to pursue it when they had better options. Today, the explanations for gender segregation are more complex. Tradition, cultural influences, societal expectations, and opportunity structures all influence both women's and men's career paths.

Although the explanations for gender segregation may be different now than in the past, one thing remains remarkably similar: the kinds of work mostly done by women tend to be lower in pay than the kinds of work mostly done by men. And although women have gained access to higher education and moved into many types of professional work that were previously closed to them, much of the work that continues to be associated with women, especially the kind that is related to caring for other people, is worth relatively little in the labor market. In fact, gender segregation in occupations is a primary explanation of the gender wage gap between women and men (Padavic and Reskin, 2002).

CONTEMPORARY EMPLOYMENT PATTERNS

A look at the current most common occupational categories for women and men shows us a great deal about the type of work that people view as customary for each. Table 1 lists the ten most common occupations for women and men in 2017. Consistent with trends in occupations for many years, nurses, elementary and middle school teachers, and secretaries are the three most common jobs for women, while truck driver continues to be one of the most common occupations for men to hold (Padavic and Reskin, 2002). What Table 1 also shows us is just how concentrated women and men are in just a small set of highly segregated occupations. Although the Bureau of Labor Statistics tracks more than 500 specific detailed occupations, 32 percent of all employed women and 27 percent of all employed men worked in just these 18 occupations. Furthermore, Table 1 shows that many of the occupations are highly segregated, especially for women. For example, the occupation of *secretary and administrative assistant* is 95 percent women. Table 1 makes it clear that the paid work most often done by women is quite different from the paid work that is most often done

by men. Women and men had only two top-10 occupations in common: first-line supervisors/managers of retail sales workers and all other managers. It is not surprising, then, that these two occupations are some of the most gender-integrated ones on the list.

Looking at the distribution of women and men in specific occupations is telling and helps create a picture of how segregation appears in employment, but it is not the best way to summarize society-wide patterns of segregation. Scholars typically use a single measure, the *index of dissimilarity* (D), to measure overall levels of segregation. The index of dissimilarity is calculated so that one number tells us what percentage of women (or men) would have to change occupations to be equally represented to men (or women) across all occupations. A score of zero would mean occupations are fully integrated, whereas a score of 100 would mean they were fully segregated. The 2017 index of dissimilarity was 49.8, meaning that almost half of all women would need to switch occupations for women and men to be equally represented across all occupations.[2] The index of dissimilarity allows researchers to compare segregation across geographic regions, across different industries, and over time, which is illustrated below.

Yet only looking at occupations and occupational characteristics can actually gloss over a great deal of segregation that occurs in the labor force. Occupations, even detailed lists of them, are, by definition, broad categories that capture only the most basic activities that workers perform, and they do not take industry, location, or employer into account. Jobs, in contrast, are much more specific categories of work, because they include more information about where and for whom people work. For example, someone may have an occupation as a teacher, but could have a job in a poor, rural school district or a more affluent suburb. A chief executive officer could have a job for a large multinational manufacturing corporation or for a small nonprofit educational organization. As these latter jobs illustrate, the industry in which a person is employed also affects the content of an occupation, as well as its compensation. Researchers also study and document gender segregation in industries and in jobs, although the bulk of research focuses on the level of occupation.

TABLE 1. TOP TEN OCCUPATIONS FOR WOMEN AND MEN, 2017

Women	Number of Women	Percentage Women
Registered nurses	2,253,000	89%
Elementary and middle school teachers	2,224,000	78%
Secretaries and administrative assistants	2,046,000	95%
Customer service representatives	1,234,000	66%
Nursing, psychiatric, and home health aides	1,223,000	88%
Managers, all other	1,163,000	39%
First-line supervisors of retail sales workers	1,013,000	42%
Cashiers	982,000	72%
Accountants and auditors	890,000	59%
First-line supervisors of office and administrative support workers	854,000	68%

Men	Number of Men	Percentage Men
Driver/sales workers and truck drivers	2,689,000	95%
Managers, all other	1,841,000	61%
Construction laborers	1,400,000	97%
First-line supervisors of retail sales workers	1,376,000	58%
Laborers and freight, stock, and material movers, hand	1,196,000	83%
Software developers, applications and systems software	1,174,000	82%
Retail salespersons	1,160,000	61%
Janitors and building cleaners	1,136,000	71%
Cooks	859,000	63%
Carpenters	851,000	98%

Source: Author calculations based on Bureau of Labor Statistics Labor Force Statistics from the Current Population Survey, 2017. Table 39. Median weekly earnings of full-time wage and salary workers by detailed occupation and gender.

HISTORICAL PRECEDENCE

Employers have been sorting women and men into different paid work since the start of the Industrial Revolution. Documents and photos from the mid-1800s through the early 1900s show that women worked in coal mines, labored as seamstresses, and assembled mechanical devices, such as watches. In each of these cases, however, women mostly worked separately from men, either on different tasks or in different rooms or departments. Employers hired women workers for these jobs in part because women were less expensive to employ, as they could not demand pay as high as men. As women, men, and children moved into industrial work, the overabundance of labor supply meant intense competition for jobs and led to low factory wages. One way for groups of men to reduce the competition was to limit women's (and children's) access to the labor market; they accomplished this through unions, most of which included only men as members. Unions in the late 19th and early 20th centuries supported protective legislation that barred women and children from certain kinds of employment, especially when working conditions were considered unsafe. The outcome of this protective legislation also removed women from some of the highest-paying industrial jobs where they had previously been employed (Padavic and Reskin, 2002).

Protective legislation and similar restrictions on women's employment (such as rules barring married women or mothers from employment) were successful at reducing women's labor force participation and pushing women out of some lines of work entirely. Thus, by the mid-20th century (with the exception of a wartime employment), most women in the labor market were concentrated in relatively low-paying jobs such as laundress, maid, sales girl, teacher, nurse, and secretary (Kessler-Harris, 1982; Padavic and Reskin, 2002).

In the United States, it was legal for employers to choose employees for jobs on the basis of their sex category until the 1960s. Prior to the passage of Civil Rights Act in 1964, newspaper advertisements for jobs were routinely separated into "Male Help" and "Female Help" sections so that employers could easily target their desired employees. For example, in 1958 an advertisement in the Male Help section of the *The State*, a South Carolina newspaper, read: "Need Assistant Manager for Westinghouse Appliances, Good Opportunity for Right Man," whereas one in the female section read: "Need one more curb girl-cashier, day shift" ("Want Ads," 1958). In this way, employers could explicitly and easily sort people into jobs based on their sex category. It is worth noting here that newspapers also commonly included separate sections for "colored help," and these sections also included separate ads for women and men, which allowed them to differentiate potential employees on the basis of race, in addition to sex.

It was not until the Civil Rights Act passed that the story began to change, and even then progress started slowly. The legacy of these earlier associations between particular types of work and gender has been powerful. What emerged throughout the 19th and early 20th centuries as ideology about which jobs were appropriate for women has had remarkable sticking power, even in the face of a number of extraordinary social changes, such as the women's movement and dramatic increases in women's labor force participation.

DECADES OF CHANGE

Title VII of the 1964 Civil Rights Act, which barred employment discrimination on the basis of sex, race, color, religion, or national origin, opened the door for decades of change in employment. Yet women's influx into work that had been traditionally performed by men proceeded at a slow and uneven pace. Because the enforcement of the new nondiscrimination legislation did not gain momentum until the 1970s, the 1960s saw little change in occupational segregation (Padavic and Reskin, 2002). The 1970s saw the greatest overall decline in segregation, according to the index of dissimilarity. The decade began with a score of 67 and ended with a score of 60 (Jacobs, 2003). Declines in segregation continued into the 1980s and the early part of the 1990s and then stalled in the middle 1990s. The current level of segregation has shown only slight declines since that time (Hegewisch et al., 2010).

A variety of factors led to notable declines in occupational segregation during the 1970s and 1980s. In large part, these changes reflected many occupations opening access to women. Occupations such as "bartender" saw large influxes of women. In 1970, only 21 percent of bartenders were women, but by 1980 it was no longer a segregated occupation—44 percent of bartenders were women—and by the end of the 1980s, women were roughly half of all bartenders (Reskin and Roos, 1990). This kind of change was not true for all occupations dominated by men, however, and women had less success gaining access to occupations like engineering, dentistry, electrician, and painter.

Although much of the change in occupational segregation during the 1970s and 1980s was a result of women moving into occupations previously dominated by men, another reason for the drop in overall levels of segregation was a result of shifts in the economic structure. Specifically, some of the occupations that had been the most segregated before this time began to decline as a share of the total labor force. For example, manufacturing work, an industry which has been consistently heavily dominated by men, took up a smaller and smaller portion of the total labor force. In 1960 the manufacturing sector employed about 30 percent of all workers and by the end of the 1980s that figure was only 17.4 percent. This trend had two implications for gender segregation. First, because of fewer opportunities available in manufacturing, it was more difficult for women to move into positions in that industry. Second, although the manufacturing industry remained heavily dominated by men, the smaller proportion of workers in this sector meant that it had a smaller impact on overall measures of employment segregation than some of the occupations that were gaining ground.

What is especially interesting about the desegregation that occurred during the 1970s and 1980s is that many occupations feminized, meaning they shifted from being dominated by men to having more women in them. For example, the occupation of insurance adjuster shifted from 30 percent women to 60 percent women during the decade (Reskin and Roos, 1990). Conversely, few occupations masculinized (changed from customarily being filled by women to include many more men). In fact, many of the occupations that were dominated by women saw little change in men's representation. Dental assistant, hairdresser, cashier, preschool and kindergarten teacher, registered nurse, and librarian remained heavily segregated occupations.

THE POWER OF TRADITION

Despite the many changes that occurred as a result of the antidiscrimination policies of the 1970s, the pace of change and occupational integration slowed in the 1980s and even more so after that. By 2010, it was clear that gender segregation had no longer been declining for quite some time, and scholars began referring to a "stalled gender revolution" in employment (England, 2010; Hegewisch et al., 2010). Women's influx into occupations previously dominated by men has slowed considerably, and many occupations, such as engineering and carpentry, seem especially impervious to women's entry.

It is worth noting that even within broad occupational categories, women and men may hold different occupational specialties. For example, although more professors are women than in the past, women are concentrated in the humanities, human sciences, and some social sciences. Moreover, many occupations may be in the process of "resegregating," meaning they are in the process of shifting from being dominated by one gender to being dominated by the other (i.e., feminized or masculinized). This is the case for the occupation of bartending. As mentioned previously, by the end of the 1980s roughly half of all bartenders were women, and now that figure stands at

62 percent. If the trend continues, bartending will be relatively dominated heavily by women in the not-so-distant future.

Before turning to explanations for continuing gender segregation in employment, it is helpful to get a sense of some of the employment patterns that did not change much during the period that saw the most transformation. As Paula England (2010) has pointed out, the declines in gender segregation in employment have been different for middle-class jobs compared to working-class jobs. Working-class jobs, like construction worker and manufacturing work, are "almost as segregated as they were in 1950!" (157). Many of the occupations that opened up to women during the 1970s and 1980s were professional jobs that required a college degree. Professors, lawyers, doctors, and managers are all increasingly likely to be women.

Furthermore, the work that is often considered "women's work" continues to be devalued—worth less in the labor market—than that work that is customarily seen as "men's work." When that is the case, women have an economic incentive to try to move into customarily male work, but men have little economic incentive to move into occupations dominated by women (England, 2010). Indeed, it is much rarer for an occupation to masculinize. In cases when men have begun doing the work that women had done, often they do so in a different occupation. For example, until the early to mid-1900s, midwives used to deliver most babies (as they do still in many other countries). The growing medical profession, dominated by men, in the 19th and 20th centuries recognized that childbirth was a potentially lucrative addition to medical practices and, in effect, created a monopoly on assisting in childbirth in the United States. Until recently, the majority of obstetrician/gynecologists were men, although that particular occupation has seen the entrance of increasing numbers of women in the past several decades.

These examples show that some kinds of work have been more impervious to change than others. They also begin to hint at some of the reasons that some occupations are less likely to change than others. How much training is needed for a job, how high status it is, and how much it pays are all linked to the reasons that some occupations remain more segregated than others.

EXPLANATIONS FOR CONTINUED SEGREGATION

It is tempting to believe that the patterns in women's and men's employment that we see in the United States simply reflect the choices that people make about their careers, especially when we see how little girls and boys seem to gravitate toward different kinds of activities. But as sociologists we know that the choices people make reflect subtle influences, many of which are beyond individuals' control. Parents, teachers, and peers influence what children believe they are good at and what they think they should pursue. Cultural expectations and stereotypes influence the way people view what is appropriate work for women and men. The availability of certain kinds of jobs, the way people are treated at work and when they search for work, and what employers are looking for in employees all influence women's and men's options and choices.

WORKERS' CHOICES AND ACTIONS

Children learn stereotypes about gender early, and these stereotypes can influence how young people imagine their futures. Indeed, these stereotypes influence the kinds of jobs that young children see as appropriate and can influence their early decisions. For example, although girls' and boys' math test scores are about the same, parents and teachers persist in believing that girls are not as good at math as boys (Gunderson et al., 2012). As a result, girls tend to believe they are not as good at math as boys, undermining their enjoyment of the field and possibly resulting in fewer girls headed toward math-related careers (Correll, 2001). Luckily, in this case, social psychologists know how to fix the problem. As years of careful research have shown, when girls are taught math in such a way that they also learn they can develop their ability (rather than seeing it as something that is innate and fixed), they actually perform better in math (Dweck, 2006). Doing well in a subject can then have the consequence of increasing girls' enjoyment and motivation in that area (Eccles and Wigfield, 2002).

Even the language we use influences children's perceptions about work. Research shows that children perceive occupations as more suited to one gender or another depending on their title. For example, children tend to envision jobs with names like "policeman" and "fireman" as appropriate for men, but not for women (Liben et al., 2002). Using gender-neutral language for such occupations (police officer and firefighter) changes children's understanding of who can occupy these jobs.

Despite the powerful lessons children learn, sociologists know that people's choices are flexible and often bend toward options that make greater sense as their circumstances change. For example, college students take different courses and change majors (often more than once) and people continue to change their ideas about jobs well into their twenties (Jacobs, 2003). This is because the situations people face when they actually try to get a job, when they begin to train for work, or as they start working for a specific company are much more powerful influences on their adult career choices than their stated preferences when they are young.

EMPLOYER PRACTICES

Cultural stereotypes do not just affect workers' decisions, of course. Many people, including employers and co-workers, continue to view women and men as fundamentally different from one another and think that those differences mean that certain kinds of work are most suitable for either men or women. Although overt discrimination is no longer legal, gender stereotypes—and the expectations that result from them—continue to influence employers' decisions. Employers can channel women and men into different work because of implicit biases, everyday business practices, and overt discrimination.

A vast and growing literature on implicit bias shows that biases that people may not even be aware of can influence their perceptions and treatment of others. For example, experimental research has shown that when people evaluate resumes, they judge the same resume differently depending on whether they think it belongs to a woman or a man (Steinpreis et al., 1999). The subtle ways that stereotypes can affect judgments of people can creep into employment decisions. An employer may view a woman who has strong negotiating skills as "aggressive," but consider a man demonstrating the same skills "assertive." A man who mentions his family may seem like a "good family man," whereas an employer may think a similar woman would be too focused on her family to do a good job. The biases may not always be this obvious, but they can influence decisions about who to hire and which position to fill with a specific applicant.

Beyond these examples of bias, sometimes employers' everyday practices tend to reproduce the gender composition of occupations. A majority of jobs (about 60 percent of them) are never advertised and thus do not use a competitive hiring process. In fact, a great deal of hiring for jobs happens through social networks. For example, when I asked students in my sociology of work course how they got their first jobs, nearly every one of them raised his or her hand to show that it was through one of their parents or parents' friends. Evidence suggests that when hiring occurs informally in this way, employers tend to hire people who are similar to themselves in both gender and race, whom they feel more comfortable with (known as "homosocial reproduction"). Ultimately, homosocial reproduction is likely to replicate the current workforce, at least demographically.

Another aspect of common employment practices that influences who is hired into an occupation is the relationship between training and occupational access. Title IX of the Educational Amendments of 1972, which protects against sex discrimination in education, opened up many opportunities for women to enter professional occupations by granting access to the formal education and training needed for those occupations. This allowed women to overcome the first hurdle to gain access to many professional occupations,

such as doctor and lawyer. However, other occupations that require people to obtain training on the job or through apprenticeships means that they first must be accepted as someone's apprentice, or even hired, to gain the skills needed to perform these jobs. Occupations like electrician, carpenter, and plumber, which operate through apprenticeships and hiring, have not opened up to women as much as occupations dominated by men in the professional arena have (Bergmann, 2011).

Although much of the bias in employer decisions may be unintended, blatant discrimination also still occurs. In recent years, more than 25,000 cases of sex discrimination per year have been reported to the Equal Employment Opportunity Commission (Equal Employment Opportunity Commission, 2018), and although they are not all hiring discrimination cases, they do show us that employers continue to use the sex category in employment decisions. In fact, some powerful evidence of employer discrimination comes from firsthand experiences. In her book based on interviews with transgender men, Kristin Schilt (2010) documented many cases where men saw firsthand just how they had been discriminated against before they transitioned, when they were women. They saw how co-workers, supervisors, managers, customers, and employers based decisions about hiring, promotion, and pay primarily—and in some cases exclusively—on the basis of gender. These "behind-the-scenes" views the men gained after transitioning support the numerous experiences women report about acts of discrimination at work.

All three of the explanations above (implicit bias, everyday hiring practices, and blatant discrimination) can help us understand why some occupations have been slower to desegregate than others. These patterns help to show the powerful role that employers have in perpetuating occupational segregation. They also demonstrate how important antidiscrimination efforts are in reducing employment discrimination.

CONSEQUENCES OF SEGREGATION

You might wonder why sociologists have paid so much attention to occupational gender segregation. Occupational segregation is one of the primary forces behind women's lower average earnings compared to men. Women's pay lags behind men's even among workers who work full time. This is in large part because the occupations and jobs in which women are concentrated pay less, on average, than those in which men are concentrated, even when they require similar levels of skills and training. These trends harken back to a long history of "women's work" being seen as less valuable than that done by men. Current employment patterns reflect that history.

Table 2 shows median earnings for men and women in several different occupations in 2017. Keep in mind that these are all wages for full-time, year-round workers. It is notable that the highest-paying occupations, near the top of the list, almost all employ many more men than women. Pharmacists are an exception and illustrate that women have made headway in some high-paying occupations. In the case of pharmacists, structural changes in the industry (more corporate-owned chains and hospital employment instead of small independent pharmacies) have meant that the occupation continues to be highly paid and is also more open to women (Goldin and Katz, 2012). In general, the occupations that are dominated by women, however, are more likely to appear near the bottom of the list.

TABLE 2.   MEDIAN WEEKLY EARNINGS FOR SELECT OCCUPATIONS, 2017

	Men	Women	Percent Women in Occupation
Chief executives	$2,415	$1,920	28
Physicians and surgeons	$2,277	$1,759	43
Pharmacists	$2,228	$1,834	58
Lawyers	$2,105	$1,753	43
Software developers, applications and systems software	$1,863	$1,543	18
Managers, all other	$1,629	$1,251	39
Registered nurses	$1,260	$1,143	89
Sales representatives, wholesale and manufacturing	$1,222	$956	28
Elementary and middle school teachers	$1,139	$987	78
Social workers	$935	$900	83
Secretaries and administrative assistants	$852	$735	95
Driver/sales workers and truck drivers	$807	$589	5
Retail salespersons	$704	$523	39
Construction laborers [a]	$667	-	3
Laborers and freight, stock, and material movers, hand	$595	$500	18
Nursing, psychiatric, and home health aides	$583	$493	88
Janitors and building cleaners	$574	$481	29
Maids and housekeeping cleaners	$508	$439	84
Cashiers	$493	$422	72
Cooks	$481	$436	37

Source: Author calculations based on Bureau of Labor Statistics Labor Force Statistics from the Current Population Survey, 2017. Table 39. Median weekly earnings of full-time wage and salary workers by detailed occupation and gender.

a   *There are too few women in the occupation to calculate reliable statistics for women's wages.*

Because much of the difference in women's and men's average earnings reflects these occupational distributions, legislation addressing pay discrimination without addressing occupational segregation is unlikely to have a substantial influence on the larger pay gap. Some policy experts have suggested that comparable worth policies would have a greater influence on the pay gap. Comparable worth policies seek to evaluate the level of skill required in particular occupations and then adjust the compensation in those occupations to directly reflect the skill involved, rather than the gender of the occupants. Such policies have the potential to reduce gender differences in pay, especially in working-class occupations. This is because many working-class "women's jobs" often require a similar level of training, but tend to pay substantially less than the jobs of working class men.

CONCLUSION

This article has intentionally boiled down the issue of occupational sex segregation to its most basic elements. Of course, many other factors complicate the picture I have painted here. For example, employment is also further segregated by race and ethnicity as a result of related historical and cultural patterns, including discrimination. Changing demographics, global economic restructuring, and shifting cultural patterns all form part of the larger context that affects gender and employment. The historical trends and contemporary patterns summarized here build a foundation for understanding the centrality of gender in shaping the institution of work.

Today's young people may enter a less segregated labor market on the whole than young people in the past, which could have long-term consequences for the composition of occupations. Even so, women and men continue to be channeled into different occupations through complex social, cultural, and business practices. The work that most people continue to view as women's work carries lower status and is paid less than work viewed as men's work. The public policies that helped advance greater gender equality in employment opportunity throughout the latter decades of the 20th century have not been not enough. Traditional antidiscrimination laws have reduced labor market segregation overall, but new equality strategies will be necessary for 21st-century women and men to have access to the work that interests them and to be fairly compensated for it.

NOTES

1. Historically, this type of occupational segregation was known as "occupational sex segregation," based on biological sex category rather than gender. More recently, researchers and activists have begun to think of it as being based on socially-constructed gender categories, rather than biological sex.
2. Author calculations based on Bureau of Labor Statistics Labor Force Statistics from the Current Population Survey, 2017. Table 39. Median weekly earnings of full-time wage and salary workers by detailed occupation and sex.

REFERENCES

Bergmann, Barbara R. 2011. "Sex Segregation in the Blue-collar Occupations: Women's Choices or Unremedied Discrimination?: Comment on England." *Gender & Society* 25:88–93.

Correll, Shelley J. 2001. "Gender and the Career Choice Process: The Role of Biased Self-Assessments." *American Journal of Sociology* 106(6):1691–1730.

Dweck, Carol S. 2006. "Is Math a Gift? Beliefs That Put Females at Risk." In S. J. Ceci and W. Williams (Eds.), *Why Aren't More Women in Science? Top Researchers Debate the Evidence*. Washington, DC: American Psychological Association.

Eccles, Jacquelynne S., and Allan Wigfield. 2002. "Motivational Beliefs, Values, and Goals." *Annual Review of Psychology* 53:109–132.

England, Paula. 2010. "The Gender Revolution: Uneven and Stalled." *Gender & Society*. 24:149–166.

Equal Employment Opportunity Commission. 2018. *Charge Statistics (Charges files with EEOC) FY 1997 through FY 2017*. Retrieved November 7, 2018. http://eeoc.gov/eeoc/statistics/enforcement/charges.cfm/.

Goldin, Claudia, and Lawrence F. Katz. 2012. "The Most Egalitarian of All Professions: Pharmacy and the Evolution of a Family-Friendly Occupation." *Working Paper 18410*. National Bureau of Economic Research.

Gunderson, Elizabeth A., Gerardo Ramirez, Susan C. Levine, and Sian L. Beilock. 2012. "The Role of Parents and Teachers in the Development of Gender-Related Math Attitudes." *Sex Roles* 66:153–166.

Hegewisch, Ariana, Hannah Lipemann, Jeffrey Hayes, and Heidi Hartmann. 2010. "Separate and Not Equal? Gender Segregation in the Labor Market and the Gender Wage Gap." *Briefing Paper IWPR C377*. Institute for Women's Policy Research.

Jacobs, Jerry. 2003. "Detours on the Road to Equality: Women, Work, and Higher Education." *Contexts* 2:32–41.

Kessler-Harris, Alice. 1982. *Out to Work: A History of Wage Earning Women in the United States*. New York: Oxford University Press.

Liben, Lynn S., Rebecca Bigler, and Holleen R. Krough. 2002. "Language at Work: Children's Gendered Interpretations of Occupational Titles." *Child Development* 73(3):810–828.

Padavic, Irene, and Barbara Reskin 2002. *Women and Men at Work*, 22nd ed. Thousand Oaks: Pine Forge Press.

Reskin, Barbara F., and Patricia A. Roos. 1990. *Job Queues, Gender Queues: Explaining Women's Inroads into Male Occupations*. Philadelphia: Temple University Press.

Schilt, Kristen. 2010. *Just One of the Guys: Transgender Men and the Persistence of Gender Inequality*. Chicago: University of Chicago Press.

Steinpreis, Rhea E., Katie A. Anders, and Dawn Ritzke. 1999. "The Impact of Gender on the Review of the Curricula Vitae of Job Applicants and Tenure Candidates: A National Empirical Study." *Sex Roles* 41:509–528.

"Want Ads." *The State*. June 1, 1958, p. 8D. Newspapers on microfilm. Published Material Division, South Carolina Library, University of South Carolina, Columbia, South Carolina.

ABOUT THOSE 79 CENTS

ADIA HARVEY WINGFIELD

Extensive research shows[1] that even when controlling for factors like education, skill, and experience, women routinely earn less than men employed in the same professions. Often, this argument is accompanied by the now-famous statistic that women earn about 79 cents for every dollar men make at work.[2] This is an important data point, but focusing on that figure alone masks the role race can play in perpetuating these disparities.

---

1   Pearson, Catherine. 2016. "No, The Gender Pay Gap Isn't a Myth—And Here's Why." *Huffington Post*, April 12.

2   Pearson, 2016.

For instance, it is important to ask: Which women? The 79 cents statistic is an average that includes all women, but it obscures the even wider gaps[3] faced by women of color. For Black women, the number is closer to 65 cents, while for Latinas it is even lower, at 54 cents. This data draws attention to the fact that while women as a group aren't paid as much as men, women of color see even more pronounced earnings gaps.

What is at the root of these disparities? In the late 1980s, the legal scholar Kimberlé Williams Crenshaw argued[4] that when it came to antidiscrimination law, looking at categories like race or gender in isolation obscured the ways gender and race intersected to create a specific, unique disadvantage for Black women. This omission rendered them an overlooked, unprotected group whose particular experiences with discrimination had little legal recourse. Crenshaw introduced the theory of intersectionality, the idea that when it comes to thinking about how inequalities persist, categories like gender, race, and class are best understood as overlapping and mutually constitutive rather than isolated and distinct.

This is particularly evident when it comes to the gender–wage gap. There are a couple of commonly offered explanations for why women of color make less than men: Some say it's the unfortunate result of the fact that women of color tend to go into different, lower-paying careers, or the fact that many of them temporarily pause their careers to care for their children. However, studies[5] looking at specific occupations show that even when controlling for professional experience, area of specialty, and educational background, disparities still persist.

In fact, sociologists have shown how racial and gender discrimination[6] plays important roles in creating and reinforcing this particular wage gap. Using data from the Ohio Civil Rights Commission, the sociologist Vincent Roscigno points out[7] that office rules are applied more harshly to women of color than to others, and that some predominantly White workplaces have racially inhospitable environments that serve to push women of color out. This effect is even more pronounced in majority-male occupations. The sociologists Ella L. J. Bell Smith and Stella Nkomo also document[8] how Black women working in male-dominated executive ranks encounter both racial and gender stereotypes as well as disparities in mentorship that limit their career trajectories.

Additionally, as the sociologist Jake Rosenfeld has shown,[9] the decline in unionization has worsened the racial wage gap, particularly for Black women working in the private sector. Rosenfeld's work indicated that Black women were joining the workforce in large numbers—at last gaining access to the benefits of unions—right around the time that organized labor began to decline in influence, scope, and power. This left collective bargaining largely unavailable to them, worsening wage gaps that still exist today. The point is that the gender–wage gap is not just a story of women making less money than men; it is indicative of how race also shapes earnings disparities, such that women of color often find themselves financially in even worse shape than their White female colleagues.

Importantly, these racial disparities exist on both sides of the gender–pay gap. While researchers and policymakers are more likely today to draw attention to how women of color are differentially affected by these gaps in pay, men of color, as the intersectional approach would suggest, are facing earnings gaps unique to them.

When it comes to hourly wages, White men earn an average of $21 an hour,[10] compared to $15 an hour for Black men and $14 an hour for Latino men. (White and Asian women actually earn more per hour, on average—$17 an hour and $18 an hour, respectively—than Black and Latino men.) Further, a recent report[11] from the Economic Policy Institute, a left-leaning think tank, showed that in 2015, after controlling for education, region, and work experience, Black men earned 22 percent less than White men working in the same occupations, a disparity that worsened in the aftermath of the Great Recession.

Other sociological research can provide some insights into the processes that enable and perpetuate these particular gaps. New York University's Deirdre Royster has shown[12] that social

3   Covert, Bryce, and Dylan Petrohilos. 2014. "The Gender Wage Gap Is a Chasm for Women of Color, in One Chart." Retrieved March 13, 2019, from https://thinkprogress.org/the-gender-wage-gap-is-a-chasm-for-women-of-color-in-one-chart-1e8824ee6707.

4   Crenshaw, Kimberle. 1989. "Demarginalizing the Intersection of Race and Sex: A Black Feminist Critique of Antidiscrimination Doctrine, Feminist Theory and Antiracist Politics." *University of Chicago Legal Forum*: Vol. 1989, Article 8.
     Available at https://chicagounbound.uchicago.edu/uclf/vol1989/iss1/8.

5   Oaklander, Mandy. 2016. "Women Doctors Are Paid $20,000 Less Than Male Doctors." *Time*. Retrieved March 13, 2019, from http://time.com/4398888/doctors-gender-wage-gap.

6   Covert, Bryce. 2014. "Here's Why We Know the Gender Wage Gap Really Does Exist." Retrieved March 13, 2019, from https://thinkprogress.org/heres-why-we-know-the-gender-wage-gap-really-does-exist-c1ed7bbadb6a.

7   Roscigno, Vincent. 2007. *The Face of Discrimination: How Race and Gender Impact Work and Home Lives*. Lanham, MD: Rowman & Littlefield.

8   Bell, Ella L. J. Edmondson, and Stella M. Nkomo. 2003. *Our Separate Ways: Black and White Women and the Struggle for Professional Identity*. Boston: Harvard Business School; McGraw-Hill.

9   Rosenfeld, Jake. 2014. *What Unions No Longer Do*. Cambridge, MA: Harvard University Press.

10   Patten, Eileen. 2016. "Racial, Gender Wage Gaps Persist in U.S. Despite Some Progress." Pew Research Center. Retrieved March 13, 2019, from http://www.pewresearch.org/fact-tank/2016/07/01/racial-gender-wage-gaps-persist-in-u-s-despite-some-progress.

11   Wilson, Valerie, and William M. Rodgers III. 2016. "Black–White Wage Gaps Expand with Rising Wage Inequality." Retrieved March 13, 2019, from https://www.epi.org/publication/black-white-wage-gaps-expand-with-rising-wage-inequality.

12   Royster, Deirdre A. 2003. *Race and the Invisible Hand: How White Networks Exclude Black Men from Blue-Collar Jobs*. Berkeley: University of California Press.

networks help White men more than Black men when it comes to looking for skilled jobs. And the sociologists Kathryn Neckerman and Joleen Kirschenman have reported that in lower-wage markets, employers are particularly loath to hire Black men,[13] often based on stereotypes about their work ethic. Further, my own work[14] on Black male professionals—specifically, lawyers—shows that they often are steered to organizational tasks that give firms the appearance of greater diversity but obscure their ability to contribute in other, more valued ways. Thus, it's important to think about how race operates in conjunction with gender when considering pay disparities not just for women, but for men as well.

Recent data from California are particularly illustrative of this. In the state's 37th congressional district, which is in Los Angeles County, data from 2015 seemed to show[15] an encouraging erasure of the gender–pay gap, with women's average earnings above men's. But it turns out that it was not so much

that the pay gap had closed as it was that the 37th district has a very high proportion of Black and Latino men relative to the rest of the country; when women's—particularly Black and brown women's—wages were being compared to those of a group of mostly non-White men, the gender–pay gap effectively disappeared—an effect that can be explained by the fact that the wage gap between men and women of color is smaller than the one between women of color and White men. A disappearance of the pay gap, in this context, likely means that the same processes that put workers of color at a disadvantage—closed social networks, stereotyping, and persistent discrimination, in particular—remain present. It is less of an egalitarian success story if gender–pay equity emerges as a result of lower average wages for men of color.

So, while the gender–pay gap certainly exists, it is a little more complicated than the basic assertion that men make more than women; an intersectional approach reveals that some groups of men—namely, men of color—actually earn less on average than White women. Therefore, any efforts to close the gender–pay gap should address not just the processes that perpetuate gender discrimination—the motherhood penalty, gender stereotypes, and a lack of policies to support working parents, to name a few—but also the mechanisms that reproduce racial inequalities. Pay gaps will still remain, but they should be driven only by differences in skill, education, and experience—not by race or gender.

13 Jencks, Christopher, and Paul E. Peterson, eds. 1991. *The Urban Underclass*. Washington, DC: Brookings Institution.

14 Wingfield, Adia Harvey. 2013. *No More Invisible Man: Race and Gender in Men's Work*. Philadelphia: Temple University Press.

15 Martin, Brittany. 2016. "One Part of L.A. Is Leading the Nation in Closing the Gender Wage Gap." *Time Out Los Angeles*. Retrieved March 13, 2019, from https://www.timeout.com/los-angeles/blog/one-part-of-l-a-is-leading-the-nation-in-closing-the-gender-wage-gap-091916.

CARMEN NOBEL

63. THE CASE AGAINST RACIAL COLORBLINDNESS IN THE WORKPLACE

Although racial colorblindness may seem like a laudable goal, Nobel discusses research and policy that indicate the approach of ignoring racial differences in the workplace may not be the best decision. Different levels of support for affirmative action and belief in the existence of discrimination can influence individuals' support for diversity in the workplace, and attempting to ignore racial difference can create awkward and damaging working environments. Nobel argues that organizations should highlight multiculturalism rather than racial colorblindness.[1]

In trying to prevent discrimination and prejudice, many companies adopt a strategy of "colorblindness"—actively trying to ignore racial differences when enacting policies and making organizational decisions. The logic is simple: if we don't even notice race, then we can't act in a racist manner. The problem is that most of us naturally do notice each other's racial differences, regardless of our employer's policy.

"It's so appealing on the surface to think that the best way to approach race is to pretend that it doesn't exist," says behavioral psychologist Michael I. Norton, an associate professor at Harvard Business School. "But research shows that it simply doesn't work. We do notice race, and there's no way of getting around this fact." Several studies by Norton and his colleagues show that attempting to overcome prejudice by ignoring race is an ineffective strategy that—in many cases—only serves to perpetuate bias. In short, bending over backward to ignore race can exacerbate rather than solve issues of race in the workplace.

"UMM, HE HAS PANTS"

In efforts to be politically correct, people often avoid mentioning race when describing a person, even if that person's race is the most obvious descriptor. (Comedian Stephen Colbert often poke[d] fun of this tendency on his TV show, The Colbert Report, claiming that he. . .[didn't] "see color.") If a manager, for example, is asked which guy Fred is, he or she may be loath to say, "Fred's Asian," even if Fred is the only Asian person in the company. "Instead, it's, 'He's that nice man who works in operations, and, umm, he has hair, and, umm, he has pants,'" Norton says. "And it keeps going on until finally someone comes out and asks, 'Oh, is he Asian?'"

Norton and several colleagues documented this phenomenon in a study that they described in an article for the journal *Psychological Science*, "Color Blindness and Interracial Interaction."[2] The researchers conducted an experiment in which White participants engaged in a two-person guessing game designed—unbeknownst to them—to measure their tendencies toward attempted racial colorblindness. Each participant was given a stack of photographs, which included 32 different faces. A partner sat across from the participant, looking at one picture that matched a picture from the participant's stack. The participants were told that the goal of the game was to determine which photo the partner was holding by asking as few

Carmen Nobel, "The Case against Racial Colorblindness in the Workplace," Working Knowledge [Harvard Business School] February 13, 2012. Reprinted with permission.

yes/no questions as possible—for example, "Is the person bald?"

Half the faces on the cards were Black, and the other half White, so asking a yes/no question about skin color was a very efficient way to narrow down the identity of the photo on the partner's card. But the researchers found that many of the participants completely avoided asking their partners about the skin color of the person in the photograph—especially when paired with a Black partner. Some 93 percent of participants with White partners mentioned race during the guessing game, as opposed to just 64 percent who were playing the game with Black partners.

BACKFIRING RESULTS

Two independent coders were hired to watch videos of the sessions on mute, rating the perceived friendliness of the White participants based on nonverbal cues. Alas, the participants who attempted colorblindness came across as especially unfriendly, often avoiding eye contact with their Black partners. And when interviewed after the experiment, Black partners reported perceiving the most racial bias among those participants who avoided mentioning race. "The impression was that if you're being so weird about not mentioning race, you probably have something to hide," Norton says.

The researchers repeated the experiment on a group of elementary school children.[3] The third graders often scored higher on the guessing game than grown-ups because, Norton says, they weren't afraid to ask if the person in the photo was Black or White. But many of the fourth and fifth graders avoided mentioning race during the game. As it turns out, racial colorblindness is a social convention that many Americans start to internalize by as young as age 10. "Very early on kids get the message that they are not supposed to acknowledge that they notice people's race—often the result of a horrified reaction from a parent when they do," Norton says.

A ZERO-SUM GAME?

In addition to an ineffective strategy at managing interracial interactions, racial colorblindness has evolved into an argument against affirmative action policies, an issue Norton addresses in a recent working paper, "Racial Colorblindness: Emergence, Practice, and Implications,"[4] cowritten with Evan P. Apfelbaum of MIT and Samuel R. Sommers of Tufts University. "Though once emblematic of the fight for equal opportunity among racial minorities marginalized by openly discriminatory practices, contemporary legal arguments for colorblindness have become increasingly geared toward combating race-conscious policies," they write. "If racial minority status confers an advantage in hiring and school admissions and in the selection of voting districts and government subcontractors—the argument goes—then Whites' right for equal protection may be violated."

In a related article, "Whites See Racism as a Zero-Sum Game That They Are Now Losing," Norton and Sommers surveyed 100 White and 100 Black respondents about their perceptions of racial bias in recent American history.[5] They found that Black respondents reported a large decrease in antiBlack bias between the 1950s and the 2000s, but perceived virtually no anti-White bias in that same period—ever. White respondents, on the other hand, perceived a large decrease in antiBlack bias over time, but also a huge increase in antiWhite bias. In fact, on average, White respondents perceive more antiWhite bias than antiBlack bias in the twenty-first century. "It's very hard to find a metric that suggests that White people actually have a worse time of it than Black people," Norton says. "But this perception is driving the current cultural discourse in race and affirmative action. It's not just that Whites think Blacks are getting some unfair breaks, it's that Whites are thinking, 'I'm actually the victim of discrimination now.'"

MULTICULTURALISM

In "Racial Colorblindness," the authors suggest that organizations might ease racial tensions among a diverse workforce by stressing multiculturalism over racial colorblindness. "Shutting our eyes to the complexities of race does not make them disappear, but it does make it harder to see that colorblindness often creates more problems than it solves," they write.

Norton points out that while many companies host "diversity days," these celebrations often focus solely on the cultures of ethnic minority employees. Excluding White employees from celebrating their cultures can breed resentment, he says, suggesting that an all-inclusive approach might work better.

"Think of having not only Black people talking about being African American, but also White people talking about their Irish or Italian heritage, for instance," he says. "Research shows that in highlighting everyone's differences you can create a kind of commonality—we are *all* different, and my difference is no more or less valued than yours. Most organizations do not manage diversity in this way, however."

For organizations, supporting multiculturalism is not just about paying lip service to cultural differences,

but—increasingly—also about forming a stronger team and improving performance, Norton says. He cites a recent incident in which several retired high-ranking US military leaders publicly supported a Supreme Court decision in favor of affirmative action[6] in university admissions. "Their point was that enlisted men and women were predominantly minorities, and that the military needed minority officers who were college graduates to lead their diverse enlistees," Norton says. "Statements like these help to reframe the general notion of why developing effective strategies for managing diversity is crucial for managers. Multiculturalism is not just about feel-good sentiments. It's about organizational effectiveness."

NOTES

1. © 2012 President & Fellows of Harvard College.
2. Norton, Michael I., Samuel R. Sommers, Evan P. Apfelbaum, Natassia Pura, and Dan Ariely. 2006. "Color Blindness and Interracial Interaction: Playing the Political Correctness Game." *Psychological Science* 17(11):949–953. http://www.people.hbs.edu/mnorton/norton%20sommers%20apfelbaum%20pura%20ariely.pdf.
3. Apfelbaum, Evan P., Kristin Pauker, Nalini Ambady, Samuel R. Sommers, and Michael I. Norton. 2008. "Learning (Not) to Talk about Race: When Older Children Underperform in Social Categorization." *Developmental Psychology* 44(5):1513–1518. http://www.people.hbs.edu/mnorton/apfelbaum%20et%20al%202008.pdf.
4. Apfelbaum, Evan P., Michael I. Norton, and Samuel R. Sommers. 2012. "Racial Color Blindness: Emergence, Practice, and Implications." *Current Directions in Psychological Science.* 21(3):205–209. http://www.people.hbs.edu/mnorton/apfelbaum%20norton%20sommers.pdf.
5. Norton, Michael I., and Samuel R. Sommers. 2011. "Whites See Racism and a Zero-Sum Game That They Are Now Losing." *Perspectives on Psychological Science.* 6(3):215–218. http://www.people.hbs.edu/mnorton/norton%20sommers.pdf.
6. Americans for a Fair Chance. 2003. "Military Leaders Speak out in Favor of Affirmative Action." *The Leadership Conference.* http://www.civilrights.org/press/2003/military-leaders-speak-out-in-favor-of-affirmative-action.html.

WHAT'S IN A NAME? DISCRIMINATION

ERIN THOMAS

Conventional wisdom suggests that when employers want to fill a position, they always choose the best candidate—the one with the most skills, knowledge, and experience. Given this conventional wisdom, applicants pore over their resumes, checking for

spelling errors and finding just the right words to represent themselves as strong candidates. But what if the thing that kept applicants from getting the job was something they wouldn't change? Researchers have found that, long before an employer sees your

Original to *Focus on Social Problems: A Contemporary Reader.*

employment history, your skills, or where you graduated from, something else may help determine which resumes make it to the callback pile and which land among the rejects—your name.

In one study, researchers sent out resumes to 1,300 job postings in Boston and Chicago. For each ad they sent four resumes—two of higher quality and two of lower quality. The only other difference in the resumes was that one lower-quality and one higher-quality resume were assigned a "Black-sounding" name, whereas the others were assigned "White-sounding" names (Bertrand & Mullainathan, 2004).[1] The researchers found that applicants with White-sounding names—like Emily and Greg—received 50 percent more callbacks for job interviews than applicants with Black-sounding names—like Lakisha and Jamal. This means generally that for every 100 applications a person with a White-sounding name has to send, applicants with Black-sounding names have to send 150 to have the same chance at getting called back.

The conventional wisdom about higher qualifications resulting in more callbacks did hold true but only for some applicants. Applicants with White-sounding names and high-quality resumes received 30 percent more callbacks than applicants with Black-sounding names and lower-quality resumes. But high-quality applicants with Black-sounding names received only a nine percent boost in callbacks over their lower-quality resume counterparts. Equal opportunity employers, such as federal contractors, were found to discriminate against Black-sounding names at similar rates (Bertrand & Mullainathan, 2004). In a more recent study where researchers submitted 9,400 resumes for online job opportunities in urban areas across the United States, researchers found that job applicants with Black-sounding names received 14 percent fewer interview requests than similar applicants with White-sounding names (Nunley et al., 2015). Other researchers have since found even more evidence of racial/ethnic discrimination for other groups. Widner andChicoine (2011) conducted a similar study using an Internet job site and found that resumes with Arab American names, like Shakir and Qahhar, also received 50 percent fewer callbacks for jobs compared to identical applicants with White-sounding names.

The trend also persists in higher education. Researchers recently found that faculty at 259 of the United States' top universities were more likely to ignore student requests for research opportunities at the doctoral level when the requests were sent by students whose names indicated that they were racial or ethnic minorities or women. This pattern was particularly evident in higher-paying disciplines, like business, and at private universities (Milkman et al., 2015).

These studies suggest that employers and educators do not blindly hire and assist the best candidates but instead regularly discriminate against candidates based, not on their visible skin color, but on the race that is implied by their name. This discrimination means that applicants and students whose names mark them as members of racial and ethnic minority groups have fewer options to choose from when seeking employment and academic opportunities and may be dissuaded from entering higher-paying fields because of a lack of guidance from university faculty. In response to this discrimination, researchers found that some minority applicants feel forced to conceal or downplay racial cues in their applications in a practice known as "resume Whitening" (Kang et al., 2016). These patterns of hiring discrimination contribute to higher levels of unemployment and poverty for members of racial and ethnic minority groups, even when they have credentials that are identical to those of White Americans. It marks a type of racial discrimination that is invisible to the victims and, thus, a challenge to address.

REFERENCES

Bertrand, Marianne, and Sendhil Mullainathan. 2004. "Are Emily and Greg More Employable than Lakisha and Jamal? A Field Experiment on Labor Market Discrimination." *American Economic Review* 94(4): 991–1013.

Kang, S. K., DeCelles, K. A., Tilcsik, A., & Jun, S. 2016. "Whitened Resumes: Race and Self-presentation in the Labor Market." *Administrative Science Quarterly*, 61(3), 469–502.

Milkman, Katherine L., Akinola, Modupe, and Dolly Chugh. 2015. "What Happens Before? A Field Experiment Exploring How Pay and Representation Differentially Shape Bias on the Pathway Into Organizations." *Journal of Applied Psychology* 100(6): 1678–712.

Nunley, J. M., Pugh, A., Romero, N., & Seals, R. A. 2015. "Racial Discrimination in the Labor Market for Recent College Graduates: Evidence from a Field Experiment." *BE Journal of Economic Analysis and Policy*, 15(3), 1093–125.

Widner, Daniel, and Stephen Chicoine. 2011. "It's All in the Name: Employment Discrimination against Arab Americans." *Sociological Forum* 26(4): 806–23.

---

1   Researchers determined distinctly Black-sounding names and distinctly White-sounding names by analyzing data from birth certificates in Massachusetts from 1974 to 1979. The date range was chosen to account for the birth year of the applicants. The names that were most frequently used by one race or the other were selected as White sounding or Black sounding for the experiment.

CHAPTER 13

SOCIAL PROBLEMS RELATED TO THE ENVIRONMENT AND FOOD SYSTEM

Social problems related to the environment and food system inspire a lot of debate and controversy, particularly among elected officials. Like many of the problems in this chapter, it is tempting to approach environmental and food systems problems from an individualist perspective: If you are unhealthy because of your food choices, you should eat better! If you live in a polluted area, you should move! Taking a sociological perspective requires looking at the role of institutions in the creation and persistence of social problems, and problems in our environment and our food system are no different. And when we look at environmental problems and closely linked problems in the food system, we can see ways in which race, gender, and class discrimination are perpetuated and how the profit motive embedded in our economic system can put our individual and societal health at risk.

As with social problems in major social institutions such as education, the criminal justice system, and the health care system, environmental problems disproportionately impact people of color and lower-income people. Hollie Nyseth Brehm and David Pellow discuss this unequal distribution, focusing on how deep cultural racism and profit-maximizing corporations combine to keep the economic benefits of industry centralized within affluent, predominantly White communities. Simultaneously, the environmental risks—toxic waste, garbage dumps, and high-pollution factories—are more likely to be located in poor communities and those with high concentrations of people of color. Because they have less social, economic, and political power, poor communities are in less of a position to prevent industry from moving into their neighborhoods, and moving is cost-prohibitive for many community members. Nyseth Brehm and Pellow argue that environmental racism and discrimination occurs on a global scale as well, and that as the climate continues to change, we will continue to see those in the least powerful positions most negatively impacted. Tracey Ross and Danyelle Solomon discuss environmental racism more specifically in the case of the lead-polluted water crisis in Flint, Michigan, and describe ways that government intervention can help alleviate the consequences of environmental racism.

While government officials debate whether climate change and global warming is real or caused by humans, David Wallace-Wells argues that the outcomes of our changing climate are likely to be far, far worse than any of us have imagined. These consequences include dramatic heating of the Earth causing serious health problems for people, the destruction of food sources as a result of heat and drought, toxic air and oceans, the release of long-dormant plagues trapped in arctic ice, war over scarce resources, and economic collapse. What used to be a "worst-case scenario," Wallace-Wells explains—dramatic heating of the atmosphere, rising sea levels, melting of polar ice caps—is now "the destruction baked into our future," and it will take more than reducing our dependence on fossil fuels to change our collective destiny.

Like Wallace-Wells, Matt Wilkins asserts that small, individual changes—reducing our fuel consumption or recycling our plastic—are unlikely to create the major changes necessary to protect our environment and reverse the impact of climate change. Wilkins argues that major marketing campaigns about environmental protection—for example, those that promote the recycling and reuse of plastic—actually obscure the role that corporations have in not only causing direct pollution of the planet, but also in preventing regulation of large corporations and single-use plastics (such as straws and plastic grocery bags). This "greenwashing," Wilkins states, has shifted the responsibility from industry and corporations to the individual, who often faces an uphill battle in reducing plastic consumption and whose efforts to reduce pollution ultimately have less impact on the state of the environment. Similarly, Eleanor Cummins discusses a ubiquitous product—bottled water—and how corporations exploit water resources, garnering huge profits while depleting groundwater, creating environmental damage, and defying the wishes of citizens and local regulators.

Government regulations not only impact our environment, but the food that we consume. Emily Stutzman takes a broad look at the food system, helping us to understand how laws, policies, regulations, and other government actions impact agricultural production, distribution, and, ultimately, our food consumption. These policies, along with trends such as industry consolidation and food advertising, Stutzman argues, shape individual choices about food by restricting the options that are available to us and are often at odds with medical knowledge about nutrition and healthy diets, consumer preference, and our long-term health outcomes. The restriction of food choice may make you think of "food deserts," a term that describes neighborhoods—typically low-income and populated by people of color—that lack access to fresh, healthy foods because they don't have grocery stores. Claudia Tillman examines the concepts of food deserts and food swamps (areas where there is an abundance of unhealthy food choices such as fast-food restaurants and convenience stores) and argues that we must examine more of the context of people's food choices and how community-based organizations can help alleviate food scarcity concerns, if we are to understand how to improve health outcomes.

Though we often blame individuals for their food choices and the related negative health outcomes from poor diets, Stutzman and Tillman's readings demonstrate that these choices are made within larger institutional contexts—often that we are unaware of or simply so used to that we no longer recognize their presence. Michael Moss discusses another factor that shapes our food choices in ways we aren't aware of: how processed foods are designed to be addictive to consumers in order to increase profits for corporations. Despite the consequences of ill health for individuals and the larger society, food corporations continue to design products—often marketed to children—that have been consciously engineered to get us hooked. Corporations, Moss argues, are exploiting our vulnerabilities not only in terms of our susceptibility to advertising, but in our biology and brain chemistry.

This chapter also examines the ways in which government regulation—or the lack thereof—can impact the safety of our food system and the food we consume. Wil S. Hylton examines the food system and finds that food safety regulations and inspections are the domain of more than a dozen government organizations, a system prone to confusion and internal conflict. When inspections and regulations break down or companies obstruct investigations, the results can be fatal for consumers, and changes in regulations and inspection policies are often driven by tragic cases and subsequent litigation. Finally, a report from the Food Chain Workers Alliance looks at the impact that consumer organizations and activists have had on the food system, calling for increased regulation, less industrialization and consolidation of food production, and more concern for the environmental impact of our food consumption practices. Despite the fact that where we live and the food we consume seem like individual choices, this chapter demonstrates that institutions, corporations, and government policies constrain and enable our choices.

DANIEL R. WILDCAT

Daniel R. Wildcat, Ph.D., is the director of the Haskell Environmental Research Studies Center and Indigenous & American Indian Studies faculty member at Haskell Indian Nations University. He is a Yuchi member of the Muscogee Nation of Oklahoma.

What is the mission of Haskell Environmental Research Studies (HERS) at Haskell Indian Nations University? What is your role in the program?

The HERS Center was founded in 1995 to address hazardous substance remediation issues in Indian Country. In addition to this specific goal, there was a broader goal of serving as an informational clearinghouse on environmental issues. Since 2005, the primary focus of the Center has been to serve as the catalyst for the formation of the American Indian and Alaska Native Climate Change Working Group now known as the Indigenous Peoples Climate Change Working Group (IPCCWG). I serve as the convener of the IPCCWG and as director of the HERS Center.

What are the most pressing environmental issues affecting indigenous populations?

There is no doubt that the most pressing issues will be the multiple and interacting problems associated with climate change. The challenge is to help the public understand that due to the geographic and ecological diversity of the Earth's biosphere, global climate change will manifest itself differently in different places of the planet. Even given this, one common denominator is that much of what we experience will be water related. As island and coastal communities can attest, they presently have more water than they can live with; in many cases, homelands are under water. At the other extreme are folks who are finding out they will have much less water than they have had in the past. These situations—combined with the rising sea level, warming, and increasing acidification of the Earth's oceans and seas—make it clear that this century may in many respects be known as the century of water.

How did you first become interested in environmental issues? Who was your inspiration?

In retrospect, I think my maternal grandfather and grandmother may be my largest influences. They were farmers—not in the agribusiness model, but in the subsistence tradition. As a teenager I loved going out and helping them in their vegetable garden. They had chickens for eggs, fruit trees, and when I was very young they had pigs and a milk cow. Somehow their simple life, although it was hard work, taught

(*continued*)

me something about the intrinsic value of the water, soil, and air. They were, in a deep experiential (and not romanticized) sense, part of nature. From an intellectual standpoint, my mentor Vine Deloria Jr., an American Indian scholar, activist, and visionary, has shaped much of my research, scholarship, and teaching.

As a scholar-activist, what are your top goals?

I want to encourage humankind to move from a dangerous and costly worldview that sees nonhuman features of nature as resources to seeing them as relatives. We need to move from legal and political systems overwhelmingly shaped by inalienable individual rights to ones that balance those rights with recognition of inalienable human responsibilities to our relatives—human and nonhuman. We cannot treat our relatives like resources, yet that is exactly what we have been doing. Much of modern humankind views nature, including other people, as ATM machines that we constantly make withdrawals from with no regard for what we deposit back into the life-system of the planet. Many Indigenous cultures do not view the world this way, instead seeing people and the natural world as interdependent. If we adopt an Indigenously informed paradigm shift, we will see some real improvement to many environmental situations that, on a global scale, only seem to be getting worse. Overall, I would say it is time to replace the anthropocentric notion of progress, where humans are the center of existence, with the promotion and enactment of systems of life-enhancement.

What strategies do you use to enact social change in your area of study? How do you take the results of your research and apply them to enact change?

I use community engagement, partnerships, publications, books,[1] journal articles, workshops and, just as importantly, popular journalistic efforts to educate the public. Most importantly, I infuse all of my teaching with a focus on the practical questions we face today in creating nonanthropocentric systems of life enhancement.

What are the major challenges activists in your field face?

There are too few of us.

What are major misconceptions the public has about activism in general and in your area of advocacy, specifically?

There are two really: first, many think activism is something only "activists" do, and to me that view is fundamentally wrong. Activism is "choice"—one promotes something with every choice one makes in their daily lives. This first misconception leads to the second: because most activism and advocacy movements work within real physical, political, and economic institutional landscapes that they did not construct, they often engage in activities that appear contradictory, for example, compromising and making concessions that seem counter to their goals. Critics who use that charge "being contradictory" as an indictment of activism are disingenuous, as we all are in the "belly of the beast," so to speak. We all live with contradictions; the goal is to reduce the number we encounter daily. To some extent, activists can bring this latter criticism upon themselves when they take a "holier-than-thou" attitude regarding environmental issues.

What would you consider to be your greatest success as an activist?

I am not comfortable talking about my accomplishments as if they are "my own," because everything I do is a result of collaboration and partnerships. But the work I am proudest of is serving as the convener of the Indigenous Peoples Climate Change Working Group (IPCCWG). That working group, which has always been a tribal college and university-centered network, was designed to be very agile and dynamic. We have been meeting twice annually for nine years, engaging and partnering with federal agencies, our tribal nations, mainstream universities and colleges, nongovernmental organizations (NGOs), private-sector partners, intertribal and tribal organizations, and some of the leading scientific labs in the United States (such as the National Center for Atmospheric Research, the National Renewable Energy Lab, and even the National

Aeronautics and Space Administration [NASA]). We brought a bunch of really good people together and let the interaction and ideas percolate. What emerged is a dynamic group that has moved from evaluating, assessing, and sharing information about climate change to one that is rolling up its sleeves and creating a working agenda for change. I am proud that we maintained the tribal colleges' and universities' centrality to the network (many people are unaware that there are 37 tribal colleges and universities in the United States). Again, this was not my accomplishment alone. I had a lot of good partners, co-workers, and co-conveners that helped make it possible.

Climate change is such a monumental issue to tackle; what are ways to break the problem down and begin to think about steps we can take?

There are three areas that faculty and students in tribal colleges are focusing on and researching that we should all understand better in order to engage in change. The first area is taking better care of and reevaluating our relationship with water. We take water for granted, and people will need to consider water conservation, reuse, and desalination, for example, and be mindful of their use of water. I think we would all prefer to conserve water voluntarily, before governmental entities force us to restrict our use. The second area to think about is land use. We have a lot of students studying land use (planning, economic development, zoning). We could make incredible improvements in our use of carbon energy if we rethought our land-use strategies, avoiding energy-depleting forms like suburban sprawl. Even people living on reservations are looking at ways to use land more effectively, thinking about strategic

building placement to avoid the environmental costs of transportation to and from those buildings. The third area is my "pet" area—one I would work in if I ever had an opportunity for a second career—and that's architecture and design. American houses are horrible in terms of energy consumption; they are poorly designed, built, and sized, and are terribly energy inefficient. We could probably have the most immediate and practical impact on carbon energy savings if we would simply take the time and energy to innovate and adapt existing technologies to create greener homes. We need to think about the intersection between water, land, and our housing—there are many practical opportunities for change. We need to get to work building greener, more sustainable structures.

What are the best ways that students can contribute?

The site for students to do their work is the school they are in! We need to really start thinking about the kinds of campuses we inhabit. Students have a tremendous amount of power if they can get organized. I recommend that students who are in school make their campus their site of engagement (join the Student Senate and prioritize environmental issues, make environmental issues the focus of your research projects for school, etc.). Use your campus and make a difference right there.

NOTE

1. Dr. Wildcat's most recent book is *Red Alert: Saving the Planet with Indigenous Knowledge* (Fulcrum Publishing).

HOLLIE NYSETH BREHM AND DAVID PELLOW

64. ENVIRONMENTAL INEQUALITIES

Nyseth Brehm and Pellow discuss environmental inequality, or the unequal distribution of exposure to hazards in the environment, and the connection this issue has to other major social problems. They argue that environmental inequalities impact racial minorities and those living in poor communities the most and outline possible causes of this disparity, including economic and discrimination-based explanations. Nyseth Brehm and Pellow discuss activism related to environmental inequality and how national and international responses are needed to reduce the impact on communities around the world.

Think back to the movie *Erin Brockovich*. The basic plot, based on a true story, goes like this: A woman with no legal training learns that many residents in a small town have gotten cancer due to exposure to contaminated groundwater. After investigating a large factory believed to be responsible for the contamination, Brockovich proceeds to kick ass. She files a lawsuit against the company, bringing justice to the sick families.

It's the perfect drama-filled Hollywood plot. Yet what is even more dramatic is that the basic story of communities living in contamination isn't rare at all. In many places around the world and in the U.S., people share their neighborhoods with hazardous waste, toxic incinerators, and health-threatening chemical contamination. Moreover, some people are much more likely to be affected by these environmental hazards than others—namely, people of color, working class people, immigrants, and indigenous communities.

This uneven exposure to environmental risks and hazards, often coupled with the systematic exclusion of people from environmental decision-making processes, is called environmental racism or environmental inequality. But, don't be fooled by the terms—the causes of environmental inequality are social and political. In other words, environmental inequality is not, at its core, an environmental issue. Rather, it is rooted in our discourses, structures, and political and economic institutions, and it is intertwined with the other inequalities that permeate our daily lives.

THE EMERGENCE OF ENVIRONMENTAL (IN)JUSTICE

Although *Erin Brockovich* hit the theaters in 2000, environmental inequalities are far from new and far from over. Native Americans, African Americans, Latinos, and European immigrants in the United States have long been disproportionately exposed to the harmful

Hollie Nyseth Brehm and David Pellow, "Environmental Inequalities," The Society Pages White Paper, September 19, 2013 (https://thesocietypages.org/papers/environmental-inequalities/). Reprinted with permission of the authors.

effects of living near city dumps, working in coal mines and on farms picking pesticide-drenched produce, and bearing the brunt of undemocratic and destructive land use decisions. But it wasn't until researchers, activists, and government officials began documenting patterns of social inequality and environmental harm in the 1970s and early 1980s that the concept of environmental inequality emerged.

For example, the U.S. General Accounting Office conducted one of the earliest studies of environmental inequality in 1983. The study examined the racial composition of communities near four major hazardous waste landfills in the South. In three of the four cases, the communities around the landfills were predominantly African American (in the fourth, the community was disproportionately African American). Several other groundbreaking studies in the 1980s and 1990s confirmed these patterns at the local, regional, national, and even international scales.

In response, scholars and activists began calling for environmental justice. According to sociologist Robert Bullard, environmental justice is the notion that all people and communities are entitled to equal protection by environmental health laws and regulations. Many researchers and advocates have rallied around this concept, which has influenced a body of scholarship on environmental inequalities as well as an ever-growing social movement to combat them.

INITIAL DOCUMENTATION AND RESPONSE TO ENVIRONMENTAL INEQUALITIES

Scholars and movement activists began to address environmental inequalities by first documenting their existence. Since the 1980s, there have literally been thousands of studies that have provided strong evidence of racial inequalities in exposure to environmental hazards. Many other scholars have argued that environmental inequalities do not just disproportionately affect racial minorities. Other social categories, like gender, age, class, immigration status/citizenship, and indigeneity, are also associated with disproportionate exposure to hazards. Taken together, these effects overlap and are difficult to disentangle. Here, we focus on race and class, as these are the most prominent in existing studies.

Rather than reviewing these studies (which could fill books), we turn to two examples in the city of Chicago. The Southeast portion of Chicago is known locally as "the Toxic Doughnut" because it is surrounded on all sides by hundreds of polluting industrial facilities, including paint manufacturers, landfills, a sewage treatment plant, a steel manufacturing company, incinerators, and several dumps. Each year, these local industries emit hundreds of thousands of pounds of chemicals into the air. Local residents, who are predominantly African Americans living in public housing, report high incidences of asthma, chronic obstructive pulmonary disease, skin rashes, and cancer.

Scholars like Bullard, Beverly Wright, Bunyan Bryant, and Dorceta Taylor (among others) founded the field of environmental justice studies in order to document inequalities like these. Yet, unlike the Hollywood portrayal, it is actually very difficult to link health problems to specific chemical or industrial sites, especially when several exist in the same area. While this means the resolution depicted in *Erin Brockovich* is not representative, it also means that there are many other responses to environmental inequalities. In the mid-1980s in the Toxic Doughnut, for example, several activists engaged in an act of civil disobedience against a chemical waste incinerator operator. They coordinated a "lock down" and chained themselves to vehicles placed in the path of trucks transporting hazardous materials for incineration. By the end of the day, the coalition had turned away no less than 57 waste trucks.

Such acts of civil disobedience have been common responses to perceived environmental injustices, though this particular story doesn't end at the incinerator gates. The activists involved in the lock down joined a broader network of organizations that comprise the environmental justice movement, and they collectively pushed then-president Bill Clinton to sign an Executive Order (12898), directing federal agencies to develop and implement plans to guard against the production of environmental inequalities. It was an historic accomplishment for the environmental justice movement, though the fight for environmental justice was (and is) far from over.

In fact, 20 years later in the same city, things hadn't changed much. Many of Chicago's Latino communities are concentrated in the neighborhoods of Pilsen and Little Village on the city's West Side. In the early 2000s, activists in these communities began a campaign to shut down two coal-fired power plants. Pollution from the Fisk (in Pilsen) and Crawford (in Little Village) plants are, according to researchers from Chicago's Clean Air Task Force, largely responsible for 42 premature deaths, 66 heart attacks, and 720 asthma attacks each year. Community organizations from environmental, faith, health, and labor movements across the city came together to form the Clean Power Coalition (CPC) not only to phase out the power plants, but also to make Chicago a coal-free city. The CPC eventually received support from 35 aldermen and the mayor. In 2012, the organization achieved its goal. An agreement was signed to close the Fisk plant within the year and the Crawford plant in 2014. It was a major victory for the environmental justice movement and for one of the lead organizations in the CPC, the Little Village Environmental Justice Organization.

CAUSES OF ENVIRONMENTAL INEQUALITIES

As the fight for environmental justice rages on, scholars have turned their attention to better understanding why environmental inequalities exist. Various explanations have been proposed, and here we focus on two—economic and discrimination-based explanations. Socio-political explanations are also at play, but since power and politics are everywhere, we integrate them into the first two. As noted above, none of these are fundamentally environmental causes—they are rooted in society.

ECONOMIC EXPLANATIONS

Social and economic benefits are unevenly distributed in favor of businesses and affluent communities, while the environmental risks are disproportionately concentrated among the most vulnerable groups: the poor, unskilled laborers, and skilled blue-collar residents.

A common explanation for environmental inequality is that polluting corporations do not intentionally discriminate. Instead, they place facilities where land is cheap and where labor pools are available. Both help companies in their quest to maximize profits. Often, marginalized communities already live in such areas, and once a hazardous facility is present, they likely lack the resources to move.

Focusing on the broader social system, sociologists Allan Schnaiberg and Kenneth Gould developed a related economic-based explanation called the treadmill of production thesis. Under this model, there is an ever-growing need for capital investment to generate goods for sale in the marketplace, and that requires continuous inputs of energy and expansion. This expansion of the economy drives two fundamental dynamics: the creation of economic wealth and the creation of the negative by-products of the production process. The social and economic benefits are unevenly distributed in favor of businesses and affluent communities, while the environmental risks and other negative by-products are disproportionately concentrated among the groups of people with the least ability to resist the location of polluting facilities in their community. Thus, polluting facilities are sited among the most vulnerable groups: the poor, unskilled laborers, and skilled blue-collar residents. . . .

DISCRIMINATION-BASED EXPLANATIONS

Other researchers focus more directly on racism and institutional discrimination as drivers of environmental inequality. As evidence, they point to the persistent and stark racial divides in environmental policy making. For example, scholars like Charles Mills and Robert Higgins point to the ways that racism informs environmental decision making on a deeper cultural register. Mills draws on philosophy and historical texts to connect racism to a psychological, cultural, and legal framework linking images of people of color (specifically people of African descent) with barbarism, filth, dirt, and pollution. According to Mills, many White people view African peoples as a form of pollution, making it morally easier to contain industrial waste and factory pollution in their segregated, already-"polluted" neighborhoods. This link between non-European peoples and symbols associated with nature, such as danger, disease, and the primitive savage, is common throughout European history and literature, as well as within contemporary politics in the global North, whether one is speaking of Africans, African Americans, Indigenous peoples, Asians, Latin Americans, or the Roma of Europe.

Like Mills, environmental philosopher Robert Higgins argues that "minority" environments are seen as "appropriately polluted" spaces. Immigrants, indigenous populations, and people of color are viewed by many policymakers, politicians, and ecologists as a source of environmental contamination. That view influences and supports decisions to place noxious facilities and toxic waste in the spaces these populations occupy or relegate these groups to spaces where environmental quality is low and undesirable.

Racial disparities are also mirrored in myriad other aspects of environmental justice—relevant U.S. institutions, including education, health care, and criminal justice, revealing how environmental inequality's impacts can multiply and ripple across the social terrain far beyond those spaces traditionally associated with "environmental" issues. Often, however, particular acts of racism and discrimination cannot easily be located and measured . . . so scholars must continue to explore creative approaches to study this problem.

As we consider economic- and discrimination-based explanations for environmental injustice, politics are clearly at play in both. The political power of communities, states, and industries is inseparable from racial and economic forces driving environmental inequalities. For one, industries and corporations might purposefully seek the path of least resistance. As affluent, and often White, communities have the resources and social capital to oppose the placement of hazardous facilities in or near their neighborhoods, companies place hazards in locations where they believe they will meet little or no local political resistance. Communities that are already socially marginalized are often excluded from participation in policymaking, zoning, and urban planning, while industries, corporations, and similar entities are highly involved in these processes. It's just easier to . . . [place] industrial operations in neighborhoods where the residents have long held little political clout. In addition, working class communities and communities of color are relatively invisible in mainstream environmental movements. If the voices of disadvantaged communities are not heard or respected in political or protest circles, they can be overlooked. Multiple forms of hierarchy and politics drive environmental inequalities.

EXPANDING ENVIRONMENTAL JUSTICE

Though the scholarly field (and related social movements) of environmental justice studies began by focusing on unequal exposure to environmental hazards, some scholars and activists have expanded its boundaries. . . . More recently, scholars have analyzed how other aspects of social life (beyond race and class) influence environmental inequalities. For example, environmental hazards can affect women differently than men. In places like Silicon Valley, where the electronics industry boom began decades ago, the majority of workers in the most chemically intensive jobs were immigrant women (some were exposed to upwards of 700–1,000 different chemicals in a single workstation). Gender also plays a strong role in how people confront environmental hazards. As research by Phil Brown and Faith Ferguson and Celene Krauss demonstrates, women have been the most visible and vocal advocates for the environmental justice movement. This is largely because of their social structural position as likely caretakers of children and the elderly (often the first members of families and communities to show signs of environmental illness) and because they are most likely to have strong connections to community-based institutions like schools, churches, health clinics, and salons—sites where information and concerns about environmental threats are shared and where people are often mobilized.

Environmental justice scholars are working to expand the concept in other ways as well. Notably, while we have focused on the United States in this piece, scholars are increasingly seeing environmental inequalities as global issues. For example, the practice of hazardous waste dumping across national borders is a form of transnational environmental inequality. Every year, wealthy nations and corporations produce

FOCUS ON SOCIAL PROBLEMS

millions of tons of toxic waste from industry, consumers, municipalities, state institutions, computers and electronics products, and agricultural practices. These hazards directly and indirectly contribute to high rates of human and non-human morbidity and mortality and to ecosystem damage on every continent and in every ocean system. Dumping waste in other people's "backyards" is reflective of economically, racially, and politically unequal relations between and within global North and South communities.

Climate change is another example of global environmental inequality. While contributing the least to the causes of climate disruption, people of color, women, indigenous communities, and global South nations often feel the brunt of climate disruption. They bear the burdens of ecological, economic, and health effects, thereby giving rise to the concept of climate injustice. These communities are among the first to experience the effects of climate disruption, which can include "natural" disasters, rising levels of respiratory illness and infectious disease, heat-related morbidity and mortality, and large increases in energy costs. Flooding from severe storms, rising sea levels, and melting glaciers affects millions in Asia and Latin America, while sub-Saharan Africa is experiencing sustained droughts. Yet, nearly 75 percent of the world's annual CO_2 emissions come from the global North, where only 15 percent of the earth's population resides.

The ability to adapt to climate change is also highly uneven across social groups within countries. For example, African Americans have fewer resources to cope with or recover from a host of negative health impacts that might result from climate change. For example, they are 50 percent more likely than non-African Americans to lack health insurance. The delivery of disaster relief is less available to African Americans, too. This was made evident in the aftermath of Hurricane Katrina [in 2005], when the Federal Emergency Management Agency failed to provide services to thousands of African Americans in the Gulf region who were without shelter, food, or drinkable water for days. Research demonstrates that racial stereotypes continue to contribute to reduced disaster relief aid for African Americans in the wake of all manner of climate-related emergencies.

Gender inequalities impact the ability to adapt to climate change as well. In Bangladesh, for instance, women's domestic duties have historically made them especially vulnerable to extreme weather events like storms and floods. Responsibilities as the primary child care givers, primary gatherers of food, fuel, water, and the primary cooks and tenders of livestock have typically tied women to low-lying residences, which are more vulnerable to the rising waters associated with extreme weather events. The relative poverty of women in Bangladesh also makes them less resilient in the face of climate change, since they have poorer nutrition, limited health care, and, in the case of divorced and widowed women, fewer sources of social support. . . .

A GLOBAL RESPONSE

Today, the real Erin Brockovich continues to participate in other environmental justice lawsuits, and activists living in the Toxic Doughnut and on Chicago's West Side are still orchestrating grassroots campaigns for environmental justice, including a push to improve the city's public transit system and promote sustainable energy production. The movement is much broader, with grassroots activists, scholars, governmental and even corporate actors, converging around these pressing issues. At the global level, too, international treaties have come to recognize global environmental injustices tied to climate change and the transfer of hazardous waste to the global South. Yet, despite some of the successes of these transnational advocacy movements, environmental inequalities persist.

Multiple solutions at all levels are needed to comprise a global response to environmental inequality. The United States can and should do its part. While new laws may be needed over time, right now we believe we must start with the enforcement of existing laws that are relevant to environmental justice. The Executive Order referenced earlier was intended to ensure that federal agencies function in a way that protects communities against environmental inequalities. Unfortunately, as the U.S. government's own Inspector General has concluded, federal agencies are doing a poor job of implementing Order 12898, and there have been varying and uneven levels of commitment from the White House, Congress, and the U.S. Environmental Protection Agency since it was signed in 1994 . . . .

The first of many needed responses to environmental injustice, then, is for the federal government to enforce a host of existing laws intended to protect the environment, human health, and vulnerable communities. Laws like the National Environmental Policy Act, the Clean Air Act, and the Fair Housing Act have been under attack by industry and special interest groups since their passage, and each has been weakened over the years. As a result, it has become more difficult—not less—for working class people and people of color to find jobs, homes, and recreational spaces that are free from toxic hazards. Many other solutions—far more than we can review here—are needed, but enforcing the laws already on the books is a good start.

FLINT ISN'T THE ONLY PLACE WITH RACISM IN THE WATER

TRACEY ROSS AND DANYELLE SOLOMON

. . . [In January 2016], Michigan Governor Rick Snyder (R) delivered his fifth State of the State address,[1] a ceremonious speech that typically presents the governor's legislative priorities and vision for the year ahead. But instead of talking about pressing priorities—such as the need to reform the state's public education system, improve its job market, or invest in its infrastructure—Governor Snyder was forced to apologize for his government's failure to provide clean, safe water to the people of Flint, Michigan.

The Flint water crisis began in April 2014 with an effort to cut the budget. Government officials chose to switch water access from the clean Lake Huron to the more corrosive and polluted Flint River. As Curt Guyette, a journalist for the ACLU explained[2] . . . almost immediately residents began complaining of hair loss, rashes, and tap water that looked and tasted strange. Yet, despite calls from concerned residents, city and state officials assured the community[3] that the water was fine. Former Flint mayor Dayne Walling . . . even drank the water on television to dissuade any further concerns. For months, nothing was done.

At the heart of the current national outrage is the impact that tainted water will have on Flint residents—especially the city's children. A study by the Centers for Disease Control and Prevention found that even minimal lead exposure can cause cognitive and behavioral issues,[4] including an increased propensity toward violent behavior. In fact, children with lead poisoning are seven times[5] more likely to drop out of school and six times[6] more likely to become involved in the juvenile justice system than those not exposed to lead. Moreover, the impact of lead exposure is irreversible.

The long history of environmental racism

In the midst of this knowledge, it is hard to ignore the facts that 56 percent of Flint's population is African American and most of the city's residents live paycheck to paycheck. According to the 2015 Census, more than 40 percent of residents are living below the federal poverty level. Once the booming Vehicle City where General Motors was born, Flint has since lost its industrial base and, with it, government investment in all forms of infrastructure. Support for the city's schools, public transportation, and employment has fallen by the wayside.[7] Still, how is it possible that, in 2016, low-income, Black Americans are denied access to clean, safe water?

---

1   State of the State 2016. Retrieved on March 15, 2019, from https://www.michigan.gov/formergovernors/0,4584,7-212-90815_74857_74858—,00.html.

2   *TalkPoverty.org.* "Flint." Retrieved on March 15, 2019, from talkpoverty.org/podcast/flint.

3   Bellware, Kim. 2016. "State Gave Its Workers in Flint Clean Water as It Assured Residents Taps Were Safe." *Huffington Post*, January 28. Retrieved on March 15, 2019, from https://www.huffingtonpost.com/entry/flint-government-water-coolers_us_56aaa4a5e4b077d4fe8d8135.

4   Advisory Committee on Childhood Lead Poisoning Prevention. 2012. "Low Level Lead Exposure Harms Children: A Renewed Call for Primary Prevention." Centers for Disease Control and Prevention. Retrieved on March 15, 2019, from https://www.cdc.gov/nceh/lead/acclpp/final_document_030712.pdf.

5   Green & Healthy Homes Initiative. N.d. "Home & Health: Lead." Retrieved on March 15, 2019, from https://www.greenandhealthyhomes.org/hazard/lead.

6   Green & Healthy Homes Initiative. N.d.

7   Smith, Jay Scott. 2011. "Flint's Economic Fall Like None Other in the Country." *The Grio*, September 26. Retrieved on March 15, 2019, from https://thegrio.com/2011/09/26/flints-economic-fall-like-none-other-in-the-country.

(*continued*)

Danyelle Solomon and Tracey Ross, "Protecting America from Racism in the Water." February 3, 2016. This material was created by the Center for American Progress (www.americanprogress.org).

Unfortunately, the roots of this injustice run deep.[8] Environmental racism is entwined with the country's industrial past. At the beginning of the twentieth century, zoning ordinances emerged as a way to separate land uses in order to protect people from health hazards. Over time, however, city planning and zoning ordinances focused less on public health and more on creating idyllic communities, protecting property rights, and excluding "undesirables."[9] In other words: The least desirable communities were reserved for discarding waste and marginalized people alike.

By the 1930s,[10] federal leaders began to make large investments in creating stable, affluent, and White communities in the suburbs, while giving local governments the autonomy to neglect low-income communities and communities of color. New highways and waste facilities were constructed in marginalized communities, where they cut through businesses or homes and exposed residents to excessive pollution.

In his seminal book, *Dumping in Dixie: Race, Class, and Environmental Quality*, Professor Robert Bullard, considered the father of environmental justice,[11] wrote,[12] "The problem of polluted Black communities is not a new phenomenon. Historically, toxic dumping and the location of locally unwanted land uses (LULUs) have followed the 'path of least resistance,' meaning Black and poor communities have been disproportionately burdened with these types of externalities."

Environmental racism is an issue of political power: The negative externalities of industrialization—pollution and hazardous waste—are placed where politicians expect little or no political backlash. For this reason, ZIP codes often have more of an effect on health than genetic codes. Despite legislative efforts to dismantle segregation, it remains[13] a pernicious problem[14]

in America today. Affluent communities still adopt exclusionary zoning codes[15] that keep less affluent households from moving in, and African American home buyers are still shown fewer homes than Whites[16] and are often steered away from predominantly White neighborhoods. "African Americans, even affluent African Americans are more likely to live closer to and in communities that are more polluted than poor White families that make $10,000 a year," according to Bullard.[17] In essence, the nation's laws are executed mostly to protect White households and leave the rest of the country to inhale the toxic fumes of racism.

A recent study[18] in *Environmental Research Letters* noted that the highest polluting facilities in the country are disproportionately located near communities of color. One of the most notorious examples of this disparity is Cancer Alley,[19] the 85-mile stretch between Baton Rouge, Louisiana, and New Orleans that is home to more than 150 industrial plants and refineries. The deadly corridor earned its disreputable name due to the sheer number of cancer cases, inexplicable illnesses, and deaths that have afflicted its residents. The ExxonMobil refinery in Baton Rouge alone is 250 times the size of the Superdome, with a surrounding population that is 78 percent people of color.[20] Black communities and industrial sites are so closely intertwined that a number of Cancer Alley refineries include old Black cemeteries[21] that hold the remains of former slaves—a blunt reminder of just how little Black lives matter on these grounds.

8 "Mock, Brentin. 2016. "If You Want Clean Water, Don't Be Black in America." *CityLab*, January 26. Retrieved on March 15, 2019, from https://www.citylab.com/equity/2016/01/if-you-want-clean-water-dont-be-black-in-america/426927.

9 Wilson, Sacoby, Malon Hutson, and Mahasin Mujahid. 2008. "How Planning and Zoning Contribute to Inequitable Development, Neighborhood Health, and Environmental Injustice." *Environmental Justice*, 1(4): 211-216.

10 Badger, Emily. 2015. "Redlining: Still a Thing." *The Washington Post*, May 28. Retrieved March 15, 2019, from https://www.washingtonpost.com/news/wonk/wp/2015/05/28/evidence-that-banks-still-deny-black-borrowers-just-as-they-did-50-years-ago/?utm_term=.954c6ba69c9d.

11 Dicum, Gregory. 2006. "Meet Robert Bullard, the Father of Environmental Justice." *The Grist*. Retrieved on March 15, 2019, from https://grist.org/article/dicum.

12 Bullard, Robert D. 1990. *Dumping in Dixie: Race, Class, and Environmental Quality* (Boulder, CO: Westview Press, 2019). Retrieved on March 15, 2019, from http://www.ciesin.org/docs/010–278/010-278chpt1.html.

13 Semuels, Alana. 2015. "White Flight Never Ended." *The Atlantic*, July 30.

14 Millhiser, Ian. 2015. "American Schools Are More Segregated Than They Were in 1968 and the Supreme Court Doesn't Care." *ThinkProgress*, August 13. Retrieved on March 15, 2019, from https://thinkprogress.org/american-schools-are-more-segregated-now-than-they-were-in-1968-and-the-supreme-court-doesnt-care-cc7abbf6651c.

15 Hertz, Daniel. 2014. "One of the Best Ways to Fight Inequality in Cities: Zoning." *The Washington Post*, August 13. Retrieved on March 15, 2019, from https://www.washingtonpost.com/posteverything/wp/2014/08/13/the-best-way-to-fight-inequality-in-cities-is-through-zoning/?noredirect=on&utm_term=.d25a6d226500.

16 The Urban Institute, Margery Austin Turner, Diane K. Levy, Doug Wissoker, Claudia K. Aranda, Rob Pitingolo, and Rob Santos. 2013. "Housing Discrimination Against Racial and Ethnic Minorities 2012." U.S. Department of Housing and Urban Development. Retrieved on March 15, 2019, fom https://www.huduser.gov/portal/publications/fairhsg/hsg_discrimination_2012.html.

17 Lee, Trymaine. 2015. "Cancer Alley: Big Industry, Big Problems." *MSNBC.com*. Retrieved on March 15, 2019, from http://www.msnbc.com/interactives/geography-of-poverty/se.html.

18 Collins, Mary B., Ian Munoz, and Joseph JaJa. 2016. "Linking 'Toxic Outliers' to Environmental Justice Communities." *Environmental Research Letters* 11(1): 1–9.

19 Lee, 2015.

20 Sharp, Robert. 2009. "Environmental Injustice: Minorities and Poor at Greatest Risk from Refinery Pollution." *The Barrel Blog*. Retrieved March 15, 2019, from https://blogs.platts.com/2009/05/08/environmental_injustice_minorities_and_poor_at_greatest_risk_from_refinery_pollution.

21 Lee, 2015.

Standing up for environmental justice in FLINT and in the nation

The road ahead for Flint is a very long one. After the immediate crisis has been addressed, it will be years before the nation can fully realize how the state affected the lives of the children it poisoned. These families need and deserve a lifetime of support. And while the country's outrage is correct, the injustice in Flint must be viewed as one example of a widespread problem. In order to address the root causes of environmental racism, the nation must demand government accountability and effective industry regulations, support clean energy, and commit to furthering fair housing.

All levels of government must focus on investing in and modernizing infrastructure that will protect the building blocks of our society—specifically in areas where there is historic underinvestment. A $1 billion investment in infrastructure creates about 18,000 jobs, while the same-size tax cut would generate 14,000 jobs and no new public asset.[22] There is much work to be done to ensure that all communities are safe, stable places where people can thrive.

Many Americans believe that racism can be boiled down to a sin marked by slurs and men burning crosses under the cover of night. Flint serves as a stark reminder that racism is in the air we breathe, flowing freely into our homes and down the stretch of blocks riddled with liquor stores but begging for a supermarket. There is a societal cost to this reality.

The crisis in Flint has refocused the public spotlight on environmental justice. Voters and policymakers across the country should seize this moment to address the environmental racism that persists in too many communities. If the nation does not stand up against the injustice of environmental racism, communities of color will continue to be targeted. As the country becomes more ethnically and racially diverse, communities of color must have equity in the level and quality of government-provided services. Americans must lend their voices to support not just Flint residents, but also the residents of countless other communities where racism still takes a physical toll.

22 Treuhaft, Sarah. 2013. "Infrastructure: Supporting Communities So All Can Thrive." Pp. 54–78 in *All-In Nation: An American that Works for Everyone*, edited by Vanessa Cárdenas and Sarah Treuhaft. Center for American Progress and PolicyLink.

DAVID WALLACE-WELLS

65. THE UNINHABITABLE EARTH

Much of the focus on climate change has been on rising sea levels, but as Wallace-Wells points out, that is not the only way that the environment we live in is being changed because of our dependence on fossil fuels. Climate change will radically reshape the Earth and human society, exacerbating existing social problems like food scarcity, war and conflict, the spread of preventable diseases and illnesses, and pollution of the air and soil. Unless we take radical action now, Wallace-Wells argues, these changes are destined to leave many parts of the Earth uninhabitable by humans.

"Doomsday"

It is, I promise, worse than you think. If your anxiety about global warming is dominated by fears of sea-level rise, you are barely scratching the surface of what terrors are possible, even within the lifetime of a teenager today. And yet the swelling seas—and the cities they will drown—have so dominated the picture of global warming, and so overwhelmed our capacity for climate panic, that they have occluded our perception of other threats, many much closer at hand. Rising oceans are bad, in fact very bad; but fleeing the coastline will not be enough. "indeed, absent a significant adjustment to how billions of humans conduct their lives, parts of the Earth will likely become close to uninhabitable, and other parts horrifically inhospitable, as soon as the end of this century.

Even when we train our eyes on climate change, we are unable to comprehend its scope. This past winter, a string of days 60 and 70 degrees warmer than normal baked the North Pole, melting the permafrost that encased Norway's Svalbard seed vault—a global food bank nicknamed "Doomsday," which was designed to ensure that our agriculture survives any catastrophe, and which appeared to have been flooded by climate change less than 10 years after being built.

The Doomsday vault is fine, for now: The structure has been secured and the seeds are safe. But treating the episode as a parable of impending flooding missed the more important news. Until recently, permafrost was not a major concern of climate scientists because, as the name suggests, it was soil that stayed permanently frozen. But Arctic permafrost contains 1.8 trillion tons of carbon, more than twice as much as is currently suspended in the Earth's atmosphere. When it thaws and is released, that carbon may evaporate as methane, which is 34 times as powerful a greenhouse-gas warming blanket as carbon dioxide when judged on the timescale of a century; when judged on the timescale of two decades, it is 86 times as powerful. In other words, we have, trapped in Arctic permafrost, twice as much carbon as is currently wrecking the atmosphere of the planet, all of it scheduled to be released at a date that keeps getting moved up, partially in the form of a gas that multiplies its warming power 86 times over.

Maybe you know that already—there are alarming stories in the news every day, like those . . . that seemed to suggest satellite data showed[1] the globe warming since 1998 more than twice as fast as scientists had thought (in fact, the underlying story was considerably less alarming than the headlines). Or the

---

Excerpts from David Wallace-Wells, "The Uninhabitable Earth." New York Magazine, July 2017. Reprinted by permission.

news from Antarctica this past May, when a crack[2] in an ice shelf grew 11 miles in six days, then kept going; the break now has just three miles to go —by the time you read this, it may already have met the open water,[3] where it will drop into the sea one of the biggest icebergs ever, a process known poetically as "calving." [*Editor's Note*: This section of the Antarctic, which is the size of Delaware and weighs a trillion tons, eventually did break off in 2017].

But no matter how well informed you are, you are surely not alarmed enough. Over the past decades, our culture has gone apocalyptic with zombie movies and Mad Max dystopias, perhaps the collective result of displaced climate anxiety, and yet when it comes to contemplating real-world warming dangers, we suffer from an incredible failure of imagination. The reasons for that are many: the timid language of scientific probabilities, which the climatologist James Hansen once called "scientific reticence" in a paper chastising scientists for editing their own observations so conscientiously that they failed to communicate how dire the threat really was; the fact that the country is dominated by a group of technocrats who believe any problem can be solved and an opposing culture that doesn't even see warming as a problem worth addressing; the way that climate denialism has made scientists even more cautious in offering speculative warnings; the simple speed of change and, also, its slowness, such that we are only seeing effects now of warming from decades past; our uncertainty about uncertainty, which the climate writer Naomi Oreskes in particular has suggested stops us from preparing as though anything worse than a median outcome were even possible; the way we assume climate change will hit hardest elsewhere, not everywhere; the smallness (two degrees) and largeness (1.8 trillion tons) and abstractness (400 parts per million) of the numbers; the discomfort of considering a problem that is very difficult, if not impossible, to solve; the altogether incomprehensible scale of that problem, which amounts to the prospect of our own annihilation; simple fear. But aversion arising from fear is a form of denial, too.

In between scientific reticence and science fiction is science itself. This [reading] is the result of dozens of interviews and exchanges with climatologists and researchers in related fields and reflects hundreds of scientific papers on the subject of climate change. What follows is not a series of predictions of what will happen—that will be determined in large part by the much-less-certain science of human response. Instead, it is a portrait of our best understanding of where the planet is heading absent aggressive action. It is unlikely that all of these warming scenarios will be fully realized, largely because the devastation along the way will shake our complacency. But those scenarios, and not the present climate, are the baseline. In fact, they are our schedule.

The present tense of climate change—the destruction we've already baked into our future—is horrifying enough. Most people talk as if Miami and Bangladesh still have a chance of surviving; most of the scientists I spoke with assume we'll lose them within the century, even if we stop burning fossil fuel in the next decade. Two degrees of warming used to be considered the threshold of catastrophe: tens of millions of climate refugees unleashed upon an unprepared world. Now two degrees is our goal, per the Paris Climate Accords, and experts give us only slim odds of hitting it. The United Nations Intergovernmental Panel on Climate Change [(IPCC)] issues serial reports, often called the "gold standard" of climate research; the most recent one projects us to hit four degrees of warming by the beginning of the next century, should we stay the present course. But that's just a median projection. The upper end of the probability curve runs as high as 8 degrees—and the authors still haven't figured out how to deal with that permafrost melt. The IPCC reports also don't fully account for the albedo effect (less ice means less reflected and more absorbed sunlight, hence more warming); more cloud cover (which traps heat); or the dieback of forests and other flora (which extract carbon from the atmosphere). Each of these promises to accelerate warming, and the history of the planet shows that temperature can shift as much as 5 degrees Celsius within 13 years. The last time the planet was even four degrees warmer, Peter Brannen points out in *The Ends of the World*, his new history of the planet's major extinction events, the oceans were hundreds of feet higher.

The Earth has experienced five mass extinctions before the one we are living through now, each so complete a slate-wiping of the evolutionary record that it functioned as a resetting of the planetary clock, and many climate scientists will tell you they are the best analog for the ecological future we are diving headlong into. Unless you are a teenager, you probably read in your high school textbooks that these extinctions were the result of asteroids. In fact, all but the one that killed the dinosaurs were caused by climate change produced by greenhouse gas. The most notorious was 252 million years ago; it began when carbon warmed the planet by 5 degrees, accelerated when that warming triggered the release of methane in the Arctic, and ended with 97 percent of all life on Earth dead. We are currently adding carbon to the atmosphere at a considerably faster rate; by most estimates, at least 10 times faster. The rate is accelerating. This is what Stephen Hawking had in mind when he said[4] . . . that the species needs to colonize other planets in the next century to survive, and what drove Elon Musk . . . to unveil his plans[5] to build a Mars habitat in 40 to 100 years.

These are nonspecialists, of course, and probably as inclined to irrational panic as you or I. But the many sober-minded scientists I interviewed . . . the most credentialed and tenured in the field, few of them inclined to alarmism and many advisers to the IPCC who nevertheless criticize its conservatism—have quietly reached an apocalyptic conclusion, too: No plausible program of emissions reductions alone can prevent climate disaster. . . .

HEAT DEATH

Humans, like all mammals, are heat engines; surviving means having to continually cool off, like panting dogs. For that, the temperature needs to be low enough for the air to act as a kind of refrigerant, drawing heat off the skin so that the engine can keep pumping. At 7 degrees of warming, that would become impossible for large portions of the planet's equatorial band, and especially the tropics, where humidity adds to the problem. In the jungles of Costa Rica, for instance, where humidity routinely tops 90 percent, simply moving around outside when it's over 105 degrees Fahrenheit would be lethal. And the effect would be fast: Within a few hours, a human body would be cooked to death from both inside and out.

Climate-change skeptics point out that the planet has warmed and cooled many times before, but the climate window that has allowed for human life is very narrow, even by the standards of planetary history. At 11 or 12 degrees of warming, more than half the world's population, as distributed today, would die of direct heat. Things almost certainly won't get that hot this century, though models of unabated emissions do bring us that far eventually. This century, and especially in the tropics, the pain points will pinch much more quickly even than an increase of 7 degrees. The key factor is something called wet-bulb temperature, which is a term of measurement as home-laboratory-kit as it sounds: the heat registered on a thermometer wrapped in a damp sock as it's swung around in the air (since the moisture evaporates from a sock more quickly in dry air, this single number reflects both heat and humidity). At present, most regions reach a wet-bulb maximum of 26 or 27 degrees Celsius; the true red line for habitability is 35 degrees. What is called heat stress comes much sooner.

Actually, we're about there already. Since 1980, the planet has experienced a 50-fold increase in the number of places experiencing dangerous or extreme heat; a bigger increase is to come. The five warmest summers in Europe since 1500 have all occurred since 2002, and soon, the IPCC warns, simply being outdoors that time of year will be unhealthy for much of the globe. Even if we meet the Paris goals of two degrees warming, cities like Karachi and Kolkata will become close to uninhabitable, annually encountering deadly heat waves like those that crippled them in 2015. At 4 degrees, the deadly European heat wave of 2003, which killed as many as 2,000 people a day, will be a normal summer. At 6, according to an assessment focused only on effects within the United States. from the National Oceanic and Atmospheric Administration, summer labor of any kind would become impossible in the lower Mississippi Valley, and everybody in the country east of the Rockies would be under more heat stress than anyone, anywhere, in the world today. As Joseph Romm has put it in his authoritative primer *Climate Change: What Everyone Needs to Know*, heat stress in New York City would exceed that of present-day Bahrain, one of the planet's hottest spots, and the temperature in Bahrain "would induce hyperthermia in even sleeping humans"[6] The high-end IPCC estimate, remember, is two degrees warmer still. By the end of the century, the World Bank has estimated, the coolest months in tropical South America, Africa, and the Pacific are likely to be warmer than the warmest months at the end of the twentieth century. Air-conditioning can help but will ultimately only add to the carbon problem; plus, the climate-controlled malls of the Arab Emirates aside, it is not remotely plausible to wholesale air-condition all the hottest parts of the world, many of them also the poorest. And indeed, the crisis will be most dramatic across the Middle East and Persian Gulf, where in 2015 the heat index registered temperatures as high as 163 degrees Fahrenheit. As soon as several decades from now, the hajj will become physically impossible for the 2 million Muslims who make the pilgrimage each year.

It is not just the hajj, and it is not just Mecca; heat is already killing us. In the sugarcane region of El Salvador, as much as one-fifth of the population has chronic kidney disease, including over a quarter of the men, the presumed result of dehydration from working the fields they were able to comfortably harvest as recently as two decades ago. With dialysis, which is expensive, those with kidney failure can expect to live five years; without it, life expectancy is in the weeks. Of course, heat stress promises to pummel us in places other than our kidneys, too. As I type that sentence, in the California desert in mid-June, it is 121 degrees outside my door. It is not a record high.

THE END OF FOOD

Climates differ and plants vary, but the basic rule for staple cereal crops grown at optimal temperature is that for every degree of warming, yields decline by 10 percent. Some estimates run as high as 15 or even 17 percent. Which means that if the planet is five degrees warmer at the end of the century, we may have as many as 50 percent more people to feed and 50 percent less grain to give them. And proteins are worse: It takes 16 calories of grain to produce just a single calorie of hamburger meat, butchered from a cow that spent its life polluting the climate with methane farts.

Pollyannaish plant physiologists will point out that the cereal-crop math applies only to those regions already at peak growing temperature, and they are right—theoretically, a warmer climate will make it easier to grow corn in Greenland. But as the pathbreaking work by Rosamond Naylor and David Battisti has shown,[7]

the tropics are already too hot to efficiently grow grain, and those places where grain is produced today are already at optimal growing temperature—which means even a small warming will push them down the slope of declining productivity. And you can't easily move croplands north a few hundred miles, because yields in places like remote Canada and Russia are limited by the quality of soil there; it takes many centuries for the planet to produce optimally fertile dirt.

Drought might be an even bigger problem than heat, with some of the world's most arable land turning quickly to desert. Precipitation is notoriously hard to model, yet predictions for later this century are basically unanimous: unprecedented droughts nearly everywhere food is today produced. By 2080, without dramatic reductions in emissions, southern Europe will be in permanent extreme drought, much worse than the American Dust Bowl ever was. The same will be true in Iraq and Syria and much of the rest of the Middle East; some of the most densely populated parts of Australia, Africa, and South America; and the breadbasket regions of China. None of these places, which today supply much of the world's food, will be reliable sources of any. As for the original Dust Bowl: The droughts in the American plains and Southwest would not just be worse than in the 1930s, a 2015 NASA study predicted,[8] but worse than any droughts in a thousand years—and that includes those that struck between 1100 and 1300, which dried up all the rivers East of the Sierra Nevada mountains and may have been responsible for the death of the Anasazi civilization. Remember, we do not live in a world without hunger as it is. Far from it: Most estimates put the number of undernourished at 800 million globally. In case you haven't heard, spring [2017] . . . brought an unprecedented quadruple famine to Africa and the Middle East; the UN has warned that separate starvation events in Somalia, South Sudan, Nigeria, and Yemen could kill 20 million this year alone.

CLIMATE PLAGUES

Rock, in the right spot, is a record of planetary history, eras as long as millions of years flattened by the forces of geological time into strata with amplitudes of just inches, or just an inch, or even less. Ice works that way, too, as a climate ledger, but it is also frozen history, some of which can be reanimated when unfrozen.

There are now, trapped in Arctic ice, diseases that have not circulated in the air for millions of years—in some cases, since before humans were around to encounter them. Which means our immune systems would have no idea how to fight back when those prehistoric plagues emerge from the ice. The Arctic also stores terrifying bugs from more recent times. In Alaska, already, researchers have discovered remnants of the 1918 flu that infected as many as 500 million and killed as many as 100 million—about 5 percent of the world's population and almost six times as many as had died in the world war for which the pandemic served as a kind of gruesome capstone.

As the BBC reported[9] in [2017], scientists suspect smallpox and the bubonic plague are trapped in Siberian ice, too—an abridged history of devastating human sickness, left out like egg salad in the Arctic sun. Experts caution that many of these organisms won't actually survive the thaw and point to the fastidious lab conditions under which they have already reanimated several of them—the 32,000-year-old "extremophile" bacteria revived in 2005, an 8 million-year-old bug brought back to life in 2007, the 3.5 million-year-old one a Russian scientist self-injected just out of curiosity—to suggest that those are necessary conditions for the return of such ancient plagues. But already last year, a boy was killed and 20 others infected by anthrax released when retreating permafrost exposed the frozen carcass of a reindeer killed by the bacteria at least 75 years earlier; 2,000 present-day reindeer were infected, too, carrying and spreading the disease beyond the tundra. What concerns epidemiologists more than ancient diseases are existing scourges relocated, rewired, or even re-evolved by warming. The first effect is geographical. . . . You don't worry much about dengue or malaria if you are living in Maine or France. But as the tropics creep northward and mosquitoes migrate with them, you will. You didn't much worry about Zika a couple of years ago either.

As it happens, Zika may also be a good model[10] of the second worrying effect—disease mutation. One reason you hadn't heard about Zika until recently is that it had been trapped in Uganda; another is that it did not, until recently, appear to cause birth defects. Scientists still don't entirely understand what happened, or what they missed. But there are things we

do know for sure about how climate affects some diseases: Malaria, for instance, thrives in hotter regions not just because the mosquitoes that carry it do, too, but because for every degree increase in temperature, the parasite reproduces 10 times faster. Which is one reason that the World Bank estimates that, by 2050, 5.2 billion people will be reckoning with it.

UNBREATHABLE AIR

Our lungs need oxygen, but that is only a fraction of what we breathe. The fraction of carbon dioxide is growing: It just crossed 400 parts per million, and high-end estimates extrapolating from current trends suggest it will hit 1,000 ppm by 2100. At that concentration, compared to the air we breathe now, human cognitive ability declines by 21 percent.

Other stuff in the hotter air is even scarier, with small increases in pollution capable of shortening lifespans by 10 years. The warmer the planet gets, the more ozone forms, and by midcentury, Americans will likely suffer a 70 percent increase in unhealthy ozone smog, the National Center for Atmospheric Research has projected. By 2090, as many as 2 billion people globally will be breathing air above the World Health Organization "safe" level; one paper . . . .showed that, among other effects, a pregnant mother's exposure to ozone raises the child's risk of autism (as much as tenfold, combined with other environmental factors). . . .

Already, more than 10,000 people die each day from the small particles emitted from fossil fuel burning; each year, 339,000 people die from wildfire smoke, in part because climate change has extended forest-fire season (in the United States, it has increased by 78 days since 1970). By 2050, according to the U.S. Forest Service,[11] wildfires will be twice as destructive as they are today; in some places, the area burned could grow fivefold. What worries people even more is the effect that would have on emissions, especially when the fires ravage forests arising out of peat. Peatland fires in Indonesia in 1997, for instance, added to the global CO_2 release by up to 40 percent, and more burning only means more warming only means more burning. There is also the terrifying possibility that rain forests like the Amazon, which in 2010 suffered its second "hundred-year drought" in the space of five years, could dry out enough to become vulnerable to these kinds of devastating, rolling forest fires—which would not only expel enormous amounts of carbon into the atmosphere but also shrink the size of the forest. That is especially bad because the Amazon alone provides 20 percent of our oxygen.

Then there are the more familiar forms of pollution. In 2013, melting Arctic ice remodeled Asian weather patterns, depriving industrial China of the natural ventilation systems it had come to depend on, which blanketed much of the country's north in an unbreathable smog. Literally unbreathable. A metric called the Air Quality Index categorizes the risks and tops out at the 301–to–500 range, warning of "serious aggravation of heart or lung disease and premature mortality in persons with cardiopulmonary disease and the elderly" and, for all others, "serious risk of respiratory effects"; at that level, "everyone should avoid all outdoor exertion." The Chinese "airpocalypse" of 2013 peaked at what would have been an Air Quality Index of over 800. That year, smog was responsible for a third of all deaths in the country.

PERPETUAL WAR

Climatologists are very careful when talking about Syria. They want you to know that while climate change did produce a drought that contributed to civil war, it is not exactly fair to say that the conflict is the result of warming; next door, for instance, Lebanon suffered the same crop failures. But researchers like Marshall Burke and Solomon Hsiang have managed to quantify some of the nonobvious relationships between temperature and violence: For every half-degree of warming, they say, societies will see between a 10 and 20 percent increase in the likelihood of armed conflict. In climate science, nothing is simple, but the arithmetic is harrowing: A planet five degrees warmer would have at least half again as many wars as we do today. Overall, social conflict could more than double this century.

This is one reason that, as nearly every climate scientist I spoke to pointed out, the U.S. military is obsessed with climate change: The drowning of all American Navy bases by sea-level rise is trouble enough, but being the world's policeman is quite a bit harder when the crime rate doubles. Of course, it's not just Syria where climate has contributed to conflict. Some speculate that the elevated level of strife

across the Middle East over the past generation reflects the pressures of global warming—a hypothesis all the more cruel considering that warming began accelerating when the industrialized world extracted and then burned the region's oil.

What accounts for the relationship between climate and conflict? Some of it comes down to agriculture and economics; a lot has to do with forced migration, already at a record high, with at least 65 million displaced people wandering the planet right now. But there is also the simple fact of individual irritability. Heat increases municipal crime rates, and swearing on social media, and the likelihood that a major league pitcher, coming to the mound after his teammate has been hit by a pitch, will hit an opposing batter in retaliation. And the arrival of air-conditioning in the developed world, in the middle of the past century, did little to solve the problem of the summer crime wave.

PERMANENT ECONOMIC COLLAPSE

The murmuring mantra of global neoliberalism, which prevailed between the end of the Cold War and the onset of the Great Recession, is that economic growth would save us from anything and everything. . . . Before fossil fuels, nobody lived better than their parents or grandparents or ancestors from 500 years before, except in the immediate aftermath of a great plague like the Black Death, which allowed the lucky survivors to gobble up the resources liberated by mass graves. After we've burned all the fossil fuels, these scholars suggest, perhaps we will return to a "steady-state" global economy. Of course, that one-time injection has a devastating long-term cost: climate change.

The most exciting research on the economics of warming has also come from Hsiang and his colleagues . . . who offer some very bleak analysis of their own: Every degree Celsius of warming costs, on average, 1.2 percent of GDP (an enormous number, considering we count growth in the low single digits as "strong"). This is the sterling work in the field, and their median projection is for a 23 percent loss in per capita earning globally by the end of this century (resulting from changes in agriculture, crime, storms, energy, mortality, and labor). Tracing the shape of the probability curve is even scarier: There is a 12 percent chance that climate change will reduce global output by more than 50 percent by 2100, they say, and a 51 percent chance that it lowers per capita GDP by 20 percent or more by then, unless emissions decline. By comparison, the Great Recession lowered global GDP by about 6 percent, in a onetime shock; Hsiang and his colleagues estimate a one-in-eight chance of an ongoing and irreversible effect by the end of the century that is eight times worse.

The scale of that economic devastation is hard to comprehend, but you can start by imagining what the world would look like today with an economy half as big, which would produce only half as much value, generating only half as much to offer the workers of the world. . . . [A]mong other things, it makes the idea of postponing government action on reducing emissions and relying solely on growth and technology to solve the problem an absurd business calculation. Every round-trip ticket on flights from New York to London, keep in mind, costs the Arctic three more square meters of ice.

POISONED OCEANS

That the sea will become a killer is a given. Barring a radical reduction of emissions, we will see at least 4 feet of sea-level rise and possibly 10 by the end of the century. A third of the world's major cities are on the coast, not to mention its power plants, ports, navy bases, farmlands, fisheries, river deltas, marshlands, and rice-paddy empires, and even those above 10 feet will flood much more easily, and much more regularly, if the water gets that high. At least 600 million people live within 10 meters of sea level today.

But the drowning of those homelands is just the start. At present, more than a third of the world's carbon is sucked up by the oceans—thank God, or else we'd have that much more warming already. But the result is what's called "ocean acidification," which, on its own, may add a half a degree to warming this century. It is also already burning through the planet's water basins—you may remember these as the place where life arose in the first place. You have probably heard of "coral bleaching"—that is, coral dying—which is very bad news, because reefs support as much as a quarter of all marine life and supply food for half a billion people. Ocean acidification will fry fish populations directly, too, though scientists aren't yet sure

how to predict the effects on the stuff we haul out of the ocean to eat; they do know that in acid waters, oysters and mussels will struggle to grow their shells, and that when the pH of human blood drops as much as the oceans' pH has over the past generation, it induces seizures, comas, and sudden death.

That isn't all that ocean acidification can do. Carbon absorption can initiate a feedback loop in which underoxygenated waters breed different kinds of microbes that turn the water still more "anoxic," first in deep-ocean "dead zones," then gradually up toward the surface. There, the small fish die out, unable to breathe, which means oxygen-eating bacteria thrive, and the feedback loop doubles back. This process, in which dead zones grow like cancers, choking off marine life and wiping out fisheries, is already quite advanced in parts of the Gulf of Mexico and just off Namibia, where hydrogen sulfide is bubbling out of the sea along a thousand-mile stretch of land known as the "Skeleton Coast." The name originally referred to the detritus of the whaling industry, but today it's more apt than ever. Hydrogen sulfide is so toxic that evolution has trained us to recognize the tiniest, safest traces of it, which is why our noses are so exquisitely skilled at registering flatulence. Hydrogen sulfide is also the thing that finally did us in that time 97 percent of all life on Earth died, once all the feedback loops had been triggered and the circulating jet streams of a warmed ocean ground to a halt—it's the planet's preferred gas for a natural holocaust. Gradually, the ocean's dead zones spread, killing off marine species that had dominated the oceans for hundreds of millions of years, and the gas the inert waters gave off into the atmosphere poisoned everything on land. Plants, too. It was millions of years before the oceans recovered.

THE GREAT FILTER

So why can't we see it? In his recent book-length essay *The Great Derangement*, the Indian novelist Amitav Ghosh wonders why global warming and natural disaster haven't become major subjects of contemporary fiction—why we don't seem able to imagine climate catastrophe, and why we haven't yet had a spate of novels in the genre he basically imagines into half-existence and names "the environmental uncanny." "Consider, for example, the stories that congeal around questions like, 'Where were you when the Berlin Wall fell?' or 'Where were you on 9/11?'" he writes. "Will it ever be possible to ask, in the same vein, 'Where were you at 400 ppm?' or 'Where were you when the Larsen B ice shelf broke up?'" His answer: Probably not, because the dilemmas and dramas of climate change are simply incompatible with the kinds of stories we tell ourselves about ourselves, especially in novels, which tend to emphasize the journey of an individual conscience rather than the poisonous miasma of social fate.

Surely this blindness will not last—the world we are about to inhabit will not permit it. In a 6-degree-warmer world, the Earth's ecosystem will boil with so many natural disasters that we will just start calling them "weather": a constant swarm of out-of-control typhoons and tornadoes and floods and droughts, the planet assaulted regularly with climate events that not so long ago destroyed whole civilizations. The strongest hurricanes will come more often, and we'll have to invent new categories with which to describe them; tornadoes will grow longer and wider and strike much more frequently, and hail rocks will quadruple in size. . . .

. . . Many people perceive climate change as a sort of moral and economic debt, accumulated since the beginning of the Industrial Revolution and now come due after several centuries—a helpful perspective, in a way, since it is the carbon-burning processes that began in eighteenth-century England that lit the fuse of everything that followed. But more than half of the carbon humanity has exhaled into the atmosphere in its entire history has been emitted in just the past three decades; since the end of World War II, the figure is 85 percent. Which means that, in the length of a single generation, global warming has brought us to the brink of planetary catastrophe, and that the story of the industrial world's kamikaze mission is also the story of a single lifetime. My father's, for instance: born in 1938, among his first memories the news of Pearl Harbor and the mythic Air Force of the propaganda films that followed, films that doubled as advertisements for imperial-American industrial might; and among his last memories the coverage of the desperate signing of the Paris Climate Accords on cable news, 10 weeks before he died of lung cancer [in July 2017]. Or my mother's: born in 1945, to German Jews fleeing the smokestacks through which their relatives were incinerated, now enjoying her 72nd year in an American commodity paradise, a paradise supported by the supply chains of an industrialized developing world. She has been smoking for 57 of those years, unfiltered. . . .

Several of the scientists I spoke with proposed global warming as the solution to Fermi's famous paradox, which asks, If the universe is so big, then why haven't we encountered any other intelligent life in it? The answer, they suggested, is that the natural lifespan of a civilization may be only several thousand years, and the lifespan of an industrial civilization perhaps only several hundred. In a universe that is many billions of years old, with star systems separated as much by time as by space, civilizations might emerge and develop and burn themselves up simply too fast to ever find one another. Peter Ward, a charismatic paleontologist among those responsible for discovering that the planet's mass extinctions were caused by greenhouse gas, calls this the "Great Filter": "Civilizations rise, but there's an environmental filter that causes them to die off again and disappear fairly quickly," he told me. "If you look at planet Earth, the filtering we've had in the past has been in these mass extinctions." The mass extinction we are now living through has only just begun; so much more dying is coming. And yet, improbably, Ward is an optimist. So are . . . many of the other scientists I spoke to. We have not developed much of a religion of meaning around climate change that might comfort us, or give us purpose, in the face of possible annihilation. But climate scientists have a strange kind of faith: We will find a way to forestall radical warming, they say, because we must.

It is not easy to know how much to be reassured by that bleak certainty, and how much to wonder whether it is another form of delusion; for global warming to work as parable, of course, someone needs to survive to tell the story. The scientists know that to even meet the Paris goals, by 2050, carbon emissions from energy and industry, which are still rising, will have to fall by half each decade; emissions from land use (deforestation, cow farts, etc.) will have to zero out; and we will need to have invented technologies to extract, annually, twice as much carbon from the atmosphere as the entire planet's plants now do. Nevertheless, by and large, the scientists have an enormous confidence in the ingenuity of humans—a confidence perhaps bolstered by their appreciation for climate change, which is, after all, a human invention, too. They point to the Apollo project, the hole in the ozone we patched in the 1980s, the passing of the fear of mutually assured destruction. Now we've found a way to engineer our own doomsday, and surely we will find a way to engineer our way out of it, one way or another. The planet is not used to being provoked like this, and climate systems designed to give feedback over centuries or millennia prevent us—even those who may be watching closely—from fully imagining the damage done already to the planet. But when we do truly see the world we've made, they say, we will also find a way to make it livable. For them, the alternative is simply unimaginable.

NOTES

1. Hausfather, Zeus. 2017. "Major Correction to Satellite Data Shows 140% Faster Warming Since 1998." *Carbon Brief: Clear on Climate*, June 30. Retrieved on March 16, 2019, from https://www.carbonbrief.org/major-correction-to-satellite-data-shows-140-faster-warming-since-1998.

2. Osborne, Hannah. 2017. "Giant Crack in Antarctica's Larsen C Ice Shelf Grew 11 Miles in Just 6 Days." *Newsweek*, June 1. Retrieved on March 15, 2019, from https://www.newsweek.com/antarctica-ice-shelf-larsen-c-crack-grown-618676.

3. Levitz, Eric. 2017. "Trillion-Ton Iceberg Breaks Off Antarctic Ice Shelf." *New York Magazine*, July 12. Retrieved on March 15, 2019, from http://nymag.com/intelligencer/2017/07/trillion-ton-iceberg-breaks-off-antarctic-ice-shelf.html?gtm=bottom.

4. Knapton, Sarah. 2017. "Tomorrow's World Returns to BBC with Startling Warning from Stephen Hawking—We Must Leave Earth." *The Telegraph*, May 2. Retrieved on March 15, 2019, from http://nymag.com/intelligencer/2017/07/trillion-ton-iceberg-breaks-off-antarctic-ice-shelf.html?gtm=bottom.

5. Osborne, Hannah. 2017. "Elon Musk Reveals Vision for a SpaceX City on Mars." *Newsweek*, June 15. Retrieved on March 16, 2019, from https://www.newsweek.com/elon-musk-mars-spacex-martian-city-625994.

6. Romm, Joseph. *Climate Change: What Everyone Needs to Know*, 2e. New York: Oxford University Press.

7. Battisti, David. S. and R. L. Naylor. 2009. "Historical Warnings of Future Food Insecurity with Unprecedented Seasonal Heat." *Science* 323(5911): 240–44.

8. 2015. "NASA Study Finds Carbon Emissions Could Dramatically Increase Risk of U.S. Megadroughts." NASA. Retrieved March 16, 2019, from https://www.nasa.gov/press/2015/february/nasa-study-finds-carbon-emissions-could-dramatically-increase-risk-of-us.

9. Fox-Skelly, Jasmin. 2017. "There Are Diseases Hidden in Ice, and They Are Waking Up." *BBC*, May 4. Retrieved on March 15, 2019, from http://www.bbc.com/earth/story/20170504-there-are-diseases-hidden-in-ice-and-they-are-waking-up.

10. Wallace-Wells, David, 2016. "Welcome to the Age of Robot Animals." *The Cut*, February 9. Retrieved on March 15, 2019, from https://www.thecut.com/2016/02/zika-virus-gmo-mosquitoes.html.

11. Vose, James M., David L. Peterson, and Toral Patel-Weynand, eds. 2012. "Effects of Climate Variability and Change on Forest Ecosystems: A Comprehensive Science Synthesis for the U.S. Forest Sector." United States Department of Agriculture, Forest Service. Retrieved on March 16, 2019, from https://www.usda.gov/oce/climate_change/effects_2012/FS_Climate1114%20opt.pdf.

MATT WILKINS

66. MORE RECYCLING WON'T SOLVE PLASTIC POLLUTION

Many Americans believe that recycling household plastics such as bottles and bags is an essential part of reducing pollution. The ubiquity of recycling bins is a testament to our interest in reducing plastic waste in the environment. But is the emphasis on individual effort to recycle misplaced? Wilkins discusses the marketing of plastic recycling campaigns, which obscure the role that industry and corporations have in not only creating plastic pollution, but in obstructing efforts to regulate plastic use and distribution. While individual waste reduction is important, we must examine the role of institutions and corporations as well if we hope to stem the tide of plastic pollution in our environment.

The only thing worse than being lied to is not knowing you're being lied to. It's true that plastic pollution is a huge problem, of planetary proportions. And it's true we could all do more to reduce our plastic footprint. The lie is that blame for the plastic problem is wasteful consumers and that changing our individual habits will fix it.

Recycling plastic is to saving the Earth what hammering a nail is to halting a falling skyscraper. You struggle to find a place to do it and feel pleased when you succeed. But your effort is wholly inadequate and distracts from the real problem of why the building is collapsing in the first place. The real problem is that single-use plastic—the very idea of producing plastic items like grocery bags, which we use for an average of 12 minutes[1] but can persist in the environment for half a millennium—is an incredibly reckless abuse of technology. Encouraging individuals to recycle more will never solve the problem of a massive production of single-use plastic that should have been avoided in the first place.

As an ecologist and evolutionary biologist, I have had a disturbing window into the accumulating literature on the hazards of plastic pollution. Scientists have long recognized that plastics biodegrade slowly, if at all, and pose multiple threats to wildlife through entanglement and consumption. More recent reports highlight dangers posed by absorption of toxic chemicals[2] in the water and by plastic odors that mimic some species' natural food.[3] Plastics also accumulate up the food chain, and studies now show that we are likely ingesting it ourselves in seafood.[4] If we consumers are to blame, how is it possible that we fail to react when a study reports that there will be more plastic than fish in the oceans by 2050?[5] I would argue the simple answer is that it is hard. And the reason why it is hard has an interesting history.

Beginning in the 1950s, big beverage companies like Coca-Cola and Anheuser-Busch, along with Phillip Morris and others, formed a nonprofit called Keep America Beautiful. Its mission is/was to educate and encourage environmental stewardship in the public. Joining forces with the Ad Council (the public service announcement geniuses behind Smokey the Bear and McGruff the Crime Dog), one of their first and most lasting impacts was bringing "litterbug" into the American lexicon[6] through their marketing campaigns against thoughtless individuals. Two decades later, their "Crying Indian" PSA,[7] would become hugely influential for the U.S. environmental movement. In the ad, a Native American man canoes up to a highway, where a motorist tosses a bag of trash. The camera pans up to show a tear rolling down the man's cheek. By tapping into a shared national guilt for the history of mistreatment of Native Americans and the sins of a throwaway society, the PSA became a powerful symbol to motivate behavioral change. More recently, the Ad Council and Keep America Beautiful teams produced the "I Want to Be Recycled"[8] campaign, which urges consumers to imagine the reincarnation of shampoo bottles and boxes, following the collection and processing of materials to the remolding of the next generation of products.

At face value, these efforts seem benevolent, but they obscure the real problem, which is the role that corporate polluters play in the plastic problem. This clever misdirection has led journalist and author Heather Rogers to describe Keep America Beautiful as the first corporate greenwashing front,[9] as it has helped shift the public focus to consumer recycling behavior and actively thwarted legislation[10] that would increase extended producer responsibility for waste management.

For example, back in 1953, Vermont passed a piece of legislation called the Beverage Container Law,[11] which outlawed the sale of beverages in nonrefillable containers. Single-use packaging was just being developed, and manufacturers were excited about the much higher profit margins associated with selling containers along with their products, rather than having to be in charge of recycling or cleaning and reusing them. Keep America Beautiful was founded that year and began working to thwart such legislation. Vermont lawmakers allowed the measure to lapse after four years, and the single-use container industry expanded, unfettered, for almost 20 years. In 1971 Oregon reacted to a growing trash problem by becoming the first U.S. state to pass a "bottle bill," requiring a five-cent deposit on beverage containers that would be refunded upon the container's return. Bottle bills provide a strong incentive for container reuse and recycling, and the 10 states with bottle deposit laws have around 60 percent container recovery rates compared to 24 percent in states without them.[12] Yet Keep America Beautiful and other industrial lobbying groups have publicly opposed or marketed against bottle deposit legislation for decades, as it threatens their bottom line. Between 1989 and 1994 the beverage industry spent $14 million to defeat the National Bottle Bill.

In fact, the greatest success of Keep America Beautiful[13] has been to shift the onus of environmental responsibility onto the public while simultaneously becoming a trusted name in the environmental movement. This psychological misdirect has built public support for a legal framework that punishes individual litterers with hefty fines or jail time, while imposing almost no responsibility on plastic manufacturers for the numerous environmental, economic and health hazards imposed by their products.

Because of a legal system that favors corporate generation of plastic, plus public acceptance of single-use items as part of the modern economy, consumers who want to reduce their plastic footprint are faced with a host of challenges. We should carry around reusable beverage and takeout containers. We should avoid bottled water or sodas at all costs. When we have to accept a single-use plastic container, we should inform ourselves about the complex nuances of which types of plastic are acceptable (No. 1–3, but not No. 5?), which forms are acceptable (bottles and jugs, but not bags?) and where they can be deposited (curbside or at a special location?).

In the case of most restaurants and gas stations, which almost never have customer-facing recycling facilities even where required by law,[14] we should transport recyclables to another location that does recycle. Even then, we must live with the knowledge that plastics generally degrade with recycling, such that plastic bottles are more often turned into nonrecyclable carpets and synthetic clothes than more bottles.[15]

Effectively, we have accepted individual responsibility for a problem we have little control over. We can swim against this plastic stream with all our might and fail to make much headway. At some point we need to address the source. According to a 2016 Pew Research poll,[16] 74 percent of Americans think the government should do "whatever it takes to protect the environment." So what would swift, informed, and effective governmental action to stop the pollution of our water, food,[17] and bodies[18] look like?

Legislators could make laws that incentivize and facilitate recycling, like the national bottle deposit and bag tax bills[19] that were proposed in 2009. These bills would have created a nationwide five-cent deposit on plastic bottles and other containers, and a nonrefundable five-cent charge on plastic bags at checkout. The UK launched a similar charge on all single-use grocery bags in 2015[20] and announced a nationwide bottle deposit requirement in March of [2018].[21] Within six months of the plastic bag charge being in place, usage dropped over 80 percent. Similarly, in Germany, where a nationwide bottle bill was put in place in 2003, recycling rates have exceeded 98 percent.[22] In the United States. these actions would go a long way toward recovering the estimated $8 billion yearly economic opportunity[23] cost of plastic waste.

Other actions could include a ban or "opt-in" policy on single-use items like plastic straws. That is, single-use plastic items would not be available or only upon request. A small tweak like this can lead to huge changes in consumer behavior, by making wastefulness an active choice rather than the status quo. Such measures were . . . adopted by several U.S. cities,[24] and are under consideration in California[25] and the UK.[26] [*Editor's Note*: In 2018, California passed legislation that banned restaurants from giving customers plastic straws unless the customer requested them. In January 2019, Washington, DC also banned plastic straws in restaurants.]

And yet, some plastic producers continue to oppose legislation that would eat into their profit margins. Though California and Hawaii have banned the free distribution of plastic bags at checkout, a result of lobbying is that 10 U.S. states now have preemption laws[27] preventing municipalities from regulating plastic at the local level. [*Editor's Note*: As of March 2019, 11 states have "preemption laws" that prevent the regulation of plastic, and six additional states are considering legislation.[28]] Plastic producers see their profits threatened and have taken a familiar tactic, forming the Save the Plastic Bag Coalition and the American Progressive Bag Alliance[29] to fight bag bans under the guise of defending customers' finances and freedom to choose.

So what can we do to make responsible use of plastic a reality? First: reject the lie. Litterbugs are not responsible for the global ecological disaster of plastic. Humans can only function to the best of their abilities, given time, mental bandwidth, and systemic constraints. Our huge problem with plastic is the result of a permissive legal framework that has allowed the uncontrolled rise of plastic pollution, despite clear evidence of the harm it causes to local communities and the world's oceans. Recycling is also too hard in most parts of the United States and lacks the proper incentives to make it work well.

Second: talk about our plastic problem loudly and often. Start conversations with your family members and friends. Call your local and federal representatives to support bottle bills, plastic bag taxes, and increased producer responsibility for reuse and recycling. Stand up against preemptive bans on local plastic regulation. There are signs that corporations are listening to consumer opinions, too. After numerous petitions from customers and environmental organizations, McDonald's has pledged to use only sustainable packaging materials by 2025[30] and to phase out Styrofoam by the year's end.

Third: think bigger. There is now serious talk of zero waste. Instead of trying to reduce waste by a small fraction, some individuals and communities[31] are shifting their lifestyles to ensure that nearly everything is reused, recycled, or composted. Nonrecyclable straws and to-go cup lids do not fit into this system. Though inspiring, a zero waste lifestyle will be impractical or impossible for most of us within current economic systems.

A better alternative is the circular economy model, where waste is minimized by planning in advance how materials can be reused and recycled at a product's end of life rather than trying to figure that out after the fact. To make this happen, we can support groups like the Ellen MacArthur Foundation that are partnering with industry to incorporate "cradle-to-cradle" (i.e., circular economic) design into their products.

This could be our future—a future of clean cities, rivers, and beaches but also simpler, more responsible choices for consumers. There are now too many humans and too much plastic on this pale blue dot to continue planning our industrial expansions on a quarterly basis. It's time to stop blaming consumers for our plastic crisis and demand a better system.

NOTES

1. "Take Action: Plastic Bags." N.d. 5 Gyres. Retrieved on March 18, 2019, from https://www.5gyres.org/plastic-bags.

2. Barclay, Eliza. 2013. "How Plastic in the Ocean Is Contaminating Your Seafood." *National Public Radio*, December 13. Retrieved on March 18, 2019, from https://www.npr.org/sections/thesalt/2013/12/12/250438904/how-plastic-in-the-ocean-is-contaminating-your-seafood.

3. Perkins, Sid. 2016. "Why Do Seabirds Eat Plastic? They Think It Smells Tasty." *Science*, November 9. Retrieved on March 18, 2019, from https://www.sciencemag.org/news/2016/11/why-do-seabirds-eat-plastic-they-think-it-smells-tasty?r3f_986=https://blogs.scientificamerican.com/observations/more-recycling-wont-solve-plastic-pollution.

4. Johnston, Ian. 2017. "Plastic Microparticles Found in Flesh of Fish Eaten by Humans." *The Independent*, July 26. Retrieved on March 18, 2019, from https://www.independent.co.uk/environment/plastic-microparticles-fish-flesh-eaten-humans-food-chain-mackerel-anchovy-mullet-a7860726.html.

5. Kaplan, Sarah. 2016. "By 2050, There Will Be More Plastic Than Fish in the World's Oceans, Study Says." *The Washington Post*, January 20. Retrieved on March 18, 2019, from https://www.washingtonpost.com/news/morning-mix/wp/2016/01/20/by-2050-there-will-be-more-plastic-than-fish-in-the-worlds-oceans-study-says/?utm_term=.0e06c4c8b274.

6. Plumer, Bradford. 2006. "The Origins of Anti-Litter Campaigns." *Mother Jones*, May 22. Retrieved on March 18, 2019, from https://www.motherjones.com/politics/2006/05/origins-anti-litter-campaigns.

7. https://www.youtube.com/watch?v=j7OHG7tHrNM

8. http://iwanttoberecycled.org/journey

9. Conrad, Ariane. 2005. "Litterbug World." *AlterNet*, April 1. Retrieved on March 18, 2019, from https://www.alternet.org/2005/04/litterbug_world.

10. "Keep America Beautiful." N.d. The Center for Media and Democracy. Retrieved on March 18, 2019, from https://www.sourcewatch.org/index.php/Keep_America_Beautiful.

11. "Bottle Bills." 2012. James M. Jeffords Center's Vermont Legislative Research Service, University of Vermont. Retrieved on March 18, 2019, from https://www.uvm.edu/~vlrs/Environment/Bottle%20Bills.pdf.

12. "Bottle Bills." The Container Recycling Institute. Retrieved on March 18, 2019, from http://www.container-recycling.org/index.php/issues/bottle-bills.

13. Strand, Ginger. 2008. "The Crying Indian." *Orion Magazine*. Retrieved on March 18, 2019, from https://orionmagazine.org/article/the-crying-indian.

14. Faulkner, Tim. 2014. "Gas Stations, Coffee Shops Must Recycle; Most Don't." *EcoRI News*, August 16. Retrieved on March 18, 2019, from https://www.ecori.org/composting/2014/8/16/gas-stations-coffee-shops-must-recycle-most-dont.html.

15. Wong, Vanessa. 2017. "Almost No Plastic Bottles Get Recycled into New Bottles." *Buzzfeed News*, April 23. Retrieved on March 18, 2019, from https://www.buzzfeednews.com/article/venessawong/plastic-drinking-problem#.nvveDDK4G.

16. Anderson, Monica. 2017. "For Earth Day, Here's How Americans View Environmental Issues." Pew Research Center. Retrieved on March 18, 2019, from http://www.pewresearch.org/fact-tank/2017/04/20/for-earth-day-heres-how-americans-view-environmental-issues.

17. Clean Water Action. "The Problem of Marine Plastic Pollution." N.d. Retrieved on March 18, 2019, from https://www.cleanwater.org/problem-marine-plastic-pollution.

18. "Exposure to Chemical Found in Plastics 'Hard to Avoid' in Everyday Life." 2018. College of Medicine and Health. Medicine, Nursing, and Allied Health Professions, University of Exeter. Retrieved on March 18, 2019, from https://medicine.exeter.ac.uk/news/articles/exposuretochemicalfoundin.html.

19. Boyle, Katherine. 2009. "New Bottle Deposit, Bag Tax Bills Touted for Combating Pollution." *The New York Times*, April 23. Retrieved on March 18, 2019, from https://archive.nytimes.com/www.nytimes.com/gwire/2009/04/23/23greenwire-new-bottle-deposit-and-bag-tax-bills-touted-fo-10641.html?scp=1&sq=New%2520bottle%2520deposit%252C%2520bag%2520tax%2520bills%2520touted%2520for%2520combating%2520pollution&st=cse.

20. "Carrier Bags: Why There's a Charge." 2018. Department for Environment Food and Rural Affairs. Retrieved on March 18, 2019, from https://www.gov.uk/government/publications/single-use-plastic-carrier-bags-why-were-introducing-the-charge/carrier-bags-why-theres-a-5p-charge.

21. Carrington, Damian. 2018. "Bottle and Can Deposit Return Scheme Gets Green Light in England." *The Guardian*, March 27. Retrieved on March 18, 2019, from https://www.theguardian.com/environment/2018/mar/27/bottle-and-can-deposit-return-scheme-gets-green-light-in-england.

22. Simon, Joan Marc. 2010. "Beverage Packing and Zero Waste." Zero Waste Europe. Retrieved on March 18, 2019, from https://zerowasteeurope.eu/2010/09/beverage-packaging-and-zero-waste.

23. Woodring, Doug. 2013. "Plastic Waste is Worth $8 Billion a Year." Ocean Health Index. Retrieved on March 18, 2019, from http://www.oceanhealthindex.org/news/Plastic_Waste_is_Worth_8B_a_Year.

24. Victor, Daniel. 2018. "Ban of Plastic Straws in Restaurants Expand to More Cities." *The New York Times*, March 3. Retrieved on March 18, 2019, from https://www.nytimes.com/2018/03/03/climate/plastic-straw-bans.html.

25. Daniels, Jeff. 2018. "California Looks to Ban Removable Plastic Bottle Caps, Restrict Plastic Straws." *CNBC.com*, March 7. Retrieved on March 18, 2019, from https://www.cnbc.com/2018/03/07/california-targets-removable-plastic-bottle-caps-plastic-straws.html.

26. Perkins, Anne. 2018. "Cotton Buds and Plastic Straws Could Be Banned in England Next Year." *The Guardian*, April 19. Retrieved on March 18, 2019, from https://www.theguardian.com/environment/2018/apr/18/single-use-plastics-could-be-banned-in-england-next-year.

27. "State Plastic and Paper Bag Legislation." 2019. National Conference of State Legislatures. Retrieved on March 18, 2019, from http://www.ncsl.org/research/environment-and-natural-resources/plastic-bag-legislation.aspx.

28. "State Plastic and Paper Bag Legislation." 2019.

29. Luna, Taryn. 2016. "Environmental Nuisance or Grocery-Store Necessity? California Voters to Decide Fate of Plastic Bags." *The Sacramento Bee*, October 8. Retrieved on March 18, 2019, from https://www.sacbee.com/news/politics-government/capitol-alert/article106779332.html.

30. Geier, Ben. 2018. "McDonald's is Going Green." *CNN Business*, January 16. Retrieved on March 18, 2019, from https://money.cnn.com/2018/01/16/news/companies/mcdonalds-packaging-green/index.html.

31. Longest, Molly. 2017. "A Beginner's Guide to Zero Waste Living (PS, It Doesn't Happen Overnight)." Trash Is for Tossers. Retrieved on March 18, 2019, from http://trashisfortossers.com/a-beginners-guide-to-zero-waste-living-ps-it-doesnt-happen-overnight.

MAKING A PROFIT ON BOTTLED WATER

ELEANOR CUMMINS

For the thousands of tourists who take to the Great Lakes[1] each summer, Michigan seems like a waterlogged oasis in the middle of an otherwise crusty continent. But for all its soggy splendor (the mitt-shaped midwestern state is surrounded on three sides by water), the last few years have read like an unmitigated disaster.

In 2014, officials moved the residents of Flint, Michigan[2] off their historic water source—treated H20 from Lake Huron and the Detroit River—to improperly treated liquid pulled from the Flint River.[3] Two years later, Michigan's governor declared a state of emergency when it could no longer be denied that drinking and otherwise using the water piped in from Flint River had exposed thousands of children to high levels of the neurotoxin lead[4] and may have triggered a deadly outbreak of Legionnaires' disease.[5] Since January 2016, Flint residents have lived on bottles of water delivered by the state government by the thousands. On April 6 [2018], officials announced the water drops would stop, saying the lead levels in Flint tap water had been meeting federal limits for almost two years.[6] The move was criticized by locals, many of whom expressed their distrust of the water—and the people in charge of it.

At the same time, another water bottling issue has been brewing in the state. Just four days earlier, on April 2, the Michigan Department of Environmental Quality approved a widely-protested plan[7] that would allow the snack company Nestlé to pump 250 gallons of water a minute from White Pine Springs, which the company would then bottle, brand like Nestlé Pure Life Purified Water or Ice Mountain 100 percent Natural Spring Water, and sell (at least in New York) for about $2.50 a pop. The timing, though coincidental, brings to the forefront an issue of increasing international importance: the privatization of water.

The history of bottled water is actually rather murky. Some say it was Holy Well bottling in the United Kingdom, which first began selling spring water in 1622, under the reign of King James I. Others trace it to Jackson's Spa[8] in Boston, which began selling its allegedly medicinal water in 1767. The intervening 150 years saw hundreds of other companies get into the water game, including Nestlé, which got in the bottling game in 1843 in Switzerland. By 2016, bottled water sales hit $16 billion in the United States alone[9] and are expected to keep rising around the world. At the same time water bottle sales have shot up, access to clean and affordable water has declined. La Paz in Bolivia, Cape Town in Africa, and numerous other cities are hitting the rocky bottom[10] of their natural aquifers and glacial reserves. While there's certainly enough water on the planet—Earth has an estimated 326 million trillion gallons of it—it's not always in the right places or in the right form. (Most of Earth's water is stored in its oceans, which humans cannot directly consume due to high saline content.)

1   Hsu, Jeremy. 2010. "Obama Pledges $475 Million to Rescue Great Lakes." *Popular Science*, February 22. Retrieved on March 18, 2019, from https://www.popsci.com/technology/article/2010–02/iobama-administration-unveils-475-million-plan-rescue-us-great-lakes.

2   Ossola, Alexandra. 2016. "Lead in Water: What Are the Health Effects and Dangers?" *Popular Science*, January 18. Retrieved on March 18, 2019, from https://www.popsci.com/lead-water-what-are-health-effects-dangers.

3   *Popular Science*. 2016."How Did Lead Get Into Flint River Water?"January 26, Retrieved on December 2, 2019, from https://www.popsci.com/whats-wrong-with-flint-river/.

4   Pierre-Louis, Kendra. 2017. "The Devastating Effects of Childhood Lead Exposure Could Last a Lifetime." *Popular Science*, March 29. Retrieved on March 18, 2019, from https://www.popsci.com/lead-effects-can-last-lifetime.

5   Pierre-Louis, Kendra. 2017. "Michigan Health Director Charged with Involuntary Manslaughter Due to Flint Water Woes." *Popular Science*, June 14. Retrieved on March 18, 2019, from https://www.popsci.com/health-director-involuntary-manslaughter-flint.

6   Fortin, Jacey. 2018. "Michigan Will No Longer Provide Free Bottled Water to Flint." *The New York Times*, April 8. Retrieved on March 18, 2019, from https://www.nytimes.com/2018/04/08/us/flint-water-bottles.html.

7   Chappell, Bill. 2018. "Michigan OKs Nestlé Water Extraction, Despite 80K+ Public Comments Against It." *National Public Radio*, April 3. Retrieved on March 18, 2019, from https://www.npr.org/sections/thetwo-way/2018/04/03/599207550/michigan-oks-nestl-water-extraction-despite-over-80k-public-comments-against-it.

8   "A Brief History of Bottled Water in America." 2009. Great Lakes Law. Retrieved on March 18, 2019, from https://www.greatlakeslaw.org/blog/2009/03/a-brief-history-of-bottled-water-in-america.html.

9   Winter, Caroline. 2017. "Nestlé Makes Billions Bottling Water It Pays Nearly Nothing For." *Bloomberg Businessweek*, September 21. Retrieved on March 18, 2019, from https://www.bloomberg.com/news/features/2017-09-21/nestl-makes-billions-bottling-water-it-pays-nearly-nothing-for.

10 Ahmed, Amal. 2018. "The People of Cape Town Are Running Out of Water—and They're Not Alone." *Popular Science*, March 13. Retrieved on March 18, 2019, from https://www.popsci.com/water-crisis-cape-town-world.

Water bottling companies like Nestlé and Coca-Cola may seem like the solution to many of these problems. Their product is potable and portable. In some areas, like the northeastern United States, there has been an uptick in rainfall just as other cities have become more arid, which makes water redistribution a tantalizing thought. The same is true for communities like Flint, where waters are so contaminated locals had no choice but to bus in some liquid life from off-site.

But experts continue to urge caution. For one, the companies that bottle water often do so cheaply, which means companies are pocketing the vast majority of those billions, instead of sharing them with the cities from which they take water. In the case of Nestlé's operations in Michigan, the company was paying just $200 in extraction fees, according to a 2017 investigation by *Bloomberg*.[11] And a price tag was conspicuously absent from news reports on the additional bottling rights Nestlé secured in Michigan. . . . In other states like Maine and Texas, the *Bloomberg* article notes, absolute capture laws allow landowners—whether they're an average joe or a multinational corporation—to suck every ounce of groundwater beneath their property, free of charge.

In already-arid places like Texas, these loosey-goosey water rights pose clear problems. As groundwater is rapidly depleted across the United States, drought looms ever larger. But the Great Lakes states aren't immune just because they have abundant H20. In advance of . . . [the] permit approval for new Nestlé pumping, 80,945 Michiganders wrote to their officials in opposition to the permit.[12] Just 75 public comments were in favor. Among those who dissented, concerns over corporate greed were cited regularly. Many people also stated their belief that water is a right, not a commodity.

Other concerns center on the environment. Even in a place where water appears to flow aplenty, these concerns appear to be founded. Numerous studies, including those conducted by Nestlé itself, suggest aggressive pumping[13] can and already has caused ecological damages.[14] One attempted solution has been to cap the gallons pumped each day, thereby conserving the watershed. But Nestlé has been accused of pumping beyond the permit in the past. In the midst of a recent drought, the company appears to have taken more than its legal allotment of water from California's San Bernardino National Forest,[15] where the company was operating with little environmental oversight.[16] Between 1947 and 2015, the state's water board reported, Nestlé pumped an average of 62.6 million gallons a year,[17] but may have only had permits to extract 8.5 million gallons annually.

When juxtaposed against the crisis in Flint, the promise and peril of bottled water seem particularly stark. After public officials made disastrous decisions, bottled water was the only thing keeping residents safe and their thirst slaked. But now that the government-subsidized shipments are done, it's questionable whether the people of Flint will be able to pay for bottled water on their own. Flint is one of the poorest cities in the nation,[18] and many residents have wracked up thousands of dollars in water bills[19] despite being unable to safely drink the liquid sent to their homes and schools. Meanwhile, mere miles away, premium Michigan water is being pumped for profit.

Instead of offering us a sideways glance at tragedy, Flint seems to provide a glimpse into the future. As Environmental Protection Agency programs protecting our waters from pollution are rolled back,[20] for-profit companies gobble up pumping permits, and freshwater becomes harder to access,[21] bottled water sales will only grow. While many will find some refuge from thirst in Nestlé Pure Life or Coca Cola's Dasani bottles, the industry's increasing relevance will require equal scrutiny.

11 Winter, 2017.
12 Chappell, 2018.
13 Ellison, Garret. 2017. "More Pumping Could Harm Wetlands, Suggests Nestlé's Own Study." *Michigan Live*, April 9. Retrieved on March 18, 2019, from https://www.mlive.com/news/2017/04/nestle_evart_wetlands_impact.html.
14 Winter, 2017.
15 Chappell, Bill. 2017. "California Says Nestlé Lacks Permits to Extract Millions of Gallons of Water." *National Public Radio*, December 27. Retrieved on March 18, 2019, from https://www.npr.org/sections/thetwo-way/2017/12/27/573774328/california-says-nestle-lacks-permits-to-extract-millions-of-gallons-of-water.
16 James, Ian. 2015. "Bottling Water Without Scrutiny." *Desert Sun*, March 8. Retrieved on March 18, 2019, from https://www.desertsun.com/story/news/2015/03/05/bottling-water-california-drought/24389417.
17 California Water Boards, State Water Resources Control Board. 2017. https://www.waterboards.ca.gov/waterrights/water_issues/programs/enforcement/complaints/docs/nestle/roi_transmittal_letter.pdf
18 Johnson, Jiquanda. 2015. "Flint, Detroit among Nation's Poorest Cities, New Census Data Show." *Michigan Live*, September 17. Retrieved on March 18, 2019, from https://www.mlive.com/news/flint/2015/09/flint_detroit_among_nations_po.html.
19 Baxter, Anthony. 2018. "Flint Residents Are Being Punished for Not Paying for Poisoned Water. *The Guardian*, April 4. Retrieved on March 18, 2019, from https://www.theguardian.com/commentisfree/2018/apr/04/flint-residents-punished-poisoned-water.
20 Davenport, Coral. 2018. "E.P.A. Blocks Obama-Era Clean Water Rule." *The New York Times*, January 31. Retrieved on March 18, 2019, from https://www.nytimes.com/2018/01/31/climate/trump-water-wotus.html.
21 Ahmed, 2018.

EMILY STUTZMAN

67. WHY BEEF IS WHAT'S FOR DINNER

Agricultural Policy And Its Implications

Think about what you had for dinner last night. Do you know where your food came from or how it fits into the larger food system? If you don't, you're not alone. The system that supports and constrains our food choices—including a wide variety of federal and state policies and regulations—is largely hidden from the American consumer, but it affects the types of foods available to us, their affordability, their production's impact on the environment, and our individual and public health. Stutzman discusses the origins, motivations, and effects of these policies and how they might be redesigned to keep the consumer's needs and desires in mind.

What might a political conflict in Washington, DC, over a proposed border wall in the southwestern United States have to do with the monitoring of bacteria living on romaine lettuce in Georgia? The U.S. food system is complex, and the federal government plays a large role in inspecting, regulating, purchasing, and supplying food for millions of people every day. This role became clearer with the government shutdown of 2018–2019, which lasted 35 days, the longest federal government shutdown in the history of the United States. During this shutdown, aspects of food policy that are normally hidden from the public eye, or at least operating in the background of our society, came into sharper focus. While the federal government's role in the food system doesn't typically make flashy headlines, sociologists and those who work in food policy, who have an eye for the social dimensions of food and agriculture, were reading the news and inferring how the sudden cutoff of government funding would impact the food system. Government policies, regulations, and actions (or inaction) impact the food system directly (e.g., by funding school lunch programs that feed 30 million children daily, by monitoring and regulating the safety of the food supply, and by implementing social safety net programs that prevent hunger and food insecurity) and indirectly (by employing millions of workers and contractors who, when faced without paychecks during the shutdown, were forced to seek assistance at food pantries).

The government shutdown highlighted the behind-the-scenes work that the government provides to make our food system safer and to distribute food to those in need. Yet governmental policies do not always protect consumers, and certain policies may have detrimental effects. Governmental programs and policies have direct ramifications for the food system and consumers, demonstrating just one example of the ways in which what we eat is not simply a "personal choice." Individuals make choices based on available options (or "food access"), and those available options are strongly affected by U.S. food and agricultural policy. Food policy is the cumulative effect of laws, regulations,

Original to *Focus on Social Problems: A Contemporary Reader*.

decisions, and actions by governments that influence agricultural production, distribution, and consumption. Reflecting American values of individualism and capitalism, food policy both reflects and reinforces the social and economic context of the nation.[1]

In this reading, I highlight several federal policies that contribute to the limited food options in food consumption in the United States and offer some explanations as to why these policies exist and persist. Although there are many food-related policies (regulating food safety, food aid to foreign countries, and immigrant laborers in the agricultural system, for example), in this reading I focus on agricultural subsidies that contradict recommendations for a healthy diet as well as those policies that influence eaters' ability to make informed choices about their food. Sadly, some policies lead to poor health outcomes that hurt individuals and our society. The health food industry's meager impact on health and well-being is dwarfed by the messages and choices dictated by U.S. food policy. As a result, more people are shopping for food primarily at Dollar General, which sells overwhelmingly low-nutrient value, shelf-stable convenience food and snack foods, than at Whole Foods. Such a shift displays both a rural/urban divide and a socioeconomic one.[2] The real problem is that profit-motivated businesses drive both the health food industry and U.S. food policy. There are opportunities for positive change, and below I will identify some contemporary efforts to achieve better food policy, access, and health outcomes. Changing the food system for the better isn't simply about convincing individuals to buy better food products. Rather, such change involves a paradigm shift about what food is and what we can do, collectively, to improve food access by bringing policy in line with our national interest in a healthy population, potentially refocusing the role of the federal government in the food system on ensuring the well-being of people living in the United States.

NUTRITIONAL RECOMMENDATIONS AND FOOD SUBSIDIES: AT ODDS

In the more than 35 years since various arms of the U.S. government[3] began publishing dietary recommendations based on food and nutrition science,

these instructions can be summed up as follows: eat vegetables, fruits, nuts, seeds, lean meats, and whole grains, but limit processed starches, red meat, salt, and refined sugar.[4] These recommendations are based entirely on promoting health and avoiding disease, not on the economics of food or consumer preferences, much less the profitability of food production and processing. However, agricultural policies are created with economic interests in mind. Not surprisingly, these economic interests do not always align with public health goals. The result is that the foods we're told to avoid are the easiest to find and the least expensive for consumers to purchase.

The federal government has long offered direct subsidies for certain food producers in an attempt to control production and prices. Yet the government also has a vested interest in preserving the health of the population and educating the populace on how to live healthy, productive lives. To achieve those goals simultaneously, agricultural subsidies would have to increase production of and lower prices of health-promoting foods. However, the direct opposite is currently true. Processed starches, animal products, and sugars are the three categories that receive the greatest direct and indirect economic incentives for production, called subsidies, from the government, whereas fruit, vegetable, and nut production (called "specialty crops") do not receive payments. These subsidies affect the production and price of unhealthy foods, making them plentiful and artificially cheap. Food processing and specialized packaging (like frozen dinners, for example) lengthens the shelf life of these less healthy food products, making them more convenient as well. But why are processed starches, animal products, and sugar subsidized in the first place? To understand why our system functions the way it does today, let's explore the roots of our current agri-food system with a brief agricultural history of the United States.

HISTORY OF AGRICULTURE

The major trend in agriculture in the United States over the past century has been consolidation and specialization—farms are getting larger, as corporate-owned farms buy out smaller, diversified family-owned ones. Farms today are more likely to produce only a few crops on land that once produced a wide variety. These trends are a result of top-down agricultural policy that fostered the growth of agribusiness to the detriment of small family farms, policy that was designed and implemented by the federal government, and policy that has only escalated as these grown-up agribusinesses exert political influence.

"Get big or get out" was the command Earl Butz (Secretary of Agriculture under Presidents Nixon and Ford) gave U.S. farmers in the 1970s. His agricultural policy prioritized large farm scale and agribusiness, facilitating the growth of corporate farms and increasing subsidized[5] production of grains for export. As these policies took effect, the small, family-run farms we had relied on for food production began to disappear. Our agrarian society began to vanish, as small, family-owned farms with diverse crops couldn't compete with specialized corporate farms, whose profits were based on economies of scale as well as the growing subsidization of the production of agricultural commodities. Changes in farming coincided with the rise of the number of men and women in the industrial workforce as farm- and home-based work shifted to wage-based work. These changes set the stage for the economic dominance of the processed food and fast-food industries. Food provision was no longer under the control of individual families; it was increasingly industrialized. Consolidation and specialization meant that food now traveled long distances between farmer and eater. This travel, and thus the whole food system, was built on the consistent availability of cheap fossil fuels.

Agricultural policy intersected with the technological, economic, and social context of the post–World War II era. Some of the factors that made large specialized farms profitable were technological advances that replaced large amounts of farm labor with machines. Much of the research behind these technological developments happened at public land grant universities with a combination of public and corporate funding. Other factors supporting the industrial model of agriculture have been cheap fossil fuels and the development of the interstate highway system. At the federal level, lowering previous trade barriers meant that larger farms growing mass quantities of grain had greatly expanded markets. Large grain farmers

also benefited from agricultural subsidies, expanding the production of corn, wheat, and soy, making these grains plentiful and inexpensive. The goal of these subsidies was to standardize production, encouraging farmers to produce a stable food supply by removing some of the risk inherent in farming, where crops and thus livelihoods are vulnerable to weather and pests. Over time, farmers planted according to the payout they'd receive, which meant producing more and more feed grain, much of which was fed to animals. The subsidy program therefore took on a life of its own—becoming more and more enmeshed with corporate food and agriculture and the trade groups and lobbyists that represent their commercial interests. In contrast to small, diversified farms with grass-grazing herds of livestock, confined animal feeding operations (CAFOs) became economically advantageous after World War II. Americans considered meat from grain-fed animals preferable (fattier, more consistent quality, etc.). As a result of the postwar economic boom, consumers had larger disposable incomes. At that time, meat consumption in the United States was a sign of affluence, a form of conspicuous consumption that demonstrated high social status; with rising incomes came increased spending on animal-based foods.[6] Food policy has shaped what is available by shaping what farmers and corporations produce. Thus, the explosion of CAFOs and the subsequent increase in animal product consumption was a result of changes in agricultural technology and what consumer markets supported.

Although it dramatically shapes the eating options of the 318 million people in the United States, agricultural policy is not on most people's minds. That's partially because only 2 percent of adults in the United States are farmers. Every five or so years when a new Farm Bill moves through the wheels of government, we may hear about it on the news, but farms don't register high on the list of what's important for most people. Yet they should. Only a small group stands to benefit from subsidies, although the costs of food production are shared by all, including direct costs as a portion of taxes and hidden costs in the form of poor health outcomes. The agricultural lobby is so strong because of how our legislative branch is set up: whereas the House of Representatives is determined by population of the 50 states, the Senate is composed of two senators per state. Thus, senators representing states that are small in population, but where agriculture is an economically important industry (read: influenced highly by agribusinesses and their lobbyists) have a disproportionately loud voice in setting agricultural policy. One strategy for catching the attention of a larger group of Americans is to refer to this piece of legislation as the "Food Bill," instead of the "Farm Bill." After all, it determines funding for agricultural programs and antihunger programs (including the Supplemental Nutritional Access Program, or SNAP, formerly called food stamps) as well as conservation on farmland, issues that many nonfarmers care about but may be overlooked, hidden in the Farm Bill.

SUGAR: NOT SO SWEET

It's no secret that a major factor in chronic diseases including diabetes, obesity, and heart disease is sugar consumption. Agricultural policy runs counter to nutritional recommendations when it comes to sugar production. One of the reasons we consume so much sugar is because it is cheap and readily available. We pour it directly into our iced tea, coffee, and Kool-Aid. Yet it is also hidden, added to processed foods where it is harder to visualize, which thus makes it harder for people to realize how much sugar they're actually eating. This cheap sugar isn't just ending up in candy and cookies; it's also added to foods that few would count as "sugary" or "sweets," like yogurt, jarred pasta sauce, and peanut butter. Why is there sugar in pasta sauce? Humans have an evolutionary preference toward sweet fruits. This was important for our hunter–gatherer ancestors for whom sweet fruits were in short supply and only seasonally available, but were filled with vital nutrients. Now that sugar is everywhere and doesn't come attached to vitamins and fiber, like it does in an apple or a grapefruit, our human predilection toward sugar can be harmful, leading to negative health outcomes like diabetes, heart disease, high blood pressure, and cancer, not to mention tooth decay.

Agricultural policy artificially props up sugar, making it inexpensive to consumers. Growing cane sugar is ecologically destructive and economically unprofitable without the direct payment of federal dollars to the sugar industry in the United States, especially because sugar can be more cheaply grown in tropical countries. The government's direct payments for corn production influence the production and price of corn-based syrups, including high-fructose corn syrup, which we rely on far more than cane sugar. If you've ever had the pleasure to travel and sip a Coca-Cola in another country, you may have noticed that in addition to being served room temperature (that's cultural), it has a different sweet taste (that's a result of U.S. agricultural policy). In the United States, the sugar in our soft drinks is corn based because our corn is subsidized and therefore artificially cheap; elsewhere, Coca-Cola and other soft drinks are made with cane- or beet-based sugar. Although added sugars are unhealthy in all forms, corn-based sweeteners are plentiful and cheap as a direct result of our agricultural policy.

The influence of money on politics, including the politics of public health, is perhaps the largest impact of agricultural industrialization and consolidation. This is clearly evidenced with the sugar industry (including corn-based sugars). One source of the sugar lobby's power is that sugar is prevalent in such a diversity of processed foods and is thus closely connected with other food and agricultural industries and trade groups. The World Health Organization (WHO) conducted a meta-analysis of research on the connection between sugar consumption and public health to develop a standard recommendation for sugar consumption, similar to daily recommendations for calories, fat, sodium, and other public health concerns. In response, multiple Big Food trade associations[7] threatened the WHO with political retribution.[8] At the urging of two senators, the Health and Human Services secretary, Tommy G. Thompson, submitted comments in 2003 attempting to suppress the draft report, saying in part, "Evidence that soft drinks are associated with obesity is not compelling."[9] You read that right: when a global nongovernmental organization with a public health mission made a dietary recommendation regarding sugar consumption, they were threatened by U.S. trade groups because the implications of this WHO report so compromised their economic interests.

BIG FEED GRAINS = BIG ANIMAL AG

Although it was never the original design, feed grains (led by corn) have become the largest category of commodity receiving subsidies. The availability of this artificially cheap feed was a contributing factor to the development of highly concentrated animal feeding operations. You may have seen the label Certified Grass-Fed on ground beef at the supermarket and thought, "Wait, I thought all cattle ate grass!" In fact, conventionally raised animals eat grain for much of their lives. This misunderstanding is largely an issue of visibility. If you drive by a cow pasture, what you're likely viewing is a herd of cows used for breeding. After calves are old enough to stop nursing from their mothers and eat a diet only of grain, they are sold to CAFOs to grow as large and quickly as possible before slaughter and butchering. These CAFOs are invisible to most U.S. eaters because they are located geographically far from urban and suburban residential areas, because the sheer amount of animal waste (65 percent of all animal manure in the United States is produced by CAFOs[10]) is so odorous and takes the form of dust, impacting air quality and health for neighbors. Communities near CAFOs are likely rural as well as socially and economically disadvantaged, and the addition of a nearby CAFO only further decreases the quality of life for the people who live there, forcing residents inside away from the stench and contributing to respiratory diseases.[11] Although it's difficult to pin down the growth of CAFOs, 50 percent of U.S. food animals were estimated to be in CAFOs in 2008,[12] including cattle, chickens, pigs, and turkeys. The sheer scale of these operations presents unique environmental obstacles. Large volumes of fecal matter are treated in lagoons. Inevitably, pathogens and chemicals like nitrates and ammonia seep into soil and waterways. Worse, these lagoons often burst, disturbing ecosystems and nearby communities.[13]

Animal welfare is also a concern. As the name implies, animals are confined because the purpose of CAFOs is feeding and fattening. "Confined" often translates to "so cramped that they can't turn around," and thus the animals are unable to behave naturally. Scientific measurements of animal welfare include health (disease, pain, and injury), behavior (for example, the space and ability to do grooming behaviors), and physiology (for example, stress responses), and the results of measurements raise questions about the ethics and safety of CAFOs. As a result of the inherent stress and unsanitary environments of CAFOs, animals are routinely given antibiotics, a major contributor to antibiotic resistance and a source of water pollution. In all of these areas, CAFOs present many issues with animal welfare. Will Harris, a South Georgia rancher, described his distaste for the conventional process of raising healthy calves and selling them to the CAFO: "It's like raising your daughter to be a princess and then sending her to the whorehouse."[14] His family has managed a cattle herd on the same piece of land for five generations, and he effectively transitioned from conventional practices to a grass-fed, humane operation, from conception to slaughter. He went against the current and took some risks, but he is now able to practice ranching in a way that makes him proud. It turns out that cattle, too, are what they eat: the nutritional content of meat from cattle fattened on grain is inferior to grass-fed beef, which is higher in Omega 3's and lower in fat and calories. Thus, grass-fed meat lines up better with nutritional recommendations that lead to heart health. Increasingly, choosy consumers (often affluent urban and suburban residents) are paying a premium to access this meat.[15] It's become common to say that consumers "vote with their forks." Although consumers do have purchasing power, class inequality ensures that some people are disproportionately powerful, leaving economically disadvantaged people with an unequal "vote."

Consumers are increasingly wary of foods from genetically modified organisms (GMOs). To develop GMOs, agricultural scientists alter plants' and animals' genes directly. This represents a major technological leap from selective breeding, the centuries-old practice of saving seed from individual plants with desired characteristics for next season's crop, crossing plants to develop hybrids, or even using genetic sciences (a la Gregor Mendel) to achieve higher yields and bigger, tastier, more uniform products. Those practices model nature, as plants are cross-pollinated. However, genetic engineering involves going beyond designing crops to have high yields and be more uniform, as in the example of Bt crops (including potatoes, corn, and soybeans, with more crops added as they are developed).[16] Genes are inserted from the bacterium *Bacillus thuringiensis* into the genetic structure of these crop plants, imbuing the crop with pest resistance. This particular gene does not naturally exist in corn and would not have been generated through millennia-old selective breeding techniques. Other examples of genetic engineering include Roundup Ready crops that have been modified to withstand applications of Monsanto's herbicide, Roundup. Critics refer to GMO foods as "Frankenfoods," referencing Mary Shelley's cautionary tale of the consequences of meddling with nature and life.

Perhaps most disconcerting about the practice of developing GMO crops is the unknown impact of their use on both the environment and human health. Although there is scientific consensus that GMO crops do not pose immediate human health risks, health impacts throughout time and over generations are difficult to predict. To be sure, all forms of agriculture involve humans engaged creatively with nature, and unintended consequences are almost certain. However, these consequences may be more severe when our interactions with nature become more sophisticated. One already-apparent environmental impact is that weeds are becoming resistant to a particular herbicide (glyphosate) that is frequently used with GMO crops. This necessitates the development of increasingly strong herbicides (in this case, an herbicide called 2-4D), and a new set of genetically engineered seeds resistant to 2-4D. Thus, farmers must use harsher and harsher agricultural chemicals, and new GMO crops must be constantly developed, continuing a vicious cycle with no end in sight.

Also troubling is the proprietary nature of genetically engineered (GE) crops, resulting from the specialization and corporatization of food commodities.[17] Agribusiness corporations hold patents on particular seeds, along with their accompanying agricultural chemicals (such as the aforementioned herbicides), that the farmers must buy each year.[18] Advocates of GMOs argue that the profit motivation is the impetus for corporations to innovate and that restricting profits will have a negative impact on technological advancement. However, this corporate control puts farmers on a technology treadmill, where to stay competitive they must adopt the innovative, production-increasing technology. But as production increases for all farmers, prices (and financial returns to the farmer) fall, and the farmer is stuck in a cycle of relying increasingly on off-farm inputs (nutrient fertilizer, seed, synthetic pesticides, etc.) to maintain a slim margin of profitability.[19] This treadmill largely explains the fact that, although agricultural technology has improved and farm size has grown, farmers' profits have not risen proportionately, as corporations capture the lion's share of agricultural profits. The regulation of GMO crops and foods is an important policy issue and one that (unsurprisingly) is closely tied to corporate agriculture.

Although regulatory agencies in the United States have deemed genetically engineered crops and foods "functionally equivalent" to their non-GMO counterparts, citizen groups have focused their efforts on mandatory labeling of GMO foods so that consumers wishing to avoid them will have ready access to that information. That battle has largely been waged at the state level. In 2014, Vermont was the first state in the United States to mandate GMO labels, and the Grocery Manufacturers Association promptly filed suit to reverse this legislation before it had a chance to go into effect.[20] Also in 2014, an Oregon statewide measure for mandatory GMO labeling was narrowly defeated by just 837 votes, or 0.056 percent.[21] The focus of these citizen actions is on accessing information about how food was produced and giving consumers the information they need to differentiate between products made from agricultural practices they support and those they oppose.

FOOD LABELS: HOW CONSUMERS GET INFORMATION

When you pick up a box of cereal, what do you see? Much of what there is to read at the grocery store is a result of food policy. In fact, it's a pretty safe bet that if it is boring and doesn't read like an advertisement, it's a policy-related food label. But like most areas where money and market share are involved, the food industry has a loud voice in the political debate about what consumers know about their food.

The most important health-related information is usually on one of the narrow sides of the box. Nutrition Facts labels on processed foods are federally mandated and overseen by the Food and Drug Administration (FDA). Nutrition labels include information related to public health concerns. In other words, the goal of nutrition labels is to reduce the risk of chronic diseases such as cardiovascular disease, obesity, high blood pressure, and stroke and to encourage people to consume enough vital nutrients.[22] Although these familiar Black and White boxes on food packaging may seem pretty straightforward, in the U.S. context of agribusiness and politics, the issue of which nutrients are included on the label is contentious.

Mandatory nutrition facts labels are the result of the Nutrition Labeling and Education Act of 1990 and went into effect in 1994.[23] The FDA proposed the first wave of revisions late in 2014, and they will be implemented around 2016.[24] The clearer and easier to understand food labels are, the more useful they are to regular people weighing day-to-day food decisions. Several upcoming changes clarify nutritional recommendations. One change simply makes food labels bigger and thus easier to read. Another does away with some of the confusing "serving size" issues of the present. How bizarre is it for a 20-ounce bottle of soda to give nutrition recommendations as "per serving," but the bottle is actually 2.5 servings? New labels will eliminate the need to multiply, presenting the package as a serving size (per bottle, per can, and so on), considering how people eat. Another proposed major change in labeling is the per-gram distinction between sugars that naturally occur in foods or ingredients (for example, sugars present in whole milk and fruit juice or in cereal containing dried fruit) and sugars added to foods. Although consumers have always been able to glance at an ingredients list to see the added sugar content relative to other ingredients (because ingredients are listed from greatest to least), we've never been able to differentiate between the total amount of sugar and the amount of processed or refined sugar that's been added to foods. This was a hotly debated issue because the sugar industry (discussed earlier) fought to keep added sugars essentially hidden on nutrition facts labels by adding their quantities to total grams of sugar.

Although I applaud this change as a step in the right direction, what I'd really like to see is a daily value recommendation for added sugars based in sound nutrition science. Percentage daily values can really stand out (they're even bolded). But quantifying a dietary recommendation for added sugars is a politically charged question. For some other important dietary considerations like calories, fat, carbohydrates, and sodium, our bodies require some, but too much is a problem. Added sugar isn't like fat or sodium in that way. Dietitians and food scientists know that human bodies do not require any added sugars. However, powerful sugar interests (in corn and sugar agriculture as well as the food and beverage industry) are working to keep that information off the nutrition facts labels. Additionally, they work hard to push countermessages through advertising.

ADVERTISING: START 'EM YOUNG

Corporate interests drive agricultural policy from production and processing to marketing and advertising. Industry self-regulation is the standard, with little government intervention. Jim Gaffigan pokes fun at our conflicted, somewhat embarrassing relationship with fast food and advertising in his standup routine. "We know those McDonald's commercials aren't realistic. I'd like to see a McDonald's commercial show someone five minutes after they ate McDonald's. 'Ughhhhhh. Now I need a cigarette. I deserve a cigarette break today.'" I don't think it's an accident that Gaffigan presents the image of cigarette smoking alongside McDonald's consumption: these are behaviors that are commonly recognized as unhealthy but that people choose for a variety of short-term reasons. Advertising commonly sells an experience or emotion, not just a product. Just like the Marlboro Man was designed to sell us the image of the rugged, independent cowboy, food and beverage companies sell us on an image, too. Why do you think McDonald's labels children's meals as "Happy Meals"? We, as adults, can usually critique the message that drinking the right brand of soda will magically make us cool, happy, and energetic. We even know from experience how eating junk food makes us feel. Unfortunately, kids don't have that ability.

Research shows that children under the age of 8 do not understand that advertising is trying to sell them something, much less understand the increasingly sophisticated tactics that the advertisers are using. Kids under age 4 can't even determine the difference between the cartoon program they're watching and the cartoon advertisement.[25] Advertisements targeted at kids are almost exclusively for junk food.[26] This is an issue that could be regulated by smart government policies. As a society, we protect children from images and information they're not yet emotionally and intellectually prepared to handle—for example, visual content in a movie may warrant an R (for "restricted") rating. The daily deluge of food advertising to kids is drowning out the nutritional messages they desperately need to hear.

Jim Gaffigan paints a humorous picture of some of the reaction that McDonald's withstands: "I just love the societal outrage at McDonald's. 'McDonald's, there's no nutritional value! There's no vitamins!' McDonald's is just like, 'Excuse me, we sell burgers and fries. We never said we were a farmer's market. Heck, our spokesman is a pedophile clown from the 70s. What do you want from us, America?'" The absurdity is not that people are outraged; it's that this emotional energy is directed at the wrong target. McDonald's is operating within the current policy context. This outrage needs to be channeled into rewriting the rules to prohibit corporations from using clowns and cartoons to market harmful food to children, just as people took on and beat Big Tobacco, killing cartoon Joe Camel. An incredibly easy place to start is to do away with food advertising to children in schools and the sale of junk foods in school vending machines and snack lines. In the world I want to live in, public schools are sacred spaces, where children learn and are safe from violence, coercion, and the targeted advertising and sale of foods that lead to diet-related diseases and mortality. Industry self-regulation is not working, and the time has come for stricter regulations on food advertising, especially advertising targeting children. McDonald's and other retailers and brands are carefully crafting lifelong, brand-loyal customers by selling the positive experience of Happy Meals (and their equivalents), complete with cartoons and

toys in the box, knowing that these flavors, smells, and emotions are psychologically linked and incredibly powerful. It's important that children have a chance to develop choices that aren't influenced by predatory advertising for foods that will likely contribute to health conditions, and possibly their deaths, as adults.

CONCLUSION

Jim Gaffigan's concluding summation of McDonald's is "Momentary pleasure, followed by incredible guilt, eventually leading to cancer." A fantastic corollary to food policy that's not of the people, by the people, and for the people is tobacco policy. Until the major legal and political battles of the 1990s, tobacco companies employed many of the techniques that corporate food producers use: advertising to children (enticing lifelong customers), squelching research about the health impacts of smoking, and lobbying elected officials to maintain their economic power. This tobacco comparison also matches Gaffigan's progression: pleasure, guilt, and cancer. The tobacco victory required mobilization of a social movement (backed by strong medical research) to debunk Big Tobacco's message that tobacco use was cool, sophisticated, and safe. The fight (and victory) of the American people over Big Tobacco is a template for the changes, at a policy level, that are possible with food. The exciting difference between tobacco and food is that we have agricultural options that, unlike the production of refined grains, sugars, and animal products, are actually health promoting. Fruit and vegetable producers in the United States are, as a whole, profitable without subsidies. How easy would it be to redirect some federal money into an already-profitable sector to make nutritious food financially competitive with calorie-dense but nutrient-poor foods? For cash-strapped families, it can be tough to afford the cost of an organic bag of spinach, especially when a more filling option is to order from a fast-food chain's value meal. What if we subsidized organic foods, making foods that are pesticide free (good for our bodies and our environment) cost the same (or less) compared to conventional foods?

Consider the potential positive impacts of subsidizing ecologically restorative agricultural production[27] for the long-term productivity of our soils and food system. Consider the impact of reinvesting current subsidies of the production of food that makes us sick into the production of food that fulfills our health needs and protects water, soil, and our atmosphere. How restorative, healing, and positive would that be? Some applications that are already being developed and tested include payment for ecosystem services arrangements, where instead of slapping farmers who pollute water or destroy habitat of threatened and endangered species with fines, farmers are economically rewarded for taking actions to manage their lands in ways that improve water and soil health, sequester carbon in trees and other plants, and provide on-farm habitat for vulnerable wildlife species. Another idea is providing economic incentives for the production of nutrient-dense foods like sweet potatoes, spinach, nuts, and seeds. What if federal subsidies went to farmers who grew the healthiest foods, thus lowering the retail cost and increasing their availability to consumers? What if legislation required that full-service grocery stores be sited like schools—based on where people live, not profit driven and based on the financial demographics of the zip code, as is currently done, leaving out low-income and impoverished neighborhoods? If that were the case, low-income communities in rural and urban America would have access to foods beyond the limited fare of Dollar General and other convenience-food retailers. The exciting thing is that the problem is so far-reaching—literally touching every person—that the solutions are equally diverse.

The growing food movement is challenging attitudes about food and the food system that do not serve people well. This movement is made up of many groups, including farmers, parents, people who have dealt with food-related diseases, chefs, nutritionists and health care professionals, and food and agricultural research scientists (both social scientists and natural scientists). Change is in the wind, but the mobilization of social energies, a true social movement, is needed to overcome the power of Big Ag and Big Food to establish policies that honor the true value of good food. Some of these attitudes are deep seated, and challenging them involves examining commonly held beliefs that are often taken for granted. The first of these attitudes is the notion that food is just like any other commodity or product; it's made, valued, and traded based on what consumers are willing to pay for it. In contrast, the new food movement regards food as qualitatively different from other consumer goods. Food is not like toasters or t-shirts. We require it to live. It is also part of our humanity because of the cultural, spiritual, and emotional meaning that people across time and culture have imbued in food and eating. A second belief is that access to safe, nutritious, and adequate food (termed "food security") is a human right. Treating food as any other consumer good leads to ignoring social problems related to the food system (e.g., diet-related diseases, childhood obesity, lack of affordable healthy food for people in poverty) in favor of focusing on inefficiencies and/or overreach of government.

In our capitalist economy, we treat the basics of food, health care and medicine, and education the same as other consumer goods and services. But economic systems are not outside the realm of human influence; in fact, they only persist because societies, and the people who make up societies, subscribe to them. What if we examined our economic system using measurements of health and well-being—human and ecological? What if we treated food, health care, and medicine—these foundations of human life and society—as the strong foundation on which to build an economy, not solely as economic industries themselves? Do we really want diet-related health care to be a positive contributor to our gross domestic product and a major economic driver? Improved food access does not just rest on everyone in the United States having access to safe, affordable, healthy food; it also includes a reorientation of our beliefs about food and a transformation of our economic and political systems to treat food differently. Profits cannot, and should not, be the ultimate goal of a food system. The development, implementation, and normalization of human- and earth-centric goals of our food system, as well as effective policy to achieve these goals, are the key to a healthy food system for all.

NOTES

1. Parke Wilde, *Food Policy in the United States: An Introduction*. Abingdon, UK: Routledge, 2013.
2. Delaney, Arthur. 2018. "Dollar Stores Sell More Food than Whole Food." *Huffington Post*, December 7. Retrieved on March 20, 2019, from https://www.huffingtonpost.com/entry/dollar-store-sells-more-food-whole-foods-monopoly_us_5c0ac57ae4b0ab8cf6931e80.
3. U.S. Department of Agriculture (USDA) Department of Health and Human Services, Office of Disease Prevention and Health Promotion, USDA Food, Nutrition, and Consumer Services, USDA Center for Nutrition Policy and Promotion.
4. http://health.gov/dietaryguidelines.
5. The government pays agricultural subsidies to farmers and agribusinesses to augment income and to moderate cost and supply of commodities. Commodities are primary, interchangeable agricultural products that can be bought and sold. Most often, commodities are used to produce other goods. Wheat is a commodity, whereas a box of Wheaties is not.
6. Before industrial agriculture, low-cost meals included staple grains like corn, wheat, or rice, beans, and greens, with meat used for flavoring (for example, beans and greens, with ham used to flavor both). The Western dietary pattern is meat- and sweet-centric, and the Western standard of living is the aspiration of the citizens of many developing countries.
7. Corn Refiners Association, International Dairy Foods Association, National Corn Growers Association, Snack Food Association, the Sugar Association, Wheat Foods Council, and U.S. Council for International Business.
8. Juliet Eilperin, U.S. Sugar Industry Targets New Study; Lawmakers' Aid Sought in Halting WHO Report JO. *The Washington Post*, April 23, 2003.
9. *The Washington Post*, April 23, 2003.
10. Doug Gurian-Sherman, *CAFOs Uncovered* (Union of Concerned Scientists, April 2008), p. 94. Retrieved April 22, 2015, from http://vegetarian.procon.org/sourcefiles/cafos_uncovered.pdf.
11. Wendee Nicole, "CAFOs and Environmental Justice: The Case of North Carolina," *Environmental Health Perspectives*, 121 (2013), 182–189. http://dx.doi.org/10.1289/ehp.121-a182/.
12. Gurian-Sherman, 2008.
13. Nicole, 2013.
14. Kim Severson, "At White Oak Pastures, Grass-Fed Beef Is Only the Beginning," *The New York Times*, March 10, 2015. http://www.nytimes.com/2015/03/11/dining/at-white-oak-pastures-grass-fed-beef-is-only-the-beginning.html.
15. Wendy J. Umberger, Peter C. Boxall, and R. Curt Lacy, "Role of Credence and Health Information in Determining US Consumers' Willingness-to-Pay for Grass-Finished Beef," *Australian Journal of Agricultural and Resource Economics*, 53 (2009), 603–623. http://dx.doi.org/10.1111/j.1467-8489.2009.00466.x.
16. Ric Bessin, *Bt-Corn: What It Is and How It Works*. University of Kentucky: UK Cooperative Extension Service. Retrieved April 26, 2015, from http://www2.ca.uky.edu/entomology/entfacts/entfactpdf/ef130.pdf.
17. GMO crops are also referred to as genetically engineered (GE) crops, and the foods produced from these crops, including meat and animal products fed GMO crops, are referred to as GMO or GE foods.
18. Monsanto's Roundup Ready soy is glyphosate resistant and thus coupled with Monsanto's Roundup (glyphosate) herbicide.

19. Richard A. Levins, and Willard W. Cochrane, "The Treadmill Revisited," *Land Economics*, 72 (1996), 550–553. http://dx.doi.org/10.2307/3146915.

20. "Judge Considers Halting Vermont GMO Labeling Law," *USA Today*. April 27, 2015. http://www.usatoday.com/story/news/nation/2015/01/07/judge-considers-halting-vermont-gmo-law/21422959/. At the time this book went to press, the judge had just required that the labeling law go into effect while the lawsuit continues.

21. Michelle Brence, The Oregonian/Oregon-Live, "Oregon Certifies Defeat of Measure 92; GMO Labeling Loses by 837 Votes," *OregonLive.com*, 2014. Retrieved April 27, 2015, from http://www.oregonlive.com/politics/index.ssf/2014/12/oregon_certifies_defeat_of_mea.html.

22. Center for Food Safety and Applied Nutrition, "Labeling & Nutrition—Factsheet on the New Proposed Nutrition Facts Label." Retrieved April 5, 2015, from http://www.fda.gov/Food/GuidanceRegulation/GuidanceDocumentsRegulatoryInformation/LabelingNutrition/ucm387533.htm.

23. Center for Food Safety and Applied Nutrition, 2015.

24. Center for Food Safety and Applied Nutrition, 2015.

25. Food and Water Watch, *It Pays to Advertise: Junk Food Marketing to Children*. Washington, DC: Food & Water Watch, 2012, p. 23.

26. Food and Water Watch, 2012.

27. Restorative agriculture is a fascinating area because it is necessarily ecological and site specific. It involves really understanding a mix of plant and animal species as well as having intimate knowledge of land. Some categories of restorative agricultural practices include agroforestry (combining trees and agricultural crops or livestock), perennial crops (as opposed to annual crops, which require soil disturbance and thus erosion each year), practice of no-till methods for annual crops, and practice of integrated pest management (where pesticides are avoided by introducing natural plant-based deterrents or predators of pests). The on-farm application of these practices is always nuanced, contrasted with large-scale monocropped agribusinesses.

REFERENCES

Bessin, Ric. *Bt-Corn: What It Is and How It Works*. University of Kentucky: UK Cooperative Extension Service. Retrieved April 26, 2015, from http://www2.ca.uky.edu/entomology/entfacts/entfact-pdf/ef130.pdf.

Brence, Michelle. 2014. "Oregon Certifies Defeat of Measure 92; GMO Labeling Loses by 837 Votes. *OregonLive.com*. Retrieved April 27, 2015, from http://www.oregonlive.com/politics/index.ssf/2014/12/oregon_certifies_defeat_of_mea.html.

Center for Food Safety and Applied Nutrition. "Labeling & Nutrition—Factsheet on the New Proposed Nutrition Facts Label." Retrieved April 5, 2015, from http://www.fda.gov/Food/GuidanceRegulation/GuidanceDocumentsRegulatoryInformation/LabelingNutrition/ucm387533.htm.

Food and Water Watch. 2012. *It Pays to Advertise: Junk Food Marketing to Children*. Washington, DC: Food & Water Watch, p. 23.

Gurian-Sherman, Doug. 2008. *CAFOs Uncovered*. Union of Concerned Scientists, p. 94. Retrieved April 22, 2015, from https://www.ucsusa.org/sites/default/files/2019-10/cafos-uncovered-full-report.pdf.

"Judge Considers Halting Vermont GMO Labeling Law," *USA Today*. Retrieved April 27, 2015. From http://www.usatoday.com/story/news/nation/2015/01/07/judge-considers-halting-vermont-gmo-law/21422959.

Levins, Richard A., and Willard W. Cochrane. 1996. "The Treadmill Revisited." *Land Economics* 72:550–553. http://dx.doi.org/10.2307/3146915.

Nicole, Wendee. 2013. "CAFOs and Environmental Justice: The Case of North Carolina." *Environmental Health Perspectives* 121:a182–a189. http://dx.doi.org/10.1289/ehp.121-a182.

Severson, Kim. 2015. "At White Oak Pastures, Grass-Fed Beef Is Only the Beginning." *The New York Times*, March 10, 2015. Retrieved April 5, 2015, from http://www.nytimes.com/2015/03/11/dining/at-white-oak-pastures-grass-fed-beef-is-only-the-beginning.html.

Umberger, Wendy J., Peter C. Boxall, and R. Curt Lacy. 2009. "Role of Credence and Health Information in Determining US Consumers' Willingness-to-Pay for Grass-Finished Beef." *Australian Journal of Agricultural and Resource Economics* 53:603–623. http://dx.doi.org/10.1111/j.1467-8489.2009.00466.x.

Wilde, Parke. 2013. *Food Policy in the United States: An Introduction*. Abingdon, UK: Routledge.

DESERTS AND SWAMPS: Inhospitable Foodscapes and Health

CLAUDIA TILLMAN

It is easy to think that what we consume for nourishment every day is highly individualized and logical. The 70 billion dollar diet industry banks on marketing this premise, and shows like *The Biggest Loser* highlight the entertainment value produced by the elusiveness of this popular narrative. The intrigue of fat to thin "success" stories exists, in part, because more than one in three people living in the United States are medically obese—not only do we want to consume these stories as entertainment, but their ubiquity in the popular media makes them almost impossible to avoid. Associated with various medical complications. including type 2 diabetes, stroke, high cholesterol, sleep apnea, asthma, liver disease, osteoarthritis, gallbladder disease, cancer, body pain, and depression, obesity is widely considered a public health epidemic (CDC 2018; U.S. Department of Health and Human Services 2018).[1] How could so many people "fail" to maintain a healthy weight in this country despite the risk factors of obesity? A closer look finds that different groups of people are more or less likely to be obese, and as sociologists, we have evidence that many social factors such as environment, income/wealth, and even discrimination can play a role. For instance, African Americans and Latinx Americans, particularly women, experience higher rates of obesity than White men. Similarly, living in poverty increases the rate of obesity across all demographics (U.S. Department of Health and Human Services 1998).

Foodscapes

Since the early 2000s, scholars, activists, and policymakers have discussed the impact of "food deserts" on health. Food deserts are low-income dense geographic locations where residents lack reasonable access to fresh, healthy foods such as the produce provided by large-scale grocers. Most research definitions indicate that the majority of the residents of food deserts live one mile away from a commercial food source in an urban area. In some neighborhoods, this means that the only accessible fresh produce can be found in the form of apples and bananas placed by the cash register at convenience stores. The food desert phenomenon received high-profile attention when First Lady Michelle Obama raised awareness of the problem through her 2010 initiative to eliminate food deserts in the United States by 2017. A substantial effort to bring healthier options to areas that lacked them ensued. This strategy seemed like a solid solution at the time and certainly offers opportunity to improve overall health in affected communities, but recent research suggests a more complicated food terrain exists than was previously understood. A 2012 study found that not only are regional rates of obesity and proximity to grocery retailers uncorrelated, but many urban communities instead have an *abundance* rather than a *lack* of food availability (Lee 2012). More precisely, which food is readily available to residents of a particular neighborhood has emerged as an important piece of the food inequity puzzle.

"Food swamps" are geographic areas saturated with establishments like fast-food restaurants and convenience stores that offer highly caloric, yet nutritionally deficient, food options relative to healthier, fresh, whole-food, and less processed

---

1 Despite the American Medical Association labeling obesity as a disease, obesity is not necessarily an indicator of poor health. See, for example, Tomiyama, A. J., J. M. Hunger, J. Nguyen-Cuu, and C. Wells. 2016. "Misclassification of Cardiometabolic Health When Using Body Mass Index Categories in NHANES 2005–2012." *International Journal of Obesity* 40(5):883–86.

(Continued)

Original to *Focus on Social Problems: A Contemporary Reader*.

options. You may have noticed the plethora of fast-food joints operating in poorer areas of cities and outlying neighborhoods. Similarly, in some rural areas, fast food represents the only option available for prepared foods. A large-scale study using nationwide data on food merchants along with health and sociodemographic data found that food swamps better predict obesity rates than food deserts (Cooksey-Stowers, Schwartz, & Brownell 2017). The 2017 study measured rates of adult obesity at the county level based on various food availability measures, including the Retail Food Environmental Index (a ratio of healthy to unhealthy food establishments in a particular area). In order to parse out the specific effects of food swamps on obesity rates, the study took into account a range of other variables in the environment like the presence of food deserts; fitness and recreation amenities; sociodemographic characteristics, including median household income, poverty rate, metropolitan versus nonmetropolitan status, and where individuals "choose" to live.[2] The results illuminated multiple links between access to healthy *and* unhealthy food and detrimental health outcomes at the county level. Researchers found that food swamps had a clear association with obesity rates across all measures and that people are healthier when they have greater access to basic grocery stores and reduced access to fast-food and convenience stores. The strong findings also contributed to evidence that food deserts and food swamps are two influential but distinct concepts.

The distinction between food swamps and food deserts is just one example of the complex factors involved in why people eat the food that they do. Much of the food justice work up to this point is aimed at changing behaviors based on the introduction of healthy food options for purchase as a solution for improving health outcomes. Recent research investigating improving foodscapes helps illuminate why such campaigns largely miss the mark by providing evidence that availability alone is not responsible for individual consumption. For example, a recent study on convenience store interventions in two Latinx food swamps found that, while limited physical modifications (like adding more fresh fruits and produce throughout the store) created greater opportunity for healthy food purchases and improved general perceptions of convenience store quality, actual sales of fruits and vegetables remained unchanged (Ortega et al. 2016). To explain this finding, researchers suggest that these relatively minor changes at a few establishments cannot combat the extensive unhealthy offerings embedded in an established urban food swamp. Unsuccessful attempts to battle obesity in

the larger population by simply bringing healthy foods to urban and rural areas underscore the need for multilevel approaches and community-based change.

Cooksey-Stowers and colleagues dug deeper into why food swamps are challenging environments for maintaining health. They found that individuals who lacked their own transportation or access to public transportation are at greater risk of experiencing the negative impacts of residing in a food swamp (2017). If going to the grocery store requires substantial planning, time, and effort, it makes sense that an abundance of fast-food options (inexpensive, convenient, and generally considered quite tasty) and the persistent advertising of other unhealthy products (like cheap beer and cigarettes) along the way might derail the best intentions of adopting and sticking to healthy habits. Gaining community support at multiple levels through the development of interdependent local partnerships among government, residents, and businesses to alter foodscapes is a potential strategy in countering this reality.

The importance of community-based responses

A promising multidimensional health improvement initiative in San Francisco casts a wide net across many community aspects and is locally originated and powered. The development of the initiative included community-based participatory research and the formation of a coalition of residents, community leaders, health department workers, and academics that led to the implementation of a healthy retail ordinance (set of laws and regulations for business) (Minkler et al. 2018). The project included educating store owners and the community about both the overall initiative and the importance of fresh food and also provided ongoing support. The program not only promoted adding healthy options to convenience store fare but also advocated decreasing the window advertisements of unhealthy offerings. Preliminary results suggest this comprehensive and collective approach rooted in community commitment increased sales of healthy products and even reduced the sale of tobacco in some participating stores (Minkler et al. 2018).

From food deserts to food swamps, the complex relationship between the foodscape and health outcomes like obesity are inextricably (and unequally) woven into our built world. Resources like money, transportation, time, and energy all interact with these conditions and are influential in the daily and ongoing work of feeding ourselves and our families. While the mechanisms responsible for connecting the environment to obesity await full exploration, it is clear that marginalized populations in the United States are more likely to live in food deserts and/or food swamps and are also more likely to incur the burden of obesity and the negative health conditions that come with it (U.S. Department of Health and Human Services 1998).

---

2   Most people are constrained by economic factors in acquiring housing. As such, calculated decisions are based on these factors, rather than free choices related purely to preference.

Macrosocial factors beyond foodscapes

Foodscapes are definitely an important factor in the health out-come equation, yet research indicates that enduring macro-level social factors may be even more influential. Eating is a necessity, and what we eat is a crucial component of long-term health and well-being. At the same time, eating can provide temporary stress relief and pleasure within a contemporary economy and culture that exhausts bodies and offers little time to enjoy life, much less prepare healthy meals (Berlant 2010). When living in a perpetual state of survival, depleted and stressed from work demands, finding ways to cover the bills with small paychecks, or even responding to the stressors of discrimination, food becomes a reliable—if fleeting—way to feel better. Thus, along with environmental factors related to obesity like food deserts and food swamps, the fundamental causes of health inequalities like poverty and discrimination must also be addressed (Phelan, Link, & Tehranifar 2010). Meanwhile, traditional nutrition education, along with an awareness of the impact of accessibility, is foundational, and what seems most useful in promoting healthy eating is optimizing community networks to implement and maintain sustainable change. This is the more holistic goal of future work directed at lessening the health effects of compromised foodscapes on the people who call them home.

REFERENCES

Berlant, Lauren. 2010. "Risky Bigness: On Obesity, Eating, and the Ambiguity of 'Health'." Pp. 26–39 in *Against Health: How Health Became the New Morality*, edited by Johnathan M. Metzl and Anna Kirkland. New York: New York University Press.

CDC Centers for Disease Control and Prevention. Healthy Weight. "The Health Effects of Overweight and Obesity." Retrieved December 18, 2018, from https://www.cdc.gov/healthyweight/effects/index.html.

Cooksey-Stowers, K., Schwartz, M.B., and K.D. Brownell. 2017. "Food Swamps Predict Obesity Rates Better Than Food Deserts in the United States." *International. Journal of Environmental Research and Public Health* 14: 1366.

Lee, Helen. 2012. "The Role of Local Food Availability in Explaining Obesity Risk among School-aged Children." *Social Science and Medicine* 74(8): 1193–203.

Minkler, M., Estrada, J., Thayer, R., Juachon, L, Wakimoto, P, and J. Falbe. 2018. "Bringing Healthy Retail to Urban "Food Swamps": a Case Study of CBPR-Informed Policy and Neighborhood Change in San Francisco." *Journal of Urban Health* 95(6): 850–858.

Ortega, A.N., Albert, S.L., Chan-Golston, A.M., Langellier, Brent A., Glik, Deborah C., Belin, Thomas R., Garcia, Rosa Elena, Brookmeyer, Ron, Sharif, Mienah Z., and Michael L. Prelip. 2016. "Substantial improvements not seen in health behaviors following corner store conversions in two Latino food swamps." *BMC Public Health* 16: 389.

Phelan, Jo C., Bruce Link, and Parisa Tehranifar. 2010. "Social Conditions as Fundamental Causes of Health Inequalities: Theory, Evidence, and Policy Implications." *Journal of Health and Social Behavior*, 51(S): S28–40.

Pudrovska, Tetyana, Eric N. Reither, Ellis S. Logan, and Kyler J. Sherman-Wilkins. 2014. "Gender and Reinforcing Associations between Socioeconomic Disadvantage and Body Mass over the Life Course." *Journal of Health and Social Behavior*, 55(3): 283–301.

U.S. Department of Health and Human Services. National Heart Lung and Blood Institute. "NIH Overweight and Obesity—Complications." Retrieved December 18, 2018, from https://www.nhlbi.nih.gov/health-topics/overweight-and-obesity.

U.S. Department of Health and Human Services. National Heart, Lung, and Blood Institute. Obesity Education Initiative. 1998. *Clinical Guidelines on the Identification, Evaluation, and Treatment of Overweight and Obesity in Adults: The Evidence Report. (NIH publication No.98-4083)*. Washington, DC: National Institutes of Health.

MICHAEL MOSS

68. THE EXTRAORDINARY SCIENCE
OF ADDICTIVE JUNK FOOD

Have you ever wondered why processed foods that are not good for us taste so good and remain so popular despite the growing evidence that they damage our health? Relying on interviews with industry insiders and featuring case studies for products like Dr Pepper and Lunchables, Moss discusses how processed foods are designed and marketed to be addictive to consumers, despite the health risks resulting from regular consumption.

On the evening of April 8, 1999, a long line of Town Cars and taxis pulled up to the Minneapolis headquarters of Pillsbury and discharged 11 men who controlled America's largest food companies. Nestlé was in attendance, as were Kraft and Nabisco, General Mills and Procter & Gamble, Coca-Cola and Mars. Rivals any other day, the C.E.O.'s and company presidents had come together for a rare, private meeting. On the agenda was one item: the emerging obesity epidemic and how to deal with it. While the atmosphere was cordial, the men assembled were hardly friends. Their stature was defined by their skill in fighting one another for what they called "stomach share"—the amount of digestive space that any one company's brand can grab from the competition.

James Behnke, a 55-year-old executive at Pillsbury, greeted the men as they arrived. He was anxious but also hopeful about the plan that he and a few other food-company executives had devised to engage the C.E.O.'s on America's growing weight problem. "We were very concerned, and rightfully so, that obesity was becoming a major issue," Behnke recalled. "People were starting to talk about sugar taxes, and there was a lot of pressure on food companies." Getting the company chiefs in the same room to talk about anything, much less a sensitive issue like this, was a tricky business, so Behnke and his fellow organizers had scripted the meeting carefully, honing the message to its barest essentials. "C.E.O.'s in the food industry are typically not technical guys, and they're uncomfortable going to meetings where technical people talk in technical terms about technical things," Behnke said. "They don't want to be embarrassed. They don't want to make commitments. They want to maintain their aloofness and autonomy."

A chemist by training with a doctoral degree in food science, Behnke became Pillsbury's chief technical officer in 1979 and was instrumental in creating a long line of hit products, including microwaveable popcorn. He deeply admired Pillsbury but in recent years had grown troubled by pictures of obese children suffering from diabetes and the earliest signs of hypertension and heart disease. In the months leading up to the C.E.O. meeting, he was engaged in conversation with a group of food-science experts who were painting an increasingly grim picture of the public's ability to cope with the industry's formulations—from the body's fragile controls on overeating to the hidden power of some processed foods to make people feel hungrier still. It was time, he and a handful of others felt, to warn the C.E.O.'s that their companies may have gone too far in creating and marketing products that posed the greatest health concerns.

The discussion took place in Pillsbury's auditorium. The first speaker was a vice president of Kraft named Michael Mudd. "I very much appreciate this opportunity to talk to you about childhood obesity and the growing challenge it presents for us all," Mudd began. "Let me say right at the start, this is not an easy subject. There are no easy answers—for what the public health community must do to bring this problem under control or for what the industry should do as others seek to hold it accountable for what has happened. But this much is clear: For those of us who've looked hard at this issue, whether they're public health professionals or staff specialists in your own companies, we feel sure that the one thing we shouldn't do is nothing."

As he spoke, Mudd clicked through a deck of slides—114 in all—projected on a large screen behind him. The figures were staggering. More than half of American adults were now considered overweight, with nearly one-quarter of the adult population—40 million people—clinically defined as obese. Among children, the rates had more than doubled since 1980, and the number of kids considered obese had shot past 12 million. (This was still only 1999; the nation's obesity rates would climb much higher.) Food manufacturers were now being blamed for the problem from all sides—academia, the Centers for Disease Control and Prevention, the American Heart Association and the American Cancer Society. The secretary of agriculture, over whom the industry had long held sway, had recently called obesity a "national epidemic."

Mudd then did the unthinkable. He drew a connection to the last thing in the world the C.E.O.'s wanted linked to their products: cigarettes. First came a quote from a Yale University professor of psychology and public health, Kelly Brownell, who was an especially vocal proponent of the view that the processed-food industry should be seen as a public health menace: "As a culture, we've become upset by the tobacco companies advertising to children, but we sit idly by while the food companies do the very same thing. And we

could make a claim that the toll taken on the public health by a poor diet rivals that taken by tobacco." "If anyone in the food industry ever doubted there was a slippery slope out there," Mudd said, "I imagine they are beginning to experience a distinct sliding sensation right about now."

Mudd then presented the plan he and others had devised to address the obesity problem. Merely getting the executives to acknowledge some culpability was an important first step, he knew, so his plan would start off with a small but crucial move: the industry should use the expertise of scientists—its own and others—to gain a deeper understanding of what was driving Americans to overeat. Once this was achieved, the effort could unfold on several fronts. To be sure, there would be no getting around the role that packaged foods and drinks play in overconsumption. They would have to pull back on their use of salt, sugar and fat, perhaps by imposing industrywide limits. But it wasn't just a matter of these three ingredients; the schemes they used to advertise and market their products were critical, too. Mudd proposed creating a "code to guide the nutritional aspects of food marketing, especially to children."

"We are saying that the industry should make a sincere effort to be part of the solution," Mudd concluded. "And that by doing so, we can help to defuse the criticism that's building against us." What happened next was not written down. But according to three participants, when Mudd stopped talking, the one C.E.O. whose recent exploits in the grocery store had awed the rest of the industry stood up to speak. His name was Stephen Sanger, and he was also the person—as head of General Mills—who had the most to lose when it came to dealing with obesity. Under his leadership, General Mills had overtaken not just the cereal aisle but other sections of the grocery store. The company's Yoplait brand had transformed traditional unsweetened breakfast yogurt into a veritable dessert. It now had twice as much sugar per serving as General Mills' marshmallow cereal Lucky Charms. And yet, because of yogurt's well-tended image as a wholesome snack, sales of Yoplait were soaring, with annual revenue topping $500 million. Emboldened by the success, the company's development wing pushed even harder, inventing a Yoplait variation that came in a squeezable tube—perfect for kids. They called it Go-Gurt and rolled it out nationally in the weeks before the C.E.O. meeting. (By year's end, it would hit $100 million in sales.)

According to the sources I spoke with, Sanger began by reminding the group that consumers were "fickle." (Sanger declined to be interviewed.) Sometimes they worried about sugar, other times fat. General Mills, he said, acted responsibly to both the public and shareholders by offering products to satisfy dieters and other concerned shoppers, from low sugar to added whole grains. But most often, he said, people bought what they liked, and they liked what tasted good. "Don't talk to me about nutrition," he reportedly said, taking on the voice of the typical consumer. "Talk to me about taste, and if this stuff tastes better, don't run around trying to sell stuff that doesn't taste good." To react to the critics, Sanger said, would jeopardize the sanctity of the recipes that had made his products so successful. General Mills would not pull back. He would push his people onward, and he urged his peers to do the same. Sanger's response effectively ended the meeting.

"What can I say?" James Behnke told me years later. "It didn't work. These guys weren't as receptive as we thought they would be." Behnke chose his words deliberately. He wanted to be fair. "Sanger was trying to say, 'Look, we're not going to screw around with the company jewels here and change the formulations because a bunch of guys in White coats are worried about obesity.' "

The meeting was remarkable, first, for the insider admissions of guilt. But I was also struck by how prescient the organizers of the sit-down had been. [In 2013], one in three adults is considered clinically obese, along with one in five kids, and 24 million Americans are afflicted by type 2 diabetes, often caused by poor diet, with another 79 million people having pre-diabetes. Even gout, a painful form of arthritis once known as "the rich man's disease" for its associations with gluttony, now afflicts eight million Americans.

The public and the food companies have known for decades now—or at the very least since this meeting—that sugary, salty, fatty foods are not good for us in the quantities that we consume them. So why are the diabetes and obesity and hypertension numbers still spiraling out of control? It's not just a matter of poor willpower on the part of the consumer and a give-the-people-what-they-want attitude on the part of the food manufacturers. What I found, over four years of research and reporting, was a conscious effort—taking place in labs and marketing meetings and grocery-store aisles—to get people hooked on foods that are convenient and inexpensive. I talked to more than 300 people in or formerly employed by the processed-food industry, from scientists to marketers to C.E.O.'s. Some were willing whistle-blowers, while others spoke reluctantly when presented with some of the thousands of pages of secret memos that I obtained from inside the food industry's operations. What follows is a series of small case studies of a handful of characters whose work then, and perspective now, sheds light on how the foods are created and sold to people who, while not powerless, are extremely vulnerable to the intensity of these companies' industrial formulations and selling campaigns.

"IN THIS FIELD, I'M A GAME CHANGER."

John Lennon couldn't find it in England, so he had cases of it shipped from New York to fuel the "Imagine" sessions. The Beach Boys, ZZ Top and Cher all stipulated in their contract riders that it be put in their dressing rooms when they toured. Hillary Clinton asked for it when she traveled as first lady, and ever after her hotel suites were dutifully stocked.

What they all wanted was Dr Pepper, which until 2001 occupied a comfortable third-place spot in the soda aisle behind Coca-Cola and Pepsi. But then a flood of spinoffs from the two soda giants showed up on the shelves—lemons and limes, vanillas and coffees, raspberries and oranges, Whites and blues and clears—what in food-industry lingo are known as "line extensions," and Dr Pepper started to lose its market share. Responding to this pressure, Cadbury Schweppes created its first spin-off, other than a diet version, in the soda's 115-year history, a bright red soda with a very un-Dr Pepper name: Red Fusion . . . . But consumers hated Red Fusion. "Dr Pepper is my all-time favorite drink, so I was curious about the Red Fusion," a California mother of three wrote on a blog to warn other Peppers away. "It's disgusting. Gagging. Never again."

Stung by the rejection, Cadbury Schweppes in 2004 turned to a food-industry legend named Howard Moskowitz. Moskowitz, who studied mathematics and holds a Ph.D. in experimental psychology from Harvard, runs a consulting firm in White Plains, where for more than three decades he has "optimized" a variety of products for Campbell Soup, General Foods, Kraft and PepsiCo. "I've optimized soups," Moskowitz told me. "I've optimized pizzas. I've optimized salad dressings and pickles. In this field, I'm a game changer."

In the process of product optimization, food engineers alter a litany of variables with the sole intent of finding the most perfect version (or versions) of a product. Ordinary consumers are paid to spend hours sitting in rooms where they touch, feel, sip, smell, swirl and taste whatever product is in question. Their opinions are dumped into a computer, and the data are sifted and sorted through a statistical method called conjoint analysis, which determines what features will be most attractive to consumers. Moskowitz likes to imagine that his computer is divided into silos, in which each of the attributes is stacked. But it's not simply a matter of comparing Color 23 with Color 24. In the most complicated projects, Color 23 must be combined with Syrup 11 and Packaging 6, and on and on, in seemingly infinite combinations . . . .

Moskowitz's work on Prego spaghetti sauce was memorialized in a 2004 presentation by the author Malcolm Gladwell at the TED conference in Monterey, California:

> After . . . months and months, he had a mountain of data about how the American people feel about spaghetti sauce . . . . And sure enough, if you sit down and you analyze all this data on spaghetti sauce, you realize that all Americans fall into one of three groups. There are people who like their spaghetti sauce plain. There are people who like their spaghetti sauce spicy. And there are people who like it extra-chunky. And of those three facts, the third one was the most significant, because at the time, in the early 1980s, if you went to a supermarket, you would not

find extra-chunky spaghetti sauce. And Prego turned to Howard, and they said, 'Are you telling me that one-third of Americans crave extra-chunky spaghetti sauce, and yet no one is servicing their needs?' And he said, 'Yes.' And Prego then went back and completely reformulated their spaghetti sauce and came out with a line of extra-chunky that immediately and completely took over the spaghetti-sauce business in this country . . . . That is Howard's gift to the American people . . . . He fundamentally changed the way the food industry thinks about making you happy.

Well, yes and no. One thing Gladwell didn't mention is that the food industry already knew some things about making people happy—and it started with sugar. Many of the Prego sauces—whether cheesy, chunky or light—have one feature in common: The largest ingredient, after tomatoes, is sugar. A mere half-cup of Prego Traditional, for instance, has the equivalent of more than two teaspoons of sugar, as much as two-plus Oreo cookies. It also delivers one-third of the sodium recommended for a majority of American adults for an entire day. In making these sauces, Campbell supplied the ingredients, including the salt, sugar and, for some versions, fat, while Moskowitz supplied the optimization. "More is not necessarily better," Moskowitz wrote in his own account of the Prego project. "As the sensory intensity (say, of sweetness) increases, consumers first say that they like the product more, but eventually, with a middle level of sweetness, consumers like the product the most (this is their optimum, or 'bliss,' point)."

I first met Moskowitz on a crisp day in the spring of 2010 at the Harvard Club in Midtown Manhattan. As we talked, he made clear that while he has worked on numerous projects aimed at creating more healthful foods and insists the industry could be doing far more to curb obesity, he had no qualms about his own pioneering work on discovering what industry insiders now regularly refer to as "the bliss point" or any of the other systems that helped food companies create the greatest amount of crave. "There's no moral issue for me," he said. "I did the best science I could. I was struggling to survive and didn't have the luxury of being a moral creature. As a researcher, I was ahead of my time."

. . . Thirty-two years after he began experimenting with the bliss point, Moskowitz got the call from Cadbury Schweppes asking him to create a good line extension for Dr Pepper. I spent an afternoon in his White Plains offices as he and his vice president for research, Michele Reisner, walked me through the Dr Pepper campaign. Cadbury wanted its new flavor to have cherry and vanilla on top of the basic Dr Pepper taste. Thus, there were three main components to play with. A sweet cherry flavoring, a sweet vanilla flavoring and a sweet syrup known as "Dr Pepper flavoring."

Finding the bliss point required the preparation of 61 subtly distinct formulas—31 for the regular version and 30 for diet. The formulas were then subjected to 3,904 tastings organized in Los Angeles, Dallas, Chicago and Philadelphia. The Dr Pepper tasters began working through their samples, resting five minutes between each sip to restore their taste buds. After each sample, they gave numerically ranked answers to a set of questions: How much did they like it overall? How strong is the taste? How do they feel about the taste? How would they describe the quality of this product? How likely would they be to purchase this product?

Moskowitz's data—compiled in a 135-page report for the soda maker—is tremendously fine-grained, showing how different people and groups of people feel about a strong vanilla taste versus weak, various aspects of aroma and the powerful sensory force that food scientists call "mouth feel." This is the way a product interacts with the mouth, as defined more specifically by a host of related sensations, from dryness to gumminess to moisture release. These are terms more familiar to sommeliers, but the mouth feel of soda and many other food items, especially those high in fat, is second only to the bliss point in its ability to predict how much craving a product will induce.

. . . On page 83 of the report, a thin blue line represents the amount of Dr Pepper flavoring needed to generate maximum appeal. The line is shaped like an upside-down U . . . [a]nd at the top of the arc, there is not a single sweet spot but instead a sweet range, within which "bliss" was achievable. This meant that Cadbury could edge back on its key ingredient, the sugary Dr Pepper syrup, without falling out of the range and losing the bliss. Instead of using

2 milliliters of the flavoring, for instance, they could use 1.69 milliliters and achieve the same effect. The potential savings is merely a few percentage points, and it won't mean much to individual consumers who are counting calories or grams of sugar. But for Dr Pepper, it adds up to colossal savings. "That looks like nothing," Reisner said. "But it's a lot of money. A lot of money. Millions."

The soda that emerged from all of Moskowitz's variations became known as Cherry Vanilla Dr Pepper, and it proved successful beyond anything Cadbury imagined. In 2008, Cadbury split off its soft-drinks business, which included Snapple and 7-Up. The Dr Pepper Snapple Group has since been valued in excess of $11 billion.

"LUNCHTIME IS ALL YOURS"

Sometimes innovations within the food industry happen in the lab, with scientists dialing in specific ingredients to achieve the greatest allure. And sometimes, as in the case of Oscar Mayer's bologna crisis, the innovation involves putting old products in new packages.

The 1980s were tough times for Oscar Mayer. Red-meat consumption fell more than 10 percent as fat became synonymous with cholesterol, clogged arteries, heart attacks and strokes. Anxiety set in at the company's headquarters in Madison, Wis., where executives worried about their future and the pressure they faced from their new bosses at Philip Morris. Bob Drane was the company's vice president for new business strategy and development when Oscar Mayer tapped him to try to find some way to reposition bologna and other troubled meats that were declining in popularity and sales . . . .

Drane's first move was to try to zero in not on what Americans felt about processed meat but on what Americans felt about lunch. He organized focus-group sessions with the people most responsible for buying bologna—mothers—and as they talked, he realized the most pressing issue for them was time. Working moms strove to provide healthful food, of course, but they spoke with real passion and at length about the morning crush, that nightmarish dash to get breakfast on the table and lunch packed and kids out the door. He summed up their remarks for me like this: "It's awful. I am scrambling around. My kids are asking me for stuff. I'm trying to get myself ready to go to the office. I go to pack these lunches, and I don't know what I've got." What the moms revealed to him, Drane said, was "a gold mine of disappointments and problems."

He assembled a team of about 15 people with varied skills, from design to food science to advertising, to create something completely new—a convenient prepackaged lunch that would have as its main building block the company's sliced bologna and ham. They wanted to add bread, naturally, because who ate bologna without it? But this presented a problem: There was no way bread could stay fresh for the two months their product needed to sit in warehouses or in grocery coolers. Crackers, however, could—so they added a handful of cracker rounds to the package. Using cheese was the next obvious move, given its increased presence in processed foods. But what kind of cheese would work? Natural cheddar, which they started off with, crumbled and didn't slice very well, so they moved on to processed varieties, which could bend and be sliced and would last forever, or they could knock another two cents off per unit by using an even lesser product called "cheese food," which had lower scores than processed cheese in taste tests. The cost dilemma was solved when Oscar Mayer merged with Kraft in 1989 and the company didn't have to shop for cheese anymore; it got all the processed cheese it wanted from its new sister company, and at cost.

Drane's team moved into a nearby hotel, where they set out to find the right mix of components and container. They gathered around tables where bagfuls of meat, cheese, crackers and all sorts of wrapping material had been dumped, and they let their imaginations run. After snipping and taping their way through a host of failures, the model they fell back on was the American TV dinner—and after some brainstorming about names (Lunch Kits? Go-Packs? Fun Mealz?), Lunchables were born.

The trays flew off the grocery-store shelves. Sales hit a phenomenal $218 million in the first 12 months, more than anyone was prepared for. This only brought Drane his next crisis. The production costs were so

high that they were losing money with each tray they produced. So Drane flew to New York, where he met with Philip Morris officials who promised to give him the money he needed to keep it going. "The hard thing is to figure out something that will sell," he was told. "You'll figure out how to get the cost right." Projected to lose $6 million in 1991, the trays instead broke even; the next year, they earned $8 million.

With production costs trimmed and profits coming in, the next question was how to expand the franchise, which they did by turning to one of the cardinal rules in processed food: When in doubt, add sugar. "Lunchables with Dessert is a logical extension," an Oscar Mayer official reported to Philip Morris executives in early 1991. The "target" remained the same as it was for regular Lunchables—"busy mothers" and "working women," ages 25 to 49—and the "enhanced taste" would attract shoppers who had grown bored with the current trays. A year later, the dessert Lunchable morphed into the Fun Pack, which would come with a Snickers bar, a package of M&M's or a Reese's Peanut Butter Cup, as well as a sugary drink. The Lunchables team started by using Kool-Aid and cola and then Capri Sun after Philip Morris added that drink to its stable of brands. Eventually, a line of the trays, appropriately called Maxed Out, was released that had as many as nine grams of saturated fat, or nearly an entire day's recommended maximum for kids, with up to two-thirds of the max for sodium and 13 teaspoons of sugar.

When I asked Geoffrey Bible, former C.E.O. of Philip Morris, about this shift toward more salt, sugar and fat in meals for kids, he smiled and noted that even in its earliest incarnation, Lunchables was held up for criticism. "One article said something like, 'If you take Lunchables apart, the most healthy item in it is the napkin.'" Well, they did have a good bit of fat, I offered. "You bet," he said. "Plus cookies."

The prevailing attitude among the company's food managers—through the 1990s, at least, before obesity became a more pressing concern—was one of supply and demand. "People could point to these things and say, 'They've got too much sugar, they've got too much salt,'" Bible said. "Well, that's what the consumer wants, and we're not putting a gun to their head to eat it. That's what they want. If we give them less, they'll buy less, and the competitor will get our market. So you're sort of trapped." (Bible would later press Kraft to reconsider its reliance on salt, sugar and fat.)

When it came to Lunchables, they did try to add more healthful ingredients. Back at the start, Drane experimented with fresh carrots but quickly gave up on that, since fresh components didn't work within the constraints of the processed-food system, which typically required weeks or months of transport and storage before the food arrived at the grocery store. Later, a low-fat version of the trays was developed, using meats and cheese and crackers that were formulated with less fat, but it tasted inferior, sold poorly and was quickly scrapped.

When I met with Kraft officials in 2011 to discuss their products and policies on nutrition, they had dropped the Maxed Out line and were trying to improve the nutritional profile of Lunchables through smaller, incremental changes that were less noticeable to consumers. Across the Lunchables line, they said they had reduced the salt, sugar and fat by about 10 percent, and new versions, featuring mandarin-orange and pineapple slices, were in development. These would be promoted as more healthful versions, with "fresh fruit," but their list of ingredients—containing upward of 70 items, with sucrose, corn syrup, high-fructose corn syrup and fruit concentrate all in the same tray—have been met with intense criticism from outside the industry.

One of the company's responses to criticism is that kids don't eat the Lunchables every day—on top of which, when it came to trying to feed them more healthful foods, kids themselves were unreliable. When their parents packed fresh carrots, apples and water, they couldn't be trusted to eat them. Once in school, they often trashed the healthful stuff in their brown bags to get right to the sweets. This idea—that kids are in control—would become a key concept in the evolving marketing campaigns for the trays. In what would prove to be their greatest achievement of all, the Lunchables team would delve into adolescent psychology to discover that it wasn't the food in the trays that excited the kids; it was the feeling of power it brought to their lives. As Bob Eckert, then the C.E.O. of Kraft, put it in 1999: "Lunchables aren't about lunch. It's about kids being able to put together what they want to eat, anytime, anywhere."

Kraft's early Lunchables campaign targeted mothers. They might be too distracted by work to make a lunch, but they loved their kids enough to offer them this prepackaged gift. But as the focus swung toward kids, Saturday-morning cartoons started carrying an ad that offered a different message: "All day, you gotta do what they say," the ads said. "But lunchtime is all yours."

With this marketing strategy in place and pizza Lunchables—the crust in one compartment, the cheese, pepperoni and sauce in others—proving to be a runaway success, the entire world of fast food suddenly opened up for Kraft to pursue. They came out with a Mexican-themed Lunchables called Beef Taco Wraps; a Mini Burgers Lunchables; a Mini Hot Dog Lunchable, which also happened to provide a way for Oscar Mayer to sell its wieners. By 1999, pancakes—which included syrup, icing, Lifesavers candy and Tang, for a whopping 76 grams of sugar—and waffles were, for a time, part of the Lunchables franchise as well.

Annual sales kept climbing, past $500 million, past $800 million; at last count, including sales in Britain, they were approaching the $1 billion mark. Lunchables was more than a hit; it was now its own category. Eventually, more than 60 varieties of Lunchables and other brands of trays would show up in the grocery stores. In 2007, Kraft even tried a Lunchables Jr. for three to five-year-olds.

In the trove of records that document the rise of the Lunchables and the sweeping change it brought to lunchtime habits, I came across a photograph of Bob Drane's daughter, which he had slipped into the Lunchables presentation he showed to food developers. The picture was taken on Monica Drane's wedding day in 1989, and she was standing outside the family's home in Madison, a beautiful bride in a White wedding dress, holding one of the brand-new yellow trays . . . . Monica Drane had three of her own children by the time we spoke, ages 10, 14 and 17. "I don't think my kids have ever eaten a Lunchable," she told me. "They know they exist and that Grandpa Bob invented them. But we eat very healthfully."

Drane himself paused only briefly when I asked him if, looking back, he was proud of creating the trays. "Lots of things are trade-offs," he said. "And I do believe it's easy to rationalize anything. In the end, I wish that the nutritional profile of the thing could have been better, but I don't view the entire project as anything but a positive contribution to people's lives."

Today Bob Drane is still talking to kids about what they like to eat, but his approach has changed. He volunteers with a nonprofit organization that seeks to build better communications between school kids and their parents, and right in the mix of their problems, alongside the academic struggles, is childhood obesity. Drane has also prepared a précis on the food industry that he used with medical students at the University of Wisconsin. And while he does not name his Lunchables in this document, and cites numerous causes for the obesity epidemic, he holds the entire industry accountable. "What do University of Wisconsin M.B.A.'s learn about how to succeed in marketing?" his presentation to the med students asks. "Discover what consumers want to buy and give it to them with both barrels. Sell more, keep your job! How do marketers often translate these 'rules' into action on food? Our limbic brains love sugar, fat, salt . . . . So formulate products to deliver these. Perhaps add low-cost ingredients to boost profit margins. Then 'supersize' to sell more . . . . And advertise/promote to lock in 'heavy users.' Plenty of guilt to go around here!"

"THESE PEOPLE NEED A LOT OF THINGS, BUT THEY DON'T NEED A COKE."

The growing attention Americans are paying to what they put into their mouths has touched off a new scramble by the processed-food companies to address health concerns. Pressed by the Obama administration and consumers, Kraft, Nestlé, Pepsi, Campbell and General Mills, among others, have begun to trim the loads of salt, sugar and fat in many products. And with consumer advocates pushing for more government intervention, Coca-Cola made headlines in January by releasing ads that promoted its bottled water and low-calorie drinks as a way to counter obesity. Predictably, the ads drew a new volley of scorn from critics who pointed to the company's continuing drive to sell sugary Coke.

One of the other executives I spoke with at length was Jeffrey Dunn, who, in 2001, at age 44, was directing more than half of Coca-Cola's $20 billion in annual sales as president and chief operating officer in both North and South America. In an effort to control as much market share as possible, Coke extended its aggressive marketing to especially poor or vulnerable areas of the U.S., like New Orleans—where people were drinking twice as much Coke as the national average—or Rome, Ga., where the per capita intake was nearly three Cokes a day. In Coke's headquarters in Atlanta, the biggest consumers were referred to as "heavy users." "The other model we use was called 'drinks and drinkers,'" Dunn said. "How many drinkers do I have? And how many drinks do they drink? If you lost one of those heavy users, if somebody just decided to stop drinking Coke, how many drinkers would you have to get, at low velocity, to make up for that heavy user? The answer is a lot. It's more efficient to get my existing users to drink more."

One of Dunn's lieutenants, Todd Putman, who worked at Coca-Cola from 1997 to 2001, said the goal became much larger than merely beating the rival brands; Coca-Cola strove to outsell every other thing people drank, including milk and water. The marketing division's efforts boiled down to one question, Putman said: "How can we drive more ounces into more bodies more often?" (In response to Putman's remarks, Coke said its goals have changed and that it now focuses on providing consumers with more low- or no-calorie products.)

In his capacity, Dunn was making frequent trips to Brazil, where the company had recently begun a push to increase consumption of Coke among the many Brazilians living in *favelas*. The company's strategy was to repackage Coke into smaller, more affordable 6.7-ounce bottles, just 20 cents each. Coke was not alone in seeing Brazil as a potential boon; Nestlé began deploying battalions of women to travel poor neighborhoods, hawking American-style processed foods door to door. But Coke was Dunn's concern, and on one trip, as he walked through one of the impoverished areas, he had an epiphany. "A voice in my head says,

'These people need a lot of things, but they don't need a Coke.' I almost threw up."

Dunn returned to Atlanta, determined to make some changes. He didn't want to abandon the soda business, but he did want to try to steer the company into a more healthful mode, and one of the things he pushed for was to stop marketing Coke in public schools. The independent companies that bottled Coke viewed his plans as reactionary. A director of one bottler wrote a letter to Coke's chief executive and board asking for Dunn's head. "He said what I had done was the worst thing he had seen in 50 years in the business," Dunn said. "Just to placate these crazy leftist school districts who were trying to keep people from having their Coke. He said I was an embarrassment to the company, and I should be fired." In February 2004, he was.

Dunn told me that talking about Coke's business today was by no means easy and, because he continues to work in the food business, not without risk. "You really don't want them mad at you," he said. "And I don't mean that, like, I'm going to end up at the bottom of the bay. But they don't have a sense of humor when it comes to this stuff. They're a very, very aggressive company."

When I met with Dunn, he told me not just about his years at Coke but also about his new marketing venture. In April 2010, he met with three executives from Madison Dearborn Partners, a private-equity firm based in Chicago with a wide-ranging portfolio of investments. They recently hired Dunn to run one of their newest acquisitions—a food producer in the San Joaquin Valley. As they sat in the hotel's meeting room, the men listened to Dunn's marketing pitch. He talked about giving the product a personality that was bold and irreverent, conveying the idea that this was the ultimate snack food. He went into detail on how he would target a special segment of the 146 million Americans who are regular snackers—mothers, children, young professionals—people, he said, who "keep their snacking ritual fresh by trying a new food product when it catches their attention."

He explained how he would deploy strategic storytelling in the ad campaign for this snack, using a key phrase that had been developed with much calculation: "Eat 'Em Like Junk Food." After 45 minutes, Dunn clicked off the last slide and thanked the men for coming . . . . The snack that Dunn was proposing to sell: carrots. Plain, fresh carrots. No added sugar. No creamy sauce or dips. No salt. Just baby carrots, washed, bagged, then sold into the deadly dull produce aisle. "We act like a snack, not a vegetable," he told the investors. "We exploit the rules of junk food to fuel the baby-carrot conversation. We are pro-junk-food behavior but anti-junk-food establishment."

The investors were thinking only about sales. They had already bought one of the two biggest farm producers of baby carrots in the country, and they'd hired Dunn to run the whole operation. Now, after his pitch, they were relieved. Dunn had figured out that using the industry's own marketing ploys would work better than anything else. He drew from the bag of tricks that he mastered in his 20 years at Coca-Cola, where he learned one of the most critical rules in processed food: The selling of food matters as much as the food itself. Later, describing his new line of work, Dunn told me he was doing penance for his Coca-Cola years. "I'm paying my karmic debt," he said.

WIL S. HYLTON

69. A BUG IN THE SYSTEM

Why Last Night's Chicken Made You Sick

If you've ever had even a mild case of food poisoning, you know just how terrible it can be. Although many of us have gotten sick from food, many consumers believe that our food is generally safe and that, in general, a system of strict government regulations and inspections of manufacturing plants protects us from contamination and pathogens in our meat, produce, and frozen foods. It may surprise you, then, to read Hylton's investigation of the broken food safety system. Hylton argues that the system designed to protect consumers is convoluted and often ineffective, putting American consumers at risk on a regular basis.

Late one night in September of 2013, Rick Schiller awoke in bed with his right leg throbbing. Schiller, who is in his fifties, lives in San Jose, California. He had been feeling ill all week, and, as he reached under the covers, he found his leg hot to the touch. He struggled to sit upright, then turned on a light and pulled back the sheet. "My leg was about twice the normal size, maybe even three times," he told me. "And it was hard as a rock, and bright purple." Schiller roused his fiancée, who helped him hobble to their car. He dropped into the passenger seat, but he couldn't bend his leg to fit it through the door. "So I tell her, 'Just grab it and shove it in,'" he recalled. "I almost passed out in pain."

At the hospital, five employees helped move Schiller from the car to a consulting room. When a doctor examined his leg, she warned him that it was so swollen there was a chance it might burst. She tried to remove fluid with a needle, but nothing came out. "So she goes in with a bigger needle—nothing comes out," Schiller said. "Then she goes in with a huge needle, like the size of a pencil lead—nothing comes out."

When the doctor tugged on the plunger, the syringe filled with a chunky, meatlike substance. "And then she gasped," Schiller said.

That night, he drifted in and out of consciousness in his hospital room. His temperature rose to a hundred and three degrees and his right eye oozed fluid that crusted over his face. Schiller's doctors found that he had contracted a form of the salmonella bacterium, known as Salmonella Heidelberg, which triggered a cascade of conditions, including an inflamed colon and an acute form of arthritis. The source of the infection was most likely something he had eaten, but Schiller had no idea what. He spent four days in intensive care before he could stand again and navigate the hallways. On the fifth day, he went home, but the right side of his body still felt weak, trembly, and sore, and he suffered from constant headaches. His doctors warned that he might never fully recover.

Three weeks later, Schiller received a phone call from the Centers for Disease Control and Prevention. An investigator wanted to know whether he had eaten chicken before he became sick. Schiller remembered that he'd bought two packages of raw Foster Farms chicken thighs just before the illness. He'd eaten a few pieces from one of the packages; the other package was still in his freezer. Several days later, an investigator from the U.S. Department of Agriculture stopped by to pick it up. She dropped the chicken into a portable cooler and handed him a slip of paper that said "Property Receipt." That was the last time Schiller heard from the investigators. More than a year later, he still wasn't sure what was in the chicken: "I don't know what the Department of Agriculture found."

Each year, contaminated food sickens forty-eight million Americans, of whom a hundred and twenty-eight thousand are hospitalized, and three thousand die. Many of the deadliest pathogens, such as *E. coli* and listeria, are comparatively rare; many of the most widespread, such as norovirus, are mercifully mild. Salmonella is both common and potentially lethal. It infects more than a million Americans each year, sending nineteen thousand victims to the hospital, and killing more people than any other foodborne pathogen. A recent U.S.D.A study found that twenty-four per cent of all cut-up chicken parts are contaminated by some form of salmonella. Another study, by *Consumer Reports*, found that more than a third of chicken breasts tainted with salmonella carried a drug-resistant strain.

By the time Schiller became infected by salmonella, federal officials had been tracking an especially potent outbreak of the Heidelberg variety for three months—it had sent nearly forty per cent of its victims to the hospital. The outbreak began in March, but investigators discovered it in June, when a cluster of infections on the West Coast prompted a warning from officials at the C.D.C.'s PulseNet monitoring system, which tracks illnesses reported by doctors. Scientists quickly identified the source of the outbreak as Foster Farms facilities in California, where federal inspectors had discovered the same strain of pathogen during a routine test. Most of the victims of the outbreak confirmed that they'd recently eaten chicken, and many specifically named the Foster Farms brand. On August 9th, investigators joined a conference call with Foster Farms executives to inform them of the outbreak and its link to the company.

Identifying the cause of an outbreak is much simpler than trying to stop one. Once officials have traced

the contamination to a food producer, the responsibility to curb the problem falls to the U.S.D.A.'s Food Safety and Inspection Service, or F.S.I.S. In the summer of 2013, as the outbreak spread, F.S.I.S. officials shared the C.D.C.'s conclusion that Foster Farms meat was behind the outbreak, but they had no power to force a recall of the tainted chicken. Federal law permits a certain level of salmonella contamination in raw meat. But when federal limits are breached, and officials believe that a recall is necessary, their only option is to ask the producer to remove the product voluntarily. Even then, officials may only request a recall when they have proof that the meat is already making customers sick. As evidence, the F.S.I.S. typically must find a genetic match between the salmonella in a victim's body and the salmonella in a package of meat that is still in the victim's possession, with its label still attached. If the patient has already eaten the meat, discarded the package, or removed the label, the link becomes difficult to make, and officials can't request a voluntary recall.

As the Heidelberg outbreak continued into the fall, F.S.I.S. investigators tracked down dozens of patients and asked them to search their homes for contaminated chicken. In some cases, they discovered Foster Farms chicken that tested positive for salmonella—but they could not find a genetic match. David Goldman, who oversees public health at the F.S.I.S., told me, "We started about a hundred and forty traceback efforts. And we failed in every case."

Meanwhile, Foster Farms was still producing chicken. By mid-September, on the week that Schiller checked into the hospital, at least fifty new patients had been infected—the most of any week since the outbreak began. On October 8th, the C.D.C. issued its first warning to the public: two hundred and seventy-eight patients had now been infected with Heidelberg in seventeen states, the agency reported, and Foster Farms chicken was the "likely source" of the outbreak. On November 15th, the C.D.C. raised the number to three hundred and eighty-nine victims in twenty-three states. By early July, 2014, there were six hundred and twenty-one cases. Scientists estimate that for each reported case twenty-eight go unreported, which meant that the Foster Farms outbreak had likely sickened as many as eighteen thousand people.

Finally, on July 3, 2014, more than a year after the outbreak began, officials at the F.S.I.S. announced a genetic match that would allow the agency to request a recall. Foster Farms executives agreed to withdraw the fresh chicken produced in its California facilities during a six-day period in March of that year. All other Foster Farms chicken would remain in distribution.

A few days later, I stopped by the office of Representative Rosa DeLauro, a Democrat from Connecticut and one of the most vocal advocates for food safety in Congress. After twenty-five years in the capital, DeLauro is not easily surprised, but when I mentioned the Foster Farms outbreak she slammed a fist on the table. "They're getting a tainted product out!" she said. "What in the hell is going on?" Rick Schiller wondered the same thing. Last spring, as his leg healed and the headaches faded, he searched newspapers for signs of a recall. Then he started calling lawyers. Eventually, he found Bill Marler.

During the past twenty years, Marler has become the most prominent and powerful food-safety attorney in the country. He is fifty-seven years old, with neat gray hair and a compact physique; he tends to speak in a high, raspy voice, as though delighted by what he's about to say. His law firm, on the twenty-eighth floor of a Seattle office building, has filed hundreds of lawsuits against many of the largest food producers in the world. By his estimate, he has won more than six hundred million dollars in verdicts and settlements, of which his firm keeps about twenty per cent.

Given the struggles of his clients—victims of organ failure, sepsis, and paralysis—Marler says it can be tempting to dismiss him as a "bloodsucking ambulance chaser who exploits other people's personal tragedies." But many people who work in food safety believe that Marler is one of the few functioning pieces in a broken system. Food-borne illness, they point out, is pervasive but mostly preventable when simple precautions are taken in the production process. In Denmark, for instance, after a surge of salmonella cases in the 1980s, poultry workers were made to wash their hands and change clothing on entering the plant and to perform extensive microbiological testing. Sanctions—including recalls—are imposed as soon as a pathogen is found. As a result, salmonella contamination has fallen to less than two per cent.

Similar results have been achieved in other European countries.

In the U.S., responsibility for food safety is divided among fifteen federal agencies. The most important, in addition to the F.S.I.S., is the Food and Drug Administration, in the Department of Health and Human Services. In theory, the line between these two should be simple: the F.S.I.S. inspects meat and poultry; the F.D.A. covers everything else. In practice, that line is hopelessly blurred. Fish are the province of the F.D.A.—except catfish, which falls under the F.S.I.S. Frozen cheese pizza is regulated by the F.D.A., but frozen pizza with slices of pepperoni is monitored by the F.S.I.S. Bagel dogs are F.D.A.; corn dogs, F.S.I.S. The skin of a link sausage is F.D.A., but the meat inside is F.S.I.S. "The current structure is there not because it's what serves the consumer best," Elisabeth Hagen, a former head of the F.S.I.S., told me. "It's there because it's the way the system has grown up." Mike Taylor, the highest-ranking food-safety official at the F.D.A., said, "Everybody would agree that if you were starting on a blank piece of paper and designing the food-safety system for the future, from scratch, you wouldn't design it the way it's designed right now."

Both the F.S.I.S. and the F.D.A. are also hampered by internal tensions. The regulatory function at the F.S.I.S. can seem like a distant afterthought at the U.S.D.A., whose primary purpose is to advance the interests of American agriculture. "We're the red-headed stepchild of the U.S.D.A.," one senior F.S.I.S. official told me. When regulation fails, private litigation can be the most powerful force for change. As Marler puts it, "If you want them to respond, you have to make them." Robert Brackett, who directed food safety at the F.D.A. during the George W. Bush Administration, told me that Marler has almost single-handedly transformed the role that lawsuits play in food policy: "Where people typically thought of food safety as this three-legged stool—the consumer groups, the government, and the industry—Bill sort of came in as a fourth leg and actually was able to effect changes in a way that none of the others really had." Hagen said the cost that Marler extracts from food makers "can be a stronger incentive or disincentive than the passing of any particular regulation." Mike Taylor called litigation such as Marler's "a central element of accountability."

Bill Marler lives with his wife and three daughters on Bainbridge Island, just west of Seattle. He commutes to work on a public ferry and spends the time walking in circles. He leaves his briefcase with friends in the cabin, climbs to the upper level, and steps outside, into the mist of Puget Sound. By the time the ferry reaches Seattle, forty minutes later, Marler has usually logged about two and a half miles. A few years ago, realizing that most of his clients were too sick or too far away to visit him at work, he stopped wearing office attire, leaving on the wicking fabrics he wears on the ferry. It can be jarring for a first-time visitor to pass through the wood-paneled lobby of his firm, down a long hallway of offices filled with paralegals and junior attorneys, only to discover a small man in damp gym clothes reclining at Marler's desk.

Marler rarely uses the fiery rhetoric one might expect from a lifelong litigator. His preference is the soft sell, the politician's lure—cajoling insurance adjusters, health officials, microbiologists, and opposing counsel. He developed his coaxing manner early on. In 1977, as a sophomore at Washington State University, in the small town of Pullman, he ran for the city council on a whim, and won by fifty-three votes. During the next four years, he sponsored a fair-housing bill, tightened snow-removal laws, established a bus service for drunk drivers (critics called it Bill's Booze Bus), and helped to manage the seven-member council's six-million-dollar budget. "All these skills that I use every day—how to deal with the media, how to deal with complex interpersonal relationships to try to get a deal done—I learned between the ages of nineteen and twenty-two, when everybody else was smoking dope," he told me. Jeff Miller, an attorney in New York, recalled the first time he faced Marler in federal court, on a day that Miller had to leave early for a charity event. The judge was notoriously thorny and Miller was terrified to request an early dismissal, which seemed like an invitation for Marler to object and score points. Miller told me, "And as I was in court, telling the judge that I needed to get out of there, Bill just cut a significant check and said, 'Bring this with you.'"

Marler became involved in food safety in 1993, as a thirty-five-year-old lawyer at a big Seattle firm, when a client called with a food-poisoning referral. An outbreak of E. coli, seemingly caused by contaminated burgers from Jack in the Box, was spreading through the state. Marler's client had a friend whose daughter had become ill, and Marler took her case. During the next several months, the outbreak sickened more than five hundred Jack in the Box customers. Four children died. Marler plunged into microbiological research on E. coli. After reading scientific papers and talking to experts, he discovered that the bacterium, which typically lives in the intestines of cattle, can enter the food supply in meat or when vegetables are contaminated by fecal matter. The outbreak had been caused by a variant of the bug known as O157:H7, which secretes a powerful toxin in a victim's body. In some cases, the toxin can induce a reaction called hemolytic–uremic syndrome, in which the individual's face and hands swell, bruises cover the body, and blood begins to trickle from the nose. One in twenty patients dies. The only way to kill the bacteria in food is to cook it thoroughly.

Attorneys for Jack in the Box responded to Marler's lawsuit by sending him more than fifty cardboard boxes of discovery material. Marler moved the boxes to his firm's conference room and spent nights and weekends sifting through every page. He found letters sent by the Washington State Department of Health to Jack in the Box, announcing a new, mandatory cooking temperature for ground beef. He discovered that the chain had not followed the new standards, undercooking its meat, and he studied suggestion forms submitted by employees to corporate headquarters indicating that Jack in the Box executives knew they were cutting corners.

Marler spent the next two years immersed in discovery and settlement negotiations. He turned down multimillion-dollar offers, and demanded a hundred million dollars, an unprecedented sum at the time. He courted food and health reporters at major news organizations and publicly accused the company's executives of killing children. To defuse the tension, he would meet the Jack in the Box attorneys at a hotel bar and buy them drinks. (Hours later, he might call a reporter to pass along gossip he had gleaned.) As the outbreak became national news, more than a hundred victims came forward to be represented by Marler. The settlement, of more than fifty million dollars, included $15.6 million for a ten-year-old girl named Brianne Kiner, who spent forty days in a coma. It was the largest individual food-poisoning claim in American history.

Prompted by public outrage, federal officials took a dramatic step. On September 29, 1994, at a convention of the American Meat Institute, Mike Taylor, at that time the administrator of the F.S.I.S., announced that his agency would adopt a zero-tolerance policy toward *E. coli* in ground beef. There would be no acceptable level of contamination; anytime the agency detected the bacterium, it would remove the product from distribution. To do so, Taylor would classify the outbreak strain of *E. coli* as an "adulterant," which in meat and poultry is normally reserved for toxic industrial chemicals. It was the first time that the agency had applied the designation to a food-borne microbe. Although a consortium of meat producers and retailers sued the U.S.D.A. that December, a federal court affirmed the change. Five years later, officials expanded the rule to banish the same strain of *E. coli* in other beef products. In 2011, they declared six additional strains of *E. coli* to be adulterants. The lesson, Taylor told me, is that "having accountability for prevention in the government regulatory system works." Yet, twenty years after Taylor's landmark *E. coli* decision, officials at the F.S.I.S. have failed to declare any other foodborne pathogen to be an adulterant in raw meat.

People who work with Marler are accustomed to e-mails landing in the night, with links and attachments and an abundance of exclamation points. At least twice a month, he flies across the country to speak with advocacy groups and at food-industry events. He will not accept payment from any food company, and has turned down thousands of dollars to deliver a short lecture, only to pay his own way to the venue and present the speech for free. Sometimes, when Marler takes the stage, members of the audience walk out. At a meeting of the Produce Manufacturers Association, in the summer of 2013, he approached the lectern as loudspeakers blared the Rolling Stones song "Sympathy for the Devil."

Marler rarely has trouble getting companies to concede when their product has caused illness, but occasionally one of his cases involves more complicated legal questions. In 2011, thirty-three people died of listeriosis after eating cantaloupe produced in Colorado by Jensen Farms. Listeria is a rare but deadly bacterium. It infects about sixteen hundred U.S. residents per year, and kills one in five victims. The disease can take up to seventy days to manifest symptoms, and, when it does, the initial signs—a sudden onset of chills, fever, diarrhea, headache, or vomiting—can resemble those of the flu. Since the 1980s, it has caused three of the deadliest food-borne outbreaks on record.

Because listeria can grow in cold temperatures, it is perfectly suited to the era of prepared foods. "One of the reasons that we still have a lot of food-borne illness is because we've created these environments of convenience," Marler told me one morning, as we barreled down the highway in his pickup, a 1951 Chevy with the license plate "ECOLI." The truck rattled and reeked of gasoline; his golden retriever, Rowan, slept in the truck bed. "Bagged salad, refrigerators with secret drawers that are supposed to keep things fresh for longer," Marler said, shaking his head. "We get so wrapped up with production and convenience, and nobody pays any attention to bacteriology." Indeed, at the Jensen Farms plant, where the contaminated cantaloupes originated, a mechanized system had been washing the melons with tap water, rather than the antimicrobial solution recommended by the F.D.A. The C.D.C. counts a hundred and forty-seven victims in the cantaloupe case. Sixty-six have filed suit, and forty-six of them have hired Marler. He is using a novel legal argument that could set a precedent in food law.

Unlike the F.S.I.S., the F.D.A. does not have a large army of inspectors for the products under its purview. Years can elapse between official inspections at a given food producer. In place of federal inspections, most reviews are conducted by private companies known as auditors. These audits are demanded by retailers who want to be sure they are buying clean food. In the case of the 2011 listeria outbreak, auditors had actually been inside the plant just a few days before the first contaminated cantaloupes were shipped. Subcontractors working for the company PrimusLabs noted the absence of antimicrobial wash but gave the facility a rating of "superior" and a score of ninety-six per cent.

Marler has filed suit against Jensen Farms and retailers like Walmart and Kroger, but he is also suing PrimusLabs on behalf of listeria victims. There is no clear legal basis for doing so. Because PrimusLabs is a private company, hired by another private company for a private purpose, its lawyers contend that its only legal duty is to the producer that commissioned its audit—not to the consumers who bought a cantaloupe several steps down the supply chain. Attorneys for PrimusLabs have tried repeatedly to have Marler's lawsuit dismissed. In most jurisdictions, they have failed. Marler says that the PrimusLabs attorneys have made a strategic blunder. An early settlement would have kept the outbreak relatively quiet, he told me, but each time the court rejects a motion by Primus to dismiss the case a precedent is set. "There was an empty desert between us, and I wasn't even sure they were there," he said. "Then they started leaving bread crumbs. They're creating a road map for how to try a case against them."

Privately, officials at the F.S.I.S. say that they would like to take a more aggressive stand on salmonella. But an agency ruling like the one twenty years ago on *E. coli* would almost certainly fail in court today. In the past forty years, federal judges have severely limited the agency's power. That history began, by most accounts, with a 1974 lawsuit in which the American Public Health Association sued the U.S.D.A. to demand that it print bacterial warnings on raw meat. An appellate court ruled that the warnings were unnecessary, because customers already knew that meat carries bacteria. "American housewives and cooks normally are not ignorant or stupid," the judge wrote.

When another court ruled in favor of the F.S.I.S. decision to declare *E. coli* an adulterant, the ruling included a passage to prevent the F.S.I.S. from applying the same label to other bacteria: "Courts have held that other pathogens, such as salmonella, are not adulterants." In response to that decision, in 1996 the F.S.I.S. enacted a series of new rules to curb pathogens like salmonella. For whole chickens, the salmonella "performance standard" was set at twenty percent, meaning that one in every five bird carcasses could be contaminated. That standard has since been lowered to 7.5 per cent, but the performance standard for salmonella in ground chicken is much higher—44.6 per cent—and for ground turkey it is 49.9 per cent. "Which means that almost half of all your ground chicken that goes off the line can actually test positive

for salmonella," Urvashi Rangan, the director of food safety at *Consumer Reports*, told me. Some products, such as cut-up chicken parts, have no performance standard at all. A hundred per cent of the product in supermarkets may be contaminated without running afoul of federal limits. Rangan told me that she was stunned when she discovered this, just recently: "We've asked the U.S.D.A. point blank, 'So does that mean there aren't standards for lamb chops and pork ribs?' And they said, 'Yeah, we don't have standards for those.'"

When I asked David Goldman, of the F.S.I.S.'s public-health program, why a common product like chicken parts has no contamination limit, he said, "We're in the process of doing just that." [In 2015], the agency announced plans to establish its first performance standard for chicken parts, limiting salmonella contamination to 15.4 per cent of packages. I asked Phil Derfler, the deputy administrator, why it had taken the agency twenty years. "It's not like there is anybody else in the world who is pursuing what we're doing, and so it is a bit of trial and error," he said. "If there was a font of wisdom that said, 'You should be doing this,' maybe we would be doing it." I mentioned Denmark's success in combatting salmonella, and Derfler said, "I mean, it would be a major kind of almost top-to-bottom kind of thing. And I don't know what the costs would be in economics."

Even when the agency sets a pathogen limit and a producer exceeds it, officials have few options. Under the terms of a 1999 lawsuit, inspectors may not shut down a facility because of a failure to meet contamination limits. Instead, officials must use indirect measures to put pressure on the company, such as posting news of the violation on the F.S.I.S. Web site, which could embarrass company executives. Derfler told me that the agency's work-arounds have been effective. "We have tried to do it," he said.

In December of 2013, officials at the F.S.I.S. unveiled a new "Salmonella Action Plan." At the heart of the plan was a "poultry-slaughter rule," which would reduce the number of federal inspectors observing the production line at slaughterhouses. Derfler told me that this will allow the agency to place "a greater emphasis on microbiology" and added that the rule also requires plants to do their own testing. Critics of the plan wonder how it is possible to improve food safety by removing inspectors. On March 13th of [2014], Representative Louise Slaughter, who is the only member of Congress with a degree in microbiology, and ten other members of the House, including Rosa DeLauro, wrote a letter to the F.S.I.S., calling certain aspects of the new plan "pernicious" and asking that it be suspended. Nevertheless, the fiscal budget for 2015 assume[d] that it [would] go into effect, and cut the funding for several hundred federal meat inspectors.

Marler opposes the new poultry rule, but he says that the real issue is the inspectors' inability to close a plant when they detect high levels of food-borne pathogens. "If you're allowing the product to become contaminated, having more or less inspectors is beside the point," he said. In 2011, the Center for Science in the Public Interest, a nonprofit advocacy group, submitted a petition to the F.S.I.S. arguing that the four most vicious types of salmonella should be declared adulterants, like *E. coli*. The agency issued no response and, in May of last year, Marler consulted with the center on a lawsuit demanding a reply to the petition. On July 31st, officials formally rejected the proposal, claiming that "more data are needed." Marler scoffed at the claim. "One part of the meat industry is just ignoring twenty years of progress on the other side," he said. "They're using the same words, the same press releases, the same language that they used twenty years ago, when they were saying, 'Oh, my God, the sky will fall if you label *E. coli* O157 as an adulterant.'"

When Marler's litigation becomes complicated and protracted, his firm can go months without generating income. Marler routinely lends money to the firm to keep the operation afloat. One morning, his longtime office manager, Peggy Paulson, stepped into his office with a sheepish look. When Marler glanced up, Paulson said quietly, "I could use a check for half a million bucks." Marler's jaw dropped with feigned horror. "So could I!" he said with a laugh. Then he promised to write a check. Later, he told me, "That's partly why I don't buy a vacation home. I've never been in a position that I settled a case because I needed the money."

During the past five years, Marler has begun to move from litigation to activism. In 2009, frustrated by the short attention span of the mass media, he founded an online newsletter, *Food Safety News*, which employs four full-time reporters and costs Marler a quarter of a million dollars a year to underwrite. On July 25, 2014, the editor of the site, Dan Flynn, and two of its employees received subpoenas in a defamation lawsuit against ABC News by the meat producer Beef Products, Inc. The lawsuit also names two former employees of the F.S.I.S., who spoke critically about the company in the ABC segment. Marler is defending those employees pro bono; two weeks ago, he received a subpoena in the case himself. Late at night, Marler also scribbles entries for the MarlerBlog, his personal Web site, where he has posted more than five thousand commentaries on food safety in recent years.

Sometimes, when Marler encounters critics who charge him with having predatory motives, he challenges them to "put me out of business." David Acheson, a former Associate Commissioner for Foods at the F.D.A., told me, "That's just become a bit of a trademark. He doesn't want that." Still, Acheson told me that he has seen an evolution in Marler. "In the early days, Bill was just on a mission to sue large food companies—he was on a mission to make money," Acheson said. "But I think during the course of that he realized that there are problems with the food-safety system, and I think progressively, philosophically, he changed from just being a plaintiff attorney to being somebody who believes that changing food safety for the betterment of public health is a laudable goal." Acheson added, with no small measure of distaste, "He still sues food companies."

In April, 2014, Marler filed a suit against Foster Farms on behalf of Rick Schiller. On July 31st, the C.D.C. announced that the outbreak "appears to be over." Foster Farms has implemented new controls to reduce salmonella, but Marler hopes that a successful lawsuit will pressure other producers to take similar precautions. Meanwhile . . . an eight-year-old boy in Braintree, Massachusetts, died of complications from *E. coli* after eating ground beef from a Whole Foods market. Six weeks later, an epidemiologist with the Massachusetts Department of Public Health, in an e-mail to the boy's mother, accused Whole Foods executives of "grasping at straws and dragging their feet in an attempt to avoid doing a recall." On August 15th, the F.S.I.S. announced that its testing had "determined that there is a link between ground beef purchased at Whole Foods Market and this illness cluster." The company agreed to issue a recall of three hundred and sixty-eight pounds of ground beef, but it continues to assert that "our thorough and ongoing investigation of the circumstances has not shown any clear link to our business." On December 17th, Marler filed suit against Whole Foods on behalf of the boy's parents.

"Fifteen years ago, almost all the cases I had were *E. coli* linked to hamburger, and now I have maybe two or three," he told me over the phone in mid-January. He was sitting in his office overlooking the Seattle harbor. "It shows how much progress we've made. You might hate lawyers, you might not want us to make money, but look what the beef industry did." Marler said he had recently eaten a hamburger for the first time in twenty years. "Ground beef has learned its lesson—but chicken is still, in many respects, unregulated. So we have to keep fighting."

CONSUMERS FIGHT BACK

FOOD CHAIN WORKERS ALLIANCE

Consumers have been responding to the food system's domination by large corporations for almost 100 years. In the early twentieth century, Jewish immigrant housewives in New York City's Lower East Side challenged a growing kosher meat trust among butchers.[1] In the late 1960s, a small group of suburban Chicago housewives, including U.S. Representative Jan Schakowsky, then a young stay-at-home mother, took on the National Tea Company, a large supermarket chain based in Chicago, and demanded transparency in their food labeling. Until their campaign, foods did not have a clear expiration date. Instead, only the grocery stores and the distributors were able to decipher the codes to reveal the expiration dates on foods such as bologna and baby formula. Through a campaign of pressuring local stockboys at area grocery stores, the women were able to break the codes. Using this information, they wrote a "codebook" that drew national attention. Housewives across the country began to send in 50 cents to purchase the codebook. The national media attention encouraged A&P Grocery, National Tea Company's competitor, to mount an ad campaign that their products were stamped with clear and transparent expiration dates. The National Tea Company quickly followed suit.[2]

The most recent national consumer movement around food, emerging over the last 30 years, is both a response to corporate consolidation in the food system and rising environmental concerns. Since the early 1970s, the movement to challenge the consolidation of the food industry has been growing. With the publication of Frances Moore Lappe's *Diet for a Small Planet* in 1971, food activists have called for a more sustainable way to live.[3] However, greater consumer concern with fresh, local, organic, and sustainable food practices can also, in part, be traced back to these historical moments when members of the public began to raise serious concerns about the threats posed by the use of pesticides, particularly DDT, in the cultivation of foods.[4]

Emboldened by the actions of activists like Ralph Nader, consumer rights activists took on large corporations seeking greater regulation of their business practices for the protection of the public;[5] this movement extended to the food industry and resulted in a recalibrated orientation to vegetarianism and organic foods. One of the first restaurants that integrated an environmentalist ethos into its selections was Alice Waters's Chez Panisse, which opened in Berkeley, California, in 1971.[6] Today, a hallmark of the food movement is the commitment, implicit or explicit, to environmental issues. Publications such as Eric Schlosser's

1   Frank, Dana. "Housewives, Socialists, and the Politics of Food: The 1917 New York Cost-of-Living Protests." *Feminist Studies* 11.2 (1985); Hyman, Paula E. "Immigrant Women and Consumer Protest: The New York City Kosher Meat Boycott of 1902." Ed. Pozzetta, George A. *American Immigration and Ethnicity.* New York: Garland Publishers, 1991; "Fight for Cheap Kosher Meat." *Chicago Daily Tribune.* 13 May 1902.

2   Twarog, Emily E. LaBarbera. *Beyond the Strike Kitchen: Housewives and Domestic Politics, 1935–1973.* Diss. University of Illinois at Chicago, 2011.

3   Lappé, Frances Moore. *Diet for a Small Planet.* New York: Ballantine Books, 1991.

4   Levenstein, Harvey A. "Chapter Three: The Rise of Giant Food Processors." *Revolution at the Table: The Transformation of the American Diet.* Berkeley: University of California Press, 2003.

5   McClean, Tom. "Ralph Nader, Lone Crusader? The Role of Consumer and Public Interest Advocates in the History of Freedom of Information." *Southwestern Journal of International Law* 24:41–71 (2018).

2001 *Fast Food Nation: The Dark Side of the All-American Meal* and Michael Pollan's 2006 *The Omnivore's Dilemma: A Natural History of Four Meals* have directed increased attention to eco-friendly domestic and restaurant practices.

As concerns over the environmental impact of food production catalyzed the turn toward locally grown foods and sustainable culinary practices—a staple of the food movement—these issues have transformed otherwise apolitical individuals into activists. Participants in the growing food movement express "concern about the industrial food system, and its implication in health problems, ecological devastation, and social injustices." In this sense, the time and care given to selecting locally grown food or seeking out organic eateries has become a form of social protest that is "more alluring than conventional political channels, particularly in a political climate where many people feel disenfranchised from traditional political processes and institutions."[7] Likewise, "In terms of the rhythms of daily life, it is often easier to express one's politics through a food purchase, than it is to find the time to write a letter, attend a protest, or participate in social movement politics."[8]

6   Johnston, Josée, and Shyon Baumann. *Foodies: Democracy and Distinction in the Gourmet Foodscape.* New York: Routledge. 2010; Kamp, David. *The United States of Arugula: The Sun-Dried, Cold-Pressed, Dark-Roasted, Extra Virgin Story of the American Food Revolution.* New York: Random House. 2007.
7   Johnston & Baumann, 2010.
8   Johnston & Baumann, 2010

Consumer activism around locally grown, fresh, and organic foods has successfully changed the food supply to include more of these food items. . . . [E]mployers note that they have maintained or grown their business by focusing on this niche market. However, the food movement of the last several decades has not focused on sustainable labor practices within the food system, with some notable exceptions, particularly with regard to farmworkers. For example, the United Farm Workers (UFW) realized that the only way they would win justice for farmworkers was through a collaborative effort with consumers. At its peak, the UFW grape boycott claimed that 10 percent of U.S. consumers were boycotting grapes. The boycott worked and farmworkers won collective bargaining in the fields.

. . . Pineros y Campesinos Unidoes del Noroeste (PCUN), an Oregon-based farmworker union, called on consumers to boycott NORPAC foods, a large grower cooperative in the Northwest that employs both farmworkers and packers, by boycotting Gardenburger, which was distributed by NORPAC. Given the popularity of Gardenburger on college campuses, PCUN organized a campaign to target key college campuses and their food service companies. In 1999, PCUN was successful in getting Gardenburger to find another distributor. These and other examples of consumer activism having broad influence on the food system demonstrate the potential for consumer activism with regard to working conditions along the food chain. In fact, the members of the Food Chain Workers Alliance have engaged in significant consumer engagement work over the last decade, unanimously promoting the concept that a sustainable food system must include sustainable labor practices for food workers.

CHAPTER 14

STRATEGIES FOR SOCIAL CHANGE

N ow that you've learned so much about social problems—how they are caused, their consequences, and how they are often intertwined with each other—you might be wondering what can be done to create change. Is there anything that individuals can do to change the nature and experience of social problems? What's the best way to become active in a social change organization? And how do activist organizations improve social conditions? In an era with some of the largest public protests in history, such as the March for Our Lives gun control protest in 2018 (with 1.25 million people participating) and the Women's March in 2017 (with 4.15 million participants),[1] how can activists seize upon this collective desire for change? You have read interviews with activists working at a variety of organizational levels at the beginning of each chapter in this book—some working for large national organizations, others for small, grassroots organizations. Their stories, and the readings in this chapter, help us to understand how activism functions on a broader social level.

In today's social media and technology-driven world, when more and more of our collective time is spent online, can low-risk social activism campaigns—"click here to donate"—really gain as much traction and have as much impact as high-risk forms of activism like the civil rights campaigns of the 1960s? Malcolm Gladwell examines this question, using the sociological concepts of strong and weak ties (essentially, how closely knit together social actors are) to understand the distinction between these two types of activism and how they can each be used to create a particular kind of social change.

Rosa Parks is regarded as "the mother of the civil rights movement," and rightly so. But Paul Rogat Loeb argues that the way that her activism is characterized—as a lone woman, acting on a sudden urge to do something heroic at just the right historical moment—obscures the real truth of her role in the civil rights movement, as well as a more powerful moral. The real story, Loeb argues, is one of hard work, perseverance, and collective action

---

1   Dockery, Heather. 2018. "The March for Our Lives Was One of the Biggest Protests in History—Get Ready for More." *Mashable*, March 27. Retrieved on March 21, 2019, from https://mashable.com/2018/03/27/largest-protests-american-history/#i8B6QsWYpsqB.

by Parks and many others, for more than a decade before her refusal to move from her seat—a more powerful moral, he argues, because it emphasizes that everyday people can create great movements in social justice through incremental change.

It can seem difficult to imagine how to create change in a political climate as polarized as contemporary America's. Megan M. Tesene examines the trends in political polarization among political leaders as well as the average American, discussing the ways in which our political ideologies influence our individual social lives as well as our political system. In the past, political polarization was largely found among political leaders and media figures; now, the electorate has become increasingly polarized, which will likely have long-term effects on the functioning of our government and the policies that result.[2] Tesene also outlines the possible paths that our political polarization may take us down and how changes in our national demographics may impact our political system. One path of social change is through the ballot box, but legislation in a number of states has suppressed voter turnout and made it harder to vote. Zachary Roth and Wendy R. Weiser detail these partisan measures, as well as their ramifications for our democracy, and argue that large-scale efforts are needed to reform election and voting laws.

Finally, acknowledging the structural sources of social problems, while important, can also be discouraging. But there are ways that students can participate in social change. Allan G. Johnson provides practical tools to target oppression in our everyday lives. By confronting inequalities within ourselves, our inner circles, our social institutions, and our nation, we can create positive social change.

---

2   Abramowitz, Alan I. 2018. *The Great Alignment: Race, Party Transformation, and the Rise of Donald Trump*. New Haven, CT: Yale University Press.

ALICIA GARZA

Alicia Garza is co-creator of #BlackLivesMatter. Started as a social media campaign, Black Lives Matter moved beyond a hashtag to become a rallying cry of social protestors and a new movement for social change.

Could you describe how #BlackLivesMatter developed? Did you anticipate how strongly it would strike a chord with people all around the country?

#BlackLivesMatter was developed in 2013 after George Zimmerman was acquitted in the murder of a Black teenager, Trayvon Martin, who was walking through the neighborhood. When the verdict was announced, I just felt sick to my stomach.

When I saw how some people online were responding to the verdict, I felt that a large part of our experience was missing. People were either really cynical about the ability of Black people to ever receive any justice from the U.S. criminal justice system or there was a blaming and "personal responsibility" narrative being directed at Black people—as if we created these conditions under which so many of us suffer. I have a brother who is 25; he's tall, brilliant, and Black and was raised in a predominantly White suburban area. I just couldn't help thinking that he could have been Trayvon.

So I wrote a love letter to Black people that challenged the notion that if Trayvon had just been more "respectable," that his life would not have been lost. Instead, I wrote that we all deserve to live dignified

lives and that what happened to Trayvon wasn't about the hoodie he was wearing—it was about a system of racism in this country that renders Black people and our lives without value. I celebrated our love for each other and for our willingness to still fight for freedom and justice, even though that fight gets harder and harder. And I ended it with Black lives matter.

Patrisse Cullors placed a hashtag in front of it and together we decided to build it out as an organizing project. Opal Tometi then built out our online engagement platforms using her skills and resources. We developed it as an organizing project nationally that used social media to connect people online so that they could take action together offline.

I think we had some sense that #BlackLivesMatter was resonating with people in a different way than what we'd seen before, but we had no idea that it would explode in this way.

What do you mean (more broadly) when you say "Black Lives Matter"?

Black Lives Matter is a principle by which we organize our lives and a principle we use in order to organize our communities to build the political and economic power that we need to determine our own futures. Black Lives Matter means that we have value and deserve to live with dignity. This country was built off of the backs and blood of our ancestors and has yet to reckon with its brutal and bloody beginnings. The lasting impacts of slavery and the structural racism that was built after slavery was "abolished" in this country to limit Black people's access to opportunities and resources and the democratic process has not yet been dealt with. It's not just police killings that comprise the heart and soul of #BlackLivesMatter. We are calling attention to the conditions of Black people across all social institutions throughout the United States and throughout the world.

It is important to us that we lift up the notion of "All Black Lives" rather than a much more common notion where Black lives = Black men. When we visualize the experiences of those who are often left out of the narratives, we can see not only the conditions of our people much more clearly, but we can devise better strategies and tools to get us closer to the world that we dream of.

As an activist and organizer, what did you do once you realized the level of attention and momentum that the social media campaign developed?

#BlackLivesMatter never was solely a social media campaign. We used it on social media, but immediately after we developed it, we took it out into our communities. We have always tried to use the momentum that social media generates to have provocative conversations and to take bold steps together that test the limits of what's possible in this moment.

One thing that is really important to us as organizers is that we are vigilant in our quest not to become "activist celebrities." To the degree that we have a platform, we want to use it to lift up the courage and hard work of so many people who never get recognition for the bold steps they are taking for all of us. We want to use our platforms to push our country to engage in real dialogue and meaningful action that eliminates racism, patriarchy, and heteronormativity, and takes on capitalism in a real way as an unsustainable economic system responsible for the degradation of our communities and our democracy.

Black Lives Matter was visible in ferguson, missouri, following the killing of unarmed Black teenager, michael brown, by a police officer. How did you participate in social activism in ferguson?

Patrisse and Darnell Moore organized a #BlackLivesMatter freedom ride that brought together more than 400 Black people from around the country in support of communities in St. Louis that were fighting back against the impact of racism in their communities, particularly Black communities. I personally spent over five weeks in St. Louis (Ferguson is a small suburb of St. Louis) supporting the development and training of local community members in community based organizing work. I worked with a team of almost 20 people to learn how to increase long-term participation and leadership of a growing movement against racism there.

Who is your activist inspiration and why?

My activist inspiration is Harriet Tubman, mostly because she organized the Underground Railroad to lead Black people to freedom in the North during slavery. Her courage and tenacity against the toughest odds really inspire me. Tubman once said, "If you hear the dogs, keep going. If you see the torches in the woods, keep going. If there's shouting after you, keep going. Don't ever stop. Keep going. If you want a taste of freedom, keep going." "Keep going" is something I tell myself every day.

You now work for the national domestic workers alliance. Do you plan on continuing to organize specific actions around Black Lives Matter?

Of course! I joined the National Domestic Workers Alliance (NDWA) just a short while after we launched #BlackLivesMatter, and for me, the work is really integrated. In fact, we just launched our new Black domestic workers organizing project, called We Dream in Black. This project invests in the leadership capacity of Black domestic workers to support their ability to lead the movement for a new democracy and a new economy. So much of the work I do at NDWA is really living the vision that we have for #BlackLivesMatter.

How much control do you have over the Black Lives Matter movement and actions?

#BlackLivesMatter is an organized network of people united under a vision and set of guiding principles and practices. The corporate media really are the ones responsible for naming this movement the #BlackLivesMatter movement, not us. At the same time, we see ourselves as a part of a Black liberation movement whose time has come. It's exciting that so many people are using #BlackLivesMatter to describe what a world can look like when Black people are free.

What are the major challenges that activists face?

Some of the challenges that activists in our chapters have are figuring out how to work with new configurations of people, how to bring together different approaches and strategies, and also how to navigate conflict that can arise as a result of trying to do things differently.

I think the other challenge activists and organizers face is that outside of our world, people don't really know what this work is, what it entails, and more importantly, why it's important. We sometimes tell stories that are incredibly ahistorical about how change happens. People end up looking at our history as if there weren't the same kinds of challenges and conflicts.

What are major misconceptions the public has about activism in general?

I remember seeing this episode of Seinfeld once that depicted an activist as a dreary communist wearing an old green army uniform and carrying around a newspaper to sell and who was, of course, a White man. But the reality is that most activists are not that. There isn't a typical profile of an activist, and activism comes in many forms—I think we're seeing that now in really important and beautiful ways. Commonalities amongst us include a passion and a commitment to making the impossible possible.

What would you consider to be your greatest successes as an activist?

I think my greatest success is yet to come! One thing I'm proud of has been connecting with and celebrating the leadership of young queer Black women. That's something that's important to me and something I think is so important to our movement.

I had the amazing opportunity to support the work of a fantastic organization known as Millennial Activists United, founded by a brilliant group of mostly queer Black women working to engage young people in the ongoing fight against state-sanctioned violence. I was honored to be present when they founded the organization! I continue to be incredibly inspired by them each and every day.

Why should students get involved in your line of activism?

I would encourage students to be involved in something that supports the empowerment of the communities that they come from and to do something every day that is about the "we." I would encourage students to get involved in something that they are passionate about and committed to—it doesn't need to be what I do, but it should be something that ensures that we leave this world much better than we found it.

If an individual has little money and time, are there other ways they can contribute? What ways can students enact social change in their daily lives?

There are a million ways to contribute to this movement, and while you don't have to have a lot of money, investing your time is important! Having conversations with your friends and family about the movement's goals and objectives is a big one. Writing to your local decision makers and letting them know you support the demands of the #BlackLivesMatter network is also important. You can find out if there is a local chapter in your area and see how you can be helpful there as well.

MALCOLM GLADWELL

70. SMALL CHANGE

Why the Revolution Will Not Be Tweeted

Is social media radically changing the way we fight to bring about social change? Gladwell argues no, that accounts of social media revolutionizing successful activism and social change are over-hyped. Gladwell acknowledges the strength of social media in generating large networks of individuals, but argues that these networks are built around weak ties to others in the network, without clear leaders. He contends that strong ties and a hierarchal organization are needed for a successful social change agenda because networks generated by social media succeed at increasing participation in social change movements precisely because so little needs to be done to participate; the type of activism that will cause meaningful social change lies in more traditional forms of activism that combine closely connected and strongly motivated individuals.

At four-thirty in the afternoon on Monday, February 1, 1960, four college students sat down at the lunch counter at the Woolworth's in downtown Greensboro, North Carolina. They were freshmen at North Carolina A. & T., a Black college a mile or so away.

"I'd like a cup of coffee, please," one of the four, Ezell Blair, said to the waitress.

"We don't serve Negroes here," she replied.

The Woolworth's lunch counter was a long L-shaped bar that could seat sixty-six people, with a standup snack bar at one end. The seats were for Whites. The snack bar was for Blacks. Another employee, a Black woman who worked at the steam table, approached the students and tried to warn them away. "You're acting stupid, ignorant!" she said. They didn't move. Around five-thirty, the front doors to the store were locked. The four still didn't move. Finally, they left by a side door. Outside, a small crowd had gathered, including a photographer from the Greensboro *Record*. "I'll be back tomorrow with A. & T. College," one of the students said.

By next morning, the protest had grown to twenty-seven men and four women, most from the same dormitory as the original four. The men were dressed in suits and ties. The students had brought their schoolwork, and studied as they sat at the counter. On Wednesday, students from Greensboro's "Negro" secondary school, Dudley High, joined in, and the number of protesters swelled to eighty. By Thursday, the protesters numbered three hundred, including three White women, from the Greensboro campus of the University of North Carolina. By Saturday, the sit-in had reached six hundred. People spilled out onto the street. White teenagers waved Confederate flags. Someone threw a firecracker. At noon, the A. & T. football team arrived. "Here comes the wrecking crew," one of the White students shouted.

By the following Monday, sit-ins had spread to Winston–Salem, twenty-five miles away, and

Durham, fifty miles away. The day after that, students at Fayetteville State Teachers College and at Johnson C. Smith College, in Charlotte, joined in, followed on Wednesday by students at St. Augustine's College and Shaw University, in Raleigh. On Thursday and Friday, the protest crossed state lines, surfacing in Hampton and Portsmouth, Virginia, in Rock Hill, South Carolina, and in Chattanooga, Tennessee. By the end of the month, there were sit-ins throughout the South, as far west as Texas. "I asked every student I met what the first day of the sitdowns had been like on his campus," the political theorist Michael Walzer wrote in *Dissent*. "The answer was always the same: 'It was like a fever. Everyone wanted to go.'" Some seventy thousand students eventually took part. Thousands were arrested and untold thousands more radicalized. These events in the early sixties became a civil-rights war that engulfed the South for the rest of the decade—and it happened without e-mail, texting, Facebook, or Twitter.

The world, we are told, is in the midst of a revolution. The new tools of social media have reinvented social activism. With Facebook and Twitter and the like, the traditional relationship between political authority and popular will has been upended, making it easier for the powerless to collaborate, coordinate, and give voice to their concerns. When ten thousand protesters took to the streets in Moldova in the spring of 2009 to protest against their country's Communist government, the action was dubbed the Twitter Revolution, because of the means by which the demonstrators had been brought together. A few months after that, when student protests rocked Tehran, the State Department took the unusual step of asking Twitter to suspend scheduled maintenance of its Web site, because the Administration didn't want such a critical organizing tool out of service at the height of the demonstrations. "Without Twitter the people of Iran would not have felt empowered and confident to stand up for freedom and democracy," Mark Pfeifle, a former national-security adviser, later wrote, calling for Twitter to be nominated for the Nobel Peace Prize. Where activists were once defined by their causes, they are now defined by their tools. Facebook warriors go online to push for change. "You are the best hope for us all," James K. Glassman, a former senior

State Department official, told a crowd of cyber activists at a recent conference sponsored by Facebook, AT&T, Howcast, MTV, and Google. Sites like Facebook, Glassman said, "give the U.S. a significant competitive advantage over terrorists. Some time ago, I said that Al Qaeda was 'eating our lunch on the Internet.' That is no longer the case. Al Qaeda is stuck in Web 1.0. The Internet is now about interactivity and conversation."

These are strong, and puzzling, claims. Why does it matter who is eating whose lunch on the Internet? Are people who log on to their Facebook page really the best hope for us all? As for Moldova's so-called Twitter Revolution, Evgeny Morozov, a scholar at Stanford who has been the most persistent of digital evangelism's critics, points out that Twitter had scant internal significance in Moldova, a country where very few Twitter accounts exist. Nor does it seem to have been a revolution, not least because the protests—as Anne Applebaum suggested in *The Washington Post*—may well have been a bit of stagecraft cooked up by the government. (In a country paranoid about Romanian revanchism, the protesters flew a Romanian flag over the Parliament building.) In the Iranian case, meanwhile, the people tweeting about the demonstrations were almost all in the West. "It is time to get Twitter's role in the events in Iran right," Golnaz Esfandiari wrote, this past summer, in *Foreign Policy*. "Simply put: There was no Twitter Revolution inside Iran." The cadre of prominent bloggers, like Andrew Sullivan, who championed the role of social media in Iran, Esfandiari continued, misunderstood the situation. "Western journalists who couldn't reach—or didn't bother reaching?—people on the ground in Iran simply scrolled through the English-language tweets post with tag #iranelection," she wrote. "Through it all, no one seemed to wonder why people trying to coordinate protests in Iran would be writing in any language other than Farsi."

Some of this grandiosity is to be expected. Innovators tend to be solipsists. They often want to cram every stray fact and experience into their new model. As the historian Robert Darnton has written, "The marvels of communication technology in the present have produced a false consciousness about the past—even a sense that communication has no history, or had nothing of importance to consider before the days of television and the Internet." But there is something else at work here, in the outsized enthusiasm for social media. Fifty years after one of the most extraordinary episodes of social upheaval in American history, we seem to have forgotten what activism is.

Greensboro in the early nineteen-sixties was the kind of place where racial insubordination was routinely met with violence. The four students who first sat down at the lunch counter were terrified. "I suppose if anyone had come up behind me and yelled 'Boo,' I think I would have fallen off my seat," one of them said later. On the first day, the store manager notified the police chief, who immediately sent two officers to the store. On the third day, a gang of White toughs showed up at the lunch counter and stood ostentatiously behind the protesters, ominously muttering epithets such as "burr-head nigger." A local Ku Klux Klan leader made an appearance. On Saturday, as tensions grew, someone called in a bomb threat, and the entire store had to be evacuated.

The dangers were even clearer in the Mississippi Freedom Summer Project of 1964, another of the sentinel campaigns of the civil-rights movement. The Student Nonviolent Coordinating Committee recruited hundreds of Northern, largely White unpaid volunteers to run Freedom Schools, register Black voters, and raise civil-rights awareness in the Deep South. "No one should go *anywhere* alone, but certainly not in an automobile and certainly not at night," they were instructed. Within days of arriving in Mississippi, three volunteers—Michael Schwerner, James Chaney, and Andrew Goodman—were kidnapped and killed, and, during the rest of the summer, thirty-seven Black churches were set on fire and dozens of safe houses were bombed; volunteers were beaten, shot at, arrested, and trailed by pickup trucks full of armed men. A quarter of those in the program dropped out. Activism that challenges the status quo—that attacks deeply rooted problems—is not for the faint of heart.

What makes people capable of this kind of activism? The Stanford sociologist Doug McAdam compared the Freedom Summer dropouts with the participants who stayed, and discovered that the key difference wasn't, as might be expected, ideological fervor. "*All* of the applicants—participants and withdrawals alike—emerge as highly committed, articulate supporters of the goals and values of the summer

program," he concluded. What mattered more was an applicant's degree of personal connection to the civilrights movement. All the volunteers were required to provide a list of personal contacts—the people they wanted kept apprised of their activities—and participants were far more likely than dropouts to have close friends who were also going to Mississippi. Highrisk activism, McAdam concluded, is a "strong-tie" phenomenon.

This pattern shows up again and again. One study of the Red Brigades, the Italian terrorist group of the nineteen-seventies, found that seventy per cent of recruits had at least one good friend already in the organization. The same is true of the men who joined the mujahideen in Afghanistan. Even revolutionary actions that look spontaneous, like the demonstrations in East Germany that led to the fall of the Berlin Wall, are, at core, strong-tie phenomena. The opposition movement in East Germany consisted of several hundred groups, each with roughly a dozen members. Each group was in limited contact with the others: at the time, only thirteen per cent of East Germans even had a phone. All they knew was that on Monday nights, outside St. Nicholas Church in downtown Leipzig, people gathered to voice their anger at the state. And the primary determinant of who showed up was "critical friends"—the more friends you had who were critical of the regime the more likely you were to join the protest.

So one crucial fact about the four freshmen at the Greensboro lunch counter—David Richmond, Franklin McCain, Ezell Blair, and Joseph McNeil— was their relationship with one another. McNeil was a roommate of Blair's in A. & T.'s Scott Hall dormitory. Richmond roomed with McCain one floor up, and Blair, Richmond, and McCain had all gone to Dudley High School. The four would smuggle beer into the dorm and talk late into the night in Blair and McNeil's room. They would all have remembered the murder of Emmett Till in 1955, the Montgomery bus boycott that same year, and the showdown in Little Rock in 1957. It was McNeil who brought up the idea of a sit-in at Woolworth's. They'd discussed it for nearly a month. Then McNeil came into the dorm room and asked the others if they were ready. There was a pause, and McCain said, in a way that works only with people who talk late into the night with one another, "Are you guys chicken or not?" Ezell Blair worked up the courage the next day to ask for a cup of coffee because he was flanked by his roommate and two good friends from high school.

The kind of activism associated with social media isn't like this at all. The platforms of social media are built around weak ties. Twitter is a way of following (or being followed by) people you may never have met. Facebook is a tool for efficiently managing your acquaintances, for keeping up with the people you would not otherwise be able to stay in touch with. That's why you can have a thousand "friends" on Facebook, as you never could in real life.

This is in many ways a wonderful thing. There is strength in weak ties, as the sociologist Mark Granovetter has observed. Our acquaintances—not our friends—are our greatest source of new ideas and information. The Internet lets us exploit the power of these kinds of distant connections with marvellous efficiency. It's terrific at the diffusion of innovation, interdisciplinary collaboration, seamlessly matching up buyers and sellers, and the logistical functions of the dating world. But weak ties seldom lead to high-risk activism.

In a new book called "The Dragonfly Effect: Quick, Effective, and Powerful Ways to Use Social Media to Drive Social Change," the business consultant Andy Smith and the Stanford Business School professor Jennifer Aaker tell the story of Sameer Bhatia, a young Silicon Valley entrepreneur who came down with acute myelogenous leukemia. It's a perfect illustration of social media's strengths. Bhatia needed a bone-marrow transplant, but he could not find a match among his relatives and friends. The odds were best with a donor of his ethnicity, and there were few South Asians in the national bone-marrow database. So Bhatia's business partner sent out an e-mail explaining Bhatia's plight to more than four hundred of their acquaintances, who forwarded the e-mail to their personal contacts; Facebook pages and YouTube videos were devoted to the Help Sameer campaign. Eventually, nearly twenty-five thousand new people were registered in the bone-marrow database, and Bhatia found a match.

But how did the campaign get so many people to sign up? By not asking too much of them. That's the only way you can get someone you don't really know to do something on your behalf. You can get thousands of people to sign up for a donor registry, because doing so is pretty easy. You have to send in a cheek swab and—in the highly unlikely event that your bone marrow is a good match for someone in need—spend a few hours at the hospital. Donating bone marrow isn't a trivial matter. But it doesn't involve financial or personal risk; it doesn't mean spending a summer being chased by armed men in pickup trucks. It doesn't require that you confront socially entrenched norms and practices. In fact, it's the kind of commitment that will bring only social acknowledgment and praise.

The evangelists of social media don't understand this distinction; they seem to believe that a Facebook friend is the same as a real friend and that signing up for a donor registry in Silicon Valley today is activism in the same sense as sitting at a segregated lunch counter in Greensboro in 1960. "Social networks are particularly effective at increasing motivation," Aaker and Smith write. But that's not true. Social networks are effective at increasing *participation*—by lessening the level of motivation that participation requires. The Facebook page of the Save Darfur Coalition has 1,282,339 members, who have donated an average of nine cents apiece. The next biggest Darfur charity on Facebook has 22,073 members, who have donated an average of thirty-five cents. Help Save Darfur has 2,797 members, who have given, on average, fifteen cents. A spokesperson for the Save Darfur Coalition told *Newsweek*, "We wouldn't necessarily gauge someone's value to the advocacy movement based on what they've given. This is a powerful mechanism to engage this critical population. They inform their community, attend events, volunteer. It's not something you can measure by looking at a ledger." In other words, Facebook activism succeeds not by motivating people to make a real sacrifice but by motivating them to do the things that people do when they are not motivated enough to make a real sacrifice. We are a long way from the lunch counters of Greensboro.

The students who joined the sit-ins across the South during the winter of 1960 described the movement as a "fever." But the civil-rights movement was more like a military campaign than like a contagion. In the late nineteen-fifties, there had been sixteen sit-ins in various cities throughout the South, fifteen of which were formally organized by civil-rights organizations like the [National Association for the Advancement of Colored People] N.A.A.C.P. and [Congress for Racial Equality] CORE. Possible locations for activism were scouted. Plans were drawn up. Movement activists held training sessions and retreats for would-be protesters. The Greensboro Four were a product of this groundwork: all were members of the N.A.A.C.P. Youth Council. They had close ties with the head of the local N.A.A.C.P. chapter. They had been briefed on the earlier wave of sit-ins in Durham, and had been part of a series of movement meetings in activist churches. When the sit-in movement spread from Greensboro throughout the South, it did not spread indiscriminately. It spread to those cities which had preexisting "movement centers"—a core of dedicated and trained activists ready to turn the "fever" into action.

The civil-rights movement was high-risk activism. It was also, crucially, strategic activism: a challenge to the establishment mounted with precision and discipline. The N.A.A.C.P. was a centralized organization, run from New York according to highly formalized operating procedures. At the Southern Christian Leadership Conference, Martin Luther King, Jr., was the unquestioned authority. At the center of the movement was the Black church, which had, as Aldon D. Morris points out in his superb 1984 study, "The Origins of the Civil Rights Movement," a carefully demarcated division of labor, with various standing committees and disciplined groups. "Each group was task-oriented and coordinated its activities through authority structures," Morris writes. "Individuals were held accountable for their assigned duties, and important conflicts were resolved by the minister, who usually exercised ultimate authority over the congregation."

This is the second crucial distinction between traditional activism and its online variant: social media are not about this kind of hierarchical organization. Facebook and the like are tools for building *networks*, which are the opposite, in structure and character, of hierarchies. Unlike hierarchies, with their rules and procedures, networks aren't controlled by a single central authority. Decisions are made through consensus, and the ties that bind people to the group are loose.

This structure makes networks enormously resilient and adaptable in low-risk situations. Wikipedia is a perfect example. It doesn't have an editor, sitting in New York, who directs and corrects each entry. The effort of putting together each entry is self-organized. If every entry in Wikipedia were to be erased tomorrow, the content would swiftly be restored, because that's what happens when a network of thousands spontaneously devote their time to a task.

There are many things, though, that networks don't do well. Car companies sensibly use a network to organize their hundreds of suppliers, but not to design their cars. No one believes that the articulation of a coherent design philosophy is best handled by a sprawling, leaderless organizational system. Because networks don't have a centralized leadership structure and clear lines of authority, they have real difficulty reaching consensus and setting goals. They can't think strategically; they are chronically prone to conflict and error. How do you make difficult choices about tactics or strategy or philosophical direction when everyone has an equal say?

The Palestine Liberation Organization [PLO] originated as a network, and the international-relations scholars Mette Eilstrup-Sangiovanni and Calvert Jones argue in a recent essay in *International Security* that this is why it ran into such trouble as it grew: "Structural features typical of networks—the absence of central authority, the unchecked autonomy of rival groups, and the inability to arbitrate quarrels through formal mechanisms—made the P.L.O. excessively vulnerable to outside manipulation and internal strife."

In Germany in the nineteen-seventies, they go on, "the far more unified and successful left-wing terrorists tended to organize hierarchically, with professional management and clear divisions of labor. They were concentrated geographically in universities, where they could establish central leadership, trust, and camaraderie through regular, face-to-face meetings." They seldom betrayed their comrades in arms during police interrogations. Their counterparts on the right were organized as decentralized networks, and had no such discipline. These groups were regularly infiltrated, and members, once arrested, easily gave up their comrades. Similarly, Al Qaeda was most dangerous when it was a unified hierarchy. Now that it has dissipated into a network, it has proved far less effective.

The drawbacks of networks scarcely matter if the network isn't interested in systemic change—if it just wants to frighten or humiliate or make a splash—or if it doesn't need to think strategically. But if you're taking on a powerful and organized establishment you have to be a hierarchy. The Montgomery bus boycott required the participation of tens of thousands of people who depended on public transit to get to and from work each day. It lasted a *year*. In order to persuade those people to stay true to the cause, the boycott's organizers tasked each local Black church with maintaining morale, and put together a free alternative private carpool service, with forty-eight dispatchers and forty-two pickup stations. Even the White Citizens Council, King later said, conceded that the carpool system moved with "military precision." By the time King came to Birmingham, for the climactic showdown with Police Commissioner Eugene (Bull) Connor, he had a budget of a million dollars, and a hundred full-time staff members on the ground, divided into operational units. The operation itself was divided into steadily escalating phases, mapped out in advance. Support was maintained through consecutive mass meetings rotating from church to church around the city.

Boycotts and sit-ins and nonviolent confrontations—which were the weapons of choice for the civil-rights movement—are high-risk strategies. They leave little room for conflict and error. The moment even one protester deviates from the script and responds to provocation, the moral legitimacy of the entire protest is compromised. Enthusiasts for social media would no doubt have us believe that King's task in Birmingham would have been made infinitely easier had he been able to communicate with his followers through Facebook, and contented himself with tweets from a Birmingham jail. But networks are messy: think of the ceaseless pattern of correction and revision, amendment and debate, that characterizes Wikipedia. If Martin Luther King, Jr., had tried to do a wiki-boycott in Montgomery, he would have been steamrollered by the White power structure. And of what use would a digital communication tool be in a town where ninety-eight per cent of

the Black community could be reached every Sunday morning at church? The things that King needed in Birmingham—discipline and strategy—were things that online social media cannot provide.

The bible of the social-media movement is Clay Shirky's "Here Comes Everybody." Shirky, who teaches at New York University, sets out to demonstrate the organizing power of the Internet, and he begins with the story of Evan, who worked on Wall Street, and his friend Ivanna, after she left her smart phone, an expensive Sidekick, on the back seat of a New York City taxicab. The telephone company transferred the data on Ivanna's lost phone to a new phone, whereupon she and Evan discovered that the Sidekick was now in the hands of a teenager from Queens, who was using it to take photographs of herself and her friends.

When Evan e-mailed the teenager, Sasha, asking for the phone back, she replied that his "White ass" didn't deserve to have it back. Miffed, he set up a Web page with her picture and a description of what had happened. He forwarded the link to his friends, and they forwarded it to their friends. Someone found the MySpace page of Sasha's boyfriend, and a link to it found its way onto the site. Someone found her address online and took a video of her home while driving by; Evan posted the video on the site. The story was picked up by the news filter Digg. Evan was now up to ten e-mails a minute. He created a bulletin board for his readers to share their stories, but it crashed under the weight of responses. Evan and Ivanna went to the police, but the police filed the report under "lost," rather than "stolen," which essentially closed the case. "By this point millions of readers were watching," Shirky writes, "and dozens of mainstream news outlets had covered the story." Bowing to the pressure, the N.Y.P.D. reclassified the item as "stolen." Sasha was arrested, and Evan got his friend's Sidekick back.

Shirky's argument is that this is the kind of thing that could never have happened in the pre-Internet age—and he's right. Evan could never have tracked down Sasha. The story of the Sidekick would never have been publicized. An army of people could never have been assembled to wage this fight. The police wouldn't have bowed to the pressure of a lone person who had misplaced something as trivial as a cell phone. The story, to Shirky, illustrates "the ease and speed with which a group can be mobilized for the right kind of cause" in the Internet age.

Shirky considers this model of activism an upgrade. But it is simply a form of organizing which favors the weak-tie connections that give us access to information over the strong-tie connections that help us persevere in the face of danger. It shifts our energies from organizations that promote strategic and disciplined activity and toward those which promote resilience and adaptability. It makes it easier for activists to express themselves, and harder for that expression to have any impact. The instruments of social media are well suited to making the existing social order more efficient. They are not a natural enemy of the status quo. If you are of the opinion that all the world needs is a little buffing around the edges, this should not trouble you. But if you think that there are still lunch counters out there that need integrating it ought to give you pause.

Shirky ends the story of the lost Sidekick by asking, portentously, "What happens next?"—no doubt imagining future waves of digital protesters. But he has already answered the question. What happens next is more of the same. A networked, weak-tie world is good at things like helping Wall Streeters get phones back from teenage girls. *Viva la revolución*.

71. THE REAL ROSA PARKS

Many of the stories that we hear about social activists such as Rosa Parks can lead us to believe that in order to create social change, courageous individuals must take heroic stands without doubts or fear. This inaccurate telling of history and of the reality of social activism, Loeb argues, obscures the fact that most social movements begin, and succeed, with small steps—steps that all of us can take in order to create social change.

We learn much from how we present our heroes. A few years ago, on Martin Luther King Day, I was interviewed on CNN. So was Rosa Parks, by phone from Los Angeles. "We're very honored to have her," said the host. "Rosa Parks was the woman who wouldn't go to the back of the bus. She wouldn't get up and give her seat in the White section to a White person. That set in motion the year-long bus boycott in Montgomery. It earned Rosa Parks the title of 'mother of the civil rights movement.'"

I was excited to hear Parks's voice and to be part of the same show. But it occurred to me that the host's description—the story's standard rendition—stripped the Montgomery boycott of all of its context. Before refusing to give up her bus seat, Parks had been active for 12 years in the local NAACP chapter, serving as its secretary. The summer before her arrest, she had attended a 10-day training session at Tennessee's labor and civil rights organizing school, the Highlander Center, where she'd met an older generation of civil rights activists, including South Carolina teacher Septima Clark, and discussed the recent Supreme Court decision banning "separate-but-equal" schools. During this period of involvement and education, Parks had become familiar with previous challenges to segregation: Another Montgomery bus boycott, 50 years earlier, successfully eased some restrictions; a bus boycott in Baton Rouge won limited gains two years before Parks was arrested; and the previous spring, a young Montgomery woman had also refused to move to the back of the bus, causing the NAACP to consider a legal challenge until they realized that she was unmarried and pregnant, and therefore a poor symbol for a campaign.

In short, Rosa Parks didn't make a spur-of-the-moment decision. She didn't singlehandedly give birth to the civil rights efforts, but she was part of an existing movement for change, at a time when success was far from certain. We all know Parks's name, but few of us know about Montgomery NAACP head E. D. Nixon, who served as one of her mentors and first got Martin Luther King Jr. involved. Nixon carried people's suitcases on the trains and was active in the Brotherhood of Sleeping Car Porters, the union founded by legendary civil rights activist A. Philip Randolph. Nixon played a key role in the campaign. But no one talks of him, any more than they talk of JoAnn Robinson, who taught nearby at an underfunded and segregated Black college and whose Women's Political Council distributed the initial leaflets following Parks's arrest. Without the often lonely work of people like Nixon, Randolph, and Robinson, Parks would likely have never taken her stand, and if she had, it would never have had the same impact.

This in no way diminishes the power and historical importance of Parks's refusal to give up her seat.

But it reminds us that this tremendously consequential act, along with everything that followed, depended on all the humble and frustrating work that Parks and others undertook earlier on. It also reminds us that Parks's initial step of getting involved was just as courageous and critical as the stand on the bus that all of us have heard about.

People like Parks shape our models of social commitment. Yet the conventional retelling of her story creates a standard so impossible to meet that it may actually make it harder for us to get involved, inadvertently stripping away Parks's most powerful lessons of hope.

The conventional portrayal suggests that social activists come out of nowhere, to suddenly take dramatic stands. It implies that we act with the greatest impact when we act alone, at least initially. And that change occurs instantly, as opposed to building on a series of often-invisible actions. The myth of Parks as lone activist reinforces a notion that anyone who takes a committed public stand, or at least an effective one, has to be a larger-than-life figure—someone with more time, energy, courage, vision, or knowledge than any normal person could ever possess. This belief pervades our society, in part because the media tend not to represent historical change as the work of ordinary human beings, which it almost always is.

Once we enshrine our heroes on pedestals, it becomes hard for mere mortals to measure up in our eyes. However individuals speak out, we're tempted to dismiss their motives, knowledge, and tactics as insufficiently grand or heroic. We fault them for not being in command of every fact and figure, or for being unable to answer every question put to them. We fault ourselves as well, for not knowing every detail, or for harboring uncertainties and doubts. We find it hard to imagine that ordinary human beings with ordinary flaws might make a critical difference in worthy social causes.

Yet those who act have their own imperfections and ample reasons to hold back. "I think it does us all a disservice," says a young African American activist in Atlanta named Sonya Tinsley, "when people who work for social change are presented as saints—so much more noble than the rest of us. We get a false sense that from the moment they were born they were

called to act, never had doubts, were bathed in a circle of light. But I'm much more inspired learning how people succeeded despite their failings and uncertainties. It's a much less intimidating image. It makes me feel like I have a shot at changing things too."

Sonya had recently attended a talk given by one of Martin Luther King's Morehouse professors in which he mentioned how much King had struggled when he first came to college, getting only a C, for example, in his first philosophy course. "I found that very inspiring, when I heard it," Sonya said, "given all that King achieved. It made me feel that just about anything was possible."

Our culture's misreading of the Rosa Parks story speaks to a more general collective amnesia, where we forget the examples that might most inspire our courage, hope, and conscience. Apart from obvious times of military conflict, most of us know next to nothing of the many battles ordinary men and women fought to preserve freedom, expand the sphere of democracy, and create a more just society. Of the abolitionist and civil rights movements, we at best recall a few key leaders—and often misread their actual stories. We know even less about the turn-of-the-century populists who challenged entrenched economic interests and fought for a "cooperative commonwealth." Who these days can describe the union movements that ended 80-hour work weeks at near-starvation wages? Who knows the origin of the Social Security system, now threatened by systematic attempts to privatize it? How did the women's suffrage movement spread to hundreds of communities and gather enough strength to prevail?

As memories of these events disappear, we lose the knowledge of mechanisms that grassroots social movements have used successfully in the past to shift public sentiment and challenge entrenched institutional power. Equally lost are the means by which their participants managed to keep on and eventually prevail in circumstances at least as harsh as those we face today.

Think again about the different ways one can frame Rosa Parks's historic action. In the prevailing myth, Parks decides to act almost on a whim, in isolation. She's a virgin to politics, a holy innocent. The lesson seems to be that if any of us suddenly got the urge to do something equally heroic, that would be great. Of course most of us don't, so we wait our entire lives to find the ideal moment.

Parks's real story conveys a far more empowering moral. She begins with seemingly modest steps. She goes to a meeting, and then another, helping build the community that in turn supported her path. Hesitant at first, she gains confidence as she speaks out. She keeps on despite a profoundly uncertain context, as she and others act as best they can to challenge deeply entrenched injustices, with little certainty of results. Had she and others given up after her tenth or eleventh year of commitment, we might never have heard of Montgomery.

Parks's journey suggests that change is the product of deliberate, incremental action, whereby we join together to try to shape a better world. Sometimes our struggles will fail, as did many earlier efforts of Parks, her peers, and her predecessors. Other times they may bear modest fruits. And at times they will trigger a miraculous outpouring of courage and heart—as happened with her arrest and all that followed. For only when we act despite all our uncertainties and doubts do we have the chance to shape history.

MEGAN M. TESENE

72. POLITICAL POLARIZATION IN CONTEMPORARY AMERICAN SOCIETY

The political system in America has become marked by polarization, ideological differences, and partisanship; it seems our political parties, leaders, and citizens have grown farther apart over time, leading to animosity and political gridlock. Tesene examines this trend, explaining how, in what ways, and why this shift has occurred, as well as its effects on our political system and on the average American. She also discusses major cultural and social trends predicted to occur within the next generation and their potential to change polarization in the political system (e.g., the growth of minority and immigrant populations, the decline of the working class, and the resolution of the "culture wars") and outlines strategies to begin to improve the current political climate.

Although partisanship and animosity between Republicans and Democrats have long contextualized the American sociopolitical landscape, the ideological distinction between the two parties has grown more prevalent since the 1970s (Cohn, 2014; DeSilver, 2014; Fiorina, 2014; Haidt & Hetherington, 2012; Levendusky, 2009). Prior to this shift, the Republican and Democratic parties both had strong liberal and conservative representation among their constituents and elected officials (Cohn, 2014; Haidt & Hetherington, 2012; Levendusky, 2009). Whereas liberal Republicans and conservative Democrats were once commonplace, the present-day political arena has become increasingly segregated on the basis of political ideology (Cohn, 2014; DeSilver, 2014; Fiorina, 2014; Haidt & Hetherington, 2012; Levendusky, 2009). Beginning in the 1960s, the Democratic Party began more closely associating with the civil rights movement, whereas Republicans aligned themselves with the Religious Right (Haidt & Hetherington, 2012),

creating distinct partisan homogeneity that previously did not exist (Fiorina, 2014). Issues that once divided the diverse membership of each political party—such as abortion, homosexuality, immigration, or gun ownership—now serve as points of unification and as a means to rally the base behind specific, common goals.

With each election cycle, political leaders take clearly defined "liberal" or "conservative" positions on social, cultural, and economic issues (Cohn, 2014; Fiorina, 2014; Levendusky, 2009). They distinguish themselves from the opposing party, delineating their own party's platform along clearly conservative or liberal lines. As political leaders define their parties as explicitly conservative or liberal, Americans are better able to sort themselves into the party that most represents their values (Cohn, 2014; Levendusky, 2009). These hard-and-fast ideological party lines have led liberals to the Democratic Party and conservatives to the Republican Party. Political analysts refer to this

Original to *Focus on Social Problems: A Contemporary Reader* process as "political sorting," and in addition to dramatically shaping partisan affiliation, it occurs geographically and socially (Abdullah, 2013, 2014; Cohn, 2014; DeSilver, 2014; Fiorina, 2014; Levendusky, 2009; Tuschman, 2014). Compared to their counterparts from the mid- to late twentieth century, present-day Americans are more likely to socialize with, marry, and live near those who are like themselves on a variety of social measures, including political affiliation (Abdullah, 2013, 2014; DeSilver, 2014; Pew Research Center, 2014; Tuschman, 2014); this is true for both conservatives and liberals, although self-segregating appears to be more common among conservatives than it is among liberals (Pew Research Center, 2014).

Such trends should not be misconstrued to imply that Americans are becoming more extreme or radical in their political views (Fiorina, 2014). Rather, they are using conservative and liberal ideology to gradually sort themselves into two distinct political "camps" (Abdullah, 2013, 2014; Fiorina, 2014; Levendusky, 2009). In this reading, I discuss how increasing political polarization is shaping the American public in a myriad of ways. In addition, I examine the effects of polarization on elected officials, governing bodies, and the broader sociopolitical landscape in general. I further describe the potential forms that political polarization may take in our country's future and highlight some of the bipartisan policy changes that may aid in creating a more efficient government and politically engaged electorate.

A POLARIZED PUBLIC

In 2014, the Pew Research Center carried out one of the largest nationally representative studies on American politics. The study sought to understand "the nature and scope of political polarization in the American public, and how it interrelates with government, society, and people's personal lives" (Pew Research Center, 2014). The study consists of data collected from two independent surveys. The first surveyed 10,013 American adults via telephone using 10 policy-oriented questions, which were dichotomously indexed as liberal or conservative positions (Doherty, 2014; Fiorina, 2014; Pew Research Center, 2014). Questions focused on issues such as health care, abortion, immigration,

gun control, and other social, economic, and political issues (Pew Research Center, 2014). The second survey recruited a subset ($n = 3,308$) of the original respondents who identified themselves as active Internet users. The data discussed within this article highlight Pew's first and third reports on political polarization. The first report examines growing ideological uniformity and partisan antipathy among the American public using both independent surveys (Pew Research Center, 2014). The third report focuses on American media habits within the context of increasing political polarization (Mitchell et al., 2014), and relies upon data solely from the subset of active Internet users.

It is important to emphasize that this research does not focus on extremism or intensity of liberal–conservative ideology. Rather, it identifies and analyzes ideological consistency—that is, whether Americans' political views are consistently liberal, consistently conservative, or a mix of liberalism and conservatism (Fiorina, 2014; Pew Research Center, 2014). Consistent liberals and consistent conservatives are not necessarily on the far left or the far right ideologically. Rather, they are those who consistently supported liberal or conservative positions when presented with policy-related questions. Those that the study identifies as being in the center should not be understood to be centrist or moderate on the political spectrum (Fiorina, 2014; Pew Research Center, 2014). Instead, they are those who expressed mixed views that span the political ideology spectrum. For instance, someone may have conservative views on gun control but a liberal position on abortion. Such views may be extreme, moderate, or weak; however, the study does not measure the intensity of those views. Ultimately, the findings should be understood to reflect ideological consistency, not intensity.

Perhaps the most significant trend identified within the Pew Report (2014) is in regard to increased ideological consistency. According to the report, the proportion of Americans who are consistently liberal or conservative has doubled from 10 percent in 1994 to 21 percent in 2014. As highlighted above, an ideological sorting has been taking place since the 1970s with liberals identifying as Democrats and conservatives identifying as Republican (Cohn, 2014; DeSilver, 2014; Fiorina, 2014; Haidt & Hetherington,

2012; Levendusky, 2009). Ideological overlap is diminishing within each party and the data reflect these trends, showing that today's median Republican is 97 percent more conservative than the median Democrat and median Democrats are 95 percent more liberal than median Republicans (Kiley, 2017). This gap has been increasing over time; in 1994, those percentages were at 70 and 64, respectively (Doherty, 2014; Pew Research Center, 2014). Whereas liberals and conservatives once constituted both parties, they are now segregated into distinct partisan camps (Abdullah, 2013, 2014).

As the two parties become more ideologically distinct from one another, their mutual feelings of distrust and antipathy have grown stronger toward those across the political aisle (Doherty, 2014; Pew Research Center, 2014). In fact, the number of Americans who view members of the "opposing" political party in a negative light has more than doubled in the past two decades (Pew Research Center, 2014). An earlier study confirms this trend, noting that since the Clinton administration, Republicans' and Democrats' dislike for one another has become more intense (Haidt & Hetherington, 2012). What's even more telling of the growing animosity and distrust between the two parties is that 27 percent of Democrats and 36 percent of Republicans view the other party and its policies as a "threat to the nation's well-being" (Doherty, 2014; Pew Research Center, 2014). Antipathy appears to be connected to ideological consistency because those who have the most partisan views are the ones most likely to express negativity toward the other party (Pew Research Center, 2014).

The report further notes that partisan antipathy, as well as ideological consistency, appears to drive the desire to be politically engaged and active. If one views the opposing party and its policies as inherently threatening, one may be more inclined to participate in the political process. Consequently, compromise and bipartisan politics are considered less desirable among consistent conservatives and liberals (Doherty, 2014; Pew Research Center, 2014). According to Pew Research Center (2014), these groups view the goal of compromise as getting what they want, while not giving in to the other party. For those who view the opposing party and its beliefs as inherently dangerous,

bipartisanship itself appears to be a threat because it would enable those presumably harmful values to be implemented.

In addition to propelling a liberal–conservative segregation of the two parties, polarization also serves to sort liberals and conservatives both geographically and socially (Abdullah, 2013, 2014; Cohn, 2014; DeSilver, 2014; Fiorina, 2014; Levendusky, 2009; Pew Research Center, 2014; Tuschman, 2014). Both Republicans and Democrats prefer to live in communities where people share their ideological beliefs; however, this expressed desire is stronger among Republicans (Pew Research Center, 2014). Political ideology further shapes the type of neighborhoods and communities one hopes to live in. Whereas conservatives want to live in large homes that are far apart, liberals prefer smaller houses that are closer together in neighborhoods that are "walkable" (Doherty, 2014; Pew Research Center, 2014). Conservatives also have a stronger preference to live among people who share their religious faith. This difference was the most pronounced between consistent conservatives and liberals, with 57 percent of consistent conservatives and 17 percent of consistent liberals expressing such a desire (Pew Research Center, 2014). Liberals as a whole are more likely to desire living in neighborhoods that are racially and ethnically diverse; however, the contrast between consistent liberals and conservatives is once again stark. Whereas 76 percent of consistent liberals preferred racial and ethnic diversity in their communities, only 20 percent of consistent conservatives responded in kind (Pew Research Center, 2014).

Political polarization is also associated with media consumption habits as outlined in the third Pew report (Mitchell et al., 2014). Both conservatives and liberals tend to consume media that is consistent with their own ideological perspective, and there is little overlap between the two in terms of their choices of news sources (Mitchell et al., 2014). One of the more marked differences is that whereas conservatives tend to rely on one primary media source (Fox News), liberals have more diverse media consumption patterns, relying on a handful of news media outlets such as CNN, MSNBC, NPR, and PBS (Mitchell et al., 2014). Another important difference is that conservatives were more likely than liberals to express distrust of the media sources identified in the study. Whereas conservatives are more likely to have social media communities that are ideologically similar, liberals are more likely to "defriend" someone for political reasons (Mitchell et al., 2014). This trend is not particularly surprising, considering that conservatives are more likely than liberals to have friends who are ideologically similar on issues of politics and government (Mitchell et al., 2014).

These self-segregating patterns help to create what Pew regards as "ideological silos" or "echo chambers" where conservatives and liberals are isolated from one another and surrounded by friends, family, and communities that are ideologically homogeneous. In consuming media and creating personal, political, and social media communities that are ideologically similar, they are less likely to interact with those who have differing values and beliefs (Doherty, 2014; Mitchell et al., 2014; Pew Research Center, 2014). Immersion in these ideological silos can further exacerbate ideological homogeneity and partisan antipathy (Pew Research Center, 2014). In fact, in 2018, 53 percent of Americans reported that talking about politics with people they disagreed with was stressful and frustrating (rather than interesting and informative), an increase from spring 2016 (during the primaries leading up the 2016 presidential election) (Pew Research Center, 2018). Moreover, despite the common adage that talking with people who differ in political stance can reveal that the two sides have more in common than previously believed, 63 percent of American reported that after talking with someone they disagreed with politically, they actually felt they had *less* in common with them (Pew Research Center, 2018).

As this political sorting takes place, the center—made up of those with mixed ideological views—continues to narrow (Doherty, 2014; Pew Research Center, 2014). Whereas almost half (49 percent) of the U.S. adult population expressed a combination of conservative and liberal ideology in 1994 and 2004, that number has decreased to 39 percent by 2014 and continued to decline to 32 percent by 2017. They also differ from those who have more partisan political perspectives. They tend to have more politically diverse friends and live in politically mixed communities; they express less negativity and antipathy toward either political party; they are less inclined to view

partisan policies as a "threat to the nation;" and they are more likely to prefer congressional compromise and bipartisanship rather than "getting their way." Although they constitute the majority, they are often the least interested and least engaged at each stage of the political process (Doherty, 2014: Pew Research Center, 2014).

On the other hand, those who are the most consistent ideologically are the most active and engaged politically (Doherty, 2014; Pew Research Center, 2014)—they also make up just 21 percent of American adults. Despite their smaller numbers, their active engagement at every stage of the political process significantly shapes the broader sociopolitical landscape in America. They fund campaigns and candidates of their liking, help elect those candidates to positions of power, and actively work to ensure that the only candidates who remain in office are those who toe the party line (Abdullah, 2013, 2014). Their disproportionate representation during caucus, primary, and general elections ensures that their preferred candidates are the ones who are elected and reelected. Compounded with the inactive and somewhat apathetic position of those with mixed political ideologies, they have helped to create and sustain one of the most politically polarized Congresses since the Civil War and Reconstruction (DeSilver, 2014; Haidt & Hetherington, 2012; Hare et al., 2014).

CONGRESSIONAL POLARIZATION: TRENDS AND OUTCOMES

Although it is not clear whether congressional polarization started before or after public polarization (DeSilver, 2014), there does appear to be a cyclical relationship between congressional and public polarization: (1) polarizing political leaders shape the ideological party platform—aligning with either conservative or liberal values (Cohn, 2014; Fiorina, 2014; Levendusky, 2009); (2) the public then sorts itself into the party that best fits their views—liberals become Democrats and conservatives become Republican (Abdullah, 2013, 2014; Cohn, 2014; DeSilver, 2014; Fiorina, 2014; Levendusky, 2009; Tuschman, 2014); (3) partisans support, elect, and reelect political leaders who strictly follow the party line (Abdullah,

2013, 2014); (4) those leaders continue to push their party's increasingly rigid ideological agenda—indeed, if they do not, they will lose their positions (Abdullah, 2013, 2014); and (5) the process continues.

A consequence of this cyclical process is that congressional polarization is currently at an all-time high. Using scores that identify and track congressional roll call votes on a liberal–conservative scale, Keith Poole and Howard Rosenthal (2015) mapped congressional polarization trends from 1879 to the present (DeSilver, 2014; Haidt & Hetherington, 2012; Hare et al., 2012; Matthews, 2013). Their analysis indicates that congressional leadership was significantly polarized just after the Civil War and Reconstruction; polarization dramatically decreased after World War I, remaining low through World War II and its postwar era; during the 1960s and 1970s, Congress started becoming polarized once more; and in the 1980s, the parties became more ideologically homogeneous, leading to political sorting, and this trend has continued to the present day (Haidt & Hetherington, 2012).

The most recent Congresses have been described as the most polarized to date (Hare et al., 2014; Matthews, 2013). Not surprisingly, they've also been the least effective in congressional history (Bump, 2014), no doubt one of the causes for their "all-time low" ratings (Bipartisan Policy Center, 2014; Riffkin, 2014). As Democratic and Republican leaders grow apart ideologically, they become less capable of compromise and consequently, less capable of passing legislation and doing the jobs they were elected to do (DeSilver, 2014; Haidt & Hetherington, 2012; Hare et al., 2014; Matthews, 2013). Interestingly, congressional leaders' inability to push through legislation—often because of gridlock and a lack of bipartisanship—hasn't caused voters to push them out of office. In fact, although American voters "overwhelmingly disapprove of the job Congress" is currently doing, they continue to reelect most members back into office each election cycle (Mendes, 2013). Polls show that despite broader congressional approval ratings—or rather, a lack thereof—most Americans have a positive view of their own representatives (Mendes, 2013). Each election term, they reelect their local and regional representatives (Mendes, 2013) and thus contribute to the perpetuation of congressional discord.

Those voters who are consistently conservative or liberal actually prefer that their elected officials avoid bipartisan compromise (Doherty, 2014; Pew Research Center, 2014). As mentioned earlier, these individuals tend to view the goal of compromise as getting what they want, rather than giving in and working with those across the aisle (Doherty, 2014; Pew Research Center, 2014). However, as a whole, most Americans do not agree with this sentiment (Pew Research Center, 2014) and prefer that their elected leaders work together rather than against one another (Bipartisan Policy Center, 2014; Pew Research Center, 2014). But without substantial change, such as an increase in political engagement among the majority or a decrease in partisan political ideology, it is likely that these trends will persist (Haidt & Hetherington, 2012; Hare et al., 2014).

A LOOK TO THE FUTURE

In their discussion of increasing political polarization and its effects, Hare et al. (2014) outline four distinct pathways polarization may take. The first, and most unlikely, is what they describe as a "hot decline in polarization." This would take place if our current two-party system simply broke down, much like it did just before the Civil War. Another possibility is that polarization could become even worse. If Democrats were to shift drastically to the left—embracing more European-style or social democratic principles—compromise and bipartisanship would become even less likely (Hare et al., 2014). The two more realistic options are that "polarization will stabilize at or near current levels for the foreseeable future" or we will instead witness what the researchers deem a "cooling-off period," where both parties shift back toward the ideological center (Hare et al., 2014). If such a shift took place, candidates with moderate or mixed conservative–liberal ideologies would become more commonplace (Hare et al., 2014).

In an analysis of demographic and geographic shifts taking place in the United States, Ruy Teixeira (2008) argues that the "cultural wars" that currently shape the contemporary American politicosphere are nearing their end. As these social and cultural issues become less important to a changing American electorate, the political polarization we are currently accustomed to will gradually decline, taking its grid-locking and lack of congressional productivity along with it (Teixeira, 2008). According to Teixeira (2008), ongoing demographic and geographic changes will likely take us back to the ideological center, and that center will likely shift as well—causing both Democratic and Republican parties to reassess their platforms and goals to remain relevant to an ever-evolving American people.

Teixeira (2008) highlights several important trends that will significantly shape the face of the American electorate and, in doing so, will alter the American political landscape. As the population ex-pands, we'll see emergent suburbs and exurbs grow on the "metropolitan fringes" of urban cities (Lang et al., 2008; Teixeira, 2008). Older suburbs will grow at a slower rate, urbanizing and becoming home to increasingly diverse communities (Lang et al., 2008; Teixeira, 2008). In doing so, they will likely become increasingly liberal (Lang et al., 2008; Teixeira, 2008). Traditionally, the farther out a community is from an urban core, the more likely it is to be both conserva-tive and Republican (Teixeira, 2008). Although com-munities on the metropolitan fringe are expanding more rapidly, population densities of the urban core and urbanizing suburbs are significantly higher, thus retaining their political and electorate power.

Another important trend that will shape the politi-cal landscape is the growing minority and immigrant populations who tend to lean more Democratic (Frey, 2008; Teixeira, 2008). Hispanic, Asian, and Black communities are growing at much faster rates than are non-Hispanic Whites. However, it must be noted that the electoral impact of Hispanics and Asians is weakened because many are either younger than 18 or currently not citizens (Frey, 2008; Teixeira, 2008). In addition, the current tendency of minority and im-migrant communities to align themselves with the Democratic Party should not be taken for granted or assumed to be stable over the long haul (Frey, 2008; Teixeira, 2008). Region can play an important role in shaping voting patterns among minority communi-ties. For instance, Hispanics living in the South vote more conservatively than their counterparts on the West Coast (Frey, 2008; Teixeira, 2008).

As communities of color expand, the White work-ing class—a group that has long existed as a large and powerful voting bloc of the American electorate—is both transforming and declining in number (Abramowitz & Teixeira, 2008; Teixeira, 2008). Once characterized by blue-collar and manufacturing posi-tions, today's White working class is seeing increases in level of education and in median income (Abramowitz & Teixeira, 2008; Teixeira, 2008). Changes in the eco-nomic structure have also led to a shift toward the ser-vice sector and low-level White-collar service positions (Abramowitz & Teixeira, 2008; Teixeira, 2008). In the past, White working-class communities tended to vote primarily Democratic; however, in recent decades they have more closely affiliated with the Republican Party. Although the working class is on the decline, the upper middle class—those households making $100,000 or more—is growing. These educated pro-fessionals tend to have mixed political ideologies—being socially liberal and economically moderate (Abramowitz & Teixeira, 2008; Teixeira, 2008). Thus, both political parties will need to vie for their support or shift their political ideology to be more palatable to this expanding voting bloc (Abramowitz & Teixeira, 2008; Teixeira, 2008).

Smith (2008) and Teixeira (2008) also identify the shifting American family structure as a potential source of the changing political landscape. The institu-tion of marriage is no longer as dominant as it once was. Divorce, single-parent households, cohabitation, and never-married and same-sex families are all be-coming more prevalent. In fact, those families who are described as "married with children" constitute less than 25 percent of American households (Smith, 2008; Teixeira, 2008). Whereas married voters are more likely to vote Republican, never-married persons are more likely to vote Democratic (Smith, 2008; Teixeira, 2008). Married couples with children are more likely to vote Republican, whereas single-parent households are significantly more likely to vote Democratic. As cul-tural mores change, we should expect an increase in the number of nontraditional families who will likely be more politically liberal (Smith, 2008; Teixeira, 2008).

Another change we are seeing is an increase in both secular and Evangelical populations (Green & Dionne, 2008; Teixeira, 2008). Secular voters are often liberal, whereas Evangelicals are overwhelmingly conservative. The researchers also note how Americans, as a whole, are becoming less religiously observant and that one's level of observance significantly shapes whether he or she votes Republican or Democrat (Green & Dionne, 2008; Teixeira, 2008). Those who are more religiously observant tend to vote Republican, whereas those who are less observant often vote for the Democratic Party (Green & Dionne, 2008; Teixeira, 2008). Noting the diverse range of issues facing Americans today, such as global warming, increasing economic inequality, and America's role in foreign policy, the researchers speculate that the cultural issues that often pit conservatives and liberals against one another are going to become less important over time (Green & Dionne, 2008; Teixeira, 2008). Along with other demographic changes, which will likely liberalize views on social and cultural issues, debate on such issues will become less heated and less polarized.

It is also possible that political polarization could decrease with generational changes (Haidt & Hetherington, 2012; Keeter, 2008; Teixeira, 2008). Indeed, each consecutive generational cohort becomes increasingly liberal, with Millennials being the most liberal of any age group (Kiley & Dimock, 2014; Lauter, 2014). As younger generations become older, start taking on political leadership positions, and begin constituting the majority of active voters, we could likely see a gradual decrease in polarization and, ultimately, an increase in legislative compromise (Haidt & Hetherington, 2012). Although each of these trends may help to lessen the current antagonisms between political parties, additional efforts will be needed to create substantive change.

STRATEGIES FOR CHANGE

In 2013, the Bipartisan Policy Center brought together engaged citizens, elected officials, and various "issue experts" from across the political spectrum to form a Commission on Political Reform (Bipartisan Policy Center, 2014). The commission worked toward identifying various strategies that might be implemented to help remedy some of the diverse social problems exacerbated by political polarization. According to the commission's report, there is a growing sense of

distrust between Republicans and Democrats. Each party fears that the other is making extensive efforts to manipulate the electoral and legislative processes. In addition, many Americans are frustrated with legislators and their inability to do the job they were elected to do. The antagonism between parties and the distrust for the electoral process and, by extension, our government, has carried over into the American psyche—creating an apathetic and unengaged electorate (Bipartisan Policy Center, 2014).

Given these concerns, the commission identifies three key areas to focus on: electoral system reform, congressional reform, and encouraging Americans' civic engagement (Bipartisan Policy Center, 2014). Although they make several suggestions for how to address these key areas, I will highlight only a handful of their proposals. To improve the electoral system, they suggest making efforts to increase voter registration and participation and to develop new forms of candidate selection. In addition, they argue that trust for the electoral process can be improved if there is more transparency in political contributions. Americans have the right to know how politicians, their campaigns, and their political action committees (PACs) are being funded.

In regard to congressional reform, the report identifies many strategies for ensuring the government becomes more functional than it is at present. Many suggestions address increasing communication and interaction between the two parties. They propose that the House and Senate synchronize their schedules and be required to have regular five-day workweeks. Since Newt Gingrich changed the legislative calendar in the mid-1990s, most legislators live in their home states rather than in Washington—thus preventing them from having face time and developing positive working relationships with other legislators (Haidt & Hetherington, 2012). Many fly in on Tuesday and out on Thursday, wasting time in transit instead of building relationships and networking with colleagues face-to-face (Haidt & Hetherington, 2012). Increasing expectations of fundraising further exacerbates this distance between congressional parties. Instead of performing their legislative responsibilities and connecting with their colleagues, congressional leaders spend a significant portion of their workdays fundraising and campaigning (Grim & Siddiqui, 2013; Kroll, 2013).

They also propose that the president meet with congressional leaders at least once a month—a practical approach, but one not currently implemented. In addition, they argue it is important that congressional committees pay special attention to minority members because all members should have a voice and the opportunity to structure legislative bills (Bipartisan Policy Center, 2014).

Values that once defined a publicly engaged American electorate are falling by the wayside. Fewer and fewer Americans are volunteering. Charitable donations are decreasing, and few see the appeal or benefit of pursuing office themselves. The commission contends that to have a strong democratic society, we must have an educated and engaged American citizenry. Some suggestions include efforts at the collegiate and university levels. By offering diverse resources, curricula, and developmental opportunities to their students, institutions of higher learning can cultivate a student body that is politically informed, impassioned, and engaged. They also suggest that all Americans aged 18 to 28 years give "one year of full service to their communities or nation" via civilian, military, volunteer, or other nonprofit organizations (Bipartisan Policy Center, 2014:9). Furthermore, they argue that the federal government must increase opportunities and funding to organizations such as Ameri-Corps, Vista, and the Peace Corps. These efforts, in addition to those highlighted above, are just some of the ways that we can begin instituting change, making both our government and its citizenry better suited to address the diverse and challenging issues that our country faces today.

REFERENCES

Abdullah, Halimah. 2013. "It's Your Fault: How Our 'Tribes' Help Create Gridlock in Congress." *CNN News*. Retrieved March 21, 2015, from http://www.cnn.com/2013/02/06/politics/congress-redistrict-fault.

Abdullah, Halimah. 2014. "Partisan Politics in Congress the Product of a More Polarized Electorate." *CNN News*. Retrieved March 20, 2015, from http://www.cnn.com/2014/06/12/politics/pew-survey-society-polarization.

Abramowitz, Alan, and Ruy Teixeira. 2008. ""The Decline of the White Working Class and the Rise of a Mass Upper-Middle Class." Pp. 109–143 in *Red, Blue & Purple America: The Future of Election Demographics*, edited by Ruy Teixeira. Washington, DC: Brookings Institution Press.

Bipartisan Policy Center. 2014. "Governing in a Polarized America: A Bipartisan Blueprint to Strengthen Our Democracy, Executive Summary." *Bipartisan Policy Center*. Retrieved March 20, 2015, from http://bipartisanpolicy.org/wp-content/uploads/sites/default/files/files/BPC%20CPR%20Executive%20Summary.pdf.

Bump, Philip. 2014. "The 113th Congress Is Historically Good at Not Passing Bills." *The Washington Post*. Retrieved March 23, 2015, from http://www.washingtonpost.com/blogs/the-fix/wp/2014/07/09/the-113th-congress-is-historically-good-at-not-passing-bills.

Cohn, Nate. 2014. "Polarization Is Dividing American Society, Not Just Politics." *The New York Times*. Retrieved March 20, 2015, from http://www.nytimes.com/2014/06/12/upshot/polarization-is-dividing-american-society-not-just-politics.html?_r=0&abt=0002&abg=0.

DeSilver, Drew. 2014. "The Polarized Congress of Today Has Its Roots in the 1970s." *Pew Research Center*. Retrieved March 20, 2015, from http://www.pewresearch.org/fact-tank/2014/06/12/polarized-politics-in-congress-began-in-the-1970s-and-has-been-getting-worse-ever-since.

Doherty, Carroll. 2014. "7 Things to Know about Polarization in America." *Pew Research Center*. Retrieved March 20, 2015, from http://www.pewresearch.org/fact-tank/2014/06/12/7-things-to-know-about-polarization-in-america.

Fiorina, Morris. 2014. "Americans Have Not Become More Politically Polarized." *The Washington Post*. Retrieved March 20, 2015, from http://www.washingtonpost.com/blogs/monkey-cage/wp/2014/06/23/americans-have-not-become-more-politically-polarized.

Frey, William. 2008. ""Race, Immigration, and America's Changing Electorate." Pp. 79–108 in *Red, Blue & Purple America: The Future of Election Demographics*, edited by Ruy Teixeira. Washington, DC: Brookings Institution Press.

Green, John, and E. J. Dionne Jr. 2008. "Religion and American Politics: More Secular, More Evangelical, or Both?" Pp. 194–224 in *Red, Blue & Purple America: The Future of Election Demographics*, edited by Ruy Teixeira. Washington, DC: Brookings Institution Press.

Grim, Ryan, and Sabrina Siddiqui. 2013. "Call Time for Congress Shows How Fundraising Dominates Bleak Work Life." *Huffington Post*. Retrieved April 27, 2015, from http://www .huffingtonpost.com/2013/01/08/call-time-congressional-fundraising_n_2427291.html.

Haidt, Jonathan, and Marc Hetherington. 2012. "Look How Far We've Come Apart." *The New York Times*. Retrieved March 20, 2015, from http://campaignstops.blogs.nytimes.com/2012/09/17/ look-how-far-weve-come-apart/?_r=0&assetType=opinion.

Hare, Christopher, Keith Poole, and Howard Rosenthal. 2014. "Polarization in Congress Has Risen Sharply. Where Is It Going Next?" *The Washington Post*. Retrieved March 20, 2015, from http:// www.washingtonpost.com/blogs/monkey-cage/wp/2014/02/13/polarization-in-congress-has-risen-sharply-where-is-it-going-next/.

Keeter, Scott. 2008. ""The Aging of the Boomers and the Rise of the Millennials." Pp. 225–257 in *Red, Blue & Purple America: The Future of Election Demographics*, edited by Ruy Teixeira. Washington, DC: Brookings Institution Press.

Kiley, Jocelyn. 2017. "In Polarized Era, Fewer Americans Hold a Mix of Conservative and Liberal Views." *Pew Research Center*. Retrieved January 21, 2019, from http://www.pewresearch.org/ fact-tank/2017/10/23/in-polarized-era-fewer-americans-hold-a-mix-of-conservative-and-liberal-views.

Kiley, Jocelyn, and Michael Dimock. 2014. "The GOP's Millennial Problem Runs Deep." *Pew Research Center*. Retrieved March 21, 2015, from http://www.pewresearch.org/fact-tank/2014/09/25/ the-gops-millennial-problem-runs-deep.

Kroll, Andy. 2013. "Retiring Senator: Congress Doesn't Work Because We Fundraise Way Too Much." *Mother Jones*. Retrieved April 27, 2015, from http://www.motherjones.com/mojo/2013/01/ tom-harkin-retire-senator-fundraise-money.

Lang, Robert, Thomas Sanchez, and Alan Berube. 2008. ""The New Suburban Politics: A County-Based Analysis of Metropolitan Voting Trends since 2000." Pp. 25–49 in *Red, Blue & Purple America: The Future of Election Demographics*, edited by Ruy Teixeira. Washington, DC: Brookings Institution Press.

Lauter, David. 2014. "Millennial Generation Less Religious, More Liberal Than Older Ones." *Los Angeles Times*. Retrieved March 21, 2015, from http://articles.latimes.com/2014/mar/07/news/ la-pn-millennials-liberal-views-pew-poll-20140306.

Levendusky, Matthew. 2009. *The Partisan Sort: How Liberals Became Democrats and Conservatives Became Republicans*. Chicago: University of Chicago Press.

Matthews, Dylan. 2013. "It's Official: The 112th Congress Was the Most Polarized Ever." *The Washington Post*. Retrieved March 20, 2015, from http://www.washingtonpost.com/blogs/ wonkblog/wp/2013/01/17/its-official-the-112th-congress-was-the-most-polarized-ever.

Mendes, Elizabeth. 2013. "Americans Down on Congress, OK with Own Representatives." *Gallup*. Retrieved March 30, 2015, from http://www.gallup.com/poll/162362/americans-down-congress-own-representative.aspx.

Mitchell, Amy, Jeffrey Gottfried, Jocelyn Kiley, and Katerina Eva Matsa. 2014. "Political Polarization & Media Habits." *Pew Research Center*. Retrieved March 20, 2015, from http://www.journalism. org/2014/10/21/political-polarization-media-habits.

Pew Research Center. 2014. "Political Polarization in the American Public: How Increasing Ideological Uniformity and Partisan Antipathy Affect Politics, Compromise and Everyday Life." *Pew Research Center*. Retrieved March 20, 2015, from http://www.people-press.org/2014/06/12/political-polarization-in-the-american-public.

Pew Research Center, 2018. "More Now Say It's 'Stressful' to Discuss Politics with People They Disagree With." *Pew Research Center*. Retrieved January 21, 2019, from http://www.people-press.org/2018/11/05/more-now-say-its-stressful-to-discuss-politics-with-people-they-disagree-with.

Poole, Keith, and Howard Rosenthal. 2015. "Polarized America." *The Voteview Website (1995– Present), University of Georgia, Department of Political Science*. Retrieved March 30, 2015, from http://www.polarizedamerica.com/.

Riffkin, Rebecca. 2014. "2014 U.S. Approval of Congress Remains near All-Time Low." *Gallup*. Retrieved March 21, 2015, from http://www.gallup.com/poll/180113/2014-approval-congress-remains-near-time-low.aspx.

Smith, Tom. 2008. ""Changes in Family Structure, Family Values, and Politics, 1972–2006." Pp. 147–193 in *Red, Blue & Purple America: The Future of Election Demographics*, edited by Ruy Teixeira. Washington, DC: Brookings Institution Press.

Teixeira, Ruy. 2008. ""Beyond Polarization? The Future of Red, Blue, and Purple America." Pp. 1–22 in *Red, Blue & Purple America: The Future of Election Demographics*, edited by Ruy Teixeira. Washington, DC: Brookings Institution Press.

Tuschman, Avi. 2014. "Why Americans Are So Polarized: Education and Evolution." *The Atlantic*. Retrieved March 20, 2015, from http://www.theatlantic.com/politics/archive/2014/02/why-americans-are-so-polarized-education-and-evolution/284098.

THE WORST VOTER SUPPRESSION WE'VE SEEN IN THE MODERN ERA

ZACHARY ROTH AND WENDY R. WEISER

Large-scale voter purges from Florida to Maine. Ultra-strict registration rules keeping voters off the rolls in Georgia and other states. Cuts to early voting sites in North Carolina. A North Dakota voter ID law that could keep Native Americans from the polls. False voting information being spread online.[1]

Since the modern-day push to create barriers to voting got underway around a decade ago, the Brennan Center has been tracking restrictive voting laws and practices as closely as any organization in the country—as well as speaking out against them and challenging many in court. In the 2018 election, citizens in 24 states faced new laws making it harder for them to vote than in 2010.[1] And in nine of those states, it was harder to vote than in 2016. By our assessment, the range of voter suppression efforts was more widespread, intense, and brazen in the 2018 cycle than in any other since the modern-day assault on voting began,

especially when viewed in combination with the accumulated new hurdles to voting.[2]

Reasons for the uptick in voter suppression

A number of factors have converged to turn up the volume on voter suppression. First, by consistently and falsely stoking fear about illegal voting for over two years—including the lie that he'd have won the popular vote if it weren't for millions of noncitizen voters—President Trump helped make the issue central to the far right's agenda. Trump's short-lived voter fraud commission collapsed in January 2018 after drawing bipartisan outrage, but it nonetheless acted as a signal to supportive states that efforts to make voting harder would be welcomed at the highest levels. It's no coincidence that in the first few months of Trump's

---

1   https://www.brennancenter.org/analysis/voting-laws-roundup-2018

2   For a range of voter problems that we observed: https://www.brennancenter.org/blog/voting-problems-2018.

Zachary Roth, Wendy R. Weiser, "This Is the Worst Voter Suppression We've Seen in the Modern Era," Brennan Center for Justice, November 2, 2018.

presidency, a slew of states proposed or passed new restrictions, after several years during which the pace had seemed to slow.[3]

The courts also have played a key role. The Supreme Court's 2013 ruling in *Shelby County v. Holder*, which neutered the most effective plank of the Voting Rights Act, offered a green light to a host of election rules changes in parts of the country whose voting rules previously had been under federal supervision. The Court's new staunchly conservative majority may be encouraging even states not directly affected by *Shelby* to lean forward on voter suppression, confident—we hope falsely—that the justices won't stop them. In October 2018, the Court declined to block North Dakota's voter ID law, despite evidence that thousands of Native Americans who live on reservations could be stymied by its requirement that their IDs include a residential mailing address.

Of course, the courts have also been major players in stemming the growth of voting restrictions. The number of court decisions against new restrictions has ballooned in recent years,[4] with several finding that officials had intentionally tried to keep minorities from voting. But despite these victories, another troubling reality has emerged: Even when courts rule against restrictive voting measures, it isn't enough to deter those looking to limit access to the ballot.

Challenges fighting voter suppression efforts

Litigation is typically time consuming, and so these harsh laws often stay in place, fully intact and disenfranchising voters, for one or more election before a court rules against them. And even if that ruling does come, it may only weaken the law rather than striking it down fully—as happened with Texas's and Wisconsin's strict voter ID laws, among other examples. Such limited outcomes give would-be vote suppressors little incentive to think twice about their strategy. And in the cases when a court scraps a law entirely, the confusion and misinformation surrounding the process can often still keep some voters from the polls.[5]

Equally troubling, those who seek to restrict access to voting do not seem to pay much of a political price. For example, the authors of North Carolina's sweeping voter suppression law, struck down by a federal court which found it "targeted African Americans with almost surgical precision," did not lose their political perches—indeed, one of its key legislative champions now sits in the U.S. Senate, and the lawyer who defended the law was nominated to be a federal judge (though his nomination failed to pass the Senate). Put bluntly: In the absence of a broad Supreme Court ruling enforcing voting rights—something that is now an uphill battle at best—or strong federal legislation expanding the

legal tools available to voters, the courts simply aren't enough to combat voter suppression.

The role of race and partisanship in voter suppression efforts

Then there's race. There's evidence that states in which the political clout of minorities is growing—where the ruling majority perceives a threat to its power—are more likely to see restrictive voting laws than are more demographically homogeneous states.[6] And as the salience of race in our politics has increased, so too has voter suppression.

A decade ago, there was a national spike in voter suppression efforts in the 2008 election cycle, when Barack Obama, backed by a multiracial coalition, was bidding to become the nation's first African American president. That spurred unfounded fears that ACORN, a community group serving mostly minority communities, and its allied voter registration group for which Obama once worked, was plotting to steal the election on his behalf. Two years later, this resulted in the first massive wave of new laws cutting back on voting access.[7] In the age of Trump, politicians have grown more comfortable openly playing to these fears. . . .

Partisanship plays a role too. Voting restrictions have almost exclusively been promoted and supported by Republicans. As our country becomes more polarized, the partisan divide on voting rights has taken on greater import. That's what explains the targeting of another group of voters beyond racial minorities: college students, who tend to vote Democratic. Texas's voter ID law allowed people to vote with a gun license but not an ID from a state university. Since 2017, New Hampshire, where students make up a significant slice of the Democratic base, has passed two[8] separate[9] laws that will make it harder for students to vote. And several states including North Carolina[10] and Florida[11] have tried to close polling places on college campuses, sometimes successfully.

Causes aside, here's the grim reality: The scope and sophistication of efforts to make voting more difficult make clear that voting advocates can't respond solely by playing a defensive whack-a-mole against the worst laws and practices. That crucial work will continue, but it must be paired with a positive reform

---

3   https://www.brennancenter.org/analysis/voting-laws-roundup-2017

4   https://www.brennancenter.org/sites/default/files/publications/2018_06_StateOfVoting_v5%20%281%29.pdf

5   http://www.brennancenter.org/publication/voting-law-changes-election-update

6   https://www.brennancenter.org/analysis/election-2016-restrictive-voting-laws-numbers#raceandvoting

7   https://www.brennancenter.org/publication/voting-law-changes-2012

8   https://www.brennancenter.org/blog/new-hampshires-new-voting-law-threatens-student-voters

9   http://www.thedartmouth.com/article/2017/09/new-hampshire-judge-lets-sb3-stand

10   https://www.wral.com/advocates-say-politics-motivates-moving-polling-places-off-campus/13511385/

11   https://www.orlandosentinel.com/features/education/school-zone/os-early-voting-college-campuses-20180724-story.html

agenda—one that is gaining momentum at the state level—that bolsters protections for the right to vote and expands access to the ballot. Adding to this momentum, in 2018 voters in four states approved ballot initiatives to expand access to voting (in addition to four ballot initiatives to improve the redistricting process).[12] The most important of these was in Florida, where voters overwhelmingly supported a measure that reenfranchised around 1.4 million Floridians, disproportionately racial minorities, with past criminal convictions. And Congress underlined its commitment to the issue by introducing a sweeping bill to protect and expand voting, along with other democracy reforms, as its first order of business in 2019.

We faced even worse voter suppression schemes before the 1965 Voting Rights Act, and we responded by making our democracy stronger. We should do so again.

[*Editor's Note*: In March of 2019, the United States House of Representatives passed H.R. 1, For the People Act of 2019. This Act:

> This bill addresses voter access, election integrity, election security, political spending, and ethics for the three branches of government. . . . [It] expands voter registration and voting access, makes Election Day a federal holiday, and limits removing voters from voter rolls. The bill provides for states to establish independent, nonpartisan redistricting commissions [and] . . . sets forth provisions related to election security, including sharing intelligence information with state election officials, protecting the security of the voter rolls, supporting states in securing their election systems, developing a national strategy to protect the security and integrity of U.S. democratic institutions, establishing in the legislative branch the National Commission to Protect United States Democratic Institutions, and other provisions to improve the cybersecurity of election systems. This bill addresses campaign spending, including by expanding the ban on foreign nationals contributing to or spending on elections; expanding disclosure rules pertaining to organizations spending money during elections, campaign advertisements, and online platforms; and revising disclaimer requirements for political advertising. This bill establishes an alternative campaign funding system for certain federal offices. The system involves federal matching of small contributions for qualified candidates. This bill sets forth provisions related to ethics in all three branches of government. Specifically, the bill requires a code of ethics for federal judges and justices, prohibits Members of the House from serving on the board of a for-profit entity, expands enforcement of regulations governing foreign agents, and establishes additional conflict-of-interest and ethics provisions for federal employees and the White House. The bill also requires candidates for President and Vice President to submit 10 years of tax returns.[13]

It remains to be seen whether or not the United States Senate will pass a version of this legislation.]

---

12   https://www.brennancenter.org/publication/state-voting-2018

13   https://www.congress.gov/bill/116th-congress/house-bill/1/text

ALLAN G. JOHNSON

73. WHAT CAN WE DO? BECOMING PART OF THE SOLUTION

Students who study the structural sources of our many social problems may feel discouraged about the potential for social change. Johnson recognizes the challenges of social change, but argues the tools are at our disposal. To begin, Johnson contends we must acknowledge and target systems of privilege and oppression. For students, this may mean recognizing your own participation in these systems and advocating for change in a variety of ways. Johnson grants risks are involved, but that the rewards of social change far outweigh them.

The challenge we face is to change patterns of exclusion, rejection, privilege, harassment, discrimination, and violence that are everywhere in this society and have existed for hundreds (or, in the case of gender, thousands) of years. We have to begin by thinking about the trouble and the challenge in new and more productive ways. . . . Here is a summary of the tools we have to start with.

Large numbers of people have sat on the sidelines and seen themselves as neither part of the problem nor the solution. Beyond this shared trait, however, they are far from homogeneous. Everyone is aware of the [people, often] Whites, heterosexuals, and men who intentionally act out in oppressive ways. But there is less attention to the millions of people who know inequities exist and want to be part of the solution. Their silence and invisibility allow the trouble to continue. Removing what silences them and stands in their way can tap an enormous potential of energy for change.

The problem of privilege and oppression is deep and wide, and to work with it we have to be able to see it clearly so that we can talk about it in useful ways. To do that, we have to reclaim some difficult language

that names what's going on, language that has been so misused and maligned that it generates more heat than light. We can't just stop using words like racism, sexism, and privilege, however, because these are tools that focus our awareness on the problem and all the forms it takes. Once we can see and talk about what's going on, we can analyze how it works as a system. We can identify points of leverage where change can begin.

Reclaiming the language takes us directly to the core reality that the problem is privilege and the power that maintains it. Privilege exists when one group has something that is systematically denied to others not because of who they are or what they've done or not done, but because of the social category they belong to.

Privilege is a feature of social systems, not individuals. People have or don't have privilege depending on the system they're in and the social categories other people put them in. To say, then, that I have race privilege says less about me personally than it does about the society we all live in and how it is organized to assign privilege on the basis of a socially defined set of racial categories that change historically and often overlap. The challenge facing me as an individual has more to do with how I participate in society as a recipient of race privilege and how those choices oppose or support the system itself.

In dealing with the problem of privilege, we have to get used to being surrounded by paradox. Very often those who have privilege don't know it, for example, which is a key aspect of privilege. Also paradoxical is the fact that privilege doesn't necessarily lead to a "good life," which can prompt people in privileged groups to deny resentfully that they even have it. But privilege doesn't equate with being happy. It involves having what others don't have and the struggle to hang on to it at their expense, neither of which is a recipe for joy, personal fulfillment, or spiritual contentment. . . .

To be an effective part of the solution, we have to realize that privilege and oppression are not a thing of the past. It's happening right now. It isn't just a collection of wounds inflicted long ago that now need to be healed. The wounding goes on as I write these words and as you read them, and unless people work to change the system that promotes it, personal healing by itself cannot be the answer. Healing wounds is no more a solution to the oppression that causes the wounding than military hospitals are a solution to war. Healing is a necessary process, but it isn't enough. . . .

Since privilege is rooted primarily in systems—such as families, schools, and workplaces—change isn't simply a matter of changing people. People, of course, will have to change in order for systems to change, but the most important point is that changing people isn't enough. The solution also has to include entire systems, such as capitalism, whose paths of least resistance shape how we feel, think, and behave as individuals, how we see ourselves and one another.

As they work for change, it's easy for members of privileged groups to lose sight of the reality of privilege and its consequences and the truth that the trouble around privilege is their trouble as much as anyone else's. This happens in large part because systems of privilege provide endless ways of seeing and thinking about the world that make privilege invisible. These include denying and minimizing the trouble; blaming the victim; calling the trouble something else; assuming everyone prefers things the way they are; mistaking intentions with consequences; attributing the trouble to others and not their own participation in social systems that produce it; and balancing the trouble with troubles of their own. The more aware people can be of how these behaviors limit their effectiveness, the more they can contribute to change both in themselves and the systems where they work and live. With these tools in hand, we can begin to think about how to make ourselves part of the solution to the problem of privilege and oppression. . . .

. . . WHAT CAN WE DO?

There are no easy answers to the question of what can we do about the problem of privilege. There is no twelve-step program, no neat set of instructions. Most important, there is no way around or over it: the only way out is through it. We won't end oppression by pretending it isn't there or that we don't have to deal with it.

Some people complain that those who work for social change are being "divisive" when they draw attention to gender or race or social class and the oppressive systems organized around them. But when members of dominant groups mark differences by excluding or discriminating against subordinate groups and treating them as "other," they aren't accused of being divisive. Usually it's only when someone calls attention to how differences are used for oppressive purposes that the charge of divisiveness comes up.

In a sense, it is divisive to say that oppression and privilege exist, but only insofar as it points to divisions that already exist and to the perception that the status quo is normal and unremarkable. Oppression promotes the worst kind of divisiveness because it cuts us off from one another and, by silencing us about the truth, cuts us off from ourselves as well. Not only must we participate in oppression by living in an oppressive society, we also must act as though oppression didn't exist, denying the reality of our own experience and its consequences for people's lives, including our own.

What does it mean to go out by going through? What can we do that will make a difference? I don't have the answers, but I do have some suggestions.

ACKNOWLEDGE THAT THE TROUBLE EXISTS

A key to the continued existence of every oppressive system is unawareness, because oppression contradicts so many basic human values that it invariably arouses opposition when people know about it. The Soviet Union and its East European satellites, for example, were riddled with contradictions so widely known among their people that the oppressive regimes fell apart with an ease and speed that astonished the world. An awareness of oppression compels people to speak out, to break the silence that continued oppression depends on.

This is why most oppressive cultures mask the reality of oppression by denying its existence, trivializing it, calling it something else, blaming it on those most victimized by it, or diverting attention from it. Instead of treating oppression as a serious problem, we go to war or get embroiled in controversial "issues" such as capital gains tax cuts or "family values" or immigrant workers. There would be far more active opposition to racism, for example, if White people lived with an ongoing awareness of how it actually affects the everyday lives of those it oppresses as "not White." As we have seen, however, the vast majority of White people don't do this.

It's one thing to become aware and quite another to stay that way. The greatest challenge when we first become aware of a critical perspective on the world is simply to hang on to it. Every system's paths of least resistance invariably lead away from critical awareness of how the system works. In some ways . . . [it is] harder and more important to pay attention to systems of privilege than it is to people's behavior and the paths of least resistance that shape it. . . .

PAY ATTENTION

Understanding how privilege and oppression operate and how you participate in them is where the work for change begins. It's easy to have opinions, but it takes work to know what you're talking about. The simplest way to begin is by reading, and making reading about privilege part of your life. Unless you have the luxury of a personal teacher, you can't understand this issue without reading, just as you'd need to read about a foreign country before you traveled there for the first

time, or about a car before you tried to work under the hood. Many people assume they already know what they need to know because it's part of everyday life. But they're usually wrong. Just as the last thing a fish would discover is water, the last thing people discover is society itself and something as pervasive as the dynamics of privilege.

We also have to be open to the idea that what we think we know is, if not wrong, so deeply shaped by systems of privilege that it misses most of the truth. This is why activists talk with one another and spend time reading one another's writing: seeing things clearly is tricky. This is also why people who are critical of the status quo are so often self-critical as well: they know how complex and elusive the truth really is and what a challenge it is to work toward it. . . .

LITTLE RISKS: DO SOMETHING

The more you pay attention to privilege and oppression, the more you'll see opportunities to do something about them. You don't have to mount an expedition to find those opportunities; they're all over the place, beginning in yourself. As I became aware of how male privilege encourages me to control conversations, for example, I also realized how easily men dominate group meetings by controlling the agenda and interrupting, without women's objecting to it. This pattern is especially striking in groups that are mostly female but in which most of the talking nonetheless comes from a few men. I would find myself sitting in meetings and suddenly the preponderance of male voices would jump out at me, an unmistakable sign of male privilege, in full bloom.

As I've seen what's going on, I've had to decide what to do about this little path of least resistance and my relation to it that leads me to follow it so readily. With some effort, I've tried out new ways of listening more and talking less. At times my methods have felt contrived and artificial, such as telling myself to shut up for a while or even counting slowly to ten (or more) to give others a chance to step into the space afforded by silence. With time and practice, new paths have become easier to follow and I spend less time monitoring myself. But awareness is never automatic or permanent, for paths of least resistance will be there to choose or not as long as male privilege exists.

As you become more aware, questions will arise about what goes on at work, in the media, in families, in communities, in religious institutions, in government, on the street, and at school—in short, just about everywhere. The questions don't come all at once (for which we can be grateful), although they sometimes come in a rush that can feel overwhelming. If you remind yourself that it isn't up to you to do it all, however, you can see plenty of situations in which you can make a difference, sometimes in surprisingly simple ways. Consider the following possibilities:

MAKE NOISE, BE SEEN.

Stand up, volunteer, speak out, write letters, sign petitions, show up. Every oppressive system feeds on silence. Don't collude in silence. Breaking the silence is especially important for dominant groups, because it undermines the assumption of solidarity that dominance depends on. If this feels too risky, you can practice being aware of how silence reflects your investment in solidarity with other dominant-group members. This can be a place to begin working on how you participate in making privilege and oppression happen: "Today I said nothing, colluded in silence, and this is how I benefited from it. Maybe tomorrow I can try something different."

FIND LITTLE WAYS TO WITHDRAW SUPPORT FROM PATHS OF LEAST RESISTANCE AND PEOPLE'S CHOICES TO FOLLOW THEM, STARTING WITH YOURSELF.

It can be as simple as not laughing at a racist or heterosexist joke or saying you don't think it's funny, or writing a letter to your senator or representative or the editor of your newspaper, objecting to an instance of sexism in the media. When my local newspaper ran an article whose headline referred to sexual harassment as "earthy behavior," for example, I wrote a letter pointing out that harassment isn't "earthy."

The key to withdrawing support is to interrupt the flow of business as usual. We can subvert the assumption that we're all going along with the status quo by simply not going along. When we do this, we stop the flow, if only for a moment, but in that moment other people can notice and start to think and question. It's

a perfect time to suggest the possibility of alternatives, such as humor that isn't at someone else's expense, or of ways to think about discrimination, harassment, and violence that do justice to the reality of what's going on and how it affects people. . . .

DARE TO MAKE PEOPLE FEEL UNCOMFORTABLE, BEGINNING WITH YOURSELF.

At the next local school board meeting, for example, you can ask why principals and other administrators are almost always White and male (unless your system is an exception that proves the rule), while the teachers they supervise are mostly women and people of color. Or look at the names and mascots used by local sports teams and see if they exploit the heritage and identity of Native Americans; if that's the case, ask principals and coaches and owners about it.[1] Consider asking similar kinds of questions about privilege and difference in your place of worship, workplace, and local government. . . .

Some will say it isn't "nice" to make people uncomfortable, but oppressive systems do a lot more than make people feel uncomfortable, and there isn't anything "nice" about allowing that to continue unchallenged. Besides, discomfort is an unavoidable part of any meaningful process of education. We can't grow without being willing to challenge our assumptions and take ourselves to the edge of our competencies, where we're bound to feel uncomfortable. If we can't tolerate ambiguity, uncertainty, and discomfort, then we'll never get beneath superficial appearances or learn or change anything of much value, including ourselves.

And if history is any guide, discomfort—to put it mildly—is also an unavoidable part of changing systems of privilege. As sociologist William Gamson noted in his study of social movements, "the meek don't make it."[2] To succeed, movements must be willing to disrupt business as usual and make those in power as uncomfortable as possible. Women didn't win the right to vote, for example, by reasoning with men and showing them the merits of their position. To even get men's attention, they had to take to the streets in large numbers at considerable risk to themselves. At the very least they had to be willing to suffer ridicule and ostracism, but it often got worse than that. In England, for example, suffragettes were jailed and, when they went on hunger strikes, were force fed through tubes run down their throats. The modern women's movement has had to depend no less on the willingness of women to put themselves on the line in order to make men so uncomfortable that they've had to pay attention and, eventually, to act.

It has been no different with the civil rights movement. Under the leadership of men like Martin Luther King, the movement was dedicated to the principle of nonviolence. As with the movement for women's suffrage, however, they could get White people's attention only through mass demonstrations and marches. Whites typically responded with violence and intimidation.[3] As Douglas McAdam showed in his study of that period, the Federal government intervened and enacted civil rights legislation only when White violence against civil rights demonstrators became so extreme that the government was compelled to act.[4] . . .

OPENLY CHOOSE AND MODEL ALTERNATIVE PATHS.

As we identify paths of least resistance, we can identify alternatives and then follow them openly so that other people can see what we're doing. Paths of least resistance become more visible when people choose alternatives, just as rules become more visible when someone breaks them. Modeling new paths creates tension in a system, which moves toward resolution. . . .

ACTIVELY PROMOTE CHANGE IN HOW SYSTEMS ARE ORGANIZED AROUND PRIVILEGE.

The possibilities here are almost endless, because social life is complicated and privilege is everywhere. You can, for example,

- Speak out for equality in the workplace.
- Promote diversity awareness and training.
- Support equal pay and promotion.
- Oppose the devaluing of women and people of color and the work they do, from dead-end jobs to glass ceilings.

- Support the well-being of mothers and children and defend women's right to control their bodies and their lives.
- Object to the punitive dismantling of welfare and attempts to limit women's access to reproductive health services.
- Speak out against violence and harassment wherever they occur, whether at home, at work, or on the street.
- Support government and private services for women who are victimized by male violence. Volunteer at the local rape crisis center or battered-women's shelter. Join and support groups that intervene with and counsel violent men.
- Call for and support clear and effective anti-harassment policies in workplaces, unions, schools, professional associations, religious institutions, and political parties, as well as public spaces such as parks, sidewalks, and malls.
- Object to theaters and video stores that carry violent pornography. This doesn't require a debate about censorship—just the exercise of freedom of speech to articulate pornography's role in the oppression of women and to express how its opponents feel about it.
- Ask questions about how work, education, religion, and family are shaped by core values and principles that support race privilege, gender privilege, and other forms of privilege. You might accept women's entry into combat branches of the military or the upper reaches of corporate power as "progress," for example. But you could also raise questions about what happens to people and societies when political and economic institutions are organized around control, domination, "power over," and, by extension, competition and the use of violence. Is it progress to allow selected women to share control with men over oppressive systems?

SUPPORT THE RIGHT OF WOMEN AND MEN TO LOVE WHOMEVER THEY CHOOSE.

Raise awareness of homophobia and heterosexism. For example, ask school officials and teachers about what's happening to gay and lesbian students in local schools. If they don't know, ask them to find out, since it's a safe bet these students are being harassed, suppressed, and oppressed by others at one of the most vulnerable stages of life. When sexual orientation is discussed, whether in the media or among friends, raise questions about its relation to patriarchy. Remember that it isn't necessary to have answers to questions in order to ask them.

PAY ATTENTION TO HOW DIFFERENT FORMS OF OPPRESSION INTERACT WITH ONE ANOTHER.

There has been a great deal of struggle within women's movements, for example, about the relationship between gender oppression and other forms of oppression, especially those based on race and social class. White middle- and upper-middle-class feminists have been criticized for pursuing their own agenda to the detriment of women who aren't privileged by class or race. Raising concerns about glass ceilings that keep women out of top corporate and professional positions, for example, does little to help working-or lower-class women. There has also been debate over whether some forms of oppression are more important to attack first or produce more oppressive consequences than other forms.

One way out of this conflict is to realize that patriarchy isn't problematic just because it emphasizes male dominance, but because it promotes dominance and control as ends in themselves. In that sense, all forms of oppression draw support from common roots, and whatever we do that calls attention to those roots undermines all forms of oppression. If working against patriarchy is seen simply as enabling some women to get a bigger piece of the pie, then some women probably will "succeed" at the expense of others who are disadvantaged by race, class, ethnicity, and other characteristics. One could make the same argument about movements for racial justice: If it just means enabling well-placed Blacks to get ahead, then it won't end racial oppression for the vast majority. But if we identify the core problem as any society organized around principles of domination and privilege, then changing that requires us to pay attention to all the forms of oppression those principles promote. Whether we begin with race or gender or ethnicity or

class or the capitalist system, if we name the problem correctly we'll wind up going in the same general direction.

WORK WITH OTHER PEOPLE.

This is one of the most important principles of participating in social change. From expanding consciousness to taking risks, being in the company of people who support what you're trying to do makes all the difference in the world. For starters, you can read and talk about books and issues and just plain hang out with other people who want to understand and do something about privilege and oppression. The roots of the modern women's movement were in consciousness-raising groups where women did little more than talk about themselves and try to figure out how they were shaped by a patriarchal society. It may not have looked like much at the time, but it laid the foundation for huge social change. . . .

It is especially important to form alliances across difference—for men to ally with women, Whites with people of color, heterosexuals with lesbians and gay men. What does this mean? As Paul Kivel [author of *Uprooting Racism* (1996)] argues, one of the keys to being a good ally is a willingness to listen—for Whites to listen to people of color, for example—and to give credence to what people say about their own experience.[5] This isn't easy to do, of course, since Whites, heterosexuals, and men may not like what they hear about their privilege from those who are most damaged by it. It is difficult to hear anger about privilege and oppression and not take it personally, but that is what allies have to be willing to do. It's also difficult for members of privileged groups to realize how mistrusted they are by subordinate groups and to not take that personally as well. . . .

DON'T KEEP IT TO YOURSELF.

A corollary of looking for company is not to restrict your focus to the tight little circle of your own life. It isn't enough to work out private solutions to social problems like oppression and keep them to yourself. It isn't enough to clean up your own act and then walk away, to find ways to avoid the worst consequences of oppression and privilege at home and inside yourself and think that's taking responsibility. Privilege and oppression aren't a personal problem that can be solved through personal solutions. At some point, taking responsibility means acting in a larger context, even if that means letting just one other person know what you're doing. It makes sense to start with yourself, but it's equally important not to end with yourself.

A good way to convert personal change into something larger is to join an organization dedicated to changing the systems that produce privilege and oppression. Most college and university campuses, for example, have student organizations that focus on issues of gender, race, and sexual orientation. There are also national organizations working for change, often through local and statewide branches. . . .

DON'T LET OTHER PEOPLE SET THE STANDARD FOR YOU.

Start where you are and work from there. Make lists of all the things you could actually imagine doing—from reading another book about inequality to suggesting policy changes at work to protesting against capitalism to raising questions about who cleans the bathroom at home—and rank them from the most risky to the least. Start with the least risky and set reasonable goals ("What small risk for change will I take today?"). As you get more experienced at taking risks, you can move up your list. You can commit yourself to whatever the next steps are for you, the tolerable risks, the contributions that offer some way—however small it might seem—to help balance the scales. As long as you do something, it counts.

In the end, taking responsibility doesn't have to involve guilt and blame, letting someone off the hook, or being on the hook yourself. It simply means acknowledging an obligation to make a contribution to finding a way out of the trouble we're all in, and to find constructive ways to act on that obligation. You don't have to do anything dramatic or earth-shaking to help change happen. As powerful as oppressive systems are, they cannot stand the strain of lots of people doing something about it, beginning with the simplest act of naming the system out loud.

WHAT'S IN IT FOR ME?

It's risky to promote change. You risk being seen as odd, being excluded or punished for asking questions and setting examples that make people uncomfortable or threaten privilege. We've all adapted in one way or another to life in a society organized around competition, privilege, and difference. Paths of least resistance may perpetuate oppression, but they also have the advantage of being familiar and predictable and therefore can seem preferable to untried alternatives and the unknown. There are inner risks—of feeling lost, confused, and scared—along with outer risks of being rejected or worse. Obviously, then, working for change isn't a path of least resistance, which raises the question of why anyone should follow Gandhi's advice and do it anyway.

It's an easier question to answer for subordinate groups than it is for dominants, which helps explain why the former have done most of the work for change. Those on the losing end have much to gain by striving to undo the system that oppresses them, not only for themselves in the short run, but for the sake of future generations. The answer comes less easily for those in dominant groups, but they don't have to look very far to see that they have much to gain—especially in the long run—that more than balances what they stand to lose.[6]

When Whites, heterosexuals, and men join the movement against privilege and oppression, they can begin to undo the costs of participating in an oppressive system as the dominant group. Few men, for example, realize how much they deaden themselves in order to support (if only by their silence) a system that privileges them at women's expense, that values maleness by devaluing femaleness, that makes women invisible in order to make men appear larger than life. Most men don't realize the impoverishment to their emotional and spiritual lives, the price they pay in personal authenticity and integrity, how they compromise their humanity, how they limit the connections they can have with other people, how they distort their sexuality to live up to core patriarchal values of control. They don't realize how much they have to live a lie in order to interact on a daily basis with their mothers, wives, sisters, daughters, women friends and co-workers—all members of the group male privilege oppresses. So the first thing men can do is claim a sense of aliveness and realness that doesn't depend on superiority and control, and a connection to themselves and the world—which they may not even realize was missing until they begin to feel its return.

In similar ways, most Whites don't realize how much energy it takes to defend against their continuing vulnerability to guilt and blame and to avoid seeing how much trouble the world is in and the central role they play in it. When Whites do nothing about racial privilege and oppression, they put themselves on the defensive, in the no-safe-place-to-hide position of every dominator class. But when White people make a commitment to participate in change, to be more than part of the problem, they free themselves to live in the world without feeling open to guilt simply for being White.

In perhaps more subtle ways, homophobia and heterosexism take a toll on heterosexuals. The persecution of lesbians, for example, is a powerful weapon of sexism that encourages women to silence themselves, to disavow feminism, and tolerate male privilege for fear that if they speak out, they'll be labeled as lesbians and ostracized.[7] In similar ways, the fear of being called gay is enough to make men conform to masculine stereotypes that don't reflect who they really are

and to go along with an oppressive gender system they may not believe in. And because homosexuals all come from families, parents and siblings may also pay a huge emotional price for the effects of prejudice, discrimination, and persecution directed at their loved ones. . . .

When people join together to end any form of oppression, they act with courage to take responsibility to do the right thing, and this empowers them in ways that can extend to every corner of their lives. Whenever we act with courage, a halo effect makes that same courage available to us in other times and places. . . . As we do the work, we build a growing store of experience to draw on in figuring out how to act with courage again and again. As our inner and outer lives become less bound by the strictures of fear and compromise, we can claim a deeper meaning for our lives than we've known before.

The human capacity to choose how to participate in the world empowers all of us to pass along something different from what's been passed to us. With each strand of the knot of privilege that we help to work loose and unravel, we don't act simply for ourselves, we join a process of creative resistance to oppression that's been unfolding for thousands of years. We become part of the long tradition of people who have dared to make a difference—to look at things as they are, to imagine something better, and to plant seeds of change in themselves, in others, and in the world.

NOTES

1. For more on this, see Ward Churchill, "Crimes against Humanity," *Z Magazine* 6 (March 1993): 43–47. Reprinted in Margaret L. Andersen and Patricia Hill Collins (eds.), *Race, Class, and Gender*, 3d ed. (Belmont, CA: Wadsworth, 1998), pp. 413–20.
2. William A. Gamson, "Violence and Political Power: The Meek Don't Make It," *Psychology Today* 8 (July 1974): 35–41.
3. For more on this, see the excellent PBS documentary of the civil rights movement, *Eyes on the Prize.*
4. Doug McAdam, *Political Process and the Development of Black Insurgency 1930–1970* (Chicago: University of Chicago Press, 1982).
5. See Kivel, *Uprooting Racism: How White People Can Work for Racial Justice* (Philadelphia: New Society Publishers, 1996), part 3, "Being Allies."
6. A lot of what follows came out of a brainstorming session with my friend and colleague Jane Tuohy as we worked out the design for a gender workshop.
7. See Suzanne Pharr, *Homophobia: A Weapon of Sexism* (Inverness, CA: Chardon Press, 1988).